MODERN CRIMINAL LAW

CASES, COMMENTS AND QUESTIONS

Third Edition

By

Wayne R. LaFave

*David C. Baum Professor of Law Emeritus and
Center for Advanced Study Professor Emeritus,
University of Illinois*

AMERICAN CASEBOOK SERIES®

**WEST
GROUP**

A THOMSON COMPANY

ST. PAUL, MINN., 2001

American Casebook Series, and the West Group symbol
are registered trademarks used herein under license.

COPYRIGHT © 1978, 1988 By WEST PUBLISHING CO.
COPYRIGHT © 2001 By WEST GROUP
        610 Opperman Drive
        P.O. Box 64526
        St. Paul, MN 55164–0526
        1–800–328–9352

All rights reserved
Printed in the United States of America

ISBN 0–314–24721–1

 TEXT IS PRINTED ON 10% POST CONSUMER RECYCLED PAPER

1st Reprint — 2002

To
Marissa Grace

*"Perfect love sometimes does not
come until grandchildren"*

~Welsh proverb

*

Preface to the Third Edition

This new third edition of *Modern Criminal Law* represents a rather substantial revision of the previous edition. The revision was undertaken in order to provide a casebook with an even richer and more contemporary set of materials, thus permitting examination in greater breadth and depth than before of those issues in the field of criminal law that are of current major importance. Approximately one-third of the principal cases are new and, with rare exception, were decided since publication of the second edition. The notes following the principal cases have been enriched with the discussion of over 180 newer court decisions, as well as with excerpts from about 170 very recent books and law review articles. At the same time, most of the previous material in the notes and questions has been retained because of its continuing value, yet by judicious editing the entire collection of materials still lends itself to coverage within the confines of a single three-hour course.

These additions and deletions, it must be emphasized, have not been undertaken simply to replace previous material with other material, whether cases or secondary authority, of more recent vintage. On the contrary, older materials were retained except when the substituted (and, typically, more recent) item appeared to better serve the objectives of this book (further discussed herein). New cases were added where they exposed and examined new problems, where they reexamined old problems in an interesting new way, or when the problems considered were presented in a more contemporary context, thus making it easier for students to appreciate their exact nature and current importance. New excerpts from books and articles were added so that students could benefit from the illuminating and provocative writings which, collectively, make up a very impressive body of contemporary criminal law scholarship.

In keeping with the Book's title of *Modern Criminal Law*, one major purpose of this revision has been to ensure that students are exposed to those criminal law issues that are on the forefront today or are likely to be in the future. Thus, together with those difficult issues that have been with us for centuries (e.g., when should the law permit one to take another life to save his or her own?), this Book also exposes the student to a host of modern-day questions and practices of some difficulty. Illustrative is this random sampling of a dozen issues of this latter type, which are either relatively "new" or which have taken on much greater importance or meaning in contemporary society: (1) When if ever should criminal liability result from the transmission of AIDS to another party? (2) When if ever should criminal liability be imposed for failure to come to the aid of an endangered stranger? (3) When if ever should homicide or other criminal liability be imposed because of a doctor's termination of an unconscious anencephalic neonate in order to facilitate the harvesting of transplantable organs? (4) When if ever should mothers or expectant mothers be subject to criminal prosecution for prenatal drug abuse resulting in physical harm to the fetus? (5) When if ever should a murder prosecution result in acquittal or conviction of a lesser offense because the conduct causing the death was prompted by a nonviolent homosexual advance by the victim? (6) When if ever should a woman be acquitted for killing her physically abusive husband in order to avoid further physical harm on some future occasion? (7) When technological advances in genetics make it possible to find and identify genes responsible for a person's predisposition to violent behavior, should such a genetic makeup constitute a defense to a criminal prosecution based upon the occurrence of such violence? (8) If a person whose conduct is otherwise a violation of the criminal law establishes that the conduct in question is by custom tolerated within the subculture where it occurred, should that constitute a defense? (9) When and by what means, if ever, should a doctor or friend of a terminally ill person be entitled, upon the purported consent of that person, to end that person's life? (10) When if ever should deception concerning a matter deemed material by the other party be deemed a sufficient basis for conviction of rape should the deception lead to sexual intercourse? (11) Should the "default position" of the criminal law be that sexual intercourse is nonconsensual, so that such intercourse constitutes rape except when there has been an affirmative manifestation of consent by the other party? (12) When if ever should parents be held criminal liable for failure to prevent the offenses committed by their children?

This casebook is intended for use in a basic course on the substantive criminal law, which at most law schools is a required part of the first year curriculum. In selecting, editing, and organizing these materials, I have sought to bring together a collection of cases and secondary sources which will serve what I perceive to be the primary functions of such a course. These are: (1) together with the other first-year courses, to provide training in the case method and techniques of legal analysis; (2) also with the other first year courses, to afford the student with new insights into the fundamental question of how and to what extent the law can be effectively utilized as an instrument of social control; (3) to compare and evaluate the actual and potential contributions of legislatures (through codification), courts (through the common law and by "interpretation" of statutes) and administrators (by certain enforcement policies) in defining and grading crimes; (4) to provide the fundamental information and impart those skills which are the necessary foundation for criminal law practice, either as a prosecutor or defense counsel; (5) to provide an awareness of the inherent difficulties in trying to control antisocial behavior through the criminal law without encroaching upon basic democratic values, an appropriate matter of concern to all members of the legal profession.

This Book does not attempt to cover both substantive criminal law and criminal procedure. This is not to suggest that criminal procedure is unimportant. Rather, the assumption here is that both subjects are important parts of the law school curriculum, and that neither substantive criminal law nor criminal procedure should be shortchanged by compaction into a single course. There has been a growing realization that there is no particular advantage in teaching the two subjects together (any more than, say, combining torts and civil procedure); in recent years more and more schools have chosen to offer them separately.

It is important, however, for the student studying criminal law to have a general understanding of how the criminal process works. Thus, I have included herein textual material on that subject (Chapter 1, Section 1). Also, there are some aspects of substantive criminal law that simply cannot be meaningfully understood unless they are considered together with certain matters which, literally speaking, fall within the realm of criminal procedure. When this is the case, I have included the relevant procedural material.[1] Thus, for example, Chapter 6, dealing with mental disease or defect, treats incompetency to stand trial (which often is a "substitute" for an insanity defense) and various procedural aspects of the insanity defense.

---

1. On the other hand, I have not covered the subject of entrapment in this Book. Though strictly speaking it is a matter of substantive criminal law, it is more meaningfully studied in the context of that part of criminal procedure dealing with restrictions upon police investigative practices.

The reach of the substantive criminal law is constantly expanding, and thus today's law student is much more likely than his counterpart of some years ago to find himself engaged to some extent in the practice of criminal law after graduation. This practice may involve the prosecution of or defense against charges of such familiar crimes as robbery, battery and rape; it may instead or in addition be concerned with the increasing body of regulatory crimes which have been enacted in response to such contemporary concerns as consumer protection and environmental control. An adequate preparation for such practice requires an *understanding* of the fundamental bases of our system of substantive criminal law, rather than *knowledge* of the precise definitions of the growing list of crimes. Consequently the major emphasis in this casebook is upon what is usually referred to as the "general part" of the criminal law: mental state (Chapter 3) and act (Chapter 4); responsibility (Chapters 6 and 7); justification and excuse (Chapter 8); inchoate crimes (Chapters 10 and 11); and liability for the conduct of another (Chapter 12).

It is my belief that imparting detailed information about many different crimes is not the goal of a basic course in criminal law. It is sometimes useful, however, to focus upon certain specific crimes or a category of crimes, which is why three of the twelve chapters in this casebook take such an approach. Chapter 2 looks mainly at cases concerning the so-called "crime against nature"; Chapter 5 has to do with criminal homicide; and Chapter 9 examines the law of rape. In each instance the focus serves to advance inquiry into matters of considerable importance– respectively, the sources and purposes of criminal law; the challenge in drawing meaningful differentiations between related crimes; and the dilemmas confronted in undertaking reform of the substantive criminal law.

Over the years, the so-called "crime against nature" has been the subject of frequent and intense litigation about the meaning of this common law crime, about often-ambiguous statutes replacing or adding to the common law offense, and about the proper role of courts in broadening or elaborating upon either the judicially—or legislatively-created version of the crime. In more recent times, constitutional considerations have often played a part; the due process void-for—vagueness doctrine has been invoked in an effort to have some of these statutes invalidated, and various provisions in the Bill of Rights have been relied upon in an effort to support the claim that the conduct covered by certain "crime against nature" formulations cannot constitutionally be made punishable at all or in a certain degree or manner. As judicial elaborations and legislative reformulations of the "crime against nature" have occurred, there has naturally arisen the additional question of whether either detrimental or beneficial changes in either the definition of the crime or the extent of authorized punishment can or should be applied retroactively. So too, this offense has not infrequently been the object of litigation concerning the respective authority of state, federal and local lawmakers. What all the forgoing issues have in common is that they have to do with the sources and limits of the criminal law, which is why Chapter 2, aimed at those problems, relies mainly upon the "crime against nature" offense category in dealing with this array of problems.

With regard to Chapter 5, focusing upon criminal homicide, the rationale here is that it is important for students of the criminal law to consider not only the question of what conduct should be made criminal, but also the question of how various forms of criminal conduct should be classified into separate crimes so as to reflect their respective seriousness. Although this problem of classification arises in a great many areas of the criminal law, undoubtedly the courts and legislatures have experienced the greatest difficulty in articulating intelligent classifications in the area of homicide. Moreover, study of homicide provides a useful background to consideration of certain doctrines which come into play almost exclusively in a homicide context (e.g., the insanity defense) or which raise the most difficult issues in that context (e.g., the defenses of duress or self-defense).

In order to demonstrate some of the difficulties encountered in efforts at reform of the criminal law, Chapter 9 looks at the crime of rape, the focus of a great many reform efforts in the last decade or more. Both feminists and other law reformers have raised serious questions about the traditional substantive and procedural law on the subject of rape; they have complained that this body of law (a) reflects perspectives about the crime which have no contemporary legitimacy, and (b) contributes to low rates of arrest, prosecution and conviction for this offense. Much useful reform has occurred on the procedural side, and some has also occurred with respect to the substantive law of rape as well, although the changes there tend to be more controversial. The question of just how the substantive law of rape ought to be stated remains a live topic in many jurisdictions. Chapter 6, using highly controversial principal cases enriched with a great many excerpts from critical commentary, mostly from just the past few years, takes a look at the three areas of major continuing conflict: (i) what nature and degree of imposition–force, other coercion, fraud, or what–should suffice? (ii) when should either consent or nonconsent be presumed, and in other cases what should be taken to constitute a sufficient manifestation of nonconsent? (iii) what mental state, if any, should be required for the crime, especially with respect to a defendant's mistaken belief in consent?

In Chapter 9 as well as elsewhere in this Book, I have attempted to place special emphasis upon the actual and potential contributions of the legislative branch in resolving the difficult policy questions which exist in the field of criminal law. (The matter is first confronted in Chapter 2, but is a recurring theme in the rest of the Book as well.) This emphasis takes proper account of the contributions which legislatures have made to the criminal law in recent years; a total of thirty- eight states have adopted new substantive criminal law codes.[2] Moreover, this emphasis aids in presenting the first-year student, often preoccupied with the common law in his other courses, with a more balanced picture of our legal system. Thus, while it is my belief that this Book is readily adaptable to a wide range of teaching styles, it is especially suited to those professor who have found it useful to require their students to work intensively with the Model Penal Code (major portions of which appear in the Appendix) and/or with the code of some particular jurisdiction.[3]

Although the subject of criminal law has not been "constitutionalized" to the same extent as criminal procedure, it is fair to say that there is some degree of overlap between the law school subjects of constitutional law and substantive criminal law. This gives rise to the very difficult question of how much constitutional law to include in a first-year criminal law course, which the authors of extant casebooks have resolved in quite different ways. It is my judgment that the constitutional limits on the substantive criminal law cannot be ignored in a criminal law course, for without some appreciation of those limitations the student cannot evaluate in a meaningful way alternative legislative proposals for dealing with various issues. On the other hand, it is hardly appropriate to subsume most of constitutional law into the criminal law offering, if for no other reason than that the beginning law student would probably be overwhelmed as a consequence. I have attempted to strike a fair balance. As noted earlier, I have in Chapter 2 focused on "crimes against nature" in inquir-

---

2. Efforts directed toward similar reform have been undertaken but have faltered in some other states and on the federal level.

3. I have not infrequently required my students to have and work with the Illinois Criminal Code, not because I want them to learn the specifics of the law in this state, but rather because I want to give them some experience in working closely with a *real* criminal code. (The Illinois code, like that in many of the states that have accomplished a complete recodification, has been heavily influenced by the Model Penal Code, but has over the years taken on considerable additional baggage as a result of frequent legislative revision.) Examination of such a warts-and-all code, I have found, presents the students with an experience closer to real life than exclusive examination of the Model Penal Code.

ing into the constitutional limits of penal legislation. Beyond this, I have included a few Supreme Court decisions (e.g., *Powell v. Texas; Montana v. Egelhoff*) that raise very basic issues about the permissible reach of the substantive criminal law.[4]

The introductory chapter concludes with an inquiry into the purposes of the criminal law and, in particular, the considerations which ought to bear upon the imposition of a criminal sentence. This is done by a close examination of the sentencing decision in a pre-Sentencing Guidelines case by a federal judge who had theretofore written thoughtfully about the subject; the case is then revisited in light of procedures required under the Guidelines, and then capped off by some very recent and sharp differences of opinion by other federal judges on the respective merits of Guidelines and pre-Guidelines sentencing law. Some sentencing issues are occasionally raised later in the Book, but in the main the matter of sentencing–or, indeed, the broader subject of corrections–is not given major emphasis in this Book. This reflects the fact that the law of corrections has developed to the point where at many law schools it has become the basis of a separate course.[5] Where such an offering is not available, an expanded treatment of corrections within the context of these materials can be readily achieved by examination of relevant parts of the Model Penal Code or some state penal or corrections code.

In selecting the major cases which appear in this Book, I have included those which, in my judgment, are most likely to stimulate an interesting and profitable classroom dialogue. That is, inclusion of a particular case does not necessarily rest upon the conclusion that it was rightly decided or that the court's analysis was in all respects sound, but rather is grounded in the belief that the facts or the analysis or both provide a useful vehicle for classroom discussion.[6] The book is intended as a teaching too, not a research tool, and thus the primary objective throughout has been to provide the teacher and student with a common source of material upon which they may interact in the classroom. As for the notes and questions following the principal cases, their purpose is not to upstage the teacher, but rather to direct the student's thoughts down certain avenues prior to class so that the class time may be utilized more effectively and efficiently. Sometimes this supplementary material will summarize another case either reflecting a somewhat different approach or point of view or presenting a somewhat different fact situation for "testing" the doctrines accepted in the principal cases.[7] On many occasions the supplementary material consists of excerpts from illuminating or provocative writings in the law reviews, which either elaborate upon the doctrines of the principal case or present a different perspective on the matters at issue. Here again, there has been no attempt to select only excerpts that completely square with my own thinking about the topics under discussion.

4. One important constitutional limitation unique to criminal law is the requirement that the prosecution prove the defendant's guilt beyond a reasonable doubt. Consequently, I have given attention at several points in these materials to the constitutionality of putting some proof burdens on the defendant (i.e., the impact of *Mullaney v. Wilbur* and its progeny) or of "lightening" the prosecutor's burden by resort to inferences and presumptions (i.e., the impact of *Barnes v. United States* and related cases). However, a professor who feels that these matters should be reserved until later in the student's legal education will find it easy to omit the aforementioned cases and the few others of the same character without interrupting the flow of the remaining material.

5. Teaching materials on the subject are available. See, e.g., Lynn S. Branham, & Sheldon Krantz, *The*

Law of Sentencing, Corrections, and Prisoners' Rights (5th ed.1997).

6. I have been less than successful over the years in convincing even my own students that this is the case, for some of them view a casebook as some collection of ultimate truths. Indeed, I've had difficulties of this kind with some professors as well!

7. Not infrequently, there will be an inquiry as to what the result should be on the facts stated, followed by or footnoted with a citation to the case containing those or similar facts. This is not intended to suggest that it is either necessary or desirable that the student consult the cited case in preparing for class. An evaluation of the fact situation provided should be possible on the basis of the immediately preceding material in this Book.

Students desiring to do additional reading on the subject may wish to consult other sources. Many materials written specifically for students are available; I would mention here Wayne R. LaFave, *Criminal Law* (3rd ed.2000), a 1046-page hardcover text with considerable footnoting, which understandably matches up most closely with the coverage of this casebook; Joshua Dressler, *Understanding Criminal Law* (2d ed.1995), a 556-page paperback text with limited footnoting; Arnold H. Loewy, *Criminal Law in a Nutshell* (3d ed.2000), a 329-page paperback; and Paul H. Robinson, *Criminal Law* (1997), an 853-page hardcover text with footnotes. Also very useful are the many outstanding articles on a variety of substantive criminal law topics appearing in the four-volume *Encyclopedia of Crime and Justice* (1983). On the question of how the problems discussed herein may best be dealt with through recodification, a primary source is the updated *Model Penal Code and Commentaries* published by the American Law Institute commencing in1980 and ending in 1985.

Case citations in opinions and footnotes of the courts and commentators have been omitted without so specifying. Numbered footnotes are from the original materials; my footnotes are lettered.

I wish to extend my thanks to the many users of the second edition of this Book who provided helpful advice and suggestions; to the many copyright holders who graciously permitted me to include herein excerpts from various works (see list of Acknowledgments on pages following); to Dean Thomas Mengler and others at the College of Law, University of Illinois, for continuing support of my research endeavors; and to my wife Loretta, without whose ongoing support and encouragement I would not have completed this Book (or, for that matter, much of anything else), and who would have this Book dedicate to her but for the fact that I have chosen a much younger lady to whom we are both devoted.

WAYNE R. LaFAVE

January, 2001

Acknowledgments

I am especially grateful to THE AMERICAN LAW INSTITUTE for permission to include as an Appendix the *Model Penal Code*, copyright 1985 by The American Law Institute, and to include portions of the updated Commentary, copyright 1980 and 1985, reprinted with permission of the American Law Institute. I am also grateful to the following for permission to reproduce extracts from the works indicated:

ALBANY LAW REVIEW: Steven Belenko, *The Challenges of Integrating Drug Treatment Into the Criminal Justice Process*, 63 Alb.L.Rev. 833 (2000).

AMERICAN BAR ASSOCIATION JOURNAL: George Goldberg, *Misprision of Felony: An Old Concept in a New Context*, 52 A.B.A.J. 148 (1966); Herbert Wechsler, *The American Law Institute: Some Observations on Its Model Penal Code*, 42 A.B.A.J. 321 (1956).

AMERICAN BAR FOUNDATION: Samuel J. Brakel et al., *The Mentally Disabled and the Law* (3d ed.1985); Arnold Enker, *Mens Rea and Criminal Attempt*, 1977 A.B.F.Res.J. 845; Arthur A. Matthews, *Mental Disability and the Criminal Law* (1970).

AMERICAN CRIMINAL LAW REVIEW: Ronald Allen & Lee Ann DeGrazia, *The Constitutional Requirement of Proof Beyond a Reasonable Doubt in Criminal Cases*, 20 Am.Crim.L.Rev. 1 (1982); Stephen Saltzburg, *Burdens of Persuasion in Criminal Cases: Harmonizing the Views of the Justices*, 20 Am.Crim.L.Rev. 393 (1983).

AMERICAN JOURNAL OF CRIMINAL LAW: David M. Treiman, *Recklessness and the Model Penal Code*, 9 Am.J.Crim.L. 281 (1981); David Robinson, Jr., *Powell v. Texas: The Case of the Intoxicated Shoeshine Man–Some Reflections a Generation Later by a Participant*, 26 Am.J.Crim.L. 401 (1999).

AMERICAN JOURNAL OF TRIAL ADVOCACY: Note, 20 Am.J.Trial Advoc. 381 (1997).

ARIZONA LAW REVIEW: David L. Faigman & Amy J. Wright, *The Battered Woman Syndrome in the Age of Science*, 39 Ariz.L.Rev. 67 (1997), copyright © 1997 by the Arizona Board of Regents; reprinted by permission.

THE BOBBS-MERRILL COMPANY: Jerome Hall, *General Principles of Criminal Law* (2d ed.1960); Roy Moreland, *Law of Homicide* (1952).

BRIGHAM YOUNG UNIVERSITY LAW REVIEW: Stanislaw Pomorski, *On Multiculturism, Concepts of Crime, and the "De Minimis" Defense*, 1997 B.Y.U.L.Rev. 51.

BROOKLYN LAW REVIEW: Patricia J. Falk, *Rape by Fraud and Rape by Coercion*, 64 Brook.L.Rev. 39 (1998).

BUFFALO CRIMINAL LAW REVIEW: Vivian Berger, *Rape Law Reform at the Millenium*, 3 Buff.Crim.L.Rev. 513 (2000); David P. Bryden, *Redefining Rape*, 3 Buff.Crim.L.Rev. 317 (2000); Alan Wertheimer, *What is Consent? And is It Important?*, 3 Buff.Crim.L.Rev. 557 (2000).

BUTTERWORTHS: K.J.M. Smith, *A Case of Reckless Murder*, 123 New L.J. 792 (1973); G.R. Sullivan, *Self Induced and Recurring Automatism*, 123 New.L.J. 1093 (1973).

PROF. NAOMI CAHN: Naomi R. Cahn, *Pragmatic Questions About Parental Liability Statutes*, 1996 Wis.L.Rev. 399.

CALIFORNIA LAW REVIEW: Larry Alexander, *Insufficient Concern: A Unified Conception of Criminal Culpability*, 88 Calif.L.Rev. 931 (2000); Anne E. Coughlin, *Excusing Women*,

82 Calif.L.Rev. 1 (1994); Meir Dan-Cohen, *Basic Values and the Victim's State of Mind*, 88 Calif.L.Rev. 759 (2000); Joshua Dressler, *Does One Mens Rea Fit All? Thoughts on Alexander's Unified Conception of Criminal Culpability*, 88 Calif.L.Rev. 955 (2000); Kent Greenawalt, *Dignity and Victimhood*, 88 Calif.L.Rev. 779 (2000); Phillip E. Johnson, *The Unnecessary Crime of Conspiracy*, 61 Calif.L.Rev. 1137 (1973); Sanford H. Kadish, *Fifty Years of Criminal Law: An Opinionated Review*, 87 Calif.L.Rev. 943 (1999), © 2000, 1999, 1994 and 1973 by California Law Review, Inc., reprinted by permission.

CLEVELAND STATE LAW REVIEW: Joshua Dressler, *Where We Have Been, and Where We Might be Going: Some Cautionary Reflections on Rape Law Reform*, 46 Clev.St.L.Rev. 409 (1998).

COLUMBIA LAW REVIEW: Francis B. Sayre, *Public Welfare Offenses*, 33 Colum.L.Rev. 55 (1933); Notes, 93 Colum.L.Rev. 1223 (1993); 86 Colum.L.Rev. 348 (1986); 75 Colum.L.Rev. 1517 (1975); 75 Colum.L.Rev. 1122 (1975); 47 Colum.L.Rev. 1332 (1947).

CORNELL LAW REVIEW: Nelson E. Roth & Scott E. Sundby, *The Felony-Murder Rule: A Doctrine at Constitutional Crossroads*, 70 Cornell L.Rev. 446 (1985).

CRIMINAL LAW FORUM: James J. Gobert, *The Fortuity of Consequence*, 4 Crim.L.F. 1 (1993),

CUMBERLAND LAW REVIEW: Comment, 27 Cumb.L.Rev. 1279, 1281-83 (1997).

DEPAUL LAW REVIEW: Dierdre A. Burgman, *Unilateral Conspiracy: Three Critical Perspectives*, 29 DePaul L.Rev. 75 (1979).

DUKE UNIVERESITY SCHOOL OF LAW: Christopher H. Schroeder, *Two Methods for Evaluating Duty to Rescue Proposals*, 49 Law & Contemp.Probs 181 (1986); Kent Greenawalt, *Distinguishing Justifications from Excuses*, 49 Law & Contemp.Probs. 89 (1986).

EMORY LAW JOURNAL: Donald A. Dripps, *Bowers v. Hardwick and the Law of Standing: Noncases Make Bad Law*, 44 Emory L.J. 1417 (1995).

FOOD DRUG COSMETIC LAW JOURNAL: Marsha Cohen, *Enforcement Under the Food, Drug and Cosmetic Act*, 30 Food Drug Cosmetic L.J. 5 (1975).

FORDHAM LAW REVIEW: Christopher Slobogin & Amy Mashburn, *The Criminal Defense Lawyer's Fiduciary Duty to Clients with Mental Disability*, 68 Fordham L.Rev. 1641 (2000); Comment, 45 Fordham L.Rev. 553 (1976); Note, 66 Fordham L.Rev. 1029 (1997).

GEORGETOWN LAW JOURNAL: Notes, 87 Geo.L.J. 2431 (1999); 87 Geo.L.J. 139 (1998); 60 Geo.L.J. 667 (1972).

HARCOURT BRACE JOVANOVICH, INC: Benjamin Cardozo, *Law and Literature* (1931).

HARVARD CIVIL RIGHTS-CIVIL LIBERTIES LAW REVIEW: Christopher R. Leslie, *Creating Criminals: The Injuries Inflicted by "Unenforced" Sodomy Laws*, 35 Harv.C.R.-C.L.L.Rev. 103 (2000), © 2000 by the President and Fellows of Harvard College and the Harvard Civil Rights Civil Liberties Law Review.

HARVARD LAW REVIEW: Dan M. Kahan, *Is Chevron Relevant to Federal Criminal Law?*, 110 Harv.L.Rev. 469 (1996); James M. Landis, *A Note on "Statutory Interpretation,"* 43 Harv.L.Rev. 886 (1930); Alan C. Michaels, *Constitutional Innocence*, 112 Harv.L.Rev. 828 (1999); *Developments in the Law–Criminal Conspiracy*, 72 Harv.L.Rev. 920 (1968); *Developments–Sexual Orientation and the Law*, 102 Harv.L.Rev. 1508 (1989), copyright © 1930, 1968, 1989, 1996, and 1999 by the Harvard Law Review Association.

HILL AND WANG (NOW A DIVISION OF FARRAR, STRAUS & GIROUX, INC.): Marvin E. Frankel, *Criminal Sentences* (1972), copyright © 1972, 1973 by Marvin E. Frankel.

INDIANA LAW REVIEW: Daniel R. Karon, *Winning Isn't Everything, It's the Only Thing: Violence in Professional Sports: The Need for Federal Regulation and Criminal Sanctions*, 25 Ind.L.Rev. 147 (1991).

JOURNAL OF APPELLATE PRACTICE AND PROCESS: Brent E. Newton, *The Antiquated "Slight Evidence Rule" in Federal Conspiracy Cases*, 1 J.App.Prac. & Process 49 (1999).

JOURNAL OF CRIMINAL LAW AND CRIMINOLOGY: Ronald J.Allen, *Montana v. Egelhoff–Reflections on the Limits of Legislative Imagination and Judicial Authority*, 87 J.Crim.L. & Crimin. 633 (1997); Douglas N. Husak, *Justifications and the Criminal Liability of Accessories*, 80 J.Crim.L. & Criminology 491 (1989); Sanford H. Kadish, *Reckless Complicity*, 87 J.Crim.L. & Criminology 369 (1997); Yale Kamisar, *Physician Assisted Suicide: The Problems Presented by the Compelling, Heartwrenching Case*, 88 J.Crim.L.& Criminology 1121 (1998); Ira Robbins, *The Ostrich Instruction: Deliberate Ignorance as a Criminal Mens Rea*, 81 J.Crim.L. & Criminology 191 (1990), all reprinted by special permission of Northwestern University School of Law, Journal of Criminal Law and Criminology.

JOURNAL OF TRANSNATIONAL LAW & POLICY: Alan Reed, *Duress and Provocation as Excuses to Murder: Salutary Lessons from Recent Anglo-American Jurisprudence*, 6 J.Trans.L.& Pol'y 51 (1996).

KANSAS LAW REVIEW: Note, Kan.L.Rev. 272 (1974).

KENTUCKY LAW JOURNAL: Roy Moreland, *A Reexamination of the Law of Homicide in 1971: the Model Penal Code*, 59 Ky.L.J. 788 (1971).

MACMILLAN REFERENCE USA: Geoffrey C. Hazard, Jr., *Criminal Justice System*, in 2 Encyclopedia of Crime and Justice 450 (1983).

PROF. PAUL MARCUS: Paul Marcus, *Criminal Conspiracy: The State of Mind Crime*, 1976 U.Ill.L.F. 627.

MCGEORGE LAW REVIEW: J. Cross Creason, *Eliminating the Use of Civil Compromise in Cases of Domestic Violence, Elder Abuse, and Child Abuse*, 29 McGeorge L.Rev. 641 (1998).

MICHIGAN LAW REVIEW: Dan M. Kahan, *Ignorance of the Law is an Excuse–But Only for the Virtuous*, 96 Mich.L.Rev. 127 (1997).

MINNESOTA LAW REVIEW: Beverly Balos & Mary Louise Fellows, *Guilty of the Crime of Trust: Nonstranger Rape*, 75 Minn.L.Rev. 599 (1991); Arnold Enker, *Impossibility in Criminal Attempts–Legality and the Legal Process*, 53 Minn.L.Rev. 665 (1969).

MODERN LAW REVIEW: Alec Samuels, *Excusable Loss of Self-Control in Homicide*, 34 Mod.L.Rev. 163 (1971).

NATIONAL LAW JOURNAL: Austin Wehrwein, *'Samaritan' Law Poses Difficulties*, Nat'l L.J., Aug. 22, 19083.

NEBRASKA LAW REVIEW: Frederick J. Ludwig, *Responsibility for Young Offenders*, 29 Neb.L.Rev. 521 (1950).

THE NEW YORK TIMES: Editorial, June 18, 1976; Articles, June 17, June 19, July 3, Sept. 2, Sept. 15, Sept. 17, 1976, copyright © by The New York Times Company.

NEW YORK UNIVERSITY REVIEW OF LAW AND SOCIAL CHANGE: Richard Uviller, *Seizure by Gunshot: the Riddle of the Fleeing Felon*, 14 N.Y.U.Rev.L. & Soc.Chg. 705 (1986) .

NORTH CAROLINA LAW REVIEW: Richard A. Rosen, *Self-Defense, Imminence, and Women Who Kill Their Batterers*, 71 N.C.L.Rev. 371 (1993).

NORTHERN ILLINOIS UNIVERSITY LAW REVIEW: Comment, 20 No.Ill.U.L. Rev. 219 (2000)

NORTHWESTERN UNIVERSITY LAW REVIEW: Kate Stith & Jose A. Cabranes, *Judging Under the Federal Sentencing Guidelines*, 91 Nw.U.L.Rev. 1247 (1997), reprinted by special permission of Northwestern University School of Law.

NOTRE DAME LAW REVIEW: Recent Decision, 59 Notre Dame L.Rev. 253 (1983).

PROF. IRA ROBBINS: Ira P. Robbins, *Double Inchoate Crimes*, 26 Harv.J.Legis. 1 (1989).

ROGER WILLIAMS UNIVERSITY LAW REVIEW: Harold J. Krent, *Should Bouie v. Buoyed?: Judicial Retroactive Lawmaking and the Ex Post Facto Clause*, 3 Roger Williams U.L.Rev. 35 (1997).

RUTGERS LAW JOURNAL: Note, 21 Rutgers L.J. 669 (1990).

SOUTHERN CALIFORNIA LAW REVIEW: Joshua Dressler, *Exegesis of the Law of Duress: Justifying the Excuse and Searching for its Proper Limits*, 62 So.Cal.L.Rev. 1331 (1989), reprinted with the permission of the Southern California Law Review.

STANFORD LAW REVIEW: Mark Kelman, *Interpretive Construction in the Substantive Criminal Law*, 33 Stan.L.Rev. 591 (1981); Robert Misner, *The New Attempt Laws: Unsuspected Threat to the Fourth Amendment*, 33 Stan.L.Rev. 201 (1981), copyright 1981 by the Board of Trustees of the Leland Stanford Junior University.

ST. JOHN'S LAW REVIEW: Elizabeth Holtzman, *Premenstrual Symptoms: No Legal Defense*, 60 St.John's L.Rev. 712 (1986).

ST. LOUIS UNIVERSITY LAW JOURNAL: Frank O. Bowman, *Fear of Law: Thoughts on Fear of Judging and the State of the Federal Sentencing Guidelines*, 44 St.Louis U.L.J. 299 (2000).

SUPREME COURT REVIEW: Dan M. Kahan, *Lenity and Federal Common Law Crimes*, 1994 Sup.Ct.Rev. 345; Larry Alexander, *The Supreme Court, Dr. Jekyll, and the Due Process of Proof*, 1996 Sup.Ct.Rev. 191, copyright by the University of Chicago Press.

SWEET & MAXWELL, LTD.: Glanville Williams, *Criminal Law-The General Part* (2d ed.1961); Richard Buxton, *Incitement and Attempt*, 1973 Crim.L.Rev. 656; D.W. Elliott, *Offences Against the Person–Murder*, 1977 Crim.L.Rev. 70; Donald Stuart, *The Actus Reus in Attempts*, 1970 Crim.L.Rev. 505.

TEMPLE LAW REVIEW: Daniel G. Moriarty, *Extending the Defense of Renunciation*, 62 Temple L.Rev. 1 (1989).

TEXAS JOURNAL OF WOMEN AND THE LAW: Nancy Kubasek, *The Case Against Prosecutions for Prenatal Drug Abuse*, 8 Tex.J.Women & L. 167 (1999), © Texas Journal of Women and the Law, 1999.

UNIVERSITY OF CALIFORNIA DAVIS LAW REVIEW: Grant H. Morris & Reid Meloy, *Out of Mind? Out of Sight: The Uncivil Commitment of Permanently Incompetent Criminal Defendants*, 27 U.C. Davis L.Rev. 1 (1993), copyright 1993 by The Regents of the University of California; reprinted with permission.

THE UNIVERSITY OF CHICAGO PRESS: Herbert Packer, *Mens Rea and the Supreme Court*, 1962 Sup.Ct.Rev. 107, copyright © 1962 by The University of Chicago.

UNIVERSITY OF CHICAGO LAW REVIEW: Robert A. Burt & Norval Morris, *A Proposal for the Abolition of the Incompetency Plea*, 40 U.Chi.L.Rev. 66 (1972); Edward H. Levi, *An*

Introduction to Legal Reasoning, 15 U.Chi.L.Rev. 501 (1948); Dan M. Kahan, *Gentle Nudges vs. Hard Shoves: Solving the Sticky Norms Problem*, 67 U.Chi.L.Rev. 607 (2000).

U.C.L.A. Law Review and Fred B. Rothman & Co.: Norman Abrams, *Criminal Liability of Corporate Officers for Strict Liability Offenses–A Comment on Dotterweich and Park*, 28 U.C.L.A.L.Rev. 463 (1981); Comments, 33 U.C.L.A.L.Rev. 1679 (1986).

University of Illinois Law Review: Richard Epstein, *Living Dangerously: A Defense of Mortal Peril*, 1998 U.Ill.L.Rev. 909; William N. Eskridge, *Hardwick and Historiography*, 1999 U.Ill.L.Rev. 631; David Orentlicher, *The Alleged Distinction Between Euthanasia and the Withdrawal of Life-Sustaining Treatment: Conceptually Incoherent and Impossible to Maintain*, 1998 U.Ill.L.LRev. 837; Monrad Paulsen, *Intoxication as a Defense to Crime*, 1961 U.Ill.L.F. 1; Frank J. Remington & Victor G. Rosenblum, *The Criminal Law and the Legislative Process,* 1960 U.Ill.L.F. 481.

University of Pennsylvania Law Review: Leo Katz, *Proximate Cause in Michael Moore's Act and Crime*, 142 U.Pa.L.Rev. 1513 (1994); Stephen J. Schulhofer, *The Feminist Challenge in Criminal Law,* 143 U.Pa.L.Rev. 2151 (1995); Comments, 143 U.Pa.L.Rev. 2251 (1995); 121 U.Pa.L.Rev. 120 (1972); Notes, 109 U.Pa.L.Rev. 67 (1960); 106 U.Pa.L.Rev. 1021 (1958).

University of Pittsburgh Law Review: Robert A. Skilton, *The Requsite Act in a Criminal Attempt*, 3 U.Pitt.L.Rev. 308 (1937).

Virginia Environmental Law Journal: Note, 14 Va.Envtl.L.J. 151 (1994).

Virginia Journal of Social Policy & the Law: Robert Batey, *Vagueness and the Construction of Criminal Statutes–Balancing Acts*, 5 Va.J.Soc.Pol.& L. 1 (1997); Heidi Kitrosser, *Meaningful Consent: Toward New Generation of Statutory Rape Laws*, 4 Va.J.Soc.Pol'y & L. 287 (1997).

Virginia Law Review: P. Browning Hoffman & Robert C. Dunn, *Beyond Rouse and Wyatt: An Administrative Law Model for Expanding and Implementing the Mental Patient's Right to Treatment*, 161 Va.L.Rev. 297 (1975); John Calvin, Jeffries, *Legality, Vagueness, and the Construction of Penal Statutes*, 71 Va.L.Rev. 189 (1985); Charles H. Whitebread and Ronald Stevens, *Constructive Possession in Narcotics Cases; To Have and Have Not*, 58 Va.L.Rev. 751 (1972); Note, 72 Va.L.Rev. 619 (1986).

Warren, Gorham & Lamont: Donald T. Lunde & Thomas E. Wilson, *Brainwashing as a Defense to Criminal Liability: Patty Hearst Revisited*, 13 Crim.L.Bull. 341 (1977).

Washington Law Review Association: Notes, 52 Wash.L.Rev. 142 (1976).

Willamette Law Review: Robert Misner, *Minimalism, Desuetude, and Fornication*, 35 Willamette L.Rev. 1 (1999)

William and Mary Bill of Rights Journal: Paul Marcus, *Criminal Conspiracy Law: Time to Turn Back From an Ever Expanding, Ever More Troubling Area*, 1 Wm. & Mary Bill Rts. J. 1 (1992).

William and Mary Law Review: Note, 26 Wm. & Mary L.Rev. 645 (1985).

Wisconsin Law Review: Frank J. Remington & Orrin L. Helstad, *The Mental Element in Crime–A Legislative Problem*, 1952 Wis.L.Rev. 644; Comment, 1956 Wis.L.Rev. 641, copyright by the University of Wisconsin.

John Wright & Sons, Ltd.: D. O'Connor, *The Voluntary Act*, 15 Med.Sci. Law 31 (1975)

YALE LAW JOURNAL: Susan Estrich, *Teaching Rape Law*, 102 Yale L.J. 509 (1992); Susan Estrich, *Rape*, 95 Yale L.J. 1087 (1986); Herbert Fingarette, *Addiction and Criminal Responsibility*, 84 Yale. L.J. (1975); Abraham Goldstein, *Conspiracy to Defraud the United States*, 68 Yale L.J. 405 (1959); Graham Hughes, *Criminal Omissions*, 67 Yale L.J. 590 (1958); Notes, 101 Yale L.J. 919 (1992); 70 Yale L.J. 916 (1958), reprinted by permission of The Yale Law Journal Company and William S. Hein Company from The Yale Law Journal.

YALE UNIVERSITY PRESS: Abraham Goldstein, *The Insanity Defense* (1967).

Summary of Contents

CHAPTER 12.   PARTIES; LIABILITY FOR THE CONDUCT OF ANOTHER

*

Table of Contents

*[Principal cases and extracts from secondary authorities listed to the left;
cases and extracts quoted or discussed in Notes listed to the right;
titles of secondary authorities sometimes shortened]*

Page

CHAPTER 4. THE ACT REQUIREMENT

CHAPTER 8. JUSTIFICATION AND EXCUSE

*

Table of Cases

The principal cases are in bold type. Cases cited or discussed in the text are roman type. References are to pages. Cases cited in principal cases and within other quoted materials are not included.

*

Table of Other Authorities

References are to pages. Except with respect to the Model Penal Code, authorities cited in principal cases or within other quoted materials are not included.

Books

Brakel, Samuel J., John Parry & Barbara A. Weiner, *The Mentally Disabled and the Law* (3d ed.1985), 378, 412, 425, 434

Burdick, William L., *The Law of Crime* (1946), 619

Cardozo, Benjamin, *Law and Literature and Others Essays and Addresses* (1931), 297

Dalton, Katherina, *Once a Month* (1983), 226

Estrich, Susan, *Real Rape* (1987), 585

Frankel, Marvin E., *Criminal Sentences* (1973), 18

Goldstein, Abraham, *The Insanity Defense* (1967), 427

Hall, Jerome, *General Principles of Criminal Law* (2d ed.1960), 358

LaFave, Wayne R., *Criminal Law* (3d ed.2000), 639, 642

LaFave, Wayne R., Jerold H. Israel & Nancy J. King, *Criminal Procedure* (3d ed.2000), 2

Llewellyn, Karl, *The Common Law Tradition* (1960), 53

Matthews, Arthur R., *Mental Disability and the Criminal Law* (1970), 379, 413, 420

Moore, Michael S., *Act and Crime: The Philosophy of Action and Its Implications for Criminal Law* (1993), 220

Morris, Norval, & Gordon Hawkins, *The Honest Politician's Guide to Crime Control* (1970), 412

Schulhofer, Stephen J., *Unwanted Sex: The Culture of Intimidation and the Failure of Law* (1998), 585

Smith, John C., & Brian Hogan, *Criminal Law* (1965), 654

Articles

Abrams, Norman, *Criminal Liability of Corporate Officers for Strict Liability Offenses—A Comment on Dotterweich and Park*, 28 U.C.L.A.L.Rev. 463 (1981), 884

Alexander, Larry, & Kimberly D. Kessler, *Mens Rea and Inchoate Crimes*, 87 J.Crim.L. & Criminology 1138 (1997), 658

Alexander, Larry, *Insufficient Concern: A Unified Conception of Criminal Culpability*, 88 Calif.L.Rev. 931 (2000), 165, 173

Alexander, Larry, *The Supreme Court, Dr. Jekyll, and the Due Process of Proof*, 1996 Sup.Ct.Rev. 191, p. 475

Allen, Ronald J., & Lee Ann DeGrazia, *The Constitutional Requirement of Proof Beyond a Reasonable Doubt in Criminal Cases: A Comment Upon Incipient Chaos in the Lower Courts*, 20 Am.Crim.L.Rev. 1 (1982), 139, 243

Allen, Ronald J., *Montana v. Egelhoff—Reflections on the Limits of Legislative Imagination and Judicial Authority*, 87 J.Crim.L. & Criminology 633 (1997), 475

Althouse, Ann, *The Lying Woman, the Devious Prostitute, and Other Stories From the Evidence Casebook*, 88 Nw.U.L.Rev. 914 (1994), 636

Anderson, Michelle J., *Reviving Resistance in Rape Law*, 1998 U.Ill.L.Rev. 953, p. 613

Ashworth, A. J., *Self-Defence and the Right to Life*, 34 Camb.L.J. 282 (1975), 500

Backman, Ronet, & Raymond Paternoster, *A Contemporary Look at the Effects of Rape Law Reform: How Far Have We Really Come?*, 84 J.Crim.L. & Criminology 554 (1993), 584

Balos, Beverly & Mary Louise Fellows, *Guilty of the Crime of Trust: Nonstranger Rape*, 75 Minn.L.Rev. 599, 609 (1991), 590, 618

Batey, Robert, *Vagueness and the Construction of Criminal Statutes—Balancing Acts*, 5 Va.J.Soc.Pol. & L. 1 (1997), 77

Student–Authored Works

Newspapers

Model Penal Code
[To locate full text of a specific section, see Table of Contents at the beginning of the Appendix]

*

MODERN
CRIMINAL LAW
CASES, COMMENTS AND QUESTIONS
Third Edition

*

Chapter 1

PROCESS AND PURPOSES

This course has to do with the *substantive* criminal law. Substantive criminal law consists of that body of law which declares what conduct is criminal and prescribes the punishment to be imposed for such conduct.

This field of law includes not only the definition of specific offenses (e.g., murder, robbery, rape), but also a good many general principles of liability. Those general principles, which receive primary emphasis in this Book, are of two types. One, represented by the principles that an insane person cannot be guilty of a crime, or that one coerced into committing what would otherwise be criminal conduct cannot be guilty of most crimes, has to do with *defenses to liability*. The second concerns principles of the *affirmative liability* sort—for example, those having to do with accomplice liability (who, other than the person who pulled the trigger, may be convicted of a murder?) or with the "inchoate crimes" of attempt, conspiracy and solicitation.

The criminal justice process consists of that series of procedures through which the substantive criminal law is enforced. In the typical law school curriculum, that process is the subject of intense study in one or more courses often labeled *criminal procedure*. It is important, however, that students commencing their study of substantive criminal law have at least a general appreciation of how the criminal justice process is structured and how it operates. One of the objectives of this Chapter is to provide a general overview of the steps in the criminal justice process.[a]

Broadly stated, the purpose of the substantive criminal law and of the criminal justice process is to prevent people from doing what society considers to be undesirable. But, exactly how does the criminal law, with its threat of punishment to violators, operate to influence human conduct away from the undesirable and toward the desirable? There are a number of theories of punishment, and each theory has or has had its enthusiastic adherents. The choice of one theory over the others can have a profound effect upon one's view of what the sentence should be in a particular case, and also as to exactly how the sentencing step in the criminal justice process should be structured. These matters are considered in Section 2 of this Chapter.

a. There is, of course, no single criminal justice system in this country. The United States consists of 51 jurisdictions (federal, plus the individual states), and thus it is fair to say that there are many systems which are quite similar but yet have individual uniqueness. Because that is so and because the description which follows is necessarily brief, some degree of overgeneralization is inevitable. The reader is forewarned.

1

SECTION 1. THE CRIMINAL JUSTICE PROCESS[b]

This section describes the major steps taken in the processing of a criminal case. The focus is on the processing of a "typical case" in a "typical jurisdiction" (i.e., those procedures employed by most states in processing most of their criminal cases). The processing of both felony and misdemeanor cases is covered, but primary concentration is upon felony cases.[c]

Step 1. The Report of the Crime. The criminal justice process usually starts with the event that brings to the attention of the police the possible commission of a crime, for that event commonly triggers the administrative steps that may lead to the eventual enforcement of the criminal law against the offender. It has been estimated that of all the crimes committed, substantially less than half are brought to the attention of the police.

Police learn about crimes from reports of citizens (usually victims), discovery in the field (usually observation on patrol), or from investigative and intelligence work. Where the police conclude a crime may well have been committed, it will be recorded as a "known offense." The longstanding tradition of police departments is to devote the vast bulk of their investigative efforts to solving "known offenses" and to at least initially attempt to investigate the vast majority of such offenses. Accordingly, the distribution of "known offenses" provides a fairly accurate general picture of the types of crimes that are investigated (albeit sometimes minimally) by police. The dominant offenses among the reported-crimes are those involving the taking or destruction of property (likely to approximate 50%), offenses relating to the use of alcohol or drugs, and assaults of various types. The most serious violent offenses (e.g., robbery, rape, aggravated assault, and homicide) are likely to constitute as a group no more than 7% of all reported crimes.

Step 2. Prearrest Investigation. (a) On–Scene Arrests. A substantial percentage of arrests for a wide variety of crimes are made by police with little or no prearrest investigation. These are arrests made during the course of the crime or immediately thereafter either at the place where the crime occurred or in its immediate vicinity. Ordinarily, on-scene arrests will be based on the officer's own observation (leading to the alternative description of such arrests as "on-view"), although they will sometimes be based on the directive of a witness who has just viewed the crime. For some offenses, on-scene arrests typically are the product of prearrest investigative activities designed to place the police in a position where they will be able to view the crime as it is committed. That usually is the case, for example, with crimes which ordinarily involve willing participants, such as vice crimes or narcotics-transfer offenses. For other offenses, most on-scene arrests come about with basically no investigative activity beyond the immediate response to the event that calls the commission of the crime to the officer's attention. In these cases, a prompt response to a victim's call for assistance or a burglar alarm may place the officer in a position to make an arrest while the crime is in progress or immediately following its completion. So too, the officer may simply come across a crime, open to his view, in the course of regular patrol activities.

(b) Reactive Investigations. Where the police learn of the possible commission of a crime, but are not in a position to make an "on-scene" arrest, their responsibility then is to

---

b. The material in this section is abridged from Wayne R. LaFave, Jerold H. Israel & Nancy J. King, *Criminal Procedure* § 1.3 (3d ed.2000), where Prof. Israel has very effectively and thoroughly described these steps with greater precision and detail.

c. American jurisdictions commonly use one of two different standards in distinguishing between felonies and misdemeanors. Some classify as felonies all of-fenses punishable by a maximum term of imprisonment of more than one year; offenses punishable by imprisonment for one year or less are then misdemeanors. Others look to the location of the possible imprisonment: if the offense is punishable by incarceration in a penitentiary, it is a felony; if punishable only by a jail term, it is a misdemeanor.

"solve" that crime. This involves (1) determining whether there actually was a crime committed, (2) if so, determining who committed the crime, (3) collecting evidence of that person's guilt, and (4) locating the offender so that he can be taken into custody. Investigations directed at performing these crime-solving functions commonly are described as "reactive" or "retrospective" in nature because they focus on past criminal (or presumably criminal) activity. They reflect what is characterized as an "incident-driven" or "complaint-responsive" style of policing which has long dominated the deployment of police investigative resources. A wide variety of investigative activities may be utilized prearrest in the course of a reactive investigation. These include: (1) the interviewing of victims; (2) the interviewing of witnesses at the crime scene; (3) canvassing the neighborhood for (and interviewing) other witnesses; (4) the interviewing of suspects, which may require a physical stopping of the suspect on the street and a frisking of the suspect (i.e., pat-down of the outer clothing) for possible weapons; (5) the examination of the crime scene and the collection of physical evidence found there; (6) checking departmental records and computer files; (7) seeking information from informants; (8) searching for physical evidence of the crime (e.g., stolen property or weapons) in places accessible to the suspect (e.g., his home or automobile) and seizing any evidence found there; (9) surveillance of a suspect (including electronic surveillance) aimed at obtaining leads to evidence or accomplices; (10) using undercover operatives to gain information from the suspect.

Where the traces of the crime are very weak and the offense is not of an especially serious nature, the police are likely to terminate their investigation after having done little more than interview the victim and any other witnesses available at the scene. Police are aware that, for most crimes, the odds of arresting the offender are slim unless there are witnesses at the scene who can provide information that either specifically identifies the offender or makes that identification readily determinable. While the absence of such information from witnesses will not necessarily lead to an immediate termination of the investigation, it will certainly work against a substantial extension of the investigation (unless further steps are especially fruitful). The end result is that for a great many crimes, including even offenses as serious as burglary, very little is done besides interviewing the person reporting the crime.

On the other side, a prearrest investigation also may be ended without exploring all possible leads because the police feel that they have a sufficiently strong case without the corroboration that might be produced through further investigation. An eyewitness who can identify the offender provides a strong basis for an arrest, although not necessarily a strong case for conviction. The investigating officer in such a case may well seek (though not necessarily prearrest) the corroboration of an additional eyewitness or tangible physical evidence (e.g., the stolen property) that might tie the suspect to the offense. However, corroborating evidence is likely to be sought only up to a certain point. Thus, an officer with two or more eyewitnesses and corroborating physical evidence may well decline to explore further avenues for collecting evidence (e.g., latent fingerprints or secondary witnesses), especially if that would involve considerable effort and the offense is not extremely serious.

While the variation among investigations is far too great to characterize any single combination of investigative procedures as "average," even for a particular type of offense, it is clear that prearrest investigations rarely take on the characteristics of popular depictions of the crime solving process. In general, investigations do not involve the use of scientific methods of investigation, confrontations with crafty criminals, or reliance upon informants. A study of robbery and burglary investigations found, for example, that the interviewing of the victim and the examination of the crime scene were by far the most common steps in the process. Aside from the canvassing for and interviewing of additional witnesses, no other procedure was used in as many as a third of all cases.

(c) Proactive Investigations. General purpose police agencies, who employ over 85% of all full-time police officers in this country, devote the vast majority of their investigative efforts to the solving of known crimes. However, those agencies also have a long tradition of engaging as well in proactive investigations, and in recent years, many local police agencies have sought to make greater use of proactive investigative procedures. Also, many special-function police agencies (such as the federal Drug Enforcement Administration) traditionally have devoted a substantial portion of their resources to proactive investigations.

Proactive investigations are aimed at uncovering criminal activity that is not specifically known to the police. The investigation may be aimed at placing the police in a position where they can observe ongoing criminal activity that otherwise would both be hidden from public view and not reported (as typically is the case with offenses that prohibit the possession of contraband or proscribe transactions between willing participants). It may be aimed at inducing persons who have committed crimes of a certain type, including many unknown to the police, to reveal themselves (as in a "fencing sting"). Proactive investigations also often are aimed at anticipating future criminality and placing police in a position to intercept when the crime is attempted. Here, the investigative technique may be designed simply to gain information that will permit the police to predict when and where a crime is likely to be committed, or it may be designed to "instigate" or "induce" the criminal attempt at a particular time and place by creating a setting likely to spur into action those prone to criminality.

While deception is a common element of many proactive procedures, other proactive techniques rely on intrusive confrontations designed to place police in a position where they can observe what otherwise would be hidden or to elicit nervous or unthinking incriminatory responses that will provide a legal grounding for taking further investigative action (e.g., an arrest or stop). Thus, police following an aggressive motorized patrol strategy will fully utilize traffic laws to maximize stops of motorists, thereby gaining greater opportunity to peer into car windows, to ask questions, and to request consent to a search of the vehicle. Similarly, under a practice of heavy field interrogation, police will frequently approach pedestrians and initiate questions to determine who they are and what they are doing. Such intrusive confrontations are most often used on a selective basis, with police concentrating their efforts on those characteristics of the social environment that suggest to them possible criminality (e.g., high-crime neighborhood, suspicious class of persons, unusual behavior).

(d) Prosecutorial Investigations. For certain types of crimes, and with certain types of traces of crime, the best investigatory tool is the subpoena—a court order directing a person to appear in a particular proceeding for the purpose of testifying and presenting specified physical evidence (e.g., documents) within his possession. The subpoena authority generally is available for the investigation of crime only through the grand jury, which has authority to conduct investigations into the possible commission of crimes within the judicial district in which it sits. In carrying out this function, the grand jurors, being a group of laypersons with no special expertise in investigation, quite naturally rely heavily on the direction provided by their legal advisor, who is the prosecutor. Thus, grand jury investigations become, for all practical purposes, investigations by the prosecutor.

Compared to police investigations, grand jury investigations are expensive, time consuming, and logistically cumbersome. Accordingly, the grand jury investigation ordinarily is used by the prosecutor only in those special settings where a grand jury investigation has a distinctive advantage over a police investigation. Such an advantage is present: (1) where witnesses will not cooperate with the police (as they can be compelled by subpoena to testify before the grand jury and given immunity to replace their self-incrimination privilege should they refuse to testify on that ground); (2) where the critical evidence of the crime is likely to be a "paper trail" buried in voluminous records of business dealings (as the subpoena can be used to require production of such records where the police lack the necessary probable cause predicate for obtaining those documents through a search); and (3) where the area of investigation is especially sensitive, reflecting a strong need to keep the ongoing investigation from the public gaze (an objective facilitated by grand jury secrecy requirements) or to ensure public confidence in the integrity of the investigation (an objective facilitated by the participation of the lay grand jurors). Criminal investigations imposing such special needs are likely to deal with crimes of public corruption (e.g., bribery), misuse of economic power (e.g., price-fixing), and widespread distribution of illegal services or goods (e.g., organized crime operations).

Step 3. Arrest. Once a police officer has obtained sufficient information to justify arresting a suspect (i.e., probable cause to believe the person has committed a crime), the arrest ordinarily becomes the next step in the criminal justice process. This involves the detention of the suspect (by force if necessary) for the purpose of first transporting him to a police facility and then requesting that charges be filed against him. As an alternative to such a "full custody" arrest, many jurisdictions authorize the officer in some situations to briefly detain the suspect and then release him upon issuance of an official document (commonly titled a "citation," "notice to appear" or "appearance ticket") which directs the suspect to appear in court on a set date to respond to the charge specified in the document. This release-on-citation alternative commonly is authorized only for minor offenses, with the choice between the release procedure and the custodial arrest then lying in the discretion of the individual officer. In many localities the standard practice is to use the citation alternative for a wide range of minor offenses, while in others, police generally prefer arrests and largely confine their regular use of the citation alternative to a few minor offenses, primarily regulatory in character. Where citations regularly are used for even a handful of the more common minor offenses, the number of citations issued can readily equal a quarter or a third of the total number of misdemeanor arrests.

Where there is no immediate need to arrest a suspect, an officer may seek to obtain an arrest warrant (a court order authorizing the arrest) prior to taking the person into custody. Arrest warrants are issued by magistrates on probable cause to believe that the prospective arrestee committed the crime for which he will be arrested. The showing of probable cause may be made by affidavits or live testimony of either the investigating officer or a witness (usually the victim). Arrests also can be made without a warrant, and that is the predominant practice even where the investigating officer, after establishing probable cause, expects a lapse of a day or more before making an arrest.

Officers obtain a warrant instead only where the special setting makes a warrant legally necessary or otherwise advantageous. The most common of those settings are: (1) cases in which the offender is located in another jurisdiction (as a warrant is needed to utilize procedures for having the person arrested by officers of another state and later extradited); (2) cases in which the person cannot be found and his name therefore will be entered into the computerized state or local law enforcement information network as someone who is subject to an arrest on the basis of an outstanding warrant; (3) cases in which there will probably be a need to enter into a dwelling without consent in order to make the arrest (a situation that requires a warrant); (4) cases in which the offense was a misdemeanor not committed in the officer's presence (a situation requiring a warrant in some states); and (5) cases in which the police have sought the advice of the prosecutor before deciding to proceed (where the prosecutor responds affirmatively, a complaint typically will be filed immediately, with a warrant then obtained prior to the arrest).

The vast majority of arrests (60–80%) will be for misdemeanors. Among felony arrests, property offenses will account for roughly a third, and drug offenses for 25–30%, and crimes of violence for another 25%. A substantial percentage of all of the persons arrested (e.g., 10–20%) will be juveniles, with that percentage varying considerably with the offense. Ordinarily, juvenile arrestees will be separated from adult arrestees shortly after they are taken into custody, and will be processed through the juvenile justice system, although some will later be returned to the regular criminal justice process and be prosecuted as adults.

Step 4. Booking. Immediately after arrest, the arresting officer usually will search the arrestee's person and remove any weapons, contraband, or evidence relating to a crime. If the arrested person was driving a vehicle, the officer may also search the passenger compartment of the vehicle for the same items. The arrestee will then be taken, either by the arresting officer or other officers called to the scene, to the police station, a centrally located jail, or some similar "holding" facility. It is at this facility that the arrestee will be taken through a process known as "booking." Initially, the arrestee's name, the time of his arrival, and the offense for which he was arrested are noted in the police "blotter" or "log." This is strictly a clerical procedure, and it does not control whether the arrestee will be charged or what charge might be brought. As part of the booking process, the arrestee also will be photographed and fingerprinted.

In many jurisdictions, an arrestee booked on a minor misdemeanor will be given the opportunity to obtain his immediate release by posting what is described as "stationhouse bail." This involves posting a specified amount of cash, as prescribed for the particular offense in a judicially approved bail schedule, and agreeing to appear in court on a specified date. Persons arrested for more serious offenses and those eligible to post stationhouse bail but lacking the resources will remain at the holding facility until presented before a magistrate (see step 9). Ordinarily they will be placed in a "lockup," which usually is some kind of cell. Before entering the lockup, they will be subjected to another search, more thorough than that conducted at the point of arrest. This search is designed primarily to inventory the arrestee's personal belongs and to prevent the introduction of contraband into the lockup.

Step 5. Post–Arrest Investigation. The initial post-arrest investigation by the police consists of the search of the person (and possibly the interior of the automobile) as discussed above. The extent of any further post-arrest investigation will vary with the fact situation. In some cases, such as where the arrestee was caught "red-handed," there will be little left to be done. In others, police will utilize many of the same kinds of investigative procedures as are used before arrest (e.g., interviewing witnesses, searching the suspect's home, and viewing the scene of the crime). Post-arrest investigation does offer one important investigative source, however, that ordinarily is not available prior to the arrest—the person of the arrestee. Thus, the police may seek to obtain an eyewitness identification of the arrestee by placing him in a lineup, having the witness view him individually (a "showup"), or taking his picture and showing it to the witness (usually with the photographs of several other persons in a "photographic lineup"). They may also require the arrestee to provide handwriting or hair samples that can be compared with evidence the police have found at the scene of the crime. The arrest similarly facilitates questioning the arrestee at length about either the crime for which he was arrested or other crimes thought to be related (although warnings must be given prior to the custodial interrogation).

Step 6. The Decision to Charge. The decision to charge a person with a crime has four components: (1) the decision of the investigating officer to arrest and charge; (2) the police review of that decision prior to filing charges; (3) prosecutorial review prior to filing; and (4) ongoing prosecutorial review after the filing. The first component has already been noted in step 3; the others are considered here.

(a) Pre–Filing Police Screening. Sometime between booking and the point at which the arrestee is to be taken before the magistrate, there will be an internal police review of a

warrantless arrest. When the arresting officer prepares an arrest report to be given to his or her supervisor, the supervisor may approve the bringing of charges at the level recommended in the police report, raise or reduce the level of the recommended charges, or decide against bringing charges. A decision not to bring charges ordinarily will be based on the supervisor's conclusion either that the evidence is insufficient to charge or that the offense can more appropriately be handled by a "stationhouse adjustment" (e.g., in the case of a fight among acquaintances, a warning and lecture may be deemed sufficient). Studies report police decisions to release arrestees and forego prosecution in the range of 4% to 10%; the percentage of misdemeanor arrestees released by the police without charging is likely to be somewhat higher.

(b) Pre–Filing Prosecutor Screening. Prosecutors' offices vary substantially in their approach to pre-filing review of the decision to charge. In many jurisdictions, all arrests, both for misdemeanors and felonies, will be screened, and no charges will be filed except upon approval of the prosecutor. In many others, however, particularly in urban districts, police often file charges on their own initiative for at least some types of offenses. Typically, prosecutors here will screen the vast majority of the felony charges, but there will be districts in which prosecutors review only the most serious felony charges before they are filed. In those districts, the initial prosecutorial screening of most felony charges occurs sometime between the first appearance and the preliminary hearing or grand jury review (see steps 9 and 10 infra). Prosecutors are more likely to permit police to file misdemeanor charges without advance prosecutorial screening. When that occurs, prosecutors may not review a misdemeanor charge until it is scheduled for trial (and thus may never screen those charges that result in a guilty plea at the first appearance).

Prosecutorial decisions not to proceed are based upon: (1) insufficient evidence; (2) witness difficulties (e.g., where the victim was acquainted with the offender and does not desire to proceed, the victim fears reprisal and is reluctant to pursue prosecution, or the victim cannot be located); (3) due process problems (e.g., critical evidence was obtained illegally and will not be admissible at trial); (4) adequate disposition will be provided by other criminal proceedings (e.g., prosecution by another jurisdiction, probation revocation, or prosecution for another offense); (5) the "interests of justice"; and (6) anticipated use of a diversion program.

A diversion program offers the arrestee the opportunity to avoid conviction if he or she is willing to perform prescribed "rehabilitative steps" (e.g., making restitution to the victim, undertaking a treatment program). The diversion agreement operates, in effect, to place the arrestee on a probationary status without conviction. In many jurisdictions, this is achieved by the prosecutor promising not to file charges if the arrestee complies with the prescribed conditions. In others, charges initially are filed with the court, then held in abeyance for the period during which the arrestee is to meet the prescribed conditions, and dismissed with prejudice once the arrestee meets those conditions. If the arrestee fails to meet the prescribed conditions, the prosecution against the arrestee proceeds (with the charges filed, if that had not been done previously). Pretrial diversion tends to be used mostly with first-offense, non-violent misdemeanor arrestees.

Where the prosecutor decides to charge, pre-filing screening involves another important prosecutorial decision—setting the level of the charge. Although an arrest was made on a felony charge, the prosecutor may decide to go forward on a lesser charge. Prosecutors most often reduce the recommended charge because they believe that the evidence only supports a lower charge, but reductions also may be based on the prosecutor's determination that the penalty for the higher charges is too severe for the nature of the crime or that the additional process costs involved in proceeding on a felony (rather than a misdemeanor) are not justified.

(c) Post–Filing Prosecutorial Screening. Post-filing prosecutorial review of the charging decision is inherent in the many post-filing procedures that require the prosecutor to review the facts of the case. If the prosecutor should determine that the charge is not justified, a dismissal can be obtained through a nolle prosequi motion (noting the prosecutor's desire to relinquish prosecution), which ordinarily will be granted in a perfunctory fashion by the court. Similarly, if the prosecutor considers the charge to be too high, a motion can be entered to reduce the charges. In deciding whether to make such motions, the prosecutor will look to basically the same grounds that might justify a pre-filing rejection or reduction of the charge recommended by the police. Even where a charge was carefully screened and approved prior to filing, post-filing review can readily lead to a contrary conclusion as circumstances change (e.g., evidence becomes unavailable) or the prosecutor learns more about the facts of the case. Of course, where the charge was not previously screened or was screened only on a skimpy arrest report, post-filing review is even more likely to lead to a decision to drop or reduce the charges.

What is the end product of the combined pre-filing screening by police and prosecutor and post-filing screening by the prosecutor? The best source on that question is a series of studies on the attrition of felony arrests. A 1988 study, using a dozen urban prosecutorial districts, found that those districts screened out of the criminal justice system from 31% to 46% of all felony arrests, with a jurisdictional mean of 39%. When diversions were added, no jurisdiction removed from prosecution less than 33% of their felony arrests, all but three removed in excess of 40%, and one removed 50%. A 1992 study, drawing information from 11 states, provides data suggesting removal by screening (including diversion) fell in the range of 31–36% for those states as a group. The end product of screening on misdemeanor arrests is more difficult to measure, but it is likely that prosecutorial screening of misdemeanor arrest cases equals (or even exceeds) the impact of prosecutorial screening of felony cases, particularly if the heavier use of diversion for misdemeanor cases is taken into account.

Step 7. Filing the Complaint. Assuming that the pre-charge screening results in a decision to prosecute, the next step is the filing of charges with the magistrate court. Typically, the initial charging instrument will be called a "complaint." In misdemeanor cases, which are triable before the magistrate court, the complaint will serve as the charging instrument throughout the proceedings. In felony cases, on the other hand, the complaint serves to set forth the charges only before the magistrate court; an information or indictment will replace the complaint as the charging instrument when the case reaches the general trial court.

For most offenses, the complaint will be a fairly brief document. Its basic function is to set forth concisely the allegation that the accused, at a particular time and place, committed specified acts constituting a violation of a particular criminal statute. The complaint will be signed by a "complainant," a person who swears under oath that he or she believes the factual allegations of the complaint to be true. The complainant usually will be either the victim or the investigating officer. When an officer-complainant did not observe the offense being committed, but relied on information received from the victim or other witnesses, the officer ordinarily will note that the allegations in the complaint are based on "information and belief." With the filing of the complaint, the person accused in the complaint will have become a "defendant" in a criminal proceeding. The formal charge initiates a judicial record keeping procedure that puts his case on the docket and follows it through to its termination.

Step 8. Magistrate Review of the Arrest. Following the filing of the complaint and prior to or at the start of the first appearance (see step 9), the magistrate must, if the accused was arrested without a warrant and remains in custody, determine that there exists probable cause for the continued detention of the arrestee for the offense charged in the complaint. This ordinarily is an ex parte determination, similar to that made in the issuance of an arrest warrant and relying on the same sources of information. If the magistrate finds that probable cause has not been established, he will direct the prosecution to promptly produce more information or release the arrested person. Such instances are exceedingly rare, however.

Step 9. The First Appearance. Once the complaint is filed, the case is before the magistrate court, and the accused must appear before the court within a specified period. This appearance of the accused is usually described as the "first appearance," although the terminology varies, with jurisdictions also using "preliminary appearance," "initial presentment," "preliminary arraignment," "arraignment on the warrant," and "arraignment on the complaint." The timing of the first appearance varies with the custodial status of the accused. Where the accused was not taken into custody, but was released on issuance of a citation, there is likely to be a gap of at least several days between the issuance of the citation and the first appearance date as specified in the citation. The same is often true also of the first appearance set for the arrestee who gained his release by posting stationhouse bail.

Almost all felony arrestees and many misdemeanor arrestees will have been held in custody following their arrest, however, and here the time span between the arrest and the first appearance is much shorter. All jurisdictions require that an arrestee held in custody be brought before the magistrate court in a fairly prompt fashion. Ordinarily, the time consumed in booking, transportation, limited post-arrest investigation, reviewing the decision to charge, and preparing and filing the complaint makes it unlikely that the arrestee will be presented before the magistrate until at least several hours after his arrest. Thus, if the magistrate court does not have an evening session, a person arrested in the afternoon or evening will not be presented before the magistrate until the next day. Many jurisdictions do not allow much longer detention than this, as they impose a 24 hour limit on pre-appearance detention, requiring both the filing of the complaint and the presentation of the detained arrestee within that period. Others, desiring to limit weekend sessions of the court, allow up to 48 hours of pre-appearance detention.

The first appearance often is a quite brief proceeding. Initially, the magistrate will make certain that the person before him is the person named in the complaint. The magistrate then will inform the defendant of the charge in the complaint and will note various rights that the defendant may have in further proceedings. The range of rights mentioned will vary from one jurisdiction to another. Commonly, the magistrate will inform the defendant of his right to remain silent and warn him that anything he says in court or to the police may be used against him at trial. Further advice as to rights may depend upon whether the defendant is charged with a felony or misdemeanor. In felony cases, the magistrate will advise the defendant of the next step in the process, the preliminary hearing, and will set a date for that hearing unless the defendant desires to waive it. If the defendant is charged with a misdemeanor, he will not be entitled to a preliminary hearing or a subsequent grand jury review (see steps 10 and 11).

At least where the defendant is not represented by counsel at the first appearance, the magistrate will inform the defendant of his right to be represented by retained counsel, and, if indigent, his right to court-appointed counsel. The scope of the right to appointed counsel may vary with the level of the offense. In some jurisdictions, appointed counsel will not be available for defendants who are charged with low-level misdemeanors if they will not be sentenced to incarceration if convicted. Where there is a right to appointed counsel, which will be the case in all jurisdictions for indigent defendants charged with felonies and serious misdemeanors, the magistrate usually will have the responsibility for at least initiating the appointment process. This involves first determining that the defendant is indigent and that he desires the assistance of counsel. The magistrate then will either directly appoint counsel or notify a judge in charge of appointments that an appointment should be made.

Appointed counsel will be required for a substantial percentage of all felony defendants. Three basic systems are used to provide counsel for indigent defendants. In counties containing roughly 70% of the country's population, counsel is provided primarily through a state or county public defender service. In counties containing roughly 25% of the population, reliance is placed primarily upon an assigned counsel system. Here private attorneys are selected from a list of available attorneys, either on an ad hoc basis (with individual judges choosing attorneys as they please) or through a coordinated selection system (with selection by a single administrator according to established guidelines). A smaller group of counties, containing less than 10% of the population, rely primarily upon contract systems under which a private law firm, a group of private practitioners, or a nonprofit organization (such as a bar association) contracts to provide representation for the bulk of the indigent defendants for an extended period of time.

Since a misdemeanor charge will be triable to the magistrate court, the magistrate at the first appearance may also ask the misdemeanor defendant to enter a plea to the charge contained in the complaint. Indeed, at one time, it was the common practice to dispose of almost all misdemeanor cases at the first appearance in a fashion similar to that still prevailing in traffic courts. With the general recognition of the misdemeanor defendant's right to the assistance of counsel at trial, however, that practice has largely been discarded.

One of the most important first-appearance functions of the magistrate is to set bail (i.e., the conditions under which the defendant can obtain his release from custody pending the final disposition of the charges against him). In many misdemeanor cases, there will be no need to set bail. The defendant will already have been released on the police issuance of a citation or on the posting of stationhouse bail or the defendant will enter a guilty plea at the first appearance and be promptly sentenced. However, a bail determination ordinarily must be made in all felony and serious misdemeanor cases and in a substantial portion of the lesser misdemeanor cases.

At one time, bail was limited almost entirely to the posting of cash or a secured bond purchased from a professional bondsman. Today, those are only two of several alternatives available to the magistrate. Others are: (1) release upon a promise to appear (release on "personal recognizance"); (2) release on making a personal promise to forfeit a specified dollar amount upon a failure to appear (an "unsecured" personal bond); (3) release upon the imposition of one or more nonfinancial conditions (e.g., restrictions on defendant's associations or travel); and (4) the posting with the court of a percentage of the bail forfeiture amount (commonly 10%), which will be returned to the defendant if he appears as scheduled. In a few states, the 10% alternative has basically replaced the secured bond, resulting in the elimination of professional bondsmen.

In general, the magistrate is directed to impose such bail conditions as appear reasonably needed to assure that the defendant will make court appearances as scheduled throughout the proceedings. In making that determination, the magistrate looks to a variety of factors that might indicate a likelihood of flight (e.g., severity of possible punishment if convicted). Most jurisdictions also direct the magistrate to consider community safety in setting bail conditions, and approximately half of our fifty-two jurisdictions authorize preventive detention—a procedure under which the magistrate orders that the accused be detained because no bail condition will provide satisfactory assurance against his commission of an offense posing danger to the community.

In misdemeanor cases, magistrates most commonly utilize release on personal recognizance or personal bonds, and even where a secured bond is required, the amount is sufficiently low so that only a small percentage of defendants fail to gain their release. As a result, studies that cover both misdemeanor and felony arrestees report overall release rates of 85% or higher, with the vast majority of defendants released on nonfinancial conditions.

Step 10. Preliminary Hearing. Following the first appearance, the next scheduled step in a felony case ordinarily is the preliminary hearing (sometimes called a preliminary "examination"). All but a few jurisdictions grant the felony defendant a right to a preliminary hearing, to be held within a specified period (typically, within a week or two if the defendant does not gain pretrial release and within a few weeks if released). This hardly means, however, that the preliminary hearing will be held in almost all or even most cases. Post-arrest prosecutorial screening of charges in the period prior to the scheduled preliminary hearing results in dismissal of 15–30% of the felony cases. Where the charges are not dismissed, two additional decisions—one by the prosecutor and one by the defense—can sharply reduce the number of preliminary hearings.

In almost all jurisdictions, if the prosecutor obtains a grand jury indictment prior to the scheduled preliminary hearing, the preliminary hearing will not be held, as the grand jury's finding of probable cause has rendered irrelevant any contrary finding that the magistrate might make at the preliminary hearing. Prosecutorial bypassing of the preliminary hearing by immediately obtaining a grand jury indictment is most likely to occur in those twenty jurisdictions that require prosecution by indictment (see step 11 infra). In some of these jurisdictions, prosecutors make such frequent use of the bypass option as to preclude preliminary hearings in 50–80% of the felony cases that reach the felony trial court. In many others, however, the bypass procedure is used sparingly, and this is the norm in jurisdictions that ordinarily prosecute by information.

Finally, where the preliminary hearing is made available to the defendant, there nonetheless may not be a preliminary hearing because the defendant prefers to waive the hearing and move directly to the trial court. That is often the strategy employed where the defendant intends to plead guilty. Thus, a number of jurisdictions report a waiver rate exceeding 50%, although there also are jurisdictions in which defendants ask for the hearing in the vast majority of cases.

Where the preliminary hearing is held, the magistrate must determine whether, on the evidence presented, there is probable cause to believe that defendant committed the crime charged. Jurisdictions vary in the evidentiary rules applicable to the preliminary hearing, but most require that the parties rely primarily on live witnesses rather than affidavits. Typically, the prosecution will present its key witnesses and the defense will limit its response to the cross-examination of those witnesses. The defendant has the right to present his own evidence at the hearing, but traditional defense strategy advises against subjecting defense witnesses to prosecution cross-examination in any pretrial proceeding.

If the magistrate concludes that the evidence presented establishes probable cause, he will "bind the case over" to the next stage in the proceedings. In an indictment jurisdiction (see step 11), the case is bound over to the grand jury, and in a jurisdiction that permits the direct filing of an information (see step 12), the case is bound over directly to the general trial court. If the magistrate finds that the probable cause supports only a misdemeanor charge, he will reject the felony charge and allow the prosecutor to substitute the lower charge, which will then be set for trial in the magistrate court. If the magistrate finds that the prosecution's evidence does not support any charge, he will order that the defendant be released.

Step 11. Grand Jury Review. Although almost all jurisdictions still have provisions authorizing grand jury screening of felony charges, such screening is mandatory only in those jurisdictions requiring felony prosecutions to be instituted by an indictment, a charging instrument issued by the grand jury. In a majority of the states, the prosecution is now allowed to proceed either by grand jury indictment or by information at its option. Because prosecutors in these states most often choose to prosecute by information, the states providing this option commonly are referred to as "information" states. Eighteen states, the federal system, and the District of Columbia currently require grand jury indictments for all felony prosecutions. These jurisdictions commonly are described as "indictment" jurisdictions. Four additional states are "limited indictment" jurisdictions, requiring prosecution by indictment only for their most severely punished offenses (capital, life imprisonment, or both).

Indictment and limited indictment jurisdictions commonly make prosecution by indictment an absolute mandate only for capital offenses. As to other offenses, the defendant may waive the right to be proceeded against by indictment, thereby allowing the prosecution to proceed by information. As in the case of the preliminary hearing, defendants may prefer to waive when intending to plead guilty. Waiver rates vary from one jurisdiction to another but waivers are likely to be made by at least 10% of all felony defendants. Where a potential charge is brought to the grand jury for its possible issuance of an indictment, the grand jury is in no way bound by any prior ruling at a preliminary hearing on that charge. The grand jury may indict even though the magistrate dismissed the charge at the preliminary hearing, and may refuse to indict even though the magistrate bound over to the grand jury.

The grand jury is composed of a group of private citizens who are selected to review cases presented over a term that may range from one to several months. Traditionally the grand jury consisted of 23 persons with the favorable vote of a majority needed to indict. Today, many states use a somewhat smaller grand jury (e.g., 12) and some require more than a simple majority to indict. As in the case of the magistrate at the preliminary hearing, the primary function of the grand jury is to determine whether there is sufficient evidence to justify a trial on the charge sought by the prosecution. The grand jury, however, participates in a screening process quite different from the preliminary hearing. It meets in a closed session and hears only the evidence presented by the prosecution. The defendant has no right to offer his own evidence or to be present during grand jury proceedings. If a majority of the grand jurors conclude that the prosecution's evidence is sufficient, the grand jury will issue the indictment requested by the prosecutor. The indictment will set forth a brief description of the offense charged, and the grand jury's approval of that charge will be indicated by its designation of the indictment as a "true bill." If the grand jury majority refuses to approve a proposed indictment, the charges against the defendant will be dismissed. In indictment jurisdictions, grand juries typically refuse to indict in less than 10% of the cases presented before them.

Step 12. The Filing of the Indictment or Information. If an indictment is issued, it will be filed with the general trial court and will replace the complaint as the accusatory instrument in the case. Where grand jury review either is not required or has been waived, an information will be filed with the trial court. Like the indictment, the information is a charging instrument which replaces the complaint, but it is issued by the prosecutor rather than the grand jury. In most information states, the charge in the information must be supported by a preliminary hearing bindover (unless the preliminary hearing was waived).

Step 13. Arraignment on the Information or Indictment. After the indictment or information has been filed, the defendant is arraigned—i.e., he is brought before the trial court, informed of the charges against him, and asked to enter a plea of guilty, not guilty, or, as is permitted under some circumstances, nolo contendere. In the end, most of those felony defendants whose cases reach the trial court will plead guilty.

At the arraignment, however, they are likely to enter a plea of not guilty. Where there has not been a preliminary hearing, defense counsel probably will not be fully apprised of the strength of the prosecution's case at this point in the proceedings. Also, in most jurisdictions, guilty pleas in felony cases are the product of plea negotiations with the prosecution, and in many places, that process does not start until after the arraignment. When the defendant enters a plea of not guilty at the arraignment, the judge will set a trial date, but the expectation generally is that the trial will not be held.

Between the arraignment and the scheduled trial date, three possible dispositions can result in the termination of the case without trial. Although there will have been extensive prosecutorial screening by this point, changed circumstances and new information typically will lead to dismissals on a prosecutor's nolle prosequi motion in roughly 5–15% of the cases. A smaller percentage of the informations or indictments will be dismissed on motion of the defense, as discussed in step 14. The vast majority of the dispositions without trial will be the product of guilty pleas.

Guilty pleas in felony cases commonly will be entered in response to a plea agreement under which the prosecution offers certain concessions in return for the defendant's entry of the plea. Those concessions may take the form of a reduction of the charges (sometimes to a misdemeanor and sometimes to a lesser felony charge), a dismissal of related charges where the defendant faces multiple charges, a recommendation on sentence, or a specific sentence (when agreed to by the trial court). Prosecutors' offices vary in the concessions they offer and their willingness to bargain over concessions (as opposed to presenting a take-it-or-leave-it offer). The guilty plea remains the primary mode of disposition for felony indictments and informations in all jurisdictions; most jurisdictions appear to fall within the range of 60–85%. The guilty plea rate is as high or higher as to misdemeanor charges in the magistrate court, although there tends to be less plea negotiation on charges originally filed as misdemeanors.

Step 14. Pretrial Motions. In most jurisdictions, a broad range of objections must be raised by a pretrial motion. Those motions commonly present challenges to the institution of the prosecution (e.g., claims regarding the grand jury indictment process), attacks upon the sufficiency of the charging instrument, requests for disclosure of evidence within the government's possession that has not been made available through discovery, and requests for the suppression of evidence allegedly obtained through a constitutional violation. While some pretrial motions are made only by defendants who intend to go to trial, other motions (e.g., discovery) may benefit as well defendants who expect in the end to plead guilty. Nevertheless, pretrial motions are likely to be made in only a small portion of the felony cases that reach the trial court. Their use does vary considerably, however, with the nature of the case. In narcotics cases, for example, motions to suppress are quite common. In the typical forgery case, on the other, pretrial motions of any type are quite rare.

As a group, pretrial motions are unlikely to result in the dismissal of more than 5% of the felony cases before the trial court, and quite often will produce a dismissal rate of less than 2.5%. The pretrial motion most likely to produce a dismissal is the motion to suppress. Quite frequently, if the defendant gains suppression of unconstitutionally obtained evidence, there will be insufficient remaining evidence to continue with the prosecution. In misdemeanor cases before the magistrate court, motions tend to be made only in cases slated for trial and even there, they are uncommon. Thus, the percentage of cases dismissed on the basis of a successful defense motion probably will fall below two percent.

Step 15. The Trial. Assuming that there has not been a dismissal and the defendant has not entered a guilty plea (or a nolle contendere plea), the next step in the criminal process is the trial. In most respects, the criminal trial resembles the civil trial. There are, however, several distinguishing features that are either unique to criminal trials or of special importance in such trials. These include (1) the presumption of defendant's innocence, (2) the requirement of proof beyond a reasonable doubt, (3) the right of the defendant not to take the stand, (4) the exclusion of evidence obtained by the state in an illegal manner, and (5) the more frequent use of incriminating statements of defendants. In most jurisdictions, the misdemeanor trial will be almost indistinguishable from a felony trial. In some jurisdictions, however, misdemeanor trials tend to be less formal, with rules of evidence applied in a rather loose fashion.

As noted previously, most felony and misdemeanor cases are likely to be disposed of either by a guilty plea or by a dismissal. Typically, only 4% to 8% of all felony complaints are resolved by a trial. Because a substantial portion of felony complaints are likely to be resolved at the magistrate level, the percentage of trials will be somewhat higher for the disposition of the smaller group of felony informations or indictments filed in the general trial court, but even so, that percentage will not ordinarily exceed 15%. For misdemeanor cases resolved at the magistrate level (including both cases originally filed as misdemeanors and felony complaints reduced to misdemeanors) the percentage of trials is likely to fall in the range of 3% to 7% on a statewide basis. The median time frame from the arrest of the defendant to the start of the felony trial can exceed a year in judicial districts with slow moving dockets, but for most judicial districts, it is likely to fall within the range of 5–8 months.

The trial itself tends to be relatively short. Misdemeanor trials typically last less than a day. Felony jury trials are somewhat longer, but most will be completed within 2–3 days. One variable will be the local practice governing voir dire (the questioning of prospective jurors, either by judge or counsel), as some jurisdictions tend to spend considerably more time on jury selection than others. Another will be the type of case, as certain types of offense (e.g., complex white collar offenses and capital homicide cases) produce trials substantially longer than the typical felony. In general trials to the bench are considerably shorter, and unlikely to last more than a day.

The defendant has a right to a jury trial for all felony offenses and for misdemeanors punishable by more than 6 months imprisonment. Most states also provide a jury trial for lesser misdemeanors as well (although that right may exist only through the opportunity to seek a trial de novo in the general trial court after an initial bench trial before the magistrate court). Juries traditionally were composed of 12 persons, but most states now utilize 6 person juries in misdemeanor cases and several use the smaller juries in non-capital felony cases as well. Of course, the right to a jury trial can be waived, and in most jurisdictions, a significant number of defendants will waive the jury in favor of a bench trial. Over the country as a whole, roughly 70% of all felony trials are tried to a jury. In misdemeanor cases, in contrast, bench trials, typically predominate (often accounting for 95% or more of all trials). In all but a few jurisdictions, the jury verdict in both misdemeanor and felony cases, whether for acquittal or conviction, must be unanimous. Where the jurors cannot agree, no verdict is entered and the case may be retried. For most communities, such "hung juries" occur in only a very small percentage of all jury trials (e.g., 3–6%).

Whether a criminal case is tried to the bench or the jury, the odds favor conviction over acquittal. A fairly typical ratio for felony charges will be 3 convictions for every acquittal. That ratio may vary significantly, however, with the nature of the offense. In some jurisdictions, the rate of conviction at trial tends to be substantially lower (though still well above 50%) for some crimes (e.g., rape and murder) than for others (e.g., drug trafficking).

Step 16. Sentencing. In all but a few jurisdictions (which allow for jury sentencing, even apart from capital punishment), the sentence determination is the function of the court. Basically three different types of sentences may be used: financial sanctions (e.g., fines, restitution orders); some form of release into the community (e.g., probation, unsupervised release, house arrest); and incarceration in a jail (for lesser sentences) or prison (for longer sentences). The process applied in determining the sentence is shaped in considerable part by the sentencing options made available to the court by the legislature. For a particular offense, the court may have no choice. The legislature may have prescribed that conviction automatically carries with it a certain sentence and there is nothing left for the court to do except impose that sentence. Most frequently, however, legislative narrowing of options on a particular offense does not go beyond eliminating the community release option (by requiring incarceration) and setting maximums (and sometimes mandatory minimums) for incarceration and financial sanctions.

The sentence of incarceration for a felony offense probably presents the widest diversity of approach to judicial sentencing authority. Initially, jurisdictions divide on the use of determinate and indeterminate sentences. In states utilizing indeterminate sentences, the sentencing structure calls for a maximum and minimum term of imprisonment, with the parole board determining the actual release date within the span set by those the two terms. The legislature always sets the outer limit for the maximum term, but beyond that point, division of sentencing authority between the court and the legislature varies with the jurisdiction and the offense. Possibilities include: judicial authority to set both the maximum term (within the legislatively prescribed outer-limit) and the minimum term; judicial authority to set only the minimum (with the maximum and sometimes a mandatory minimum prescribed by the legislature); and judicial authority to set only a maximum within the prescribed outer-limit (with the minimum then set by law as certain percentage of the judicially set maximum).

The federal system and roughly a dozen states largely utilize determinate sentences. Those jurisdictions have eliminated for all or most offenses the discretionary release authority of the parole board. The sentence imposed by the court sets a fixed term which the prisoner will serve (subject to gaining earlier release through credits earned for "good time"). In all determinate sentencing jurisdictions, as in all indeterminate sentencing jurisdictions, the legislature sets the maximum sentence possible. In a few, the legislature sets a presumptive prison term (or narrow range of terms) which the sentencing judge is directed to use for the typical offense of a particular character (e.g., burglary), absent a finding of specific aggravating or mitigating factors calling for upward and downward adjustments. Typically, however, the setting of the specific sentence within the maximum is left either to unfettered judicial discretion or to judicial discretion operating within the restraints of guidelines formulated by a sentencing commission.

A second major division in felony sentencing structures relates to the use of legislatively mandated penalties. The legislature may mandate a specific penalty, as where it specifies that conviction for a specific crime automatically carries a sentence of life imprisonment. More frequently, however, the mandatory penalty consists of a mandated sentence of at least a certain term of incarceration. The judge in an indeterminate sentencing jurisdiction then must set a minimum term at least equal to the mandatory penalty and the judge in a determinate sentencing jurisdiction must set a fixed term at least equal to the mandatory penalty. All fifty-two jurisdictions make some use of mandatory penalties, but there is substantial variation in the frequency of their use.

Insofar as the legislature leaves the judge authority to choose, a third major division is found in felony sentencing structures. Most states do not seek to direct the trial court in its choice of a sentence that would fit within statutorily prescribed limits, but the federal system and a growing number of states are relying on sentencing guidelines promulgated by a sentencing commission to channel the exercise of such discretion. Those guidelines serve to establish a presumptively correct sentence of incarceration for a particular offense in accordance with the circumstances of the offense and the criminal history of the offender. Where the jurisdiction utilizes determinate sentences, the guideline presumption sets the fixed sentence; where the jurisdiction uses indeterminate sentences, the guideline ordinarily sets the minimum sentence. Typically, the guidelines also specify where a sentence other than incarceration would be appropriate, although they do not direct that such a sentence be used. In some states, the guidelines are "voluntary," and the court is free to disregard them. In most guideline jurisdictions, however, the court can depart from the guidelines only if it finds good reason to do so. Jurisdictions vary in their toleration of "departures" from the guidelines, but even where most lenient in this regard, a substantial majority of the sentences (e.g., in excess of 80%) are likely to fit within the guidelines.

The process utilized in felony sentencing varies to some extent according to whether judicial discretion is broad or is channeled or limited by guideline or legislative reference to specific sentencing circumstances. In all jurisdictions, the process is designed to obtain for the court information beyond that which will have come to its attention in the course of trial or in the acceptance of a guilty plea. The primary vehicle here is the presentence report prepared by the probation department, although the prosecution and defense commonly will be allowed to present additional information and to challenge the information contained in the presentence report. The presentation of this information is not subject to the rules governing the presentation of information at trial. The rules of evidence do not apply, and neither the prosecution nor the defense has a right to call witnesses or to cross-examine the sources of adverse information presented in the presentence report or in any additional documentation presented by the opposing side. However, where the sentencing authority of the judge is restricted by guidelines or legislatively set presumptive sentences that require findings of fact as to specific factors, the sentencing process tends to be more formal. Here, the court often will find it necessary to hold an evidentiary hearing and utilize trial-type procedures if the presence of a critical factor is controverted.

The sentencing structure and procedure for misdemeanor offenses is far less complex and varied. Ordinarily the court is free to choose among financial sanctions, conditional release, incarceration within the maximum term set by the legislature. A sentence of incarceration will be to fixed term (i.e., a specified number of days) and will be served in jail. In assessing the sentence, the court will ordinarily seek some background information, but presentence reports of the type used in felony sentencing commonly are utilized only for the most serious misdemeanors. Evidentiary hearings on sentencing matters are even more unusual. Indeed, the sentence commonly is set immediately upon conviction.

Although the length of the prison sentence set by the court has quite different significance in different sentencing structures, nationwide sentence lengths are usually assessed by reference to the maximum term that can be served under the court's sentence. Under this standard, in 1992, the nationwide mean prison sentence was 164 months for persons convicted in state courts of rape, 117 months for persons convicted of robbery, 76 months for persons convicted of burglary, 53 months for persons convicted of larceny, and 55 months for persons convicted of drug possession. Since most of those terms merely set the maximum length in an indeterminate sentencing structure, the more important measurement is the minimum term that determines when the individual becomes eligible for parole. Moreover, many jurisdictions provide for extensive "good time credits" that will reduce that minimum term or the fixed term of a determinate sentence. As a result, prisoners nationwide tend to serve between 40% and 60% of the mean maximum sentence, with the percentage varying with the nature of the offense. Thus, while the mean term for rape is 164 months, the mean time actually served is likely to be in the range of 91 months, and while the mean term for larceny is 53 months, the mean time actually to be served will be about 17 months.

Step 17. Appeals. For criminal cases disposed of in the general trial court, the initial appeal is to the intermediate appellate court. If the state has no intermediate appellate court, then the initial and final appeal within the state system is to the state's court of last resort. Initial appeals in cases disposed of by the magistrate court will be to the general trial court. In some jurisdictions, the appeal procedure from a conviction in the magistrate court is a trial de novo before the general trial court, rather than that court exercising appellate review of the lower court record.

Although all convicted defendants are entitled to appeal their convictions, appeals are taken predominantly by convicted defendants who were sentenced to imprisonment on a felony conviction. Imprisoned defendants convicted pursuant to a guilty plea are included in this group, but they account for only a narrow slice of all appeals. Though the trial court's acceptance of a guilty plea may be challenged on appeal, such appellate challenges are limited to exceptional cases, so that appeals by guilty plea defendants tend to be sentencing challenges, which usually are significant only in jurisdictions that use sentencing guidelines or legislatively mandated presumptive sentences. In those jurisdictions, challenges to the sentence can constitute a substantial portion (e.g., 15–30%) of all appeals.

Appeals challenging the conviction itself come primarily from imprisoned defendants who are seeking review of a trial conviction. Indeed, in some jurisdictions, as many as 90%

of the defendants who were convicted after trial and sentenced to prison will appeal their convictions. Even with almost automatic appeal by this group, however, the total number of appeals to the intermediate appeals court is likely to amount to less than 10% of all convictions entered by the state's general trial court. Of course, where the jurisdiction provides for extensive appellate review of sentencing, the overall percentage of appeals is likely to be somewhat higher. Appeals from misdemeanor convictions before the magistrate courts, on the other hand, can very well amount to less than 1% of the number of convictions entered in the magistrate courts.

Appeals challenging convictions raise a wide range of issues, usually relating to some action or inaction of the trial judge. The court's admission of evidence challenged as unconstitutionally obtained stands out in several jurisdictions as by far the most frequently raised appellate objection, but in others, that objection is raised no more frequently than several other claims, such as the alleged insufficiency of the evidence and incompetency of counsel.

Step 18. Postconviction Remedies. After the appellate process is exhausted, imprisoned defendants may be able to use postconviction remedies to challenge their convictions on limited grounds. In particular, federal postconviction remedies are available to state as well as federal prisoners to challenge their convictions in the federal courts on most constitutional grounds. The federal district courts currently receive roughly 18,000 such postconviction applications. Relief is granted on less than 3 percent of these petitions, however, and the relief often is limited to requiring a further hearing. In the state system, annual postconviction challenges typically fall below 5% of all felony filings.

SECTION 2. THE PURPOSES OF THE CRIMINAL LAW

JUDGE MARVIN E. FRANKEL—CRIMINAL SENTENCES

7–8, 23–24, 105–111 (1973).

Why do we impose punishment? Or is it properly to be named "punishment"? Is our purpose retributive? Is it to deter the defendant himself or others in the community from committing crimes? Is it for reform? rehabilitation? incapacitation of dangerous people? Questions like these have engaged philosophers and students of the criminal law for centuries. There are no easy—probably no single, simple—answers. But perhaps differing from concerns about angels and pins, these problems as to the purposes of criminal sanctions are, or should be, at the bedrock of any rational structure of criminal law. It makes all the difference in the world, for instance, whether we think, as it is fashionable nowadays to say, that only rehabilitation of the offender can justify confinement. It is impossible on that premise to order a week in jail for the elderly official finally caught after years of graft, now turned out of office and disgraced, and neither in need of nor susceptible to any extant kinds of rehabilitation. Leaving this subject for the time being * * *, I make the point that our legislators have not done the most rudimentary job of enacting meaningful sentencing "laws" when they have neglected even to sketch democratically determined statements of basic purpose. Left at large, wandering in deserts of uncharted discretion, the judges suit their own value systems insofar as they think about the problem at all. * * *

Beyond the random spreads of judicial attitudes, there is broad latitude in our sentencing laws for kinds of class bias that are commonly known, never explicitly acknowledged, and at war with the superficial neutrality of the statute as literally written. Judges are on the whole more likely to have known personally tax evaders, or people just like tax evaders, than car thieves or dope pushers. Dichotomies of a similar kind are obvious beyond the need to multiply examples. Can such items of personal experience fail to have effects upon sentencing? I do not stop at simpleminded observations about the substantial numbers of judges who simply do not impose prison sentences for tax evasion though the federal law, for example, provides a maximum of five years per count (and tax-evasion prosecutions frequently involve several tax years, with each a separate count). There are more things at stake than judicial "bias" when tax evaders average relatively rare and brief prison terms, while more frequent and much longer average terms (under a statute carrying the same five-year maximum) are imposed for interstate transport of stolen motor vehicles.* Whatever other factors may be operating, however, it is not possible to avoid the impression that the judges' private senses of good and evil are playing significant parts no matter what the law on the books may define as the relative gravity of the several crimes. And, although it anticipates a later subject, this is certainly the focus of the familiar jailhouse complaint that "the more you steal, the less of a sentence you get." I believe the complaint has a basis in the fundamental realities and in the way justice is seen to be dispensed. The latter aspect is important in itself; among our sounder aphorisms is the one teaching that justice must not only be done, but must appear to be done. Both objectives are missed by a system leaving to individual preferences and value judgments the kind of discretion our judges have over sentencing. * * *

A Supreme Court opinion in 1958 made the obvious point that the "apportionment of punishment," its "severity," "its efficacy or its futility," all "are peculiarly questions of legislative policy."** Fully agreeing that this *ought to be* so, I have been saying at some length that the legislature has for too long abdicated this basic function. To begin at the elementary beginning, we have an almost entire absence in the United States of legislative determinations—of "law"—governing the basic questions as to the purposes and justifications of criminal sanctions. Without binding guides on such questions, it is inevitable that individual sentencers will strike out on a multiplicity of courses chosen by each decision-maker for himself. The result is chaos.

The writings of philosophers and lawyers about sentencing have identified a familiar small list of purposes to be sought through the imposition of criminal sanctions. There is not universal agreement on the list. There are bookshelves of disputation concerning the feasibility or moral propriety of one asserted objective or another. Skirting that interesting subject, let me just note for present uses the main ends of criminal sentences that have been posited at one time or another:

Retribution, the exaction of payment—"an eye for an eye."

Deterrence, which may be "general" (i.e., discouraging others than the defendant from committing the wrong), "special" (discouraging the specific defendant from doing it again), or both.

Denunciation, or condemnation—as a symbol of distinctively criminal "guilt," as an affirmation and re-enforcement of moral standards, and as reassurance to the law-abiding.

Incapacitation, during the time of confinement.

Rehabilitation or *reformation* of the offender.

* It may serve only to confirm a priori hunches, but consider these illustrative figures for federal sentences in the fiscal year 1969. Of 502 defendants convicted for income tax fraud, 95, or 19 percent, received prison terms, the average term being three months. Of 3,791 defendants sentenced for auto theft, 2,373, or 63 percent, went to prison, the average term being 7.6 months. From the Administrative Office of the U.S. Courts' publication, *Federal Offenders in the United States District Courts,* 1969, pp. 146–7 (1971).

** *Gore v. United States,* 357 U.S. 386, 393 (1958).

Different scholars would shorten or lengthen the list, or prefer other terminology. While the academic debate continues, it is ignored by those empowered (and expected) to make uniform rules of law. We have in our country virtually no legislative declarations of the principles justifying criminal sanctions. It will take only a minute or two to show that this is much more than an aesthetically regrettable lack. It is the omission of foundation stones, without which no stable or reliable structure is possible.

To begin at the first item on the debatable list, there is in contemporary jurisprudential literature a large majority for, but a vocal minority against, the view that retribution is not an acceptable aim of sentencing. There are judges, naturally, on both sides of the issue. While that is to be expected, the power of the judges to go their variable and conflicting ways in sentencing is not tolerable. And it is perfectly clear that divergent opinions on the purposes of punishment will lead to divergent decisions as to the appropriate sentence. We expect judges, like others, to hold varying opinions on many things—on the scope and limits of permissible wiretapping, on the desirability of outlawing gambling, on bank loans for securities purchases, on prostitution, whatever. But we neither expect nor permit that each judge should follow his private judgment in deciding the legal consequences of these— or any—forms of conduct. The consequences are matters of law, prescribed legislatively and equally for all.

It seems clear to me that judgments affecting consequences so grave as the length and character of sentences should similarly be matters of law. Whatever our individual preferences may be, it is for the legislature in our system to decide and prescribe the legitimate bases for criminal sanctions. Accordingly, while it may remain a matter for debate and amendment in the future, there ought to be one uniform rule now on such questions as whether retribution is a legitimate concept to be entertained by a judge in determining a sentence. There should be at a minimum a basic provision of the criminal code listing and defining the legislatively decreed purposes or objectives the community has chosen to pursue, for the time being, by means of criminal sanctions. * * *

To illustrate these points, let us hypothesize a sentencing code with an initial section declaring the permissible objects of sentencing. Suppose the list is the one I tendered awhile ago: retribution, deterrence ("general" and "special"), denunciation, incapacitation, and rehabilitation. Assume that the sentencer must decide and state which of these purposes underlie the judgment in each individual case. Assume, finally, that the system is to include both definite and indeterminate sentences—i.e., some to be fixed in length at the time of sentencing, others to be fixed finally by later decisions of a parole board.

One clear benefit of such provisions would be a long step toward sense and rationality in choosing for the particular case between the two kinds of sentences. If the sentencer determines that the particular case implicates the goals of general deterrence and, perhaps, retribution—and determines at the same time that the defendant is neither dangerous nor a suitable candidate for rehabilitation—there should be no occasion for an indeterminate sentence. Whatever complexities and imponderables there are—and there are plenty, some to be touched upon below—there is none that is not knowable on the day of sentencing. Or, to note the other side of the coin, there is none that is justifiably postponed for, or assigned to, parole-board consideration. There are no factors or questions peculiarly suited—or, indeed, suited at all—to handling by the supposed expertise of parole officials. The impact of the sentence in such a case is presumably achieved in the very fact, and at the very time, of its pronouncement. Assuming, of course, that sentences are known to be carried out, the effect of the example on other people is achieved and the desire for vengeance is satisfied without regard to the kinds of treatment and observation to which the prisoner is thereafter subjected. It is arguable, in fact, that indeterminacy in such a case is unsound, quite apart from its oppressive impact upon the defendant. Since the effects for general deterrence and retribution are really aimed at people other than the defendant himself, uncertainty in the sentence tends to diminish or dissipate its impact.

To elaborate this simple analysis a little more, take the case where the sentencer has studied the defendant and found concrete needs for incapacitation and rehabilitation. This, of course, presents the arguable occasion for an indeterminate sentence. In this sort of case, the intended effect is upon the defendant and is to be achieved, in considerable measure at least, over some period of time, not at the instant of sentencing. The questions presented at the time of the sentence entail predictions: when, if ever, will the defendant's dangerous propensities subside? How soon may we hope to cure or alleviate the defects disposing him to violate the criminal law? Being in their nature risky predictions, the answers to such questions must be tentative, subject to later verification or correction.

It should be obvious that the purpose or purposes of a sentence are first steps toward deciding whether a definite or indeterminate term is appropriate. However obvious, the point is systematically ignored both in existing statutes prescribing penalties and in the current judgments of the courts. Existing codes, buttressed by still prevalent professional opinion, rarely make distinctions along the lines of purpose. They tend simply to provide for indeterminacy across the board. They do not call upon the sentencer even to consider, let alone to state, whether any rehabilitative or incapacitating goal is involved. There is no suggestion of what a parole board is to be looking at or looking for as it hears the prisoner's application for release. Small wonder that our parole boards characteristically never tell the prisoner—or anyone—the grounds of their decisions. Who knows if they know?

Without pretending to follow the whole course of implications and issues, we can readily see further stages of judgment after the choice between a definite and an indefinite sentence has been made. Where we seek only general deterrence, say, of tax evaders or bribetakers, we may come to see that relatively short but substantially inexorable sentences to prison are the prescription. More complex questions present themselves when we think the case involves a need or a desire for rehabilitation. It does not follow as a matter of good sense—though it appears currently to be a matter of practice—that such a sentence must or should be indeterminate. First off, it is not definitive that a judge (perhaps echoing, without deep insight, the debatable views of others) is led to say there is a need for rehabilitation. He may be wrong. If he is right, there is still the question whether and where appropriate rehabilitative resources may be found. It is a familiar kind of well-intended mockery for our judges to imagine vaguely, or to say, that psychotherapy or some other form of treatment is the proper course for a defendant, to impose a supposedly rehabilitative sentence, and to ignore that there is no pertinent treatment available where the defendant is sent or anywhere else in the state's penal facilities.

Compelled to focus on what he thinks he means by rehabilitation, the sentencer should be better able to know whether he really means it at all. He should be able to see with some clarity whether and why the sentence should be indeterminate. He should be moved to ask insistently where the defendant will be taken from the courtroom, what will be done to or for him, and why that course is thought to present realistic prospects of rehabilitation.

BERGMAN URGES JUDGE TO "SHOW MERCY" AND NOT JAIL HIM FOR AGED–HOME FRAUD

New York Times, June 17, 1976, at 39, col. 1.

Bernard Bergman, the nursing home promoter, appealed to a Federal judge yesterday not to send him to prison for his confessed role in a $1.2 million Medicaid and tax fraud.

Mr. Bergman, with his voice breaking, asked Judge Marvin Frankel to "spare me more suffering" and "show me mercy." The judge, who expressed impatience with defense arguments minimizing the crime, said he would pass sentence this morning. Mr. Bergman faces a maximum term in prison of eight years.

"I pleaded guilty to those charges because I permitted my business to be conducted in a manner that violated the law," he said. "I intended no evil and I am not the monster I was portrayed as being."

Nathan Lewin, one of three lawyers appearing for Mr. Bergman at the presentence hearing in United States District Court at Foley Square, argued that the major fraud had been committed by an accountant and that the offenses admitted by Mr. Bergman were "technical."

Judge Frankel retorted that the defendant had pleaded guilty to "a serious Federal offense" that indeed had cost the Government money in the form of a "no-show" job by Mr. Bergman's wife and a contract with a company secretly controlled by Mr. Bergman for services paid by Medicaid.

"At this point," the judge said, "I begin to wonder whether there has been a failure to plead guilty. Now you tell me that although he admitted these facts, there were no untoward effects."

Mr. Bergman's lawyers disclosed that they had suggested to the court alternatives to imprisonment, such as assigning him to teach high school students about the lessons of the Holocaust, or visiting the sick and incapacitated.

Sentencing had originally been set for last Monday, but had been postponed during negotiations between Mr. Bergman and Federal and state prosecutors over the amount of restitution. Monroe Friedman, another of Mr. Bergman's lawyers, revealed that he had offered to pay back about one-third of a million dollars.

The New York State Health Department has claimed overpayments of more than $2 million for capital costs alone at Mr. Bergman's Park Crescent Nursing Home at 87th Street and Riverside Drive in Manhattan. Other large claims are pending for allegedly padded operating costs at the Park Crescent and the now closed Towers Nursing Home, at 106th Street and Central Park West.

Following plea bargaining, Mr. Bergman pleaded guilty three months ago to the Federal conspiracy indictment and to a state indictment alleging that he had bribed Albert H. Blumenthal, the Assembly majority leader, to obtain his influence in getting a license for the Park Crescent. In return, he and his family were granted immunity from further prosecution. * * *

Mr. Friedman told the court yesterday that Mr. Bergman had cooperated with the prosecution in testifying about his relations with politicians, adding that the plea-bargain had excused the operator from testifying about other nursing homes. Jeremy Epstein, an Assistant United States Attorney, said the defendant's information had been of little value aside from the Blumenthal case.

[Mr. Friedman] argued also that other nursing-home operators who had pleaded guilty had not been sent to prison. Mr. Lewin, the lawyer, cited the cases of Eugene Hollander and Frank Trippi. Mr. Hollander was sentenced to spend five nights a week for six months in a Federal treatment center. Mr. Trippi, of Buffalo, drew 10 years, but is free on bail pending appeal.

Mr. Hollander agreed to withdraw from the nursing home business and to make restitution, but officials said yesterday that he had not yet begun to pay back the more than $1 million he was committed to pay nor the nearly $6 million in other overpayments claimed by the state. * * *

UNITED STATES v. BERGMAN

United States District Court, Southern District of New York, 1976.

416 F.Supp. 496.

SENTENCING MEMORANDUM

FRANKEL, DISTRICT JUDGE.

Defendant is being sentenced upon his plea of guilty to two counts of an 11–count indictment. The sentencing proceeding is unusual in some respects. It has been the subject of more extensive submissions, written and oral, than this court has ever received upon such an occasion. The court has studied some hundreds of pages of memoranda and exhibits, plus scores of volunteered letters. A broad array of issues has been addressed. Imaginative suggestions of law and penology have been tendered. A preliminary conversation with counsel, on the record, preceded the usual sentencing hearing. Having heard counsel again and the defendant speaking for himself, the court postponed the pronouncement of sentence for further reconsideration of thoughts generated during the days of studying the briefs and oral pleas. It seems fitting now to report in writing the reasons upon which the court concludes that defendant must be sentenced to a term of four months in prison.[1]

I. Defendant and His Crimes

Defendant appeared until the last couple of years to be a man of unimpeachably high character, attainments, and distinction. A doctor of divinity and an ordained rabbi, he has been acclaimed by people around the world for his works of public philanthropy, private charity, and leadership in educational enterprises. Scores of letters have come to the court from across this and other countries reporting debts of personal gratitude to him for numerous acts of extraordinary generosity. (The court has also received a kind of petition, with fifty-odd signatures, in which the signers, based upon learning acquired as newspaper readers, denounce the defendant and urge a severe sentence. Unlike the pleas for mercy, which appear to reflect unquestioned facts inviting compassion, this document should and will be disregarded.) In addition to his good works, defendant has managed to amass considerable wealth in the ownership and operation of nursing homes, in real estate ventures, and in a course of substantial investments.

Beginning about two years ago, investigations of nursing homes in this area, including questions of fraudulent claims for Medicaid funds, drew to a focus upon this defendant among several others. The results that concern us were the present indictment and two state indictments. After extensive pretrial proceedings, defendant embarked upon elaborate plea negotiations with both state and federal prosecutors. A state guilty plea and the instant plea were entered in March of this year. (Another state indictment is expected to be dismissed after defendant is sentenced on those to which he has pled guilty.) As part of the

---

1. The court considered, and finally rejected, imposing a fine in addition to the prison term. Defendant seems destined to pay hundreds of thousands of dollars in restitution. The amount is being worked out in connection with a state criminal indictment. Apart from defendant's further liabilities for federal taxes, any additional money exaction is appropriately left for the state court.

detailed plea arrangements, it is expected that the prison sentence imposed by this court will comprise the total covering the state as well as the federal convictions.[2]

For purposes of the sentence now imposed, the precise details of the charges, and of defendant's carefully phrased admissions of guilt, are not matters of prime importance. Suffice it to say that the plea on Count One (carrying a maximum of five years in prison and a $10,000 fine) confesses defendant's knowing and wilful participation in a scheme to defraud the United States in various ways, including the presentation of wrongfully padded claims for payments under the Medicaid program to defendant's nursing homes. Count Three, for which the guilty plea carries a theoretical maximum of three more years in prison and another $5,000 fine, is a somewhat more "technical" charge. Here, defendant admits to having participated in the filing of a partnership return which was false and fraudulent in failing to list people who had bought partnership interests from him in one of his nursing homes, had paid for such interests, and had made certain capital withdrawals.

The conspiracy to defraud, as defendant has admitted it, is by no means the worst of its kind; it is by no means as flagrant or extensive as has been portrayed in the press; it is evidently less grave than other nursing-home wrongs for which others have been convicted or publicized. At the same time, the sentence, as defendant has acknowledged, is imposed for two federal felonies including, as the more important, a knowing and purposeful conspiracy to mislead and defraud the Federal Government.

II. The Guiding Principles of Sentencing

Proceeding through the short list of the supposed justifications for criminal sanctions, defense counsel urge that no licit purpose could be served by defendant's incarceration. Some of these arguments are plainly sound; others are not.

The court agrees that this defendant should not be sent to prison for "rehabilitation." Apart from the patent inappositeness of the concept to this individual, this court shares the growing understanding that no one should ever be sent to prison *for rehabilitation.* That is to say, nobody who would not otherwise be locked up should suffer that fate on the incongruous premise that it will be good for him or her. Imprisonment is punishment. Facing the simple reality should help us to be civilized. It is less agreeable to confine someone when we deem it an affliction rather than a benefaction. If someone must be imprisoned—for other, valid reasons—we should seek to make rehabilitative resources available to him or her. But the goal of rehabilitation cannot fairly serve in itself as grounds for the sentence to confinement.[3]

Equally clearly, this defendant should not be confined to incapacitate him. He is not dangerous. It is most improbable that he will commit similar, or any, offenses in the future. There is no need for "specific deterrence."

Contrary to counsel's submissions, however, two sentencing considerations demand a prison sentence in this case:

First, the aim of *general deterrence,* the effort to discourage similar wrongdoing by others through a reminder that the law's warnings are real and that the grim consequence of imprisonment is likely to follow from crimes of deception for gain like those defendant has admitted.

---

2. This is not absolutely certain. Defendant has been told, however, that the imposition of any additional prison sentence by the state court will be an occasion for reconsidering today's judgment.

3. This important point, correcting misconceptions still widely prevalent, is developed more fully by Dean Norval Morris in *The Future of Imprisonment* (1974).

Second, the related, but not identical, concern that any lesser penalty would, in the words of the *Model Penal Code,* § 7.01(1)(c), "depreciate the seriousness of the defendant's crime."

Resisting the first of these propositions, defense counsel invoke Immanuel Kant's axiom that "one man ought never to be dealt with merely as a means subservient to the purposes of another."[4] In a more novel, but equally futile, effort, counsel urge that a sentence for general deterrence "would violate the Eighth Amendment proscription against cruel and unusual punishment." Treating the latter point first, because it is a short subject, it may be observed simply that if general deterrence as a sentencing purpose were now to be outlawed, as against a near unanimity of views among state and federal jurists, the bolt would have to come from a place higher than this.[5]

As for Dr. Kant, it may well be that defense counsel mistake his meaning in the present context.[6] Whether or not that is so, and without pretending to authority on that score, we take the widely accepted stance that a criminal punished in the interest of general deterrence is not being employed *"merely* as a means * * *." Reading Kant to mean that every man must be deemed *more* than the instrument of others, and must "always be treated as an end in himself,"[7] the humane principle is not offended here. Each of us is served by the enforcement of the law—not least a person like the defendant in this case, whose wealth and privileges, so long enjoyed, are so much founded upon law. More broadly, we are driven regularly in our ultimate interests as members of the community to use ourselves and each other, in war and in peace, for social ends. One who has transgressed against the criminal laws is certainly among the more fitting candidates for a role of this nature. This is no arbitrary selection. Warned in advance of the prospect, the transgressor has chosen, in the law's premises, "between keeping the law required for society's protection or paying the penalty."[8]

But the whole business, defendant argues further, is guesswork; we are by no means certain that deterrence "works." The position is somewhat overstated; there is, in fact, some reasonably "scientific" evidence for the efficacy of criminal sanctions as deterrents, at least as against some kinds of crimes.[9] Moreover, the time is not yet here when all we can "know" must be quantifiable and digestible by computers. The shared wisdom of generations teaches meaningfully, if somewhat amorphously, that the utilitarians have a point; we do, indeed, lapse often into rationality and act to seek pleasure and avoid pain.[10] It would be better, to be sure, if we had more certainty and precision. Lacking these comforts, we continue to include among our working hypotheses a belief (with some concrete evidence in its support) that crimes like those in this case—deliberate, purposeful, continuing, non-impulsive, and committed for profit—are among those most likely to be generally deterrable by sanctions most shunned by those exposed to temptation.[11]

The idea of avoiding depreciation of the seriousness of the offense implicates two or three thoughts, not always perfectly clear or universally agreed upon, beyond the idea of

---

4. Quoting from I. Kant, *Philosophy of Law* 1986 (Hastie Trans.1887).

5. To a large extent the defendant's eighth amendment argument is that imprisoning him because he has been "newsworthy" would be cruelly wrong. This thought is accepted by the court without approaching the Constitution. (See below.) The reference at this point is meant to acknowledge, if only to reject, a seemingly broader submission.

6. See H.L.A. Hart, *Punishment and Responsibility* 243–44 (1968).

7. Andenaes, *The Morality of Deterrence,* 37 U.Chi. L.Rev. 649 (1970). See also O. Holmes, *Common Law* 43–44, 46–47 (1881).

8. H.L.A. Hart, supra note 6, at 23.

9. See, e.g., F. Zimring and G. Hawkins, *Deterrence* 168–71, 282 (1973).

10. See Andenaes, supra note 7, at 663–64.

11. For some supporting evidence that "white-collar" offenses are somewhat specially deterrable, see Chambliss, *Types of Deviance and the Effectiveness of Legal Sanctions,* 1967 Wis.L.Rev. 703, 708–10.

deterrence. It should be proclaimed by the court's judgment that the offenses are grave, not minor or purely technical. Some attention must be paid to the demand for equal justice; it will not do to leave the penalty of imprisonment a dead letter as against "privileged" violators while it is employed regularly, and with vigor, against others. There probably is in these conceptions an element of retributiveness, as counsel urge. And retribution, so denominated, is in some disfavor as a reason for punishment. It remains a factor, however, as Holmes perceived,[12] and as is known to anyone who talks to judges, lawyers, defendants, or people generally. It may become more palatable, and probably more humanely understood, under the rubric of "deserts" or "just deserts."[13] However the concept is formulated, we have not yet reached a state, supposing we ever should, in which the infliction of punishments for crime may be divorced generally from ideas of blameworthiness, recompense, and proportionality.

III. An Alternative, "Behavioral Sanction"

Resisting prison above all else, defense counsel included in their thorough memorandum on sentencing two proposals for what they call a "constructive," and therefore a "preferable" form of "behavioral sanction." One is a plan for Dr. Bergman to create and run a program of Jewish vocational and religious high school training. The other is for him to take charge of a "Committee on Holocaust Studies," again concerned with education at the secondary school level.

A third suggestion was made orally at yesterday's sentencing hearing. It was proposed that Dr. Bergman might be ordered to work as a volunteer in some established agency as a visitor and aide to the sick and the otherwise incapacitated. The proposal was that he could read, provide various forms of physical assistance, and otherwise give comfort to afflicted people.

No one can doubt either the worthiness of these proposals or Dr. Bergman's ability to make successes of them. But both of the carefully formulated "sanctions" in the memorandum involve work of an honorific nature, not unlike that done in other projects to which the defendant had devoted himself in the past. It is difficult to conceive of them as "punishments" at all. The more recent proposal is somewhat more suitable in character, but it is still an insufficient penalty. The seriousness of the crimes to which Dr. Bergman has pled guilty demands something more than "requiring" him to lend his talents and efforts to further philanthropic enterprises. It remains open to him, of course, to pursue the interesting suggestions later on as a matter of unforced personal choice.

IV. "Measuring" the Sentence

In cases like this one, the decision of greatest moment is whether to imprison or not. As reflected in the eloquent submissions for defendant, the prospect of the closing prison doors is the most appalling concern; the feeling is that the length of the sojourn is a lesser question once that threshold is passed. Nevertheless, the setting of a term remains to be accomplished. And in some respects it is a subject even more perplexing, unregulated, and unprincipled.

Days and months and years are countable with a sound of exactitude. But there can be no exactitude in the deliberations from which a number emerges. Without pretending to a nonexistent precision, the court notes at least the major factors.

---

12. See O. Holmes, *Common Law* 41–42, 45 (1881).

13. See A. von Hirsch, *Doing Justice* 45–55 (1976); see also N. Morris, *The Future of Imprisonment* 73–77 (1974).

The criminal behavior, as has been noted, is blatant in character and unmitigated by any suggestion of necessitous circumstance or other pressures difficult to resist. However, metaphysicians may conjure with issues about free will, it is a fundamental premise of our efforts to do criminal justice that competent people, possessed of their faculties, make choices and are accountable for them. In this sometimes harsh light, the case of the present defendant is among the clearest and least relieved. Viewed against the maxima Congress ordained, and against the run of sentences in other federal criminal cases, it calls for more than a token sentence.[14]

On the other side are factors that take longer to enumerate. Defendant's illustrious public life and works are in his favor, though diminished, of course, by what this case discloses. This is a first, probably a last, conviction. Defendant is 64 years old and in imperfect health, though by no means so ill, from what the court is told, that he could be expected to suffer inordinately more than many others of advanced years who go to prison.

Defendant invokes an understandable, but somewhat unworkable, notion of "disparity." He says others involved in recent nursing home fraud cases have received relatively light sentences for behavior more culpable than his. He lays special emphasis upon one defendant whose frauds appear indeed to have involved larger amounts and who was sentenced to a maximum of six months' incarceration, to be confined for that time only on week nights, not on week days or weekends. This court has examined the minutes of that sentencing proceeding and finds the case distinguishable in material respects. But even if there were a threat of such disparity as defendant warns against, it could not be a major weight on the scales.

Our sentencing system, deeply flawed, is characterized by disparity. We are to seek to "individualize" sentences, but no clear or clearly agreed standards govern the individualization. The lack of meaningful criteria does indeed leave sentencing judges far too much at large. But the result, with its nagging burdens on conscience, cannot be meaningfully alleviated by allowing any handful of sentences in a short series to fetter later judgments. The point is easy, of course, where Sentence No. 1 or Sentences 1–5 are notably harsh. It cannot be that a later judge, disposed to more leniency, should feel in any degree "bound." The converse is not identical, but it is not totally different. The net of this is that this court has considered and has given some weight to the trend of the other cited sentences (though strict logic might call for none), but without treating them as forceful "precedents" in any familiar sense.

How, then, the particular sentence adjudged in this case? As has been mentioned, the case calls for a sentence that is more than nominal. Given the other circumstances, however—including that this is a first offense, by a man no longer young and not perfectly well, where danger of recidivism is not a concern—it verges on cruelty to think of confinement for a term of years. We sit, to be sure, in a nation where prison sentences of extravagant length are more common than they are almost anywhere else. By that light, the term imposed today is not notably long. For this sentencing court, however, for a nonviolent first offense involving no direct assaults or invasions of others' security (as in bank robbery, narcotics, etc.), it is a stern sentence. For people like Dr. Bergman, who might be disposed to engage in similar wrongdoing, it should be sufficiently frightening to serve the major end of general deterrence. For all but the profoundly vengeful, it should not depreciate the seriousness of his offenses.

---

14. Despite Biblical teachings concerning what is expected from those to whom much is given, the court has not, as his counsel feared might happen, held Dr. Bergman to a higher standard of responsibility because of his position in the community. But he has not been judged under a lower standard either.

V. Punishment in or for the Media

Much of defendant's sentencing memorandum is devoted to the extensive barrage of hostile publicity to which he has been subjected during the years before and since his indictment. He argues, and it appears to be undisputed, that the media (and people desiring to be featured in the media) have vilified him for many kinds of evildoing of which he has in fact been innocent. Two main points are made on this score with respect to the problem of sentencing.

First, as has been mentioned, counsel express the concern that the court may be pressured toward severity by the force of the seeming public outcry. That the court should not allow itself to be affected in this way is clear beyond discussion. Nevertheless, it is not merely permissible, but entirely wholesome and responsible, for counsel to bring the expressed concern out in the open. Whatever our ideals and mixed images about judges, it would be naive to doubt that judges have sometimes been swept by a sense of popular demand toward draconian sentencing decisions. It cannot hurt for the sentencing judge to be reminded of this and cautioned about it. There can be no guarantees. The sentencer must confront and regulate himself. But it bears reaffirmance that the court must seek to discount utterly the fact of notoriety in passing its judgment upon the defendant. Defense counsel cite reported opinions of this court reflecting what happens in a large number of unreported cases, by the present sentencer and many others, in which "unknown" defendants have received prison sentences, longer or shorter than today's, for white-collar or comparably nonviolent crimes. The overall run of cases, with all their individual variations, will reflect, it is hoped, earnest efforts to hew to the principle of equal treatment, with or without publicity.

Defendant's second point about his public humiliation is the frequently heard contention that he should not be incarcerated because he "has been punished enough." The thought is not without some initial appeal. If punishment were wholly or mainly retributive, it might be a weighty factor. In the end, however, it must be a matter of little or no force. Defendant's notoriety should not in the last analysis serve to lighten, any more than it may be permitted to aggravate, his sentence. The fact that he has been pilloried by journalists is essentially a consequence of the prestige and privileges he enjoyed before he was exposed as a wrongdoer. The long fall from grace was possible only because of the height he had reached. The suffering from loss of public esteem reflects a body of opinion that the esteem had been, in at least some measure, wrongly bestowed and enjoyed. It is not possible to justify the notion that this mode of nonjudicial punishment should be an occasion for leniency not given to a defendant who never basked in such an admiring light at all. The quest for both the appearance and the substance of equal justice prompts the court to discount the thought that the public humiliation serves the function of imprisonment.

Writing, as judges rarely do, about a particular sentence concentrates the mind with possibly special force upon the experience of the sentencer as well as the person sentenced. Consigning someone to prison, this defendant or any other, "is a sad necessity." There are impulses of avoidance from time to time—toward a personally gratifying leniency or toward an opposite extreme. But there is, obviously, no place for private impulse in the judgment of the court. The course of justice must be sought with such objective rationality as we can muster, tempered with mercy, but obedient to the law, which, we do well to remember, is all that empowers a judge to make other people suffer.

SUPPLEMENTAL SENTENCING MEMORANDUM ON ADJOURNMENT OF SURRENDER

The defendant moves to adjourn his surrender on the ground that interrelated plea bargains by state and federal prosecutors contemplate coordinated sentencing decisions in this and the state court. Apparently recognizing the soundness of defendant's basic position, the United States Attorney agreed last week that this court should not even impose sentence until the state court was ready to sentence on the same day. Now, however, citing the court's refusal to postpone sentencing, the United States Attorney takes a fundamentally changed position on surrender. But it was or should have been plain that this court's decision to impose sentence, and the simultaneous delay of surrender, was meant to leave time for an intervening state sentence, since it was understood that an additional state sentence might warrant some further application here. In any case, as events have developed, the propriety of postponing surrender is obvious. The reasons why this is so, given the history of these proceedings, merit some explication.

This is a case in which two prosecutors, state and federal, brought indictments charging monstrous frauds and larcenies, but then chose to deal away most of the charges in two narrowly drawn plea bargains. It is highly probable that if either prosecutor had proved even a substantial part of his charges in open court, Dr. Bergman would have faced a heavy sentence indeed. Instead of taking these charges to trial, however, the prosecutors entered into interrelated plea bargains with the defendant's counsel. Both agreements were reduced to writing, signed by the parties, and made a part of the public record.

The federal and state plea bargains provided that the Special State Prosecutor was to drop his fraud and larceny indictment altogether and only require the defendant to plead to a much narrower one charging bribery of a state legislator. (That indictment was dismissed as against the legislator. The dismissal is being appealed.) Both plea agreements provided that Dr. Bergman was to plead guilty to only Counts One and Three of the 11–count federal indictment. Although these are serious crimes, they are moderate in comparison to the full panoply of the offenses originally charged. Under the federal agreement, the defendant was permitted to plead guilty by reading a prepared statement of narrowly drawn, tightly limited admissions of fact, which were to be all the defendant would confess (and all he could justly be sentenced for). This statement contained nothing, for example, about $1.2 million or $2.5 million or any other astronomical sums of allegedly fraudulent Medicaid claims. There was certainly nothing about whether the Bergman nursing homes had given good or bad nursing care.

This court's duty was, of course, to sentence defendant for what he had admitted, not upon accusations that were not only unproved, but that the prosecutors had agreed to drop as criminal charges. The general public could easily have misunderstood this. But the plea bargainers certainly had no reason to misunderstand. It appears, however, that there have been, putting the best face upon things, some possible misunderstandings.

As part of the plea bargain, though his case has been scheduled as the first and primary one, the Special State Prosecutor agreed to have the problem of sentencing handled by the federal court.[1] He further agreed to "recommend to the Judge of the New York State Supreme Court who will sentence Bernard Bergman on his plea of guilty to

---

1. Implementing the understanding that the state case would go to trial first, and might well obviate a trial of the federal case altogether, this court on September 29, 1975, deferred the federal prosecution, noting "that the central concerns of the two prosecutions relate primarily to matters of state interest." The adjournment was granted on papers that included an affidavit by the Special State Prosecutor, who pointed out that his office had conducted "a thorough investigation into alleged abuses and fraudulent practices in the nursing home industry." There was every reason to expect that the results of that investigation would be made the subjects of lawful proof, under familiar safeguards, in the state prosecution. On that anticipation, a month later this court disposed very briefly of a substantial motion in which the defendant urged that the federal indictment alleged essentially state claims and was not a valid indictment at all. In thus deciding that the motion should not be granted, this court observed that the case might well have a different aspect after the completion of the state prosecution, and that it might well prove unnecessary to consider whether there was any sufficient federal interest to pursue.

making unlawful payments to [a state legislator] that, in light of Bernard Bergman having voluntarily disclosed the facts of the crime to the Special Prosecutor and since the Federal Judge will know of these facts when he imposes sentence on the Federal charges, no sentence additional to that imposed by the United States District Court Judge on the federal indictment be imposed here."

The occasion for the application to postpone surrender is an unresolved dispute, evidently in progress for some time, over the restitution aspect of the state plea bargain. It has been agreed that the defendant "will pay to the State of New York, voluntarily, without any civil action or litigation of any kind, whatever sums of money are owing to the State of New York * * *," the amount to be determined after accountants representing the United States, the State of New York, and the defendant have consulted and examined the relevant financial records. The Special Prosecutor has argued in the state court that the main fault for failing to reach an agreement as to the amount to be paid lies on Dr. Bergman's side. He has said that the plea agreement might well become "a nullity" if the defendant's resistance continues, and might amount after all only to "froth."

If the state plea bargain, for any reason, becomes "a nullity," serious questions will arise as to the closely connected federal bargain. If the Special Prosecutor is forced, after all, to go first, as had been planned, and prove his charges in open court, as he has thus far chosen not to do, there may be an issue as to whether the secondary federal case is barred by double jeopardy or other defenses. More significantly, the federal plea bargain and the state plea bargain are tied inseparably together. The court may not overlook the evident possibility that nullification of the state plea bargain may lead to nullification of the one here and a substantial motion to withdraw the guilty plea and vacate the sentence.

Nobody should be made to begin serving a sentence in such circumstances. Courts serve the public, to be sure. That cannot mean bowing to passing waves of popular frenzy goaded by misunderstanding.

The motion to postpone surrender is granted. Defendant will surrender to begin service of his sentence at 10:30 a.m. on July 7, 1976.

It is so ordered.[2]

BERGMAN SENTENCE IS DISCUSSED

New York Times, June 19, 1976, at 46, col. 2.

When former Vice President Spiro T. Agnew pleaded "no contest" to an income tax evasion charge in 1973 and received no prison sentence, large segments of the public reacted with shock, disbelief and outrage. Similarly, many felt that sentences meted out to several Watergate figures were too lenient. Those same reactions were evident yesterday— from taxi drivers, dozens of irate individuals who telephoned newspapers, politicians, lawyers and judges—following the four-month prison term given Bernard Bergman, the central figure in the New York nursing home scandal. * * *

While expressing admiration for Judge Frankel, Morris B. Abram, the lawyer who headed the state's Moreland Act Commission that investigated nursing homes, said: "The sentence failed to meet society's justified expectations."

---

2. Defendant has also applied to have the court recommend that his sentence be served in a halfway house. The Government opposes on seemingly sound grounds. Halfway houses serve special purposes, none of which appears pertinent to this case. The recommen- dation defendant seeks will not be made. Ultimately, of course, the place of confinement is for the Attorney General, through his Bureau of Prisons, not for the court.

"The 'Bergman' has become a new unit of sentencing," said Justice James J. Leff of State Supreme Court. "This becomes the standard. Every lawyer will ask that his client be treated no more harshly than Mr. Bergman." * * *

Coming to Judge Frankel's defense, Adrian W. DeWind, president of the Association of the Bar of the City of New York said:

"Judge Frankel had better access to all matters relevant to the Bergman sentencing than anyone else. He obviously was not motivated by whether or not his sentence would be popular. In this situation, his reputation as a fair-minded, conscientious jurist of unquestioned integrity should not be overlooked."

But Mr. Abram said: "If the public perceives a wide disparity between sentences inflicted upon the rich and the poor, the cement that holds the society together is impaired."

EDITORIAL—EQUAL JUSTICE?

New York Times, June 18, 1976, at A. 22, col. 2.

Bernard Bergman was brought to justice yesterday. He got four months.

In imposing sentence, United States District Judge Marvin Frankel said, "I've undertaken to impose sentence on what you did and admitted, and not what was reported and rumored." It therefore is hardly useful, in discussing the sentence, to rehearse the history of Mr. Bergman's involvement in the nursing-home business. It is worth noting, however, that after his arrest, Mr. Bergman entered into negotiations with the prosecutor which resulted in his plea of guilty to a charge of conspiring to commit fraud against the United States, a felony carrying a top sentence of five years, and of filing a false income-tax return, another felony, carrying a top sentence of three years.

Judge Frankel said that Mr. Bergman's "imperfect health," the fact that he was a first offender and had been "pilloried in the press," along with considerations of his earlier "unimpeachable high character, attainments and distinction," had an impact on the sentencing process. As a result, on charges of defrauding the Government of $1.2 million and filing a false return, Mr. Bergman was sentenced to four months in prison.

One of the most prominent current theories is that sentences should serve to deter others from committing similar crimes. Though this view is most regularly applied to street crime, it would seem to be substantially more applicable to white-collar criminals to whom prison is much more jarring than to criminals who live at society's economic and social margins. Yet, Mr. Bergman now joins a parade of formerly respectable white-collar criminals who have received sentences which make the odds on white-collar crime look rather good.

A second popular notion about sentencing is that it should show the criminal justice system to be even-handed. At a time when the Legislature is moving toward mandatory sentences of three years for juveniles convicted of serious crimes, a four-month sentence for a rich felon, guilty of a million-dollar fraud, can only reinforce cynicism about the realities of equal justice under law.

———

At a hearing in state court on July 2, the defendant and the special prosecutor both requested a deferral of sentencing on the plea of guilty to bribery pending an audit which would determine the amount of restitution Bergman was to make. As reported in *N.Y. Times,* July 3, 1976, at 18, col. 1:

"At the close of the hearing, Justice Melia, reading from notes, commented sharply on the pressures that he said had been brought upon him in this case. He said he had received 400 letters in favor of Mr. Bergman, many of them apparently 'solicited.' In the last 24 hours, he continued, he received 19 telegrams, 250 letters and many telephone calls, mostly demanding a harsh sentence.

"Most of these, the judge said, were 'in response to a call by a public official.' The reference was to Assemblyman Andrew Stein, Democrat of Manhattan, who visited Justice Melia on Wednesday and, in a news conference, called for measures by the public to urge a maximum sentence of four years.

" 'This is an indecent assault on the court,' Justice Melia said. 'I hope we will not have a repetition of that kind of thing.'

"Mr. Stein, who attended the court session, said in a statement later:

" 'The courts belong to the people and they have a right to air their views. * * * ' "

On July 9, the federal sentence was again stayed pending sentencing in the state court. *N.Y. Times,* July 10, 1976, at 21, col. 4.

———

When the fall term commenced at Hofstra University law school, Dean Monroe Freedman appeared before the student body to explain why he had defended Mr. Bergman. As reported in *N.Y. Times,* Sept. 2, 1976, at 35, col. 1:

"He was not a 'hired gun' who represented anyone who could afford his services, the dean said. Nor did he represent 'only those he loved.'

"Rather, he agreed to help with the Bergman defense because it was 'a cause I believe in.'

" 'Should a 64–year–old man, broken in spirit, broken in health serve time in prison?' he asked.

"The question was rhetorical and not meant to be answered, but many of the students muttered, 'Yes.'

"The dean asked angrily if any students had been inside prisons, which he described as 'cages.'

"A student shot back, 'Have you ever been inside a nursing home?'

"Mr. Freedman replied that his client was the 'victim of some of the most irresponsible and malicious character assassination I have ever seen.'

"But the chief reason for his helping in the case, the dean said, was that it provided an opportunity for him to argue that the theory of general deterrence—punishing an individual so that others would be deterred from committing similar crimes—was an improper rationale for sentencing.

" 'Judge Frankel did not write the opinion I had hoped for,' the dean said. * * *

" 'I think Bernard Bergman should have spent no time at all,' he said."

On Sept. 14th, Bergman was sentenced in state court to one year in a city prison for bribery. The sentencing judge "said Mr. Bergman's long 'shilly-shallying' about the debt [i.e., the amount owed the state because of his Medicaid fraud, which he acknowledged on the date of sentencing was $2.5 million] confirmed a probation report that he appeared to be 'an unscrupulous and corrupt individual,' warped by greed, and with 'no compunction' and 'little or no remorse.' * * *

"Taking in consideration, on the one hand, the prosecutor's recommendation for no additional time and, on the other, 'concern for the proper effect of a sentence on society,' Justice Melia said he was imposing a sentence of one year, rather than the maximum of four years. In reply to a question from the defense, he added, 'consecutive.' " *N.Y. Times,* Sept. 15, 1976, at 1, col. 4.

The following day, Judge Frankel ordered Bergman to begin his federal sentence. He rejected a defense motion to suppress the sentence on the ground that the state plea bargain had been breached, saying that the place to settle that issue was in state court. *N.Y. Times,* Sept. 16, 1976, at 31, col. 3. Bergman was sent to the minimum-security federal prison in Allenwood, Pa. "The 400–acre Allenwood prison was described by its Superintendent, L. Eldon Jensen, as 'a very-minimum-security prison.'

" 'There are fences,' he said, 'but they are not designed to keep people in or out, they're just designed to let us know where our property ends.'

"He added that the prisoners—about 500 of them—live in open, dormitorylike accommodations and have access to a game room, television and a library. They work either in the prison's furniture factory or on its farm.

" 'It doesn't have the feel of a prison in a James Cagney sense,' Mr. Jensen said. 'It's the opposite end of the scale from Lewisburg and Terre Haute and the others.' " *N.Y. Times,* Sept. 17, 1976, at 12, col. 3.

Bergman was released from the federal prison after serving three and a half months of his federal sentence. *N.Y. Times,* Jan. 6, 1977, at 27, col. 5. He sought unsuccessfully to recover his assets from a receivership which was set up as part of his plea bargain with the state, *People v. Bergman,* 55 A.D.2d 542, 389 N.Y.S.2d 589 (1976), and to withdraw his state guilty plea, *N.Y. Times,* Sept. 17, 1976, at 12, col. 3. The state sentence, which he was scheduled to commence serving in mid-January, was stayed pending his appeal, *N.Y. Times,* Dec. 7, 1976, at 45, col. 6, which was unsuccessful, 395 N.Y.S.2d 872 (1977). On the day he was scheduled to commence serving the state sentence, he obtained a stay from federal judge Robert Ward pending a hearing in federal court on the state conviction. "Alan Dershowitz, a lawyer for Mr. Bergman, contended that Mr. Bergman's agreement to plead guilty in both cases had been violated by Charles J. Hynes, the special state prosecutor on nursing homes. Mr. Dershowitz said that Mr. Hynes had broken the agreement by criticizing the four-month Federal sentence imposed on Mr. Bergman by Judge Marvin E. Frankel." *N.Y. Times,* July 13, 1977, at 59, col. 4. That contention was rejected by the federal district court and court of appeals. See *Bergman v. Lefkowitz,* 569 F.2d 705 (2d Cir.1977).

Bergman then surrendered to serve his state sentence, *N.Y. Times,* Feb. 7, 1978, at 24, col. 5, but even thereafter some two dozen lawyers and numerous state and federal officials struggled to untangle Bergman's business affairs. *N.Y. Times,* Oct. 20, 1979, at 26, col. 1. A few years later, the nursing home reopened despite the efforts of community groups contending that Bergman and his family owned the holding company that sold the home to Beth Rifka, a Hasidic organization which assumed operation of the home. *N.Y. Times,* May 17, 1981, at 48, col. 1. At the age of 73, Bernard Bergman died of a heart attack. *N.Y. Times,* June 22, 1984, § 4, p. 6, col. 1.

Notes and Questions

1. Do you agree with Judge Frankel's sentence? Does it square with the points made by author Frankel?

2. Largely because of concerns of the kind raised in the Frankel book, Congress adopted the Comprehensive Crime Control Act of 1984, creating a Sentencing Commission and assigning to that body the responsibility to develop sentencing guidelines. The Commission thereafter approved a set of United States Sentencing Guidelines (U.S.S.G.); they took effect on November 1, 1987, and have subsequently been revised from time to time.

3. Assess, to the extent you can, what Bergman's fate would have been regarding the conspiracy to defraud the government charge had these guidelines been applicable to his case.

The first step under the guidelines is to determine the "base offense level and apply any appropriate specific offense characteristics."[a] For conspiracy, the base offense level is determined from the object offense[b] or most analogous offense,[c] except that it is necessary to "decrease by 3 levels, unless the defendant or a co-conspirator completed all the acts the conspirators believed necessary on their part for the successful completion of the substantive offense or the circumstances demonstrate that the conspirators were about to complete all such acts but for apprehension or interruption by some similar event beyond their control."[d]

Because the object of the conspiracy was fraud, applicable here is the guideline regarding such conduct, which reads in relevant part:

"(a) Base Offense Level: 6

"(b) Specific Offense Characteristics

"(1) If the loss exceeded $2,000, increase the offense level as follows:

	Loss(Apply the Greatest)	Increase in Level
(A)	$2,000 or less	no increase
(B)	More than $2,000	add 1
(C)	More than $5,000	add 2
(D)	More than $10,000	add 3
(E)	More than $20,000	add 4
(F)	More than $40,000	add 5
(G)	More than $70,000	add 6
(H)	More than $120,000	add 7
(I)	More than $200,000	add 8
(J)	More than $350,000	add 9
(K)	More than $500,000	add 10
(L)	More than $800,000	add 11
(M)	More than $1,500,000	add 12 * * *

"(2) If the offense involved (A) more than minimal planning, or (B) a scheme to

a. U.S.S.G. § 1B1.1(b).   **c.** U.S.S.G. § 2X5.1.

b. U.S.S.G. § 2X1.1(a).   **d.** U.S.S.G. § 2X1.1(b)(2).

defraud more than one victim, increase by 2 levels.''[e]

The next step is to "apply the adjustments as appropriate related to victim, role, and obstruction of justice.''[f] The only adjustments arguably possible here have to do with the defendant's role in the offense, as follows:

"Based on the defendant's role in the offense, increase the offense level as follows:

"(a) If the defendant was an organizer or leader of a criminal activity that involved five or more participants or was otherwise extensive, increase by 4 levels.

"(b) If the defendant was a manager or supervisor (but not an organizer or leader) and the criminal activity involved five or more participants or was otherwise extensive, increase by 3 levels.

"(c) If the defendant was an organizer, leader, manager, or supervisor in any criminal activity other than described in (a) or (b), increase by 2 levels.

"If the defendant abused a position of public or private trust, or used a special skill, in a manner that significantly facilitated the commission or concealment of the offense, increase by 2 levels. This adjustment may not be employed if an abuse of trust or skill is included in the base offense level or specific offense characteristic. If this adjustment is based upon an abuse of a position of trust, it may be employed in addition to an adjustment under § 3B1.1 (Aggravating Role); if this adjustment is based solely on the use of a special skill, it may not be employed in addition to an adjustment under § 3B1.1 (Aggravating Role).''[g]

The third step is to "apply the adjustment as appropriate for the defendant's acceptance of responsibility,''[h] as follows:

"(a) If the defendant clearly demonstrates acceptance of responsibility for his offense, decrease the offense level by 2 levels.

"(b) If the defendant qualifies for a decrease under subsection (a), the offense level determined prior to the operation of subsection (a) is level 16 or greater, and the defendant has assisted authorities in the investigation or prosecution of his own misconduct by taking one or more of the following steps:

(1) timely providing complete information to the government concerning his own involvement in the offense; or

(2) timely notifying authorities of his intention to enter a plea of guilty, thereby permitting the government to avoid preparing for trial and permitting the court to allocate its resources efficiently,

decrease the offense level by 1 additional level.''[i]

The fourth step is to "determine the defendant's criminal history category,''[j] and where (as here) there are no prior convictions the category is 0.[k]

The fifth step is to "determine the guideline range * * * that corresponds to the offense level and criminal history category.''[l] For criminal history category 0, this table, stated in terms of months of imprisonment, applies:

Offense Level	Guideline Range	Offense Level	Guideline Range
1	0–6	23	46–57

e. U.S.S.G. § 2F1.1.

f. U.S.S.G. § 1B1.1(c).

g. U.S.S.G. §§ 3B1.1, 3B1.3.

h. U.S.S.G. § 1B1.1(e).

i. U.S.S.G. § 3E1.1.

j. U.S.S.G. § 1B1.1(f).

k. U.S.S.G. § 4A1.1.

l. U.S.S.G. § 1B1.1(g).

Offense Level	Guideline Range	Offense Level	Guideline Range
2	0–6	24	51–63
3	0–6	25	57–71
4	0–6	26	63–78
5	0–6	27	70–87
6	0–6	28	78–97
7	0–6	29	87–108
8	0–6	30	97–121
9	4–10	31	108–135
10	6–12	32	121–151
11	8–14	33	135–168
12	10–16	34	151–188
13	12–18	35	168–210
14	15–21	36	188–235
15	18–24	37	210–262
16	21–27	38	235–293
17	24–30	39	262–327
18	27–33	40	292–365
19	30–37	41	324–405
20	33–41	42	360–life
21	37–46	43	life[m]
22	41–51		

The last step is to apply the sentencing requirements "for the particular guideline range."[n] For criminal history category 0, probation is permissible for offense levels 1–8, or, if the court imposes a condition or combination of conditions requiring intermittent confinement, community confinement, or home detention, offense levels 9–10.[o] "A sentence [of imprisonment] conforms with the guidelines for imprisonment if it is within the minimum and maximum terms of the guideline range,"[p] expressed in the above table in terms of months. (For example, if you were to conclude the offense level was 10, then a sentence anywhere from 6 to 12 months of imprisonment would be within the guidelines.) But, the sentence imposed may not exceed any maximum or minimum set for that crime by statute.[q] "The court shall impose a fine in all cases, except where the defendant establishes that he is unable to pay and is not likely to become able to pay any fine,"[r] usually per this table:

"Fine Table

Offense Level	A Minimum	B Maximum
3 and below	$100	$5,000
4–5	$250	$5,000
6–7	$500	$5,000
8–9	$1,000	$10,000
10–11	$2,000	$20,000
12–13	$3,000	$30,000
14–15	$4,000	$40,000
16–17	$5,000	$50,000

m. U.S.S.G. Ch. 5, Part A.

n. U.S.S.G. § 1B1.1(h).

o. U.S.S.G. § 5B1.1(a).

p. U.S.S.G. § 5C2.1.

q. U.S.S.G. § 5G1.1.

r. U.S.S.G. § 5E1.2(a).

Offense Level	A Minimum	B Maximum
18–19	$6,000	$60,000
20–22	$7,500	$75,000
23–25	$10,000	$100,000
26–28	$12,500	$125,000
29–31	$15,000	$150,000
32–34	$17,500	$175,000
35–37	$20,000	$200,000
38 and above	$25,000	$250,000"[s]

In the event of a plea agreement, it is still necessary that the recommended or agreed to sentence fall within the applicable guideline range,[t] subject to the qualification that a court may depart from a guideline-specified sentence only when it finds "an aggravating or mitigating circumstance * * * that was not adequately taken into consideration by the Sentencing Commission."[u]

4. Would these guidelines have produced a "wiser" sentence in the *Bergman* case? Will they in other cases? Consider the following commentary:

(a) Professor Kate Stith & Federal Court of Appeals Judge Jose A. Cabranes, *Judging Under the Federal Sentencing Guidelines*, 91 Nw.U.L.Rev. 1247, 1254–57, 1263 (1997): "[T]he federal trial judge in today's sentencing ritual has little or no opportunity to consider the overall culpability of the defendant before him. The Guidelines themselves determine not only which factors are relevant (and irrelevant) to criminal punishment, but also, in most circumstances, the precise quantitative relevance of each factor. * * *

"This * * * offers little opportunity for judicial reasoning. The judge's role is largely limited to factual determinations and rudimentary arithmetic operations. Moreover, the Sentencing Commission has taken pains to limit sharply the judge's authority to depart from the sentencing range that these arithmetic calculations yield. * * * One judge has recently likened his role in sentencing to that of a 'notary public'; another has likened the sentencing judge's role under the new dispensation to that of 'an accountant.'

"The hallmark of judging in the common-law tradition is the judge's application of general principles to specific facts, a process by which the general principles are themselves refined, explained, and, indeed, reconsidered. In sentencing, the Guidelines have minimized the opportunities and removed the authority for judges to do what they do best—to reason and to apply general principles of law to particular circumstances. Instead, the Guidelines require judges to address many quantitative and definitional issues in excruciating detail, while staying away from larger questions relating to culpability and the purposes of criminal punishment. Every hour a judge spends analyzing the Guidelines is an hour that might instead be directed toward application, and thus further refinement and development, of common principles and standards of criminal sentencing. * * *

"At the same time that the Guidelines have greatly reduced the authority and role of the judge, they have enhanced the roles of two other actors in the ritual: the prosecutor and the probation officer. Many critics of the Guidelines have insisted that the new system has, at bottom, simply transferred sentencing authority from the judge to the prosecutor. Wary of this possibility, both the Sentencing Commission and the Department of Justice have sought to limit prosecutorial power to plea bargain around the Guidelines, thereby

s.   U.S.S.G. § 5E1.2(c)(3).

t.   U.S.S.G. § 6B1.2.

u.   18 U.S.C.A. § 3553(b).

ensuring the hegemony of the Commission itself. Even so, there is little doubt that the Guidelines have augmented the authority of the prosecutor relative to that of the judge.

"What is clear beyond doubt is that the role of the probation officer has been transformed. Rather than providing guidance to the court in its exercise of sentencing discretion, probation officers now undertake a kind of preliminary adjudication of all issues made relevant by the Sentencing Guidelines. No longer serving merely as a conduit for the parties to present their respective versions of the offense to the judge, the presentence report today gives a single version—one determined, in principle, by the probation officer herself. The officer then provides her Guidelines calculus—applying the Guidelines to the facts as she finds them and computing a recommended sentencing range. Together, these two functions—independent fact-finding and autonomous Guidelines calculation—make the probation officer the ' "special master" of guidelines facts' and the primary enforcer of the Guidelines. * * *

"The sentencing proceeding itself has been recast from a discretionary into a formal adjudicatory process, in which the court makes findings of fact that translate into sentencing requirements under the Guidelines. By largely eliminating from the sentencing proceeding the power of any individual to consider the circumstances of the crime and of the defendant in their entirety and to form a judgment on that basis, the Guidelines threaten to transform the venerable ritual of sentencing into a puppet theater in which defendants are not persons, but kinds of persons, abstract entities to be defined by a chart, their concrete existence systematically ignored and thus nullified. The judge who conducts the sentencing is now, by design, little more than the instrument of a distant bureaucracy. Like the law in Kafka's parable, the real power of the court has receded into an impenetrable state agency, nearly inaccessible to the courtroom observer. The defendant may implore the court to consider the full circumstances of his crime and his humanity, but the judge generally is not permitted to consider most of these circumstances in sentencing. Indeed, the range of attitudes and gestures we commonly associate with sentencing—defiance or contrition on the part of the defendant; vengeance or forgiveness on the part of his victims, condemnation; admonition, or forbearance on the part of the judge—become strangely inappropriate, even cruelly farcical in this setting.

"Without moral authority, neither mercy nor moral condemnation are possible. Under the Guidelines, mercy, by which the full application of the law is relaxed in furtherance of the law's ends, has been rendered largely obsolete. Without the possibility of mercy, however, rigid adherence to the law cannot express severity of judgment. No moral judgment can be expressed at all."

(b) Federal Court of Appeals Judge Frank O. Bowman III, *Fear of Law: Thoughts on Fear of Judging and the State of the Federal Sentencing Guidelines,* 44 St.Louis U.L.J. 299, 314–18 (2000): "The rise of an extensive federal criminal justice system coincided with the rise of the rehabilitative ideal in sentencing in both state and federal courts. The one period in U.S. history in which broad judicial sentencing discretion had the most theoretical and statutory support, state and federal, was the period when the rehabilitative model was in the ascendant, from the late 1800s to the enactment of the Sentencing Reform Act of 1984. But Stith and Cabranes gloss over two critical points about the role of judges in the rehabilitative sentencing model.

"First, judges were granted access to the widest possible range of information about offenders and allowed to fix punishments anywhere in the spectrum from probation to the statutory maximum because they were conceived to be experts in choosing the strength and combination of remedies from the penological armamentarium most likely to effect rehabilitation. Second, the apparently unlimited scope of judicial sentencing power in the rehabilitative period was always something of an illusion. Although federal judges may have had broad power to choose between an incarcerative sentence and pure probation, once the decision to impose any period of imprisonment was made, the picture changed. In all such cases, rather than being lord of the sentencing manor, the judge was both in theory and in fact no more than an equal partner with the parole authorities. The parole authority's regulations and post-conviction case-by-case administrative decisions set the true length of sentence—the actual months and years the defendant would spend behind bars—within the maximum stated by the court.

"Stith and Cabranes repeatedly deride the Guidelines as the misbegotten offspring of excessive rationalism, a sort of bastard child of the Enlightenment. The Guidelines, they say, are 'pseudo-scientific,' and represent a calamitous departure from what they characterize as a long tradition of allowing judges broad exercise of their moral intuition. In fact, this characterization turns history on its head. It was the rehabilitative sentencing model that relied on 'pseudo-science' and unsustainable claims about the power of human rationality. The rehabilitative model rested on the proposition that probation officers, correctional workers, parole authorities, and judges armed with the diagnostic tools and behavior modification techniques of psychology, sociology, and other behavioral sciences could predict and treat anti-social conduct. Thus, in the period which Stith and Cabranes claim as precedent for broad judicial discretion, judges were allowed great sentencing latitude largely because they were viewed as part of a treatment team of criminological professionals whose purpose was protection of society through cure (or, if necessary, lengthy quarantine) of the criminal deviant.

"But the rehabilitative model collapsed in the absence of evidence that its goals were being (or perhaps ever could be) achieved. The Federal Sentencing Guidelines, far from being a product of devotion to 'science' in sentencing, are a reaction against the notion that science has very much to say about criminal punishment. In the place of the claim of rehabilitationists that punishment can be individualized to maximize the odds of 'curing' criminal conduct, the Guidelines substitute three simple, but powerful, ideas—one moral and the other two pragmatically utilitarian. First, the moral lodestar of the Guidelines is that criminals should be punished in proportion to their blameworthiness, which is in turn a function of the degree of harm inflicted and the defendant's state of mind, and to a lesser degree of the defendant's personal circumstances. Second, the two pragmatic generalizations about human behavior the Guidelines have substituted for individualized criminal diagnostics are: (1) The more blameworthy the criminal conduct, the greater risk the defendant poses to society, and the greater is the need for deterrence and incapacitation; and (2) The best measure of the likelihood of recidivism, and thus of the necessity for deterrence and incapacitation, is prior criminal behavior. The interaction of these three ideas produces a sentencing system that determines punishments based on three considerations, in descending order of influence: (a) offense seriousness (an approximation of blameworthiness embodied in the vertical Offense Level axis of the sentencing grid), (b) criminal history (the horizontal axis), and (c) personal circumstances (primarily relevant to choice of sentence within the guideline range and to departures). * * *

"[S]ome commentators who complain about a lack of clearly-stated purposes in the Guidelines (including Professor Stith and Judge Cabranes) are really concerned about who gets to choose the dominant purposes in sentencing rather than with the particular choices the Sentencing Commission made in writing the Guidelines. This group favors a regime in which judges are permitted to decide which purpose shall predominate in each case. In effect, such commentators advocate a system in which a judge is free to decide, for example, that for drug dealer A, the dominant sentencing purpose should be rehabilitation, and thus the sentence will be probation, while for drug dealer B, the dominant sentencing purpose should be deterrence/incapacitation, and thus the sentence will be five years in prison. The Guidelines largely preclude this sort of judicial choice. Instead, they embody an a priori 'legislative' choice by the Sentencing Commission and the Congress that the predominant sentencing purpose in virtually all cases of commercially significant quantities of narcotics is to prevent crime by deterring or incapacitating offenders, and therefore that all drug sellers should go to prison.

"The second complaint that often appears clothed in the contention that the purposes of the Guidelines are unclear comes from commentators whose real beef is not lack of clarity, but the Guidelines' achingly clear emphasis on purposes with which the commentators do not agree. Commentators who have never quite reconciled themselves to the current devaluation of rehabilitation as a sentencing goal often fall into this group."

Chapter 2

THE ABOMINABLE AND DETESTABLE CRIME AGAINST NATURE NOT TO BE NAMED AMONG CHRISTIANS: SOURCES AND LIMITS OF THE CRIMINAL LAW

SECTION 1. THE COMMON LAW

Introductory Notes

1. "In the original common law, which began its development with the Norman domination of England after 1066, crimes and civil wrongs were not clearly distinguished. Moreover, there was no systematic body of criminal prohibitions. Rather, the original common-law offenses consisted of the use of force by the offender in violation of the King's peace and could result in both punitive and compensatory sanctions. It was the use of violence as such, rather than the particular consequences of a violent act, that constituted the wrong. From this foundation, the common law of crimes evolved over the course of centuries. Development took place through judicial decisions interpreting and elaborating the concept of violence into such specific categories as homicide, robbery, arson, and assault. In the later years of the common law's development, particularly from the sixteenth century onward, enactments of Parliament added specific crimes to the array of common-law offenses.

"There was, however, no penal code or official systemization of the law of crimes. Commentaries by jurists * * * undertook to group the array of offenses, common-law and statutory, into coherent order according to the nature of the harm inflicted and the intensity and severity of the violation. The law of crimes thus unofficially systematized was nevertheless essentially common law, that is, the pronouncements of courts defining conduct that constituted a crime. In the colonization of British North America, the common law of crimes was received and applied. With the rupture of sovereignty in the colonies at the time of the American Revolution, however, a strong movement arose to establish all law, including the criminal law, on the foundations of legislative enactments that simply declared the common law, including the common law of crimes, to be in effect except as displaced by particular statutory provisions." Geoffrey C. Hazard, Jr., *Criminal Justice System*, in 2 *Encyclopedia of Crime and Justice* 450, 451 (1983).

2. "At the behest of Henry VIII, the Reformation Parliament of 1533 temporarily criminalized 'the detestable and abominable vice of buggery committed with mankind or

41

beast.' Elizabeth I's second Parliament reenacted the Act of 1533, including its penalty of death for buggery. These statutes secularized offenses that had traditionally been called 'sodomy' and had been regulated by the Roman Catholic Church, which Henry and Elizabeth were renouncing. As applied by the English courts, buggery was understood to include anal intercourse between two men or between a man and a woman ('sodomy'), any sexual intercourse between a human male or female and an animal ('bestiality'), but not oral intercourse between humans (neither sodomy nor bestiality, nor any other species of buggery). Sexual intercourse between women was not regulated by the Act of 1533.

"The English criminal prohibition of buggery and its punishment as a capital crime were generally applicable in the American colonies—either as a matter of common law or by statutory enactment. For example, although Virginia did not formally have a buggery law in place, the colony in 1624–25 tried and executed Richard Cornish, a ship's master, for attacking and sodomizing a steward. Explicitly invoking biblical injunctions, the New England colonies alone considered expanding the coverage of the Act of 1533. The Massachusetts Bay Colony debated but ultimately declined to adopt Reverend John Cotton's 1636 proposal that woman-woman intercourse be included as sodomy. The New Haven Colony in 1656 prohibited under pain of death men lying with men, women lying with women, masturbation (if aggravating circumstances), and any other 'carnall knowledge.' Masturbation and women lying with women were dropped as offenses when the New Haven Colony was annexed by Connecticut in 1665. On the other hand, the authorities in Connecticut and Massachusetts, like those in Virginia, were willing to prosecute men and on at least one occasion women for same-sex lewdness without a specific statutory basis. Altogether, there are records for perhaps as many as twenty sodomy prosecutions and four executions during the colonial period.

"Between independence and 1830, the original thirteen states all adopted laws making buggery or sodomy a serious offense, but most eliminated the death penalty. None of the early statutes defined what precisely was meant by buggery or sodomy, for this remained 'a detestable and abominable sin, amongst Christians not to be named,' as Sir Edward Coke put it in 1644. New states adopted similar laws, usually deploying terminology such as 'sodomy, or the crime against nature, with mankind or beast.' Most of the early statutes were revised by the middle of the century to criminalize what Coke and Blackstone had termed 'the infamous crime against nature.' (Again, note the shift in terminology.) Courts and commentators in the nineteenth century read the sodomy, buggery, carnal knowledge, and crime against nature statutes—hereinafter collectively described simply as sodomy laws—to criminalize 'unnatural' intercourse between men and women as well as men and men, but not between women and women. Although there were only a handful of reported cases * * *, sodomy prosecutions occurred episodically throughout the century." William N. Eskridge, *Hardwick and Historiography*, 1999 U.Ill.L.Rev. 631, 643–46.

COMMONWEALTH v. POINDEXTER

Court of Appeals of Kentucky, 1909.

133 Ky. 720, 118 S.W. 943.

SETTLE, C.J.

The appellees, C. H. Poindexter and Frank Moore, * * * were indicted in the court below for the crime of sodomy. Upon being arraigned for trial they severally entered a plea of guilty, and the trial jury by the verdict returned found them guilty, and fixed their punishment at confinement in the penitentiary two years each. After the return of the verdict appellees entered a motion and grounds for a new trial. The principal ground urged for the new trial was that in entering the plea of guilty on the trial they and their counsel labored under a misapprehension of the law, in that he and they believed the acts charged in the indictment, of which they still admitted their guilt, constituted the crime of sodomy, whereas they did not as they were advised after the trial constitute that crime or any other under the law. The circuit court set aside the verdict, and granted appellees a new trial. Thereupon they, by counsel, interposed a demurrer to the indictment, which the court sustained on the ground that the acts charged therein did not constitute sodomy, and dismissed the indictment. From the judgment entered pursuant to that ruling the commonwealth has appealed.

The acts charged against the appellees are so disgusting that we refrain from copying the indictment in the opinion. They, however, manifest the perpetration between appellees and by each against the other of an offense against nature committed by the insertion of the private part of the one into the mouth of the other and thereby producing an emission. The question for decision is: Did these acts constitute the crime of sodomy? We have in this state a statute which makes sodomy a felony, and prescribes the punishment to be inflicted for its commission, but the statute does not define the crime. As it is nevertheless a crime at common law in this state, we must look to that source to ascertain its constituent elements and meaning. However, the word "sodomy" is derived from the city of Sodom, where the crime against nature had its origin, and was universally prevalent until that city was destroyed by the wrath of God.

In 2 *Bishop's New Criminal Law*, § 1191, it is thus defined: "Sodomy is a carnal copulation by human beings with each other against nature, or with a beast." By many of the common-law writers sodomy is spoken of as "the infamous crime against nature"; the terms "sodomy," "buggery" and "crime against nature" being often used as synonymous. Strictly speaking, however, sodomy is the crime when committed between two human beings, or man and man, while buggery is the same offense committed by a man with a beast. Sodomy *in ano* is the most common form of the offense between man and man; penetration being necessary to complete the crime. Unlike the crime of rape, the consent of the victim in the crime of sodomy does not remove the criminal element, but simply makes the consenting party an accomplice.

After thus considering the derivation and meaning of the word "sodomy," it remains to be seen whether the form of carnal copulation adopted by appellees, viz., penetration of the mouth, constituted sodomy in the meaning of the law. With one accord the authorities hold that it does not. Again referring to *Bishop's New Criminal Law*, we find in volume 2, § 1194, this statement from the learned author: "A penetration of the mouth is not sodomy." The same conclusion is expressed in [other treatises], and likewise announced in [American and English] cases * * *. We must confess that we are unable to see why the act with which appellees stand charged is not as much a crime against nature as if done in the manner sodomy is usually committed; but as the only authorities we have been able to discover decide otherwise, we regard it our duty to follow precedent, and for this reason alone we hold that the circuit court properly held the indictment bad, and dismissed it. It is to be hoped, however, that the Legislature will by proper enactment make such an infamous act as that of which appellees confess themselves guilty a felony and punishable as such.

For the reasons indicated, the judgment is affirmed.

Notes and Questions

1. Having found a statute on the subject which, however, was deemed defective for lack of a definition, was the court correct in presuming that the common law offense still

existed in Kentucky? Compare a case decided nearly 50 years earlier, *Estes v. Carter*, 10 Iowa 400 (1860), which, as the court stated, "presents the question, not before raised in this court, that we are aware of, whether the courts of this State may take cognizance of and punish offenses at common law, which are not included and specified by name in our Criminal Code. The statute does not expressly adopt or repeal the common law in this State; yet its principles are recognized in the Code, as well as by our courts, and are made the rules of decision both in civil and criminal cases. Indeed it would be a most difficult matter to administer criminal justice under our Code of procedure without the aid of the common law, in the light of which statutory crimes are to be interpreted, and their definitions, if defective, to be expounded and explained. Whilst, therefore, the principles of the common law do enter into all our criminal adjudications when the jurisdiction of our courts over criminal offenses has been established by law, still they do not confer upon the courts in this State the power to try and punish an offense that is such at common law, but which has not been ordained as such by the supreme law making power of the State. Art. 5, section 6 of the Constitution declares, that the District Courts of this State shall have jurisdiction in civil and criminal matters arising in their respective districts in such manner as shall be prescribed by law. The mode thus prescribed is contained in our Code of criminal procedure, and is limited, we think, to the prosecution and punishment of the offenses therein enumerated. This is inferable from the powers and duties of the grand jury and the court, therein expressed. Besides, the statutory offenses so nearly cover all the common law offenses, that it is reasonable to infer that those which are omitted were intended to be excluded. * * * In this State the mode of punishing the crime of sodomy is not prescribed by law, and in the absence of such statutory authority the court can exercise no such power."

Can *Estes* and *Poindexter* be reconciled?

2. If the *Poindexter* court felt this strongly about the conduct of the defendants, then why did the court decide to leave the problem to the legislature? Isn't the virtue of the common law of crimes that courts can intervene in the event of legislative default? Consider Note, 47 Colum.L.Rev. 1332, 1336 (1947): "The most obvious argument favoring the retention of common law is that, in its breadth, it effectively precludes the possibility of those lacunae which must appear to some extent in even the best code. The existence of such lacunae is said to constitute a threat to the public security,[35] and, moreover, to do violence to that retributive instinct of society which Holmes once called ' * * * a felt necessity that punishment should follow wrongdoing.'[36] Supporting arguments are that today the operation of the common law is so restricted to the field of petty offenses as not to be sufficiently important to merit legislative treatment; and that within this field history has shown the common law technique to be adequate."

3. Compare the attitude of the *Poindexter* court with that expressed in the following two cases, and consider how the courts in those two cases would have resolved the issue presented in *Poindexter*.

4. In *State v. Egan*, 287 So.2d 1 (Fla.1973), the court upheld a charge of "the common-law offense of nonfeasance" in light of a state statute providing: "The common law of England in relation to crimes * * * shall be of full force in this state where there is no existing provision by statute on the subject." As to an objection regarding the vagueness of that provision, the court responded that the statute was not vague because (i) "the

---

35. "It is impossible to find precedents for all offenses. The malicious ingenuity of mankind is constantly producing new inventions in the art of disturbing their neighbors. To this invention must be opposed general principles. * * *"; *Commonwealth v. Taylor*, 5 Binn. 276, 281 (Pa.1812).

36. Holmes, *The Common Law* 42 (1881).

legislative intent * * * is plain and unambiguous," and (ii) it is not objectionable that "the statute imposes the duty upon the reader thereof to ascertain for himself what the common law is." As for the claim that there was no longer any need for common law crimes, the court replied: "Whenever a principle of the common law has been once clearly established, the courts of this country must enforce it until repealed by the legislature, as long as there is a subject matter for the principle to operate on, and although the reason, in the opinion of the court, which induced its original establishment may have ceased to exist. Of course, when the rules of the common law are in doubt, or when a factual situation is presented which is not within the established precedents, courts are called upon to determine what general principles are to be applied, and, in so doing, of necessity, must exercise a broad judicial discretion. The courts of this jurisdiction do, and properly so, take into account the changes in our social and economic customs and present day conceptions of right and justice. But the fact remains, as this Court said in *Ripley v. Ewell,* [61 So.2d 420 (Fla.1952)] 'When the common law is clear we have no power to change it.' "

5. In *Commonwealth v. Mochan,* 177 Pa.Super. 454, 110 A.2d 788 (1955), the defendant was indicted and convicted for a common law misdemeanor on evidence that on numerous occasions he telephoned a married woman to suggest sexual intercourse and sodomy. The court affirmed, reasoning:

"It is of little importance that there is no precedent in our reports which decides the precise question here involved. The test is not whether precedents can be found in the books but whether the alleged crimes could have been prosecuted and the offenders punished under the common law. In *Commonwealth v. Miller,* 94 Pa.Super. 499, 507, the controlling principles are thus stated: 'The common law is sufficiently broad to punish as a misdemeanor, although there may be no exact precedent, any act which directly injures or tends to injure the public to such an extent as to require the state to interfere and punish the wrongdoer, as in the case of acts which injuriously affect public morality, or obstruct, or pervert public justice, or the administration of government.' * * *

"To endeavor merely to persuade a married woman to commit adultery is not indictable. *Smith v. Commonwealth,* [p. 788 of this Book]. The present defendant's criminal intent was evidenced by a number of overt acts beyond the mere oral solicitation of adultery. The vile and disgusting suggestions of sodomy alone and the otherwise persistent lewd, immoral and filthy language used by the defendant, take these cases out of the principle of the *Smith* case. Moreover potentially at least, defendant's acts injuriously affected public morality. The operator or any one on defendant's four-party telephone line could have listened in on the conversations, and at least two other persons in Mrs. Zivkovich's household heard some of defendant's immoral and obscene language over the telephone."

A dissenting judge objected: "There is no doubt that the common law is a part of the law of this Commonwealth, and we punish many acts under the common law. But after nearly two hundred years of constitutional government in which the legislature and not the courts have been charged by the people with the responsibility of deciding which acts do and which do not injure the public to the extent which requires punishment, it seems to me we are making an unwarranted invasion of the legislative field when we arrogate that responsibility to ourselves by declaring now, for the first time, that certain acts are a crime."

6. In 1962 the American Law Institute adopted the Model Penal Code, portions of which appear as an Appendix to this Book. As the Chief Reporter explained in Herbert Wechsler, *The American Law Institute: Some Observations on Its Model Penal Code,* 42 A.B.A.J. 321 (1956): "Our belief that such a model can contribute to the sound develop-

ment of the criminal law does not, of course, imply that we are seeking uniformity in penal law throughout the country or that we wish to standardize the law of crimes. Uniformity is not as such a value of importance in this field, as it is, for example, in the case of the commercial code. It is to be expected that substantial differences of social situation or of point of view among the states should be reflected in substantial variation in their penal laws. But what is generally needed, we believe, is systematic re-examination of the subject—to the end that the law may represent the mature sentiment of our respective jurisdictions—sentiment formed after a fresh appraisal of the situation, with attention to the goals to be achieved, the legislative possibilities for their attainment and the knowledge or experience that bears upon the choices to be made."

The Code has had a very significant impact. A total of 38 states have enacted comprehensive new criminal codes, although similar efforts have been undertaken but faltered in several other states and on the federal level. These new codes draw heavily upon the Model Penal Code, and most of them have followed its lead (see § 1.05) in abolishing common law crimes. In these jurisdictions, however, as noted in *Estes*, the common law definitions are relevant to the interpretation of statutes using common law terminology.

7. "Few major controversies have ended with as slight a whimper as the battle over federal common law crimes that raged in the first two decades of the American republic. In the 1812 case *United States v. Hudson & Goodwin*,[2] the Marshall Court dispensed in just eight paragraphs with what Thomas Jefferson had regarded thirteen years earlier as 'the most formidable' of doctrines that had 'ever been broached by the federal government.' Through a 'course of reasoning' it boldly characterized as 'simple, obvious, and admitting of but little illustration,' the *Hudson* Court held that before one can suffer a federal conviction, the 'legislative authority of the Union must first make an act a crime, affix a punishment to it, and declare the Court that shall have jurisdiction of the offence.'

"*Hudson*'s apparent unwillingness to treat the issue of federal common law criminal jurisdiction as worthy of serious contemplation has led courts and commentators to assume erroneously that *Hudson* merely restated what had always been, that '[t]here were no common-law punishments in the federal system.' Indeed, precisely because we take the *Hudson* doctrine as such a tired truth today—'Federal crimes, of course,' the Supreme Court recently yawned, citing *Hudson*, ' "are solely creatures of statute" '[7]—we often fail to see just what a considerable revision of the early republic's practice it represents. For without acknowledging it, the *Hudson* Court disapproved at least eight circuit court cases, brushed off the views of all but one Justice who sat on the Court prior to 1804, and departed from what was arguably the original understanding of those who framed the Constitution and penned the Judiciary Act of 1789. * * *

" * * * When, for example, the Jeffersonians denounced the Sedition Act of 1798, which threatened their ability to mount an effective opposition campaign, one Federalist expressed 'astonishment that gentlemen should raise such an outcry against a law so perfectly analogous to the laws and usages under which they had all been born and bred.' The abolition of common law crimes in 1812 represents a moment when the implications of the Constitution's structure ultimately caught up with lived experience. It crystallized the realization—first suggested in 1798—that the Constitution and the common law could not coexist, that the American system of government had broken off from its English antecedents more sharply than anyone had quite realized. * * *

---

2. 11 U.S. (7 Cranch) 32, 3 L.Ed. 259 (1812).

7. *Dowling v. United States*, 473 U.S. 207, 213 (1985) (quoting *Liparota v. United States*, 471 U.S. 419, 424 (1985) (citing *Hudson*)).

"[T]he principal arguments supporting common law criminal jurisdiction * * * had been decisively rejected in the political and constitutional struggle known as the Jeffersonian 'Revolution of 1800': *Hudson* simply outlined some of the basic principles of this victorious Jeffersonian constitutional vision. Rather than being doctrinally innovative or politically venturesome, then, *Hudson* performed a 'codifying' function, writing into constitutional law that which the political branches of government and the political public had already decided. By holding that the federal courts lacked inherent common law powers, the Court gave formal definition to the notion that the common law would operate only within the interstices of the Constitution's structure." Note, 101 Yale L.J. 919–23 (1992).

8. Consider, however, Dan M. Kahan, *Lenity and Federal Common Law Crimes*, 1994 Sup.Ct.Rev. 345, 347, 369–70, concluding "that federal criminal law is most appropriately viewed as a species of federal common law. Federal common law is commonplace in various statutory domains, including antitrust, labor law, and securities regulation. In these fields, broad statutory language is understood to constitute an implicit delegation of lawmaking power to courts. But the existence of delegated judicial lawmaking has never been formally recognized in federal criminal jurisprudence, a central principle of which is that there are and can be no 'federal common law crimes.' Nonetheless, any close examination reveals that federal criminal law, no less than other statutory domains, is dominated by judge-made law crafted to fill the interstices of open-textured statutory provisions."

As Kahan explains, while "the proposition that Congress might want to delegate criminal lawmaking to the judiciary (or anyone else) might seem implausible," because "Congress faces the same time constraints when it makes criminal law that it does when it makes civil law, it has the same incentive to maximize the return on its legislative investment by drafting criminal statutes broadly. * * *"

"Congress also faces political constraints when it makes criminal law. Just like civil regulatory legislation, criminal legislation can provoke intense controversy among powerful interest groups. Such controversy makes it politically perilous for Congress to proceed and can thus block legislation. Thus, in criminal lawmaking no less than civil lawmaking, Congress has every incentive to avail itself of the 'virtue of vagueness,' resorting to highly general language that facilitates legislative consensus by deferring resolution of controversial points to the moment of judicial application."

SECTION 2. CRIMINAL STATUTES AND THEIR JUDICIAL AND ADMINISTRATIVE INTERPRETATION

STATE v. WHITMARSH

Supreme Court of South Dakota, 1910.
26 S.D. 426, 128 N.W. 580.

Whiting, P. J.

Appellant was tried upon an information charging that he did "willfully, unlawfully, and feloniously make an assault upon one * * * a boy of six years of age, with the intent then and there to commit in and upon the person of the said * * * the detestable and abominable crime against nature, in violation of section 351 of the Penal Code of the state of South Dakota and contrary to the statute. * * * " The jury returned a verdict of guilty, the court rendered judgment, and appellant was sentenced, on February 1, 1909, to imprisonment in the state's prison for a period of three years commencing that date. Appellant appealed from the judgment and from the order of the trial court denying a new trial. * * *

Appellant [questions] the correctness of the trial court's ruling upon a motion made by appellant for a directed verdict.

We regret that the importance of this question, covering as it does a matter wherein the courts of other states are in conflict, renders it necessary to soil the pages of our reports with a discussion of a subject so loathsome and disgusting as the one confronting us. The question presented is, whether or not the crime against nature when committed by one male person upon another male person can be committed through the mouth, or whether it can only be committed through the anus. It must be conceded that under the common law sodomy could not be committed by means of the mouth; the reason given by all the authorities being that given in *Russell on Crimes* *937: "To constitute this offense, the act must be in that part where sodomy is usually committed." The mere statement of the above reason shows the unsoundness of such a distinction. It concedes that the act is sometimes committed in some other part, and, by conceding that the act committed in such other part is not the usual offense, the statement concedes that the act, if committed in such other part, would be still more unnatural, because, if not more unnatural, it would not be more unusual. Certainly this unusual act is many times more "detestable and abominable" than that made criminal at common law. As was well said by the court in *State v. Vicknair*, 52 La. Ann. 1921, 28 South. 273: "But why in the common-law courts the use of the mouth should not have been considered as much against nature as though the act were committed *per anum* is incomprehensible." If it should be conceded that our statute, which refers to the crime, not by the use of word "sodomy," but by the use of the phrase "detestable and abominable crime against nature," does not, by such words, include more than is included in the one word "sodomy," yet should we feel bound by a construction based upon no sounder reasoning? What would we think of the reasoning of a court that should hold that the killing of a human being in some peculiar and practically unheard of manner was not murder simply because such killing was committed in an unusual way? It would certainly be as sensible as to say that sodomy is not sodomy when committed in an unusual way of committing sodomy. What is sodomy according to modern lexicographers? Webster defines it as "carnal copulation in a manner against nature." Such definition is certainly broad enough to include the act proven in this case. Texas, California, and Nebraska have held that their statutes include simply those acts that were sodomy under the common law. The Texas court enters into no discussion of the question, but merely bases its decision upon *Russell on Crimes* and the case of *Rex v. Jacobs*, Russ. & R. C. C. 331, saying that, the offense "being undefined, we must look to the common law for the elements of this crime." *Prindle v. State*, 31 Tex. Cr. R. 551, 21 S. W. 360, 37 Am. St. Rep. 833. It is quite possible that the Texas court was influenced in its decision by the use of the word "sodomy" in the statute of that state which reads: "If any person shall commit with mankind or beast the abominable and detestable crime against nature, he shall be deemed guilty of sodomy. * * *" In California, however, the offense is stated in the language of our statute (section 351, Rev. Pen. Code S. D.), and is similar to the Texas statute omitting from such statute, "he shall be deemed guilty of sodomy." In the case of *People v. Boyle*, 116 Cal. 658, 48 Pac. 800, the California court followed the above Texas decision without any discussion whatsoever, simply saying: "It has been so held in at least two cases"—and citing the Texas case and 1 *Wharton, Cr. Law*, § 575. The Nebraska court in *Kinnan v. State*, 86 Neb. 234, 125 N. W. 594, discusses the question before us quite fully, and inasmuch as their statute is similar to ours, and, like ours, does not use the word "sodomy," we should ordinarily give their decision great weight. It will be seen, however, that, after citing the old common law and the California and Texas decisions in support of their position, they attempt to strengthen their position by reference to decisions in Indiana, Iowa, Ohio, and Kentucky, stating: "In *Commonwealth v. Poindexter* [p. 42 of this

Book], the Supreme Court of Kentucky considered this question, and in a very able opinion reached the same conclusion. * * *." The only one of these cases bearing in the remotest degree upon the question before the Nebraska court is *Commonwealth v. Poindexter*, and the statute of Kentucky is not similar to that of this state or of Nebraska. The Kentucky statute (section 91, c. 182, Laws 1893) reads: "Whoever shall be convicted of the crime of sodomy or buggery with man or beast, shall be. * * *" * * *

In Illinois they have a statute setting forth this offense by the use of the words, "the infamous crime against nature, either with man or beast," and not using the word "sodomy." In *Honselman v. People*, 168 Ill. 172, 48 N. E. 304, the court says: "But it is also contended that the evidence for the people, if true, did not prove the offense, because the defendant made use of his mouth. The evidence was that he was the principal actor in the transaction, and by his efforts the act was consummated by that means. The claim is that the evidence must prove the crime of sodomy, and that the crime against nature, as defined in our statute, embraces nothing but sodomy, or buggery, as denominated in the English statute. With this we cannot agree. While the 'crime against nature' and 'sodomy' have often been used as synonymous terms, paragraph 279 of our Criminal Code, defining infamous crimes, plainly shows that the Legislature included in the crime against nature other forms of the offense than sodomy or buggery. It is there enacted: 'Every person convicted of the crime of * * * sodomy or other crime against nature * * * shall be deemed infamous,' etc. The method employed in this case is as much against nature, in the sense of being unnatural and against the order of nature, as sodomy or any beastial or unnatural copulation that can be conceived. It is within the statute." The Nebraska court in referring to the Illinois decision maintains that it cannot be considered as authority in other states owing to "paragraph 279" referred to by the Illinois court. There can be no question, however, but that the Illinois court held that the term "crime against nature" is not necessarily synonymous with the word "sodomy."

We believe the clause "crime against nature" as used in our statute was so used intending to include therein every unnatural carnal copulation. The statute of this state (section 10, Rev. Penal Code) provides: "The rule of common law that penal statutes are to be strictly construed, has no application to this Code. All its provisions are to be construed according to the fair import of their terms, with a view to effect its objects and promote justice." It would be an insult to the Legislature which enacted our statute to hold that from the words of our statute it appears it intended to allow the most heinous form of the crime against nature to go unpunished simply because it was an unusual form of such crime. Even if our Legislature had in such statute used the term "sodomy," still we would feel bound to give to such word the broad meaning given it by lexicographers, which meaning was given it by at least one common-law authority, as is evidenced by 1 *Hawk. Pleas of the Crown*, p. 357, wherein it was said: "All unnatural carnal copulations, whether with man or beast, seem to come under the notion of sodomy, which was a felony by the ancient common law." And we would say with the Georgia court: "After much reflection, we are satisfied that, if the baser form of the abominable and disgusting crime against nature-i. e., by the mouth-had prevailed in the days of the early common law, the courts of England could well have held that that form of the offense was included in the current definition of the crime of sodomy. And no satisfactory reason occurs to us why the lesser form of this crime against nature should be covered by our statute, and the greater excluded, when both are committed in a like unnatural manner, and when either might well be spoken of and understood as being 'the abominable crime not fit to be named among Christians.'" *Herring v. State*, 119 Ga. 709, 46 S. E. 876.

The judgment of the trial court and order denying a new trial are affirmed.

Corson, J., dissents [without opinion].

Notes and Questions

1. Did the court in *Whitmarsh* convincingly distinguish *Poindexter*? Is a more convincing distinction the fact that *Whitmarsh* concerns the interpretation of a statute, while in *Poindexter* the court was concerned with the dimensions of a common law crime? To what extent is a court's activity in construing a statute different than interpretation of prior case law? Consider Edward H. Levi, *An Introduction to Legal Reasoning*, 15 U.Chi.L.Rev. 501, 521 (1948): "[It is necessary] to reexamine whether there is any difference between case-law and statutory interpretation. It is not enough to show that the words used by the legislature have some meaning. Concepts created by case law also have some meaning, but the meaning is ambiguous. It is not clear how wide or narrow the scope is to be. Can it be said that the words used by the legislature have any more meaning than that, or is there the same ambiguity? One important difference can be noted immediately. Where case law is considered, there is a conscious realignment of cases; the problem is not the intention of the prior judge. But with a statute the reference is to the kind of things intended by the legislature. All concepts suggest, but case-law concepts can be re-worked. A statutory concept, however, is supposed to suggest what the legislature had in mind; the items to be included under it should be of the same order. We mean to accomplish what the legislature intended. * * * The difficulty is that what the legislature intended is ambiguous. In a significant sense there is only a general intent which preserves as much ambiguity in the concept used as though it had been created by case law."

2. Compare *Whitmarsh* with *State v. Morrison*, 25 N.J.Super. 534, 96 A.2d 723 (1953), similarly involving the question whether defendant's fellatio was covered by a state statute reading: "Sodomy, or the infamous crime against nature, committed with man or beast, is a high misdemeanor, and shall be punished by a fine of not more than $5,000, or by imprisonment for not more than 20 years, or both." The court concluded: "Sodomy was known by that name at common law and as 'the infamous crime against nature.' There can be no doubt, therefore, that our legislative declaration, using the same terminology, is rooted in the common-law concept of sodomy, and that a fair appraisal of the legislative intendment does not take us beyond such concept. Therefore, while the case law of other jurisdictions contains much that is instructive and thought-provoking, it is obvious that their pronouncements in expansion of the common-law doctrine cannot be accepted as sound precedents. Two principles must be accorded paramount importance in resolving the present problem: (1) penal statutes must be strictly construed; and (2) if a change in the common law is to be effected by statute, the legislative intent to accomplish the change must be clearly and plainly expressed."

3. Can the different results in *Whitmarsh* and *Morrison* be explained on the ground that New Jersey but not South Dakota followed the rule of strict construction? If so, is that rule a sound or unsound approach? Consider John Calvin Jeffries, Jr., *Legality, Vagueness, and the Construction of Penal Statutes*, 71 Va.L.Rev. 189, 219–20 (1985): "I find the rejection of strict construction in itself unobjectionable. The notion that every statutory ambiguity should be resolved against the government, no matter what the merits of the case, seems to me simplistic and wrong. Certainly, no such rule is required by a concern for political legitimacy. Separation of powers might be taken to mean that courts should make law only interstitially, but not that all change must move in one direction. Nor is strict construction required for fair warning. Of course, unfair surprise must be avoided, but that concern is rarely in issue. It does not apply to the generality of cases where there is no plausible suggestion that the actor either knew or cared what the law was. Finally, strict

construction bears no necessary or dependable relation to the rule of law. In a great many cases the resolution of statutory ambiguity is very far removed from a concern for abusive enforcement."

Are there varieties of strict construction? For example, how would *Morrison* have come out if the court had embraced the following language from *United States v. Hartwell,* 73 U.S. (6 Wall.) 385, 18 L.Ed. 830 (1868): "The rule does not exclude the application of common sense to the terms made use of in the act in order to avoid an absurdity, which the legislature ought not to be presumed to have intended. * * * The rule of strict construction is not violated by permitting the words of the statute to have their full meaning, or the more extended of two meanings, as the wider popular instead of the more narrow technical one; but the words should be taken in such a sense, bent neither one way nor the other, as will best manifest the legislative intent."

4. In *Morrison,* the court noted that the statute it was dealing with (as is equally true of the statute in *Whitmarsh*) "offers no direct guidance as to the kind or kinds of acts forbidden" because the "enactment suffers in this respect from the great concern for delicacy that has usually marked the treatment of this crime both at common law and in legislation." But legislative ambiguity is more widespread; as Levi, supra, at 521–22, explains: "This is not the result of inadequate draftsmanship, as is so frequently urged. Matters are not decided until they have to be. For a legislature perhaps the pressures are such that a bill has to be passed dealing with a certain subject. But the precise effect of the bill is not something upon which the members have to reach agreement. If the legislature were a court, it would not decide the precise effect until a specific fact situation arose demanding an answer. Its first pronouncement would not be expected to fill in the gaps. But since it is not a court, this is even more true. It will not be required to make the determination in any event, but can wait for the court to do so. * * *

"Controversy does not help. Agreement is then possible only through escape to a higher level of discourse with greater ambiguity. This is one element which makes compromise possible. Moreover, from the standpoint of the individual member of the legislature there is reason to be deceptive. He must escape from pressures at home. Newspapers may have created an atmosphere in which some legislation must be passed. Perhaps the only chance to get legislation through is to have it mean something not understood by some colleagues. * * * And if all this were not sufficient, it cannot be forgotten that to speak of legislative intent is to talk of group action, where much of the group may be ignorant or misinformed."

5. Given the ambiguity in the *Whitmarsh* and *Morrison* statutes,[a] should not the court in each instance have examined and interpreted relevant legislative records? Consider James M. Landis, *A Note on "Statutory Interpretation,"* 43 Harv.L.Rev. 886, 888–89, (1930): "The assumption that the meaning a representative assembly attached to the words used in a particular statute is rarely discoverable, has little foundation in fact. The records of legislative assemblies once opened and read with a knowledge of legislative procedure often reveal the richest kind of evidence. To insist that each individual legislator besides his aye vote must also have expressed the meaning he attaches to the bill as a condition precedent to predicating an intent on the part of the legislator, is to disregard the

---

a. Absent such ambiguity, the Supreme Court concluded in *Caminetti v. United States,* 242 U.S. 470, 37 S.Ct. 192, 61 L.Ed. 442 (1917), "the duty of interpretation does not arise," for then the words of the statute "must be taken as the final expression of the legislative intent, and are not to be added to or subtracted from" by examination of legislative history. And thus the defendant there, who was convicted of violating the Mann Act by transporting his mistress across state lines, was not permitted to show by extraneous sources that the Act was intended to reach only commercialized vice, as the critical statutory words (for "any * * * immoral purpose") were "free from doubt."

realities of legislative procedure. Through the committee report, the explanation of the committee chairman, and otherwise, a mere expression of assent becomes in reality a concurrence in the expressed views of another. A particular determinate thus becomes the common possession of the majority of the legislature, and as such a real discoverable intent."

Compare Robert A. Leflar, *Statutory Construction: The Sound Law Approach* (remarks delivered to Federal Appellate Judges Conference, Federal Judicial Center, Washington, D.C., May 13, 1975): "We say frequently that in interpreting a statute we want to discover the intent of the legislature. I think that it was Chief Justice Hingham, I'm not sure, who said that the devil himself 'knoweth not the mind of man.' It is difficult to discover intent; and when you cannot discover with any authority the state of mind of one man, the process of discovering the states of mind, the intent of 535 men, who make up the Federal Congress, becomes an extremely difficult matter. The United States Supreme Court, as I said a few moments ago, has time and again referred back to legislative debates, to discussions in committee and to all other background sources. We could cite dozens of U.S. cases in which that has occurred. But if you have to work with state law few legislatures have transcripts of proceedings comparable to those that are available at the federal level. The problem of legislative intent as such seems to me to involve as much in the way of possibility of being misled as almost anything one can get into. There are bits of legislative record that are devised peculiarly by congressmen or senators for the purpose of misleading judges. And sometimes it is difficult to know which of those you are looking at."

6. Perhaps because of a dearth of legislative records, the court in *Whitmarsh* turned to Webster's Dictionary to determine what the word "sodomy" means. Is that a legitimate means of statutory construction? Consider Note, 107 Harv.L.Rev. 1437, 1452 (1994): "There is nothing wrong with employing dictionaries to identify the general outlines of word meanings and then relying on contextual arguments from text, structure, history, or policy to determine which meaning is appropriate. Difficulties arise from assuming that dictionaries provide perfect category boundaries and then applying those boundaries to contexts never considered by the authors of the dictionaries. Dictionaries can, in some cases, provide valuable assistance to Justices seeking to distill the essence of statutory terms. But dictionaries should occupy a space at the beginning rather than at the end of the interpretive process."

7. The Court in *Whitmarsh*, although declining to adopt the Nebraska position on the matter at issue, noted it would "ordinarily" give Nebraska decisions "great weight" because of the similarities between the two statutes. What would/should the court have done if the connection were even closer, that is, if the Nebraska statute was the source of language used in the local statute? Consider *State v. Dietz*, 135 Mont. 496, 343 P.2d 539 (1959), where the dissent, relying upon the "fundamental principle and universal rule that where a statute is taken from another state it is taken subject to the interpretation placed upon it by the courts of that state" prior to the borrowing, concluded that because the Montana statute was taken word-for-word from the California statute, the court should conform to the California view that the "crime against nature" does not include fellatio.

8. That argument did not prevail in *Dietz* because of another consideration the majority deemed more important: 43 years earlier it had held that the Montana statute *did* include fellatio, and thus the "rule of stare decisis should control." That rule, the court elaborated, is "the principle that the decisions of this court should stand as precedents for future guidance," so that it "is not necessary that we be concerned with how good or how bad the first pronouncement of the highest appellate court of the state might be in construing * * * the enactments of our state Legislative Assembly so long as that

construction holds and is adhered to until such time as * * * the Legislature sees fit to change the laws enacted by it." Would/should the court have felt the same way in *Dietz* if the interval had been 3 years instead of 43? In any event, is the rule of stare decisis overstated in *Dietz*? Compare *People v. Mitchell*, 189 Ill.2d 312, 245 Ill.Dec. 1, 727 N.E.2d 254 (2000): "Our most important duty * * *, to which all other considerations are subordinate, is to reach the correct decision under the law. * * * Stare decisis should not preclude us from admitting our mistake, interpreting the statute correctly, and bringing some stability and reason to this area of the law. As Justice Frankfurter once observed, 'Wisdom too often never comes, and so one ought not to reject it merely because it comes late.'"

On the other hand, is *Dietz* correct because legislative inaction in the interim manifests legislative approval of the court's interpretation? Consider *People v. Morante*, 20 Cal.4th 403, 84 Cal.Rptr.2d 665, 975 P.2d 1071 (1999) ("Legislative silence after a court has construed a statute gives rise at most to an arguable inference of acquiescence or passive approval," but "something more than mere silence is required before that acquiescence is elevated into a species of implied legislation"). As for the "something more," consider *Delaney v. State*, 190 So.2d 578 (Fla.1966), where, regarding that court's prior interpretation of the "crime against nature" statute as covering fellatio, the court observed: "In this state, as in most others, the rule prevails that in reenacting a statute the legislature is presumed to be aware of constructions placed upon it by the highest court of the state, and, in the absence of clear expressions to the contrary, is presumed to have adopted these constructions. Indeed, there is substantial authority for the proposition that such reenactment of the statute bars the court from subsequently changing its earlier construction."

9. In construing criminal statutes, courts often make use of various canons of construction, including the three considered in the following cases dealing with sexual activity falling somewhat outside the "crime against nature" category. In considering whether resort to a canon in each of these cases helped or hindered the court's effort to reach the correct result, assess this observation of Karl Llewellyn in *The Common Law Tradition* 522 (1960): "Plainly, to make any canon take hold in a particular instance, the construction contended for must be sold, essentially, by means other than the use of the canon: The good sense of the situation and a *simple* construction of the available language to achieve that sense, *by tenable means, out of the statutory language*."

(a) *In pari materia*. Defendant was convicted of gross sexual imposition, defined by the statute under which he was prosecuted as "hav[ing] sexual contact" with a person under 13, on proof that he rubbed the bare feet of two boys against his "fully clothed pubic region." In *State v. Baker*, 50 Ohio App.2d 68, 361 N.E.2d 519 (1976), the court found defendant's conduct to be "sordid and potentially dangerous" and thus was "unable to believe that it was not the purpose and intent of the legislature to proscribe acts such as those committed herein," but yet felt compelled to construe the statute otherwise because another statute defined "sexual contact" as "any touching of an erogenous zone of another." As the court explained: "Rules of construction require that these enactments, passed and becoming effective at the same time and being *in pari materia*, be construed together."

(b) *Ejusdem generis*. Defendant was convicted of felonious sexual penetration, defined by statute as forcibly "insert[ing] any instrument, apparatus or other object into the vaginal or anal cavity of another," upon proof the defendant penetrated the victim with his finger. On appeal, the prosecutor argued that the dictionary definition of object, "anything visible or tangible," certainly included a finger, but in *State v. Hooper*, 57 Ohio St.2d 87,

386 N.E.2d 1348 (1979), the court found such reasoning not determinative: "The statute lists three nouns two specific and the third, general. The general term is immediately preceded by the word 'other,' a word which refers to the two specific nouns in the list and suggests legislative intent to limit the scope of the general noun to those objects having the characteristics of those specific nouns," meaning the statute is "subject to the doctrine of *Ejusdem generis.* * * *

"Once the doctrine of *Ejusdem generis* is applied to Ohio's sexual-penetration statute, it becomes clear that a finger is not an 'object' within [its] purview. In general, dictionaries define instruments and apparatuses as implements or tools, or groups of implements or tools. One characteristic common to instruments and apparatuses is that they are inanimate. * * * Since, under the doctrine of *Ejusdem generis*, nothing may be construed to fall within the catchall term 'object' unless it shares the characteristics of instruments and apparatuses, only inanimate objects fall within the purview of [the statute]. A finger is not inanimate. It is part of the human body. Therefore, a finger is not an object under [the statute]."

(c) *Expressio unius est exclusio alterius.* Defendant was convicted of incest upon proof he had sexual intercourse with his stepgranddaughter. The incest statute provides: "A person commits the offense of incest when he engages in sexual intercourse with a person to whom he knows he is related either by blood or by marriage as follows: (1) Father and daughter or stepdaughter; (2) Mother and son or stepson; (3) Brother and sister of the whole blood or of the half blood; (4) Grandparent and grandchild; (5) Aunt and nephew; or (6) Uncle and niece." In *Glisson v. State*, 188 Ga.App. 152, 372 S.E.2d 462 (1988), the court reversed on the ground that "since the statute does not include a prohibition against sexual intercourse between a 'stepgrandfather' and 'stepgranddaughter,' it is excluded under the maxim *expressio unius est exclusio alterius*.

" 'The fact that the ... sexual act[s] here involved [are] fully as loathsome and disgusting as the acts proscribed by the Code does not justify us in reading into the statutory prohibition something which the General Assembly either intentionally or inadvertently omitted.' Since the relationship between appellant and the alleged victim is not one which is expressly enumerated in the statute, any sexual relationship between them would not be incestuous."

NOTES AND QUESTIONS ON ADMINISTRATIVE INTERPRETATION

1. *Delegation.* A legislature may delegate to an administrative agency the power to make rules, the violation of which is punishable as a crime by virtue of penalties set by statute. However, it has often been held that such delegation is proper only if the legislature, in its delegation statute, sets forth sufficient standards to guide the administrative agency. There is considerable difference of opinion in the cases as to what standards will suffice. In *State v. Boyajian*, 344 A.2d 410 (Me.1975), the court upheld a statute making it unlawful to sell "any drug designated by the Board [of Commissioners of the Profession of Pharmacy] as a 'potent medicinal substance.' " The court noted that a companion statute said such designation could be made as to any "central nervous system stimulants or depressants, psychic energizers or any other drugs having a tendency to depress or stimulate which are likely to be injurious to health if improperly used," and concluded that this statute "contains limitations, readily understandable by experienced pharmacists, on the type of materials to be designated."

But in *Sundberg v. State*, 234 Ga. 482, 216 S.E.2d 332 (1975), a statute prohibiting the possession of a "depressant or stimulant drug" as designated by the State Board of Pharmacy was struck down. Though the statute went on to say that such a drug is "[a]ny substance which the State Board shall determine to be habit-forming because of its stimulant effect on the central nervous system or any drug which the State Board shall determine to contain any quantity of a substance having a potential for abuse because of its depressant or stimulant effect on the central nervous system or its hallucinogenic effect,'' the court concluded that ''this paragraph says a depressant or stimulant drug is anything the State Board of Pharmacy says it is.''

2. *Administrative Interpretation.* Absent such delegation, should the views of those who are responsible for administering the criminal law (especially prosecutors) be taken into account by courts when they are interpreting criminal statutes? Consider:

(a) In *Chevron U.S.A., Inc. v. Natural Resources Defense Council, Inc.,* 467 U.S. 837, 104 S.Ct. 2778, 81 L.Ed.2d 694 (1984), upholding the Environmental Protection Agency's interpretation of ambiguous language in the Clean Air Act Amendments of 1977, the Court stated: ''When a court reviews an agency's construction of the statute which it administers, it is confronted with two questions. First, always, is the question whether Congress has directly spoken to the precise question at issue. If the intent of Congress is clear, that is the end of the matter; for the court, as well as the agency, must give effect to the unambiguously expressed intent of Congress. If, however, the court determines Congress has not directly addressed the precise question at issue, the court does not simply impose its own construction on the statute, as would be necessary in the absence of an administrative interpretation. Rather, if the statute is silent or ambiguous with respect to the specific issue, the question for the court is whether the agency's answer is based on a permissible construction of the statute.''

(b) Dan M. Kahan, *Is Chevron Relevant to Federal Criminal Law?*, 110 Harv.L.Rev. 469, 470–71 (1996): ''My target in this Article is the orthodox understanding of institutional roles in federal criminal law. This view gives pride of place to separation of powers. Combining the authority to make, enforce, and interpret law in the hands of a single actor, it is said, is a blueprint for tyranny. Yet it is exactly this concentration of functions that I want to defend. Federal criminal law would be better by any conceivable measure, I will argue, if the executive branch were treated as an authoritative law-expositor, and not merely an authoritative law-enforcer. The proper mechanism for integrating these powers is the so-called *Chevron* doctrine, which requires courts to defer to administrative interpretations of ambiguous statutes as binding exercises of delegated lawmaking authority.

''My dissent from conventional wisdom relates to means, not ends. I defend the integration of lawmaking and law-enforcement functions not because I reject the values that separation of powers is meant to secure, but because I believe that these values along with a host of others would be better served by the kind of executive branch 'interpretive lawmaking' that *Chevron* contemplates.

''The orthodox defense of separation of powers rests on a profoundly mistaken understanding of the nature of federal criminal law. The conventional account treats substantive criminal law as exclusively legislative in origin; there are and can be no federal common law crimes. But this view is impossible to sustain on close inspection. What forms of behavior fall within the ambit of criminal fraud statutes, what kinds of interests count as 'property' for purposes of federal anti-theft provisions, what types of legal and factual mistakes negate the mens rea element of various offenses—all are the products of judicial invention. Such inventiveness, moreover, does not reflect a lawless usurpation of legislative prerogative; rather, it is a response to the deliberate incompleteness of the criminal statutes that Congress enacts. For this reason, federal criminal law, as a whole, is best conceptualized as a regime of delegated common law-making.

"This state of affairs is not all bad; indeed, the system of federal common law crimes no doubt exists (in part) because it works so much better than the imaginary regime of legislative crimes ever would. But still, there are obvious problems associated with federal common law-making in this field. Federal judges frequently lack sufficient consensus to make the law uniform, sufficient expertise to make it rational, and sufficient democratic accountability to make it legitimate.

"The way to conserve the benefits of delegated criminal law-making while avoiding the costs associated with criminal common law-making is to change the identity of the delegate. Applying *Chevron* to federal criminal law would transfer to the executive branch the de facto criminal law-making authority that courts now exercise. Such a shift is desirable in criminal law for exactly the same reasons that it is desirable in other regulatory domains. Because the executive branch is more unified than the judiciary, its readings are more likely to be consistent. Because it has more experience with criminal law enforcement than does any court, its readings are more likely to be wise. And because it is ultimately accountable to the people at the polls, its readings are more likely to reflect popular sentiment than are those of unelected judges."

3. *Discretionary enforcement.* In *Poe v. Ullman,* 367 U.S. 497, 81 S.Ct. 1752, 6 L.Ed.2d 989 (1961), Justice Frankfurter, after noting that the criminal statute there challenged apparently had never been enforced, commented: "What was said in another context is relevant here. 'Deeply embedded traditional ways of carrying out state policy * * *'—or not carrying it out—'are often tougher and truer law than the dead words of the written text.'" In that sense, it may be said that those responsible for enforcing the criminal law determine, within the statutory limits, what the actual content of the criminal law will be. This subject is helpfully discussed in Frank J. Remington & Victor G. Rosenblum, *The Criminal Law and the Legislative Process,* 1960 U.Ill.L.F. 481. They note that "[w]here the substantive law is ambiguous there is an opportunity, indeed a necessity, for the exercise of discretion by enforcement agencies and courts as to what conduct ought to be subjected to the criminal process," and observe that such ambiguity may be: (i) "by default" [i.e., resulting from "inadequacies of legislative draftsmanship in the criminal law"]; (ii) "unavoidable" [i.e., resulting from "theoretical and practical limitations upon the capacity for precise legislative formulation"]; or (iii) "by design." As to the latter, they comment at 490–94:

"One who sets out to eliminate ambiguity in the substantive law very soon is confronted with the argument that he thus creates loopholes through which the guilty can escape.

"The effort to be explicit as to the precise mental state required is often resisted by law enforcement agencies, not on the grounds that persons ought to be convicted who lack the prescribed mental state, but rather on the ground that the explicit requirement will create a loophole through which some of the guilty can escape.

"If the legislative contribution is to be a major one, clarity as an objective ought to prevail even at the cost of creating opportunity of escape for some who ought to be convicted. There are, however, some situations in which the line is not easily drawn in a way that will exempt conduct which it is not desired to proscribe without seriously hindering enforcement against conduct which it is desirable to proscribe. In this case the temptation is strong to overgeneralize, leaving it to enforcement agencies not to invoke the process against conduct which is not serious. The consequence is, of course, the delegation of broad discretion. For example, this problem confronted the draftsmen of the Model Anti–Gambling Act:

'The Commission has also had great difficulty with this problem of finding a formula which would exclude the social or casual gambler from prosecution and punishment, yet which would not result in opening a large breach in the statute for the benefit of professional gamblers and their patrons. The Commission recognizes that it is unrealistic to promulgate a law literally aimed at making a criminal offense of the friendly election bet, the private, social card game among friends, etc. Nevertheless, it is imperative to confront the professional gambler with a statutory facade that is wholly devoid of loopholes.'[27]

"The combination of the attitude that loopholes might result and that overgeneralization has not been abused in practice tends to support a continuation of the ambiguity created by criminal statutes which are intended to proscribe a much narrower range of conduct than that defined by the terms of the statute.

"In the field of regulation of economic activity it is assumed that the legislature is incapable of dealing with the details of regulation and that these are best left to administrative agencies staffed by persons expert in the particular aspect of the economy involved. The legislature contents itself with a broad policy directive, leaving to the administrative agency the task of taking steps to implement that policy. The actions of the administrative agency are subject to judicial review to determine whether the action was arbitrary.

"In the field of criminal law, the regulation of social behavior, there has been little explicit recognition given to the role of administrative expertness in determining, within a legislative policy framework, what conduct ought to be treated as criminal. The tradition of the criminal law, in recent years, has been to assume that the legislature is responsible for the definition of criminal conduct and the administrative agencies are responsible for discovering such conduct and subjecting persons who engage in it to arrest, prosecution, and conviction. Expertise relates to efficiency of investigation, apprehension, and conviction rather than to issues relating to whether it is desirable, under particular circumstances, to subject conduct to part or all of the criminal process. * * *

"Perhaps there is a difference in principle between the exercise of discretion by an agency primarily responsible for economic regulation which uses the criminal sanction as an incident to regulation and the exercise of discretion by the police, but the difference, if one, is not easy to see or to formulate. It is not clear, for example, why the Supreme Court's per curiam support of the discretionary power of the Federal Trade Commission to select the businessmen against whom the Robinson–Patman Act is to be enforced should not apply equally to similar problems of enforcement of criminal law by the police. In *Moog Industries v. FTC*,[29a] the Supreme Court upheld the power of the FTC to put into operation a cease and desist order against a single firm, despite the firm's offer to show that its competitors engaged in the same proscribed practices and that it would suffer serious financial loss if prohibited from engaging in these practices that remained open to their competitors. Stressing the 'specialized experienced judgment,' the 'expert understanding,' and the 'special competence' of the Commission, the Court concluded that 'the Commission alone is empowered to develop that enforcement policy best calculated to achieve the ends contemplated by Congress and to allocate its available funds and personnel in such a way as to execute its policy efficiently and economically.'

"When a Pennsylvania court was faced recently with a similar assertion of discretionary power by Philadelphia's Police Commissioner in enforcing the city's Sunday Blue Law, the court held his action a violation of the fourteenth amendment's equal protection clause.

---

27. 2 ABA Comm'n on Organized Crime, *Organized Crime and Law Enforcement* 57 (1952).

29a. 355 U.S. 411, 78 S.Ct. 377, 2 L.Ed.2d 370 (1958).

Apparently, the Commissioner's mistake was to assert that, for lack of funds and personnel, he would limit initial enforcement of the Sunday closing law to large retail establishments.[29b]

"A careful study of legislative attitude in relation to certain kinds of criminal conduct might well disclose a legislative willingness to delegate a measure of discretion to an enforcement agency thought to be expert in the matter involved. One explanation, and perhaps justification, of current, broadly formulated gambling statutes is that they are a delegation of discretion to police, who have expert knowledge, to apply the statute with the objective of eliminating organized commercial gambling. The continuation of broadly phrased gambling statutes may well be on the assumption that the wide discretion thus conferred has not been abused.

"It is well known that some criminal statutes reflect the hope rather than the expectation that the community will conform to the standard set forth in the statute. Vigorous enforcement is not resorted to because, although there is general support for proscribing the conduct, there is no such support for a program of systematic enforcement. Thus statutes prohibiting fornication and adultery, for example, stand relatively immune from repeal although it can be demonstrated that they are seldom invoked in practice. In part their continued existence undoubtedly reflects a desire to reassert the validity of certain standards of morality by keeping them in the criminal code. In part this also undoubtedly reflects the fact that it is difficult to repeal such statutes because of practical legislator's judgment that his vote for repeal is likely to be interpreted as a vote in favor of the conduct of which most of his constituents disapprove. Perhaps the most important reason is the lack of an adequate demonstration that harm results from the continued existence of such legislation. The assertion that such statutes give enforcement agencies the power to invoke the statute only against those whom they desire to convict rests upon an assumption that the existence of such power, within the prescribed limits, is necessarily undesirable.[30] For example, a recent Wisconsin case involved a situation where a woman was charged and convicted of fornication. It appears quite clearly that the prosecution resulted primarily because she had agreed, and then refused, to testify against her hoodlum boyfriend. Is this different from the situation where an Al Capone is prosecuted for income tax violation primarily because of his gangster activities which are more difficult to prove? There is no consensus that the income tax penalty ought to be repealed. Is there a difference in regard to the offense of fornication? If so, it is one so subtle in nature it is not surprising that it is not reflected in typical state legislative action. It is obvious that the issue may be one of degree and that the power to invoke the income tax penalty selectively against persons suspected of other criminal conduct does not necessitate the conclusion that the fornication statute must be retained. But, it does mean that opposition to a fornication-type statute on the ground that it creates a discretionary power in law enforcement agencies is not a completely persuasive one when the total system is, realistically viewed, characterized by broad discretionary power."

4. *Nonenforcement of "crime against nature" statutes.* "Although all fifty states and the District of Columbia had sodomy laws on their books in the mid-twentieth century,

---

29b. *Bargain City v. Dilworth,* 29 U.S.L.Week 2002 (Pa.Ct.Com.Pls. June 10, 1960).

30. The position that criminal statutes are the arsenal available to enforcement officials is advanced in Arnold, *The Symbols of Government* (1935). In omitting some sex offenses, the Model Penal Code advances the argument that such offenses are used for purposes of discriminatory enforcement. See *Model Penal Code* 204–10 (Tent.Draft No. 4, 1955). Yet, there is no adequate empirical basis for concluding that these offenses are more susceptible to selective enforcement than certain other kinds of offenses, like worthless checks, which are retained as crimes.

since then over half of the states have discarded their sodomy laws.[8] This leaves approximately twenty states with sodomy laws in effect. The net result is that the United States is 'the only major Western industrial democracy where same-sex relations continue to be illegal in a significant part of the country.' However, because sodomy laws are perceived as unenforced, most courts and scholars assert that they are harmless. * * *

" * * * [T]here appears to be a consensus among courts and commentators that sodomy laws are not regularly enforced. While this perception represents an over-simplification,[31] this Article focuses on the * * * assumption that sodomy laws are benign because unenforced laws are without consequence. Courts and commentators routinely assert that because sodomy laws are not enforced through criminal prosecutions, they inflict no harm. * * *

" * * * While sodomy laws are not routinely enforced by means of criminal prosecution, they are nonetheless enforced through a system of collateral enforcement. Sodomy laws provide the underlying justification for much physical violence, harassment, and discrimination by civilians and police. This indirect enforcement occurs through both legal and extralegal means. 'Legal' enforcers of sodomy laws include police (e.g., when enforcement is through arrests for solicitation to commit sodomy) and the courts (e.g., when judges deny custody to gay parents based on sodomy laws). Examples of extralegal enforcement include employment discrimination by private actors (when based on the illegality of sodomy), vigilante gay bashing, and police harassment, including blackmail. Even in the absence of enforcement through criminal prosecution, the overall effect of this harassment, violence, and discrimination is to put gay citizens under siege, which weighs heavily on the individual psyche and inhibits the growth of meaningful community in some regions. Thus, in response to the discrimination facilitated by sodomy laws, many gay people are forced into the closet, isolating them from society and from each other." Christopher R. Leslie, *Creating Criminals: The Injuries Inflicted by "Unenforced" Sodomy Laws*, 35 Harv.C.R.-C.L.L.Rev. 103, 106, 108–09, 178 (2000).

5. *Repeal by Nonenforcement?* Especially in light of that experience, should not general nonenforcement of a criminal statute, such as one dealing with the "crime against nature," operate as a repeal of that statute? Consider:

8. Elimination has occurred in two ways. In a majority of states, the state legislature repealed the sodomy statute. For example, during the 1970s, twenty state legislatures repealed their state sodomy laws. See Paula A. Brantner, *Removing Bricks from a Wall of Discrimination: State Constitutional Challenges to Sodomy Laws*, 19 Hastings Const. L.Q. 495, 498 (1992). In the remainder, state courts struck down sodomy laws as unconstitutional.

31. It is true that sodomy laws do not appear to be enforced against private, noncommercial sodomy between consenting adults. See William N. Eskridge, Jr., *Challenging the Apartheid of the Closet: Establishing Conditions for Lesbian and Gay Intimacy, Nomos, and Citizenship*, 1961–1981, 25 Hofstra L.Rev. 817, 852 (1997). However, sodomy laws are enforced in at least four ways. First, because most sodomy laws make no distinctions based on consent, place, or age, the same sodomy laws that proscribe private sodomy between consenting adults are used in cases of public sodomy, forcible sodomy, or sodomy with a minor. * * * Of course, forcible sodomy, public sodomy, and sodomy with a minor should be illegal, but they can be pro-

scribed through more narrowly tailored statutes that do not reach private sodomy between consenting adults.

Second, sodomy laws have historically been used to imprison gay men for their private, consensual conduct. * * *

Third, sodomy laws are used as leverage in plea bargain negotiations. There are hundreds of Americans currently incarcerated for violating sodomy law proscriptions on consensual sexual conduct between adults. In rape and sexual assault cases, prosecutors often charge defendants with consensual sodomy as a lesser included offense for many reasons, including use as a negotiating tool to force plea bargains. * * *

Fourth, and most importantly, sodomy laws are enforced by government officials (other than prosecutors) and by private action primarily through a system of collateral punishments that do not lead to incarceration, but also does not provide the constitutional guarantees that go along with the traditional process of arrest, trial, and conviction.

(a) "One can find very little support in American case law for the doctrine of desuetude, which allows that 'under some circumstances statutes may be abrogated or repealed by a long-continued failure to enforce them.' Although one may find the odd federal or state case that seemingly supports the doctrine's existence or commentators who have supported the need for the doctrine, desuetude currently appears to be a viable defense to criminal prosecution only in West Virginia. In most jurisdictions, there simply are no reported cases that adopt or reject desuetude; the majority of states that have faced the issue of desuetude have rejected it. These state courts have followed the lead of the United States Supreme Court in *District of Columbia v. John R. Thompson Co.*, in which a restaurateur was convicted for refusing to serve an African–American.[81] The defendant was convicted under a statute that had been unenforced for seventy-eight years. In rejecting the defendant's claim of desuetude, the Supreme Court intimated that disuse of a statute might be 'an ameliorating factor' but concluded that 'repeal of laws is as much a legislative function as their enactment.' * * *

" * * * The doctrine of desuetude * * * does not center on the fairness of prosecution of a particular defendant but rather questions the vitality of the law by re-testing legislative consensus. The doctrine tramples notions of state allocation of power and misconstrues the manner in which state legislatures operate. It is unconstitutional and unnecessary for the judiciary to set the legislative agenda, and doing so goes far beyond traditional cooperative ventures. Indeed, the wide assertion of the doctrine of desuetude, a doctrine accepted by very few American jurisdictions, would likely have the consequence of forcing state legislatures to invade traditional areas preserved to prosecutors." Robert Misner, *Minimalism, Desuetude, and Fornication*, 35 Willamette L. Rev. 1, 16, 55 (1999).

(b) "The depth of the American commitment to the abrogation of enacted law by desuetude is perhaps best revealed by analogy to the due-process fair-notice or fair-warning cases. Where both the community and its law-enforcement agencies have notoriously ignored an enactment for an unduly protracted period, it should be constitutionally impermissible to suddenly prosecute its violation because the act's proscriptions have disappeared from the legal consciousness of the body politic. The statute has neither been obeyed nor applied for such an extended period that ample justification has long existed for the public's feeling that the act has lost the force of binding law." Arthur E. Bonfield, *The Abrogation of Penal Statutes by Nonenforcement,* 49 Iowa L.Rev. 389, 415–16 (1964).

SECTION 3. STATUTORY INTERPRETATION AND THE VOID–FOR–VAGUENESS DOCTRINE

LOCKE v. STATE

Court of Criminal Appeals of Tennessee, 1973.

501 S.W.2d 826.

Russell, Judge.

Harold Locke was charged and convicted of committing a "crime against nature" as proscribed by T.C.A. § 39–707 against Minnie R. Rogers, and his punishment set at not less than five (5) nor more than seven (7) years in the penitentiary. The State's theory of the case was that Locke entered the apartment of a neighbor, Mrs. Rogers, late at night on the pretext of using the telephone, presented a butcher knife, and forced Mrs. Rogers to submit to two episodes of cunnilingus. This theory is adequately supported by the evidence * * *.

---

81. 346 U.S. 100, 102 (1953).

We next confront the question of whether or not cunnilingus is an act made unlawful as a "crime against nature" by T.C.A. § 39–707. We hold that it is. Our Supreme Court has heretofore held that fellatio is such a crime. *Fisher v. State,* 197 Tenn. 594, 277 S.W.2d 340. And, in *Sherrill v. State,* 204 Tenn. 427, 321 S.W.2d 811, our Supreme Court has specifically adopted the liberal Maine doctrine defining crimes against nature as bringing "all unnatural copulation with mankind or a beast, including sodomy, within its scope", as first pronounced in the Maine case of *State v. Cyr,* 135 Me. 513, 198 A. 743. Maine has since broadened its case law to specifically hold cunnilingus included. *State v. Townsend,* 145 Me. 384, 71 A.2d 517. It would be a paradox of legal construction to say that fellatio, "which in common language means sexual perversion committed with the male sexual organ and the mouth", *Sherrill v. State,* supra, is proscribed as a crime against nature, but cunnilingus is not. We recognize that many states limit crimes against nature strictly to sodomy; but the weight of authority supports the view which we follow, said to be the better reasoned in 48 Am.Jur. 549, *Sodomy* § 2. This court used the following language in *Stephens v. State,* Tenn.Cr.App., 489 S.W.2d 542 (1972):

" * * * In its narrower sense sodomy is the carnal copulation between two human beings per anus, or by a human being in any manner with a beast. In its broader sense it is the carnal copulation by human beings with each other against nature or with a beast in which sense it includes all acts of unnatural copulation. Our Courts probably accept the broader meaning since they have held that the proscribed acts may be per os as well as per anus. * * * "

Finally, T.C.A. § 39–707 is said to be unconstitutionally vague and indefinite. We disagree.

We express no opinion as to the constitutionality of the application of this statute to the private acts of married couples, a question inapplicable to the facts of this case, and not briefed herein. Nor does the case sub judice involve the application of the statute to consenting adults.

Affirmed.

WALKER, P.J., concurs.

GALBREATH, JUDGE (dissenting).

I must with all due respect for my colleagues in the majority point out that cursory research does not appear to substantiate the holding that "the weight of authority supports the view" that oral caressing of the vagina, or cunnilingus, is included in the acts proscribed by Section 39–707 of our criminal code which sets out:

"Crimes against nature, either with mankind or any beast, are punishable by imprisonment in the penitentiary not less than five (5) years nor more than fifteen (15) years."

Less than one half of the jurisdictions in the nation have a statute such as ours which is a reiteration of the common law definition of sodomy. In at least two states the statute has been declared unconstitutional. See *Harris v. State* (Alaska), 457 P.2d 638, and *Franklin v. State* (Fla.), 257 So.2d 21. From a review of the many cases cited in West's Fifth through Seventh Decennial Digests under Key Number 1 for Sodomy, nature and elements of offenses, the courts of six states have ruled that cunnilingus is not a form of sodomy while four states seem to have adopted the view expressed by the majority.

To hold that cunnilingus (an act approved by almost 90% of adults between 18 and 34 according to an exhaustive study)[2] is a crime would seem to me to be judicial legislation of

---

2. "Sexual Behavior in the 1970's" *Playboy Magazine,* October, 1973, p. 85. See also Kinsey's *Sexual* *Behavior in the Human Female,* p. 257 (1942).

the plainest kind. The writer of this opinion is a strict constructionist. I firmly believe courts must take the law as it is made up for us by legislative bodies and higher judicial authority. One of the most basic canons of judicial behavior is incorporated in the doctrine of stare decisis. Although the issue involved in this case has never been passed on by either our Supreme Court or made the subject of legislation, we are firmly bound by many decisions which hold that when a statute is based on the common law, courts must look to the common law to determine the elements of the offense. Our own Court has emphasized this in pointing out that acts of sexual deviation other than sodomy could never be the subject of prosecution under the statute:

> "Since crime against nature means the common law offense of sodomy and the crime is well defined and described at common law, T.C.A. 39–707 is not unconstitutionally vague. There is no danger that some kind of sexual perversion apart from unnatural carnal copulation, unnatural sexual intercourse, could be embraced in the definition and description as plaintiff in error contends." *Stephens v. State,* Tenn.Cr. App., 489 S.W.2d 542.

Affirmation of the conviction here for a perversion that did not involve copulation or sexual intercourse, natural or unnatural, is a direct refutation of what this Court said in *Stephens,* supra, and points up the danger inherent in judicial legislation. Where do we stop if we decree that any form of sexual activity is the equivalent of copulation or sexual intercourse so as to be unlawful if not confined to penis-vaginal connection? Even if we had the authority to legislate on the subject, where would we draw the line? * * *

From what has been pointed out above, it is clear that the laws in this State dealing with sexual perversions are in need of clarification. What is, or is not, illegal sexual activity could be, and in my view should be, set out in clear and precise terms so as to remove the present confusion and uncertainty. Surely we have progressed some from the dim past when Lord Coke spoke of sodomy as being "a detestable and abominable sin among Christians not to be named," although affirmation here would seem to be a regression since not even Lord Coke and his fellow English jurists through the centuries have felt it legally permissible to include cunnilingus, or even fellatio, within the definition of sodomy. See *Rex v. Jacobs,* 168 Eng.Rep. 830 (1817), construing 25 Henry VIII, C 6, 1533, the first statutory enactment of the common law offense Crime Against Nature.

The reticence expressed by Lord Coke and the framers of our statute to deal explicitly with the offense involved is a singular departure from one of the most basic rules of criminal procedure, i.e., that an accused is entitled to be notified of just what he has allegedly done to violate the law, usually by an indictment. To hold as has the puritanical court in Illinois would not seem to even slightly conform to this long established rule of law:

> "It was never the practice to describe the particular manner or the details of the commission of the act, but the offense was treated in the indictment as the abominable crime not fit to be named among Christians. * * * The existence of such an offense is a disgrace to human nature. The legislature has not seen fit to define it further than by the general term, and the records of the courts need not be defiled with the details of different acts which may go to constitute it. A statement of the offense in the language of the statute, or so plainly that its nature may be easily understood by the jury, is all that is required." *Honselman v. People,* 168 Ill. 172, 48 N.E. 304 (1897).

This reasoning seems to suggest two fallacies to me. Firstly, that sodomy is the most abhorrent of all crimes, so much so that it may not even be defined in writing. Any person who believes that sodomy is more abhorrent than murder, which is sharply defined by statute, in my opinion has a misplaced sense of priority. Secondly, the attitude of the Maine Court, now adopted by the majority, seems to be "everyone knows what a crime against nature is, so why spell it out? "In the first place, there have been so many disagreements as to what constitutes the offense that such reasoning falls under its own weight. (The legal paradox mentioned by the majority has not prevented some few states, at least two, from holding that while fellatio is proscribed as a crime against nature, cunnilingus is not. *State v. Tarrant,* 83 Ohio App. 199, 80 N.E.2d 509, and *Riley v. Garrett,* 219 Ga. 345, 133 S.E.2d 367.) Secondly, if there is no need to define this offense, why should it be necessary to define every other offense in our statutes exacting penal sanctions? Are arson, rape, robbery, burglary, forgery, etc. so little understood that they must be carefully defined while the never before in this State judicially encountered activity involved here is so familiar to all that one accused of committing a "crime against nature" must of necessity know what he is supposed to have done so as to be able to prepare a defense? The defendant here has the dubious distinction of being the only person in the history of this State, so far as reference to our case law is concerned, who has ever been sentenced to prison for committing this act which, as aforesaid, has been statistically attributed to some 46% of the adult population.

Cunnilingus, unlike fellatio, does not involve the virile male organ of reproduction. It would seem that it is the penis that must penetrate in order to accomplish the offense. Regardless of how loathsome one might view such conduct, surely, inserting any other part of the body against, or even in, the vagina would not be an offense under the common law or our statute. For instance, if the defendant had forced his victim onto the bed as the proof shows and had her remove her clothing and then placed his hand or one of his fingers against her vagina, this would not be punishable under the statute. Even if penetration should be made with the finger, or nose, toe, lips, tongue, or some foreign object, it is doubtful if this would meet the test under the common law or statute.

Proof of penetration is lacking.

"Penetration has been held an essential element of the crime of sodomy both at common law and under a number of the statutes defining and punishing the offense, but any penetration, however slight, is sufficient, and on penetration the crime becomes complete. The view that cunnilingus is not within the crime against nature, as discussed supra subdivision b(1) of this section, has been based on the lack of penetration of the body." 81 C.J.S. *Sodomy* § 1(4). * * *

Under the evidence the defendant is certainly guilty of an aggravated assault and battery since the proof is that he employed a deadly weapon to force his will on the prosecutrix, but under the present posture of the law in this State, in my considered opinion, he did not commit sodomy. I would reverse with a suggestion that a more appropriate prosecution be considered.

LOCKE v. ROSE

United States Court of Appeals, Sixth Circuit, 1975.

514 F.2d 570.

Per Curiam.

Plaintiff-appellant ("appellant") was convicted in state court of committing a "crime against nature," by forcibly performing cunnilingus on a neighbor. The Tennessee court of criminal appeals (2:1) affirmed the conviction, rejecting appellant's claim that section 39–

707 was unconstitutionally vague, *Locke v. State,* and the Tennessee Supreme Court denied certiorari (November 28, 1973).

Thereafter, appellant filed, *pro se,* the instant petition for writ of habeas corpus in the district court. That court, by order, rejected appellant's claim of unconstitutional vagueness in light of *Wainwright v. Stone,* 414 U.S. 21, 94 S.Ct. 190, 38 L.Ed.2d 179 (1973), and denied relief. We reverse.

We do not understand defendant-appellee ("appellee") as arguing that the statutory term, "crimes against nature," could in and of itself withstand a charge of unconstitutional vagueness. Neither could appellee so argue, *Harris v. State,* 457 P.2d 638 (Alaska 1969), see *Perkins v. State,* 234 F.Supp. 333, 336 (W.D.N.C.1964), *Hogan v. State,* 84 Nev. 372, 441 P.2d 620, 621 (1968), particularly since courts have differed widely in construing the reach of "crimes against nature" to cunnilingus.

Although *Stone* upheld the constitutionality of Florida's "crime[s] against nature statute," as applied to copulation per os and per anum, the Court noted that the Florida statute had long been construed as proscribing "[t]hese very acts." Conversely, no reported Tennessee opinion had previously applied the Tennessee statute to cunnilingus. Section 39–707 had been applied exclusively as proscribing copulation per anum.

Appellee, however, argues that language in prior state court opinions, particularly in *Sherrill,* supra, has cured the unconstitutional vagueness of section 39–707 as applied to cunnilingus. Though *Sherrill* explicitly adopted the "liberal" statutory construction of *State v. Cyr,* 135 Me. 513, 198 A. 743 (1938), *Cyr* involved fellatio rather than cunnilingus. Moreover, *Sherrill* failed to cite *State v. Townsend,* 145 Me. 384, 71 A.2d 517, 518 (1950), which applied the Maine statute to cunnilingus. Even had *Sherrill* cited *Townsend,* however, such citation most likely would still have failed in putting "[m]en of common intelligence," *Winters v. New York,* 333 U.S. 507, 515, 68 S.Ct. 665, 92 L.Ed. 840 (1948), on notice of the court's cunnilingus-reaching interpretation. Likewise, *Stephens,* supra, even assuming that it preceded appellant's challenged act[3] cannot preclude "men of common intelligence [from] necessarily guess[ing] at its meaning and differ[ing] [at] its application" as applied to cunnilingus. *Bouie v. Columbia,* 378 U.S. 347, 351, 84 S.Ct. 1697, 1701, 12 L.Ed.2d 894 (1964).

Stephens, the Tennessee courts' most candid attempt at outlining the scope of section 39–707, defined the statutory "crime against nature" as

> "a euphemism for the particular acts that constitute the offense of sodomy at common law. * * * In its narrower sense sodomy is the carnal copulation between two human beings per anus, or by a human being in any manner with a beast. In its broader sense it is the carnal copulation by human beings with each other against nature or with a beast in which sense it includes all acts of unnatural copulation. Our courts *probably* accept the broader meaning * * *." (Emphasis added.)

First, sodomy at common law included only copulation per anum. Second, *Stephens* only hinted that Tennessee "probably" accepts the broader view of crimes against nature. Moreover, even had the court expressly adopted the broader view, such view, as described, proscribing "carnal copulation by human beings with each other against nature * * * includ[ing] all acts of unnatural copulation," would still fail to give "fair warning," *Bouie,* supra, of the proscription of cunnilingus.

---

3. *Stephens* was filed on September 28, 1972. Appellant's petition for writ of habeas corpus indicates that he was convicted on October 3, 1972, the forced cunnilingus thereby virtually certainly occurring prior to September 28, 1972.

In accordance with the foregoing, the judgment of the district court is reversed and the case is remanded to the district court for remand to the Criminal Court of Knox County for such further proceedings as may be deemed appropriate and permissible under the applicable law, such as a prosecution for aggravated assault and battery; and provided further that if no such proceedings are instituted within sixty days of such remand, the writ shall issue and appellant shall stand discharged.

ROSE v. LOCKE

Supreme Court of the United States, 1975.

423 U.S. 48, 96 S.Ct. 243, 46 L.Ed.2d 185.

PER CURIAM. * * *

It is settled that the fair-warning requirement embodied in the Due Process Clause prohibits the States from holding an individual "criminally responsible for conduct which he could not reasonably understand to be proscribed." *United States v. Harriss,* 347 U.S. 612, 617, 74 S.Ct. 808, 812, 98 L.Ed. 989 (1954); see *Wainwright v. Stone,* 414 U.S. 21, 94 S.Ct. 190, 38 L.Ed.2d 179 (1973). But this prohibition against excessive vagueness does not invalidate every statute which a reviewing court believes could have been drafted with greater precision. Many statutes will have some inherent vagueness, for "[i]n most English words and phrases there lurk uncertainties." *Robinson v. United States,* 324 U.S. 282, 286, 65 S.Ct. 666, 668, 89 L.Ed. 944 (1945). Even trained lawyers may find it necessary to consult legal dictionaries, treatises, and judicial opinions before they may say with any certainty what some statutes may compel or forbid. Cf. *Nash v. United States,* 229 U.S. 373, 33 S.Ct. 780, 57 L.Ed. 1232 (1913); *United States v. National Dairy Corp.,* 372 U.S. 29, 83 S.Ct. 594, 9 L.Ed.2d 561 (1963). All the Due Process Clause requires is that the law give sufficient warning that men may conform their conduct so as to avoid that which is forbidden.[3]

Viewed against this standard, the phrase "crime against nature" is no more vague than many other terms used to describe criminal offenses at common law and now codified in state and federal penal codes. The phrase has been in use among English-speaking people for many centuries, see 4 W. Blackstone, *Commentaries* * 216, and a substantial number of jurisdictions in this country continue to utilize it. Anyone who cared to do so could certainly determine what particular acts have been considered crimes against nature, and there can be no contention that the respondent's acts were ones never before considered as such.

Respondent argued that the vice in the Tennessee statute derives from the fact that jurisdictions differ as to whether "crime against nature" is to be narrowly applied to only those acts constituting the common-law offense of sodomy, or is to be broadly interpreted to encompass additional forms of sexual aberration. We do not understand him to contend that the broad interpretation is itself impermissibly vague; nor do we think he could successfully do so. We have twice before upheld statutes against similar challenges. In *State v. Crawford,* 478 S.W.2d 314 (Mo.1972), the Supreme Court of Missouri rejected a claim that its crime against nature statute was so devoid of definition as to be unconstitutional, pointing out its provision was derived from early English law and broadly embraced sodomy, bestiality, buggery, fellatio, and cunnilingus within its terms. We dismissed the appeal from this judgment as failing to present a substantial federal question. *Crawford v.*

---

3. This is not a case in which the statute threatens a fundamental right such as freedom of speech so as to call for any special judicial scrutiny, see *Smith v.* *Goguen,* 415 U.S. 566, 572–573, 94 S.Ct. 1242, 1246, 39 L.Ed.2d 605 (1974).

Missouri, 409 U.S. 811, 93 S.Ct. 176, 34 L.Ed.2d 66 (1972); see *Hicks v. Miranda,* 422 U.S. 332, 343–345, 95 S.Ct. 2281, 2289, 45 L.Ed.2d 223 (1975). And in *Wainwright v. Stone,* supra, we held that a Florida statute proscribing "the abominable and detestable crime against nature" was not unconstitutionally vague, despite the fact that the State Supreme Court had recently changed its mind about the statute's permissible scope.

The Court of Appeals, relying on language in *Stone,* apparently believed these cases turned upon the fact that the state courts had previously construed their statutes to cover the same acts with which the defendants therein were charged. But although *Stone* demonstrated that the existence of previous applications of a particular statute to one set of facts forecloses lack-of-fair-warning challenges to subsequent prosecutions of factually identical conduct, it did not hold that such applications were a prerequisite to a statute's withstanding constitutional attack. If that were the case it would be extremely difficult ever to mount an effective prosecution based upon the broader of two reasonable constructions of newly enacted or previously unapplied statutes, even though a neighboring jurisdiction had been applying the broader construction of its identically worded provision for years.

Respondent seems to argue instead that because some jurisdictions have taken a narrow view of "crime against nature" and some a more broad interpretation, it could not be determined which approach Tennessee would take, making it therefore impossible for him to know if § 39–707 covered forced cunnilingus. But even assuming the correctness of such an argument if there were no indication of which interpretation Tennessee might adopt, it is not available here. Respondent is simply mistaken in his view of Tennessee law. As early as 1955 Tennessee had expressly rejected a claim that "crime against nature" did not cover fellatio, repudiating those jurisdictions which had taken a "narrow restrictive definition of the offense." *Fisher v. State,* 197 Tenn. 594, 277 S.W.2d 340. And four years later the Tennessee Supreme Court reiterated its view of the coverage intended by § 39–707. Emphasizing that the Tennessee statute's proscription encompasses the broad meaning, the court quoted from a Maine decision it had earlier cited with approval to the effect that " 'the prohibition brings all unnatural copulation with mankind or a beast, including sodomy, within its scope.' " *Sherrill v. State,* 204 Tenn. 427, 429, 321 S.W.2d 811, 812 (1959), quoting from *State v. Cyr,* 135 Me. 513, 198 A. 743 (1938). And the Maine statute, which the Tennessee court had at that point twice equated with its own, had been applied to cunnilingus before either Tennessee decision. *State v. Townsend,* 145 Me. 384, 71 A.2d 517 (1950). Thus, we think the Tennessee Supreme Court had given sufficiently clear notice that § 39–707 would receive the broader of two plausible interpretations, and would be applied to acts such as those committed here when such a case arose.

This also serves to distinguish this case from *Bouie v. City of Columbia,* 378 U.S. 347, 84 S.Ct. 1697, 12 L.Ed.2d 894 (1964), a decision the Court of Appeals thought controlling. In *Bouie,* the Court held that an unforeseeable judicial enlargement of a criminal statute narrow and precise on its face violated the Due Process Clause. It pointed out that such a process may lull "the potential defendant into a false sense of security, giving him no reason even to suspect that conduct clearly outside the scope of the statute as written will be retroactively brought within it by an act of judicial construction." But as we have noted, respondent can make no claim that § 39–707 afforded no notice that his conduct might be within its scope. Other jurisdictions had already reasonably construed identical statutory language to apply to such acts. And given the Tennessee court's clear pronouncements that its statute was intended to effect broad coverage, there was nothing to indicate, clearly or otherwise, that respondent's acts were outside the scope of § 39–707. There is no possibility of retroactive lawmaking here. Accordingly, the petition for certiorari and respondent's motion to proceed *in forma pauperis* are granted, and the judgment of the Court of Appeals is reversed.

Judgment of Court of Appeals reversed.

So ordered.

MR. JUSTICE BRENNAN, with whom MR. JUSTICE MARSHALL concurs, dissenting.

I dissent from the Court's summary reversal. The offense of "crimes against nature" at common law was narrowly limited to copulation *per anum*. American jurisdictions, however, expanded the term—some broadly and some narrowly—to include other sexual "aberrations." Of particular significance for this case, as the Court of Appeals accurately stated, "courts have differed widely in construing the reach of 'crimes against nature' to cunnilingus."

The Court holds, however, that because "other jurisdictions had already reasonably construed identical statutory language to apply to [cunnilingus] * * * given the Tennessee court's clear pronouncements that its statute was intended to effect broad coverage, there was nothing to indicate, clearly or otherwise, that respondent's acts were outside the scope of § 39–707." In other words the traditional test of vagueness—whether the statute gives fair warning that one's conduct is criminal—is supplanted by a test whether there is anything in the statute "to indicate, clearly or otherwise, that respondent's acts were outside the scope of" the statute. This stands the test of unconstitutional vagueness on its head. And this startling change in vagueness law is accompanied by the equally startling holding that, although the Tennessee courts had not previously construed "crimes against nature" to include cunnilingus, respondent can not be heard to claim that § 39–707, therefore afforded no notice that his conduct fell within its scope, because he was on notice that Tennessee courts favored a broad reach of "crimes against nature" and other state courts favoring a broad reach had construed their state statutes to include cunnilingus.

Yet these extraordinary distortions of the principle that the Due Process Clause prohibits the States from holding an individual criminally responsible for conduct when the statute did not give fair warning that the conduct was criminal, are perpetrated without plenary review affording the parties an opportunity to brief and argue the issues orally. It is difficult to recall a more patent instance of judicial irresponsibility. For without plenary review the Court announces today, contrary to our prior decisions, that even when the statute he is charged with violating fails of itself to give fair warning, one acts at his peril if the state court has indicated a tendency to construe the pertinent statute broadly, and some other state court of like persuasion has construed its state statute to embrace the conduct made the subject of the charge. I simply cannot comprehend how the fact that one state court has judicially construed its otherwise vague criminal statute to include particular conduct can, without explicit adoption of that state court's construction by the courts of the charging State, render an uninterpreted statute of the latter State also sufficiently concrete to withstand a charge of unconstitutional vagueness. But apart from the merits of the proposition, surely the citizens of this country are entitled to plenary review of its soundness before being required to attempt to conform their conduct to this drastically new standard. Today's holding surely flies in the face of the line of our recent decisions that have struck down statutes as vague and overbroad, although other state courts had previously construed their like statutes to withstand challenges of vagueness and overbreadth.

Nor will the Court's assertions that the Tennessee courts had in any event in effect construed the Tennessee statute to include cunnilingus withstand analysis. The Court relies on a 1955 Tennessee decision that had held that "crimes against nature" include fellatio, the Tennessee court rejecting the contention that the statute was limited to the common-law copulation *per anum* scope of the phrase. The Tennessee court in that opinion cited a Maine case, decided in 1938, *State v. Cyr,* where the Maine court had applied a "crimes against nature" statute to fellatio. But the Tennessee court did not also cite a 1950 Maine decision, *State v. Townsend,* 145 Me. 384, 71 A.2d 517 (1950), that applied Maine's "crimes against nature" statute to cunnilingus. *Fisher v. State,* 197 Tenn. 594, 277 S.W.2d 340 (1955). Four years later, in 1959, in another fellatio case, the Tennessee court again made no mention of *Townsend,* although quoting from *Cyr's* holding that the Maine statute applies to "all unnatural copulation with mankind or a beast, including sodomy." *Sherrill v. State,* 204 Tenn. 427, 321 S.W.2d 811, 812 (1959). Despite this significant failure of the Tennessee court to cite *Townsend,* and solely on the strength of the Tennessee court's general "equating" of the Maine statute with the Tennessee statute, this Court holds today that respondent had sufficient notice that the Tennessee statute would receive a "broad" interpretation that would embrace cunnilingus.

This 1974 attempt to bootstrap 1950 Maine law for the first time into the Tennessee statute must obviously fail if the principle of fair warning is to have any meaning. When the Maine court in 1938 applied its statute broadly to all "unnatural copulation," nothing said by the Maine court suggested that that phrase reached cunnilingus. The common-law "crimes against nature," limited to copulation *per anum,* required penetration as an essential element. In holding that a "broad" reading of that phrase should encompass all unnatural copulation including fellatio—copulation *per os*—Maine could not reasonably be understood as including cunnilingus in that category. Other jurisdictions, though on their States' particular statutory language, have drawn that distinction. Thus, when the Tennessee court in 1955 adopted the language of Maine's 1938 *Cyr* case, a Tennessee citizen had at most notice of developments in Maine law through 1938. That Maine subsequently in 1950 applied its statute to cunnilingus is irrelevant, for such subsequent developments were not "adopted" by the Tennessee court until the case before us. Indeed, the Tennessee court's failure in its 1955 *Fisher* opinion to cite *Townsend,* Maine's 1950 cunnilingus decision, although citing *Cyr,* Maine's 1938 fellatio decision, more arguably was notice that the Tennessee courts considered fellatio but not cunnilingus as within the nebulous reach of the Tennessee statute.

Moreover, I seriously question the Court's assumption that the "broad interpretation" of the phrase "crimes against nature" is not unconstitutionally vague. The Court's assumption rests upon two supposed precedents, (1) this Court's dismissal for want of a substantial federal question of the appeal in *Crawford v. Missouri,* 409 U.S. 811, 93 S.Ct. 176, 34 L.Ed.2d 66 (1972), and (2) the Court's *per curiam* opinion in *Wainwright v. Stone,* 414 U.S. 21, 94 S.Ct. 190, 38 L.Ed.2d 179 (1973). That reliance is plainly misplaced.

In *Crawford,* the appellant had been convicted of coercing a mentally retarded individual to perform fellatio on appellant. The Supreme Court of Missouri did not, as the Court implies, for the first time in that case adopt a "broad" construction of its statute and apply that construction in appellant's case. Rather, the Supreme Court of Missouri first noted that the original statute, probably reaching only common-law "crimes against nature," had been legislatively amended in express terms to expand the offense to conduct committed "with the sexual organs or with the mouth," thereby "enlarg[ing] the common law definition of the crime * * *." *State v. Crawford,* 478 S.W.2d 314, 317 (Mo.1972). Moreover, the court, observing that a "court's construction of statutory language becomes a part of the statute 'as if it had been so amended by the legislature,'", stated that in the 60 years since that amendment, the Missouri courts had "adjudicated" that the statute embraced "bestiality, buggery, fellatio * * * and cunnilingus," and that "[a]t least five [Missouri] cases have specifically held that the act charged [against appellant] is within the statute." In light of that prior judicial and legislative construction of the statutory phrase, and its specific prior application to acts identical to the appellant's, the dismissal in *Crawford* simply cannot be treated as holding that the phrase "crimes against nature" is not in itself vague.

Wainwright v. Stone, as MR. JUSTICE STEWART correctly observes, also involved a statute already construed to cover the conduct there in question. Indeed, it was for that very reason that we held that the "judgment of federal courts as to the vagueness or not of a state statute must be made in the light of prior state constructions of the statute." The reversal of the Court of Appeals' holding finding the statute unconstitutional was explicitly based on the fact that the state statute had previously been applied to identical conduct, which decisions "require[d] reversal" in *Wainwright* since they put the particular conduct expressly within the statute.

No spectre of increasing caseload can possibly justify today's summary disposition of this case. The principle that due process requires that criminal statutes give sufficient warning to enable men to conform their conduct to avoid that which is forbidden is one of the great bulwarks of our scheme of constitutional liberty. The Court's erosion today of that great principle without even plenary review reaches a dangerous level of judicial irresponsibility. I would have denied the petition for certiorari, but now that the writ has been granted would affirm the judgment of the Court of Appeals or at least set the case for oral argument.

MR. JUSTICE STEWART, with whom MR. JUSTICE MARSHALL concurs, dissenting.

I would have denied the petition for certiorari in this case, but, now that the writ has been granted, I would affirm the judgment of the Court of Appeals. * * *

As the Court of Appeals pointed out, the defendant in this case could, and probably should, be prosecuted for aggravated assault and battery. But I think the Court of Appeals was correct in holding that the Tennessee statute under which the defendant was in fact prosecuted was unconstitutionally vague as here applied.

Notes and Questions

1. Did Locke *really* receive the warning to which he was entitled? Would the case have come out the same way if the sodomy had been consensual? Consider the following.

2. Meir Dan–Cohen, *Decision Rules and Conduct Rules: An Accoustic Separation in Criminal Law,* 97 Harv.L.Rev. 625, 660 (1984): "Couched as it is in the rhetoric of 'fair warning,' the Court's reasoning has a surreal quality: it implies that the defendant could have been expected, before engaging in sexual activities, to canvass the law libraries of various jurisdictions in search of the relevant decisions and then to anticipate the convoluted process of legal reasoning that ultimately led even Supreme Court Justices to opposite conclusions. When determining the meaning of a statute requires such refined legal skills, the notion of 'fair warning' is distorted beyond recognition."

3. Note, 62 Harv.L.Rev. 77, 80 (1948): "In general, it would seem fair to charge the individual with such knowledge of a statute's meaning and application as he could obtain through competent legal advice, provided that the statute gives him enough warning that he ought reasonably to see the need of obtaining such advice."

4. Justice Holmes, in *Nash v. United States,* 229 U.S. 373, 33 S.Ct. 780, 57 L.Ed. 1232 (1913): "[T]he law is full of instances where a man's fate depends on his estimating rightly, that is, as the jury subsequently estimates it, some matter of degree. If his judgment is wrong, not only may he incur a fine or a short imprisonment, as here; he may incur the

penalty of death. 'An act causing death may be murder, manslaughter, or misadventure, according to the degree of danger attending it' by common experience in the circumstances known to the actor. 'The very meaning of the fiction of implied malice in such cases at common law was, that a man might have to answer with his life for consequences which he neither intended nor foresaw.' 'The criterion in such cases is to examine whether common social duty would, under the circumstances, have suggested a more circumspect conduct.' "

5. Justice Frankfurter, dissenting in *Winters v. New York,* 333 U.S. 507, 68 S.Ct. 665, 92 L.Ed. 840 (1948): "There is no such thing as 'indefiniteness' in the abstract, by which the sufficiency of the requirement expressed by the term may be ascertained. The requirement is fair notice that conduct may entail punishment. But whether notice is or is not 'fair' depends upon the subject matter to which it relates. Unlike the abstract stuff of mathematics, or the quantitatively ascertainable elements of much of natural science, legislation is greatly concerned with the multiform psychological complexities of individual and social conduct. Accordingly, the demands upon legislation, and its responses, are variable and multiform. [It is thus necessary to ask, in the particular case, such questions as:] How easy is it to be explicitly particular?"

6. Mark Kelman, *Interpretive Construction in the Substantive Criminal Law,* 33 Stan.L.Rev. 591, 662 (1981): "Vagueness doctrine is *predominantly* used when the conduct that is *ambiguously* covered by the statute, conduct that the court fears will be deterred because citizens are unsure whether or not it falls within the ambit of the statute, is either affirmatively constitutionally protected or at least desirable. When this 'nearby' conduct is unprotected or affirmatively undesirable in the judge's eyes, courts are less likely to overturn. Naturally, the court's interpretation of the breadth of conduct that may be deterred is quite flexible. For instance, does a facially vague statute outlawing vexatious phone-calling chill protected 'speech' or less protected 'telephoning to strangers'?"

7. Note, 109 U.Pa.L.Rev. 67, 73–75 (1960): "[W]here the opinions do attempt to expound some policy bases for the doctrine, the holdings often fail to bear these bases out: it is common ground, for example, to explain the antivagueness prescription as a constitutional mandate that 'no one may be required at peril of life, liberty or property to speculate as to the meaning of penal statutes. All are entitled to be informed as to what the State commands or forbids.'[33] Yet the Supreme Court, in passing on these penal statutes, has invariably allowed them the benefit of whatever clarifying gloss state courts may have added in the course of litigation of the very case at bar. This would indicate, inconsistently with the 'warning' rationale, that 'the defendant, at the time he acted, was chargeable with knowledge of the scope of subsequent interpretation.'[34] Nor is this practice of the Court— 'for the purpose of deciding the constitutional questions * * * [taking] the statute as though it read precisely as the highest court of the State has interpreted it'[35]—quite compatible with another claimed foundation for the vagueness doctrine: that 'it would certainly be dangerous if the legislature could set a net large enough to catch all possible offenders and leave it to the courts to step inside and say who could be rightfully detained and who should be set at large.'[36] These several circumstances indicate that vagueness alone, although helpful and important, does not provide a full and rational explanation of the case development in which it appears so prominently. Together with certain further

33. *Lanzetta v. New Jersey,* 306 U.S. 451, 453 (1939).

34. *Winters v. New York,* 333 U.S. 507, 514–15 (1948) (dictum). As *Winters* and *Kunz v. New York,* 340 U.S. 290 (1951), demonstrate, *post hoc* state construction may be heavily relied on by the Court in striking down, as well as in sustaining, a challenged statute.

Such reliance for purposes of voiding is of course not, as is saving reliance, inconsistent with the fair warning rationale.

35. *Minnesota ex rel. Pearson v. Probate Court,* 309 U.S. 270, 273 (1940).

36. *United States v. Reese,* 92 U.S. 214, 221 (1875).

indications which may be derived from the history of the doctrine and from the settings in which it is invoked successfully, they rather compel the conclusion that in the great majority of instances the concept of vagueness is an available instrument in the service of other more determinative judicially felt needs and pressures."

8.   Justice Douglas, in *Papachristou v. City of Jacksonville,* 405 U.S. 156, 92 S.Ct. 839, 31 L.Ed.2d 110 (1972): "Another aspect of the [vagrancy] ordinance's vagueness appears when we focus, not on the lack of notice given a potential offender, but on the effect of the unfettered discretion it places in the hands of the Jacksonville police. * * *

"Those generally implicated by the imprecise terms of the ordinance—poor people, nonconformists, dissenters, idlers—may be required to comport themselves according to the life style deemed appropriate by the Jacksonville police and the courts. Where, as here, there are no standards governing the exercise of the discretion granted by the ordinance, the scheme permits and encourages an arbitrary and discriminatory enforcement of the law. It furnishes a convenient tool for 'harsh and discriminatory enforcement by local prosecuting officials, against particular groups deemed to merit their displeasure.'"

9.   The significance of this consideration is highlighted by *City of Chicago v. Morales,* 527 U.S. 41, 119 S.Ct. 1849, 144 L.Ed.2d 67 (1999), involving an ordinance defining loitering as "remain[ing] in any one place with no apparent purpose" and then failing to disperse upon a police order to do so. Only three Justices found the statute vague for failure of notice to offenders, but a total of five held, as an independent ground, that the ordinance was void because it created a potential for police abuse. As Justice Stevens' plurality opinion explained, the ordinance failed to provide "any guidance" because "the 'no apparent purpose' standard for making the [dispersal] decision is inherently subjective because its application depends on whether some purpose is 'apparent' to the officer on the scene." Justice Scalia objected in dissent: "No one in his right mind would read the phrase 'without any apparent purpose' to mean anything other than without any apparent lawful purpose."

How would the Supreme Court rule as to an ordinance reading: "Any person loitering in the immediate vicinity of a cash-dispensing machine, who disobeys a police order to leave that vicinity, shall be guilty of a misdemeanor"? See Alfred Hill, *Vagueness and Police Discretion: The Supreme Court in a Bog,* 51 Rutgers U.L.Rev. 1289 (1999).

10.   The application of the *Bouie* case in *Locke* and other contexts will be considered in connection with the *Wilson* case, following.

SECTION 4. RETROACTIVE APPLICATION OF DETRIMENTAL AND BENEFICIAL LAW REGARDING A CRIME'S DEFINITION AND PUNISHMENT

WILSON v. STATE

Supreme Court of Florida, 1974.

288 So.2d 480.

McCain, Justice: * * *

The appellants, together with certain others, were charged with sodomy in violation of Florida Statutes, § 800.01 (1971), F.S.A., by informations filed in the Circuit Court in and for Bradford County. The incident giving rise to the charges and convictions occurred in Raiford prison. The appellants and their victim were prison inmates. The victim was threatened at knife point after an initial beating and forced to submit to sexual copulation *per anum.* Following a jury trial, defendants were found guilty as charged. The Court adjudged them guilty and sentenced Brinson to 20 years imprisonment and Wilson to 15 years. In the interim between the adjudication of guilt and the subsequent appeal, this Court ruled in *Franklin v. State*, 257 So.2d 21 (1971) that the statute, Fla.Stat. § 800.01, F.S.A. was "void on its face as unconstitutional for vagueness and uncertainty in its language, ... ". On May 17, 1973, the District Court[a] reversed defendant's convictions and remanded the case to the trial court for "further proceedings under Section 794.01, Florida Statutes, on charges of rape and forcible carnal knowledge." Thereupon timely appeal was taken to this Court.

Florida Statutes, § 794.01, F.S.A., specifically provided the following generic language: "Whoever ravishes and carnally knows a *female* of the age of ten years or more, by force and against *her* will, or unlawfully or carnally knows and abuses a *female* child under the age of ten years, shall be guilty of a capital felony, ..." (Emphasis supplied.)

The District Court in reversing the conviction based upon the now unconstitutional Section 800.01 was correct in light of the decision in *Franklin,* supra, since the appellate court in reviewing a judgment, is bound by the interpretation of the constitutionality of the statute prevailing at the time of the appellate disposition. Had the District Court elected to restrict its action to only that course of action, the need for additional appellate review would have been unnecessary, however, that Court further held that the defendant could be tried under the provisions of Florida Statutes, § 794.01, F.S.A., for rape.

The Court seeks sanctity in the decision of *Deas v. State*, 119 Fla. 839, 161 So. 729 (1935). In 1921, a companion statute to Section 794.01, Chapter 8596, Acts of 1921, (now Fla.Stat. § 794.05, F.S.A.[b]) was amended, changing in effect the word "female" to the word "person". This Court said of that change:

"The purpose of the 1921 amendment (passed at the first session of the Legislature elected after the ratification of the national woman's suffrage amendment) was to abolish the distinction as to sex, and thereupon to provide for the protection of the chastity of all unmarried persons, whether male or female, under the age of eighteen years when of previous chaste character."

This Court was operating with the express legislative pronouncement and not with its own interpretation of the prevailing popular morality. Had the Legislature elected to conform Section 794.01 to that language found in Section 794.05 we would have less difficulty with the District Court's decision; or if this Court were solely a court of justice and not a court of justice under the law, the moral merit of the District Court's determination that this heinous crime must not go unpunished would force a different result. However, this is not the case. It is not the province of the judiciary to legislate; therefore, for the Court to change the definition of "female" found in Florida Statutes, § 794.01, F.S.A., to be the same as the more inclusive word "person" is to invade the province of the Legislature. It is just such an expansion the District Court undertook:

"We hold therefore that any verbiage contained in Section 794.01 that purports to limit the protective provisions of the law to females while such verbiage withholds that same protection from males is violative of Sections 2, 9 and 21 of Article 1 of the Florida Constitution F.S.A. and Section 1 of the Fourteenth Amendment of the United States Constitution."

a. That is, the intermediate appellate court.

b. As amended, that statute provided: "Any person who has unlawful carnal intercourse with any unmar-ried person, of previous chaste character, who at the time of such intercourse is under the age of 18 years, shall be guilty of a felony of the second degree."

Clearly from this language, the lack of a protective statute has affected the judicial conscience, as well it should, but the courts should not shoulder the burden and responsibility of the Legislature. The Legislature has had two years to fill the void created by the holding of the sodomy statute unconstitutional. The wording has been changed in Section 794.01, Florida Statutes, F.S.A. to read "person" but related crimes classified at common law as "sodomy" are as yet uncovered.

Finally, the District Court considered the denial of equal protection to all males while in the same breath denied equal protection to the defendants in this action. As stated above, the statute did not cover a rape of a male, but the radically new interpretation of Section 794.01, punishes as criminal conduct that which was not criminal under the existing statutes at the time of the incident, thus violating the Due Process Clause of the United States Constitution and the Florida Constitution as being ex post facto in its application. *Bouie v. City of Columbia*, [p. 66 of this Book]; * * *. The State, in fact, concedes this point:

> "Therefore, it is with great reluctance that the Appellee (State of Florida) admits that in the face of the controlling cases of *Bouie*[, etc.], it can make no supportive argument that to apply the provisions of Section 794.01, Florida Statutes to these Appellants would not be ex post facto in application."

For these reasons, Florida Statutes Section 794.01, F.S.A., shall not be applied to the actions of these defendants; however, the record reveals that the reprehensible conduct might be supportive of prosecution, but that is not for us to decide.

Therefore the decision of the District Court is reversed and remanded with instructions not to proceed inconsistently with this decision. * * *

Notes and Questions

1. It might be thought that in any judicial proceedings in which a conviction of these defendants for their attack upon a fellow inmate was sought or was challenged, any legal developments occurring subsequent to the time of the defendants' conduct would not be relevant. This is generally not the case, however, as to subsequent judicial decisions, or at least as to those which purport to have "found" what the law is and was back to the time of that conduct. Thus, it is quite common for a judicial decision finding a constitutional defect in the statute under which the prosecution was brought to be applied retroactively. This is why the *Wilson* court said that the District Court quite properly relied upon the *Franklin* case, decided between these defendants' conviction and their appeal, in deciding their sodomy convictions could not stand.

The same is true of a judicial decision giving a new interpretation to a criminal statute, as with *Bailey v. United States*, 516 U.S. 137, 116 S.Ct. 501, 133 L.Ed.2d 472 (1995), holding that conviction for use of a firearm during drug trafficking requires evidence that defendant "actively employed the firearm." *Bailey* can be invoked even in the context of a post-conviction collateral attack by a defendant challenging his pre-*Bailey* conviction under the same statute. See *Bousley v. United States*, 523 U.S. 614, 118 S.Ct. 1604, 140 L.Ed.2d 828 (1998).

In both of these illustrations, of course, the subsequent judicial decision being applied retroactively to defendant's conduct was one which was beneficial to the defendant. But application of a new decision, perhaps even one reached in the defendant's own case, which is detrimental to the defendant obviously raises different concerns, concerns that prompted the Supreme Court's *Bouie* decision, relied upon by the defendants in both *Locke* and *Wilson* (but with quite different results). A closer look at *Bouie* is now in order.

2.   *Bouie* arose out of a "sit-in" demonstration at Eckerd's Drug Store in Columbia, South Carolina. Two blacks took seats in a booth in the store's restaurant area; no notices were posted restricting the area to whites only. When they refused to leave upon demand, they were arrested and convicted of violating a criminal trespass statute prohibiting entry on the property of another "after notice" forbidding such conduct. While prior South Carolina decisions emphasized the necessity or proving such advance notice, the state supreme court affirmed theses convictions by construing the statute to prohibit not only the act of entering after notice not to do so but also the act of remaining on the property after receiving notice to leave. The Supreme Court, per Brennan, J., after noting this was unlike the usual void-for-vagueness case because the statute here "was admirably narrow and precise," continued: "The thrust of the distinction, however, is to produce a potentially greater deprivation of the right to fair notice in this sort of case, where the claim is that a statute precise on its face has been unforeseeably and retroactively expanded by judicial construction, than in the typical 'void for vagueness' situation. When a statute on its face is vague or overbroad, it at least gives a potential defendant some notice, by virtue of this very characteristic, that a question may arise as to its coverage, and that it may be held to cover his contemplated conduct. When a statute on its face is narrow and precise, however, it lulls the potential defendant into a false sense of security, giving him no reason even to suspect that conduct clearly outside the scope of the statute as written will be retroactively brought within it by an act of judicial construction. If the Fourteenth Amendment is violated when a person is required 'to speculate as to the meaning of penal statutes,' * * * or to 'guess at (the statute's) meaning and differ as to its application,' * * * the violation is that much greater when, because the uncertainty as to the statute's meaning is itself not revealed until the court's decision, a person is not even afforded an opportunity to engage in such speculation before committing the act in question.

"There can be no doubt that a deprivation of the right of fair warning can result not only from vague statutory language but also from an unforeseeable and retroactive judicial expansion of narrow and precise statutory language. * * * Indeed, an unforeseeable judicial enlargement of a criminal statute, applied retroactively, operates precisely like an ex post facto law, such as Art. I, § 10, of the Constitution forbids. * * * If a state legislature is barred by the Ex Post Facto Clause from passing such a law, it must follow that a State Supreme Court is barred by the Due Process Clause from achieving precisely the same result by judicial construction. * * *. If a judicial construction of a criminal statute is 'unexpected and indefensible by reference to the law which had been expressed prior to the conduct in issue,' it must not be given retroactive effect. * * *

"We think it clear that the South Carolina Supreme Court, in applying its new construction of the statute to affirm these convictions, has deprived petitioners of rights guaranteed to them by the Due Process Clause. If South Carolina had applied to this case its new statute prohibiting the act of remaining on the premises of another after being asked to leave, the constitutional proscription of ex post facto laws would clearly invalidate the convictions. The Due Process Clause compels the same result here, where the State has sought to achieve precisely the same effect by judicial construction of the statute. While such a construction is of course valid for the future, it may not be applied retroactively, any more than a legislative enactment may be, to impose criminal penalties for conduct committed at a time when it was not fairly stated to be criminal. Application of this rule is particularly compelling where, as here, the petitioners' conduct cannot be deemed improper or immoral."

3.   In light of that language, what is your assessment of *Locke* and *Wilson*? Can it be said that *Locke* is correct but that *Wilson* is wrong because the conduct in both instances, unlike that in *Bouie*, was "improper and immoral"? What then if in *Locke* and *Wilson* the

conduct had been consensual? Or, should a court's assessment of defendant's conduct have nothing to do with whether or not there is a *Bouie* violation? Consider: "In sum, for constitutional purposes, courts measure the permissible degree of retroactivity against the perceived 'moral quality of the [defendant's] conduct' rather than against some abstract legal yardstick. Which is to say that courts do exactly what the proponents of the liberal conception of nonretroactivity say no official should ever be trusted to do—namely, make ex post decisions about what forms of conduct are sufficiently immoral to be treated as criminal." Dan M. Kahan, *Some Realism About Retroactive Criminal Lawmaking*, 3 Roger Williams U.L.Rev. 95, 110 (1997).

4. Consider *Locke* and *Wilson* from a different standpoint, namely, the assertion in *Bouie* that a judicial construction cannot be retroactive when it is "unexpected and indefensible by reference to the law which had been expressed prior to the conduct in issue." If that is the point, then can it be said that both *Locke* and *Wilson* end up on the wrong side of this line because any foreseeability in *Locke* required speculation about adoption of a view accepted in a few other states, while in *Wilson* it was foreseeable a court might read the rape statute to square with its closest companion in the criminal code and with principles well established within the state regarding equal protection of the sexes?

5. Is the error in *Bouie* as written and applied a failure to be as strict with judicial decisions as with legislation? Consider Harold J. Krent, *Should Bouie be Buoyed?: Judicial Retroactive Lawmaking and the Ex Post Facto Clause*, 3 Roger Williams U.L.Rev. 35, 36–39 (1997): "Despite the Supreme Court's strictures on retroactive lawmaking in the criminal context, the Court has declined to impose ex post facto restrictions on judicial decision-making. The language of the Clause apparently refers only to the legislature, for it forbids states and the federal government from 'pass[ing]' any 'ex post facto law.' Indeed, as early as the 1798 United States Supreme Court decision in *Calder v. Bull*,[14] several Justices opined that the Ex Post Facto Clause did not apply to judicial decisions, and the Court has never struck down any judicial act on that basis.

"From the perspective of the criminally accused, however, it is not obvious why judicial action should be exempt from ex post facto scrutiny. * * * To the extent that the Ex Post Facto Clause protects reliance interests, the identity of the governmental actor causing the injury seems irrelevant.

"In light of these realities, the Supreme Court in *Bouie v. City of Columbia* held that ex post facto principles as read into the Due Process Clause applied to judicial decision-making. * * *

"But the promise of *Bouie* has been largely illusory. Courts have resorted to a number of devices to curtail drastically the impact of applying ex post facto principles to judicial action. First, they have limited the due process inquiry to unforeseeable judicial changes in the law. In contrast, courts do not permit legislative change to be applied retroactively even when that change * * * can be considered foreseeable."

14. 3 U.S. (3 Dall.) 386 (1798). [In this case, the Court provided this much-quoted list of ex post facto laws: "1st. Every law that makes an action done before the passing of the law, and which was innocent when done, criminal; and punishes such action. 2nd. Every law that aggravates a crime, or makes it greater than it was, when committed. 3d. Every law that changes the punishment, and inflicts a greater punishment, than the law annexed to the crime, when committed. 4th. Every law that alters the legal rules of evidence, and receives less, or different testimony, than the law required at the time of the commission of the offense, in order to convict the offender." The first three are restrictions on the substantive law. As to the fourth, a limitation on procedural law, the Court has more recently held that extending the ex post facto prohibition to the area of procedure was not "consistent with the understanding of the term 'ex post facto' at the time the Constitution was adopted." *Collins v. Youngblood*, 497 U.S. 37, 110 S.Ct. 2715, 111 L.Ed.2d 30 (1990).]

6. In *People v. Sobiek,* 30 Cal.App.3d 458, 106 Cal.Rptr. 519 (1973), the state appealed the quashing of an indictment for theft which alleged that the defendant had embezzled or stolen partnership property. The applicable statute reads: "Every person who shall feloniously steal, take, carry, lead, or drive away the personal property of another, or who shall fraudulently appropriate property which has been entrusted to him, or who shall knowingly and designedly, by any false or fraudulent representation or pretense, defraud any other person of money, labor or real or personal property, * * * is guilty of theft." The court acknowledged that in *People v. Brody,* 29 Cal.App.2d 6, 83 P.2d 952 (1938), it had been held, relying upon dictum in two California Supreme Court cases, that it was "settled law" that it was not theft for a partner to take partnership property. But the *Sobiek* court, noting that this view had been rejected in the Model Penal Code and in the recent recodifications in other jurisdictions, concluded it was "both illogical and unreasonable to hold that a partner cannot steal from his partners merely because he has an undivided interest in the partnership property" and that there was nothing in the statute quoted above "which requires an interpretation different from that in [the] Model Penal Code." The defendant objected that such a construction of the statute, if applied to him, would violate the principles of the *Bouie,* but the court responded that this was not so because "in the case at bar, 'common social duty' would have forewarned respondent that 'circumspect conduct' prohibited robbing his partners and also would have told him that he was stealing 'property of another.'"

7. Does *Sobiek* fit the following characterization by Krent, supra, at 74, and, if so, is that a basis for praise or criticism? "*Bouie* is best understood as a means of limiting judicial vindictiveness rather than protecting offenders' reliance interests or ensuring repose. The foreseeability analysis acts as a crude filter to separate judicial reinterpretations animated by retributive impulses from the more familiar common law evolutionary process.

"Indeed, a survey of recent appellate decisions addressing *Bouie* claims suggests that *Bouie* has been applied to those ends. The real inquiry is not whether the judicial change was foreseeable, but rather whether the change was motivated by impermissible reasons."

8. Consider also the following views regarding *Sobiek*:

(a) "[N]ecessity plays a significant role in the construction of criminal statutes. Prosecutors frequently argue that a particular statutory interpretation is necessary to fulfill the legislature's intent to ensure that a wrongdoer who is within the contemplation of the drafters of the crime will receive adequate punishment. This contention has most potency when the defendant will go unpunished unless the court reads the statute as the prosecution requests, a class of cases exemplified by an academic chestnut, *People v. Sobiek*.

"* * * *Though the court [in *Sobiek*] cited some unsatisfactory reasons for its decision, a better one, and one that surely influenced the result, would have been that if Sobiek's conduct did not constitute theft, his behavior would go unpunished because no other existing statute seemed even remotely applicable. Extending the theft statute to include the embezzlement of partnership property was necessary to effectuate the state's purpose to protect victims like Sobiek's partners and to punish those who victimize them.

"The California case usually paired with *Sobiek* in casebooks and in scholarly analysis, *Keeler v. Superior Court,*[204] reflects the flipside of the necessity argument. In *Keeler,* the California Supreme Court suggested that it was unwilling to extend its murder statute to include the intentional killing of a viable but unborn fetus by the estranged husband of the

---

204.   470 P.2d 617 (Cal. 1970); * * *.

fetus' mother because there was another crime covering the same conduct—the state law against abortion. While the court included this reference in a rather tortured discussion of why the proposed extension of the murder statute would deprive *Keeler* of fair notice, a more persuasive argument would have been that the extension was not necessary to guarantee Keeler's criminal punishment, as a jury could have convicted him of abortion and of battery on the mother of the fetus, even if the jury was not allowed to consider a murder charge. In other words, the extension of the murder statute to include viable but unborn fetuses was not required in order to adequately punish wrongdoers." Robert Batey, *Vagueness and the Construction of Criminal Statutes–Balancing Acts*, 5 Va.J.Soc.Pol. & L. 1, 44–46 (1997).

(b) "[O]n the issue of fairness to the accused (which is what notice is all about), *Sobiek* seems essentially sound. This conclusion rests in part on the sheer unreality of assuming that the conduct of *Keeler* or *Sobiek* or others similarly situated depended on an expectation about the fact or grade of criminal liability. In the great run of cases, the picture of a citizen relying to his or her detriment on highly technical legal sources is simply not credible. More important, the claim of such hypothetical persons to our moral sympathies is unconvincing and obscure. If by some chance Keeler had consulted the statute, identified the uncertainty in 'human being,' and tracked his way back through the precedents to the restrictive pronouncements of Blackstone and Hale, he would not, in my view, have established the kind of reliance interest that society would be obliged to respect. Rather it seems that a person who embarks on obviously wrongful conduct takes his chances on just how seriously the rest of society may view the matter. Thus, even if it were true, the fact that Keeler thought he was merely committing an assault or that *Sobiek* believed he had found a loophole in the law of theft would not, in my judgment, make punishment unjust. This is not to say, of course, that society has no obligation to treat wrongdoers fairly, but only that fairness, at least in any sense even roughly congruent with our penal law, does not turn on the wrongdoer's own conception of the legal consequences of his act." John Calvin Jeffries, Jr., *Legality, Vagueness, and the Construction of Penal Statutes*, 71 Va.L.Rev. 189, 230–31 (1985).

STATE v. MULLEN

Supreme Court of Rhode Island, 1999.

740 A.2d 783.

PER CURIAM. * * *

The defendant was charged, inter alia, with nine counts of abominable and detestable crimes against nature pursuant to § 11–10–1. The indictment alleged that defendant committed sexual acts upon the victim between February 22, 1992, and February 22, 1995, when the victim was between the ages of fourteen and seventeen. However, the state, upon a request for a bill of particulars, stated that the alleged acts took place between April 10, 1994, and February 22, 1995, when the victim was over sixteen years of age.

While this indictment was pending, the Legislature repealed certain provisions of § 11–10–1. The statute as amended reads as follows:

"SECTION 1. Section 11–10–1 of the General Laws in Chapter 11–10 entitled 'Crime Against Nature' is hereby amended to read as follows:

11–10–1. Abominable and detestable crime against nature.—Every person who shall be convicted of the abominable and detestable crime against nature, either with mankind or with any beast, shall be imprisoned not exceeding twenty (20) years nor less than seven (7) years." P.L.1998, ch. 24, § 1.

A justice of the Superior Court dismissed nine counts charging abominable and detestable crimes against nature on the ground that the Legislature repealed that portion of the statute prohibiting such conduct with mankind. The motion justice reasoned that the thrust of the repeal was to decriminalize sodomy between persons who had attained the age of consent (sixteen years) and "the manifest intent of the General Assembly was to end prosecutions, convictions, and perhaps even sentencing, * * * of persons who engage in no other criminal conduct than that of sodomy."

On appeal the state argues that * * * it would not contravene the intent of the Legislature to apply the general savings statute and prosecute defendant for alleged violations of § 11–10–1.

The parties agree that "[a]t common law the general rule was that in the absence of an effective saving clause, the repeal of a penal statute operated to bar prosecution for prior violations of the statute." *State v. Babbitt*, 457 A.2d 1049, 1053–54 (R.I.1983). "The rule was founded on the theory that the Legislature by its repeal determined that the conduct in question should no longer be prosecuted as a crime."

Rhode Island's general savings statute, G.L.1956 § 43–3–23, provides that "[n]o suit, prosecution, or indictment pending at the time of the repeal of any statute for any offense committed * * * shall in any case be affected by the repeal, but the suit, prosecution, or indictment may be proceeded with, and the act shall be deemed to be in force for the purpose of prosecuting the act to final judgment and execution or sentence, as the case may be." "[I]t was the legislative intent that [§ 43–3–23] was to have the effect of saving criminal proceedings pending at the time of the repeal of any penal statute unless such construction would be clearly repugnant to the express provisions of the repealing statute." *State v. Lewis*, 91 R.I. 110, 115, 161 A.2d 209, 212 (1960).

In *Babbitt* this Court held that the effect of a simultaneous repeal and reenactment of a common-law rape statute into one for sexual assault did not deprive the trial court of jurisdiction to prosecute the defendant for a violation of the repealed statute. Applying the simultaneous-repeal-and-reenactment exception to the common-law abatement doctrine, this Court stated that "the effect of the change in the law as it relates to the crime of rape was merely amendatory in nature; there was never a time when the elements of the offense were not considered criminal." There the crime of common-law rape was embodied in the new sexual-assault statute.

The defendant in *Babbitt* was also charged with violating G.L.1956 § 11–34–5, which made unlawful the "transport[ing of] * * * another for the purpose of prostitution * * *. [T]he Legislature amended § 11–34–5 by adding the requirement that the proscribed conduct be conducted for pecuniary gain.' "This Court concluded that because the defendant did not act in the interests of pecuniary gain, the acts of the defendant were not made criminal under the amended statute and a "contrary ruling would be inconsistent with the legislative intent."

In the case at bar we are of the opinion that the trial justice was correct in determining that it was the manifest intention of the Legislature to decriminalize the act of sodomy between consenting adults. Having repealed that portion of § 11–10–1 that proscribed sodomy "with mankind," the Legislature clearly intended that such activity be regulated by the criminal statute on sexual assault. The definitional provisions of that statute explicitly include those acts that formerly composed the "crime against nature" provision, so that those acts are punishable when they are carried out in such a way as to violate the statute. The sexual-assault statute further provides that the age of consent is sixteen, and this age of consent is applicable to sodomy as well as to other forms of sexual behavior. Consequently for purposes of this statute a person who has attained the age of sixteen years may be considered a consenting adult. In applying the savings statute, § 43–3–23, one must also consider § 43–3–2, which reads as follows:

"Application of rules of construction. In the construction of statutes the provisions of this chapter shall be observed, unless the observance of them would lead to a construction *inconsistent with the manifest intent of the general assembly, or be repugnant to some other part of the statute*." (Emphasis added.)

We are of the opinion that the trial justice was correct in determining that the preservation of these charges would have been inconsistent with the manifest intention of the General Assembly to decriminalize sodomy between consenting adults and that it would be repugnant to the statute as amended.

The dissent suggests that the effect of the Court's ruling in this case will be to revive the common-law rule extinguishing all pending prosecutions upon repeal of a criminal statute. Nothing could be further from the intent of this opinion.

We believe that when the Legislature repeals or amends a portion of a criminal statute, the effect of such repeal or amendment upon pending prosecutions should be considered on a case-by-case basis, taking into account the provisions of § 43–3–2 in the light of the intent of the Legislature in enacting the repeal or amendment. In the case at bar we are of the opinion that it is inconsistent with the intent of the Legislature to prosecute acts that are no longer criminal offenses. It is fundamentally unfair to prosecute an individual for prior conduct that would now not constitute a violation of law. A major purpose of a criminal statute is to deter conduct deemed unacceptable and either *malum in se* or at least *malum prohibitum* by the Legislature.

When by virtue of amendment or repeal such conduct is no longer prohibited, prosecution can have no deterrent effect. The sole purpose of prosecution in such a situation is pure punishment for its own sake. We believe that such nondeterrent punitive action would be inconsistent with and repugnant to the express provisions of the repealing statute.

For the reasons stated, the state's appeal is denied. * * *

FLANDERS, JUSTICE, with whom JUSTICE BOURCIER joins, dissenting. * * *

Here the terms of the repealing statute, see P.L.1998, ch. 24, § 1, contain no such clear repugnance to the General Assembly's manifest intent to preserve pending prosecutions from being "affected by the repeal." See § 43–3–23. Although it is obvious that the General Assembly intended to decriminalize sodomy as of the effective date of the repeal, the Legislature said nothing whatsoever about preserving or quashing pending prosecutions for acts of sodomy committed before the repeal. Indeed, in light of the default provisions of the saving statute, it would have been superfluous for the General Assembly to do so unless it intended to quash pending prosecutions for the repealed offense. But having given us no indication of any manifest intent to achieve such a result, such prosecutions are saved by the plain language of § 43–3–23.

Although the brief explanation attached to this repeal is not pellucid, it does provide some insight concerning the Legislature's intention. In two brief sentences, the explanation states that

"1. This act would de-criminalize sodomy between two consenting adults.

"2. This act would take effect upon passage."

In our opinion, these sentences, read together or separately, contain no indication that the "manifest intent" of the General Assembly was to override the general saving statute's preservation of criminal prosecutions that are pending when the underlying criminal statute is repealed. Nor does this explanation somehow indicate that to apply the general saving statute and to preserve the state's pending prosecution of defendant would be "clearly repugnant" to the "express provisions of the repealing statute."

The explanation states that the repeal would decriminalize sodomy. But the act says nothing about whether this decriminalization should apply to pending prosecutions. On the contrary, the second sentence states that "the act would take effect upon passage." Thus, if the repealing statute manifests any legislative intent at all, it seems to us that this sentence indicates that the repeal was intended only to have had a prospective application. * * *

[*Babbitt*] is not the situation we face in this case. Here the Legislature has not acted to clarify what elements are needed to establish a preexisting criminal offense nor to impose additional elements of proof upon a preexisting crime. Rather it has repealed outright, as of an effective date, that portion of a criminal statute that outlawed sodomy. In these circumstances, § 43–3–23 preserves pending prosecutions for acts of sodomy committed before the effective date of the repeal.

The majority also suggests that "[i]t is fundamentally unfair to prosecute an individual for prior conduct that would now not constitute a violation of law. * * * When by virtue of amendment or repeal such conduct is no longer prohibited, prosecution can have no deterrent effect." We respectfully disagree.

First, we do not believe it is unfair to prosecute an individual who has engaged in criminal misconduct that was unlawful at the time the criminal acts were committed. Merely because such acts would not now be deemed unlawful if they had been committed at a different, later time does not mean that it is unfair to prosecute the individual who committed the crimes in question when such conduct was against the law. If the majority truly believes that "[i]t is fundamentally unfair to prosecute an individual for prior conduct that would not now constitute a violation of law," then why is it not also "fundamentally unfair" to keep those who have been convicted of such offenses behind bars after the conduct that led to their convictions has been decriminalized via a later repeal of the underlying criminal statute? Does the majority also subscribe to the belief that the continued incarceration of such individuals "can have no deterrent effect" after the conduct for which they were convicted and incarcerated has been decriminalized? We hope not, but the logic of their reasoning leads to answering such questions in the affirmative.

Second, the fact that the conduct in question is no longer unlawful does not mean that prosecuting the individual who committed the offense "can have no deterrent effect." We believe that would-be lawbreakers are more likely to be deterred from committing crimes in the future if individuals who break the law are prosecuted for their offenses even when the conduct in question is no longer prohibited because of a subsequent repeal of the pertinent criminal statute. Otherwise would-be lawbreakers could be encouraged to believe that they may be able to skate free of their crimes if they are fortunate enough to benefit from a later legislative decriminalization of the offending conduct. Thus the result in this case encourages disrespect for the law as it exists at any given time.

Third, by means of the saving statute, § 43–3–23, the Legislature enacted into law its policy preference that pending prosecutions shall be unaffected by the later decriminalization of the conduct in question absent an expressed and clear legislative intention to the contrary. Accordingly we as judges have no business overriding this legislative policy choice in favor of enforcing a judicial belief that it is "fundamentally unfair to prosecute acts which are no longer criminal offenses" and that such prosecutions "can have no deterrent effect." The short answer to these sentiments is that the General Assembly decided otherwise when it enacted the saving statute. * * *

Unfortunately, we believe that the effect of the Court's ruling in this case will be to revive the common-law rule extinguishing all pending prosecutions upon repeal of a criminal statute, notwithstanding the absence of any indication in the repealing statute that the Legislature intended to do so. * * *

Notes and Questions

1. Is the dissent correct in concluding that the majority has, in effect, repealed the savings statute and returned to the common law position? If not, then precisely what remains of the statute? If so, then is that not itself a sufficient basis for concluding that the majority has overstepped its authority?

2. As a matter of policy, when should a criminal defendant be allowed to take advantage of decriminalization occurring after his conduct? Consider Comment, 121 U.Pa.L.Rev. 120, 148–49 (1972): "A criminal statute might be repealed due to a present legislative determination that the conduct proscribed should never have been criminal,[176] that a change in societal mores demands that the conduct be decriminalized,[177] or that a sudden change in circumstances or conditions renders the proscription unnecessary.[178] In each of the cases, the prudence of retroactivity or nonretroactivity must be measured in terms of serving the possible goals of punishment: prevention, restraint, rehabilitation, deterrence, education, and retribution. For example, if upon repeal of a law a determination that the proscribed conduct should never have been criminal can be attributed to the legislature, the 'no benefit' rule clearly does not advance the goals of punishment. Prevention or particular deterrence is not served since the defendant cannot commit the same crime again once the conduct has been decriminalized. Further restraint is unnecessary to protect society from the now legalized conduct, and to the extent that rehabilitation is aimed at eliminating any predisposition to repeat the same criminal act, decriminalization completes rehabilitation. General deterrence is not fostered since decriminalization ends the need to dissuade others from committing the previously proscribed act.[180] Public education about the criminality of the act becomes anachronistic. The only remaining goal, retribution, *is* served by continued punishment, but is a generally discredited goal."

3. It is common for a savings statute or some other statute to provide that if the penalty is reduced the defendant is entitled to be sentenced under the new penalty provisions. See, e.g., *State v. Easton*, 203 W.Va. 631, 510 S.E.2d 465 (1998) (applying provision that "sentencing court shall apply the penalties imposed by the statute in effect at the time of the offense, except where the amended penal statute provides for lesser penalties").

SECTION 5. OTHER CONSTITUTIONAL LIMITATIONS ON DEFINING CRIMINAL BEHAVIOR

BOWERS v. HARDWICK

Supreme Court of the United States, 1986.

478 U.S. 186, 106 S.Ct. 2841, 92 L.Ed.2d 140.

176. Repeal of prohibition by the 21st amendment is illustrative of such a change.

177. The absolute decriminalization of abortions performed in New York by licensed physicians on women less than 24 weeks pregnant is such an example.

178. This type of change is illustrated by the repeal of a variety of price controls at the end of World War II.

180. Of course, one possible objective of punishment may be the deterrence of law-breaking in general. Under this rationale, it is a disregard for law, and not a substantive offense, that is punished.

JUSTICE WHITE delivered the opinion of the Court.

In August 1982, respondent was charged with violating the Georgia statute criminalizing sodomy[1] by committing that act with another adult male in the bedroom of respondent's home. After a preliminary hearing, the District Attorney decided not to present the matter to the grand jury unless further evidence developed.

Respondent then brought suit in the Federal District Court, challenging the constitutionality of the statute insofar as it criminalized consensual sodomy.[2] He asserted that he was a practicing homosexual, that the Georgia sodomy statute, as administered by the defendants, placed him in imminent danger of arrest, and that the statute for several reasons violates the Federal Constitution. The District Court granted the defendants' motion to dismiss for failure to state a claim.

A divided panel of the Court of Appeals for the Eleventh Circuit reversed. * * * Relying on our decisions in *Griswold v. Connecticut,* 381 U.S. 479, 85 S.Ct. 1678, 14 L.Ed.2d 510 (1965), *Eisenstadt v. Baird,* 405 U.S. 438, 92 S.Ct. 1029, 31 L.Ed.2d 349 (1972), *Stanley v. Georgia,* 394 U.S. 557, 89 S.Ct. 1243, 22 L.Ed.2d 542 (1969), and *Roe v. Wade,* 410 U.S. 113, 93 S.Ct. 705, 35 L.Ed.2d 147 (1973), the court went on to hold that the Georgia statute violated respondent's fundamental rights because his homosexual activity is a private and intimate association that is beyond the reach of state regulation by reason of the Ninth Amendment and the Due Process Clause of the Fourteenth Amendment. The case was remanded for trial, at which, to prevail, the State would have to prove that the statute is supported by a compelling interest and is the most narrowly drawn means of achieving that end.

Because other Courts of Appeals have arrived at judgments contrary to that of the Eleventh Circuit in this case, we granted the State's petition for certiorari questioning the holding that its sodomy statute violates the fundamental rights of homosexuals. We agree with the State that the Court of Appeals erred, and hence reverse its judgment.

This case does not require a judgment on whether laws against sodomy between consenting adults in general, or between homosexuals in particular, are wise or desirable. It raises no question about the right or propriety of state legislative decisions to repeal their laws that criminalize homosexual sodomy, or of state court decisions invalidating those laws on state constitutional grounds. The issue presented is whether the Federal Constitution confers a fundamental right upon homosexuals to engage in sodomy and hence invalidates the laws of the many States that still make such conduct illegal and have done so for a very long time. The case also calls for some judgment about the limits of the Court's role in carrying out its constitutional mandate.

---

1. Ga.Code Ann. § 16–6–2 (1984) provides, in pertinent part, as follows:

"(a) A person commits the offense of sodomy when he performs or submits to any sexual act involving the sex organs of one person and the mouth or anus of another. * * *

"(b) A person convicted of the offense of sodomy shall be punished by imprisonment for not less than one nor more than 20 years. . . ."

2. John and Mary Doe were also plaintiffs in the action. They alleged that they wished to engage in sexual activity proscribed by § 16–6–2 in the privacy of their home, and that they had been "chilled and deterred" from engaging in such activity by both the existence of the statute and Hardwick's arrest. The District Court held, however, that because they had neither sustained, nor were in immediate danger of sustaining, any direct injury from the enforcement of the statute, they did not have proper standing to maintain the action. The Court of Appeals affirmed the District Court's judgment dismissing the Does' claim for lack of standing, and the Does do not challenge that holding in this Court.

The only claim properly before the Court, therefore, is Hardwick's challenge to the Georgia statute as applied to consensual homosexual sodomy. We express no opinion on the constitutionality of the Georgia statute as applied to other acts of sodomy.

We first register our disagreement with the Court of Appeals and with respondent that the Court's prior cases have construed the Constitution to confer a right of privacy that extends to homosexual sodomy and for all intents and purposes have decided this case. The reach of this line of cases was sketched in *Carey v. Population Services International,* 431 U.S. 678, 97 S.Ct. 2010, 52 L.Ed.2d 675 (1977). *Pierce v. Society of Sisters,* 268 U.S. 510, 45 S.Ct. 571, 69 L.Ed. 1070 (1925), and *Meyer v. Nebraska,* 262 U.S. 390, 43 S.Ct. 625, 67 L.Ed. 1042 (1923), were described as dealing with child rearing and education; *Prince v. Massachusetts,* 321 U.S. 158, 64 S.Ct. 438, 88 L.Ed. 645 (1944), with family relationships; *Skinner v. Oklahoma ex rel. Williamson,* 316 U.S. 535, 62 S.Ct. 1110, 86 L.Ed. 1655 (1942), with procreation; *Loving v. Virginia,* 388 U.S. 1, 87 S.Ct. 1817, 18 L.Ed.2d 1010 (1967), with marriage; *Griswold v. Connecticut, supra,* and *Eisenstadt v. Baird, supra,* with contraception; and *Roe v. Wade, supra,* with abortion. The latter three cases were interpreted as construing the Due Process Clause of the Fourteenth Amendment to confer a fundamental individual right to decide whether or not to beget or bear a child. *Carey v. Population Services International, supra.*

Accepting the decisions in these cases and the above description of them, we think it evident that none of the rights announced in those cases bears any resemblance to the claimed constitutional right of homosexuals to engage in acts of sodomy that is asserted in this case. No connection between family, marriage, or procreation on the one hand and homosexual activity on the other has been demonstrated, either by the Court of Appeals or by respondent. Moreover, any claim that these cases nevertheless stand for the proposition that any kind of private sexual conduct between consenting adults is constitutionally insulated from state proscription is unsupportable. Indeed, the Court's opinion in *Carey* twice asserted that the privacy right, which the *Griswold* line of cases found to be one of the protections provided by the Due Process Clause, did not reach so far.

Precedent aside, however, respondent would have us announce, as the Court of Appeals did, a fundamental right to engage in homosexual sodomy. This we are quite unwilling to do. It is true that despite the language of the Due Process Clauses of the Fifth and Fourteenth Amendments, which appears to focus only on the processes by which life, liberty, or property is taken, the cases are legion in which those Clauses have been interpreted to have substantive content, subsuming rights that to a great extent are immune from federal or state regulation or proscription. Among such cases are those recognizing rights that have little or no textual support in the constitutional language. *Meyer, Prince,* and *Pierce* fall in this category, as do the privacy cases from *Griswold* to *Carey.*

Striving to assure itself and the public that announcing rights not readily identifiable in the Constitution's text involves much more than the imposition of the Justices' own choice of values on the States and the Federal Government, the Court has sought to identify the nature of the rights qualifying for heightened judicial protection. In *Palko v. Connecticut,* 302 U.S. 319, 326, 58 S.Ct. 149, 152, 82 L.Ed. 288 (1937), it was said that this category includes those fundamental liberties that are "implicit in the concept of ordered liberty," such that "neither liberty nor justice would exist if [they] were sacrificed." A different description of fundamental liberties appeared in *Moore v. East Cleveland,* 431 U.S. 494, 97 S.Ct. 1932, 52 L.Ed.2d 531 (1977) (opinion of POWELL, J.), where they are characterized as those liberties that are "deeply rooted in this Nation's history and tradition."

It is obvious to us that neither of these formulations would extend a fundamental right to homosexuals to engage in acts of consensual sodomy. Proscriptions against that conduct have ancient roots. Sodomy was a criminal offense at common law and was forbidden by the laws of the original thirteen States when they ratified the Bill of Rights. In 1868, when the Fourteenth Amendment was ratified, all but 5 of the 37 States in the Union had criminal sodomy laws. In fact, until 1961, all 50 States outlawed sodomy, and today, 24 States and the District of Columbia continue to provide criminal penalties for sodomy performed in private and between consenting adults. Against this background, to claim that a right to engage in such conduct is "deeply rooted in this Nation's history and tradition" or "implicit in the concept of ordered liberty" is, at best, facetious.

Nor are we inclined to take a more expansive view of our authority to discover new fundamental rights imbedded in the Due Process Clause. The Court is most vulnerable and comes nearest to illegitimacy when it deals with judge-made constitutional law having little or no cognizable roots in the language or design of the Constitution. That this is so was painfully demonstrated by the face-off between the Executive and the Court in the 1930's, which resulted in the repudiation of much of the substantive gloss that the Court had placed on the Due Process Clause of the Fifth and Fourteenth Amendments. There should be, therefore, great resistance to expand the substantive reach of those Clauses, particularly if it requires redefining the category of rights deemed to be fundamental. Otherwise, the Judiciary necessarily takes to itself further authority to govern the country without express constitutional authority. The claimed right pressed on us today falls far short of overcoming this resistance.

Respondent, however, asserts that the result should be different where the homosexual conduct occurs in the privacy of the home. He relies on *Stanley v. Georgia*, where the Court held that the First Amendment prevents conviction for possessing and reading obscene material in the privacy of his home: "If the First Amendment means anything, it means that a State has no business telling a man, sitting alone in his house, what books he may read or what films he may watch."

Stanley did protect conduct that would not have been protected outside the home, and it partially prevented the enforcement of state obscenity laws; but the decision was firmly grounded in the First Amendment. The right pressed upon us here has no similar support in the text of the Constitution, and it does not qualify for recognition under the prevailing principles for construing the Fourteenth Amendment. Its limits are also difficult to discern. Plainly enough, otherwise illegal conduct is not always immunized whenever it occurs in the home. Victimless crimes, such as the possession and use of illegal drugs do not escape the law where they are committed at home. *Stanley* itself recognized that its holding offered no protection for the possession in the home of drugs, firearms, or stolen goods. And if respondent's submission is limited to the voluntary sexual conduct between consenting adults, it would be difficult, except by fiat, to limit the claimed right to homosexual conduct while leaving exposed to prosecution adultery, incest, and other sexual crimes even though they are committed in the home. We are unwilling to start down that road.

Even if the conduct at issue here is not a fundamental right, respondent asserts that there must be a rational basis for the law and that there is none in this case other than the presumed belief of a majority of the electorate in Georgia that homosexual sodomy is immoral and unacceptable. This is said to be an inadequate rationale to support the law. The law, however, is constantly based on notions of morality, and if all laws representing essentially moral choices are to be invalidated under the Due Process Clause, the courts will be very busy indeed. Even respondent makes no such claim, but insists that majority sentiments about the morality of homosexuality should be declared inadequate. We do not agree, and are unpersuaded that the sodomy laws of some 25 States should be invalidated on this basis.[8]

Accordingly, the judgment of the Court of Appeals is

Reversed.

CHIEF JUSTICE BURGER, concurring.

I join the Court's opinion, but I write separately to underscore my view that in constitutional terms there is no such thing as a fundamental right to commit homosexual sodomy.

To hold that the act of homosexual sodomy is somehow protected as a fundamental right would be to cast aside millennia of moral teaching.

This is essentially not a question of personal "preferences" but rather of the legislative authority of the State. I find nothing in the Constitution depriving a State of the power to enact the statute challenged here.

JUSTICE POWELL, concurring.

I join the opinion of the Court. I agree with the Court that there is no fundamental right—*i.e.,* no substantive right under the Due Process Clause—such as that claimed by respondent, and found to exist by the Court of Appeals. This is not to suggest, however, that respondent may not be protected by the Eighth Amendment of the Constitution. The Georgia statute at issue in this case authorizes a court to imprison a person for up to 20 years for a single private, consensual act of sodomy. In my view, a prison sentence for such conduct—certainly a sentence of long duration—would create a serious Eighth Amendment issue. Under the Georgia statute a single act of sodomy, even in the private setting of a home, is a felony comparable in terms of the possible sentence imposed to serious felonies such as aggravated battery, first degree arson, and robbery.

In this case, however, respondent has not been tried, much less convicted and sentenced.[2] Moreover, respondent has not raised the Eighth Amendment issue below. For these reasons this constitutional argument is not before us.

JUSTICE BLACKMUN, with whom JUSTICE BRENNAN, JUSTICE MARSHALL, and JUSTICE STEVENS join, dissenting.

This case is no more about "a fundamental right to engage in homosexual sodomy," as the Court purports to declare, than *Stanley v. Georgia* was about a fundamental right to watch obscene movies, or *Katz v. United States,* 389 U.S. 347, 88 S.Ct. 507, 19 L.Ed.2d 576 (1967), was about a fundamental right to place interstate bets from a telephone booth. Rather, this case is about "the most comprehensive of rights and the right most valued by civilized men," namely, "the right to be let alone." *Olmstead v. United States,* 277 U.S. 438, 478, 48 S.Ct. 564, 572, 72 L.Ed. 944 (1928) (Brandeis, J., dissenting).

The statute at issue denies individuals the right to decide for themselves whether to engage in particular forms of private, consensual sexual activity. The Court concludes that

---

8. Respondent does not defend the judgment below based on the Ninth Amendment, the Equal Protection Clause or the Eighth Amendment.

2. It was conceded at oral argument that, prior to the complaint against respondent Hardwick, there had been no reported decision involving prosecution for private homosexual sodomy under this statute for several decades. Moreover, the State has declined to present the criminal charge against Hardwick to a grand jury, and this is a suit for declaratory judgment

brought by respondents challenging the validity of the statute. The history of nonenforcement suggests the moribund character today of laws criminalizing this type of private, consensual conduct. Some 26 states have repealed similar statutes. But the constitutional validity of the Georgia statute was put in issue by respondents, and for the reasons stated by the Court, I cannot say that conduct condemned for hundreds of years has now become a fundamental right.

§ 16–6–2 is valid essentially because "the laws of * * * many States * * * still make such conduct illegal and have done so for a very long time." But the fact that the moral judgments expressed by statutes like § 16–6–2 may be "natural and familiar * * * ought not to conclude our judgment upon the question whether statutes embodying them conflict with the Constitution of the United States." *Roe v. Wade.* Like Justice Holmes, I believe that "[i]t is revolting to have no better reason for a rule of law than that so it was laid down in the time of Henry IV. It is still more revolting if the grounds upon which it was laid down have vanished long since, and the rule simply persists from blind imitation of the past." I believe we must analyze respondent's claim in the light of the values that underlie the constitutional right to privacy. If that right means anything, it means that, before Georgia can prosecute its citizens for making choices about the most intimate aspects of their lives, it must do more than assert that the choice they have made is an " 'abominable crime not fit to be named among Christians.' "

First, the Court's almost obsessive focus on homosexual activity is particularly hard to justify in light of the broad language Georgia has used. Unlike the Court, the Georgia Legislature has not proceeded on the assumption that homosexuals are so different from other citizens that their lives may be controlled in a way that would not be tolerated if it limited the choices of those other citizens. Rather, Georgia has provided that "[a] person commits the offense of sodomy when he performs or submits to any sexual act involving the sex organs of one person and the mouth or anus of another." Ga.Code Ann. § 16–6–2(a). The sex or status of the persons who engage in the act is irrelevant as a matter of state law. In fact, to the extent I can discern a legislative purpose for Georgia's 1968 enactment of § 16–6–2, that purpose seems to have been to broaden the coverage of the law to reach heterosexual as well as homosexual activity. I therefore see no basis for the Court's decision to treat this case as an "as applied" challenge to § 16–6–2, or for Georgia's attempt, both in its brief and at oral argument, to defend § 16–6–2 solely on the grounds that it prohibits homosexual activity. Michael Hardwick's standing may rest in significant part on Georgia's apparent willingness to enforce against homosexuals a law it seems not to have any desire to enforce against heterosexuals. But his claim that § 16–6–2 involves an unconstitutional intrusion into his privacy and his right of intimate association does not depend in any way on his sexual orientation.

Second, I disagree with the Court's refusal to consider whether § 16–6–2 runs afoul of the Eighth or Ninth Amendments or the Equal Protection Clause of the Fourteenth Amendment. Respondent's complaint expressly invoked the Ninth Amendment, and he relied heavily before this Court on *Griswold v. Connecticut,* which identifies that Amendment as one of the specific constitutional provisions giving "life and substance" to our understanding of privacy. More importantly, the procedural posture of the case requires that we affirm the Court of Appeals' judgment if there is *any* ground on which respondent may be entitled to relief. This case is before us on petitioner's motion to dismiss for failure to state a claim. It is a well settled principle of law that "a complaint should not be dismissed merely because a plaintiff's allegations do not support the particular legal theory he advances, for the court is under a duty to examine the complaint to determine if the allegations provide for relief on any possible theory." Thus, even if respondent did not advance claims based on the Eighth or Ninth Amendments, or on the Equal Protection Clause, his complaint should not be dismissed if any of those provisions could entitle him to relief. I need not reach either the Eighth Amendment or the Equal Protection Clause issues because I believe that Hardwick has stated a cognizable claim that § 16–6–2 interferes with constitutionally protected interests in privacy and freedom of intimate association. But neither the Eighth Amendment nor the Equal Protection Clause is so clearly irrelevant that a claim resting on either provision should be peremptorily dismissed.[3] The Court's cramped reading of the issue before it makes for a short opinion, but it does little to make for a persuasive one.

"Our cases long have recognized that the Constitution embodies a promise that a certain private sphere of individual liberty will be kept largely beyond the reach of government." In construing the right to privacy, the Court has proceeded along two somewhat distinct, albeit complementary, lines. First, it has recognized a privacy interest with reference to certain *decisions* that are properly for the individual to make. Second, it has recognized a privacy interest with reference to certain *places* without regard for the particular activities in which the individuals who occupy them are engaged. The case before us implicates both the decisional and the spatial aspects of the right to privacy.

The Court concludes today that none of our prior cases dealing with various decisions that individuals are entitled to make free of governmental interference "bears any resemblance to the claimed constitutional right of homosexuals to engage in acts of sodomy that is asserted in this case." While it is true that these cases may be characterized by their connection to protection of the family, the Court's conclusion that they extend no further than this boundary ignores the warning in *Moore v. East Cleveland,* 431 U.S. 494, 501, 97 S.Ct. 1932, 1936, 52 L.Ed.2d 531 (1977) (plurality opinion), against "clos[ing] our eyes to the basic reasons why certain rights associated with the family have been accorded shelter under the Fourteenth Amendment's Due Process Clause." We protect those rights not because they contribute, in some direct and material way, to the general public welfare, but because they form so central a part of an individual's life. * * *

Only the most willful blindness could obscure the fact that sexual intimacy is "a sensitive, key relationship of human existence, central to family life, community welfare, and the development of human personality." The fact that individuals define themselves in a significant way through their intimate sexual relationships with others suggests, in a

3. In *Robinson v. California,* the Court held that the Eighth Amendment barred convicting a defendant due to his "status" as a narcotics addict, since that condition was "apparently an illness which may be contracted innocently or involuntarily." In *Powell v. Texas,* where the Court refused to extend *Robinson* to punishment of public drunkenness by a chronic alcoholic, one of the factors relied on by JUSTICE MARSHALL, in writing the plurality opinion, was that Texas had not "attempted to regulate appellant's behavior in the privacy of his own home." JUSTICE WHITE wrote separately:

"Analysis of this difficult case is not advanced by preoccupation with the label 'condition.' In *Robinson* the Court dealt with 'a statute which makes the "status" of narcotic addiction a criminal offense. * * * ' By precluding criminal conviction for such a 'status' the Court was dealing with a condition brought about by acts remote in time from the application of the criminal sanctions contemplated, a condition which was relatively permanent in duration, and a condition of great magnitude and significance in terms of human behavior and values * * *. If it were necessary to distinguish between 'acts' and 'conditions' for purposes of the Eighth Amendment, I would adhere to the concept of 'condition' implicit in the opinion in *Robinson* * * *. The proper subject of inquiry is whether volitional acts brought about the 'condition' and whether those acts are sufficiently proximate to the 'condition' for it to be permissible to impose penal sanctions on the 'condition.' "

Despite historical views of homosexuality, it is no longer viewed by mental health professionals as a "disease" or disorder. But, obviously, neither is it simply a matter of deliberate personal election. Homosexual orientation may well form part of the very fiber of an individual's personality. Consequently, under JUSTICE WHITE's analysis in *Powell,* the Eighth Amendment may pose a constitutional barrier to sending an individual to prison for acting on that attraction regardless of the circumstances. An individual's ability to make constitutionally protected "decisions concerning sexual relations," is rendered empty indeed if he or she is given no real choice but a life without any physical intimacy.

With respect to the Equal Protection Clause's applicability to § 16–6–2, I note that Georgia's exclusive stress before this Court on its interest in prosecuting homosexual activity despite the gender-neutral terms of the statute may raise serious questions of discriminatory enforcement, questions that cannot be disposed of before this Court on a motion to dismiss. The legislature having decided that the sex of the participants is irrelevant to the legality of the acts, I do not see why the State can defend § 16–6–2 on the ground that individuals singled out for prosecution are of the same sex as their partners. Thus, under the circumstances of this case, a claim under the Equal Protection Clause may well be available without having to reach the more controversial question whether homosexuals are a suspect class.

Nation as diverse as ours, that there may be many "right" ways of conducting those relationships, and that much of the richness of a relationship will come from the freedom an individual has to *choose* the form and nature of these intensely personal bonds. * * *

The behavior for which Hardwick faces prosecution occurred in his own home, a place to which the Fourth Amendment attaches special significance. The Court's treatment of this aspect of the case is symptomatic of its overall refusal to consider the broad principles that have informed our treatment of privacy in specific cases. * * *

The Court's interpretation of the pivotal case of *Stanley v. Georgia* is entirely unconvincing. *Stanley* held that Georgia's undoubted power to punish the public distribution of constitutionally unprotected, obscene material did not permit the State to punish the private possession of such material. According to the majority here, *Stanley* relied entirely on the First Amendment, and thus, it is claimed, sheds no light on cases not involving printed materials. But that is not what *Stanley* said. Rather, the *Stanley* Court anchored its holding in the Fourth Amendment's special protection for the individual in his home. * * *

The central place that *Stanley* gives Justice Brandeis' dissent in *Olmstead,* a case raising *no* First Amendment claim, shows that *Stanley* rested as much on the Court's understanding of the Fourth Amendment as it did on the First. Indeed, in *Paris Adult Theatre I v. Slaton,* 413 U.S. 49, 93 S.Ct. 2628, 37 L.Ed.2d 446 (1973), the Court suggested that reliance on the Fourth Amendment not only supported the Court's outcome in *Stanley* but actually was *necessary* to it: "If obscene material unprotected by the First Amendment in itself carried with it a 'penumbra' of constitutionally protected privacy, this Court would not have found it necessary to decide *Stanley* on the narrow basis of the 'privacy of the home,' which was hardly more than a reaffirmation that 'a man's home is his castle.' " "The right of the people to be secure in their * * * houses," expressly guaranteed by the Fourth Amendment, is perhaps the most "textual" of the various constitutional provisions that inform our understanding of the right to privacy, and thus I cannot agree with the Court's statement that "[t]he right pressed upon us here has no * * * support in the text of the Constitution." Indeed, the right of an individual to conduct intimate relationships in the intimacy of his or her own home seems to me to be the heart of the Constitution's protection of privacy.

The Court's failure to comprehend the magnitude of the liberty interests at stake in this case leads it to slight the question whether petitioner, on behalf of the State, has justified Georgia's infringement on these interests. I believe that neither of the two general justifications for § 16–6–2 that petitioner has advanced warrants dismissing respondent's challenge for failure to state a claim.

First, petitioner asserts that the acts made criminal by the statute may have serious adverse consequences for "the general public health and welfare," such as spreading communicable diseases or fostering other criminal activity. Inasmuch as this case was dismissed by the District Court on the pleadings, it is not surprising that the record before us is barren of any evidence to support petitioner's claim. In light of the state of the record, I see no justification for the Court's attempt to equate the private, consensual sexual activity at issue here with the "possession in the home of drugs, firearms, or stolen goods," to which *Stanley* refused to extend its protection. None of the behavior so mentioned in *Stanley* can properly be viewed as "[v]ictimless:" drugs and weapons are inherently dangerous, and for property to be "stolen," someone must have been wrongfully deprived of it. Nothing in the record before the Court provides any justification for finding the activity forbidden by § 16–6–2 to be physically dangerous, either to the persons engaged in it or to others.[4]

The core of petitioner's defense of § 16–6–2, however, is that respondent and others who engage in the conduct prohibited by § 16–6–2 interfere with Georgia's exercise of the " 'right of the Nation and of the States to maintain a decent society,' "Essentially, petitioner argues, and the Court agrees, that the fact that the acts described in § 16–6–2 "for hundreds of years, if not thousands, have been uniformly condemned as immoral" is a sufficient reason to permit a State to ban them today.

I cannot agree that either the length of time a majority has held its convictions or the passions with which it defends them can withdraw legislation from this Court's scrutiny. As Justice Jackson wrote so eloquently for the Court in *West Virginia Board of Education v. Barnette,* 319 U.S. 624, 63 S.Ct. 1178, 87 L.Ed. 1628 (1943), "we apply the limitations of the Constitution with no fear that freedom to be intellectually and spiritually diverse or even contrary will disintegrate the social organization. . . .[F]reedom to differ is not limited to things that do not matter much. That would be a mere shadow of freedom. The test of its substance is the right to differ as to things that touch the heart of the existing order." It is precisely because the issue raised by this case touches the heart of what makes individuals what they are that we should be especially sensitive to the rights of those whose choices upset the majority.

The assertion that "traditional Judeo–Christian values proscribe" the conduct involved cannot provide an adequate justification for § 16–6–2. That certain, but by no means all, religious groups condemn the behavior at issue gives the State no license to impose their judgments on the entire citizenry. The legitimacy of secular legislation depends instead on whether the State can advance some justification for its law beyond its conformity to religious doctrine. Thus, far from buttressing his case, petitioner's invocation of Leviticus, Romans, St. Thomas Aquinas, and sodomy's heretical status during the Middle Ages undermines his suggestion that § 16–6–2 represents a legitimate use of secular coercive power. A State can no more punish private behavior because of religious intolerance than it can punish such behavior because of racial animus. * * *

Nor can § 16–6–2 be justified as a "morally neutral" exercise of Georgia's power to "protect the public environment." Certainly, some private behavior can affect the fabric of society as a whole. Reasonable people may differ about whether particular sexual acts are moral or immoral, but "we have ample evidence for believing that people will not abandon morality, will not think any better of murder, cruelty and dishonesty, merely because some private sexual practice which they abominate is not punished by the law." Petitioner and the Court fail to see the difference between laws that protect public sensibilities and those that enforce private morality. Statutes banning public sexual activity are entirely consistent with protecting the individual's liberty interest in decisions concerning sexual rela-

---

4. Although I do not think it necessary to decide today issues that are not even remotely before us, it does seem to me that a court could find simple, analytically sound distinctions between certain private, consensual sexual conduct, on the one hand, and adultery and incest (the only two vaguely specific "sexual crimes" to which the majority points), on the other. For example, marriage, in addition to its spiritual aspects, is a civil contract that entitles the contracting parties to a variety of governmentally provided benefits. A State might define the contractual commitment necessary to become eligible for these benefits to include a commitment of fidelity and then punish individuals for breaching that contract. Moreover, a State might conclude that adultery is likely to injure third persons, in particular, spouses and children of persons who engage in extramarital affairs. With respect to incest, a court might well agree with respondent that the nature of familial relationships renders true consent to incestuous activity sufficiently problematical that a blanket prohibition of such activity is warranted. Notably, the Court makes no effort to explain why it has chosen to group private, consensual homosexual activity with adultery and incest rather than with private, consensual heterosexual activity by unmarried persons or, indeed, with oral or anal sex within marriage.

tions: the same recognition that those decisions are intensely private which justifies protecting them from governmental interference can justify protecting individuals from unwilling exposure to the sexual activities of others. But the mere fact that intimate behavior may be punished when it takes place in public cannot dictate how States can regulate intimate behavior that occurs in intimate places.

This case involves no real interference with the rights of others, for the mere knowledge that other individuals do not adhere to one's value system cannot be a legally cognizable interest, let alone an interest that can justify invading the houses, hearts, and minds of citizens who choose to live their lives differently. * * *

JUSTICE STEVENS, with whom JUSTICE BRENNAN and JUSTICE MARSHALL join, dissenting.

Like the statute that is challenged in this case, the rationale of the Court's opinion applies equally to the prohibited conduct regardless of whether the parties who engage in it are married or unmarried, or are of the same or different sexes. * * *

Because the Georgia statute expresses the traditional view that sodomy is an immoral kind of conduct regardless of the identity of the persons who engage in it, I believe that a proper analysis of its constitutionality requires consideration of two questions: First, may a State totally prohibit the described conduct by means of a neutral law applying without exception to all persons subject to its jurisdiction? If not, may the State save the statute by announcing that it will only enforce the law against homosexuals? The two questions merit separate discussion. * * *

Society has every right to encourage its individual members to follow particular traditions in expressing affection for one another and in gratifying their personal desires. It, of course, may prohibit an individual from imposing his will on another to satisfy his own selfish interests. It also may prevent an individual from interfering with, or violating, a legally sanctioned and protected relationship, such as marriage. And it may explain the relative advantages and disadvantages of different forms of intimate expression. But when individual married couples are isolated from observation by others, the way in which they voluntarily choose to conduct their intimate relations is a matter for them—not the State—to decide.[10] The essential "liberty" that animated the development of the law in cases like *Griswold, Eisenstadt,* and *Carey* surely embraces the right to engage in nonreproductive, sexual conduct that others may consider offensive or immoral.

Paradoxical as it may seem, our prior cases thus establish that a State may not prohibit sodomy within "the sacred precincts of marital bedrooms," *Griswold,* or, indeed, between unmarried heterosexual adults. *Eisenstadt.* In all events, it is perfectly clear that the State of Georgia may not totally prohibit the conduct proscribed by § 16–6–2 of the Georgia Criminal Code.

If the Georgia statute cannot be enforced as it is written—if the conduct it seeks to prohibit is a protected form of liberty for the vast majority of Georgia's citizens—the State must assume the burden of justifying a selective application of its law. Either the persons to whom Georgia seeks to apply its statute do not have the same interest in "liberty" that others have, or there must be a reason why the State may be permitted to apply a generally applicable law to certain persons that it does not apply to others.

---

10. Indeed, the Georgia Attorney General concedes that Georgia's statute would be unconstitutional if applied to a married couple. See Tr. of Oral Arg. 8 (stating that application of the statute to a married couple "would be unconstitutional" because of the "right of marital privacy as identified by the Court in Griswold"). Significantly, Georgia passed the current statute three years after the Court's decision in *Griswold.*

The first possibility is plainly unacceptable. Although the meaning of the principle that "all men are created equal" is not always clear, it surely must mean that every free citizen has the same interest in "liberty" that the members of the majority share. From the standpoint of the individual, the homosexual and the heterosexual have the same interest in deciding how he will live his own life, and, more narrowly, how he will conduct himself in his personal and voluntary associations with his companions. State intrusion into the private conduct of either is equally burdensome.

The second possibility is similarly unacceptable. A policy of selective application must be supported by a neutral and legitimate interest—something more substantial than a habitual dislike for, or ignorance about, the disfavored group. Neither the State nor the Court has identified any such interest in this case. The Court has posited as a justification for the Georgia statute "the presumed belief of a majority of the electorate in Georgia that homosexual sodomy is immoral and unacceptable." * * *

Nor, indeed, does the Georgia prosecutor even believe that all homosexuals who violate this statute should be punished. This conclusion is evident from the fact that the respondent in this very case has formally acknowledged in his complaint and in court that he has engaged, and intends to continue to engage, in the prohibited conduct, yet the State has elected not to process criminal charges against him. As JUSTICE POWELL points out, moreover, Georgia's prohibition on private, consensual sodomy has not been enforced for decades. The record of nonenforcement, in this case and in the last several decades, belies the Attorney General's representations about the importance of the State's selective application of its generally applicable law. * * *

The Court orders the dismissal of respondent's complaint even though the State's statute prohibits all sodomy; even though that prohibition is concededly unconstitutional with respect to heterosexuals; and even though the State's *post hoc* explanations for selective application are belied by the State's own actions. At the very least, I think it clear at this early stage of the litigation that respondent has alleged a constitutional claim sufficient to withstand a motion to dismiss.[13]

I respectfully dissent.

Notes and Questions

1. Consider Donald A Dripps, *Bowers v. Hardwick and the Law of Standing: Noncases Make Bad Law*, 44 Emory L.J. 1417 (1995):

"*Bowers v. Hardwick* has provoked more scholarly debate than any Supreme Court decision of the last two decades. This is entirely appropriate, for *Hardwick* itself was not a case but a debate. Hardwick was not contesting a pending charge of sodomy, because the state had dropped the prosecution for that offense. Nor was Hardwick complaining of his arrest, for he sought declaratory relief, not damages. In any case, Hardwick's arrest would have been perfectly legal even if the Georgia statute was invalid; the arresting officer had a facially valid warrant for the arrest and also had discovered Hardwick in possession of marijuana. Nor could Hardwick complain of the threat of future prosecution, because all knew that the charge against him was a unique aberration from a deliberate pattern of

---

13. Indeed, at this stage, it appears that the statute indiscriminately authorizes a policy of selective prosecution that is neither limited to the class of homosexual persons nor embraces all persons in that class, but rather applies to those who may be arbitrarily selected by the prosecutor for reasons that are not revealed either in the record of this case or in the text of the statute. If that is true, although the text of the statute is clear enough, its true meaning may be "so intolerably vague that evenhanded enforcement of the law is a virtual impossibility." *Marks v. United States,* 430 U.S. 188, 198, 97 S.Ct. 990, 996, 51 L.Ed.2d 260 (1977) (STEVENS, J., concurring in part and dissenting in part).

nonenforcement. The vote of the Justices did not cost any party to the case anything. In doctrinal terms, Hardwick had no standing to challenge Georgia's sodomy law.

"*Bowers v. Hardwick*, then, is not a case, but an advisory opinion. If this thesis is correct, the judgment was rendered without a constitutional prerequisite of jurisdiction. Whether the jurisdictional defect authorizes a subsequent Supreme Court to treat the judgment as void is debatable, but all courts should recognize how the absence of standing influenced the decision. Not only did Justice Powell, the fifth Justice in the majority, write a concurring opinion to the effect that the result would have differed had the state actually prosecuted Hardwick for sodomy.[a] Other Justices—including Justice White, the author of *Hardwick*—turned a far more sympathetic ear to the claims of gay men facing actual injury in other cases."

2. *Right to privacy.* (a) Consider *The Supreme Court—Leading Cases,* 100 Harv. L.Rev. 100, 217–18 (1986): "In declining to view the right to privacy as protecting the right to make personal decisions in intimate relationships, the *Hardwick* Court also refused to declare a new fundamental right, because the claimed right lacked a historical or traditional basis. The Court's use of history and tradition, rather than the underlying values protected by the right of privacy, to analyze Hardwick's claim is nothing less than an abdication of judicial responsibility. The Court apparently assumed that because intrusive and oppressive legislation is long-standing, it is no longer oppressive and is in fact justified. However, the long history of restrictions on homosexuals, like the long history of state-sanctioned racial discrimination before it, illustrates the need for judicial intervention, not the legitimacy of the oppression. To cite a shameful history of prejudice, and to adopt it as support for the constitutionality of Georgia's law, is to relegate constitutional analysis to preserving the status quo without regard for those who cannot vindicate their rights through the political process. As numerous observers have noted, the case for active judicial review is especially compelling when the Court is evaluating a statute penalizing a minority group with a long history of political powerlessness and social stigmatization."

(b) How would the Court have come out as to John and Mary Doe (fn. 2 in *Hardwick*) had they not lacked standing? How would the Court come out on the facts of *Lovisi v. Slayton,* 539 F.2d 349 (4th Cir.1976), where Margaret Lovisi performed fellatio upon her husband and Earl Dunn (who had answered the Lovisis' ad in "Swinger's Life") in the Lovisis' bedroom?

3. In that regard, reconsider the scope of the Georgia statute, quoted in footnote 1, and note the criticism in William N. Eskridge, Jr., *Hardwick and Historiography*, 1999 U.Ill.L.Rev. 631, 632–35: "The Court's decision in *Hardwick* has become infamous, partly because Justice White went out of his way to focus on and disrespect 'homosexual sodomy' and 'homosexuality.' * * *.

"Institutionally, the Court sought to atone for *Hardwick* in *Romer v. Evans,*[147] which invalidated a Colorado initiative preventing state and local government units from carrying out laws or policies whereby 'homosexual ... orientation' could be the basis for any positive legal claim. The Court emphasized two features of the initiative, either assertedly fatal to its constitutionality even under the easy-to-pass rational basis standard of review.

---

a. Note, 19 Hastings Const'l L.Q. 495, 506 n.94 (1992), observes: "Justice Powell's position on this case is an interesting one, worthy of further analysis. It was reported that Justice Powell initially voted to invalidate the statute. Al Kamen, *Powell Changed Vote in Sodomy Case*, Wash. Post, July 13, 1986, at A1. He later changed his vote, resulting in the majority upholding the Georgia statute. Justice Powell, now retired from the Court, has since commented that he 'made a mistake' in *Bowers v. Hardwick* because he feels the decision is inconsistent with the Court's other privacy decisions. Anand Agneshwar, *Powell Concedes Error in Key Privacy Ruling*, N.Y.L.J., Oct. 26, 1990, at 1."

147. 517 U.S. 620 (1996).

On the one hand, the initiative, 'unprecedented in our jurisprudence,' sought to accomplish something the state could not do, namely, 'singl[e] out a certain class of citizens for disfavored legal status or general hardships.' On the other hand, 'laws of the kind now before us raise the inevitable inference that the disadvantage imposed is born of animosity toward the class of persons affected.' *Evans* not only situates the Supreme Court in a more neutral position as regards homosexuality, but calls *Hardwick* itself into question. * * *

"Because *Evans* involved an unusually targeted denial of rights to gay people as a class, 'unprecedented in our jurisprudence,' and focused on homosexual status rather than conduct (sodomy), it is inaccurate to say that the decision overrules *Hardwick,* even implicitly; the Georgia sodomy law did not on its face focus on same-sex sodomy. But the two decisions do not rest easily together in the same logic set. Stigmatizing an entire class of peaceful citizens as criminals because of their private, consensual behavior has a more pronounced effect on gay people than Colorado's antigay initiative probably would have had, and *Evans*'s rhetoric of inclusion suggests a broader reading. Justice Antonin Scalia recognized this in his *Evans* dissent. 'If it is constitutionally permissible for a State to make homosexual conduct criminal [*Hardwick*], surely it is constitutionally permissible for a State to enact other laws merely disfavoring homosexual conduct,' or 'merely prohibiting all levels of state government from bestowing special protections upon homosexual conduct [*Evans*].' The six-Justice *Evans* majority failed to deny, much less refute, this assertion. Now that *Evans* has been decided, the assertion can be reversed: If it is constitutionally impermissible for the state to enact laws disfavoring people who engage in 'homosexual conduct,' then is it not impermissible to penalize the conduct itself?"

4. *State right to privacy.* (a) Note, 14 N.Y.U.Rev.L. & Soc.Chg. 973, 994 (1986): "Many state constitutions provide either explicit or court-inferred privacy guarantees, and state courts present a forum in which to pursue sodomy law reform. * * * State constitutional privacy guarantees offer an exciting and largely untapped opportunity to meet the important goal of sodomy law reform."

(b) This has now occurred in some states, and even the statute at issue in *Hardwick* has now been found unconstitutional in part in *Powell v. State*, 270 Ga. 327, 510 S.E.2d 18 (1998):

"Today, we are faced with whether the constitutional right of privacy screens from governmental interference a non-commercial sexual act that occurs without force in a private home between persons legally capable of consenting to the act. While [our prior cases] do not set out the full scope of the right of privacy in connection with sexual behavior, it is clear that unforced sexual behavior conducted in private between adults is covered by the principles espoused [therein] since such behavior between adults in private is recognized as a private matter by '[a]ny person whose intellect is in a normal condition....' Adults who 'withdraw from the public gaze' to engage in private unforced sexual behavior are exercising a right 'embraced within the right of personal liberty.' We cannot think of any other activity that reasonable persons would rank as more private and more deserving of protection from governmental interference than unforced, private, adult sexual activity. * * *

" * * * As judicial consideration of the right to privacy has developed, this Court has concluded that the right of privacy is a fundamental right and that a government-imposed limitation on the right to privacy will pass constitutional muster if the limitation is shown to serve a compelling state interest and to be narrowly tailored to effectuate only that compelling interest. * * * Implicit in our decisions curtailing the assertion of a right to privacy in sexual assault cases involving sexual activity taking place in public, performed with those legally incapable of giving consent, performed in exchange for money, or performed with force and against the will of a participant, is the determination that the State has a role in shielding the public from inadvertent exposure to the intimacies of others, in protecting minors and others legally incapable of consent from sexual abuse, and in preventing people from being forced to submit to sex acts against their will. * * *

"The State also maintains that the furtherance of 'social morality,' giving 'due regard to the collective will of the citizens of Georgia,' is a constitutional basis for legislative control of the non-commercial, unforced, private sexual activity of those legally capable of consenting to such activity. It is well within the power of the legislative branch to establish public policy through legislative enactment. It is also without dispute that oftentimes the public policy so established and the laws so enacted reflect the will of the majority of Georgians as well as the majority's notion of morality. However, * * * [w]hile many believe that acts of sodomy, even those involving consenting adults, are morally reprehensible, this repugnance alone does not create a compelling justification for state regulation of the activity."

5. *Scope of state right.* (a) Is there a middle ground between *Hardwick* and *Powell*? Consider Arthur A. Murphy & John P. Ellington, *Homosexuality and the Law: Tolerance and Containment*, 97 Dick.L.Rev. 693, 697–98 (1993), proposing a statute "meant to strike a fair and humane balance between the state's concerns and the individual's autonomy and privacy interests. It gives due weight to competing social, moral, psychological and political considerations. The statute would say: A person who has consensual oral or anal intercourse with someone of the same sex is guilty of a crime (a misdemeanor, not a felony) with one major exception. That person is not guilty if he or she and the other party are true homosexuals or if he or she is a true homosexual and reasonably but mistakenly believes that the partner is of similar persuasion. A 'true homosexual' is defined as an individual whose sexual orientation is predominantly toward individuals of the same sex.

"A society which enacts the proposed statute announces that heterosexuality is one of its core values—a preferred moral and social characteristic of both men and women and of the family. The homosexual lifestyle is not a desirable alternative for anyone who is substantially free to avoid it. Homosexual acts should be kept within bounds—confined to persons for whom, depending upon one's viewpoint, such conduct is natural and right, an unfortunate compulsion or merely a tolerable evil. Homosexuals are told not to seduce straight or potentially straight individuals. The sexually uncertain, the curious and the libertine are warned not to experiment with homosexual behavior. The bisexual is directed to make a choice."

(b) Assuming a ruling along the lines of *Powell*, must the activity occur within a private residence to be protected, or can there be zones of privacy within a public place? What would be the result, for example, on the facts of *United States v. Lemons*, 697 F.2d 832 (8th Cir.1983), where a park ranger entered the men's section of the public rest room at Hot Springs National Park, saw the legs of two persons beneath the partition of one stall, and then opened the door and found the two individuals engaged in fellatio. Was that a private place because it is unreasonably intrusive to open the door of a stall known to be occupied? Even if the answer to that is no, what then of the argument of the defendant in *Lemons* "that his right to privacy claim does not rest on the location of his acts, but on his right to freely decide matters of affectional choice," so that "the location of his acts is irrelevant"?

6. *Substantive due process.* (a) Comment, 45 Fordham L.Rev. 553, 580–81 (1976), though noting that the Supreme Court "has found no difficulty in upholding federal and state laws legislating morality," made this pre-AIDS observation:

"Since it can be demonstrated that deviate sexual practices carried out in private by willing adults result in no mental or physical danger to the health or safety of the participants or of others, the only possible interest capable of being safeguarded by the prohibition of such conduct is the moral interest. Adult consensual sodomy, if it does any harm at all, harms the soul of the actor, as Plato would say. But while the welfare of its citizens' souls may have been the most important concern of Plato's ideal state, it is questionable whether such a concern is proper to a secular, pluralistic society.[147] Critics of sodomy laws argue that majority opinion as to what is moral and rational should not carry the sanction of the criminal law. Indeed, they point out that such moral condemnation cannot satisfy the rational basis test required by substantive due process."

(b) When there is no recognized privacy right in the picture, is it sufficient to establish an adequate state interest to say that the law is intended to "discourage immoral behavior"? What then of the added point that the statute concerns a "public health issue"? Consider Janet M. LaRue & Rory K. Nugent, *Williams v. State: The Constitutionality and Necessity of Sodomy Laws*, 29 U.Balt.L.F. 6, 13 (1999), asserting both grounds and stating, as to the latter: "The most recent statistics available from the Centers for Disease Control and Prevention highlight the need to control 'high-risk' sexual behavior. Homosexual men represent fifty-seven percent of the cumulative total number of AIDS cases through 1998 in the United States, a far larger percentage than any other category. Furthermore, sodomy, whether heterosexual, homosexual, or bisexual, inevitably leads to rectal and prostate damage which may lead to the onset of AIDS, hepatitis B, and other sexually transmitted diseases. Former Surgeon General C. Everett Koop has stated that 'anal intercourse, even with a condom, is simply too dangerous a practice.' "

7. *Equal protection of the laws.* (a) Note, 14 N.Y.U.Rev.L. & Soc.Chg. 995, 1014 (1986): "Ironically, had Hardwick decided to press an equal protection claim, a showing of a history of discrimination would have been required for a finding that lesbian and gay litigants deserve special protection. But even an equal protection claim would have left Hardwick pleading for rights this Court would not grant. An equal protection argument would have required Hardwick to jump through legal hoops, meeting the required 'indicia of suspectness': a history of discrimination against lesbians and gay men, their discreteness and insularity today, and a biological basis of same-sex attraction. Again Hardwick would have been forced to analogize the lesbian and gay experience to that of the few other groups to whom the Court has begrudgingly granted special protection status."

---

147. After all, whose morals are to be enforced? In 1957 England's Wolfenden Committee recommended that private homosexual acts between consenting adults be decriminalized, reasoning that, unless crime is to be made synonymous with sin, "there remains a realm of private morality and immorality which is, in brief and crude terms, not the law's business." *Report of the Committee on Homosexual Offenses and Prostitution* ¶ 62 (Stein & Day eds. 1963) (Wolfenden Report).

On the other hand, many of our legal writers and judges have expressed the view that morality is the source and inspiration of lawmaking. "Dean Pound has said that 'the attempt to make law and morals identical by covering the whole field of morals with legal precepts, and by conforming existing precepts to the requirements of a reasoned system of morals, made the modern law.' In a similar generalization, Justice Cardo-

zo held that 'The scope of legal duty has expanded in obedience to the urge of morals.' " S. Stumpf, *Morality and the Law* 9 (1966) (footnotes omitted); see U.C.L.A. Comment, supra note 144, at 582.

Lord Devlin, one of the most vigorous advocates of society's right to use the law to prevent moral harm, has relied on two principal arguments. The first is that a set of shared moral values is essential to society and, therefore, private conduct that threatens a moral principle, though it may not be a menace to particular individuals, is a threat to the existence of society. The second argument holds that a sincere moral conviction that certain activity is wrong justifies the individual or community in seeking to outlaw it. Sartorius, *The Enforcement of Morality*, 81 Yale L.J. 891, 892–93 (1972). * * *

(b) Comment, 45 Fordham L.Rev. 553, 585–87 (1976): "Justice Holmes once characterized the equal protection challenge as 'the usual last resort of Constitutional arguments.' It is an attack, not upon what a law directs, but upon the classification of citizens to whom it is or is not to be applied. Thus, as concerns a statute making consensual sodomy illicit, the issue is whether the distinction between married people and single people or between heterosexuals and homosexuals is the type of 'invidious discrimination' that offends the Constitution. * * *

"If single people or homosexuals can be deemed to form a suspect class, they will qualify for the added protection of the compelling state interest test. Suspect classes are those composed of 'discrete and insular minorities,' groups therefore meriting judicial protection. These groups must be readily definable. Thus the category 'poor people' has been held not to qualify inasmuch as it was 'a large, diverse, and amorphous class.' To date, only race, alienage, and national origin have been specifically denominated as suspect classes. It may be noted that these are congenital attributes, over which the individual has no control and to which opprobrium has frequently attached."

(c) *People v. Onofre*, 51 N.Y.2d 476, 434 N.Y.S.2d 947, 415 N.E.2d 936 (1980), involved an appeal of several sodomy convictions under a statute proscribing "sexual conduct between persons not married to each other consisting of contact between the penis and the anus, the mouth and penis, or the mouth and the vulva." After finding the statute violated the defendants' right to privacy, the court continued:

"As to the denial of defendants' right to equal protection. Section 130.38 of the Penal Law on its face discriminates between married and unmarried persons, making criminal when done by the latter what is innocent when done by the former. With that distinction drawn, we look to see whether there is, as a minimum, 'some ground of difference that rationally explains the different treatment accorded married and unmarried persons' under the statute (*Eisenstadt v. Baird*, 405 U.S. 438, 447, 92 S.Ct. 1029, 1035, 31 L.Ed.2d 349, supra).[6] In our view, none has been demonstrated or identified by the People in any of the cases before us. In fact, the only justifications suggested are a societal interest in protecting and nurturing the institution of marriage and what are termed 'rights accorded married persons'. As has been indicated, however, no showing has been made as to how, or even that, the statute banning consensual sodomy between persons not married to each other preserves or fosters marriage. Nor is there any suggestion how consensual sodomy relates to rights accorded married persons; certainly it is not evident how it adversely affects any such rights. Thus, even if it be assumed that the objectives tendered by the prosecution are legitimate matters of public concern, no relationship much less rational relationship between those objectives and the proscription of section 130.38 of the Penal Law is manifested. The statute therefore must fall as violative of the right to equal protection enjoyed by persons not married to each other."

The dissent in *Onofre* responded: "Inasmuch as I conclude that there is no 'fundamental right' to sexual gratification, I must also consider whether section 130.38 of the Penal Law represents an irrational classification on the basis of marital status in violation of the equal protection clause of the Fourteenth Amendment. Since marital status has never been recognized as a 'suspect classification', the legislative distinction between marrieds and

---

6. If we are correct in the view earlier expressed in this opinion that section 130.38 of the Penal Law infringes on defendants' right of privacy which is a fundamental right, then, as observed, in *Eisenstadt*, the statutory classification "would have to be not merely rationally related to a valid public purpose but necessary to the achievement of a compelling state interest" As was so in *Eisenstadt*, however, we do not need to measure the statute by that test inasmuch as it fails to satisfy even the more lenient rational basis standard.

unmarrieds may stand if it bears some rational relation to a legitimate governmental interest.

"Unlike my colleagues in the majority, I have no trouble concluding that the legislative decision to permit married individuals to engage in conduct that is forbidden to the unmarried is rationally based. While the State may prefer that none if its citizens engage in the proscribed forms of sexual gratification, it may properly limit its statutory prohibition to those that are unmarried on the theory that the institution of marriage is so important to our society that even offensive intimacies between married individuals should be tolerated. The statute at issue in this case is thus distinguishable from the statute at issue in *Eisenstadt v. Baird*, where the Supreme Court concluded that a ban on the sale of contraceptives to unmarrieds only had no relation to any legitimate government interest."

(d) In *Sawatzky v. City of Oklahoma City*, 906 P.2d 785 (Okla.Crim.1995), the defendant was convicted under a city ordinance proscribing the soliciting of a private nonconsensual act of lewdness (sodomy) in a public place from a member of the same gender. Because the ordinance defined lewdness in terms of fellatio and various other acts "with any person not his or her spouse," the defendant raised an *Onofre*-style equal protection challenge. The court responded "that the married person exception is rationally related to a legitimate governmental interest and does not violate the right to equal protection." Can *Sawatzky* and *Onofre* be reconciled?

(e) Consider Note, 26 Wm. & Mary L.Rev. 645, 678–80 (1985): "The courts that have invalidated state sodomy statutes on equal protection grounds have failed to apply this analysis properly. The court in *Baker*[1] struck down the Texas sodomy statutes both because it could find no legitimate state interest behind the statute and because the heterosexual-homosexual distinction was impermissible. The court was incorrect, however, on both points. First, the 'public distaste' " for homosexual sodomy that the court found not to be a legitimate state interest is a legitimate interest if it represents the expression of the general public morality. Further, most cases have held that the regulation of morals is within the police power.

"Second, the heterosexual-homosexual distinction should have passed rational basis scrutiny. Because sodomy is the only form of sexual expression available to homosexuals, they necessarily are more likely to perform sodomy than heterosexuals. So long as homosexuals are more likely to engage in prohibited conduct, a statute applied only to them is rationally related to the legitimate state goal of preventing, or at least reducing, sodomy. Admittedly the Texas statute and all sodomy statutes have the effect of discriminating against homosexuals by denying them their only sexual outlet while not so denying heterosexuals. In *Washington v. Davis*,[243] however, the Supreme Court held that disproportionate impact alone is insufficient to render a statute constitutionally defective. Some discriminatory intent must exist.

1. The reference is to *Baker v. Wade*, 553 F.Supp. 1121 (N.D.Tex.1982). However, the case was reversed on appeal, 769 F.2d 289 (5th Cir.1985), where it was held: "Because we have held that engaging in homosexual conduct is not a constitutionally protected liberty interest and because Baker has not cited any cases holding, and we refuse to hold, that homosexuals constitute a suspect or quasi-suspect classification, the standard of review is whether section 21.06 is rationally related to a legitimate state end. In view of the strong objection to homosexual conduct, which has prevailed in Western culture for the past seven centuries, we cannot say that section 21.06 is "totally unrelated to the pursuit of" implementing morality, a permissible state goal. Therefore, section 21.06 does not deprive Baker of equal protection of the laws."

243. 426 U.S. 229 (1976). The Supreme Court upheld a District of Columbia police department's requirement for all applicants to pass Federal Test 21 despite the fact that a disproportionate number of blacks failed the test. Effect, by itself, is not a constitutional violation. See also *Mobile v. Bolden*, 446 U.S. 55 (1980).

"The court in *Onofre* discovered a different equal protection defect, finding that the New York statute distinguished impermissibly between married and unmarried persons. The court apparently held the view that *Griswold* protects all sexual activity between married persons and that *Eisenstadt* extended that range of sexual freedom to all persons, married or unmarried. Consequently, the court believed that no distinction could be drawn between married and unmarried persons without a rational justification. * * *

"This married-unmarried distinction, like the 'pure' heterosexual-homosexual distinction, should not make sodomy statutes defective. Because homosexual couples by definition are unmarried, and homosexuals are more likely to engage in sodomy, a statute applied only to unmarried couples rationally furthers the legitimate state interest in preventing sodomy. * * *

"*Baker* [and] *Onofre* * * * demonstrate that the courts which invalidate sodomy statutes do so by distorting the equal protection analysis. In the absence of a suspect class or fundamental right, they are in reality applying a strict scrutiny analysis rather than the proper rational basis scrutiny. * * * These courts are ignoring totally the state's long-recognized ability to define and to protect morality. As a result, the decisions reached by these courts conflict with a proper equal protection analysis of the sodomy statutes."

(f) Compare Note, 87 Geo.L.J. 139, 192–93 (1998): "A standard of judicial deference that refuses to subject such laws to rational scrutiny, and refuses to invalidate those laws as failing such scrutiny, should not be praised, especially not by legal conservatives, as a prudent exercise of judicial restraint. Judicial deference to such state-approved irrationality and injustice only undermines the rule of law, decreases law's normative authority, encourages disrespect for the legal system, and destabilizes the civic order that conservatives hold dear. As Justice Kennedy remarked in *Romer* [p. 92 of this Book]:

> [E]ven in the ordinary equal protection case calling for the most deferential of standards, we insist on knowing the relation between the classification adopted and the object to be attained. The search for the link between classification and objective gives substance to the Equal Protection Clause; it provides guidance and discipline for the legislature, which is entitled to know what sorts of laws it can pass; and it marks the limits of our own authority.

The question, of course, remains as to how courts are to determine whether a given objective of the state is legitimate, and whether the classification under review is rationally related to realizing that objective.

"This discussion has responded that in order to determine whether a government interest is legitimate, the courts must look to empirical effects on the public welfare. Where the interest in question is unrelated to such effects, or the legislative classification designed as a means of achieving that interest does not realize such effects, the law is rationally unrelated to a legitimate government purpose.

"The underlying thesis of this discussion has been that laws that discriminate against people on the basis of sexual orientation cannot pass that test. Defenders of such laws, lacking any other argument, must resort to bare assertions that homosexuality is wrong. Depriving that bare moral argument of its constitutional legitimacy brings the controversy over homosexuality closer to concluding that laws that burden lesbian and gay people violate the guarantee of equal protection because they have no rational relationship to a legitimate government interest. Such laws are no more than an expression of private bias."

SECTION 6. OTHER CONSTITUTIONAL LIMITS ON PUNISHMENT OF CRIME

PERKINS v. STATE OF NORTH CAROLINA

United States District Court, W.D. North Carolina, 1964.

234 F.Supp. 333.

CRAVEN, CHIEF JUDGE.

On January 8, 1962, Max Doyle Perkins and Robert Eugene McCorkle were jointly indicted by the grand jury of Mecklenburg County, North Carolina. It was charged that they "did unlawfully, willfully, maliciously and feloniously commit the abominable and detestable crime against nature with each other." McCorkle pleaded nolo contendere, received a sentence of five to seven years, served a portion of it, and has been released. Perkins, after conviction by a jury upon his plea of not guilty, was sentenced to a term of not less than twenty nor more than thirty years. The disparate sentences were passed by the same judge.

* * * There has been sufficient exhaustion of state remedies to make it appropriate for a federal court to entertain Perkins' petition for writ of habeas corpus.

Perkins was convicted of a violation of N.C.G.S. § 14–177, which reads in its entirety as follows: "If any person shall commit the abominable and detestable crime against nature, with mankind or beast, he shall be imprisoned in the State's prison not less than five nor more than sixty years."

The statute is copied from the first English statute on the subject passed in the year 1533 during the reign of King Henry VIII. It was adopted in North Carolina in 1837 with only one difference. The words "vice of buggery" which appeared in the ancient English statute were omitted and instead there was substituted the delightful euphemism "crime against nature, not to be named among Christians." It then read in its entirety: "Any person who shall commit the abominable and detestable crime against nature, not to be named among Christians, with either mankind or beast, shall be adjudged guilty of a felony, and shall suffer death without the benefit of clergy."

By 1854 Christians had become more articulate and less clergical. The phrases "not to be named among Christians" and "without benefit of clergy" were deleted from the statute. Finally, in 1869, the death penalty was limited to murder and the like. The punishment for crime against nature was limited to sixty years maximum. Since 1869 the statute has remained unchanged—in itself a shocking example of the unfortunate gulf between criminal law, and medicine and psychiatry.

The evidence against Perkins tended to show that his criminal conduct consisted of fellatio. * * *

The prohibition of cruel and unusual punishment contained in the Eighth Amendment of the United States Constitution applies to the states through the due process clause of the Fourteenth Amendment.

In *Trop v. Dulles*, 356 U.S. 86, 78 S.Ct. 590, 2 L.Ed.2d 630 (1958), the Court said "the exact scope of the constitutional phrase 'cruel and unusual' has not been detailed by this Court. * * * The Amendment must draw its meaning from the evolving standards of decency that mark the progress of a maturing society." And in *Weems v. U.S.*, 217 U.S. 349, 30 S.Ct. 544, 54 L.Ed. 793 (1910), the Court said that the inhibition was directed "against all punishments which, by their excessive length or severity, are greatly dispro- portioned to the offenses charged."

Imprisoning Perkins for his homosexual conduct is not unlike putting a person in jail for being addicted to the use of narcotics, as was done in *Robinson v. California*, [p. 448 of this Book]. In that case the United States Supreme Court held that the statute inflicted a cruel and unusual punishment, but it is important to note that the statute had been interpreted to condemn the status of narcotic addiction as a criminal offense. Perkins was convicted of an overt act—a distinction more important to law than medicine and one which conveniently ignores causative factors of homosexuality—but nevertheless a legally valid distinction.

Does the mere duration of sentence—twenty to thirty years—make it "cruel and unusual" within the prohibition of the Constitution? The Attorney General of North Carolina, although requested to do so, has not called to the court's attention any sentence under this statute in excess of five years where the offenders were both adult males. It may be judicially noticed, certainly within the last decade, that sentences imposed on adult homosexual offenders in the North Carolina courts, absent special circumstances, seldom if ever exceeded the five year statutory minimum. The moderation of North Carolina judges in this respect is probably the reason why the Legislature has not long since felt required to amend the statute. If the usual five year sentence is "right", then twenty to thirty years is "wrong". Certainly twenty to thirty years is unusual. There can be no justification for such disparity of punishment. But the sentence is within the astounding statutory limit of "not less than five nor more than sixty years", and it is well settled that within statutory limits even the harshest sentence, absent exceptional circumstances, is not cruel and unusual within the meaning of the Constitution.

Is such as exceptional circumstance present here? The co-defendant in the same indictment who pleaded nolo contendere was sentenced to five to seven years; whereas Perkins who pleaded not guilty and subjected the court to affording him trial by jury was sentenced to twenty to thirty years. It is easy to suspect that Perkins may have been punished for insisting upon his right to trial by jury. Indeed, court-appointed counsel concedes that Perkins may have been punished in part for pleading not guilty. But the inference is of doubtful validity. Perkins and his co-defendant, McCorkle, were apparently quite different in background and in previous homosexual conduct. Although the difference is not enough to justify the extreme disparity of punishment, it is enough to cast doubt upon what otherwise might be inferred: that his not guilty plea inconvenienced the court and that he was punished for it. * * *

Indictment by the grand jury occurred on Monday, January 8, 1962. At about 4:00 P.M. on Tuesday afternoon, because of indigency, counsel was appointed for Perkins. At 9:00 A.M. on Wednesday morning the trial was begun, completed that day, and sentence and judgment imposed. Previous to the appointment of counsel, Perkins himself had asked the court for a continuance, and it had been denied. Perkins asked his court-appointed lawyer to attempt to get a postponement, and the lawyer talked with the Solicitor, but was unable to get his consent to it. Apparently, counsel decided that a formal motion to the court would be futile, and none was made. * * *

Plainly counsel was not afforded reasonable opportunity to investigate and prepare for trial. In the light of these attendant circumstances, there was "such expedition as to deprive" Perkins "of the effective aid and assistance of counsel."

It will be ordered that the petitioner be released within sixty days unless the State elects to try him again.

In all probability Perkins will be tried again, found guilty, and resentenced.

Putting Perkins into the North Carolina prison system is a little like throwing Brer Rabbit into the briarpatch. Most doctors who have studied homosexuality agree that prison environment, including close, continuous, and exclusive contact with other men, aggravates and strengthens homosexual tendencies and provides unexcelled opportunity for homosexual practices. For the confirmed homosexual, imprisonment can accomplish no rehabilitative function; instead, it provides an outlet for the gratification of sexually-deviate desires. * * *

* * * Is there any public purpose served by a possible sixty year maximum or even five year minimum imprisonment of the occasional or one-time homosexual without treatment, and if so, what is it? Are homosexuals twice as dangerous to society as second-degree murderers—as indicated by the maximum punishment for each offense? Is there any good reason why a person convicted of a single homosexual act with another adult may be imprisoned six times as long as an abortionist, thirty times as long as one who takes indecent liberties with children, thirty times as long as the drunk driver-even though serious personal injury and property damage results, twice as long as an armed bank robber, three times as long as a train robber, six times as long as one who feloniously breaks and enters a store, and 730 times as long as the public drunk?

These questions, and others like them, need to be answered.

Notes and Questions

1.   Courts have not deemed it necessary to delve into such questions in pursuing an Eighth Amendment proportionality inquiry. A typical case is *Carter v. State*, 255 Ark. 225, 500 S.W.2d 368 (1973): "Appellants also argue that since a maximum sentence of 21 years may be imposed upon consenting adults for sodomy, and the maximum punishment for a husband and wife engaging in normal sexual intercourse under the same circumstances [in an automobile at a well-lighted public rest area adjacent to an interstate highway] would constitute nothing more than disorderly conduct, [for which the greatest possible punishment would be a fine of $300 and a jail sentence of one year,] enforcement of the statute constitutes cruel and unusual punishment. * * * It is within the province of the legislative branch to classify crimes and determine the punishment therefor. No punishment authorized by statute, even though severe, is cruel and unusual unless barbarous or unknown to the law, or so wholly disproportionate to the nature of the offense as to shock the moral sense of the community. We cannot say that either appellants' eight-year sentence or the 21–year maximum fails to meet any of these tests for constitutionality."

2.   *Proportionality revisited.* Is the "serious Eighth Amendment issue" noted by Justice Powell in *Hardwick* still with us in light of *Harmelin v. Michigan*, 501 U.S. 957, 111 S.Ct. 2680, 115 L.Ed.2d 836 (1991)? In that case, Scalia, J., joined by the Chief Justice, concluded after study of historical sources that "the Eighth Amendment contains no proportionality guarantee." Kennedy, J., joined by O'Connor and Souter, JJ., took note of four principles—(i) "that the fixing of prison terms for specific crimes involves a substantive penological judgment that, as a general matter, is 'properly within the province of legislatures, not courts' "; (ii) "that the Eighth Amendment does not mandate adoption of any one penological theory"; (iii) that "marked divergences both in underlying theories of sentencing and in the length of prescribed prison terms are the inevitable, often beneficial, result of the federal structure," meaning "the circumstance that a State has the most severe punishment for a particular crime does not by itself render the punishment grossly disproportionate"; and (iv) "that proportionality review by federal courts should be informed by 'objective factors to the maximum possible extent' "–and concluded that those

four principles "inform the final one: the Eighth Amendment does not require strict proportionality between crime and sentence. Rather, it forbids only extreme sentences that are 'grossly disproportionate' to the crime." White, J., joined by Blackmun and Stevens, JJ., and separately joined by Marshall, J., favored continued use of the three factors that *Solem v. Helm*, 463 U.S. 277, 103 S.Ct. 3001, 77 L.Ed.2d 637 (1983), found relevant to the proportionality determination: (1) the inherent gravity of the offense, (2) the sentences imposed for similarly grave offenses in the same jurisdiction, and (3) sentences imposed for the same crime in other jurisdictions.

3. *Robinson revisited.* Christopher R. Leslie, *Creating Criminals: The Injuries Inflicted by "Unenforced" Sodomy Laws*, 35 Harv.C.R.-C.L.L.Rev 103, 169–70 (2000), argues that to dismiss the *Robinson* case as Judge Craven did "ignores the manner in which sodomy laws are actually enforced": "Judges have conflated sexual orientation with the criminal conduct of sodomy by holding that homosexuality is a 'status defined by conduct.' Courts have repeatedly held that an individual's acknowledgment of homosexual orientation operates as an admission that one has committed sodomy. Justice Scalia explicitly conflated conduct with status in his dissent in *Romer v. Evans* [p. 92 of this Book] when he opined that '[i]f it is rational to criminalize the conduct, surely it is rational to deny special favor and protection to those with a self-avowed tendency or desire to engage in the conduct. Indeed, where criminal sanctions are not involved, homosexual "orientation" is an acceptable stand-in for homosexual conduct.' Scalia's limitation that such conflation is limited to instances not involving criminal sanctions provides scant relief in cases involving noncriminal sanctions (e.g., termination or refusal of state employment), in which courts have treated gay and lesbian citizens as criminals because of the existence of sodomy laws in state criminal codes. For example, one Texas court succinctly noted: 'Donald Baker is a homosexual.... Therefore, Donald Baker is also a criminal under § 21.06 of the Texas Penal Code.' Even those courts that have sought to protect the equal rights of gay men and lesbians have reasoned that the terms 'orientation' and 'conduct' 'provide[ ] nothing more than a different way of identifying the same class of persons.' In short, 'judges equate homosexuality with sodomy.' "

4. *Creative sentencing.* In *Williams v. State*, 234 Ga.App. 37, 505 S.E.2d 816 (1998), the defendant, convicted of soliciting sodomy, was placed on twelve months probation on the condition that he "walk that portion of Findley Street located between Hancock and Broad Streets [in Athens, Georgia, where the solicitation occurred] in 4 hour intervals on ten (10) days between the hours of 7:00 p.m. and 11:00 p.m. displaying a sign containing the language 'BEWARE HIGH CRIME AREA' which is to be large enough for citizens in the area to view same." On appeal, the defendant claimed this condition constituted cruel and unusual punishment, to which the court responded:

"The trial judge in this case is to be commended for having the initiative to adopt a new and creative form of sentencing which might very well have a positive effect on Williams and be beneficial to the public. The law does not permit, however, the imposition of a condition of probation where compliance would result in the probationer being placed in danger. We therefore vacate the sentence and remand the case to the trial court for resentencing, consistent with this opinion."

5. *Sex offender registration and notification.* "Michael was a distinguished Korean War veteran, twenty-three years old and only sixteen days away from an honorable discharge. His arrest one night in 1956, for having sex with another man in a San Diego 'lover's lane,' however, changed that. He was convicted of the felony crime of 'sexual perversion,' sentenced to five years of probation, fined, and given an undesirable military

discharge. As he walked through a gauntlet of Navy officers who ripped the medals off his chest, he probably assumed that his troubles with the law were, at least, now behind him.

"Michael's actions, however, took on unexpected significance nearly forty years later. In 1995, at the age of sixty-one, a letter from the Los Angeles Police Department ordered him to register with the state as a convicted sex offender. After a two-year struggle with hundreds of attorneys' hours spent on his case, Michael finally was allowed to clear his name from the registry.

"[S]ex offender registration statutes [are] overly broad tools that reinforce patterns of anti-gay harassment by the police. When the nation's first sex offender registration law was enacted in California more than fifty years ago, it was created in large part as a tool to harass gay men. Police in the state, like those in the rest of the country, engaged in unrelenting ploys to ensnare closeted gay men and expose them. The registration statute perpetuated this harassment by requiring persons to register with the police for such minor and victimless crimes as consensual adult sodomy and gay solicitation.

"Now, in the 1990s, similar registration laws have blossomed across the nation. After prodding from Congress and from public pressure, every state has enacted a 'Megan's Law,' a statute that requires certain sex offenders to register with law enforcement agencies and potentially be the subject of public notification. Although the statutes are nominally designed to protect the public from dangerous sexual offenders, many of them have returned full circle to their roots of California's anti-gay harassment. Several of the states require registration for consensual sodomy, purposefully branding gay men and lesbians as sex criminals. Many more states have unintentionally added to the harassment by requiring registration for minor crimes which are often enforced disproportionately against gay men. Still more states compound the problem by making their statutes retroactive, requiring registration for convictions from decades before, a time when police harassment of gay men was particularly severe." Note, 87 Geo.L.J. 2431, 2431–31 (1999) (with Appendix at 2467 surveying the extent to which each state's registration statute applies to nonviolent offenses).

Because these provisions are deemed to be remedial rather than punitive, they are not subject to challenge as cruel and unusual punishment. See, e.g., *Doe v. Poritz*, 142 N.J. 1, 662 A.2d 367 (1995). However, as discussed in Note, supra, at 2464, one court has found another basis upon which to deal with this problem: "The Massachusetts Supreme Judicial Court mandated an expansive procedural change in 1997, stating that every low-risk sexual offender, regardless of the charge on which the person was convicted, is entitled to an administrative hearing to determine whether registration is appropriate. In *Doe v. Attorney General*,[218] the petitioner had pled guilty in 1990 to indecent assault and battery for fondling a decoy police officer in a wooded area known for consensual sex between men. Under Massachusetts law, all persons convicted of that crime were automatically required to register as sex offenders for at least fifteen years. The petitioner, a bisexual man, sought an injunction to prevent the state from making him register, believing that registration as a sexual offender would destroy his marriage, make him a pariah in his community, and destroy his business as a self-employed carpenter. He conceded that registration might be appropriate for some convictions of indecent assault and battery, but argued that the circumstances of his conviction showed that he did not pose a threat to anyone, particularly children.

"The court assumed that the petitioner would be classified as a low-risk, 'level one' offender. Under the Massachusetts registration act, police do not engage in any affirmative

---

218.   426 Mass. 136, 686 N.E.2d 1007 (1997).

community notification for level-one offenders, but information about them is available to the public upon request. The court found that this availability of information could stigmatize him as a sex offender and expose him to adverse economic consequences and held that these risks triggered a liberty and privacy interest under the Massachusetts constitution. Given these interests, the court held that procedural due process entitled the petitioner to a hearing to determine whether the state's interest in protecting the public justified registering him. The Court found that nothing inherent in a conviction for indecent assault and battery, or in the circumstances of the plaintiff's arrest, demonstrated that registering him would serve the purposes of the state's registration act-protecting vulnerable individuals from sexual predators."

SECTION 7. STATE AUTHORITY VERSUS FEDERAL AND LOCAL AUTHORITY

PIERCE v. COMMONWEALTH

Supreme Court of Kentucky, 1989.

777 S.W.2d 926.

LAMBERT, JUSTICE.

The question in this case is whether a city, by local ordinance proscribing solicitation to commit sodomy, may redefine the elements of the offense and impose criminal penalties four times greater than allowed by state statute for the same violation. We have determined that it may not.

Appellant Pierce was convicted in the Boone District Court of criminal solicitation to commit sodomy under City of Florence Ordinance No. 0–33–85. Appellant was fined $500.00 and sentenced to six months in the county jail. He was also convicted, fined and sentenced for escape, but this conviction is not before us. Upon appeal to the Boone Circuit court, both convictions were affirmed. The Court of Appeals denied Pierce's motion for discretionary review. Appellant sought review before this Court. We granted discretionary review to consider the conviction for violation of the sodomy ordinance.

Appellant contends, as he did in each of the courts below, that Florence Ordinance No. 0–33–85 conflicts with KRS 506.030, and thus is invalid. The statute states:

"(1) A person is guilty of criminal solicitation when, with the intent of promoting or facilitating the commission of a crime, he commands or encourages another person to engage in specific conduct which would constitute that crime or an attempt to commit that crime or which would establish the other's complicity in its commission or attempted commission.

(2) A criminal solicitation is a:

(a) Class B felony when the crime solicited is a class A felony or capital offense;

(b) Class C felony when the crime solicited is a Class B felony;

(c) Class A misdemeanor when the crime solicited is a Class C or D felony;

(d) Class B misdemeanor when the crime solicited is a misdemeanor." Id. (Emphasis added.)

Unlike the state statute quoted above, the ordinance under attack addresses itself specifically to solicitation to violate KRS 510.100, the offense of Sodomy in the Fourth Degree, which is a Class A misdemeanor. Under KRS 506.030(d), solicitation to commit a misdemeanor is punishable as a Class B misdemeanor for which the maximum penalty is ninety days imprisonment and a $250.00 fine. KRS 532.090(2) and KRS 534.040. Upon his conviction for violation of the ordinance, appellant was sentenced to six months in jail and a fine of $500.00, twice the period of imprisonment and twice the amount of fine which could have been imposed under the statute.

In addition to enlarged penalties, Florence Ordinance No. 0–33–85 also attempts to prohibit local sodomy solicitation by defining the offense more broadly than the state penal code provisions. The ordinance is as follows:

"Section I

It shall be a criminal offense for a person to solicit, invite, influence or encourage another person *by speech, gesture, or any other form of communication*, to engage in or attempt to engage in conduct which would constitute a violation of the provisions of K.R.S. 510.100, in the City of Florence, Kentucky, with the intent to promote or facilitate such conduct.

Section II

Any person convicted of the offense hereinabove established *shall be fined not less than $100.00 nor more than $500.00, and/or imprisoned for not more than one (1) year*." (Emphasis added.)

As can be seen, the ordinance prohibits sodomy solicitation more explicitly than does KRS 506.030 in combination with KRS 510.100, but in either instance, solicitation of the same illegal act is condemned and made unlawful. Thus the ordinance enacted by the City of Florence directly addresses criminal conduct which is comprehensively addressed by state statutes. Moreover, the ordinance is subject to a more expansive interpretation allowing for the possibility of abusive arrest and prosecution not likely under state law. As the General Assembly chose the language used in the statute, we must conclude it did so intentionally and we cannot approve an ordinance which amounts to an enlargement of the conduct proscribed by the act of the General Assembly. We are also concerned that under the expansive language of the ordinance there is a possibility that an inadvertent act would appear to be a violation when in fact it is but an innocent behavioral idiosyncrasy.

Under KRS 82.082, the so-called "Home Rule" statute, municipalities may act in furtherance of a public purpose, so long as the exercise of power is "not in conflict with a constitutional provision or statute." KRS 82.082(1).

"A power or function is in conflict with a statute if it is expressly prohibited by a statute or *there is a comprehensive scheme of legislation on the same general subject embodied in the Kentucky Revised Statutes*." KRS 82.082(2) (emphasis added).

Appellee argues that the ordinance neither permits or licenses acts or conduct the statute prohibits, nor forbids or prohibits things the statute permits. Further, it contends, KRS 506.030 is merely a general prohibition against criminal solicitation and not a comprehensive scheme which preempts local authority to enact an ordinance dealing with the same subject matter. Appellee concludes that the ordinance does not conflict with KRS 506.030. We disagree.

In enacting KRS 506.030, the General Assembly designed a comprehensive approach to prohibiting the solicitation of criminal acts, which includes a coherent classification scheme for determining the range of penalties from which an appropriate punishment may be imposed. The Florence Ordinance conflicts with the statute by its description of the proscribed conduct and by the excessive penalty it authorizes. For this reason, it is an invalid exercise of the power granted to cities under KRS 82.082.

Because Florence Ordinance No. 0–33–85, under which appellant was convicted, is invalid, we reverse appellant's conviction and remand this cause to the Boone District Court for further proceedings consistent with this opinion. * * *

WINTERSHEIMER, JUSTICE, dissenting.

I respectfully dissent from the majority opinion because the Florence ordinance does not conflict with the statute and the statute does not preempt the field of criminal solicitation of sodomy.

Pursuant to K.R.S. 82.082, the Home Rule statute, the statutory authority which forms the basis for the enactment of the city ordinance is a valid exercise of municipal legislative authority in furtherance of a public purpose of the city. The test for determining whether a city ordinance conflicts with a state statute is whether the ordinance is in conflict with a constitutional provision or statute. K.R.S. 82.082(2) provides that a power is in conflict with a statute if it is expressly prohibited by a statute or there is a comprehensive scheme of legislation on the same general subject. The city ordinance is valid because there is no comprehensive system of legislation on the same general subject in the statutes. K.R.S. 506.030 is a general prohibition against criminal solicitation while the city ordinance is a specific prohibition against criminal solicitation of sodomy. *Commonwealth v. Do, Inc.*, Ky., 674 S.W.2d 519 (1984) recognized that there are many individual situations where local police power may operate on the same subject matter to supplement the general law by providing for additional reasonable requirements. [The] Florence ordinance is an example of application of local police power to the specific problem of activities at certain restrooms in a shopping mall and at an interstate rest stop. The ordinance was an appropriate response to numerous complaints and repeated incidents of activities which the ordinance has attempted to curtail.

The ordinance is not invalid because of preemption of the subject matter. *Do, Inc.,* supra, indicates that in areas of the public health, a state statute may not necessarily preempt the entire field and local communities could enact ordinances dealing with the same subject matter. The constitutional limitations on the exercise of police power to regulate health is a matter of reasonableness. The mere presence of the state in a particular area of the law will not automatically eliminate local authority to regulate. Concurrent local regulation was held valid in *City of Ashland v. Ashland Supply Co.*, 225 Ky. 123, 7 S.W.2d 833 (1928), unless it is unreasonable and oppressive and conflicts with state law.

The doctrine of preemption is often confused with the doctrine that provides there should be no conflict between state and local regulations. Municipal regulation is not always precluded simply because the legislature has taken some action in regard to the same subject matter. The true test of concurrent authority is absence of conflict. The state statute prohibits criminal solicitation and the city ordinance specifically prohibits criminal solicitation to commit sodomy. The specific state statute is a general description of solicitation which may be applied to any crime. The ordinance deals specifically with solicitation for sodomy and is directed to a local problem. The city ordinance does not conflict with the statute and therefore is not preempted by it.

The ordinance is not invalid because it imposes a penalty greater than that imposed by the legislature. K.R.S. 534.040(2) specifically exempts offenses defined outside the penal code from the penalty limiting provisions of the code. This principal is clearly stated in *Commonwealth v. Schindler*, Ky., 685 S.W.2d 544 (1984) which certified the law in regard to an alleged conflict in state statute. This ordinance creates an offense defined outside the penal code and the penalties are not controlled by the code.

Kentucky Constitution Section 168 provides that a city ordinance may not fix a penalty less than the statute for the same offense. This section does not prohibit a municipal corporation from fixing by ordinance a penalty for a violation thereof above the minimum fixed by statute. Obviously, the Kentucky Constitution recognizes the authority of both state and city to operate in the same general field of the law absent any conflict. The constitutional provision specifically forbids the city from imposing any lesser penalty for the same offense. There is no constitutional prohibition for the establishment of a higher penalty for the same offense.

However, it is not necessary to reach that situation because the Florence ordinance does not prohibit an act that the statute permits and the state statute does not preempt the entire field of criminal solicitation because it is a general and not a comprehensive system of legislation. The city ordinance deals specifically with sodomy as a question of criminal solicitation in that it affects public health and it is outside the area defined by the penal code. The application of any of these principles clearly indicates that the city of Florence can act in the manner it has chosen to act.

Therefore I would affirm the conviction.

Notes and Questions

1.   Pursuant to authorization from the legislature, local governmental units have the police power to regulate for the protection of the lives, health and property of their inhabitants and the preservation of good order and morals. In most states the typical municipality has numerous ordinances on local traffic matters, on local nontraffic matters (e.g., regulating garbage disposal), and on matters also covered by state criminal laws (e.g., assault and battery). These ordinances frequently provide for fines or imprisonment or both for their violation, although sometimes the power to imprison is limited to imprisonment for failure to pay a fine. While the prevailing view is that violation of a municipal ordinance is a civil wrong rather than a crime, the modern trend is in the direction of calling such violations criminal, at least where imprisonment is authorized or where the ordinance prohibits the same conduct as does the state criminal law.

2.   Why shouldn't the City of Florence be able to take measures to deal with a local problem–the solicitations at the shopping mall and rest stop? If in *Pierce* the penalties for the ordinance violation had been the same as for violation of the state statute, would the ordinance have been struck down nonetheless? If so, is that because of preemption or because of conflict, which the dissent notes are often confused?

3.   Assume that in a state where the criminal code makes possession of marijuana a misdemeanor punishable by up to a year in jail and/or a fine of $500, and sale of marijuana a felony punishable by up to 5 years in the penitentiary, the students at the state university manage to elect a majority of the city council in the city where the university is located, after which the council adopts an ordinance making possession or sale of marijuana an offense punishable by not more than a fine of $5. Absent an express constitutional prohibition, as in Kentucky, against lower penalties for ordinance violations, is the ordinance valid? Of what relevance, if any, is *Waller v. Florida*, 397 U.S. 387, 90 S.Ct. 1184, 25 L.Ed.2d 435 (1970), holding that the constitutional protection against double jeopardy bars a state prosecution of a defendant for the "same acts" for which he was previously tried under a city ordinance.

NOTES AND QUESTIONS ON THE LIMITS OF STATE POWER

1. Just as a city ordinance and state criminal statute may proscribe identical or substantially identical conduct, so too it sometimes happens that a state criminal statute and federal criminal statute will match up in this way. In such a case, the state law may be upheld on the theory that the two statutes do not conflict and that Congress did not intend to make its law exclusive, or the state legislation may be held unconstitutional under the supremacy clause, art. VI of the Constitution, on the theory that the federal legislation has occupied the field. While "[n]o simple formula can capture the complexities of this determination," *Goldstein v. California,* 412 U.S. 546, 93 S.Ct. 2303, 37 L.Ed.2d 163 (1973), the Supreme Court in *Pennsylvania v. Nelson,* 350 U.S. 497, 76 S.Ct. 477, 100 L.Ed. 640 (1956), set forth three tests for determining the pre-emption issue: (1) Is the federal legislative scheme as to the subject matter in question so pervasive as to indicate that Congress must have meant the states were not to supplement the federal legislation? (2) Is the federal interest in the subject matter so dominant that Congress must have meant to preclude the states from dealing with the matter? (3) Would state enforcement in the matter present a serious danger to effective federal enforcement?

2. Definition of the power of a state to declare conduct criminal requires consideration of (1) the subject matter which a state may regulate, and (2) the territory which the laws may encompass. As for the first of these, the important point is that while the federal government, as discussed below, is a government of limited powers, this is not so as to the states, and consequently a state, unlike the federal government, may declare activities to be criminal without the necessity of finding some express or implied authority therefor in its constitution. It is commonly said that a state has regulatory power (usually termed its "police power") to regulate its internal affairs for the protection or promotion of public health, safety and morals, or—somewhat more vaguely—for the protection or promotion of the public welfare. This police power is the purported basis of the various "crime against nature" type statutes heretofore discussed in this chapter. As we have seen, there are constitutional limits on this power, and so criminal statutes must serve a valid public interest (substantive due process), must be sufficiently clear (the void-for-vagueness doctrine), must not be so broad as to encroach on protected rights (e.g., the right to privacy), and must not be too narrow in the sense of drawing an arbitrary line between what is included and excluded (equal protection).

3. As for the second aspect of state power, one would expect that if this police power is being exercised for the promotion of the public welfare of the citizens of the state, then ordinarily this would mean that the enforcement of these criminal statutes would be limited to activities inside the state. If the legislature of state X has made the judgment that protection of its citizens' morals required adoption of a statute prohibiting consensual sodomy, one would not as a general rule expect that this statute could be applied to such acts of sodomy occurring in state Y. If state Y has not made such consensual acts a crime, then those participating in them in state Y should not be prosecuted at all; or, if state Y has made such acts criminal, then it is for state Y rather than state X to enforce its statute if it chooses. And so it is that the common law adopts as the principal basis of jurisdiction a territorial theory of jurisdiction over crimes: a state has power to make conduct or the results of conduct a crime if the conduct takes place or the results happen within its territorial limits. Modern statutes, without departing from the territorial principle of jurisdiction, have sometimes enlarged their criminal jurisdiction by making other local conduct or results (other than the one particular act or omission or result which the common law considered vital) the basis for jurisdiction.

4. Such enlargement of the criminal jurisdiction of states can result in the situation where two states have jurisdiction over the same crime, as in *Heath v. Alabama*, 474 U.S. 82, 106 S.Ct. 433, 88 L.Ed.2d 387 (1985). In that case, Georgia prosecuted and convicted defendant for murder of his wife, whose body was found in Alabama, on the basis that time-of-death evidence showed the killing occurred in Georgia, after which Alabama tried and convicted defendant of the murder on the basis of the victim's body being found in the state. The Supreme Court rejected defendant's claim that the second prosecution was barred and concluded that each state with concurrent jurisdiction is free to prosecute, for "their powers to undertake criminal prosecutions derive from separate and independent sources of power and authority." The Court declined the invitation "to restrict the applicability of the dual sovereignty principle to cases in which two governmental entities, having concurrent jurisdiction and pursuing quite different interests, can demonstrate that allowing only one entity to exercise jurisdiction over the unvindicated interests of the second entity." Frequently, however, a statutory provision will prohibit a second prosecution in a concurrent jurisdiction situation,[a] and even absent such a statute the prosecuting officials may, in their discretion, decided not to prosecute in such circumstances.

5. Just how far do you think the territorial principle can fairly be expanded in the interest of allowing a state to fully protect its citizens? For example, what should the result be in each of the following examples, assuming in all instances that state *X* has made consensual sodomy a crime but that state *Y* has not: (1) *A* and *B*, both citizens of state *X*, meet for the first time in state Y and there engage in consensual sodomy, resulting in a charge of sodomy in state *X*. Consider *State ex rel. Chandler v. Main*, 16 Wis. 398 (1863), concluding that "the power of a state over its own citizens stands upon a still stronger ground, and it may * * * pass * * * laws which are binding and obligatory upon them everywhere." (2) *C* and *D*, both citizens of state *X*, desiring to thwart the restrictions in state *X*, cross from state *X* into adjoining state *Y* for the purpose of engaging in consensual sodomy there, which they do, likewise resulting in a charge of sodomy in state *X*. Consider *Commonwealth v. Crass*, 180 Ky. 794, 203 S.W. 708 (1918), holding prosecution for betting on a state election proper though the betters traveled to an adjoining state to make the bet, as "the parties traveled to Dukedom merely for the purpose of evading the statute." (3) *E* and *F* reach an agreement in state *X* that they will travel to state *Y* and engage in sodomy there, resulting in a charge in state *X* of conspiracy to commit sodomy. (4) *G* approaches H in state X and suggests that they go to state Y and there engage in sodomy, resulting in a charge against G in state X of solicitation of conspiracy. Compare *Model Penal Code* § 1.03(1)(d), recognizing jurisdiction where "conduct occurring within the State establishes * * * solicitation or conspiracy to commit, an offense in another jurisdiction that also is an offense under the law of this State."

6. While the territorial principle would suggest that a state's criminal statutes could be applied to all conduct within the state's borders, this is not entirely correct, as is illustrated by the case of *People v. Mouse*, 203 Cal. 782, 265 P. 944 (1928). Mouse was prosecuted and convicted of violating the state's "infamous crime against nature" statute because of his conduct in Los Angeles, specifically, on the grounds of the National Home for Disabled Volunteer Soldiers. The court noted: "Exclusive jurisdiction in the United

---

a. Some states have enacted provisions identical or similar to *Model Penal Code* § 1.10, which provides that in a case of concurrent jurisdiction, a prosecution in the other jurisdiction is a bar to a subsequent prosecution in the state if: (1) the first prosecution resulted in an acquittal or a conviction and the subsequent prosecution is based on the same conduct, unless (a) the former and present offenses each require proof of a fact not required by the other and each is intended to prevent a substantially different harm or evil, or (b) the second offense was not consummated when the former trial began; or (2) the former prosecution was terminated in a way which required a determination inconsistent with a fact which must be established for conviction of the offense for which the defendant is subsequently prosecuted.

States to punish criminal offenses exists [as to] offenses committed in 'all places purchased by the consent of the Legislature of the state in which the same shall be, for the erection of forts, magazines, arsenals, dockyards, and other needful buildings.' Article 1, § 8, Constitution of the United States." Consequently the court found it necessary to reverse Mouse's conviction, as the California legislature had given the requisite consent and prior case authority established 'that a soldiers' home of the type here found is such 'needful building.' "

NOTES AND QUESTIONS ON THE LIMITS OF FEDERAL POWER

1. The federal government has the power to create statutory crimes where the Constitution expressly grants Congress the power (e.g., art. I, § 8, power to punish counterfeiting; art. III, § 3, power to punish treason). In addition, art. I, § 8 of the Constitution provides that the Congress has the power "to make all Laws which shall be necessary and proper for carrying into Execution the foregoing [express] Powers, and all other Powers vested by this Constitution in the Government of the United States." Thus, many federal criminal statutes have been enacted on the theory that they are "necessary and proper" to such powers as the power to regulate interstate commerce, to establish post offices, and to tax. It has been noted that in fact the federal criminal law is utilized to punish antisocial conduct primarily injurious to the federal government (e.g., bribery of federal officers) and also to punish antisocial conduct of primarily local concern with which local officials are unable or unwilling to cope (e.g., use of the mails to defraud, kidnaping across state lines). See Louis B. Schwartz, *Federal Criminal Jurisdiction and Prosecutors' Discretion*, 13 Law & Contemp. Prob. 64 (1948).

2. The Supreme Court has occasionally held that the Congress has overstepped its bounds, as in *United States v. Lopez*, 514 U.S. 549, 115 S.Ct. 1624, 131 L.Ed.2d 626 (1995), holding that the Gun–Free School Zones Act, making it a federal offense for any individual knowingly to possess a firearm at a place that individual knows or has reasonable cause to believe is a school zone, exceeds Congress' commerce clause authority, since possession of a gun in a local school zone was not economic activity that substantially affected interstate commerce. After noting the government's concession that "[n]either the statute nor its legislative history contain[s] express congressional findings regarding the effects upon interstate commerce of gun possession in a school zone, the Court concluded:

"The Government's essential contention, *in fine*, is that we may determine here that § 922(q) is valid because possession of a firearm in a local school zone does indeed substantially affect interstate commerce. The Government argues that possession of a firearm in a school zone may result in violent crime and that violent crime can be expected to affect the functioning of the national economy in two ways. First, the costs of violent crime are substantial, and, through the mechanism of insurance, those costs are spread throughout the population. Second, violent crime reduces the willingness of individuals to travel to areas within the country that are perceived to be unsafe. The Government also argues that the presence of guns in schools poses a substantial threat to the educational process by threatening the learning environment. A handicapped educational process, in turn, will result in a less productive citizenry. That, in turn, would have an adverse effect on the Nation's economic well-being. As a result, the Government argues that Congress could rationally have concluded that § 922(q) substantially affects interstate commerce.

"We pause to consider the implications of the Government's arguments. The Government admits, under its 'costs of crime' reasoning, that Congress could regulate not only all violent crime, but all activities that might lead to violent crime, regardless of how tenuously they relate to interstate commerce. Similarly, under the Government's 'national productivity' reasoning, Congress could regulate any activity that it found was related to the economic productivity of individual citizens: family law (including marriage, divorce, and child custody), for example. Under the theories that the Government presents in support of § 922(q), it is difficult to perceive any limitation on federal power, even in areas such as criminal law enforcement or education where States historically have been sovereign. Thus, if we were to accept the Government's arguments, we are hard pressed to posit any activity by an individual that Congress is without power to regulate."

3.　Even when the Supreme Court does not strike down a federal statute on a *Lopez* theory, it may narrowly construe the statute at issue in order to avoid a *Lopez* problem, as in *Jones v. United States*, 529 U.S. 848, 120 S.Ct. 1904, 146 L.Ed.2d 902 (2000). Jones tossed a Molotov cocktail into a home owned and occupied by his cousin as a dwelling place for everyday family living, resulting in his prosecution and conviction for violating 18 U.S.C. § 844(I), which makes it a federal crime to "maliciously damage[] or destroy[], * * * by means of fire or an explosive, any building * * * used in interstate or foreign commerce or in any activity affecting interstate or foreign commerce." In response to the government's claim that the statutory language manifested an intent by Congress to use its full power under the commerce clause, the Court concluded the "used in" language indicated that Congress had required that the *function* of the building affect interstate commerce, which was not the case here absent any showing the building was "the locus of any commercial undertaking." In support of this conclusion, the Court added:

"Given the concerns brought to the fore in *Lopez*, it is appropriate to avoid the constitutional question that would arise were we to read § 844(i) to render the 'traditionally local criminal conduct' in which petitioner Jones engaged 'a matter for federal enforcement.' Our comprehension of § 844(i) is additionally reinforced by other interpretive guides. We have instructed that 'ambiguity concerning the ambit of criminal statutes should be resolved in favor of lenity,' and that 'when choice has to be made between two readings of what conduct Congress has made a crime, it is appropriate, before we choose the harsher alternative, to require that Congress should have spoken in language that is clear and definite.' We have cautioned, as well, that 'unless Congress conveys its purpose clearly, it will not be deemed to have significantly changed the federal-state balance' in the prosecution of crimes. To read § 844(i) as encompassing the arson of an owner-occupied private home would effect such a change, for arson is a paradigmatic common-law state crime."

4.　The limited nature of federal power, as compared to state power, explains in part why all of the cases heretofore discussed in this chapter regarding "crime against nature" offenses arose in the state courts. This is not to suggest, however, that prosecutions for such conduct never occur in a federal forum. For one thing, Article 125 of the Uniform Code of Military Justice provides that "[a]ny person subject to this chapter who engages in unnatural carnal copulation with another person of the same or opposite sex or with an animal is guilty of sodomy," and court-martials for such conduct are undertaken; see, e.g., *United States v. Henderson*, 34 M.J. 174 (U.S.C.M.A.1992). Secondly, there is the flip side of the situation discussed in the *Mouse* case, supra, that is, where the conduct in question occurred within some federal enclave inside the borders of some state. Because it is important to have a complete criminal code available for use within these enclaves, Congress has enacted the Assimilative Crimes Act, 18 U.S.C.A. § 13, which incorporates by reference the criminal laws of the state in which the enclave lies as to any conduct not otherwise "punishable by any enactment of Congress." And thus, for example, the Arkansas sodomy law provides a basis for a federal prosecution for such conduct occurring in the Hot Springs National Park. *United States v. Lemons*, 697 F.2d 832 (8th Cir.1983).

5. Such federal prosecutions for the "crime against nature" are, of course, subject the same kinds of constitutional challenges as have been discussed in the preceding sections of this chapter regarding state prosecutions for like conduct. At least in some instances, however, the special character of the federal interest involved may make a challenge on some of these grounds even more difficult to sustain:

(a) In *United States v. Brewer*, 363 F.Supp. 606 (M.D. Pa. 1973), the court concluded that the justification for enforcing the consensual sodomy law against an inmate of a federal prison was especially compelling: "The interest in preventing disorder in prison and injury to prisoners is sufficient to justify the existence of a prison regulation, or a state or federal statute, prohibiting consensual acts of sodomy between prison inmates. Two additional factors to be considered in balancing the state's interest in proscribing a prisoner's conduct against asserted constitutional rights or privileges are: (1) the threats of violence which may cause a victim to 'consent' to sodomy, and as a corollary, the difficulty in proof, and (2) the very tense and potentially dangerous situation existing within the prison confines as opposed to society at large. These additional factors convince the court that 'consensual' sodomy between prison inmates may be validly prohibited."

(b) In *Beller v. Middendorf*, 632 F.2d 788 (9th Cir.1980), upholding the prohibition on consensual sodomy by military personnel, the court stated: "While it is clear that one does not surrender his or her constitutional rights upon entering the military, the Supreme Court has repeatedly held that constitutional rights must be viewed in light of the special circumstances and needs of the armed forces. As the Court [has] said * * *, the military is 'by necessity, a specialized society separate from civilian society.' Military services 'must insist upon a respect for duty and a discipline without counterpart in civilian life.' Regulations which might infringe constitutional rights in other contexts may survive scrutiny because of military necessities. * * *

"There are multiple grounds for the Navy to deem this regulation appropriate for the full and efficient accomplishment of its mission. The Navy can act to protect the fabric of military life, to preserve the integrity of the recruiting process, to maintain the discipline of personnel in active service, and to insure the acceptance of men and women in the military, who are sometimes stationed in foreign countries with cultures different from our own. The Navy, moreover, could conclude rationally that toleration of homosexual conduct, as expressed in a less broad prohibition, might be understood as tacit approval."

6. The matter of federal jurisdiction is a bit more complex than that of state jurisdiction, discussed earlier, and only a brief outline will be given here. As for the limited powers set forth in Note 1 supra, their exercise by the enactment of criminal legislation by Congress provides a basis for prosecutions for conduct occurring within the several states. In addition, the federal government has additional territorial jurisdiction by virtue of art. I, § 8 of the United States Constitution, which gives Congress full legislative authority over the District of Columbia, the Territories, and American ships and aircraft wherever they may be. Two other noteworthy bases of jurisdiction are nationality, whereby the United States has the power (sparingly exercised) to make criminal the conduct of its own nationals abroad, and the "protective principle," whereby the United States has the power (occasionally exercised) to enact substantive criminal laws dealing even with the conduct of aliens in foreign territory when the conduct threatens our security as a state or the operation of the federal government's functions.

Chapter 3

MENTAL STATE

Introductory Notes

1. It is commonly stated that a crime consists of both a physical part and a mental part; that is, both an act or omission (and sometimes also a prescribed result of action or omission, or prescribed attendant circumstances, or both) and a state of mind. This Chapter is concerned with what is required of crimes in the way of the mental part, variously called *mens rea* ("guilty mind") or *scienter* or criminal intent.

Actually, the terms "mental part" and "*mens rea*" and "state of mind" are somewhat too narrow to be strictly accurate, for they include matters that are not really mental at all. Thus we shall see that, though many crimes do require some sort of mental fault (*i.e.,* a bad mind), other crimes (which are commonly said to require *mens rea*) require only some sort of fault which is not mental.[a] The unadorned word "fault" is thus a more accurate word to describe what crimes generally require in addition to their physical elements.

2. During the early days of the development of common law crimes, the judges often declared conduct to be criminal which did not include any bad state of mind. But in more recent times (*i.e.,* since about 1600), the judges have generally defined common law crimes in terms which require, in addition to prescribed action or omission, some prescribed bad state of mind, although that state of mind has differed from one common law crime to another. The basic premise that for criminal liability some *mens rea* is required is expressed by the Latin maxim *actus not facit reum nisi mens sit rea* (an act does not make one guilty unless his mind is guilty). The words and phrases used by the judges to express the bad mind necessary for common law crimes include "maliciously" (as in murder, arson, malicious mischief), "fraudulently" (forgery), "feloniously" (larceny), "wilfully and corruptly" (perjury), and "with intent to * * *" (*e.g.,* "with intent to steal," another phrase used in defining larceny; "with intent to commit a felony therein," in burglary).[b]

3. Most crimes today, of course, are statutory crimes. In most jurisdictions common law crimes have been abolished; in others common law crimes are sparingly used. In all

---

a. In addition, some crimes require no fault at all, mental or otherwise; these impose liability without fault. But such crimes are said not to require *mens rea.*

b. The common law did occasionally depart from the requirement of a literally bad mind. Thus manslaughter could be committed by a type of negligent conduct which, in England, did not require a subjective bad mind, though it did require objective fault. In two crimes, libel and nuisance, vicarious liability was imposed upon a faultless employer for the conduct of his employee.

113

jurisdictions most of the common law crimes have been stated in the form of statutory law. And of course, in modern times, new statutory crimes, unknown to the common law, far outnumber the relatively few common law crimes originally created by the judges. The "mental" aspects of statutory crimes may be roughly classified as follows as to type:

(1) Many statutes defining conduct which is criminal employ words (usually adverbs) or phrases indicating some type of bad-mind requirement: "intentionally" or "with intent to * * *"; "knowingly" or "with knowledge that * * *"; "purposely" or "for the purpose of * * *"; "fraudulently" or "with intent to defraud"; "wilfully"; "maliciously"; "corruptly"; "designedly"; "recklessly"; "wantonly"; "unlawfully"; "feloniously" and so on. (2) Some of the statutes use words or phrases indicating a requirement of fault, but not necessarily mental fault—*e.g.*, "negligently", "carelessly", or "having reason to know * * *"(3) Some statutes define criminal conduct without any words or phrases indicating any express requirement of fault; thus "whoever does so-and-so (or: whoever omits to do so-and-so) is guilty of a crime and subject to the following punishment * * *"[c] However, although the statute may contain no adverbs or phrases indicating a requirement of fault, some fault may be inherent in a verb which the statute employs (*e.g.*, whoever "refuses" to do something or "permits" another to do something).

It may be said of statutory crimes that, so far as the mental element is concerned, (1) some crimes (like most of the common law crimes) require "subjective fault"—actually a bad mind of some sort; (2) others require only "objective fault"—fault which is not a matter of the mind; and (3) others require no fault at all, either subjective (mental) or objective (nonmental), such statutes providing instead for "liability without fault."

4. The difficulties inherent in such a variety of expressions as to *mens rea* as is used by the common law and by statutes in defining crimes have led modern thinkers to classify the mental aspects of crime into a few general types; and to urge that, in drafting penal codes, a single expression be used to express a single type of *mens rea* culpability. The Model Penal Code has thus reduced the matter to four basic types of crimes which require fault: (1) crimes requiring *intention* (or *purpose*) to do the forbidden act (omission) or cause the forbidden result; (2) crimes requiring *knowledge* of the nature of the act (omission) or of the result which will follow therefrom or of the attendant circumstances; (3) those requiring *recklessness* in doing the act (omission) or causing the result (subjective fault in that the actor must in his own mind realize the risk which his conduct involves); and (4) those requiring only *negligence* in so doing or causing (objective fault in creating an unreasonable risk; but, since the actor need not realize the risk in order to be negligent, no subjective fault is required).[d] Most of the modern criminal codes expressly provide for these four basic types of culpability. Of course, there remains the possibility that, for some crimes or for some elements of a crime, a statute may impose strict liability.

REGINA v. CUNNINGHAM

Court of Appeal, Criminal Division, England, 1957.

[1957] 2 Q.B. 396, [1957] 3 W.L.R. 56, [1957] 2 All E.R. 412.

Byrne, J.: * * *

The appellant was convicted at Leeds Assizes upon an indictment framed under section 23 of the Offences against the Person Act, 1861, which charged that he unlawfully

c. Legislatures seldom if ever expressly provide that lack of fault shall be irrelevant, by any such phrase as "without regard to fault."

d. *Model Penal Code* § 2.02(2).

and maliciously caused to be taken by Sarah Wade a certain noxious thing, namely, coal gas, so as thereby to endanger the life of the said Sarah Wade.

The facts were that the appellant was engaged to be married and his prospective mother-in-law was the tenant of a house, No. 7a, Bakes Street, Bradford, which was unoccupied but which was to be occupied by the appellant after his marriage. Mrs. Wade and her husband, an elderly couple, lived in the house next door. At one time the two houses had been one, but when the building was converted into two houses a wall had been erected to divide the cellars of the two houses, and that wall was composed of rubble loosely cemented. On the evening of January 17 last the appellant went to the cellar of No. 7a, Bakes Street, wrenched the gas meter from the gas pipes and stole it, together with its contents, and in a second indictment he was charged with the larceny of the gas meter and its contents. To that indictment he pleaded Guilty and was sentenced to six months' imprisonment. In respect of that matter he does not appeal. The facts were not really in dispute, and in a statement to a police officer the appellant said: "All right I will tell you. I was short of money, I had been off work for three days, I got eight shillings from the gas meter. I tore it off the wall and threw it away." Although there was a stop tap within two feet of the meter, the appellant did not turn off the gas, with the result that a very considerable volume of gas escaped, some of which seeped through the wall of the cellar and partially asphyxiated Mrs. Wade, who was asleep in her bedroom next door, with the result that her life was endangered.

At the close of the case for the prosecution Mr. Brodie, who appeared for the appellant at the trial and who has appeared for him again in this court, submitted that there was no case to go to the jury, but the learned judge, quite rightly in our opinion, rejected this submission. The appellant did not give evidence.

The act of the appellant was clearly unlawful and therefore the real question for the jury was whether it was also malicious within the meaning of section 23 of the Offences against the Person Act, 1861. Before this court Mr. Brodie has taken three points, all dependent upon the construction of that section. Section 23 provides as follows: "Whosoever shall unlawfully and maliciously administer to or cause to be administered to or taken by any other person any poison or other destructive or noxious thing, so as thereby to endanger the life of such person, or so as thereby to inflict upon such person any grievous bodily harm, shall be guilty of felony." Mr. Brodie argued, first, that *mens rea* of some kind is necessary. Secondly, that the nature of the *mens rea* required is that the appellant must have an intention to do the particular kind of harm that was done, or alternatively he must foresee that that harm may occur, yet nevertheless continue recklessly to do the act. Thirdly, that the learned judge misdirected the jury as to the meaning of the word "maliciously." He cited the following cases: *Pembliton* (1874) L.R. 2 C.C.R. 119; *Latimer* (1886) 17 Q.B.D. 359; and *Faulkner* (1877) 13 Cox 550. In reply Mr. Snowden, on behalf of the Crown, cited *Martin* (1881) 8 Q.B.D. 54.

We have considered those cases, and we have also considered, in the light of those cases, the following principle which was propounded by the late Professor C. S. Kenny in the first edition of his *Outlines of Criminal Law,* published in 1902, and repeated in the sixteenth edition edited by Mr. J. W. Cecil Turner and published in 1952: "In any statutory definition of a crime, malice must be taken not in the old vague sense of wickedness in general but as requiring either (1) An actual intention to do the particular kind of harm that in fact was done; or (2) Recklessness as to whether such harm should occur or not (i.e., the accused has foreseen that the particular kind of harm might be done and yet has gone on to take the risk of it). It is neither limited to nor does it indeed require any ill will towards the person injured." * * * We think that this is an accurate statement of the law.

It derives some support from the judgments of Lord Coleridge, C.J. and Blackburn, J. in *Pembliton's* case. In our opinion, the word "maliciously" in a statutory crime postulates foresight of consequence.

In his summing-up the learned judge directed the jury as follows: "You will observe that there is nothing there about 'with intention that that person should take it.' He has not got to intend that it should be taken; it is sufficient that by his unlawful and malicious act he causes it to be taken. What you have to decide here, then, is whether, when he loosed that frightful cloud of coal gas into the house which he shared with this old lady, he caused her to take it by his unlawful and malicious action. 'Unlawful' does not need any definition. It is something forbidden by law. What about 'malicious'? 'Malicious' for this purpose means wicked—something which he has no business to do and perfectly well knows it. 'Wicked' is as good a definition as any other which you would get. The facts which face you (and they are uncontradicted and undisputed; the prisoner has not gone into the box to seek to give any particular explanation) are these. Living in the house, which was now two houses but which had once been one and had been rather roughly divided, the prisoner quite deliberately, intending to steal the money that was in the meter * * * broke the gas meter away from the supply pipes and thus released the mains supply of gas at large into that house. When he did that he knew that this old lady and her husband were living next door to him. The gas meter was in a cellar. The wall which divided his cellar from the cellar next door was a kind of honeycomb wall through which gas could very well go, so that when he loosed that cloud of gas into that place he must have known perfectly well that gas would percolate all over the house. If it were part of this offence—which it is not—that he intended to poison the old lady, I should have left it to you to decide, and I should have told you that there was evidence on which you could find that he intended that, since he did an action which he must have known would result in that. As I have already told you, it is not necessary to prove that he intended to do it; it is quite enough that what he did was done unlawfully and maliciously."

With the utmost respect to the learned judge, we think it is incorrect to say that the word "malicious" in a statutory offence merely means wicked. We think the learned judge was in effect telling the jury that if they were satisfied that the appellant acted wickedly—and he had clearly acted wickedly in stealing the gas meter and its contents—they ought to find that he had acted maliciously in causing the gas to be taken by Mrs. Wade so as thereby to endanger her life.

In our view, it should have been left to the jury to decide whether, even if the appellant did not intend the injury to Mrs. Wade, he foresaw that the removal of the gas meter might cause injury to someone but nevertheless removed it. We are unable to say that a reasonable jury, properly directed as to the meaning of the word "maliciously" in the context of section 23, would without doubt have convicted.

In these circumstances this court has no alternative but to allow the appeal and quash the conviction.

Notes and Questions

1. Reassess *Cunningham* in light of the four cases the court notes were cited by counsel:

(a) *Pembliton* (1874): The defendant threw a stone at some persons with whom he had been fighting; the stone passed over their heads and broke a large plate glass window. The jury found that the defendant threw the stone intending to strike one or more of those persons and not intending to break the window. This finding, the court held per Lord

Coleridge, C.J., was not sufficient to convict under a statute making it a misdemeanor for one to "unlawfully and maliciously" commit any damage upon real or personal property: "[W]hat was intended to be provided against by the Act is the wilfully doing an unlawful Act, and that the Act must be wilfully and intentionally done on the part of the person doing it, to render him liable to be convicted. Without saying that, upon these facts, if the jury had found that the prisoner had been guilty of throwing the stone recklessly, knowing that there was a window near which it might probably hit, I should have been disposed to interfere with the conviction, yet as they have found that he threw the stone at the people he had been fighting with intending to strike them and not intending to break the window, I think the conviction must be quashed."

(b) *Faulkner* (1877): The defendant, a sailor, went into the hold of a ship to steal some rum; he lit a match to see better, but this ignited the rum and the resulting fire destroyed the ship. The defendant was convicted by a jury of violating the Malicious Damage Act by maliciously setting fire to the ship. The court, per Barry, J., reversed: "The jury were, in fact, directed to give a verdict of guilty upon the simple ground that the firing of the ship, though accidental, was caused by an act done in the course of, or immediately consequent upon, a felonious operation, and no question of the prisoner's malice, constructive or otherwise, was left to the jury. I am of opinion that, according to *Reg. v. Pembliton*, that direction was erroneous, and that the conviction should be quashed."

(c) *Martin* (1881): Shortly before the conclusion of a performance at a theatre, the defendant, with the intention and with the result of causing terror in the minds of persons leaving the theatre, put out the gaslights on a staircase which a large number of them had to descend in order to leave. He also, with the intention and with the result of obstructing the exit, placed an iron bar across the doorway. Upon the lights being extinguished a panic seized a large portion of the audience, and they rushed in fright down the staircase, forcing those in front against the iron bar and causing those persons to be injured. The defendant was indicted under a statute providing that "whosoever shall unlawfully and maliciously wound, or inflict any grievous bodily harm upon any other person, either with or without a weapon or instrument, shall be guilty of a misdemeanor." The jury was charged that if they concluded the conduct of the defendant in extinguishing the lights and putting the bar across the doorway amounted to nothing more than a mere piece of foolish mischief they might acquit, but that if they believed the acts were done with a deliberate and malicious intention they ought to convict. The defendant was convicted. The court, per Lord Coleridge, C.J., affirmed: "The prisoner must be taken to have intended the natural consequences of that which he did. He acted 'unlawfully and maliciously,' not that he had any personal malice against the particular individuals injured, but in the sense of doing an unlawful act calculated to injure, and by which others were in fact injured. Just as in the case of a man who unlawfully fires a gun among a crowd, it is murder if one of the crowd is thereby killed." Stephen, J., concurring, commented: "I wish to add that the Recorder seems to have put the case too favourably for the prisoner, for he put it to the jury to consider whether the prisoner did the act 'as a mere piece of foolish mischief.' Now, it seems to me, that if the prisoner did that which he did as a mere piece of foolish mischief unlawfully and without excuse, he did it 'wilfully,' that is 'maliciously,' within the meaning of the statute."

(d) *Latimer* (1886): The defendant, a soldier, quarreled with Chapple in a public-house, and Chapple knocked him down. The defendant left but returned about five minutes later and walked over to Chapple and swung a leather belt at him. The belt struck Chapple slightly, bounded off and struck Ellen Rolston, cutting her face open. The defendant was convicted under a statute making it a misdemeanor to "unlawfully and maliciously wound or inflict any grievous bodily harm upon any other person." The court, per Lord Coleridge,

C.J., affirmed: "It is common knowledge that a man who has an unlawful and malicious intent against another, and, in attempting to carry it out, injures a third person, is guilty of what the law deems malice against the person injured, because the offender is doing an unlawful act, and has that which the judges call general malice, and that is enough. * * * He intended to do an unlawful act, and in course of doing it the consequence was that somebody was injured." Esher, M. R., elaborated: "The only case which could be cited against the well-known principle of law applicable to this case was *Reg. v. Pembliton,* but, on examination, it is found to have been decided on this ground, viz., that there was no intention to injure any property at all. It was not a case of attempting to injure one man's property and injuring another's, which would have been wholly different."

2.   Compare *State v. Hatley,* 72 N.M. 377, 384 P.2d 252 (1963), where the defendant was convicted of mayhem. Though the defendant struck the blow which put out the victim's eye, he claimed there was no proof he intended to maim the victim and that the harm resulted from the victim turning his head at the moment of the blow. The court affirmed: "We think the conduct of appellant falls well within the rule so as to make him liable for the consequences of an unlawful act, even though such consequences may not have been intended. One who, in the commission of a wrongful act, commits another wrong not meant by him, is nevertheless liable for the latter wrong. Here, the appellant deliberately committed the crime of assault and battery, and, in so doing, committed mayhem."

3.   Consider *United States v. Zapata,* 497 F.2d 95 (5th Cir.1974), where defendant, upon her entry into the United States, was found to have 2,000 grams of pure cocaine in her undergarments. Questioned concerning the possession, she indicated an awareness of wrongdoing but did not specify whether she meant she was aware (i) she was illegally importing cocaine, (ii) she had failed to declare the packages on her person, or (iii) she had tried to enter on a false passport. She was charged with "knowingly and intentionally" importing the cocaine. At trial, she testified a stranger had given her money to transport unspecified "raw material" into the country for him and that he had assured her this was perfectly legal. Query, which of the following jury instructions, if any, would be proper: (a) that requested by the government, namely, that the "test is whether there was a conscious purpose to avoid enlightenment"; (b) that requested by the defendant, namely, that there must be "proof that the defendant knew the substance she was carrying was cocaine"; or (c) that given by the court, namely, that it must be shown the defendant "was aware of the fact that he was committing some kind of wrong, or some sort of crime—not necessarily the crime of bringing in cocaine itself."

SECTION 2. INTENT

STATE v. ROCKER

Supreme Court of Hawaii, 1970.

52 Hawai'i 336, 475 P.2d 684.

RICHARDSON, CHIEF JUSTICE.

Defendants-appellants, having waived a jury trial, were tried in the circuit court of the second circuit and found guilty as charged for violation of HRS § 727–1 for creating a common nuisance. The complaint read: "That Richard Barry Rocker and Joseph Cava [defendants] at Puu Olai, Makena, District of Makawao, County of Maui, State of Hawaii, on the 26th day of February, 1969, did openly sun bathe in the nude, which was offensive and against common decency or common morality, thereby committing the offense of common nuisance, contrary to the provisions of Section 727–1 of the Hawaii Revised Statutes."

It is undisputed that on February 26, 1969, police officers of the Maui Police Department received a phone call from an anonymous person and, thereafter, on the day of the call, proceeded to the Puu Olai beach at Makena to look for nude sunbathers. On reaching their destination, the police surveyed the beach from a ridge using both their naked eyes and binoculars and saw the defendants lying on the beach completely nude, one on his stomach and the other on his back. The officers then approached the defendants and arrested them for indecent exposure. It was admitted by the police officers that defendants were not at any time engaged in any activity other than sunbathing. At the time of the arrest there were several other people on the beach where the defendants were nude. Defendant Rocker was nude at the Puu Olai beach on other days before and after he was arrested on February 26, 1969. Defendant Cava likewise frequently sunbathed in the nude at the same beach prior to his arrest on February 26, 1969. * * *

HRS § 727–1, unlike statutes of most states, incorporates indecent exposure as an example of what the legislature has defined to constitute common nuisances.[a] The statute does not specifically delineate the elements of the crime of indecent exposure, and although reference to the common law or to cases decided in other jurisdictions based upon statutes different from ours may be helpful, neither is controlling.[1] The question of whether sunbathing in the nude on a public beach is punishable as a common nuisance is one of construction of our statute. * * *

Sunbathing in the nude is not per se illegal. It must be coupled with the intent to indecently expose oneself. Intent is an element of the crime of common nuisance defined by HRS § 727–1. The intent necessary is a general intent, not a specific intent; *i.e.,* it is not necessary that the exposure be made with the intent that some particular person see it, but only that the exposure was made where it was likely to be observed by others. Thus, the intent may be inferred from the conduct of the accused and the circumstances and environment of the occurrence. The criminal intent necessary for a conviction of indecent exposure is usually established by some action by which the defendant either (1) draws attention to his exposed condition or (2) by a display in a place so public that it must be presumed it was intended to be seen by others.

The defendants argue that there is no circumstantial evidence in the record from which a trier of fact could conclude that the element of intent had been proved beyond a reasonable doubt. The issue, therefore, is whether defendants' nude sunbathing at Puu Olai beach at Makena, Maui, was at a place so *public* that a trier of fact could infer it was intended to be seen by others. The prosecution offered testimony of one of the arresting

---

a. The statute reads as follows:

"The offense of common nuisance is the endangering of the public personal safety or health, or doing, causing or promoting, maintaining or continuing what is offensive, or annoying and vexatious, or plainly hurtful to the public; or is a public outrage against common decency or common morality; or tends plainly and directly to the corruption of the morals, honesty, and good habits of the people; the same being without authority or justification by law: *what Rocker is charged with*

"As for example: * * *

"Open lewdness or lascivious behavior, or indecent exposure; * * *"

1. It should be noted that the Hawaii Penal Code (Proposed Draft) 1970 adopts the American Law Insti-

tute Model Penal Code classification and definition of indecent exposure. It is classified as a sexual offense and is defined as follows:

(1) A person commits the offense of indecent exposure if, with intent to arouse or gratify sexual desire of himself or of any person, he exposes his genitals to a person to whom he is not married under circumstances in which he knows his conduct is likely to cause affront or alarm.

(2) Indecent exposure is a petty misdemeanor.

See Hawaii Penal Code (Proposed Draft) 1970, Chapter 7, Part V, Section 738.

This classification and definition of the crime of indecent exposure takes it out of the realm of common nuisances and makes it a specific sexual offense.

police officers that the beach was a popular location for fishermen and was in fact one of his favorite fishing spots. Defendants testified that the public in general used the beach, that it was used by fishermen and local residents, and that they observed between 20 and 25 people on the beach over a two-month period. Although the Puu Olai beach is isolated by a hill and a ledge, away from the view of the public road and adjoining beaches, it is accessible by a well-worn path and known to be a favorite location of fishermen to cast and throw fish nets. In view of this and other evidence in the record, we cannot agree with defendants' argument that the trier of fact could not find the beach so public as to justify an inference of intent on the part of defendants to be seen by others. * * *

The third issue raised on this appeal is whether the trial court erred in denying the defendants' motion for judgment of acquittal at the end of the prosecution's case. * * *

At the close of the prosecution's case it had been established that the defendants were seen by two police officers sunbathing in the nude at Puu Olai beach, a beach isolated by a hill and a ledge but accessible by a well worn path. One of the officers testified that the beach was a popular location for fishermen and was in fact one of his favorite fishing spots. From these facts the trial judge ruled that a prima facie case had been established and denied the defendants' motion for acquittal. We affirm this ruling. There was sufficient evidence at the close of the prosecution's case to justify an inference beyond a reasonable doubt that the Puu Olai beach was so public that the defendants could be attributed with the necessary knowledge to know that their acts under the circumstances were likely to offend members of the general public. * * *

Affirmed.

LEVINSON, JUSTICE (dissenting).

I dissent because I think that the evidence adduced by the government at the close of the prosecution's case was insufficient to sustain a conviction of either defendant. The trial judge erroneously denied the defendants' motion for acquittal made at that time. My view of the role that the motion for acquittal plays in the criminal process leads me to conclude that in reviewing a denial of such a motion, the appellate court should consider only the record as it existed when the motion was made. The majority opinion appears to concur in this view. * * *

My reading of the majority opinion leads me to conclude that in order to prove a prima facie case against the defendants it was necessary for the prosecution to demonstrate that the defendants possessed a general intent to expose themselves in a place where it would be likely that they would be observed by others. To prove this, it would be enough for the prosecution to establish the defendants' awareness of sufficient facts and circumstances from which a trier of fact could infer such intent beyond a reasonable doubt. From the evidence in the record at the close of the prosecution's case I do not think that a trier of fact could be justified in inferring beyond a reasonable doubt that the defendants possessed the necessary general intent to be seen by others.

Although there was testimony that the beach was visited by fishermen there was no link established between the visits by the fishermen and visits to the beach by the defendants. Officer Matsunaga, one of the fishermen who used the beach, did not testify to ever having observed the defendants on this beach prior to arresting them. Thus, this evidence could not be used to support an inference that the defendants were aware that this beach was used by fishermen and therefore public.

Nor could a trier of fact infer beyond a reasonable doubt that the defendants were aware of the "well-worn" path leading over the hill to the beach and therefore knew that they were sunbathing in an area readily accessible to the public. One of the police officers testified that the beach was accessible by another trail which was *not* "well-used." There was no other evidence that would eliminate as a reasonable doubt the possibility that the defendants had used this other path and therefore inferred from its unused nature that the public would not be likely to see them. The majority opinion does not mention this possibility in assessing the adequacy of the prosecution's case. In failing to prove that the defendants were aware of the visits of the fishermen or the well-worn path I believe the State failed to prove beyond a reasonable doubt defendants' awareness of facts sufficient to establish a general intent to be seen by others. * * *

Notes and Questions

1. There is some disagreement as to what ought to be encompassed within the term "intent." Compare J.W.C. Turner, *The Mental Element in Crimes at Common Law,* 6 Camb.L.J. 31, 39 (1938) (" 'Intention' describes the state of mind of the man who not only foresaw, but also desired the possible consequences of his conduct"); with Frank J. Remington & Orrin L. Helstad, *The Mental Element in Crime—A Legislative Problem,* 1952 Wis.L.Rev. 644, 675 ("As to the meaning of intent, the word usually is identified with desire, but in the final analysis it means no more than that the person who intends something knows or believes that it is certain to result from his conduct"). How is the word being used in *Rocker* ? Which definition is preferable?[a]

2. How would the defendants have fared under the proposed statute set out in footnote 1 of *Rocker* ? Cf. *In re Smith,* 7 Cal.3d 362, 102 Cal.Rptr. 335, 497 P.2d 807 (1972), reversing the defendant's conviction for "willfully and lewdly" exposing the private parts of his body. The defendant had fallen asleep while sunbathing in the nude on a public but then vacant beach, but when he awakened several other persons were present. The court concluded there was "no doubt" that the defendant had " 'willfully'—i.e., intentionally— expose[d] himself," but that it was not shown he had done so lewdly, which the court concluded "requires proof beyond a reasonable doubt that the actor not only meant to expose himself, but intended by his conduct to direct public attention to his genitals for purposes of sexual arousal, gratification, or affront." (In *State v. Bull,* 61 Hawai'i 62, 597 P.2d 10 (1979), the court stated that the California statute so construed in *Smith* was "thus placed in the same category" as the statute quoted in footnote 1 of *Rocker.*)

3. The Hawaii indecent exposure statute was later revised to read: "A person commits the offense of indecent exposure if, the person intentionally exposes the person's genitals to a person to whom the person is not married under circumstances in which the actor's conduct is likely to cause affront." How would the *Rocker* defendants have fared under this version of the statute?

Consider *State v. Kalama,* 94 Hawai'i 60, 8 P.3d 1224 (2000), where defendant was prosecuted under that statute for nude sunbathing at an "isolated and desolate" and "unimproved" park where "there was nobody there but six nude sunbathers and the police," though in the past "people had made complaints to the police and had asked the police to watch the area." It was stipulated that defendant's exposure of his genitals to

---

a. See *Model Penal Code* § 2.02(2)(a). The Comment thereto (1985) states: "In defining the kinds of culpability, the Code draws a narrow distinction between acting purposely and knowingly, one of the elements of ambiguity in legal usage of intent. Knowledge that the requisite external circumstances exist is a common element in both conceptions. But action is not purposive with respect to the nature or the result of the actor's conduct unless it was his conscious object to perform an action of that nature or to cause such a result. * * *

"It is true, of course, that this distinction is inconsequential for most purposes of liability; acting knowingly is ordinarily sufficient. But there are areas where the discrimination is required and is made under traditional law, which uses the awkward concept of 'specific intent.' "

fellow sunbathers was not "likely to cause affront," but the court convicted defendant nonetheless on the theory "that other persons who could have been in the area would have been affronted." On appeal, the court rejected the state's contention, grounded in *Rocker*, "that a general intent 'that exposure was made where it was likely to be observed by others' suffices," noting that as a consequence of the state's adoption of the Model Penal Code approach "arguments concerning specific and general intent are no longer relevant." [See Note 3 infra.] Rather, the appellate court concluded, the case was governed by two statutory provisions, one declaring that when "the definition of an offense specifies the state of mind sufficient for the commission of that offense, without distinguishing among the elements thereof, the specified state of mind shall apply to all elements of the offense, unless a contrary purpose plainly appears," and the other defining the "intentional" state of mind as follows:

(a) A person acts intentionally with respect to his conduct when it is his conscious object to engage in such conduct.

(b) A person acts intentionally with respect to attendant circumstances when he is aware of the existence of such circumstances or believes or hopes that they exist.

(c) A person acts intentionally with respect to a result of his conduct when it is his conscious object to cause such a result.

NOTES AND QUESTIONS ON MOTIVE AND ON CRIMINAL, CONSTRUCTIVE, GENERAL, SPECIFIC, CONDITIONAL AND MULTIPLE INTENT

1. *Motive.* What is the difference between "intent" and "motive"? It has been said that when *A* kills *B* in order to obtain *B*'s money, *A*'s intent was to kill and his motive was to get the money.[a] This suggests intent is limited to one's purpose to commit the proscribed act, and that all inquiries into why one did the proscribed act are concerned with motive.[b] If this is so, then if *A* breaks into *B*'s house to get *B*'s money, it must be said that the intent was to break and enter and the motive was to get the money. But the better view is that this is not so; rather, the question of why *A* broke into *B*'s home is a matter of intent (the so-called "special intent" required for the crime of burglary) rather than motive. This suggests that intent relates to the means and motive to the ends, but that where the end is the means to yet another end, then the medial end may also be considered in terms of intent.[c] Thus, when *A* breaks into *B*'s house in order to get money to pay his debts, it is appropriate to characterize his purpose to take the money as his intent and the desire to pay his debts as the motive. Under this definition, it may be said that motive is not relevant in substantive criminal law[d] except as circumstantial evidence tending to show that defendant committed the crime.[e]

2. *"Criminal" and "constructive" intent.* The phrase "criminal intent" is often taken to be synonymous with *mens rea*, the general notion that except for strict liability offenses some form of mental state is a prerequisite to guilt. As a result, that phrase is sometimes

a. Walter Wheeler Cook, *Act, Intention, and Motive in the Criminal Law*, 26 Yale L.J. 645, 660 (1917).

b. This view has sometimes been taken; see John William Salmond, *Jurisprudence* § 134 (John Parker ed. 9th ed. 1937).

c. See Glanville Williams, *Criminal Law: The General Part* 48 (2d ed. 1961).

d. See, e.g., *United States v. Pomponio*, 429 U.S. 10, 97 S.Ct. 22, 50 L.Ed.2d 12 (1976), holding that the term "willful" in the statute prohibiting the wilful filing of a false income tax return requires only an intent to violate a known legal duty and that consequently the trial judge did not err in instructing that "[g]ood motive alone is never a defense where the act done or omitted is a crime" and that motive was thus irrelevant except as it bore on intent.

e. See, e.g., *State v. Powell*, 126 Wash.2d 244, 893 P.2d 615 (1995), holding evidence of defendant's hostile relationship with his wife was admissible in his prosecution for murdering his spouse.

used to refer to criminal negligence or recklessness. Similarly, the notion of "constructive intent" has been used by some courts; it is first asserted that intent is required for all crimes, and then it is added that such intent may be inferred from recklessness or negligence. It would make for clearer analysis if courts would merely acknowledge that for some crimes intent is not needed and that recklessness or negligence will suffice.

3. *"General" and "specific" intent.* The cases often distinguish "general" from "specific" intent, although the distinction being drawn by the use of these two terms often varies. Sometimes "general intent" is used in the same way as "criminal intent." Or, "general intent" may be used to encompass all forms of the mental state requirement, while "specific intent" is limited to the one mental state of intent. Another possibility is that "general intent" will be used to characterize an intent to do something on an undetermined occasion, and "specific intent" to denote an intent to do that thing at a particular time and place.

But the most common usage of "specific intent" is to designate a special mental element which is required above and beyond any mental state required with respect to the *actus reus* of the crime. Common law larceny, for example, requires the taking and carrying away of the property of another, and the defendant's mental state as to this act must be established, but in addition it must be shown that there was an "intent to steal" the property. Similarly, common law burglary requires a breaking and entry into the dwelling of another, but in addition to the mental state connected with these acts it must also be established that the defendant acted "with intent to commit a felony therein." The same situation prevails with many statutory crimes, such as assault "with intent to kill" or kidnaping "for the purpose of ransom or reward." Although this distinction between "general" and "specific" intent has not been without importance in the criminal law,[f] greater clarity may be accomplished by abandoning this terminology, and this has been done in the Model Penal Code[g] and in many of the modern recodifications.

4. *"Conditional" and "multiple" intent.* In *Holloway v. United States*, 526 U.S. 1, 119 S.Ct. 966, 143 L.Ed.2d 1 (1999), petitioner was charged with carjacking, defined in 18 U.S.C. § 2119 as "tak[ing] a motor vehicle * * * from * * * another by force and violence or by intimidation" "with the intent to cause death or serious bodily harm." He was convicted by a jury charged that the statute's intent element could be satisfied by a conditional intent, that is, by an intent to cause death or serious bodily harm only if the alleged victims refused to turn over their cars. The Supreme Court, per Stevens, J., in concluding that the instruction squared with "a common-sense reading of the carjacking statute," reasoned that "it is reasonable to presume that Congress was familiar with the cases and the scholarly writing that have recognized that the 'specific intent' to commit a wrongful act may be conditional. The facts of the leading case on the point are strikingly similar to the facts of this case. In *People v. Connors,* 253 Ill. 266, 97 N.E. 643 (1912), the Illinois Supreme Court affirmed the conviction of a union organizer who had pointed a gun at a worker and threatened to kill him forthwith if he did not take off his overalls and quit work. The Court held that the jury had been properly instructed that the 'specific intent to kill' could be found even though that intent was 'coupled with a condition' that the defendant would not fire if the victim complied with his demand. That holding has been

---

f. As we shall see, the traditional view was that the rules on when mistake of fact or mistake of law are a defense differ depending upon what kind of intent is involved. Also, some courts have taken the view that intent may be presumed (i.e., a person is "presumed to intend the natural and probable consequences of his acts") only as to a general intent.

g. *Model Penal Code* § 2.02, Comments (Tent.Draft No. 4, 1955): "[W]e can see no virtue in preserving the concept of 'general intent,' which has been an abiding source of ambiguity and of confusion in the penal law."

repeatedly cited with approval by other courts and by scholars. Moreover, it reflects the views endorsed by the authors of the Model [Penal] Code [in § 2.02(6)]. The core principle that emerges from these sources is that a defendant may not negate a proscribed intent by requiring the victim to comply with a condition the defendant has no right to impose; '[a]n intent to kill, in the alternative, is nevertheless an intent to kill.'

"This interpretation of the statute's specific intent element does not, as petitioner suggests, render superfluous the statute's 'by force and violence or by intimidation' element. While an empty threat, or intimidating bluff, would be sufficient to satisfy the latter element, such conduct, standing on its own, is not enough to satisfy § 2119's specific intent element.[13] In a carjacking case in which the driver surrendered or otherwise lost control over his car without the defendant attempting to inflict, or actually inflicting, serious bodily harm, Congress' inclusion of the intent element requires the Government to prove beyond a reasonable doubt that the defendant would have at least attempted to seriously harm or kill the driver if that action had been necessary to complete the taking of the car."

Scalia, J., dissenting, objected "that in customary English usage the unqualified word 'intent' does not usually connote a purpose that is subject to any conditions precedent except those so remote in the speaker's estimation as to be effectively nonexistent—and it never connotes a purpose that is subject to a condition which the speaker hopes will not occur," which "is [the] sort of 'conditional intent' that is at issue in this case." Thomas, J., dissenting, objected that while "there is some authority to support [the] view that the specific intent to commit an act may be conditional," "that authority does not demonstrate that such a usage was part of a well-established historical tradition. Absent a more settled tradition, it cannot be presumed that Congress was familiar with this usage when it enacted the statute."

Are *Connors* and *Hairston* really distinguishable? May they be explained on the ground that in *Hairston* the evidence "is insufficient to support an inference of an actual intent to kill," while in *Connors* "there was enough to support the inference that the defendants actually had homicide in mind"?[h] Does the approach taken in *Model Penal Code* § 2.02(6) help?

What should the result be in the following situations? (a) Hamil has been charged with attempted rape, which requires proof that he intended to have carnal knowledge of a female against her will by means of force. He grabbed a young woman into his car and then parked the car against a building to prevent her from opening the door. He pulled off some of her clothes and said that if she was a virgin he would let her go, but if she was not he was going to have intercourse with her. She said she was a virgin and the defendant thereafter said she was "nothing but a virgin and no good." He then started the car and pulled away, at which the girl jumped out of the car.[i]

(b) Kinnemore has been charged with assault with intent to kill. He was apprehended by department store security personnel for shoplifting. After he was taken to an office, he

---

13. In somewhat different contexts, courts have held that a threat to harm does not in itself constitute intent to harm or kill. In *Hairston v. State*, 54 Miss. 689 (1877), for example, the defendant in an angry and profane manner threatened to shoot a person if that person stopped the defendant's mules. The court affirmed the defendant's conviction for assault, but reversed a conviction of assault with intent to commit murder, explaining that "we have found no case of a conviction of assault with intent to kill or murder,

upon proof only of the levelling of a gun or pistol." * * *

h. Rollin M. Perkins & Ronald N. Boyce, *Criminal Law* 647 (3d ed. 1982).

i. See *People v. Hamil*, 20 Ill.App.3d 901, 314 N.E.2d 251 (1974), affirming the conviction on the ground that "the defendant's actions, both before and after his equivocal statement about the victim's virginity, bespeak his intent much louder than his words alone."

grabbed a female store employee around the neck and placed a scissors to her neck and stated that he would kill her if the others did not allow him to leave. At that point other store personnel intervened and disarmed him without any injury to his hostage.[j]

(c) Simonson has been charged with receiving stolen property, which requires proof that he knew the property was stolen and that he intended to deprive the owner of his property. Simonson bought tools worth $800 for $60 shortly after they had been stolen, and he then contacted the company from which they had been stolen and negotiated a reward of $125 for return of the tools. He was arrested before the exchange occurred.[k]

Sometimes a person may act with two or more intentions, in which case, so long as he had the intention required by the definition of the crime, it is immaterial that he also had some other intention as well. Illustrative is *O'Neal v. United States,* 240 F.2d 700 (10th Cir.1957), affirming defendant's conviction of a Mann Act violation where he transported a female interstate with the intent to have her work as a waitress in the day and as a prostitute at night; the court held the purpose of prostitution need not be the sole purpose of the trip.

FORD v. STATE

Maryland Court of Appeals, 1993.
330 Md. 682, 625 A.2d 984.

Chasanow, Judge.

In the early morning hours of May 27, 1990, petitioner, Maurice Edward Ford, and three other youths stood on or next to the Capital Beltway and hurled large landscaping rocks at vehicles travelling on the Beltway. A number of people in the vehicles were injured and significant damage was done to many vehicles. Ford was apprehended on June 2, 1990, and a ninety count indictment ultimately charged him with assault with intent to murder (eight counts), assault with intent to maim (one count), assault with intent to disable (twenty-eight counts), assault and battery (twenty-nine counts), and malicious destruction of property (twenty-four counts). A Prince George's County Circuit Court jury found Ford guilty of one count of assault with intent to maim, eleven counts of assault with intent to disable, seventeen counts of assault and battery, six counts of assault, fourteen counts of malicious destruction of property which the jury found to have value of $300 or more, and three counts of malicious destruction of property of value less than $300. The circuit court, Missouri, J., imposed sentences totalling thirty-nine years with additional prison terms suspended in favor of five years probation to commence upon Ford's release.

Ford appealed to the Court of Special Appeals, which reversed and remanded for resentencing on two of the malicious destruction of property counts worth less than $300, but otherwise affirmed all of the convictions. Upon his petition to this Court, we granted certiorari to consider issues relating to his remaining convictions. We find no error and affirm Ford's convictions. * * *

j. *State v. Kinnemore,* 34 Ohio App.2d 39, 295 N.E.2d 680 (1972), reversing the conviction, and noting that "the exclamation tends to show that its objective was escape—not murder. The threat was conditional, whereas an assault coupled with a present intent to kill necessarily involves continuous, sequential, and uninterrupted conduct. The state was required to prove that Kinnemore intended to kill Miss Frazier at the time of the assault, but the evidence upon this issue, which consists entirely of the exclamation of the defendant at the time of the assault, is not sufficient to sustain an essential element of the crime beyond a reasonable doubt."

k. *State v. Simonson,* 298 Minn. 235, 214 N.W.2d 679 (1974), affirming the conviction, as "with reference to the matter of intent, we believe that the rule should be that one who receives or conceals what he knows to be stolen property with the intent to restore it to the owner only if the owner pays a reward does have the requisite wrongful intent."

We now address an important, albeit somewhat collateral, issue that the Court of Special Appeals addressed in the instant case. At trial, the judge also instructed the jury on the common law doctrine of transferred intent that this Court approved in *Gladden v. State*, 273 Md. 383, 330 A.2d 176 (1974). The theory of transferred intent as explicated in *Gladden* is that " 'the state of mind which one has when about to commit a crime upon one person is considered by law to exist and to be equally applicable although the intended act affects another person.' " The judge instructed the jury that if it found Ford assaulted with intent to disable the drivers, this intent could be transferred to the passengers. Ford never objected to this instruction and, in light of our conclusion above that the evidence sufficiently supported a jury determination that Ford intended to disable both drivers and passengers in the vehicles, we decline to find the unobjected to instruction was reversible error under the plain error doctrine. Nonetheless, the Court of Special Appeals addressed at some length the issue of transferred intent. Because of the need to clarify the inapplicability of transferred intent to assault with intent to disable and related crimes, we believe it is necessary to comment upon the intermediate appellate court's discussion. The Court of Special Appeals held that the doctrine of transferred intent did not apply to the crimes with which Ford was charged. For two reasons, we believe the Court of Special Appeals was correct that transferred intent does not apply to § 386 offenses. We acknowledge that one of these reasons may be inconsistent with prior indications by this Court that transferred intent applies to attempted murder and assault with intent to murder.

Although it is clear that the doctrine of transferred intent applies to both general and specific intent crimes, the Court of Special Appeals correctly perceived that there are two types of specific intent crimes and that transferred intent may apply to only one of these types. "The first type of specific intent crimes are those that require a specific intent to cause a specific type of harm.... The second type are those which, by statutory definition, require a specific intent to cause a specific type of harm *to a specific person.* ..." (emphasis in original). We have previously indicated that transferred intent does not apply to the latter class, namely those statutory offenses which require that the defendant's criminal intent be directed towards the actual victim. *State v. Wilson*, 313 Md. 600, 606 & n. 3, 546 A.2d 1041, 1044 & n. 3 (1988). Section 386, at issue here, is of this latter type; under § 386, it is a crime to "assault or beat any person, with intent to maim, disfigure or disable *such person* ... " (Emphasis added). Professor Perkins illustrates this type of statute with an old Kentucky law which provided that " 'if any person shall wilfully and maliciously shoot at and wound another with an intention to kill him,' "he has committed a felony. * * *. The analogy could not be more direct; the plain statutory language of § 386 precludes the application of transferred intent.

Apart from these statutory grounds, the application of transferred intent to the crime of assault with intent to disable is also precluded by the underlying nature of the crime. It is a fundamental tenet of criminal law that a completed crime requires the concurrence of a *mens rea*, a guilty mind, and an *actus reus*, a bad act. The purpose of transferred intent is to link the mental state directed towards an intended victim, i.e., the intent to kill, maim, or disable that person, with the actual harm caused to another person. In effect, transferred intent makes a whole crime out of two component halves.

Any discussion of transferred intent in Maryland must focus on *Gladden v. State*, supra, in which this Court recognized the continuing viability of transferred intent. *Gladden* traced transferred intent back to its English common law heritage and the early cases it cited support the view that the doctrine was intended to enable conviction of a defendant of the crime he intended to commit *only when that crime was not committed upon the intended victim.* * * *

The underlying rationale for the doctrine also suggests that transferred intent should apply only when, without the doctrine, the defendant could not be convicted of the crime at issue because the mental and physical elements do not concur as to either the intended or the actual victim. As Dean Prosser notes, "[t]he early criminal cases were understandably preoccupied with mens rea, moral guilt, and the obvious fact that if the defendant was not convicted there would be no one to punish for the crime."

Thus, transferred intent makes a whole crime out of two halves by joining the intent as to one victim with the harm caused to another victim. Transferred intent does not make two crimes out of one. Where the crime intended has actually been committed against the intended victim, transferred intent is unnecessary and should not be applied to acts against unintended victims. * * *

* * * Because the elements of an assault with intent to disable are (1) an assault and (2) an intent to disable, the crime is complete regardless of whether the projectile reaches its target. The requisite intent has already been formed and the requisite assault has already been committed; no intent need be transferred to complete a crime.

We realize that this conclusion seems at odds with our holding in *State v. Wilson*, in which we applied transferred intent to the crime of attempted murder. In *Wilson*, the defendants, two brothers, became involved in a dispute with one Marvin Brown. Brown fled after the Wilsons threatened to pistol-whip him. Both Wilsons then drew handguns and fired multiple shots towards Brown, who managed to avoid the bullets. One of the shots hit and injured Juan Kent, an innocent bystander. This Court affirmed the defendants' attempted murder convictions for both victims, invoking the transferred intent doctrine to uphold the attempted murder of Kent, the bystander.

We believe *Wilson* should not have applied transferred intent to attempted murder. First, as we have noted, the purpose of transferred intent is not to multiply criminal liability, but to prevent a defendant who has committed all the elements of a crime (albeit not upon the same victim) from escaping responsibility for that crime. If the defendant charged with attempted murder, shot at but missed the intended victim, the defendant may still be convicted of attempted murder of that victim. The completed crime has been committed on the intended victim, and the fiction of transferred intent would not so much transfer the intent as replicate it and apply it to another victim, thus making multiple specific intent crimes from one single act intended to injure one person. * * *

A related reason why transferred intent cannot properly apply to attempted murder derives from the fact that the crime of attempted murder requires no physical injury to the victim. Although in *Wilson* the bystander was in fact injured, injury is not an essential element of attempted murder. Assuming an attempted murder scenario where the defendant fires a shot at an intended victim and no bystanders are physically injured, one sees that it is virtually impossible to decide to whom the defendant's intent should be transferred. Is the intent to murder transferred to everyone in proximity to the path of the bullet? Is the intent transferred to everyone frightened and thereby assaulted by the shot? There is no rational method for deciding how the defendant's intent to murder should be transferred.[14]

The result in *Wilson* can best be explained and justified by distinguishing between transferred intent and what is essentially concurrent intent. Although transferred intent should not have been invoked to convict the Wilsons of attempted murder of the bystander

---

14. We note that refusal to apply transferred intent to attempted murder by no means relieves a defendant of criminal liability for the harm caused to unintended victims. The defendant clearly can be convicted of attempted murder as to the primary victim and some other crime, such as criminal battery, as to other victims. * * *

because the crime of attempted murder was already complete as to the primary victim, the convictions could have been properly upheld on the basis of such concurrent intent. We elaborate.

In transferred intent, the intended harm does not occur to the intended victim, but occurs instead to a second unintended victim. The actual result is an unintended, unanticipated consequence of intended harm. For example, consider a defendant who shoots a single bullet at the head of A, standing with B and C. If the defendant misses A and instead kills B, the defendant's intent to murder A will be transferred to allow his conviction for B's murder. The intent is concurrent, on the other hand, when the nature and scope of the attack, while directed at a primary victim, are such that we can conclude the perpetrator intended to ensure harm to the primary victim by harming everyone in that victim's vicinity. For example, an assailant who places a bomb on a commercial airplane intending to harm a primary target on board ensures by this method of attack that all passengers will be killed. Similarly, consider a defendant who intends to kill A and, in order to ensure A's death, drives by a group consisting of A, B, and C, and attacks the group with automatic weapon fire or an explosive device devastating enough to kill everyone in the group. The defendant has intentionally created a "kill zone" to ensure the death of his primary victim, and the trier of fact may reasonably infer from the method employed an intent to kill others concurrent with the intent to kill the primary victim. When the defendant escalated his mode of attack from a single bullet aimed at A's head to a hail of bullets or an explosive device, the factfinder can infer that, whether or not the defendant succeeded in killing A, the defendant concurrently intended to kill everyone in A's immediate vicinity to ensure A's death. The defendant's intent need not be transferred from A to B, because although the defendant's goal was to kill A, his intent to kill B was also direct; it was concurrent with his intent to kill A. Where the means employed to commit the crime against a primary victim create a zone of harm around that victim, the factfinder can reasonably infer that the defendant intended that harm to all who are in the anticipated zone.* * *

In *Wilson*, then, the jury could have found from the nature of the attack an intent to murder Kent concurrent with the intent to murder Brown. Where the Wilsons specifically intended to kill Brown, and attempted to do so by firing multiple bullets from two handguns, they could have intended a "kill zone" around Brown akin to the automatic weapon or explosive attack described above. The factfinder could conclude that the Wilsons intended to kill everyone in the direct path of their bullets. Kent, the bystander victim, was obviously in the Wilsons' direct line of fire and the evidence permitted finding concurrent intent to kill everyone in the path of the bullets. In essence, we still believe Wilson reached the right result, although we no longer adopt its explanation. There was sufficient evidence to support convictions for the attempted murders of both Brown and Kent, but not via transferred intent theory. The sufficiency of the evidence should be based instead on the inference of a concurrent intent to murder the bystander Kent that could be drawn from the multiple shots fired towards both victims. * * *

McAuliffe, Judge, concurring. * * *

Other courts have taken a different view of the applicability of the doctrine of transferred intent where both the intended and unintended victims were injured or killed. In *State v. Worlock*, 117 N.J. 596, 569 A.2d 1314 (1990), the Supreme Court of New Jersey rejected the defendant's argument that it should follow the rationale of the California courts relied upon by the majority here. The court said:

When a defendant contemplates or designs the death of another, the purpose of deterrence is better served by holding that defendant responsible for the knowing or purposeful murder of the unintended as well as the intended victim. Hence, we reject defendant's argument that the successful killing of the intended victim prevents the 'transfer' of that intent to an unintended victim.

* * *

The Court's newly announced limitation on the doctrine of transferred intent is likely to present some interesting problems. Assume, for example, that the defendant, intending to kill *A*, shoots and wounds him, but the bullet passes through *A* and kills *B*. Under the Court's theory, I assume the defendant would be guilty of the murder of *B*, although also guilty of attempted murder or assault with intent to murder *A*. If *A* had also died, the Court would hold that the defendant could not be convicted of the murder of *B*, but only of battery, or perhaps manslaughter. What happens, then, if the defendant is convicted of the murder of *B* while *A* is still alive, but *A* dies of wounds received in the assault within a year and a day of the shooting?

In my judgment, the Court goes too far in its attempt to limit the utilization of the doctrine of transferred intent in criminal cases. * * *

Notes and Questions

1. *Ford* does not question application of the transferred intent doctrine to obtain a murder conviction in *Gladden*, a "bad aim" case in which the bullet missed the intended victim and hit and killed another person. But consider *State v. Gardner*, 57 Del. 588, 203 A.2d 77 (1964), which, though in accord with *Gladden*, asserts that "the purely logical view is that *A*, the killer, should be charged with an attempt [requiring intent to kill] to murder *B*, his intended victim, and manslaughter [requiring recklessness] of *C*, his real victim."

2. What then of a "good aim/bad luck" case, where the bullet passed through the intended victim, who survives, and strikes and kills a bystander. Can the defendant be convicted of attempted murder of the former and murder of the latter? That situation arose in *Poe v. State*, 341 Md. 523, 671 A.2d 501 (1996), where the court concluded:

"Petitioner tries to unduly stretch our holding in *Ford* that the doctrine of transferred intent is inapplicable to attempted murder. We reject Poe's argument that because he completed the crime of attempted murder of his intended victim, the doctrine of transferred intent does not apply to the death of another person. In *Ford*, we made clear that if a defendant intends to kill a specific victim and instead wounds an unintended victim without killing either, the defendant can be convicted only of the attempted murder of the intended victim and transferred intent does not apply. This is not true where, as in the case sub judice, the defendant intends to murder one victim and instead kills an unintended victim. Here, transferred intent applies because there is a death and the doctrine is necessary to impose criminal liability for the murder of the unintended victim in addition to the attempted murder of the intended victim. See *Ruffin v. United States*, 642 A.2d 1288, 1294–95 (D.C.App.1994) (discussing *Ford* and upholding the conviction of defendant for first degree murder of unintended victim under the doctrine of transferred intent where defendant only wounded intended victim). In *Ford*, this Court asserted that the doctrine is used when the defendant fails to commit the crime intended upon the targeted victim and completes it upon another. Thus, the doctrine should be applied to the instant case."

SMALLWOOD v. STATE

Maryland Court of Appeals, 1996.
343 Md. 97, 680 A.2d 512.

MURPHY, CHIEF JUDGE.

In this case, we examine the use of circumstantial evidence to infer that a defendant possessed the intent to kill needed for a conviction of attempted murder or assault with intent to murder. We conclude that such an inference is not supportable under the facts of this case.

On August 29, 1991, Dwight Ralph Smallwood was diagnosed as being infected with the Human Immunodeficiency Virus (HIV). According to medical records from the Prince George's County Detention Center, he had been informed of his HIV-positive status by September 25, 1991. In February 1992, a social worker made Smallwood aware of the necessity of practicing "safe sex" in order to avoid transmitting the virus to his sexual partners, and in July 1993, Smallwood told health care providers at Children's Hospital that he had only one sexual partner and that they always used condoms. Smallwood again tested positive for HIV in February and March of 1994.

On September 26, 1993, Smallwood and an accomplice robbed a woman at gunpoint, and forced her into a grove of trees where each man alternately placed a gun to her head while the other one raped her. On September 28, 1993, Smallwood and an accomplice robbed a second woman at gunpoint and took her to a secluded location, where Smallwood inserted his penis into her with "slight penetration." On September 30, 1993, Smallwood and an accomplice robbed yet a third woman, also at gunpoint, and took her to a local school where she was forced to perform oral sex on Smallwood and was raped by him. In each of these episodes, Smallwood threatened to kill his victims if they did not cooperate or to return and shoot them if they reported his crimes. Smallwood did not wear a condom during any of these criminal episodes.

Based upon his attack on September 28, 1993, Smallwood was charged with, among other crimes, attempted first-degree rape, robbery with a deadly weapon, assault with intent to murder, and reckless endangerment. In separate indictments, Smallwood was also charged with the attempted second-degree murder of each of his three victims. On October 11, 1994, Smallwood pled guilty in the Circuit Court for Prince George's County to attempted first-degree rape and robbery with a deadly weapon. The circuit court also convicted Smallwood of assault with intent to murder and reckless endangerment based upon his September 28, 1993 attack, and convicted Smallwood of all three counts of attempted second-degree murder.

Following his conviction, Smallwood was sentenced to concurrent sentences of life imprisonment for attempted rape, twenty years imprisonment for robbery with a deadly weapon, thirty years imprisonment for assault with intent to murder, and five years imprisonment for reckless endangerment. The circuit court also imposed a concurrent thirty-year sentence for each of the three counts of attempted second-degree murder. The circuit court's judgments were affirmed in part and reversed in part by the Court of Special Appeals[, which] found that the evidence was sufficient for the trial court to conclude that Smallwood intended to kill his victims and upheld all of his convictions. Upon Smallwood's petition, we granted certiorari to consider whether the trial court could properly conclude that Smallwood possessed the requisite intent to support his convictions of attempted second-degree murder and assault with intent to murder.

Smallwood asserts that the trial court lacked sufficient evidence to support its conclusion that Smallwood intended to kill his three victims. Smallwood argues that the fact that he engaged in unprotected sexual intercourse, even though he knew that he carried HIV, is insufficient to infer an intent to kill. The most that can reasonably be inferred, Smallwood contends, is that he is guilty of recklessly endangering his victims by exposing them to the risk that they would become infected themselves. The State disagrees, arguing that the facts of this case are sufficient to infer an intent to kill. The State likens Smallwood's HIV-positive status to a deadly weapon and argues that engaging in unprotected sex when one is knowingly infected with HIV is equivalent to firing a loaded firearm at that person.

In *Faya v. Almaraz*, 329 Md. 435, 438–440, 620 A.2d 327 (1993), we discussed HIV and the Acquired Immune Deficiency Syndrome (AIDS) in detail. There, we described HIV as a retrovirus that attacks the human immune system, weakening it, and ultimately destroying the body's capacity to ward off disease. We also noted that

> [t]he virus may reside latently in the body for periods as long as ten years or more, during which time the infected person will manifest no symptoms of illness and function normally. HIV typically spreads via genital fluids or blood transmitted from one person to another through sexual contact, the sharing of needles in intravenous drug use, blood transfusions, infiltration into wounds, or from mother to child during pregnancy or birth.

In *Faya*, we also described AIDS and its relationship to HIV:

> AIDS, in turn, is the condition that eventually results from an immune system gravely impaired by HIV. Medical studies have indicated that most people who carry the virus will progress to AIDS. AIDS patients by definition are profoundly immunocompromised; that is, they are prone to any number of diseases and opportunistic infections that a person with a healthy immune system might otherwise resist. AIDS is thus the acute clinical phase of immune dysfunction.... AIDS is invariably fatal.

In this case, we must determine what legal inferences may be drawn when an individual infected with the HIV virus knowingly exposes another to the risk of HIV-infection, and the resulting risk of death by AIDS.

As we have previously stated, "[t]he required intent in the crimes of assault with intent to murder and attempted murder is the specific intent to murder, i.e., the specific intent to kill under circumstances that would not legally justify or excuse the killing or mitigate it to manslaughter." Smallwood has not argued that his actions were performed under mitigating circumstances or that he was legally justified in attacking the three women. He was properly found guilty of attempted murder and assault with intent to murder only if there was sufficient evidence from which the trier of fact could reasonably have concluded that Smallwood possessed a specific intent to kill at the time he assaulted each of the three women.

To evaluate the sufficiency of the evidence in a non-jury trial, we must review the case on both the law and the evidence. In making this inquiry, we will not set aside the trial court's findings of fact unless they are clearly erroneous. We must determine "whether the evidence shows directly or supports a rational inference of the facts to be proved, from which the trier of fact could fairly be convinced beyond a reasonable doubt of the defendant's guilt of the offense charged."

An intent to kill may be proved by circumstantial evidence. "[S]ince intent is subjective and, without the cooperation of the accused, cannot be directly and objectively proven, its presence must be shown by established facts which permit a proper inference of its existence." Therefore, the trier of fact may infer the existence of the required intent from surrounding circumstances such as "the accused's acts, conduct and words." *State v. Raines*, 326 Md. 582, 591, 606 A.2d 265 (1992). As we have repeatedly stated, "under the proper circumstances, an intent to kill may be inferred from the use of a deadly weapon directed at a vital part of the human body."

In *Raines*, supra, we upheld the use of such an inference. In that case, Raines and a friend were traveling on a highway when the defendant fired a pistol into the driver's side window of a tractor trailer in an adjacent lane .. The shot killed the driver of the tractor trailer, and Raines was convicted of first degree murder. The evidence in the case showed that Raines shot at the driver's window of the truck, knowing that the truck driver was immediately behind the window. We concluded that "Raines's actions in directing the gun at the window, and therefore at the driver's head on the other side of the window, permitted an inference that Raines shot the gun with the intent to kill."

The State argues that our analysis in Raines rested upon two elements: (1) Raines knew that his weapon was deadly, and (2) Raines knew that he was firing it at someone's head. The State argues that Smallwood similarly knew that HIV infection ultimately leads to death, and that he knew that he would be exposing his victims to the risk of HIV transmission by engaging in unprotected sex with them. Therefore, the State argues, a permissible inference can be drawn that Smallwood intended to kill each of his three victims. The State's analysis, however, ignores several factors.

First, we must consider the magnitude of the risk to which the victim is knowingly exposed. The inference drawn in *Raines* rests upon the rule that "[i]t is permissible to infer that 'one intends the natural and probable consequences of his act.'" Before an intent to kill may be inferred based solely upon the defendant's exposure of a victim to a risk of death, it must be shown that the victim's death would have been a natural and probable result of the defendant's conduct. It is for this reason that a trier of fact may infer that a defendant possessed an intent to kill when firing a deadly weapon at a vital part of the human body. When a deadly weapon has been fired at a vital part of a victim's body, the risk of killing the victim is so high that it becomes reasonable to assume that the defendant intended the victim to die as a natural and probable consequence of the defendant's actions.

Death by AIDS is clearly one natural possible consequence of exposing someone to a risk of HIV infection, even on a single occasion. It is less clear that death by AIDS from that single exposure is a sufficiently probable result to provide the sole support for an inference that the person causing the exposure intended to kill the person who was exposed. While the risk to which Smallwood exposed his victims when he forced them to engage in unprotected sexual activity must not be minimized, the State has presented no evidence from which it can reasonably be concluded that death by AIDS is a probable result of Smallwood's actions to the same extent that death is the probable result of firing a deadly weapon at a vital part of someone's body. Without such evidence, it cannot fairly be concluded that death by AIDS was sufficiently probable to support an inference that Smallwood intended to kill his victims in the absence of other evidence indicative of an intent to kill.

In this case, we find no additional evidence from which to infer an intent to kill. Smallwood's actions are wholly explained by an intent to commit rape and armed robbery, the crimes for which he has already pled guilty. For this reason, his actions fail to provide evidence that he also had an intent to kill. As one commentator noted, in discussing a criminal case involving similar circumstances, "[b]ecause virus transmission occurs simultaneously with the act of rape, that act alone would not provide evidence of intent to transmit the virus. Some additional evidence, such as an explicit statement, would be necessary to demonstrate the actor's specific intent." Smallwood's knowledge of his HIV-infected status provides the only evidence in this case supporting a conclusion that he intended anything beyond the rapes and robberies for which he has been convicted.

The cases cited by the State demonstrate the sort of additional evidence needed to support an inference that Smallwood intended to kill his victims. The defendants in these cases have either made explicit statements demonstrating an intent to infect their victims or have taken specific actions demonstrating such an intent and tending to exclude other possible intents. In *State v. Hinkhouse*, 139 Or.App. 446, 912 P.2d 921 (1996), for example, the defendant engaged in unprotected sex with a number of women while knowing that he was HIV positive. The defendant had also actively concealed his HIV-positive status from these women, had lied to several of them by stating that he was not HIV-positive, and had refused the women's requests that he wear condoms. There was also evidence that he had told at least one of his sexual partners that "if he were [HIV-]positive, he would spread the virus to other people." The Oregon Court of Appeals found this evidence to be sufficient to demonstrate an intent to kill, and upheld the defendant's convictions for attempted murder. * * *

The evidence in *State v. Haines*, 545 N.E.2d 834 (Ind.App.1989), contained both statements by the defendant demonstrating intent and actions solely explainable as attempts to spread HIV. There, the defendant's convictions for attempted murder were upheld where the defendant slashed his wrists and sprayed blood from them on a police officer and two paramedics, splashing blood in their faces and eyes. Haines attempted to scratch and bite them and attempted to force blood-soaked objects into their faces. During this altercation, the defendant told the officer that he should be left to die because he had AIDS, that he wanted to "give it to him," and that he would "use his wounds" to spray the officer with blood. Haines also "repeatedly yelled that he had AIDS, that he could not deal with it and that he was going to make [the officer] deal with it." * * * *[4]

In contrast with these cases, the State in this case would allow the trier of fact to infer an intent to kill based solely upon the fact that Smallwood exposed his victims to the risk that they might contract HIV. Without evidence showing that such a result is sufficiently probable to support this inference, we conclude that Smallwood's convictions for attempted murder and assault with intent to murder must be reversed.

Notes and Questions

1. Compare Note, 27 U.Balt.L.Rev. 251, 277–78 (1977): "Due to the arguably spontaneous nature of rape, it may seem reasonable to imagine a person not having the specific intent to kill by committing a single act of AIDS rape. However, this was not the case with Smallwood. Smallwood raped three women on three separate occasions. It would certainly be reasonable to construe these three separate acts as the result of a contemplated, deliberate motive.

"The fact finder may consider the surrounding circumstances of the events when inferring the element of intent. However, this does not require the fact finder to view the events as if they took place in isolation. Therefore, in light of both what reasonable persons

---

4. * * * In *Commonwealth v. Brown*, 413 Pa.Super. 421, 605 A.2d 429 (1992), the defendant was convicted of aggravated assault after throwing a cup of his fecal matter into the face and mouth of a prison guard. The defendant had been diagnosed as carrying HIV and Hepatitis B and had been informed by them of the means by which these two viruses may be transmitted. The inmate testified that he intended to punish the prison guard for "messing with [his] mail." The Pennsylvania Superior Court found this evidence to be suffi-cient to demonstrate an intent to cause serious bodily injury. Although this issue was not discussed by the Pennsylvania court, Brown also dealt with the possible transmission of two distinct viruses, Hepatitis B and HIV, and therefore with a correspondingly higher probability that the defendant's actions would cause the victim to become infected with at least one of them. An increased probability of infection would strengthen the inferences that could be drawn from the defendant's knowingly exposing his victim to the risk of infection.

commonly understand about the AIDS virus and Smallwood's three separately occasioned, deliberate acts, it was reasonable for the trial judge to conclude that Smallwood possessed the specific intent to kill his victims by exposing them to the AIDS virus."

2.   Consider also Note, 106 Yale L.J. 1617, 1619–20 (1997), concluding that *Smallwood* "reached the only legally proper result"; that "the inference that Smallwood acted with reckless indifference as to whether his victims contracted HIV is a much stronger and more reasonable inference," so that "he can be convicted of reckless endangerment," which "is typically a misdemeanor"; but that "Smallwood's crime of knowingly exposing his rape victims to the risk of contracting HIV should [be] treat[ed] more seriously than a misdemeanor."

3.   "At least 25 states have passed laws that make it illegal to knowingly transmit or expose another to HIV. This legislation is aimed at reducing the spread of HIV/AIDS by penalizing certain conduct. However, using the criminal law to decrease HIV/AIDS transmission may hinder public health efforts to encourage voluntary testing, early treatment, and education. Since actual knowledge is an essential element of the crime under HIV statutes, individuals may avoid testing in order to avoid having the requisite mental state at a later prosecution. * * *

"Defendants who are unable to avoid prosecution by lack of knowledge face a variety of penalties depending on jurisdiction. A defendant who transmits HIV/AIDS is guilty of a misdemeanor in Alabama and Florida, but the same conduct is punishable in Louisiana with a possible ten-year prison sentence with hard labor and a maximum of $5,000. This disparity in sentencing makes the legislative approach to criminalizing HIV transmission appear unfair." Lori A. David, *The Legal Ramifications in Criminal Law of Knowingly Transmitting AIDS,* 19 Law & Psych.Rev. 259, 269–70 (1995).

4.   Questions as to when the defendant's intent may be inferred from the circumstances often arise when the charge is burglary, for the crime of burglary as typically defined by statute requires that the defendant have had an intent to commit a crime therein at the time of his entry of the premises. Especially when no crime occurs thereafter, there may be some question as to whether the specific criminal purpose alleged has been sufficiently proven. Consider:

(a) In *Justice v. State*, 530 N.E.2d 295 (Ind.1988), a young woman was awakened at 2:45 a.m. at the sound of a crashing noise, after which she saw a man standing in the hallway outside her room. He walked into her room and toward her bed. She noticed that he had black socks on his hands. Bryant recognized him as a former friend of her brother and said: "Terry Justice, what are you doing here? I'm Anthony's little sister." Upon hearing this, the man turned around and immediately left the house. In holding the charged burglary with intent to commit theft had not been proved, the court stated: "The State argues the intent to commit theft can be inferred from the evidence that Justice entered the premises illegally, fled when the victim recognized him and covered his hands. We do not agree.

"Intent to commit a felony may not be inferred from proof of breaking and entering alone. Similarly, evidence of flight alone may not be used to infer intent, though other factors, such as the removal of property from the premises, may combine with flight to prove the requisite intent for burglary.

"Evidence of breaking and entering, and evidence of flight are not probative unless tied to some other evidence which is strongly corroborative of the actor's intent. The evidence does not need to be insurmountable, but it must provide 'a solid basis to support a reasonable inference' that the defendant intended to commit the underlying felony. While there is evidence of breaking and entering, and evidence of flight in this case, there is no evidence that Justice touched, disturbed or even approached any valuable property.

"The State asks us to infer that the reason Justice had socks on his hands was because he intended to commit theft. * * *

"While precautions designed to avoid leaving fingerprints point to illegal intent, they do not by themselves establish intent to commit a particular felony."

(b) In *Patterson v. Commonwealth,* 215 Va. 698, 213 S.E.2d 752 (1975), a woman found a man hiding behind the shower door in her bathroom. He had entered at night through the bathroom window while she was wearing only a gown. When she screamed, he fled. She recognized the man as the same person who had trailed her home several weeks earlier. The defendant's conviction on a charge of burglary "with intent to rape" was reversed: "Here, a trier of fact could find an intent to rape only by resorting to surmise and speculation. Neither a spoken word of the defendant nor any other action on his part justifies the inference that he harbored the intent to ravish Mrs. Horton. So far as the evidence shows, the defendant's intent might just as well have been to commit larceny or any of a number of offenses other than rape."

(c) In *Lee v. State,* 489 S.W.2d 61 (Tenn.App.1972), the court quotes a leading treatise as follows: "There is a lack of unanimity of opinion among the courts on the question whether the intent to commit larceny in connection with a burglary charge must be affirmatively shown to exist as distinct from some other offense which might have been intended. Numerous cases, however, hold that an unexplained breaking and entering into a dwelling house in the nighttime is in itself sufficient to sustain a verdict that the breaking and entry was done with the intent to commit larceny rather than some other felony. The fundamental theory, in the absence of evidence of other intent or explanation for breaking and entering, is that the usual object or purpose of burglarizing a dwelling house at night is theft."

SANDSTROM v. MONTANA

Supreme Court of the United States, 1979.

442 U.S. 510, 99 S.Ct. 2450, 61 L.Ed.2d 39.

MR. JUSTICE BRENNAN delivered the opinion of the Court.

The question presented is whether, in a case in which intent is an element of the crime charged, the jury instruction, "the law presumes that a person intends the ordinary consequences of his voluntary acts," violates the Fourteenth Amendment's requirement that the State prove every element of a criminal offense beyond a reasonable doubt.

On November 22, 1976, 18–year–old David Sandstrom confessed to the slaying of Annie Jessen. Based upon the confession and corroborating evidence, petitioner was charged on December 2 with "deliberate homicide," in that he "purposely or knowingly caused the death of Annie Jessen." * * *

The prosecution requested the trial judge to instruct the jury that "[t]he law presumes that a person intends the ordinary consequences of his voluntary acts." Petitioner's counsel objected, arguing that "the instruction has the effect of shifting the burden of proof on the issue of" purpose or knowledge to the defense, and that "that is impermissible under the Federal Constitution, due process of law." He offered to provide a number of federal decisions in support of the objection, including this Court's holding in *Mullaney v. Wilbur,* [p. 264 of this Book], but was told by the judge: "You can give those to the

Supreme Court. The objection is overruled." The instruction was delivered, the jury found petitioner guilty of deliberate homicide, and petitioner was sentenced to 100 years in prison.

Sandstrom appealed to the Supreme Court of Montana, again contending that the instruction shifted to the defendant the burden of disproving an element of the crime charged, in violation of *Mullaney v. Wilbur, supra, In re Winship,* 397 U.S. 358, 90 S.Ct. 1068, 25 L.Ed.2d 368 (1970), and *Patterson v. New York,* [p. 270 of this Book]. The Montana court conceded that these cases did prohibit shifting the burden of proof to the defendant by means of a presumption, but held that the cases "do not prohibit allocation of *some* burden of proof to a defendant under certain circumstances." Since in the court's view, "[d]efendant's sole burden under instruction No. 5 was to produce *some* evidence that he did not intend the ordinary consequences of his voluntary acts, not to disprove that he acted 'purposely' or 'knowingly,' * * * the instruction does not violate due process standards as defined by the United States or Montana Constitution * * *." (emphasis added). * * *

Respondent argues, first, that the instruction merely described a permissive inference—that is, it allowed but did not require the jury to draw conclusions about defendant's intent from his actions—and that such inferences are constitutional. These arguments need not detain us long, for even respondent admits that "it's possible" that the jury believed they were required to apply the presumption. Sandstrom's jurors were told that "[t]he law presumes that a person intends the ordinary consequences of his voluntary acts." They were not told that they had a choice, or that they might infer that conclusion; they were told only that the law presumed it. It is clear that a reasonable juror could easily have viewed such an instruction as mandatory.

In the alternative, respondent urges that, even if viewed as a mandatory presumption rather than as a permissive inference, the presumption did not conclusively establish intent but rather could be rebutted. On this view, the instruction required the jury, if satisfied as to the facts which trigger the presumption, to find intent *unless* the defendant offered evidence to the contrary. Moreover, according to the State, all the defendant had to do to rebut the presumption was produce "some" contrary evidence; he did not have to "prove" that he lacked the required mental state. Thus, "[a]t most, it placed a *burden of production* on the petitioner," but "did not shift to petitioner the *burden of persuasion* with respect to any element of the offense * * *"Again, respondent contends that presumptions with this limited effect pass constitutional muster. * * *

The Supreme Court of Montana is, of course, the final authority on the legal weight to be given a presumption under Montana law, but it is not the final authority on the interpretation which a jury could have given the instruction. If Montana intended its presumption to have only the effect described by its Supreme Court, then we are convinced that a reasonable juror could well have been misled by the instruction given, and could have believed that the presumption was not limited to requiring the defendant to satisfy only a burden of production. Petitioner's jury was told that "*[t]he law presumes* that a person intends the ordinary consequences of his voluntary acts." They were not told that the presumption could be rebutted, as the Montana Supreme Court held, by the defendant's simple presentation of "some" evidence; nor even that it could be rebutted at all. Given the common definition of "presume" as "to suppose to be true without proof," Webster's New Collegiate Dictionary 911 (1974), and given the lack of qualifying instructions as to the legal effect of the presumption, we cannot discount the possibility that the jury may have interpreted the instruction in either of two more stringent ways.

First, a reasonable jury could well have interpreted the presumption as "conclusive," that is, not technically as a presumption at all, but rather as an irrebuttable direction by the court to find intent once convinced of the facts triggering the presumption. Alternatively, the jury may have interpreted the instruction as a direction to find intent upon proof of the defendant's voluntary actions (and their "ordinary" consequences), unless *the defendant* proved the contrary by some quantum of proof which may well have been considerably greater than "some" evidence—thus effectively shifting the burden of persuasion on the element of intent. * * *

In *Winship,* this Court stated:

"Lest there remain any doubt about the constitutional stature of the reasonable-doubt standard, we explicitly hold that the Due Process Clause protects the accused against conviction except upon proof beyond a reasonable doubt *of every fact* necessary to constitute the crime with which he is charged." (emphasis added).

The petitioner here was charged with and convicted of deliberate homicide, committed purposely or knowingly. It is clear that under Montana law, whether the crime was committed purposely or knowingly is a fact necessary to constitute the crime of deliberate homicide. Indeed, it was the lone element of the offense at issue in Sandstrom's trial, as he confessed to causing the death of the victim, told the jury that knowledge and purpose were the only questions he was controverting, and introduced evidence solely on those points. Moreover, it is conceded that proof of defendant's "intent" would be sufficient to establish this element. Thus, the question before this Court is whether the challenged jury instruction had the effect of relieving the State of the burden of proof enunciated in *Winship* on the critical question of petitioner's state of mind. We conclude that under either of the two possible interpretations of the instruction set out above, precisely that effect would result, and that the instruction therefore represents constitutional error.

We consider first the validity of a conclusive presumption. This Court has considered such a presumption on at least two prior occasions. In *Morissette v. United States,* 342 U.S. 246, 72 S.Ct. 240, 96 L.Ed. 288 (1952), the defendant was charged with willful and knowing theft of Government property. Although his attorney argued that for his client to be found guilty, " 'the taking must have been with felonious intent'," the trial judge ruled that " '[t]hat is presumed by his own act.' "After first concluding that intent was in fact an element of the crime charged, and after declaring that "[w]here intent of the accused is an ingredient of the crime charged, its existence is * * * a jury issue," *Morissette* held:

"*It follows that the trial court may not withdraw or prejudge the issue by instruction that the law raises a presumption of intent from an act.* It often is tempting to cast in terms of a 'presumption' a conclusion which a court thinks probable from given facts. * * * [But] [w]e think presumptive intent has no place in this case. *A conclusive presumption which testimony could not overthrow would effectively eliminate intent as an ingredient of the offense.* A presumption which would permit but not require the jury to assume intent from an isolated fact would prejudge a conclusion which the jury should reach of its own volition. A presumption which would permit the jury to make an assumption which all the evidence considered together does not logically establish would give to a proven fact an artificial and fictional effect. In either case, *this presumption would conflict with the overriding presumption of innocence with which the law endows the accused and which extends to every element of the crime.*" (Emphasis added; footnote omitted.)

Just last Term, in *United States v. United States Gypsum Co.,* 438 U.S. 422, 98 S.Ct. 2864, 57 L.Ed.2d 854 (1978), we reaffirmed the holding of *Morissette.* In that case defendants, who were charged with criminal violations of the Sherman Act, challenged the following jury instruction:

"The law presumes that a person intends the necessary and natural consequences of his acts. Therefore, if the effect of the exchanges of pricing information was to raise, fix, maintain and stabilize prices, then the parties to them are presumed, as a matter of law, to have intended that result."

After again determining that the offense included the element of intent, we held:

"[A] defendant's state of mind or *intent is an element of a criminal antitrust offense which * * * cannot be taken from the trier of fact through reliance on a legal presumption* of wrongful intent from proof of an effect on prices. Cf. *Morissette v. United States* * * *.

* * *

"Although an effect on prices may well support an inference that the defendant had knowledge of the probability of such a consequence at the time he acted, the jury must remain free to consider additional evidence before accepting or rejecting the inference. * * * [U]ltimately the decision on the issue of intent must be left to the trier of fact alone. The instruction given invaded this factfinding function." (emphasis added).

As in *Morissette* and *United States Gypsum Co.,* a conclusive presumption in this case would "conflict with the overriding presumption of innocence with which the law endows the accused and which extends to every element of the crime," and would "invade [the] factfinding function" which in a criminal case the law assigns solely to the jury. The instruction announced to David Sandstrom's jury may well have had exactly these consequences. Upon finding proof of one element of the crime (causing death), and of facts insufficient to establish the second (the voluntariness and "ordinary consequences" of defendant's action), Sandstrom's jurors could reasonably have concluded that they were directed to find against defendant on the element of intent. The State was thus not forced to prove "beyond a reasonable doubt * * * every fact necessary to constitute the crime * * * charged," and defendant was deprived of his constitutional rights as explicated in *Winship.*

A presumption which, although not conclusive, had the effect of shifting the burden of persuasion to the defendant, would have suffered from similar infirmities. If Sandstrom's jury interpreted the presumption in that manner, it could have concluded that upon proof by the State of the slaying, and of additional facts not themselves establishing the element of intent, the burden was shifted to the defendant to prove that he lacked the requisite mental state. Such a presumption was found constitutionally deficient in *Mullaney v. Wilbur.* In *Mullaney,* the charge was murder, which under Maine law required proof not only of intent but of malice. The trial court charged the jury that " 'malice aforethought is an essential and indispensable element of the crime of murder.' "However, it also instructed that if the prosecution established that the homicide was both intentional and unlawful, malice aforethought was to be implied unless the defendant proved by a fair preponderance of the evidence that he acted in the heat of passion on sudden provocation. As we recounted just two Terms ago in *Patterson v. New York,* "[t]his Court * * * unanimously agreed with the Court of Appeals that Wilbur's due process rights had been invaded by the presumption casting upon him the burden of proving by a preponderance of the evidence that he had acted in the heat of passion upon sudden provocation." And *Patterson* reaffirmed that "a State must prove every ingredient of an offense beyond a reasonable doubt, and * * * may not shift the burden of proof to the defendant" by means of such a presumption.

Because David Sandstrom's jury may have interpreted the judge's instruction as constituting either a burden-shifting presumption like that in *Mullaney,* or a conclusive presumption like those in *Morissette* and *United States Gypsum Co.,* and because either interpretation would have deprived defendant of his right to the due process of law, we hold the instruction given in this case unconstitutional.

Notes and Questions

1. In *Francis v. Franklin,* 471 U.S. 307, 105 S.Ct. 1965, 85 L.Ed.2d 344 (1985), the respondent, a state prisoner, while attempting to escape after receiving treatment at a dentist's office, shot and killed the resident of a nearby house with a stolen pistol when, at the moment the resident slammed the door as respondent demanded the key to the resident's car, the pistol fired and a bullet pierced the door, hitting the resident in the chest. At his Georgia trial for malice murder, he claimed the killing was an accident. The trial judge instructed: "The acts of a person of sound mind and discretion are presumed to be the product of a person's will, but the presumption may be rebutted. A person of sound mind and discretion is presumed to intend the natural and probable consequences of his acts, but the presumption may be rebutted. A person will not be presumed to act with criminal intention but the trier of facts * * * may find criminal intention upon a consideration of the words, conduct, demeanor, motive and all of the circumstances connected with the act for which the accused is prosecuted." Though the state supreme court had characterized this as merely a permissive inference and had upheld respondent's murder conviction, the Supreme Court held, 5–4, that this instruction was unconstitutional under *Sandstrom.* Because the "challenged sentences are cast in the language of command," they would be viewed by jurors either as a conclusive presumption or as a burden-shifting rebuttal presumption. The majority also concluded the general instructions on the prosecution's burden of proof and respondent's presumption of innocence did not dissipate the error. Nor, they concluded, did the more specific "criminal intention" instruction, but the four dissenters felt otherwise.

2. Is the Court's conclusion in *Sandstrom* and *Francis* regarding the so-called conclusive presumption correct? Consider Ronald J. Allen & Lee Ann DeGrazia, *The Constitutional Requirement of Proof Beyond a Reasonable Doubt in Criminal Cases: A Comment Upon Incipient Chaos in the Lower Courts,* 20 Am.Crim.L.Rev. 1, 13 (1982): "If the instruction is given in every case of murder, a traditional element of the definition of the crime has been removed. If the instruction accurately describes state law, intent is not included as an element of murder; rather, the state must show only a voluntary act and its ordinary consequences. Alternatively, the instruction may be read to define the crime to require either proof of intent or proof that the defendant's act was voluntary and that the ordinary consequences of that act would be death. In either case, the instruction merely provides an untraditional definition of homicide that foregoes the usual requirement of intent. This involves no burden shifting at all; the issue has simply been removed as an absolute requirement. Consequently, neither alternative should have been objectionable to the Court on the grounds that the reasonable doubt requirement was violated. Montana may very well have defined homicide in an unusual fashion, but under the Court's theory *all* it did was define the crime. Without a constitutional limitation on a state's definition of crime, Montana's statute should have been perfectly acceptable."

3. As we will see in *Patterson v. New York,* p. 270 of this Book, at least when a crime may constitutionally be defined without a particular factual matter being stated as an element, then that matter may be expressed as an affirmative defense and the burden of proof as to it placed on the defendant. Allen & DeGrazia, supra at 13–14, therefore assert that *Sandstrom,* which does not disapprove of *Patterson,* thus "appears to approve of traditionally constructed affirmative defenses, but to regard as constitutionally impermissi-

ble the unorthodox method of creating affirmative defenses through presumptions. This distinction, however, is difficult to support because placing a burden of persuasion on a defendant by a presumption is the functional equivalent of creating an affirmative defense in the conventional manner. * * * To be constitutional, the state need only use the correct words in its statute. If the state makes the mistake of effectively creating an affirmative defense through the use of mandatory presumption language rather than in the manner approved in *Patterson,* then the statute is unacceptable even though there is no functional difference between the two methods."

4. In *Holliday v. State,* 601 N.E.2d 385 (Ind.App.1992), the defendant, relying on *Sandstrom* and *Francis*, objected to an instruction stating: "You may, however, infer that every person intends the natural and probable consequences of his voluntary acts, unless the circumstances are such to indicate the absence of such intent. A determination of the Defendant's intent may be arrived at by the jury from a consideration of the Defendant's conduct and the natural and usual consequences to which such conduct logically and reasonably points." What should the result be?

SECTION 3. KNOWLEDGE

STATE v. BEALE

Supreme Court of Maine, 1973.

299 A.2d 921.

WEATHERBEE, JUSTICE.

The Defendant, who operates an antique shop in Hallowell, was convicted under 17 M.R.S.A. § 3551 of the offense of knowingly concealing stolen property. His appeal presents us for the first time with the opportunity to construe the phrase "knowing it to be stolen" found in this statute.

One Saturday during the summer of 1971, when the Defendant was absent and his store was in Mrs. Beale's care, a prospective customer, a Mrs. Johnson, noticed that some of the displayed merchandise looked familiar. On examining it further she became convinced that several items were in fact pieces of silverware and glass which had been stolen from her several months earlier.

She left and returned after a short interval with a Hallowell police officer. She then pointed out to Mrs. Beale the items which she believed to have been stolen from her. The officer told Mrs. Beale that these items were "possibly stolen" and that they should be placed aside and not displayed or sold. She then gathered these items and put them on a shelf. The officer testified that he told Mrs. Beale to tell her husband to "contact me as soon as he got back". He later testified that he said that she "would be contacted, probably, later on that day".

There was no further contact between the Beales and the police during the weekend. The following Monday morning the investigation was apparently taken over by a deputy sheriff from the county where the theft had occurred. When he called at Defendant's store Defendant informed him that he had put the articles back in the counter for sale Sunday morning and that he had sold many of these items that day in spite of knowing that the police officer had requested that they be withdrawn from sale. Among those which the Defendant said he had sold were all the articles which bore the distinctive initials by which the owner had identified them as hers.

The Defendant testified that he had purchased these items at different times from people whom he considered to be reliable, that he had receipts for many of them and that he was entitled to sell them regardless of the officer's warning. The only testimony as to the details of the complaint by Mrs. Johnson and the officer's admonitions to Mrs. Beale which were in fact related to Mr. Beale was given by Mrs. Beale (called by the State) and the Defendant himself. The Defendant and Mrs. Beale testified that Mrs. Beale told the Defendant that Mrs. Johnson claimed that these items had been stolen from her home, and that the officer had asked Mrs. Beale to put the items aside saying that he would be back later.

[Over defense counsel's objection, the trial court instructed the jury that "knowing" includes the situation in which a reasonable prudent man would be led to believe the items were stolen.]

* * * The issue is one of statutory interpretation of the words "knowing it to be stolen". Did the Legislature intend that the jury be satisfied as to the knowledge of the Defendant by testing it subjectively or objectively? To put it another way, must the State satisfy the jury that the Defendant himself actually had knowledge that the goods were stolen or is it enough that a reasonable person, with the information that was available to the Defendant, would have known that the goods were stolen?

We find a split of authority among the jurisdictions which have had the occasion to examine this issue, with the majority requiring that the State's proof should meet the subjective test. * * *

A minority of jurisdictions apply the so-called objective test as to knowledge, being impressed perhaps, by the difficulties of proof as to the actual state of a defendant's mind. * * *[1]

We consider that the distinction between the bases of the two points of view was clarified by an opinion from the Circuit Court of Appeals, 2nd Circuit, written by Judge Learned Hand. He wrote:

"The defendants ask us to distinguish between 'knowing' that goods are stolen and merely being put upon an inquiry which would have led to discovery; but they have misconceived the distinction which the decisions have made. The receivers of stolen goods almost never 'know' that they have been stolen, in the sense that they could testify to it in a court room. The business could not be so conducted, for those who sell the goods—the 'fences'—must keep up a more respectable front than is generally possible for the thieves. Nor are we to suppose that the thieves will ordinarily admit their theft to the receivers: that would much impair their bargaining power. For this reason, some decisions even go so far as to hold that it is enough, if a reasonable man in the receiver's position would have supposed that the goods were stolen. That we think is wrong; and the better law is otherwise, although of course the fact that a reasonable man would have thought that they had been stolen, is some basis for finding that the accused actually did think so. But that the jury must find that the receiver did more than infer the theft from the circumstances has never been demanded, so far as we know; and to demand more would emasculate the statute, for the evil against which it is directed is exactly that: i.e., making a market for stolen goods which the purchaser believes to have probably been stolen." *United States v. Werner*, 160 F.2d 438, 441–442 (2d Cir.1947). * * *

---

1. In some states the statutes define the offense as being committed by one who knows or who has reason-able cause to believe that the property received had been stolen.

It appears to us that the minority jurisdictions which follow the "ordinary reasonable man" test are failing to stress sufficiently the distinction between civil and criminal responsibility. In civil cases the failure of the defendant to act with the degree of care which a person of ordinary prudence would have used may be the test of his responsibility without any determination that the defendant, himself, was a person of ordinary prudence or that he had any wrongful intent. On the other hand, the very essence of this criminal offense is the intentional wrongdoing of the defendant.

Such was the case at common law and if the Legislature had intended something less than actual knowledge, more appropriate language could easily have been chosen.

The distinction is more than one of semantics. It is made necessary by the fact that while a defendant may have received information which would have convinced a person of ordinary intelligence and average capacity to comprehend and evaluate facts, a defendant may be a person of less than average intelligence, comprehension and reasoning powers. The true test is, did the *defendant* know the goods were stolen.

This is not to say that the defendant must have direct knowledge or positive proof that the goods were stolen, such as he would have gained by actually witnessing the theft or hearing the admission of the thief. It is enough if he was made aware of circumstances which caused him to believe that they were stolen.

The fact that the jury must be satisfied as to the state of the defendant's personal belief does not present the State with an insurmountable task when direct proof of his belief is absent. Juries have been instructed from time immemorial as to other offenses that they may draw rational inferences as to intent from a defendant's speech and conduct in relation to the subject matter and from evidence showing the information of which a defendant was aware. The state of a defendant's belief may be resolved by inference in the same manner.

While the objective test of what an ordinary intelligent man would have believed cannot serve as the absolute standard which determines the defendant's guilt or innocence, the jury, in making its determination as to the state of a defendant's belief, may properly take into consideration, among other things, the belief which the jury concludes a person of ordinary intellectual capacity would have formed from such facts and circumstances. The jury may consider this in the light of its evaluation of a defendant as an intelligent person, based upon what the jury has learned about the defendant from testimony and observation. * * * Appeal sustained. Remanded for new trial.

Notes and Questions

1. In *People v. Prante,* 177 Colo. 243, 493 P.2d 1083 (1972), the defendant was convicted of the crime of assaulting a police officer, defined by statute as requiring that a defendant "knew or reasonably should have known that the person assaulted was a peace officer engaged in the performance of his duties." On appeal, the defendant claimed that this language was (i) void for vagueness, and (ii) not a sufficient standard for criminal guilt. The court responded:

"The statute under consideration here states clearly the behavior sought to be proscribed. In a statute so framed as to clearly put before the public notice of what is prohibited, those who risk violation and seek escape through an exceptional fact situation are not protected by the Fourteenth Amendment * * *.

"In situations where it is difficult to determine what an actor knows or knew, there can be no better appraisal of it than for a jury to educe what a temperate and measured man would know in the same circumstances. Indeed, this is the function of the jury at any rate whether statutorily delegated or not. And framing a statute in such a way as to give this function to the jury is not arbitrary or unreasonable."

2. Compare *State v. Ware,* 27 Ariz.App. 645, 557 P.2d 1077 (1976), where defendant was convicted of the sale of stolen property. The statute provided the defendant must have dealt with the property while "knowing or having reason to believe the property was stolen." In response to defendant's assertion that this language rendered the statute unconstitutional, the court stated:

"We hold that [the statute] requires a finding and proof that the defendant *himself* possessed actual knowledge or belief that the goods he retained were stolen. We reject the 'reasonable man' approach which attempts to integrate the civil negligence standard into the criminal law, primarily for the reason that implementation of this test would allow juries to return guilty verdicts against those who may be less circumspect and intelligent than the average man. * * *

"No legislative history has been presented by counsel as to the specific reason why the phrase 'having reason to believe' was added to the statute when it was amended in 1969 to raise the monetary amount from \$50 to \$100, differentiating a felony from a misdemeanor. In light of our holding regarding the impropriety of a 'reasonable man standard', it is our view that the language added in 1969 * * * merely codified the law in Arizona as set down by the Arizona Supreme Court in *Reser v. State* [27 Ariz. 43, 229 P. 936 (1924), adopting the subjective test]. Change in statutory language is presumed to be a change in form only, unless it is clearly shown that the Legislature intended to change the meaning of the law."

3. *State v. Jantzi,* 56 Or.App. 57, 641 P.2d 62 (1982): "The trial court stated for the record at the close of the evidence that it believed defendant's version of what occurred in the incident from which this charge arose. Defendant testified that he was asked to accompany Diane Anderson, who shared a house with defendant and several other people, to the home of her estranged husband, Rex. While Diane was in the house talking with Rex, defendant was using the blade of his knife to let the air out of the tires on Rex's van. Another person put sugar in the gas tank of the van.

"While the Andersons were arguing, Diane apparently threatened damage to Rex's van and indicated that someone might be tampering with the van at that moment. Rex's roommate ran out of the house and saw two men beside the van. He shouted and began to run toward the men. Rex ran from the house and began to chase defendant, who ran down a bicycle path. Defendant, still holding his open knife, jumped into the bushes beside the path and landed in the weeds. He crouched there, hoping that Rex would not see him and would pass by. Rex, however, jumped on top of defendant and grabbed his shirt. They rolled over and Rex was stabbed in the abdomen by defendant's knife. Defendant could not remember making a thrusting or swinging motion with the knife; he did not intend to stab Rex.

"The indictment charged that defendant 'did unlawfully and knowingly cause physical injury to Rex Anderson by means of a deadly weapon, to-wit: knife, by stabbing the said Rex Anderson with said knife.' ORS 163.175 provides that:

'(1) A person commits the crime of assault in the second degree if he:
' * * *

'(b) Intentionally or knowingly causes physical injury to another by means of a deadly or dangerous weapon;
' * * *

'Knowingly' is defined in ORS 161.085(8):

' "Knowingly" or "with knowledge" when used with respect to conduct or to a circumstance described by a statute defining an offense, means that a person acts with an awareness that his conduct is of a nature so described or that a circumstance so described exists.'[1]

The trial court stated:

> 'Basically, the facts of this case are: that Defendant was letting air out of the tires and he has an open knife. He was aware of what his knife is like. He is aware that it is a dangerous weapon. He runs up the bicycle path. He has a very firm grip on the knife, by his own admission, and he knows the knife is dangerous. It is not necessary for the state to prove that he thrust it or anything else. Quite frankly, this could have all been avoided if he had gotten rid of the knife, so he "knowingly caused physical injury to Rex Anderson." And, therefore, I find him guilty of that particular charge.'

"Although the trial judge found defendant guilty of 'knowingly' causing physical injury to Anderson, what he described in his findings is recklessness. The court found that defendant knew he had a dangerous weapon and that a confrontation was going to occur. The court believed that defendant did not intend to stab Anderson. The court's conclusion seems to be based on the reasoning that because defendant knew it was possible that an injury would occur, he acted 'knowingly.' However, a person who 'is aware of and consciously disregards a substantial and unjustifiable risk' that an injury will occur acts 'recklessly,' not 'knowingly.' Recklessly causing physical injury to another is assault in the third degree."

UNITED STATES v. JEWELL

United States Court of Appeals, Ninth Circuit, 1976.

532 F.2d 697.

BROWNING, CIRCUIT JUDGE.[a] * * *

It is undisputed that appellant entered the United States driving an automobile in which 110 pounds of marihuana worth $6,250 had been concealed in a secret compartment between the trunk and rear seat. Appellant testified that he did not know the marijuana was present. There was circumstantial evidence from which the jury could infer that appellant had positive knowledge of the presence of the marihuana, and that his contrary testimony was false.[1] On the other hand there was evidence from which the jury could

---

1. The commentary to the Oregon Criminal Code of 1971 (1975 ed.) indicates that the definitions of the culpable mental states set out in ORS 161.085 are derived from the New York Revised Penal Law §§ 15.00–15.05, and that

"[t]he definition of 'knowingly' or 'with knowledge' in subsection (8) was changed by the New York reporters to eliminate any reference to result of conduct and to restrict the term to awareness of the nature of one's conduct or of the existence of specified circumstances (*e.g.*, that property is stolen, that one has no right to enter a building, etc.).

The New York commentary has this to say:

" 'Under the formulations of the Model Penal Code (§ 2.02[2bii]) and the Illinois Criminal Code (§ 4–5[b]), "knowingly" is, in one phase, almost synonymous with "intentionally" in that a person achieves a given result "knowingly" when he "is practically certain" that his conduct will cause that result. This

distinction between "knowingly" and "intentionally" in that context appears highly technical or semantic, and the Revised Penal Law does not employ the word "knowingly" in defining *result* offenses. Murder of the common law variety, for example, is committed *intentionally* or not at all.' (Commentary § 15.05, New York Revised Penal Law)."

a. Joined by 8 other members of the court, which heard the case en banc.

1. Appellant testified that a week before the incident in question he sold his car for $100 to obtain funds "to have a good time." He then rented a car for about $100, and he and a friend drove the rented car to Mexico. Appellant and his friend were unable to adequately explain their whereabouts during the period of about 11 hours between the time they left Los Angeles and the time they admitted arriving in Mexico.

Their testimony regarding acquisition of the load car follows a pattern common in these cases: they were conclude that appellant spoke the truth—that although appellant knew of the presence of the secret compartment and had knowledge of facts indicating that it contained marijuana, he deliberately avoided positive knowledge of the presence of the contraband to avoid responsibility in the event of discovery.[2] If the jury concluded the latter was indeed the situation, and if positive knowledge is required to convict, the jury would have no choice consistent with its oath but to find appellant not guilty even though he deliberately contrived his lack of positive knowledge. Appellant urges this view. The trial court rejected the premise that only positive knowledge would suffice, and properly so.

Appellant tendered an instruction that to return a guilty verdict the jury must find that the defendant knew he was in possession of marihuana. The trial judge rejected the instruction because it suggested that "absolutely, positively, he has to know that it's there." * * *

* * * The court told the jury that the government must prove beyond a reasonable doubt that the defendant "knowingly" brought the marihuana into the United States (count 1: 21 U.S.C. § 952(a)), and that he "knowingly" possessed the marihuana (count 2: 21 U.S.C. § 841(a)(1)). The court continued:

> The Government can complete their burden of proof by proving, beyond a reasonable doubt, that if the defendant was not actually aware that there was marijuana in the vehicle he was driving when he entered the United States his ignorance in that regard was solely and entirely a result of his having made a conscious purpose to disregard the nature of that which was in the vehicle, with a conscious purpose to avoid learning the truth.

The legal premise of these instructions is firmly supported by leading commentators here and in England. Professor Rollin M. Perkins writes, "One with a deliberate antisocial purpose in mind * * * may deliberately 'shut his eyes' to avoid knowing what would otherwise be obvious to view. In such cases, so far as criminal law is concerned, the person acts at his peril in this regard, and is treated as having 'knowledge' of the facts as they are

approached in a Tijuana bar by a stranger who identified himself only by his first name—"Ray." He asked them if they wanted to buy marihuana, and offered to pay them $100 for driving a car north across the border. Appellant accepted the offer and drove the load car back, alone. Appellant's friend drove appellant's rented car back to Los Angeles.

Appellant testified that the stranger instructed him to leave the load car at the address on the car registration slip with the keys in the ashtray. The person living at that address testified that he had sold the car a year earlier and had not seen it since. When the Customs agent asked appellant about the secret compartment in the car, appellant did not deny knowledge of its existence, but stated that it was in the car when he got it.

There were many discrepancies and inconsistencies in the evidence reflecting upon appellant's credibility. Taking the record as a whole, the jury could have concluded that the evidence established an abortive scheme, concocted and carried out by appellant from the beginning, to acquire a load of marihuana in Mexico and return it to Los Angeles for distribution for profit.

2. Both appellant and his companion testified that the stranger identified as "Ray" offered to sell them marihuana and, when they declined, asked if they

wanted to drive a car back to Los Angeles for $100. Appellant's companion "wanted no part of driving the vehicle." He testified, "It didn't sound right to me." Appellant accepted the offer. The Drug Enforcement Administration agent testified that appellant stated "he thought there was probably something wrong and something illegal in the vehicle, but that he checked it over. He looked in the glove box and under the front seat and in the trunk, prior to driving it. *He didn't find anything, and, therefore, he assumed that the people at the border wouldn't find anything either*". (Emphasis added.) Appellant was asked at trial whether he had seen the special compartment when he opened the trunk. He responded, "Well, you know, I saw a void there, but I didn't know what it was." He testified that he did not investigate further. The Customs agent testified that when he opened the trunk and saw the partition he asked appellant "when he had that put in." Appellant told the agent "that it was in the car when he got it."

The jury would have been justified in accepting all of the testimony as true and concluding that although appellant was aware of facts making it virtually certain that the secret compartment concealed marihuana, he deliberately refrained from acquiring positive knowledge of the fact.

ultimately discovered to be."[4] J. Ll. J. Edwards, writing in 1954, introduced a survey of English cases with the statement, "For well-nigh a hundred years, it has been clear from the authorities that a person who deliberately shuts his eyes to an obvious means of knowledge has sufficient *mens rea* for an offence based on such words as * * * 'knowingly.' "[5] Professor Glanville Williams states, on the basis [of] both English and American authorities, "To the requirement of actual knowledge there is one strictly limited exception. * * * [T]he rule is that if a party has his suspicion aroused but then deliberately omits to make further enquiries, because he wishes to remain in ignorance, he is deemed to have knowledge."[6] Professor Williams concludes, "The rule that wilful blindness is equivalent to knowledge is essential, and is found throughout the criminal law."[7]

The substantive justification for the rule is that deliberate ignorance and positive knowledge are equally culpable. The textual justification is that in common understanding one "knows" facts of which he is less than absolutely certain. To act "knowingly," therefore, is not necessarily to act only with positive knowledge, but also to act with an awareness of the high probability of the existence of the fact in question. When such awareness is present, "positive" knowledge is not required.

This is the analysis adopted in [§ 2.02(7) of] the Model Penal Code. * * * As the Comment to this provision explains, "Paragraph (7) deals with the situation British commentators have denominated 'wilful blindness' or 'connivance,' the case of the actor who is aware of the probable existence of a material fact but does not satisfy himself that it does not in fact exist."[9] * * *

Appellant's narrow interpretation of "knowingly" is inconsistent with the Drug Control Act's general purpose to deal more effectively "with the growing menace of drug abuse in the United States." Holding that this term introduces a requirement of positive knowledge would make deliberate ignorance a defense. It cannot be doubted that those who traffic in drugs would make the most of it. This is evident from the number of appellate decisions reflecting conscious avoidance of positive knowledge of the presence of contraband—in the car driven by the defendant or in which he is a passenger, in the suitcase or package he carries, in the parcel concealed in his clothing.

---

4. R. Perkins, *Criminal Law* 776 (2d ed. 1969).

5. Edwards, *The Criminal Degrees of Knowledge*, 17 Modern L.Rev. 294, 298 (1954). * * *

6. G. Williams, *Criminal Law: The General Part*, § 57 at 157 (2d ed.1961).

7. Id. at 159. Mr. Williams' concluding paragraph reads in its entirety:

The rule that wilful blindness is equivalent to knowledge is essential, and is found throughout the criminal law. It is, at the same time, an unstable rule, because judges are apt to forget its very limited scope. A court can properly find wilful blindness only where it can almost be said that the defendant actually knew. He suspected the fact; he realised its probability; but he refrained from obtaining the final confirmation because he wanted in the event to be able to deny knowledge. This, and this alone, is wilful blindness. It requires in effect a finding that the defendant intended to cheat the administration of justice. Any wider definition would make the doctrine of wilful blindness indistinguishable from the civil doctrine of negligence in not obtaining knowledge.

9. *Model Penal Code* 129–30 (Tent.Draft No. 4, 1955). Comment 9 reads in full as follows:

Paragraph (7) deals with the situation British commentators have denominated "wilful blindness" or "connivance," the case of the actor who is aware of the probable existence of a material fact but does not satisfy himself that it does not in fact exist. Whether such cases should be viewed as instances of acting recklessly or knowingly presents a subtle but important question.

The draft proposes that the case be viewed as one of acting knowingly when what is involved is a matter of existing fact, but not when what is involved is the result of the defendant's conduct, necessarily a matter of the future at the time of acting. The position reflects what we believe to be the normal policy of criminal enactments which rest liability on acting "knowingly," as is so commonly done. The inference of "knowledge" of an existing fact is usually drawn from proof of notice of substantial probability of its existence, unless the defendant establishes an honest, contrary belief. The draft solidifies this usual result and clarifies the terms in which the issue is submitted to the jury.

It is no answer to say that in such cases the fact finder may infer positive knowledge. It is probable that many who performed the transportation function, essential to the drug traffic, can truthfully testify that they have no *positive* knowledge of the load they carry. Under appellant's interpretation of the statute, such persons will be convicted only if the fact finder errs in evaluating the credibility of the witness or deliberately disregards the law. * * *

It is worth emphasizing that the required state of mind differs from positive knowledge only so far as necessary to encompass a calculated effort to avoid the sanctions of the statute while violating its substance. "A court can properly find wilful blindness only where it can almost be said that the defendant actually knew." In the language of the instruction in this case, the government must prove, "beyond a reasonable doubt, that if the defendant was not actually aware * * * his ignorance in that regard was *solely* and *entirely* a result of * * * a conscious purpose to avoid learning the truth."[21]

No legitimate interest of an accused is prejudiced by such a standard, and society's interest in a system of criminal law that is enforceable and that imposes sanctions upon all who are equally culpable requires it.

The conviction is affirmed.

ANTHONY M. KENNEDY, CIRCUIT JUDGE, with whom ELY, HUFSTEDLER and WALLACE, CIRCUIT JUDGES, join (dissenting). * * *

One problem with the wilful blindness doctrine is its bias towards visual means of acquiring knowledge. We may know facts from direct impressions of the other senses or by deduction from circumstantial evidence, and such knowledge is nonetheless "actual." Moreover, visual sense impressions do not consistently provide complete certainty.

Another problem is that the English authorities seem to consider wilful blindness a state of mind distinct from, but equally culpable as, "actual" knowledge. When a statute specifically requires knowledge as an element of a crime, however, the substitution of some other state of mind cannot be justified even if the court deems that both are equally blameworthy.

Finally, the wilful blindness doctrine is uncertain in scope. There is disagreement as to whether reckless disregard for the existence of a fact constitutes wilful blindness or some lesser degree of culpability. Some cases have held that a statute's scienter requirement is satisfied by the constructive knowledge imputed to one who simply fails to discharge a duty to inform himself. There is also the question of whether to use an "objective" test based on the reasonable man, or to consider the defendant's subjective belief as dispositive.

The approach adopted in section 2.02(7) of the Model Penal Code clarifies, and, in important ways restricts, the English doctrine. * * *

In light of the Model Penal Code's definition, the "conscious purpose" jury instruction is defective in three respects. First, it fails to mention the requirement that Jewell have been aware of a high probability that a controlled substance was in the car. It is not culpable to form "a conscious purpose to avoid learning the truth" unless one is aware of facts indicating a high probability of that truth. To illustrate, a child given a gift-wrapped

21. We do not suggest that the instruction given in this case was a model in all respects. The jury should have been instructed more directly (1) that the required knowledge is established if the accused is aware of a high probability of the existence of the fact in question, (2) unless he actually believes it does not exist.

The deficiency in the instruction does not require reversal, however. Appellant did not object to the instruction on this ground either below or in this court. Since both of the elements referred to are implied in the instruction, the deficiency in the instructions is not so substantial as to justify reversal for plain error. * * *

package by his mother while on vacation in Mexico may form a conscious purpose to take it home without learning what is inside; yet his state of mind is totally innocent unless he is aware of a high probability that the package contains a controlled substance. Thus, a conscious purpose instruction is only proper when coupled with a requirement that one be aware of a high probability of the truth.

The second defect in the instruction as given is that it did not alert the jury that Jewell could not be convicted if he "actually believed" there was no controlled substance in the car. The failure to emphasize, as does the Model Penal Code, that subjective belief is the determinative factor, may allow a jury to convict on an objective theory of knowledge—that a reasonable man should have inspected the car and would have discovered what was hidden inside. * * *

Third, the jury instruction clearly states that Jewell could have been convicted even if found ignorant or "not actually aware" that the car contained a controlled substance. This is unacceptable because true ignorance, no matter how unreasonable, cannot provide a basis for criminal liability when the statute requires knowledge. A proper jury instruction based on the Model Penal Code would be presented as a way of defining knowledge, and not as an alternative to it. * * *

We do not agree with the majority that we can only reverse if the conscious purpose instruction constituted "plain error." Before the instruction was given, the defense counsel objected "strenuously" on the basis that the jury could convict Jewell for failure to make an adequate attempt to check out the car. When the trial judge rejected this argument, the defense counsel further requested that he "add an addendum" to the charge so the jury would understand it properly. * * *

* * * We believe these objections were sufficient to require reversal on appeal unless the deficiencies in the instruction were harmless error. * * *

Notes and Questions

1. Compare *State v. Nations*, 676 S.W.2d 282 (Mo.App.1984), where defendant was convicted under a statute making punishable one who "knowingly encourages, aids or causes a child less than seventeen years old to engage in any conduct" tending to injure the child's welfare. The evidence was that police found a scantily clad 16–year-old girl dancing for tips in the Main Street Disco, operated by the defendant. The defendant claimed on appeal that the state had failed to prove she knew the girl was under 17. After taking note of *Model Penal Code* § 2.02(7), the court stated:

"Our legislature, however, did not enact this proposed definition of 'knowingly'. Although the definitions of 'knowingly' and 'recklessly' in our Criminal Code are almost identical to the primary definitions of these terms as proposed in the Model Penal Code, *see* Model Penal Code § 2.02(2)(b)–(c) (Proposed Official Draft 1962), the Model Penal Code's proposed expanded definition of 'knowingly', encompassing wilful blindness of a fact, is absent from our Criminal Code. The sensible, if not compelling, inference is that our legislature rejected the expansion of the definition of 'knowingly' to include wilful blindness of a fact and chose to limit the definition of 'knowingly' to actual knowledge of the fact. Thus, in the instant case, the state's burden was to show defendant actually was aware the child was under seventeen, a heavier burden than showing there was a 'high probability' that defendant was aware the child was under seventeen. In short, the state's burden was to prove defendant acted 'knowingly', not just 'recklessly'. The state proved, however, that defendant acted 'recklessly', not 'knowingly'."

2. Compare also *United States v. Bright*, 517 F.2d 584 (2d Cir.1975), where the defendant was convicted of knowing possession of stolen mail. The trial judge instructed:

"You may also find that the defendant had the requisite knowledge if you find that she acted with reckless disregard as to whether the checks were stolen, but with a conscious effort to avoid learning the truth, even though you may find that she was not specifically aware of the fact which would establish the stolen character of the checks." Accepting the definition in *Model Penal Code* 2.02(7) as applicable, the court reversed because the above instruction "was in no way balanced by an instruction that if the jury nevertheless found that 'the defendant actually believed that the bills were not stolen' they should acquit."

3. The federal cases often caution against giving the wilful blindness (or "ostrich") instruction except "in those comparatively rare cases where * * * there are facts that point in the direction of deliberate ignorance," as the "danger of a very liberal use of such an instruction in an inappropriate case is that juries will convict on a basis akin to a standard of negligence." *United States v. Rivera*, 944 F.2d 1563 (11th Cir.1991). Consider in this regard *United States v. Giovannetti*, 919 F.2d 1223 (7th Cir.1990), where Janis was convicted of aiding and abetting an illegal gambling business in that he, himself a gambler, rented his house to persons he knew were professional gamblers "knowing" they would use it as a wireroom. There was no direct evidence of such knowledge, but it was shown he made no inquiries about the use his lessees were going to make of the premises, and the jury was given an "ostrich" instruction. In holding this was not an appropriate case for such an injunction, the court stated:

"The most powerful criticism of the ostrich instruction is, precisely, that its tendency is to allow juries to convict upon a finding of negligence for crimes that require intent. The criticism can be deflected by thinking carefully about just what it is that real ostriches do (or at least are popularly supposed to do). They do not just fail to follow through on their suspicions of bad things. They are not merely careless birds. They bury their heads in the sand so that they will not see or hear bad things. They deliberately avoid acquiring unpleasant knowledge. The ostrich instruction is designed for cases in which there is evidence that the defendant, knowing or strongly suspecting that he is involved in shady dealings, takes steps to make sure that he does not acquire full or exact knowledge of the nature and extent of those dealings. A deliberate effort to avoid guilty knowledge is all the guilty knowledge the law requires. A good example of a case in which the ostrich instruction was properly given is *United States v. Diaz*, 864 F.2d 544, 550 (7th Cir.1988). The defendant, a drug trafficker, sought 'to insulate himself from the actual drug transaction so that he could deny knowledge of it,' which he did sometimes by absenting himself from the scene of the actual delivery and sometimes by pretending to be fussing under the hood of his car.

"The government points out that the rented house in Bridgeview was a short way down a side street from the thoroughfare on which Janis commuted to work daily. It would have been easy for him to drive by the house from time to time to see what was doing, and if he had done so he might have discovered its use as a wireroom. He did not do so. But this is not the active avoidance with which the ostrich doctrine is concerned. It would be if the house had been on the thoroughfare, and Janis, fearful of what he would see if he drove past it, altered his commuting route to avoid it. Janis failed to display curiosity, but he did nothing to prevent the truth from being communicated to him. He did not act to avoid learning the truth.

"The critical question so far as Janis's guilt or innocence was concerned is simple (to pose, not necessarily to answer): what did Janis know? Did he know that he was renting his house for use as a wireroom, or did he believe that he was renting his house to the Orlando crew for some private purpose of theirs unconnected with gambling? (Even criminals have private lives.) The ostrich instruction did not advance this inquiry; it confused it, by pointing the jury to circumstances of deliberate avoidance of knowledge that did not exist. [T]he deliberate effort to avoid guilty knowledge that we said is all the guilty knowledge the law requires can be a mental, as well as a physical, effort—a cutting off of one's normal curiosity by an effort of will. There is no evidence of either sort of effort here."

4. Consider Ira Robbins, *The Ostrich Instruction: Deliberate Ignorance as a Criminal Mens Rea*, 81 J.Crim.L. & Criminology 191, 231–33 (1990): "The Model Penal Code formulation should be rejected as a model for deliberate-ignorance jury instructions. The high-probability/unless standard describes recklessness rather than knowledge, and its adoption by the judiciary instead of the legislature infringes on the legislature's province of defining criminal conduct. Furthermore, it violates the defendant's right to proof beyond a reasonable doubt of each element of the crime charged. Finally, despite the precision of the Model Penal Code language, inadequate statement and application of this standard often leads to conviction for mere negligence. In light of these deficiencies, further manipulation of the definition of knowledge to eliminate the deliberate-ignorance defense must be rejected.

"Statutory revision-the addition of recklessness or specific deliberate-ignorance provisions as a basis of conviction for particular crimes-could simultaneously answer these concerns and effectively limit the deliberate-ignorance defense."

BARNES v. UNITED STATES

Supreme Court of the United States, 1973.

412 U.S. 837, 93 S.Ct. 2357, 37 L.Ed.2d 380.

MR. JUSTICE POWELL delivered the opinion of the Court.

Petitioner Barnes was convicted in United States District Court on two counts of possessing United States Treasury checks stolen from the mails, knowing them to be stolen, two counts of forging the checks, and two counts of uttering the checks, knowing the endorsements to be forged. * * *

The evidence at petitioner's trial established that on June 2, 1971, he opened a checking account using the pseudonym "Clarence Smith." On July 1, and July 3, 1971, the United States Disbursing Office at San Francisco mailed four Government checks in the amounts of $269.02, $154.70, $184, and $268.80 to Nettie Lewis, Albert Young, Arthur Salazar, and Mary Hernandez, respectively. On July 8, 1971, petitioner deposited these four checks into the "Smith" account. Each check bore the apparent endorsement of the payee and a second endorsement by "Clarence Smith."

At petitioner's trial the four payees testified that they had never received, endorsed, or authorized endorsement of the checks. A Government handwriting expert testified that petitioner had made the "Clarence Smith" endorsement on all four checks and that he had signed the payees' names on the Lewis and Hernandez checks. Although petitioner did not take the stand, a postal inspector testified to certain statements made by petitioner at a post-arrest interview. Petitioner explained to the inspector that he received the checks in question from people who sold furniture for him door to door and that the checks had been signed in the payees' names when he received them. Petitioner further stated that he could not name or identify any of the salespeople. Nor could he substantiate the existence of any furniture orders because the salespeople allegedly wrote their orders on scratch paper that had not been retained. Petitioner admitted that he executed the Clarence Smith endorsements and deposited the checks but denied making the payees' endorsements.

The District Court instructed the jury that "[p]ossession of recently stolen property, if not satisfactorily explained, is ordinarily a circumstance from which you may reasonably draw the inference and find, in the light of the surrounding circumstances shown by the evidence in the case, that the person in possession knew the property had been stolen."[33] * * *

The teaching of [our prior] cases is not altogether clear. To the extent that the "rational connection," "more likely than not," and "reasonable doubt" standards bear ambiguous relationships to one another, the ambiguity is traceable in large part to variations in language and focus rather than to differences of substance. What has been established by the cases, however, is at least this: that if a statutory inference submitted to the jury as sufficient to support conviction satisfies the reasonable-doubt standard (that is, the evidence necessary to invoke the inference is sufficient for a rational juror to find the inferred fact beyond a reasonable doubt) as well as the more-likely-than-not standard, then it clearly accords with due process.[a]

In the present case we deal with a traditional common-law inference deeply rooted in our law. * * * This long-standing and consistent judicial approval of the instruction, reflecting accumulated common experience, provides strong indication that the instruction comports with due process.

This impressive historical basis, however, is not in itself sufficient to establish the instruction's constitutionality. Common-law inferences, like their statutory counterparts, must satisfy due process standards in light of present-day experience. In the present case the challenged instruction only permitted the inference of guilt from *unexplained* possession of recently stolen property.[9] The evidence established that petitioner possessed

---

33. The full instruction on the inference arising from possession of stolen property stated:

"Possession of recently stolen property, if not satisfactorily explained is ordinarily a circumstance from which you may reasonably draw the inference and find, in the light of the surrounding circumstances shown by the evidence in the case, that the person in possession knew the property had been stolen.

"However, you are never required to make this inference. It is the exclusive province of the jury to determine whether the facts and circumstances shown by the evidence in this case warrant any inference which the law permits the jury to draw from the possession of recently stolen property.

"The term 'recently' is a relative term, and has no fixed meaning. Whether property may be considered as recently stolen depends upon the nature of the property, and all the facts and circumstances shown by the evidence in the case. The longer the period of time since the theft the more doubtful becomes the inference which may reasonably be drawn from unexplained possession.

"If you should find beyond a reasonable doubt from the evidence in the case that the mail described in the indictment was stolen, and that while recently stolen the contents of said mail here, the four United States Treasury checks, were in the possession of the defendant you would ordinarily be justified in drawing from those facts the inference that the contents were possessed by the accused with knowledge that it was stolen property, unless such possession is explained by

facts and circumstances in this case which are in some way consistent with the defendant's innocence.

"In considering whether possession of recently stolen property has been satisfactorily explained, you are reminded that in the exercise of constitutional rights the accused need not take the witness stand and testify.

"Possession may be satisfactorily explained through other circumstances, other evidence, independent of any testimony of the accused."

a. While *Barnes* thus left open the question of whether all presumptions were to be tested by a beyond a reasonable doubt standard, the Court later decided this was the case as to conclusive presumptions, as we saw in *Sandstrom v. Montana*, p. 135 of this Book, but not as to permissible presumptions, as we shall see in *County Court of Ulster County v. Allen*, p. 236 of this Book, where it was decided that for a permissible presumption it is only necessary that the presumption meet the "rational connection" test, which is met when the presumed fact is more likely than not to flow from the proved fact.

9. Of course, the mere fact that there is some evidence tending to explain a defendant's possession consistent with innocence does not bar instructing the jury on the inference. The jury must weigh the explanation to determine whether it is "satisfactory." The jury is not bound to accept or believe any particular explanation any more than it is bound to accept the correctness of the inference. But the burden of proving beyond a reasonable doubt that the defendant did have knowledge that the property was stolen, an essential element of the crime, remains on the Government.

recently stolen Treasury checks payable to persons he did not know, and it provided no plausible explanation for such possession consistent with innocence. On the basis of this evidence alone common sense and experience tell us that petitioner must have known or been aware of the high probability that the checks were stolen. Such evidence was clearly sufficient to enable the jury to find beyond a reasonable doubt that petitioner knew the checks were stolen. Since the inference thus satisfies the reasonable doubt standard, the most stringent standard the Court has applied in judging permissive criminal law inferences, we conclude that it satisfies the requirements of due process.[11]

Petitioner also argues that the permissive inference in question infringes his privilege against self-incrimination. The Court has twice rejected this argument, and we find no reason to re-examine the issue at length. The trial court specifically instructed the jury that petitioner had a constitutional right not to take the witness stand and that possession could be satisfactorily explained by evidence independent of petitioner's testimony. Introduction of any evidence, direct or circumstantial, tending to implicate the defendant in the alleged crime increases the pressure on him to testify. The mere massing of evidence against a defendant cannot be regarded as a violation of his privilege against self-incrimination.

Petitioner further challenges his conviction on the ground that there was insufficient evidence that he knew the checks were stolen *from the mails*. He contends that 18 U.S.C. § 1708 requires knowledge not only that the checks were stolen, but specifically that they were stolen from the mails. The legislative history of the statute conclusively refutes this argument[14] and the courts of appeals that have addressed the issue have uniformly interpreted the statute to require only knowledge that the property was stolen. * * *

Affirmed.

MR. JUSTICE DOUGLAS, dissenting. * * *

[W]ithout a nexus with the "mails" there is no federal offense. How can we rationally say that "possession" of a stolen check allows a judge or jury to conclude that the accused knew the check was *stolen from the mails?* * * *

[W]e have no evidence whatsoever showing what amount of stolen property, let alone stolen checks, *implicates the mails*. Without some evidence or statistics of that nature we have no way of assessing the likelihood that this petitioner knew that these checks were

---

11. It is true that the practical effect of instructing the jury on the inference arising from unexplained possession of recently stolen property is to shift the burden of going forward with evidence to the defendant. If the Government proves possession and nothing more, this evidence remains unexplained unless the defendant introduces evidence, since ordinarily the Government's evidence will not provide an explanation of his possession consistent with innocence. In *Tot v. United States*, 319 U.S. 463, 63 S.Ct. 1241, 87 L.Ed. 1519 (1943), the Court stated that the burden of going forward may not be freely shifted to the defendant. *Tot* held, however, that where there is a "rational connection" between the facts proved and the fact presumed or inferred, it is permissible to shift the burden of going forward to the defendant. Where an inference satisfies the reasonable-doubt standard, as in the present case, there will certainly be a rational connection between the fact presumed or inferred (in this case, knowledge) and the facts the Government must prove in order to shift the burden of going forward (possession of recently stolen property).

We do not decide today whether a judge-formulated inference of less antiquity or authority may properly be emphasized by a jury instruction.

14. Prior to 1939 the statute required proof of possession of articles stolen from the mail "knowing the same to have been *so* stolen." In 1939 Congress eliminated the word "so" preceding the word "stolen." H.R.Rep. No. 734, 76th Cong., 1st Sess., 1 (1939), explains the change:

"The reported bill amends the existing law so that it will sustain a conviction for the Government to prove that the property was in fact stolen from the mails and that the defendant knew the property he received had been stolen. The committee feel that this should be sufficient without requiring the Government to prove also that the defendant knew the property received had been stolen from the mails." See also S.Rep. No. 864, 76th Cong., 1st Sess. (1939).

stolen from the mails. We can take judicial notice that checks are stolen from the mails. But it would take a large degree of assumed omniscience to say with "substantial assurance" that this petitioner more likely than not knew from the realities of the underworld that this stolen property came *from the mails.* But without evidence of that knowledge there would be no federal offense of the kind charged. * * *

Mr. Justice Brennan, with whom Mr. Justice Marshall joins, dissenting. * * *

We held in *In re Winship,* 397 U.S. 358, 364, 90 S.Ct. 1068, 1073, 25 L.Ed.2d 368 (1970), that the Due Process Clause requires "proof beyond a reasonable doubt of every fact necessary to constitute the crime * * *." Thus, in *Turner v. United States,* 396 U.S. 398, 417, 90 S.Ct. 642, 653, 24 L.Ed.2d 610 (1970), we approved the inference of "knowledge" from the fact of possessing smuggled heroin because " '[c]ommon sense' * * * tells us that those who traffic in heroin will *inevitably* become aware that the product they deal in is smuggled * * *." (Emphasis added.) The basis of that "common sense" judgment was, of course, the indisputable fact that all or virtually all heroin in this country is necessarily smuggled. Here, however, it cannot be said that all or virtually all endorsed United States Treasury checks have been stolen. Indeed, it is neither unlawful nor unusual for people to use such checks as direct payment for goods and services. Thus, unlike *Turner,* "common sense" simply will not permit the inference that the possessor of stolen Treasury checks *"inevitably"* knew that the checks were stolen.

* * * The instruction thereby violated the principle of *Winship* that every essential element of the crime must be proved beyond a reasonable doubt.

Notes and Questions

1. Compare *State v. Attardo,* 263 S.C. 546, 211 S.E.2d 868 (1975), where defendant was convicted under a statute making it a crime to "knowingly" possess a controlled substance. The trial judge instructed the jury that "normally where a person is in possession of contraband, there is a factual presumption that he knows what it is, and the burden is then on him to prove that he did not have actual knowledge." Reversed: "In this case, knowledge, the element in question, *must* be established by the State before the accused has to put forth *any* defenses. Even where the State establishes a prima facie case, the burden of proof in a criminal case does *not* shift but the accused is only required to overcome inferences the State has established. A shifting of the burden of proof would impose a significantly greater onus on the defendant and, even more significantly, it would obliterate the presumption of innocence."

2. In *State v. Keihn,* 542 N.E.2d 963 (Ind.1989), the court, in interpreting the statute defining the offense of driving while under suspension as requiring the state to prove that the defendant had "actual knowledge that his license was suspended," concluded: "We do not find the prosecution's difficulty in showing the defendant's knowledge of his license suspension to be a strong enough consideration to obviate knowledge as a required element of proof. When the Bureau of Motor Vehicles mails notice of license suspension to the defendant's last known address, proof of such notice would allow the trial court to infer a defendant's knowledge."

3. In *People v. Hodogbey,* 306 Ill.App.3d 555, 239 Ill.Dec. 775, 714 N.E.2d 1072 (1999), defendant was convicted of knowingly possessing of heroin. After customs agents found heroin inside a package from Thailand addressed to defendant, a police officer dressed as a mailman made personal delivery of that package to defendant at his apartment, after which the police executed a warrant and found the package therein. In reversing defendant's conviction, the court explained: "At trial, the evidence established

that defendant accepted a package addressed to him. Defendant did not open the package. Neither did he hide the package within his apartment. Rather, he left it, unopened, in the middle of his living room floor as he went about other business. The evidence also established that defendant did not attempt to flee when the officers approached him on the street, nor did he otherwise resist them. In fact, he gave the officers the keys to his apartment, as requested.

"While it is true defendant left his apartment after receiving the package, looked up and down Sheridan Road and then returned inside, that evidence was also insufficient to prove his knowledge of the heroin beyond a reasonable doubt. '[S]uspicious behavior in the vicinity of narcotics will not suffice as proof of knowledge as to their presence.' "

4. In *Whitney v. State*, 726 N.E.2d 823 (Ind.App.2000), defendant was arrested for driving on a suspended license, after which the officer smelled the odor of marijuana in the car and saw in plain view a partially smoked marijuana cigarette on the floor of the driver's compartment. During a search of the vehicle for other contraband, the officer noticed a loose panel above the glove compartment, opened it and discovered a brown paper bag containing marijuana and cocaine. After defendant's conviction for knowing possession of marijuana and knowing possession of cocaine, defendant appealed the latter conviction. Rejecting defendant's claim that because he had borrowed the car he lacked exclusive possession of it, the appellate court then noted that while such "exclusive possession of the car is some evidence from which it might ordinarily be inferred that he was aware of the cocaine," here there was the added factor that "the drugs were hidden in a secret compartment. * * * We find the Fifth Circuit's opinion in *United States v. Richardson*, 848 F.2d 509 (5th Cir.1988) instructive. There, the court held that in hidden compartment cases, knowledge may not be inferred solely from the defendant's control of the vehicle in which the contraband is hidden. * * * Thus, we conclude that additional evidence of guilty knowledge is necessary to establish intent where narcotics are found in a hidden compartment.

"While Whitney's exclusive possession of the vehicle is insufficient to support a conviction, we conclude there is sufficient additional circumstantial evidence from which the trier of fact could reasonably infer that Whitney knew that the marijuana and cocaine were concealed in the vehicle he was driving. During the traffic stop, Officer Benner noticed a marijuana cigarette on the floor of the driver's compartment and he smelled the odor of marijuana. Marijuana and cocaine were found in a secret compartment of the car. Based on Whitney's use of marijuana and the fact that marijuana was found in the secret compartment, the trier of fact could reasonably infer that Whitney knew the drugs were in the vehicle. Furthermore, the panel behind which the drugs were hidden was popped open on one side. This is further circumstantial evidence of Whitney's guilty knowledge."

5. In *State v. Reed*, 125 N.M. 552, 964 P.2d 113 (1998), during a computer check following a traffic stop, the driver gave passenger Reed a pack of cigarettes at his request. The officer thereafter asked them both to empty their pockets, at which Reed removed from his pockets and handed to the officer a cellophane cigarette wrapper and a cigarette pack. The wrapper was later found to have a trace amount of cocaine on its inside surface.[a]

---

a. As the court noted: "A chemist from the State crime laboratory, who was qualified as an expert witness, testified lab tests confirmed that the residue was cocaine, and the amount in the wrapper was so small that he was unable to weigh it without destroying it. He estimated the weight to be approximately two milligrams, which he equated to about five or six grains of salt. To see the trace amount, one would have to turn the wrapper under a good light or a strong flashlight. The chemist opined that at one time the wrapper contained a larger quantity of crack cocaine and that the residue tested had rubbed off or remained in the wrapper after other cocaine had been removed from the wrapper."

Reed was convicted of knowing possession of cocaine, but the conviction was reversed on appeal:

"There was no evidence to indicate Reed knew the wrapper had a white residue in it or that the residue was cocaine. The amount of cocaine in the wrapper was not immediately apparent to the human eye. Reed did not flee or otherwise act in a suspicious manner. Cf. *Sizemore*, 115 N.M. at 757, 858 P.2d at 424 (listing cases permitting inference of guilt from unexplained flight). Durham found no drug paraphernalia or other drugs in the vehicle or on Reed's person. Cf. *State v. Wood*, 117 N.M. 682, 686, 875 P.2d 1113, 1117 (Ct.App.1994) (trace amount of cocaine and drug paraphernalia in defendant's pocket sufficed to prove knowledge that substance was cocaine). Nor was there an admission by Reed that might support an inference of knowledge. Finally, there was no evidence of intoxication or otherwise suspicious behavior by Reed or Taylor. * * *

"The State argues that Reed's possession of a wrapper with cocaine residue inside provides 'corroboration [of Reed's knowledge]' in the same way that finding trace amounts of a controlled substance on other types of drug paraphernalia has been found to corroborate a defendant's knowledge.' Reed counters that a cellophane cigarette wrapper is used to protect the freshness of a pack of cigarettes and therefore has a 'legitimate common purpose.' *Lord v. State*, 616 So.2d 1065, 1066 (Fla.Dist.Ct.App.1993) (adopting the legitimate common purpose rule and noting that microscopic amounts of cocaine can be found on much of the currency circulating in south Florida). The State argues that, far from having a legitimate common purpose, cellophane cigarette wrappers 'are commonly used to transport and store controlled substances and particularly crack cocaine.' However, the State presented no evidence at trial to support this assertion; therefore, it will not be considered on appeal."

A dissent stated: "Reed had only a small amount of cocaine on his person. However, possession of even a trace of illegal drugs will support a conviction. See *State v. Wood*, 117 N.M. 682, 686, 875 P.2d 1113, 1117 (Ct.App.1994) (finding that knowledge of possession may be inferred where a defendant had a syringe on his person that tested positive for .0001 grams of contraband). Here, the record clearly permitted the jury to infer that Reed knowingly possessed cocaine. Contrary to the majority's suggestion, the cocaine residue was not invisible. The arresting officer testified that he saw the residue in the bag when Reed handed it to him. * * * If the officer could see the cocaine, the jury was free to infer that Reed also could see it and that Reed knew the cocaine was there when he put the wrapper in his pocket."

SECTION 4. RECKLESSNESS AND NEGLIGENCE

STATE v. HAZELWOOD

Supreme Court of Alaska, 1997.

946 P.2d 875.

RABINOWITZ, JUSTICE. * * *

Respondent's conviction stems from the Exxon Valdez incident. On March 24, 1989, Captain Joseph Hazelwood ran his ship aground off Bligh Reef and reported he was "evidently leaking some oil." Eventually, eleven million gallons poured into Prince William Sound. A jury subsequently convicted Hazelwood of negligent discharge of oil.

The Court of Appeals reversed Hazelwood's conviction on the basis that * * * Hazelwood should have been tried under a criminal negligence theory rather than the civil negligence standard of culpability. * * *

The difference between criminal and civil negligence although not major is distinct. Under both standards, a person acts "negligently" when he fails to perceive a substantial and unjustifiable risk that a particular result will occur.

The two tests part ways in their descriptions of the relevant unobserved risk. Under ordinary negligence, "the risk must be of such a nature and degree that the failure to perceive it constitutes a deviation from the standard of care that a reasonable person would observe in the situation." Criminal negligence requires a greater risk. This standard is met only when the risk is

> of such a nature and degree that the failure to perceive it constitutes a *gross* deviation from the standard of care that a reasonable person would observe in the situation. *Criminal negligence is something more than the slight degree of negligence necessary to support a civil action for damages and is negligence of a degree so gross as to be deserving of punishment.*

(emphasis added).

In essence, then, the criminal negligence standard requires the jury to find negligence so gross as to merit not just damages but also punishment. It does not spill over into recklessness; there is still no requirement that the defendant actually be aware of the risk of harm. However, criminal negligence does require a more culpable mental state than simple, ordinary negligence.

The statute under which Hazelwood was convicted provides in relevant part:

> A person may not discharge, cause to be discharged, or permit the discharge of petroleum ... into, or upon the waters or land of the state except in quantities, and at times and locations or under circumstances and conditions as the department may by regulation permit....

At the time of the alleged crime, a person who "negligently" violated this provision was guilty of a class B misdemeanor.[2] * * *

In defense of the Court of Appeals' ruling, Hazelwood presents two lines of argument. First, he contends the guarantee of due process demands that criminal penalties be predicated on more than just ordinary negligence. He reads our precedents as requiring a mens rea of at least reckless culpability for criminal offenses. Second, Hazelwood maintains that the statute under which he was convicted itself incorporates the criminal negligence standard. We address each argument in turn.

[I]t is firmly established in our jurisprudence that a mental state of simple or ordinary negligence can support a criminal conviction. Further decisions reveal, however, that in some situations more will be required, and sometimes less. *Speidel* [*v. State*, 460 P.2d 77 (Alaska 1969)], found a denial of due process where the defendant had been convicted of "simple neglectful or negligent failure to return a rented automobile." In that case, we insisted on at least a finding of reckless culpability in order for criminal sanctions to be imposed.

On the other hand, elsewhere we have allowed the mens rea element to be dispensed with entirely. We have allowed strict liability to be read into "public welfare offenses." * * *

An appropriate place to begin an explanation for objective fault crimes is with the objections of those who would abolish them altogether. In Jerome Hall, *Negligent Behavior*

---

2. A person convicted of a class B misdemeanor at the time of Hazelwood's offense could be "sentenced to a term of imprisonment of not more than 90 days."

Should Be Excluded from Penal Liability, 63 Colo. L.Rev. 632 (1963), Professor Hall challenges the alleged utility of sanctions based on negligence and strict liability. He contends crimes that are not based on subjective awareness of wrongdoing are, by their terms, not addressed to "the extremely important degree of individual freedom, autonomy, and awareness ... expressed in (voluntary) action by a normal adult." Merely negligent harm doers, contends Professor Hall, "have not in the least thought of their duty, their dangerous behavior, or any sanction."

The difficulty with this thesis is that it assumes legal regulations can operate only through the offender's conscious reason. A rebuttal is supplied by Professor Hart:

> the connexion between the threat of punishment and subsequent good behavior is not [always] of the rationalistic kind pictured in the guiding-type of case. The threat of punishment is something which causes [the offender] to exert his faculties, rather than something which enters as a reason for conforming to the law when he is deliberating whether to break it or not. It is perhaps more like a goad than a guide. But there seems to me to be nothing disreputable in allowing the law to function in this way, and it is arguable that it functions in this way rather than in the rationalistic way more frequently than is generally allowed.

H.L.A. Hart, *Punishment and Responsibility* 134 (1968).

The law's "goad," rather than its guide, is also emphasized by Professor LaFave. He asks whether more than civil negligence should be required for a criminal offense, and concludes "that there is no need to choose one answer for all crimes." His primary focus is on deterrence:

> The principal policy question is whether the threat of punishment for objective fault will deter people from conducting themselves in such a way as to create risk to others. Though the matter is disputed, it would seem that some people can be made to think, before they act, about the possible consequences of acting, so that the existence of objective-fault crimes does tend to reduce risky conduct.... The point is that the legislature might, in the exercise of its police power, require subjective fault for some crimes and objective fault for other crimes.

It is here, grounded in a theory of reasonable deterrence, that any explanation for objective fault crimes must have its origins. Despite Professor Hall's challenge, it cannot be disputed that the threat of punishment necessarily deters. Even when an offender does not of his own accord realize that his conduct is wrongful, he can in many cases be made to take care. Coercion that causes the offender to pay attention can serve important social aims that would not be achieved by proscriptions that only come into effect when the transgressor recognizes the harm in his or her behavior.

The fulcrum for deciding what level of intent is the absolute minimum for a particular offense is a question of when an expectation of individual conformity is reasonable. Due process under Alaska's Constitution requires that social interests be weighed against those of the individual. While society's interest in obtaining compliance with its regulations is strong, it can never outweigh the individual's interest in freedom from substantial punishment for a violation he or she could not reasonably have been expected to avoid. The threshold question, then, is whether the defendant's conduct is something which society could reasonably expect to deter.

The principle of reasonable deterrence allows the imposition of strict liability in some circumstances. * * *

Outside of these strict liability exceptions, though, a separate showing of simple civil negligence is both necessary and sufficient under Alaska's Constitution. Negligence, rather than gross negligence, is the minimum, not because we believe it is the necessary element of every prosecutor's case; indeed, all courts have allowed a separate showing of mental culpability to be dispensed with altogether in some circumstances. Rather, the negligence standard is constitutionally permissible because it approximates what the due process guarantee aims at: an assurance that criminal penalties will be imposed only when the conduct at issue is something society can reasonably expect to deter.[17]

Partisans of the criminal negligence approach have expressed the concern that an ordinary negligence standard gives the criminal proceeding an unseemly resemblance to tort law. *Commonwealth v. Heck*, 341 Pa.Super. 183, 491 A.2d 212, 224 (1985), aff'd, 517 Pa. 192, 535 A.2d 575 (1987), which adopts criminal negligence as a minimum, notes that the civil law standard serves purposes unsuited to the "harshness of criminal punishment." Tort aims simply to "shift the economic costs of injuries onto those responsible for them."[18]

This desire to differentiate criminal proceedings from civil proceedings appears to drive the definition of criminal negligence. That standard is typically characterized as "something more" than ordinary negligence. Thus the only consensus and precision available in the definition of criminal negligence is that it is not civil negligence.[19]

This fear of tort standards is unfounded. In response to similar allegations that civil standards do not protect, the Michigan Supreme Court has noted that "[i]t is just as much a violation of the due process clause of the Constitution to take property as it is to take the liberty of a person." *People v. McMurchy*, 249 Mich. 147, 228 N.W. 723 (1930). In other words, the same constitutional clause which governs the criminal prosecution would also govern a civil proceeding, and it is undisputed that due process is satisfied by the negligence standard in that forum.

We are not persuaded that the simple or ordinary civil negligence standard is inadequate to protect Hazelwood's interests. We conclude that the Superior Court's adoption of an ordinary civil negligence mens rea standard in its instructions to the jury did not constitute a denial of due process under article I, section 7 of the Alaska Constitution.

Hazelwood next contends that the statute under which he was convicted, former AS 46.03.790(a), itself incorporates the criminal negligence mens rea standard. His argument is unconvincing. The legislature made "negligence" the standard of liability. Unadorned, this word is commonly understood to mean ordinary negligence, not criminal or gross negligence. Nowhere in the criminal code is an ordinary negligence standard applied through the words "civil negligence" or "ordinary negligence." These added terms are used only when differentiating common negligence from criminal negligence. Otherwise,

---

17. We note also that the overwhelming majority of jurisdictions allow crimes based on ordinary negligence

18. A noteworthy aspect of *Heck* is that while the vehicular homicide statute at issue there required a negligence standard, the lower court had found there was negligence per se because the defendant had committed a minor traffic violation. While we decline to follow *Heck*'s lead in adopting the criminal negligence standard, we find that that court's due process concerns were justified. Although a jury finding of ordinary negligence is ordinarily sufficient, that finding has not been made when negligence per se is invoked; such an approach does not satisfy the requirement of criminal intent.

19. The Model Penal Code also adopts the criminal negligence standard. The commentators concede, however, that

> it is quite impossible to avoid tautological articulation of the final question. The tribunal must evaluate the actor's failure of perception and determine whether, under all the circumstances, it was serious enough to be condemned. The jury must find fault, and must find that it was substantial and unjustified. That is the heart of what can be said in legislative terms.

Model Penal Code, § 2.02, cmt. 4.

criminal negligence is always referred to specifically, and "negligence" always denotes ordinary, civil negligence. * * *

COMPTON, CHIEF JUSTICE, dissenting. * * *

In my view, notions of fundamental fairness, which underlie all due process issues, require a showing of something more than "failure to act reasonably" before a defendant may be subjected to imprisonment. Professor LaFave notes that a "general feeling" has arisen among judges that

> [S]omething more [i]s required for criminal liability than the ordinary negligence which is sufficient for tort liability. The thought [i]s this: When it comes to compensating an injured person for damages suffered, the one who has negligently injured an innocent victim ought to pay for it; but when the problem is one of whether to impose criminal punishment on the one who caused the injury, then something extra—beyond ordinary negligence—should be required.

1 Wayne R. LaFave & Austin W. Scott, *Substantive Criminal Law* 326 (1986). This position is persuasive. Civil negligence provides an acceptable standard of fault for allocating any burden which neglectful conduct creates. However, that standard does not provide an adequate basis for levying a separate punishment on a neglectful person. In particular, a punishment of imprisonment is sufficiently severe that it should not be imposed, with the possible exception of the cases noted, for conduct which involves only civil negligence. The right to due process would support imprisonment for a truly gross deviation from "reasonable" conduct. It does not, in my view, support imprisonment for every deviation whatsoever from "reasonableness." * * *

Notes and Questions

1. How would the *Hazelwood* court feel about *State v. Williams*, 4 Wash.App. 908, 484 P.2d 1167 (1971), where the defendants, husband and wife (respectively, a 24–year–old laborer with a sixth grade education and a 20–year–old with an eleventh grade education) were convicted of manslaughter for negligently failing to supply their 17–month–old child with necessary medical attention, as a result of which he died. The trial court expressly found:

"That both defendants were aware that William Joseph Tabafunda was ill during the period September 1, 1968 to September 12, 1968. The defendants were ignorant. They did not realize how sick the baby was. They thought that the baby had a toothache and no layman regards a toothache as dangerous to life. They loved the baby and gave it aspirin in hopes of improving its condition. They did not take the baby to a doctor because of fear that the Welfare Department would take the baby away from them. They knew that medical help was available because of previous experience. They had no excuse that the law will recognize for not taking the baby to a doctor."

The applicable statute provided that "homicide, not being excusable or justifiable, is manslaughter." In affirming the convictions, the court noted:

"The concept of simple or ordinary negligence describes a failure to exercise the 'ordinary caution' necessary to make out the defense of excusable homicide. Ordinary caution is the kind of caution that a man of reasonable prudence would exercise under the same or similar conditions. If, therefore, the conduct of a defendant, regardless of his ignorance, good intentions and good faith, fails to measure up to the conduct required of a man of reasonable prudence, he is guilty of ordinary negligence because of his failure to use 'ordinary caution'"

2. Compare *Hazelwood* with *Santillanes v. State*, 115 N.M. 215, 849 P.2d 358 (1993), where defendant was convicted of the felony of child abuse, defined by statute as "negligently" placing a child in a dangerous situation. The trial court instructed the jury in terms of civil negligence rather than, as defendant requested, the definition in *Model Penal Code* § 2.02(2)(d). The court first noted that several other criminal statutes in the state used the undefined term "negligence" as well, but noted that "each of them is punishable as a petty misdemeanor, which is consistent with the view that only a showing of ordinary civil negligence is required." By contrast, the court concluded, the child abuse statute was intended "to punish conduct that is morally culpable, not merely inadvertent," and consequently "the mens rea element of negligence in the child abuse statute" must be interpreted "to require a showing of criminal negligence instead of ordinary civil negligence."

3. Is the need for civil negligence in the criminal law increasing or decreasing? Consider Leslie Y. Garfield, *A More Principled Approach to Criminalizing Negligence: A Presumption for the Legislature*, 65 Tenn.L.Rev. 875 (1998): "As society advances beyond the current frontiers of the technological revolution, we are increasingly prone to more distractions. While the new millennium offers the potential for new safety devices, technological advances, and activities involving equipment or substances yet to be discovered, careless use of these instruments or participation in particular activities involving these discoveries is likely to yield a significant type of harm against which criminal law must protect."

4. *Hazelwood* suggests that even the Model Penal Code's criminal negligence standard is somewhat ambiguous as to what the "something more" is that raises it above the civil standard. Consider in that regard *Walker v. Superior Court*, 47 Cal.3d 112, 253 Cal.Rptr. 1, 763 P.2d 852 (1988), holding that defendant could be put on trial for involuntary manslaughter of the criminal negligence type based upon the following facts:

"Defendant Laurie Grouard Walker is a member of the Church of Christ, Scientist (hereafter the Church). Her four-year-old daughter, Shauntay, fell ill with flu-like symptoms on February 21, 1984, and four days later developed a stiff neck. Consistent with the tenets of her religion, defendant chose to treat the child's illness with prayer rather than medical care.[43] Defendant contacted an accredited Christian Science prayer practitioner who thereafter prayed for Shauntay and visited the child on two occasions. Defendant also engaged a Christian Science nurse who attended Shauntay on February 27 and again on March 6 and 8. Shauntay nevertheless lost weight, grew disoriented and irritable during the last week of her illness, and died on March 9 of acute purulent meningitis after a period of heavy and irregular breathing. During the 17 days she lay ill, the child received no medical treatment."

STATE v. LARSON

Supreme Court of South Dakota, 1997.
582 N.W.2d 15.

SABERS, JUSTICE. * * *

On September 16, 1996, a highway construction crew was working in the right lane of eastbound Interstate 90 in Lyman County. The construction area stretched between mile

---

43. Members of the Church "believe that disease is a physical manifestation of errors of the mind." The use of medicine is believed to perpetuate such error and is therefore discouraged. Nonetheless, "the Church sets up no abstract criteria for determining what diseases or injuries should be treated by prayer or other methods but, rather, leaves such questions to individual decision in concrete instances. . . . If some turn in what they think is an urgent time of need to medical treatment for themselves or their children, they are not—contrary to some recent charges—stigmatized by their church."

markers 212 and 234 and was separated from the driving lane by "candlestick" dividers. These dividers were generally placed about a foot inside the closed lane, but placed on the center line where the crew was actually working. The highway had a posted speed limit of 75 m.p.h. but a posted recommended speed of 55 m.p.h. through the construction zone.

There was expert testimony that Brian Larson was traveling between 62 and 68 m.p.h. when his 1996 Ford Explorer crossed over the center line and drove about one and one-half feet into the closed lane for approximately 101 feet. At this estimated speed, Larson would have traveled that 101 feet in just over one second. In that one second, he struck and killed two construction workers, Julie Smith, age 20, and Brandon Koehn, age 18.

Three crew members, Ryan Kotz, Dave Solmonson, and Koehn were breaking up bad concrete with jackhammers near the on-ramp of Exit 214. Once there was an accumulation of chipped concrete, Smith would remove the debris using first an air hose and then a shovel. At about 9:30 a.m., Kotz was working in the first, westernmost cutout area, Solmonson was in the first cutout east of Kotz, and Koehn was in the next cutout, approximately ten to twenty feet east of Solmonson. Solmonson's cutout became full of debris; he stopped working and went to sit in a company pickup. Smith began cleaning the cutout with an air hose and was standing somewhere between the center line and a point one and one-half feet into the driving lane.

Almost immediately after getting into the pickup, Solmonson's attention was caught by dust and debris flying through the air. When he looked up, he saw Smith on the front of the vehicle and Koehn flying off to the right. Kotz testified that he was facing the driving lane as he worked and suddenly realized a vehicle was driving in his cutout. He looked up and to his right and saw the vehicle hit Koehn, knocking him into the air. Solmonson observed Smith as she came out from under the back of the vehicle and into the median. The dent on the Explorer indicates Smith was struck in the approximate center of its hood. Both Smith and Koehn were killed instantly. As noted, the vehicle left the closed lane after 101 feet, crossed the driving lane diagonally, and entered the median. Larson first braked after he entered the median, where he traveled approximately 205 feet before the vehicle came to a stop.

At trial, the court allowed two highway patrolmen and Kotz to testify to their opinions that certain tire tracks depicted in photographs were made by Larson's Explorer. The court also admitted, over Larson's objection, two photographs of Smith's body and one of Koehn's body.

Larson was convicted of two counts of second degree manslaughter under [a statute defining the crime in terms of the reckless killing of another]. He received two consecutive 10–year penitentiary sentences. * * *

Larson claims that his conduct did not constitute "recklessness" under SDCL 22–16–20. "Recklessness" is defined in SDCL 22–1–2(1)(d):

> The words "reckless, recklessly" and all derivatives thereof, import a conscious and unjustifiable disregard of a substantial risk that the offender's conduct may cause a certain result or may be of a certain nature. A person is reckless with respect to circumstances when he consciously and unjustifiably disregards a substantial risk that such circumstances may exist[.]

He argues that under *State v. Olsen*, 462 N.W.2d 474 (S.D.1990), his motion for judgment of acquittal should have been granted.

Olsen was driving a tractor at a very low speed on a state highway. As he turned left onto a gravel road, he was struck by a car traveling in the opposite direction. The driver of the car was killed instantly. An eyewitness testified that Olsen ran from the tractor exclaiming, "I didn't see it." State charged Olsen with second degree manslaughter, which was dismissed at preliminary hearing after the magistrate determined there was not probable cause to sustain the charge.

This court affirmed the dismissal, stating, "[r]ecklessness requires more than ordinary negligent conduct. Evidence of carelessness, inadvertence or other similar behavior is insufficient to sustain a conviction where reckless conduct is required." The focus is on the state of mind of the individual, and whether his conduct is perceived as negligent or reckless depends upon his awareness of the risk his behavior creates. * * *

Larson points to State's comment in closing argument, wherein this accident was characterized as resulting from a "microsecond of recklessness." He argues this cannot constitute the requisite "conscious disregard of a known risk" as required by *Olsen*.

State responds that Larson had advance warning of the crew's presence and could have driven on the left shoulder to avoid the accident. State also claims Larson's admission that he was driving faster than he should and his failure to brake until he was out of the construction zone and in the median proves recklessness. Larson counters with the claim that the crew was not wearing bright clothing and that there were no flagpersons present as required by the construction contract and by the Manual on Uniform Traffic Control Devices (MUTCD), which has been adopted by the State of South Dakota. Therefore, he argues that the construction company and State share the blame for this accident, mitigating any "recklessness" on his part.

Larson does not claim that he was unaware of the construction zone because of inadequate signage or unaware of the crew's presence because they were not wearing bright clothing. In fact, he saw the crew working and was aware that he hit Smith. Larson did not testify at trial; however, in a conversation taped almost immediately after the accident, he told Trooper Storey that the work crew was "kinda far out ... they were pretty close to the line but I was in my lane." He also stated that he was traveling 60 m.p.h. and that he believed the construction zone speed limit was 40 m.p.h.

We cannot say, as a matter of law, that Larson's conduct did not constitute recklessness. Here, reasonable minds could certainly differ. Viewing the evidence and the inferences which may be fairly drawn therefrom in the light most favorable to the verdict, we conclude there was sufficient evidence to sustain the jury's finding of guilt beyond a reasonable doubt. Larson argues that driving in excess of the recommended speed limit cannot alone constitute recklessness. See *Olsen* ("Criminal responsibility for death resulting from the operation of a motor vehicle in violation of the law will result only if the violation is done in such a manner as to evidence a reckless disregard for the safety of others."). However, Larson's speed of 62 to 68 m.p.h. *in the presence of a visible road construction crew* constitutes a conscious disregard of the safety of the crew. "Awareness can be established if the defendant acts in a manner that indicates a reckless disregard for the safety of others."

It is Larson's speed of 62 to 68 m.p.h., maintained despite his admitted awareness of the crew's presence, coupled with his veering into the closed lane, which constitutes recklessness, and which distinguishes this case from *Olsen* and other cases relied upon by Larson. * * *

AMUNDSON, JUSTICE (dissenting). * * *

The majority states that "Larson's speed of 62 to 68 m.p.h. in the presence of a visible road construction crew constitutes a conscious disregard of the safety of the crew." (Emphasis in original.) However, the fact that the road construction crew was visible, does not mean that Larson saw them in time to take action to avoid the accident or that he consciously disregarded the safety of the crew. The evidence showed that Larson suddenly drifted from his lane. In Larson's taped conversation with Trooper Storey almost immediately after the accident, Larson sobbed uncontrollably as he told what had happened from his perspective. He stated that "I was in my lane ... [and the] next thing I know, I hit that gal, just boom, you know.... I didn't mean it, it was a total accident." He did not even know that he hit the second construction worker until after the accident had occurred. "[S]omeone cannot be reckless if they are unaware of the risk their behavior creates as they cannot disregard that risk if they are unaware of it." What caused Larson to drift out of his lane is unknown, but there is no evidence in this record that showed either a pattern of erratic driving or that Larson was under the influence of alcohol or drugs. * * *

The majority treats the standard of "conscious disregard" as if it were determined by an objective standard. According to this line of thinking, Larson should have been aware of the danger as he drove through the construction zone, because a reasonable person would have recognized it. However, a "conscious disregard" is a subjective standard resting on the particular defendant's state of mind. Thus, the question is whether Larson, himself, consciously disregarded a known risk of harm. The evidence does not begin to show as much. The majority grasps onto the fact that Larson knowingly drove his vehicle above the suggested speed limit (even though it was well below the actual speed limit) as evidence of Larson's recklessness. However, there is no evidence that if Larson would have been traveling at a more moderate speed that it would have prevented the tragedy that occurred. The tragedy occurred, not because of the speed of Larson's vehicle, but because he wandered, for whatever reason, out of his proper lane of travel. * * *

Notes and Questions

1. In *State v. Hodgdon,* 244 Or. 219, 416 P.2d 647 (1966), the defendant was convicted under a statute making it a crime to cause death by the "driving of any motor vehicle * * * in a grossly negligent manner," that is, in "reckless disregard of the rights of others." In affirming the conviction, the court concluded that the definition of recklessness in the law of torts governed, namely:

"The actor's conduct is in reckless disregard of the safety of another if he intentionally does an act or fails to do an act which it is his duty to the other to do, knowing or having reason to know of facts which would lead a reasonable man to realize that the actor's conduct not only creates an unreasonable risk of bodily harm to the other but also involves a high degree of probability that substantial harm will result to him."

2. Most of the modern recodifications contain their own definitions of such words as "recklessness" and "negligence," indicating what degree of risk is required and whether an objective or subjective test is intended. The definitions in *Model Penal Code* § 2.02(2)(c) and (d) are often but not always[44] used. See David M. Treiman, *Recklessness and the Model Penal Code,* 9 Am.J.Crim.L. 281, 375–86 (1981).

44. In *People v. Calvaresi,* 188 Colo. 277, 534 P.2d 316 (1975), the variation adopted in that state, whereby inadvertence would suffice for either recklessness or negligence, was found wanting:

"Under the manslaughter statute in question, a jury must determine if an accused acted 'recklessly,' i.e., whether he failed to perceive a risk, of which he should have been aware, and whether he acted in wanton and willful disregard of the standard of conduct that a reasonable person would observe in a given situation. Under the criminal negligence statute, the jury must determine whether the failure to perceive an unjustifia-ble risk constitutes a gross deviation from the standard of care that a reasonable person would observe in the situation. The distinction between a gross deviation from, and a wanton and willful disregard of, a standard of care is not sufficiently apparent to be intelligently and uniformly applied. The legislative attempt to distinguish between recklessness, and its purportedly less culpable counterpart, criminal negligence, constitutes a distinction without a sufficiently pragmatic difference. To base a conviction of a felony, rather than a misdemeanor, upon the shifting sands of these semantics does not constitute substantial justice."

3. To what extent are the Model Penal Code definitions of recklessness and negligence really different? In what ways should they be different? Consider Treiman, supra, at 351–69:

"The requirement that the actor *consciously disregard* the risk is probably the most significant part of the definition of recklessness. * * * It is the concept of conscious disregard that distinguishes recklessness from negligence. * * *

"Since the *Model Penal Code* defines both knowledge and recklessness in terms of awareness, this suggests that conscious and knowledge might mean the same thing. However, some writers have suggested that knowledge is broader in meaning than conscious or aware. Being aware or conscious of something suggests that the something is in the person's thoughts at the moment. Knowledge, on the other hand, may be in a person's conscious thoughts, or may be something tucked away in the person's memory. Obviously we all have considerably more knowledge than we have in our conscious thoughts at any moment. We may know something without being currently aware or conscious of that fact or idea. * * *

"Since the *Model Penal Code* concept of recklessness utilizes awareness rather than knowledge of the risk, this would appear to exclude the situation in which the actor had knowledge of a risk, but was not aware of it at the moment. Having knowledge of a risk involved in specific conduct, but not being aware of the risk at the moment, that is, not stopping to think of the consequences, may be negligent but it is not reckless. * * *

"With respect to recklessness, there is also a problem of lack of certainty. Can one claim he was not reckless because he was not certain that he was aware of the risk? Awareness of a risk involves a different mental process than awareness of an object being before one's eyes. Simple perception is sufficient to inform one of the object before his eyes. When one does not actually see the object, but is aware of a risk that the object is present, a mental process more complex than perception is required. One must reason from perceptions and previous knowledge and experience to make a judgment that something might be present. Can one be certain that there is a risk of the object being present? It is unlikely that a judgment or calculation of risks will be as fixed or clear in one's mind as perceptions. Just as requiring absolute certainty for knowledge would negate the usefulness of the concept of knowledge, requiring certain awareness or consciousness of a risk would make recklessness an almost useless concept. * * *

"In addition to the confusion resulting from proof of subjective mental states, there is also the danger that in defining consciousness of the risk the standard might be converted into an objective one. An illustration of this is found in *People v. Taylor*.[301] In finding that recklessness had not been established, the court stated the standard for recklessness as 'when the actor *has knowledge* of the highly dangerous nature of his actions or *knowledge of such facts* as under the circumstances would disclose to a reasonable man the dangerous character of his action, and despite this knowledge he so acts.' Since the prosecution's evidence was unable to meet this test, the misstatement of the standard was not harmful to Mr. Taylor, but it was a misstatement nevertheless.

"Though the standard in *Taylor* is more demanding than the definition of recklessness found in the *Restatement of Torts,* which does not even require knowledge of the circumstances, it fails to require any subjective awareness of the risk of harm. This is clearly insufficient for recklessness. The second sentence of both recklessness and negligence judge the nature and the degree of the risk based on the circumstances known to the

---

301. 31 A.D.2d 852, 297 N.Y.S.2d 192 (1969).

actor. What distinguishes recklessness from negligence is awareness of the risk itself, not just the circumstances. * * *

" * * * There is strong support for the view that the actor must be aware of a substantial risk, not just any risk. * * *

"When the actor underestimates the risk so much that he believes the risk is not substantial at all, can he be found to have consciously disregarded a substantial risk? A very cautious person might be aware of a remote risk because he carefully considers his actions, but because of mistaken judgment or evaluation of facts he *did* perceive, think that the risk is much less than it is. Unless the actor is at least aware of a substantial risk, it is difficult to separate this actor from the negligent actor. Even if this mistake were unreasonable, in terms of culpability it is difficult to see why such a cautious actor should be any more culpable than the person who unreasonably failed to see any risk whatsoever. * * *

"For the actor to be reckless with respect to a result or a circumstance, must the actor be aware that the risk he is disregarding is unjustifiable? * * *

"The *Model Penal Code* Commentary suggests that the weighing of interests to determine recklessness is an objective standard. After pointing to the factors to be weighed, the Commentary states, 'Some principle must be articulated, however, to indicate what final judgment is demanded after everything is weighed. There is no way to state this value-judgment that does not beg the question in the last analysis; the point is that the *jury must evaluate* the conduct and determine whether it should be condemned.'

"Several writers are also fairly explicit that the actor need not be conscious that his conduct is unjustifiable. This is a social judgment, determined by the trier of fact looking back at the actor's conduct and judging it by objective standards, and not by the actor's belief that the conduct is justifiable. * * *

"However, the conclusion that the unjustifiability of the risk is to be determined for purposes of recklessness by a purely objective standard is misleadingly oversimplified. * * *

"[T]he requirement for recklessness of conscious disregard should require the trier of fact to look at the purpose the actor had for engaging in the conduct, at the likelihood the actor thought existed of achieving the goal by his conduct, and at the harm he thought was risked by the conduct. However, the trier of fact should assign a value to the harm threatened and to the goal the actor sought. Finally, the trier of fact should weigh the factors, without regard to how the actor might have weighed those factors."

4. With respect to the above conclusion, consider Larry Alexander, *Insufficient Concern: A Unified Conception of Criminal Culpability*, 88 Calif.L.Rev. 931, 933–35 (2000): "The standard formulation of recklessness makes it appear that a defendant, to be deemed reckless, must consciously disregard a risk that satisfies two independent criteria: (1) the risk must be 'substantial'; and (2) the risk must be 'unjustifiable.' I believe that this appearance is mistaken both with respect to the purpose behind the formulation and with respect to a normatively attractive conception of the culpability displayed through recklessness.

"Consider the following cases:

"(1) Driver is accompanied by Passenger, who suddenly displays the symptoms of a severe heart attack. Driver speeds down city streets in order to get Passenger to a hospital in time to save his life. In doing so, Driver creates risks to bystanders' lives, limbs, and property of magnitude R.

"(2) Daniel loves to set off dynamite on city streets just for the thrill of it. In doing so, he creates risks to bystanders' lives, limbs, and property of magnitude R/100.

"(3) Deborah likes to take Sunday drives. Although she is a very careful driver, in taking Sunday drives she creates risks to bystanders' lives, limbs, and property of magnitude R/10,000.

"(4) Demented likes to expose others to risk. He has concocted his own version of Russian roulette in which, when he pulls a switch, he creates a risk of magnitude R/100,000 that an innocent person will die or be severely injured.

"Now if the substantiality criterion is truly independent of the justifiability criterion, then there must be some level of risk imposition below which the actor cannot be reckless. Suppose that level is just above R/100. In Case 1, Driver does satisfy the substantiality criterion but may escape the judgment of recklessness by failing to satisfy the justification criterion. In other words, Driver may have justifiably imposed risk R on bystanders because his purpose in doing so was to save the life of Passenger. Deborah, the Sunday driver in Case 3, also escapes the judgment of recklessness, in this case because R/10,000 is below the risk threshold.

"The problem with the independent criteria approach, however, surfaces with Cases 2 and 4. Both Daniel and Demented have imposed risks that by hypothesis fail the substantiality criterion, yet the intuition is virtually unshakable that they are being culpably reckless toward bystanders. This is perhaps clearer in the case of Demented, who subjects others to risk simply because he enjoys it. Imposing Russian roulette on others, no matter how high the ratio of empty to loaded chambers, seems a clear case of criminally culpable conduct. What is doing all the work here is, of course, the justifiability criterion, which also explains the intuition about Daniel, namely, that the mere thrill of a dynamite blast does not justify imposing more than a de minimis risk on others.

"What emerges from consideration of these cases is the proposition that the level of risk that one may permissibly impose on others is dependent on the reasons one has for imposing that risk. The reason Driver has for imposing risks on bystanders is a weightier one than the reason Deborah, the Sunday driver, has for doing so. Thus, we deem it permissible for Driver to impose a higher risk on bystanders than Deborah may impose. Daniel's reason—the thrill of explosions—may justify even less risk-imposition than Deborah is permitted. And Demented's reason—imposing risks on others for its own sake—cannot justify even the slightest increase in risk.

"The conclusion that one should draw from these examples is that recklessness consists of imposing unjustifiable risks on others. The level of risk imposed will bear on its justifiability but is not itself an independent criterion of recklessness. Even very tiny risk-impositions can be reckless if imposed for insufficient or misanthropic reasons, just as very large risk-impositions can be nonculpable if supported by weighty reasons.

"If recklessness consists of imposing unjustifiable risks on others, then it can be characterized as displaying the central moral vice of insufficient concern. It is my contention in this Essay that all recognized forms of criminal mens rea other than negligence display this single moral vice, and that they do so in ways that establish their unity rather than their separateness."

Joshua Dressler, *Does One Mens Rea Fit All? Thoughts on Alexander's Unified Conception of Criminal Culpability*, 88 Calif.L.Rev. 955, 956 (2000), who disagrees with Alexander's conclusion in the immediately preceding paragraph, notes: "A proponent of a unified conception of criminal culpability can justify this position on at least one of three grounds: (1) purposeful, knowing, and reckless wrongdoers who cause the same harm are equally blameworthy; (2) they are not equally blameworthy, but the differences in culpability are de minimis; and (3) whether or not significant differences in culpability exist, there is no reliable way to draw distinctions, so we are better off with a one-mens-rea-fits-all system." Which (if any) supports Alexander's conclusion?

5. In *In re William G.*, 192 Ariz. 208, 963 P.2d 287 (App.1998), a 15–year-old youth was adjudicated delinquent for committing the offense of criminal damage to property by colliding with a parked car while riding and "flipping" a shopping cart in a shopping center parking lot. The mental state for that offense was recklessness, defined by statute as requiring a showing "that a person is aware of and consciously disregards a substantial and unjustifiable risk that the result will occur or that the circumstance exists. The risk must be of such a nature and degree that disregard of such risk constitutes a gross deviation from the standard of conduct that a reasonable person would observe in the situation." In reversing the finding of delinquency, the court stated:

"We conclude that defining a substantial risk as one 'different in kind' from the merely unreasonable risk sufficient for civil negligence best serves the purpose of circumscribing recklessness in such a manner that a fact-finder will not be misled into criminalizing conduct which is only civilly negligent. We also conclude that, in this case, reasonable minds could not differ that the juvenile's conduct did not create a risk different in kind from the risk associated with many types of misbehavior which create no more than an unreasonable risk of harm.

"This was not a case of teenagers engaging in an inherently dangerous activity or using an inherently dangerous instrumentality. Rather, this fifteen year old and his friends were 'goofing off' with shopping carts, not going fast, '[j]ust picking up enough momentum to do what they were doing.' Moreover, '[t]hey did very good jobs' in riding the carts, indicating a proficiency which minimized the risk of harm. Two of the three concluded the activity without incident, and it was not until his last ride that this juvenile caused damage with his cart. We would concur that the juvenile's activity created an unreasonable risk of damage to cars parked in the lot. Nevertheless, to constitute reckless criminal behavior, conduct must create a risk that is not only unreasonable but also substantial. That is not the case here and no rational trier of fact could have so found. A fortiori, no rational trier of fact could have found an awareness and conscious disregard of such a risk by the juvenile.

"Recklessness requires that the conduct in question, in addition to creating a substantial risk of harm, also constitute a 'gross' deviation from the standard of conduct of a reasonable person. An initial question is how this hypothetical reasonable person is to be defined. If the conduct under consideration is that of a juvenile, should he be held to the standard of conduct of an adult or to that of juveniles of like age, intelligence and maturity? In the law of civil negligence in Arizona, the latter standard is applied. This is generally true throughout the country, absent special circumstances such as operation of an automobile, hunting, use of an inherently dangerous instrument or participation in an inherently dangerous activity.

"We conclude that in the circumstances of this case, or cases closely analogous, the civil rule is what the legislature intended to incorporate by its reference to a standard of conduct. We reserve judgment on any future case that concerns significantly different activity by juveniles. We hold only that riding a shopping cart in a parking lot when done by a fifteen year old is an activity that must be judged by the standard of fifteen year olds of like age, intelligence and experience.

"With a standard of conduct to work from, the final inquiry is whether the conduct of this juvenile was a 'gross' deviation from that standard. Since the legislature has not provided a definition of this term, we attempt to ascertain and apply the ordinary meaning of the term.

"One authority offers this relevant definition of gross: 'flagrant and extreme.' *Random House Unabridged Dictionary* 842 (2d ed.1993). Synonyms include: 'outrageous, heinous, grievous.'

"While this etymological reference is not clearly definitive, it does season the term 'gross' with sufficient semantic flavor to cause us to conclude that the deviation from acceptable behavior required for recklessness must be markedly greater than the mere inadvertence or heedlessness sufficient for civil negligence. We do not doubt that the juvenile's conduct in this case was a sufficient deviation from the standard of conduct applicable to fifteen year olds to constitute civil negligence. Where reasonable minds could not differ is that the deviation was not a flagrant, extreme, outrageous, heinous or grievous deviation from that standard. In short, the deviation was not gross."

6. What then of *Boggess v. State*, 655 P.2d 654 (Utah 1982), where the defendant, convicted of recklessness-manslaughter, objected on appeal that the trial judge should have instructed upon the lesser offense of negligent homicide. The majority reasoned: "Section 76–5–206, U.C.A. 1953 provides:

(1) Criminal homicide constitutes negligent homicide if the actor, acting with criminal negligence, causes the death of another.

"Section 76–2–103(4) provides that a person is criminally negligent when he ought to be aware of a substantial and unjustifiable risk that circumstances exist or the result will occur. The risk must be of such a nature and degree that the failure to perceive it constitutes a gross deviation from the standard of care that an ordinary person would exercise in all the circumstances as viewed from the actor's standpoint.

"The defendant did not claim that he was unaware of the danger associated with the use of guns. He admitted that he should have looked to have seen if the gun was unloaded before he fired it, but he did not. He noted that his action was a 'hell of a way to show it's unloaded.' Even though he thought the gun was unloaded, defendant knew it was dangerous to have pointed it at his wife and pulled the trigger. In view of this evidence as to the defendant's knowledge concerning the inherent danger of firearms and the recklessness of his conduct towards his wife, the evidence would not admit of a finding that he was unaware but should have been aware of a substantial and unjustifiable risk, or that he failed to perceive the nature and degree of the risk—all of which is necessary to constitute criminal negligence. To the contrary, the defendant's own testimony establishes a state of mind found in manslaughter. He repeatedly characterized his action as 'reckless' which under § 76–5–205 constitutes manslaughter. There being no evidence to support a verdict of negligent homicide under the peculiar facts of this case, it clearly was not error for the court to have failed to have given an instruction on that crime."

Stewart, J., concurring only because the defendant failed to ask for a negligent homicide instruction, responded: "In *People v. Stanfield,* 36 N.Y.2d 467, 330 N.E.2d 75, 369 N.Y.S.2d 118 (1975), a case not unlike the instant, defendant was convicted of reckless manslaughter for shooting his common law wife. The defendant had cocked the hammer of his pistol, pointed the barrel upward at about a 45 degree angle but in the direction of his wife who stood very close to him, and told her he was going to shoot her. His wife responded, '[D]on't mess with the gun like that,' and then slapped his hand or arm." The weapon discharged and inflicted the mortal wound. In holding that the trial court erred in not instructing on criminal negligence, the court stated:

[C]riminal recklessness and criminal negligence with respect to a particular result—there homicide—may in a particular case, if not hypothetically or definitionally, be but shades apart on the scale of criminal culpability. And the distinction between the two mental states is less clear practically than theoretically * * *.

[I]t seems manifest that in a practical, if not a literal definitional sense, if one acts with criminal recklessness he is at least criminally negligent. Moreover, negligence may, in a particular case, quickly, even imperceptibly, aggravate on the scale of culpability to recklessness.

"On the particular facts of this case, I think the conclusion is inescapable that there is a reasonable view of the evidence which would support an acquittal of reckless manslaughter and a conviction for criminal negligent homicide. The defendant testified, *and the State concedes, that the defendant did not think that the gun was loaded.* Thus, the State in effect concedes that defendant did not consciously disregard the risk because, if as believed, the gun was unloaded, there was no risk."

7. In *Regina v. Caldwell,* [1982] A.C. 341, [1981] 2 W.L.R. 509, [1981] 1 All E.R. 961, the House of Lords concluded that recklessness "includes not only deciding to ignore a risk of harmful consequences resulting from one's acts that one has recognised as existing, but also failing to give any thought to whether or not there is any such risk in circumstances where, if any thought were given to the matter, it would be obvious that there was." Is this to be preferred over the Model Penal Code approach? Consider:

(a) John C. Smith, *Subjective or Objective? Ups and Downs of the Test of Criminal Liability in England,* 27 Vill.L.Rev. 1179, 1201–02 (1982): "Why did the House of Lords in *Caldwell* take this step? In the first place Lord Diplock thought that there was no difference in culpability between the defendant in *Caldwell* and one who was reckless in the previously accepted sense. * * *

"Is it proper to equate the blameworthiness of a person who fails to realize that there is a risk of some harmful consequence with that of one who does realize that there is such a risk and decides to take it? It is submitted that there is a real distinction in degree of blameworthiness between the two cases."

(b) R.A. Duff, *Recklessness,* 1980 Crim.L.Rev. 282, 291: "Some failures of attention or realisation may manifest, not mere stupidity or 'thoughtlessness,' but the same indifference or disregard which characterises the conscious risk-taker as reckless. If I intend to injure someone seriously, I may not realise that this might kill them: not because I am *mistaken* about the likely effects of my assault, but because it 'just doesn't occur to me'—I am blind to that aspect of my action. But such blindness to such an essential and integral aspect of a serious assault, though possible, itself manifests a 'reckless disregard' for my victim's life no different from that of an assailant who knows he is endangering life."

8. In *State v. Smith,* 185 Conn. 63, 441 A.2d 84 (1981), the court rejected defendant's claim that his reckless homicide conviction could not stand because the evidence showed the defendant acted with intent to kill: "*State v. Rodriguez,* 180 Conn. 382, 429 A.2d 919 (1980), established that in prosecutions for homicides despite the differences between acting intentionally, acting recklessly, and acting with criminal negligence, we will deem the more culpable of those mental states to include the less culpable when both apply to actions with respect to an identical result or circumstance. Therefore the defendant could not prevent his conviction by preserving a reasonable doubt that he intentionally rather than recklessly killed Curmon and seriously injured Nichols. See Model Penal Code, § 2.02(5), comment, p. 129 (tentative draft No. 4, 1955) (applying the analysis which we adopted in *Rodriguez* to all offenses)."

STATE v. CUSHMAN

Supreme Court of Vermont, 1974.

133 Vt. 121, 329 A.2d 648.

SMITH, JUSTICE. The defendant was charged by information and warrant with the offense of recklessly engaging in conduct which placed another person in danger of death or serious bodily injury. On June 1, 1973, the defendant was tried in the District Court of Vermont, Unit No. 4, Caledonia Circuit, by a jury and was found guilty. Defendant's appeal from this conviction has been timely taken to this Court.

The appeal of the defendant is mainly premised on what he claims to be a wrongful interpretation by the trial court of the statute under which he was charged. This challenged interpretation was the source of allegedly erroneous jury instructions. Because of the points raised by the defendant, we believe it essential to quote the statute in its entirety for a proper understanding of the questions presented, as well as the resolution thereof.

§ 1025.   Recklessly endangering another person

A person who recklessly engages in conduct which places or may place another person in danger of death or serious bodily injury shall be imprisoned for not more than one year or fined not more than $1,000.00 or both. Recklessness and danger shall be presumed where a person knowingly points a firearm at or in the direction of another, whether or not the actor believed the firearm to be loaded.

Taken in the light most favorable to the State, the prevailing party below, the factual situation is not complicated. Trooper McDonald came to the home of the defendant in the evening of January 1, 1973. The visit was in response to a call made to the State Police by a Mrs. Aldrich, who lived with the defendant at his home on Bible Hill. Mrs. Aldrich was disturbed, because of her young daughter, by the presence of an individual brought to the house by the defendant, and for whom defendant had furnished bail. An argument ensued between the defendant and the trooper, the details of which are not relevant to this decision. The evidence of the State was that the defendant, during this argument, took a firearm from a rack in the kitchen and pointed it in the direction of the police officer. It was the contention of the defendant, who took the stand in his own behalf, that the weapon was of antique vintage and not loaded.

The first point briefed by the defendant is that the trial court committed error by instructing the jury that it need not find that the weapon used by the defendant was loaded in order to convict him. What defendant argues, as we understand it, is that he has not been charged with assault, but with placing another in danger of death or bodily injury. The claim of the defendant is that in order to convict him under 13 V.S.A. § 1025 it is essential that actual power to commit bodily injury must rest in the actor's hand, and the apparent power which is adequate for the finding of an assault is inadequate under the above statute.

We agree with the defendant that 13 V.S.A. § 1025 does not charge a simple assault, the definitions of which are set forth in 13 V.S.A. § 1023. The Legislature, in its general revision of the laws relative to breach of the peace in the 1971 Adjourned Session of the General Assembly, set forth a separate offense directly concerned with the use of firearms under § 1025. There is a clearly expressed legislative intent in the second sentence of this provision that even if the actor has knowledge, or is presumed to have knowledge, that the gun he is pointing in the direction of another is unloaded, the recklessness of his conduct is presumed from such action, as is the fact that he is placing the other person in danger of death or bodily injury.

We are aware of the principle cited by the defendant that, in interpreting a penal statute, the interpretation most favorable to the accused must be the one adopted. But the fundamental rule is to ascertain and give effect to the intention of the Legislature, and "construction of a statute leading to an absurd consequence must be avoided, if possible."

It can hardly be doubted that a person threatened by another with a firearm has no way of ascertaining whether or not such weapon is loaded, but the state of mind of the victim is irrelevant under this statute. The danger of death or of bodily injury is equally acute, no matter what knowledge the actor may possess on the loaded or unloaded condition of the firearm which he points in the direction of the victim. To accept the defendant's contention that the Legislature, in enacting this statute, only intended to prevent the pointing of a loaded weapon at another but not to proscribe the pointing of an unloaded weapon would require us to construe the statute to lead to an absurd result. The most dangerous weapon is the "unloaded gun", and the Legislature's intent was to proscribe the pointing of all firearms at others. * * *

The defendant next briefs a contention that the denial of his request to charge that "To find the Respondent Guilty, you must find beyond a reasonable doubt: (c) That J. Bruce McDonald was actually placed in danger" was error. He argues that the court's charge on this issue was that, "The testimony is not whether, in fact, the weapon was loaded, but whether it reasonably appeared to the person that he was placed in such danger." Taken out of context, as this quotation is, it would appear to be an instruction more favorable to the defendant than he would be entitled to under 13 V.S.A. § 1025. It would require proof on the part of the State that a person toward whom an actor pointed a firearm could reasonably believe that he was in danger of death or bodily injury from the firearm.

However, reading the charge as a whole, as we must, we find that the court correctly charged the jury. The charge was directly based on the words of the statute, and the jury was instructed several times during the charge that the crucial issue was whether or not the defendant pointed a firearm at the officer. As we have already pointed out, under the second sentence of 13 V.S.A. § 1025 the danger to the victim is presumed once the jury decides that the defendant pointed a firearm in the direction of the victim. While the loaded or unloaded condition of the firearm is irrelevant, an accused can, of course, introduce potentially exculpatory evidence for the jury's consideration that the firearm was actually a toy and incapable, under any conditions, of inflicting injury. As no such evidence was adduced below, defendant takes nothing by his exception to the charge on this issue. * * *

Judgment affirmed.

DALEY, JUSTICE (dissenting).

While I fully concur with the view of the majority that under the statute the knowledge of the actor as to the loaded or unloaded nature of the firearm is an irrelevancy, I cannot subscribe to my associates' further conclusion that the question of whether the gun is *actually* loaded or unloaded is similarly nongermane.

In my opinion, one cannot be placed in an objective state of danger when an unloaded gun is pointed at him. He may well be "in fear", but he is not, as I see it, "in danger". In cases of this nature I would recognize the presumption of danger (loaded gun) from the act of pointing, but permit the defendant to present evidence that the gun was not, in fact, loaded. The ultimate determination as to whether the gun was loaded, and thus whether the victim was placed in danger, would then properly rest with the jury.

Defendant in the case before us testified at trial that the gun was not loaded, and I feel that the trial court committed reversible error in instructing the jury that "the fact that a firearm is or is not loaded is of no importance." The jury was thereby prevented from considering an important factor bearing on the essential element of danger.

I would reverse.

Notes and Questions

1.   Is the majority correct in saying that defendant's construction of the statute would "lead to an absurd result"? Consider *State v. McLaren*, 135 Vt. 291, 376 A.2d 34 (1977), stating: "We fully recognize, as did both the majority and dissenting opinions in *Cushman*, that the statutory presumption renders irrelevant the state of mind of the actor as it relates to the loaded nature of the firearm. We cannot agree, however, with the view expressed by the majority in *Cushman* that the presumption can be likewise construed to make irrelevant the actual dangerous nature of the firearm itself. We therefore overrule *Cushman* and hold that the Legislature, when it enacted 13 V.S.A. § 1025, intended to proscribe conduct which would place the victim in actual danger of death or serious bodily injury, not mere apparent danger."

2.   Is there a difference between the unloaded antique in *Cushman* and a loaded but jammed gun? Consider *People v. Davis*, 72 N.Y.2d 32, 530 N.Y.S.2d 529, 526 N.E.2d 20 (1988), where defendant was convicted of reckless endangerment, which "is committed when a person, under circumstances evincing a depraved indifference to human life, recklessly creates a grave risk of death to another (Penal Law § 120.25). A person acts recklessly when he is aware of, but disregards, a substantial and unjustifiable risk to the degree that his behavior does not comport with the manner in which a reasonable person would have acted under the circumstances." Considering the "narrow question" whether "pointing a gun at another and pulling the trigger constitute reckless endangerment when a jammed cartridge prevents the gun from firing," the appellate court concluded "that such conduct does not, in the words of the statute, 'create a grave risk of death to another.'" The dissent objected:

"It is indisputable that the gun had just discharged in a struggle during a failed robbery attempt and that a few minutes later, and with no break in the action, defendant assumed a crouched combat stance, pointed the loaded weapon (a 9 millimeter semiautomatic with high velocity bullets) at the windshield of the pursuing police car 20 feet away and pulled the trigger. Fortuitously, at that particular instant of the confrontation, the just previously spent shell casing had lodged in the chamber and no bullet emerged. The unrebutted testimony of a police ballistics expert was that the gun showed evidence of recent discharge, that a spent round had been recovered, and that upon test-firing the weapon both the gun and the ammunition were found to be operable. Indeed, one of the responding policemen, Officer Farley, indicated in his testimony that he perceived the risk of death to be grave throughout the incident, including after defendant pulled the trigger of his gun the first time; thus, when defendant assumed the combat stance and prepared to fire a second time at Farley's fellow officer as the two officers were chasing defendant all on foot, Farley shot defendant before he could repeat his act.

"The majority's interpretation of the statute and its application in this instance are thus flawed. Even if 'operability' and 'grave risk of death' were synonymous, and even if they are to be gauged by a flash-frozen moment in eternity, which is probably too inflexible an approach, still in this case the People's direct and circumstantial evidence on grave risk of death is enough beyond a reasonable doubt. Surely, the test of reckless endangerment in the first degree cannot be that the perpetrator must succeed and that failure in accomplishing the intended act under the grave risk created by the perpetrator somehow nullifies the crime in these circumstances. The grave risk of death was unquestionably present and proven because another squeeze of the trigger, another jarring of the gun by the mere palm of a hand to dislodge the just spent shell, or any among many other intended or fortuitous instantaneous actions, could have brought death to the pursuing officers. The grave risk of death was present throughout, and the mere fact that one firing failed does not evaporate the risk intended to be punished by the statute."

3. Is *Davis* the same as or different from the hypothetical put in Larry Alexander, *Insufficient Concern: A Unified Conception of Criminal Culpability*, 88 Calif.L.Rev. 931, 935 (2000)?: "David wants to get home in time to watch the Lakers game on television. He accelerates until his speedometer reads ninety miles per hour, a speed that he believes creates a very substantial risk of death, serious bodily injury, or property damage to other drivers, passengers, and pedestrians. In fact, his speedometer is broken, and he is only going fifty-five miles per hour, a reasonable speed given the road and traffic conditions. Is David acting recklessly?" Alexander's answer is yes, that an "actor is reckless if he believes he is imposing a level of risk that would be unjustifiable regardless of the actual risk he is imposing," because risk "is always relative to someone's perspective, a perspective that is defined by possession of certain information but not other information," but he then concludes that the law "appears to be against me" on this point. Id. at 935–36.

4. In *State v. Wong,* 125 N.H. 610, 486 A.2d 262 (1984), the court ruled that defendant, who was driving while intoxicated at the time of his death-causing conduct, was properly convicted of negligent homicide despite the absence of a specific allegation or proof of criminal negligence. (The negligent homicide statute says that a "person is guilty of a class B felony when he causes the death of another: I. Negligently; or II. In consequence of his being under the influence of intoxicating liquor or controlled drug while operating a propelled vehicle.")

"The plain meaning of RSA 630:3 comports with the comments of the drafters of the statute. The statute is based, in part, on the 'determination' by the drafters that 'using an instrumentality as dangerous to human life as a vehicle . . . while in a state of intoxication is *per se* negligence.' Report of Commission to Recommend Codification of Criminal Laws, Comments, at 36 (1969). * * *

"Accordingly, it is clear that the legislature, in adopting the drafter's formulation of the negligent homicide statute, intended that the culpability requirement of negligent homicide can be satisfied *either* by showing that a person caused the death of another '[n]egligently,' *or* by establishing that the person caused the death in consequence of driving a propelled vehicle while under the influence of intoxicating liquor or a controlled drug."

5. Do *Cushman* and *Wong* involve conclusive presumptions which are invalid under *Sandstrom,* p. 135 of this Book?

SECTION 5. STRICT LIABILITY

STATE v. STEPNIEWSKI

Supreme Court of Wisconsin, 1982.
105 Wis.2d 261, 314 N.W.2d 98.

STEINMETZ, JUSTICE.

The principal issue in this case is whether the state must prove intentional conduct by a defendant in all charged circumstances of a violation of sec. 100.26(3), Stats.1977,[1] for a conviction. * * *

The defendants, Malec and Stepniewski, were each convicted of trade practice violations, Malec of six violations and Stepniewski of 12 counts. The evidence showed that the two defendants violated ch. AG 110 Wis.Adm.Code.[3] In particular, the defendants on several occasions failed to state in writing projects' starting and completion dates. On other occasions, while the defendants did enter such dates in writing, they then failed to complete the projects. In two cases where work was left undone, severe damage occurred to the homes when winter arrived. Many of the homeowners victimized by the defendants were elderly and retired citizens. * * *

The defendants interpret the focused language of sec. 100.26(3), Stats.1977, "or who intentionally refuses, neglects or fails to obey any regulation made under s. 100.19 or 100.20, shall, * * * "as meaning that "intentionally" modifies all the words following it. * * *

The words following "intentionally" are "*refuses*," "*neglects*" or "*fails*." (Emphasis added.) The Random House Dictionary of the English Language, Unabridged Edition, relevant definitions of those words as verbs are:

"refuse—* * * to express a determination not to (do something) * * * to decline to submit to * * * to decline acceptance, consent, or compliance * * * "

"neglect—to pay no attention * * * to omit, through indifference or carelessness * * * to fail to carry out or perform (order, duties, etc.) * * * "

"fail—to fall short of success or achievement in something expected, attempted, desired, or approved * * * to be or become deficient or lacking * * * "

Since "refuses" has usages ranging from an expression of determination to not do something to a more passive declination of compliance, it is apparent the legislature preceded the word "refuses" with "intentionally" to make it understood that the refusal intended was the determination to not do something. This was done so mere declination to comply would be understood to be the same as a failure to carry out or perform an order or duties, which is the meaning of *neglect*. Neglect was, therefore, not modified by "intentionally," since the conduct described was something less than determination to not act.

---

1. Sec. 100.26(3), Stats.1977, provides:

"Any person who violates s. 100.15, 100.19, 100.20 or 100.22, or who intentionally refuses, neglects or fails to obey any regulation made under s. 100.19 or 100.20, shall, for each offense, be fined not less than $25 nor more than $5,000, or imprisoned in the county jail for not more than one year or both."

3. Ch. AG 110 Wis.Adm.Code, in pertinent part, states:

"AG 110.02 **Prohibited trade practices.** No seller shall engage in the following unfair methods of competition or unfair trade practices:

" * * * *

"(7) PERFORMANCE * * *.

"(b) Fail to begin or complete work on the dates or within the time period specified in the home improvement contract, or as otherwise represented, unless the delay is for reason of labor stoppage, unavailability of supplies or materials, unavoidable casualties, or any other cause beyond the seller's control. Any changes in the dates or time periods stated in a written contract shall be agreed to in writing."

"AG 110.05 **Home improvement contract requirements.** * * *

" * * * *

"(2) Home improvement contracts and all changes in the terms and conditions thereof, required under this section to be in writing, shall be signed by all parties thereto, and shall clearly and accurately set forth in legible form all terms and conditions of the contract, and particularly the following:

" * * * *

"(d) The dates or time period on or within which the work is to begin and be completed by the seller."

The word "fails" was intended to mean a failure to obey a regulation by a lack of success or achievement, where the performance in compliance was deficient or lacking.

The legislature intended to provide for as wide a range of conduct to be included as an offense of sec. 100.26(3), Stats.1977, as penalties provided: "shall for each offense, be fined not less than $25 nor more than $5,000, or imprisoned in the county jail for not more than one year or both."

The legislature has shown its awareness of the use of intentional in respect to neglect and other words in other statutes, *i.e.*:

> "52.05 **Abandonment; uniform act.** (1) PENALTY. Any person who, without just cause, deserts or wilfully [intentionally] neglects *or* refuses to provide for the support and maintenance of his or her spouse or child under 18 years * * * ." (Emphasis added.)

> "947.15 **Contributing to the delinquency of children; neglect; neglect contributing to death.** (1) The following persons * * *

> "(a) Any person * * * who intentionally encourages *or* contributes to the delinquency * * * *or* the neglect of any child * * * ." (Emphasis added.)

When the legislature intended in those statutes that the modifying word "intentionally" apply to other words and also "neglect," it used the conjunctive word "*or*." It did not do so in sec. 100.26(3), Stats.1977, until after the word neglect and before the word "fails." Intentionally cannot modify "fails," since one who has intentionally failed to obey is one who has a mental purpose of refusal to obey and such use would be duplicitous.

The defendant argues that sec. 100.26(3), Stats.1977, was meant to include only intentional conduct or, alternatively, that it violates due process to convict a person of a crime with no *mens rea*. This idea was rejected by the U.S. Supreme Court and this court in several instances over the years. The first rejection in Wisconsin was in *State v. Hartfiel*, 24 Wis. 60 (1869), which involved the prosecution of a saloon keeper for serving a minor an intoxicating liquor when the statute did not include the words "knowingly" or "wilfully." The jurors were instructed that ignorance or mistake on the part of the accused as to the fact that the six-foot-one-inch person who was served was a minor was no defense. The court held:

> "The act in question is a police regulation, and we have no doubt that the legislature intended to inflict the penalty, irrespective of the knowledge or motives of the person who has violated its provisions. Indeed, if this were not so, it is plain that the statute might be violated times without number, with no possibility of convicting offenders, and so it would become a dead letter on the statute book, and the evil aimed at by the legislature remain almost wholly untouched. To guard against such results, the legislature has, in effect, provided that the saloon keeper, or other vendor of intoxicating liquors or drinks, must know the facts—must know that the person to whom he sells is a *qualified drinker*, within the meaning of the statute; and, if not, he acts at his peril in disobeying the requirements of the law."

The U.S. Supreme Court stated the history of crime without intent in *Morissette v. United States*, 342 U.S. 246, 72 S.Ct. 240, 96 L.Ed. 288 (1952) and declared: * * *

> "The industrial revolution multiplied the number of workmen exposed to injury from increasingly powerful and complex mechanisms, driven by freshly discovered sources of energy, requiring higher precautions by employers. Traffic of velocities, volumes and varieties unheard of came to subject the wayfarer to intolerable casualty risks if owners and drivers were not to observe new cares and uniformities of conduct.

Congestion of cities and crowding of quarters called for health and welfare regulations undreamed of in simpler times. Wide distribution of goods became an instrument of wide distribution of harm when those who dispersed food, drink, drugs, and even securities, did not comply with reasonable standards of quality, integrity, disclosure and care. Such dangers have engendered increasingly numerous and detailed regulations which heighten the duties of those in control of particular industries, trades, properties or activities that affect public health, safety or welfare.

"While many of these duties are sanctioned by a more strict civil liability, lawmakers, whether wisely or not, have sought to make such regulations more effective by invoking criminal sanctions to be applied by the familiar technique of criminal prosecutions and convictions. This has confronted the courts with a multitude of prosecutions, based on statutes or administrative regulations, for what have been aptly called 'public welfare offenses.' These cases do not fit neatly into any of such accepted classifications of common-law offenses, such as those against the state, the person, property, or public morals. Many of these offenses are not in the nature of positive aggressions or invasions, with which the common law so often dealt, but are in the nature of neglect where the law requires care, or inaction where it imposes a duty. Many violations of such regulations result in no direct or immediate injury to person or property but merely create the danger or probability of it which the law seeks to minimize. While such offenses do not threaten the security of the state in the manner of treason, they may be regarded as offenses against its authority, for their occurrence impairs the efficiency of controls deemed essential to the social order as presently constituted. In this respect, whatever the intent of the violator, the injury is the same, and the consequences are injurious or not according to fortuity. Hence, legislation applicable to such offenses, as a matter of policy, does not specify intent as a necessary element. The accused, if he does not will the violation, usually is in a position to prevent it with no more care than society might reasonably expect and no more exertion than it might reasonably exact from one who assumed his responsibilities. Also, penalties commonly are relatively small, and conviction does no grave damage to an offender's reputation. Under such considerations, courts have turned to construing statutes and regulations which make no mention of intent as dispensing with it and holding that the guilty act alone makes out the crime. This has not, however, been without expressions of misgiving. * * * "

The statement of purpose for creating sec. 100.26(3), Stats.1977, is reflected in sec. 100.20(1) and (2):

"100.20 **Methods of competition and trade practices.** (1) Methods of competition in business and trade practices in business shall be fair. Unfair methods of competition in business and unfair trade practices in business are hereby prohibited.

"(2) The department, after public hearing, may issue general orders forbidding methods of competition in business or trade practices in business which are determined by the department to be unfair. The department, after public hearing, may issue general orders prescribing methods of competition in business or trade practices in business which are determined by the department to be fair."

The statement of purpose as appears in subsecs. (1) and (2) reflect a concern of the legislature with protection of the public, and it has chosen a proper means of exercising its police power to protect the public welfare. The literal reading of the statute urged by the defendants would interfere with the substantive purpose of the legislature. * * *

The defendants held themselves out to the public as persons having an expertise in home improvement. They sought out, by advertising and referrals, those persons in society who were in need of help and for the most part uninformed as to the law and construction practices. It is reasonable and necessary for the legislative body to protect the innocent who need services by placing a burden of regularity, evenhandedness and legal guidelines on the purveyors of the services. It is as much a part of competition to be honest, forthright and fulfilling as it is to work for a lower bid. The public does not always recognize this. Good, honest entrepreneurs recognize it and are not hurt by the law holding them strictly liable in a punitive statute which requires minimum standards of behavior. It is not offensive to require starting dates and completion dates to be stated in a contract. It would appear offensive only to persons not wishing to be held to any semblance of accountability. * * *

ABRAHAMSON, JUSTICE (dissenting). * * *

The instant case differs from the usual case raising the issue of whether the legislature intended scienter to be an element of a crime, in that in the usual case, the statutory definition of the crime is silent as to the element of scienter. In the case at bar, as the state and the majority acknowledge, the legislature specifically includes scienter in the definition of the offense; scienter is required for at least one type of violation of sec. 100.26(3), namely the state must prove that a defendant intentionally refuses to obey the regulation. While in the usual case the state urges this court not to read the element of scienter into a statute which is silent as to mens rea, in this case the state urges us to read the statute to create three ways of committing a crime, only one of which requires proof of scienter. The state is in effect asking the court to read scienter out of a portion of the statute.

The cases and commentators suggest that courts consider the following factors in deciding whether a statute should be interpreted as requiring scienter as an element of the crime or as imposing liability without fault:

1. The language of the statute.

2. The legislative history of the statute.

3. The seriousness of the penalty.

4. The purpose of the statute.

5. The practical requirements of effective law enforcement. * * *

In determining legislative intent and in analyzing the five factors outlined above, a key principle is that "the element of scienter is the rule rather than the exception in our criminal jurisprudence." This court has frequently recognized that a primary ethical foundation of the criminal justice system is that criminal liability is premised on individual blameworthiness. Reviewing these factors in the context of the case at bar, I conclude that they weigh heavily in favor of holding that the legislature intended scienter to be a necessary element of sec. 100.26(3).

Language of the Statute. As the majority concedes, the statute can reasonably be read so that intentionally modifies all three verbs. The majority then labors mightily to limit "intentionally" to modifying the verb "refuses" and to define "refuses," "neglects" and "fails" as three totally separate and distinct ways of committing a single offense. There are several flaws in the majority's analysis. First, the majority defines "refuses" as meaning intentional conduct, and the majority's conclusion that the word "intentionally" modifies only the verb "refuses" renders the word "intentionally" redundant. Second, the majority's dictionary definitions of the three verbs—and especially the definitions of neglect and fail—demonstrate that the meanings of the three verbs are not totally different and in fact overlap. * * *

Legislative History. Although the legislative history does not provide a definitive answer to the proper construction of the statute, it does point toward the legislature intending scienter to be an element of the crime. As the majority points out, the original 1921 version of sec. 100.26(3) does not include any words indicating that scienter is an element of the crime. In 1923 the legislature revised sec. 100.26(3), specifically adding the element of scienter. The 1923 statute reads "wilfully violates or refuses, neglects or fails to obey any order or regulation." * * *

Severity of the Penalty. One of the principal indices courts consider to determine whether the legislature intended to require scienter is the severity of the penalty involved. Penalties imposed on the basis of strict liability "commonly are relatively small and conviction does no grave damage to an offender's reputation." *Morissette v. United States.*

In the instant case the potential maximum penalty is relatively severe in the context of criminal sanctions. The penalty under sec. 100.26(3)—up to one-year imprisonment in the county jail or a fine from $25 to $5,000, or both—is more severe—at least as to the term of imprisonment—than the penalty for the highest classification of misdemeanors in the criminal code. * * *

The state and the majority would have us look not at the maximum penalty possible but at the minimum penalty allowable, and the majority apparently reasons that the range of penalties illustrates that the legislature meant the statute to include various degrees of scienter. One way the majority opinion can be read is that it concludes that any problem caused by the severity of the sentence is cured by the prosecutors exercising discretion in selecting persons for prosecution and in charging the appropriate degree of scienter, and by the trial courts exercising discretion in imposing the severest penalties only on those who acted most culpably. This solution is not satisfactory; the solution merely dispenses with the safeguards of a trial on the critical issue of blameworthiness. The defendants in this case were charged with and convicted of "failing" to obey the regulations, the least culpable behavior under the reasoning of the majority. Yet the defendants were sentenced to one-year terms of imprisonment on each charge, several to be served consecutively. I recognize that the defendants had been previously charged with crimes involving property improvements and that execution of the present sentences was stayed pending probation. Nevertheless, if either defendant violates one of the numerous terms of probation, he will be subject to a lengthy period of imprisonment on conviction of "strict liability" offenses.

In my view, a determinative factor in the case at bar is the severity of the penalty. I do not believe the legislature intended a person who is blameless to be subjected to the harsh consequences sec. 100.26(3) imposes. It is one thing to accept the idea that a blameless person might occasionally be required to pay a fine and quite another to speak of a blameless person spending a year in county jail.

* * * Under the [Model Penal] Code a conviction resting on strict liability may result only in a civil penalty of monetary forfeiture. The rationale for the position taken in the Model Penal Code is explained as follows:

> " * * * The liabilities involved are indefensible in principle, unless reduced to terms that insulate conviction from the type of moral condemnation that is and ought to be implicit when a sentence of imprisonment may be imposed. In the absence of minimal culpability, the law has neither a deterrent nor corrective nor an incapacitative function to perform. * * * "

Purpose of the Statute. * * *

Although one purpose of sec. 100.20, pursuant to which the regulations in the case at bar were issued, is to implement a high standard of care in the public's interest of protecting competition, I conclude that an additional purpose of sec. 100.20, and the primary purpose of the regulations in the case at bar and of sec. 100.26(3), is to punish wrongdoers. If the primary purpose of sec. 100.26(3) is to punish wrongdoers, the legislature must have intended that scienter be an element of the criminal offense set forth in sec. 100.26(3). I reach these conclusions for several reasons.

First, strict liability has generally been imposed on people who engage in acts which in and of themselves are not innocent or on people who engage in unusual or highly regulated activities and who may reasonably be held to know of and conform to government regulations. Such is not the case here.

Unlike the usual strict liability statutes which affect special, highly regulated businesses or activities such as drugs, intoxicating liquors, or firearms, sec. 100.20 and the regulations adopted under sec. 100.20, the violation of which are penalized under sec. 100.26(3), Stats., affect potentially all business people in the state. * * *

Thus when the majority decides that the legislature did not intend that scienter be proved for violations of home improvement regulations, it ignores the fact that its decision governs violations not only of the regulations of home improvement contracts but also of regulations which potentially govern every person engaged in almost any trade or business in this state. I find it hard to believe that the legislature intended criminal sanctions ranging up to a $5,000 fine and one year imprisonment to be imposed on each business person in the state who without fault fails to comply with one of the multitude of administrative regulations adopted under sec. 100.20, Stats.

Second, most of the home improvement regulations deal with false statements and misrepresentations and thus prescribe offenses which are supplementary to and extensions of the common law crimes of larceny, false pretenses and cheat. The purpose of these regulations is to prevent unscrupulous, fraudulent business practices which harm individual consumers. Many other regulations adopted pursuant to sec. 100.20 have a similar purpose. It is apparent that the Department of Agriculture, Trade and Consumer Protection has interpreted sec. 100.20 to authorize regulations to protect the pocket book of the individual consumer. These regulations primarily expand common-law and statutory property offenses; they do not primarily protect the public safety or the physical welfare or economic order of the community. Because the regulations of Ag ch. 110 (as well as other regulations) proscribe in large part variants of the classic larceny offense, a traditional property offense protecting individual private property, and because ordinarily scienter is an element of such an offense at common law, I conclude that the legislature intended scienter to be an element of sec. 100.26(3).

Third, as is explained more fully below, the legislature provided a multitude of civil remedies for violation of a regulation issued under sec. 100.20 in lieu of or in addition to criminal prosecution under sec. 100.26(3). The multitude of civil remedies indicates that the legislature intended criminal prosecution to be used to punish only "intentional" offenses.

Effective enforcement of the law. The larger the number of prosecutions expected or required to enforce the law, the more likely the legislature meant to impose liability without fault; the fewer the expected or required prosecutions, the more likely the legislature meant the prosecutor to prove scienter.

The legislature did not envisage a large number of criminal prosecutions under sec. 100.26(3) which had to be quickly processed. Quick criminal trials unhindered by proof of scienter are not needed for effective enforcement of sec. 100.20 or the regulations. The Wisconsin legislature has enacted a multitude of civil administrative and judicial remedies to enable the department of agriculture, trade and consumer protection, the department of justice, the district attorneys and the injured parties to stop the prohibited practices and to afford relief to the injured parties.

With this arsenal of weapons available to the state and the injured party against the violator, the argument that requiring proof of scienter in criminal prosecutions imposes severe difficulties in enforcement of the statute and regulations is not persuasive in the instant case.

The defendant argues that if the statute does not require scienter the statute violates due process. The majority apparently rejects this argument quoting at length various cases that have upheld strict liability statutes. I recognize that this court has, as have many federal and state courts, upheld the constitutionality of legislative acts creating crimes without a requirement of intent. Nevertheless the majority errs in intentionally neglecting to acknowledge that many courts and commentators have expressed misgivings about the constitutionality of strict liability statutes and that courts have recognized that due process may be violated when imprisonment and the stigma of a conviction are imposed on acts done innocently.

Professor Packer concludes that one of the major flaws in the jurisprudence concerning mens rea is that courts have consistently avoided trying to define the constitutional limits of the problem by employing the conclusory label, "public welfare offense." Packer, *Mens Rea and The Supreme Court,* 1962 The Supreme Court Review 149–52. The majority by not tackling the constitutional issue raised by its holding that scienter is not an element of the offense does nothing to provide future guidance for the legislature, litigants or the courts. For even if it is difficult to analyze the interrelation of scienter and due process, this court should try to begin to define the limits, if any, on the legislature's power to define a crime.

Notes and Questions

1. In *Morissette,* quoted in *Stepniewski,* the defendant had been convicted of converting government bomb casings which he had found on a government target range while deer hunting. The district court had refused to instruct on the issue of intent, holding no intent was required by the statute, and the court of appeals affirmed. In reversing, the Supreme Court distinguished the instant case from those dealing with regulatory or "public welfare offenses" not requiring proof of intent. In concluding that Congress must not have intended merely by omission of fault words from the statute to make this crime a strict liability offense, the Court stressed (i) that the crime is a felony when the value of the property taken exceeds $100; (ii) that conviction of such a crime would gravely besmirch the defendant as a thief; and (iii) that the offense was taken over from the common law, which required proof of intent.

2. Stepniewski challenged his conviction in federal court via habeas corpus. The district court granted relief, relying upon *Morissette,* but the court of appeals reversed: "Although the *Morissette* court enunciated various factors, including those used by the district court, for federal courts to consider when reviewing statutes that arguably impose strict liability, the Court did not establish those factors as principles of constitutional law." *Stepniewski v. Gagnon,* 732 F.2d 567 (7th Cir.1984).

3. Frank J. Remington & Orrin L. Helstad, *The Mental Element in Crime—A Legislative Problem,* 1952 Wis.L.Rev. 644, 670: "How can these strict liability crimes be distinguished from those requiring proof of a mental element? Several tests have been suggested. Perhaps the one most frequently suggested is the determination of whether the

crime is 'malum in se' or 'malum prohibitum.' Others seem to think it depends on whether the crime is a common-law crime or a statutory one. The size of the possible penalty also has been suggested as a test. Since most of these offenses are of relatively recent origin, having resulted from the need for social regulation brought about by the industrial revolution, they usually can be recognized by their regulatory character. It has been pointed out that most of them fall into one or the other of the following categories: 1. illegal sales of intoxicating liquor; 2. sales of impure or adulterated food or drugs; 3. sales of misbranded articles; 4. violations of antinarcotic acts; 5. criminal nuisances; 6. violations of traffic regulations; 7. violations of motor-vehicle laws; and 8. violations of general police regulations, passed for the safety, health, or well-being of the community. If these categories could be depended on as being the exclusive ones where strict liability is imposed, the problem would be simplified considerably, but they cannot. The tendency is to every now and then extend strict liability to much more serious crimes. Thus, strict liability is quite frequently imposed for sex crimes committed against persons below a certain age, for adultery, and for bigamy."

4. State court decisions on the question of whether a criminal statute empty of words denoting fault was intended by the legislature to be a strict liability statute are typically based upon some or all of the factors discussed in *Stepniewski*. However, in the modern codes there is a greater likelihood that the court will find more guidance as to when absence of fault words in a statute means strict liability. Thus, in *People v. Arnold,* 3 Ill.App.3d 678, 279 N.E.2d 436 (1972), the court relied upon a criminal code provision which stated that an offense is not of the strict liability type unless it "is a misdemeanor which is not punishable by incarceration or by a fine exceeding $500, or the statute defining the offense clearly indicates a legislative purpose to impose absolute liability for the conduct described," in holding that the statute under which the defendant was charged required proof of a mental state.

5. Herbert Packer, *Mens Rea and the Supreme Court,* 1962 Sup.Ct.Rev. 107, 109: "The role of *mens rea* in the criminal law has been the subject of much discussion. The consensus can be summarily stated: to punish conduct without reference to the actor's state of mind is both inefficacious and unjust. It is inefficacious because conduct unaccompanied by an awareness of the factors making it criminal does not mark the actor as one who needs to be subjected to punishment in order to deter him or others from behaving similarly in the future, nor does it single him out as a socially dangerous individual who needs to be incapacitated or reformed. It is unjust because the actor is subjected to the stigma of a criminal conviction without being morally blameworthy. Consequently, on either a preventive or a retributive theory of criminal punishment, the criminal sanction is inappropriate in the absence of *mens rea*."

6. Compare Note, 75 Colum.L.Rev. 1517, 1537, 1564 (1975): "Punishing those in excusing conditions can have utile consequences. While the *threat* of punishment may indeed be inefficacious in deterring crimes by those in excusing conditions, the actual infliction of such punishment on *blameless* offenders may well serve to increase adherence to the law by members of the general public not in excusing conditions. Primarily, it would deter those potential offenders who *believe* (correctly or incorrectly) that their fault in committing a crime is probably unprovable in a court of law. * * *

"The retributivist reminds us that a state of affairs in which undeserved punishment is imposed is worse than one in which it is not imposed, and that since the institution of a system of strict liability leads with virtual certainty to such undeserved punishment, it is unacceptable.

"The retributivist, however, fails to consider the total context in which strict liability has been defended. It is not only undeserved punishment that is an evil, but also any undeserved *suffering*. Strict liability may well prevent undeserved suffering by victims of crime. Where some few individuals suffer undeserved punishment under a system which thereby deters many harmful offenses against individuals equally undeserving of harm, the total degree of desert requital may be greater than under a system which does not impose liability without fault."

7. The dissent in *Stepniewski* points out that strict liability statutes are selectively enforced. In assessing whether such crimes have a legitimate place in a rational system of criminal law, is this a plus or a minus?

(a) Consider the description of the enforcement of the food and drug laws by the Wisconsin Department of Agriculture in Comment, 1956 Wis.L.Rev. 641, 653–55: "The general policy of the department has been to refrain from prosecuting inadvertent violations of the food and drug sections until a specific warning has been given and the violator has had ample opportunity to cease the offending action or correct the offensive condition. The considerations underlying this policy are many. Some of the more clearly defined factors include: (1) The department believes that the most effective control and the best public relations can be achieved by co-operation with the regulated group and correction of the average offender, coupled with selective prosecution of only the uncooperative recalcitrant minority. (2) The state would incur substantial cost from large numbers of food and drug prosecutions. (3) Administrative officers and field inspectors alike share a natural reluctance to be responsible for the imposition of punishment for a wholly unintended violation by a defendant free from any subjective fault. (4) The department faces the necessity of convincing the appropriate district attorney to institute prosecution, even after the inspector has decided that prosecution is desirable and has prepared a case. Evidence that a warning has been issued to the prospective defendant and has been ignored will often encourage a district attorney, who might otherwise be hesitant to do so, to prosecute. (5) Courts and juries may be reluctant to find an offender guilty even in the face of conclusive evidence of an actual violation, unless this evidence is accompanied by some showing of moral culpability, or subjective fault, such as might be provided by proof of failure to heed an express warning issued by the department. * * *

"To a certain extent the practical effect of these enforcement policies is to nullify the significance of the liability without fault character of the food and drug sections, since prosecution under them takes place only when the defendant has demonstrated subjective fault by showing a conscious intent to violate or, at least, a wilful heedlessness in failing to respond to repeated warnings. However, the liability without fault character of these provisions is still of prime importance to successful regulation of foods and drugs because the necessity of proving guilty knowledge or intent to the satisfaction of a court or jury would in many instances present an insurmountable burden to the department and greatly hinder efforts at control and regulation. This would be true even in many cases of conscious and advertent violation."

(b) But consider John S. Wiley Jr., *Not Guilty by Reason of Blamelessness: Culpability in Federal Criminal Interpretation*, 85 Va.L.Rev. 1021, 1065–66 (1999): "In truth, the prosecutorial discretion defense for strict liability had little going for it in the first place. The argument is too extreme. It gives prosecutors the power to convict the morally innocent—and no one else can do anything about it. This power is fundamentally different than a prosecutor's usual and necessary power of deciding which culpable people to prosecute. That traditional discretion, which is unavoidable in a world of scarce resources and abundant crime, properly goes to prosecutors rather than some less flexible, less specialized, less informed, and less local decisionmaker—like Congress or the courts. But the argument in the strict liability situation is not just that Congress should cast a wide net over wrongdoers large and small and then let prosecutors choose the keepers. It is that Congress should cast a net that covers morally innocent people and then leave all the details to prosecutors. Traditional prosecutorial discretion allows prosecutors no unreviewable power to imprison the innocent. Unreviewable prosecutorial errors there can amount at most to bad priorities: ignoring big fish or fixating on fry. But under statutory construction that allows imprisonment without proof of culpability, judges become powerless to prevent imprisonment of the innocent."

8. Taking into account the reasons for and objections to strict liability in criminal law, may it be said that there are preferable alternatives? Consider:

(a) *Increased penalties.* Note, supra, at 1548, observes that Bentham's oft-quoted principle (that when "the value of the punishment falls short, either in point of certainty, or of proximity, of that of the profit of the offense, it must receive a proportionable addition in point of magnitude") "suggests that it is possible to gain conformity to law by those who would be deterred by strict liability by increasing the penalties associated with crimes. Since the deterrent effect of a punishment is a function of the severity of the threatened punishment and the probability of incurring it, in those cases in which the latter is low, we may increase the former to achieve substantial deterrence."

(b) *Shifting the burden of proof.* Francis B. Sayre, *Public Welfare Offenses,* 33 Colum.L.Rev. 55, 82 (1933): "It is fundamentally unsound to convict a defendant for a crime involving a substantial term of imprisonment without giving him the opportunity to prove that his action was due to an honest and reasonable mistake of fact or that he acted without guilty intent. If the public danger is widespread and serious, the practical situation can be met by shifting to the shoulders of the defendant the burden of proving a lack of guilty intent."

In thus proposing a "good faith defense" for strict liability crimes, Laurie L. Levenson, *Good Faith Defenses: Reshaping Strict Liability Crimes,* 78 Cornell L.Rev. 401 (1993), takes special note of *United States v. Kantor,* 858 F.2d 534 (9th Cir.1988), a prosecution of two admitted producers of pornographic films for violating the federal child pornography law, a strict liability crime prohibiting the production of materials depicting a minor engaged in sexually explicit conduct and carrying a maximum penalty of ten years in jail. The defendants had employed Traci Lords in their films, but they argued they had no reason to believe that she was underage at the time, and they sought to introduce evidence that Lords, her parents and her agent made various efforts, including producing a false birth certificate and driver's license, to deceive them into believing that Lords was old enough to make the films. Lords' physical appearance and reputation in the industry supported her agent's claim that she was an adult. The prosecution moved to preclude any such evidence and the defendants in turn moved to dismiss the charges, after which the trial judge ruled the defendants would be allowed to prove "the defense of a good faith, reasonable mistake of fact as to Lords' actual age." The appellate court affirmed, concluding that in light of the defendants' First Amendment interests they should be allowed to prove their good faith by clear and convincing evidence. The prosecution was then dropped.

(c) *Using objective negligence standard.* Packer, supra, at 109–10: "If there is no concept between *mens rea* in the conventional sense and strict liability, then the agencies of enforcement will choose strict liability when the pressure to do so exists, as it notably does in the case of offenses that are handled on an assembly-line basis. But there is a 'halfway house': criminal liability predicated upon negligence. * * * [T]he idea of criminal responsibility based upon the actor's failure to act as carefully as he should affords an important and largely unutilized means for avoiding the tyranny of strict liability in the criminal law."

9. In *United States v. Balint,* 258 U.S. 250, 42 S.Ct. 301, 66 L.Ed. 604 (1922), the defendants were charged with the sale of narcotics not in pursuance of a written order. The defendants demurred to the indictment on the ground it failed to charge they had sold the drugs knowing them to be such. The district court sustained the demurrer, but the Supreme Court reversed, holding that consistent with Fourteenth Amendment due process "the state may in the maintenance of a public policy provide 'that he who shall do them shall do them at his peril and will not be heard to plead in defense good faith or ignorance.'"

As noted in Herbert Packer, *Mens Rea and the Supreme Court,* 1962 Sup.Ct.Rev. 107, 113–16: "The Government's brief relied upon the numerous State cases in which criminal convictions had been upheld (usually without discussion of constitutionality) even though the statutes were construed to dispense with *mens rea.* There was no appearance for the defendants in the Supreme Court. So it came about that this all-important case was presented on an abstract issue and decided on the basis of an *ex parte* presentation.

"Unfortunately, the unanimous opinion of the Court, written by Mr. Chief Justice Taft, did not remedy the deficiency in the presentation. The constitutional point, only fleetingly referred to in the Government's brief, was quickly dismissed by the Court. * * *

"By a similarly obscure process of divination, the Chief Justice concluded that the omission of any reference to knowledge in the statute indicated an intention on the part of Congress to force persons dealing in narcotic drugs to do so at their peril. 'Doubtless considerations as to the opportunity of the seller to find out the facts and the difficulty of proof of knowledge contributed to this conclusion.' * * * But the Court showed no concern about the imposition of severe criminal sanctions without proof of blameworthiness. There was not a whisper in the opinion about the maximum penalty under the Act: five years' imprisonment, as it then stood. Nor was anything said about the trivial nature of the offenses dealt with in the State cases cited by the Court, although the distinction had not escaped the attention of State court judges.

"Upon this flimsy basis, dictum became holding, and the doctrine passed into our constitutional law that severe criminal punishment may be inflicted at the legislature's will, regardless of whether the defendant had any opportunity to conform his conduct to the requirements of law. And the more far-reaching doctrine that legislative silence is to be construed as a direction to dispense with *mens rea* took a firm hold. One wonders whether the result would have been the same * * * if Balint had come before the Supreme Court after conviction and sentence of five years' imprisonment, rather than in the posture of one protesting the omission of a word from an indictment."

10. Whether as a matter of constitutional law or simply sound criminal law policy, may it be concluded that serious penalties should not be imposed whenever guilt has been established on a strict liability basis? Consider Note, 75 Colum.L.Rev. 1517, 1556 (1975):

"[I]t has been suggested that strict liability may be imposed only where the possible penalty is a (nominal) fine. This basic approach is adopted by the Model Penal Code in section 2.05 and most vigorously defended in the framers' Comments. Yet, the deterrent effect of a threatened punishment depends upon its severity when compared to the anticipated gain by the potential offender from his crime. In the case of selling adulterated foods, drugs, etc., the possible financial gains are often quite high. For that reason, a commensurably high punishment may be necessary to outweigh the lure of the envisaged profits. Nor must such punishment be restricted to severe fines, as the Code suggests, particularly where the potential harm of the offense is severe and widespread. In fact, to some individuals the harm inflicted by a fine of $10,000 would be more severe than a six-month prison sentence."

11. If (at least so long as *Balint* survives) the penalty does not alone provide a basis for setting due process limits on strict liability, then how might such limits be drawn? Consider Alan C. Micheals, *Constitutional Innocence*, 112 Harv.L.Rev. 828, 901–02 (1999): "The Supreme Court has not heeded the academy's many calls for broad constitutional prohibitions on strict liability. A review of the Supreme Court's jurisprudence, including cases involving fundamental rights largely ignored by strict liability commentators, nonetheless reveals that the Court has followed a consistent and powerful, though unstated, principle regarding strict liability. Under this principle, here called constitutional innocence, strict liability is constitutional when, but only when, the intentional conduct covered by the statute (i.e., the statute minus the strict liability element) could be made criminal.

"Constitutional innocence provides a robust explanation for both the cases that have rejected and those that have accepted the constitutionality of strict liability. In addition, constitutional innocence, in both its negative and positive aspects, is well justified as a matter of constitutional interpretation. Furthermore, it has the virtue of respecting legislative primacy and allowing courts to decide strict liability cases using doctrines they already employ; under a constitutional innocence framework, courts can override legislative decisions regarding strict liability only on the basis of independently established limits on legislative power—in particular, recognized fundamental rights, void for vagueness doctrine, and the rational basis test of the Due Process Clause. From a practical perspective, because of constitutional innocence's strong precedential pedigree, its respect for legislative primacy (a longstanding special concern of the Court in matters of substantive criminal law), and its reliance on independently established limits on legislative power, courts may be expected to employ its restrictions on the use of strict liability far more readily than the broader, normative prohibitions commentators have unsuccessfully urged on them in the past."

SECTION 6. IGNORANCE OR MISTAKE OF FACT OR LAW

STATE v. SEXTON   M | F

Supreme Court of New Jersey, 1999.

160 N.J. 93, 733 A.2d 1125.

O'HERN, J. * * *

On May 10, 1993, Shakirah Jones, a seventeen-year-old friend of defendant and decedent, overheard the two young men having what she described as a "typical argument." The two young men walked from a sidewalk into a vacant lot. Jones saw defendant with a gun in his hand, but she did not see defendant shoot Matthews.

Jones heard Matthews tell defendant, "there are no bullets in that gun," and then walk away. Defendant called Matthews back and said, "you think there are no bullets in this gun?" Matthews replied, "yeah." Jones heard the gun go off. A single bullet killed Matthews.

Acting on information received from Jones, police recovered a small caliber automatic pistol near the crime scene. The police did not trace the ownership of the gun, which may have been owned by Matthews's grandmother.

A ballistics expert testified that there was a spring missing from the gun's magazine, which prevented the other bullets from going into the chamber after the first bullet was discharged. In this condition, the gun would have to be loaded manually by feeding the live cartridge into the chamber prior to firing.

The expert later clarified that, if the magazine had been removed after one round had been inserted into the chamber, it would be impossible to see whether the gun was loaded without pulling the slide that covered the chamber to the rear. The expert agreed that, for someone unfamiliar with guns, once the magazine was removed, it was "probably a possible assumption" that the gun was unloaded.

Defendant's version was that when the two young men were in the lot, Matthews showed defendant a gun and "told me the gun was empty." Defendant "asked him was he sure," and "he said yes." When Matthews asked if defendant would like to see the gun, defendant said "yes." Defendant "took the gun and was looking at it, and "it just went off." He never unloaded the gun or checked to see if there were any bullets in the gun. He had never before owned or shot a gun.

A grand jury indicted defendant for purposeful or knowing murder, possession of a handgun without a permit, and possession of a handgun for an unlawful purpose. At the close of the State's case, defendant moved to dismiss the murder charge because the victim had told him that the gun was not loaded. The court denied the motion.

The court charged murder and the lesser-included offenses of aggravated manslaughter and reckless manslaughter. Concerning defendant's version of the facts, the court said:

> Defense contends this was a tragic accident. That Alquadir [Matthews], says the defense, handed the gun to Ronald [defendant]. Alquadir told Ronald, you know, the gun was not loaded. Ronald believed the gun was not loaded. Ronald did not think the gun was pointed at Alquadir when it went off. But the gun went off accidentally and, says the defense, that is a very tragic and sad accident but it is not a crime.

> If, after considering all the evidence in this case, including the evidence presented by the defense as well as the evidence presented by the State, if you have a reasonable doubt in your mind as to whether the State has proven all the elements of any of these crimes: murder, aggravated manslaughter, or reckless manslaughter, you must find the defendant not guilty of those crimes.

The jury found defendant not guilty of murder, aggravated manslaughter, or possession of a handgun for an unlawful purpose, but guilty of reckless manslaughter and unlawful possession of a handgun without a permit.

On the charge of reckless manslaughter, the court sentenced defendant to the presumptive term of seven years, three of which were parole ineligible. For possession of a handgun without a permit, the court sentenced defendant to a concurrent four-year term with no period of parole ineligibility. The court recommended that defendant serve his sentence at the Youth Correction and Reception Center.

On appeal, the Appellate Division reversed defendant's conviction on multiple grounds. The court found that the trial judge erroneously charged the jury on first degree murder, despite the absence of any credible evidence that defendant intended to kill or seriously injure Matthews. The court concluded that the unwarranted charge had the potential of leading the jury to a compromise verdict on reckless manslaughter instead of acquitting him entirely.

The Appellate Division also held that the trial court should have charged the jury that the State bore the burden of disproving beyond a reasonable doubt defendant's mistake-of-fact defense, and that the failure to do so was plain error. The Appellate Division relied on *Wilson v. Tard*, 593 F.Supp. 1091 (D.N.J.1984), in which Judge Stern, applying New Jersey law, reversed a conviction of aggravated manslaughter because the trial court had charged the jury that defendant carried the burden of establishing his mistake-of-fact defense by a preponderance of the evidence. The Appellate Division noted that "[t]he critical holding of *Wilson* is that once the defendant, as here, presents evidence of a reasonable mistake of fact that would refute an essential element of the crime charged, the State's burden of proving each element beyond a reasonable doubt includes disproving the reasonable mistake of fact." * * *

We granted the State's petition for certification, limited to the issue of whether "mistake of fact was a defense to the charge of reckless manslaughter."

* * *To resolve the variety, disparity, and confusion concerning the mental elements of crime, the drafters of the MPC attempted to establish distinct levels of culpability applicable to all criminal offenses. The MPC "obliterated ill-defined, confusing common law language and concepts and replaced them with four specifically defined hierarchial levels of culpability in relation to the three objective element types used to define crimes."

The 1979 New Jersey Code of Criminal Justice followed the mental-state formulation of the MPC. The Code provides generally that no person should be guilty of an offense unless the person "acted purposely, knowingly, recklessly or negligently, as the law may require, with respect to each material element of the offense." * * *

The MPC [§ 2.04] also contains an express provision for mistake-of-fact defenses. "Its mistake of fact provision, while creating potential for conceptual confusion by continuing the common law characterization of the doctrine as a 'defense,' in fact sought to clarify the common law." The MPC expressly recognized that the doctrine did not sanction a true defense, but rather was an attack on the prosecution's ability to prove the requisite culpable mental state for at least one objective element of the crime. Hence, unlike enactments in many pre-MPC states, "the MPC expressly recognizes that the mistake of an accused need not be a reasonable mistake unless the Legislature has expressly decided that the requisite culpable mental state was minimal—'negligence' or perhaps, 'recklessness.'" * * *

Whether a mistake would negate a required element of the offense, depended, of course, on the nature of the mistake and the state of mind that the offense required. This led commentators to observe:

> Technically, such provisions [for a mistake of fact defense] are unnecessary. They simply confirm what is stated elsewhere: 'No person may be convicted of an offense unless each element of such offense is proven beyond a reasonable doubt.' If the defendant's ignorance or mistake makes proof of a required culpability element impossible, the prosecution will necessarily fail in its proof of the offense.

The Commentary to the Hawaii Criminal Code gives an easy example of how, under the MPC, a mistake of fact may negate culpability.

> [I]f a person is ignorant or mistaken as to a matter of fact ... the person's ignorance or mistake will, in appropriate circumstances, prevent the person from having the requisite culpability with respect to the fact ... as it actually exists. For example, a person who is mistaken (either reasonably, negligently, or recklessly) as to which one of a number of similar umbrellas on a rack is the person's and who takes another's umbrella should be afforded a defense to a charge of theft predicated on either intentionally or knowingly taking the property of another.... A reckless mistake would afford a defense to a charge requiring intent or knowledge—but not to an offense which required only recklessness or negligence. Similarly, a negligent mistake

would afford a defense to a charge predicated on intent, knowledge, or recklessness—but not to an offense based on negligence.

[*State v. Cavness*, 80 Hawai'i 460, 911 P.2d 95, 99–100 (Ct.App.1996).]

State legislatures, however, "in emulating the Model Penal Code's three culpability provisions (its culpability definitions, its guidelines for resolving the requisite culpable mental state, and its mistake of fact doctrine), have not always understood their interrelationship. Hence, these states have failed to coordinate the enactment of these three types of culpability provisions." States have restricted the mistake-of-fact doctrine by imposing a reasonableness requirement. By thinking in terms of the reasonable person while failing to appreciate that the MPC's mistake-of-fact and culpability provisions are interrelated, these states have undermined the structure of the MPC.

To explain, we may consider again the case of the absent-minded umbrella thief. If only a reasonable mistake will provide a defense to the charge of theft, the absent-minded but careless restaurant patron will have no defense to a charge of theft. *People v. Navarro*, 99 Cal.App.3d Supp. 1, 160 Cal.Rptr. 692 (1979), explains how a mistake of fact, even though it is unreasonable, may constitute a defense to a crime requiring a culpable mental state higher than recklessness or negligence. In *Navarro*, defendant took some wooden beams from a construction site. He was charged with theft. He claimed that he thought the owner had abandoned the beams. The trial court instructed the jury that this would be a valid defense only if the scavenger's belief was reasonable. The reviewing court held that such an instruction was erroneous because if the jury "concluded that defendant in good faith believed that he had the right to take the beams, even though such belief was unreasonable . . . , defendant was entitled to an acquittal since the specific intent required to be proved as an element of the offense had not been established." Otherwise, one would end up imposing liability for theft on a lesser basis than knowledge or purpose to steal the property of another.

How then shall we resolve the problem created by the selective inclusion and exclusion of the culpability provisions of the MPC?

The issue posed by our grant of certification was whether a mistake of fact was a defense to the charge of reckless manslaughter. The short answer to that question is: "It depends." The longer answer requires that we relate the type of mistake involved to the essential elements of the offense, the conduct proscribed, and the state of mind required to establish liability for the offense. Defendant insists that the State is required to disprove, beyond a reasonable doubt, his mistake-of-fact defense. Most states would agree with that statement. In *State v. Savoie*, 67 N.J. 439, 463 n. 8, 341 A.2d 598 (1975), the Court similarly said that once the defense of mistake of fact is raised, the burden of persuasion is on the State. Just what does that mean? Does it mean that the State must prove that the mistake was unreasonable? We must begin by examining the language of the statute.

N.J.S.A. 2C:2–4a allows a defense of ignorance or mistake "if the defendant reasonably arrived at the conclusion underlying the mistake and" the mistake either "negatives the culpable mental state required to establish the offense" or "[t]he law provides that the state of mind established by such ignorance or mistake constitutes a defense." The crime of manslaughter is a form of criminal homicide. "A person is guilty of criminal homicide if [the actor] purposely, knowingly [or] recklessly . . . causes the death of another human being." N.J.S.A. 2C:11–2. Criminal homicide constitutes aggravated manslaughter, a first-degree offense with special sentencing provisions, when the actor "recklessly causes death under circumstances manifesting extreme indifference to human life." N.J.S.A. 2C:11–4a. Criminal homicide constitutes manslaughter, a second-degree crime, "when . . . [i]t is committed recklessly," that is, when the actor has recklessly caused death. N.J.S.A. 2C:11–4b.

In this case, the jury has acquitted defendant of aggravated manslaughter. He can be retried only for reckless manslaughter. The culpable mental state of the offense is recklessness. N.J.S.A. 2C:2–2b(3) states:

> A person acts recklessly with respect to a material element of an offense when [the actor] consciously disregards a substantial and unjustifiable risk that the material element exists or will result from [the actor's] conduct. The risk must be of such a nature and degree that, considering the nature and purpose of the actor's conduct and the circumstances known to [the actor], its disregard involves a gross deviation from the standard of conduct that a reasonable person would observe in the actor's situation. . . .

The State argues that "[i]t is obvious that the firing of a gun at another human being without checking to see if it is loaded disregards a substantial risk." The State argues that at a minimum there must be some proof establishing that defendant "reasonably arrived at the conclusion underlying the mistake." N.J.S.A. 2C:2–4a. To return to the language of N.J.S.A. 2C:2–4a, does the mistake about whether the gun was loaded "negative[ ] the culpable mental state required to establish the offense", or does "the law provide[ ] that the state of mind established by such ignorance or mistake constitutes a defense"? Of itself, a belief that the gun is loaded or unloaded does not negate the culpable mental state for the crime of manslaughter. Thus, one who discharges a gun, believing it to be unloaded, is not necessarily innocent of manslaughter.

The State notes that under N.J.S.A. 2C:12–1b(4), a defendant is criminally liable for fourth-degree aggravated assault when the actor, "[k]nowingly under circumstances manifesting extreme indifference to the value of human life points a firearm . . . at or in the direction of another, whether or not the actor believes it to be loaded." The State contends that a defendant should not be able to assert a mistake-of-fact defense when charged with manslaughter, if such a defense would not be available against a charge of aggravated assault. In the case of certain offenses, state of mind is simply not an essential or material element. See N.J.S.A. 2C:2–2c(3).

On the other hand, the Sixth Amendment allows a defendant to assert any fact that will negate a material element of a crime. The material elements of manslaughter are the killing of another human being with a reckless state of mind. The culpable mental state is recklessness—the conscious disregard of a substantial and unjustified risk that death will result from the conduct. What mistaken belief will negate this state of mind?

> [T]he translation is uncertain at its most critical point: in determining the kind of mistake that provides a defense when recklessness, the most common culpability level, as to a circumstance is required. Recall that a negligent or faultless mistake negates . . . recklessness. While a "negligent mistake" may be said to be an "unreasonable mistake," all "unreasonable mistakes" are not "negligent mistakes." A mistake may also be unreasonable because it is reckless. Reckless mistakes, although unreasonable, will not negate recklessness. Thus, when offense definitions require recklessness as to circumstance elements, as they commonly do, the reasonable-unreasonable mistake language inadequately describes the mistakes that will provide a defense because of the imprecision of the term "unreasonable mistake." Reckless-negligent-faultless mistake language is necessary for a full and accurate description.

Thus, to disprove a reasonable mistake by proving that it is unreasonable, will turn out to be a mixed blessing for defendant. If the State may disprove a reasonable mistake by proving that the mistake was unreasonable, defendant may be convicted because he was negligent, as opposed to reckless, in forming the belief that the gun was unloaded. If recklessness is required as an element of the offense, "a merely negligent or faultless mistake as to that circumstance provides a defense."

Correctly understood, there is no difference between a positive and negative statement on the issue—what is required for liability versus what will provide a defense to liability .. What is required in order to establish liability for manslaughter is recklessness (as defined by the Code) about whether death will result from the conduct. A faultless or merely careless mistake may negate that reckless state of mind and provide a defense.

How can we explain these concepts to a jury? We believe that the better way to explain the concepts is to explain what is required for liability to be established. The charge should be tailored to the factual circumstances of the case. The court should explain precisely how the offered defense plays into the element of recklessness. Something along the following lines will help to convey to the jury the concepts relevant to a reckless manslaughter charge:

> In this case, ladies and gentlemen of the jury, the defendant contends that he mistakenly believed that the gun was not loaded. If you find that the State has not proven beyond a reasonable doubt that the defendant was reckless in forming his belief that the gun was not loaded, defendant should be acquitted of the offense of manslaughter. On the other hand, if you find that the State has proven beyond a reasonable doubt that the defendant was reckless in forming the belief that the gun was not loaded, and consciously disregarded a substantial and unjustifiable risk that a killing would result from his conduct, then you should convict him of manslaughter.

Undoubtedly, our Committee on Model Criminal Charges can improve the formulation.

To sum up, evidence of an actor's mistaken belief relates to whether the State has failed to prove an essential element of the charged offense beyond a reasonable doubt. As a practical matter, lawyers and judges will undoubtedly continue to consider a mistake of fact as a defense. When we do so, we must carefully analyze the nature of the mistake in relationship to the culpable mental state required to establish liability for the offense charged.

Despite the complexities perceived by scholars, the limited number of appeals on this subject suggests to us that juries have very little difficulty in applying the concepts involved. We may assume that juries relate the instructions to the context of the charge. For example, in the case of the carelessly purloined umbrella, we are certain that juries would have no difficulty in understanding that it would have been a reasonable mistake (although perhaps a negligent mistake) for the customer to believe that he or she was picking up the right umbrella.

To require the State to disprove beyond a reasonable doubt defendant's reasonable mistake of fact introduces an unnecessary and perhaps unhelpful degree of complexity into the fairly straightforward inquiry of whether defendant "consciously disregard[ed] a substantial and unjustifiable risk" that death would result from his conduct and that the risk was "of such a nature and degree that, considering the nature and purpose of the actor's conduct and the circumstances known to him, its disregard involve[d] a gross deviation from the standard of conduct that a reasonable person would observe in the actor's situation."

The judgment of the Appellate Division is affirmed. * * *

Notes and Questions

1. Is it not apparent that in enacting N.J.S.A. 2C:2–4 the New Jersey legislature intended to depart from the Model Penal Code approach in favor of the more traditional approach? If so, on what authority has the New Jersey Supreme Court reached the decision it did in *Sexton*?

2. On retrial for reckless manslaughter, if the jury is instructed as suggested in *Sexton*, what should the result be? If Matthews had survived and Sexton had been charged with fourth-degree aggravated assault, what should the result be?

3. In *Stagner v. State*, 842 P.2d 520 (Wyo.1992), the defendant was charged with violating a statute covering one "who buys, receives, conceals or disposes of property which he knows, believes, or has reasonable cause to believe was obtained in violation of law." Defendant testified that she received the property in question, a 1973 Lincoln Continental Mark IV, from one Kilwein, who told her he had purchased the car in Montana. The trial judge refused defendant's proposed instruction that "a person is not guilty of a crime if he commits an act or omits to act under an honest and reasonable belief in the existence of certain facts and circumstances which, if true, should make such act or omission lawful." Defendant was convicted, but the appellate court reversed on the ground that the federal and state due process clauses require an instruction on defendant's theory of defense whenever that theory is fairly supported by the evidence. A dissenting judge objected that defendant's claim "she did not know the car was stolen" related to "an element of the offense that the State had to prove beyond any reasonable doubt" and that "the jury was given all the instructions required or needed to resolve this case," including one in which "the elements of the offense were articulated" by the jury being told "that it was required to find, beyond a reasonable doubt, that Stagner knew, believed or had reason to believe the car was obtained in violation of law."

Can *Stagner* be reconciled with *Sexton*?

4. Even assuming *Sexton* is correct, there are a few instances in which it is unquestionably correct to refer to mistake of fact as a defense. One is where, as we have seen (Note 8(b), p. 183 of this Book), a court "creates" a defense to a strict liability offense that otherwise might be deemed unconstitutional. See, e.g., *Perez v. State*, 111 N.M. 160, 803 P.2d 249 (1990) (in statutory rape case, where defendant told by victim and another that victim over the age limit, court says that "while we do not hold that knowledge of the victim's age is an element of the offense, we do hold that under the facts of this case the defendant should have been allowed to present his defense of mistake of fact").

PEOPLE v. MARRERO

Court of Appeals of New York, 1987.

69 N.Y.2d 382, 515 N.Y.S.2d 212, 507 N.E.2d 1068.

BELLACOSA, JUDGE.

[Defendant, a federal corrections officer, was arrested in a Manhattan social club for possession of a loaded .38 caliber automatic pistol. The statute under which he was charged exempted "peace officers," which another statute defined to include "correction officers of any state correctional facility or of any penal correctional institution." The charge was dismissed on the ground that defendant fell within that definition, but on appeal the court ruled otherwise, and defendant was thereafter convicted at a trial where the judge refused to instruct that his reasonable belief he fell within the statutory exemption would be a defense.]

The common-law rule on mistake of law was clearly articulated in *Gardner v. People*, 62 N.Y. 299. In *Gardner*, the defendants misread a statute and mistakenly believed that their conduct was legal. The court insisted, however, that the "mistake of law" did not relieve the defendants of criminal liability. * * *

* * * This is to be contrasted with *People v. Weiss*, 276 N.Y. 384, 12 N.E.2d 514 where, in a kidnaping case, the trial court precluded testimony that the defendants acted with the honest belief that seizing and confining the child was done with "authority of law". We held it was error to exclude such testimony since a good-faith belief in the legality of the conduct would negate an express and necessary element of the crime of kidnaping, i.e., intent, without authority of law, to confine or imprison another. Subject to the mistake statute, the instant case, of course, falls within the *Gardner* rationale because the weapons possession statute violated by this defendant imposes liability irrespective of one's intent.

The desirability of the *Gardner*-type outcome, which was to encourage the societal benefit of individuals' knowledge of and respect for the law, is underscored by Justice Holmes' statement: "It is no doubt true that there are many cases in which the criminal could not have known that he was breaking the law, but to admit the excuse at all would be to encourage ignorance where the law-maker has determined to make men know and obey, and justice to the individual is rightly outweighed by the larger interests on the other side of the scales."

The revisors of New York's Penal Law intended no fundamental departure from this common-law rule in Penal Law § 15.20, which provides in pertinent part:

"§ 15.20. Effect of ignorance or mistake upon liability. * * *

"2. A person is not relieved of criminal liability for conduct because he engages in such conduct under a mistaken belief that it does not, as a matter of law, constitute an offense, unless such mistaken belief is founded upon an official statement of the law contained in (a) a statute or other enactment * * * (d) an interpretation of the statute or law relating to the offense, officially made or issued by a public servant, agency, or body legally charged or empowered with the responsibility or privilege of administering, enforcing or interpreting such statute or law."

This section was added to the Penal Law as part of the wholesale revision of the Penal Law in 1965. When this provision was first proposed, commentators viewed the new language as codifying "the established common law maxim on mistake of law, while at the same time recognizing a defense when the erroneous belief is founded upon an 'official statement of the law.' "

The defendant claims as a first prong of his defense that he is entitled to raise the defense of mistake of law under section 15.20(2)(a) because his mistaken belief that his conduct was legal was founded upon an official statement of the law contained in the statute itself. Defendant argues that his mistaken interpretation of the statute was reasonable in view of the alleged ambiguous wording of the peace officer exemption statute, and that his "reasonable" interpretation of an "official statement" is enough to satisfy the requirements of subdivision (2)(a). However, the whole thrust of this exceptional exculpatory concept, in derogation of the traditional and common-law principle, was intended to be a very narrow escape valve. Application in this case would invert that thrust and make mistake of law a generally applied or available defense instead of an unusual exception which the very opening words of the mistake statute make so clear, i.e., "A person is not relieved of criminal liability for conduct * * * unless" (Penal Law § 15.20). The momentarily enticing argument by defendant that his view of the statute would only allow a defendant to get the issue generally before a jury further supports the contrary view because that consequence is precisely what would give the defense the unintended broad practical application.

The prosecution further counters defendant's argument by asserting that one cannot claim the protection of mistake of law under section 15.20(2)(a) simply by misconstruing the meaning of a statute but must instead establish that the statute relied on actually permitted the conduct in question and was only later found to be erroneous. To buttress that argument, the People analogize New York's official statement defense to the approach taken by the Model Penal Code (MPC) [§ 2.04(3)(b)].

Although the drafters of the New York statute did not adopt the precise language of the Model Penal Code provision with the emphasized clause, it is evident and has long been believed that the Legislature intended the New York statute to be similarly construed. * * *

It was early recognized that the "official statement" mistake of law defense was a statutory protection against prosecution based on reliance of a statute that did *in fact* authorize certain conduct. "It seems obvious that society must rely on some statement of the law, and that conduct which is *in fact* 'authorized' * * * should not be subsequently condemned. The threat of punishment under these circumstances can have no deterrent effect unless the actor doubts the validity of the official pronouncement—*a questioning of authority that is itself undesirable*." While providing a narrow escape hatch, the idea was simultaneously to encourage the public to read and rely on official statements of the law, not to have individuals conveniently and personally question the validity and interpretation of the law and act on that basis. If later the statute was invalidated, one who mistakenly acted in reliance on the authorizing statute would be relieved of criminal liability. That makes sense and is fair. To go further does not make sense and would create a legal chaos based on individual selectivity.

In the case before us, the underlying statute never in fact authorized the defendant's conduct; the defendant only thought that the statutory exemptions permitted his conduct when, in fact, the primary statute clearly forbade his conduct. Moreover, by adjudication of the final court to speak on the subject in this very case, it turned out that even the exemption statute did not permit this defendant to possess the weapon. It would be ironic at best and an odd perversion at worst for this court now to declare that the same defendant is nevertheless free of criminal responsibility. * * *

Strong public policy reasons underlie the legislative mandate and intent which we perceive in rejecting defendant's construction of New York's mistake of law defense statute. If defendant's argument were accepted, the exception would swallow the rule. Mistakes about the law would be encouraged, rather than respect for and adherence to law. There would be an infinite number of mistake of law defenses which could be devised from a good-faith, perhaps reasonable but mistaken, interpretation of criminal statutes, many of which are concededly complex. Even more troublesome are the opportunities for wrong-minded individuals to contrive in bad faith solely to get an exculpatory notion before the jury. These are not in terrorem arguments disrespectful of appropriate adjudicative procedures; rather, they are the realistic and practical consequences were the dissenters' views to prevail. * * *

Accordingly, the order of the Appellate Division should be affirmed.

HANCOCK, JUDGE (dissenting).

The rule adopted by the majority prohibiting the defense of mistake of law under Penal Law § 15.20(2)(a) in the circumstances here is directly contrary to the plain dictates of the statute and a rejection of the jurisprudential reforms and legislative policies underlying its enactment. For these reasons, as more fully explained herein, we cannot agree with this decision.

The basic difference which divides the court may be simply put. Suppose the case of a man who has committed an act which is criminal not because it is inherently wrong or immoral but solely because it violates a criminal statute. He has committed the act in complete good faith under the mistaken but entirely reasonable assumption that the act does not constitute an offense because it is permitted by the wording of the statute. Does the law require that this man be punished? The majority says that it does and holds that (1) Penal Law § 15.20(2)(a) must be construed so that the man is precluded from offering a defense based on his mistake of law and (2) such construction is compelled by prevailing considerations of public policy and criminal jurisprudence. We take issue with the majority on both propositions.

There can be no question that under the view that the purpose of the criminal justice system is to punish blameworthiness or "choosing freely to do wrong", our supposed man who has acted innocently and without any intent to do wrong should not be punished. Indeed, under some standards of morality he has done no wrong at all. Since he has not knowingly committed a wrong there can be no reason for society to exact retribution. Because the man is law-abiding and would not have acted but for his mistaken assumption as to the law, there is no need for punishment to deter him from further unlawful conduct. Traditionally, however, under the ancient rule of Anglo–American common law that ignorance or mistake of law is no excuse, our supposed man would be punished.

* * * Various justifications have been offered for the rule, but all are frankly pragmatic and utilitarian—preferring the interests of society e.g., in deterring criminal conduct, fostering orderly judicial administration, and preserving the (primacy of the rule of law) to the interest of the individual in being free from punishment except for intentionally engaging in conduct which he knows is criminal.

Today there is widespread criticism of the common-law rule mandating categorical preclusion of the mistake of law defense. The utilitarian arguments for retaining the rule have been drawn into serious question, but the fundamental objection is that it is simply wrong to punish someone who, in good-faith reliance on the wording of a statute, believed that what he was doing was lawful. It is contrary to "the notion that punishment should be conditioned on a showing of subjective moral blameworthiness." * * *

It is difficult to imagine a case more squarely within the wording of Penal Law § 15.20(2)(a) or one more fitted to what appears clearly to be the intended purpose of the statute than the one before us. * * *

Nothing in the statutory language suggests the interpretation urged by the People and adopted by the majority: that Penal Law § 15.20(2)(a) is available to a defendant not when he has mistakenly read a statute but only when he has correctly read and relied on a statute which is later invalidated. Such a construction contravenes the general rule that penal statutes should be construed against the State and in favor of the accused and the Legislature's specific directive that the revised Penal Law should not be strictly construed but "must be construed according to the fair import of [its] terms to promote justice and effect the objects of the law."

More importantly, the construction leads to an anomaly: only a defendant who is not mistaken about the law when he acts has a mistake of law defense. In other words, a defendant can assert a defense under Penal Law § 15.20(2)(a) only when his reading of the statute is correct—not mistaken. Such construction is obviously illogical; it strips the statute of the very effect intended by the Legislature in adopting the mistake of law defense. * * *

Finally, the majority's disregard of the natural and obvious meaning of Penal Law § 15.20(2)(a) so that a defendant mistaken about the law is deprived of a defense under the statute amounts, we submit, to a rejection of the obvious legislative purposes and policies favoring jurisprudential reform underlying the statute's enactment. It is self-evident that in enacting Penal Law § 15.20(2) as part of the revision and modernization of the Penal Law the Legislature intended to effect a needed reform by abolishing what had long been considered the unjust archaic common-law rule totally prohibiting mistake of law as a defense. Had it not so intended it would simply have left the common-law rule intact. In place of the abandoned "ignorantia legis" common-law maxim the Legislature enacted a rule which permits no defense for ignorance of law but allows a mistake of law defense in specific instances, including the one presented here: when the defendant's erroneous belief is founded on an "official statement of the law."

Instead, the majority bases its decision on an analogous provision in the Model Penal Code and concludes that despite its totally different wording and meaning Penal Law § 15.20(2)(a) should be read as if it were Model Penal Code § 2.04(3)(b)(i). But New York in revising the Penal Law did not adopt the Model Penal Code. * * * New York followed parts of the Model Penal Code provisions and rejected others. * * *

Thus, the precise phrase in the Model Penal Code limiting the defense under section 2.04(3)(b)(i) to reliance on a statute "afterward determined to be invalid or erroneous" which, if present, would support the majority's narrow construction of the New York statute, is omitted from Penal Law § 15.20(2)(a). How the Legislature can be assumed to have enacted the very language which it has specifically rejected is not explained. * * *

Any fair reading of the majority opinion, we submit, demonstrates that the decision to reject a mistake of law defense is based on considerations of public policy and on the conviction that such a defense would be bad, rather than on an analysis of CPL 15.20(2)(a) under the usual principles of statutory construction. * * *

We believe that the concerns expressed by the majority are matters which properly should be and have been addressed by the Legislature. * * *

It is no answer to protest that the defense may become a "false and diversionary stratagem", or that "wrongminded individuals [could] contrive" an "infinite number of mistake of law defenses"; for it is the very business of the courts to separate the true claims from the false. * * *

We do not believe that permitting a defense in this case will produce the grievous consequences the majority predicts. The unusual facts of this case seem unlikely to be repeated. * * * Nor is there any reason to believe that courts will have more difficulty separating valid claims from "diversionary stratagem[s]" in making preliminary legal determinations as to the validity of the mistake of law defense than of justification or any other defense.

Notes and Questions

1. Consider Dan M. Kahan, *Ignorance of the Law is an Excuse–But Only for the Virtuous*, 96 Mich.L.Rev. 127, 131, 133, 141–42 (1997): "Who exactly is the mistake of law doctrine afraid of? The answer suggested by the classic view is the strategically heedless. Were mistake of law a defense, a person bent on violating the rights of others—Holmes's 'bad man'—could evade punishment by remaining studiously ignorant of his legal duties.

"But the specter of strategic heedlessness is a fairly obvious piece of misdirection. To be sure, strict liability for mistakes of law takes the profit out of deliberate ignorance, but it's such a wildly overinclusive solution to that problem that it's impossible to view the strategically heedless as more than a bit player in the mistake of law drama. The real protagonist is someone else; to see who, consider *People v. Marrero.* * * *

" * * * The anxiety of strategic heedlessness obviously rang false in Marrero's individual case. Marrero hadn't deliberately shielded himself from legal knowledge; rather he had tenaciously attempted to ferret it out, displaying exactly the type of dedication to legal learning that the utility of knowledge purports to value.

"Nor would an excuse for Marrero have promoted strategic heedlessness in others. Marrero sought to present a reasonable mistake of law defense. Had the court sided with Marrero, it would have been establishing, in effect, a negligence standard with respect to the existence or meaning of the law defining who counts as a 'peace officer' under the New York gun possession statute. Under such a standard, heedlessness would be a foolish strategy, for a lawbreaker who deliberately failed to take reasonable steps to learn the law would be deemed negligent and hence denied a defense.

"In fact, if the goal were truly to maximize private knowledge of law, a negligence standard would be unambiguously superior to a strict liability standard. This is so because the value of learning the law is always higher when the law excuses reasonable mistakes of law than when it doesn't.

" * * * Strict liability warns citizens not to be Holmes's bad man. It tells them that if they suspect that some species of immoral conduct may evade the reach of the law, the only sure way to avoid punishment is to do what they know is right, not what they think is legal.

"This account makes it easier to see why *Marrero* came out the way it did. Marrero ignored the law's injunction to do what's right rather than what one thinks is legal. New York's restrictive gun possession law embodies its citizens' strong antipathy toward, and fear of, handguns. But rather than defer to those norms, Marrero decided to be strategic, availing himself of what must have appeared even to him to be a largely fortuitous gap in the law. That's the attitude that made the court see in Marrero's efforts to decode the law not an earnest and laudable attempt to obey but rather a 'false and diversionary stratagem[ ],' a form of 'game playing and evasion.'

"Other facts, not even mentioned by the court, also likely played a role: that the policy of the federal prison at which Marrero worked forbade guards to carry guns either on or off duty; that Marrero had supplied his girlfriend and another companion with guns, even though they clearly had no grounds for believing their possession to be lawful; and that Marrero menacingly reached for his weapon when the police approached him in the Manhattan club. These facts might not have been formally relevant to the court's disposition, but they no doubt helped the court to see Marrero as a Holmesian bad man. And in the eyes of the court, a Holmesian bad man is plenty bad enough to be designated a criminal."

2. Under what Kahan refers to as "the negligence standard," precisely how would it be determined whether Marrero and others interposing an ignorance or mistake of law claim had acted reasonably? Consider Richard G. Singer, *The Proposed Duty to Inquire as Affected by Recent Criminal Law Decisions in the United States Supreme Court*, 3 Buff.Crim.L.Rev. 701 (2000), discussing the proposal of other theorists that *ignorantia lexis* should be an excuse for those "reasonably unaware of, or mistaken as to, the extent of the law making their conduct illegal." Singer, id. At 703–04, concludes "that there are at least two difficulties with [that] proposal: (1) even if it is true that persons 'generally' know that their ignorance of the law is no excuse, they are still not culpable unless they were on

'some' notice that their specific conduct might be surrounded by criminal law restrictions; (2) there is unacceptable ambiguity in what might it mean to ask a lay person to take 'reasonable steps' to 'know' the law. Unless, as the Model Penal Code purports to do, we establish bright line tests of conduct–did defendant contact an expressly listed independent source for his views on the law–the muddles that will arise in implementing the standard of negligence are manifold."

3.   In light of these comments, consider the following dozen mistake-of-law "classics" with a view to determining in which of them the law ought to recognize the mistake as a defense:

(a) A state statute prohibiting the sale of intoxicants was held unconstitutional by the state supreme court on the ground it was in violation of the interstate commerce clause of the federal Constitution. O'Neil, relying upon that decision, proceeded to make sales in that state for a certain brewery. Thereafter, the state supreme court overruled its prior decision, relying upon a United States Supreme Court case decided before O'Neil's conduct and upholding a similar statute of another state.[a]

(b) The municipal court held that a certain type of gum vending machine was not a gambling device. Armed with certified copies of that decree, the distributors of these machines presented themselves to Striggles, the operator of a restaurant, and induced him to allow them to install one of the machines in his place of business. Thereafter, Striggles was charged with having a gambling device in his restaurant. It now appears that the municipal court decision was in error.[b]

(c) Irwin received a letter from his draft board ordering him to report for induction on a certain date. Thereafter, he was arrested for disorderly conduct and was arraigned in municipal court. The magistrate explained that Irwin would be released on bail and that a notice would be mailed informing him of the date of his court appearance. Irwin told the magistrate that he had received his draft notice, and the magistrate responded, "You have to take care of this first." Irwin inquired, "Well, suppose this doesn't come up before I am scheduled for induction, that is December 8." The magistrate again responded that Irwin would have to take care of the charge first. Irwin, who had not yet received notice to appear in court, did not report for induction on December 8th. He was charged with knowingly failing to report for induction.[c]

(d) Goodenow married a woman before a justice of the peace who erroneously advised the couple that they were entitled to marry in light of the fact that the woman's prior spouse, whom she had not divorced, had remarried. He was thereafter charged with adultery.[d]

(e) DeMeo, who was married to Ann in New Jersey, obtain a Mexican mail order divorce from her. Thereafter, he married Josephine in New Jersey. In his application for a license to marry Josephine, DeMeo set out in full that he had been divorced by a Mexican divorce decree and gave the date it was granted and the court which granted it. The license was granted without question. In fact, the Mexican divorce has no validity in New Jersey, and this has resulted in DeMeo being charged with bigamy.[e]

---

a. *State v. O'Neil,* 147 Iowa 513, 126 N.W. 454 (1910), reversing defendant's conviction.

b. *State v. Striggles,* 202 Iowa 1318, 210 N.W. 137 (1926), affirming defendant's conviction.

c. *United States v. Irwin,* 546 F.2d 1048 (3d Cir. 1976), affirming defendant's conviction.

d. *State v. Goodenow,* 65 Me. 30 (1876), affirming defendant's conviction.

e. *State v. De Meo,* 20 N.J. 1, 118 A.2d 1 (1955), affirming defendant's conviction.

(f). Davis, a member of the county board, was a member of the board's airport committee and thereby became involved in problems encountered in the development of the airport. One of these was the forced resignation of the airport manager for inadequate performance. Davis, on behalf of the committee, acted as temporary manager while a replacement was sought. Being unable to find a qualified replacement, the airport committee, with the advice and approval of the county corporation counsel, asked Davis to accept the position of permanent airport manager. He accepted. Thereafter, a longtime political adversary swore out a complaint charging Davis with violating a statute prohibiting a public official from having a personal interest in a public contract. By law, the duties of the county corporation counsel "shall be limited to civil matters and may include giving legal opinions to the board and its committees and interpreting the powers and duties of the board and county officers."[f]

(g). Rev. Hopkins wished to erect some advertising signs. He consulted the state's attorney, who told him that the proposed signs would not violate the law. Hopkins then put up a sign at the entrance to his home and another along side the highway. About 3 years later, he was charged with violating a statute making it unlawful to erect or maintain any sign intended to aid in the solicitation or performance of marriages.[g]

(h). Insco, unsuccessful Republican candidate for Congress in 1972 against Democratic candidate Gunter, had printed and distributed 2,500 bumper stickers containing only the words "McGovern–Gunter." Insco was charged with violating a federal statute making it a crime to distribute "any card, pamphlet, circular, poster, dodger, advertisement, writing, or other statement" concerning a candidate in a federal election without indicating thereon the name of the person or organization responsible therefor. He understandably did not think his conduct was criminal, as the universal practice of federal candidates has been *not* to affix attribution clauses to bumper stickers, and there has never been a prosecution with respect to this universal practice. The legislative history of the statute indicates that this practice is consistent with the Congressional intent, which was not to cover the usual sticker which conveys only candidate identification. But the stickers distributed by Insco, by linking Gunter and McGovern, are "political statements" and thus fall within the statute.[h]

(i). Barker and others have been charged with burglary for breaking into the headquarters of the Democratic Party's National Committee in the Watergate office complex. The defendants, all Cuban refugees, were led to believe by Howard Hunt (their senior officer in the abortive CIA-sponsored invasion of the Bay of Pigs), who then had his office in the White House, that they were to work for a secretly sponsored government intelligence agency seeking to photograph documents containing financial information indicating Cuban communist money was going into the Democratic campaign.[i]

---

f. *State v. Davis,* 63 Wis.2d 75, 216 N.W.2d 31 (1974), reversing defendant's conviction.

g. *Hopkins v. State,* 193 Md. 489, 69 A.2d 456 (1949), affirming defendant's conviction.

h. *United States v. Insco,* 496 F.2d 204 (5th Cir. 1974), reversing defendant's conviction.

i. *United States v. Barker,* 514 F.2d 208 (D.C.Cir. 1975). A majority of the court, en banc, held that the district judge properly refused to allow the defendants to withdraw their pleas of guilty, and thus did not have to reach the merits of the claimed mistake of law defense. Bazelon, J., concurring, and MacKinnon and Wilkey, JJ., dissenting, all indicated they would recognize the defense on these facts.

See also *United States v. Barker,* 546 F.2d 940 (D.C.Cir.1976), reversing defendants' convictions of conspiracy to violate the civil rights of Dr. Fielding, whose office they burglarized in an effort to find records on his patient, Daniel Ellsberg. The court concluded that the district court erred in rejecting the possibility of a limited mistake of law defense where the defendants claimed they reasonably believed that Hunt, their White House superior, had authority to order such an operation. Compare *United States v. Ehrlichman,* 546 F.2d 910 (D.C.Cir.1976), holding it was no defense that a former presidential assistant mistakenly believed the break-in into Fielding's office was legal.

(j) Powers, president of a magazine distributing company, has been charged with possession of obscene literature with intent to distribute same. The publications in question were imported into the country. Though the customs authorities are authorized by statute to bar entry into the country of obscene materials, these particular publications were allowed to enter. Powers, knowing of this, claims he thus concluded these publications did not meet the legal definition of obscenity.[j]

(k) Long moved from Delaware to Arkansas and obtained a divorce from his wife; thereafter he moved back to Delaware and later remarried. Prior to the second marriage, Long consulted a Delaware attorney with respect to whether he was free to remarry. The attorney erroneously advised him that the Arkansas divorce was valid and that he was free to remarry. Long has now been charged with bigamy.[k]

(*l*). Snyder was charged with violating a state statute subjecting to criminal penalties "any person who has been convicted of a felony * * * who owns * * * any pistol, revolver, or other firearm." Snyder, who in fact had a prior felony conviction for sale of marijuana, had entered a guilty plea in that earlier case as a result of a plea bargain which ensured she would receive no jail or prison time. Her attorney told her she was pleading guilty to a misdemeanor, and Snyder thereafter conducted herself accordingly (e.g., believing she was not a felon, she registered to vote and voted).[l]

NOTES AND QUESTIONS ON MISTAKE OF LAW AND
THE UNITED STATES SUPREME COURT

In several important cases, the United States Supreme Court has had occasion to decide what bearing, if any, the defendant's ignorance or mistake of law should have upon his conviction. The first of these cases concerns a city ordinance, where the Court was assessing the conviction in due process terms; the others involved the Court's interpretation of federal criminal statutes. As to this latter group, consider whether you believe the Court faithfully interpreted the statute and whether, when mistake of law *is* deemed a defense, whether this is because the case fits within the *Weiss* exception, discussed in *Marrero*. As to all the cases, consider whether there is some sound underlying policy supporting the conclusion that the defendant's error either should or should not be taken into account.

1. *Lambert v. California*, 355 U.S. 225, 78 S.Ct. 240, 2 L.Ed.2d 228 (1957), involved a Los Angeles ordinance which made it unlawful for any person with a prior felony conviction to be or remain in the city more than 5 days without registering. Ms. Lambert, arrested on suspicion of another offense, was charged with violating this ordinance; she was convicted, fined $250 and placed on 3 years probation. The Court, per Douglas, J., reversed:

"We must assume that appellant had no actual knowledge of the requirement that she register under this ordinance, as she offered proof of this defense which was refused. The question is whether a registration act of this character violates due process where it is applied to a person who has no actual knowledge of his duty to register, and where no showing is made of the probability of such knowledge.

"We do not go with Blackstone in saying that 'a vicious will' is necessary to constitute a crime, for conduct alone without regard to the intent of the doer is often sufficient. There

---

j. *Regina v. Prairie Schooner News Ltd. and Powers*, 75 W.W.R. 585 (Manitoba C.A.1970), dismissing defendant's appeal.

k. *Long v. State*, 44 Del. 262, 65 A.2d 489 (1949), reversing defendant's conviction.

l. *People v. Snyder*, 32 Cal.3d 590, 186 Cal.Rptr. 485, 652 P.2d 42 (1982), affirming exclusion of evidence of such mistaken belief.

is wide latitude in the lawmakers to declare an offense and to exclude elements of knowledge and diligence from its definition. But we deal here with conduct that is wholly passive—mere failure to register. It is unlike the commission of acts, or the failure to act under circumstances that should alert the doer to the consequences of his deed. The rule that 'ignorance of the law will not excuse' is deep in our law, as is the principle that of all the powers of local government, the police power is 'one of the least limitable.' On the other hand, due process places some limits on its exercise. Engrained in our concept of due process is the requirement of notice. Notice is sometimes essential so that the citizen has the chance to defend charges. Notice is required before property interests are disturbed, before assessments are made, before penalties are assessed. Notice is required in a myriad of situations where a penalty or forfeiture might be suffered for mere failure to act. * * *

"Many [registration] laws are akin to licensing statutes in that they pertain to the regulation of business activities. But the present ordinance is entirely different. Violation of its provisions is unaccompanied by any activity whatever, mere presence in the city being the test. Moreover, circumstances which might move one to inquire as to the necessity of registration are completely lacking. At most the ordinance is but a law enforcement technique designed for the convenience of law enforcement agencies through which a list of the names and addresses of felons then residing in a given community is compiled. The disclosure is merely a compilation of former convictions already publicly recorded in the jurisdiction where obtained. Nevertheless, this appellant on first becoming aware of her duty to register was given no opportunity to comply with the law and avoid its penalty, even though her default was entirely innocent. She could but suffer the consequences of the ordinance, namely, conviction with the imposition of heavy criminal penalties thereunder. We believe that actual knowledge of the duty to register or proof of the probability of such knowledge and subsequent failure to comply are necessary before a conviction under the ordinance can stand. As Holmes wrote in *The Common Law*, 'A law which punished conduct which would not be blameworthy in the average member of the community would be too severe for that community to bear.' Its severity lies in the absence of an opportunity either to avoid the consequences of the law or to defend any prosecution brought under it. Where a person did not know of the duty to register and where there was no proof of the probability of such knowledge, he may not be convicted consistently with due process. Were it otherwise, the evil would be as great as it is when the law is written in print too fine to read or in a language foreign to the community."

Frankfurter, J., joined by Harlan and Whittaker, JJ., dissenting, objected that "what the Court here does is to draw a constitutional line between a State's requirement of doing and not doing. What is this but a return to Year Book distinctions between feasance and nonfeasance—a distinction that may have significance in the evolution of common-law notions of liability, but is inadmissible as a line between constitutionality and unconstitutionality."[a]

2. What, exactly, are the dimensions of the *Lambert* holding? Does it mean that the principle that ignorance of the law is no excuse simply is inapplicable to criminal omissions? Consider Graham Hughes, *Criminal Omissions*, 67 Yale L.J. 590, 600–01 (1958): "In an offense of commission, the mind of the actor is almost always to some extent addressed to the prohibited conduct, even though he may be unaware of the legal prohibition. In these offenses, *mens rea* can quite usefully be generalized as an intention to bring about the prohibited consequences or, at the least, recklessness with regard to such

---

a. In *Texaco, Inc. v. Short*, 454 U.S. 516, 102 S.Ct. 781, 70 L.Ed.2d 738 (1982), the Court observed that *Lambert*'s "application has been limited, lending some credence to Justice Frankfurter's colorful prediction in dissent that the case would stand as 'an isolated deviation from the strong current of precedents—a derelict on the waters of the law.' "

consequences. With omissions, the great difficulty is that the mind of the offender may not be addressed at all to the enjoined conduct, if he is unaware of the duty to act. One may not know that it is prohibited to place garbage cans on the sidewalk between 9:00 A.M. and 7:00 P.M., but one can hardly place such a can on the sidewalk without knowing that he is doing it. * * * This approach is clearly of no use with omissions, where the accused does not have to perform any act to incur liability. What of the offender who violates a regulation requiring garbage to be put out in suitable receptacles at certain times? If he was quite unaware of the existence of the rule, in what sense can he be said to have been addressing his mind at all to the conduct required of him by law? This is the difficulty which plagues the analysis of omissions in terms of the conventional concepts of *mens rea*."

3. *Liparota v. United States,* 471 U.S. 419, 105 S.Ct. 2084, 85 L.Ed.2d 434 (1985), concerned a federal statute governing food stamp fraud providing that "whoever knowingly uses, transfers, acquires, alters, or possesses coupons or authorization cards in any manner not authorized by [the statute] or the regulations" is subject to a fine and imprisonment. 7 U.S.C. § 2024(b). Liparota, co-owner of a Chicago sandwich shop, was indicted for acquiring and possessing food stamps in violation of § 2024(b). In submitting the case to the jury, the District Court rejected petitioner's proposed "specific intent" instruction, which would have instructed the jury that the Government must prove that "the defendant knowingly did an act which the law forbids, purposely intending to violate the law." The jury returned a verdict of guilty. The Supreme Court, per Brennan, J., concluded:

"Absent indication of contrary purpose in the language or legislative history of the statute, we believe that § 2024(b) requires a showing that the defendant knew his conduct to be unauthorized by statute or regulations.[9] 'The contention that an injury can amount to a crime only when inflicted by intention is no provincial or transient notion. It is as universal and persistent in mature systems of law as belief in freedom of the human will and a consequent ability and duty of the normal individual to choose between good and evil.' *Morissette v. United States*, 342 U.S. 246, 72 S.Ct. 240, 96 L.Ed. 288 (1952). [I]n this case, the failure of Congress explicitly and unambiguously to indicate whether *mens rea* is required does not signal a departure from this background assumption of our criminal law.

"This construction is particularly appropriate where, as here, to interpret the statute otherwise would be to criminalize a broad range of apparently innocent conduct. For instance, § 2024(b) declares it criminal to use, transfer, acquire, alter, or possess food stamps in any manner not authorized by statute or regulations. The statute provides further that '[c]oupons issued to eligible households shall be used by them only to purchase food in retail food stores which have been approved for participation in the food stamp program *at prices prevailing in such stores*.' This seems to be the *only* authorized use. A strict reading of the statute with no knowledge of illegality requirement would thus render criminal a food stamp recipient who, for example, used stamps to purchase food from a store that, unknown to him, charged higher than normal prices to food stamp program participants. Such a reading would also render criminal a nonrecipient of food stamps who 'possessed' stamps because he was mistakenly sent them through the mail due to

---

9. The Dissent repeatedly claims that our holding today creates a defense of "mistake of law." Our holding today no more creates a "mistake of law" defense than does a statute making knowing receipt of stolen goods unlawful. In both cases, there is a legal element in the definition of the offense. In the case of a receipt of stolen goods statute, the legal element is that the goods were stolen; in this case, the legal element is that the "use, transfer, acquisition," etc. were in a manner not authorized by statute or regulations. It is not a

defense to a charge of receipt of stolen goods that one did not know that such receipt was illegal, and it is not a defense to a charge of a § 2024(b) violation that one did not know that possessing food stamps in a manner unauthorized by statute or regulations was illegal. It *is*, however, a defense to a charge of knowing receipt of stolen goods that one did not know that the goods were stolen, just as it is a defense to a charge of a § 2024(b) violation that one did not know that one's possession was unauthorized. * * *

administrative error, 'altered' them by tearing them up, and 'transferred' them by throwing them away. Of course, Congress *could* have intended that this broad range of conduct be made illegal, perhaps with the understanding that prosecutors would exercise their discretion to avoid such harsh results. However, given the paucity of material suggesting that Congress did so intend, we are reluctant to adopt such a sweeping interpretation.

"[T]he Government contends that the § 2024(b) offense is a 'public welfare' offense, which the Court defined in *United States v. Morissette* to 'depend on no mental element but consist only of forbidden acts or omissions.' Yet the offense at issue here differs substantially from those ''public welfare offenses'' we have previously recognized. In most previous instances, Congress has rendered criminal a type of conduct that a reasonable person should know is subject to stringent public regulation and may seriously threaten the community's health or safety."

Justice White, in his dissent, responded: "Even accepting that 'knowingly' does extend through the sentence, or at least that we should read § 2024(b) as if it does, the statute does not mean what the Court says it does. Rather, it requires only that the defendant be aware of the relevant aspects of his conduct. A requirement that the defendant know that he is acting in a particular manner, coupled with the fact that that manner is forbidden, does not establish a defense of ignorance of the law. It creates only a defense of ignorance or mistake of fact. Knowingly to do something that is unauthorized by law is not the same as doing something knowing that it is unauthorized by law.

"This point is demonstrated by the hypothetical statute referred to by the majority, which punishes one who 'knowingly sells a security without a permit.' Even if 'knowingly' does reach 'without a permit,' I would think that a defendant who knew that he did not have a permit, though not that a permit was required, could be convicted. * * *

"The Court's opinion provides another illustration of the general point: someone who used food stamps to purchase groceries at inflated prices without realizing he was overcharged. I agree that such a person may not be convicted, but not for the reason given by the majority. The purchaser did not 'knowingly' use the stamps in the proscribed manner, for he was unaware of the circumstances of the transaction that made it illegal.

"The majority and I would part company in result as well as rationale if the purchaser knew he was charged higher than normal prices but not that overcharging is prohibited. In such a case, he would have been aware of the nature of his actions, and therefore the purchase would have been 'knowing.' I would hold that such a mental state satisfies the statute. Under the Court's holding, as I understand it, that person could not be convicted because he did not know that his conduct was illegal. * * *

"In relying on the 'background assumption of our criminal law' that *mens rea* is required, the Court ignores the equally well-founded assumption that ignorance of the law is no excuse. It is 'the conventional position that knowledge of the existence, meaning or application of the law determining the elements of an offense is not an element of that offense....' "

4. *Cheek v. United States,* 498 U.S. 192, 111 S.Ct. 604, 112 L.Ed.2d 617 (1991), concerned 26 U.S.C. § 7201, providing that any person "who willfully attempts in any manner to evade or defeat any tax imposed by this title or the payment thereof" shall be guilty of a felony, and 26 U.S.C. § 7203, providing that "[a]ny person required under this title ... or by regulations made under authority thereof to make a return ... who willfully fails to ... make such return" shall be guilty of a misdemeanor. Cheek, a pilot for American Airlines, filed federal income tax returns through 1979 but thereafter ceased to

file returns. He also claimed an increasing number of withholding allowances—eventually claiming 60 allowances by mid–1980—and for the years 1981 to 1984 indicated on his W–4 forms that he was exempt from federal income taxes. In 1983, he unsuccessfully sought a refund of all tax withheld by his employer in 1982. His income during this period at all times far exceeded the minimum necessary to trigger the statutory filing requirement. As a result, Cheek was indicted for 10 violations of federal law. At trial, the evidence established that between 1982 and 1986, he was involved in at least four civil cases that challenged various aspects of the federal income tax system. In all four of those cases, the plaintiffs were informed by the courts that many of their arguments, including that they were not taxpayers within the meaning of the tax laws, that wages are not income, that the Sixteenth Amendment does not authorize the imposition of an income tax on individuals, and that the Sixteenth Amendment is unenforceable, were frivolous or had been repeatedly rejected by the courts. In addition, there was evidence that in 1980 or 1981 an attorney had advised Cheek that the courts had rejected as frivolous the claim that wages are not income.

Cheek testified that as early as 1978, he had begun attending seminars sponsored by, and following the advice of, a group that believes, among other things, that the federal tax system is unconstitutional. Some of the speakers at these meetings were lawyers who purported to give professional opinions about the invalidity of the federal income tax laws. Cheek produced a letter from an attorney stating that the Sixteenth Amendment did not authorize a tax on wages and salaries but only on gain or profit. His defense was that, based on the indoctrination he received from this group and from his own study, he sincerely believed that the tax laws were being unconstitutionally enforced and that his actions during the 1980–1986 period were lawful, and therefore he had acted without the willfulness required for conviction. The trial court advised the jury that an objectively reasonable good-faith misunderstanding of the law would negate willfulness, but mere disagreement with the law would not. At the end of the first day of deliberation, in response to a note from the jury, the judge instructed that "[a]n honest but unreasonable belief is not a defense and does not negate willfulness," and that "[a]dvice or research resulting in the conclusion that wages of a privately employed person are not income or that the tax laws are unconstitutional is not objectively reasonable and cannot serve as the basis for a good faith misunderstanding of the law defense." Approximately two hours later, the jury returned a verdict finding Cheek guilty on all counts. The Supreme Court, per White, J., concluded:

"The general rule that ignorance of the law or a mistake of law is no defense to criminal prosecution is deeply rooted in the American legal system. Based on the notion that the law is definite and knowable, the common law presumed that every person knew the law. This common-law rule has been applied by the Court in numerous cases construing criminal statutes.

"The proliferation of statutes and regulations has sometimes made it difficult for the average citizen to know and comprehend the extent of the duties and obligations imposed by the tax laws. Congress has accordingly softened the impact of the common-law presumption by making specific intent to violate the law an element of certain federal criminal tax offenses. Thus, the Court almost 60 years ago interpreted the statutory term 'willfully' as used in the federal criminal tax statutes as carving out an exception to the traditional rule. This special treatment of criminal tax offenses is largely due to the complexity of the tax laws. In *United States v. Murdock*, 290 U.S. 389, 54 S.Ct. 223, 78 L.Ed. 381 (1933), the Court recognized that:

'Congress did not intend that a person, by reason of a bona fide misunderstanding as to his liability for the tax, as to his duty to make a return, or as to the adequacy of the records he maintained, should become a criminal by his mere failure to measure up to the prescribed standard of conduct.'

"Willfulness, as construed by our prior decisions in criminal tax cases, requires the Government to prove that the law imposed a duty on the defendant, that the defendant knew of this duty, and that he voluntarily and intentionally violated that duty. We deal first with the case where the issue is whether the defendant knew of the duty purportedly imposed by the provision of the statute or regulation he is accused of violating, a case in which there is no claim that the provision at issue is invalid. In such a case, if the Government proves actual knowledge of the pertinent legal duty, the prosecution, without more, has satisfied the knowledge component of the willfulness requirement. But carrying this burden requires negating a defendant's claim of ignorance of the law or a claim that because of a misunderstanding of the law, he had a good-faith belief that he was not violating any of the provisions of the tax laws. This is so because one cannot be aware that the law imposes a duty upon him and yet be ignorant of it, misunderstand the law, or believe that the duty does not exist. In the end, the issue is whether, based on all the evidence, the Government has proved that the defendant was aware of the duty at issue, which cannot be true if the jury credits a good-faith misunderstanding and belief submission, whether or not the claimed belief or misunderstanding is objectively reasonable.

"In this case, if Cheek asserted that he truly believed that the Internal Revenue Code did not purport to treat wages as income, and the jury believed him, the Government would not have carried its burden to prove willfulness, however unreasonable a court might deem such a belief. Of course, in deciding whether to credit Cheek's good-faith belief claim, the jury would be free to consider any admissible evidence from any source showing that Cheek was aware of his duty to file a return and to treat wages as income, including evidence showing his awareness of the relevant provisions of the Code or regulations, of court decisions rejecting his interpretation of the tax law, of authoritative rulings of the Internal Revenue Service, or of any contents of the personal income tax return forms and accompanying instructions that made it plain that wages should be returned as income.

"We thus disagree with the Court of Appeals' requirement that a claimed good-faith belief must be objectively reasonable if it is to be considered as possibly negating the Government's evidence purporting to show a defendant's awareness of the legal duty at issue. Knowledge and belief are characteristically questions for the factfinder, in this case the jury. Characterizing a particular belief as not objectively reasonable transforms the inquiry into a legal one and would prevent the jury from considering it. It would of course be proper to exclude evidence having no relevance or probative value with respect to willfulness; but it is not contrary to common sense, let alone impossible, for a defendant to be ignorant of his duty based on an irrational belief that he has no duty, and forbidding the jury to consider evidence that might negate willfulness would raise a serious question under the Sixth Amendment's jury trial provision.

"It was therefore error to instruct the jury to disregard evidence of Cheek's understanding that, within the meaning of the tax laws, he was not a person required to file a return or to pay income taxes and that wages are not taxable income, as incredible as such misunderstandings of and beliefs about the law might be. Of course, the more unreasonable the asserted beliefs or misunderstandings are, the more likely the jury will consider them to be nothing more than simple disagreement with known legal duties imposed by the tax laws and will find that the Government has carried its burden of proving knowledge.

"Cheek asserted in the trial court that he should be acquitted because he believed in good faith that the income tax law is unconstitutional as applied to him and thus could not legally impose any duty upon him of which he should have been aware. Such a submission is unsound * * *.

"Claims that some of the provisions of the tax code are unconstitutional are submissions of a different order. They do not arise from innocent mistakes caused by the complexity of the Internal Revenue Code. Rather, they reveal full knowledge of the provisions at issue and a studied conclusion, however wrong, that those provisions are invalid and unenforceable. * * *

"We do not believe that Congress contemplated that such a taxpayer, without risking criminal prosecution, could ignore the duties imposed upon him by the Internal Revenue Code and refuse to utilize the mechanisms provided by Congress to present his claims of invalidity to the courts and to abide by their decisions. There is no doubt that Cheek, from year to year, was free to pay the tax that the law purported to require, file for a refund and, if denied, present his claims of invalidity, constitutional or otherwise, to the courts. Also, without paying the tax, he could have challenged claims of tax deficiencies in the Tax Court, with the right to appeal to a higher court if unsuccessful. Cheek took neither course in some years, and when he did was unwilling to accept the outcome. As we see it, he is in no position to claim that his good-faith belief about the validity of the Internal Revenue Code negates willfulness or provides a defense to criminal prosecution under §§ 7201 and 7203. Of course, Cheek was free in this very case to present his claims of invalidity and have them adjudicated, but like defendants in criminal cases in other contexts, who "willfully" refuse to comply with the duties placed upon them by the law, he must take the risk of being wrong.

"We thus hold that in a case like this, a defendant's views about the validity of the tax statutes are irrelevant to the issue of willfulness and need not be heard by the jury, and, if they are, an instruction to disregard them would be proper. For this purpose, it makes no difference whether the claims of invalidity are frivolous or have substance."

Justice Blackmun's dissent responded: "[I]t is incomprehensible to me how, in this day, more than 70 years after the institution of our present federal income tax system with the passage of the Income Tax Act of 1913, any taxpayer of competent mentality can assert as his defense to charges of statutory willfulness the proposition that the wage he receives for his labor is not income, irrespective of a cult that says otherwise and advises the gullible to resist income tax collections. One might note in passing that this particular taxpayer, after all, was a licensed pilot for one of our major commercial airlines; he presumably was a person of at least minimum intellectual competence. * * *

"This Court's opinion today, I fear, will encourage taxpayers to cling to frivolous views of the law in the hope of convincing a jury of their sincerity. If that ensues, I suspect we have gone beyond the limits of common sense."

Justice Scalia, though concurring, observed: "I find it impossible to understand how one can derive from the lonesome word 'willfully' the proposition that belief in the nonexistence of a textual prohibition excuses liability, but belief in the invalidity (i.e., the legal nonexistence) of a textual prohibition does not."

5.   Consider Mark D. Yochum, *Cheek is Chic: Ignorance of the Law is an Excuse for Tax Crimes—A Fashion That Does Not Wear Well*, 31 Duq.L.Rev. 249, 254–55 (1993): "The real harm of the *Cheek* decision is its effect, albeit difficult to gauge, on the wavering ethics of the citizenry and the shaky sense of justice in our world of somewhat voluntary self-assessment. Decisions which proclaim knowledge of the law as a prerequisite to incarcera-

tion must suggest to the possible tax risk-taker that ignorance is a little more valuable than seeking competent tax advice. This real problem, manifested by the virulent tax protest movement, is the reason the initial interpretation of the tax crimes was and continues to be so shortsighted. Taxpayers should be encouraged to discover the law. But the day after Cheek was issued, the picture of a sober and sadfaced Cheek topped the front page of USA Today and the headline teased: 'Sincere' Tax Evaders May Skip Jail.''

6. In *Ratzlaf v. United States*, 510 U.S. 135, 114 S.Ct. 655, 126 L.Ed.2d 615 (1994), Ratzlaf ran up a debt of $160,000 playing blackjack at the High Sierra Casino in Reno, Nevada. The casino gave him one week to pay. On the due date, Ratzlaf returned to the casino with cash of $100,000 in hand. A casino official informed Ratzlaf that all transactions involving more than $10,000 in cash had to be reported to state and federal authorities. The official added that the casino could accept a cashier's check for the full amount due without triggering any reporting requirement. The casino helpfully placed a limousine at Ratzlaf's disposal, and assigned an employee to accompany him to banks in the vicinity. Informed that banks, too, are required to report cash transactions in excess of $10,000, Ratzlaf purchased cashier's checks, each for less than $10,000 and each from a different bank. He delivered these checks to the High Sierra Casino. Ratzlaf was then charged with ''structuring transactions'' to evade the banks' obligation to report cash transactions exceeding $10,000; this conduct, the indictment alleged, violated 31 U.S.C. §§ 5322(a) and 5324(3). Regarding the ''willfully violating'' part of the statute, the trial judge instructed the jury that the Government had to prove defendant's knowledge of the banks' reporting obligation and his attempt to evade that obligation, but did not have to prove defendant knew the structuring was unlawful. Ratzlaf was convicted, fined, and sentenced to prison. The Supreme Court, per Ginsburg, J., disagreed:

'' 'Willful,' this Court has recognized, is a 'word of many meanings,' and 'its construction [is] often ... influenced by its context.' Accordingly, we view §§ 5322(a) and 5324(3) mindful of the complex of provisions in which they are embedded. In this light, we count it significant that § 5322(a)'s omnibus 'willfulness' requirement, when applied to other provisions in the same subchapter, consistently has been read by the Courts of Appeals to require both 'knowledge of the reporting requirement' and a 'specific intent to commit the crime,' i.e., 'a purpose to disobey the law.'

''A term appearing in several places in a statutory text is generally read the same way each time it appears. * * *

''The United States urges, however, that § 5324 violators, by their very conduct, exhibit a purpose to do wrong, which suffices to show 'willfulness.' * * *

''Undoubtedly there are bad men who attempt to elude official reporting requirements in order to hide from government inspectors such criminal activity as laundering drug money or tax evasion. But currency structuring is not inevitably nefarious. Consider, for example, the small business operator who knows that reports filed under 31 U.S.C. § 5313(a) are available to the Internal Revenue Service. To reduce the risk of an IRS audit, she brings $9,500 in cash to the bank twice each week, in lieu of transporting over $10,000 once each week. That person, if the united states is right, has committed a criminal offense, because she structured cash transactions 'for the specific purpose of depriving the government of the information that section 5313(a) is designed to obtain.' Nor is a person who structures a currency transaction invariably motivated by a desire to keep the government in the dark. But under the government's construction an individual would commit a felony against the united states by making cash deposits in small doses, fearful that the bank's reports would increase the likelihood of burglary, or in an endeavor to keep a former spouse unaware of his wealth.

"In light of these examples, we are unpersuaded by the argument that structuring is so obviously 'evil' or inherently 'bad' that the 'willfulness' requirement is satisfied irrespective of the defendant's knowledge of the illegality of structuring. Had Congress wished to dispense with the requirement, it could have furnished the appropriate instruction."

Blackmun, J., for the four dissenters, argued:

"Unlike other provisions of the subchapter, the antistructuring provision identifies the purpose that is required for a § 5324 violation: 'evading the reporting requirements.' The offense of structuring, therefore, requires (1) knowledge of a financial institution's reporting requirements, and (2) the structuring of a transaction for the purpose of evading those requirements. These elements define a violation that is 'willful' as that term is commonly interpreted. The majority's additional requirement that an actor have actual knowledge that structuring is prohibited strays from the statutory text, as well as from our precedents interpreting criminal statutes generally and 'willfulness' in particular.

"The Court reasons that the interpretation of the Court of Appeals for the Ninth Circuit, and that of nine other Circuits, renders § 5322(a)'s willfulness requirement superfluous. This argument ignores the generality of § 5322(a), which sets a single standard—willfulness—for the subchapter's various reporting provisions. Some of those provisions do not themselves define willful conduct, so the willfulness element cannot be deemed surplusage. Moreover, the fact that § 5322(a) requires willfulness for criminal liability to be imposed does not mean that each of the underlying offenses to which it applies must involve something less than willfulness. Thus, the fact that § 5324 does describe a 'willful' offense, since it already requires 'the purpose of evading the reporting requirements,' provides no basis for imposing an artificially heightened scienter requirement.

"The Court next concludes that its interpretation of 'willfully' is warranted because structuring is not inherently 'nefarious.' It is true that the Court, on occasion, has imposed a knowledge-of-illegality requirement upon criminal statutes to ensure that the defendant acted with a wrongful purpose. See, e.g., *Liparota*. I cannot agree, however, that the imposition of such a requirement is necessary here. First, the conduct at issue—splitting up transactions involving tens of thousands of dollars in cash for the specific purpose of circumventing a bank's reporting duty—is hardly the sort of innocuous activity involved in cases such as *Liparota*, in which the defendant had been convicted of fraud for purchasing food stamps for less than their face value. Further, an individual convicted of structuring is, by definition, aware that cash transactions are regulated, and he cannot seriously argue that he lacked notice of the law's intrusion into the particular sphere of activity. Cf. *Lambert v. California*. By requiring knowledge of a bank's reporting requirements as well as a 'purpose of evading' those requirements, the antistructuring provision targets those who knowingly act to deprive the Government of information to which it is entitled. In my view, that is not so plainly innocent a purpose as to justify reading into the statute the additional element of knowledge of illegality."

7. "*Ratzlaf* in particular has significant implications for other criminal statutes that require willfulness, and may signal a broader change in courts' previous reluctance to consider motive in determining whether an individual has committed a crime. *Ratzlaf*'s rationale arguably creates a mistake of law defense for criminal violations of federal banking laws, firearms regulations, and other crimes that are not, in Justice Ginsburg's words, 'obviously evil or inherently bad.' Though the lower federal courts could easily have limited *Ratzlaf* to its facts, many have instead extended the Supreme Court's interpretation of 'willfully' to other *mala prohibita* offenses, reaching a result to which it appears

they may have been predisposed." Comment, 62 U.Chi.L.Rev. 1301, 1302 (1995), concluding "that, in the absence of a clear legislative command to the contrary, mistake of law should be a defense to all *mala prohibita* crimes that require a mens rea of recklessness or higher for violation."

8. *Bryan v. United States*, 524 U.S. 184, 118 S.Ct. 1939, 141 L.Ed.2d 197 (1998), concerned 18 U.S.C. § 924(a)(1)(D), prohibiting anyone from "willfully" violating, inter alia, § 922(a)(1)(A), which forbids dealing in firearms without a federal license. The evidence at Bryan's unlicensed dealing trial was adequate to prove that he was dealing in firearms and knew his conduct was unlawful, but there was no evidence he was aware of the federal licensing requirement. The trial judge refused to instruct there could be no conviction absent such awareness, and instructed the jury to the contrary. Bryan was found guilty. The Supreme Court, per Stevens, J., concluded: "As a general matter, when used in the criminal context, a 'willful' act is one undertaken with a 'bad purpose.' In other words, in order to establish a 'willful' violation of a statute, 'the Government must prove that the defendant acted with knowledge that his conduct was unlawful.' *Ratzlaf*.

"Petitioner argues that a more particularized showing is required in this case for two principal reasons. First, he argues that the fact that Congress used the adverb 'knowingly' to authorize punishment of three categories of acts made unlawful by § 922 and the word 'willfully' when it referred to unlicensed dealing in firearms demonstrates that the Government must shoulder a special burden in cases like this. This argument is not persuasive because the term 'knowingly' does not necessarily have any reference to a culpable state of mind or to knowledge of the law. As Justice Jackson correctly observed, 'the knowledge requisite to knowing violation of a statute is factual knowledge as distinguished from knowledge of the law.' * * *

"With respect to the three categories of conduct that are made punishable by § 924 if performed 'knowingly,' the background presumption that every citizen knows the law makes it unnecessary to adduce specific evidence to prove that 'an evil-meaning mind' directed the 'evil-doing hand.' More is required, however, with respect to the conduct in the fourth category that is only criminal when done 'willfully.' The jury must find that the defendant acted with an evil-meaning mind, that is to say, that he acted with knowledge that his conduct was unlawful.

"Petitioner next argues that we must read § 924(a)(1)(D) to require knowledge of the law because of our interpretation of 'willfully' in two other contexts. In certain cases involving willful violations of the tax laws, we have concluded that the jury must find that the defendant was aware of the specific provision of the tax code that he was charged with violating. See, e.g., *Cheek*. Similarly, in order to satisfy a willful violation in *Ratzlaf*, we concluded that the jury had to find that the defendant knew that his structuring of cash transactions to avoid a reporting requirement was unlawful. Those cases, however, are readily distinguishable. Both the tax cases and *Ratzlaf* involved highly technical statutes that presented the danger of ensnaring individuals engaged in apparently innocent conduct. As a result, we held that these statutes 'carv[e] out an exception to the traditional rule' that ignorance of the law is no excuse and require that the defendant have knowledge of the law. The danger of convicting individuals engaged in apparently innocent activity that motivated our decisions in the tax cases and *Ratzlaf* is not present here because the jury found that this petitioner knew that his conduct was unlawful."

Scalia, J., for the three dissenters, objected: "It is enough, in my view, if the defendant is generally aware that the actus reus punished by the statute—dealing in firearms without a license—is illegal. But the Court is willing to accept a mens rea so 'general' that it is entirely divorced from the actus reus this statute was enacted to punish. That approach turns § 924(a)(1)(D) into a strange and unlikely creature. Bryan would be guilty of 'willfully' dealing in firearms without a federal license even if, for example, he had never heard of the licensing requirement but was aware that he had violated the law by using straw purchasers or filing the serial numbers off the pistols. The Court does not even limit (for there is no rational basis to limit) the universe of relevant laws to federal firearms statutes. Bryan would also be 'act[ing] with an evil-meaning mind,' and hence presumably be guilty of 'willfully' dealing in firearms without a license, if he knew that his street-corner transactions violated New York City's business licensing or sales tax ordinances."

9. Consider Sharon L. Davies, *The Jurisprudence of Willfulness: An Evolving Theory of Excusable Ignorance*, 48 Duke L.J. 341, 386–87 (1998): "In summary, the *Bryan* decision continues the modern judicial trend of defining criminal willfulness to require proof of knowledge of illegality, but simultaneously reduces the rigorousness of the prosecutor's burden of proof. Having thus handed both the government and the criminal defense bar weapons that can be used in future battles over mistake of law claims, the Court has now only to step back and watch the bloodbath that is bound to ensue. Although the government technically 'won' in *Bryan* (the defendant's conviction was upheld), in the long run it can scarcely be pleased with the weapon with which it has been left. True, the government need now only prove knowledge of general illegality in the run-of-the-mill willfulness case, but this is a burden the ignorantia legis maxim never thrust upon it. Moreover, in prosecutions brought under 'highly technical' statutes—whatever that phrase may turn out to mean—the government's burden will be significantly heavier. In the aftermath of *Bryan*, it is uncertain whether the Court will, over time, further broaden the class of criminal statutes placing this heightened burden on the government. The defense bar is likely to be more content with its weapon. *Bryan* himself may have lost, but he secured for others accused of willful criminal conduct a broad judicial statement that 'willfulness' generally will be construed to require proof of knowledge of the law. This statement reflects the judiciary's continued disaffection with the ignorantia legis principle."

Chapter 4

THE ACT REQUIREMENT

SECTION 1. VOLUNTARY ACT

STATE v. CADDELL

Supreme Court of North Carolina, 1975.

287 N.C. 266, 215 S.E.2d 348.

LAKE, JUSTICE. [Defendant, charged with kidnaping, pleaded not guilty and not guilty by reason of insanity. At trial, the victim, a 14–year–old girl, testified that he forced her into his car, drove to a wooded area, beat her and attempted to have sexual intercourse with her, and then ran away. The defendant testified that he remembered nothing about the events of that day and that his lack of recall began as of the time he drove his car over an embankment the day before the alleged kidnaping. A psychiatrist testified he had diagnosed the defendant's condition as "sociopathic personality and anti-social reaction" and that characteristics of that condition are "meanness toward other human beings," "an inability to get along with people," "an inability to abide by the rules of society," and, in defendant's case, "extreme aggressiveness toward other human beings." The defendant was convicted and sentenced to life imprisonment.]

We come now to the defendant's contention that the trial court erred in its instruction with reference to the burden of proof in connection with the defense of unconsciousness. That instruction was:

> "Now, members of the jury, a person cannot be held criminally responsible for acts committed while he is unconscious. Unconsciousness is never an affirmative defense. Where a person commits an act without being conscious thereof, such act is not criminal even though if committed by a person who was conscious it would be a crime. The defendant has no burden to prove that he was unconscious. If you find that the defendant was completely unconscious of what transpired when Catherine Sutton was taken violently from her driveway at her residence * * * then he would not be guilty, and it would be your duty to so find."

The defendant contends that the instruction that the defendant does not have the burden of proof on this issue and the instruction that the jury would find him not guilty, if it found he was "completely unconscious of what transpired" at the time of the alleged offense, are inconsistent and the court should have charged the jury to find the defendant not guilty unless they found beyond a reasonable doubt that he was conscious of what allegedly transpired.

This assignment of error has merit if, but only if, under the law of this State, a criminal defendant relying upon the defense of unconsciousness, also called automatism, does not have the burden of proof thereof. If the burden of proof is upon the defendant on this issue, the error in the charge was favorable to the defendant and does not entitle him to a new trial.

The defense of unconsciousness, or automatism, while not an entirely new development in the criminal law, has been discussed in relatively few decisions by American appellate courts, most of these being in California where the defense is expressly provided by statute. In *Bratty v. Attorney General for Northern Ireland,* All E.R. 3 (1961) 523, Lord Denning observed: "Until recently there was hardly any reference in the English books to this so-called defense of automatism. There was a passing reference to it in 1951 in *R. v. Harrison–Owen* [1951] 2 All E.R. 726." The only express reference to it which we have found in our Reports is in *State v. Mercer,* 275 N.C. 108, 165 S.E.2d 328, which we discuss below.

Unconsciousness, as a defense to a criminal charge, is discussed briefly in most of the textbooks and treatises on criminal law, the most extensive treatment of it, which has come to our attention, being in LaFave and Scott, *Criminal Law,* § 44 (1972), where it is said, "[a] defense related to but different from the defense of insanity is that of unconsciousness, often referred to as automatism: one who engages in what would otherwise be criminal conduct is not guilty of a crime if he does so in a state of unconsciousness or semi-consciousness." In *State v. Mercer,* this Court said: "Upon the present record, defendant was entitled to an instruction to the effect the jury should return verdicts of not guilty if in fact defendant was *completely* unconscious of what transpired when [the victims] were shot."

The defenses of insanity and unconsciousness are not the same in nature, for unconsciousness at the time of the alleged criminal act need not be the result of a disease or defect of the mind. As a consequence, the two defenses are not the same in effect, for a defendant found not guilty by reason of unconsciousness, as distinct from insanity, is not subject to commitment to a hospital for the mentally ill. * * *

Sources of unconsciousness, recognized as a defense by courts and textwriters, include somnambulism, somnolenture, hypnotism, cerebral concussion, delirium from fever or drugs, diabetic shock, epileptic black-outs, and drunkenness. Unconsciousness due to voluntary drunkenness was held no defense in *Lewis v. State,* 196 Ga. 755, 27 S.E.2d 659.

It is generally said that amnesia, in and of itself, is not a defense to a criminal charge. *Thomas v. State,* 201 Tenn. 645, 301 S.W.2d 358. In *Thomas* the Supreme Court of Tennessee quoted Gray, *Attorneys' Textbook of Medicine,* § 96.01 (3rd ed. 1949), as follows:

"Amnesia, loss of memory, may lead to crimes entirely unknown to the culprit at a later date. That is rare. More frequently, the accused, remembering full well what he has done, alleges amnesia in false defense. He is a malingerer. To prove his innocence or guilt may be most difficult. * * * Failure to remember later, when accused, is in itself no proof of the mental condition when crime was performed."

The principal point of difference among the few reported decisions on the defense of unconsciousness is with reference to the burden of proof. In *People v. Hardy,* supra, the California Supreme Court said:

"In *People v. Nihell,* 144 Cal. 200, 77 P. 916, where defendant claimed he was unconscious by reason of epilepsy, it was held that the burden was on him to establish the peculiar mental condition upon which he relied, and the Court stated * * * 'Men are presumed to be conscious when they act as if they were conscious, and if they would have the jury know that things are not what they seem, they must impart that knowledge by affirmative proof.' This is merely another way of saying that defendant has the duty of going forward with the evidence, and it is entirely consistent with the rule that defendant has only the burden of producing evidence which would raise a reasonable doubt in the minds of the jury."

In *Bratty v. Attorney General for Northern Ireland,* supra, the accused killed a girl, a passenger in his car, by strangling her with her own stocking. He testified that a "blackness" came over him and that "I didn't know what I was doing; I didn't realize anything," and that he had previously had "feelings of blackness and headaches." There was medical testimony that he *might have been* suffering from an attack of psychomotor epilepsy, a disease of the mind which could cause ignorance of the nature and quality of acts done. There was no medical evidence of any other pathological cause for a state of automatism. The trial judge refused to submit the defense of automatism to the jury but did submit the defense of insanity, which the jury rejected. The House of Lords held: "The trial judge was justified in not putting the defense of automatism to the jury since the evidence attributed any involuntariness in the appellant's act solely to a disease of the mind and there was no sufficient evidence of automatism, apart from insanity, to be left to the jury." The Lord Chancellor (Viscount Kilmuir) said:

"It is necessary that a proper foundation be laid before a judge can leave 'automatism' to the jury. That foundation, in my view, is not forthcoming merely from unaccepted evidence of a defect of reason from disease of the mind.

* * *

"[In *Hill v. Baxter* [1958] 1 All E.R. 193 [1958] 1 Q.B. 277] Lord Goddard expressed the view that the onus of proving the defendant was in a state of automatism was on him because automatism is akin to insanity and further is a fact exclusively within his own knowledge. The other members of the court reserved this point.

* * *

"If one subtracts the medical evidence directed to the establishment of psychomotor epilepsy, I am of the opinion that there was not any evidence on which a jury could properly have considered the existence of automatism. Counsel for the appellant directed our attention to the appellant's statement, to his evidence and to his previous conduct. In my view they do not provide evidence fit to be left to a jury on that question. They could not form the basis of reasonable doubt.

* * *

"[N]ormally the presumption of mental capacity is sufficient to prove that he acted consciously and voluntarily and the prosecution need go no further. But, if, after considering evidence properly left to them by the judge, the jury are left in real doubt whether or not the accused acted in a state of automatism, it seems to me that on principle they should acquit because the necessary mens rea—if indeed the actus reus—has not been proved beyond a reasonable doubt."

Lord Denning was of the opinion that while the ultimate burden rests on the prosecution to prove every element essential in the crime, it was entitled to rely on the presumption that every man has sufficient mental capacity to be responsible for his crimes. He said:

"[I]f the defence wish to displace that presumption they must give some evidence from which the contrary may reasonably be inferred. * * * The necessity of laying this proper foundation is on the defence: and if it is not so laid, the defence of automatism need not be left to the jury * * *. The evidence of the man himself will rarely be sufficient unless it is supported by medical evidence which points to the cause of the mental incapacity. It is not sufficient for a man to say 'I had a black-out:' for 'black-out' as Stable, J., said in *Cooper v. McKenna* [1960] Qd.R. at p. 419, 'is one of the first refuges of a guilty conscience and a popular excuse.' The words of Devlin, J., in *Hill v. Baxter* [1958], 1 All E.R. at p. 197 [1958], 1 Q.B. at p. 285, should be remembered:

" 'I do not doubt that there are genuine cases of automatism and the like, but I do not see how the layman can safely attempt without the help of some medical or scientific evidence to distinguish the genuine from the fraudulent.' "

Although unconsciousness, or automatism, is a defense separate and apart from insanity, in that it may not be the result of a disease or defect of the mind, it does not necessarily follow that the two defenses are different in law with respect to the burden of proof. Somnambulism and epilepsy, two sources of the defense of unconsciousness, have been said to be like unto insanity.

In *State v. Davis,* 214 N.C. 787, 1 S.E.2d 104, Justice Barnhill, later Chief Justice, speaking for this Court, said:

"[It has long been settled in this State that although the burden of establishing the *corpus delicti* is upon the state, when defendant relies upon some, independent, distinct, substantive matter of exemption, immunity or defense, beyond the essentials of the legal definition of the offense itself, the *onus* of proof as to such matter is upon the defendant." * * *

An affirmative defense is one in which the defendant says, "I did the act charged in the indictment, but I should not be found guilty of the crime charged because * * *." In *Bratty v. Attorney General for Northern Ireland,* supra, the House of Lords, and in *People v. Hardy,* supra, the California Court, were of the opinion that, once the defendant has introduced substantial evidence of unconsciousness, or automatism, the ultimate burden of proving consciousness, beyond a reasonable doubt, rests upon the prosecution, because an element of crime is the presence of *mens rea* at the time the act was done. The defense of insanity is said to be distinguishable because the law presumes sanity. We are unable to perceive a reasonable basis for distinction, in this respect, between *insanity* and *intoxication* on the one hand and *unconsciousness* from a different cause, on the other. In all three defenses the contention is the same—the defendant did the act, but should not be convicted because the requisite mental element was not present. The same presumption, which casts upon the defendant, claiming insanity, the burden of proving it to the satisfaction of the jury, and thus to negative the presence of *mens rea,* applies also to the defendant who asserts a temporary mental lapse due to concussion, somnolentia, epilepsy or the like.

In *State v. Mercer,* supra, the defendant, according to the State's evidence, went to the home of his estranged wife, armed with a pistol. When she refused to admit him, upon his knocking at the locked door, he kicked the door open, entered and immediately shot and killed his wife, her woman companion and the infant son of the other woman. His testimony was that he became "blank in his mind" when his wife ordered him off the porch and "when he became conscious, he was standing on the porch and the pistol, which was beside his head clicked." There was no medical, or other, evidence establishing any pathological explanation of the alleged "black-out." This Court, saying there was no evidence of insanity, held, as one of several grounds for a new trial, that the trial court's charge to the jury was deficient in that it limited the jury's consideration of the alleged unconsciousness to its bearing upon the matter of premeditation and deliberation. We said, "Unconsciousness is never an affirmative defense."

Upon further reflection, we are convinced that we erred in *State v. Mercer,* supra, in saying, "Unconsciousness is never an affirmative defense." In that respect, *State v. Mercer,* supra, is hereby overruled.

Our research has disclosed no decision, other than *State v. Mercer,* supra, in which any court has held that the defendant's uncorroborated and unexplained testimony that, at the moment of his otherwise criminal act, he "blacked-out," and so does not remember what, if anything, he did, is sufficient to carry to the jury the question of unconsciousness as a defense. * * *

We now hold that, under the law of this State, unconsciousness, or automatism, is a complete defense to a criminal charge, separate and apart from the defense of insanity; that it is an affirmative defense; and that the burden rests upon the defendant to establish this defense, unless it arises out of the State's own evidence, to the satisfaction of the jury.

In the present case, the learned trial judge fell into error, in his instruction as to the burden of proof on the question of unconsciousness, by reason of our own error in *State v. Mercer,* supra, but his error therein was in the defendant's favor and could not have prejudiced him in any way. It does not, therefore, afford a basis for granting him a new trial. * * *

SHARP, CHIEF JUSTICE (concurring in result and dissenting in part). * * *

[I]t seems to me utterly impossible that any juror could have construed this charge to place the burden of proof on defendant to establish his plea of unconsciousness.

As heretofore noted, at the beginning of the charge the jury were told the defendant had *no* burden to prove his innocence; that the burden was on the State to prove his guilt beyond a reasonable doubt. Later, in words too plain to be misunderstood, the judge charged that a person cannot be held criminally responsible for acts committed while he is unconscious even though such acts would be criminal if committed by a conscious person, and that *unconsciousness is never an affirmative defense.* He then said, *"The defendant has no burden to prove that he was unconscious.* If you find that the defendant was completely unconscious of what transpired when Catherine Sutton was taken violently from her driveway * * * put in an automobile [etc.] * * * he would not be guilty and it would be your duty to so find." (Emphasis added.) * * *

I can perceive no conflict between the judge's charge in this case and our decision in *Mercer.* On the contrary, the judge meticulously followed the law as laid down in that case. Hence, upon the present record, there is no need to consider whether the *Mercer* holding that unconsciousness is never an affirmative defense should be reaffirmed or overruled. Notwithstanding, the majority purport to overrule it upon the grounds stated in that opinion. Since I consider those grounds unsound, I am constrained to express my contrary view.

In writing the well documented opinion in *Mercer,* Chief Justice Bobbitt pointed out that if a person is actually unconscious when he does an act which would otherwise be criminal, the absence of consciousness not only excludes the existence of any specific mental state, but also excludes the *possibility of a voluntary act* without which there can be no criminal liability. Unconsciousness, therefore, can never be an affirmative defense, which imposes the burden of proof upon the defendant, because the State has the burden of proving the essential elements of the offense charged, and "a voluntary act is an absolute requirement for criminal liability." Although the defense of unconsciousness "is sometimes explained on the ground that such a person could not have the requisite mental state for commission of the crime, the better rationale is that the individual has not engaged in a voluntary act." * * *

Whether the offense charged be a specific-intent or a general-intent crime, in order to convict the accused the State must prove that he voluntarily did the forbidden act. Here I note that in *In Re Winship,* 397 U.S. 358, 90 S.Ct. 1068, 25 L.Ed.2d 368 (1970), in an opinion expressing the views of five members of the Court, Mr. Justice Brennan said: "Lest, there remain any doubt about the constitutional stature of the reasonable-doubt standard, we explicitly hold that the Due Process Clause protects the accused against conviction except upon proof beyond a reasonable doubt of every fact necessary to constitute the crime with which he is charged."

The plea of unconsciousness is analogous to a plea of accident or of alibi, neither of which is an affirmative defense. Each plea merely negates an essential element of the crime charged. The plea of accidental homicide imposes no burden upon the defendant because the State cannot convict unless it first proves that the killing was culpable. "The claim that the killing was accidental goes to the very gist of the charge, and denies all criminal intent, and throws on the prosecution the burden of proving such intent beyond a reasonable doubt." When proof of defendant's presence at the scene of the crime charged is essential to his guilt, his plea that he was elsewhere and therefore could not have committed the crime is merely a denial of guilt, not an affirmative defense. To convict, the State must prove beyond a reasonable doubt that he was present at the scene and participating. "Such proof, of course, would demolish an alibi." Similarly, proof of a voluntary act negates unconsciousness; voluntary action and unconsciousness cannot coexist.

When the State's evidence tends to show that, at the time in question, a defendant was "up and about," acting as if he had full possession of his faculties and knew what he was doing, it makes out a prima facie case of consciousness, and nothing else appearing, the law will assume he was conscious. Thus no issue of unconsciousness or automatism arises until some evidence of it is adduced. If the defendant offers such evidence, or if it is elicited from the State's own witnesses, the jurors must determine whether they are satisfied beyond a reasonable doubt that defendant voluntarily committed the act. From the beginning of the case and throughout the trial the burden remains upon the State to establish defendant's guilt beyond a reasonable doubt. This rule is supported by both reason and authority.

In *Government of the Virgin Islands v. Smith,* 278 F.2d 169 (3d Cir.1960), defendant, who was charged with involuntary manslaughter by automobile, defended on the ground that he was suddenly stricken by an epileptic seizure and was unconscious at the time of the accident which resulted in a death. In its findings, the trial court said that the question was whether defendant's evidence convinces the court that he had a seizure which rendered him unconscious. In awarding a new trial, the Court of Appeals said: "This was an erroneous statement of the law for the defendant did not have the burden of convincing the court he had an epileptic seizure. On the contrary, his burden was merely to go forward with the evidence to the extent necessary to raise a doubt * * * as to the defendant's consciousness * * *." In arriving at this conclusion the Third Circuit Court of Appeals relied heavily upon the reasoning of the Supreme Court of California in *People v. Hardy,* 33 Cal.2d 52, 198 P.2d 865 (1948), which is briefed below.

In *Hardy,* the defendant, whose defense was unconsciousness, was convicted of first degree murder. On appeal she assigned as error the trial court's charge that when the evidence shows a defendant acted as if he was conscious the law presumes he was then conscious, and that presumption remains until overcome by a preponderance of evidence to the contrary. In ordering a new trial the court said that this instruction deprived the defendant of the benefit of the "cardinal rule in criminal cases that the burden rests on the prosecution to prove the offense beyond a reasonable doubt."

"The mere fact that there is a presumption which tends to support the prosecution's case does not change the amount or quantum of proof which the defendant must produce. * * * The prosecution is required to prove the offense beyond a reasonable doubt and, in so doing, may rely on any applicable presumptions. The defendant, on the other hand, is not required to prove his innocence by a preponderance of the evidence, but only to produce sufficient evidence to raise a reasonable doubt in the minds of the jury. * * * 'Men are presumed to be conscious when they act as if they were conscious, and if they would have the jury know that things are not what they seem, they must impart that knowledge by affirmative proof.' This is merely another way of saying that defendant has the duty of going forward with the evidence, and it is entirely consistent with the rule that defendant has only the burden of producing evidence which would raise a reasonable doubt in the minds of the jury."

In *Bratty v. A.–G. for N. Ireland,* 3 All E.R. 523 (1961), a case from which the majority opinion quotes extensively but which does not support its conclusion, the Lord Chancellor and each of the four Lords who considered the case with him, expressed views in accord with those of *Hardy.*

The Lord Chancellor (Viscount Kilmuir), while noting that "a defence of automatism is very near a defence of insanity," said, "Nevertheless, one must not lose sight of the overriding principle, laid down by this House in *Woolmington's* case, that it is for the prosecution to prove every element of the offence charged. One of these elements is the accused's state of mind; normally the presumption of mental capacity is sufficient to prove that he acted consciously and voluntarily and the prosecution need go no further. But, if, after considering evidence properly left to them by the judge, the jury are left in real doubt whether or not the accused acted in a state of automatism, it seems to me that on principle they should acquit because the necessary mens rea—if indeed the actus reus—has not been proved beyond reasonable doubt. * * * "

"My conclusion is, therefore, that once the defence have surmounted the initial hurdle to which I have referred and have satisfied the judge that there is evidence fit for the jury's consideration, the proper direction is that, if that evidence leaves them in a real state of doubt, the jury should acquit."

Lord Morris agreed that if, during the trial, defendant advanced the defense of unconsciousness in explanation of the act, "and if such explanation was so supported that it had sufficient substance to merit consideration by the jury, then the onus which is on the prosecution would not be discharged unless the jury, having considered the explanation, were sure that guilt in regard to the particular crime charged was established so that they were left in no reasonable doubt."

Lords Tucker and Hodson each agreed with the views of both the Lord Chancellor and Lord Morris.

Lord Denning began his remarks by saying, " 'When dealing with a murder case the Crown must prove (a) death as the result of a voluntary act of the accused and (b) malice of the accused.' The requirement that it should be a voluntary act is essential, not only in a murder case, but also in every criminal case. No act is punishable if it is done involuntarily. * * * "He then noted that (1) an act is not involuntary "simply because the doer does not remember it * * * (or) could not control his impulse to do it" or "because it is unintentional or its consequences are unforeseen"; (2) automatism which results from drunkenness cannot lead "to a complete acquittal"; (3) "if the involuntary act proceeds from a disease of the mind, it gives rise to a defence of insanity, but not to a defence of automatism." These exceptions noted, Lord Denning perceived that "the category of involuntary acts is very limited."

While Lord Denning did not doubt that there were "genuine cases of automatism and the like" he observed that "black-out" was a popular excuse and "one of the first refuges of a guilty conscience," and he doubted that without the help of scientific evidence the layman-juror could distinguish the genuine from the fraudulent. In his opinion the evidence of the defendant himself would *rarely* be a sufficient foundation for the defense unless supported by medical evidence which pointed to the cause of the unconsciousness. He was convinced, however, that "[o]nce a proper foundation is thus laid for automatism, the matter becomes at large and must be left to the jury. As the case proceeds, the evidence may weigh first to one side and then to the other; and so the burden may appear to shift to and fro. *But at the end of the day the legal burden* comes into play and requires that the jury should be satisfied beyond reasonable doubt that the act was a voluntary act." (Emphasis added.)

The *decision* in *Bratty* was that the trial judge had not erred when he refused to submit to the jury defendant's defense of unconsciousness. In my view this was clearly correct, for the evidence was that the defendant remembered and gave the police a detailed account of the manner in which he had murdered his victim, and his only explanation for his conduct was that "something terrible" came over him and that he "didn't mean to do what really happened." Obviously such testimony constituted neither a "proper foundation" nor "evidence fit to be left to the jury on the question."

In discussing the relationship between the defenses of automatism and insanity, the "Law Lords" noted that the defendant acquitted by reason of insanity could be detained in a hospital where he was not a continuing danger to the public, whereas one acquitted on the ground of unconsciousness was unconditionally released. LaFave and Scott have noted the judicial tendency to characterize instances in which the condition of unconsciousness is likely to recur as insanity rather than automatism so that the defendant may be committed.

It is quite obvious that judges everywhere distrust the plea of unconsciousness and apprehend that jurors may repose hasty confidence in it. I think, however, there is no need for such concern, since jurors are sensible people too. For example, the jurors who tried this case were no more impressed with defendant's plea of automatism than is this Court. In my view we can safely assume that ordinarily a defendant's unsupported plea of blackout will aid the prosecution rather than the defense. But however that may be, were we to deny a defendant the defense of unconsciousness unless his testimony tending to establish unconsciousness be corroborated by medical testimony, we would violate fundamental and long-established principles of our criminal jurisprudence—that defendant has no burden to prove his innocence and that he is entitled to testify in his own behalf. * * *

It is quite possible that to require corroboration of a defendant's testimony that he was unconscious at the time the act with which he is charged was committed would, in effect, deprive an accused, who was actually unconscious at the time in question, of that plea. Presumably such a person would have no recollection of the acts with which he is charged. In such a case if his automatism resulted from a concussion of the brain caused by an injury or attack which he does not remember, he might well be in no position to provide the testimony upon which to base a hypothetical question an expert medical witness might answer in his favor. Unconsciousness resulting from unknown causes, or as the first manifestation or symptom of a previously undiagnosed condition or disease, might create similar problems.

In support of its thesis that the defense of automatism should be equated with the affirmative defense of insanity, the majority opinion says, "An affirmative defense is one in which the defendant says, 'I did the act charged in the indictment, but I should not be found guilty of the crime charged because * * *.'" "A plea of unconsciousness, however, is not routinely one of confession and avoidance. Assuming a genuine case of unconsciousness—and the majority opinion concedes the possibility—the defendant who had been unconscious could not always know for certain whether he committed the act charged, and it therefore seems most unlikely he would admit having done so. Of course, until the jury is satisfied beyond a reasonable doubt that the defendant indeed committed the act charged, his mental condition at the time is irrelevant. In this case the defendant did not admit he kidnapped Catherine. On the contrary he denied having done so. * * *

The opinions in both *Mercer* and *Bratty* point out the fundamental difference in the pleas of insanity and automatism. A plea of insanity raises this question: Was the defendant, at the time he committed the offense charged, so incapacitated from *a disease of the mind* that he was incapable of knowing the nature and quality of his act, or if he did know, was he incapable of distinguishing between right and wrong with relation thereto? No such question arises upon a plea of unconsciousness. One who is completely unconscious *cannot* know the nature and quality of his act or judge whether it is right or wrong. He is incapable of any voluntary action. Automatism "means unconscious involuntary action, and it is a defence because the mind does not go with what is being done." Automatism is action by one who has no knowledge of action, "no consciousness of doing what was being done." *Bratty.*

For the reasons stated herein I concur in the decision of the Court that there is no reversible error in the trial below, but I dissent from the statement in the majority opinion that unconsciousness is an affirmative defense. In my view unconsciousness, as held in *Mercer,* is never an affirmative defense.

Notes and Questions

1. Compare *People v. Newton,* 8 Cal.App.3d 359, 87 Cal.Rptr. 394 (1970), where defendant was convicted of the murder of police officer Frey. Prosecution witnesses testified that an altercation ensued after Frey stopped the defendant's car; that defendant had drawn a gun and that it had fired, wounding another officer; that this officer then fired at defendant's midsection; and that the defendant then wrested the gun away and fired point blank at Frey. The defendant testified that he carried no gun, that he felt a sensation like "boiling hot soup had been spilled on my stomach" and heard an "explosion," and that he remembered nothing else until he found himself at the entrance to a hospital some time later. A doctor testified on behalf of the defendant that "it is not at all uncommon for a person shot in the abdomen to lose consciousness and go into this reflex shock condition for short periods of time up to half an hour or so." Held, "that the trial court should have given appropriate unconsciousness instructions upon its own motion in the present case, and that its omission to do so was prejudicial error."

2. In *People v. Grant,* 46 Ill.App.3d 125, 4 Ill.Dec. 696, 360 N.E.2d 809 (1977), reversed 71 Ill.2d 551, 17 Ill.Dec. 814, 377 N.E.2d 4 (1978), defendant was charged with battery of a policeman. When the officer made an arrest at a tavern altercation, the defendant leaped out of the crowd and struck the officer in the face. He appeared to be very agitated and upset at the time, and great force was required to restrain him. An hour later, defendant was found on his jail cot gasping for breath. His eyes were fixed and his back formed a rigid reversed arch, typical symptoms of a grand mal convulsive seizure. He was hospitalized for 10 days. It was established that he suffers from psychomotor epilepsy and

has a history of violent attacks on other persons. At trial, he interposed an insanity defense, but the jury returned a guilty verdict. The appellate court—in the course of holding that "the interests of justice require reversal of the defendant's conviction because the jury instructions are substantially defective in that they do not contain an instruction on the defense of involuntary conduct"—noted that defendant's "past history is replete with emotional outbursts and he has been convicted on separate occasions of involuntary manslaughter and aggravated assault."

Green, J., dissenting, concluded that such an instruction should have been given if tendered, but that since it was not tendered justice did not require the "extraordinary step of granting a new trial so that another jury can make a new determination upon the proof rejected by the first jury" when it failed to find the defendant not guilty by reason of insanity. He added: "I share with Lord Denning and the majority of commentators on the subject a belief in the need for protective custody for persons who repeatedly attack others while in a state of automatism. The situation merits an attempt by the legislature to devise a procedure balancing the rights of the public to be protected against the rights of the person subject to automatism to be at liberty and basing any deprivation of that liberty upon the degree of danger presented by that individual."

3. Is the solution to draw the line between the insanity and unconsciousness defenses in terms of whether there is a need for post-acquittal commitment of the defendant? Consider *Fulcher v. State,* 633 P.2d 142 (Wyo.1981), holding that unconsciousness due to a concussion, when it involves "simple brain trauma with no permanent after effects," properly falls within the automatism defense, because commitment for treatment "is not suited to unconscious behavior resulting from a bump on the head," but that "brain damage" which amounts to "some serious and irreversible condition having an impact upon the ability of the person to function" is properly viewed as falling within the insanity defense.

4. On the burden of proof issue, compare *Caldwell* with *State v. Pierson,* 201 Conn. 211, 514 A.2d 724 (1986): "There are some basic aspects of criminal liability [e.g., absence of unconsciousness, insanity, duress, and entrapment] that may be presumed and thus need not be discussed in a charge to the jury, at least in the absence of a request or some evidence casting doubt upon the presumption. * * * Though the state bears the burden of disproving these defenses, once they are raised by the presentation of some evidence supporting them, there is no requirement that evidence negating them be produced as part of the state's prima facie case. A fortiori there is no requirement that a court suo motu instruct a jury upon these defenses in cases where the evidence produced by both parties contains not the remotest hint of their applicability."

5. In *People v. Decina,* 2 N.Y.2d 133, 157 N.Y.S.2d 558, 138 N.E.2d 799 (1956), defendant was convicted of negligent homicide after his automobile struck and killed four children. On appeal, he claimed his demurrer should have been sustained because the indictment (stating defendant knowing "that he was subject to epileptic attacks or other disorder rendering him likely to lose consciousness for a considerable period of time" was culpably negligent "in that he consciously undertook to and did operate his Buick sedan on a public highway" and "while so doing" suffered such an attack which caused said auto "to travel at a fast and reckless rate of speed, jumping the curb and driving over the sidewalk" causing the death of four persons) failed to charge a crime. The court of appeals disagreed:

"Assuming the truth of the indictment, as we must on a demurrer, this defendant knew he was subject to epileptic attacks and seizures that might strike *at any time.* He also knew that a moving motor vehicle uncontrolled on a public highway is a highly dangerous instrumentality capable of unrestrained destruction. With this *knowledge,* and without anyone accompanying him, he deliberately took a chance by making a conscious choice of a course of action, in disregard of the consequences which he knew might follow from his conscious act, and which in this case did ensue. How can we say as a matter of law that this did not amount to culpable negligence within the meaning of section 1053–a?

" * * * His awareness of a condition which he knows may produce such consequences as here, and his disregard of the consequences, renders him liable for culpable negligence, as the courts below have properly held. To have a sudden sleeping spell, an unexpected heart or other disabling attack, without any prior knowledge or warning thereof, is an altogether different situation, and there is simply no basis for comparing such cases with the flagrant disregard manifested here."

Desmond, J., dissenting, objected: "Just what is the court holding here? No less than this: that a driver whose brief blackout lets his car run amuck and kill another has killed that other by reckless driving. But any such 'recklessness' consists necessarily not of the erratic behavior of the automobile while its driver is unconscious, but of his driving at all when he knew he was subject to such attacks. Thus, it must be that such a blackout-prone driver is guilty of reckless driving, whenever and as soon as he steps into the driver's seat of a vehicle. Every time he drives, accident or no accident, he is subject to criminal prosecution for reckless driving or to revocation of his operator's license. And how many of this State's 5,000,000 licensed operators are subject to such penalties for merely driving the cars they are licensed to drive?"

How would Judge Desmond deal with *George v. State,* 681 S.W.2d 43 (Tex.Crim.App. 1984), where defendant was convicted of aggravated assault, defined by statute as intentionally, knowingly or recklessly shooting another? "In his confession and testimony at trial appellant described in greater detail that after he asked Martin a second time for a dollar he cocked the hammer back short of its locked position; that he 'struck [the gun] up in [Martin's] face;' that Martin 'turned his face away;' and then 'the hammer slipped off my thumb' and the gun 'went off.' Appellant further told the jury that he did not know the gun would nor did he mean for it to go off 'when he cocked the hammer back;' he denied ever pulling the trigger and stated that he did not intend to shoot Martin or harm him in any way—it was an accident." Was the Texas court correct in asserting, on the issue of whether a voluntary act had been proved, that "factually whether appellant's precise bodily movement that released the hammer of his handgun was voluntary or involuntary is of little moment"?

6. In defense of *Decina,* it has been said that the act requirement means that if "the court can find a voluntary act by the defendant, accompanied *at that time* by whatever culpable *mens rea* that is required, which act in fact and proximately causes some legally prohibited state of affairs, then the defendant is prima facie liable for that legal harm." Michael S. Moore, *Act and Crime: The Philosophy of Action and Its Implications for Criminal Law* 35 (1993). Leo Katz, *Proximate Cause in Michael Moore's Act and Crime,* 142 U.Pa.L.Rev. 1513, 1516–17 (1994), responds that this is not inevitably the case, even absent any justification or excuse for defendant's conduct, as with the instance of "ducking":

"In their article *Ducking Harm,*[22] two philosophers, Christopher Boorse and Roy Sorensen, offer a series of startling examples to illustrate the dramatically different treatment we accord deaths caused by (what they call) 'ducking' and deaths caused by (what they call) 'shielding.' Their essay opens with a joke that captures the distinction especially memorably:

22. Christopher Boorse & Roy A. Sorensen, *Ducking Harm, 85 J.Phil. 115 (1988).*

[T]wo campers, Alex and Bruce, meet a ravenous bear. As Alex grabs his running shoes, Bruce points out that no one can outrun a bear. "I don't have to outrun him," Alex replies. "I only have to outrun you." Few ... will criticize Alex for running away full tilt, or even for using his new Sauconys. But suppose Alex instead ties Bruce's ankles, or knocks Bruce unconscious and throws him to the bear. Alex is now blameworthy in ethics and in law. The result is the same in both cases: Bruce's death. Further, Alex may know the result to be the same if he knows he can outrun Bruce. Nonetheless most people sharply distinguish the two acts.

"The joke is followed with a potpourri of further illustrations:

(a1) Angela, at the end of a movie ticket line, sees X about to shoot a .22 automatic at her. Angela knows that a .22 bullet will kill one person but not two. Angela leaps aside; the bullet kills Brenda, who is next in line.

(a2) Same as (a1), but Angela grabs Brenda and moves her in front as a shield; the bullet kills Brenda.

. . . .

(c1) Alison is one of 25 U.S. government officials on an airplane, each with a briefcase bearing an official seal. Terrorist hijackers announce they will kill one American per hour until their demands are met. Surreptitiously Alison covers her seal with a Libya Air sticker. The terrorists pass her briefcase and shoot Beatrice, the next American.

(c2) Same as (c1), but Alison has no Libyan sticker. Instead she switches briefcases with Babette, a French novelist, while she is in the bathroom. The terrorists shoot Babette."

7. In *State v. Boleyn,* 328 So.2d 95 (La.1976), defendant was convicted of escape, defined by statute as "the intentional departure of a person, while imprisoned, * * * from any place where he is lawfully detained." He and Manuel were discovered missing at 2:30 p.m. but were apprehended less than 12 hours later when police stopped a car defendant was driving. The trial judge excluded (i) evidence relating to defendant's state of consciousness at the time of the purported escape (i.e., that he fell asleep in the parked truck by which Manuel made his escape) and (ii) evidence of his consumption of alcohol and drugs immediately prior thereto. On appeal, the court first held that the latter exclusion was proper under the rule that "voluntary intoxication can be considered as a defense only in cases where specific intent is a necessary element of the crime," and then concluded that it was error to exclude the other evidence because it "would indicate to the jury that defendant did not *voluntarily* escape."

Marcus, J., dissenting, asserted: "Under the circumstances of the instant case, defendant's criminal intent is found in the accused's intention to become intoxicated or drugged, i.e., the accused is held to have intended, in law, all the consequences of his intoxicated or drugged condition. Therefore, the criminal act of escape is a consequence of defendant's voluntary intoxicated or drugged condition."

Is the dissent sound? Is it supported by *Decina?* Consider G. R. Sullivan, *Self Induced and Recurring Automatism,* 123 New L.J. 1093, 1094 (1973), commenting on *Regina v. Quick,* [1973] 3 W.L.R. 26, holding it was error not to instruct on the defense of automatism where defendant, a diabetic, assaulted another while in a hypoglycaemic episode after taking insulin but very little food:

"The law is unsatisfactory in that it would probably provide for an acquittal, despite the fact that Q., with a history of violent blackouts, negligently induced his automatous state. [T]he court was reluctant to concede that the defence would have succeeded if the condition had been caused by insulin. It was felt that much would have depended on the answers to the following questions: 'to what extent had he brought about his condition by not following his doctor's instructions about taking regular meals? Did he know he was getting into a hypoglycaemic episode? If yes, why did he not use the antidote of eating a lump of sugar as he had been advised to?' The court felt that Q. might have had difficulty in answering these questions in a manner which would have relieved him of responsibility for his acts.

"Yet, even though Q. may have been clearly responsible for his condition the defence of automatism may still have succeeded at trial. The charge was assault, [which requires] 'any act which intentionally—or possibly recklessly—causes another person to apprehend immediate and unlawful physical violence.' So, *at the very least,* the prosecution would have had to prove that Q. foresaw he would attack someone."

Compare D. O'Connor, *The Voluntary Act,* 15 Med.Sci.Law 31, 35 (1975), arguing that any "distinction between self-induced and other-induced malfunction is not useful in the criminal law. If it is a necessary part of the [prosecution's] case to show a voluntary act, and the [prosecution] is unable to prove it beyond a reasonable doubt because there is evidence of involuntary conduct, the question whether the involuntarism resulted from the accused's own conduct or was induced by some external cause does not seem to be relevant."

8. *Decina* is often referred to in order to illustrate another point, that when a crime is defined in terms of a certain mental state plus an act producing a certain result, the act and mental state must "concur," for the court's theory was that the mental state (recklessness) and act (driving in a manner that caused death) both preceded the defendant's blackout. Issues of concurrence can arise even when there is no voluntary act problem. That fact, as well as the fact that sometimes the defendant's acts must be assessed for yet another reason, to determine how many crimes have occurred, are illustrated by *Clay v. Commonwealth*, 30 Va.App. 254, 516 S.E.2d 684 (1999). Clay approached pedestrians Guise and Vandegrift, pulled a gun and pointed it at Guise's chest and said "Just give me all your stuff," and then removed Guise's coat, after which Clay turned the gun toward Vandegrift and patted him down but found nothing to take, and then left with Guise's coat. Because the coat contained two twenty-dollar bills belonging to Vandegrift, Clay was charged and convicted of two counts of robbery–one for robbing Guise, and one for robbing Vandegrift. The appellate court noted that it was well established that in robbery cases "the appropriate 'unit of prosecution' was determined by the number of persons from whose possession property is taken separately,"[a] and then concluded that here there had been two takings–the taking of the jacket and the taking of the money in the jacket pocket. The court continued:

"Clay further argues that the taking and the required mental state for that taking were not contemporaneous. The issue is not whether the *mens rea* and the *actus rea* are

a. Consider also *State v. Morro,* 127 N.M. 763, 987 P.2d 420 (App.1999), where defendant in "an undifferentiated rage" and in "one continuous episode" albeit by separate acts damaged ten tombstones with a sledgehammer. In upholding defendant's conviction on ten counts of defacing tombs, the court emphasized that while "the injury to general community sensibilities is essentially the same for each gravestone," nonetheless "each gravestone represents distinct interests protected by the statute," for "injury to each gravestone causes injury to the memory of a different person and is likely to cause emotional distress to a different collection of living persons." The court found "ground for pause" in the "single-larceny doctrine," under which "the taking of property belonging to different owners at the same time and place should be prosecuted as one larceny." but concluded that was merely an exception to the general rule, explainable in part by the fact that an "additional feature of the larceny statute is that the penalty for the offense depends on the value of the goods taken."

contemporaneous; rather, it is whether the *mens rea* and the *actus rea* concur. However, 'concurrence in time ... is neither required nor sufficient; the true meaning of the requirement that the mental fault concur with the act or omission is that the former actuates the latter.' * * *

" * * * Clay intended to rob both Vandegrift and Guise of their possessions and his state of mind was not abandoned at the time he committed the physical act of taking Guise's jacket that contained Vandegrift's money. Clay's mental state actuated the taking and his intent to rob both men was not abandoned at the time he committed the physical act of taking Guise's jacket that contained Vandegrift's money."

The dissenters objected: "To hold that the taking of a single item from the actual possession of a single victim–which item, unbeknowst to the robber, happens to contain property that is owned by some other person present at the scene and that remains constructively in that other person's possession–also implied the *animus furandi* to support a second robbery conviction would improperly relieve the Commonwealth of its burden of proving that intent to steal from the second victim actuated the taking from the first."

Under the majority's theory, what would the result have been had the robber started with Vandergrift and then turned to Guise?

9.　Donald T. Lunde & Thomas E. Wilson, *Brainwashing as a Defense to Criminal Liability: Patty Hearst Revisited,* 13 Crim.L.Bull. 341, 341–42, 370 (1977): "The recent trial and conviction of Patricia Hearst for bank robbery has raised anew within American society, and the legal and psychiatric communities more specifically, the question of 'brainwashing' as a defense of exculpation or mitigation to criminal liability. The facts of the *Hearst* case are well known: On April 15, 1974 Hearst participated in a San Francisco bank robbery together with members of the Symbionese Liberation Army who had kidnapped Hearst some ten weeks before, on February 4, 1974. The central issue at trial was whether Hearst had joined her abductors subsequent to her kidnaping and participated in the robbery voluntarily, or whether she was forced to participate—either by threats of death if she refused or as a result of beliefs inculcated in her through an indoctrination process of the SLA.

"The jury in the *Hearst* case was faced with the question of where coerced behavior ends and truly voluntary action begins for persons who appear to have changed their loyalties and values while held in captivity. The answer to that question was thought to reside in a misunderstood, potentially powerful, yet quite simple, process developed by the Chinese Communists and called 'brainwashing.' Because of the term's popularization during the Korean War years, and its reappearance in everyday parlance, a widely held belief was that it was a recognized legal doctrine. In fact, the term 'brainwashing' was not used or defended to any extent during the trial itself and the jury rejected the implied brainwashing defense while convicting Hearst. Most important, brainwashing is not a presently recognized defense to criminal liability. * * *

"Bringing coercive persuasion under this legal rubric [of automatism] has the advantage of not faltering on the disease or defect hurdle that the insanity defense does because the unconsciousness defense applies to persons of sound mind. However, coercive persuasion simply does not rise to the factual sufficiency necessary. In none of the prisoner of war cases, nor in the *Hearst* case would it be possible to argue that the defendants were not aware of what they were doing. All remembered their crimes and did not contend otherwise, when an allegation of lack of memory is usually the necessary, but not sufficient, condition for raising an unconsciousness defense."

10. Without regard to whether brainwashing fits within the traditional definition of automatism, should it be recognized as a defense? Compare: (a) Richard Delgado, *Ascription of Criminal States of Mind: Toward a Defense Theory for the Coercively Persuaded ("Brainwashed") Defendant*, 63 Minn.L.Rev. 1, 11 (1978): "The victim of thought reform typically commits criminal acts fully aware of their wrongfulness. He acts consciously, even enthusiastically, and without overt coercion. Yet, in an important sense, the guilty mind with which he acts is not his own. Rather, his mental state is more appropriately ascribed to the captors who instilled it in him for their own purposes. Explication of the concept of transferred or superimposed mens rea—criminal intent that is not the actor's own—is thus the principal task of this Article."

(b) Joshua Dressler, *Professor Delgado's "Brainwashing" Defense: Courting A Deterministic Legal System*, 63 Minn.L.Rev. 335, 343 (1979): "Such a proposal is doctrinally untenable. All ideas and intents originate outside the individual, in the sense that they are shaped by experiences and environment. As we have seen, however, the law nevertheless considers intent to be personal—to be a product of each individual's free will. This is true whether the intent to commit the crime is initiated by an inanimate object ('I saw the painting and it made me think of killing'), an innocent third party ('X told me the victim had a lot of money so I killed the victim'), or a guilty third party. If this were not the case, one could plausibly argue that all mental states—for example, criminal intentions, or political or religious views—are inauthentic, thus unacceptably blurring concepts of moral and legal responsibility."

11. *Caddell* lists "hypnotism" as one source of unconsciousness, and Model Penal Code § 2.01(c) says "conduct during hypnosis or resulting from hypnotic suggestion" does not constitute a voluntary act. Compare Comment, 39 Wayne L.Rev. 1299, 1333–34 (1993): "The strands of hypnotic phenomena are now unraveled. Yet, questions about hypnotism as a valid defense remain unanswered. For the reasons discussed in this Comment, the hypnotism defense should not be allowed. The questions which remain unanswered persist because of the numerous fallacies and unsolved debates about hypnotic effect. Before a hypnotism defense can successfully accomplish the proper goals of excuse, a narrower scientific inquiry must examine whether a hypnotized person can resist criminal or antisocial suggestion. This, of course, may never occur because of the obvious problems in experimenting with criminal suggestion under hypnosis. Additionally, even with conclusive proof of induced hypnotic crime, the overwhelming legal considerations that naturally flow from such a defense should still preclude the defense.

"As one commentator proclaimed, '[a] plea of hypnosis as a defense should be received with the greatest caution, and should be clearly demonstrated before the subject is held to be irresponsible and absolved from the consequences of his crime.' Many uncertainties exist about hypnosis. Perhaps that is why so many states restrict the practice of hypnotism. But until these uncertainties become provable facts, a hypnotism defense is unwise and dangerous. Many states have realized the inherent problems associated with hypnotism and have, therefore, refrained from taking the giant leap of faith in allowing the hypnotism defense. Such a leap may bode well for the criminal, but it sounds a potential death knell to acceptable substantive criminal defense law."

12. In *McClain v. State*, 678 N.E.2d 104 (Ind.1997), where defendant was charged with aggravated battery on two police officers, the trial court granted the state's motion to bar the defense from offering expert testimony on sleep disorders and dissociative states. Such testimony was sought by defendant, who claimed to have been without sleep for all but three of the 48 hours preceding the incident, to support his claim "that his violent behavior towards police was a form of automatism caused by sleep deprivation." On appeal,

the court ruled that the tendered evidence "goes to the voluntariness of his actions" and should have been received.

13. In *Hazelwood*, p. 155 of this Book, the court commented: "Had terrorists boarded the Exxon Valdez, for example, and demanded that Hazelwood run his vessel onto Bligh Reef, the fact that he did so even with knowledge and purpose would be irrelevant. He could defend on the basis that his act was not voluntary." Compare *State v. Daoud*, 141 N.H. 142, 679 A.2d 577 (1996), where defendant claimed that because of duress she had not engaged in a voluntary act, and "in support of her position * * * focuse[d]on comments written by the 1969 commission charged with codifying New Hampshire's criminal laws" to the effect that the voluntary act statute "ought to be broad enough to preclude criminal liability under circumstances of duress." But the court ruled otherwise, noting that "commentators agree that duress does not make criminal conduct involuntary." Why?

14. In *Baird v. State*, 604 N.E.2d 1170 (Ind.1992), defendant introduced evidence that because of a mental illness the homicides he committed were the result of an irresistible impulse and, upon appeal of his conviction, claimed that this evidence tended to show his actions were not voluntary and that the prosecution had not shown otherwise beyond a reasonable doubt. The court disagreed: "The evidence appellant points to as raising the issue of voluntariness thus actually would bear on the issue of 'irresistible impulse,' were that test still recognized as part of the insanity defense, but fails to provide a factual basis which would require the prosecution to prove beyond a reasonable doubt that appellant acted voluntarily."

15. C. Peter Erlinder, *Paying the Price for Vietnam: Post–Traumatic Stress Disorder and Criminal Behavior*, 25 B.C.L.Rev. 305, 310–11, 329 (1984): "Following the traumatic event, a person who suffers from PTSD may have a number of symptoms that include: self medication through substance or alcohol abuse, memory loss, loss of sleep, nightmares reliving the original traumatic event, intrusive thoughts, exaggerated startle response, reduction in emotional response, a feeling of alienation, and, 'disassociative states' during which the original event is relived and *the individual behaves as though experiencing the event of the moment.'* * * * The more difficult aspect of PTSD for many to accept is that the *symptoms of PTSD can occur long after the original traumatic event has ended*. Thus, long after the traumatic event, persons affected by PTSD may react as though they were back in the original traumatic situation.

"This tendency to 'reexperience' or 'relive' the original event is common to those who experience PTSD symptoms after a traumatic event, regardless of its source. For those trained to survive in combat, a 'reexperiencing' of the original event may include combat-like reactions. * * *

"Perhaps the most likely alternative theory for the introduction of PTSD at trial lies in the well accepted, but little used defense of automatism."

In *State v. Jerrett*, 309 N.C. 239, 307 S.E.2d 339 (1983), defendant burglarized a farmhouse, shot and killed the owner, and then kidnapped the owner's wife. At trial, defendant testified he had been blacked out during those events and that he had been experiencing blackouts since his Vietnam service. His parents testified about his many blackouts. A state psychiatrist testified defendant was not suffering from PTSD, while a defense psychiatrist testified the state had not adequately tested the defendant. Relying on *Caddell*, the court ruled defendant should have had an automatism instruction "because here there was corroborating evidence tending to support the defense of unconsciousness. In addition to the testimonial corroborating evidence, defendant's very peculiar actions in permitting the kidnapped victim to repeatedly ignore his commands and finally lead him docilely into the presence and custody of a police officer lends credence to his defense of unconsciousness."

16. In *State v. Grimsley,* 3 Ohio App.3d 265, 444 N.E.2d 1071 (1982), an appeal of defendant's conviction for driving while intoxicated, the defendant, who had a multiple personality disorder, contended she should not have been convicted because at the time of her conduct she was disassociated from her primary personality (Robin) and in the state of consciousness of a secondary personality (Jennifer, who is impulsive, angry, fearful and anxious). The court responded:

"We disagree. Assuming *arguendo* that the evidence was sufficient to establish such a complete break between appellant's consciousness as Robin and her consciousness as Jennifer that Jennifer alone was in control (despite years of therapy), nevertheless the evidence fails to establish the fact that Jennifer was either unconscious or acting involuntarily. There was only one person driving the car and only one person accused of drunken driving. It is immaterial whether she was in one state of consciousness or another, so long as in the personality then controlling her behavior, she was conscious and her actions were a product of her own volition. The evidence failed to demonstrate that Jennifer was unconscious or otherwise acting involuntarily."

17. Consider the following comments on the premenstrual syndrome: (a) Recent Decision, 59 Notre Dame L.Rev. 253, 257–58, 264–65 (1983): "Although medical experts disagree on the diagnosis, cause, and treatment of PMS, they do agree that the syndrome causes marked psychological anomalies. These psychological anomalies have significantly affected the behavioral patterns of thousands of women. These women demonstrate the greatest potential for PMS-induced criminal behavior. Medical studies have linked PMS to an increased number of suicide attempts, automobile accidents, and miscellaneous criminal acts. Nonetheless, the legal community has not yet paid sufficient attention to the correlation between PMS and crime. * * *

"Because PMS is not a disease or defect of the mind, it might fit more appropriately within the automatism defense. * * *

"American courts might find it equally appropriate to exclude PMS-induced conduct from the reach of the criminal law. Although a PMS sufferer may be conscious of her actions and devoid of any mental disease or defect, she is no more able to control her actions than the automaton or the legally insane. Physiological anomalies render the PMS sufferer unable to control her actions during the short time PMS symptoms surface. These symptoms surface, however, at regular, predictable intervals which doctors can effectively control under appropriate medical supervision."

(b) Elizabeth Holtzman, *Premenstrual Symptoms: No Legal Defense,* 60 St. John's L.Rev. 712, 713 (1986), concludes "that there is no scientific evidence for the proposition that the onset of the menstrual cycle provokes aggressive or violent behavior in women. The scientific evidence is confirmed by common sense experience—if women became violent each month our jails would be filled with women. But, as it is, the overwhelming number of jail inmates are men; no menstrual cycle caused their aggression."

(c) Katherina Dalton, *Once a Month* 207 (1983): "Those few women who lose control of themselves for a day or two, month after month, need help and help is available. However, they must not be confused with the other 99.9 percent of women who are well able to control their actions. PMS is not a universal defense, nor should it be allowed to become one. Medical evidence is required by the court and the doctor must become fully conversant with the recognition, diagnosis and treatment of the syndrome."

18. Glanville Williams, *Criminal Law: The General Part* § 9 (2d ed. 1961): "At the present day the exception from responsibility, such as it is, given by the 'act' doctrine could, in respect of the requirement of will, just as well be put on the ground of absence of mens rea." Why?

19. Compare the following three cases and consider whether they all involve applications of the same principle:

(a) *Martin v. State,* 31 Ala.App. 334, 17 So.2d 427 (1944): Police arrested defendant at his home and took him onto the highway, where he was boisterous. Defendant was convicted under a statute covering any "person who, while intoxicated or drunk, appears in any public place where one or more persons are present, * * * and manifests a drunken condition by boisterous or indecent conduct." Reversed, as "an accusation of drunkenness in a designated public place cannot be established by proof that the accused, while in an intoxicated condition, was involuntarily and forcibly carried to that place by the arresting officer."

(b) *People v. Newton,* 72 Misc.2d 646, 340 N.Y.S.2d 77 (1973): The defendant was a passenger on a commercial flight originating in the Bahamas and destined for Luxembourg. The defendant was unruly on the plane, and the captain feared he might be armed, so he diverted the plane from over international waters and made an unscheduled landing in New York. Police came aboard and found defendant had a loaded gun on his person. Defendant was charged with the felony of carrying a loaded weapon. The court found that the defendant "did not subject himself to criminal liability by virtue of a voluntary act. Flight #101 was not scheduled to terminate in or pass through the territorial jurisdiction of the United States. The landing at John F. Kennedy International Airport on December 8, 1972 was merely an interruption of flight not attributable to a voluntary action by the petitioner."

(c) *People v. Shaughnessy,* 66 Misc.2d 19, 319 N.Y.S.2d 626 (1971): The defendant was a passenger in a car she understood was headed for a certain public park. The driver instead pulled into private premises across the street from the park, where the car was stopped by a watchman. The occupants waited 20 minutes for a police officer to arrive, during which time the defendant never left the vehicle. The defendant was prosecuted for violating an ordinance forbidding entry on private property without permission of the owner or occupant. In granting the defendant's motion to dismiss, the court stated:

"In the case at bar, the People have failed to establish any act on the part of the Defendant. She merely was a passenger in a vehicle. Any action taken by the vehicle was caused and guided by the driver thereof and not by the Defendant. If the Defendant were to be held guilty under these circumstances, it would dictate that she would be guilty if she had been unconscious or asleep at the time or even if she had been a prisoner in the automobile. There are many situations which can be envisioned and in which the trespass statute in question would be improperly applied to an involuntary act. One might conceive of a driver losing control of a vehicle through mechanical failure and the vehicle proceeding onto private property which is the subject of a trespass.

"Although the Court need not pass on the question, it might very well be proper to hold the driver responsible for his act even though he was under the mistaken belief that he was on his way to Christopher Morley Park. The legislature has provided statutes which make mistakes of fact or lack of knowledge no excuse in a criminal action. However, if the driver had been a Defendant, the People could have established an act on the part of the Defendant driver, to wit, turning his vehicle into the private property."

20.   In *Williams v. City of Petersburg,* 216 Va. 297, 217 S.E.2d 893 (1975), defendant was convicted of violating an ordinance providing that "[n]o person shall drive or operate any automobile * * * in the city while under the influence of alcohol." At 4 a.m. a police officer was attracted to a car with the engine running in a parking lot. The defendant, intoxicated, was slumped over the wheel. All the doors were locked, but the officer managed to get defendant's attention, and the defendant then turned off the car. On appeal, the court held that "the trial court could properly find beyond a reasonable doubt that the defendant was in actual physical control of the vehicle and that he had engaged the machinery of the vehicle which alone, or in sequence, would have activated its motive power. Therefore, the defendant was 'operating' the vehicle within the meaning of the ordinance.

"The trial court was not required to accept the defendant's account of the incident, which was that he had started the engine merely for the purpose of using the car heater to keep warm and not for the purpose of driving the vehicle."

The dissenters objected: "Defendant did exactly what others should do upon finding that they have consumed too much alcohol to operate a vehicle—stop drinking and go to sleep. For security purposes he locked his car doors. To keep from getting too cold he started the heater. He did nothing with his car that was a menace to himself or to the public. For us to hold that what the defendant did in this case amounts to operating a car within the purview of Code § 18.1–54, or the Petersburg ordinance, is unrealistic and unreasonable."

Compare *State v. Bugger,* 25 Utah 2d 404, 483 P.2d 442 (1971) (where intoxicated person was asleep in a car on the shoulder of the road and the car was not running, he is not guilty of violating a statute making it unlawful "for any person who is under the influence of intoxicating liquor to drive or be in actual physical control of any vehicle within the state"); with *Wiyott v. State,* 284 Ark. 399, 683 S.W.2d 220 (1985) (defendant guilty under such a statute where he intoxicated and asleep in the car, parked in grocery store parking lot but, when a policeman banged on the window and hollered at him, defendant reached for key in ignition switch).

SECTION 2. THE "ACT" OF POSSESSION

PEOPLE v. GORY

Supreme Court of California, 1946.
28 Cal.2d 450, 170 P.2d 433.

SPENCE, JUSTICE.

In an information filed by the District Attorney of Los Angeles County, defendant was accused of * * * violating section 11160 of the Health and Safety Code in that he did, on or about June 2, 1944, "willfully, unlawfully and feloniously have in his possession flowering tops and leaves of Indian Hemp (cannabis sativa)," commonly called marijuana. * * * From the judgment of conviction entered upon this verdict and from an order denying his motion for a new trial, defendant prosecutes this appeal. * * *

There is practically no conflict in the testimony. At the time of the alleged possession of marijuana, defendant was a prisoner at the Los Angeles County Honor Farm near Castaic. He shared living quarters with some thirty odd prisoners in one of the camp's bunkhouses, to which he had been assigned in April, 1944. As part of the equipment issued to each prisoner, defendant received a metal box—18 inches long, 12 inches wide, 8 inches deep—in which he kept his toilet articles and small personal effects. There was no way of locking these boxes, each of which bore a number corresponding to the bed number of the space occupied by the particular prisoner. Each prisoner's box was placed on the floor near the head of his bed. During the day when the prisoners were engaged in their duties on the farm, one man was left in charge of the bunkhouse to "keep the inmates from monkeying with other people's property."

About 9:30 p.m. on June 2, 1944, Officer Gunderson and several accompanying officers entered the bunkhouse. While his associates searched the boxes of other prisoners in the bunkhouse, Officer Gunderson went to defendant's bed—on which defendant was lying—picked up the metal box bearing the number of defendant's bed, opened the box and found marijuana "scattered from the top down to the bottom * * * just loose in the box." Said officer took off defendant's clothes and examined them, turning the pockets "wrong side out," but found no marijuana either on his person or in his clothes. Deputy Sheriff Huber, who was present at the time, testified at the trial that he asked defendant what he knew about this marijuana, stating: "This is your marijuana; where did you get it?" and that defendant did not answer. In his own testimony at the trial, defendant admitted that the material which the officers identified as marijuana was taken from his box, but stated that he had never seen it before the officers removed it from the box.

With the evidence so presented at the trial, defendant challenges the propriety of the trial Court's action in reading, rereading, and then expressly withdrawing from the jury's consideration the following instructions, hereinafter designated "instruction 12" and "instruction 13."

Instruction 12: "In order for defendant to have in his possession the objects charged in the information, you must be convinced by the evidence and beyond a reasonable doubt that he *knowingly* had such objects in his possession. The meaning of the word 'possession' includes the exercise of dominion and control over the thing possessed."

Instruction 13: "Even if you find from the evidence beyond a reasonable doubt that the defendant had in his possession, flowering tops of Indian Hemp or locoweed, before you can find the defendant guilty of possessing the same, you must also be convinced beyond a reasonable doubt that the defendant had a *guilty knowledge* of the character of said flowering tops of Indian Hemp and possessed a *guilty intent*. If you find that the defendant was innocent of the *knowledge of the character* of the flowering tops of Indian Hemp or did not have a *guilty knowledge* of possessing said flowering tops of Indian Hemp, then you will find the defendant not guilty and must acquit him." * * *

So far as pertinent to defendant's argument, section 20 of the Penal Code provides that "In every crime or public offense there must exist a union, or joint operation of act and intent * * *." But this does not mean that a positive, wilful intent to violate the law is an essential ingredient of every offense. Sometimes an act is expressly prohibited by statute, in which case the *intentional doing of the act*, regardless of good motive or ignorance of its criminal character, constitutes the offense denounced by law. * * * Speaking to this point, the court in *People v. Sweeney*, 66 Cal.App.2d 855, 153 P.2d 371, a case concerning violation of the same code section here involved, said: "Neither intent nor knowledge is an element of the offense herein charged. The mere possession, except as authorized by the provisions of the Health and Safety Code, is a violation of the act. * * *"

While it thus appears that "mere possession, except as authorized" is sufficient to constitute the statutory offense in question, without regard for *scienter* or specific intent to violate the law as would follow from evidence establishing defendant's *knowledge of the contraband character* of the property, the law makes the matter of knowledge in relation to *defendant's awareness of the presence* of the object a basic element of the offense of possession. It has been repeatedly held that the term "possession" as used in the State Poison Act (now embraced in the Health and Safety Code) means an "immediate and exclusive possession and one under the dominion and control of defendant." Thus it was said in *People v. Noland,* 61 Cal.App.2d 364, 366, 143 P.2d 86, 87: "A person has 'possession' of a chattel who has physical control with the intent to exercise such control, or, having had such physical control, has not abandoned it and no other person has obtained possession. (Restatement Torts, section 216.)" But knowledge of the *existence* of the object is essential to "physical control thereof with the intent to exercise such control" and such knowledge must necessarily precede the intent to exercise, or the exercise of, such control. * * *

The distinction which must be drawn, from a reading of the foregoing authorities, is the distinction between (1) *knowledge of the character of the object and the unlawfulness of possession thereof* as embraced within the concept of a specific intent to violate the law, and (2) *knowledge of the presence of the object* as embraced within the concept of "physical control with the intent to exercise such control," which constitutes the "possession" denounced by the statute. It is "knowledge" in the first sense which is mentioned in the authorities as being immaterial but "knowledge" in the second sense is the essence of the offense.

In line with these authorities, it plainly appears in this case that instruction 13, as above quoted, in requiring the finding of a "guilty knowledge" and a "guilty intent" on the part of defendant to sustain his conviction, was properly withdrawn from the jury as an improper matter for consideration.

But instruction 12, as above quoted, in its predication of a finding of guilt upon defendant's "*knowingly*" having "in his possession the objects charged in the information," should have been given to the jury. "The word 'knowingly' imports only a knowledge that the facts exist which bring the act or omission within the provisions of this code. It does not require any knowledge of the unlawfulness of such act or omission." Thus instruction 12 invoked the element of knowledge in the sense of defendant's *awareness of the presence* of the marijuana in the box given him for the storage of his personal effects at the prison farm and so presented to the jury an issue of fact determinative of defendant's guilt or innocence of the possession prohibited by statute. * * *

The judgment and the order denying defendant's motion for a new trial are reversed.

SCHAUER, JUSTICE.

I concur in the judgment and agree that it was prejudicial error to fail to give (to withdraw) instruction number 12. I do not agree to the implication, if there be such, that mere conscious possession of an object, not knowing its true character (as, for example, possession of marijuana believed in good faith to be ordinary tobacco), any more than conscious possession of an object lawful in itself but within which, unknown to the possessor, contraband is concealed, constitutes a criminal act.

Notes and Questions

1. Assume that defendant is arrested moments after he has received a package from postal authorities and that the police then open the package and find narcotics. In one such case, *Commonwealth v. Lee,* 331 Mass. 166, 117 N.E.2d 830 (1954), the court affirmed defendant's conviction for possession of narcotics, stating: "Before the package was opened the defendant had received it from the mail carrier and had claimed it as hers. She indicated no intent not to exercise control of it on her own behalf.

"We need not consider whether there was sufficient evidence that the defendant knew or had reason to believe that the package contained marijuana, until she opened it. And we need not consider cases in other jurisdictions, where a statute made criminal the possession of a drug or other harmful thing, in which it has been held that a defendant cannot be convicted unless he knowingly had possession of the forbidden thing, illustrated by *People v. Gory*."

Compare *Commonwealth v. Rambo,* 488 Pa. 334, 412 A.2d 535 (1980), noting that a statute in the criminal code defined possession as "an act, within the meaning of this section, if the possessor knowingly procured or received the thing possessed or was aware of his control thereof for a sufficient period to have been able to terminate his possession," and concluding from this that defendant's conviction must be reversed because there was no "evidence which would establish, beyond a reasonable doubt, that appellant knew the packages contained hashish."

Are *Lee* and *Rambo* in conflict as to what constitutes the "act" of possession, or as to whether the particular possession crime also has a mental state element?

2. In *State v. Flaherty,* 400 A.2d 363 (Me.1979), defendant was convicted of unlawful possession of a firearm because a rifle owned by another person was found in defendant's car. Defendant claimed the owner of the rifle had mistakenly put it there and that he had just discovered it there shortly before. On appeal, the court ruled defendant should have received an instruction in the language of the statute (essentially like that in *Rambo*) because with such an instruction "the jury might reasonably have concluded that the Defendant had not been aware of his control of the rifle for a sufficient period to have been able to terminate his possession." The court explained such a provision provides a " 'grace' period * * * designed to separate illegal possession from temporary control incidental to the lawful purpose of terminating possession. Thus a 'sufficient period' is not always the absolute minimum time required to get rid of the contraband. So long as the Defendant's control of the contraband remains incidental to the lawful purpose of terminating his possession and, viewed under the circumstances, remains 'temporary,' it falls within the 'sufficient period' permitted him by" the statute.

3. In *People v. Norris,* 40 Mich.App. 45, 198 N.W.2d 430 (1972), police raided defendant's home, where gambling was allegedly occurring, and arrested him for possession of a blackjack, for which he was thereafter convicted. Defendant, who testified he had taken the blackjack from a customer to ensure it would not be used and then had thrown it on the couch after a few minutes, was refused an instruction on "the difference between temporary custody and possession." The court affirmed, concluding "that the defendant's reason for having the blackjack was immaterial, and that his proffered defense was in reality no defense at all."

WHEELER v. UNITED STATES

District of Columbia Court of Appeals, 1985.

494 A.2d 170.

MACK, ASSOCIATE JUDGE: * * *

Viewing the evidence in the light most favorable to the government, the facts of this case are as follows. On January 17, 1982, a search warrant was executed for Room 201 of the Logan Inn at 1338 R Street, N.W. In an affidavit in support of the warrant, Detective Alan Penberg stated that a source had informed him that female occupants of Room 201 were selling heroin from that room. The police knocked on the door to Room 201, identifying themselves, but received no response. Instead, they heard what they described as "scurrying" noises behind the door. After at least a minute, they succeeded in breaking down the door. They found appellant and two other women coming out of the bathroom; the toilet had just been flushed. A fourth woman was sitting in a chair next to the bathroom. Two of the women were dressed in street clothes, but appellant and another woman, Mary Sales, were wearing sleeping attire. Luggage and clothes belonging to appellant were found in the room along with other personal effects. Appellant and Sales both gave aliases to the police. Both admitted, however, that they lived in Room 201. There were two beds in the hotel room, at opposite ends of the room. Sales retrieved some slippers from underneath a bed at one end. Under the second bed's pillow, the police found 3550 milligrams of 2.7% heroin. Sales and appellant were arrested. While the charges against Sales were subsequently dismissed, appellant was found guilty of possession of heroin after a bench trial. This appeal followed. * * *

This case was submitted to the trial court on a theory of constructive possession. An individual has constructive possession of an illegal substance when he is knowingly in a position or has the right to exercise dominion and control over it, and has some appreciable ability to guide its destiny. The right to exercise dominion and control may be jointly shared. In evaluating the sufficiency of the evidence submitted by the government, no distinction is made between direct and circumstantial evidence, and the trier may infer knowledge from circumstantial evidence.

Appellant contends that the heroin could have been placed under the pillow by any one of the three other women present in the room at the time the police arrived, and that to hold her responsible for the drug is mere speculation. The case law on the question of who may be held responsible when the police find an illegal item in a location together with more than one individual demonstrates some inconsistency. Several general principles may be extracted from the cases, however. Mere proximity to an illegal substance will be insufficient to uphold a conviction on a theory of constructive possession when an individual is one of several people found by the authorities on the premises together with the substance. *Cook v. United States,* 272 A.2d 444, 447 (D.C.1971) (conviction for possession of narcotics paraphernalia reversed where the government did not show appellant to be a resident of the premises and the actual tenant and other occupants were also present on the scene at the time of the raid); *United States v. Holland,* 144 U.S.App.D.C. 225, 227, 445 F.2d 701, 703 (1971) (conviction for possession of heroin reversed where drugs were found in codefendant's apartment, and although appellant was present when drugs were found the government did not show that he was residing there); *see United States v. Pardo,* 204 U.S.App.D.C. 263, 277, 636 F.2d 535, 549 (1980) (conviction for possession with intent to distribute narcotics reversed where appellant was merely present while a drug transaction was consummated between other individuals); *United States v. Watkins,* 171 U.S.App.D.C. 158, 162, 519 F.2d 294, 298 (1975) (conviction for possession of narcotics reversed even though police found appellant and narcotics in the same room, where two other individuals were found on the premises and insufficient evidence of appellant's residency at that location was adduced).[1] A common theme running

---

1. *See also Easley v. United States,* 482 A.2d 779, 781 (D.C.1984) (conviction for possession of an unregistered gun and ammunition reversed where the gun was hidden under the front seat of the car and appellants were sitting in the back seat); *Hack v. United States, supra,* 445 A.2d at 639–40 (conviction for possession of narcotics reversed where appellant and a co-defendant had been transported by the police in a squad car and the police subsequently found the drugs under the seat where the co-defendant had been sitting); *United States v. Bethea,* 143 U.S.App.D.C. 68, 71, 442 F.2d 790, 793 (1971) (conviction for distribution of heroin reversed where drugs were found together with a gun hidden behind the back seat of a car, appellant had been sitting in the front seat, and the police had observed another passenger place the gun in the rear hiding place); *United States v. Whitfield,* 203 U.S.App. D.C. 102, 109, 629 F.2d 136, 143 (1980) (conviction for through many of these cases is the courts' reluctance to hold an individual responsible for controlled substances or drug paraphernalia found in a home absent some proof that he is something other than a visitor. In this case, however, the government's evidence showed that appellant admitted that she was living in Room 201.

Even where the government proves that the defendant is a resident of the place where illegal items are seized, the courts are wary of imputing possession to the defendant absent proof of his involvement in some criminal enterprise. *Thompson v. United States,* 293 A.2d 275, 276 (D.C.1972) (conviction for possession of marijuana reversed where drug was found, along with four individuals, in living room and appellant was found in bedroom); *United States v. Bonham,* 477 F.2d 1137, 1138–40 (3d Cir.1973) (en banc) (conviction for acquisition of heroin reversed where drugs were found hidden behind a false wall panel in a room appellant shared with his half-brother; informant's tip did not mention appellant; and half-brother was an addict).

On the other hand, where there are circumstances giving rise to an inference of a concert of illegal action involving drugs by the occupants of the premises where the drugs are found, those circumstances tend to dispel any fear that the "constructive possession" doctrine has cast too wide a net. We have held that proximity may establish a supportable case of constructive possession of narcotics when colored by evidence linking the accused to an ongoing criminal operation of which that possession is a part. Other circumstances that will buttress the "constructive possession" inference include attempts to hide or destroy evidence. *See Logan v. United States,* 489 A.2d 485, 491–92 (D.C.1985) (joint constructive possession of weapon affirmed where appellants were observed jointly throwing something out of car and gun was thereafter recovered from roadbed); *United States v. Smith,* 171 U.S.App.D.C. 342, 344, 520 F.2d 74, 76 (1975) (constructive possession of phencyclidine found in closet affirmed despite fact that appellant was not sole occupant of apartment, where police had found appellant in bathroom and had discovered bag of marijuana directly below open bathroom window).

While this is a close case, we think that the government's evidence, albeit circumstantial, gives rise to sufficient inferences to support the judgment of conviction. As mentioned previously, appellant admitted to the police that she lived in the room, and the government's proof permitted the inference that appellant occupied the bed from which the heroin was recovered. Appellant failed to open the door or to respond in any way to the knock by the police. The observation by the officers that the toilet was flushed while three of the room's occupants, including appellant, were standing in the bathroom simultaneously, permitted the trier to infer that appellant used the period of time that the police required to break down the door to eliminate evidence. In addition, the fact that appellant identified herself to the police using an alias carries some weight on the question of whether she was involved in a criminal enterprise.

In sum, this is not a case in which the defendant's conduct, other than a shared proximity to the illegal item, is entirely innocent. It is unnecessary for the government either to adduce evidence that would compel a finding of guilt, or to negate every possible inference of innocence. The inference that appellant knew of the presence of the drug is not wholly speculative, and that inference, combined with the other circumstances outlined above, suffice to attribute to appellant a measure of control over the heroin and thus to support a finding of constructive possession.

possession of an unregistered pistol reversed where appellant had taken a 5–10 minute car ride with his co-defendant, sitting in the front seat, and although the pistol was found under that front seat it was hidden and there was no evidence that appellant knew of its presence), *cert. denied,* 449 U.S. 1086, 101 S.Ct. 875, 66 L.Ed.2d 812 (1981).

Affirmed.

Notes and Questions

1.   Compare *In the Interest of K.S.*, 500 N.W.2d 603 (N.D.1993), where police respond-ing to a loud party complaint saw, when the door was opened, that juveniles were fleeing upstairs. Various alcoholic beverages were observed within, apparently accessible to anyone in the house. K.S., a 15–year-old girl, was found hiding in a closet with a male youth who had been drinking; she denied having brought alcoholic beverages to the party or consum-ing any there. The juvenile court set aside a referee's finding that K.S. was a juvenile in possession of alcohol, and the state appealed. The court concluded:

"The law, in general, recognizes two kinds of possession: actual possession and constructive possession. * * *

"A juvenile's responsibility for conduct prohibited by NDCC 5–01–08, then, depends on the kind of 'possession' prohibited. The 'manifest purpose and design' of NDCC 5–01–08 is to dissuade minors from consuming alcohol. While the legislative history of NDCC 5–01–08 is unrevealing on the kind of 'possession' prohibited, it is difficult to imagine how this statute's objective would be effectuated by convicting minors of a crime when they have not actually taken alcohol into their control. The plain language of this statute, together with its purpose, lead us to the conclusion that, under these circumstances, a minor is culpable only for actual, not constructive, possession of alcohol.

"By confining this strict liability offense to actual possession of alcohol, we avoid any implication that a minor may be chargeable when parents or guardians keep alcoholic beverages in the home for their own use. There would be an obvious enforcement difficulty in a broader construction that included 'constructive possession,' because a minor might exercise dominion and control over numerous places in a home where alcohol is kept, and could thus be said to be in possession."

A concurring Justice cautioned: "I write separately to emphasize that the circum-stances in this case are significantly different from those in which alcohol is found in an automobile full of minors." Note, 70 N.D.L.Rev. 1059, 1071 (1994), observes: "this raises the question of why the definition of possession differs for minors in a house than minors in a car." Why should it?

2.   In *State v. Lewis*, 394 N.W.2d 212 (Minn.App.1986), defendant sustained injuries in an automobile accident and was taken to a hospital, where he consented to a taking of a urine sample when a police officer invoked the implied consent law. Analysis of the sample revealed traces of morphine, and on that basis defendant was tried and convicted of possession of a controlled substance. On appeal, the conviction was reversed: "We adopt a 'common-sense interpretation' of the term 'possession.' The usual and ordinary meaning of the term 'possession' does not include substances injected into the body and assimilated into the system. After a controlled substance is within a person's system the power to exercise dominion and control necessary to establish possession no longer exists. Moreover, the particular terms of the statute suggest a legislative intent to regulate the physical movement and transfer of controlled substances between different persons. Consequently, once a controlled substance is within a person's system the substance is beyond the scope of regulation contemplated by the statute."

3.   In *People v. Konrad*, 449 Mich. 263, 536 N.W.2d 517 (1995), after defendant was arrested on another matter, a police officer was at his home awaiting a search warrant when Joel Hamp arrived with a package he said was for defendant. When the officer identified himself, Hamp fled, abandoning the package on the lawn. When the officer found

over 880 grams of cocaine in the package, he went to the station and questioned defendant, who said he had already paid $40,000 for the cocaine and that Hamp had called and said he would be delivering it that evening. Defendant, convicted of possession with intent to deliver that cocaine, claimed on appeal that there was not sufficient proof of possession, to which the court responded:

"The essential question is whether the defendant had dominion or control over the controlled substance. In the foremost discussion of what is necessary to have dominion or control over drugs, Judge Posner explained that a defendant 'need not have them literally in his hands or on premises that he occupies but he must have the right (not the legal right, but the recognized authority in his criminal milieu) to possess them, as the owner of a safe deposit box has legal possession of the contents even though the bank has actual custody.' *United States v. Manzella*, 791 F.2d 1263, 1266 (C.A.7, 1986).* * *

"In the present case, there is ample evidence from which a rational trier of fact could conclude beyond a reasonable doubt that the defendant constructively possessed the cocaine through his agent, Joel Hamp. The evidence permits the conclusion that the defendant had paid for the drugs and that they were his—that is, that he had the intention and power, in the sense referred to by Judge Posner, to exercise control over them. There is evidence that the defendant made a prior arrangement with Joel Hamp and others to purchase a kilogram of cocaine, that he had already paid for the cocaine, that he told Joel to come to his house about seven that evening, and that, after he had been arrested, he had instructed his wife to direct Joel not to come. Joel arrived after 6:30 p.m. and acknowledged that he had something for the defendant.[7]

"Although most cases discussing constructive possession through a defendant's agents involve agents who have sold controlled substances, Michigan courts have recognized that defendants also may constructively possess substances that their agents have bought for them."

4.   In Charles H. Whitebread & Ronald Stevens, *Constructive Possession in Narcotics Cases: To Have and Have Not,* 58 Va.L.Rev. 751, 766 (1972), the authors are critical of how courts typically establish constructive possession. They propose that "the prosecution should have to show either: (a) defendant's exclusive control over the area in which the drug is found, or (b) substantial evidence of the defendant's past possession of the drug on his person. Failure to meet one of these two standards should justify a directed verdict of acquittal at the close of the prosecution's evidence."

5.   Steven married Kathy in May, and they moved into a house trailer. Kathy came from a wealthy family, and when in November the couple's financial picture darkened she told Steven she was considering selling marijuana. Steven told her he was against the idea, but a few weeks later he came home from work to find 200 pounds of marijuana in the trailer. When he questioned Kathy, she became very upset and threatened to go to England

---

7.   The dissenting opinion argues that "[t]here was no evidence produced at trial from which a reasonable jury could conclude beyond a reasonable doubt that" Hamp was an agent of the defendant for the purpose of this transaction. The dissent appears to assume that if Hamp was not the criminal equivalent of the defendant's full-time exclusive employee, then the defendant cannot be found responsible for any of his acts. This is not the case, even under formal agency principles, which provide for agents "authorized to conduct a single transaction or a series of transactions not involving continuity of service." *Restatement Agency, 2d,* § 3(2), p. 15. A "special agent" can bind a principal by contracts or conveyances that he is authorized to make. See *Restatement Agency, 2d,* § 161 A, pp 382–383.

We do not hold that Joel Hamp was the criminal equivalent of the defendant's general agent, which might render the defendant liable for any cocaine Hamp possessed during that time. We hold only that there is sufficient evidence to convict the defendant of possessing cocaine that had been procured by Hamp but that belonged to the defendant. Assuming arguendo that the Restatement principles govern, it provides that wide discretion regarding the assigned transaction is consistent with special, as opposed to general, agency. *Restatement Agency, 2d,* comment to § 3, p 16.

alone, as she had planned to do before they met. Steven then relented and did nothing further. In December police raided the trailer and found over 100 pounds of marijuana.[a] Is *Steven* guilty of possession of marijuana?

6.   Harmon stopped at a border checkpoint near Sarita, Texas, at 4 a.m. A border patrol agent detected the smell of marijuana and asked Harmon to open his trunk; Harmon answered that he did not have the trunk key. Martinez arrived at the checkpoint in another car. The agent asked Harmon if he knew Martinez and Harmon answered in the affirmative. The agent asked Martinez if he had the key to Harmon's trunk; Martinez said yes and handed over a key ring. The agent opened the trunk of Harmon's car and found locked chests, which he opened with keys on Martinez's key ring. Marijuana was found within. Is *Martinez* guilty of possession of marijuana?[b]

7.   Martorano, not knowing Raiton was an undercover informant for federal agents, arranged to buy controlled substance P–2–P from him. Raiton rented a van and turned it over to the FBI; FBI agents loaded it with P–2–P, placed a special padlock on the rear doors, and then parked it near Rittenhouse Square in Philadelphia. Raiton met Martorano at the Square as planned and received $100,000 from him upon revealing the location of the van. Martorano remained there with Raiton while accomplices Vadino and DeTullio were dispatched to "check out" the van's location. After they left, Raiton gave Martorano the van and padlock keys. Martorano later gave them to DeTullio, who returned to the van, unlocked it and entered the van. He sat there for less than two minutes before he was arrested by FBI agents, who were maintaining continued surveillance of the van to prevent its removal. Is *Martorano* guilty of possessing P–2–P?[c]

COUNTY COURT OF ULSTER COUNTY v. ALLEN

Supreme Court of the United States, 1979.

442 U.S. 140, 99 S.Ct. 2213, 60 L.Ed.2d 777.

Mr. Justice Stevens delivered the opinion of the Court.

A New York statute provides that, with certain exceptions, the presence of a firearm in an automobile is presumptive evidence of its illegal possession by all persons then occupying the vehicle.[1] The United States Court of Appeals for the Second Circuit held that respondents may challenge the constitutionality of this statute in a federal habeas corpus proceeding and that the statute is "unconstitutional on its face." We granted certiorari to

a. *People v. Ireland*, 38 Ill.App.3d 616, 348 N.E.2d 277 (1976), reversing the conviction because of insufficient jury instructions.

b. *United States v. Martinez*, 588 F.2d 495 (5th Cir.1979), affirming the conviction.

c. *United States v. Martorano*, 709 F.2d 863 (3d Cir.1983), a 2–1 affirmance of the conviction.

1. New York Penal Law § 265.15(3) (McKinney 1967):

"The presence in an automobile, other than a stolen one or a public omnibus, of any firearm, defaced firearm, firearm silencer, bomb, bombshell, gravity knife, switchblade knife, dagger, dirk, stiletto, billy, blackjack, metal knuckles, sandbag, sandclub or slungshot is presumptive evidence of its possession by all persons occupying such automobile at the time such weapon, instrument or appliance is found, except under the following circumstances:

"(a) if such weapon, instrument or appliance is found upon the person of one of the occupants therein; (b) if such weapon, instrument or appliance is found in an automobile which is being operated for hire by a duly licensed driver in the due, lawful and proper pursuit of his trade, then such presumption shall not apply to the driver; or (c) if the weapon so found is a pistol or revolver and one of the occupants, not present under duress, has in his possession a valid license to have and carry concealed the same."

In addition to the three exceptions delineated in §§ 265.15(3)(a)–(c) above as well as the stolen-vehicle and public-omnibus exception in § 265.15(3) itself, § 265.20 contains various exceptions that apply when weapons are present in an automobile pursuant to certain military, law enforcement, recreational, and commercial endeavors.

review these holdings and also to consider whether the statute is constitutional in its application to respondents.

Four persons, three adult males (respondents) and a 16–year–old girl (Jane Doe, who is not a respondent here), were jointly tried on charges that they possessed two loaded handguns, a loaded machinegun, and over a pound of heroin found in a Chevrolet in which they were riding when it was stopped for speeding on the New York Thruway shortly after noon on March 28, 1973. The two large-caliber handguns, which together with their ammunition weighed approximately six pounds, were seen through the window of the car by the investigating police officer. They were positioned crosswise in an open handbag on either the front floor or the front seat of the car on the passenger side where Jane Doe was sitting. Jane Doe admitted that the handbag was hers. The machinegun and the heroin were discovered in the trunk after the police pried it open. The car had been borrowed from the driver's brother earlier that day; the key to the trunk could not be found in the car or on the person of any of its occupants, although there was testimony that two of the occupants had placed something in the trunk before embarking in the borrowed car. The jury convicted all four of possession of the handguns and acquitted them of possession of the contents of the trunk.

Counsel for all four defendants objected to the introduction into evidence of the two handguns, the machinegun, and the drugs, arguing that the State had not adequately demonstrated a connection between their clients and the contraband. The trial court overruled the objection, relying on the presumption of possession created by the New York statute. Because that presumption does not apply if a weapon is found "upon the person" of one of the occupants of the car, see n. 1, *supra,* the three male defendants also moved to dismiss the charges relating to the handguns on the ground that the guns were found on the person of Jane Doe. Respondents made this motion both at the close of the prosecution's case and at the close of all evidence. The trial judge twice denied it, concluding that the applicability of the "upon the person" exception was a question of fact for the jury.

At the close of the trial, the judge instructed the jurors that they were entitled to infer possession from the defendants' presence in the car. He did not make any reference to the "upon the person" exception in his explanation of the statutory presumption, nor did any of the defendants object to this omission or request alternative or additional instructions on the subject.

Defendants filed a post-trial motion in which they challenged the constitutionality of the New York statute as applied in this case. The challenge was made in support of their argument that the evidence, apart from the presumption, was insufficient to sustain the convictions. The motion was denied, and the convictions were affirmed by the Appellate Division without opinion.

The New York Court of Appeals also affirmed. It rejected the argument that as a matter of law the guns were on Jane Doe's person because they were in her pocketbook. Although the court recognized that in some circumstances the evidence could only lead to the conclusion that the weapons were in one person's sole possession, it held that this record presented a jury question on that issue. Since the defendants had not asked the trial judge to submit the question to the jury, the Court of Appeals treated the case as though the jury had resolved this fact question in the prosecution's favor. It therefore concluded that the presumption did apply and that there was sufficient evidence to support the convictions. It also summarily rejected the argument that the presumption was unconstitutional as applied in this case.

Respondents filed a petition for a writ of habeas corpus in the United States District Court for the Southern District of New York contending that they were denied due process of law by the application of the statutory presumption of possession. The District Court issued the writ, holding * * * that the mere presence of two guns in a woman's handbag in a car could not reasonably give rise to the inference that they were in the possession of three other persons in the car.

The Court of Appeals for the Second Circuit affirmed, but for different reasons. [T]he majority of the court, without deciding whether the presumption was constitutional as applied in this case, concluded that the statute is unconstitutional on its face because the "presumption obviously sweeps within its compass (1) many occupants who may not know they are riding with a gun (which may be out of their sight), and (2) many who may be aware of the presence of the gun but not permitted access to it." * * *

Without determining whether the presumption in this case was mandatory, the Court of Appeals analyzed it on its face as if it were. In fact, it was not, as the New York Court of Appeals had earlier pointed out.

The trial judge's instructions make it clear that the presumption was merely a part of the prosecution's case,[19] that it gave rise to a permissive inference available only in certain circumstances, rather than a mandatory conclusion of possession, and that it could be ignored by the jury even if there was no affirmative proof offered by defendants in rebuttal.[20] The judge explained that possession could be actual or constructive, but that constructive possession could not exist without the intent and ability to exercise control or dominion over the weapons. He also carefully instructed the jury that there is a mandatory presumption of innocence in favor of the defendants that controls unless it, as the exclusive trier of fact, is satisfied beyond a reasonable doubt that the defendants possessed the handguns in the manner described by the judge. In short, the instructions plainly directed the jury to consider all the circumstances tending to support or contradict the inference that all four occupants of the car had possession of the two loaded handguns and to decide the matter for itself without regard to how much evidence the defendants introduced.

Our cases considering the validity of permissive statutory presumptions such as the one involved here have rested on an evaluation of the presumption as applied to the record before the Court. None suggests that a court should pass on the constitutionality of this kind of statute "on its face." It was error for the Court of Appeals to make such a determination in this case.

---

19. "It is your duty to consider all the testimony in this case, to weigh it carefully and to test the credit to be given to a witness by his apparent intention to speak the truth and by the accuracy of his memory to reconcile, if possible, conflicting statements as to material facts and in such ways to try and get at the truth and to reach a verdict upon the evidence."

"To establish the unlawful possession of the weapons, again the People relied upon the presumption and, in addition thereto, the testimony of Anderson and Lemmons who testified in their case in chief."

"Accordingly, you would be warranted in returning a verdict of guilt against the defendants or defendant if you find the defendants or defendant was in possession of a machine gun and the other weapons and that the fact of possession was proven to you by the People beyond a reasonable doubt, and an element of such proof is the reasonable presumption of illegal possession of a machine gun or the presumption of illegal possession of firearms, as I have just before explained to you."

20. "Our Penal Law also provides that the presence in an automobile of any machine gun or of any handgun or firearm which is loaded is presumptive evidence of their unlawful possession.

"In other words, these presumptions or this latter presumption upon proof of the presence of the machine gun and the hand weapons, you may infer and draw a conclusion that such prohibited weapon was possessed by each of the defendants who occupied the automobile at the time when such instruments were found. The presumption or presumptions is effective only so long as there is no substantial evidence contradicting the conclusion flowing from the presumption, and the presumption is said to disappear when such contradictory evidence is adduced."

"The presumption or presumptions which I discussed with the jury relative to the drugs or weapons in this case need not be rebutted by affirmative proof or affirmative evidence but may be rebutted by any evidence or lack of evidence in the case."

As applied to the facts of this case, the presumption of possession is entirely rational. Notwithstanding the Court of Appeals' analysis, respondents were not "hitchhikers or other casual passengers," and the guns were neither "a few inches in length" nor "out of [respondents'] sight." The argument against possession by any of the respondents was predicated solely on the fact that the guns were in Jane Doe's pocketbook. But several circumstances—which, not surprisingly, her counsel repeatedly emphasized in his questions and his argument—made it highly improbable that she was the sole custodian of those weapons.

Even if it was reasonable to conclude that she had placed the guns in her purse before the car was stopped by police, the facts strongly suggest that Jane Doe was not the only person able to exercise dominion over them. The two guns were too large to be concealed in her handbag. The bag was consequently open, and part of one of the guns was in plain view, within easy access of the driver of the car and even, perhaps, of the other two respondents who were riding in the rear seat.

Moreover, it is highly improbable that the loaded guns belonged to Jane Doe or that she was solely responsible for their being in her purse. As a 16–year–old girl in the company of three adult men she was the least likely of the four to be carrying one, let alone two, heavy handguns. It is far more probable that she relied on the pocketknife found in her brassiere for any necessary self-protection. Under these circumstances, it was not unreasonable for her counsel to argue and for the jury to infer that when the car was halted for speeding, the other passengers in the car anticipated the risk of a search and attempted to conceal their weapons in a pocketbook in the front seat. The inference is surely more likely than the notion that these weapons were the sole property of the 16–year–old girl.

Under these circumstances, the jury would have been entirely reasonable in rejecting the suggestion—which, incidentally, defense counsel did not even advance in their closing arguments to the jury—that the handguns were in the sole possession of Jane Doe. Assuming that the jury did reject it, the case is tantamount to one in which the guns were lying on the floor or the seat of the car in the plain view of the three other occupants of the automobile. In such a case, it is surely rational to infer that each of the respondents was fully aware of the presence of the guns and had both the ability and the intent to exercise dominion and control over the weapons. The application of the statutory presumption in this case therefore comports with the standard laid down in *Tot v. United States*, 319 U.S. 463, 63 S.Ct. 1241, 87 L.Ed. 1519, and restated in *Leary v. United States*, 395 U.S. 6, 89 S.Ct. 1532, 23 L.Ed.2d 57. For there is a "rational connection" between the basic facts that the prosecution proved and the ultimate fact presumed, and the latter is "more likely than not to flow from" the former.

Respondents argue, however, that the validity of the New York presumption must be judged by a "reasonable doubt" test rather than the "more likely than not" standard employed in *Leary*. Under the more stringent test, it is argued that a statutory presumption must be rejected unless the evidence necessary to invoke the inference is sufficient for a rational jury to find the inferred fact beyond a reasonable doubt. Respondents' argument again overlooks the distinction between a permissive presumption on which the prosecution is entitled to rely as one not necessarily sufficient part of its proof and a mandatory presumption which the jury must accept even if it is the sole evidence of an element of the offense.

In the latter situation, since the prosecution bears the burden of establishing guilt, it may not rest its case entirely on a presumption unless the fact proved is sufficient to support the inference of guilt beyond a reasonable doubt. But in the former situation, the prosecution may rely on all of the evidence in the record to meet the reasonable-doubt standard. There is no more reason to require a permissive statutory presumption to meet a reasonable-doubt standard before it may be permitted to play any part in a trial than there is to require that degree of probative force for other relevant evidence before it may be admitted. As long as it is clear that the presumption is not the sole and sufficient basis for a finding of guilt, it need only satisfy the test described in *Leary*.

The permissive presumption, as used in this case, satisfied the *Leary* test. And, as already noted, the New York Court of Appeals has concluded that the record as a whole was sufficient to establish guilt beyond a reasonable doubt.

The judgment is reversed.

MR. CHIEF JUSTICE BURGER, concurring.

I join fully in the Court's opinion reversing the judgment under review. In the necessarily detailed step-by-step analysis of the legal issues, the central and controlling facts of a case often can become lost. The "underbrush" of finely tuned legal analysis of complex issues tends to bury the facts.

On this record, the jury could readily have reached the same result without benefit of the challenged statutory presumption; here it reached what was rather obviously a compromise verdict. Even without relying on evidence that two people had been seen placing something in the car trunk shortly before respondents occupied it, and that a machinegun and a package of heroin were soon after found in that trunk, the jury apparently decided that it was enough to hold the passengers to knowledge of the two handguns which were in such plain view that the officer could see them from outside the car. Reasonable jurors could reasonably find that what the officer could see from outside, the passengers within the car could hardly miss seeing. Courts have long held that in the practical business of deciding cases the factfinders, not unlike negotiators, are permitted the luxury of verdicts reached by compromise.

MR. JUSTICE POWELL, with whom MR. JUSTICE BRENNAN, MR. JUSTICE STEWART and MR. JUSTICE MARSHALL join, dissenting. * * *

In sum, our decisions uniformly have recognized that due process requires more than merely that the prosecution be put to its proof. In addition, the Constitution restricts the court in its charge to the jury by requiring that, when particular factual inferences are recommended to the jury, those factual inferences be accurate reflections of what history, common sense, and experience tell us about the relations between events in our society. Generally, this due process rule has been articulated as requiring that the truth of the inferred fact be more likely than not whenever the premise for the inference is true. Thus, to be constitutional a presumption must be at least more likely than not true. * * *

Undeniably, the presumption charged in this case encouraged the jury to draw a particular factual inference regardless of any other evidence presented: to infer that respondents possessed the weapons found in the automobile "upon proof of the presence of the machine gun and the hand weapon" and proof that respondents "occupied the automobile at the time such instruments were found." I believe that the presumption thus charged was unconstitutional because it did not fairly reflect what common sense and experience tell us about passengers in automobiles and the possession of handguns. People present in automobiles where there are weapons simply are not "more likely than not" the possessors of those weapons.

Under New York law, "to possess" is "to have physical possession or otherwise to exercise dominion or control over tangible property." N.Y.Penal Law § 10.00(8). Plainly, the mere presence of an individual in an automobile—without more—does not indicate that he exercises "dominion or control over" everything within it. As the Court of Appeals noted, there are countless situations in which individuals are invited as guests into vehicles the contents of which they know nothing about, much less have control over. Similarly, those who invite others into their automobile do not generally search them to determine what they may have on their person; nor do they insist that any handguns be identified and placed within reach of the occupants of the automobile. Indeed, handguns are particularly susceptible to concealment and therefore are less likely than are other objects to be observed by those in an automobile.

In another context, this Court has been particularly hesitant to infer possession from mere presence in a location, noting that "[p]resence is relevant and admissible evidence in a trial on a possession charge; but absent some showing of the defendant's function at the [illegal] still, its connection with possession is too tenuous to permit a reasonable inference of guilt—'the inference of the one from proof of the other is arbitrary * * *.' *Tot v. United States*, 319 U.S. 463, 467, 63 S.Ct. 1241, 1245, 87 L.Ed. 1519." *United States v. Romano*.[a] We should be even more hesitant to uphold the inference of possession of a handgun from mere presence in an automobile, in light of common experience concerning automobiles and handguns. Because the specific factual inference recommended to the jury in this case is not one that is supported by the general experience of our society, I cannot say that the presumption charged is "more likely than not" to be true. Accordingly, respondents' due process rights were violated by the presumption's use.

As I understand it, the Court today does not contend that in general those who are present in automobiles are more likely than not to possess any gun contained within their vehicles. It argues, however, that the nature of the presumption here involved requires that we look, not only to the immediate facts upon which the jury was encouraged to base its inference, but to the other facts "proved" by the prosecution as well. The Court suggests that this is the proper approach when reviewing what it calls "permissive" presumptions because the jury was urged "to consider all the circumstances tending to support or contradict the inference."

It seems to me that the Court mischaracterizes the function of the presumption charged in this case. As it acknowledges was the case in *Romano, supra,* the "instruction authorized conviction even if the jury disbelieved all of the testimony except the proof of presence" in the automobile.[7] The Court nevertheless relies on all of the evidence

---

a. 382 U.S. 136, 86 S.Ct. 279, 15 L.Ed.2d 210 (1965), where the defendant, found within a few feet of a still, was convicted of being in "possession, custody and control" of an illegal still. 26 U.S.C. § 5601(b)(1) provides that presence at the site of an illegal still "shall be deemed sufficient evidence to authorize conviction, unless the defendant explains such presence to the satisfaction of the jury." The Court, distinguishing *United States v. Gainey*, 380 U.S. 63, 85 S.Ct. 754, 13 L.Ed.2d 658 (1965) (upholding a provision that such presence suffices to prove the offense of carrying on a distilling business), reversed:

"Presence at an operating still is sufficient evidence to prove the charge of 'carrying on' because anyone present at the site is very probably connected with the illegal enterprise. Whatever his job may be, he is at the very least aiding and abetting the substantive crime of carrying on the illegal distilling business. Section 5601(a)(1), however, proscribes possession, custody or control. This is only one of the various aspects of the total undertaking, many of which have nothing at all to do with possession * * *. Presence tells us only that

the defendant was there and very likely played a part in the illicit scheme. But presence tells us nothing about what the defendant's specific function was and carries no legitimate, rational or reasonable inference that he was engaged in one of the specialized functions connected with possession, rather than in one of the supply, delivery or operational activities having nothing to do with possession."

7. In commending the presumption to the jury, the court gave no instruction that would have required a finding of possession to be based on anything more than mere presence in the automobile. Thus, the jury was not instructed that it should infer that respondents possessed the handguns only if it found that the guns were too large to be concealed in Jane Doe's handbag; that the guns accordingly were in the plain view of respondents, *ibid.*; that the weapons were within "easy access of the driver of the car and even, perhaps, of the other two respondents who were riding in the rear seat"; that it was unlikely that Jane Doe was solely responsible for the placement of the weapons in her purse; or that the case was "tantamount to

introduced by the prosecution and argues that the "permissive" presumption could not have prejudiced defendants. The possibility that the jury disbelieved all of this evidence, and relied on the presumption, is simply ignored.

I agree that the circumstances relied upon by the Court in determining the plausibility of the presumption charged in this case would have made it reasonable for the jury to "infer that each of the respondents was fully aware of the presence of the guns and had both the ability and the intent to exercise dominion and control over the weapons." But the jury was told that it could conclude that respondents possessed the weapons found therein from proof of the mere fact of respondents' presence in the automobile. For all we know, the jury rejected all of the prosecution's evidence concerning the location and origin of the guns, and based its conclusion that respondents possessed the weapons solely upon its belief that respondents had been present in the automobile.[8] For purposes of reviewing the constitutionality of the presumption at issue here, we must assume that this was the case. * * *

In sum, it seems to me that the Court today ignores the teaching of our prior decisions. By speculating about what the jury may have done with the factual inference thrust upon it, the Court in effect assumes away the inference altogether, constructing a rule that permits the use of any inference—no matter how irrational in itself—provided that otherwise there is sufficient evidence in the record to support a finding of guilt. Applying this novel analysis to the present case, the Court upholds the use of a presumption that it makes no effort to defend in isolation. In substance, the Court—applying an unarticulated harmless-error standard—simply finds that the respondents were guilty as charged. They may well have been but rather than acknowledging this rationale, the Court seems to have made new law with respect to presumptions that could seriously jeopardize a defendant's right to a fair trial. Accordingly, I dissent.

Notes and Questions

1. Stephen Saltzburg, *Burdens of Persuasion in Criminal Cases: Harmonizing the Views of the Justices,* 20 Am.Crim.L.Rev. 393, 418–19 (1983): "The majority and the dissent differ more in their reading of what the trial judge did than in their approach to presumptions and inferences. Both appear to have examined exactly what the trial judge said and to have asked whether it was a fair statement of what the evidence actually offered could be said to have proved.

"Had the trial judge said to the jury, 'If you believe that the defendants were in the car and weapons were in open view, you could reason from this that the defendants were jointly in possession of the weapons; but this is not the only way to view the evidence, and the important thing is that you must believe beyond a reasonable doubt that a defendant possessed the weapons before voting to convict the defendant,' the entire Court might have viewed this as a fair statement of a possible way of looking at the evidence. Alternatively, had the trial judge said to the jury, 'If you believe that the defendants were in the car

one in which the guns were lying on the floor or the seat of the car in the plain view of the three other occupants of the automobile."

8. The Court is therefore mistaken in its conclusion that, because "respondents were not 'hitchhikers or other casual passengers,' and the guns were neither 'a few inches in length' nor 'out of [respondents'] sight,' "reference to these possibilities is inappropriate in considering the constitutionality of the presumption as charged in this case. To be sure, respondents' challenge is to the presumption as charged to the jury in

this case. But in assessing its application here, we are not free, as the Court apparently believes, to disregard the possibility that the jury may have disbelieved all other evidence supporting an inference of possession. The jury may have concluded that respondents—like hitchhikers—had only an incidental relationship to the auto in which they were traveling, or that, contrary to some of the testimony at trial, the weapons were indeed out of respondents' sight.

where weapons were found, this is sufficient for you to convict them of possession, unless there is some adequate explanation for the defendants' presence,' all members of the Court might have agreed that this statement overstated the significance of evidence of presence in the car, and that the instruction may have produced a conviction for the wrong reason because the jury may have believed the judge was saying that as a matter of law the evidence proved guilt unless some explanation for presence was present.

"Both opinions in *Allen* support the first principle identified above, which complements *Mullaney* and *Patterson*. The government may not evade its responsibility to prove guilt of the offense it charges by relying on a judicial comment that goes beyond a fair assessment of the proof actually presented. In other words, the government may not prove guilt by having a judge tell a jury that something has been proved when it has not. The proof must be evident in the record, and any instruction may not go beyond the proof offered."

2. Ronald J. Allen & Lee Ann DeGrazia, *The Constitutional Requirement of Proof Beyond a Reasonable Doubt in Criminal Cases: A Comment Upon Incipient Chaos in the Lower Courts*, 20 Am.Crim.L.Rev. 1, 11 (1983): "One result of the *Ulster* Court's heavy emphasis on the evidence adduced at trial appears to be to transform the analysis of the instructions into a harmless error analysis. * * * A harmless error standard that looks heavily to the facts in the record can permit an instruction to be upheld, and a conviction affirmed, primarily on the basis of facts that a jury did not believe beyond reasonable doubt. The effect is to undercut both the right to a jury trial and the reasonable doubt standard."

SECTION 3. OMISSIONS

STATE v. WILLIQUETTE

Supreme Court of Wisconsin, 1986.

129 Wis.2d 239, 385 N.W.2d 145.

STEINMETZ, JUSTICE.

The issue in the case is whether a parent who allegedly knew her husband had repeatedly abused her two children both physically and sexually, but who took no action to stop the abuse and instead left the children in the father's sole physical custody for hours at a time, can be tried for the direct commission of the crime of child abuse under sec. 940.201, Stats.[1] * * *

In a criminal complaint issued on November 15, 1983, Terri Williquette, the defendant, was charged with two counts of child abuse, contrary to sec. 940.201, Stats. Count one was based on the defendant's alleged failure to take any action to prevent her husband, Bert Williquette, from repeatedly "sexually abusing, beating, and otherwise mistreating" her seven year old son, B.W. Count two was based on the defendant's alleged failure to take any action to prevent her husband from committing similar acts against the defendant's eight year old daughter, C.P. * * *

On June 6, 1984, the defendant filed a motion to dismiss the information. She claimed that she could not be charged with child abuse because she did not directly commit the

1. Sec. 940.201, Stats., provides as follows:

"**940.201 Abuse of children.** Whoever tortures a child or subjects a child to cruel maltreatment, including, but not limited to, severe bruising, lacerations, fractured bones, burns, internal injuries or any injury constituting great bodily harm under s. 939.22(14) is guilty of a Class E felony. In this section, 'child' means a person under 16 years of age."

abusive conduct. The circuit court granted the motion to dismiss. The court concluded that sec. 940.201, Stats., applies only to the intentional acts of a defendant who directly abuses a child. Accordingly, the mother's alleged failure to take any action to prevent her husband from abusing the children was not covered by the statute. * * *

The parties disagree as to whether sec. 940.201, Stats., requires a person to directly inflict child abuse in order to violate the statute. The defendant contends that the legislature intended the statute to apply only to persons who directly abuse children. She maintains that the statute does not impose a duty on her to protect her own children from abuse. The state, however, argues that the statute is susceptible to an interpretation which includes persons having a special relationship to children who expose them to abuse. The state relies on the statutory language "subjects a child to cruel maltreatment." The state urges the court to construe this language to cover situations in which a parent knowingly exposes a child to abuse by placing the child in a situation where abuse has occurred and is likely to recur. * * *

There is no statutory definition of "subjects" in sec. 940.201, Stats. We therefore turn to standard dictionary definitions for guidance. Webster's Third New International Dictionary (1967) defines "subject" when used as a verb to mean: "a: to bring under control or dominion * * * b. to reduce to subservience or submission * * * 2a: to make liable * * * 4: to cause to undergo or submit to: make submit to a particular action or effect: expose." * * *

We conclude that the ordinary and accepted meaning of "subjects" does not limit the application of sec. 940.201, Stats., only to persons who actively participate in abusing children. The common meaning of "subjects" is broader than directly inflicting abuse on children. It covers situations in which a person with a duty toward a child exposes the child to a foreseeable risk of abuse. * * *

A person exposes a child to abuse when he or she causes the child to come within the influence of a foreseeable risk of cruel maltreatment. * * * In this case, Bert Williquette's conduct obviously was a direct cause of the abuse his children suffered. However, the defendant's alleged conduct, as the mother of the children, also was a contributing cause of risk to the children. She allegedly knew that the father abused the children in her absence, but she continued to leave the children and to entrust them to his exclusive care, and she allegedly did nothing else to prevent the abuse, such as notifying proper authorities or providing alternative child care in her absence. We conclude that the defendant's conduct, as alleged, constituted a substantial factor which increased the risk of further abuse. * * *

The court also expressly rejects the defendant's claim that an act of commission, rather than omission, is a necessary element of a crime. The essence of criminal conduct is the requirement of a wrongful "act." This element, however, is satisfied by overt acts, as well as omissions to act where there is a legal duty to act. LaFave and Scott, *Criminal Law* sec. 26 at 182, states the general rule applicable to omissions:

> "Some statutory crimes are specifically defined in terms of omission to act. With other common law and statutory crimes which are defined in terms of conduct producing a specified result, a person may be criminally liable when his omission to act produces that result, but only if (1) he has, under the circumstances, a legal duty to act, and (2) he can physically perform the act. The trend of the law has been toward enlarging the scope of duty to act."

The comments to this section then state the traditional rule that a person generally has no duty to rescue or protect an endangered person unless a special relationship exists between the persons which imposes a legal duty to protect:

"For criminal liability to be based upon a failure to act it must first be found that there is a duty to act—a legal duty and not simply a moral duty. As we have seen, some criminal statutes themselves impose the legal duty to act, as with the tax statute and the hit-and-run statute. With other crimes the duty must be found outside the definition of the crime itself—perhaps in another statute, or in the common law, or in a contract.

"Generally one has no legal duty to aid another person in peril, even when that aid can be rendered without danger or inconvenience to himself. He need not shout a warning to a blind man headed for a precipice or to an absent-minded one walking into a gunpowder room with a lighted candle in hand. He need not pull a neighbor's baby out of a pool of water or rescue an unconscious person stretched across the railroad tracks, though the baby is drowning or the whistle of an approaching train is heard in the distance. A doctor is not legally bound to answer a desperate call from the frantic parents of a sick child, at least if it is not one of his regular patients. A moral duty to take affirmative action is not enough to impose a legal duty to do so. But there are situations which do give rise to a duty to act:

"(1) *Duty based upon relationship.* The common law imposes affirmative duties upon persons standing in certain personal relationships to other persons—upon parents to aid their small children, upon husbands to aid their wives, upon ship captains to aid their crews, upon masters to aid their servants. Thus a parent may be guilty of criminal homicide for failure to call a doctor for his sick child, a mother for failure to prevent the fatal beating of her baby by her lover, a husband for failure to aid his imperiled wife, a ship captain for failure to pick up a seaman or passenger fallen overboard, and an employer for failure to aid his endangered employee. Action may be required to thwart the threatened perils of nature (*e.g.*, to combat sickness, to ward off starvation or the elements); or it may be required to protect against threatened acts by third persons."

The requirement of a legal duty to act is a policy limitation which prevents most omissions from being considered the proximate cause of a prohibited consequence. In a technical sense, a person's omission, *i.e.*, whether the person fails to protect, warn or rescue, may be a substantial factor in exposing another person to harm. The concept of causation, however, is not solely a question of mechanical connection between events, but also a question of policy. A particular legal cause must be one of which the law will take cognizance. The rule that persons do not have a general duty to protect represents a public policy choice to limit criminal liability.

The requirement of an overt act, therefore, is not inherently necessary for criminal liability. Criminal liability depends on conduct which is a substantial factor in producing consequences. Omissions are as capable of producing consequences as overt acts. Thus, the common law rule that there is no general duty to protect limits criminal liability where it would otherwise exist. The special relationship exception to the "no duty to act" rule represents a choice to retain liability for some omissions, which are considered morally unacceptable. * * *

We next address the scope of the "legal duty" exception to the rule regarding criminal liability for omissions. Like most jurisdictions, Wisconsin generally does not require a person to protect others from hazardous situations. When a special relationship exists between persons, however, social policy may impose a duty to protect. The relationship between a parent and a child exemplifies a special relationship where the duty to protect is imposed. We stated the rule applicable to the parent and child relationship in *Cole v. Sears, Roebuck & Co.*, 47 Wis.2d 629, 634, 177 N.W.2d 866 (1970):

" 'It is the right and duty of parents under the law of nature as well as the common law and the statutes of many states to protect their children, to care for them in sickness and in health, and to do whatever may be necessary for their care, maintenance, and preservation, including medical attendance, if necessary. An omission to do this is a public wrong which the state, under its police powers, may prevent. The child has the right to call upon the parent for the discharge of this duty, and public policy for the good of society will not permit or allow the parent to divest himself irrevocably of his obligations in this regard or to abandon them at his mere will or pleasure.... ' "

From the above discussion, we conclude that a parent who fails to take any action to stop instances of child abuse can be prosecuted as a principal for exposing the child to the abuse, contrary to sec. 940.201, Stats. Consistent with the common law rule, however, we do not hold that all persons, regardless of their relationship or lack of relationship to an abused child, violate the child abuse statute by failing to take remedial action to protect the child. Finally, when liability under sec. 940.201, depends on a breach of the parent's duty to protect, the parent must knowingly act in disregard of the facts giving rise to a duty to act. The "knowingly" requirement is necessary for a breach of the parent's duty to protect; it is not imposed as an element of sec. 940.201. * * *

The enactment of sec. 940.34, Stats.,[6] subsequent to the commencement of this prosecution also does not indicate that the defendant was previously immune from criminal liability for her conduct. Section 940.34 is a "Good Samaritan" law which imposes criminal liability on "[a]ny person who knows that a crime is being committed and that a victim is exposed to bodily harm" but fails to summon help or provide assistance to the victim. The new statute does not deny the prior existence of a parent's duty to protect. We acknowledge that a parent now could be charged under either statute. Section 939.65, however, provides that if an act forms the basis for a crime punishable under more than one statutory provision, then the state can prosecute under any or all such provisions. * * *

HEFFERNAN, CHIEF JUSTICE (dissenting). * * *

The majority correctly asserts the criminal conduct can be predicated upon the failure to act when action is required by law. The problem is that nothing in the statutes remotely suggests that a parent has the legislatively prescribed legal duty to act in the instant circumstances or that the omission of the alleged duty will result in criminal sanctions. Certainly, I agree with the majority who, after reciting the catalog of horrors perpetrated upon these children, asserts, citing *Cole v. Sears, Roebuck & Co.*:

"An omission to do this [care for and protect children] is a public wrong which the state, under its police powers, may prevent."

The problem with this position is that it begs the question. Of course, the state has the police powers which may be exercised for that very purpose. The omission can be categorized as a public wrong which the legislature *may* prevent. But the police power is a

---

6. Sec. 940.34, Stats., provides as follows:

"940.34 Duty to aid endangered crime victim. (1) Whoever violates sub. (2) is guilty of a Class C misdemeanor.

"(2) Any person who knows that a crime is being committed and that a victim is exposed to bodily harm shall summon law enforcement officers or other assistance or shall provide assistance to the victim. A person need not comply with this subsection if any of the following apply:

"(a) Compliance would place him or her in danger.

"(b) Compliance would interfere with duties the person owes to others.

"(c) Assistance is being summoned or provided by others.

"(3) If a person renders emergency care for a victim, s. 895.48 applies. Any person who provides other reasonable assistance under this section is immune from civil liability for his or her acts or omissions in providing the assistance. This immunity does not apply if the person receives or expects to receive compensation for providing the assistance."

power of the legislature. It is not an independent power conferred upon courts. Courts may validate a legislature's conduct by recognizing the legislature's police power, but courts cannot supply that exercise of power where there is no evidence that the legislature so intended to act.

We return to the fundamental defect in the position of the state. There is no evidence that the legislature intended to exercise its police power in the manner urged here. I reiterate, if it desired to do so, the appropriate statutory language was not beyond the capabilities of the legislature. * * *

One real problem revealed here is that the court does not have the investigative facilities to decide what ought to be done in a broad spectrum of cases involving child abuse. We do not have the legislature's fact-finding process to justify our determination of what the criminal law should be. We are assuming, without being sure, that the legislature, had it confronted the problem posed here, would have concluded, as the majority guesses it would have concluded, that the conduct of Terri Williquette was just as culpable as that of her husband, who was overtly and cruelly sodomizing and torturing the children. While that assumption could be correct, it is not an assumption that a court should make. We do not know how the legislature would have treated the present facts. Nor do we have the authority as a court to reach that conclusion. We are not the branch of the government that has been designated by the constitution to determine what conduct is criminal. Yet, in this case, we come forward with our own definition of criminality. While to do so may give the proponents of this court-made legislation a self-satisfied glow of rectitude, in reality we are by this opinion usurping the legislative prerogative to make the criminal law. While we have responsibilities in the formulation of the common law, the wise sages of our jurisprudence have long recognized that, unless conduct is clearly and unequivocally declared to be criminal by the legislature, a court should restrain itself—even from the impulse to do what it believes to be morally justified. * * *

Notes and Questions

1. Considering the principles discussed in *Williquette,* did the court err in *Commonwealth v. Konz,* 498 Pa. 639, 450 A.2d 638 (1982), in reversing the conviction of Mrs. Konz and Erikson for involuntary manslaughter (causing death by reckless conduct) on the following facts?

"Reverend Konz was a thirty-four year old diabetic and had, for seventeen years, administered to himself daily doses of insulin. On March 4, 1974, however, following an encounter on campus with a visiting evangelist speaker, Reverend Konz publicly proclaimed his desire to discontinue insulin treatment in reliance on the belief that God would heal the diabetic condition. He assured the president of the College and members of the student body that he would carefully monitor his condition and would, if necessary, take insulin. On only one or two occasions did the Reverend thereafter administer insulin. On March 18, 1974, however, Erikson and Reverend Konz formed a pact to pray together to enable the latter to resist the temptation to administer insulin.

"Mrs. Konz was informed of the prayer pact, and, on the morning of Saturday, March 23, 1974, when her husband evidenced symptoms of insulin debt, she removed his insulin from the refrigerator and concealed it.[2] Later that day, the Reverend attempted to obtain insulin from the refrigerator, and, upon discovering that the medicine had been removed, strongly indicated that it should be returned. He then attempted to proceed from room to room but his passage was blocked by Erikson. Harsh words were exchanged, and Erikson,

---

2. The insulin was returned to the refrigerator sometime prior to Sunday night.

after kneeling in prayer, forced the Reverend into a bedroom where, accompanied by Mrs. Konz, Erikson and the Reverend conversed for approximately one half hour. During that time, the Reverend tried to telephone police to obtain assistance but was prevented from doing so by Erikson and Mrs. Konz, who, during a struggle with the Reverend, rendered at least that telephone permanently inoperable.[3] Immediately after this confrontation, the Reverend, his wife, and Erikson returned amicably to the kitchen for coffee, and no further request for insulin was ever made. In addition, the Reverend approached his aunt who resided in the same household and stated, in an apparent reference to the preceding confrontation with Erikson, that 'It's all settled now,' and told her that there was no cause for concern. He also told his eleven year old daughter that 'Everything is fine,' and indicated to her that he did not intend to take insulin. The Reverend then departed from the house, accompanied by Erikson, and returned an hour later. As the day progressed, Reverend Konz cancelled his speaking commitment for the following day and drove his wife to an institution having hospital facilities to pick up a close friend who was a practical nurse. Late on Saturday night, while waiting inside the institution for the nurse to complete her duties, the Reverend appeared very fatigued and complained that he was developing an upset stomach. Both of these conditions were symptomatic of lack of insulin, but neither the Reverend nor his wife requested that insulin, which was available at the institution, be administered. With regard to the Reverend's condition at that time, the nurse observed that he travelled with unimpaired mobility, and that he was conversant, rational, and cognizant of his environs. Nevertheless, he made no mention of a need for insulin, and the nurse made no inquiry as to such a need because the Reverend had on a previous day become very upset at her inquiry as to his diabetic condition.

"Upon returning home from this errand, Reverend Konz experienced increasing illness, vomiting intermittently Saturday night and Sunday morning, and remained in bed all day Sunday except for trips into the bathroom. On Sunday afternoon visitors arrived at the Konz residence. The Reverend, recognizing their voices, called to them from his room to inquire whether they wished to see him; having been informed of the Reverend's nausea, however, the visitors declined to stay. As the Reverend's condition worsened and he became restless, his wife and Erikson administered cracked ice but did not summon medical aid. The Konz's eleven year old daughter then inquired as to why a doctor had not been summoned but Mrs. Konz responded that her husband was 'going to be getting better.' Late Sunday night or early Monday morning everyone in the household fell asleep. On Monday morning at approximately 6 AM, while the others were still asleep, Reverend Konz died of diabetic ketoacidosis."

2. Should the duty of parents, discussed in *Williquette*, sometimes extend to others who have or assume some sort of relationship with the children? Consider *State v. Miranda*, 245 Conn. 209, 715 A.2d 680 (1998), noting that "in addition to biological and adoptive parents and legal guardians, there may be other adults who establish familial relationships with and assume responsibility for the care of a child, thereby creating a legal duty to protect that child from harm," and that such was the case with regard to the defendant, who "had established a family-like relationship with the mother and her two children, * * * had voluntarily assumed responsibility for the care and welfare of both children, and * * * had considered himself the victim's stepfather." How, if at all, could defendant have ended his legal duty?

3. In *State v. Tennant*, 173 W.Va. 627, 319 S.E.2d 395 (1984), the defendant, convicted under a hit-and-run statute requiring that the "driver of any vehicle involved in an accident resulting in injury shall immediately stop such vehicle" and identify himself

---

3. There was testimony as to the existence of two   telephones in the residence.

and give aid, successfully argued on appeal that the jury should have been instructed that the defendant must have known of the accident. "A commonly given reason for this interpretation is summarized in [a case] where the Alaska Supreme Court concluded: '[W]e cannot believe that the legislature could have intended that persons who unknowingly fail to stop and render assistance could be subject to serious criminal penalties.' Similarly, the Virginia Supreme Court stated:

"The duty imposed upon the driver of a vehicle involved in an accident is not passive. It requires positive, affirmative action; that is, to stop and give the aid and information specified.

"How can a person perform these affirmative acts unless he knows that his vehicle has struck a person or an object? Knowledge necessarily is an essential element of the crime."

4. In *United States v. Spingola,* 464 F.2d 909 (7th Cir.1972), the defendant, secretary-treasurer of a trade union, was convicted on three counts of failing to file timely annual financial reports for the fiscal years 1966, 1967 and 1968 on behalf of the union. The trial court excluded evidence by which the defendant sought to show that the late filings were due to the inability of the union's office staff to bring its accounting records up to date, as was necessary in order to prepare the reports, that the needed records were in the possession of the government for extended periods, and that he was unable to complete the reports by himself. In reversing, the court of appeals noted that defendant's defense "is perhaps best characterized as the defense of physical impossibility—that, while the law imposed upon him a duty to file the annual financial report of his union, he possessed neither the sophistication necessary to prepare it himself nor the ability to compel its timely preparation by others. Genuine impossibility is a proper defense to a crime of omission."

Indeed, due process bars imposition of a duty that is impossible to perform. See, e.g., *United States v. Dalton,* 960 F.2d 121 (10th Cir.1992) (thus defendant may not be convicted for possessing and transferring an unregistered machine gun, as registration precluded by law, and thus these crimes "have as an essential element his failure to do an act that he is incapable of performing").

5. In *Davis v. Commonwealth,* 230 Va. 201, 335 S.E.2d 375 (1985), the defendant was convicted of involuntary manslaughter on a finding that the death of her senile and disabled mother, Emily Carter, resulted from defendant's failure to provide heat, food, liquids and other necessities. In response to defendant's claim on appeal that she violated "at most a moral duty," the court stated: "The evidence makes clear that Davis accepted sole responsibility for the total care of Carter. This became her full-time occupation. In return, Carter allowed Davis to live in her home expense free and shared with Davis her income from social security. Additionally, Carter authorized Davis to act as her food stamp representative, and for this Davis received food stamp benefits in her own right. From this uncontroverted evidence, the trial court reasonably could find the existence of an implied contract. Clearly, Davis was more than a mere volunteer; she had a legal duty, not merely a moral one, to care for her mother."

6. In *People v. Wong,* 182 A.D.2d 98, 588 N.Y.S.2d 119 (1992), the defendants' manslaughter convictions, obtained on evidence that someone had violently and repeatedly shaken the 3-month-old victim, were affirmed on this analysis: "In this case, since the incident occurred while the baby was in the sole control of defendants in their home, with no one else present other than their 3 year old child, no specific proof could be obtained as to which defendant actually shook the baby. Thus, there could be no basis upon which to

proceed against either defendant individually on the theory that he or she physically committed the homicidal act.

"However, while criminal liability will normally be imposed only for a defendant's culpable act, it may also be imposed when a defendant, with the requisite mental culpability for the crime charged—in this case, recklessness—fails to perform an act as to which a duty of performance is imposed by law. There is no question that the contractual babysitting agreement involved in this case, as well as the voluntary assumption of complete and exclusive care of a helpless child, created legal duties of care which were substantially coextensive with those which would be borne by a parent. These clearly included the duties which the defendants were charged with breaching, i.e., the duty to provide necessary emergency medical care as well as the duty to protect the child, if possible, from physical harm. Moreover, it is clear that in this case, both defendants legally owed such duties to the infant. Although Mrs. Wong was meant to be the primary caretaker, both defendants contractually assumed responsibility for the child's care at the time the babysitting arrangement was entered into. Further support for this conclusion is found in the fact that, according to both defendants' statements, on the night of Kwok–Wei's death, Eugene Wong was just as involved in 'attending to' the crying child as was his wife."

7. *State ex rel. Kuntz v. Montana Thirteenth Judicial District Court*, 298 Mont. 146, 995 P.2d 951 (2000), involved these facts: Police were called to the home of Bonnie and Warren, who had lived together about six years, to investigate a report of a stabbing and found Warren dead from a single stab wound in the chest. Bonnie said that several hours earlier Warren had physically attack her, that she did not remember what happened next except that she left for a while to "cool off," that when she returned she found Warren face-down unconscious on the porch, and that she then drove to a friend's house and called her mother. (Her sister-in-law, a neighbor of her mother, thereafter summoned the police.) Bonnie was charged with negligent homicide, but when she admitted the stabbing but entered a not guilty plea based upon justified use of force in self-defense, the prosecutor filed an amended information with the same charge, but now on the theory that Bonnie caused the death by stabbing Warren and failing to call for medical assistance. When her motion to dismiss was denied, Bonnie appealed. The appellate court first noted that the most relevant duty on these facts was the one "based on 'creation of the peril,'" whereby "when a person places another in a position of danger, and then fails to safeguard or rescue that person, and the person subsequently dies as a result of this omission, such an omission may be sufficient to support criminal liability." But since duties "are not absolute," the court proceeded to consider two significant questions: (i) whether the duty to summon aid extended to one who inflicted the harm in justified self-defense; and (ii) if so, whether a person who fails to summon aid for her attacker is thus criminally culpable:

"Whether inflicted in self-defense or accidentally, a wound that causes a loss of blood undoubtedly places a person in some degree of peril, and therefore gives rise to a legal duty to either 1) personally provide assistance; or 2) summon medical assistance. Even so, the performance of this legal duty, as discussed above, does not require that a person place herself at risk of serious bodily injury or death.

"Accordingly, based on the legal principles gleaned from our analysis thus far, we hold that when a person justifiably uses force to fend off an aggressor, that person has no duty to assist her aggressor in any manner that may conceivably create the risk of bodily injury or death to herself, or other persons. This absence of a duty necessarily includes any conduct that would require the person to remain in, or return to, the zone of risk created by the original aggressor. We find no authority that suggests that the law should require a person, who is justified in her use of force, to subsequently check the pulse of her attacker, or immediately dial 9–1–1, before retreating to safety.

"Under the general factual circumstances described here, we conclude that the victim has but one duty after fending off an attack, and that is the duty owed to one's self—as a matter of self-preservation—to seek and secure safety away from the place the attack occurred. Thus, the person who justifiably acts in self-defense is temporarily afforded the same status as the innocent bystander under the American rule.

"Finally, we conclude that the duty to summon aid may in fact be 'revived' as the State contends, but only after the victim of the aggressor has fully exercised her right to seek and secure safety from personal harm. Then, and only then, may a legal duty be imposed to summon aid for the person placed in peril by an act of self-defense. We further hold that preliminary to imposing this duty, it must be shown that 1) the person had knowledge of the facts indicating a duty to act; and 2) the person was physically capable of performing the act.

"[I]f the duty to summon aid may be revived, as we have just held, may the failure to perform this legal duty give rise to criminal liability, even though the underlying use of force was justified?

"Our holding as to the first issue consequentially narrows the issue here. Accordingly, to find a person who justifiably acts in self-defense criminally culpable for negligently causing the death of the aggressor, the failure to summon medical aid must be the "cause in fact" of the original aggressor's death, not the justified use of force. * * *

"We therefore hold that a person, who is found to have used justifiable force, but who nevertheless fails to summon aid in dereliction of the legal duty as defined here, may be found criminally negligent only where the failure to summon aid is the cause-in-fact of death, rather than the use of force itself.

"Furthermore, it is important to emphasize that even where such a duty 'revives' under the foregoing analysis, the breach of this duty should not be construed as constituting criminal negligence per se. To the contrary, it is entirely conceivable that in circumstances where such a legal duty may rightfully be imposed, a failure to summon medical assistance—due to fear, shock, or some other manifestation resulting from the confrontation—would not be a gross deviation from an ordinary standard of care as required by Montana's negligent homicide statute."

8. In most of the foregoing cases, the court has "found" the duty by looking outside the jurisdiction's criminal code. Sometimes, of course, the statute penalizing the inaction also imposes the duty, as in *Tennant*, note 3 supra. But even in such cases, a court may find it necessary to define those having the duty more clearly and narrowly than does the statute. See, e.g., *People v. Heitzman*, 9 Cal.4th 189, 37 Cal.Rptr.2d 236, 886 P.2d 1229 (1994) (offense of failure to prevent another from abusing an elder deemed not to impose duty on everyone, as then it would cover even a delivery person who failed to intervene upon seeing disheveled elder while making a delivery). Exactly how, then, should the statute be judicially narrowed?

9. George P. Fletcher, *On the Moral Irrelevance of Bodily Movements*, 142 U.Pa. L.Rev. 1443, 148–49 (1994): "The Model Penal Code provides that 'liability for the commission of an offense may not be based on an omission ... unless ... a duty to perform the omitted act is otherwise imposed by law.' 'Law' in this context means case law, law as principle, not law as statutory enactment. Therefore, the punishment of commission by omission raises serious problems under the principle *nulla poena sine lege*.

"One would think that commentators would be shocked by the wholesale breach of legality in the judicial development of duties that supplement the law of homicide. My sense of the literature is that most observers are concerned about condemning the injustice of not punishing immoral omissions. There is little concern about the issue of legality in letting courts roam freely about our moral sentiments."

10.   Austin Wehrwein, *"Samaritan" Law Poses Difficulties,* Nat'l L.J., Aug. 22, 1983, p. 5, col. 1: "Minnesota's new law that imposes a fine on bystanders who don't aid people in peril could pose some problems for prosecutors and insurance companies—if it is ever put to use. * * *

"The law, which took effect Aug. 1, requires a bystander to render 'reasonable assistance' during an emergency to anyone who is 'exposed to or has suffered grave physical harm.' The statute includes in its definition of reasonable assistance such acts as calling the police and getting medical help, but it does not require a bystander to do anything that involves 'danger or peril to himself or others.' * * *

"The bill's sponsor, Democratic state Rep. Randy Staten, said he was moved to introduce the bill by reports of the gang rape earlier this year of a woman in a New Bedford, Mass., barroom who was hoisted onto a pool table and repeatedly assaulted while spectators stood by and some reportedly shouted 'go for it! 'More recently, a 14–year–old St. Louis girl was raped last month while bystanders did nothing for 40 minutes until an 11–year–old boy called police. Last week, Mr. Staten also cited this incident as an example of the kind of conduct his bill would prevent.

"The traditional common-law rule that a bystander has no duty to aid an endangered person would permit 'totally unacceptable conduct for civilized society,' Mr. Staten said. One example of such conduct, he said, would be an expert swimmer ignoring the plight of a drowning child. * * *

"France, the Netherlands, West Germany and other European countries impose the duty to assist in their criminal statutes and hold those who fail to render help civilly liable."

11.   Christopher H. Schroeder, *Two Methods for Evaluating Duty to Rescue Proposals,* 49 Law & Contemp.Probs. 181, 192, 194 (1986): "The relative lack of causal cut-offs between failures to act and harms, as compared with those available in our normal understanding of actions, places tremendous pressure on the concept of 'reasonable expectations' within the definition of failures to act, because that limiting concept may be about all that will stand between us and legal responsibility for many, many harms that we could have prevented. The usual hypotheticals enter in here to press our intuitions about whether that line can be held. As Richard Epstein questions, if a strong swimmer is legally liable for failure to make an easy rescue of a drowning infant in a swimming pool, will you be similarly liable for failure to donate $10 to African relief if you are substantially certain that that $10 will prevent a death through starvation? Similarly, as a note pinned recently to a bulletin board at Duke University Law School queried, if you make $45,000 per year as an entry level associate at a corporate law firm and can live securely on $20,000, are you legally answerable for the deaths of one hundred Africans, on the assumption that $250 per year would sustain a life indefinitely? Or, as someone asked in a penned response to the original note, if you go to work for legal services at $20,000 a year, but could have taken a job with a corporate law firm and then donated your surplus $25,000 to relief organizations, are you still culpable? * * *

"[W]hile it may be true that a firm, albeit somewhat arbitrary, line delimiting rescues to which a legal duty attaches would be superior to a legal regime wholly without such a duty * * *, it is nevertheless important to isolate those criteria that influence where that line ought to be drawn. These criteria serve at the least as counsel to a conscientious legislator, and also clarify what we actually believe separates the case involving the drowning child and the strong swimmer from the ten dollar charitable contribution. What functions, in other words, to make certain expectations about rescue reasonable to a degree that warrants legal sanction for a failure to rescue? * * *

"Some of those principles appear in the Vermont statute requiring easy rescue, which is often cited as a model. It reads:

A person who knows that another is exposed to grave physical harm shall, to the extent that the same can be rendered without danger or peril to himself or without interference with important duties owed to others, give reasonable assistance to the exposed person unless that assistance or care is being provided by others."

Chapter 5

HOMICIDE: USING MENTAL STATE
AND OTHER FACTORS TO
CLASSIFY CRIMES

SECTION 1. "HUMAN BEING" AS THE PROTECTED INTEREST

HUGHES v. STATE

Court of Criminal Appeals of Oklahoma, 1994.

868 P.2d 730.

CHAPEL, JUDGE:

On August 2, 1990, Appellant, Treva LaNan Hughes, while intoxicated, drove her vehicle into oncoming traffic and collided with another vehicle. The driver of the other vehicle, Reesa Poole, was nine months pregnant and expected to deliver in four days. The collision caused Poole's stomach to hit the steering wheel of her car with such force that the steering wheel broke. Poole was taken to a hospital where an emergency cesarean section was performed. When the baby was delivered, the only sign of life was an extremely slow heartbeat. A pediatrician immediately began resuscitation efforts, which were unsuccessful.

After a jury trial * * *, Hughes was convicted * * *, of First Degree Manslaughter under 21 O.S.1981, § 711(1) ("[h]omicide is manslaughter in the first degree ... [w]hen perpetrated without a design to effect death by a person while engaged in the commission of a misdemeanor"). The jury also convicted Hughes of Driving Under the Influence While Involved in a Personal Injury Accident. Hughes received an eight-year prison sentence for the manslaughter conviction and a six-month suspended sentence for the driving under the influence conviction. * * *

Hughes argues as her sole proposition of error that her manslaughter conviction should be reversed on the basis of the common law "born alive" rule. Because Oklahoma has neither altered nor abolished this remnant of the common law, it remains in effect pursuant to 22 O.S.1981, § 9. Under the "born alive" rule, "[a] child can not be the subject of homicide until its complete expulsion from the body of the mother, and must be alive and have independent existence." In this case of first impression, Hughes claims that the fetus Ms. Poole was carrying was not born alive and that its death cannot be considered a homicide. We now abandon the common law approach and hold that whether or not it is

254

ultimately born alive, an unborn fetus that was viable at the time of injury is a "human being" which may be the subject of a homicide under 21 O.S.1981, § 691 ("Homicide is the killing of one human being by another").

The dissent adopts the State's position that the "born alive" rule would not prohibit a manslaughter conviction in this case because the fetus in question was born alive. It is asserted that the fetus had a heartbeat at birth and the Legislature has determined that any fetus born with a heartbeat is in fact born alive. While this argument is superficially appealing, it has no merit. The evidence presented at trial established that the baby was dead when delivered. The fetus did have a weak heartbeat. It was, however, brain dead according to the doctor to whom it was handed immediately upon delivery. Additionally, according to the testimony, the fetus had no blood pressure, no respiration and did not respond to any resuscitative efforts. We are not prepared to hold that a brain dead fetus was alive when born simply because its heart was beating weakly. Moreover, the statute relied upon by the State is a "vital statistics" statute. See 63 .S.Supp.1986, § 1–301(e). The State has an interest in reporting high incidence of live births. We will not overreach and extend a statute intended for statistical purposes to a homicide case where an individual's liberty is at stake.

Today's decision abandoning the "born alive" rule is based in significant part upon its origins, history and purpose. Common law authorities refer to the born alive rule as early as the 1300's. The born alive rule was necessitated by the state of medical technology in earlier centuries.

In fact, as late as the nineteenth century, prior to quickening "it was virtually impossible for either the woman, a midwife, or a physician to confidently know that the woman was pregnant, or, it follows, that the child in utero was alive." Hence, there was no evidence of life until quickening.

Yet, the quickening of a fetus did not constitute proof that the fetus was alive in the womb at any particular moment thereafter. The health of a child within the womb could not be determined until the child was observed after birth. "As a result, live birth was required to prove that the unborn child was alive and that the material acts were the proximate cause of death, because it could not otherwise be established if the child was alive in the womb at the time of the material acts."

Advances in medical and scientific knowledge and technology have abolished the need for the born alive rule. Specifically, the medical and scientific evidence before us establishes that the child within Poole's womb was a living, viable fetus at the time of the collision and that this child died as a result of the placental abruption which occurred when Poole's stomach hit and broke the steering wheel of her car.

Although in the minority, two states have expressly rejected the born alive rule: Massachusetts and South Carolina. The Massachusetts court addressed the question of whether a viable fetus is a "person" under that state's vehicular homicide statute in *Commonwealth v. Cass*, 392 Mass. 799, 467 N.E.2d 1324 (1984). In reaching its decision, the *Cass* court first acknowledged that it had previously held that a viable fetus was a person under the Massachusetts wrongful death statute. The court also noted that the legislature was presumed to have knowledge of judicial decisions and that the words of a statute are to be given their ordinary meaning. The *Cass* court then reasoned that:

> In keeping with approved usage, and giving terms their ordinary meaning, the word "person" is synonymous with the term "human being." *An offspring of human parents cannot reasonably be considered to be other than a human being, and therefore a person, first within, and then in normal course outside, the womb.* As will be shown

later in this opinion, heretofore the law has not recognized that the pre-born could be the victims of homicide because of difficulties in proving the cause of death; but problems in proving causation do not detract from the personhood of the victim.

(Emphasis added). The court then concluded that, since the legislature was presumed to have knowledge of the court's earlier decision regarding the personhood of a viable fetus under the wrongful death statute, the legislature contemplated that a viable fetus would be a person under the subsequently enacted vehicular homicide statute.

The *Cass* court also established an alternative rationale to support its decision, assuming that the legislature had not considered the issue. In that event, the court reasoned, the legislature intended the term "person" be defined by "reference to established and developing common law." The court then rejected the born alive rule, stating:

> The rule has been accepted as the established common law in every American jurisdiction that has considered the question. But the antiquity of a rule is no measure of its soundness. 'It is revolting to have no better reason for a rule of law than that so it was laid down in the time of Henry IV. It is still more revolting if the grounds upon which it was laid down have vanished long since, and the rule simply persists from blind imitation of the past.' ... It is time to reexamine the grounds upon which this ancient rule was laid down.
>
> The rationale offered for the rule since 1348 is that 'it is difficult to know whether [the defendant] killed the child or not....' ... That is, one could never be sure that the fetus was alive when the accused committed his act. However, difficulty of proving causation is no sound reason for denying criminal liability. Medical science now may provide competent proof as to whether the fetus was alive at the time of a defendant's conduct and whether his conduct was the cause of death. ...We do not consider [fear of speculation] a sufficient reason for refusing to consider the killing of a fetus a homicide.
>
> We think that the better rule is that infliction of prenatal injuries resulting in the death of a viable fetus, before or after it is born, is homicide. If a person were to commit violence against a pregnant woman and destroy the fetus within her,[3] we would not want the death of the fetus to go unpunished. We believe that our criminal law should extend its protection to viable fetuses.

One day later, South Carolina also rejected the born alive rule in *State v. Horne*, 282 S.C. 444, 319 S.E.2d 703 (1984). As in *Cass*, the *Horne* court acknowledged that it had previously held that a viable fetus was a person in the context of a wrongful death action. The *Horne* court then stated that "[i]t would be grossly inconsistent for us to construe a viable fetus as a 'person' for the purposes of imposing civil liability while refusing to give it a similar classification in the criminal context." Accordingly, the court held that:

> This Court has the right and the duty to develop the common law of South Carolina to better serve an ever-changing society as a whole. In this regard, the criminal law has been the subject of change. ...The fact this particular issue has not been raised or ruled on before does not mean we are prevented from declaring the common law as it should be. Therefore, we hold an action for homicide may be maintained in the future when the state can prove beyond a reasonable doubt the fetus

---

3. The Oklahoma Legislature criminalized this type of conduct in 21 O.S.1981, § 713. Section 713 provides that "[t]he willful killing of an unborn quick child by any injury committed upon the person of the mother of such child, ... is manslaughter in the first degree." The defendant in our recent opinion *Hooks v. State*, 862 P.2d 1273 (Okl.Cr.1993), was convicted under section 713 for having killed an unborn, viable fetus by fatally injuring its mother. Our holding today is not inconsistent with our holding in *Hooks*, because Hughes was charged and convicted under 21 O.S.1981, § 711 rather than section 713.

involved was viable, i.e., able to live separate and apart from its mother without the aid of artificial support.

This Court also has the right and duty to develop the common law of Oklahoma to serve the evolving needs of our citizens.

To that end, we believe that the citizens of Oklahoma would be best served by a definition of "human being" in the context of Section 691 which does not rely upon an obsolete, antiquated common law rule. Rather, the meaning of that term should be determined by the plain language and purpose of the statute. The purpose of Section 691 is, ultimately, to protect human life. A viable human fetus is nothing less than human life. As stated by the court in *Cass*, "[a]n offspring of human parents cannot reasonably be considered to be other than a human being ... first within, and then in normal course outside, the womb." Thus, the term "human being" in Section 691—according to its plain and ordinary meaning—includes a viable human fetus. * * *

We wish to make it absolutely clear that our holding shall not affect a woman's constitutional right to choose a lawful abortion based upon her constitutional right to privacy or a physician's right to perform one. Neither state statute nor caselaw can render a constitutionally protected abortion unlawful. Accordingly, today's decision to bestow upon viable human fetuses the legal status of "human being" under Oklahoma law, cannot and shall not be used as the basis for bringing homicide charges against either a woman who chooses a lawful abortion or a physician who performs a lawful abortion.

[The court then concluded that its ruling should be prospective only in light of *Bouie v. City of Columbia*, p. 66 of this Book.]

Lumpkin, Presiding Judge: concurs in part/dissents in part.

I concur in the Court's well-reasoned determination the term "human being" pursuant to 21 O.S.1981, § 691, includes a viable human fetus. * * *

[M]y dissent to the Court's decision to reverse and dismiss the conviction of Manslaughter relates to the determination the child was dead upon delivery. The evidence indicates that as a result of an automobile accident between Appellant and an expectant mother, a viable unborn child was injured. The accident occurred on August 2, 1990. The mother had been examined by her obstetrician on July 30, the unborn child was viable and the due date for delivery was set at August 6, four (4) days after the accident. At the time of the accident, the mother was thrown forward and her stomach hit and broke the steering wheel. Upon arrival at the hospital, a fetal heartbeat of 70–90 beats per minute was detected. After an emergency caesarean section was performed, the baby was delivered at 9:02 p.m. The baby had a heartbeat, but was not breathing on its own or moving. A placenta abruption was observed by the attending physician. Upon delivery, the baby was given to a pediatrician, who attempted resuscitation efforts; however, the baby's condition deteriorated rapidly and the heartbeat did not improve. The baby was pronounced dead at 10:10 p.m., over an hour after delivery. The medical examiner testified the child would have lived absent the trauma. It must also be noted, the physician who made the statement the child was brain dead when born did so only on the basis of a visual observation. The child was not placed on a monitor to determine activity in the brain.

I find the Court has erred in its scope of review. The opinion seems to forget this Court is not to substitute its view of the evidence for the jury's; rather, "the relevant question is whether, after viewing the evidence in the light most favorable to the prosecution, any rational trier of fact could have found the essential elements of the crime beyond a reasonable doubt." In the light most favorable to the prosecution, a baby who had a heartbeat before and after delivery, and who was not pronounced dead until over an hour after delivery, was alive. Thus, the verdict of the trier of fact should be affirmed. This is made clear by our Legislature's definition of "live birth" as it is used in connection with vital statistics governing birth and death:

> The term "live birth" means the complete expulsion or extraction from its mother of a product of human conception, irrespective of the duration of pregnancy, which, after such expulsion of extraction, breathes *or shows any other evidence of life such as beating of the heart*, pulsation of the umbilical cord or definite movement of voluntary muscles, whether or not the umbilical cord has been cut or the placenta is attached.

63 O.S.Supp.1986, § 1–301(e) (emphasis added). The Court seeks to avoid this statute by limiting its application based on it being a "vital statistic statute". However, * * * "[i]n general, the location of statutes in particular places in codes does not affect their force or validity". This is an action of the Legislature to provide a definition for the term "live birth" which is sufficient to abrogate the application of common law definitions. * * *

While the baby may not have had much of a chance, there was clearly a "live birth" as our Legislature has defined it. Under the evidence presented here, the baby was born alive, then died as a result of injuries sustained by Appellant's actions. The Court can arrive at this result by applying existing common law precepts and statutory language in place at the time Appellant committed the offense. * * *

Notes and Questions

1. "The case most widely cited for a discussion of the born alive rule is *Keeler v. Superior Court*.[20] In *Keeler*, the defendant blocked his ex-wife's car on a narrow mountain road and forced her out of the car. At the time his ex-wife was pregnant with a viable fetus, later determined to have a seventy-five to ninety-six percent chance of survival if born uninjured. The defendant had warned her of the consequences if she were pregnant with another man's child. After realizing that she was pregnant, the defendant threatened 'I'm going to stomp it out of you,' and then 'pushed her against the car, shoved his knee into her abdomen, and struck her in the face.' The woman survived, but the fetus was stillborn and the defendant was charged with murder. Writing for the majority, Justice Mosk discussed the history of the born alive rule extensively and evaluated the legislature's intent in enacting the state's murder statute. The majority determined that the legislature 'did not intend the act of feticide-as distinguished from abortion-to be' a crime." Note, 41 Wm. & Mary L.Rev. 1845, 1848 (2000).

A closer look at *Keeler* reflects the sharp contrast between that decision and *Hughes*. The court in *Keeler* relied mainly on the following propositions: (i) when the state legislature in 1850 first enacted the statute in question concerning murder of a "human being," that term had "the settled common law meaning of a person who had been born alive"; (ii) California at that time borrowed much of its penal law from New York, but did not borrow its feticide statute; (iii) later systematic revision of the criminal laws neither made any change in the murder statute nor added a feticide statute, by then common in other states; (iv) even if there are good policy reasons for abandoning the "born alive" rule, that "is a determination solely within the province of the Legislature"; (v) even if the court had the power to change the rule, under *Bouie* such a change "could operate only prospectively, and thus could not in any event reach the conduct of petitioner"; and (vi) the fact an unborn child has various rights on the civil side of the law does not support a different result, considering that "such rules coexisted for centuries with the common law requirement of live birth to support a conviction of homicide."

20. 470 P.2d 617 (Cal. 1970).

2. The response of the California legislature to *Keeler* was to revise the murder statute to read: "Murder is the unlawful killing of a human being, or a fetus, with malice aforethought." That statute is different from the legislation discussed in footnote 3 in *Hughes* in several ways: (a) the former deals only with murder and the latter only with manslaughter; (b) the former merely adds the killing of a fetus to existing criminal legislation, while the latter treats feticide as a separate criminal offense; (c) the former protects the fetus without any stated limitation,[a] while the latter protects from the time of quickening. (As explained in Note, supra, at 1851, 1855, viability—the beginning of protection under some feticide statutes—is usually defined as "that period at the end of the second trimester of pregnancy when the fetus is capable of surviving outside the womb," while quickening "is the period prior to viability when the mother first feels the fetus move in the womb, normally between the sixteenth and eighteenth week of pregnancy.")

Note, supra, at 1846–76, describes in considerable detail the extent and nature of the protection of the fetus by the criminal law today. In summary: (i) 18 states still subscribe to the born alive rule,[b] either by express statutory language or through judicial interpretation; (ii) 24 states, either by expansion of existing crimes or by separate feticide statutes, criminalize actions against the fetus, 6 from the point of viability, 6 from the point of quickening, 2 from specified weeks of fetal development, 7 from the point of fertilization or conception, and 3 without specifying a threshold; (iii) several states penalize actions against pregnant women that result in miscarriage or, in some states, injury to the fetus.

Did the court in *Hughes* give sufficient attention to the existing feticide statute in that state?

3. On the civil side of the law, "every jurisdiction in the United States has recognized a cause of action for prenatal injury, at least when the injury is to a viable fetus later born alive." Note, 48 Drake L.Rev. 741, 750 (2000). On the criminal side, several of those states still following the born alive rule "have held that if fetuses are injured before birth, are born alive, and then die, their deaths can be prosecuted as homicides." Note, 41 Wm. & Mary L.Rev. 1845, 1850 (2000). *Keeler* acknowledged that this was the rule at common law, and this was likewise the position taken by the *Hughes* dissent, rejected by the majority only on the ground that the fetus there had been brain dead at birth and thus was not born alive.

Where the injured fetus actually is later born alive but then dies from the prenatal injuries, should there be criminal homicide liability under the born alive rule? Should the answer depend at all upon who the defendant is? Consider *State v. Deborah J.Z.*, 228 Wis.2d 468, 596 N.W.2d 490 (App.1999), where one week before her due date, Deborah was drinking in a local tavern when she believed she was going to have her baby. At the hospital she was uncooperative, belligerent at times, and very intoxicated. Her blood alcohol concentration exceeded 0.30 percent. She allegedly told a nurse, "if you don't keep me here, I'm just going to go home and keep drinking and drink myself to death, and I'm

a. However, in *People v. Davis*, 7 Cal.4th 797, 30 Cal.Rptr.2d 50, 872 P.2d 591 (1994), the court prospectively interpreted the statute to mean that viability was not a requirement for fetal murder and that it suffices that "the state can show that the fetus has progressed beyond the embryonic stage of seven to eight weeks." "Since the *Davis* ruling, there have been several convictions under the fetal murder statute, with fetal developments ranging from fifteen weeks to eight months." Note, supra, at 1860.

b. This is not to suggest that these states are necessarily in precise agreement as to what constitutes

being "born alive." In *Keeler*, the court asserted that it agreed with *People v. Chavez*, 77 Cal.App.2d 621, 176 P.2d 92 (1947), "that a viable fetus 'in the process of being born' is a human being within the meaning of the homicide statutes," even though infanticide cases of an earlier era "had not reached uniformity on whether breathing, heart action, severance of the umbilical cord, or some combination of these or other factors established the status of 'human being' for purposes of the law of homicide."

going to kill this thing because I don't want it anyways." Deborah consented to a Cesarean section and gave birth to a baby girl. At birth the baby was extremely small, her physical features presented fetal alcohol effects, and her blood alcohol level was .199 percent. After a few weeks the baby was discharged to a foster family. Deborah, charged with attempted first-degree intentional homicide and first-degree reckless injury, appealed from the denial of a motion to dismiss the charges for lack of probable cause. On appeal, the State argued "that after the birth of M.M.Z., the applicable criminal statutes for a 'born alive' child take effect. However, the State fails to point to a case with a situation, similar to this, in which the rule has been applied for self-abuse by the mother which negatively impacts an unborn child, later 'born alive.'

"Specifically, the State posits that holding mothers accountable for injuries they inflict on their children prenatally is the next logical step beyond the courts' application of the 'born alive' rule to third parties in *State v. Cornelius*, 152 Wis.2d 272, 282–83, 448 N.W.2d 434, 438 (Ct.App.1989). In *Cornelius*, the defendant was charged with homicide by intoxicated use of a motor vehicle for the subsequent death of an unborn child after it was involved in an automobile accident resulting from the defendant's intoxicated driving. Immediately after the accident, the unborn child was delivered at the hospital, but it died soon thereafter from injuries suffered in the auto accident. We upheld the homicide charge, reasoning that the unborn child qualified as a 'human being' under § 939.22(16), Stats., because it was alive at birth. We also stated, 'Our decision does not reach the issue of the rights of a fetus, and certainly does not discuss its rights vis-a-vis the mother. [The victim] was born alive and died as a result of injuries sustained in utero, and our decision should not be read more broadly than to allow a homicide charge under these circumstances.' "

The court in *Deborah J.Z.* then concluded that "to be convicted of attempted first-degree intentional homicide and first-degree reckless injury, Deborah must attempt to kill or injure someone who has been born alive. This is not what Deborah was charged with doing. The decision whether to include an unborn child in the definition of a 'human being' is a policy issue best addressed by our legislature." As for why the instant case might be viewed differently than *Cornelius*, the court earlier noted:

"Even though Deborah's actions were egregious, we decline the State's overture to give the statute such a broad construction. Under such a construction, a woman could risk criminal charges for any perceived self-destructive behavior during her pregnancy that may result in injuries to her unborn child. Any reckless or dangerous conduct, such as smoking heavily or abusing legal medications, could become criminal behavior because the actions were taken while the woman was pregnant. 'Taken to its extreme, prohibitions during pregnancy could also include the failure to act, such as the failure to secure adequate prenatal medical care, and overzealous behavior, such as excessive exercising or dieting.'

"Additionally, the prosecution of a pregnant woman for prenatal behavior which affects the health of the unborn child reveals significant public policy implications. Many health officials agree that substance abuse in pregnant women is better addressed through treatment rather than the threat of punishment. Another area of concern is that the imposition of criminal sanctions on pregnant women for prenatal conduct may hinder many women from seeking prenatal care and needed medical treatment because any act or omission on their part may render them criminally liable to the subsequently born child. Obviously, these are complex and controversial public policy considerations; therefore, it is appropriate for the courts to defer to the legislature. We do so because 'the legislature is in a better position than the courts to gather, weigh, and reconcile the competing policy proposals addressed to this sensitive area of the law.' "

4.   Compare *Whitner v. State*, 328 S.C. 1, 492 S.E.2d 777 (1997), holding that a viable fetus is a "child" within the meaning of the child abuse and endangerment statute, so that Whitner could be charged under that statute for ingesting crack cocaine during the third trimester of pregnancy, causing her baby to born with cocaine metabolites in its system:

"Whitner also argues an interpretation of the statute that includes viable fetuses would lead to absurd results obviously not intended by the legislature. Specifically, she claims if we interpret 'child' to include viable fetuses, every action by a pregnant woman that endangers or is likely to endanger a fetus, whether otherwise legal or illegal, would constitute unlawful neglect under the statute. For example, a woman might be prosecuted under section 20–7–50 for smoking or drinking during pregnancy. Whitner asserts these 'absurd' results could not have been intended by the legislature and, therefore, the statute should not be construed to include viable fetuses.

"We disagree for a number of reasons. First, the same arguments against the statute can be made whether or not the child has been born. After the birth of a child, a parent can be prosecuted under section 20–7–50 for an action that is likely to endanger the child without regard to whether the action is illegal in itself. For example, a parent who drinks excessively could, under certain circumstances, be guilty of child neglect or endangerment even though the underlying act—consuming alcoholic beverages—is itself legal. Obviously, the legislature did not think it 'absurd' to allow prosecution of parents for such otherwise legal acts when the acts actually or potentially endanger the 'life, health or comfort' of the parents' born children. We see no reason such a result should be rendered absurd by the mere fact the child at issue is a viable fetus.

"Moreover, we need not address this potential parade of horribles advanced by Whitner. In this case, which is the only case we are called upon to decide here, certain facts are clear. Whitner admits to having ingested crack cocaine during the third trimester of her pregnancy, which caused her child to be born with cocaine in its system. Although the precise effects of maternal crack use during pregnancy are somewhat unclear, it is well documented and within the realm of public knowledge that such use can cause serious harm to the viable unborn child. There can be no question here Whitner endangered the life, health, and comfort of her child. We need not decide any cases other than the one before us.

"[W]e do not think any fundamental right of Whitner's—or any right at all, for that matter—is implicated under the present scenario. It strains belief for Whitner to argue that using crack cocaine during pregnancy is encompassed within the constitutionally recognized right of privacy. Use of crack cocaine is illegal, period. No one here argues that laws criminalizing the use of crack cocaine are themselves unconstitutional. If the State wishes to impose additional criminal penalties on pregnant women who engage in this already illegal conduct because of the effect the conduct has on the viable fetus, it may do so. We do not see how the fact of pregnancy elevates the use of crack cocaine to the lofty status of a fundamental right.

"Moreover, as a practical matter, we do not see how our interpretation of section 20–7–50 imposes a burden on Whitner's right to carry her child to term. [D]uring her pregnancy after the fetus attained viability, Whitner enjoyed the same freedom to use cocaine that she enjoyed earlier in and predating her pregnancy—none whatsoever. Simply put, South Carolina's child abuse and endangerment statute as applied to this case does not restrict Whitner's freedom in any way that it was not already restricted. The State's imposition of an additional penalty when a pregnant woman with a viable fetus engages in the already proscribed behavior does not burden a woman's right to carry her pregnancy to term; rather, the additional penalty simply recognizes that a third party (the viable fetus or newborn child) is harmed by the behavior."

5.   Consider Nancy Kubasek, *The Case Against Prosecution for Prenatal Drug Abuse*, 8 Tex. J. Women & L. 167 (1999): "Approximately eleven percent of pregnant women use illegal drugs during their pregnancy. The effects on the fetus of drug abuse during pregnancy include low birth weight, short body length, smaller head size, other physical abnormalities and defects, and learning disabilities. The federal government has calculated that the average cost of an infant exposed to illegal drugs as a fetus is about one million dollars. In an attempt to reduce the number of infants exposed in utero to illegal drugs, many states have begun to prosecute women for prenatal drug use. Since 1985, at least 240 women from more than thirty-five states have been prosecuted for using illegal drugs during their pregnancy. These women have been charged with a variety of offenses, including drug possession, drug distribution, delivery of a controlled substance to a minor, criminal child abuse, and criminal child neglect.

"Despite all of these prosecutions, the only state supreme court to uphold such a conviction is the Supreme Court of South Carolina, in *Whitner v. State*. The courts have generally concluded that the word 'child' cannot be interpreted to encompass a 'viable fetus'. The majority of these rulings show that this form of prosecution is not the intent of either drug-use or child-protection legislation. The prosecutions also have constitutional implications in that they potentially limit the right of reproductive freedom and implicate the equal protection clause. Furthermore, the threat of prosecution may keep many women from seeking prenatal care or carrying their child to term. We need to question whether these prosecutions reflect the intent of the legislature to protect children or are the result of a prejudice toward certain groups and beliefs concerning the reproductive obligations of women."

6.   *Hughes* is an unusual case in that it involves questions of when life begins (born alive or some alternative) and of when life ends (brain death or some alternative). The latter issue more commonly arises in situations like that in *People v. Eulo*, 63 N.Y.2d 341, 482 N.Y.S.2d 436, 472 N.E.2d 286 (1984), where the defendant in each of two similar cases shot his victim in the head, the victim was taken to the hospital unconscious and placed on a respirator, and when it was later determined the victim's brain had irreversibly ceased to function and upon consent of the next of kin, the victim was declared dead and removed from the respirator and bodily organs were removed for transplantation purposes. As to the claim of these defendants that the trial judge erred in not giving the jury the traditional definition of death, irreversible cessation of breathing and heartbeat, the court responded:

"It has been called to this court's attention that the Legislature has, on a number of occasions, had bills before it that would expressly recognize brain-based criteria for determining death and has taken no affirmative action. This legislative void in no way impedes this court from fulfilling its obligation to construe laws of the State. Indeed, advances made in medical science have caused a focus on the issues of when a jury may find criminal responsibility for homicide, of when physicians may transfer donated organs, and of when a person's body may be accorded the dignity of final repose. It is incumbent upon this court to instill certainty and uniformity in these important areas.

"We hold that a recognition of brain-based criteria for determining death is not unfaithful to prior judicial definitions of 'death,' as presumptively adopted in the many statutes using that term. Close examination of the common-law conception of death and the traditional criteria used to determine when death has occurred leads inexorably to this conclusion. * * *

"Considering death to have occurred when there is an irreversible and complete cessation of the functioning of the entire brain, including the brain stem, is consistent with the common-law conception of death. Ordinarily, death will be determined according to the traditional criteria of irreversible cardiorespiratory repose. When, however, the respiratory and circulatory functions are maintained by mechanical means, their significance, as signs of life, is at best ambiguous. Under such circumstances, death may nevertheless be deemed to occur when, according to accepted medical practice, it is determined that the entire brain's function has irreversibly ceased.

"Death remains the single phenomenon identified at common law; the supplemental criteria are merely adapted to account for the 'changed conditions' that a dead body may be attached to a machine so as to exhibit demonstrably false indicia of life. It reflects an improved understanding that in the complete and irreversible absence of a functioning brain, the traditional loci of life—the heart and the lungs—function only as a result of stimuli originating from outside of the body and will never again function as part of an integrated organism."

7. "Currently, all fifty states and the District of Columbia accept brain death as a legal definition of death." Samantha Weyrauch, *Acceptance of Whole–Brain Death Criteria for Determination of Death: A Comparative Analysis of the United States and Japan*, 17 UCLA Pac.Basin L.J. 91, 104 (1999). This is not to suggest, however, that the question of what should constitute death for purposes of the criminal law is no longer disputed. Consider Comment, 27 Cumb.L.Rev. 1279, 1281–83 (1997): "One recent attempt to expand the legal definition of death, and in turn increase the supply of transplantable organs, was adopted in June 1994 by the American Medical Association's Council on Ethical and Judicial Affairs (CEJA). This seven-member AMA policy-making body stated as the AMA's new policy on procuring organs from anencephalic infants:

"Anencephaly is a congenital absence of a major portion of the brain, skull, and scalp. Neonates with this condition are born without a forebrain and without a cerebrum. While anencephalic neonates are born with a rudimentary functional brain stem, their lack of a functioning cerebrum permanently forecloses the possibility of consciousness.

"*It is ethically permissible to consider the anencephalic neonate as a potential organ donor, although still alive under the current definition of death....*

"*It is normally required that a person be legally dead before removal of [his] life-necessary organs (the 'dead donor rule'). The use of the anencephalic neonate as a live donor is a limited exception to the general standard because of the fact that the infant has never experienced, and will never experience, consciousness.*

"If legally accepted, the AMA's position would allow organ harvesting from any human who permanently lacks consciousness. While this pragmatic attempt to force legal change would remedy some transplantable organ shortages, the AMA's proposal would expand the definition of death to allow organ harvesting from live, birthed children who suffer anencephaly. The AMA further asserted that after determining that an unborn child is anencephalic, the physician should counsel the mother that the 'noble' act to perform, provided she carries the child to term, is to have the child's organs harvested so that other children may receive organ transplants. At birth, transplant surgeons would take the anencephalic child to an operating room and remove the child's vital organs. Throughout the procedure, the child would still be alive under the current legal definitions of life. Following the AMA's rationale, 'permanently' comatose patients or persons in a persistent vegetative state could become organ donors even while still legally alive because they, too, have severely limited brain functions with no chance of ever gaining consciousness.

"In December 1995, the CEJA temporarily suspended the AMA policy at the repeated requests of many AMA members. Though agreeing to suspend temporarily its policy, the CEJA held firm to its original justification that: '[R]espect for the essential worth of life ... is not an absolute value. Rather, it must be balanced with other important social values, including ... the fundamental social value of saving lives.' Saving a life under this reasoning is paradoxical because it would require the destruction of another life. The AMA's proposal would give physicians the power to decide whose life should be prematurely ended so that another may continue. In essence, this policy advocates legal infanticide of a specific class of persons: anencephalic infants. The CEJA recognizes that if physicians followed the former AMA policy, they would face criminal prosecution for murder, but contends that within a few years the law will catch up with biomedical advances and allow the proposed acts."

SECTION 2. INTENTIONAL KILLING: THE "HEAT OF PASSION" TEST

MULLANEY v. WILBUR

Supreme Court of the United States, 1975.

421 U.S. 684, 95 S.Ct. 1881, 44 L.Ed.2d 508.

MR. JUSTICE POWELL delivered the opinion of the Court.

The State of Maine requires a defendant charged with murder to prove that he acted "in the heat of passion on sudden provocation" in order to reduce the homicide to manslaughter. We must decide whether this rule comports with the due process requirement, as defined in *In re Winship*, 397 U.S. 358, 364, 90 S.Ct. 1068, 1072, 25 L.Ed.2d 368 (1970), that the prosecution prove beyond a reasonable doubt every fact necessary to constitute the crime charged.

In June 1966 a jury found respondent Stillman E. Wilbur, Jr., guilty of murder. The case against him rested on his own pretrial statement and on circumstantial evidence showing that he fatally assaulted Claude Hebert in the latter's hotel room. Respondent's statement, introduced by the prosecution, claimed that he had attacked Hebert in a frenzy provoked by Hebert's homosexual advance. The defense offered no evidence, but argued that the homicide was not unlawful since respondent lacked criminal intent. Alternatively, Wilbur's counsel asserted that at most the homicide was manslaughter rather than murder, since it occurred in the heat of passion provoked by the homosexual assault.

The trial court instructed the jury that Maine law recognizes only two kinds of homicide, murder and manslaughter, and that these offenses are not subdivided into different degrees. The common elements of both are that the homicide be unlawful—i.e., neither justifiable nor excusable[1]—and that it be intentional.[2] The prosecution is required

---

1. As examples of justifiable or excusable homicides, the court mentioned a soldier in battle, a policeman in certain circumstances, and an individual acting in self-defense.

2. The court elaborated that an intentional homicide required the jury to find "either that the defendant intended death, or that he intended an act which was calculated and should have been understood by [a] person of reason to be one likely to do great bodily harm and that death resulted."

[*Editor's note:* Consider in this regard the following observation in *United States v. Paul*, 37 F.3d 496 (9th Cir.1994): "While most voluntary manslaughter cases involve intent to kill, it is possible that a defendant who killed unintentionally but recklessly with extreme disregard for human life may have acted in the heat of passion with adequate provocation. In such a case, the defendant would be guilty of voluntary manslaughter, not murder. Otherwise, a defendant who killed in the heat of passion with intent to kill would only be liable for voluntary manslaughter, whereas a defendant who killed in the heat of passion without intent to kill, but acted recklessly with extreme disregard for human life (e.g., shoots at victim to frighten, not kill), would still be liable for murder."]

to prove these elements by proof beyond a reasonable doubt, and only if they are so proved is the jury to consider the distinction between murder and manslaughter.

In view of the evidence the trial court drew particular attention to the difference between murder and manslaughter. After reading the statutory definitions of both offenses,[3] the court charged that "malice aforethought is an essential and indispensable element of the crime of murder," without which the homicide would be manslaughter. The jury was further instructed, however, that if the prosecution established that the homicide was both intentional and unlawful, malice aforethought was to be conclusively implied unless the defendant proved by a fair preponderance of the evidence that he acted in the heat of passion on sudden provocation.[4] The court emphasized that "malice aforethought and heat of passion on sudden provocation are inconsistent things," thus, by proving the latter the defendant would negate the former and reduce the homicide from murder to manslaughter. The court then concluded its charge with elaborate definitions of "heat of passion"[5] and "sudden provocation."[6] * * *

Respondent appealed to the Maine Supreme Judicial Court, arguing that he had been denied due process because he was required to negate the element of malice aforethought by proving that he had acted in the heat of passion on sudden provocation. * * *

The Maine Supreme Judicial Court rejected this contention, holding that in Maine murder and manslaughter are not distinct crimes but rather different degrees of the single generic offense of felonious homicide. * * * With respect to *Winship*, which was decided after respondent's trial,[8] the court noted that it did not anticipate the application of the *Winship* principle to a "reductive factor" such as the heat of passion on sudden provocation.

Respondent next successfully petitioned for a writ of habeas corpus in federal district court. The District Court ruled that * * * *Winship* requires the prosecution to prove malice aforethought beyond a reasonable doubt; it cannot rely on a presumption of implied malice which requires the defendant to prove that he acted in the heat of passion on sudden provocation.

3. The Maine murder statute, Me.Rev.Stat., Tit. 17, § 2651, provides:

"Whoever unlawfully kills a human being with malice aforethought, either express or implied, is guilty of murder and shall be punished by imprisonment for life."

The manslaughter statute, Tit. 17, § 2551, in relevant part provides:

"Whoever unlawfully kills a human being in the heat of passion, on sudden provocation, without express or implied malice aforethought * * * shall be punished by a fine of not more than $1,000 or by imprisonment for not more than 20 years * * *."

4. The trial court also explained the concept of express malice aforethought, which required a "premeditated design to kill" thereby manifesting "a general malignancy and disregard of human life which proceeds from a heart void of social duty and fatally bent on mischief." Despite this instruction, the court repeatedly made clear that express malice need not be established since malice would be implied unless the defendant proved that he acted in the heat of passion. Hence, the instruction on express malice appears to have been wholly unnecessary, as the Maine Supreme

Judicial Court subsequently held. *State v. Lafferty*, 309 A.2d 647 (1973).

5. "Heat of passion * * * means that at the time of the act the reason is disturbed or obscured by passion to an extent which might [make] ordinary men of fair, average disposition liable to act irrationally without due deliberation or reflection, and from passion rather than judgment."

6. "[H]eat of passion will not avail unless upon sudden provocation. Sudden means happening without previous notice or with very brief notice; coming unexpectedly, precipitated, or unlooked for * * *. It is not every provocation, it is not every rage of passion that will reduce a killing from murder to manslaughter. The provocation must be of such a character and so close upon the act of killing, that for a moment a person could be—that for a moment the defendant could be considered as not being the master of his own understanding."

8. The Maine court concluded that *Winship* should not be applied retroactively. We subsequently decided, however, that *Winship* should be given complete retroactive effect. *Ivan v. City of New York*, 407 U.S. 203, 92 S.Ct. 1951, 32 L.Ed.2d 659 (1972).

The Court of Appeals for the First Circuit affirmed, subscribing in general to the District Court's analysis and construction of Maine law. * * *

The Maine law of homicide, as it bears on this case, can be stated succinctly: Absent justification or excuse, all intentional or criminally reckless killings are felonious homicides. Felonious homicide is punished as murder—i.e., by life imprisonment—unless the defendant proves by a fair preponderance of the evidence that it was committed in the heat of passion on sudden provocation, in which case it is punished as manslaughter—i.e., by a fine not to exceed $1,000 or by imprisonment not to exceed 20 years. The issue is whether the Maine rule requiring the defendant to prove that he acted in the heat of passion on sudden provocation accords with due process.

Our analysis may be illuminated if this issue is placed in historical context.

At early common law only those homicides committed in the enforcement of justice were considered justifiable; all others were deemed unlawful and were punished by death. Gradually, however, the severity of the common-law punishment for homicide abated. Between the 13th and 16th centuries the class of justifiable homicides expanded to include, for example, accidental homicides and those committed in self-defense. Concurrently, the widespread use of capital punishment was ameliorated further by extension of the ecclesiastic jurisdiction. Almost any person able to read was eligible for "benefit of clergy," a procedural device that effected a transfer from the secular to the ecclesiastic jurisdiction. And under ecclesiastic law a person who committed an unlawful homicide was not executed; instead he received a one-year sentence, had his thumb branded and was required to forfeit his goods. At the turn of the 16th century, English rulers, concerned with the accretion of ecclesiastic jurisdiction at the expense of the secular, enacted a series of statutes eliminating the benefit of clergy in all cases of "murder of malice prepensed." Unlawful homicides that were committed without such malice were designated "manslaughter" and their perpetrators remained eligible for the benefit of clergy.

Even after ecclesiastic jurisdiction was eliminated for all secular offenses the distinction between murder and manslaughter persisted. It was said that "manslaughter (when voluntary)[14] arises from the sudden heat of passions, murder from the wickedness of the heart." 4 Blackstone's *Commentaries* 190. Malice aforethought was designated as the element that distinguished the two crimes, but it was recognized that such malice could be implied by law as well as proved by evidence. Absent proof that an unlawful homicide resulted from "sudden and sufficiently violent provocation," the homicide was "presumed to be malicious." Id., at 201. In view of this presumption, the early English authorities, relying on the case of *The King v. Onerby*, 92 Eng.Rep. 465 (KB 1727), held that once the prosecution proved that the accused had committed the homicide, it was "incumbent on the prisoner to make out * * * all * * * circumstances of justification, excuse or alleviation * * * to the satisfaction of the court and jury." 4 Blackstone's *Commentaries* 201. Thus, at common law the burden of proving heat of passion on sudden provocation appears to have rested on the defendant.

In this country the concept of malice aforethought took on two distinct meanings: in some jurisdictions it came to signify a substantive element of intent, requiring the prosecution to prove that the defendant intended to kill or to inflict great bodily harm; in other jurisdictions it remained a policy presumption, indicating only that absent proof to

---

14. Blackstone also referred to a class of homicides called involuntary manslaughter. Such homicides were committed by accident in the course of perpetrating another unlawful, although not felonious, act. 4 Black- stone's *Commentaries* 192–193. This offense, with some modification and elaboration, generally has been recognized in this country.

the contrary a homicide was presumed not to have occurred in the heat of passion.[17] In a landmark case, *Commonwealth v. York,* 9 Met. (50 Mass.) 93 (1845), Chief Justice Shaw of the Massachusetts Supreme Judicial Court held that the defendant was required to negate malice aforethought by proving by a preponderance of the evidence that he acted in the heat of passion. Initially, *York* was adopted in Maine as well as several other jurisdictions. In 1895, however, in the context of deciding a question of federal criminal procedure, this Court explicitly considered and unanimously rejected the general approach articulated in *York. Davis v. United States,* 160 U.S. 469, 16 S.Ct. 353, 40 L.Ed. 499.[21] And, in the past half century, the large majority of States have abandoned *York* and now require the prosecution to prove the absence of the heat of passion on sudden provocation beyond a reasonable doubt.

This historical review establishes two important points. First, the fact at issue here—the presence or absence of the heat of passion on sudden provocation—has been, almost from the inception of the common law of homicide, the single most important factor in determining the degree of culpability attaching to an unlawful homicide. And, second, the clear trend has been toward requiring the prosecution to bear the ultimate burden of proving this fact.

Petitioners, the warden of the Maine Prison and the State of Maine, argue that despite these considerations *Winship* should not be extended to the present case. They note that as a formal matter the absence of the heat of passion on sudden provocation is not a "fact necessary to constitute the *crime*" of felonious homicide in Maine. *In re Winship* (emphasis supplied). This distinction is relevant, according to petitioners, because in *Winship* the facts at issue were essential to establish criminality in the first instance whereas the fact in question here does not come into play until the jury already has determined that the defendant is guilty and may be punished at least for manslaughter. In this situation, petitioners maintain, the defendant's critical interests in liberty and reputation are no longer of paramount concern since, irrespective of the presence or absence of the heat of passion on sudden provocation, he is likely to lose his liberty and certain to be stigmatized.[23] In short, petitioners would limit *Winship* to those facts which, if not proved, would wholly exonerate the defendant.

This analysis fails to recognize that the criminal law of Maine, like that of other jurisdictions, is concerned not only with guilt or innocence in the abstract but also with the degree of criminal culpability. Maine has chosen to distinguish those who kill in the heat of passion from those who kill in the absence of this factor. Because the former are less "blameworth[y]," *State v. Lafferty,* 309 A.2d, at 671, 673 (concurring opinion), they are subject to substantially less severe penalties. By drawing this distinction, while refusing to

---

17. Several jurisdictions also divided murder into different degrees, typically limiting capital punishment to first-degree murder and requiring the prosecution to prove premeditation and deliberation in order to establish that offense.

21. In *Leland v. Oregon,* 343 U.S. 790, 72 S.Ct. 1002, 96 L.Ed. 1302 (1952), the Court declined to apply the specific holding of *Davis*—that the prosecution must prove sanity beyond a reasonable doubt—to the States.

23. Relying on *Williams v. New York,* 337 U.S. 241, 69 S.Ct. 1079, 93 L.Ed. 1337 (1949), and *McGautha v. California,* 402 U.S. 183, 196, 91 S.Ct. 1454, 1461, 28 L.Ed.2d 711 (1971), petitioners seek to buttress this contention by arguing that since the presence or absence of the heat of passion on sudden provocation

affects only the extent of punishment it should be considered a matter within the traditional discretion of the sentencing body and therefore not subject to rigorous due process demands. But cf. *United States v. Tucker,* 404 U.S. 443, 92 S.Ct. 589, 30 L.Ed.2d 592 (1972). There is no incompatibility between our decision today and the traditional discretion afforded sentencing bodies. Under Maine law the jury is given no discretion as to the sentence to be imposed on one found guilty of felonious homicide. If the defendant is found to be a murderer, a mandatory life sentence results. On the other hand, if the jury finds him guilty only of manslaughter it remains for the trial court in the exercise of *its* discretion to impose a sentence within the *statutorily defined* limits.

require the prosecution to establish beyond a reasonable doubt the fact upon which it turns, Maine denigrates the interests found critical in *Winship*.

The safeguards of due process are not rendered unavailing simply because a determination may already have been reached that would stigmatize the defendant and that might lead to a significant impairment of personal liberty. The fact remains that the consequences resulting from a verdict of murder, as compared with a verdict of manslaughter, differ significantly. Indeed, when viewed in terms of the potential difference in restrictions of personal liberty attendant to each conviction, the distinction established by Maine between murder and manslaughter may be of greater importance than the difference between guilt or innocence for many lesser crimes.

Moreover, if *Winship* were limited to those facts that constitute a crime as defined by state law, a State could undermine many of the interests that decision sought to protect without effecting any substantive change in its law. It would only be necessary to redefine the elements that comprise different crimes, characterizing them as factors that bear solely on the extent of punishment. An extreme example of this approach can be fashioned from the law challenged in this case. Maine divides the single generic offense of felonious homicide into three distinct punishment categories—murder, voluntary manslaughter, and involuntary manslaughter. Only the first two of these categories require that the homicidal act either be intentional or the result of criminally reckless conduct. But under Maine law these facts of intent are not general elements of the crime of felonious homicide. Instead, they bear only on the appropriate punishment category. Thus, if petitioners' argument were accepted, Maine could impose a life sentence for any felonious homicide—even those that traditionally might be considered involuntary manslaughter—unless the *defendant* was able to prove that his act was neither intentional nor criminally reckless.[24]

Winship is concerned with substance rather than this kind of formalism. * * *

In *Winship* the Court emphasized the societal interests in the reliability of jury verdicts:

> "The requirement of proof beyond a reasonable doubt has [a] vital role in our criminal procedure for cogent reasons. The accused during a criminal prosecution has at stake interests of immense importance, both because of the possibility that he may lose his liberty upon conviction and because of the certainty that he would be stigmatized by the conviction.

* * *

> "Moreover, use of the reasonable-doubt standard is indispensable to command the respect and confidence of the community in applications of the criminal law. It is critical that the moral force of the criminal law not be diluted by a standard of proof that leaves people in doubt whether innocent men are being condemned."

These interests are implicated to a greater degree in this case than they were in *Winship* itself. Petitioner there faced an 18–month sentence, with a maximum possible extension of an additional four and one-half years, whereas respondent here faces a differential in sentencing ranging from a nominal fine to a mandatory life sentence. Both the stigma to the defendant and the community's confidence in the administration of the criminal law are also of greater consequence in this case, since the adjudication of delinquency involved

---

24. Many States impose different statutory sentences on different degrees of assault. If *Winship* were limited to a State's definition of the elements of a crime, these States could define all assaults as a single offense and then require the defendant to disprove the elements of aggravation—*e.g.*, intent to kill or intent to rob. But see *State v. Ferris,* 249 A.2d 523 (Me.1969) (prosecution must prove elements of aggravation in criminal assault case by proof beyond a reasonable doubt).

in *Winship* was "benevolent" in intention, seeking to provide "a generously conceived program of compassionate treatment."

Not only are the interests underlying *Winship* implicated to a greater degree in this case, but in one respect the protection afforded those interests is less here. In *Winship* the ultimate burden of persuasion remained with the prosecution, although the standard had been reduced to proof by a fair preponderance of the evidence. In this case, by contrast, the State has affirmatively shifted the burden of proof to the defendant. The result, in a case such as this one where the defendant is required to prove the critical fact in dispute, is to increase further the likelihood of an erroneous murder conviction. Such a result directly contravenes the principle articulated in *Speiser v. Randall,* 357 U.S. 513, 525–526, 78 S.Ct. 1332, 1342, 2 L.Ed.2d 1460 (1958):

> "[W]here one party has at stake an interest of transcending value—as a criminal defendant his liberty—th[e] margin of error is reduced as to him by the process of placing on the [prosecution] the burden * * * of persuading the factfinder at the conclusion of the trial * * *."

It has been suggested that because of the difficulties in negating an argument that the homicide was committed in the heat of passion the burden of proving this fact should rest on the defendant. No doubt this is often a heavy burden for the prosecution to satisfy. The same may be said of the requirement of proof beyond a reasonable doubt of many controverted facts in a criminal trial. But this is the traditional burden which our system of criminal justice deems essential.

Indeed, the Maine Supreme Judicial Court itself acknowledged that most States require the prosecution to prove the absence of passion beyond a reasonable doubt.[28] Moreover, the difficulty of meeting such an exacting burden is mitigated in Maine where the fact at issue is largely an "objective, rather than a subjective, behavioral criterion." In this respect, proving that the defendant did not act in the heat of passion on sudden provocation is similar to proving any other element of intent; it may be established by adducing evidence of the factual circumstances surrounding the commission of the homicide. And although intent is typically considered a fact peculiarly within the knowledge of the defendant, this does not, as the Court has long recognized, justify shifting the burden to him.

Nor is the requirement of proving a negative unique in our system of criminal jurisprudence. Maine itself requires the prosecution to prove the absence of self-defense beyond a reasonable doubt. See *State v. Millett,* 273 A.2d 504 (1971).[30] Satisfying this burden imposes an obligation that, in all practical effect, is identical to the burden involved in negating the heat of passion on sudden provocation. Thus, we discern no unique hardship on the prosecution that would justify requiring the defendant to carry the burden of proving a fact so critical to criminal culpability.[31]

---

28. Many States do require the defendant to show that there is "some evidence" indicating that he acted in the heat of passion before requiring the prosecution to negate this element by proving the absence of passion beyond a reasonable doubt. Nothing in this opinion is intended to affect that requirement.

30. In *Millett* the Maine Supreme Judicial Court adopted the "majority rule" regarding proof of self-defense. The burden of producing "some evidence" on this issue rests with the defendant, but the ultimate burden of persuasion by proof beyond a reasonable doubt remains on the prosecution.

31. This conclusion is supported by consideration of a related line of cases. Generally in a criminal case the prosecution bears both the production burden and the persuasion burden. In some instances, however, it is aided by a presumption, see *Davis v. United States,* 160 U.S. 469, 16 S.Ct. 353, 40 L.Ed. 499 (1895) (presumption of sanity), or a permissible inference, see *United States v. Gainey,* 380 U.S. 63, 85 S.Ct. 754, 13 L.Ed.2d 658 (1965) (inference of knowledge from presence at an illegal still). These procedural devices require (in the case of a presumption) or permit (in the case of an inference) the trier of fact to conclude that the prosecution has met its burden of proof with respect to the

Maine law requires a defendant to establish by a preponderance of the evidence that he acted in the heat of passion on sudden provocation in order to reduce murder to manslaughter. Under this burden of proof a defendant can be given a life sentence when the evidence indicates that it is *as likely as not* that he deserves a significantly lesser sentence. This is an intolerable result in a society where, to paraphrase Mr. Justice Harlan, it is far worse to sentence one guilty only of manslaughter as a murderer than to sentence a murderer for the lesser crime of manslaughter. We therefore hold that the Due Process Clause requires the prosecution to prove beyond a reasonable doubt the absence of the heat of passion on sudden provocation when the issue is properly presented in a homicide case. Accordingly, the judgment below is affirmed.

Affirmed.

MR. JUSTICE REHNQUIST, with whom THE CHIEF JUSTICE joins, concurring. * * *

I agree with the Court that *In re Winship* does require that the prosecution prove beyond a reasonable doubt every element which constitutes the crime charged against a defendant. I see no inconsistency between that holding and the holding of *Leland v. Oregon,* 343 U.S. 790, 72 S.Ct. 1002, 96 L.Ed. 1302 (1952). In the latter case this Court held that there was no constitutional requirement that the State shoulder the burden of proving the sanity of the defendant.

The Court noted in *Leland* that the issue of insanity as a defense to a criminal charge was considered by the jury only after it had found that all elements of the offense, including the *mens rea* if any required by state law, had been proven beyond a reasonable doubt. Although as the state court's instructions in *Leland* recognized, evidence relevant to insanity as defined by state law may also be relevant to whether the required *mens rea* was present, the existence or nonexistence of legal insanity bears no necessary relationship to the existence or nonexistence of the required mental elements of the crime. For this reason, Oregon's placement of the burden of proof on insanity on Leland, unlike Maine's redefinition of homicide in the instant case, did not effect an unconstitutional shift in the State's traditional burden of proof beyond a reasonable doubt of all necessary elements of the offense. Both the Court's opinion and the concurring opinion of Mr. Justice Harlan in *In re Winship,* supra, stress the importance of proof beyond a reasonable doubt in a criminal case as "bottomed on a fundamental value determination of our society that it is far worse to convict an innocent man than to let a guilty man go free." Having once met that rigorous burden of proof that, for example, in a case such as this, the defendant not only killed a fellow human being, but did it with malice aforethought, the State could quite consistently with such a constitutional principle conclude that a defendant who sought to establish the defense of insanity, and thereby escape any punishment whatever for a heinous crime, should bear the laboring oar on such an issue.

PATTERSON v. NEW YORK

Supreme Court of the United States, 1977.
432 U.S. 197, 97 S.Ct. 2319, 53 L.Ed.2d 281.

MR. JUSTICE WHITE delivered the opinion of the Court. * * *

Patterson was charged with second-degree murder. In New York there are two elements of this crime: (1) "intent to cause the death of another person"; and (2)

presumed or inferred fact by having satisfactorily established other facts. Thus, in effect they require the defendant to present some evidence contesting the otherwise presumed or inferred fact. See *Barnes v. United States,* 412 U.S. 837, 846 n. 11, 93 S.Ct. 2357, 2363, 37 L.Ed.2d 380 (1973). Since they shift the production burden to the defendant, these devices must satisfy certain due process requirements. See e.g.,

Barnes v. United States, supra; *Turner v. United States,* 396 U.S. 398, 90 S.Ct. 642, 24 L.Ed.2d 610 (1970).

In each of these cases, however, the ultimate burden of persuasion by proof beyond a reasonable doubt remained on the prosecution. See, e.g., *Barnes v. United States, Davis v. United States.* Shifting the burden of persuasion to the defendant obviously places an even greater strain upon him since he no longer need only present some evidence with respect to the fact at issue;

"caus[ing] the death of such person or of a third person." Malice aforethought is not an element of the crime. In addition, the State permits a person accused of murder to raise an affirmative defense that he "acted under the influence of extreme emotional disturbance for which there was a reasonable explanation or excuse."

New York also recognizes the crime of manslaughter. A person is guilty of manslaughter if he intentionally kills another person "under circumstances which do not constitute murder because he acts under the influence of extreme emotional disturbance." Appellant confessed before trial to killing Northrup, but at trial he raised the defense of extreme emotional disturbance.

The jury was instructed as to the elements of the crime of murder. * * * The jury was further instructed, consistently with New York law, that the defendant had the burden of proving his affirmative defense by a preponderance of the evidence. The jury was told that if it found beyond a reasonable doubt that appellant had intentionally killed Northrup but that appellant had demonstrated by a preponderance of the evidence that he had acted under the influence of extreme emotional disturbance, it must find appellant guilty of manslaughter instead of murder.

The jury found appellant guilty of murder. * * *

In convicting Patterson under its murder statute, New York did no more than *Leland* and *Rivera*[a] permitted it to do without violating the Due Process Clause. Under those cases, once the facts constituting a crime are established beyond reasonable doubt, based on all the evidence including the evidence of the defendant's mental state, the State may refuse to sustain the affirmative defense of insanity unless demonstrated by a preponderance of the evidence.

The New York law on extreme emotional disturbance follows this pattern. This affirmative defense, which the Court of Appeals described as permitting "the defendant to show that his actions were caused by a mental infirmity not rising to the level of insanity, and that he is less culpable for having committed them," does not serve to negative any facts of the crime which the State is to prove in order to convict for murder. It constitutes a separate issue on which the defendant is required to carry the burden of persuasion; and unless we are to overturn *Leland* and *Rivera*, New York has not violated the Due Process Clause, and Patterson's conviction must be sustained.

We are unwilling to reconsider *Leland* and *Rivera*. But even if we were to hold that a State must prove sanity to convict once that fact is put in issue, it would not necessarily follow that a State must prove beyond a reasonable doubt every fact, the existence or nonexistence of which it is willing to recognize as an exculpatory or mitigating circumstance affecting the degree of culpability or the severity of the punishment. Here, in revising its criminal code, New York provided the affirmative defense of extreme emotional disturbance, a substantially expanded version of the older heat of passion concept; but it was willing to do so only if the facts making out the defense were established by the defendant with sufficient certainty. The State was itself unwilling to undertake to establish the absence of those facts beyond reasonable doubt, perhaps fearing that proof would be too difficult and that too many persons deserving treatment as murderers would escape that punishment if the evidence need merely raise a reasonable doubt about the defen-

---

he must affirmatively establish that fact. Accordingly, the Due Process Clause demands more exacting standards before the State may require a defendant to bear

this ultimate burden of persuasion.

 a. *Rivera* is discussed at p. 420 of this Book.

dant's emotional state. It has been said that the new criminal code of New York contains some 25 affirmative defenses which exculpate or mitigate but which must be established by the defendant to be operative. The Due Process Clause, as we see it, does not put New York to the choice of abandoning those defenses or undertaking to disprove their existence in order to convict for a crime which otherwise is within its constitutional powers to sanction by substantial punishment. * * *

[I]n each instance of a murder conviction under the present law, New York will have proved beyond reasonable doubt that the defendant has intentionally killed another person, an act which it is not disputed the State may constitutionally criminalize and punish. If the State nevertheless chooses to recognize a factor that mitigates the degree of criminality or punishment, we think the State may assure itself that the fact has been established with reasonable certainty. To recognize at all a mitigating circumstance does not require the State to prove its nonexistence in each case in which the fact is put in issue, if in its judgment this would be too cumbersome, too expensive, and too inaccurate.[11]

We thus decline to adopt as a constitutional imperative, operative country-wide, that a State must disprove beyond reasonable doubt every fact constituting any and all affirmative defenses related to the culpability of an accused. Traditionally, due process has required that only the most basic procedural safeguards be observed; more subtle balancing of society's interests against those of the accused have been left to the legislative branch. We therefore will not disturb the balance struck in previous cases holding that the Due Process Clause requires the prosecution to prove beyond reasonable doubt all of the elements included in the definition of the offense of which the defendant is charged. Proof of the nonexistence of all affirmative defenses has never been constitutionally required; and we perceive no reason to fashion such a rule in this case and apply it to the statutory defense at issue here.

This view may seem to permit state legislatures to reallocate burdens of proof by labeling as affirmative defenses at least some elements of the crimes now defined in their statutes. But there are obviously constitutional limits beyond which the States may not go in this regard. "[I]t is not within the province of a legislature to declare an individual guilty or presumptively guilty of a crime." The legislature cannot "validly command that the finding of an indictment, or mere proof of the identity of the accused, should create a presumption of the existence of all the facts essential to guilt." * * *

It is urged that *Mullaney v. Wilbur* necessarily invalidates Patterson's conviction. * * *

Mullaney's holding, it is argued, is that the State may not permit the blameworthiness of an act or the severity of punishment authorized for its commission to depend on the presence or absence of an identified fact without assuming the burden of proving the presence or absence of that fact, as the case may be, beyond reasonable doubt. In our view, the *Mullaney* holding should not be so broadly read. The concurrence of two Justices in *Mullaney* was necessarily contrary to such a reading; and a majority of the Court refused to

---

11. The drafters of the Model Penal Code would, as a matter of policy, place the burden of proving the nonexistence of most affirmative defenses, including the defense involved in this case, on the prosecution once the defendant has come forward with some evidence that the defense is present. The drafters recognize the need for flexibility, however, and would, in "some exceptional situations," place the burden of persuasion on the accused.

"Characteristically these are situations where the defense does not obtain at all under existing law and the Code seeks to introduce a mitigation. Resistance to the mitigation, based upon the prosecution's difficulty in obtaining evidence, ought to be lowered if the burden of persuasion is imposed on the defendant. Where that difficulty appears genuine and there is something to be said against allowing the defense at all, we consider it defensible to shift the burden in this way." ALI, Model Penal Code § 1.13, Comment, p. 113 (Tentative Draft No. 4, 1955). * * *

so understand and apply *Mullaney* when *Rivera* was dismissed for want of a substantial federal question.

Mullaney surely held that a State must prove every ingredient of an offense beyond a reasonable doubt, and that it may not shift the burden of proof to the defendant by presuming that ingredient upon proof of the other elements of the offense. This is true even though the State's practice, as in Maine, had been traditionally to the contrary. Such shifting of the burden of persuasion with respect to a fact which the State deems so important that it must be either proved or presumed is impermissible under the Due Process Clause.

It was unnecessary to go further in *Mullaney*. The Maine Supreme Court made it clear that malice aforethought, which was mentioned in the statutory definition of the crime, was not equivalent to premeditation and that the presumption of malice traditionally arising in intentional homicide cases carried no factual meaning insofar as premeditation was concerned. Even so, a killing became murder in Maine when it resulted from a deliberate, cruel act committed by one person against another, "suddenly, and without any, or without considerable, provocation." Premeditation was not within the definition of murder; but malice, in the sense of the absence of provocation, was part of the definition of that crime. Yet malice, i.e., lack of provocation, was presumed and could be rebutted by the defendant only by proving by a preponderance of the evidence that he acted with heat of passion upon sudden provocation. In *Mullaney* we held that however traditional this mode of proceeding might have been, it is contrary to the Due Process Clause as construed in *Winship*.

As we have explained, nothing was presumed or implied against Patterson; and his conviction is not invalid under any of our prior cases. The judgment of the New York Court of Appeals is

Affirmed.

Mr. Justice Powell, with whom Mr. Justice Brennan and Mr. Justice Marshall join, dissenting. * * *

[The majority's] explanation of the *Mullaney* holding bears little resemblance to the basic rationale of that decision. But this is not the cause of greatest concern. The test the Court today establishes allows a legislature to shift, virtually at will, the burden of persuasion with respect to any factor in a criminal case, so long as it is careful not to mention the nonexistence of that factor in the statutory language that defines the crime. The sole requirement is that any references to the factor be confined to those sections that provide for an affirmative defense. * * *

With all respect, this type of constitutional adjudication is indefensibly formalistic. A limited but significant check on possible abuses in the criminal law now becomes an exercise in arid formalities. What [*In re Winship*, 397 U.S. 358, 90 S.Ct. 1068, 25 L.Ed.2d 368 (1970),] and *Mullaney* had sought to teach about the limits a free society places on its procedures to safeguard the liberty of its citizens becomes a rather simplistic lesson in statutory draftsmanship. Nothing in the Court's opinion prevents a legislature from applying this new learning to many of the classical elements of the crimes it punishes.[8] It

---

8. For example, a state statute could pass muster under the only solid standard that appears in the Court's opinion if it defined murder as mere physical contact between the defendant and the victim leading to the victim's death, but then set up an affirmative defense leaving it to the defendant to prove that he acted without culpable *mens rea*. The State, in other words, could be relieved altogether of responsibility for proving *anything* regarding the defendant's state of mind, provided only that the face of the statute meets the Court's drafting formulas.

To be sure, it is unlikely that legislatures will rewrite their criminal laws in this extreme form. The Court would be preferable, if the Court has found reason to reject the rationale of *Winship* and *Mullaney,* simply and straightforwardly to overrule those precedents.

The Court understandably manifests some uneasiness that its formalistic approach will give legislatures too much latitude in shifting the burden of persuasion. And so it issues a warning that "there are obviously constitutional limits beyond which the States may not go in this regard." The Court thereby concedes that legislative abuses may occur and that they must be curbed by the judicial branch. But if the State is careful to conform to the drafting formulas articulated today, the constitutional limits are anything but "obvious." This decision simply leaves us without a conceptual framework for distinguishing abuses from legitimate legislative adjustments of the burden of persuasion in criminal cases.

It is unnecessary for the Court to retreat to a formalistic test for applying *Winship.* Careful attention to the *Mullaney* decision reveals the principles that should control in this and like cases. *Winship* held that the prosecution must bear the burden of proving beyond a reasonable doubt "the existence of every fact necessary to constitute the crime charged." In *Mullaney* we concluded that heat of passion was one of the "facts" described in *Winship*—that is, a factor as to which the prosecution must bear the burden of persuasion beyond a reasonable doubt. We reached that result only after making two careful inquiries. First, we noted that the presence or absence of heat of passion made a substantial difference in punishment of the offender and in the stigma associated with the conviction. Second, we reviewed the history, in England and this country, of the factor at issue. Central to the holding in *Mullaney* was our conclusion that heat of passion "has been, almost from the inception of the common law of homicide, the single most important factor in determining the degree of culpability attaching to an unlawful homicide."

Implicit in these two inquiries are the principles that should govern this case. The Due Process Clause requires that the prosecutor bear the burden of persuasion beyond a reasonable doubt only if the factor at issue makes a substantial difference in punishment and stigma. The requirement of course applies *a fortiori* if the factor makes the difference between guilt and innocence. But a substantial difference in punishment alone is not enough. It also must be shown that in the Anglo–American legal tradition the factor in question historically has held that level of importance. If either branch of the test is not met, then the legislature retains its traditional authority over matters of proof. But to permit a shift in the burden of persuasion when both branches of this test are satisfied would invite the undermining of the presumption of innocence, "that bedrock 'axiomatic and elementary' principle whose 'enforcement lies at the foundation of the administration of our criminal law.'"

I hardly need add that New York's provisions allocating the burden of persuasion as to "extreme emotional disturbance" are unconstitutional when judged by these standards. "Extreme emotional disturbance" is, as the Court of Appeals recognized, the direct descendant of the "heat of passion" factor considered at length in *Mullaney.* I recognize, of course, that the differences between Maine and New York law are not unimportant to the defendant; there is a somewhat broader opportunity for mitigation. But none of those distinctions is relevant here. The presence or absence of extreme emotional disturbance makes a critical difference in punishment and stigma, and throughout our history the

seems to think this likelihood of restraint is an added reason for limiting review largely to formalistic examination. But it is completely foreign to this Court's responsibility for constitutional adjudication to limit the scope of judicial review because of the expectation—however reasonable—that legislative bodies will exercise appropriate restraint.

resolution of this issue of fact, although expressed in somewhat different terms, has distinguished manslaughter from murder. * * *

The *Winship/Mullaney* test identifies those factors of such importance, historically, in determining punishment and stigma that the Constitution forbids shifting to the defendant the burden of persuasion when such a factor is at issue. *Winship* and *Mullaney* specify only the procedure that is required when a State elects to use such a factor as part of its substantive criminal law. They do not say that the State must elect to use it. For example, where a State has chosen to retain the traditional distinction between murder and manslaughter, as have New York and Maine, the burden of persuasion must remain on the prosecution with respect to the distinguishing factor, in view of its decisive historical importance. But nothing in *Mullaney* or *Winship* precludes a State from abolishing the distinction between murder and manslaughter and treating all unjustifiable homicide as murder. In this significant respect, neither *Winship* nor *Mullaney* eliminates the substantive flexibility that should remain in legislative hands.

Moreover, it is unlikely that more than a few factors—although important ones—for which a shift in the burden of persuasion seriously would be considered will come within the *Mullaney* holding. With some exceptions, then, the State has the authority "to recognize a factor that mitigates the degree of criminality or punishment" without having "to prove its nonexistence in each case in which the fact is put in issue". New ameliorative affirmative defenses,[14] about which the Court expresses concern, generally remain undisturbed by the holdings in *Winship* and *Mullaney*—and need not be disturbed by a sound holding reversing Patterson's conviction.

Furthermore, as we indicated in *Mullaney,* even as to those factors upon which the prosecution must bear the burden of persuasion, the State retains an important procedural device to avoid jury confusion and prevent the prosecution from being unduly hampered. The State normally may shift to the defendant the burden of production, that is, the burden of going forward with sufficient evidence "to justify [a reasonable] doubt upon the issue." If the defendant's evidence does not cross this threshold, the issue—be it malice, extreme emotional disturbance, self-defense, or whatever—will not be submitted to the jury. * * *

PEOPLE v. WASHINGTON

Court of Appeals, Second District, 1976.
58 Cal.App.3d 620, 130 Cal.Rptr. 96.

ALLPORT, ASSOCIATE JUSTICE.

Following trial by jury defendant was convicted of murder in violation of Penal Code section 187, which was found to be in the second degree. The allegation of use of a firearm was found to be true. He was sentenced to state prison and now appeals from the judgment.

In view of the contentions made on appeal a plenary statement of the facts surrounding this sordid affair is not necessary. Suffice to say that the victim Owen Wilson Brady

---

14. Numerous examples of such defenses are available: New York subjects an armed robber to lesser punishment than he would otherwise receive if he proves by a preponderance of the evidence that the gun he used was unloaded or inoperative. A number of States have ameliorated the usual operation of statutes punishing statutory rape, recognizing a defense if the defendant shows that he reasonably believed his partner was of age. Formerly the age of the minor was a strict liability element of the crime. The Model Penal Code also employs such a shift in the burden of persuasion for a limited number of defenses. For example, a corporation can escape conviction of an offense if it proves by a preponderance of the evidence that the responsible supervising officer exercised due diligence to prevent the commission of the offense. § 2.07(5) (Proposed Official Draft 1962).

met his death when shot by his homosexual partner Merle Francis Washington on August 10, 1974, while the two were riding in the victim's car. The killing resulted from a lover's quarrel, claimed to have been provoked by unfaithfulness on the part of the victim and his expressed desire to terminate the relationship.

It is contended on appeal that because of instructional error and inadequacy of defense trial counsel, the conviction should either be reversed or reduced to voluntary manslaughter by this court. * * *

It is next suggested that, in defining "heat of passion" necessary to reduce murder to manslaughter in a case involving a homosexual, it is error to use the standard of "an ordinarily reasonable person of average disposition" but rather should be tested by a standard applicable to a female or to the average servient homosexual.

In this respect the jury was instructed that to reduce the homicide from murder to manslaughter upon the ground of sudden quarrel or heat of passion, the conduct must be tested by the ordinarily reasonable man test. Defendant argues without precedent that to so instruct was error because, "Homosexuals are not at present a curiosity or a rare commodity. They are a distinct third sexual class between that of male and female, are present in almost every field of endeavor, and are fast achieving a guarded recognition not formerly accorded them. The heat of their passions in dealing with one another should not be tested by standards applicable to the average man or the average woman, since they are aberrant hybrids, with an obvious diminished capacity.

"Defendant submits that since the evidence disclosed that he was acting as a servient homosexual during the period of his relationship with the victim, that his heat of passion should have been tested, either by a standard applicable to a female, or a standard applicable to the average homosexual, and that it was prejudicial error to instruct the jury to determine his heat of passion defense by standards applicable to the average male." We do not agree. In *People v. Bridgehouse,* 47 Cal.2d 406, 413, 303 P.2d 1018, 1022, it was said:

> "To be sufficient to reduce a homicide to manslaughter, the heat of passion must be such as would naturally be aroused in the mind of an ordinary, reasonable person, under the given facts and circumstances, or in the mind of a person of ordinary self-control."

In *People v. Morse,* 70 Cal.2d 711, 734–735, 76 Cal.Rptr. 391, 405, 452 P.2d 607, 613, the test announced in *Bridgehouse,* supra, was applied, the court saying in addition that "the evidence of defendant's extraordinary character and environmental deficiencies was manifestly irrelevant to the inquiry." In *People v. Logan,* 175 Cal. 45, 48–49, 164 P. 1121, 1122, the applicable test is clearly stated where the court said:

> "In the present condition of our law it is left to the jurors to say whether or not the facts and circumstances in evidence are sufficient to lead them to believe that the defendant did, or to create a reasonable doubt in their minds as to whether or not he did, commit his offense under a heat of passion. The jury is further to be admonished and advised by the court that this heat of passion must be such a passion as would naturally be aroused in the mind of an ordinarily reasonable person under the given facts and circumstances, and that, consequently, no defendant may set up his own standard of conduct and justify or excuse himself because in fact his passions were aroused, unless further the jury believe that the facts and circumstances were sufficient to arouse the passions of the ordinarily reasonable man. Thus no man of extremely violent passion could so justify or excuse himself if the exciting cause be not adequate, nor could an excessively cowardly man justify himself unless the circum-

stances were such as to arouse the fears of the ordinarily courageous man. Still further, while the conduct of the defendant is to be measured by that of the ordinarily reasonable man placed in identical circumstances, the jury is properly to be told that the exciting cause must be such as would naturally tend to arouse the passion of the ordinarily reasonable man."

In the instant case the jury was properly instructed to use the ordinarily reasonable man test. * * *

The judgment is affirmed.

Notes and Questions

1. In *Bedder v. Director of Public Prosecutions*, [1954] 1 W.L.R. 1119, [1954] 2 All E.R. 801, the House of Lords dismissed the appeal of an 18–year–old youth who was convicted of murdering a prostitute. The facts, as set out by Lord Simonds, are: "The appellant has the misfortune to be sexually impotent, a fact which he naturally well knew and, according to his own evidence, had allowed to prey upon his mind. On the night of the crime he saw the prostitute with another man and when they had parted went and spoke to her and was led by her to a quiet court off a street in Leicester. There he attempted in vain to have intercourse with her, whereupon—and I summarise the evidence in the way most favourable to him—she jeered at him and attempted to get away. He tried still to hold her, and then she slapped him in the face and punched him in the stomach: he grabbed her shoulders and pushed her back from him whereas (I use his words), 'She kicked me in the privates. Whether it was her knee or foot, I do not know. After that I do not know what happened till she fell.' She fell, because he had taken a knife from his pocket and stabbed her with it twice, the second blow inflicting a mortal injury."

The House concluded the Court of Criminal Appeal was correct in ruling that the trial judge had properly instructed that the provocation must be sufficient to cause a "reasonable person * * * to lose his self-control" and that "an unusually excitable or pugnacious individual, or a drunken one or a man who is sexually impotent is not entitled to rely on provocation which would not have led an ordinary person to have acted in the way which was in fact carried out." Stated Lord Simonds:

"I am at a loss to know what other direction than that which he gave could properly have been given by the learned judge to the jury in the present case. The argument, as I understood it, for the appellant was that the jury, in considering the reaction of the hypothetical reasonable man to the acts of provocation, must not only place him in the circumstances in which the accused was placed but must also invest him with the personal physical peculiarities of the accused. Learned counsel, who argued the case for the appellant with great ability, did not, I think, venture to say that he should be invested with mental or temperamental qualities which distinguished him from the reasonable man * * *. But he urged that the reasonable man should be invested with the peculiar physical qualities of the accused, as in the present case with the characteristic of impotence, and the question should be asked what would be the reaction of the impotent reasonable man in the circumstances? For that proposition I know of no authority nor can I see any reason in it. It would be plainly illogical not to recognize an unusually excitable or pugnacious temperament in the accused as a matter to be taken into account but yet to recognize for that purpose some unusual physical characteristic, be it impotence or another. Moreover, the proposed distinction appears to me to ignore the fundamental fact that the temper of a man which leads him to react in such and such a way to provocation, is or may be itself conditioned by some physical defect. It is too subtle a refinement for my mind or, I think, for that of a jury to grasp that the temper may be ignored but the physical defect taken into account.

"It was urged upon your Lordships that the hypothetical reasonable man must be confronted with all the same circumstances as the accused and that this could not be fairly done unless he was also invested with the peculiar characteristics of the accused. But this makes nonsense of the test. Its purpose is to invite the jury to consider the act of the accused by reference to a certain standard or norm of conduct and with this object the 'reasonable' or the 'average' or the 'normal' man is invoked. If the reasonable man is then deprived in whole or in part of his reason or the normal man endowed with abnormal characteristics, the test ceases to have any value."

2. In *R. v. Raney*, 29 Crim.App. 14 (1942), the court reduced defendant's murder conviction to manslaughter, saying: "To a one-legged man like the appellant, who is dependent on his crutches, it is obvious that a blow to a crutch, whether it is a blow that knocks the crutch away or not, is something very different from mere words. It seems to us that, if the Judge had repeated that part of the appellant's evidence, it would have been very proper to do so, because a blow to a one-legged man's crutch might well be regarded by a jury as an act of provocation." Peter English, *What Did Section Three do to the Law of Provocation?*, [1970] Crim.L.Rev. 249, 254, concludes that *Raney* cannot be squared with *Bedder*. Is this so?

3. Alec Samuels, *Excusable Loss of Self–Control in Homicide*, 34 Mod.L.Rev. 163, 166, 170–71 (1971): "Each man has a different level of tolerance, or threshold of uncontrollable anger, in respect of each and every given situation.[a] An assault, a sexual overture, a family or personal insult, a racial discrimination, a moral aspersion, cruelty to a child, or anything imaginable, will at a certain level of intensity break self-control. Each 'provocative' item will break that self-control at a different point on the graph of provocation set against loss of control. But [the reasonable man test] suggests that the direction of the line on the graph is the same for all persons, that although the threshold of uncontrollable anger differs according to the provocation it does not differ in respect of each different person. The fallacy is to deny that one average man may be impervious to moral aspersions but instantly enraged by a sexual overture and another average man may be impervious to a sexual overture but instantly enraged by a moral aspersion. Who is the average man here? The first man would be open to condemnation if in fact he unexpectedly lost control in the face of a moral aspersion, the second in the face of a sexual overture. Neither should be open to condemnation in the converse case.

" * * * There is a lot to be said for the judge not attempting to describe the reasonable man but simply leaving the issue to the jury, provided that there is some evidence of loss of self-control. The jury might then take account of the virility or size or colour or psychological make-up of the accused and ask themselves what would be the effect of this provocation upon a person having these physical or mental characteristics but having that degree of

---

a. Consider Peter Brett, *The Physiology of Provocation*, [1970] Crim.L.Rev. 634, 637–38: "The degree of response to a stress situation varies considerably from one individual to another. Some men are highly vulnerable to stress, others are strikingly resistant to it. This fact has been demonstrated both by clinical observation and by experiment though it is as yet unknown why these differences should occur. It seems likely, however, that a number of factors, some genetic, others environmental, combine to produce the differences of susceptibility and response.

"It would be perverse for the law to ignore these teachings of science, and absurd for it to doubt their validity. But if we pay attention to them, it at once becomes clear that the reasonable man of provocation law is a figment of the imagination.

"Plainly we cannot sensibly talk of the ordinary man in any meaningful way. There is a whole range of types of men, and it would be pointless and cruel to penalise a particular man merely because his type occurs nearer to one or other end of the range than to the centre of it."

self-control that can properly be expected from that person. The inscrutability of the jury verdict would then remove the matter from the ambit of the law. * * *

"Provocation as a head of manslaughter could be abolished and replaced with the offence of criminal loss of self-control causing the death of another person, sentence being for culpable failure to exercise self-control. Proposed new statutory offence:

"If the jury are satisfied that the accused lost his self-control so as to form the intent to kill [or to cause grievous bodily harm] and so caused the death of the deceased they shall return a verdict of criminal [culpable] killing [manslaughter] if, having regard to all the circumstances, including in particular the standard of self-control properly to be expected of the accused, they are satisfied that the act was to some degree excusable."

4. Consider the comments of Wilkie, J., concurring in *State v. Hoyt*, 21 Wis.2d 284, 128 N.W.2d 645 (1964):

"The majority would retain the 'ordinarily-constituted man' or the 'reasonable man' test of provocation. Yet critical issues in the administration of even this test remain unanswered. The 'reasonable man' concept in the law generally has two distinct meanings. There is the statistical concept under which the reasonable man does what most people do in fact under the circumstances. Yet if this is the meaning of the test, it is clear that as a matter of fact a great majority of people will never commit murder no matter how violently provoked by another. A consistent application of this test, viewing the reasonable man as the statistical *factual* norm would, in effect, read [the manslaughter statute] out of existence.

"However, in other contexts, there is the ethical concept under which the reasonable man functions as the person the law *expects* everyone to be, regardless of whether a majority, in fact, fall short of the *moral* norm in actual conduct. To take this view of the reasonable man for the purposes of the provocation test would propel courts and juries into the strange task of deciding when a person, taken as the ethical ideal, would commit murder. This may well result in reading [the manslaughter statute] out of existence. The person we *expect* people to be like would not likely solve his problems by murder. If we conclude that an ethical ideal—that person whom all others aspire to emulate—would be driven to kill under the circumstances of a given case, logically the verdict should be not guilty, nor morally blameworthy to any degree. Again, manslaughter, as conduct less blameworthy than non-provoked intentional killing but not guiltless, is practically eliminated from the code.

"This analysis brings me to the heart of my disagreement with the majority. The objective, the 'ordinarily-constituted man' or the 'reasonable man' test leads juries and courts into inquiries which are not relevant to the issue at hand. In assessing the manslaughter defense to a charge of a more serious homicide, we are not concerned with how most people would act under the circumstances of the case, nor are we concerned with what the defendant 'ought' to have done comparing him with the morally ideal response under the circumstances. * * * The manslaughter defense assumes that the defendant is morally blameworthy to some degree. The basic question is whether he is as culpable as a person who kills solely for self-aggrandizement or out of sheer malevolence. To answer this question, we must place ourselves empathetically in the actual situation in which the defendant was placed, a situation which may be relatively unique. Therefore, an inquiry into what *most* people would do in such circumstances cannot be completely determinative of the issue. The test cannot be wholly objective or wholly subjective. A person may become filled with murderous hate for another which can be discharged only by acting out the feeling and killing that person. The victim's conduct, in relation to the defendant, from the point of view of most people, may have been neutral if not benign. The sheer intensity of the defendant's hostile feeling cannot alone justify the manslaughter verdict. The victim's conduct must be such that we conclude that the feeling and conduct of the defendant can be understood sympathetically, albeit not condoned. The trier-of-fact must be able to say, 'although I would have acted differently, and I believe most persons would have acted differently, I can understand why this person gave way to the impulse to kill. He is different from the person who kills for personal gain alone.'

"To come to this judgment, the trier-of-fact must focus upon the defendant's total life experience in relation to the victim, and attempt to understand, in emotional as well as cognitive terms, the defendant's feelings toward the victim. Under the wholly objective test, the defendant's state of mind immediately before the act of homicide, and the victim's conduct at this precise moment, are the crucial objects of inquiry. Although the majority notes that the prior experience of the defendant and victim in relation to one another is relevant to the state of mind of the defendant at the moment of the homicide, the objective test shifts the focus of inquiry in a manner which is misleading. The total life experience of the defendant in relation to the victim determines the justification of the lesser verdict. As the majority notes, the act of homicide may be the culmination of a pattern of pressures of long duration. That the defendant may have been less angry with the victim at the moment of murder than at some time in the past (when he checked the impulse to kill) is irrelevant, if the trier-of-fact can conclude that, given the total experience of the defendant with the victim, the act of violence can be understood in terms which lessen the defendant's blameworthiness.

"The instances in which the issue of manslaughter or a more serious offense is sharply posed, are relatively predictable. Outside of murder for personal gain or murder by organized criminals, most homicides involve one family member killing another, against a background of personal insult, humiliation, and bullying, such as is present in the instant case. It is important that the legal standards defining the dimensions of the crime and defenses and thereby determining the relevancy and probative worth of lines of evidence and modes of argument, focus the attention of the trier-of-fact upon the basic issues. By providing gradations of intentional homicide, the legislature has announced that not all persons who consciously and purposively kill another are equally blameworthy. Some person's act of homicide can be understood as a very human response to a desperate condition.

"The wholly objective ordinarily-constituted-man test, by failing to take account of the emotional dimensions of a concrete individual's specific situation, fails, in my view, to define sharply the issue posed by the legislatively-provided manslaughter defense.

"The provocation test formulated in the *Model Penal Code* [§ 210.3(1)(b)] of the American Law Institute, I believe, gives proper weight to all relevant factors. It is neither wholly objective or wholly subjective. * * *

"This test would enable the trier-of-fact to evaluate the defendant's conduct in a specific situation. The trier-of-fact is called upon to determine a degree of blameworthiness. This task cannot be accomplished by means of either a wholly objective or wholly subjective test. The Model Penal Code formulation permits the trier-of-fact to decide 'whether the actor's loss of self-control can be understood in terms that arouse sympathy enough to call for mitigation in the sentence.'[6] This is the critical issue surrounding the manslaughter defense."

---

6. *Model Penal Code*, Comment p. 48, Tentative Draft No. 9 (1959).

5.   Under any test which is not "either wholly objective or wholly subjective," is there any principled way to tell the jury just how subjective the test is? What of the instruction requested but rejected in *State v. Little,* 123 N.H. 433, 462 A.2d 117 (1983), that "ordinary human nature, or the nature of a man of fair, average mind and disposition, should be taken as a standard, unless you find that the defendant is shown to have some peculiar weakness of mind or emotion not arising from wickedness of heart."

6.   In light of Judge Wilkie's observation that the reasonable man does not kill, consider Joshua Dressler, *Rethinking Heat of Passion: A Defense in Search of a Rationale,* 73 J.Crim.L. & Criminology 421, 466–67 (1982): "The point of the partial defense should be that if the ordinarily law-abiding person would be expected to be in sufficient control of his emotions so as to respond in an inner directed fashion, or to respond externally, but non-violently, then homicidal conduct by the actor may be fairly perceived as an unreasonable response to reasonable anger. This homicidal conduct would not be entitled to any mitigation. If, however, the provocation is so great that the ordinarily law-abiding person would be expected to lose self-control to the extent that he could not help but act violently, yet he would still have sufficient self-control so that he could avoid using force likely to cause death or great bodily harm in response to the provocation, then we are saying that the actor's moral blameworthiness is found not in his violent response, but in his *homicidal* violent response. He did not control himself as much as he *should* have, or as much as common experience tells us he *could* have, nor as much as the ordinarily law-abiding person *would* have. Thus, his choice-capabilities were partially undermined by severe and understandable, non-blameworthy anger, but he was not sufficiently in control of his actions so as to merit total acquittal. It is in this case that the traditional defense should apply."

PEOPLE v. BERRY

Supreme Court of California, 1976.

18 Cal.3d 509, 134 Cal.Rptr. 415, 556 P.2d 777.

SULLIVAN, JUSTICE.

Defendant Albert Joseph Berry was charged by indictment with one count of murder and one count of assault by means of force likely to produce great bodily injury. * * * In each count, the alleged victim was defendant's wife, Rachel Pessah Berry. A jury found defendant guilty as charged and determined that the murder was of the first degree. Defendant was sentenced to state prison for the term prescribed by law. He appeals from the judgment of conviction. * * *

Defendant, a cook, 46 years old, and Rachel Pessah, a 20–year–old girl from Israel, were married on May 27, 1974. Three days later Rachel went to Israel by herself, returning on July 13, 1974. On July 23, 1974, defendant choked Rachel into unconsciousness. She was treated at a hospital where she reported her strangulation by defendant to an officer of the San Francisco Police Department. On July 25, Inspector Sammon, who had been assigned to the case, met with Rachel and as a result of the interview a warrant was issued for defendant's arrest.

While Rachel was at the hospital, defendant removed his clothes from their apartment and stored them in a Greyhound Bus Depot locker. He stayed overnight at the home of a friend, Mrs. Jean Berk, admitting to her that he had choked his wife. On July 26, he telephoned Mrs. Berk and informed her that he had killed Rachel with a telephone cord on that morning at their apartment. The next day Mrs. Berk and two others telephoned the police to report a possible homicide and met Officer Kelleher at defendant's apartment.

They gained entry and found Rachel on the bathroom floor. A pathologist from the coroner's office concluded that the cause of Rachel's death was strangulation. Defendant was arrested on August 1, 1974, and confessed to the killing.

At trial defendant did not deny strangling his wife, but claimed through his own testimony and the testimony of a psychiatrist, Dr. Martin Blinder, that he was provoked into killing her because of a sudden and uncontrollable rage so as to reduce the offense to one of voluntary manslaughter. He testified that upon her return from Israel, Rachel announced to him that while there she had fallen in love with another man, one Yako, and had enjoyed his sexual favors, that he was coming to this country to claim her and that she wished a divorce. Thus commenced a tormenting two weeks in which Rachel alternately taunted defendant with her involvement with Yako and at the same time sexually excited defendant indicating her desire to remain with him. Defendant's detailed testimony, summarized below, chronicles this strange course of events.

After their marriage, Rachel lived with defendant for only three days and then left for Israel. Immediately upon her return to San Francisco she told defendant about her relationship with and love for Yako. This brought about further argument and a brawl that evening in which defendant choked Rachel and she responded by scratching him deeply many times. Nonetheless they continued to live together. Rachel kept taunting defendant with Yako and demanding a divorce. She claimed she thought she might be pregnant by Yako. She showed defendant pictures of herself with Yako. Nevertheless, during a return trip from Santa Rosa, Rachel demanded immediate sexual intercourse with defendant in the car, which was achieved; however upon reaching their apartment, she again stated that she loved Yako and that she would not have intercourse with defendant in the future.

On the evening of July 22d defendant and Rachel went to a movie where they engaged in heavy petting. When they returned home and got into bed, Rachel announced that she had intended to make love with defendant, "But I am saving myself for this man Yako, so I don't think I will." Defendant got out of bed and prepared to leave the apartment whereupon Rachel screamed and yelled at him. Defendant choked her into unconsciousness.

Two hours later defendant called a taxi for his wife to take her to the hospital. He put his clothes in the Greyhound bus station and went to the home of his friend Mrs. Berk for the night. The next day he went to Reno and returned the day after. Rachel informed him by telephone that there was a warrant for his arrest as a result of her report to the police about the choking incident. On July 25th defendant returned to the apartment to talk to Rachel, but she was out. He slept there overnight. Rachel returned around 11 a.m. the next day. Upon seeing defendant there, she said, "I suppose you have come here to kill me." Defendant responded, "yes," changed his response to "no," and then again to "yes," and finally stated "I have really come to talk to you." Rachel began screaming. Defendant grabbed her by the shoulder and tried to stop her screaming. She continued. They struggled and finally defendant strangled her with a telephone cord.

Dr. Martin Blinder, a physician and psychiatrist, called by the defense, testified that Rachel was a depressed, suicidally inclined girl and that this suicidal impulse led her to involve herself ever more deeply in a dangerous situation with defendant. She did this by sexually arousing him and taunting him into jealous rages in an unconscious desire to provoke him into killing her and thus consummating her desire for suicide. Throughout the period commencing with her return from Israel until her death, that is from July 13 to July 26, Rachel continually provoked defendant with sexual taunts and incitements, alternating acceptance and rejection of him. This conduct was accompanied by repeated references to her involvement with another man; it led defendant to choke her on two occasions, until finally she achieved her unconscious desire and was strangled. Dr. Blinder testified that as a result of this cumulative series of provocations, defendant at the time he fatally strangled Rachel, was in a state of uncontrollable rage, completely under the sway of passion.

We first take up defendant's claim that on the basis of the foregoing evidence he was entitled to an instruction on voluntary manslaughter as defined by statute which is "the unlawful killing of a human being, without malice * * * upon a sudden quarrel[a] or heat of passion." In *People v. Valentine* (1946) 28 Cal.2d 121, 169 P.2d 1, this court, in an extensive review of the law of manslaughter, specifically approved the following quotation from *People v. Logan* (1917) 175 Cal. 45, 48–49, 164 P. 1121 as a correct statement of the law: "In the present condition of our law *it is left to the jurors* to say whether or not the facts and circumstances in evidence are sufficient to lead them to believe that the defendant did, or to create a reasonable doubt in their minds as to whether or not he did, commit his offense under a heat of passion. The jury is further to be admonished and advised by the court that this heat of passion must be such a passion as would naturally be aroused in the mind of an ordinarily reasonable person under the given facts and circumstances, and that, consequently, no defendant may set up his own standard of conduct and justify or excuse himself because in fact his passions were aroused, unless further the jury believe that the facts and circumstances were sufficient to arouse the passions of the ordinarily reasonable man. * * * "

We further held in *Valentine* that there is no specific type of provocation required by section 192 and that verbal provocation may be sufficient. In *People v. Borchers* (1958) 50 Cal.2d 321, 329, 325 P.2d 97 in the course of explaining the phrase "heat of passion" used in the statute defining manslaughter we pointed out that " 'passion' need not mean 'rage' or 'anger' "but may be any "[v]iolent, intense, high-wrought or enthusiastic emotion" and concluded there "that defendant was aroused to a heat of 'passion' by a series of events over a considerable period of time * * *." Accordingly we there declared that evidence of admissions of infidelity by the defendant's paramour, taunts directed to him and other conduct, "supports a finding that defendant killed in wild desperation induced by [the woman's] long continued provocatory conduct." We find this reasoning persuasive in the case now before us. Defendant's testimony chronicles a two-week period of provocatory conduct by his wife Rachel that could arouse a passion of jealousy, pain and sexual rage in an ordinary man of average disposition such as to cause him to act rashly from this passion. It is significant that both defendant and Dr. Blinder testified that the former was in the heat of passion under an uncontrollable rage when he killed Rachel.

a. In *United States v. Martinez*, 988 F.2d 685 (7th Cir.1993), dealing with the definition of voluntary manslaughter in 18 U.S.C.A. § 1112(a) as being the unlawful killing of another, without malice, "upon a sudden quarrel or heat of passion," the defendants "objected to the proposed instruction on manslaughter, arguing that the instruction should treat a killing which occurs 'upon a sudden quarrel' as a matter distinct from heat of passion, so as to be proved beyond a reasonable doubt as an element of manslaughter, or more importantly in this case, disproved beyond a reasonable doubt before there can be a conviction of murder." The lower court, however, declined to include the requested language.

On appeal, the court ultimately found the defendants otherwise not entitled to such an instruction, but nonetheless examined the origins of the sudden quarrel language—concluding: "(1) the 'sudden quarrel' or 'chance medley' doctrine developed in response to the circumstances of the times; (2) those circumstances—such as the custom of wearing sidearms and the harsh death sentence imposed on anyone who killed—are no longer prevalent; (3) as circumstances changed, the doctrine fell out of disuse; and (4) heat of passion appears to be a more refined and expanded 'chance medley' doctrine, and not a separate and distinct theory in itself"–and stated that "it may be arguable that the 'sudden quarrel' term is an anachronism with no meaning not adequately served by a proper definition of heat of passion." The court noted that states with similar statutes often so interpret those statute, although a few seem to treat the "sudden quarrel" and "heat of passion" terms distinction, while the California decisions reveal "inconsistent interpretations."

The Attorney General contends that the killing could not have been done in the heat of passion because there was a cooling period, defendant having waited in the apartment for 20 hours. However, the long course of provocatory conduct, which had resulted in intermittent outbreaks of rage under specific provocation in the past, reached its final culmination in the apartment when Rachel began screaming. Both defendant and Dr. Blinder testified that defendant killed in a state of uncontrollable rage, of passion, and there is ample evidence in the record to support the conclusion that this passion was the result of the long course of provocatory conduct by Rachel, just as the killing emerged from such conduct in *Borchers*. * * *

Notes and Questions

1. More and more jurisdictions, especially under modern code substitutes for the "heat of passion" test, are taking the view, as stated in *Berry*, "that there is no specific type of provocation required." But it is still true in many states that the "application by the courts of an objective doctrine has led to the establishment of certain concrete standards of conduct which a reasonable man is said to adhere to. Unfortunately many of these incidents have ossified into ironclad rules originally evolved in the nineteenth century. Under modern law, the categories of things which provoked the nineteenth century reasonable man continue to provoke the reasonable man of the twentieth century with the addition of a few new but rigid categories.

"In general, he is said to be provoked into taking human life when he is violently assaulted; when an unlawful attempt is made to arrest him; when he kills in mutual combat;[a] or when he sees his wife in an act of adultery and kills her or her paramour. On the other hand, he is said not to be provoked by insulting words[b] or gestures, nor, according to some authorities, is he provoked by a trespass against his land or goods. The outcome of the case which *clearly* falls within one of these rules may be predicted with a high degree of accuracy. However, the situations which develop are seldom clear cut. Some courts carefully scrutinize the evidence to determine if the facts can be forced into any of the established categories; if they cannot, the case is not one for manslaughter regardless of evidence of actual provocation or passion. The result has been an unrealistic interpretation of the facts to fit an appealing case neatly within an established category, thus leading to confusion as to the breadth of the categories and lack of uniformity in the application of the law. Other jurisdictions have refused to saddle themselves with the 'nineteenth century

---

a. This does not necessarily cover all cases in which a fight ensues. At least one court has held that if one person uses lawful force on another to prevent a trespass and the individuals then begin to fight, culminating in a killing by the latter person, this is not manslaughter. *State v. Smith*, 123 N.H. 46, 455 A.2d 1041 (1983).

b. But, "while words of an insulting and scandalous nature are not sufficient cause of provocation, words conveying information of a fact which constitutes adequate provocation when that fact is observed would constitute sufficient provocation." *Commonwealth v. Berry*, 461 Pa. 233, 336 A.2d 262 (1975). The court thus held it was error to instruct that there would be sufficient provocation only if defendant actually witnessed the assault of his mother instead of being told of it by her immediately after the culmination of the attack. *Berry* thus recognizes one common expansion of the categories; as the court explained: "The threatened

or immediate infliction of serious injury upon a parent, spouse or child because of the relationship of the parties and the expected concern of one for the well being of the other, has occasioned courts to hold this conduct may be sufficient provocation to reduce the killing to voluntary manslaughter." In some jurisdictions, this expansion has gone further and encompasses assault of a "close friend" as well. *State v. Coyle*, 119 N.J. 194, 574 A.2d 951 (1990).

With respect to insulting words, consider *People v. Pouncey*, 437 Mich. 382, 471 N.W.2d 346 (1991), where the court held there had been insufficient provocation where there had been an argument without blows struck but in which the victim referred to defendant and his friends as "punks, cowards, whores, bitches," etc. The court added this caution: "Nonetheless, we decline to issue a rule that insulting words per se are never adequate provocation."

four' and have created some few new categories of adequate provocation as the cases arise." Note, 106 U.Pa.L.Rev. 1021, 1023–24 (1958).

2. Should the number and breadth of the categories be increasing or decreasing? In *Holmes v. Director of Public Prosecutions,* [1946] A.C. 588, 62 T.L.R. 466, [1946] 2 All E.R. 124, Viscount Simon reasoned that "the application of common law principles in matters such as this must to some extent be controlled by the evolution of society. For example, the instance given by Blackstone that if a man's nose was pulled and he thereupon struck his aggressor so as to kill him, this was only manslaughter, may very well represent the natural feelings of a past time, but I should doubt very much whether such a view should necessarily be taken nowadays. The injury done to a man's sense of honour by minor physical assaults may well be differently estimated in differing ages. And, in the same way, one can imagine in these days at any rate, words of a vile character which might be calculated to deprive a reasonable man of his customary self-control even more than would an act of physical violence. But, on the other hand, as society advances, it ought to call for a higher measure of self-control in all cases."

3. As noted in *Holmes,* the significance of the common law categories was that they served as a means of controlling the jury, as only if there was evidence fitting the case within an established category would the jury be given the alternative of finding the defendant guilty of manslaughter. But, as noted in *Brown v. United States,* 584 A.2d 537 (D.C.App.1990), "this traditional view of provocation as a set of rigid categories of recognized conduct has been abandoned by a growing number of state legislatures,[c] courts,[d] and commentators," so that it may be asked how much of this control remains? Should every defendant charged with murder be entitled to a manslaughter instruction?[e] If, as Justice Wilkie said in *Hoyt,* the "basic question is whether he is as culpable as a person who kills solely for self-aggrandizement or out of sheer malevolence," should the jury be given the manslaughter alternative whenever there is some evidence of some other motive? Specifically, should the jury be given the opportunity to return a manslaughter verdict where:

(a) the defendant shot his wife, who had recently commenced divorce proceedings against him, because he had long believed she had committed adultery and because, just before the killing, she did not respond when the defendant asked her to give him custody of their three children?[f]

(b) the defendant and two friends went to David's apartment where they all drank beer, whiskey and rum and watched porno films, but when the two friends left to buy cigarettes David grabbed defendant's testicles and said, "You know you want it," at which defendant pushed David away and then choked and kicked him, resulting in David's death?[g]

c. Typically by adoption of a statutory provision at least similar to *Model Penal Code* § 210.3(1)(b).

d. As in *Berry,* supra.

e. In *United States ex rel. Matthews v. Johnson,* 503 F.2d 339 (3d Cir.1974), the court held that where, under Pennsylvania law, the jury had the power and prerogative to return a verdict of voluntary manslaughter in any murder prosecution, even in the absence of any evidence of provocation or passion which would require an instruction on voluntary manslaughter, and where there were no legal standards to guide the judge in determining whether to submit a voluntary manslaughter instruction in the absence of such evidence,

due process was denied in refusing a request for a voluntary manslaughter instruction.

f. See *People v. Arnold,* 17 Ill.App.3d 1043, 309 N.E.2d 89 (1974), holding defendant was not entitled to a manslaughter instruction on such facts.

g. See *Commonwealth v. Pierce,* 419 Mass. 28, 642 N.E.2d 579 (1994), where on similar facts the court upheld the trial judge's determination not to instruct on manslaughter, explaining: "Although the gesture was perhaps offensive, it was not the type of behavior that would provoke a reasonable person into a homicidal response." Compare *Mullaney v. Wilbur,* p. 264 of this Book, where the judge *did* instruct on manslaughter (but erroneously placed the burden of proof on

(c) the defendant shot a woman, with whom he had been out earlier that evening, who "was jealous of [him] and did not want him to stop at another bar to drink before going home," and who "threatened to follow him and raise a commotion at his home if he did stop, and she did, in fact, follow him everywhere he went" until he stopped and approached her car, when she "laughed and appeared to be taunting him"?[h]

(d) the defendant was part of a mob which beat a police officer to death after the officer, assigned to an area which had just experienced serious racial rioting, sought to arrest defendant's friend Williams and wounded Williams in the process?[i]

(e) the defendant, a probationary postal worker, shot and killed his supervisor after she lowered his rating because of an unexcused absence, which he feared would result in him losing his job?[j]

(f) the defendant made a sharp right turn from the left lane, cutting off another car, and then the other car passed defendant and slowed down to 15–20 m.p.h. in a 35 m.p.h. zone, but when the road became 4–lane defendant passed and then slowed down in front of the other car and would not let it pass, so the other car drove very close to defendant's rear bumper, and when both vehicles reached a shopping center parking lot the driver of the other car parked his car and approached defendant's car when defendant, "enmeshed in a fit of 'road rage,' " drove into the other person and killed him?[k]

(g) the defendant testified that he invited a young lady to go for a ride, that they drove to a secluded area where she seduced him, redressed herself and then calmly informed him she was going to "cry rape" because she needed an excuse for arriving home late, at which he "panicked" and shot her.[l]

defendant) where the defendant claimed "that he had attacked Herbert in a frenzy provoked by Herbert's homosexual advance."

Which view is correct? Compare *Developments–Sexual Orientation and the Law*, 102 Harv.L.Rev. 1508, 1547 (1989) (merely "experiencing fear or hatred of gay people in response to a homosexual overture should not suffice to provoke a reasonable person to lose his or her self-control and resort to deadly force"); with Joshua Dressler, *When "Heterosexual" Men Kill "Homosexual" Men: Reflections on Provocation Law, Sexual Advances, and the "Reasonable Man" Standard*, 85 J.Crim.L. & Criminology 726, 737, 753 (1995) (when provocation viewed in terms of "a person who possesses ordinary human weaknesses," it becomes apparent that there is no compelling reason why "a homicide motivated by a [nonviolent homosexual advance should] be treated any differently" than other "out-of-control homicides in responses to provocations" that the criminal justice system "punishe[s] less severely than ordinary intentional killing").

h. See *State v. Harwood*, 110 Ariz. 375, 519 P.2d 177 (1974), holding it was error not to instruct on manslaughter on these facts.

i. See *State v. Madden*, 61 N.J. 377, 294 A.2d 609 (1972), where the defendant was convicted of murder notwithstanding the fact the jury was also instructed on manslaughter.

"Defendants now urge that the jury should have been told (1) that racial or like antagonism or grievances may constitute provocation, and may so serve whether or not the officer was acting in the execution

of his duty; and (2) that the illegal arrest or the shooting of Williams could constitute a provocation of bystanders.

"The first proposition is frivolous. It is no more than this: that racial, ethnic, religious, economic, political, or like grievances within our social order should be deemed sufficient to provoke a member of one group to kill a member of a group he deems opposed to him, or to kill every police officer as a symbol of the social order within which such grievances exist. The proposition is foreign to the subject of voluntary manslaughter. * * *

"And as to the wounding of Williams, which for the purpose of the present discussion is assumed to have involved excessive force, we * * * think provocation should not be recognized in those circumstances, for two reasons. The first is that we believe a man of ordinary firmness would not be provoked to a deadly attack. The second reason, which buttresses the first, is that the protection a police officer should have in the public interest might be diluted if his mistaken use of force were accepted as an affront to a bystander."

j. See *United States v. Collins*, 690 F.2d 431 (5th Cir.1982), holding defendant was not entitled to a manslaughter instruction on such facts.

k. See *Canipe v. Commonwealth*, 25 Va.App. 629, 491 S.E.2d 747 (1997), holding defendant properly convicted of murder on such facts.

l. See *State v. Butler*, 277 S.C. 452, 290 S.E.2d 1 (1982), holding defendant was not entitled to a manslaughter instruction on such facts.

(h) the defendant stabbed and killed another man with whom he had just had sex because the other man then told the defendant that he had AIDS.[m]

4. Under the traditional "heat of passion" doctrine, a provoked defendant cannot have his homicide reduced to voluntary manslaughter where the time elapsing between the provocation and the death blow is such that a reasonable man thus provoked would have cooled; and this is so even though the defendant, being slower to cool off than the ordinary person, has not in fact cooled off by the time he delivers the lethal blow.[n] What constitutes a reasonable cooling time in a particular case depends upon the nature of the provocation and the circumstances surrounding its occurrence—a matter to be determined by the jury as a question of fact, unless the time is so short or so long that the court may hold, as a matter of law, that it was reasonable or unreasonable.

Berry follows the prevailing but not unanimous view that some act immediately preceding the killing may rekindle a passion originally aroused by some earlier provocation.

How useful is the "cooling time" concept? Consider whether the jury should be allowed to consider the alternative of manslaughter on these facts: Parker was standing in front of a drug store conversing with friends when Fraley walked up, immediately fired six shots into Parker, and said: "You damned son of a bitch! I told you I'd kill you. You killed my boy." Parker had shot and killed Fraley's son some 10 months ago and had been tried and acquitted.[o]

5. Is the case for relaxing somewhat the sudden provocation requirement, as in *Berry*, more compelling in some circumstances than others? Is *Berry* such a case? Consider Comment, 33 U.C.L.A.L.Rev. 1679, 1719–20 (1986): "When women kill men, cumulative provocation (terror) involves physical abuse and threats from the men with whom the women live, yet these women struggle to admit evidence of continual physical abuse and expert testimony to explain their reactions. For men who kill women, cumulative provocation (rage) often occurs in a similar domestic setting, but this provocation is verbal, usually involving taunts of sexual infidelity, and courts find sufficient provocation in a long course of mere verbal abuse.

"Cumulative terror should serve as an emotion adequate for heat-of-passion manslaughter and cumulative rage should not. Affronts to dignity and sexual pride should be coped with over time. The law should not mitigate culpability—thus considering a passionate reaction 'reasonable'—when the defendant 'brood[s] over his hurt' until a relatively trivial event—usually words, which traditionally do not serve as adequate provocation—triggers his rage.[p] On the other hand, when affronts to physical safety occur repeatedly, the

---

m. *N.Y. Times*, March 4, 1987, p. 16, col. 1, reporting such an incident, stating "the case was the first in the country in which a man accused of murder was using AIDS in connection with this line of defense, described as the classic 'heat of passion' reasoning. * * *

" 'It is an outrageous defense,' the executive director of the Lamba Legal Defense and Education Fund, Thomas B. Stoddard, said. 'And if it were ever accepted by a court, it would set very dangerous legal and social precedents.' * * *

"According to [defense counsel] Lewis, the reaction of his client was not unwarranted.

" 'He had been handed a death sentence,' Mr. Lewis said. 'This kid won't know for the next seven years whether he is going to die. * * *' "

The defendant was permitted to plead guilty to manslaughter. *N.Y. Times*, March 24, 1987, p. 15, col. 2.

n. A minority view eliminates the reasonable-time test, so that if there is a reasonable and actual provocation, the defendant's crime is manslaughter if in fact, because of his particular temperament, he has not cooled off, though a reasonable man's passion would have subsided.

o. *Ex parte Fraley*, 3 Okl.Cr. 719, 109 P. 295 (1910), upholding denial of bail on the ground this was murder and not manslaughter.

p. Consider also Donna K. Coker, *Heat of Passion and Wife Killing: Men Who Batter/Men Who Kill*, 2 So.Cal.L.Rev.L. & Women's Stud. 71, 77, 129 (1992), asserting that *Berry* "demonstrates the deleterious effect of the resonance between the excuses and justifications given by abusive men and the cultural (mis)understandings that underlie modern heat-of-passion/adultery doctrine," and concluding that "modern law should recognize that they need not be forgotten over time. The common pattern of violence against women by their male intimates demonstrates that earlier 'trivial' episodes of physical abuse are reliable predictors of future violence and that the violence is likely to escalate until it becomes life-threatening. When a woman kills a man in response to such physical abuse, whether she claims heat of passion or self-defense, she is acting reasonably, and the accumulated abuse is relevant to her degree of guilt."

6.   Tilson became involved in a fight in the Cue Lounge with Solomon, Jennings and Ellison. Tilson hurried to his car, obtained a pistol, returned to the club minutes later and shot and killed King, a friend of Tilson's assailants. Though Tilson was convicted of murder, the court of appeals reduced the crime to voluntary manslaughter. In *State v. Tilson*, 503 S.W.2d 921 (Tenn.1974), the court reversed the appellate ruling:

"To sustain the Court of Criminal Appeals would add a new dimension to the definition of voluntary manslaughter. That is, if the Court of Criminal Appeals holding was sustained, it would now constitute voluntary manslaughter for a defendant, under reasonable and legal provocation, such as sudden combat, to kill a non-combatant by-stander, provided either by association or friendship, or both, with the other combatant, the by-stander could be characterized as 'on the side' of the one actually provoking the fight."

Do you agree? Does it follow that the manslaughter alternative should *never* be available except when the defendant kills the provoking party? What if: (a) Tilson killed King in the mistaken belief that King had been one of his assailants? (b) Tilson killed King accidently while shooting at Solomon, one of his assailants? (c) Tilson killed King while shooting at Solomon, but under circumstances such that his firing at Solomon created a known and substantial risk that King might be hit instead?

7.   In *Berry*, the defendant's objection on appeal was that the court failed to instruct the jury on manslaughter. Sometimes, where the instruction is given without having been requested by the defendant and defendant is convicted of manslaughter, the appeal will be based upon the claim that it was error to give the instruction and that without the manslaughter alternative the jury might have acquitted him. See, e.g., *Elmore v. Commonwealth*, 520 S.W.2d 328 (Ky.1975) (manslaughter conviction reversed because instruction on that crime, given over defendant's objection, was improper, there being no evidence "which would in any way indicate that Taylor met his death * * * in a sudden affray or a sudden heat of passion").

analysis of wife-beating belongs in today's legal analysis of wife-murder [in order to] eliminate two dangerous myths: first, that men who kill their wives or girlfriends do so in the heat of 'uncontrolled passion'; second, that men who kill are not likely to kill again"; and Note, 51 Rutgers L.Rev. 193, 224 (1998), concluding that "the heat of passion defense should be eliminated altogether in spousal infidelity cases" because it "reinforc[es] the relegation of women to traditional roles, * * * sanctions a man's use of extreme violence in response to a personal attack to his masculinity," "condones revenge," and "does not demand that those harmed by the knowledge that their spouses have been unfaithful show restraint—a demand the law should make."

In *State v. Shane*, 63 Ohio St.3d 630, 590 N.E.2d 272 (1992), the court disapproved "of a rule which does not allow 'mere words' to be sufficient provocation to reduce murder to manslaughter generally, but which makes a specific exception where the provocation consists of mere words by one spouse informing the other spouse of infidelity. This exception to the general rule has its foundation in the ancient common-law concept that the wife is the property of the husband. See *Regina v. Mawgridge* (1707), Kelyng, J. 119, 137, 84 Eng.Rep. 1107, 1115: '[W]hen a man is taken in adultery with another man's wife, if the husband shall stab the adulterer, or knock out his brains, that is bare manslaughter: for jealousy is the rage of a man, and adultery is the highest invasion of property * * *.' This archaic rule has no place in modern society. Words informing another of infidelity should not be given special treatment by courts trying to determine what provocation is reasonably sufficient provocation. The killing of a spouse (usually a wife) by a spouse (usually a husband) who has just been made aware of the victim spouse's adultery simply is not an acceptable response to the confession of infidelity."

NOTES AND QUESTIONS ON ASSISTING SUICIDE[a]

1. Note, 86 Colum.L.Rev. 348, 350–52 (1986): "A survey of the criminal codes of the fifty states and three United States territories reveals that no jurisdiction defines suicide, by statute, as a criminal act. Nor does any state, by statute, criminalize attempts to commit suicide. While there is some logical difficulty in punishing one who aids an act that is not itself a crime, many states nonetheless punish suicide assistance. States that do make suicide assistance an offense generally follow one of two approaches.

"A minority of states have statutes that punish aiding a suicide, causing a suicide or both as manslaughter or murder. * * * It appears to be generally accepted, however, that actual participation in suicide, as opposed to facilitating or aiding the act, is murder. The simple form of this doctrine is: '"Murder is no less murder because the homicide is committed at the desire of the victim." 'No jurisdiction in the United States recognizes consent to homicide.

"The majority of states that have statutes imposing criminal liability for assisting a suicide, however, make the act a unique offense, as contrasted with making it a type of murder or manslaughter."

2. Is it sensible to treat as murder every case in which the assistance reached the level of active participation, or—perhaps by analogy to the heat-of-passion doctrine—should at least some instances be characterized as some lesser offense, either manslaughter or aiding suicide? Note, supra, at 355, 361, 363, notes that "psychological studies of suicide suggest that many persons who assist suicide may do so in response to active and relentless pressure created by a victim's dependent or aggressive behavior" and that defendants have "sought to plead assistance to suicide as an affirmative defense akin to the defense of provocation," and concludes that "if a defendant has acted, not from malice, but from compassion or fear, insisting on a charge of first-degree murder is unnecessarily harsh." Consider, in this regard, what result should be reached in the following two fact situations.

3. "In September of 1980, John Wamsley approached his friend, Dexter Mays, and asked him if he knew of anyone who could do him a favor. When Mays asked the nature of the favor he was told that Wamsley wanted someone 'to shoot somebody.' Mays agreed to do Wamsley this 'favor' for the sum of $300.00.

"On the evening of 14 October 1980, Wamsley, Mays and a third individual, a blonde-haired man, drove from Huntington to Gallipolis. On the way back, they stopped in Mason County and Mays learned that the man whom Wamsley had targeted for death was Wamsley himself. Mays claims that he was unwilling to shoot his friend and acquiesced only because he feared for his own life. With Wamsley kneeling on the ground, Mays pulled the trigger and fired three bullets into his willing victim.

"Wamsley was a homosexual and a drug dealer. His religious beliefs created within him a strong feeling of self-disdain. He was also deeply in debt and had taken out a life insurance policy which would not pay the death benefit if Wamsley committed suicide. Therefore, he had arranged his own death and had sought Mays' assistance in carrying out his ghoulish plan."[b]

a. Whether there should be a "consent defense" to a charge of causing or aiding suicide is discussed in Chapter 8, § 7.

b. *State v. Mays*, 172 W.Va. 486, 307 S.E.2d 655 (1983), rejecting defendant's argument "that there was no evidence of malice" because "his actions were motivated either by a fear for his own life or simple heat of passion."

4. "The minor and his friend, Jeff W., both 16 years old, drove to the Fillmore library one evening and joined a number of their friends who had congregated there. During the course of the two hours they spent at the library talking, mention was made of a car turnout on a curve over-looking a 300 to 350–foot precipice on a country road known as 'the cliff.' Both the minor and Jeff declared that they intended to 'fly off the cliff' and that they meant to kill themselves. * * * Jeff repeatedly encouraged the minor by urging, 'let's go, let's go' whenever the minor spoke. * * *

* * * The minor then drove off in the direction of the cliff with Jeff in the passenger seat * * *.

"Two other vehicles were parked in the turnout, from which vantage point their occupants watched the minor's car plummeting down the hill at an estimated 50 mph. The car veered off the road without swerving or changing course; the witnesses heard the car accelerate and then drive straight off the cliff. No one saw brakelights flash. The impact of the crash killed Jeff and caused severe injuries to the minor, resulting in the amputation of a foot."[c]

SECTION 3. INTENTIONAL KILLING: THE "DELIBERATE"—"PREMEDITATED" TEST

STATE v. GUTHRIE

Supreme Court of Appeals of West Virginia, 1995.

194 W.Va. 657, 461 S.E.2d 163.

CLECKLEY, JUSTICE:

The defendant, Dale Edward Guthrie, appeals the January, 1994, jury verdict of the Circuit Court of Kanawha County finding him guilty of first degree murder. In May of 1994, the defendant was sentenced to serve a life sentence with a recommendation of mercy. * * *

It is undisputed that on the evening of February 12, 1993, the defendant removed a knife from his pocket and stabbed his co-worker, Steven Todd Farley, in the neck and killed him. The two men worked together as dishwashers at Danny's Rib House in Nitro and got along well together before this incident. On the night of the killing, the victim, his brother, Tracy Farley, and James Gibson were joking around while working in the kitchen of the restaurant. The victim was poking fun at the defendant who appeared to be in a bad mood. He told the defendant to "lighten up" and snapped him with a dishtowel several times. Apparently, the victim had no idea he was upsetting the defendant very much. The dishtowel flipped the defendant on the nose and he became enraged.

The defendant removed his gloves and started toward the victim. Mr. Farley, still teasing, said: "Ooo, he's taking his gloves off." The defendant then pulled a knife from his

---

c. *In re Joseph G.*, 34 Cal.3d 429, 194 Cal.Rptr. 163, 667 P.2d 1176 (1983), reversing the minor's juvenile court adjudication of murder, where the court stressed that "the minor and Jeff, because of the instrumentality chosen, necessarily were to commit their suicidal acts simultaneously and were subject to identical risks of death. The potential for fraud is thus absent in a genuine suicide pact executed simultaneously by both parties by means of the same instrumentality. The traditional rationale for holding the survivor of the pact guilty of murder is thus not appropriate in this limited factual situation.

" * * * To make the distinction between criminal liability for first degree murder and merely aiding and abetting suicide turn on the fortuitous circumstance of which of the pair was actually driving serves no rational purpose. The illogic of such a distinction has been similarly recognized in the classic example of the parties to the pact agreeing to commit suicide by gassing themselves in a closed room. If the party who turns on the gas survives, he is guilty of murder; if on the other hand, the other person survives, that person's criminal liability is only that of an aider and abettor."

pocket and stabbed the victim in the neck. He also stabbed Mr. Farley in the arm as he fell to the floor. Mr. Farley looked up and cried: "Man, I was just kidding around." The defendant responded: "Well, man, you should have never hit me in my face." The police arrived at the restaurant and arrested the defendant. He was given his *Miranda* rights. The defendant made a statement at the police station and confessed to the killing. The police officers described him as calm and willing to cooperate.

It is also undisputed that the defendant suffers from a host of psychiatric problems. He experiences up to two panic attacks daily and had received treatment for them at the Veterans Administration Hospital in Huntington for more than a year preceding the killing. He suffers from chronic depression (dysthymic disorder), an obsession with his nose (body dysmorphic disorder), and borderline personality disorder. The defendant's father shed some light on his nose fixation. He stated that dozens of times a day the defendant stared in the mirror and turned his head back and forth to look at his nose. His father estimated that 50 percent of the time he observed his son he was looking at his nose. The defendant repeatedly asked for assurances that his nose was not too big. This obsession began when he was approximately seventeen years old. The defendant was twenty-nine years old at the time of trial.

The defendant testified he suffered a panic attack immediately preceding the stabbing. He described the attack as "intense"; he felt a lot of pressure and his heart beat rapidly. In contrast to the boisterous atmosphere in the kitchen that evening, the defendant was quiet and kept to himself. He stated that Mr. Farley kept irritating him that night. The defendant could not understand why Mr. Farley was picking on him because he had never done that before. Even at trial, the defendant did not comprehend his utter overreaction to the situation. In hindsight, the defendant believed the better decision would have been to punch out on his time card and quit over the incident. However, all the witnesses related that the defendant was in no way attacked, as he perceived it, but that Mr. Farley was playing around. The defendant could not bring himself to tell the other workers to leave him alone or inform them about his panic attacks. In contrast to his written statement, the defendant testified he was unable to recall stabbing the victim. After he was struck in the nose, he stated that he "lost it" and, when he came to himself, he was holding the knife in his hand and Mr. Farley was sinking to the floor.

A psychiatrist, Dr. Sidney Lerfald, testified on behalf of the defendant. He diagnosed the various disorders discussed above. Dr. Lerfald felt the defendant's diagnoses "may have affected his perception somewhat." Nevertheless, it was his opinion the defendant was sane at the time of the offense because he was able to distinguish between right and wrong and could have conformed his actions accordingly.

It was the State's position that the facts supported a first degree murder conviction. At the close of the State's case-in-chief, the defense moved for a directed verdict contending the State failed to present evidence of malice and premeditation. This motion was denied. The defense argued the facts of the case supported voluntary manslaughter or, at worse, second degree murder. The jury returned a verdict finding the defendant guilty of first degree murder with a recommendation of mercy. * * *

First, the defendant strives to persuade us that the record in this case does not support the verdict of guilty of first degree murder beyond a reasonable doubt. Because this exhortation challenges the sufficiency of evidence to support a jury's verdict, our authority to review is limited. * * * Accordingly, we proceed to consider whether on the record made in the trial court any rational trier of fact could have found the defendant guilty beyond a reasonable doubt. * * *

We begin by emphasizing that our review is conducted from a cold appellate transcript and record. For that reason, we must assume that the jury credited all witnesses whose testimony supports the verdict. The essential facts of this case—those that the jury was unquestionably entitled to find—are rather simple: The defendant became irritated with the "horseplay" of the victim; when the victim in jest hit the defendant with a wet dishtowel on his nose, the defendant became angry and drew a four-inch-long lock blade knife from his pocket and stabbed the victim fatally in the neck. After the defendant was confronted with his deed, he made a statement that could be interpreted to mean he was not remorseful but, to the contrary, was unconcerned about the welfare of the victim. In addition to the jury hearing testimony from eyewitnesses to the killing, the defendant confessed.

There is no doubt what inferences and findings of fact the jury had to draw in order to convict the defendant of first degree murder. The jury must have believed that: (1) The "horseplay" provocation was not sufficient to justify a deadly attack; (2) the defendant was under no real fear of his own from being attacked; (3) the stabbing was intentional; and (4) the time it took the defendant to open his knife and inflict the mortal wound was sufficient to establish premeditation.[11]

The difficult factual question must have been the mental state of the defendant at the time of the stabbing. The evidence was somewhat conflicting on this point. While the evidence offered by the defendant is not impossible to believe, some of his explanations seem unlikely. Guilt beyond a reasonable doubt cannot be premised on pure conjecture. However, a conjecture consistent with the evidence becomes less and less conjecture and moves gradually toward proof, as alternative innocent explanations are discarded or made less likely. The beyond a reasonable doubt standard does not require the exclusion of every other hypothesis or, for that matter, every other reasonable hypothesis. It is enough if, after considering all the evidence, direct and circumstantial, a reasonable trier of fact could find the evidence established guilt beyond a reasonable doubt.

After reviewing the record, this Court has some doubt as to whether this is a first degree murder case; but, at this point, [it] makes absolutely no difference whether we on the appellate bench as jurors would have voted to convict the defendant of a lesser-included offense or whether we would have thought there was some reasonable doubt. To the contrary, the question * * * is whether any rational jury could on the evidence presented think the defendant premeditated and intentionally killed the victim. We do not find the evidence so weak as to render the verdict irrational. A rational jury may well have found the defendant guilty of some lesser-included crime without violating its oath; but, drawing all favorable inferences in favor of the prosecution, a rational jury could also convict. We end by suggesting that variations in human experience suggest it is not unexpected to see a considerable range of reasonable verdicts or estimates about what is likely or unlikely. Thus, we find the evidence sufficient * * *.

The principal question before us under this assignment of error is whether our instructions on murder when given together deprive a criminal defendant of due process or are otherwise wrong and confusing. * * *

The purpose of instructing the jury is to focus its attention on the essential issues of the case and inform it of the permissible ways in which these issues may be resolved. If

---

11. The evidence shows the victim's actions were irritating to the defendant well before the stabbing took place. His anger was building with each comment and flip of the towel. Furthermore, witnesses testified the defendant attempted to stab the victim a second time as he fell to the ground. The evidence shows the victim was slashed in the arm during this attempt. Finally, the defendant's statement that he "had the right to respond, finally, to this act of aggression that was perpetrated against [him]" is considered probative evidence of premeditation and deliberation.

instructions are properly delivered, they succinctly and clearly will inform the jury of the vital role it plays and the decisions it must make. "Without [adequate] instructions as to the law, the jury becomes mired in a factual morass, unable to draw the appropriate legal conclusions based on the facts." This is, in essence, what the defendant argues in this case, i.e., the instructions were inadequate and failed to inform the jury of the difference between first and second degree murder. More precisely, the defendant asserts the trial court's instructions regarding the elements of first degree murder were improper because the terms wilful, deliberate, and premeditated were equated with a mere intent to kill.[17]

The jury was instructed that in order to find the defendant guilty of murder it had to find five elements beyond a reasonable doubt: "The Court further instructs the jury that murder in the first degree is when one person kills another person unlawfully, willfully, maliciously, deliberately and premeditatedly[.]" In its effort to define these terms, the trial court gave three instructions. State's Instruction No. 8, commonly referred to as the *Clifford* instruction, stated:

> "The Court instructs the jury that to constitute a willful, deliberate and premeditated killing, it is not necessary that the intention to kill should exist for any particular length of time prior to the actual killing; it is only necessary that such intention should have come into existence for the first time at the time of such killing, or at any time previously."

State's Instruction No. 10 stated: "The Court instructs the jury that in order to constitute a 'premeditated' murder an intent to kill need exist only for an instant." State's Instruction No. 12 stated: "The Court instructs the jury that what is meant by the language willful, deliberate and premeditated is that the killing be intentional." State's Instruction Nos. 10 and 12 are commonly referred to as *Schrader* instructions.

The linchpin of the problems that flow from these instructions is the failure adequately to inform the jury of the difference between first and second degree murder. Of particular concern is the lack of guidance to the jury as to what constitutes premeditation and the manner in which the instructions infuse premeditation with the intent to kill.

At common law, murder was defined as the unlawful killing of another human being with "malice aforethought." Because the common law definition of "malice aforethought" was extremely flexible, "it became over time an 'arbitrary symbol' used by trial judges to signify any of the number of mental states deemed sufficient to support liability for murder." Nevertheless, most American jurisdictions maintained a law of murder built around common law classifications. Pertinent to this case, the most significant departure from the common law came on April 22, 1794, when the Pennsylvania Legislature enacted a statute dividing murder into degrees.[20] It decreed that the death penalty would be inflicted only for first degree murder. West Virginia, like most other states, followed the Pennsylvania practice. Indeed, the 1794 Pennsylvania statute is nearly identical to W.Va. Code, 61–2–1 (1991), our murder statute.

---

17. A form of this argument was made to this Court before when similar instructions were challenged and we found the contention to be without merit. See *State v. Schrader*, 172 W.Va. 1, 302 S.E.2d 70 (1982). * * *. For purposes of convenience, we will refer to instructions regarding the length of time necessary to form an intent to kill as the *Clifford* instruction, see *State v. Clifford*, 59 W.Va. 1, 52 S.E. 981 (1906), and those equating the intent to kill with premeditation as the *Schrader* instruction.

20. The 1794 Pennsylvania statute provided that "all murder, which shall be perpetrated by means of poison, or by lying in wait, or by any other kind of willful, deliberate and premeditated killing, or which shall be committed in the perpetration or attempt to perpetrate any arson, rape, robbery, or burglary, shall be deemed murder of the first degree; and all other kinds of murder shall be deemed murder in the second degree [.]"

The West Virginia Legislature chose not to define the term "premeditated" in W.Va.Code, 61–2–1. As a result, this Court consistently has resorted to the common law.

In addition to *Clifford*, there are several cases that have made specific attempts to further define premeditation. In *State v. Dodds*, 54 W.Va. 289, 297–98, 46 S.E. 228, 231 (1903), we said:

> " 'The next ingredient of the crime is that it must be deliberate. To deliberate is to reflect, with a view to make a choice. If a person reflects, though but for a moment before he acts, it is unquestionably a sufficient *deliberation* within the meaning of the statute. The last requisite is that the killing must be *premeditated*. *To premeditate is to think of a matter before it is executed. The word, premeditated, would seem to imply something more than deliberate, and may mean that the party not only deliberated, but had formed in his mind the plan of destruction.*' " (Emphasis added to last sentence).

In *State v. Hatfield*, 169 W.Va. 191, 286 S.E.2d 402 (1982), we made an effort to distinguish the degrees of murder by indicating that the elements that separate first degree murder and second degree murder are deliberation and premeditation in addition to the formation of the specific intent to kill. Deliberation and premeditation mean to reflect upon the intent to kill and make a deliberate choice to carry it out. Although no particular amount of time is required, there must be at least a sufficient period to permit the accused to actually consider in his or her mind the plan to kill. In this sense, murder in the first degree is a calculated killing as opposed to a spontaneous event. After noting the above language in *Dodds*, Justice Miller stated in *Hatfield*:

> "The terms 'deliberate' and 'premeditated' have not often been defined in our cases but do carry a certain degree of definitional overlap. This point is made in LaFave & Scott, *Criminal Law* § 73, at 563 (1972 ed.):
>
> > " 'To be guilty of this form of first degree murder the defendant must not only intend to kill but in addition he must premeditate the killing and deliberate about it. It is not easy to give a meaningful definition of the words "premeditate" and "deliberate" as they are used in connection with first degree murder. Perhaps the best that can be said of "deliberation" is that it requires a cool mind that is capable of reflection, and of "premeditation" that it requires that the one with the cool mind did in fact reflect, at least for a short period of time before his act of killing.' (Footnotes omitted)
>
> "But, as LaFave & Scott also point out: 'The intention may be finally formed only as a conclusion of prior premeditation and deliberation.' "

Although we approved the jury instruction from *Clifford* that "it is only necessary that the intention to kill should have come into existence for the first time at the time of the killing" in *Hatfield*, Justice Miller explained this instruction was merely intended to convey the notion that it is possible for deliberation and premeditation to precede the formation of the actual intent to kill. Justice Miller further stated:

> "Here, the *Clifford* instruction refers primarily to the intention to kill not existing for any particular time and arising at the moment of the killing. This means the specific intent to kill and is to be distinguished from the elements of deliberation and premeditation which are the state of mind conveying the characteristics of reflection."

This is the meaning of the so-called *Clifford* instruction and, when it is given, its significance should be explained to the jury.

The source of the problem in the present case stems from language in *State v. Schrader*, 172 W.Va. 1, 302 S.E.2d 70 (1982). While this Court elaborated on the meaning of premeditation, we gave it a different definition than that approved in *Hatfield* and *Dodds*. In *Schrader*, we stated:

> "Hence, when the West Virginia Legislature adopted the Virginia murder statute in 1868, the meaning of 'premeditated' as used in the statute was essentially 'knowing' and 'intentional.' Since then, courts have consistently recognized that the mental process necessary to constitute 'willful, deliberate and premeditated' murder can be accomplished very quickly or even in the proverbial 'twinkling of an eye.' ... *The achievement of a mental state contemplated in a statute such as ours can immediately precede the act of killing. Hence, what is really meant by the language 'willful, deliberate and premeditated' in W.Va.Code, 61–2–1 [1923] is that the killing be intentional.*" (Emphasis added).

The language emphasized above supplied the legal authority and basis for State's Instruction Nos. 10 and 12.

While many jurisdictions do not favor the distinction between first and second degree murder,[22] given the doctrine of separation of powers, we do not have the judicial prerogative to abolish the distinction between first and second degree murder and rewrite the law of homicide for West Virginia; unless, of course, we were to declare this classification a violation of due process and force the Legislature to rewrite the law—a bold stroke that we refuse to do. On the other hand, we believe within the parameters of our current homicide statutes the *Schrader* definition of premeditation and deliberation is confusing, if not meaningless. To allow the State to prove premeditation and deliberation by only showing that the intention came "into existence for the first time at the time of such killing" completely eliminates the distinction between the two degrees of murder. Hence, we feel compelled in this case to attempt to make the dichotomy meaningful by making some modifications to our homicide common law.

Premeditation and deliberation should be defined in a more careful, but still general way to give juries both guidance and reasonable discretion. Although premeditation and deliberation are not measured by any particular period of time, there must be some period between the formation of the intent to kill and the actual killing, which indicates the killing is by prior calculation and design. As suggested by the dissenting opinion in *Green v. State*, 1 Tenn.Crim.App. 719, 735, 450 S.W.2d 27, 34 (1970): "True, it is not necessary to prove premeditation existed for any definite period of time. But it is necessary to prove that it did exist." This means there must be an opportunity for some reflection on the intention to kill after it is formed. The accused must kill purposely after contemplating the intent to kill. Although an elaborate plan or scheme to take life is not required, our *Schrader* 's notion of instantaneous premeditation and momentary deliberation is not satisfactory for proof of first degree murder. In *Bullock v. United States*, 74 App.D.C. 220, 221, 122 F.2d 213, 214 (1941), the court discussed the need to have some appreciable time elapse between the intent to kill and the killing:

> "To speak of premeditation and deliberation which are instantaneous, or which take no appreciable time, is a contradiction in terms. It deprives the statutory

---

22. The Model Penal Code and many of the modern state criminal codes abolish the first and second degree murder distinction in favor of classifications based on more meaningful criteria. Interestingly, defining premeditation in such a way that the formation of the intent to kill and the killing can result from successive impulses, see *Schrader*, supra (intent equals premeditation formula), grants the jury complete discretion to find more ruthless killers guilty of first degree murder regardless of actual premeditation. History teaches that such unbridled discretion is not always carefully and thoughtfully employed, and this case may be an example. In 1994, the Legislature raised the penalty for second degree murder to ten-to-forty years (from five-to-eighteen years), making it less important to give juries the unguided discretion to find the aggravated form of murder in the case of more ruthless killings, irrespective of actual premeditation. The penalties are now comparable.

requirement of all meaning and destroys the statutory distinction between first and second degree murder. At common law there were no degrees of murder. If the accused had no overwhelming provocation to kill, he was equally guilty whether he carried out his murderous intent at once or after mature reflection. Statutes like ours, which distinguish deliberate and premeditated murder from other murder, reflect a belief that one who meditates an intent to kill and then deliberately executes it is more dangerous, more culpable or less capable of reformation than one who kills on sudden impulse; or that the prospect of the death penalty is more likely to deter men from deliberate than from impulsive murder. The deliberate killer is guilty of first degree murder; the impulsive killer is not. The quoted part of the charge was therefore erroneous."

Thus, there must be some evidence that the defendant considered and weighed his decision to kill in order for the State to establish premeditation and deliberation under our first degree murder statute.[23] This is what is meant by a ruthless, cold-blooded, calculating killing. Any other intentional killing, by its spontaneous and nonreflective nature, is second degree murder.[24]

We * * * agree with the defendant that the language in our opinion in *Schrader* virtually eliminates the distinction in this State between first and second degree murder, equating as it does premeditation with the formation of the intent to kill. We have tried to clarify the difference between the degrees of murder in the preceding paragraphs. We find that *Schrader* wrongly equated premeditation with intent to kill and in so doing undermined the more meaningful language of *Hatfield* and *Dodds*. To the extent that the *Schrader* opinion is inconsistent with our holding today, it is overruled. * * *

Overturning precedent with a long standing in the law that has become an integrated fabric in the law is different. Therefore, we leave in tact the *Clifford* rule as amplified by *Hatfield*. So by refusing to follow *Schrader* but continuing *Clifford* and *Hatfield*, "we do not depart from the fabric of the law; we restore it."

Finally, we feel obligated to discuss what instruction defining premeditation is now acceptable. What came about as a mere suggestion in *Hatfield*, we now approve as a proper instruction under today's decision:

"A more appropriate instruction for first degree murder, paraphrased from 2 Devitt and Blackmar, *Federal Jury Practice and Instructions* § 41.03, at 214, is:

" 'The jury is instructed that murder in the first degree consists of an intentional, deliberate and premeditated killing which means that the killing is done after a period of time for prior consideration. The duration of that period cannot be arbitrarily fixed. The time in which to form a deliberate and premeditat-

---

23. In the absence of statements by the accused which indicate the killing was by prior calculation and design, a jury must consider the circumstances in which the killing occurred to determine whether it fits into the first degree category. Relevant factors include the relationship of the accused and the victim and its condition at the time of the homicide; whether plan or preparation existed either in terms of the type of weapon utilized or the place where the killing occurred; and the presence of a reason or motive to deliberately take life. No one factor is controlling. Any one or all taken together may indicate actual reflection on the decision to kill. This is what our statute means by "willful, deliberate and premeditated killing."

24. As examples of what type of evidence supports a finding of first degree murder, we identify three

categories: (1) "planning" activity—facts regarding the defendant's behavior prior to the killing which might indicate a design to take life; (2) facts about the defendant's prior relationship or behavior with the victim which might indicate a motive to kill; and (3) evidence regarding the nature or manner of the killing which indicate a deliberate intention to kill according to a preconceived design. The California courts evidently require evidence of all three categories or at least extremely strong evidence of planning activity or evidence of category (2) in conjunction with either (1) or (3). See *People v. Anderson*, 70 Cal.2d 15, 73 Cal.Rptr. 550, 447 P.2d 942 (1968). These examples are illustrative only and are not intended to be exhaustive.

ed design varies as the minds and temperaments of people differ, and according to the circumstances in which they may be placed. Any interval of time between the forming of the intent to kill and the execution of that intent, which is of sufficient duration for the accused to be fully conscious of what he intended, is sufficient to support a conviction for first degree murder.' "

Having approved a new instruction in the area of homicide law, we do not believe today's decision should be applied retroactively. * * * Nevertheless, we need not apply the "new rule" to the defendant's case on this appeal because this case is being reversed on other grounds. The defendant is entitled, however, to the benefit of this decision on remand. * * *

WORKMAN, JUSTICE, concurring:

I concur with the holding of the majority, but write this separate opinion to reiterate that the duration of the time period required for premeditation cannot be arbitrarily fixed. Neither the jury instruction approved by the majority, created from our past decisions, nor the new instruction approved in the majority opinion affix any specific amount of time which must pass between the formation of the intent to kill and the actual killing for first degree murder cases. Given the majority's recognition that these concepts are necessarily incapable of being reduced formulaically, I am concerned that some of the language in the opinion may indirectly suggest that some appreciable length of time must pass before premeditation can occur.

I agree with the majority in its conclusion that our decision in *Schrader* incorrectly equated premeditation with intent to kill. However, I must point out that the majority's suggested basis for defining premeditation and deliberation in terms of requiring some "appreciable time elapse between the intent to kill and the killing" and "some period between the formation of the intent to kill and the actual killing which indicates that the killing is by prior calculation and design" may create confusion in suggesting that premeditation must be the deeply thoughtful enterprise typically associated with the words reflection[2] and contemplation.[3] The majority's interpretation may create ambiguity, if not clarified, by adding arguably contradictory factors to the law enunciated by the majority in the approved instruction, as well as the language in the *Hatfield* and *Dodds* cases that the majority upholds. * * *

Notes and Questions

1. Benjamin Cardozo, *Law and Literature and Other Essays and Addresses* 99–101 (1931): "I think the distinction is much too vague to be continued in our law. There can be no intent unless there is a choice, yet by the hypothesis, the choice without more is enough to justify the inference that the intent was deliberate and premeditated. The presence of a sudden impulse is said to mark the dividing line, but how can an impulse be anything but sudden when the time for its formation is measured by the lapse of seconds? Yet the decisions are to the effect that seconds may be enough. What is meant, as I understand it, is that the impulse must be the product of an emotion or passion so swift and overmastering as to sweep the mind from its moorings. A metaphor, however, is, to say the least, a shifting test whereby to measure degrees of guilt that mean the difference between life and death. I think the students of the mind should make it clear to the lawmakers that the statute is framed along the lines of a defective and unreal psychology. If intent is deliberate and premeditated whenever there is choice, then in truth it is always deliberate and

---

2. The word "reflect" is defined by Webster's as "to think quietly and calmly."

3. The word "contemplate" is defined by Webster's as "to view or consider with continued attention."

premeditated, since choice is involved in the hypothesis of the intent. What we have is merely a privilege offered to the jury to find the lesser degree when the suddenness of the intent, the vehemence of the passion, seems to call irresistibly for the exercise of mercy. I have no objection to giving them this dispensing power, but it should be given to them directly and not in a mystifying cloud of words. The present distinction is so obscure that no jury hearing it for the first time can fairly be expected to assimilate and understand it.[a] I am not at all sure that I understand it myself after trying to apply it for many years and after diligent study of what has been written in the books. Upon the basis of this fine distinction with its obscure and mystifying psychology, scores of men have gone to their death.''

2.   In light of this criticism, would you say that the court in *Guthrie* did just the right thing, too much, or too little? Compare *People v. Smithey*, 20 Cal.4th 936, 86 Cal.Rptr.2d 243, 978 P.2d 1171 (1999), upholding as sufficiently clear the following instruction, consisting of the previously-used standard instruction plus the italicized language added in light of legislative abrogation of *People v. Wolff* (1964) 61 Cal.2d 795, 40 Cal.Rptr. 271, 394 P.2d 959 (1964), which had imposed such a requirement:

"All murder which is perpetrated by any kind of willful, deliberate and premeditated killing with express malice aforethought is murder of the first degree. The word 'willful,' as used in these instructions, means intentional. The word 'deliberate' means formed or arrived at or determined upon as a result of the careful thought and weighing and consideration for and against the proposed course of action. The word 'premeditated' means considered beforehand. If you find that the killing was preceded and accompanied by a clear, deliberate intent on the part of the defendant to kill, which was the result of deliberation and premeditation, so it must have been formed upon pre-existing reflection and not under a sudden heat of passion or other condition precluding the idea of deliberation, it is murder in the first degree. *To prove the killing was deliberate and premeditated, it shall not be necessary to prove the defendant maturely and meaningfully reflected upon the gravity of this act.* The law does not undertake to measure in units of time the length of the period during which the thought must be pondered before it can ripen into an intent to kill which is truly deliberate and premeditated. The time will vary with different individuals and under varying circumstances. The true test is not the duration of time, but rather the extent of the reflection. A cold, calculated judgment and decision may be arrived at in a short period of time, but a mere unconsidered and rash impulse, even though it include an intent to kill, is not such deliberation and premeditation as will fix an unlawful killing as murder of the first degree. To constitute a deliberate and premeditated killing, the slayer must weigh and consider the question of killing and the

---

a.   Consider, in this regard, *People v. Sneed*, 183 Colo. 96, 514 P.2d 776 (1973). The trial court dismissed a charge of first degree murder on the ground that the murder statute was unconstitutionally vague. The statute defined first degree murder as causing death "with premeditated intent to cause the death," second degree murder as causing death "intentionally, but without premeditation," and premeditation as "a design formed to do something at any time before it is done." The trial court emphasized that under *Van Houten v. People*, 22 Colo. 53, 43 P. 137 (1895), the length of time needed for premeditation is the time sufficient for "one thought to follow another." In reversing the trial court, the court asserted:

"It is true that if we apply the rule in *Van Houten* that premeditation occurs as fast as one thought follows another, then there does not seem to be much difference between 'premeditated intent' and 'intentionally.' But as we have said, the legislature certainly intended that there be a meaningful distinction between first degree and second degree murder. Accordingly, it is clear that it, as it had the power to do, rejected the definition of premeditation as announced in *Van Houten*. In effect, by emphasizing that 'premeditated intent' and 'intentionally, but without premeditation' were different, and that premeditation required design before the act, it indicated deliberation and reflection were necessary to create the premeditated intent.

"This means that between the forming of the intent to do the act and the act itself, an appreciable length of time must have elapsed to allow deliberation, reflection and judgment.''

reasons for and against such a choice and, having in mind the consequences, he decides to and does kill."

3. *Model Penal Code* § 210.6, Comment (1980): "It seems clear that the deliberation standard ought to exclude from the capital category cases where the homicide is committed under the influence of an extreme mental or emotional disturbance produced by causes that give rise to proper sympathy for the defendant. * * * Given this recognition of the role of mental or emotional disturbance, the case for a mitigated sentence on conviction of murder does not depend on a distinction between impulse and deliberation. Prior reflection may reveal the uncertainties of a tortured conscience rather than exceptional depravity. The very fact of a long internal struggle may be evidence that the homicidal impulse was deeply aberrational and far more the product of extraordinary circumstances than a true reflection of the actor's normal character. Thus, for example, one suspects that most mercy killings are the consequence of long and careful deliberation, but they are not especially appropriate cases for imposition of capital punishment. The same is likely to be true with respect to suicide pacts, many infanticides and cases where a provocation gains in its explosive power as the actor broods about his injury.[b]

"It also seems clear, moreover, that some purely impulsive murders will present no extenuating circumstance. The suddenness of the killing may simply reveal callousness so complete and depravity so extreme that no hesitation is required. As Stephen put the point long ago:

> As much cruelty, as much indifference to the life of others, a disposition at least as dangerous to society, probably even more dangerous, is shown by sudden as by premeditated murders. The following cases appear to me to set this in a clear light. A, passing along the road, sees a boy sitting on a bridge over a deep river and, out of mere wanton barbarity, pushes him into it and so drowns him. A man makes advances to a girl who repels him. He deliberately but instantly cuts her throat. A man civilly asked to pay a just debt pretends to get the money, loads a rifle and blows out his creditor's brains. In none of these cases is there premeditation unless the word is used in a sense as unnatural as 'aforethought' in 'malice aforethought', but each represents even more diabolical cruelty and ferocity than that which is involved in murders premeditated in the natural sense of the word.[62]"

b. Consider, for example, *People v. Gibson*, 23 Cal. App.3d 917, 101 Cal.Rptr. 620 (1972), affirming a first degree murder conviction on these facts: "On January 4, 1971, the defendant fired a single shot into the head of his twelve-year-old son causing his almost immediate death. He called the police, informed them of the killing and was taken into custody at the scene. At the initial meeting with the arresting officers the defendant appeared to be calm and rational and in possession of his faculties. His constitutional rights were read to him from a '*Miranda*' advisement card, and he again stated that he had killed his son. He did not appear, at this time, to be confused, irrational, or in any type of trance or pain.

"The deceased son was described by his mother as an autistic child who was unable to speak, had no empathy, failed to relate to sadness, was self-destructive and hyperactive, with a sexual orientation which was causing his parents concern because of fear that he might harm someone.

"A psychiatrist described infantile autism as one of the most severe, if not the most severe form of childhood mental disorder. It is characterized by failure to talk, severe motor disturbances, compulsive repetitious behavior, inability to learn, and problems with interpersonal relationships. The autistic child frequently becomes the focal point of his family because of the needs and demands he generates. Many times the family structure is severely disturbed by the intense and constant preoccupation with the problems of the autistic child.

"Defendant had suffered from a severe heart condition since approximately 1958 and had suffered an attack as recently as the day before the killing of the son. The years of hopeless search for assistance for the autistic son, coupled with physical deterioration of the defendant as a consequence of his heart disease, was proffered by defense to prove that defendant's mental state at the time of the offense was such that he could not by reason of diminished mental capacity form the degree of intent requisite for first degree murder."

62. 3 J. Stephen, *History of the Criminal Law* 94 (1883).

4. What is the best solution to the problems set out in the preceding notes? Should the premeditation-deliberation test and, indeed, any division of murder into degrees be abandoned, as a number of jurisdictions have done? Or, should a new test be devised? Consider *State v. Jenkins,* 48 Ohio App.2d 99, 355 N.E.2d 825 (1976), commenting upon the new provision that the defendant must have purposely caused the death of another with "prior calculation and design":

"Prior calculation and design sets up a more demanding standard than the old first degree murder standard of 'deliberate and premeditated malice.' Prior calculation and design requires the accused to have killed purposefully after devising a plan or scheme to kill. There must be some kind of studied analysis with its object being the means by which to kill. The kind of momentary deliberation or instantaneous premeditation that was the accepted standard under the old statute is no longer sufficient or acceptable.

"The trier of fact must look to the context in which the killing occurred to determine whether there was prior calculation and design. Some of the important factors to be examined and considered in deciding whether a homicide was committed with prior calculation and design include: whether the accused knew the victim prior to the crime, as opposed to a random meeting, and if the victim was known to him whether the relationship had been strained; whether thought and preparation were given by the accused to the weapon he used to kill and/or the site on which the homicide was to be committed as compared to no such thought or preparation; and whether the act was drawn out over a period of time as against an almost instantaneous eruption of events. These factors must be considered and weighed together and viewed under the totality of all circumstances of the homicide."

5. In *Anderson,* discussed in footnote 24 of *Guthrie,* the facts, as recited by the court, were as follows: "Defendant, a San Jose cab driver, had been living for about eight months with a Mrs. Hammond and her three children, Cynthia, aged 17, Kenneth, aged 13, and the victim, Victoria, aged 10. On the morning of the day of the murder, December 7, 1962, Mrs. Hammond left for work at 7:30 a.m., leaving only Victoria at home with the defendant. Defendant was still in bed. He had been home from work for the previous two days, during which time he had been drinking heavily, and apparently he did not go to work on the day of the murder.

"The owner of a nearby liquor store testified that defendant purchased a quart of whisky from him sometime between 1 and 2 p.m. on December 7, 1962. The only other witness who testified as to defendant's whereabouts that day prior to the discovery of the murder was the victim's 13–year–old brother Kenneth.

"Kenneth testified that he arrived home from school at 3:30 p.m. on December 7. He found the front door locked, which was not unusual, so he went around to the back of the house and down to the basement. Kenneth stayed there awhile working with his microscope. In a short time he heard noise coming from upstairs in the house which sounded like boxes and other things being moved around, like someone was cleaning up. He then heard the shower water running. A police officer later verified that a person in the basement could hear water running in the shower and movement in Victoria's bedroom.

"Kenneth testified further that he then came up from the basement and went to the back porch screen door. The screen door was locked, which also was not unusual, so Kenneth jerked on it so the hook would pop out. Kenneth then went from the back porch directly into his bedroom to change his clothes. He then returned through the back porch to the kitchen door which was also locked. Kenneth knocked on the door and the defendant opened it. Kenneth testified that the defendant was wearing slacks only. Kenneth went into the kitchen and asked defendant for $1.00 for a teen club dance he intended to attend that evening. Defendant obtained a dollar for him out of the pocket of another pair of slacks hanging on the knob of a bedroom door. When Kenneth noticed the blood on the kitchen floor and asked defendant about it, the defendant told Kenneth that he had cut himself. This explanation apparently satisfied Kenneth, as he finished dressing and left the house sometime before 4 p.m.

"Kenneth testified that no one else was at his house when he was there between 3:30 and 4 p.m. He further testified that about 6:30 he realized that he had forgotten his wallet and returned home. As he approached the front door, his mother came out and asked to see the cut on his arm, and Kenneth explained that he had no cut. His mother then asked defendant about the blood she had noticed and defendant told her that Victoria had cut herself, but that the mother should not worry, as the cut was not serious. After defendant told her that Victoria was at a friend's for dinner, the mother wanted to take Kenneth with her to get Victoria. Kenneth went back to his room to get a jacket. Because he had a "weird" feeling, he looked into Victoria's room. He found her nude, bloody body under some boxes and blankets on the floor near her bed. Kenneth ran out of the room screaming that defendant had killed her. Mrs. Hammond, after seeing Victoria's body, went next door to phone the police.

"Mrs. Hammond testified that she returned home from work at 4:45 p.m. The front door was locked, she rang the doorbell, and defendant answered. Mrs. Hammond noticed blood on the couch in the living room, and when she asked defendant about it, he told her that Kenneth had cut himself playing with a knife and that he was at a teenage dance. Mrs. Hammond then went to the grocery store and returned about 5:30 p.m. She testified that at both times she arrived home defendant was drinking a highball. She also testified as to examining Kenneth's arm for a cut when he returned home for his wallet and as to defendant's subsequent explanation that Victoria had been cut, but not seriously. Mrs. Hammond discovered Victoria's body after Kenneth came out of Victoria's room.

"A classmate of Victoria, who was the last person to see Victoria alive, testified that she left Victoria in front of the Hammond house about 3:45 p.m. after the two of them had walked home from school.

"When the police arrived at 7 p.m. the shades were down on all the windows and the doors were locked. Defendant finally opened the front door for one of the officers who arrested and handcuffed defendant. The arresting officer testified that defendant was wearing slacks, no shirt or shoes, and that there was no blood on him.

"The arresting officer found Victoria's body on the floor near her bed. He found defendant's blood-spotted shorts on a chair in the living room, and a knife and defendant's socks, with blood encrusted on the soles, in the master bedroom. The evidence established that the victim's torn and blood-stained dress had been ripped from her, that her clothes, including her panties out of which the crotch had been ripped, were found in various rooms of the house, that there were bloody footprints matching the size of the victim's leading from the master bedroom to Victoria's room, and that there was blood in almost every room including the kitchen, the floor of which appeared to have been mopped.

"The TV cameraman who covered the murder story for channel 11, the officer who drove defendant to the police station, and the officer who "observed" defendant for four hours at the station the night of December 7, 1962, all testified that defendant did not appear intoxicated. The officers who talked to defendant testified, however, that they smelled alcohol on his breath; a blood test taken at 7:45 p.m. indicated that the alcohol content in defendant's blood was .34 percent, which was more than necessary for an automobile driver to be classified as 'under the influence.'

"Over 60 wounds, both severe and superficial, were found on Victoria's body. The cuts extended over her entire body, including one extending from the rectum through the vagina, and the partial cutting off of her tongue. Several of the wounds, including the vaginal lacerations, were post mortem. No evidence of spermatozoa was found in the victim, on her panties, or on the bed next to which she was found."

The court, in reducing defendant's conviction from first degree murder to second degree murder, explained: "[W]e find that the only evidence of (1) defendant's behavior prior to the killing which could be described as 'planning' activity related to a killing purpose was defendant's sending the victim's brother on an errand and apparently returning home alone with the decedent. Such evidence is highly ambiguous in terms of the various inferences it could support as to defendant's purpose in so behaving. The evidence of (2) defendant's prior behavior with the victim (alleged sexual molestation and his question as to her virginity) is insufficient to support a reasonable inference that defendant had a 'motive' to kill the girl, which could in turn support an inference that the striking with the machete was the result of a 'preconceived design' and 'forethought.' Finally, the evidence of (3) the manner of killing (brutal hacking) does not support a reasonable inference of deliberately placed blows, which could in turn support an inference that the act of killing was premeditated rather than 'hasty and impetuous.' * * *

"Finally, the defendant * * * attempted to 'cover up' the crime * * *. Although this type of evidence may possibly bear on defendant's state of mind *after* the killing, it is irrelevant to ascertaining defendant's state of mind immediately prior to, or during, the killing. Evasive conduct shows fear: it cannot support the double inference that defendant planned to hide his crime at the time he committed it and that therefore defendant committed the crime with premeditation and deliberation."

Do you agree? In which of the following four cases should a conviction for first degree murder be affirmed on appeal?

6. The fully-clothed body of Mrs. Mesa was found in her home, where she had bled to death from 38 knife wounds to the head, face, neck, back and arms, none to a vital organ. Two different knives had been used, including the one found broken under her body. There were blood drops throughout the master bedroom, and drops of blood were found inside jewelry boxes and on clothing inside open drawers. In the kitchen, many of the cupboards and drawers were open, and drops of blood were found inside some drawers, including one containing knives. Mr. Mesa found nothing missing from the house except one of his dress shirts. Defendant, who had attended high school with Mrs. Mesa and her husband, was charged with the murder when his fingerprints were found in the house, his father produced the missing shirt, defendant was found to have a cut on his hand, and defendant's blood matched that found about the Mesa's house.[c]

7. The defendant told someone the morning of the murder that he would "like to have a little loving." On the evening of the murder he went to a bar where he threatened a woman who refused to dance with him. Later that evening he left another bar with a man who saw the victim approaching the intersection where he parted company with the defendant. The victim was found the next morning under a car at a service station near that intersection. She apparently had been dragged there. She was wearing a raincoat with only a slip and panties on underneath. All three garments were ripped open so that the front part of her body was exposed. She was lying on her back with her legs spread apart. She had suffered multiple contusions, caused by an estimated 20 to 80 blows. Four heel

c. *People v. Perez,* 2 Cal.4th 1117, 9 Cal.Rptr.2d 577, 831 P.2d 1159 (1992), holding the evidence was sufficient under the *Anderson* formula.

marks were found on her body, and a key to the defendant's hotel room was found in her clothing. The morning after the murder defendant told someone that "I beat up a woman" and that when he hit them "they stayed hit."[d]

8.   Defendant was an acquaintance of Mrs. Southerland and had been an occasional visitor at her home. He stopped by unexpectedly one evening while Mrs. Southerland and her 10–year–old grandson were watching television. They talked for more than an hour, laughing and chatting amicably with no heated discussions, arguments, or threats. Defendant walked back and forth to the window on several occasions, and repeatedly asked when Mr. Southerland would be home. Some time after the grandson had retired, Mrs. Southerland gently suggested to defendant that she wished to go to sleep, but defendant did not take the hint. At about 10:40 p.m., as she began to doze off, she was struck on the head by a succession of blows. She heard quick footsteps which she thought were headed toward the front door, and she then managed to drag herself out the back door. She then heard her grandson scream from his upstairs bedroom. When the police arrived, they found the grandson on the bed in his bedroom. The lad, his bed, the walls, and the floor all were covered with blood. He had been hit repeatedly with a blunt instrument and the blows to his head killed him. The defendant was later arrested at his home. The police found in his closet a hammer with the victim's blood on it.[e]

9.   Four eyewitnesses testified that defendant forced his way into the victim's automobile, parked on the pow-wow ground of the Rosebud Indian Reservation, put a butcher knife to her throat, and then stabbed her in the back as she attempted to escape his grasp. Defendant then threw the knife into the woods as he fled; it was recovered and was determined to be the knife which had disappeared from the residence of defendant's aunt several days earlier. Two witnesses placed defendant in the vicinity of the victim's parked car 30 minutes prior to the stabbing. The vehicle had been in good working order prior to its arrival, but some time during the celebration it had been disabled through disconnection of a coil wire. The victim, who had been defendant's wife during a brief and unstable marriage, died from the stab wound.[f]

SECTION 4. RECKLESS AND NEGLIGENT KILLING

HYAM v. DIRECTOR OF PUBLIC PROSECUTIONS

House of Lords, 1974.

[1975] A.C. 55, [1974] 2 W.L.R. 607, [1974] 2 All E.R. 41.

LORD HAILSHAM OF ST. MARYLEBONE. My Lords, in my view the one point in this case is the intention which it is necessary to impute to an accused person in order to find him guilty of the crime of murder. * * *

The facts are simple, and not in dispute. In the early hours of Saturday, July 15, 1972, the appellant set fire to a dwelling house in Coventry by deliberately pouring about half a gallon of petrol through the letter box and igniting it by means of a newspaper and a match. The house contained four persons, presumably asleep. They were a Mrs. Booth and her three children, a boy and the two girls who were the subjects of the charges. Mrs.

---

d. *People v. Craig*, 49 Cal.2d 313, 316 P.2d 947 (1957), holding the evidence only established second degree murder.

e. *Hemphill v. United States*, 402 F.2d 187 (D.C.Cir.1968), holding the evidence only established second degree murder.

f. *United States v. Blue Thunder*, 604 F.2d 550 (8th Cir.1979), affirming defendant's conviction of first degree murder.

Booth and the boy escaped alive through a window. The two girls died as the result of asphyxia by the fumes generated by the fire. The appellant's motive (in the sense in which I shall use the word 'motive') was jealousy of Mrs. Booth whom the appellant believed was likely to marry a Mr. Jones of whom the appellant herself was the discarded, or partly discarded, mistress. Her account of her actions, and her defence, was that she had started the fire only with the intention of frightening Mrs. Booth into leaving the neighbourhood, and that she did not intend to cause death or previous bodily harm. The judge directed the jury:

> "The prosecution must prove, beyond all reasonable doubt, that the accused intended to (kill or) do serious bodily harm to Mrs. Booth the mother of the deceased girls. If you are satisfied that when the accused set fire to the house she knew that it was highly probable that this would cause (death or) serious bodily harm then the prosecution will have established the necessary intent. It matters not if her motive was, as she says, to frighten Mrs. Booth."

The judge explained that he had put brackets round the words "kill or" and "death or" because he advised the jury to concentrate on the intent to do serious bodily harm rather than the intent to kill. * * *

* * * I do not think that foresight as such of a high degree of probability is at all the same thing as intention, and, in my view, it is not foresight but intention to kill or cause grievous bodily harm which absolves the heart surgeon in the case of the transplant, notwithstanding that he foresees as a matter of high probability that he action will probably actually kill the patient. It is the presence of an actual intention to kill or cause grievous bodily harm which convicts the murderer who takes a very long shot at his victim and kills him notwithstanding that he thinks correctly as he takes his aim that the odds are very much against his hitting him at all.

But what are we to say of the state of mind of a defendant who knows that a proposed course of conduct exposes a third party to a serious risk of death or grievous bodily harm, without actually intended those consequences, but nevertheless and without lawful excuse deliberately pursues that course of conduct regardless whether the consequences to his potential victim take place or not? In that case, if my analysis be correct, there is not merely actual foresight of the probable consequences, but actual intention to expose his victim to the risk of those consequences whether they in fact occur or not. Is that intention sufficient t6o reduce the crime to manslaughter notwithstanding a jury's finding that they are sure that it was the intention with which the act was done? In my opinion, it is not * * *. The heart surgeon exposes his patient to the risk, but does everything he can to save his life, regarding his actions as the best or only means of securing the patient's survival. He is, therefore, not exposing his patient to the risk without lawful excuse or regardless of the consequences. The reckless motorist who is guilty of manslaughter, but not murder, is not at least ordinarily aiming his actions at anyone * * *. If he were, it is quite possible that * * * he might be convicted of murder. In the field of guilty knowledge it has long been accepted both for the purposes of criminal and civil law that "a man who deliberately shuts his eyes to the truth will not be heard to say that he did not know it." Cannot the same be said of the state of intention of a man who, with actual appreciation of the risks and without lawful excuse, wilfully decides to expose potential victims to the risk of death or really serious injury regardless of whether the consequences take place or not? This seems to me to be the truth underlying the statement * * * that a rational man must be taken to intend the consequences of his acts. It is not a revival of the doctrine of constructive malice or the substitution of an objective for a subjective test of knowledge or intention. It is the man's actual state of knowledge and intent which, as in all other cases, determines his criminal responsibility. Nor, for the like reason, does this set up an irrebuttable presumption. It simply proclaims the moral truth that if a man, in full knowledge of the danger involved, and without lawful excuse, deliberately does that which exposes a victim to the risk of the probable grievous bodily harm (in the sense explained!) Or death, and the victim dies, the perpetrator of the crime is guilty of murder and not manslaughter to the same extent as if he had actually intended the consequence to follow, and irrespective of whether he wishes it. This is because the two types of intention are morally indistinguishable, although factually and logically distinct, and because it is therefore just that they should bear the same consequences to the perpetrator as they have the same consequences for the victim if death ensues.

This is not very far from the situation in this case. * * * Once it is conceded that [the defendant] was actually and subjectively aware of the danger to the sleeping occupants of the house in what she did, and that was the point which the judge brought to the jury's attention, it must surely follow naturally that she did what she did with the intention of exposing them to the danger of death or really serious injury regardless of whether such consequences actually ensued or not. * * * for this reason I do not think the summing up can be faulted, since the judge drew the jury's attention to the only debatable question in the case, and gave them a correct direction with regard to it. * * *

VISCOUNT DILHORNE. * * *

In this House Mr. McCullough for the appellant * * * submitted that knowledge that a certain consequence was a highly probable consequence does not establish an intent to produce that result. "All consequences that are foreseen are not," he said, "necessarily intended."

He also contended that the direction given by Ackner J. was erroneous in another respect, namely, that * * * intent to do grievous bodily harm did not, nor did knowledge that such harm was the probable result, suffice to make a killing murder. For it to be murder, he contended that the intent must be to kill or to endanger life or, if knowledge was enough, knowledge that the act would kill or endanger life.

With regard to his first contention, [i]n his *Digest of the Criminal Law*, published in 1877, in art. 223, Sir James Stephen defined "malice aforethought" as involving the following states of mind:

"(*a*) An intention to cause the death of, or grievous bodily harm to, any person, whether such person is the person actually killed or not;

(*b*) Knowledge that the act which causes death will probably cause the death of, or grievous bodily harm to, some person, whether such person is the person actually killed or not, although such knowledge is accompanied by indifference whether death or grievous bodily harm is caused or not, or by a wish that it may not be caused;
* * *."

Whether or not it be that the doing of the act with the knowledge that certain consequences are highly probable is to be treated as establishing the intent to bring about those consequences, I think it is clear that for at least 100 years such knowledge has been recognised as amounting to malice aforethought. * * *

I now turn to the second contention advanced on behalf of the appellant. This has two facets: first, that the reference to the intent to cause grievous bodily harm has been based on the law that killing in the course or furtherance of a felony is murder, and that when the Homicide Act 1957 was enacted abolishing constructive malice it meant that it no longer sufficed to establish intent to do grievous bodily harm; and, secondly, that, if intent to do grievous bodily harm still made a killing murder, it must be intent to do grievous bodily harm of such a character that life was likely to be endangered.

* * * But when one looks at the cases and the old textbooks, one does not find any indication that proof of intent to do grievous bodily harm was an ingredient of murder only on account of the doctrine of constructive malice. Indeed, one finds the contrary. * * *

Killing with intent to do grievous bodily harm has thus for many years been regarded as murder, quite apart from the doctrine of constructive malice. * * *

I now turn to the second facet of the appellant's contention, namely, that the words "grievous bodily harm" are to be interpreted as meaning harm of such a character as is likely to endanger life. * * *

If the words bore the meaning now contended for, there must have been many murder cases in which that was not explained to the jury and in which there was consequently a substantial misdirection. The Royal Commission on Capital Punishment in their review of the law did not suggest that the words had this limited meaning. Indeed, in paragraph 472 of the report [(1953) (Cmd. 8932)] the following appears:

> "We should therefore prefer to limit murder to cases where the act by which death is caused is intended to kill or to 'endanger life' or is known to be likely to kill or endanger life. But we do not believe that, if this change were made, it would lead to any great difference in the day-to-day administration of the law."

In the same paragraph it is stated that Stephen expressed the opinion that to substitute "bodily injury known to the offender to be likely to cause death" would to some extent narrow the definition. * * *

Our task is to say what, in our opinion, the law is, not what it should be. In the light of what I have said, in my opinion, the words "grievous bodily harm" must, as Viscount Kilmuir said, be given their ordinary and natural meaning and not have the gloss put on them for which the appellant contends. * * *

To change the law to substitute "bodily injury known to the offender to be likely to cause death" for "grievous bodily harm" is a task that should, in my opinion, be left to Parliament if it thinks such a change expedient. If it is made, an accused will be able to say: "True it is that I intended grievous bodily harm or that I knew such harm was likely to result but I never intended to kill the dead man or to put his life in danger and I did not know that by doing him serious bodily harm I would put his life in danger." But I share the view of the majority of the Royal Commission that such a change would not lead to any great difference in the day-to-day administration of the law.

For these reasons in my opinion this appeal should be dismissed.

Lord Diplock. * * *

Upon the first question I do not desire to say more than that I agree with those of your Lordships who take the uncomplicated view that in crimes of this class no distinction is to be drawn in English law between the state of mind of one who does an act because he desires it to produce a particular evil consequence, and the state of mind of one who does the act knowing full well that it is likely to produce that consequence although it may not be the object he was seeking to achieve by doing the act. What is common to both these states of mind is willingness to produce the particular evil consequence: and this, in my view, is the mens rea needed to satisfy a requirement, whether imposed by statute or existing at common law, that in order to constitute the offence with which the accused is charged he must have acted with "intent" to produce a particular evil consequence or, in the ancient phrase which still survives in crimes of homicide, with "malice aforethought."

I turn then to the second question. I believe that all your Lordships are agreed that if the English law of homicide were based on concepts that are satisfactory, both intellectually and morally, the crime of murder ought to be distinguished from less heinous forms of homicide by restricting it to cases where the consequence of his act, which the accused desired or foresaw as likely, was the death of a human being. * * *

If what was written before the 19th century about the degree of violence that must have been intended by the accused in order to support a charge of murder is to be properly understood, there are several matters to be borne in mind.

(1) It must be remembered that, judged by present day standards, we are dealing with a violent age. Men were used to carrying deadly weapons and not slow to resort to them. * * *

(2) Medical and surgical science were in a very primitive state. Any bodily injury, particularly if it involved risk of sepsis through an open wound, might well prove mortal although today the likelihood of its resulting in death would be insignificant. It was not until the last quarter of the 19th century that antiseptics came into general use.

(3) Until the 19th century the common law did not recognise unconsummated attempts to commit a crime as being criminal offences in themselves. So in relation to the crime of murder judges were dealing with bodily injuries which had in fact been fatal, and so demonstrated to have been of a kind which could endanger life.

(4) As stated by Foster J. it was accepted law in the 18th century that once the fact of killing was proved the onus lay upon the prisoner to prove facts negativing malice aforethought unless such facts arose out of the evidence produced against him.

(5) Until as late as 1898 persons accused of murder were incompetent to give evidence in their own defence. So the actual intent with which they had done the act which had in fact caused death could only be a matter of inference from the evidence of other witnesses as to what the accused had done or said. In drawing this inference from what he had done it was necessary to assume that the accused was gifted with the foresight and reasoning capacity of a "reasonable man" and, as such, must have foreseen as a possible consequence of his act, and thus within his intention, anything which, in the ordinary course of events, might result from it.

Bearing these considerations in mind, I for my part find it impossible to say with confidence whether or not by the close of this period judges, when in connection with malice aforethought they used various expressions connoting physical injuries, did so with the unexpressed major premise in mind: "All physical injuries, at any rate if they are serious, are likely to endanger life" and so equated intent to cause serious physical injuries with intent to endanger life. * * *

Since the first Commissioners on the Criminal Law issued their Fourth Report in 1839, it has been the uniform view of those who have assumed or been charged with the task of codifying the law of homicide that the relevant intention on a charge of murder should be an intention to kill or to cause any bodily injury which is known to the offender to be likely to endanger life. Such was the view expressed by the Criminal Code Commissioners in 1879, by Stephen in 1877 and 1833, by the Royal Commission on Capital Punishment in 1953 and by the Law Commission in 1966. [Report No. 10, Imputed Criminal Intention (*Director of Public Prosecutions v. Smith*)]. The significance of the citations that I have already made from all but the last of these is that they show that it was the opinion of these eminent lawyers at the various dates when they were writing that this would involve a rationalisation of the existing common law rather than any change in it. I have no doubt that the judges in the course of the 19th and 20th centuries would have held this to be the law as to express malice had they not been diverted from doing so by the doctrine of constructive malice. * * *

For my part I would allow the appeal and substitute a verdict of guilty of manslaughter for the verdict of guilty of murder.

Lord Cross of Chelsea. * * * I agree with my noble and learned friend, Lord Kilbrandon, that now that murder no longer attracts the death penalty it would be logical to replace the two crimes of murder and manslaughter by a single offence of unlawful homicide; but there are considerations, in which logic plays little part, which tell against the making of such a change—and as long as one has the two separate crimes one has to decide on which side of the line any given state of mind falls. Stephen's definition covers four states of mind. A(1) an intent to kill, (2) knowledge that the act in question will probably cause death. B(1) an intent to cause grievous bodily harm, (2) knowledge that the act in question will probably cause grievous bodily harm. Counsel for the appellant argued strenuously that there was a great gulf fixed between A(1) and B(1) on the one hand, and A(2) and B(2) on the other, and that unless the accused believed that the consequences in question were certain to ensue, one ought not to equate mere foresight of consequences with an intention to produce them. Even if one views the matter simply from the point of view of linguistics I am not sure that the ordinary man would agree. If, for example, someone parks a car in a city street with a time bomb in it which explodes and injures a number of people I think that the ordinary man might well argue as follows: "The man responsible for this outrage did not injure these people unintentionally; he injured them intentionally. So he can fairly be said to have intentionally injured them—that is to say, to have intended to injure them. The fact that he was not certain that anyone would be injured is quite irrelevant (after all, how could he possibly be certain that anyone would be injured?); and the fact that, although he foresaw that it was likely that some people would be injured, it was a matter of indifference to him whether they were injured or not (his object being simply to call attention to Irish grievances and to demonstrate the power of the I.R.A.) is equally irrelevant." But I can see that a logician might object that the ordinary man was using the word "intentionally" with two different shades of meaning, and I am prepared to assume that as a matter of the correct use of language the man in question did not intend to injure those who were in fact injured by his act. But we are not debating a problem of linguistics; we are asking ourselves whether Stephen was right in saying that the states of mind labelled A(2) and B(2) constitute "malice aforethought." The first question to be answered is whether if an intention to kill—using intention in the strict sense of the word—is murder—as it plainly is—doing an unlawful act with knowledge that it may well cause death ought also to be murder. I have no doubt whatever that it ought to be. * * * Turning now to the states of mind labelled B(1) and (2)—*if* it is the law that an intention to cause grievous bodily harm—using intention in the strict sense of the word—is "malice aforethought," whether or not one realises that one's act may endanger life, then I think that it is right that the doing of an act which one realises may well cause grievous bodily harm should also constitute malice aforethought whether or not one realises that one's act may endanger life. * * *

Lord Kilbrandon. * * *

My Lords, it is not so easy to feel satisfaction at the doubts and difficulties which seem to surround the crime of murder and the distinguishing from it of the crime of manslaughter. There is something wrong when crimes of such gravity, and I will say of such familiarity, call for the display of so formidable a degree of forensic and judicial learning as the present case has given rise to. I believe this to show that a more radical look at the problem is called for, and was called for immediately upon the passing of the Act of 1967.

Until that time the content of murder—and I am not talking about the definition of murder—was that form of homicide which is punishable with death. (It is not necessary to notice the experimental period during which capital murder and non-capital murder existed side by side.) Since no homicides are now punishable with death, these many hours and days have been occupied in trying to adjust a definition of that which has no content. There does not appear to be any good reason why the crimes of murder and manslaughter should not both be abolished, and the single crime of unlawful homicide substituted; one case will differ from another in gravity, and that can be taken care of by variation of sentences downwards from life imprisonment. It is no longer true, if it was ever true, to say that murder as we now define it is necessarily the most heinous example of unlawful homicide. The present case could form an excellent example exhibiting as it does, assuming it to be capable of classification as manslaughter, a degree of cold-blooded cruelty exceeding that to be found in many an impulsive crime which could never, on our present law, be so classified.

My Lords, since the passage in the summing up of the learned judge which was particularly noticed is not consistent with the common law as it has now, as I agree, been shown to be, and the proviso was not relied on, it follows that this appeal should be allowed.

Appeal dismissed.

NOTES AND QUESTIONS ON KILLING BY GROSS RECKLESSNESS (DEPRAVED HEART)

1. Claire Finkelstein, *The Inefficiency of Mens Rea*, 88 Calif.L.Rev. 895, 909 (2000): "It is not surprising that having adopted the curious position that the mens rea requirement for murder is intent, Hailsham then ended up distorting the meaning of intent in order to reach the result he would have reached under a broader interpretation of malice aforethought. This attests to the firmness of the intuition that the knowing or egregiously reckless killer is as bad as the intentional one. One might wonder why it matters which approach one takes—the narrow definition of malice aforethought coupled with the broad view of intent (Hailsham's approach), or the broad definition of malice aforethought coupled with the narrow view of intent (my argument and the more standard approach to both murder and intent). The result appears to be the same either way. But there are several reasons why the standard approach is preferable to Hailsham's." Such as?

2. K. J. M. Smith, *A Case of Reckless Murder*, 123 New L.J. 792, 793 (1973), written before *Hyam* was decided by the House of Lords, expressed the fear that if the instructions were upheld juries "would then need to be very carefully directed that they must ascertain exactly what the accused foresaw, at the time he carried out his fateful act, as regards harm and the likelihood of such harm occurring. A great difficulty would be trying to communicate to the jury the meaning of 'highly probable', and how the jury could deduce the extent of danger apparent to the accused. It does not require much imagination to see that anything resembling a uniform standard of approach and result would be hard to achieve. The consequential danger of this could be a considerable blurring of the distinction between murder and manslaughter with the probable further effect of diluting the odium which is usually attached to murder.

"Having hinted at some of the dangers involved in embracing recklessness in the context of murder, one must put the question: should recklessness form the basis of a murder charge in any circumstances? A familiar example is that of the person who plants in an aircraft a bomb primed to explode at 25,000 feet in order to collect the insurance money on his fake Old Master being carried as freight. In such a case the chances of life not being lost are of course infinitesimal, but if such a person had no intention of seriously harming anyone he would not (without the aid of some form of liability based on recklessness) be liable for murder even though he had foreseen the virtual certainty of death. Such an extreme example of recklessness is only a hair's breadth away from intent to kill and certainly it manifests such a similar degree of 'wickedness' (to borrow Lord Denning's terminology) as to warrant the stigma reserved for murder.

"The problem then is not one of possible fundamental ethical objections to accepting something other than direct intent to kill or cause grievous bodily harm as a basis of liability for murder, but rather where and how one is to draw the line between a reckless murder and manslaughter by recklessness, so as to be able to differentiate between cases equivalent to the bomb in the aircraft example from less extreme forms of recklessness."

3.   D. W. Elliott, *Offences Against the Person—Murder,* [1977] Crim.L.Rev. 70, 74–75, 77, comments critically on the proposals of the Criminal Law Revision Committee which would limit the *Hyam* rule:

"A definition of murder which includes risk-taking they regard as too wide, partly because it would include cases which are in practice dealt with as manslaughter (or were until the decision in *Hyam v. D.P.P.*) and partly because it would include a person who takes the risk of serious injury with no foresight of death. It 'would have the effect that the motorist who drives recklessly and kills someone, and the architect who designs a building involving the use of material which he knows to be highly inflammable and who thus causes a death in a fire, will be classed as murderers together with the bomber who places a bomb in a supermarket, killing a shopper, and the bank robber who fires over the heads of people in the bank but kills someone when a bullet ricochets'.

"One notes that it is not the fact that some of these four cases will be classified as murder which bothers the committee; it is the fact that *all* of them will be. It is bracketing the motorist and the architect with the supermarket bomber and the bank robber which the committee assume is objectionable, although how that can be *assumed* when *ex hypothesi* they all exhibit the same mental attitude is not at all made plain. The committee recognise that what distinguishes these people from true murderers is their lack of knowledge of the likelihood of death. They agree that they could exclude all of them by a requirement of foresight of death, but rule that out because foresight of death would then mean foresight that death would *probably* or *very probably* ensue and that would be an uncertain test for a jury to apply. * * *

"To catch such cases they propose that it should be murder to cause death by an unlawful act intended to cause fear and known to the defendant to involve a risk of causing death.

" * * * Murder is about contempt for life or safety, not about causing fear. The line they draw is tortuous, and unattractive in leaving many imaginable cases on what will seem to many to be the wrong side. Challenged to do better and propose a more appropriate factor than intent to cause fear, a critic might decline, rejecting the whole approach as a futile attempt to distinguish cases by rule in a field where experience and intuition unite in affirming that the only tool is, not rule, but discretion."

4.   The *Hyam* instruction regarding whether the defendant "knew that it was highly probable" that her conduct would cause death has not prevailed. As explained in Alan Norrie, *After Woollin,* [1999] Crim.L.Rev. 532: "The recent decision of the House of Lords in *Woollin*[1] appears to end a long-running saga concerning indirect intention for murder. The House has rejected the conclusion of the Court of Appeal that foresight of a substantial

1.   [1998] 3 W.L.R. 382.

risk of death or serious bodily harm could in certain circumstances be an alternative *mens rea* to intention. It has endorsed with slight amendments the law as stated in the earlier Court of Appeal case of *Nedrick*,[2] accepting the need for foresight of a 'virtual certainty (barring some unforeseen intervention)'. It has also distanced itself, in the lead judgment of Lord Steyn, from the earlier *Hyam* formulation of foresight of a probable, or highly probable, consequence as the *mens rea* for murder. * * * The judgment seems to bring the law finally into line with the weight of intellectual opinion."

Is *Woollin* an improvement over *Hyam*? That is, what degree of probability should it take to make death-causing conduct murder? Can the line between murder and manslaughter be meaningfully drawn in terms of probabilities, or is Norrie correct in concluding, id. at 544, that "*neither* approach adequately embodies the moral judgments required by the murder label"? On these questions, consider *Commonwealth v. Ashburn,* 459 Pa. 625, 331 A.2d 167 (1975), where the appellant contended "that the court's discussion of *Commonwealth v. Malone,* 354 Pa. 180, 47 A.2d 445 (1946), in its charge to the jury was tantamount to a direction to return a verdict of guilty of murder in the second degree. There is no merit to this contention.

"The *Malone* case bears certain striking factual similarities to the case at bar. Malone and Long, two adolescents on friendly terms with each other, procured a five chamber pistol and one cartridge, and decided to play 'Russian poker'. Malone then placed the muzzle of the pistol against Long's body and pulled the trigger three times, fatally discharging the pistol on the third pull. Malone was convicted of murder in the second degree. On appeal, this Court affirmed his conviction, remarking:

'The killing of William H. Long by this defendant resulted from an act intentionally done by the latter, in reckless and wanton disregard of the consequences which were at least sixty per cent certain from his thrice attempted discharge of a gun known to contain one bullet and aimed at a vital part of Long's body. This killing was, therefore, murder, for malice in the sense of a wicked disposition is evidenced by the intentional doing of an uncalled-for act in callous disregard of its likely harmful effects on others.'

"It was Ashburn's counsel who first broached the subject of the *Malone* case to the jury. Seizing on the passage quoted above, he argued that the odds that Ashburn's second pull of the trigger would result in Santagada's death were significantly less than three in five. In making this argument, counsel suggested that this Court in *Malone* had defined murder in the second degree as any act at least sixty per cent certain to result in the death of another.

"This was a misstatement of the law which the court was duty-bound to correct. This the court did in a fair and judicious manner. After defining the elements of murder in the second degree, the court delivered the standard charge, based on *Malone,* relative to acts of gross recklessness resulting in death. The court then briefly described the *Malone* case, and pointed out that the application of the general principles of law announced therein does not depend on any precise mathematical calculation of the probable consequences of the defendant's acts. This was an accurate statement of the law. Taken as a whole, the court's instructions clearly indicated that the task of applying the law to the facts of Ashburn's case was the jury's and the jury's alone. We find no error in it."

5. Some statutes and cases describe this variety of murder in more flowery language, such as that it is murder if "all the circumstances of the killing show an abandoned and malignant heart." E.g., *Mayes v. People,* 106 Ill. 306 (1883), affirming a murder conviction where the defendant threw a beer glass at his wife and the glass struck an oil lamp she was

2. [1986] 1 W.L.R. 1025.

carrying, causing a fire which brought about her death. Is this language less or more helpful than the probability formula in *Hyam?* See *People v. Phillips,* 64 Cal.2d 574, 51 Cal.Rptr. 225, 414 P.2d 353 (1966), holding that the jury should not be instructed in such language, though it appears in the statutory definition of murder, because "it could lead the jury to equate the malignant heart with an evil disposition or a despicable character."

6. Would it be more meaningful to draw the murder-manslaughter distinction in terms of the means by which the killing was done? In *State v. Chalmers,* 100 Ariz. 70, 411 P.2d 448 (1966), reversing defendant's murder conviction for a death resulting from his driving between 80 and 100 m.p.h., the court took note of the statutory provision "that in the crime of murder malice may be implied 'when the circumstances attending the killing show an abandoned and malignant heart.' This term also occurs in many other jurisdictions in defining the offense of murder. However, we have found no case which would indicate that gross negligence alone would constitute such conduct as appears to be contemplated when referring to *'an abandoned and malignant heart.'* The latter phrase seems to mean conduct by the use of a weapon or other appliance likely to produce death, and by the brutal and blood-thirsty use of such instrumentality."

7. Consider *Model Penal Code* § 210.2. In support, the draftsmen state in *Model Penal Code* § 210.2, Comment (1980): "Since risk * * * is a matter of degree and the motives for risk creation may be infinite in variation, some formula is needed to identify the case where recklessness may be found and where it should be assimilated to purpose or knowledge for purposes of grading. * * * In a prosecution for murder, * * * the Code calls for the further judgment whether the actor's conscious disregard of the risk, under the circumstances, manifests extreme indifference to the value of human life. The significance of purpose or knowledge as a standard of culpability is that, cases of provocation or other mitigation apart, purposeful or knowing homicide demonstrates precisely such indifference to the value of human life. Whether recklessness is so extreme that it demonstrates similar indifference is not a question, it is submitted, that can be further clarified. It must be left directly to the trier of fact under instructions."

8. Note, 85 Colum.L.Rev. 786, 789–90 (1985), observes that "four distinct approaches dominate the modern treatment of unintended murder": (1) the objective circumstances approach, which focuses upon the circumstances surrounding the crime rather than the defendant's attitude toward the victim's life, such as with the New York requirement that the jury determine whether the defendant's acts were themselves "brutal, callous, dangerous and inhuman"; (2) the degree of risk approach, which limits murder to cases in which the defendant's acts created a particularly significant chance of causing a death; (3) the multiple victim approach, whereunder a defendant is guilty only if his reckless act endangers more than one individual; and (4) the mens rea approach, which requires some state of mind more culpable than recklessness. This note concludes at 807 that the latter approach is best; that in jurisdictions where this approach obtains we "have failed to put the question of indifference to courts and juries in a sufficiently concrete and definite manner"; and that extreme indifference can best be discovered "by asking the finder of fact whether the actor would have committed the act had he known it would cause a death." Do you agree?

9. "Test" the approach you favor by applying it to these situations: (a) Randolph and Smith supplied heroin to seller Barnhill, who sold one gram to Jones on August 14th. Barnhill knew this was "pure" or "uncut" heroin, and claims to have warned Jones not to take quantities or injections as great as on previous occasions in that the heroin was uncut because she had not had an opportunity to dilute it. Jones died from a self-injected overdose on August 15th. On August 17th, an undercover agent recorded a conversation in

which Smith said to Barnhill, "You can't say that I didn't tell you that that definitely needed to be cut before it went out on the street," and Randolph observed that the same thing had happened to one of his customers two weeks earlier. Randolph, Smith and Barnhill have been charged with murder.[a]

(b) Ibn was pursued by police while he was driving a stolen Mercedes, but they were unable to catch up to him despite speeds of 100 m.p.h. Ibn drove through one roadblock, and an officer had to jump off the road to avoid being hit. Ibn then drove through a second roadblock when an officer moved his car onto the shoulder to avoid a collision. Ibn then drove through a third roadblock and at that moment had a blowout. The car continued down the road until it hit a hay truck and then swerved about 50 feet into a field, where it struck and killed Cross, who was visible from the road. Ibn has been charged with murder.[b]

(c) Watson drove to a bar, where he consumed a large quantity of beer. At one a.m. he drove through a red light and barely missed a vehicle and then continued on into another intersection (apparently through a green light) at 70 m.p.h. He skidded and swerved into the only other car on the otherwise deserted streets. Two occupants of that car were killed. Watson's blood alcohol content was .23, more than twice the amount necessary to support a finding that he was legally intoxicated. Watson has been charged with murder.[c]

(d) Berry's pit bull dog Willy killed a 2 ½ year old child; the dog was tethered near Berry's house, but no obstacle prevented access to the dog's area. There is no evidence that Willy had ever before attacked a human being, but there is considerable evidence that he was bred and trained to be a fighting dog. Berry bought Willy from a breeder of fighting dogs, who informed Berry of the dog's fighting abilities, his gameness, wind, and exceptionally hard bite. Berry raised dogs for fighting purposes and had fought pit bulls. An animal control officer has stated that pit bulls are selectively bred to be aggressive toward other animals, and that they give no warning of their attack and attack swiftly, silently and tenaciously. The officer says that while many recently bred pit bulls have good dispositions near human being and are bred and raised to be pets, even pit bulls with no prior history of aggression have been known to become highly aggressive in unpredictable situations, as when confronted by a small child. Berry has been charged with murder.[d]

(e) Markowski, knowing that he had tested positive for the AIDS virus, sold some of his blood to a commercial blood bank. As a result, one recipient of Markowski's blood contracted AIDS and died.[e]

(f) Moore, a prison inmate who knew he had tested positive for the AIDS virus, got into a dispute with a prison guard and, in the course of an altercation, bit the guard. Though there had not theretofore been any documented cases in which the virus had been transmitted by bites, the guard contracted AIDS and died.[f]

---

a. *State v. Randolph,* 676 S.W.2d 943 (Tenn.1984), reversing dismissal of the murder charge.

b. *State v. Ibn Omar–Muhammad,* 102 N.M. 274, 694 P.2d 922 (1985), reversing the murder conviction for an erroneous jury instruction stating an objective standard of knowledge of risk.

c. *People v. Watson,* 30 Cal.3d 290, 179 Cal.Rptr. 43, 637 P.2d 279 (1981), reversing dismissal of the murder charge. *Watson* is criticized in Note, 71 Calif.L.Rev. 1298 (1983). Compare *Essex v. Commonwealth,* 228 Va. 273, 322 S.E.2d 216 (1984), reversing a murder conviction on somewhat similar facts because the "jury could only speculate, upon this evidence, whether the defendant embarked upon his ill-fated

course of conduct wilfully and with a malicious purpose."

d. *Berry v. Superior Court,* 256 Cal.Rptr. 344 (Cal. App. 1989), denying writ of prohibition seeking dismissal of murder charge.

e. *Nat'l L.J.,* July 20, 1987, p. 3, col. 1, reporting such a sale of blood without fatal consequences, resulting in the defendant being charged with attempted murder.

f. Id., reporting such a case without fatal consequences. The defendant was convicted of assault with a deadly weapon.

NOTES AND QUESTIONS ON KILLING WITH INTENT TO DO SERIOUS BODILY INJURY

1.   D. W. Elliott, *Offences Against the Person—Murder,* [1977] Crim.L.Rev. 70, 73–74, discusses the proposals of the Criminal Law Revision Committee on this subject:

"A minority of the Committee, who were in favour of an intent to cause serious injury, *simpliciter,* remaining a sufficient intent in murder, argued, first, that a person who inflicts serious injury on another intentionally must know that there is a real chance that the victim will die, so if he does die, it is right that the killer should be convicted of murder, and, secondly, that a person who is minded to use violence in achieving an unlawful purpose may take more care to refrain from inflicting serious injury if he knows that a murder conviction awaits him if the victim dies. The majority notice these arguments only to reject them, saying 'The majority of us, however, think that if an intent to cause serious injury is to remain part of the *mens rea* of murder, it should be limited in some way so that it is related more closely to the fact of death.' This is apparently because for a person to be convicted of murder if he caused death with the intention of inflicting serious harm but without knowing or foreseeing that death was likely would be unacceptable to them. They do not say why it would be unacceptable.

"Having decided that some limiting factor is needed, the majority disagree on whether objective likelihood of death or subjective knowledge in the accused of likelihood of death should be chosen."

2.   Peter English, *Homicides Other than Murder,* [1977] Crim.L.Rev. 79, asks: "Is someone who causes death intending only serious injury more culpable than someone who causes death recklessly?" Consider Sally Lloyd–Bostock & Cheryl Thomas, *Decline of the "Little Parliament": Juries and Jury Reform in England and Wales*, 62 Law & Contemp.Probs. 7, 38 (Spring 1999): "In some cases, juries may be refusing to apply what they see as bad law. For instance, the legal definition of murder in England does not require an intention to kill. In a case heard before Lord Goff, the jury appeared to reject this definition of murder. The defendant had rammed a jagged glass into his victim's face and severed the man's jugular vein. The defendant did not intend to kill him, and indeed, was horrified at his victim's death. He did, however, clearly intend to cause 'really serious harm' which constituted sufficient mens rea for murder. The jury, despite being directed to that effect, acquitted him of murder. According to Lord Goff, the jurors could not bring themselves to call him a murderer, a position with which Lord Goff himself entirely sympathised."

3.   Although the intent-to-do-serious-bodily-injury type of murder is generally to be found in American jurisdictions, some of the modern codes have abandoned the doctrine, as does the Model Penal Code. As explained in *Model Penal Code* § 210.2, Comment (1980), "it is preferable to handle such cases under the standards of extreme recklessness and recklessness contained in Sections 210.2(1)(b) and 210.3(1)(a). That the actor intended to cause injury of a particular nature or gravity is, of course, a relevant consideration in determining whether he acted with 'extreme indifference to the value of human life' under Section 210.2(1)(b) or 'recklessly' with respect to death of another under Section 210.3(1)."

4.   It has often been held that an "intent to kill or to do great bodily harm [is] inferable from the intentional use of a deadly weapon upon the body of the deceased." *Bantum v. State,* 46 Del. 487, 85 A.2d 741 (1952). Moreover, while "[o]rdinarily blows inflicted by one person on another with bare fists do not demonstrate the malice requisite to sustain a conviction of second degree murder[,] * * * a protracted and continued beating with bare hands by a stronger person upon a weaker person can evince the malice

necessary for a conviction of murder." *State v. Bias,* 156 W.Va. 569, 195 S.E.2d 626 (W.Va.1973).

UNITED STATES v. ESCAMILLA

United States Court of Appeals, Fourth Circuit, 1972.

467 F.2d 341.

WINTER, CIRCUIT JUDGE:

Defendant, Mario Jaime Escamilla, was convicted of involuntary manslaughter, in violation of 18 U.S.C.A. § 1112, perpetrated on Fletcher's Ice Island T–3, an unclaimed island of ice in the Arctic Ocean, and sentenced to imprisonment for three years. * * *

T–3 is an island of glacial ice, composed of approximately 99% ice and less than 1% land matter, which meanders slowly about the general area of the Arctic Ocean. First sighted by an American in 1947, T–3 has been occupied since 1952 under the auspices of the United States Government, particularly the Departments of the Air Force and Navy, except for part of the years 1961–1962 when the island was grounded on the coastline of Alaska near Point Barrow. T–3 is used as a research station—a platform for scientific study * * *.

Discipline and order on the island depend upon the cooperation of all of the men and the effectiveness of the group leader, particularly in the summer months when it is virtually impossible to remove any wrongdoer from the ice. There are no medical facilities on the island, no doctor and, indeed, during the summer of 1970, no person trained in any aspect of medical science.

In May of 1970, a group of men arrived on T–3 expecting to remain there until late September or early October. Included were (a) the deceased, Bennie Lightsey, an employee of the United States Weather Bureau, who had been designated as station manager by the Arctic Research Laboratory, (b) the defendant, an employee of General Motors Defense Research Laboratory, (c) Donald Leavitt, who was an employee of the Arctic Research Laboratory, and whose nickname was "Porky," and (d) sixteen others. During the summer an acute problem arose from Porky's excessive drinking and resultant uncontrolled behavior. Prior to July 16, 1970, the date on which Lightsey was killed, Porky, at least three times, attacked various personnel at the station, including defendant, with butcher cleavers, mainly in an effort to obtain access to alcoholic beverages.

On July 16, while defendant was working at the General Motors camp, approximately one mile from the main camp where he lived in a trailer, he received a telephone call from his roommate, Charles Parodi, who told him that Porky was drunk and had taken some wine from their trailer. It should be noted that locked doors on T–3 were unknown because of potential fire hazard. Parodi pleaded with defendant to return to the trailer and defendant undertook to do so. He took with him a rifle selected from the common store to protect himself from the drunken Porky when he arrived back at the camp and later he loaded it. When defendant returned to the trailer he left his rifle and went to the next trailer to warn Porky to stay away from the raisin wine which was stored in defendant's trailer. Defendant found Porky and the station manager, Lightsey, consuming 190 proof Ethyl alcohol cut with grape juice and home made raisin wine. Defendant then returned to his trailer and soon thereafter heard footsteps approaching. Believing that it was Porky, he raised the rifle, put the safety off, opened the bolt, and assuring himself that the rifle was loaded, returned the bolt to the firing position and pointed the gun at the door. It was not Porky, but Lightsey, who entered the trailer.

A discussion of increasing intensity then ensued between the two over whether or not Porky should be allowed some of defendant's raisin wine. Parodi was present for part of the discussion, but after he left defendant ordered Lightsey out of the trailer, waving the gun back and forth at him. The gun discharged and Lightsey was hit. Lightsey died a short time after the wound, despite the efforts of members of the camp, including defendant, to save him. There was no witness to the actual shooting, except the two participants, but there was evidence, on which the defense heavily relied, that the rifle was defective in an unforeseeable but most deadly way, i.e., it could be discharged without pulling the trigger by banging it, dropping it, by putting the safety on and off, by ramming the bolt handle down, and by applying slight pressure to the bolt handle when holding it.

[D]efendant contends that these reversible errors were committed: * * * (b) the district court failed to charge the jury correctly on the necessary elements of the crime of involuntary manslaughter * * *.

We agree with defendant that nowhere in either [the original or supplementary] charge did the district judge tell the jury that they must find, as a necessary element of involuntary manslaughter by the commission of a lawful act without due caution and circumspection, that defendant must be shown to have actual knowledge that his conduct was a threat to the lives of others. In *United States v. Pardee*, 368 F.2d 368 (4 Cir.1966), we had occasion to discuss the crime of involuntary manslaughter. After concluding that it requires proof of *gross* negligence, and not simple negligence, we added:

"Gross negligence" is to be defined as exacting proof of a wanton or reckless disregard for human life. *Furthermore, to convict, the slayer must be shown to have had actual knowledge that his conduct was a threat to the lives of others, or to have knowledge of such circumstances as could reasonably be said to have made foreseeable to him the peril to which his acts might subject others.* The reason of the latter comment is that awareness of the tendency to danger, or the foreseeability of injury, from the act or omission is an indispensable element of negligence. This requirement of proof gains stature when it is recalled that death as a result of an accident, that is an occurrence unpurposed and unattributable to negligence, does not give rise to civil or criminal liability. (Emphasis added.)

There can be no doubt that the omission of a charge in accordance with *Pardee* was reversible error in this case. The evidence showed that defendant brandished a gun at the decedent and that the gun fired and killed him. But there was additional uncontroverted evidence from the government's experts that the gun was defective and could be discharged other than by pulling the trigger. Without the instruction, the jury may have convicted on the theory that pointing a gun capable of accidental discharge was an act of gross negligence even though it found that defendant did not discharge it, without consideration of whether defendant knew the gun was defective and thus capable of accidental discharge. If these were its findings, the conclusion of involuntary manslaughter could not follow unless the jury considered and concluded that defendant was aware that the gun was defective. On this ground alone, a new trial is required.

In a second aspect, we conclude that the charge was also defective in that it unduly restricted the jury in its consideration of the special circumstances obtaining on T–3 in its consideration of whether defendant committed an act which constituted gross negligence from which involuntary manslaughter could be found. Defendant requested that the jury be instructed:

In determining whether or not the defendant is guilty of involuntary manslaughter, the jury must measure his conduct against all of the existing circumstances and determine therefrom whether what he did was in its nature dangerous to life or grossly negligent. Some of the special circumstances you may consider in this case are the location of the alleged act, and its lack of law enforcement and medical facilities and the good character of Mario Escamilla.

This instruction was not given * * *.

This we think was error. Gross negligence or even simple negligence is to be determined by all of the facts and circumstances surrounding an act which is asserted to be either. It would seem plain that what is negligent or grossly negligent conduct in the Eastern District of Virginia may not be negligent or grossly negligent on T–3 when it is remembered that T–3 has no governing authority, no police force, is relatively inaccessible from the rest of the world, lacks medical facilities and the dwellings thereon lack locks—in short, that absent self-restraint on the part of those stationed on T–3 and effectiveness of the group leader, T–3 is a place where no recognized means of law enforcement exist and each man must look to himself for the immediate enforcement of his rights. Certainly, all of these factors are ones which should be considered by a jury given the problem of determining whether defendant was grossly negligent. This is not to say that the standards of civilized conduct and the law of the United States do not prevail even on T–3, but those standards and that law admit of consideration of the circumstances surrounding alleged involuntary manslaughter both in the continental United States and on T–3. While defendant's request for instruction, particularly the aspect invoking defendant's good character, need not have been granted exactly as requested, the district court should have instructed in accordance with the principle of the request. * * *

Reversed and remanded.

Notes and Questions

1. Courts and legislatures have experienced considerable difficulty in identifying precisely what standard should govern in determining what unintentional homicides are criminal. Considerable variation is to be found from jurisdiction to jurisdiction. As noted in Frank J. Remington & Orrin L. Helstad, *The Mental Element in Crime—A Legislative Problem,* 1952 Wis.L.Rev. 644, 663–64, "there are several distinct bases upon which liability may rest. 1. It may be sufficient that the actor should have realized that his act created an unreasonable risk of some harm to another. This is ordinary negligence, which is completely objective, and has generally been held to be insufficient for purposes of criminal liability. 2. It may be sufficient that the actor should have realized that his act creates, not only unreasonable risk, but also a substantial probability that serious harm will result. This is an objective standard which differs from ordinary negligence to the extent that the risk created is more serious. 3. The state may be required to show that the actor was aware of the circumstances, and being aware of the circumstances should have realized that his act created a serious risk. 4. Finally, the state may be required to show that the actor was aware, not only of the circumstances, but also of the fact that his act created a serious risk of harm to another.

"Seldom is there any clear indication on the face of a statute as to which of these bases is intended. The lack of clarity at the present time is amply demonstrated by the fact that 'gross negligence' in Wisconsin is equivalent to 'wanton or reckless' conduct in Massachusetts; 'wanton or reckless' conduct in Massachusetts apparently means something quite different than 'wilful and wanton' conduct in New Jersey; 'culpable negligence,' 'high degree of negligence,' and 'gross negligence' may all mean the same thing, or may mean three distinct things depending upon the jurisdiction chosen as the basis for comparison."

2. In many of the modern codes an effort has been made to be more specific, and this has necessitated more careful attention to the question of what the "bottom line" should

be with respect to criminal liability for unintentional homicides. Which of the aforementioned four standards is to be preferred? As an aid to making that judgment, consider (i) in which of the following fact situations (Notes 3–6) there should be criminal liability; and (ii) what standard would have to be applicable to produce the desired result.

3. "[T]he defendant, 57 years old at the time of trial, had left his native Arabia at the age of 19, emigrating first to China and then coming to the United States three years later. He had lived in Rochester only a short time before committing the acts which formed the basis for this homicide charge. He testified that he had been of the Sudan Muslim religious faith since birth, and had become one of the sect's leaders, claiming a sizable following. Defendant articulated the three central beliefs of this religion as 'cosmetic consciousness, mind over matter and psysiomatic psychomatic consciousness.' He stated that the second of these beliefs, 'mind over matter', empowered a 'master', or leader, to lie on a bed of nails without bleeding, to walk through fire or on hot coals, to perform surgical operations without anesthesia, to raise people up off the ground, and to suspend a person's heartbeat, pulse, and breathing while that person remained conscious. In one particular type of ceremony, defendant, purportedly exercising his powers of 'mind over matter', claimed he could stop a follower's heartbeat and breathing and plunge knives into his chest without any injury to the person. There was testimony from at least one of defendant's followers that he had successfully performed this ceremony on previous occasions. Defendant himself claimed to have performed this ceremony countless times over the previous 40 years without once causing an injury. Unfortunately, on January 28, 1972, when defendant performed this ceremony on Kenneth Goings, a recent recruit, the wounds from the hatchet and three knives which defendant had inserted into him proved fatal."[a]

4. "The defendant shot and killed Richard Levine while target practicing at a theater which he managed. The incident occurred at about 4:00 A.M. The defendant and Orberry Jackson, Dennis Martin and Richard Levine (the victim), three sailors, then stationed at the Great Lakes Naval Station, whom he employed as part-time helpers, were present in the theater at that time.

"The defendant was in the spotlight room, approximately 100 feet from the stage, and was shooting at a wicker basket placed about 2 or 3 feet from an open curtain on the right-hand side of the stage. Levine was on the stage. He, along with the rest of the parties present, had been drinking. He crossed in front of the target area several times to change a tape recorder which was located behind the curtain, and then played the drums which were near the stage. Levine then started dancing on the stage and Jackson played the drums for a while; and then Jackson went upstairs to the spotlight room. Several times when Levine walked near the target area, Jackson would guide him away—to the left of the stage—by means of the spotlight. The stage floodlights and footlights were turned off, apparently by Levine. Whenever Levine would change the tape on the tape recorder, he would walk near the target area and Jackson would use the spotlight to guide him away and then return the spotlight to the target.

"Ultimately, Levine changed a tape but did not cross back through the spotlight which was focused on the target. The defendant waited a while and then resumed firing. Jackson noted a heavy movement behind the curtain and ran to the stage. Some shots were fired while he was running to the stage. He found Levine lying on his back, partially in front of the curtain, with blood covering his face and legs."[b]

a. *People v. Strong*, 37 N.Y.2d 568, 376 N.Y.S.2d 87, 338 N.E.2d 602 (1975), reversing defendant's conviction for second degree manslaughter (subjective standard) because the jury was not given an instruction on the lesser offense of negligent homicide (objective standard).

b. *People v. Arndt*, 50 Ill.2d 390, 280 N.E.2d 230 (1972), affirming defendant's conviction for involun-

5. "On July 1, 1950, the defendant was driving a Cadillac car at a speed of approximately 40 miles per hour in a southerly direction on Route 9–W. One Carl W. Larsen, who was driving his automobile in the opposite direction, testified that when he was about two miles north of Tenafly he saw the approaching car of the defendant with apparently no driver at the wheel; that the defendant's car crossed the white line separating the lanes approximately 240 to 300 feet to the north of Larsen's car, whereupon Larsen swung sharply to his right, but the defendant's car struck Larsen's car in the left rear portion thereof; that the defendant's car continued in the same direction and crashed head-on into a Studebaker automobile approximately 40 feet in the rear of the Larsen car; that the latter collision caused the death of Glory Morrow Flobeck. When Mr. Larsen reached the defendant's car, he found that he had collapsed at the wheel and was in a semiconscious condition, so that it was necessary to assist him from the car; the defendant stated he had 'blacked out,' whereupon he collapsed and was taken to a hospital in an ambulance. It is conceded that defendant was not under the influence of intoxicating liquor nor was there any evidence thereof upon his person. In late February, 1949, the defendant, while at home, suffered a sudden attack of dizziness or unconsciousness; subsequent thereto he was treated by his family physician and shortly thereafter by one Dr. Moses Madonick, Assistant Professor of Clinical Neurology in the College of Physicians and Surgeons, Columbia University, who diagnosed the defendant's condition as Meniere's Syndrome. After treating him on two or three occasions, Dr. Madonick discharged him on July 26, 1949, advising him that he might suffer a recurrence of the disease and that if he should drive an automobile he should not drive alone, but someone should accompany him. The defendant testified that he remembers nothing about the accident; that immediately prior thereto he was proceeding at 35 to 40 miles per hour when all of a sudden he just 'blacked out' and remembered nothing until he came out of the 'black out' in the hospital. Dr. Madonick testified further that he examined the defendant after the accident on August 2, 1950, at which time he concluded there was a recurrence of the ailment and that in his opinion it was the cause of the defendant's 'black out' or loss of consciousness without warning on the date of the accident. [Prior to that date, the defendant] had been pursuing his ordinary occupations one year and three months without any recurrence of the attack."[c]

6. "The defendant was accustomed to spend his evenings at [his] night club, inspecting the premises and superintending the business. On November 16, 1942, he became suddenly ill, and was carried to a hospital, where he was in bed for three weeks and remained until discharged on December 11, 1942. * * *

"A little after ten o'clock on the evening of Saturday, November 28, 1942, the night club was well filled with a crowd of patrons. It was during the busiest season of the year. An important football game in the afternoon had attracted many visitors to Boston. Witnesses were rightly permitted to testify that the dance floor had from eighty to one hundred persons on it, and that it was 'very crowded.' * * *

"A bartender in the Melody Lounge noticed that an electric light bulb which was in or near the coconut husks of an artificial palm tree in the corner had been turned off and that the corner was dark. He directed a sixteen year old bar boy who was waiting on customers at the tables to cause the bulb to be lighted. A soldier sitting with other persons near the light told the bar boy to leave it unlighted. But the bar boy got a stool, lighted a match in

tary manslaughter under a subjective awareness-high risk type of statute; Schaefer, J., dissented.

c. *State v. Gooze,* 14 N.J.Super. 277, 81 A.2d 811 (1951), affirming defendant's conviction for causing

"the death of another by driving any vehicle carelessly and heedlessly in willful or wanton disregard of the rights or safety of others."

order to see the bulb, turned the bulb in its socket, and thus lighted it. The bar boy blew the match out, and started to walk away. Apparently the flame of the match had ignited the palm tree and that had speedily ignited the low cloth ceiling near it, for both flamed up almost instantly. The fire spread with great rapidity across the upper part of the room, causing much heat. The crowd in the Melody Lounge rushed up the stairs, but the fire preceded them. People got on fire while on the stairway. The fire spread with great speed across the foyer and into the Caricature Bar and the main dining room, and thence into the Cocktail Lounge. Soon after the fire started the lights in the night club went out. The smoke had a peculiar odor. The crowd were panic stricken, and rushed and pushed in every direction through the night club, screaming, and overturning tables and chairs in their attempts to escape.

"The door at the head of the Melody Lounge stairway was not opened until firemen broke it down from outside with an axe and found it locked by a key lock, so that the panic bar could not operate. Two dead bodies were found close to it, and a pile of bodies about seven feet from it. The door in the vestibule of the office did not become open, and was barred by the clothing rack. The revolving door soon jammed, but was burst out by the pressure of the crowd. The head waiter and another waiter tried to get open the panic doors from the main dining room to Shawmut Street, and succeeded after some difficulty. The other two doors to Shawmut Street were locked, and were opened by force from outside by firemen and others. Some patrons escaped through them, but many dead bodies were piled up inside them. A considerable number of patrons escaped through the Broadway door, but many died just inside that door. Some employees, and a great number of patrons, died in the fire. Others were taken out of the building with fatal burns and injuries from smoke, and died within a few days."[d]

SECTION 5. KILLING BY UNLAWFUL ACT

STATE v. GOODSEAL

Supreme Court of Kansas, 1976.
220 Kan. 487, 553 P.2d 279.

HARMAN, COMMISSIONER.

This is an appeal from a conviction of first degree murder.

Appellant Charles Goodseal, also known as Charles Jones, was initially charged and tried upon three separate counts arising from the same incident: Unlawful possession of a firearm, aggravated robbery, and felony murder. The murder count charged that the homicide occurred during the perpetration of the crimes of unlawful possession of a firearm and aggravated robbery. At this first trial appellant was convicted of unlawful possession of a firearm (from which no appeal has been taken), he was acquitted upon the aggravated robbery count and the jury was unable to agree as to the murder charge. Upon a second trial appellant was convicted of murder in the first degree, done in the commission of a felony, unlawful possession of a firearm after a felony conviction. Appellant brings the murder conviction here for review.

The evidence revealed the following. In August, 1969, appellant Goodseal was released from the Kansas state industrial reformatory where he had been serving sentences imposed upon two counts of forcible rape. In December, 1973, he left his home in Wichita to seek employment in Denver, Colorado. While there he stayed with a friend, Carl Davis. Davis

d. *Commonwealth v. Welansky*, 316 Mass. 383, 55 N.E.2d 902 (1944), affirming defendant's conviction under a manslaughter statute requiring proof of "wanton and reckless conduct."

testified appellant handled a .38 caliber revolver during his Colorado stay and that appellant stated during their return trip to Wichita in appellant's automobile he, appellant, had a gun in the car trunk. The two arrived in Wichita December 19, 1973. The next day they met a girl called "Silky" whose real name was either Diana Warren or Dianna Coleman. The three spent much of the day together drinking gin. Silky was to commence working that night as a topless dancer in a club in Wichita called the Golddigger's Lounge. She displayed a .22 caliber pistol which she was carrying in her purse and said she had another gun hidden at the club and that both guns were for her protection. There were generally from seven to ten girls at the club who worked as dancers, some of whom doubled as well as prostitutes.

At the club that evening appellant told his friend Davis that he had a gun but Davis did not see him with one at any time during the afternoon or early evening. Late in the evening appellant intervened in an argument between the club bartender and the girl who was the manager of the dancers, offering to help the latter. At one point he commented, "If you're having some trouble I got a heater in my back pocket that will straighten it out".

The victim of the homicide, James Warren Hunter, arrived at the lounge about 10:30 p.m. During the evening he was seen talking to Silky and at one point fondled her breasts. At a time when Hunter paid five dollars to get some of the girls to pose for pictures the bartender noticed other currency in his billfold. Hunter, Davis and appellant remained in the lounge until closing time, which was 12:30 a.m. Outside the lounge appellant told Davis he was waiting to give Silky a ride home and that she was in a car in the parking lot. Davis assumed Silky was "turning a trick". Appellant and Silky had previously agreed appellant would pretend to be her husband and pull her from the car so that she would not actually have to have sexual relations with the man she was with. Appellant testified that after this agreement Silky handed him a .38 caliber revolver which she said was not loaded.

Appellant got out of his car and went to the other automobile in the parking lot. There were no lights on inside but the motor was running. Appellant tapped the back glass with the gun butt, Silky unlocked the door and appellant opened the passenger side door. Hunter and Silky were in the back seat. Silky got out of the car immediately, pulling on her pants and asking appellant to get her shoes. Appellant asked Hunter what he was doing with his "wife" and Hunter replied he had paid her. Hunter then pulled on his pants, turned the pockets partially inside out and said, "Hey, she got my money". Appellant testified he remembered saying, "No wonder she wanted me to play this little trick so she could steal somebody's money". Appellant further testified he then bent over to pick up Silky's shoes, he slipped in the snow, bumped into the door and the gun discharged. The bullet struck Hunter in the armpit beneath his right shoulder and penetrated the lung area, causing his death. Appellant's version was that the shooting was accidental and the only reason he took the gun was to scare Hunter with it.

After appellant returned to his car he told his friend Davis he had shot the victim in the chest. Davis had witnessed the shooting. As appellant left the area he took a cartridge out of the gun and threw it away. The next day appellant left for Denver and en route he threw the gun away. Silky vanished immediately after the shooting. In January, 1974, appellant was apprehended in Olathe, Kansas. * * *

Appellant's principal point upon appeal is that the trial court erroneously denied his motions for acquittal and new trial because the offense of felonious possession of a firearm is not inherently dangerous to human life and therefore cannot be the basis for felony murder. K.S.A. 21–3401, under which appellant was convicted, provides:

"Murder in the first degree is the killing of a human being committed maliciously, willfully, deliberately and with premeditation or *committed in the perpetration or attempt to perpetrate any felony. * * * "*(Emphasis supplied.)

Possession of a firearm with a barrel less than twelve inches long by a person who within five years has been released from imprisonment for a felony, is one form of unlawful possession of a firearm and is a class D felony.

Here there is no question that appellant within five years after his release from confinement for a felony had in his hand a firearm with a barrel less than twelve inches long at a time when a bullet from that weapon caused Hunter's death. Appellant's argument is this. He says that to sustain a conviction for felony murder the collateral felony must be one inherently dangerous to human life; that this court recognized and applied this rule in *State v. Moffitt,* 199 Kan. 514, 431 P.2d 879, and held that unlawful possession of a firearm by an ex-felon is inherently dangerous to human life as a matter of law; further that in reaching this conclusion in *Moffitt* we cited a line of California decisions holding that unlawful possession of a firearm constitutes a felony inherently dangerous to human life and, where causal connection is shown, a resulting homicide constitutes felony murder in the second degree under California law; that in 1971 the California supreme court receded from this position and in *People v. Satchell,* 6 Cal.3d 28, 98 Cal.Rptr. 33, 489 P.2d 1361, 50 A.L.R.3d 383, ruled that the unlawful possession of a firearm by a convicted felon, viewed in the abstract, is not a felony inherently dangerous to human life for purposes of the felony murder rule, and this court should similarly reverse its decision in *Moffitt* and so hold.

Appellee first responds that our present statute does not require that a felony be one inherently dangerous to human life in order to support a felony murder conviction. We cannot agree. At the time *Moffitt* was decided and prior to 1970, our felony murder statute (K.S.A. 21–401 [Corrick 1964]) provided:

"Every murder which shall be committed by means of poison or by lying in wait, or by any kind of willful, deliberate and premeditated killing, or *which shall be committed in the perpetration or an attempt to perpetrate any arson, rape, robbery, burglary, or other felony, shall be deemed murder in the first degree."* (Emphasis supplied.) * * *

In *Moffitt* we were dealing with the "other felony" clause of the then felony murder statute and we concluded that to come within the clause such a felony must be one inherently dangerous to human life. Our present statute, and the one under which appellant is being prosecuted, uses the term "any felony". We see no significant distinction between the two expressions for purposes of determining the applicability of the felony murder rule and no reason to depart from the traditional requirement that the felony must be one inherently or foreseeably dangerous to human life. This limitation has always been imposed even in the absence of specific statutory mention and we adhere to that requirement. To go further could lead to manifestly unjust and even absurd results. In reaching the same conclusion the Delaware supreme court in *Jenkins v. State,* 230 A.2d 262, commented:

" * * * The only rational function of the felony-murder rule is to furnish an added deterrent to the perpetration of felonies which, by their nature or by the attendant circumstances, create a foreseeable risk of death. This function is not served by application of the rule to felonies not foreseeably dangerous. The rule should not be extended beyond its rational function. Moreover, application of the rule to felonies not foreseeably dangerous would be unsound analytically because there is no logical basis for imputing malice from the intent to commit a felony not dangerous to human life."

The next question is whether unlawful possession of a firearm by an ex-felon is an offense inherently dangerous to human life. In *Moffitt* we said that it was. In reaching this conclusion we did not specifically state whether we were viewing the felony in the abstract or, as several courts have done, were considering both the nature of the felony and the circumstances of its commission. In *Moffitt* the facts were that the defendant, a convicted felon, fired a pistol while assaulting two pedestrians and inadvertently killed a woman sitting on a motorcycle some distance down the street. We did comment in *Moffitt* upon legislative recognition that persons who had once committed a felony were dangerous to society and should not have in their possession concealable weapons. Beyond this, where doubt may exist, we see nothing wrong in considering both the nature of the offense in the abstract and the circumstances of its commission in determining whether a particular felony was inherently dangerous to human life. Some felonies, such as aggravated robbery, viewed in the abstract alone, are of such nature as to be inherently dangerous to human life, while another which seems of itself not to involve any element of human risk may be committed in such a dangerous manner as to be of the same character.

Hence we hold that the nature of the felony and, where necessary for determination, the circumstances of its commission are relevant factors in considering whether the particular felony was inherently and foreseeably dangerous to human life so as to support a conviction of felony murder. These are questions for the trial court and jury to decide in appropriate cases. In the case at bar appellant's own testimony was that he used the pistol to scare the victim. However, there was no evidence he made any presentment of the pistol in an offer to do corporal hurt to the victim so as to amount to an assault constituting an integral part of a murder charge as prohibited by *State v. Clark,* 204 Kan. 38, 460 P.2d 586. Under appellant's undisputed admissions the trial court in effect correctly held as a matter of law that the collateral felony, unlawful possession of a firearm, was a sufficient basis for application of the felony murder rule. * * *

PRAGER, JUSTICE (dissenting):

The issue before us in this case was determined by the Supreme Court of California in 1971 in *People v. Satchell*. In that case the California court pointed out that the felony-murder rule is a highly artificial concept and warned that "it should not be extended beyond any rational function that it is designed to serve." The court further held that the determination as to whether a felony is inherently dangerous for purposes of the felony-murder rule must be based upon an assessment of that felony in the abstract and not on the particular facts of a case. * * * It is important that we examine closely the rationale of the California court in *Satchell* where the court stated:

> "It is manifest that the range of antisocial activities which are criminally punishable as felonies in this state is very wide indeed. Some of these felonies, such as certain well-known crimes against the person of another, distinctly manifest a propensity for acts dangerous to human life on the part of the perpetrator. Others * * * just as distinctly fail to manifest such a propensity. Surely it cannot be said that a person who has committed a crime in this latter category, when he arms himself with a concealable weapon, presents a danger to human life so significantly more extreme than that presented by a non-felon similarly armed as to justify the imputation of malice to him if a homicide should result. Accordingly, because we can conceive of such a vast number of situations wherein it would be grossly illogical to impute malice, we must conclude that the violation of section 12021 by one previously convicted of a felony is not itself a felony *inherently* dangerous to human life which will support a second degree felony-murder instruction."

The California court recognized that possession of a firearm is a passive act which in and of itself, is not inherently dangerous. The weapon becomes inherently dangerous when it is *used* in such a manner as to endanger a human life. The California court in its opinion stated as follows in this regard:

"Viewing the matter from the standpoint of inherent danger, we find it difficult to understand how any offense of mere passive possession can be considered to supply the element of malice in a murder prosecution. To be sure, if such possession is of an extremely reckless nature manifesting a conscious disregard for human life, malice may be imputed by means of basic murder principles. * * * Moreover, if passive possession ripens into a felonious *act* in which danger to human life is inherent, the purpose of the felony-murder rule is served by its application—for it is the deterrence of such acts by felons which the rule is designed to accomplish. However, mere possession *in itself*—ignoring the propensities and conduct of the possessor—is essentially neutral in its intentional aspect and should not serve as the basis for the imputation of malice."

The rule adopted by the majority in the case before us is not sound for several reasons. In the first place, in my judgment, it is a rule which would be impossible for the trial courts of this state to apply. * * * The majority opinion has furnished no guidelines to assist the trial court in instructing the jury. This in my judgment places a difficult burden upon the district courts of this state in applying the rule adopted by the majority.

The rule of the majority opinion also may result in a serious conflict with the established principle of law that in a first-degree murder prosecution the felony-murder rule may not properly be invoked when it is based upon a felony which is an integral part of the homicide. * * * In the case now before us the majority relies upon the fact that the defendant had a gun in his hand in order to scare the deceased and thereby to coerce him into involuntary action. In order to avoid a conflict with the rule of *State v. Clark,* supra, the majority opinion emphasizes that there was no evidence the defendant made any presentment of the pistol in an offer to do corporal hurt to the victim so as to amount to an assault constituting an integral part of the murder charge as prohibited by *Clark.* The clear implication is that if the defendant had actually assaulted the deceased with a gun, then the felony-murder rule would not have been applicable since in that situation the assault would have been an integral part of the homicide. It would seem to follow that if a defendant unlawfully possessing a firearm does not commit an assault upon his victim but accidently kills him, then he may be found guilty of felony-murder. If, however, he assaults his victim then the felony-murder rule cannot be applied and in order to convict the defendant of murder the state must prove that the defendant intentionally and with malice committed the homicide. The irrationality of this distinction is obvious on its face.

Furthermore, I wish to point out that the practical application of the rule approved by the majority can produce other absurd results. For example, let us assume that a defendant, having been previously convicted of felony for writing an insufficient fund check, purchases a firearm to protect himself and his family against criminal invaders of his home. He accidently drops the gun, causing it to strike the floor and be discharged, killing a guest in his home. Since the killing occurred during commission of a felony, possession of the gun unlawfully, defendant would be precluded from interposing the defense of accident. Under the rule adopted by the majority defendant would be guilty of murder in the first degree and possibly subjected to a term of life imprisonment in the state penitentiary. * * *

Assuming that the rule of the majority should be adopted, it would still be necessary to reverse this case and grant the defendant a new trial. * * * The majority rule would, of necessity, require an instruction to the jury that before the felony-murder rule should be applied it must find that the factual circumstances of the case made felony possession an inherently dangerous crime. * * * In this case the jury was * * * not instructed to take into consideration the factual circumstances present in the case. Even the majority would appear opposed to this result. * * *

Notes and Questions

1. In *State v. Underwood*, 228 Kan. 294, 615 P.2d 153 (1980), also involving a felony-murder conviction where the underlying felony was possession of a firearm by an ex-felon, the court in a 4–3 decision concluded: "A majority of this court now are convinced that the logic, reasoning and rule urged by Mr. Justice Prager in the dissent in *State v. Goodseal*, should be adopted for Kansas. Accordingly, we hold that in determining whether a particular collateral felony is inherently dangerous to human life so as to justify a charge of felony murder under K.S.A. 21–3401, the elements of the collateral felony should be viewed in the abstract, and the circumstances of the commission of the felony should not be considered in making the determination."

2. In *State v. Lashley*, 233 Kan. 620, 664 P.2d 1358 (1983), the defendant was convicted of felony murder on a jury instruction that the alleged felony, theft, "must be proved" by a showing that the homicide victim owned the property in question, that defendant obtained unauthorized control over it, that defendant intended to personally deprive the deceased of it, and that the property was worth over $100. On appeal, the defendant invoked *Underwood*. The court responded: "There are three statutes that deal with the offense of theft: (1) theft—K.S.A. 21–3701; (2) theft of lost or mislaid property—K.S.A. 21–3703; and (3) theft of services—K.S.A. 21–3704. If the value of the stolen item or service is $100.00 or more, then the offense is a felony under each statute.

"Theft, K.S.A. 21–3701, became effective July 1, 1969. The legislature consolidated the offenses of larceny, embezzlement, false pretense, extortion, and receiving stolen property into the single crime of theft. The prior law was unduly complex, and created unnecessary problems in pleading and proof. All involved the common element of obtaining property by dishonest means. Though consolidated into a single statute of theft, the former offenses retained a portion of their former identity in the subdivisions contained within K.S.A. 21–3701.

"Theft is not one of the specified forcible felonies included in K.S.A. 21–3110(8). Does theft therefore fall into the categories of '*any other felony which involves the use or threat of physical force or violence against any person?*' Emphasis supplied. Viewing the separate statutes and the subdivisions of theft in the abstract, we can determine that the following crimes are not inherently dangerous to human life: (1) theft of lost or mislaid property—K.S.A. 21–3703; (2) unlawful deprivation of property—K.S.A. 21–3705; (3) theft, obtaining by deception control over property—K.S.A. 21–3701(*b*); and (4) theft by control over stolen property knowing the property to have been stolen by another—K.S.A. 21–3701(*d*).

"K.S.A. 21–3701 incorporates two sections that are, when viewed in the abstract, offenses that are inherently dangerous to human life: (1) theft by obtaining or exerting unauthorized control over property—K.S.A. 21–3701(*a*); and (2) theft by obtaining control over property by threat—K.S.A. 21–3701(*c*).

"Theft by obtaining or exerting unauthorized control over property (K.S.A. 21–3701[*a*]) is generally committed by stealth, but secrecy, or the owner's ignorance, is not a necessary element of the crime. The thief's intent is to deprive the owner of his property and to appropriate the property to his own use. The act of taking may be open, with a reckless disregard of the consequences, and even with knowledge of the owner.

"Theft—obtaining by threat control over property (K.S.A. 21–3701[c]), is taking property by putting the owner in fear of personal injury or injury to his property through fear induced by threats. The taking is without the voluntary consent of the owner and the owner allows the property to be taken as a result of actual fear induced by threats calculated to excite a reasonable apprehension of harm.

"The offense of theft set forth in the court's instruction is a felony when viewed in the abstract inherently dangerous to human life and is a proper felony to sustain a conviction for murder in the first degree under the felony murder rule. However, we wish to emphasize that theft may be the underlying felony in a charge of felony murder only in cases where the discovery of the thief during the course of the theft results in the death of a person."

Did the court reach a sound result? Was the court faithful to *Underwood*?

3. As noted in Comment, 48 U.Kan.L.Rev. 1047, 1055 (2000), the "legislature amended the statute in 1992, and for the first time, section 21–3401 referred to a separate section for enumeration of inherently dangerous felonies."

NOTES AND QUESTIONS ON THE RATIONALE AND STATUS OF THE FELONY–MURDER RULE

1. Consider Nelson E. Roth & Scott E. Sundby, *The Felony–Murder Rule: A Doctrine at Constitutional Crossroads,* 70 Cornell L.Rev. 446, 450–58 (1985):

"The deterrence rationale consists of two different strains. The first approach views the felony-murder rule as a doctrine intended to deter negligent and accidental killings during commission of felonies. Proponents argue that co-felons will dissuade each other from the use of violence if they may be liable for murder. Justice Holmes attempted to justify the rule on this basis by arguing that the rule would be justified if experience showed that death resulted disproportionately from the commission of felonies.[26] * * *

"The second view focuses not on the killing, but on the felony itself, and endorses the felony-murder rule as a deterrent to dangerous felonies. From this perspective, punishing both accidental and deliberate killings that result from the commission of a felony is 'the strongest possible deterrent' to 'undertaking inherently dangerous felonies.' * * *

"The felony-murder rule may be conceptualized as a theory of 'transferred or constructive intent.' This theory posits that the intent to commit the felony is 'transferred' to the act of killing in order to find culpability for the homicide. The rule thus serves 'the purpose of ... reliev[ing] the state of the burden of proving premeditation or malice.' * * *

" 'Constructive malice' is closely related to the concept of transferred intent and is also frequently used to describe the operation of the felony-murder rule. * * *

"Constructive malice, however, appears to be more akin to the legal concept of a presumption. Whereas transferred intent would allow the mental state required for Act A

---

26. Still the law is intelligible as it stands. . . .

Now, if experience shows, or is deemed by the lawmaker to show, that somehow or other deaths which the evidence makes accidental happen disproportionately often in connection with other felonies, or with resistance to officers, or if on any other ground of policy it is deemed desirable to make special efforts for the prevention of such deaths, the law-maker may

consistently treat acts which, under the known circumstances, are felonious, or constitute resistance to officers, as having a sufficiently dangerous tendency to be put under a special ban. The law may, therefore, throw on the actor the peril, not only of the consequences foreseen by him, but also of consequences which, although not predicted by common experience, the legislator apprehends.

See O.W. Holmes, The Common Law 58–59 (1881).

to substitute for the mental state required for Act B, constructive malice would 'impute' or presume the mental state required for Act B from the commission of Act A. The felony-murder rule thus acts as a *'mens rea*-imposing mechanism.'

"As a form of constructive malice, the felony-murder rule is viewed as conclusively presuming homicidal mens rea from the commission of the felony. This approach allows the courts to avoid characterizing felony murder as a strict liability crime, because, at least in theory, the mens rea for the homicide is formally retained separate and apart from the mens rea for the felony." * * *

"Courts and commentators viewing the felony-murder rule as a conclusive presumption retain a separate mens rea element for the homicide, which is irrebuttably attributed to the defendant from the commission of the felony. An alternative approach is to view the rule as not requiring a separate mens rea element for the homicide, but as justifying conviction for murder simply on the basis that the defendant committed a felony and a killing occurred.

"Courts adopting this view see felony murder as a distinct form of homicide: '[T]he elements of felony-murder are simply the intentional commission of a felony and the killing of a human being in the course thereof.' The justifications advanced for this conceptualization are deterrence of the underlying felony, and the notion that the felon has exhibited an 'evil mind' justifying severe punishment. [handwritten: → Moral forfeiture]

"The 'evil mind' theory of felony murder finds its roots in seventeenth and eighteenth century English notions of criminology. Mens rea was a less developed concept and judges focused on the harm resulting from a defendant's illegal act, rather than the maliciousness of his intent. The felony-murder rule thus partly operated on an unarticulated rationale that one who does bad acts cannot complain about being punished for their consequences, no matter how unexpected. Moreover, the felony-murder rule conceived from an 'evil mind' perspective comported with the retribution theory of punishment prevailing at the time of the rule's development, which focused on the resulting harm, not on the actor's mental state, in deciding the appropriate punishment. A convict, therefore, bore responsibility for his felony and for any harmful result arising from the crime regardless of his specific intentions."

2. Which (if any) of the foregoing rationalizations provides a justification for the felony-murder rule? Can the rule be squared with *Regina v. Cunningham,* p. 114 of this Book? With the fact, as noted in *Model Penal Code* § 210.3, Comment (1980), that "there is no basis in experience for thinking that homicides *which the evidence makes accidental* occur with disproportionate frequency in connection with specified felonies"[96]

96. In fact, the number of all homicides which occur in the commission of such crimes as robbery, burglary, or rape is lower than might be expected. For example, comparison of the figures for solved and unsolved homicides from M. Wolfgang, Criminal Homicide (1958), with statistics on basic felonies taken from the FBI Uniform Crime Reports reveals the following for Philadelphia from 1848–1952:

RELATION OF TOTAL FELONIES TO HOMICIDES OCCURRING DURING THE FELONY PHILADELPHIA 1948–1952

Offense	No. of Crimes Reported	No. Accompanied by Homicide	%	No. per 1000
Robbery	6,432	38	0.59	5.9
Rape	1,133	4	0.35	3.5
Burglary	27,669	1	0.0036	.36
Auto Theft	10,315	2	0.019	1.9

Similar figures are found in Cook County, Illinois, robbery statistics from 1926–1930. There were 71 murders committed during robberies in Cook County during 1926 and 1927. Illinois Crime Survey 610 (1929). Although robbery statistics for those years are not available, 7,196 robberies were committed in the county in 1930. Assuming this number of robberies in 1926 and 1927, it appears that only .49 per cent of the robberies in those two years resulted in homicide. More recent statistics derived from N.J. State Police, Crime in New Jersey: Uniform Crime Reports 42–45 (1975) reveal strikingly similar percentages. In 1975, 16,273 robberies were committed in New Jersey, and 66 homicides resulted from these robberies, only .41 per cent, a figure even lower than the earlier statistics from Cook County and Philadelphia. When other violent felonies are taken into account, this percentage drops even lower. In 1975, there were 1,382 forcible rapes and 111,264 forcible breaking-and-enterings in New Jersey in addition to the 16,273 robberies. These crimes resulted in 136 deaths. Thus only .10 per cent of these serious felonies resulted in homicide.

3. Only one state has judicially abandoned the felony-murder rule. In *People v. Aaron,* 409 Mich. 672, 299 N.W.2d 304 (1980), the court concluded: "We believe that it is no longer acceptable to equate the intent to commit a felony with the intent to kill, intent to do great bodily harm, or wanton and willful disregard of the likelihood that the natural tendency of a person's behavior is to cause death or great bodily harm. In *People v. Hansen,* 368 Mich. 344, 350, 118 N.W.2d 422 (1962), this Court said that '[m]alice requires an intent to cause the very harm that results or some harm of the same general nature, or an act done in wanton or wilful disregard of the plaintiff and strong likelihood that such harm will result.' In a charge of felony murder, it is the murder which is the harm which is being punished. A defendant who only intends to commit the felony does not intend to commit the harm that results and may or may not be guilty of perpetrating an act done in wanton or willful disregard of the plain and strong likelihood that such harm will result. Although the circumstances surrounding the commission of the felony may evidence a greater intent beyond the intent to commit the felony, or a wanton and willful act in disregard of the possible consequence of death or serious injury, the intent to commit the felony, of itself, does not connote a 'man-endangering-state-of-mind'. Hence, we do not believe that it constitutes a sufficient *mens rea* to establish the crime of murder.

"Accordingly, we hold today that malice is the intention to kill, the intention to do great bodily harm, or the wanton and willful disregard of the likelihood that the natural tendency of defendant's behavior is to cause death or great bodily harm. We further hold that malice is an essential element of any murder, as that term is judicially defined, whether the murder occurs in the course of a felony or otherwise. The facts and circumstances involved in the perpetration of a felony may evidence an intent to kill, an intent to cause great bodily harm, or a wanton and willful disregard of the likelihood that the natural tendency of defendant's behavior is to cause death or great bodily harm; however, the conclusion must be left to the jury to infer from all the evidence. Otherwise, 'juries might be required to find the fact of malice where they were satisfied from the whole evidence it did not exist'.

"From a practical standpoint, the abolition of the category of malice arising from the intent to commit the underlying felony should have little effect on the result of the majority of cases. In many cases where felony murder has been applied, the use of the doctrine was unnecessary because the other types of malice could have been inferred from the evidence."

4. Compare *People v. Dillon,* 34 Cal.3d 441, 194 Cal.Rptr. 390, 668 P.2d 697 (1983): "[A] thorough review of legislative history convinces us that in California—in distinction to Michigan—the first degree felony-murder rule is a creature of statute. However much we may agree with the reasoning of *Aaron,* therefore, we cannot duplicate its solution to the problem: this court does not sit as a super-legislature with the power to judicially abrogate a statute merely because it is unwise or outdated."

5. What then of a *constitutional* attack upon the felony-murder rule? In *Dillon,* in response to the defendant's reliance upon *Mullaney v. Wilbur,* p. 264 of this Book, and

Sandstrom v. Montana, p. 135 of this Book, the court stated: "Addressing the issue for the first time, we start with the indisputable fact that if the effect of the felony-murder rule on malice is indeed a 'presumption,' it is a 'conclusive' one. It does not simply shift to the defendant the burden of proving that he acted without malice, as in *Mullaney;* rather, in a felony-murder prosecution the defendant is not permitted to offer any such proof at all. Yet it does not necessarily follow that he is denied the presumption of innocence with regard to an element of the crime, as in *Sandstrom.* We are led astray if we treat the 'conclusive presumption of malice' as a true presumption; to do so begs the question whether malice is an element of felony murder. And to answer that question, we must look beyond labels to the underlying reality of this so-called 'presumption.'

" * * * In every case of murder other than felony murder the prosecution undoubtedly has the burden of proving malice as an element of the crime. Yet to say that (1) the prosecution must also prove malice in felony-murder cases, but that (2) the existence of such malice is 'conclusively presumed' upon proof of the defendant's intent to commit the underlying felony, is merely a circuitous way of saying that in such cases the prosecution need prove only the latter intent. In Wigmore's words, the issue of malice is therefore 'wholly immaterial for the purpose of the proponent's case' when the charge is felony murder. In that event the 'conclusive presumption' is no more than a procedural fiction that masks a substantive reality, to wit, that as a matter of law malice is not an element of felony murder. * * *

"Because the felony-murder rule thus does not in fact raise a 'presumption' of the existence of an element of the crime, it does not violate the due process clause as construed in *Mullaney* or *Sandstrom.* This is also the holding of each of our sister jurisdictions that has addressed the issue.

"For the same reason we need not be detained by defendant's second due process claim, i.e., that the felony-murder doctrine violates the rule that a statutory presumption affecting the People's burden of proof in criminal cases is invalid unless there is a 'rational connection' between the fact proved (here, felonious intent) and the fact presumed (malice). (See *County Court of Ulster v. Allen* [p. 236 of this Book]). If, as we here conclude, the felony-murder doctrine actually raises no 'presumption' of malice at all, there is no occasion to judge it by the standard that governs the validity of true presumptions."

6. Roth & Sundby, supra, at 470–71, conclude that a challenge "based upon *Sandstrom* * * * would require a court either to eliminate a mens rea element for the homicide aspect of felony murder or to find the rule an unconstitutional presumption of the ultimate fact of culpability for the killing." The former course, they suggest at 478, cannot be squared with Supreme Court holdings which "indicate that imposition of severe punishments for nonregulatory crimes without a finding of culpability violates constitutional guarantees of the eighth amendment and the due process clause." They rely firstly upon *Enmund v. Florida,* p. 375 of this Book, asserting at 484 that "the Court's concern with severe punishment of unintended crime applies with equal force whether the defendant's actions or a co-defendant's actions directly lead to the victim's death"; and secondly upon *United States v. Bailey,* 444 U.S. 394, 100 S.Ct. 624, 62 L.Ed.2d 575 (1980), which they assert at 489 arguably "stands for the proposition that certain crimes must contain a mens rea element."

7. What is your assessment of the "solution" provided by *Model Penal Code* § 210.2(1)(b)? Consider Roy Moreland, *A Re-examination of the Law of Homicide in 1971: The Model Penal Code,* 59 Ky.L.J. 788, 803–04 (1971): "The 1957 English Homicide Act

expressly abolished the felony murder rule in England.[a] This is the logical and proper way to handle the felony murder * * *. To one who is no friend of 'presumptions of law,' the device in the Model Code appears as an attempt to preserve a portion of the historic survivor, the felony murder rule. Taken as a compromise, as a transition statute, it may well serve a temporary purpose. It would be better to abolish the felony murder rule and prosecute such killings as negligent murders. Then if the fact was that the killing was committed in the commission of a felony, the determining factors would be the amount of danger in the act and the indifference to human life and safety shown in its perpetration."

8. The felony-murder doctrine is well entrenched in American law.[b] Though two-thirds of the states have enacted modern codes, only two of them (Kentucky and Hawaii) have totally abolished the rule, though two others (Arkansas and Delaware) have expressly added a requirement of some mental state such as recklessness.[c] Only one (New Hampshire) has adopted the Model Penal Code approach.

NOTES AND QUESTIONS ON THE DIMENSIONS OF THE FELONY–MURDER RULE

The dimensions of the felony-murder rule vary considerably from jurisdiction to jurisdiction. To some extent, especially in jurisdictions with modern codes, this may be attributable to the precise way in which the rule is set out by statute. In large measure, however, the differences may be explained by the fact that the courts in some jurisdictions are more determined than those in others to limit the reach of the felony-murder rule.

1. *What felonies will suffice?* As indicated by *Goodseal,* one important issue is that of what type of felony must have been committed in order for the felony-murder rule to be applicable. Query, which of the following alternatives is preferable:

(a) only such felonies which, when viewed in the abstract rather than upon the facts of the particular case, are inherently dangerous to human life (so that, as held in *People v. Burroughs,* 35 Cal.3d 824, 201 Cal.Rptr. 319, 678 P.2d 894 (1984), the felony-murder rule does not apply where defendant's felony of practicing medicine without a license hastened a leukemia victims' death).

(b) also such felonies which, upon the facts of the particular case, are dangerous to human life (so that, as held in *Commonwealth v. Matchett,* 386 Mass. 492, 436 N.E.2d 400 (1982), the felony-murder rule will apply to a death incidental to an extortion scheme if the extortion was committed in such a fashion).

(c) any felony (so that, as held in *State v. Chambers,* 524 S.W.2d 826 (Mo.1975), the felony of theft of a vehicle will suffice even if it was not "inherently or foreseeably dangerous to human life").

a. English Homicide Act of 1957, 5 & 6 Eliz. 2, c. 11, § 1:

"Where a person kills another in the course or furtherance of another offense, the killing shall not amount to murder unless done with the same malice aforethought (express or implied) as is required for a killing to amount to murder when not done in the course or furtherance of another offense."

b. See James J. Tomkovicz, *The Endurance of the Felony–Murder Rule: A Study of the Forces that Shape Our Criminal Law,* 51 Wash. & Lee L.Rev. 1429 (1994), exploring the various reasons, especially that the "felony-murder rule is compatible with the law and order mentality" that is "the controlling popular attitude in our society today," for "one of the more re-

markable legal phenomena of our time–the survival of the felony-murder rule."

c. Consider also *State v. Ortega,* 112 N.M. 554, 817 P.2d 1196 (1991) (construing felony-murder statute to mean that "there must be proof that the defendant intended to kill (or was knowingly heedless that death might result from his conduct)" because the statute "does not expressly negate any such requirement"); *State v. Bacon,* 163 Vt. 279, 658 A.2d 54 (1995) (since statute speaks of "murder" during perpetration of felony as first degree murder, this means, "at minimum, the prosecution must show a mental state of wanton disregard for human life with respect to the murder itself").

2. *Merger.* In *State v. Thompson,* 88 Wash.2d 13, 558 P.2d 202 (1977), defendant was convicted of the felony-murder of her husband on the theory that his death had resulted from her felonious assault upon him. On appeal, the court recognized that virtually all "states which have considered the question have adopted the merger rule, resulting in a holding that only felonies independent of the homicide can support a felony murder conviction," but declined to reject earlier Washington authority to the contrary. Utter, J., dissenting, objected:

"The only act of the appellant relied upon to establish the felony necessary for conviction of murder in the second degree was the shooting itself, which, standing alone, constitutes the crime of second-degree assault. The application of the felony-murder rule thus eliminated the necessity for proof by the state of the element of specific intent, which is the distinguishing aspect, in our statutory scheme, of murder in the second degree. Absent the proof of acts constituting an assault, the appellant could not have been found guilty of murder. In this situation it is apparent that the single act of shooting the victim can constitute one crime and one crime only. There exists no general malicious intent based upon proof of the commission of a separate felony which may be 'transferred' from that crime to an independent homicide committed in the course thereof. The existence of such a separate intent is an analytical necessity to an inference of intent to kill. For this reason the felony-murder rule should not apply where the underlying felony sought to be used as a basis for the operation of the rule is an offense included in fact in the homicide itself. To hold otherwise constitutes, as Chief Justice Cardozo observed, 'a futile attempt to split into unrelated parts an indivisible transaction.'

"[T]he use of the rule approved by the majority would effectively convert into second-degree murder any crime properly viewed as manslaughter, because manslaughter itself is a felony * * *."

Is the merger rule sound? If so, which predicate felonies merge because not sufficiently independent of the homicide? Consider, for example, *Commonwealth v. Claudio,* 418 Mass. 103, 634 N.E.2d 902 (1994), where defendant was convicted of felony murder on the predicate felony of an unlawful breaking and entering into a dwelling in the night time with intent to commit an armed assault on a lawful occupant of the dwelling:

"The minority view is represented by *People v. Wilson,* 1 Cal.3d 431, 82 Cal.Rptr. 494, 462 P.2d 22 (1969), in which the Supreme Court of California considered a case where the defendant, estranged from his wife, broke into his wife's apartment and shot her. The instructions given to the jury permitted them to find that the defendant had entered 'with an intent to commit an assault with a deadly weapon and thereby committed a burglary, in the course of which he killed his wife and thus committed first degree felony murder.' The court concluded that a jury should not be instructed that 'the intent to assault makes the [illegal] entry burglary and that the burglary raises the homicide resulting from the assault to first degree murder without proof of malice aforethought and premeditation.' The court went on to state the following: 'To hold otherwise, we would have to declare that because burglary is not technically a lesser offense included within a charge of murder, burglary constitutes an independent felony which can support a felony-murder instruction. ...[We think that] a burglary based on intent to assault with a deadly weapon is included in fact within a charge of murder, and cannot support a felony-murder instruction.'

"The majority, and, in our opinion, better reasoned view is to the contrary. In the leading case of *People v. Miller,* 32 N.Y.2d 157, 344 N.Y.S.2d 342, 297 N.E.2d 85 (1973), the New York Court of Appeals rejected the argument that a breaking and entering with the intent to commit an armed assault could not serve as the felony underlying a conviction for felony-murder. Under the Penal Law of New York, only certain enumerated felonies (which, in general, would be classified under the Commonwealth's criminal law as felonies inherently dangerous to human life) may serve as the basis for a charge of felony-murder. Burglary, defined as an unlawful entry into a building with intent to commit a crime in the building entered, is one of these enumerated felonies.

"In the *Miller* decision, the court commented that, in imposing greater punishment for a criminal act committed within a domicil than for the same act committed on the street, the New York Legislature had 'recognized that persons within domiciles are in greater peril from those entering the domicile with criminal intent, than persons on the street who are being subjected to the same criminal intent,' and that this principle applies with equal force to a person entering a domicil with the intent to commit an assault as it does to the person entering a domicil with the intent to commit, for example, an armed robbery. The court observed that, '[w]hen the assault takes place within the domicile, the victim may be more likely to resist the assault [and] less likely to be able to avoid the consequences of the assault, since his paths of retreat and escape may be barred.... Further, it is also more likely that when the assault occurs in the victim's domicile, there will be present family or close friends who will come to the victim's aid and be killed.' The court concluded that the New York Legislature intended its codification of the felony-murder rule to encompass, as a predicate felony, an unlawful entry with intent to commit armed assault, and that this interpretation of the statutory criminal law was entirely consistent with the rationale underlying the felony-murder rule, which seeks 'to reduce the disproportionate number of accidental homicides which occur during the commission of the enumerated predicate felonies by punishing the party responsible for the homicide not merely for manslaughter, but for murder.' "

Note, 22 Stan.L.Rev. 1059, 1067 (1970), concluded that under the analysis of *Wilson* "neither forcible rape nor armed robbery—two other felonies enumerated in the first degree felony-murder statute—will support the application of the felony-murder rule" because each of those offenses consists of two distinct elements, one of which is the assault element. But, as it turned out, the California Supreme Court did not go this far; see *People v. Burton*, 6 Cal.3d 375, 99 Cal.Rptr. 1, 491 P.2d 793 (1971) (armed robbery resulting in death is felony murder). Is there any rationale by which the results in *Wilson* and *Burton* may be reconciled?

Under *Claudio*, what should the result be if the prosecutor had instead relied upon a different predicate felony, namely, assault in dwelling house, which under state law is defined as covering one who, "being armed with a dangerous weapon, enters a dwelling house and while therein assaults another with intent to commit a felony"? Should it make any difference whether the assault constituting that felony included or was limited to the occupant of the premises who was the homicide victim? See *Commonwealth v. Gunter*, 427 Mass. 259, 692 N.E.2d 515 (1998).

3. *Double jeopardy.* The merger rule should not be confused with the double jeopardy question of whether a defendant may be prosecuted and punished for both felony murder and the underlying felony. Under *Brown v. Ohio*, 432 U.S. 161, 97 S.Ct. 2221, 53 L.Ed.2d 187 (1977), separate *prosecutions* are ordinarily barred unless "each provision requires proof of an additional fact which the other does not." The bar thus covers the felony-murder—felony situation. *Harris v. Oklahoma*, 433 U.S. 682, 97 S.Ct. 2912, 53 L.Ed.2d 1054 (1977). As for separate *punishment* for the two offenses, the constitutional question is simply that "of what punishment the Legislative Branch intended to be imposed." *Albernaz v. United States*, 450 U.S. 333, 101 S.Ct. 1137, 67 L.Ed.2d 275 (1981). In some states the courts have concluded the legislature had authorized cumulative punishment for

the felony murder and underlying felony, but the prevailing view is to the contrary. See *People v. Wilder,* 411 Mich. 328, 308 N.W.2d 112 (1981), and cases cited therein.

4. *Duration of the felony.* (a) In *People v. Gladman,* 41 N.Y.2d 123, 390 N.Y.S.2d 912, 359 N.E.2d 420 (1976), defendant was convicted of felony murder on evidence that he robbed a delicatessen of $145 at 8:10 p.m., left the shopping center and walked through the surrounding neighborhood, and thereafter hid under a car at a bowling alley parking lot when he saw a police car enter the lot. When the defendant crawled out upon orders of a police officer, he shot and mortally wounded the officer. This occurred 15 minutes after and less than one-half mile from the robbery. In affirming the conviction, the court commented:

"Under older statutes which did not specifically address the issue, it was early held that a killing committed during an escape could, under some circumstances, constitute a felony murder. * * * [The analysis in the earlier cases] led to the development of some rather arbitrary rules. If the defendant left the premises without the loot, the criminal action was deemed either terminated or abandoned and a subsequent homicide would not be a felony murder. * * * On the other hand, both presence on the premises and retention of loot were not regarded as conclusive proof of felony continuation, but were merely evidence that the felony was continuing.[a] The term premises was rather strictly confined to 'within the four walls of the building' and a killing on an immediately adjoining public street would not be a killing on the 'premises'.

"The later New York cases indicate some dissatisfaction with the strict legal rules that had developed and tended to leave the question of escape killings to the jury as a question of fact, under appropriate instructions. The change was to point out 'generally that the killing to be felony murder must occur while the actor or one or more of his confederates is engaged in securing the plunder or in doing something immediately connected with the underlying crime; that escape may, under certain unities of time, manner and place, be a matter so immediately connected with the crime as to be part of its commission; but that, where there is no reasonable doubt of a complete intervening desistance from the crime, as by the abandonment of the loot and running away, the subsequent homicide is not murder in the first degree without proof of deliberation and intent.' The question of termination of the underlying felony was then left to the jury as a fact question.

"The New York approach was more rigid than that developed in other jurisdictions. The majority of the States tended to follow the '*res gestae*' theory—i.e., whether the killing was committed in, about and as a part of the underlying transaction. California had adopted the *res gestae* theory, at least insofar as robbery is concerned, holding that a robbery is not complete if the 'conspirators have not won their way even momentarily to a place of temporary safety and the possession of the plunder is nothing more than a scrambling possession. In such a case the continuation of the use of arms which was necessary to aid the felon in reducing the property to possession is necessary to protect him in its possession and in making good his escape * * * The escape of the robbers with the loot, by means of arms, necessarily is as important to the execution of the plan as gaining possession of the property. Without revolvers to terrify, or, if occasion requires, to kill any person who attempts to apprehend them at the time of or immediately upon gaining possession of said property, their plan would be childlike.' (*People v. Boss,* 210 Cal. 245,

---

a. Sometimes the argument is that the offense is by its nature a continuing one. For example, in *Doane v. Commonwealth,* 218 Va. 500, 237 S.E.2d 797 (1977), where defendant stole a car at noon on July 7th and ran over and killed someone with it at 6:15 p.m. on July 8th, the prosecutor relied upon established state law that larceny is a continuing offense which "is being committed every moment of the time during which the thief deprives the owner of the stolen property or its possession." The court responded that while this fiction was accepted for purposes of establishing venue for prosecution wherever the property was taken, it would not be embraced as a means for broadening felony-murder liability.

250–251, 290 P. 881 [1930].) Subsequent case law indicates that, in California, the robbery is ongoing simply if the culprit had failed to reach a place of temporary safety. (*People v. Salas*, 7 Cal.3d 812, 103 Cal.Rptr. 431, 500 P.2d 7.) The comparative rigidity of the New York approach has been explained as stemming from the fact that, at the time, New York, with a minority of other States, provided that all felonies would support a conviction for felony murder. Of course, felony murder was also a capital offense and the cases attempted to narrow the scope of liability, particularly where it was an accomplice that did the actual killing.

"The 1967 Penal Law limited the application of the felony murder concept to nine serious and violent predicate felonies. At the same time, it was provided that the doctrine would apply to a killing committed in 'immediate flight'. This change was intended to do away with many of the old technical distinctions relating to 'abandonment' or 'completion'.

"Under the new formulation, the issue of whether the homicide occurred in 'immediate flight' from a felony is only rarely to be considered as a question of law for resolution by the court. Only where the record compels the inference that the actor was not in 'immediate flight' may a felony murder conviction be set aside on the law. Rather, the question is to be submitted to the jury, under an appropriate charge. The jury should be instructed to give consideration to whether the homicide and the felony occurred at the same location or, if not, to the distance separating the two locations. Weight may also be placed on whether there is an interval of time between the commission of the felony and the commission of the homicide. The jury may properly consider such additional factors as whether the culprits had possession of the fruits of criminal activity, whether the police, watchmen or concerned citizens were in close pursuit, and whether the criminals had reached a place of temporary safety. These factors are not exclusive; others may be appropriate in differing factual settings. If anything, past history demonstrates the fruitlessness of attempting to apply rigid rules to virtually limitless factual variations. No single factor is necessarily controlling; it is the combination of several factors that leads to a justifiable inference.

"In this case, the jury could properly find, as a question of fact, that the killing of Officer Rose occurred in immediate flight from the delicatessen robbery. The shooting occurred less than 15 minutes after the robbery and less than a half mile away. The defendant had made off with cash proceeds and was attempting to secure his possession of the loot. The police had reason to believe that the robber was still in the immediate vicinity and had taken steps to seal off avenues of escape. In this regard, the absence of proof as to why Officer Rose turned into the bowling alley parking lot is no deficiency. The standard is not whether the police officer subjectively believed that the defendant was the robber. Indeed, the defendant's own apprehension may be more valuable. The defendant's response to the observation of the police car was to seek an immediate hiding place. This indicates that the defendant perceived that the police were on his trail. The record does not indicate that the officer knew or supposed, that defendant committed a crime; it does indicate that the defendant feared that the officer possessed such knowledge. Additionally, the defendant had not reached any place of temporary safety. In short, there is evidence from which the jury could conclude, as it did, that the defendant was in immediate flight from the robbery and that he shot the officer in order to make good his escape with the loot."

(b) Similar problems arise with respect to a predicate attempted felony, which can otherwise suffice for felony-murder. Consider what the result should be based upon these facts from *State v. McNeill*, 83 Ohio St.3d 438, 700 N.E.2d 596 (1998): Fulton and Rushinsky drove about seeking to purchase crack cocaine and ultimately picked up McNeill, who directed them to where he stated he kept his supply. Upon their arrival,

McNeill pulled a gun and said, "This is a stickup"; Fulton jumped from the car and ordered McNeill out, and as Rushinsky opened his door McNeill grabbed the keys from the ignition and jumped out. McNeill aimed his gun at Rushinsky and asked if he had any money; Rushinsky replied he had none. McNeill then pointed the gun at Fulton, who told McNeill to return his keys. After further argument, McNeill walked away. Fulton, who was a locksmith, got into his car and attempted to start it using his locksmith's tools. While Fulton was trying to start the car, McNeill returned and shot and killed him.

(c) What if, on the other hand, the defendant contends that the act causing death came too soon, as in *Higginbotham v. State*, 104 Md.App. 145, 655 A.2d 1282 (1995)? There the evidence was that defendant, while a passenger in a cab, fatally stabbed the driver and then, after the vehicle crashed, took a bag belonging to the driver and fled; the jury was instructed that defendant could be convicted of felony murder even if the intent to commit the robbery was not formed until after the stabbing: "We hold that the trial judge's instructions in the case sub judice correctly stated Maryland law. [I]f a person commits an act of force that causes the death of the victim and then forms the intent to deprive the victim permanently of his property, the taking of the property with that intent may constitute robbery if the act causing the death and the 'taking with intent to steal [are] part of the same general occurrence or episode.' Under these circumstances, the robbery could also serve as the underlying felony supporting a first degree felony murder conviction. Pursuant to Maryland Code Art. 27, § 410, the act causing the death of the victim must have occurred 'in the perpetration of, or attempt to perpetrate' the felony. If the act causing the death of the victim constituted the element of force in the robbery conviction, that act was part of the underlying felony. Thus, 'logic dictates that the murder was committed in the perpetration of the felony' of robbery. * * *

"In support of his contention that 'if a defendant forms the intent to commit the felony after the killing has already occurred, the killing cannot have occurred "in the perpetration of" the felony' because 'it would have occurred prior to the commission of the felony,' appellant cites *People v. Green*, 27 Cal.3d 1, 164 Cal.Rptr. 1, 609 P.2d 468 (1980), [where] the Supreme Court of California held that Green did not commit a murder 'during the commission' of robbery because it found that the intent to rob the victim was not formed until after Green had performed the act of force that caused the death of the victim. This holding, however, was explicitly based on the fact that, under California law, 'the act of force . . . by which the taking is accomplished in robbery must be motivated by the intent to steal. . . .' In contrast with Maryland law, in California, 'if the larcenous purpose does not arise until after the force has been used against the victim, there is no "joint operation of act and intent" necessary to constitute robbery.' In other words, the robbery is not considered to have begun until the defendant forms the intent to rob. As a result, once it found that the intent to rob was formed subsequent to the act of force, the California court could only conclude that under the law of that state the murder occurred prior to, and not during the commission of, the felony."

5. *Liability of co-felon.* If *A* and *B* commit an armed robbery of *C*, in the course of which *C* is killed by a bullet fired from a gun held by *B*, under the felony-murder rule both *A* and *B* are guilty of murder. Although *A* did not fire the shot, he was a party to the felony and thus is deemed equally guilty of murder. Because this is essentially a matter of accomplice liability, further discussion of this aspect of the felony-murder rule will be deferred until Chapter 12.

6. *Felon or non-felon status of the deceased or the person directly causing the death.* The typical felony-murder case is as stated in the preceding Note. It is not uncommon, however, for deaths to occur during dangerous felonies in other ways. Illustrative is *People*

v. Dekens, 182 Ill.2d 247, 230 Ill.Dec. 984, 695 N.E.2d 474 (1998), where defendant attempted to rob an undercover officer during a drug transaction, after which the officer was grabbed by defendant's accomplice, who the officer then shot and killed. In upholding defendant's murder conviction, the majority stated:

"In *People v. Lowery*, 178 Ill.2d 462, 227 Ill.Dec. 491, 687 N.E.2d 973 (1997), this court recently reviewed the nature of the felony-murder doctrine and the opposing theories on which liability may be based. As *Lowery* explains, Illinois follows the 'proximate cause' theory of liability for felony murder. Under that theory, liability attaches 'for any death proximately resulting from the unlawful activity—notwithstanding the fact that the killing was by one resisting the crime.' The other principal theory of liability under the felony-murder doctrine is the agency theory, which is followed by a majority of jurisdictions. Under the agency theory, 'the doctrine of felony murder does not extend to a killing, although growing out of the commission of the felony, if directly attributable to the act of one other than the defendant or those associated with him in the unlawful enterprise.' There is no liability under the agency theory when the homicide is committed by a person resisting the felony.* * *

"Although we have never addressed the precise question raised here, this court has, over the years, addressed similar questions concerning the scope of the felony-murder doctrine and the proximate cause theory. A review of these cases is instructive.[b] * * *

"Although *Lowery, Hickman, Allen,* and *Payne* did not address the precise question raised in this appeal, we believe that our case law compels application of the felony-murder doctrine to the circumstances of this case. As *Lowery* noted, Illinois follows the proximate cause theory of felony murder, as opposed to the agency theory. Consistent with the proximate cause theory, liability should lie for any death proximately related to the defendant's criminal conduct. Thus, the key question here is whether the decedent's death is the direct and proximate result of the defendant's felony. As our cases make clear, application of the felony-murder doctrine does not depend on the guilt or innocence of the person killed during the felony or on the identity of the person whose act causes the decedent's death. * * *

"The defendant also maintains that limiting the scope of the felony-murder doctrine to innocent victims is consistent with the proximate cause theory on which it rests in this state. * * * As we understand the argument, the defendant seems to be urging a sort of contributory fault theory, under which no liability could attach for the death of a cofelon because his guilty participation in the offense should preclude his own recovery. We do not agree. We do not believe that a cofelon's blameworthiness should shield the defendant from liability for the death. As we have noted, the focus of the proximate cause theory is on the chain of events set in motion by the defendant, not on the individual guilt or innocence of the decedent."

One of the two dissenters in *Dekens* concluded that "Illinois also should adopt the agency theory * * * because that theory represents a reasonable and just interpretation of the law," while the other concluded: "When a defendant's commission of a forcible felony proximately results in the death of an innocent party, I agree that charging the defendant

---

b. The majority at this point discussed *People v. Payne*, 359 Ill. 246, 194 N.E. 539 (1935) (whether robbery victim shot by one of the robbers or by fellow victim immaterial under proximate cause theory); *People v. Allen*, 56 Ill.2d 536, 309 N.E.2d 544 (1974) (felony-murder under proximate cause theory where, as here, one officer killed by shots of another officer in opposition to the attempted robbery); *People v. Hick-* *man*, 59 Ill.2d 89, 319 N.E.2d 511 (1974) (felony-murder where officer shooting at fleeing burglars killed another officer); *People v. Lowery*, 178 Ill.2d 462, 227 Ill.Dec. 491, 687 N.E.2d 973 (1997) (under proximate cause theory, felony-murder where intended victim of armed robbery shot at one of the fleeing robbers and struck and killed innocent bystander instead).

with murder may comport with notions of justice and fairness. There is, however, simply a qualitative difference between that situation and the situation presented here, where the death which resulted was that of a coparticipant in the underlying felony. As one renowned treatise on criminal law has noted:

'[I]t is now generally accepted that there is no felony murder liability when one of the felons is shot and killed by the victim, a police officer, or a bystander * * *. * * *

A more plausible explanation [for this conclusion] is the feeling that it is not justice (though it may be poetic justice) to hold the felon liable for murder on account of the death, which the felon did not intend, of a co-felon willingly participating in the risky venture. It is true that it is no defense to intentional homicide crimes that the victim voluntarily placed himself in danger of death at the hands of the defendant * * *. But with unintended killings it would seem proper to take the victim's willing participation into account * * *.' W. LaFave & A. Scott, 2 *Substantive Criminal Law* § 7.5, at 217–18 (1986).

"The majority provides no explanation for how the purpose of the felony-murder doctrine is served by applying it in cases such as this. Rather, the majority's holding is simply that the proximate cause theory 'compels' this result. * * *. I disagree with this conclusion. Where a cofelon is killed by a third party, the most direct cause of the death is the cofelon's participation in the felony, not the defendant's acts. Contrary to the majority's characterization, this distinction does not go to the 'guilt or innocence' of the decedent. Rather, this distinction pertains to the 'proximate cause' of the death. * * *

"The majority nonetheless holds that 'our cases make clear' that application of the felony-murder doctrine does not depend on the 'guilt or innocence' of the decedent. Our prior cases, however, say nothing of the sort. As the majority concedes, none of this court's prior decisions addressed a situation where the person killed was a participant in the underlying felony."

Who has the better of the argument in *Dekens*? Would it make any difference if the death of the cofelon occurred without the intervention of a third party, as in *State v. Hoang*, 243 Kan. 40, 755 P.2d 7 (1988)? In *Hoang*, two of Hoang's assistants in an arson scheme crawled through a window into the building to be burned and were handed containers of gasoline; Hoang then saw flames and smoke in the building and waited for his accomplices to return to the window, but left upon hearing the approaching sirens; one of the assistants was burned to death and the other died later of smoke inhalation.

NOTES AND QUESTIONS ON THE MISDEMEANOR–MANSLAUGHTER RULE

1. *Generally.* Under the early common law, an unintended killing occurring in the commission of an unlawful act constituted a criminal homicide. When criminal homicide was later subdivided into the separate crimes of murder and manslaughter, this type was assigned to the involuntary manslaughter category. Because the requisite unlawful act was almost always a misdemeanor,[a] this type of criminal homicide came to be known as misdemeanor manslaughter. It has been aptly characterized as "a reduced analogue of the felony-murder rule." *State v. Gerak,* 169 Conn. 309, 363 A.2d 114 (1975). It is not surprising, therefore, that some of the previously discussed court-devised limits on the felony-murder rule are also applied here. See, e.g., *State v. Light,* 577 S.W.2d 134 (Mo.App.1979) (given that felon is not held for co-felon's death due to outside agency which

---

a. But, except where statutory language provides otherwise, certain other unlawful acts (e.g., a felony which for some reason will not suffice for felony- murder, or a violation of a local ordinance) will also suffice.

thwarts the felony, same true in instant case, where during misdemeanor of theft of telephone wire defendant's partner came into contact with high voltage wire and was electrocuted).

Although the misdemeanor involved is commonly a traffic offense, such as speeding or drunken driving, another common type of misdemeanor causing death is simple battery, as where the defendant hits the victim a light blow but unexpectedly causes death. Illustrative are *State v. Frazier,* 339 Mo. 966, 98 S.W.2d 707 (1936) (where battery on person not known to be a hemophiliac resulted in death, defendant guilty of manslaughter); and *State v. Johnson,* 102 Ind. 247, 1 N.E. 377 (1885) (where defendant knocked victim through screen door, resulting in cuts from which victim contracted lockjaw and died, defendant guilty of manslaughter).

Such cases as *Frazier* and *Johnson* point up the harshness of the misdemeanor-manslaughter rule. As stated in *Model Penal Code* § 201.3, Comments (Tent.Draft No. 9, 1959): "Whether the matter is viewed in relation to the just condemnation of the actor's conduct or in relation to deterrence or correction, and all are relevant perspectives, neither the terminology nor the sanctions appropriate for homicide may fairly be applied when the fatality is thus fortuitous. The actor's conduct is a crime and should be dealt with as such, but as a crime defined in reference to the specific evil it portends, e.g., bodily injury. The inequality involved in treating homicides as manslaughter, when they are accidental in the sense supposed, serves no proper purpose of the penal law and is abusive in itself."

2. *The required causal connection.* Mere coincidence of time and place between the misdemeanor and the causing of death will not suffice. Illustrative is *People v. Mulcahy,* 318 Ill. 332, 149 N.E. 266 (1925), holding it is not enough that the death was caused "while" the defendant was engaged in an unlawful act, and thus it was not manslaughter where a policeman's gun accidentally discharged and killed a hatcheck girl while he was committing the unlawful act of failing to arrest drunks and gamblers who were disturbing the peace and gambling in his presence in a cabaret.

3. *Malum in se or malum prohibitum.* In many but not all jurisdictions with misdemeanor manslaughter, it is significant whether the misdemeanor is of the *malum in se* or *malum prohibitum* type. "An offense malum in se is properly defined as one which is naturally evil as adjudged by the sense of a civilized community, whereas an act malum prohibitum is wrong only because made so by statute." *State v. Horton,* 139 N.C. 588, 51 S.E. 945 (1905). When the defendant's unlawful act was only *malum prohibitum,* courts tended to narrow the scope of the misdemeanor-manslaughter doctrine in various ways:

(a) Sometimes it is said the defendant is not guilty unless the death was the foreseeable or natural consequence of the defendant's unlawful conduct. For example, in *Commonwealth v. Williams,* 133 Pa.Super. 104, 1 A.2d 812 (1938), where the defendant struck and killed the victim while driving with an expired driver's license, the manslaughter conviction was reversed because for manslaughter liability "the death must be the natural result or probable consequence of the unlawful act."

(b) Sometimes it is said the defendant is not guilty unless the death was in fact caused by his conduct's unlawful excess, that is, that portion of the defendant's whole conduct which makes the conduct unlawful. Illustrative is *State v. Gerak,* supra, reversing a conviction for manslaughter based upon defendant's violation of a statute proscribing the discharge of a firearm within city limits without obtaining a permit from the mayor. "The unlawful act, then, is having no permit to discharge a firearm, not the discharge per se. Had the defendant obtained a permit, and assuming he fired the fatal shot as alleged, the discharge of the firearm would not be an unlawful act and since it cannot reasonably be said that failure to obtain a permit was the proximate cause of death, the doctrine cannot apply."

(c) Sometimes it is said the defendant is not guilty unless his unlawful conduct amounted to criminal negligence. Thus, in *People v. Stuart,* 47 Cal.2d 167, 302 P.2d 5 (1956), the court held that a manslaughter conviction could not be grounded upon a violation of the strict liability offense of misbranding drugs unless it was shown, which would not be necessary for conviction of the misdemeanor, that the defendant "had intentionally or through criminal negligence prepared, compounded or sold an adulterated or misbranded drug."

4. *The current trend.* The Model Penal Code rejected the misdemeanor-manslaughter doctrine in its entirety. The great majority of the recodifications adopted in recent years have followed the lead of the Model Penal Code in this regard.

SECTION 6. CAUSATION

Introductory Notes

1. Whenever a crime is defined in such a way that the occurrence of a certain specific result of conduct is required for its commission (e.g., death of a human being for any criminal homicide), it is necessary that the defendant's conduct be the "legal" or "proximate" cause of the result. For one thing, that conduct must be the cause in fact of the result, which usually means that but for the conduct the result would not have occurred.[a] In addition, even when cause in fact is established, it must be determined whether the variation between the result intended or hazarded and the actual result is so extraordinary that it would be unfair to hold the defendant responsible for the result.

2. In a very significant sense the subject of causation fits within the major theme of this Chapter: the classification of crimes in terms of their seriousness. This is because, as noted in *Model Penal Code* § 2.03, Comment (1985): "What will usually turn on determinations under this section is not the criminality of the defendant's conduct, but the gravity of his offense. For example, when the actor's purpose is to cause the death of another, the lack of an adequate relation between his conduct and the death of his intended victim results in conviction for attempted murder rather than murder. Similarly, when the actor recklessly creates a risk of death, escape from responsibility for criminal homicide under the present section does not bar criminal liability for lesser offenses. Thus, the issue in penal law is quite different from that in torts. Ordinarily, it is only in form a question of the actor's liability. In substance, it is a question of the severity of the sentence the court may impose."

3. It is very unusual for a criminal code to define proximate cause or even to articulate principles for courts to utilize in deciding causation issues; the law on this

a. The "but for" test does not work where two causes, each alone sufficient to bring about the harmful result, operate together to cause it (e.g., A shoots X in the chest and B acting independently shoots X in the head; X dies following these separate fatal wounds). As stated in *State v. Batiste,* 410 So.2d 1055 (La.1982), involving such facts: "The law will not stop, in such a case, to measure which wound is the more serious, and to speculate upon which actually caused the death." Thus, the test for cause in fact is more accurately worded: Was the defendant's conduct a substantial factor in bringing about the forbidden result? *State v. Serebin,* 119 Wis.2d 837, 350 N.W.2d 65 (1984).

Moreover, there is also authority that one of several independent injuries may be a cause of death even if it "alone would not have been sufficient to cause the death." *Commonwealth v. McLeod,* 394 Mass. 727, 477 N.E.2d 972 (1985). It is enough if it "caused, contributed to, or accelerated" the death. *Holsemback v. State,* 443 So.2d 1371 (Ala.Crim.App.1983). But a few states by statute have provided that the defendant is not the cause of death if the other cause was sufficient to cause death but defendant's was not. See *State v. Crocker,* 431 A.2d 1323 (Me.1981).

subject is almost exclusively a product of the courts. Consider, as you read the following materials, whether the subject lends itself to legislation. In particular, "test" *Model Penal Code* § 2.03 against the cases which follow.[b]

4. Consider also, in assessing the following cases, the criticism in Patricia Hassett, *Absolutism in Causation,* 38 Syrac.L.Rev. 683, 686, 710, 712–13 (1987), that while there are gradations of responsibility with respect to the other elements of criminal offenses (e.g., as to the mental element, intentionally causing a harm is deemed more serious than recklessly causing the same harm; as to results, a completed crime is deemed more serious than an attempt), "the causation element has been uniformly treated as an absolute that either exists (thus imposing full liability), or does not exist (thus resulting in exoneration). * * * No mechanism exists for adjusting either the grade of the defendant's offense or the authorized penalties to reflect the partial nature of the defendant's contribution to the harm, or the existence of contributing causal forces. * * * [T]he estimation of foreseeability is not an exact science and the transition from foreseeable to unforeseeable may be gradual rather than abrupt. A doctrine of partial causal responsibility would permit the reality of the gradual transition to be incorporated into the adjudication of criminal liability * * *."

STATE v. ROSE

Supreme Court of Rhode Island, 1973.

112 R.I. 402, 311 A.2d 281.

ROBERTS, CHIEF JUSTICE. * * *

[Defendant's conviction of manslaughter] followed the death of David J. McEnery, who was struck by defendant's motor vehicle at the intersection of Broad and Summer Streets in Providence at about 6:30 p.m. on April 1, 1970. According to the testimony of a bus driver, he had been operating his vehicle north on Broad Street and had stopped at a traffic light at the intersection of Summer Street. While the bus was standing there, he observed a pedestrian starting to cross Broad Street, and as the pedestrian reached the middle of the southbound lane he was struck by a "dirty, white station wagon" that was proceeding southerly on Broad Street. The pedestrian's body was thrown up on the hood of the car. The bus driver further testified that the station wagon stopped momentarily, the body of the pedestrian rolled off the hood, and the car immediately drove off along Broad Street in a southerly direction. The bus operator testified that he had alighted from his bus, intending to attempt to assist the victim, but was unable to locate the body.

Subsequently, it appears from the testimony of a police officer, about 6:40 p.m. the police located a white station wagon on Haskins Street, a distance of some 610 feet from the scene of the accident. The police further testified that a body later identified as that of David J. McEnery was wedged beneath the vehicle when it was found and that the vehicle had been registered to defendant.

Testifying on behalf of the state was a Robert Buckley, who stated that he had worked with defendant and that about 5 p.m. on the day of the accident he had gone to a place located in Central Falls that he identified as The Palms where he met defendant about 5:15 p.m. Buckley further testified that about 7 p.m. that evening defendant phoned him, told him that he had been involved in an accident, and asked Buckley to help him look for his car. According to Buckley, he picked up defendant's girl friend, identified as Pat, and went

b. For a critique of the Code approach, see Note, 78 Colum.L.Rev. 1249 (1978).

to the vicinity of the accident and drove around for some time but was unable to locate the car.

Buckley testified that later he picked up defendant, who asked him to take him to a café in Central Falls known as The Well, where he would attempt to establish an alibi. After arriving at The Well, defendant asked Buckley to take him to the Central Falls police station, where defendant reported that his car had been stolen from in front of The Well sometime between 5:30 p.m. and 9 p.m. on that day. Buckley later drove defendant to Pat's home, and while there defendant answered a telephone call. After the telephone call had been completed, defendant told Buckley that "a guy had been killed." According to Buckley, defendant "was denying it on the 'phone" during the conversation. * * *

The defendant * * * directs our attention to the fact that the court charged the jury that there was no evidence in the case of culpable negligence on the part of defendant up to and including the time at which Mr. McEnery was struck by the station wagon. He further charged the jury that, in order to find defendant guilty of manslaughter, it would be necessary to find that McEnery was alive immediately after the impact and that the conduct of defendant following the impact constituted culpable negligence.

The defendant is contending that if the evidence is susceptible of a finding that McEnery was killed upon impact, he was not alive at the time he was being dragged under defendant's vehicle and defendant could not be found guilty of manslaughter. An examination of the testimony of the only medical witness makes it clear that, in his opinion, death could have resulted immediately upon impact by reason of a massive fracture of the skull. The medical witness also testified that death could have resulted a few minutes after the impact but conceded that he was not sure when it did occur.

We are inclined to agree with defendant's contention in this respect. Obviously, the evidence is such that death could have occurred after defendant had driven away with McEnery's body lodged under his car and, therefore, be consistent with guilt. On the other hand, the medical testimony is equally consistent with a finding that McEnery could have died instantly upon impact and, therefore, be consistent with a reasonable conclusion other than the guilt of defendant. It is clear, then, that, the testimony of the medical examiner lacking any reasonable medical certainty as to the time of the death of McEnery, we are unable to conclude that on such evidence defendant was guilty of manslaughter beyond a reasonable doubt. Therefore, we conclude * * * that it was error to deny defendant's motion for a directed verdict of acquittal. * * *[a]

Notes and Questions

1. Bush shot Geller in the chest several times with a .38 caliber revolver. Shortly thereafter, Dlugash shot Geller in the face five times with his .25 caliber revolver. Though the trial court dismissed that portion of the indictment which alleged that Dlugash and Bush acted in concert, Dlugash was convicted of murder. The conviction was reversed in *People v. Dlugash*, 41 N.Y.2d 725, 395 N.Y.S.2d 419, 363 N.E.2d 1155 (1977): "While the defendant admitted firing five shots at the victim approximately two to five minutes after Bush had fired three times, all three medical expert witnesses testified that they could not, with any degree of medical certainty, state whether the victim had been alive at the time the latter shots were fired by the defendant. Thus, the People failed to prove beyond a reasonable doubt that the victim had been alive at the time he was shot by the defendant. Whatever else it may be, it is not murder to shoot a dead body."[b]

---

a. The court went on to conclude that the evidence was sufficient to sustain the findings that defendant had knowledge that he struck a pedestrian and that the pedestrian had sustained injuries, and that such evidence supported defendant's conviction for leaving the scene of an accident.

2. Compare with *Rose* the similar case of *State v. Southern*, 304 N.W.2d 329 (Minn.1981): "We disagree with the state's contention that the evidence established beyond a reasonable doubt that defendant was driving in a grossly negligent manner up to the point of impact.

"Defendant's conduct in accelerating and leaving the scene clearly was gross negligence, however, and we are satisfied that the state's evidence sufficiently established that gross negligence to be a substantial factor causing the child's death. There was testimony that defendant's gross negligence resulted in the child being dragged approximately 175 feet before his body came to rest, a far greater distance than he would have been dragged if defendant had stopped immediately after impact instead of fleeing. The two main injuries which led to the child's death were a head injury which probably, but not necessarily, occurred at impact and a neck injury which may have occurred at impact or while the child was being dragged. But for defendant's gross negligence, the child may well have survived. Of course, we will never know this because defendant, by her gross negligence in failing to stop and in leaving the scene, made it impossible to determine this. Further, her conduct also had the effect of ensuring the child's death. We are satisfied after a careful review of the record that the evidence established defendant's grossly negligent driving to be a substantial causal factor in the child's death."

Is this so? Does this mean that both *Rose* and *Dlugash* were wrongly decided?

3. Fine became involved in a heated argument with Hodges. Hodges became very angry when Fine said Hodges owed him $5; as Fine later testified, Hodges "had a wild, angry look on his face." Fine grabbed Hodges and shook him and then grabbed him by the throat. Fine released him in a matter of seconds, and Hodges then slumped to the ground. He never regained consciousness, and died several weeks later. At Fine's prosecution for manslaughter, the medical evidence was that Hodges had suffered a cerebral hemorrhage, that his blood pressure had been "alarmingly high," that "excitement of any kind or nature" could have caused the rupture of the blood vessel in his brain, and that "a person of that age with that blood pressure [would] be liable to have a stroke without anybody even touching them." In *Fine v. State*, 193 Tenn. 422, 246 S.W.2d 70 (1952), the court reversed the conviction. "In the light of the proven facts, including that of the medical experts bearing upon the cause of death, it cannot be said with any degree of certainty that the deceased died as the result of any criminal agency. The conclusion reached by the jury, of necessity, had to be based upon an inference upon an inference and upon a third inference which could not be thought of otherwise than a fantastic speculation."

4. Jackson shot Gloss in the back of the head; Gloss was hospitalized until his death 14 months later; the cause of death was "acute bronchopneumonia due to quadriplegia with prolonged coma due to gunshot wound of the head." The murder charge then lodged against Jackson was dismissed by the trial judge under the longstanding year-and-a-day rule, which bars prosecution for murder when the victim died more than a year and a day after being injured. On appeal, *United States v. Jackson*, 528 A.2d 1211 (D.C.App.1987), the rule was abolished prospectively:

"Since the origin and purposes of the rule are obscure, we cannot say with certainty why the rule came into existence. Most commentators suggest that it reflects the judgment that proof of causation for murder 'should not be unduly speculative.' Difficulties of proof

b. The court went on to conclude "that there is sufficient evidence in the record from which the jury could conclude that the defendant believed Geller to be alive at the time defendant fired shots into Geller's head," and therefore merely modified the judgment "to reflect a conviction for the lesser included offense of attempted murder."

arose because in early English courts, jurors decided cases by applying their own knowledge of the matter at hand or by reflecting the conviction of the community about the issue being decided. More importantly, medical technology was not capable of precisely determining the cause of death. It also has been suggested that 'the rule was intended simply to soften the old brutal law regarding homicides.' * * *

"The government argues that public policy considerations require abrogation of a rule based on scientific inadequacies and an outmoded use of jurors; because those reasons no longer exist as a result of the advances of science, the government reasons, the rule has abrogated itself. Further, the government notes the irony of a rule that insulates from full criminal responsibility persons who have committed a crime which the Council of the District of Columbia has declared so heinous that it should have no statute of limitations. Finally, Jackson's fortuitous benefit from the advances of medicine which prolonged the victim's life, the government contends, presents no barrier of unfairness to his prosecution for murder, especially where, as here, the death occurred shortly after expiration of a year and a day and the rule poses a high social cost for society, where, as here, there is no question of causation.

"Jackson's response is three-fold. He argues that notwithstanding scientific advances, the government's interest in prosecution of murder will be enhanced little, if at all, by abolition of the rule because the government now may seek life imprisonment for an armed assault. Second, the importance of finality in criminal prosecutions is a legitimate societal interest, which makes the rule necessary because of 'lingering difficulties of proof and to remove the "Sword of Damocles" hanging over a potential defendant.' Third, because views differ greatly about what is the appropriate length of time after which a prosecution should be barred, the legislature is in a better position than a court to change the rule.

"Reliance on the absence of evidence of frustrated prosecutions as a result of the year and a day rule strikes us as unpersuasive: modern medical discoveries have made life-prolonging situations a more frequent occurrence in recent years and thus the effect of the rule may not often have been presented to the prosecutor. Similarly, that the prosecutor is able to place other charges against an assailant makes the year and a day rule no less appealing in view of the legislative determination, and indeed the determination of the electorate itself by initiative, of the measure of punishment upon conviction of different kinds of assaults. Surely the windfall for the assailant is a high price for society to pay for a rule which, as persuasively reasoned by the Supreme Judicial Court of Massachusetts, appears to have become not only an anachronism but is 'capricious' and 'senselessly indulgent' in establishing a particularly short limit. * * * [18]"

KIBBE v. HENDERSON

United States Court of Appeals, Second Circuit, 1976.

534 F.2d 493.

LUMBARD, CIRCUIT JUDGE: * * *

18. Those who argue against the rule have advanced at least three alternatives as superior to the year and a day limitation. The first is to retain the proposition of an irrebuttable presumption based on a time limit, but to extend the time to a longer period. At the present time, there is no consensus as to what may be an appropriate length of time, following an assault, after which prosecution for homicide should be barred. The legislatures of California and Washington have adopted a three years and a day rule. Texas recognizes a one year rule. The traditional year and a day rule remains in effect in approximately twenty states. A second suggestion calls for retention of the year and a day time limit, but a change in the concept from an irrebuttable presumption to a rebuttable presumption with a higher burden of proof. The first two approaches are not mutually exclusive. A third alternative is complete abolition of the precept.

Kibbe and his codefendant, Roy Krall, met the decedent, George Stafford, at a bar in Rochester, New York on the evening of December 30, 1970. Stafford had been drinking heavily and by about 9:00 p.m. he was so intoxicated that the bartender refused to serve him further. Apparently the defendants saw Stafford offer a one hundred dollar bill for payment, which the bartender refused. At some point during the evening, Stafford began soliciting a ride to Canandaigua from the other patrons in the bar. Kibbe and Krall, who confessed to having already decided to rob Stafford, offered a ride and the three men left the bar together. Before starting out for Canandaigua, the three visited a second bar. When the bartender at this bar also refused to serve Stafford because of his inebriated condition, the three proceeded to a third bar, where each was served additional drinks.

Kibbe, Krall and Stafford left for Canandaigua in Kibbe's car about 9:30 that evening. According to statements of the defendants, as Krall was driving the car, Kibbe demanded Stafford's money and, upon receiving it, forced Stafford to lower his trousers and remove his boots to prove he had no more. At some time between 9:30 and 9:40 p.m., Stafford was abandoned on the side of an unlit, rural two-lane highway. His boots and jacket were also placed on the shoulder of the highway; Stafford's eyeglasses, however, remained in the car. There was testimony that it was "very cold" that night and that strong winds were blowing recently fallen snow across the highway, although the night was clear and the pavement was dry. There was an open and lighted service station in the general vicinity, but testimony varied as to its precise distance from the place where Stafford was abandoned. In any case, the station was no more than one-quarter of a mile away.

About half an hour after Kibbe and Krall had abandoned Stafford, Michael Blake, a college student, was driving his pickup truck northbound on the highway at 50 miles an hour, ten miles per hour in excess of the posted speed limit. A car passed Blake in a southbound direction and the driver flashed his headlights at Blake. Immediately thereafter, Blake saw Stafford sitting in the middle of the northbound lane with his hands in the air. Blake testified that he "went into a kind of shock" as soon as he saw Stafford, and that he did not apply his brakes. Blake further testified that he did not attempt to avoid hitting Stafford because he "didn't have time to react." After the collision, Blake stopped his truck and returned to assist Stafford, whereupon he found the decedent's trousers were around his ankles and his shirt was up to his chest. Stafford was wearing neither his jacket nor his boots.

Stafford suffered massive head and body injuries as a result of the collision and died shortly thereafter. An autopsy revealed a high alcohol concentration of .25% in his blood. The Medical Examiner testified that these injuries were the direct cause of death.

Kibbe and Krall were apprehended on December 31, 1970. They were tried for robbery and for the murder of Stafford under New York Penal Law § 125.25(2) which provides:

A person is guilty of murder in the second degree when:

* * *

(2) Under circumstances evincing a depraved indifference to human life, he recklessly engages in conduct which creates a grave risk of death to another person, and thereby causes the death of another person.

In his charge to the jury, the judge failed to define or explain the issue of causation as that term is used in § 125.25(2). No mention was made of the legal effect of intervening or supervening cause. Nevertheless, defense counsel failed to take any exception whatsoever to this omission. The jury returned guilty verdicts on the charges of second degree murder, second degree robbery, and third degree grand larceny. Kibbe was sentenced to concurrent terms of imprisonment of 15 years to life on the murder conviction, 5 to 15 years on the robbery conviction, and up to 4 years on the grand larceny conviction.

The Appellate Division affirmed the conviction on finding that there was sufficient evidence that Stafford's death was caused by appellant's acts "as well as by the acts of Blake." The court stated that while the trial judge's charge concerning causation was "lacking in detail" appellant had not questioned the sufficiency of the charge on appeal and no exceptions to or requests for a charge on causation had been made at trial. * * * The New York Court of Appeals also found sufficient evidence of causation and unanimously affirmed the convictions. * * *

Kibbe then petitioned for habeas corpus in the District Court for the Northern District. Judge Foley denied the petition and, on the question of the jury charge, noted that the correctness of instructions does not raise a constitutional claim cognizable on habeas corpus. Appeal to this court followed. * * *

In this case, by the language of the statute, the state was bound to prove to the jury beyond a reasonable doubt that appellant evinced a depraved indifference to Stafford's life, recklessly engaged in conduct that created a grave risk of Stafford's death, and thereby caused Stafford's death. The court scrupulously instructed the jury with respect to the meaning of "recklessly", "depraved", "grave", and "indifferent" as used in Penal Law § 125.25(2). The omission of any definition of causation, however, permitted the jury to conclude that the issue was not before them or that causation could be inferred merely from the fact that Stafford's death succeeded his abandonment by Kibbe and Krall.

Even if the jury were aware of the need to determine causation,[5] the court's instruction did not provide the tools necessary to that task. The possibility that jurors, as laymen, may misconstrue the evidence before them makes mandatory in every case instruction as to the legal standards they must apply. Error in the omission of an instruction is compounded where the legal standard is complex and requires that fine distinctions be made. That is most assuredly the situation in this case. It has been held that where death is produced by an intervening force, such as Blake's operation of his truck, the liability of one who put an antecedent force into action will depend on the difficult determination of whether the intervening force was a sufficiently independent or supervening cause of death. See W. LaFave & A. Scott, *Criminal Law* 257–63 (1972) (collecting cases).[6] The few

---

5. The trial judge made brief mention of the term "causation" in his charge when he stated:

"You will not consider either (first degree manslaughter or second degree manslaughter) unless you feel that these defendants or either of them, was guilty of causing the death of George Stafford recklessly." This instruction, however, was given in the context of explaining the relation between reckless conduct and manslaughter rather than in the context of a definition of causation. In fact, by emphasizing "recklessly", the judge may have implied that the jury could assume causation and had only to determine whether recklessness was involved. * * *

6. The complexity of the definition of legal causation in LaFave and Scott, supra, demonstrates that an explanation of the concept of intervening and supervening cause would have been not merely helpful (as contended by Judge Mansfield), but essential to the jury's determination here. Given the proper standard for causation, the jury could have found that Blake had been so reckless as to absolve defendants of legal responsibility for Stafford's death:

As might be expected, courts have tended to distinguish cases in which the intervening act was a *coincidence* from those in which it was a *response* to the defendant's prior action. An intervening act is a *coincidence* when the defendant's act merely put the victim at a certain place at a certain time, and because the victim was so located it was possible for him to be acted upon by the intervening cause. The case put earlier in which B, after being fired upon by A, changed his route and then was struck by lightning is an illustration of a coincidence. However, it is important to note that there may be a coincidence even when the subsequent act is that of a human agency, as where A shoots B and leaves him lying in the roadway, resulting in B being struck by C's car; or where A shoots at B and causes him to take refuge in a park, where B is then attacked and killed by a gang of hoodlums.

By contrast, an intervening act may be said to be a *response* to the prior actions of the defendant when it involves a reaction to the conditions created by the defendant.

cases that provide similar factual circumstances suggest that the controlling questions are whether the ultimate result was foreseeable to the original actor and whether the victim failed to do something easily within his grasp that would have extricated him from danger.[7]

The New York appellate courts applied these standards and found that there was sufficient evidence to uphold the convictions. We have no reason to doubt that conclusion. * * * The sufficiency of the evidence, however, is not the subject of our inquiry. Our sole concern is whether the jury was adequately instructed in order to make the same finding beyond a reasonable doubt. As this function was within the exclusive province of the jury, the appellate courts may not substitute their own findings for the jury's possible failure to consider the issue. * * * If the jury had been cognizant of the proper legal standards, this evidence, if believed, could have injected an element of reasonable doubt into the jury's deliberations as to whether defendants foresaw or could have foreseen that about one-half hour after they abandoned Stafford he would be struck in the middle of a highway lane by the driver of a speeding truck who failed to react in such a way to avoid a collision.

We are convinced that the trial judge's incomplete instructions took a necessary determination of causation of death from the jury and thereby deprived appellant of his right to due process. * * *

MANSFIELD, CIRCUIT JUDGE (dissenting): * * *

Although it might have been helpful to the jury to have a more definitive instruction on the element of causation, including an explanation of the concepts of proximate, superseding, and intervening causation, I cannot agree with the majority that such a detailed instruction was constitutionally required or that the failure to give it permitted "the jury to conclude that the issue was not before them." We are not here dealing with such fundamental unfairness as failure to advise the jury that the defendant was presumed to be innocent or the substitution by the court in its instruction of a preponderance-of-the-evidence for a reasonable doubt standard, see *In re Winship*, 397 U.S. 358, 90 S.Ct. 1068, 25 L.Ed.2d 368 (1970). Here the jury plainly was made aware by the summations of the necessity of finding that the defendants' conduct was the cause of the victim's death even though it may not have been the only cause. In these circumstances the court's instruction was sufficient to enable the jury intelligently to go about its business. * * *

————

Thus—though the distinction is not carefully developed in many of the decided cases—it may be said that a coincidence will break the chain of legal cause unless it was foreseeable, while a response will do so only if it is abnormal (and, if abnormal, also unforeseeable).

* * *

This kind of accident must be distinguished from a somewhat different situation, as where A, with intent to kill B, only wounds B, leaving him lying unconscious in the unlighted road on a dark night, and then C, driving along the road, runs over and kills B. Here C's act is a matter of coincidence rather than a response to what A has done, and thus the question is whether the subsequent events were foreseeable, as they undoubtedly were in the above illustration.[73]

73. *People v. Fowler*, 178 Cal. 657, 174 P. 892 (1918). Perhaps if C were driving in a reckless way, A would not be liable. If A in the Fowler case had

merely an intent to injure, but not to kill, A would be guilty of manslaughter, but no doubt A, having put B in an unconscious or helpless position on a dark road, has an affirmative duty to act to pull him off the road, and failure to act under the circumstances where A knows death is substantially certain to occur (or even where he realizes there is a very high risk though no certainty of such death) should make him guilty of murder of the intent to kill (or of the depraved heart) variety.

Without a proper definition of causation, the jury, if it considered causation at all, could have found that Blake's conduct, no matter how reckless, could merely supplement and not supervene defendants' culpability.

7. See *State v. Preslar*, 48 N.C.Rep. 421 (1856) (deliberate choice of victim to forego place of safety exonerates defendant of liability for victim's subsequent death from exposure).

In *Henderson v. Kibbe,* 431 U.S. 145, 97 S.Ct. 1730, 52 L.Ed.2d 203 (1977), the Court, per Stevens, J., reversed:

"The burden of demonstrating that an erroneous instruction was so prejudicial that it will support a collateral attack on the constitutional validity of a state court's judgment is even greater than the showing required to establish plain error on direct appeal. The question in such a collateral proceeding is 'whether the ailing instruction by itself so infected the entire trial that the resulting conviction violates due process', not merely whether ' * * * the instruction is undesirable, erroneous, or even "universally condemned." '

"In this case, the respondent's burden is especially heavy because no erroneous instruction was given; his claim of prejudice is based on the failure to give any explanation—beyond the reading of the statutory language itself—of the causation element. An omission, or an incomplete instruction, is less likely to be prejudicial than a misstatement of the law. Since this omission escaped notice on the record until Judge Cardamone filed his dissenting opinion at the intermediate appellate level, the probability that it substantially affected the jury deliberations seems remote.

"Because respondent did not submit a draft instruction on the causation issue to the trial judge, and because the New York courts apparently had no previous occasion to construe this aspect of the murder statute, we cannot know with certainty precisely what instruction should have been given as a matter of New York law. We do know that the New York Court of Appeals found no reversible error in this case; and its discussion of the sufficiency of the evidence gives us guidance about the kind of causation instruction that would have been acceptable.

"The New York Court of Appeals concluded that the evidence of causation was sufficient because it can be said beyond a reasonable doubt that the 'ultimate harm' was 'something which should have been foreseen as being reasonably related to the acts of the accused.' It is not entirely clear whether the court's reference to 'ultimate harm' merely required that Stafford's death was foreseeable, or, more narrowly, that his death by speeding vehicle was foreseeable. In either event, the court was satisfied that the 'ultimate harm' was one which 'should have been foreseen.' Thus, an adequate instruction would have told the jury that if the ultimate harm should have been foreseen as being reasonably related to defendants' conduct, that conduct should be regarded as having caused the death of Stafford.

"The significance of the omission of such an instruction may be evaluated by comparison with the instructions that were given. One of the elements of respondent's offense is that he acted 'recklessly.' By returning a guilty verdict, the jury necessarily found, in accordance with its instruction on recklessness, that respondent was 'aware of and consciously disregard[ed] a substantial and unjustifiable risk'[15] that death would occur. A person who is 'aware of and consciously disregards' a substantial risk must also foresee the ultimate harm that the risk entails. Thus, the jury's determination that the respondent acted recklessly necessarily included a determination that the ultimate harm was foreseeable to him.

"In a strict sense, an additional instruction on foreseeability would not have been cumulative because it would have related to an element of the offense not specifically covered in the instructions given. But since it is logical to assume that the jurors would

15. In charging the jury on recklessness the trial judge quoted the statutory definition of that term in   New York Penal Law § 15.00.

have responded to an instruction on causation consistently with their determination of the issues that were comprehensively explained, it is equally logical to conclude that such an instruction would not have affected their verdict.[16] Accordingly, we reject the suggestion that the omission of more complete instructions on the causation issue 'so infected the entire trial that the resulting conviction violated due process.' Even if we were to make the unlikely assumption that the jury might have reached a different verdict pursuant to an additional instruction, that possibility is too speculative to justify the conclusion that constitutional error was committed."

REGINA v. BLAUE

Court of Appeal, Criminal Division, England, 1975.

[1975]   1 W.L.R. 1411, [1975] 3 All E.R. 446 (C.A.).

LAWTON L.J. read the following judgment of the court. On October 17, 1974, at Teesside Crown Court after a trial before Mocatta J. the defendant was acquitted of the murder of Jacolyn Woodhead but was convicted of her manslaughter on the ground of diminished responsibility. * * *

The victim was aged 18. She was a Jehovah's Witness. She professed the tenets of that sect and lived her life by them. During the late afternoon of May 3, 1974, the defendant came into her house and asked her for sexual intercourse. She refused. He then attacked her with a knife inflicting four serious wounds. One pierced her lung. The defendant ran away. She staggered out into the road. She collapsed outside a neighbour's house. An ambulance took her to hospital, where she arrived at about 7:30 p.m. Soon after she was admitted to the intensive care ward. At about 8:30 p.m. she was examined by the surgical registrar who quickly decided that serious injury had been caused which would require surgery. As she had lost a lot of blood, before there could be an operation there would have to be a blood transfusion. As soon as the girl appreciated that the surgeon was thinking of organising a blood transfusion for her, she said that she should not be given one and that she would not have one. To have one, she said, would be contrary to her religious beliefs as a Jehovah's Witness. She was told that if she did not have a blood transfusion she would die. She said that she did not care if she did die. She was asked to acknowledge in writing that she had refused to have a blood transfusion under any circumstances. She did so. The prosecution admitted at the trial that had she had a blood transfusion when advised to have one she would not have died. She did so at 12:45 a.m. the next day. The evidence called by the prosecution proved that at all relevant times she was conscious and decided as she did deliberately, and knowing what the consequences of her decision would be. In his final speech to the jury, Mr. Herrod for the prosecution accepted that her refusal to have a blood transfusion was *a* cause of her death. The prosecution did not challenge the defence evidence that the defendant was suffering from diminished responsibility.

Towards the end of the trial and before the summing up started counsel on both sides made submissions as to how the case should be put to the jury. Counsel then appearing for the defendant invited the judge to direct the jury to acquit the defendant generally on the

16. In fact, it is not unlikely that a complete instruction on the causation issue would actually have been favorable to the prosecution. For example, an instruction might have been patterned after the following example given in W. LaFave & A. Scott, *Criminal Law* 260 (1972):

"* * * A, with intent to kill B, only wounds B, leaving him lying unconscious in the unlighted road on a dark night, and then C, driving along the road, runs over and kills B. Here C's act is a matter of coincidence rather than a response to what A has done, and thus the question is whether the subsequent events were foreseeable, as they undoubtedly were in the above illustration."

Such an instruction would probably have been more favorable to the prosecution than the instruction on recklessness which the court actually gave.

count of murder. His argument was that her refusal to have a blood transfusion had broken the chain of causation between the stabbing and her death. As an alternative he submitted that the jury should be left to decide whether the chain of causation had been broken. Mr. Herrod submitted that the judge should direct the jury to convict, because no facts were in issue and when the law was applied to the facts there was only one possible verdict, namely, manslaughter by reason of diminished responsibility.

When the judge came to direct the jury on this issue he did so by telling them that they should apply their common sense. He then went on to tell them they would get some help from the cases to which counsel had referred in their speeches. He reminded them of what Lord Parker C.J. had said in *Reg. v. Smith* [1959] 2 W.B. 35, 42 and what Maule J. had said 133 years before in *Reg. v. Holland* (1841) 2 Mood. & R. 351, 352. He placed particular reliance on what Maule J. had said. The jury, he said, might find it "most material and most helpful." He continued:

"This is one of those relatively rare cases, you may think, with very little option open to you but to reach the conclusion that was reached by your predecessors as members of the jury in *Reg. v. Holland,* namely, 'yes' to the question of causation that the stab was still, at the time of this girl's death, the operative cause of death—or a substantial cause of death. However, that is a matter for you to determine after you have withdrawn to consider your verdict."

Mr. Comyn has criticised that direction on three grounds: first, because *Reg. v. Holland* should no longer be considered good law; secondly, because *Reg. v. Smith,* when rightly understood, does envisage the possibility of unreasonable conduct on the part of the victim breaking the chain of causation; and thirdly, because the judge in reality directed the jury to find causation proved although he used words which seemed to leave the issue open for them to decide.

In *Reg. v. Holland,* 2 Mood. & R. 351, the defendant in the course of a violent assault, had injured one of his victim's fingers. A surgeon had advised amputation because of the danger to life through complications developing. The advice was rejected. A fortnight later the victim died of lockjaw. Maule J. said, at p. 352: "the real question is, whether in the end the wound inflicted by the prisoner was the cause of death." That distinguished judge left the jury to decide that question as did the judge in this case. They had to decide it as juries always do, by pooling their experience of life and using their common sense. They would not have been handicapped by a lack of training in dialectic or moral theology.

Maule J.'s direction to the jury reflected the common law's answer to the problem. He who inflicted an injury which resulted in death could not excuse himself by pleading that his victim could have avoided death by taking greater care of himself: see *Hale's Pleas of the Crown* (1800 ed.), pp. 427–428. The common law in Sir Matthew Hale's time probably was in line with contemporary concepts of ethics. A man who did a wrongful act was deemed *morally* responsible for the natural and probable consequences of that act. Mr. Comyn asked us to remember that since Sir Matthew Hale's day the rigour of the law relating to homicide has been eased in favour of the accused. It has been—but this has come about through the development of the concept of intent, not by reason of a different view of causation. * * *

There have been two cases in recent years which have some bearing upon this topic: *Reg. v. Jordan* (1956) 40 Cr.App.R. 152 and *Reg. v. Smith* [1959] 2 Q.B. 35. In *Reg. v. Jordan* the Court of Criminal Appeal, after conviction, admitted some medical evidence which went to prove that the cause of death was not the blow relied upon by the prosecution but abnormal medical treatment after admission to hospital. This case has been criticised but it was probably rightly decided on its facts. Before the abnormal treatment started the injury had almost healed. We share Lord Parker C.J.'s opinion that *Reg. v. Jordan* should be regarded as a case decided on its own special facts and not as an authority relaxing the common law approach to causation. In *Reg. v. Smith* [1959] 2 Q.B. 35 the man who had been stabbed would probably not have died but for a series of mishaps. These mishaps were said to have broken the chain of causation. Lord Parker C.J., in the course of his judgment, commented as follows:

> "It seems to the court that if at the time of death the original wound is still an operating cause and a substantial cause, then the death can properly be said to be the result of the wound, albeit that some other cause of death is also operating. Only if it can be said that the original wounding is merely the setting in which another cause operates can it be said that the death does not flow from the wound. Putting it another way, only if the second cause is so overwhelming as to make the original wound merely part of the history can it be said that the death does not flow from the wound."

The physical cause of death in this case was the bleeding into the pleural cavity arising from the penetration of the lung. This had not been brought about by any decision made by the deceased but by the stab wound.

Mr. Comyn tried to overcome this line of reasoning by submitting that the jury should have been directed that if they thought the deceased's decision not to have a blood transfusion was an unreasonable one, then the chain of causation would have been broken. At once the question arises—reasonable by whose standards? Those of Jehovah's Witnesses? Humanists? Roman Catholics? Protestants of Anglo–Saxon descent? The man on the Clapham omnibus? But he might well be an admirer of Eleazar who suffered death rather than eat the flesh of swine (2 Maccabees, ch. 6, vv. 18–31) or of Sir Thomas More who, unlike nearly all his contemporaries, was unwilling to accept Henry VIII as Head of the Church in England. Those brought up in the Hebraic and Christian traditions would probably be reluctant to accept that these martyrs caused their own deaths.

As was pointed out to Mr. Comyn in the course of argument, two cases, each raising the same issue of reasonableness because of religious beliefs, could produce different verdicts depending on where the cases were tried. A jury drawn from Preston, sometimes said to be the most Catholic town in England, might have different views about martyrdom to one drawn from the inner suburbs of London. Mr. Comyn accepted that this might be so: it was, he said, inherent in trial by jury. It is not inherent in the common law as expounded by Sir Matthew Hale and Maule J. It has long been the policy of the law that those who use violence on other people must take their victims as they find them. This in our judgment means the whole man, not just the physical man. It does not lie in the mouth of the assailant to say that his victim's religious beliefs which inhibited him from accepting certain kinds of treatment were unreasonable. The question for decision is what caused her death. The answer is the stab wound. The fact that the victim refused to stop this end coming about did not break the causal connection between the act and death.

If a victim's personal representatives claim compensation for his death the concept of foreseeability can operate in favour of the wrongdoer in the assessment of such compensation: the wrongdoer is entitled to expect his victim to mitigate his damage by accepting treatment of a normal kind. As Mr. Herrod pointed out, the criminal law is concerned with the maintenance of law and order and the protection of the public generally. A policy of the common law applicable to the settlement of tortious liability between subjects may not be, and in our judgment is not, appropriate for the criminal law.

The issue of the cause of death in a trial for either murder or manslaughter is one of fact for the jury to decide. But if, as in this case, there is no conflict of evidence and all the jury has to do is to apply the law to the admitted facts, the judge is entitled to tell the jury what the result of that application will be. In this case the judge would have been entitled to have told the jury that the defendant's stab wound was an operative cause of death. The appeal fails.

Notes and Questions

1. The distinguished English criminal law scholar Glanville Williams comments on *Blaue* as follows in 35 Camb.L.J. 15–16 (1976): "Although the case follows the precedents, * * * it fails to notice that all of them dated from a time when medical science was in its infancy, and when operations performed without hygiene carried great danger to life. It was therefore open to the court for the benefit of the defendant to consider the question afresh, and there were several reasons for doing so.

"It had been held in *Roberts* (1971) 56 Cr.App.R. 95 that the test of imputable causation (where the victim had sustained injury in an attempt to escape) was one of reasonable foresight. It is a useful test, and one might have hoped that it would be generalised; yet we are now told that it does not apply to the circumstances in *Blaue*. Why not?

"It had been held in the law of tort that the test of reasonable foresight applies to facts like those in *Blaue*, but the court refused to bring the criminal law into line. The criminal law should avoid the appearance of harshness, and to make it more stringent than the civil law in the matter of causation is surprising.[a] Lawton L.J., speaking for the court, explained the difference between crime and tort by saying that 'the criminal law is concerned with the maintenance of law and order and the protection of the public generally.' This overlooks that Blaue was in any event punishable severely for wounding with intent. What social purpose is served by giving an attacker *extra* punishment because the person attacked unreasonably refused treatment?"

2. Consider also James J. Gobert, *The Fortuity of Consequence*, 4 Crim.L.F. 1, 14–15 (1993): "The unsatisfactory nature of the court's reasoning in *Blaue* is exposed by a hypothetical posed by Hart and Honore: 'What if the victim has called for a blood transfusion and the doctor had refused to administer one, saying that he preferred to play a round of golf, so that the victim died? In that case, too, the bleeding would have continued until death but death would surely have been caused by the doctor's callousness. . . . ' Hart and Honore offer an alternative justification for the result in *Blaue*. As a policy matter, the law should respect a choice made out of conscience to conform to the dictates of one's religion. Such a choice, whether or not foreseeable, is not unreasonable. Hart and Honore question whether the 'choice' should even be deemed voluntary once one has embraced the religion. While this analysis might be persuasive if an insurance company had refused to pay a death benefit on the victim's life on the ground that she had

a. Consider, in this regard, this statement from *Commonwealth v. Root*, 403 Pa. 571, 170 A.2d 310 (1961):

"While precedent is to be found for application of the tort law concept of 'proximate cause' in fixing responsibility for criminal homicide, the want of any rational basis for its use in determining criminal liability can no longer be properly disregarded. When proximate cause was first borrowed from the field of tort law and applied to homicide prosecutions in Pennsylvania, the concept connoted a much more direct causal relation in producing the alleged culpable result than it does to-day. Proximate cause, as an essential element of a tort founded in negligence, has undergone in recent times, and is still undergoing, a marked extension. More specifically, this area of civil law has been progressively liberalized in favor of claims for damages for personal injuries to which careless conduct of others can in some way be associated. To persist in applying the tort liability concept of proximate cause to prosecutions for criminal homicide after the marked expansion of *civil* liability of defendants in tort actions for negligence would be to extend possible *criminal* liability to persons chargeable with unlawful or reckless conduct in circumstances not generally considered to present the likelihood of a resultant death."

committed suicide, it does not explain why Blaue should be deemed criminally responsible for her death."

3. In *Blaue* it is said to have "long been the policy of the law that those who use violence on other people must take their victims as they find them." This policy most often comes into play with respect to a pre-existing physical weakness of the victim, as in *State v. Chavers*, 294 So.2d 489 (La.1974). Chavers and Simpson met Johnston, who was intoxicated, in a bar. They lured Johnston to a deserted area, struck him on the jaw, and then took his wallet and watch, after which they placed him in a parked truck at another location. Johnston was found dead in the truck two days later. The coroner determined that he had died of a heart attack two days earlier and that he had a pre-existing severe heart condition. The coroner found no evidence of any blow to the body, but stated that a blow on the jaw could have aggravated enough emotion to cause a heart attack in view of the decedent's severe pre-existing coronary condition. In affirming Chavers' conviction of manslaughter, the court stated:

"Thus, the trial jury could reasonably find that the blow to the jaw precipitated the heart attack in Johnston, due to his pre-existing unusually severe coronary condition.

"A death so caused may be entirely unforeseeable on the part of the person who hit the victim suffering with a pre-existing weakness. Nevertheless, such person's blow is regarded as being a direct cause of the victim's death, for which the person is criminally responsible, at least for purposes of the misdemeanor-manslaughter rule such as is here involved. Although the holdings to this effect have received scholarly criticism, they do represent the prevailing view in American decisional interpretations of the misdemeanor-manslaughter statutes."

4. Is the *Chavers* result sound? If so, does it follow that *Blaue* is correct? Consider Gobert, supra, at 15: "The principle of taking one's victim as one finds her is so well embedded in the criminal law that it might seem fatuous to ask why this should be so. There is, of course, legitimate concern that trials not turn into medical fishing expeditions to determine whether the victim would have survived the defendant's attack if she had had a harder head. More to the point, there is little inclination to relieve a defendant of responsibility for results that would not have occurred except for his actions simply because a less frail victim might have survived. This reasoning is defensible when the difference between victims is one of degree, one victim having a more or less sturdy constitution than another, but is less supportable when the difference is more qualitative, as in the case of the hemophiliac who bleeds to death from a cut that would have caused relatively minor injury to a person without this condition. Does a conviction for murder, rather than assault, of the defendant who did not know of the victim's hemophilia make sense, or does it unduly penalize him relative to others who commit similar offenses?

"However persuasive the rule that the frailty of the victim should have no bearing on liability in cases of physical infirmity, it makes less sense in cases like *Blaue*, where the disability (if that is the appropriate term) is not physical. If the doctors had ignored the protestations of Blaue's victim and had given her a transfusion, and she had subsequently committed suicide because of the perceived offense to her religion, who should be held in law to have caused the result—Blaue, the doctors, or the victim? What if the reason for the refusal was the victim's desire to see Blaue convicted of murder—would the victim or Blaue have caused her death, or perhaps the doctors who honored the victim's decision? These are the kinds of pointless inquiries that doctrines of causation engender. They are pointless because the moral culpability of Blaue's initial actions is in no way altered by subsequent events, and it is on these actions that his criminal responsibility should be based."

NOTES AND QUESTIONS ON INTERVENING ACTS BY THE VICTIM

1. In *Commonwealth v. Atencio,* 345 Mass. 627, 189 N.E.2d 223 (1963), Marshall, Atencio and Britch played Russian roulette. "Marshall examined the gun, saw that it contained one cartridge, and, after spinning it on his arm, pointed it at his head, and pulled the trigger. Nothing happened. He handed the gun to Atencio, who repeated the process again without result. Atencio passed the gun to [Britch], who spun it, put it to his head and pulled the trigger. The cartridge exploded, and he fell over dead." In affirming the convictions of Atencio and Marshall for manslaughter, the court stated:

"The defendants argue as if it should have been ruled, as matter of law, that there were three 'games' of solitaire and not one 'game' of 'Russian roulette.' That the defendants participated could be found to be a cause and not a mere condition of Stewart Britch's death. It is not correct to say that his act could not be found to have been caused by anything which Marshall and Atencio did, nor that he would have died when the gun went off in his hand no matter whether they had done the same. The testimony does not require a ruling that when the deceased took the gun from Atencio it was an independent or intervening act not standing in any relation to the defendants' acts which would render what he did imputable to them. It is an oversimplification to contend that each participated in something that only one could do at a time. There could be found to be a mutual encouragement in a joint enterprise. In the abstract, there may have been no duty on the defendants to prevent the deceased from playing. But there was a duty on their part not to cooperate or join with him in the 'game.' Nor, if the facts presented such a case, would we have to agree that if the deceased, and not the defendants, had played first that they could not have been found guilty of manslaughter. The defendants were much more than merely present at a crime. It would not be necessary that the defendants force the deceased to play or suggest that he play.

"We are referred in both briefs to cases of manslaughter arising out of automobiles racing upon the public highway. When the victim is a third person, there is no difficulty in holding the drivers, including the one whose car did not strike the victim (*Brown v. Thayer,* 212 Mass. 392, 99 N.E. 237), or in whose car a victim was not a passenger. *Nelson v. Nason,* 343 Mass. 220, 221, 177 N.E.2d 887.

"In two cases the driver of a noncolliding car has been prosecuted for the death of his competitor, and in both cases an appellate court has ruled that he was not guilty of manslaughter. In *Commonwealth v. Root,* 403 Pa. 571, 170 A.2d 310, the competitor drove on the wrong side of the road head-on into an oncoming truck and was killed. The court held that ' * * * the defendant's reckless conduct was not a sufficiently direct cause of the competing driver's death to make him criminally liable therefor.' In *Thacker v. State,* 103 Ga.App. 36, 117 S.E.2d 913, the defendant was indicted for the involuntary manslaughter of his competitor in a drag race who was killed when he lost control of his car and left the highway. The court said that the indictment 'fails to allege any act or acts on the part of the defendant which caused or contributed to the loss of control of the vehicle driven by the deceased, other than the fact that they were engaged in a race at the time.'

"Whatever may be thought of those two decisions, there is a very real distinction between drag racing and 'Russian roulette.' In the former much is left to the skill, or lack of it, of the competitor. In 'Russian roulette' it is a matter of luck as to the location of the one bullet, and except for a misfire (of which there was evidence in the case at bar) the outcome is a certainty if the chamber under the hammer happens to be the one containing the bullet."

Is *Atencio* really distinguishable from *Root* and *Thacker?* As for the drag-racing cases, should it really make any difference whether it is a third party or one of the competitors who is killed?[a]

2. Hallett bent a stop sign over until it was parallel with the ground. At 9 a.m. the following morning, Ms. Carley passed where the sign would ordinarily be without stopping, struck another vehicle in the intersection and was killed. Within a block of that intersection, she had passed a truck traveling at 25 m.p.h., the speed limit. The word "Stop" was printed in large block letters on the pavement leading to the intersection. Is Hallett guilty of negligent homicide?[b]

3. Bonhart, who had sold Della crack cocaine for years, threatened to burn down Della's residence if he did not pay off his drug debts. Bonhart made good on his threat shortly thereafter; Della initially escaped the burning building but then voluntarily reentered in an effort to rescue his dog, resulting in Della perishing with the dog. May Bonhart be convicted of felony-murder?[c]

4. After Armstrong obtained two $100 bills from his sister, Casper and Wilson knocked him down and went through his clothing looking for the money. When they could not find it, Wilson threatened to castrate Armstrong if he didn't hand over the money. Armstrong managed to free himself and he then ran into the Missouri River to escape his pursuers. They saw no more of him, but did find the two bills in the area the following morning. Armstrong's body was found floating downstream about 10 days later.[d] May Casper and Wilson be convicted of murder?

5. Goodman picked up Ms. Husch, an 18–year–old girl who was walking down the highway in the direction he was driving. While the car was traveling about 25 m.p.h., Goodman said to the girl that he would pay her one dollar to have sexual intercourse. She immediately opened the door of the car, hesitated a moment on the running board, and jumped. Her skull was fractured in the fall and she died.[e] May Goodman be convicted of manslaughter?

6. Mangin parked his Cadillac on a boat ramp and left the motor running and the gearshift in park. The defendants parked their cars behind the Cadillac, pulled Retzel and Griffin from that vehicle and commenced to beat them. Retzel and Griffin jumped into the Cadillac as it started to roll. The car stopped momentarily, but then plunged into the water. Retzel and Griffin drowned. Are the defendants guilty of misdemeanor-manslaughter?[f]

7. Todd entered the Lighthouse Church and stole $110 from the collection plate. The theft was witnessed by several members of the congregation, including Voegltin, who took

---

a. Also compare with *Root* and *Thacker* the case of *Jacobs v. State*, 184 So.2d 711 (Fla.App.1966): "While engaged in such unlawful activity one of the three vehicles actively participating in the race was negligently operated in such manner as to cause the death of the person who drove that vehicle, as well as another innocent party who had no connection with the race. The deaths which proximately resulted from the activities of the three persons engaged in the unlawful activity of drag racing made each of the active participants equally guilty of the criminal act which caused the death of the innocent party."

b. *State v. Hallett*, 619 P.2d 335 (Utah 1980), affirming the conviction, 4–1.

c. *Bonhart v. United States*, 691 A.2d 160 (D.C.App. 1997), affirming Bonhart's conviction following a trial

at which the judge excluded proffered evidence of Della's escape and reentry on the ground it was irrelevant.

d. *State v. Casper*, 192 Neb. 120, 219 N.W.2d 226 (1974), affirming the conviction.

e. *People v. Goodman*, 182 Misc. 585, 44 N.Y.S.2d 715 (1943), denying the motion to dismiss the indictment. Compare *State v. Selby*, 183 N.J.Super. 273, 443 A.2d 1076 (1981), a similar case except that defendant's conduct was much more aggressive, where the court approved an instruction that to convict the jury "must find that the defendant's actions and threats were such as to put a reasonably prudent person in fear of her life, serious bodily harm or an assault with intent to rape."

f. *Commonwealth v. Bianco*, 388 Mass. 358, 446 N.E.2d 1041 (1983), reversing the convictions.

off in his car in pursuit of Todd. During the pursuit, Voegltin, who had a preexisting heart condition, began to experience cardiac dysrhythmia; he lost control of his vehicle, collided with a tree at low speed and died of cardiac arrest. May Todd be convicted of misdemeanor-manslaughter?[g]

8. Feinberg operated a cigar store in the skid-row section of Philadelphia. One of the products he sold was Sterno, designed for heating purposes, from which he knew some of his customers extracted the alcohol for drinking. He had been selling Sterno containing 3.75% methanol and 71% ethanol (of the two, methanol is far more toxic if consumed internally), but on Dec. 21 he inadvertently received a shipment of new industrial Sterno which was 54% methanol. The cartons in which the new Sterno were shipped were no different, but each can lid had these words: "Institutional Sterno. Danger. Poison. For use only as a Fuel. Not for consumer use. For industrial and commercial use. Not for home use." After he had sold 400 cans of the new Sterno, Feinberg returned the unsold portion to the wholesaler. Between Dec. 23 and Dec. 30, 31 persons died in the skid-row area as a result of methanol poisoning. No other industrial Sterno had been sold in the area.[h] May Feinberg be convicted of involuntary manslaughter?

9. Guillette and others were indicted for interstate transportation of stolen firearms. LaPolla, an unindicted co-conspirator, was to be the key government witness. LaPolla and government agents feared that Guillette and his cohorts might try to kill LaPolla, so LaPolla was kept in protective custody most of the time. But just a few weeks before the scheduled start of the trial, LaPolla, ignoring instructions to stay away from his home, opened the front door and touched off a massive explosion which killed him instantly. The opening of the door had caused a switch to close and detonate several sticks of dynamite. Guillette and others were then indicted for conspiracy to deprive a citizen of his civil rights with death resulting; the "if death results" part of the statute embodies the principle of proximate cause. A witness at the trial testified that Guillette confided in him the day of the explosion that he had "just left a package for your buddy up there." At trial, the defense position was that LaPolla was killed when he accidently detonated a bomb which he himself installed as a booby trap aimed at the defendants and others who were searching for him. Guillette has asked the trial judge to instruct the jury that he may not be convicted if the jury accepts that theory as to what happened.[i] Should the instruction be given?

10. Lewis became involved in an altercation with his brother-in-law Farrell, resulting in his shooting Farrell in the abdomen. The wound severed the mesenteric artery and thus would produce death in about an hour. Farrell was put to bed where, in great pain, he procured a knife and cut his throat, inflicting a wound from which he would necessarily have died in five minutes. May Lewis be convicted of murder? Does it make any difference whether the medical testimony is (a) that Farrell died from the combined effect of both wounds, or (b) that he died from the self-inflicted wound?[j]

g. *Todd v. State*, 594 So.2d 802 (Fla.App.1992), reversing the conviction.

h. *Commonwealth v. Feinberg*, 433 Pa. 558, 253 A.2d 636 (1969), affirming defendant's several convictions of involuntary manslaughter.

i. *United States v. Guillette*, 547 F.2d 743 (2d Cir. 1976), affirming denial of such an instruction.

j. See *People v. Lewis*, 124 Cal. 551, 57 P. 470 (1899). The court upheld the conviction on the ground that Farrell died from both wounds ("Drop by drop the

life current went out from both wounds"), but seemed to indicate this was not the only basis upon which Lewis could be convicted of murder: "But, if the deceased did die from the effect of the knife wound alone, no doubt the defendant would be responsible, if it was made to appear, and the jury could have found from the evidence, that the knife wound was caused by the wound inflicted by the defendant, in the natural course of events."

NOTES AND QUESTIONS ON INTERVENING ACTS BY THIRD PARTIES AND OUTSIDE FORCES

1. In *People v. Stewart*, 40 N.Y.2d 692, 389 N.Y.S.2d 804, 358 N.E.2d 487 (1976), the defendant stabbed Smith in the stomach. Prior to an operation on Smith he was given Curare, which paralyzes the chest and makes it impossible for the patient to breathe on his own, necessitating the anesthesiologist to "breathe" for him by squeezing a bag of oxygen into the lungs. During the operation, the surgeons discovered an incarcerated hernia, so after completing the operation on the stomach they proceeded to correct the hernia. During this phase of the operation the patient went into cardiac arrest, and then suffered a loss of oxygen to the brain and massive brain damage. He died a month later without regaining consciousness. At the time of death, the stomach wound had completely healed. In reducing the defendant's manslaughter conviction to assault, the court observed:

"One of the problems in the case now before us is that there is some question as to whether the operation on the hernia was made necessary by the defendant's act. According to the testimony it was 'medically correct', arguably necessary, clearly incidental—but the hernia itself was absolutely unrelated to the stab wound. Dr. Di Maio conceded that the chances were that if it had not been performed, the patient would have survived. This type of necessity is obviously of a different order than is normally required to fix responsibility for homicide. It is, we believe, a factor we must consider in determining whether the causal relationship is sufficiently direct.

"The other difficulty in the case is that it was never determined what actually caused the cardiac arrest. Dr. Di Maio acknowledged several possibilities which individually or combined could have created the condition. Most of the factors cited would indicate that the defendant's act was responsible either because it created a physical strain or shock or created the need for an operation which had the same effect. But Dr. Di Maio conceded that there was some evidence that the anesthesiologist failed to provide oxygen to the patient and that this alone could have been the cause of death. In our view if this occurred it was a grave neglect, perhaps gross negligence, but in any event sufficient to break whatever tenuous causal relationship existed at the time of this incidental operation. There is of course no showing that this was in fact the cause of death but on this record it cannot be ruled out as a possibility, certainly not beyond a reasonable doubt."

2. When an 85–year–old woman resisted a purse snatching, she was struck from behind. She was taken to the hospital, where her condition degenerated. "Six days later, on January 19, on the basis of the patient's condition and her age, after consultation with other physicians involved in the case and upon agreement by the victim's son, the neurosurgeon discontinued all 'heroic measures' "and disconnected the respirator which was keeping the woman alive. "All agree that under any legally accepted definition of death, the victim was not dead when the 'heroic measures' were discontinued." The woman died 15 to 20 minutes later. May the purse snatcher be convicted of murder?[a]

3. Bush shot a girl with a pistol. She later died, not from the wound, but from scarlet fever communicated by her attending physician.[b] May Bush be convicted of murder? What if the girl had contracted viral hepatitis and died from that?[c]

4. Catherine Michael, with intent that her 9–month–old son be killed, gave the boy's nurse a bottle of poison, which she told the nurse was medicine to be given the baby every

---

a. *Matter of J.N.*, 406 A.2d 1275 (D.C.App.1979), affirming the murder conviction though not even an instruction on the causation issue was given; rehearing en banc granted and opinion vacated.

Note that causation problems in cases of this kind are often obviated by acceptance of the "brain death" rule, discussed in Section 1 of this Chapter.

b. *Bush v. Commonwealth*, 78 Ky. 268 (1880), reversing the murder conviction.

c. See *McKinnon v. United States*, 550 A.2d 915 (D.C.App.1988), affirming murder conviction on such facts.

night. The nurse decided that the child did not need any medicine and thus concluded she would not follow those instructions. She placed the bottle on a mantel, and some days later, during the absence of the nurse, the nurse's 5–year–old son gave the poison to the baby, resulting in the infant's death. May Catherine be convicted of murder?[d]

5. At about midnight, Wanda and her passenger Lisa met up with Kenny and his passenger Jim; both vehicles rendezvoused elsewhere, after which Wanda agreed to leave with Kenny for the Skyline Motel and told Jim and Lisa to follow in Wanda's car. Apparently some disagreement developed between Jim and Lisa, as he instead dropped her off near Wanda's residence. Lisa entered Wanda's home and told the group of men there that several men had kidnapped Wanda, and she did not admit the prevarication even after the police were contacted and some of the men, armed with a pistol, set out to look for Wanda. Shortly thereafter the group stopped Jim, who was driving Wanda's vehicle, and held him there until Wanda's husband, Keith, was summoned to the scene. Keith and Jim scuffled and the gun Keith was holding discharged, killing Jim. Keith pled guilty to involuntary manslaughter. May Lisa now also be convicted of involuntary manslaughter?[e]

NOTES AND QUESTIONS ON INTERVENING ACTS BY THE DEFENDANT

1. In *People v. Crane*, 308 Ill.App.3d 675, 242 Ill.Dec. 378, 721 N.E.2d 657 (1999), Crane was convicted of murdering Gahan, whose charred remains were found near some railroad tracks. Crane told police that Gahan, a 300–lb. homosexual, had tried to choke him, at which he struck Gahan on the head with his nunchucks until Gahan fell to the ground, and that because he mistakenly thought Gahan was dead he then burned the body. The state established that the cause of Gahan's death was burning, and that several days before Gahan's death Crane had asked a friend if he wanted to "go roll queers" and then inquired "about how much gasoline it would take to burn a body." On appeal, Crane asserted "that the jury was improperly instructed. Defendant's argument assumes the following three facts: first, that the jury has rejected defendant's self-defense argument; second, that the jury has concluded that the burning caused Gahan's death; and third, that the jury has accepted his mistake-of-fact argument. According to defendant, the instructions given erroneously allowed the jury to convict him of murder by coupling (a) the mental state defendant possessed prior to the beating with (b) burning as the cause of death. Defendant contends that the fatal burning (under a mistaken belief that Gahan was dead) could be considered a cause connected with the beating only if he beat Gahan with the intent to kill. Defendant * * * states as follows: 'The explanation has been that where the intent was not to kill, the subsequent disposal of the body could not be viewed as part of one transaction.' Defendant contends that the jury should have been instructed that the State had the burden to prove beyond a reasonable doubt that 'defendant's own subsequent acts of burning were not an intervening cause of death unconnected with the defendant's initial acts of beating.'

"We attribute no error to the instructions tendered in this case. Defendant cites no Illinois case in support of the quoted legal proposition, nor does he present an argument as to why the proposition should be the law in Illinois. Further, our independent research cannot find a case in support of defendant's argument. In fact, the cases we found defeat his argument. In *People v. Rollins*, 295 Ill.App.3d 412, 418, 230 Ill.Dec. 852, 695 N.E.2d 61 (1998), it was stated:

'If an assailant inflicts unjustified wounds to the extent that he reasonably believes he has killed someone, misapprehension of his crime's effect does not license incineration,

---

d. *Regina v. Michael*, 2 Moody 120, 169 Eng.Rep. 48 (1840), affirming the murder conviction.

e. *Gallimore v. Commonwealth*, 246 Va. 441, 436 S.E.2d 421 (1993), affirming Lisa's conviction.

drowning, or dismemberment to destroy evidence of what happened. If a defendant attempts to conceal his own criminality by further acts that actually contribute to an end defendant mistakenly thinks he has already produced, he cannot escape criminal responsibility for murder.' "

2. Compare Jerome Hall, *General Principles of Criminal Law* 189 (2d ed.1960): "In one of those rare cases which greatly stimulate academic disputation, a medical student, after an affair with a young lady who became pregnant, gave her a large dose of cocaine in the state of Ohio, intended to kill her then and there. Later, he transported what he believed was her dead body into Kentucky, where he performed a decapitation. The medical evidence established that the young woman was actually alive in Kentucky until the decapitation. Despite the Kentucky court's acceptance of the fact that the defendant believed she was dead when he performed the decapitation, he was held guilty of murder in that state.[68] He was certainly guilty of an attempt to murder in Ohio. But the mistake of fact in Kentucky excluded the *mens rea* of criminal homicide there; and the court's reliance upon the defendant's homicidal intention in Ohio was clearly violative of the principle of concurrence. [I]n the above homicide case there was no intention to kill or injure a human being at the time of the decapitation. The Kentucky court apparently believed that since the defendant set out intentionally to kill and since he did, in fact, kill, the failure of the cocaine to do that in Ohio was unimportant. But the fact remains that the *mens rea* did not concur with the actual killing. The departure from the principle of concurrence in this case can only mean that the conduct required by the law of criminal homicide was nonexistent."

SECTION 7. THE DEATH PENALTY

Introductory Notes

1. In large measure, the classification of homicides by courts and legislatures has been prompted by a desire to define more narrowly those criminal homicides which would be subject to the mandatory penalty of death. As detailed in *Mullaney v. Wilbur,* p. 264 of this Book, this explains how the distinction between murder and manslaughter came into being. And as the Court has more recently observed in *Woodson v. North Carolina,* infra, it was public dissatisfaction with the mandatory death penalty statutes which led most of the states to divide the crime of murder into degrees.

2. But even this reform was not sufficient. As noted in *Woodson:*

"Despite the broad acceptance of the division of murder into degrees, the reform proved to be an unsatisfactory means of identifying persons appropriately punishable by death. Although its failure was due in part to the amorphous nature of the controlling concepts of willfulness, deliberateness, and premeditation, a more fundamental weakness of the reform soon became apparent. Juries continued to find the death penalty inappropriate in a significant number of first-degree murder cases and refused to return guilty verdicts for that crime.

"The inadequacy of distinguishing between murders solely on the basis of legislative criteria narrowing the definition of the capital offense led the States to grant juries sentencing discretion in capital cases. Tennessee in 1838, followed by Alabama in 1841, and Louisiana in 1846, were the first States to abandon mandatory death sentences in favor of discretionary death penalty statutes. This flexibility remedied the harshness of mandatory statutes by permitting the jury to respond to mitigating factors by withholding the death penalty. By the turn of the century, 23 States and the Federal Government had made

68. *Jackson v. Commonwealth,* 100 Ky. 239, 38 S.W. 422 and 1091 (1896).

death sentences discretionary for first-degree murder and other capital offenses. * * * By 1963, all of these remaining jurisdictions had replaced their automatic death penalty statutes with discretionary jury sentencing."

3. Thus, there remains one other aspect of homicide classification to be considered, namely, the classification under contemporary law of those homicides for which the penalty shall be death. In particular, it must be asked: (a) to what extent are standards to guide the exercise of discretion necessary or desirable as to those offenses for which the death penalty is discretionary; and (b) to what extent is it permissible or desirable that the penalty of death be mandatory for certain crimes; and (c) to what offenses (or, as to murder, what bases of liability) may even the discretionary death penalty not be applied.

GREGG v. GEORGIA

Supreme Court of the United States, 1976.

428 U.S. 153, 96 S.Ct. 2909, 49 L.Ed.2d 859.

MR. JUSTICE STEWART, MR. JUSTICE POWELL, and MR. JUSTICE STEVENS announced the judgment of the Court and filed an opinion delivered by MR. JUSTICE STEWART. * * *

[Gregg was found guilty by a jury of two counts of armed robbery and two counts of murder. At the penalty stage of the trial, thereafter occurring before the same jury, the jury returned verdicts of death on each count. The jury had been instructed that it could not impose a death sentence unless it found beyond a reasonable doubt that certain specified aggravating circumstances were present. The Georgia Supreme Court affirmed the convictions and the imposition of the death sentences for murder, but vacated the death sentences for armed robbery on the ground that the death penalty had rarely been imposed for that offense.]

We address initially the basic contention that the punishment of death for the crime of murder is, under all circumstances, "cruel and unusual" in violation of the Eighth and Fourteenth Amendments of the Constitution. * * *

The Court on a number of occasions has both assumed and asserted the constitutionality of capital punishment. In several cases that assumption provided a necessary foundation for the decision, as the Court was asked to decide whether a particular method of carrying out a capital sentence would be allowed to stand under the Eighth Amendment. But until *Furman v. Georgia,* 408 U.S. 238, 92 S.Ct. 2726, 33 L.Ed.2d 346 (1972), the Court never confronted squarely the fundamental claim that the punishment of death always, regardless of the enormity of the offense or the procedure followed in imposing the sentence, is cruel and unusual punishment in violation of the Constitution. Although this issue was presented and addressed in *Furman,* it was not resolved by the Court. Four Justices would have held that capital punishment is not unconstitutional *per se;* two Justices would have reached the opposite conclusion; and three Justices, while agreeing that the statutes then before the Court were invalid as applied, left open the question whether such punishment may ever be imposed. We now hold that the punishment of death does not invariably violate the Constitution. * * *

It is clear * * * that the Eighth Amendment has not been regarded as a static concept. As Chief Justice Warren said, in an oft-quoted phrase, "[t]he Amendment must draw its meaning from the evolving standards of decency that mark the progress of a maturing society." Thus, an assessment of contemporary values concerning the infliction of a challenged sanction is relevant to the application of the Eighth Amendment. As we develop below more fully, this assessment does not call for a subjective judgment. It requires, rather, that we look to objective indicia that reflect the public attitude toward a given sanction.

But our cases also make clear that public perceptions of standards of decency with respect to criminal sanctions are not conclusive. A penalty also must accord with "the dignity of man," which is the "basic concept underlying the Eighth Amendment." This means, at least, that the punishment not be "excessive." When a form of punishment in the abstract (in this case, whether capital punishment may ever be imposed as a sanction for murder) rather than in the particular (the propriety of death as a penalty to be applied to a specific defendant for a specific crime) is under consideration, the inquiry into "excessiveness" has two aspects. First, the punishment must not involve the unnecessary and wanton infliction of pain. Second, the punishment must not be grossly out of proportion to the severity of the crime.

Of course, the requirements of the Eighth Amendment must be applied with an awareness of the limited role to be played by the courts. This does not mean that judges have no role to play, for the Eighth Amendment is a restraint upon the exercise of legislative power. * * *

But, while we have an obligation to insure that constitutional bounds are not overreached, we may not act as judges as we might as legislators. * * *

Therefore, in assessing a punishment selected by a democratically elected legislature against the constitutional measure, we presume its validity. We may not require the legislature to select the least severe penalty possible so long as the penalty selected is not cruelly inhumane or disproportionate to the crime involved. And a heavy burden rests on those who would attack the judgment of the representatives of the people.

This is true in part because the constitutional test is intertwined with an assessment of contemporary standards and the legislative judgment weighs heavily in ascertaining such standards. "[I]n a democratic society legislatures, not courts, are constituted to respond to the will and consequently the moral values of the people." The deference we owe to the decisions of the state legislatures under our federal system, is enhanced where the specification of punishments is concerned, for "these are peculiarly questions of legislative policy."

Caution is necessary lest this Court become, "under the aegis of the Cruel and Unusual Punishment Clause, the ultimate arbiter of the standards of criminal responsibility * * * throughout the country." A decision that a given punishment is impermissible under the Eighth Amendment cannot be reversed short of a constitutional amendment. The ability of the people to express their preference through the normal democratic processes, as well as through ballot referenda, is shut off. Revisions cannot be made in the light of further experience.

In the discussion to this point we have sought to identify the principles and considerations that guide a court in addressing an Eighth Amendment claim. We now consider specifically whether the sentence of death for the crime of murder is a *per se* violation of the Eighth and Fourteenth Amendments to the Constitution. We note first that history and precedent strongly support a negative answer to this question.

The imposition of the death penalty for the crime of murder has a long history of acceptance both in the United States and in England. The common-law rule imposed a mandatory death sentence on all convicted murderers. And the penalty continued to be used into the 20th century by most American States, although the breadth of the common-law rule was diminished, initially by narrowing the class of murders to be punished by death and subsequently by widespread adoption of laws expressly granting juries the discretion to recommend mercy.

It is apparent from the text of the Constitution itself that the existence of capital punishment was accepted by the Framers. At the time the Eighth Amendment was ratified, capital punishment was a common sanction in every State. Indeed, the First Congress of the United States enacted legislation providing death as the penalty for specified crimes. * * *

For nearly two centuries, this Court, repeatedly and often expressly, has recognized that capital punishment is not invalid *per se.* * * *

Four years ago, the petitioners in *Furman* and its companion cases predicated their argument primarily upon the asserted proposition that standards of decency had evolved to the point where capital punishment no longer could be tolerated. The petitioners in those cases said, in effect, that the evolutionary process had come to an end, and that standards of decency required that the Eighth Amendment be construed finally as prohibiting capital punishment for any crime regardless of its depravity and impact on society. This view was accepted by two Justices. Three other Justices were unwilling to go so far; focusing on the procedures by which convicted defendants were selected for the death penalty rather than on the actual punishment inflicted, they joined in the conclusion that the statutes before the Court were constitutionally invalid.

The petitioners in the capital cases before the Court today renew the "standards of decency" argument, but developments during the four years since *Furman* have undercut substantially the assumptions upon which their argument rested. Despite the continuing debate, dating back to the 19th century, over the morality and utility of capital punishment, it is now evident that a large proportion of American society continues to regard it as an appropriate and necessary criminal sanction.

The most marked indication of society's endorsement of the death penalty for murder is the legislative response to *Furman.* The legislatures of at least 35 States have enacted new statutes that provide for the death penalty for at least some crimes that result in the death of another person. And the Congress of the United States, in 1974, enacted a statute providing the death penalty for aircraft piracy that results in death. These recently adopted statutes have attempted to address the concerns expressed by the Court in *Furman* primarily (i) by specifying the factors to be weighed and the procedures to be followed in deciding when to impose a capital sentence, or (ii) by making the death penalty mandatory for specified crimes. But all of the post-*Furman* statutes make clear that capital punishment itself has not been rejected by the elected representatives of the people. * * *

The jury also is a significant and reliable objective index of contemporary values because it is so directly involved. The Court has said that "one of the most important functions any jury can perform in making * * * a selection [between life imprisonment and death for a defendant convicted in a capital case] is to maintain a link between contemporary community values and the penal system." It may be true that evolving standards have influenced juries in recent decades to be more discriminating in imposing the sentence of death.[26] But the relative infrequency of jury verdicts imposing the death sentence does not indicate rejection of capital punishment *per se.* Rather, the reluctance of juries in many

---

26. The number of prisoners who received death sentences in the years from 1961 to 1972 varied from a high of 140 in 1961 to a low of 75 in 1972, with wide fluctuations in the intervening years: 103 in 1962; 93 in 1963; 106 in 1964; 86 in 1965; 118 in 1966; 85 in 1967; 102 in 1968; 97 in 1969; 127 in 1970; and 104 in 1971. Department of Justice, Capital Punishment 1971–1972, National prisoner Statistics Bulletin, p. 20 (December 1974). It has been estimated that before *Furman* less than 20% of those convicted of murder were sentenced to death in those States that authorized capital punishment.

cases to impose the sentence may well reflect the humane feeling that this most irrevocable of sanctions should be reserved for a small number of extreme cases. Indeed, the actions of juries in many States since *Furman* is fully compatible with the legislative judgments, reflected in the new statutes, as to the continued utility and necessity of capital punishment in appropriate cases. At the close of 1974 at least 254 persons had been sentenced to death since *Furman,* and by the end of March 1976, more than 460 persons were subject to death sentences.

As we have seen, however, the Eighth Amendment demands more than that a challenged punishment be acceptable to contemporary society. The Court also must ask whether it comports with the basic concept of human dignity at the core of the Amendment. Although we cannot "invalidate a category of penalties because we deem less severe penalties adequate to serve the ends of penology," the sanction imposed cannot be so totally without penological justification that it results in the gratuitous infliction of suffering.

The death penalty is said to serve two principal social purposes: retribution and deterrence of capital crimes by prospective offenders.

In part, capital punishment is an expression of society's moral outrage at particularly offensive conduct. This function may be unappealing to many, but it is essential in an ordered society that asks its citizens to rely on legal processes rather than self-help to vindicate their wrongs. * * * "Retribution is no longer the dominant objective of the criminal law," but neither is it a forbidden objective nor one inconsistent with our respect for the dignity of men. Indeed, the decision that capital punishment may be the appropriate sanction in extreme cases is an expression of the community's belief that certain crimes are themselves so grievous an affront to humanity that the only adequate response may be the penalty of death.

Statistical attempts to evaluate the worth of the death penalty as a deterrent to crimes by potential offenders have occasioned a great deal of debate. The results simply have been inconclusive. * * *

Although some of the studies suggest that the death penalty may not function as a significantly greater deterrent than lesser penalties, there is no convincing empirical evidence either supporting or refuting this view. We may nevertheless assume safely that there are murderers, such as those who act in passion, for whom the threat of death has little or no deterrent effect. But for many others, the death penalty undoubtedly is a significant deterrent. There are carefully contemplated murders, such as murder for hire, where the possible penalty of death may well enter into the cold calculus that precedes the decision to act. And there are some categories of murder, such as murder by a life prisoner, where other sanctions may not be adequate.

The value of capital punishment as a deterrent of crime is a complex factual issue the resolution of which properly rests with the legislatures, which can evaluate the results of statistical studies in terms of their own local conditions and with a flexibility of approach that is not available to the courts. Indeed, many of the post-*Furman* statutes reflect just such a responsible effort to define those crimes and those criminals for which capital punishment is most probably an effective deterrent. * * *

Finally, we must consider whether the punishment of death is disproportionate in relation to the crime for which it is imposed. There is no question that death as a punishment is unique in its severity and irrevocability. When a defendant's life is at stake, the Court has been particularly sensitive to insure that every safeguard is observed. But we are concerned here only with the imposition of capital punishment for the crime of murder, and when a life has been taken deliberately by the offender,[35] we cannot say that the punishment is invariably disproportionate to the crime. It is an extreme sanction, suitable to the most extreme of crimes.

We hold that the death penalty is not a form of punishment that may never be imposed, regardless of the circumstances of the offense, regardless of the character of the offender, and regardless of the procedure followed in reaching the decision to impose it. * * *

While *Furman* did not hold that the infliction of the death penalty *per se* violates the Constitution's ban on cruel and unusual punishments, it did recognize that the penalty of death is different in kind from any other punishment imposed under our system of criminal justice. Because of the uniqueness of the death penalty, *Furman* held that it could not be imposed under sentencing procedures that created a substantial risk that it would be inflicted in an arbitrary and capricious manner. * * *

Jury sentencing has been considered desirable in capital cases in order "to maintain a link between contemporary community values and the penal system—a link without which the determination of punishment could hardly reflect 'the evolving standards of decency that mark the progress of a maturing society.' "But it creates special problems. Much of the information that is relevant to the sentencing decision may have no relevance to the question of guilt, or may even be extremely prejudicial to a fair determination of that question. This problem, however, is scarcely insurmountable. Those who have studied the question suggest that a bifurcated procedure—one in which the question of sentence is not considered until the determination of guilt has been made—is the best answer. * * * When a human life is at stake and when the jury must have information prejudicial to the question of guilt but relevant to the question of penalty in order to impose a rational sentence, a bifurcated system is more likely to ensure elimination of the constitutional deficiencies identified in *Furman*.

But the provision of relevant information under fair procedural rules is not alone sufficient to guarantee that the information will be properly used in the imposition of punishment, especially if sentencing is performed by a jury. Since the members of a jury will have had little, if any, previous experience in sentencing, they are unlikely to be skilled in dealing with the information they are given. To the extent that this problem is inherent in jury sentencing, it may not be totally correctible. It seems clear, however, that the problem will be alleviated if the jury is given guidance regarding the factors about the crime and the defendant that the State, representing organized society, deems particularly relevant to the sentencing decision. * * *

While some have suggested that standards to guide a capital jury's sentencing deliberations are impossible to formulate, the fact is that such standards have been developed. When the drafters of the Model Penal Code faced this problem, they concluded "that it is within the realm of possibility to point to the main circumstances of aggravation and of mitigation that should be weighed *and weighed against each other*, when they are presented in a concrete case." *Model Penal Code* § 201.6, Comment 3, p. 71 (Tent. Draft No. 9, 1959).[a] While such standards are by necessity somewhat general, they do provide guidance to the sentencing authority and thereby reduce the likelihood that it will impose a sentence that fairly can be called capricious or arbitrary. Where the sentencing authority is

---

35. We do not address here the question whether the taking of the criminal's life is a proportionate sanction where no victim has been deprived of life—for example, when capital punishment is imposed for rape, kidnapping, or armed robbery that does not result in the death of any human being.

a. Because of renumbering, the aggravating and mitigating circumstances proposed in the *Model Penal Code* appear in § 210.6(3) and (4).

required to specify the factors it relied upon in reaching its decision, the further safeguard of meaningful appellate review is available to ensure that death sentences are not imposed capriciously or in a freakish manner.

In summary, the concerns expressed in *Furman* that the penalty of death not be imposed in an arbitrary or capricious manner can be met by a carefully drafted statute that ensures that the sentencing authority is given adequate information and guidance. As a general proposition these concerns are best met by a system that provides for a bifurcated proceeding at which the sentencing authority is apprised of the information relevant to the imposition of sentence and provided with standards to guide its use of the information. * * *

We now turn to consideration of the constitutionality of Georgia's capital-sentencing procedures. In the wake of *Furman*, Georgia amended its capital punishment statute, but chose not to narrow the scope of its murder provisions. Thus, now as before *Furman*, in Georgia "[a] person commits murder when he unlawfully and with malice aforethought, either express or implied, causes the death of another human being." Ga.Code Ann., § 26–1101(a) (1972). All persons convicted of murder "shall be punished by death or by imprisonment for life." § 26–1101(c) (1972).

Georgia did act, however, to narrow the class of murderers subject to capital punishment by specifying 10 statutory aggravating circumstances, one of which must be found by the jury to exist beyond a reasonable doubt before a death sentence can ever be imposed.[b] In addition, the jury is authorized to consider any other appropriate aggravating or mitigating circumstances. § 27–2534.1(b) (Supp.1975). The jury is not required to find any mitigating circumstance in order to make a recommendation of mercy that is binding on

---

b. The statute provides in part:

"(a) The death penalty may be imposed for the offenses of aircraft hijacking or treason, in any case.

"(b) In all cases of other offenses for which the death penalty may be authorized, the judge shall consider, or he shall include in his instructions to the jury for it to consider, any mitigating circumstances or aggravating circumstances otherwise authorized by law and any of the following statutory aggravating circumstances which may be supported by the evidence:

"(1) The offense of murder, rape, armed robbery, or kidnapping was committed by a person with a prior record of conviction for a capital felony, or the offense of murder was committed by a person who has a substantial history of serious assaultive criminal convictions.

"(2) The offense of murder, rape, armed robbery, or kidnapping was committed while the offender was engaged in the commission of another capital felony, or aggravated battery, or the offense of murder was committed while the offender was engaged in the commission of burglary or arson in the first degree.

"(3) The offender by his act of murder, armed robbery, or kidnapping knowingly created a great risk of death to more than one person in a public place by means of a weapon or device which would normally be hazardous to the lives of more than one person.

"(4) The offender committed the offense of murder for himself or another, for the purpose of receiving money or any other thing of monetary value.

"(5) The murder of a judicial officer, former judicial officer, district attorney or solicitor or former district attorney or solicitor during or because of the exercise of his official duty.

"(6) The offender caused or directed another to commit murder or committed murder as an agent or employee of another person.

"(7) The offense of murder, rape, armed robbery, or kidnapping was outrageously or wantonly vile, horrible or inhuman in that it involved torture, depravity of mind, or an aggravated battery to the victim.

"(8) The offense of murder was committed against any peace officer, corrections employee or fireman while engaged in the performance of his official duties.

"(9) The offense of murder was committed by a person in, or who has escaped from, the lawful custody of a peace officer or place of lawful confinement.

"(10) The murder was committed for the purpose of avoiding, interfering with, or preventing a lawful arrest or custody in a place of lawful confinement, of himself or another.

"(c) The statutory instructions as determined by the trial judge to be warranted by the evidence shall be given in charge and in writing to the jury for its deliberation. The jury, if its verdict be a recommendation of death, shall designate in writing, signed by the foreman of the jury, the aggravating circumstance or circumstances which it found beyond a reasonable doubt. In non-jury cases the judge shall make such designation. Except in cases of treason or aircraft hijacking, unless at least one of the statutory aggravating circumstances enumerated in section 27–2534.1(b) is so found, the death penalty shall not be imposed." § 27–2534.1 (Supp.1975).

the trial court, see § 27–2302 (Supp.1975), but it must find a *statutory* aggravating circumstance before recommending a sentence of death.

These procedures require the jury to consider the circumstances of the crime and the criminal before it recommends sentence. No longer can a Georgia jury do as *Furman's* jury did: reach a finding of the defendant's guilt and then, without guidance or direction, decide whether he should live or die. * * *

As an important additional safeguard against arbitrariness and caprice, the Georgia statutory scheme provides for automatic appeal of all death sentences to the State's supreme court. That court is required by statute to review each sentence of death and determine whether it was imposed under the influence of passion or prejudice, whether the evidence supports the jury's finding of a statutory aggravating circumstance, and whether the sentence is disproportionate compared to those sentences imposed in similar cases. § 27–2537(c) (Supp.1975).

In short, Georgia's new sentencing procedures require as a prerequisite to the imposition of the death penalty, specific jury findings as to the circumstances of the crime or the character of the defendant. Moreover to guard further against a situation comparable to that presented in *Furman,* the Supreme Court of Georgia compares each death sentence with the sentences imposed on similarly situated defendants to ensure that the sentence of death in a particular case is not disproportionate. On their face these procedures seem to satisfy the concerns of *Furman.* No longer should there be "no meaningful basis for distinguishing the few cases in which [the death penalty] is imposed from the many cases in which it is not."

The petitioner contends, however, that the changes in the Georgia sentencing procedures are only cosmetic, that the arbitrariness and capriciousness condemned by *Furman* continue to exist in Georgia—both in traditional practices that still remain and in the new sentencing procedures adopted in response to *Furman.*

First, the petitioner focuses on the opportunities for discretionary action that are inherent in the processing of any murder case under Georgia law. He notes that the state prosecutor has unfettered authority to select those persons whom he wishes to prosecute for a capital offense and to plea bargain with them. Further, at the trial the jury may choose to convict a defendant of a lesser included offense rather than find him guilty of a crime punishable by death, even if the evidence would support a capital verdict. And finally, a defendant who is convicted and sentenced to die may have his sentence commuted by the Governor of the State and the Georgia Board of Pardons and Paroles.

The existence of these discretionary stages is not determinative of the issues before us. At each of these stages an actor in the criminal justice system makes a decision which may remove a defendant from consideration as a candidate for the death penalty. *Furman,* in contrast, dealt with the decision to impose the death sentence on a specific individual who had been convicted of a capital offense. Nothing in any of our cases suggests that the decision to afford an individual defendant mercy violates the Constitution. *Furman* held only that, in order to minimize the risk that the death penalty would be imposed on a capriciously selected group of offenders, the decision to impose it had to be guided by standards so that the sentencing authority would focus on the particularized circumstances of the crime and the defendant.

The petitioner further contends that the capital-sentencing procedures adopted by Georgia in response to *Furman* do not eliminate the dangers of arbitrariness and caprice in jury sentencing that were held in *Furman* to be violative of the Eighth and Fourteenth Amendments. He claims that the statute is so broad and vague as to leave juries free to act as arbitrarily and capriciously as they wish in deciding whether to impose the death penalty. * * *

The petitioner attacks the seventh statutory aggravating circumstance, which authorizes imposition of the death penalty if the murder was "outrageously or wantonly vile, horrible or inhuman in that it involved torture, depravity of mind, or an aggravated battery to the victim," contending that it is so broad that capital punishment could be imposed in any murder case. It is, of course, arguable that any murder involves depravity of mind or an aggravated battery. But this language need not be construed in this way, and there is no reason to assume that the Supreme Court of Georgia will adopt such an open-ended construction. In only one case has it upheld a jury's decision to sentence a defendant to death when the only statutory aggravating circumstance found was that of § 7, see *McCorquodale v. State,* 233 Ga. 369, 211 S.E.2d 577 (1974), and that homicide was a horrifying torture-murder.

The petitioner also argues that two of the statutory aggravating circumstances are vague and therefore susceptible to widely differing interpretations, thus creating a substantial risk that the death penalty will be arbitrarily inflicted by Georgia juries. In light of the decisions of the Supreme Court of Georgia we must disagree. First, the petitioner attacks that part of § 1 that authorizes a jury to consider whether a defendant has a "substantial history of serious assaultive criminal convictions." The Supreme Court of Georgia, however, has demonstrated a concern that the new sentencing procedures provide guidance to juries. It held this provision to be impermissibly vague in *Arnold v. State,* 236 Ga. 534, 540, 224 S.E.2d 386, 391 (1976), because it did not provide the jury with "sufficiently 'clear and objective standards.' "Second, the petitioner points to § 3 which speaks of creating a "great risk of death to more than one person." While such a phrase might be susceptible to an overly broad interpretation, the Supreme Court of Georgia has not so construed it. The only case in which the court upheld a conviction in reliance on this aggravating circumstance involved a man who stood up in a church and fired a gun indiscriminately into the audience. See *Chenault v. State,* 234 Ga. 216, 215 S.E.2d 223 (1975). On the other hand, the court expressly reversed a finding of great risk when the victim was simply kidnapped in a parking lot. See *Jarrell v. State,* 234 Ga. 410, 424, 216 S.E.2d 258, 269 (1975).[c]

The petitioner next argues that the requirements of *Furman* are not met here because the jury has the power to decline to impose the death penalty even if it finds that one or more statutory aggravating circumstances is present in the case. This contention misinterprets *Furman.* Moreover, it ignores the role of the Supreme Court of Georgia which reviews each death sentence to determine whether it is proportional to other sentences imposed for similar crimes. Since the proportionality requirement on review is intended to prevent caprice in the decision to inflict the penalty, the isolated decision of a jury to afford mercy does not render unconstitutional death sentences imposed on defendants who were sentenced under a system that does not create a substantial risk of arbitrariness or caprice.

---

c. A statutory aggravating factor "is unconstitutionally vague if it fails to furnish principled guidance for the choice between death and a lesser penalty." *Richmond v. Lewis,* 506 U.S. 40, 113 S.Ct. 528, 121 L.Ed.2d 411 (1992) (holding "especially heinous, cruel or depraved" factor unconstitutionally vague). Compare *Tuilaepa v. California,* 512 U.S. 967, 114 S.Ct. 2630, 129 L.Ed.2d 750 (1994) (no vagueness where jurors to be told to consider certain relevant subject matter, such as the "circumstances of the crime," as it *not* necessary that jury be required to answer specific fact questions or be told how facts it finds to be weighed); *Arave v. Creech,* 507 U.S. 463, 113 S.Ct. 1534, 123 L.Ed.2d 188 (1993) ("utter disregard for human life" not vague where construed to refer to "cold-blooded, pitiless slayer").

Consider also *Johnson v. Mississippi,* 486 U.S. 578, 108 S.Ct. 1981, 100 L.Ed.2d 575 (1988) (where aggravating circumstances relied upon by jury was prior conviction, Eighth Amendment violated where conviction invalid).

The petitioner objects, finally, to the wide scope of evidence and argument allowed at presentence hearings. We think that the Georgia court wisely has chosen not to impose unnecessary restrictions on the evidence that can be offered at such a hearing and to approve open and far-ranging argument. So long as the evidence introduced and the arguments made at the presentence hearing do not prejudice a defendant, it is preferable not to impose restrictions. We think it desirable for the jury to have as much information before it as possible when it makes the sentencing decision.[d]

Finally, the Georgia statute has an additional provision designed to assure that the death penalty will not be imposed on a capriciously selected group of convicted defendants. The new sentencing procedures require that the state supreme court review every death sentence to determine whether it was imposed under the influence of passion, prejudice, or any other arbitrary factor, whether the evidence supports the findings of a statutory aggravating circumstance, and "[w]hether the sentence of death is excessive or disproportionate to the penalty imposed in similar cases, considering both the crime and the defendant. § 27–2537(c)(3) (Supp.1975). In performing its sentence review function, the Georgia court has held that "if the death penalty is only rarely imposed for an act or it is substantially out of line with sentences imposed for other acts it will be set aside as excessive." The court on another occasion stated that "we view it to be our duty under the similarity standard to assure that no death sentence is affirmed unless in similar cases throughout the state the death penalty has been imposed generally * * *." * * *

The provision for appellate review in the Georgia capital-sentencing system serves as a check against the random or arbitrary imposition of the death penalty. In particular, the proportionality review substantially eliminates the possibility that a person will be sentenced to die by the action of an aberrant jury. If a time comes when juries generally do not impose the death sentence in a certain kind of murder case, the appellate review procedures assures that no defendant convicted under such circumstances will suffer a sentence of death. * * *

For the reasons expressed in this opinion, we hold that the statutory system under which Gregg was sentenced to death does not violate the Constitution. Accordingly, the judgment of the Georgia Supreme Court is affirmed.

It is so ordered.

MR. JUSTICE WHITE, with whom THE CHIEF JUSTICE and MR. JUSTICE REHNQUIST join, concurring in the judgment. * * *

MR. JUSTICE BLACKMUN, concurring in the judgment. * * *

MR. JUSTICE BRENNAN, dissenting. * * *

This Court inescapably has the duty, as the ultimate arbiter of the meaning of our Constitution, to say whether, when individuals condemned to death stand before our Bar, "moral concepts" require us to hold that the law has progressed to the point where we should declare that the punishment of death, like punishments on the rack, the screw and the wheel, is no longer morally tolerable in our civilized society. My opinion in *Furman v. Georgia* concluded that our civilization and the law had progressed to this point and that therefore the punishment of death, for whatever crime and under all circumstances, is "cruel and unusual" in violation of the Eighth and Fourteenth Amendments of the

---

d. For a time, the Supreme Court was of the view that the sentencing jury should not be given information in the capital sentencing context about the victim and the impact of his death because such was not relevant to the issue of defendant's blameworthiness, but those cases were overruled in *Payne v. Tennessee*, 501 U.S. 808, 111 S.Ct. 2597, 115 L.Ed.2d 720 (1991), on the ground that assessment of the harm caused by the defendant has long been an important factor in determining the appropriate punishment.

Constitution. I shall not again canvass the reasons that led to that conclusion. I emphasize only that foremost among the "moral concepts" recognized in our cases and inherent in the Clause is the primary moral principle that the State, even as it punishes, must treat its citizens in a manner consistent with their intrinsic worth as human beings—a punishment must not be so severe as to be degrading to human dignity. A judicial determination whether the punishment of death comports with human dignity is therefore not only permitted but compelled by the Clause. * * *

The fatal constitutional infirmity in the punishment of death is that it treats "members of the human race as nonhumans, as objects to be toyed with and discarded. [It is] thus inconsistent with the fundamental premise of the Clause that even the vilest criminal remains a human being possessed of common human dignity." As such it is a penalty that "subjects the individual to a fate forbidden by the principle of civilized treatment guaranteed by the [Clause]." I therefore would hold, on that ground alone, that death is today a cruel and unusual punishment prohibited by the Clause. * * *

MR. JUSTICE MARSHALL, dissenting. * * *

Since the decision in *Furman,* the legislatures of 35 States have enacted new statutes authorizing the imposition of the death sentence for certain crimes, and Congress has enacted a law providing the death penalty for air piracy resulting in death. 49 U.S.C. (Supp. IV) §§ 1472, 1473. I would be less than candid if I did not acknowledge that these developments have a significant bearing on a realistic assessment of the moral acceptability of the death penalty to the American people. But if the constitutionality of the death penalty turns, as I have urged, on the opinion of an *informed* citizenry, then even the enactment of new death statutes cannot be viewed as conclusive. In *Furman,* I observed that the American people are largely unaware of the information critical to a judgment on the morality of the death penalty, and concluded that if they were better informed they would consider it shocking, unjust, and unacceptable. * * *

The two purposes that sustain the death penalty as nonexcessive in the Court's view are general deterrence and retribution. In *Furman,* I canvassed the relevant data on the deterrent effect of capital punishment. The state of knowledge at that point, after literally centuries of debate, was summarized as follows by a United Nations Committee:

"It is generally agreed between the retentionists and abolitionists, whatever their opinions about the validity of comparative studies of deterrence, that the data which now exist show no correlation between the existence of capital punishment and lower rates of capital crime." * * *

The other principal purpose said to be served by the death penalty is retribution. The notion that retribution can serve as a moral justification for the sanction of death finds credence in the opinion of my Brothers STEWART, POWELL, and STEVENS. * * * [Their] statement is wholly inadequate to justify the death penalty. As my Brother Brennan stated in *Furman,* "[t]here is no evidence whatever that utilization of imprisonment rather than death encourages private blood feuds and other disorders." It simply defies belief to suggest that the death penalty is necessary to prevent the American people from taking the law into their own hands. * * *

Notes and Questions

1. In *Jurek v. Texas,* 428 U.S. 262, 96 S.Ct. 2950, 49 L.Ed.2d 929 (1976), petitioner, who was convicted of murder and whose death sentence was upheld on appeal, challenged the constitutionality of the Texas procedures enacted after *Furman.* The new Texas Penal Code limits capital homicides to intentional and knowing murders committed in five

situations.[a] Texas also adopted a new capital-sentencing procedure, which requires the jury to answer the following three questions in a proceeding that takes place after a verdict finding a person guilty of one of the specified murder categories: (1) whether the conduct of the defendant causing the death was committed deliberately and with the reasonable expectation that the death would result; (2) whether it is probable that the defendant would commit criminal acts of violence constituting a continuing threat to society; and (3) if raised by the evidence, whether the defendant's conduct was an unreasonable response to the provocation, if any, by the deceased. If the jury finds that the State has proved beyond a reasonable doubt that the answer to each of the three questions is affirmative the death sentence is imposed; if it finds that the answer to any question is negative a sentence of life imprisonment results. Stevens, J., joined by Stewart and Powell, JJ., announced the judgment of the Court:

"We conclude that Texas' capital-sentencing procedures, like those of Georgia and Florida, do not violate the Eighth and Fourteenth Amendments. By narrowing its definition of capital murder, Texas has essentially said that there must be at least one statutory aggravating circumstance in a first-degree murder case before a death sentence may even be considered. By authorizing the defense to bring before the jury at the separate sentencing hearing whatever mitigating circumstances relating to the individual defendant can be adduced, Texas has ensured that the sentencing jury will have adequate guidance to enable it to perform its sentencing function. By providing prompt judicial review of the jury's decision in a court with statewide jurisdiction, Texas has provided a means to promote the evenhanded, rational, and consistent imposition of death sentences under law. Because this system serves to assure that sentences of death will not be 'wantonly' or 'freakishly' imposed, it does not violate the Constitution."

White, Rehnquist and Blackmun, JJ., and the Chief Justice concurred in the judgment; Brennan and Marshall, JJ., dissented.

2. In *Proffitt v. Florida*, 428 U.S. 242, 96 S.Ct. 2960, 49 L.Ed.2d 913 (1976), petitioner, who was convicted of first-degree murder, attacked the constitutionality of the Florida capital-sentencing procedure enacted after *Furman*. Under the new statute, the trial judge (who is the sentencing authority) must weigh eight statutory aggravating factors against seven statutory mitigating factors[b] to determine whether the death penalty

---

a. They are where:

"(1) the person murdered a peace officer or fireman who was acting in the lawful discharge of an official duty and who the defendant knew was a peace officer or fireman;

"(2) the person intentionally committed the murder in the course of committing or attempting to commit kidnapping, burglary, robbery, forcible rape, or arson;

"(3) the person committed the murder for remuneration or the promise of remuneration or employed another to commit the murder for remuneration or the promise of remuneration;

"(4) the person committed the murder while escaping or attempting to escape from a penal institution;

"(5) the person, while incarcerated in a penal institution, murdered another who was employed in the operation of the penal institution."

b. The aggravating circumstances are:

"(a) The capital felony was committed by a person under sentence of imprisonment.

"(b) The defendant was previously convicted of another capital felony or of a felony involving the use or threat of violence to the person.

"(c) The defendant knowingly created a great risk of death to many persons.

"(d) The capital felony was committed while the defendant was engaged, or was an accomplice, in the commission of, or an attempt to commit, or flight after committing or attempting to commit, any robbery, rape, arson, burglary, kidnapping, or aircraft piracy or the unlawful throwing, placing, or discharging of a destructive device or bomb.

"(e) The capital felony was committed for the purpose of avoiding or preventing a lawful arrest or effecting an escape from custody.

"(f) The capital felony was committed for pecuniary gain.

"(g) The capital felony was committed to disrupt or hinder the lawful exercise of any governmental function or the enforcement of laws.

"(h) The capital felony was especially heinous, atrocious, or cruel."

should be imposed, thus requiring him to focus on the circumstances of the crime and the character of the individual defendant. Powell, J., joined by Stewart and Stevens, JJ., announced the judgment of the Court:

"Under Florida's capital-sentencing procedures, in sum, trial judges are given specific and detailed guidance to assist them in deciding whether to impose a death penalty or imprisonment for life. Moreover, their decisions are reviewed to ensure that they are consistent with other sentences imposed in similar circumstances. Thus, in Florida, as in Georgia, it is no longer true that there is 'no meaningful basis for distinguishing the few cases in which [the death penalty] is imposed from the many cases where it is not.' On its face the Florida system thus satisfies the constitutional deficiencies identified in *Furman.*"

3. In *Lockett v. Ohio,* 438 U.S. 586, 98 S.Ct. 2954, 57 L.Ed.2d 973 (1978), the Court invalidated the Ohio death penalty statute, which provided that once a defendant is found guilty of aggravated murder with at least one of seven specified aggravating circumstances present, the death penalty must be imposed absent one of three specified mitigating circumstances (victim induced or facilitated the crime; unlikely offense would have been committed but for duress, coercion or strong provocation; offense a product of defendant's mental deficiency). Chief Justice Burger, with three other members of the Court concurring and three more Justices concurring in the result, concluded that "the Eighth and Fourteenth Amendments require that the sentencer, in all but the rarest kind of capital case, not be precluded from considering, *as a mitigating factor,* any aspect of a defendant's character or record and any of the circumstances of the offense that the defendant proffers as a basis for a sentence less than death.[c] * * * [A] statute that prevents the sentencer in all capital cases from giving independent mitigating weight to aspects of the defendant's character and record and to circumstances of the offense proffered in mitigation creates the risk that the death penalty will be imposed in spite of factors which may call for a less severe penalty. When the choice is between life and death, that risk is unacceptable and incompatible with the commands of the Eighth and Fourteenth Amendments."[d]

4. At issue in *Spaziano v. Florida,* 468 U.S. 447, 104 S.Ct. 3154, 82 L.Ed.2d 340 (1984), was a sentencing scheme whereby the jury's recommendation was advisory only, so that (as occurred in this case) a jury's recommendation of life imprisonment could be overruled by the trial judge who, based upon his assessment of the aggravating and mitigating circumstances, opted for the death penalty. The Court, per Blackmun, J., concluded "that the purpose of the death penalty is not frustrated by, or inconsistent with,

---

The mitigating circumstances are:

"(a) The defendant has no significant history of prior criminal activity.

"(b) The capital felony was committed while the defendant was under the influence of extreme mental or emotional disturbance.

"(c) The victim was a participant in the defendant's conduct or consented to the act.

"(d) The defendant was an accomplice in the capital felony committed by another person and his participation was relatively minor.

"(e) The defendant acted under extreme duress or under the substantial domination of another person.

"(f) The capacity of the defendant to appreciate the criminality of his conduct or to conform his conduct to the requirements of law was substantially impaired.

"(g) The age of the defendant at the time of the crime."

c. In *McKoy v. North Carolina,* 494 U.S. 433, 110 S.Ct. 1227, 108 L.Ed.2d 369 (1990), the Court later held that a statute allowing consideration of mitigating circumstances only if the jury finds them unanimously was invalid, even though a like requirement existed for aggravating circumstances.

d. Despite *Lockett,* "[n]othing in the Constitution obligates state courts to give mitigating circumstance instructions when no evidence is offered to support them." *Delo v. Lashley,* 507 U.S. 272, 113 S.Ct. 1222, 122 L.Ed.2d 620 (1993). Moreover, while the jury may not be precluded from considering any constitutionally relevant mitigating evidence, *Penry v. Lynaugh,* 492 U.S. 302, 109 S.Ct. 2934, 106 L.Ed.2d 256 (1989), it is not necessary that the jury be provided with express guidance on the concept of mitigation or be instructed on particular statutorily-defined mitigating factors. *Buchanan v. Angelone,* 522 U.S. 269, 118 S.Ct. 757, 139 L.Ed.2d 702 (1998).

a scheme in which the imposition of the penalty in individual cases is determined by a judge.

"We also acknowledge the presence of the majority view that capital sentencing, unlike other sentencing, should be performed by a jury. As petitioner points out, 30 out of 37 jurisdictions with a capital-sentencing statute give the life-or-death decision to the jury, with only 3 of the remaining 7 allowing a judge to override a jury's recommendation of life. The fact that a majority of jurisdictions has adopted a different practice, however, does not establish that contemporary standards of decency are offended by the jury override. The Eighth Amendment is not violated every time a State reaches a conclusion different from a majority of its sisters over how best to administer its criminal laws."[e]

5. In *Woodson v. North Carolina*, 428 U.S. 280, 96 S.Ct. 2978, 49 L.Ed.2d 944 (1976), the petitioners were convicted of first-degree murder. Following *Furman*, the state law which previously had provided that in cases of first-degree murder the jury in its unbridled discretion could choose whether the convicted defendant should be sentenced to death or life imprisonment was changed to make the death penalty mandatory for that crime.[f] Stewart, J., joined by Powell and Stevens, JJ., announced the judgment of the Court reversing the judgment of the state court. Noting that when such mandatory death sentence provisions were common for first-degree murder "[j]uries continued to find the death penalty inappropriate in a significant number of first-degree murder cases and refused to return guilty verdicts for that crime," and that abandonment of such mandatory death sentence provisions commenced in 1838 until by 1963 all states had replaced them with discretionary jury sentencing, they concluded: "The two crucial indicators of evolving standards of decency respecting the imposition of punishment in our society—jury determinations and legislative enactments—both point conclusively to the repudiation of automatic death sentences." Nor did they believe that the mandatory statutes adopted by a number of states following *Furman* evinced "a sudden reversal of societal values regarding the imposition of capital punishment"; rather, "it seems evident that the post-*Furman* enactments reflect attempts by the States to retain the death penalty in a form consistent with the Constitution." They continued:

"A separate deficiency of North Carolina's mandatory death sentence statute is its failure to provide a constitutionally tolerable response to *Furman's* rejection of unbridled jury discretion in the imposition of capital sentences. Central to the limited holding in *Furman* was the conviction that the vesting of standardless sentencing power in the jury violated the Eighth and Fourteenth Amendments. It is argued that North Carolina has remedied the inadequacies of the death penalty statutes held unconstitutional in *Furman* by withdrawing all sentencing discretion from juries in capital cases. But when one considers the long and consistent American experience with the death penalty in first-degree murder cases, it becomes evident that mandatory statutes enacted in response to *Furman* have simply papered over the problem of unguided and unchecked jury discretion. * * *

---

e. Consider also *Harris v. Alabama*, 513 U.S. 504, 115 S.Ct. 1031, 130 L.Ed.2d 1004 (1995) (vesting of sentencing authority in trial judge, but not specifying weight to be given jury's recommendation, as in *Spaziano*, does not violate Eighth Amendment).

f. The statute now reads as follows:

"*Murder in the first and second degree defined; punishment.*—A murder which shall be perpetrated by means of poison, lying in wait, imprisonment, starving, torture, or by any other kind of willful, deliberate and premeditated killing, or which shall be committed in the perpetration or attempt to perpetrate any arson, rape, robbery, kidnapping, burglary or other felony, shall be deemed to be murder in the first degree and shall be punished with death. All other kinds of murder shall be deemed murder in the second degree, and shall be punished by imprisonment for a term of not less than two years nor more than life imprisonment in the State's prison."

"A third constitutional shortcoming of the North Carolina statute is its failure to allow the particularized consideration of relevant aspects of the character and record of each convicted defendant before the imposition upon him of a sentence of death. In *Furman,* members of the Court acknowledge what cannot fairly be denied—that death is a punishment different from all other sanctions in kind rather than degree. A process that accords no significance to relevant facets of the character and record of the individual offender or the circumstances of the particular offense excludes from consideration in fixing the ultimate punishment of death the possibility of compassionate or mitigating factors stemming from the diverse frailties of humankind. It treats all persons convicted of a designated offense not as uniquely individual human beings, but as members of a faceless, undifferentiated mass to be subjected to the blind infliction of the penalty of death." Brennan and Marshall, JJ., concurred in the judgment. White, J., joined by Rehnquist, J., and the Chief Justice, dissented. They contended that the change in North Carolina law had solved the problem of unfettered jury discretion which was at the heart of *Furman,* and rejected the argument "that the North Carolina statute, although making the imposition of the death penalty mandatory upon proof of guilt and a verdict of first-degree murder, will nevertheless result in the death penalty being imposed so seldom and arbitrarily that it is void under *Furman.*" Blackmun, J., dissented for the reasons set out in his *Furman* dissent.

6. In *Roberts v. Louisiana,* 428 U.S. 325, 96 S.Ct. 3001, 49 L.Ed.2d 974 (1976), petitioner was found guilty of first-degree murder and sentenced to death under amended Louisiana statutes enacted after *Furman.* This legislation mandates imposition of the death penalty whenever, with respect to five categories of homicide, the jury finds the defendant had a specific intent to kill or to inflict great bodily harm.[g] If a verdict of first-degree murder is returned, death is mandated regardless of any mercy recommendation. Every jury is instructed on the crimes of second-degree murder and manslaughter and permitted to consider those verdicts even if no evidence supports the lesser verdicts; if a lesser verdict is returned it is treated as an acquittal of all greater charges. Stevens, J., joined by Stewart and Powell, JJ., announced the judgment of the Court reversing the judgment of the state court. They concluded that neither the narrower definition of first-degree murder nor the responsive verdict device freed the Louisiana statute from the constitutional deficiencies discussed in *Woodson:*

"The constitutional vice of mandatory death sentence statutes—lack of focus on the circumstances of the particular offense and the character and propensities of the offender—is not resolved by Louisiana's limitation of first-degree murder to various categories of killings. The diversity of circumstances presented in cases falling within the single category of killings during the commission of a specified felony, as well as the variety of possible offenders involved in such crimes, underscores the rigidity of Louisiana's enactment and its similarity to the North Carolina statute. Even the other more narrowly drawn categories of first-degree murder in the Louisiana law afford no meaningful opportunity for consider-

---

g. The five categories are:

"(1) When the offender has a specific intent to kill or to inflict great bodily harm and is engaged in the perpetration or attempted perpetration of aggravated kidnapping, aggravated rape or armed robbery; or

"(2) When the offender has a specific intent to kill, or to inflict great bodily harm upon, a fireman or a peace officer who was engaged in the performance of his lawful duties; or

"(3) Where the offender has a specific intent to kill or to inflict great bodily harm and has previously been convicted of an unrelated murder or is serving a life sentence; or

"(4) When the offender has a specific intent to kill or to inflict great bodily harm upon more than one person; [or]

"(5) When the offender has specific intent to commit murder and has been offered or has received anything of value for committing the murder."

ation of mitigating factors presented by the circumstances of the particular crime or by the attributes of the individual offender.[9]

" * * * This responsive verdict procedure not only lacks standards to guide the jury in selecting among first-degree murderers, but it plainly invites the jurors to disregard their oaths and choose a verdict for a lesser offense whenever they feel the death penalty is inappropriate. There is an element of capriciousness in making the jurors' power to avoid the death penalty dependent on their willingness to accept this invitation to disregard the trial judge's instructions. The Louisiana procedure neither provides standards to channel jury judgments nor permits review to check the arbitrary exercise of the capital jury's *de facto* sentencing discretion."

Brennan and Marshall, JJ., concurred in the judgment. White, J., joined by Blackmun and Rehnquist, JJ., and the Chief Justice, dissented.

7. In a case involving a different petitioner but also styled *Roberts v. Louisiana,* 431 U.S. 633, 97 S.Ct. 1993, 52 L.Ed.2d 637 (1977), the Court held, 5–4, that the death penalty may not be mandatory for the murder of a police officer. "To be sure, the fact that the murder victim was a peace officer performing his regular duties may be regarded as an aggravating circumstance. There is a special interest in affording protection to these public servants who regularly must risk their lives in order to guard the safety of other persons and property. But it is incorrect to suppose that no mitigating circumstances can exist when the victim is a police officer. Circumstances such as the youth of the offender, the absence of any prior conviction, the influence of drugs, alcohol or extreme emotional disturbance, and even the existence of circumstances which the offender reasonably believed provided a moral justification for his conduct are all examples of mitigating facts which might attend the killing of a peace officer and which are considered relevant in other jurisdictions."

8. Similarly, in *Sumner v. Shuman,* 483 U.S. 66, 107 S.Ct. 2716, 97 L.Ed.2d 56 (1987), the Court reached the same result as to a provision mandating the death penalty for murder by a life-term inmate. The Court, per Blackmun, J., reasoned that the statutory mitigating circumstances applicable in other murder cases could "be equally applicable to a murder committed by a life-term inmate" and that the state had not shown "any legitimate state interests" that could not "be satisfied through the use of a guided-discretion statute." The mandatory death penalty, the Court explained, "is not necessary as a deterrent" because sufficient deterrence is supplied by the discretionary systems, and is not "justified because of the State's retribution interests" in that "other sanctions less severe than execution [e.g., changes in the terms of confinement] * * * can be imposed even on a life-term inmate."

White, J., joined by the Chief Justice and Scalia, J., dissenting, concluded that "a State does not violate the Eighth Amendment by maintaining the full deterrent effect of the death penalty in this kind of case and by insisting that those who murder while serving a life sentence without parole not be able to escape punishment for that crime."

9. With respect to use of the death penalty for crimes other than homicide, consider *Coker v. Georgia,* 433 U.S. 584, 97 S.Ct. 2861, 53 L.Ed.2d 982 (1977). Petitioner was convicted of rape and then sentenced to death when the jury found two of the statutory aggravating circumstances to be present, i.e., the rape was (i) by a person with prior

---

9. Only the third category of the Louisiana first-degree murder statute, covering intentional killing by a person serving a life sentence or by a person previously convicted of an unrelated murder, defines the capital crime at least in significant part in terms of the charac- ter or record of the individual offender. Although even this narrow category does not permit the jury to con- sider possible mitigating factors, a prisoner serving a life sentence presents a unique problem that may justi- fy such a law.

capital-felony convictions and (ii) in the course of committing another capital-felony, armed robbery. White, J., announcing the judgment of the Court in an opinion in which Stewart, Blackmun and Stevens, JJ., joined, concluded "that death is indeed a disproportionate penalty for the crime of raping an adult woman.

"We do not discount the seriousness of rape as a crime. It is highly reprehensible, both in a moral sense and in its almost total contempt for the personal integrity and autonomy of the female victim and for the latter's privilege of choosing those with whom intimate relationships are to be established. Short of homicide, it is the 'ultimate violation of self.' It is also a violent crime because it normally involves force, or the threat of force or intimidation, to overcome the will and the capacity of the victim to resist. Rape is very often accompanied by physical injury to the female and can also inflict mental and psychological damage. Because it undermines the community's sense of security, there is public injury as well.

"Rape is without doubt deserving of serious punishment; but in terms of moral depravity and of the injury to the person and to the public, it does not compare with murder, which does involve the unjustified taking of human life. Although it may be accompanied by another crime, rape by definition does not include the death or even the serious injury to another person. The murderer kills; the rapist, if no more than that, does not. Life is over for the victim of the murderers; for the rape victim, life may not be nearly so happy as it was, but it is not over and normally is not beyond repair. We have the abiding conviction that the death penalty, which 'is unique in its severity and revocability,' is an excessive penalty for the rapist who, as such, does not take human life.''

Brennan and Marshall, JJ., concurred on the ground that the death penalty constitutes cruel and unusual punishment in all circumstances. Burger, C.J., joined by Rehnquist, J., dissented: "Until now, the issue under the Eighth Amendment has not been the state of any particular victim after the crime, but rather whether the punishment imposed is grossly disproportionate to the evil committed by the perpetrator. As a matter of constitutional principle, that test cannot have the primitive simplicity of 'life for life, eye for eye, tooth for tooth.' Rather States must be permitted to engage in a more sophisticated weighing of values in dealing with criminal activity which consistently poses serious danger of death or grave bodily harm. If innocent life and limb is to be preserved I see no constitutional barrier in punishing by death all who engage in such activity, regardless of whether the risk comes to fruition in any particular instance. * * *

"The Court's conclusion to the contrary is very disturbing indeed. The clear implication of today's holding appears to be that the death penalty may be properly imposed only as to crimes resulting in death of the victim. This casts serious doubt upon the constitutional validity of statutes imposing the death penalty for a variety of conduct which, though dangerous, may not necessarily result in any immediate death, e.g., treason, airplane hijacking, and kidnapping. In that respect, today's holding does even more harm than is initially apparent. We cannot avoid judicial notice that crimes such as airplane hijacking, kidnapping, and mass terrorist activity constitute a serious and increasing danger to the safety of the public. It would be unfortunate indeed if the effect of today's holding were to inhibit States and the Federal Government from experimenting with various remedies—including possibly imposition of the penalty of death—to prevent and deter such crimes.''

Powell, J., concurred on the facts of the case because there was "no indication that petitioner's offense was committed with excessive brutality or that the victim sustained serious or lasting injury," but objected to the Court's broader holding: "The deliberate viciousness of the rapist may be greater than that of the murderer. Rape is never an act committed accidentally. Rarely can it be said to be unpremeditated. There also is wide variation in the effect on the victim. The plurality opinion says that '[l]ife is over for the victim of the murderer; for the rape victim, life may not be nearly so happy as it was, but it is not over and normally is not beyond repair.' But there is indeed 'extreme variation' in the crime of rape. Some victims are so grievously injured physically or psychologically that life *is* beyond repair."

10. After *Coker*, it was only a matter of time before the Court would confront the issue reached in *Enmund v. Florida*, 458 U.S. 782, 102 S.Ct. 3368, 73 L.Ed.2d 1140 (1982): "whether death is a valid penalty under the Eighth and Fourteenth Amendments for one who neither took life, attempted to take life, nor intended to take life." Enmund was convicted of two counts of felony-murder and sentenced to death on proof that he drove the getaway car in a robbery during which two of his co-felons shot and killed the two victims. The Court, per White, J., first took note of "society's rejection of the death penalty for accomplice liability in felony murders," as indicated by the fact that "only a small minority of jurisdictions—eight—allow the death penalty to be imposed solely because the defendant somehow participated in a robbery in the course of which a murder was committed," and that a survey of death penalty cases since 1954 "revealed only 6 cases out of 362 where a nontriggerman felony murderer was executed." The Court continued:

"Enmund himself did not kill or attempt to kill; and, as construed by the Florida Supreme Court, the record before us does not warrant a finding that Enmund had any intention of participating in or facilitating a murder. Yet under Florida law death was an authorized penalty because Enmund aided and abetted a robbery in the course of which murder was committed. It is fundamental that "causing harm intentionally must be punished more severely than causing the same harm unintentionally." H. Hart, *Punishment and Responsibility* 162 (1968). Enmund did not kill or intend to kill and thus his culpability is plainly different from that of the robbers who killed; yet the State treated them alike and attributed to Enmund the culpability of those who killed the Kerseys. This was impermissible under the Eighth Amendment.

"In *Gregg v. Georgia* the opinion announcing the judgment observed that '[t]he death penalty is said to serve two principal social purposes: retribution and deterrence of capital crimes by prospective offenders.' Unless the death penalty when applied to those in Enmund's position measurably contributes to one or both of these goals, it 'is nothing more than the purposeless and needless imposition of pain and suffering,' and hence an unconstitutional punishment. *Coker v. Georgia, supra*. We are quite unconvinced, however, that the threat that the death penalty will be imposed for murder will measurably deter one who does not kill and has no intention or purpose that life will be taken. * * *

"It would be very different if the likelihood of a killing in the course of a robbery were so substantial that one should share the blame for the killing if he somehow participated in the felony. But competent observers have concluded that there is no basis in experience for the notion that death so frequently occurs in the course of a felony for which killing is not an essential ingredient that the death penalty should be considered as a justifiable deterrent to the felony itself. * * *

"As for retribution as a justification for executing Enmund, we think this very much depends on the degree of Enmund's culpability—what Enmund's intentions, expectations, and actions were. American criminal law has long considered a defendant's intention—and therefore his moral guilt—to be critical to 'the degree of [his] criminal culpability,' and the Court has found criminal penalties to be unconstitutionally excessive in the absence of intentional wrongdoing.''[h]

O'Connor, J., for the four dissenters, concluded that "the petitioner and the Court have failed to show that contemporary standards, as reflected in both jury determinations and legislative enactments, preclude imposition of the death penalty for accomplice felony murder. Moreover, examination of the qualitative factors underlying the concept of proportionality do not show that the death penalty is disproportionate as applied to Earl Enmund. In contrast to the crime in *Coker,* the petitioner's crime involves the very type of harm that this Court has held justifies the death penalty. Finally, because of the unique and complex mixture of facts involving a defendant's actions, knowledge, motives, and participation during the commission of a felony murder, I believe that the factfinder is best able to assess the defendant's blameworthiness.''

11.   But later, in *Tison v. Arizona,* 481 U.S. 137, 107 S.Ct. 1676, 95 L.Ed.2d 127 (1987), the Court decided *Enmund* was not applicable to every defendant convicted of felony murder on an accomplice liability theory. The petitioners affected the escape of their father from prison and armed him and another convicted murderer with guns and later helped abduct a family and watched as the two convicts murdered that family. The state supreme court affirmed their death sentences, reasoning that under *Enmund* it was sufficient that the defendants had anticipated that lethal force might be used. The Supreme Court, per O'Connor, J., affirmed:

"A narrow focus on the question of whether or not a given defendant 'intended to kill,' however, is a highly unsatisfactory means of definitively distinguishing the most culpable and dangerous of murderers. Many who intend to, and do, kill are not criminally liable at all—those who act in self-defense or with other justification or excuse. Other intentional homicides, though criminal, are often felt undeserving of the death penalty—those that are the result of provocation. On the other hand, some nonintentional murderers may be among the most dangerous and inhumane of all—the person who tortures another not caring whether the victim lives or dies, or the robber who shoots someone in the course of the robbery, utterly indifferent to the fact that the desire to rob may have the unintended consequence of killing the victim as well as taking the victim's property. This reckless indifference to the value of human life may be every bit as shocking to the moral sense as an 'intent to kill.' Indeed it is for this very reason that the common law and modern criminal codes alike have classified behavior such as occurred in this case along with intentional murders. * * * *Enmund* held that when 'intent to kill' results in its logical though not inevitable consequence—the taking of human life—the Eighth Amendment permits the State to exact the death penalty after a careful weighing of the aggravating and mitigating circumstances. Similarly, we hold that the reckless disregard for human life implicit in knowingly engaging in criminal activities known to carry a grave risk of death represents a highly culpable mental state, a mental state that may be taken into account in making a capital sentencing judgment when that conduct causes its natural, though also not inevitable, lethal result.

"The petitioners own personal involvement in the crimes was not minor, but rather, as specifically found by the trial court, 'substantial.' Far from merely sitting in a car away from the actual scene of the murders acting as the getaway driver to a robbery, each petitioner was actively involved in every element of the kidnaping-robbery and was physically present during the entire sequence of criminal activity culminating in the

h. Article 118 of the Uniform Code of Military Justice, by authorizing the death penalty for all felony murder, is contrary to *Enmund,* and thus Rule for Courts–Martial 1004, which sets out 11 categories of aggravating circumstances and requires a unanimous finding of at least one before a death sentence may be imposed, is "necessary to save Article 118." *Loving v. United States,* 517 U.S. 748, 116 S.Ct. 1737, 135 L.Ed.2d 36 (1996).

murder of the Lyons family and the subsequent flight. The Tisons' high level of participation in these crimes further implicates them in the resulting deaths. Accordingly, they fall well within the overlapping second intermediate position which focuses on the defendant's degree of participation in the felony.

"Only a small minority of those jurisdictions imposing capital punishment for felony murder have rejected the possibility of a capital sentence absent an intent to kill and we do not find this minority position constitutionally required. We will not attempt to precisely delineate the particular types of conduct and states of mind warranting imposition of the death penalty here. Rather, we simply hold that major participation in the felony committed, combined with reckless indifference to human life, is sufficient to satisfy the *Enmund* culpability requirement. The Arizona courts have clearly found that the former exists; we now vacate the judgments below and remand for determination of the latter in further proceedings not inconsistent with this opinion."

The four dissenters asserted that "the basic flaw in today's decision is the Court's failure to conduct the sort of proportionality analysis that the Constitution and past cases require. Creation of a new category of culpability is not enough to distinguish this case from *Enmund*. The Court must also establish that death is a proportionate punishment for individuals in this category. In other words, the Court must demonstrate that major participation in a felony with a state of mind of reckless indifference to human life deserves the same punishment as intending to commit a murder or actually committing a murder. The Court does not attempt to conduct a proportionality review of the kind performed in past cases raising a proportionality question * * *."

Chapter 6

MENTAL DISEASE OR DEFECT

SECTION 1. COMPETENCY TO STAND TRIAL

Introductory Notes

1. Although the matter of principal concern in this Chapter is the defense of insanity, it is appropriate to begin with a consideration of competency to stand trial. As noted in Samuel J. Brakel, John Parry & Barbara A. Weiner, *The Mentally Disabled and the Law* 693–94 (3d ed. 1985): "While the insanity defense has received more attention from the media and has inflamed public debate, the issue of competency, or what has sometimes been called 'present insanity,' affects far greater numbers of mentally disabled defendants,[2] and some consider this issue the most significant mental health inquiry pursued in the criminal justice process. Since the previous edition of this book there has been increased recognition of the detrimental consequences of a finding of incompetency for the defendant, which has resulted in an increasing number of challenges to the state procedures for hospitalizing incompetent defendants and to provisions permitting indeterminate hospitalization without resolution of the criminal charges. As with the concept of criminal responsibility, the question of present competency engages conflicting philosophies and varying standards for application to individual cases, and it raises both substantive and procedural questions at each stage of the criminal process. * * *

"Because it is often missed by practitioners in both the legal and the psychiatric professions, it is important to keep in mind the conceptual distinction between competency to participate in the criminal justice process and criminal responsibility. Competency concerns only the defendant's present ability to assist in his defense and understand the process he is involved in or the punishment he receives, whereas criminal responsibility concerns only the mental state of the defendant at the time of the commission of the crime,

---

2. For example, a 1979 study estimated that out of more than two million felony and misdemeanor cases disposed of in the state and federal courts 6,420 were institutionalized because they were incompetent to stand trial, as compared with 1,625 who were there as a result of being found not guilty by reason of insanity. Steadman, Monahan, Hartstone, Davis, & Robbins, *Mentally Disordered Offenders: A National Survey of Patients and Facilities*, 6 Law & Hum.Behav. 31, 33 (1982).

It has been estimated that as many as 9,000 persons a year are found incompetent, a figure that reflects that not all of them are institutionalized or that a percentage of those who are institutionalized are discharged after relatively brief periods. H.J. Steadman, *Beating A Rap? Defendants Found Incompetent to Stand Trial* 4 (1979). In Illinois, for example, approximately 300 people a year are found incompetent, while only about 40 are found not guilty by reason of insanity (statistics kept by the Illinois Dep't of Mental Health & Developmental Disabilities, Statistical Branch, Springfield, Illinois).

which may have been months or years before the trial. Thus, a defendant may be competent to stand trial but be found not criminally responsible for his acts. Conversely, he could be adjudged incompetent but once restored to competency be held responsible for his criminal actions. Finally, he could be declared incompetent and once restored to competency be found not criminally responsible."

2. In practice, the competency inquiry often obviates any need for a subsequent defense of insanity. Consider Arthur R. Matthews, *Mental Disability and the Criminal Law* 90–92 (1970): "Even when there is real doubt about the accused's fitness for trial, strategical considerations are highly influential in determining whether the issue will be opened up and how it is pursued. Except where competency proceedings are initiated solely for obstruction or delay—and this accounts for a very small portion of motions for competency determination—the movant characteristically seeks expert opinion on some collateral issue. The major reason is to obtain psychiatric opinion in order to determine whether some alternative disposition is feasible, a reason common to the prosecution and the defense. The initiation of competency proceedings is the major access route in the criminal process to psychiatric intervention, a necessary prerequisite if some informal psychiatric disposition is to occur. Since competency proceedings provide that access, both sides have reasons for invoking them. When the prosecution and the defense are agreed on allowing the accused to be treated on an outpatient basis or to be civilly committed, and thus on disposing of the criminal charges, both want to know if such treatment is psychiatrically indicated and feasible. Since the prosecutor has no funds in his budget for this purpose, and the defendant typically is indigent, both sides may agree to raise the competency issue to get a medical consultation. The judge may also want some help in disposing of the offender, initially or subsequently, in a perhaps more humane and effective way than sentencing him to the county jail. Neither judges nor prosecutors have illusions about the limited sentencing alternatives available to them and both are usually eager to take advantage of any opportunity to experiment with a disposition which may 'help' the offender. In many cases this is a conscious use of competency proceedings in which the judge, the prosecutor, and defense counsel concur. Whether by plan or by accident, the psychiatric report, irrespective of its impact on the competency issue, is a highly influential factor in determining the final disposition.

"Another shared reason for initiating competency proceedings is to develop evidence on the issue of criminal responsibility. Many lawyers think the standard for incompetency is broader than that for criminal responsibility * * *. Lawyers sometimes told us they thought an incompetency disposition by a judge was more likely in certain cases than an irresponsibility disposition by a jury. The judge, in the view of his brothers in the legal profession, is less likely than a jury to be prejudiced by the fact, for example, that the offense is particularly violent or atrocious. At times the competency hearing itself (when there is one) approaches a proceeding in which the court reaches a 'summary judgment' of insanity. The prosecutor can avoid a public trial which may carry with it public pressure, usually in the direction of severity; if the accused can be found incompetent, the case can later be disposed of quietly. The result in some cases is a conscious substitution of a finding of incompetency for a trial by jury on the responsibility issue—a result tacitly agreed to by both sides. This practice tends to occur in the more serious cases, especially those involving capital crimes, and helps explain why findings of incompetency outnumber findings of not guilty by reason of insanity.

"Where prosecutor and defense attorney are not equally interested in obtaining expert opinion on the insanity issue, the psychiatric report nevertheless sometimes becomes a basis for working out a disposition short of going to trial. If the psychiatric experts seem to think that the accused did not know what he was doing when the crime was committed or that he did not understand that it was wrong to do so, the prosecutor may be willing to accept a plea to a lesser offense or an outright dismissal. Furthermore, the psychiatrist performing the examination may frequently suggest alternatives, such as civil commitment or probation on condition that the accused seek outpatient psychiatric treatment. After the psychiatric examination, both parties can forecast pretty well the course of a trial, whereas in the absence of psychiatric opinion the bargaining process must be conducted with a major variable unknown.''

PATE v. ROBINSON

Supreme Court of the United States, 1966.

383 U.S. 375, 86 S.Ct. 836, 15 L.Ed.2d 815.

MR. JUSTICE CLARK delivered the opinion of the Court.

In 1959 respondent Robinson was convicted of the murder of his common-law wife, Flossie May Ward, and was sentenced to imprisonment for life. Being an indigent he was defended by court-appointed counsel. It was conceded at trial that Robinson shot and killed Flossie May, but his counsel claimed that he was insane at the time of the shooting and raised the issue of his incompetence to stand trial. On writ of error to the Supreme Court of Illinois it was asserted that the trial court's rejection of these contentions deprived Robinson of due process of law under the Fourteenth Amendment. His conviction was affirmed * * *.

The uncontradicted testimony of four witnesses called by the defense revealed that Robinson had a long history of disturbed behavior. His mother testified that when he was between seven and eight years of age a brick dropped from a third floor hit Robinson on the head. "He blacked out and the blood run from his head like a faucet." Thereafter "he acted a little peculiar." The blow knocked him "cockeyed" and his mother took him to a specialist "to correct the crossness of his eyes." He also suffered headaches during his childhood, apparently stemming from the same event. His conduct became noticeably erratic about 1946 or 1947 when he was visiting his mother on a furlough from the Army. While Robinson was sitting and talking with a guest, "he jumped up and run to a bar and kicked a hole in the bar and he run up in the front." His mother asked "what on earth was wrong with him and he just stared at [her], and paced the floor with both hands in his pockets." On other occasions he appeared in a daze, with a "glare in his eyes," and would not speak or respond to questions. In 1951, a few years after his discharge from the service, he "lost his mind and was pacing the floor saying something was after him." This incident occurred at the home of his aunt, Helen Calhoun. Disturbed by Robinson's conduct, Mrs. Calhoun called his mother about six o'clock in the morning, and she "went to see about him." Robinson tried to prevent Mrs. Calhoun from opening the door, saying "that someone was going to shoot him or someone was going to come in after him." His mother testified that after gaining admittance, "I went to him and hugged him to ask him what was wrong and he went to pushing me back, telling me to get back, somebody was going to shoot him, somebody was going to shoot him." Upon being questioned as to Robinson's facial expression at the time, the mother stated that he "had that starey look and seemed to be just a little foamy at the mouth." A policeman was finally called. He put Robinson, his mother and aunt in a cab which drove them to Hines Hospital. On the way Robinson tried to jump from the cab, and upon arrival at the hospital he was so violent that he had to be strapped in a wheel chair. He then was taken in an ambulance to the County Psychopathic Hospital, from which he was transferred to the Kankakee State Hospital. * * *

After his release from the state hospital Robinson's irrational episodes became more serious. His grandfather testified that while Robinson was working with him as a painter's assistant, "all at once, he would come down [from the ladder] and walk on out and never say where he is going and whatnot and he would be out two or three hours, and at times he would be in a daze and when he comes out, he comes back just as fresh. He just says he didn't do anything. I noticed that he wasn't at all himself." The grandfather also related that one night when Robinson was staying at his house Robinson and his wife had a "ruckus," which caused his wife to flee to the grandfather's bedroom. Robinson first tried to kick down the door. He then grabbed all of his wife's clothes from their room and threw them out in the yard, intending to set them on fire. Robinson got so unruly that the grandfather called the police to lock him up.

In 1953 Robinson, then separated from his wife, brought their 18–month–old son to Mrs. Calhoun's home and asked permission to stay there for a couple of days. She observed that he was highly nervous, prancing about and staring wildly. While she was at work the next day Robinson shot and killed his son and attempted suicide by shooting himself in the head. * * *

Robinson served almost four years in prison for killing his son, being released in September 1956. A few months thereafter he began to live with Flossie May Ward at her home. In the summer of 1957 or 1958 Robinson "jumped on" his mother's brother-in-law and "beat him up terrible." She went to the police station and swore out a warrant for his arrest. She described his abnormalities and told the officers that Robinson "seemed to have a disturbed mind." * * *

The killing occurred about 10:30 p.m. at a small barbecue house where Flossie May Ward worked. At that time there were 10 customers in the restaurant, six of them sitting at the counter. It appears from the record that Robinson entered the restaurant with a gun in his hand. As he approached the counter, Flossie May said, "Don't start nothing tonight." After staring at her for about a minute, he walked to the rear of the room and, with the use of his hand, leaped over the counter. He then rushed back toward the front of the restaurant, past two other employees working behind the counter, and fired once or twice at Flossie May. She jumped over the counter and ran out the front door with Robinson in pursuit. She was found dead on the sidewalk. Robinson never spoke a word during the three-to-four minute episode. * * *

Four defense witnesses expressed the opinion that Robinson was insane. In rebuttal the State introduced only a stipulation that Dr. William H. Haines, Director of the Behavior Clinic of the Criminal Court of Cook County would, if present, testify that in his opinion Robinson knew the nature of the charges against him and was able to cooperate with counsel when he examined him two or three months before trial. However, since the stipulation did not include a finding of sanity the prosecutor advised the court that "we should have Dr. Haines' testimony as to his opinion whether this man is sane or insane. It is possible that the man might be insane and know the nature of the charge or be able to cooperate with his counsel. I think it should be in evidence, your Honor, that Dr. Haines' opinion is that this defendant was sane when he was examined." However, the court told the prosecutor, "You have enough in the record now. I don't think you need Dr. Haines." In his summation defense counsel emphasized "our defense is clear * * *. It is as to the sanity of the defendant at the time of the crime and also as to the present time." The court, after closing argument by the defense, found Robinson guilty and sentenced him to prison for his natural life.

The State insists that Robinson deliberately waived the defense of his competence to stand trial by failing to demand a sanity hearing as provided by Illinois law. But it is contradictory to argue that a defendant may be incompetent, and yet knowingly or intelligently "waive" his right to have the court determine his capacity to stand trial. In any event, the record shows that counsel throughout the proceedings insisted that Robinson's present sanity was very much in issue. He made a point to elicit Mrs. Robinson's opinion of Robinson's "present sanity." And in his argument to the judge, he asserted that Robinson "should be found not guilty and presently insane on the basis of the testimony that we have heard." Moreover, the prosecutor himself suggested at trial that "we should have Dr. Haines' testimony as to his opinion whether this man is sane or insane." With this record we cannot say that Robinson waived the defense of incompetence to stand trial.

We believe that the evidence introduced on Robinson's behalf entitled him to a hearing on this issue. The court's failure to make such inquiry thus deprived Robinson of his constitutional right to a fair trial. The Supreme Court of Illinois held that the evidence here was not sufficient to require a hearing in light of the mental alertness and understanding displayed in Robinson's "colloquies" with the trial judge. But this reasoning offers no justification for ignoring the uncontradicted testimony of Robinson's history of pronounced irrational behavior. While Robinson's demeanor at trial might be relevant to the ultimate decision as to his sanity, it cannot be relied upon to dispense with a hearing on that very issue. Likewise, the stipulation of Dr. Haines' testimony was some evidence of Robinson's ability to assist in his defense. But, as the state prosecutor seemingly admitted, on the facts presented to the trial court it could not properly have been deemed dispositive on the issue of Robinson's competence.

Having determined that Robinson's constitutional rights were abridged by his failure to receive an adequate hearing on his competence to stand trial, we direct that the writ of habeas corpus must issue and Robinson be discharged, unless the State gives him a new trial within a reasonable time. * * * It has been pressed upon us that it would be sufficient for the state court to hold a limited hearing as to Robinson's mental competence at the time he was tried in 1959. If he were found competent, the judgment against him would stand. But we have previously emphasized the difficulty of retrospectively determining an accused's competence to stand trial. The jury would not be able to observe the subject of their inquiry, and expert witnesses would have to testify solely from information contained in the printed record. That Robinson's hearing would be held six years after the fact aggravates these difficulties. * * *

MR. JUSTICE HARLAN, whom MR. JUSTICE BLACK joins, dissenting. * * *

I do not believe the facts known to the trial judge in this case suggested Robinson's incompetence at time of trial with anything like the force necessary to make out a violation of due process in the failure to pursue the question. * * *

The Court's affirmative answer seemingly rests on two kinds of evidence, principally adduced by Robinson to prove an insanity defense after the State rested its main case. First, there was evidence of a number of episodes of severe irrationality in Robinson's past. Among them were the slaying of his infant son, his attempted suicide, his efforts to burn his wife's clothing, his fits of temper and of abstraction, and his seven-week incarceration in a state hospital eight years before the trial. This evidence may be tempered by the State's counterarguments, for example, that Robinson was found guilty of his son's killing and that alcoholism may explain his hospitalization, but it cannot be written off entirely. The difficulty remains that while this testimony may suggest that Flossie May Ward's killing was just one more irrational act, I cannot say as a matter of common knowledge that it evidences incapacity during the trial. Indeed, the pattern revealed may best indicate that Robinson did function adequately during most of his life interrupted by periods of severe derangement that would have been quite apparent had they occurred at trial. The second class of data pertinent to the Court's theory, remarks by witnesses and counsel that Robinson was "presently insane," deserves little comment. I think it apparent that these statements were addressed to Robinson's responsibility for the killing, that is, his ability to do insane acts, and not to his general competency to stand trial.

Whatever mild doubts this evidence may stir are surely allayed by positive indications of Robinson's competence at the trial. Foremost is his own behavior in the courtroom. The record reveals colloquies between Robinson and the trial judge which undoubtedly permitted a reasonable inference that Robinson was quite cognizant of the proceedings and able to assist counsel in his defense. Turning from lay impressions to those of an expert, it was stipulated at trial that a Dr. Haines, Director of the Behavior Clinic of the Criminal Court of Cook County, had examined Robinson several months earlier and, if called, would testify that Robinson "knows the nature of the charge and is able to cooperate with his counsel." The conclusive factor is that Robinson's own lawyers, the two men who apparently had the closest contact with the defendant during the proceedings, never suggested he was incompetent to stand trial and never moved to have him examined on incompetency grounds during trial; indeed, counsel's remarks to the jury seem best read as an affirmation of Robinson's present "lucidity" which would be highly peculiar if Robinson had been unable to assist properly in his defense. * * *

Notes and Questions

1. Drope was indicted with two others for rape of his wife. Following severance of his case, he filed a motion for a continuance so that he might be further examined and receive psychiatric treatment, attaching thereto the report of a psychiatrist who had examined him at his counsel's request and had suggested such treatment. The motion was denied and the case proceeded to trial. Drope's wife, in her testimony, confirmed information in the report concerning his "strange behavior" and also stated that he had tried to kill her a few days prior to the trial. On the second day of the trial, Drope shot himself in a suicide attempt, after which the trial continued without his presence. In *Drope v. Missouri*, 420 U.S. 162, 95 S.Ct. 896, 43 L.Ed.2d 103 (1975), a unanimous Court held "that when considered together with the information available prior to trial and the testimony of petitioner's wife at trial, the information concerning petitioner's suicide attempt created a sufficient doubt of his competence to stand trial to require further inquiry on the question. * * *

"Even when a defendant is competent at the commencement of his trial, a trial court must always be alert to circumstances suggesting a change that would render the accused unable to meet the standards of competence to stand trial. Whatever the relationships between mental illness and incompetence to stand trial, in this case the bearing of the former on the latter was sufficiently likely that, in light of the evidence of petitioner's behavior including his suicide attempt, and there being no opportunity without his presence to evaluate that bearing in fact, the correct course was to suspend the trial until such an evaluation could be made."

2. Should defense counsel's responsibility be comparable to that of the judge under *Robinson* and *Drope*? "Defense counsel's dilemma is illustrated by the following example. Suppose a defendant is charged with a crime for which the maximum sentence is five years in jail, a $5,000 fine or both. Suppose further that the attorney assigned to the case discovers that the defendant is suffering from a severe mental illness that makes rational communication nearly impossible. In all probability, this defendant is constitutionally incompetent to stand trial. If the defendant is found guilty, the maximum penalty is five years and $5,000. If, however, the defendant is incompetent to stand trial, then the

defendant may be civilly committed and spend many more years in a mental institution. Should the attorney raise the issue of competency? What if the defendant insisted on a 'day in court' and commanded the attorney not to raise the issue of competency? Suppose the question is raised and a competency hearing is held. The defendant's attorney has personal knowledge whether the defendant has the requisite ability to understand the proceeding and assist in the defense. Should defense counsel testify in the hearing?" Note, 9 Geo.J.Legal Ethics 639, 939–40 (1996). Compare *Enriquez v. Procunier,* 752 F.2d 111 (5th Cir.1984) (defense counsel may, for tactical reasons, decide not to request a competency hearing); with *State v. Johnson,* 133 Wis.2d 207, 395 N.W.2d 176 (1986) ("strategic considerations do not eliminate defense counsel's duty to request a competency hearing").

3. In neither *Robinson* nor *Drope* did the Court have occasion to rule on exactly what the due process standard regarding competency is, though *Drope* does quote from *Dusky v. United States,* 362 U.S. 402, 80 S.Ct. 788, 4 L.Ed.2d 824 (1960), where it is stated: "We also agree with the suggestion of the Solicitor General that it is not enough for the district judge to find that 'the defendant [is] oriented to time and place and [has] some recollection of events,' but that the 'test must be whether he has sufficient present ability to consult with his lawyer with a reasonable degree of rational understanding—and whether he has a rational as well as factual understanding of the proceedings against him.' " (In *Godinez v. Moran,* 509 U.S. 389, 113 S.Ct. 2680, 125 L.Ed.2d 321 (1993), the Court reaffirmed the *Dusky* test and held it equally applicable on the issue of a defendant's competency to enter a plea of guilty.)

There is, however, some variation from state to state as to the standard used. Compare *State v. Champagne,* 127 N.H. 266, 497 A.2d 1242 (1985) (no competency unless defendant has "the ability to communicate *meaningfully* with his lawyer so as to be able to make informed choices regarding trial strategy"); with *State v. Ortiz,* 104 Wash.2d 479, 706 P.2d 1069 (1985) (rejecting defense contention "that a person must be able to help with trial strategy in order to be found competent to stand trial").

Because of such variations, some have concluded that "the broad definition of *Dusky* has not worked." Ira Mickenberg, *Competency to Stand Trial and the Mentally Retarded Defendant,* 17 Cal.W.L.Rev. 365, 402 (1981). What, then, is the solution?

4. In *People v. Francabandera,* 33 N.Y.2d 429, 354 N.Y.S.2d 609, 310 N.E.2d 292 (1974), defendant (charged with attempted murder, reckless endangerment and possession of a dangerous weapon) moved for a determination of his fitness to stand trial. Though it was established that he was suffering from retrograde amnesia so as to be unable to recall the events surrounding the crimes with which he was charged, the trial court concluded the defendant was not incapacitated within the meaning of the statutory definition ("a defendant who as a result of mental disease or defect lacks capacity to understand the proceedings against him or to assist in his own defense"). The defendant then entered a guilty plea to reckless endangerment. On appeal, the court affirmed: "In no case yet reported has it been held that inability to recall the events charged because of amnesia constitutes mental incapacity to stand trial. * * * In *Wilson* [*v. United States,* 391 F.2d 460 (D.C.Cir.1968),*]* a case-by-case approach to the amnesic defendant was advocated so that in each situation the Judge would have to prognosticate on the basis of all the circumstances whether defendant was likely to receive a fair trial; and then, at the conclusion of the trial and before imposition of sentence, the Judge would have to decide whether defendant did, in fact, receive a fair trial—this by the application of certain tests advocated by the court.[4] * * *

---

4. "In making these findings the court should consider the following factors:

"When it is considered that the result of an order finding defendant unfit for trial in these circumstances would be outright release, assuming the amnesia is permanent and there is no other mental defect sufficient to warrant commitment, it can be more easily understood why all the courts which have passed on this question have refused to allow amnesia to be classified as the sort of mental defect causing incapacity to stand trial. This certainly is a consideration in balancing the public safety against the individual's rights; but we do not wish to be understood as making this our prime consideration since it would not fully meet the constitutional arguments. Rather, we are in accord with the reasoning in *Wilson* which addresses itself to the question whether defendant can conceivably receive a fair trial; and, after trial, whether defendant did in fact receive a fair trial. This allows for essential case-by-case evaluation. Applying those concepts to this case we can see that the court could easily have determined (as indeed it did) that defendant's trial would be fair. The alleged crime was played out in front of an audience and the overwhelming evidence, all of which was available to defendant, pointed to his guilt. From this evidence it could be determined that defendant was probably intoxicated. Had they been willing to risk the consequences, defendant and his counsel might have gone to trial on the question of defendant's inability to form the requisite intent to commit the crimes charged because of intoxication. Coupling the prosecution's evidence on this point with defendant's history of alcoholism, which defendant was perfectly capable of supplying counsel and of course capable, also, of testifying to, would have appeared to be the only course open if the decision to stand trial were made and, indeed, this is argued to us in defendant's brief. It is not explained to us, however, how defendant's lack of memory could actually have crippled his defense in this case in light of the nature of the crime and the evidence possessed by the prosecutor. It cannot be said that the decision to plead guilty to a lesser charge would not have been the most astute decision under these circumstances even had defendant been able to recall the events. There is in this case, then, no indication that defendant was deprived of any of his constitutional rights or that the court was in error in denying defendant's motion."

5. In *Medina v. California*, 505 U.S. 437, 112 S.Ct. 2572, 120 L.Ed.2d 353 (1992), the Court held that a California statute providing for a presumption of competency and requiring that the the party asserting incompetency of the defendant to stand trial have the burden of proving such status did not violate due process. One commentator has said that the statute at issue in *Medina* "minimizes inappropriate use of the incompetency status and unnecessary delay in the resolution of the defendant's charges. It also creates therapeutic opportunities for defendants who are marginally impaired by mental illness. In addition, the statute reinforces competency by presuming it and avoiding inappropriate incompetency labeling in cases of only marginal impairment, thereby promoting the psychological well-being of those individuals affected. Furthermore, it may actually increase the accuracy of the competency determination process by avoiding a potential disincentive for the defendant to produce evidence in his possession and control." Bruce J.

"(1) The extent to which the amnesia affected the defendant's ability to consult with and assist his lawyer.

"(2) The extent to which the amnesia affected the defendant's ability to testify in his own behalf.

"(3) The extent to which the evidence in suit could be extrinsically reconstructed in view of the defendant's amnesia. Such evidence would include evidence relating to the crime itself as well as any reasonably possible alibi.

"(4) The extent to which the Government assisted the defendant and his counsel in that reconstruction.

"(5) The strength of the prosecution's case. Most important here will be whether the Government's case is such as to negate all reasonable hypotheses of innocence. If there is any substantial possibility that the accused could, but for his amnesia, establish an alibi or other defense, it should be presumed that he would have been able to do so.

"(6) Any other facts and circumstances which would indicate whether or not the defendant had a fair trial."

Winick, *Presumptions and Burden of Proof in Determining Competency to Stand Trial*, 47 U. Miami L.Rev. 817, 863 (1993).

As for the extent of this burden of proof, the preponderance-of-the-evidence standard is usually utilized, but some states require clear and convincing evidence. The Supreme Court held in *Cooper v. Oklahoma*, 517 U.S. 348, 116 S.Ct. 1373, 134 L.Ed.2d 498 (1996), that the latter standard, if imposed on the defendant, allows a defendant to be put on trial even though it is more likely than not that he is incompetent, and that consequently it violates due process.

6. In *Riggins v. Nevada*, 504 U.S. 127, 112 S.Ct. 1810, 118 L.Ed.2d 479 (1992), the Court held that a defendant's interest in avoiding compelled medication is a liberty interest protected by the due process clause, such that such medication "is impermissible absent a finding of overriding justification and a determination of medical appropriateness." The Court went on to assert that due process would be satisfied if the court below "had found that treatment with antipsychotic medication was medically appropriate and, considering less intrusive alternatives, essential for the sake of [the defendant's] own safety or the safety of others." The Court took note of but had no occasion to decide the more critical issue of "whether a competent criminal defendant may refuse antipsychotic medication if cessation of medication would render him incompetent at trial."

In *State v. Garcia*, 233 Conn. 44, 658 A.2d 947 (1995), the court concluded: "The state's ability to bring an accused criminal to trial is fundamental to our system of law because it is essential to the effectuation of the state's vital interest in the enforcement of its criminal laws. 'The safeguards that the Constitution accords to criminal defendants presuppose that government has a sovereign prerogative to put on trial those accused in good faith of violating valid laws. Constitutional power to bring an accused to trial is fundamental to a scheme of "ordered liberty" and prerequisite to social justice and peace' In balancing the rights of the accused against state interests in enforcement of criminal laws, the United States Supreme Court has made reference to 'the community's vital interests in law enforcement' and has noted that 'the community's interest in fairly and accurately determining guilt or innocence . . . is of course of great importance.'

"Other courts facing the issue now before us have similarly determined that the state's interest in enforcing its criminal laws by bringing a defendant to trial is significant and, under certain circumstances, can override the liberty and privacy interests of the defendant. In *Khiem v. United States*, 612 A.2d 160 (D.C.App.1992), the District of Columbia Court of Appeals rejected a claim that the state's interests in involuntarily medicating a defendant for the purpose of rendering him competent to stand trial were 'largely symbolic.' As under our statutory scheme, the incompetent defendant could be held only for a limited time before the government was required either to release him or begin civil commitment proceedings. Because civil commitment required the government to prove that the defendant presents a present danger to himself or others, and, as in this case, there had been no such allegation, the government would be forced to release the defendant if it could not restore him to competency to stand trial. Even if the defendant could be civilly committed he would have to be released as soon as he no longer presented a risk to himself or others, which might be many years before he would have been eligible for release if he had been tried and convicted. * * * We agree with the conclusion of the District of Columbia Court of Appeals that the state's interest in bringing a defendant to trial can be an 'overriding justification' for involuntary medication under *Riggins*."

JACKSON v. INDIANA

Supreme Court of the United States, 1972.

406 U.S. 715, 92 S.Ct. 1845, 32 L.Ed.2d 435.

Mr. Justice Blackmun delivered the opinion of the Court.

We are here concerned with the constitutionality of certain aspects of Indiana's system for pretrial commitment of one accused of crime.

Petitioner, Theon Jackson, is a mentally defective deaf mute with a mental level of a pre-school child. He cannot read, write, or otherwise communicate except through limited sign language. In May 1968, at age 27, he was charged in the Criminal Court of Marion County, Indiana, with separate robberies of two women. The offenses were alleged to have occurred the preceding July. The first involved property (a purse and its contents) of the value of four dollars. The second concerned five dollars in money. The record sheds no light on these charges since, upon receipt of not-guilty pleas from Jackson, the trial court set in motion the Indiana procedures for determining his competency to stand trial.

As the statute requires, the court appointed two psychiatrists to examine Jackson. A competency hearing was subsequently held at which petitioner was represented by counsel. The court received the examining doctors' joint written report and oral testimony from them and from a deaf-school interpreter through whom they had attempted to communicate with petitioner. The report concluded that Jackson's almost nonexistent communication skill, together with his lack of hearing and his mental deficiency, left him unable to understand the nature of the charges against him or to participate in his defense. One doctor testified that it was extremely unlikely that petitioner could ever learn to read or write and questioned whether petitioner even had the ability to develop any proficiency in sign language. He believed that the interpreter had not been able to communicate with petitioner to any great extent and testified that petitioner's "prognosis appears rather dim." The other doctor testified that even if Jackson were not a deaf mute, he would be incompetent to stand trial, and doubted whether petitioner had sufficient intelligence ever to develop the necessary communication skills. The interpreter testified that Indiana had no facilities that could help someone as badly off as Jackson to learn minimal communication skills.

On this evidence, the trial court found that Jackson "lack[ed] comprehension sufficient to make his defense," and ordered him committed to the Indiana Department of Mental Health until such time as that Department should certify to the court that "the defendant is sane."

Petitioner's counsel then filed a motion for a new trial, contending that there was no evidence that Jackson was "insane," or that he would ever attain a status which the court might regard as "sane" in the sense of competency to stand trial. * * * On appeal the Supreme Court of Indiana affirmed, with one judge dissenting. * * *

I. Indiana Commitment Procedures

Section 9–1706a contains both the procedural and substantive requirements for pretrial commitment of incompetent criminal defendants in Indiana. If at any time before submission of the case to the court or jury the trial judge has "reasonable ground" to believe the defendant "to be insane,"[2] he must appoint two examining physicians and

2. The section refers at several points to the defendant's "sanity." This term is nowhere defined. In con- text, and in the absence of a contrary statutory construction by the state courts, it appears that the term

schedule a competency hearing. The hearing is to the court alone, without a jury. The examining physicians' testimony and "other evidence" may be adduced on the issue of incompetency. If the court finds the defendant "has not comprehension sufficient to understand the proceedings and make his defense," trial is delayed or continued and the defendant is remanded to the state department of mental health to be confined in an "appropriate psychiatric institution." The section further provides that "[w]henever the defendant shall become sane" the superintendent of the institution shall certify that fact to the court, and the court shall order him brought on to trial. The court may also make such an order *sua sponte*. There is no statutory provision for periodic review of the defendant's condition by either the court or mental health authorities. * * *

Petitioner's central contention is that the State, in seeking in effect to commit him to a mental institution indefinitely, should have been required to invoke the standards and procedures of Ind.Ann.Stat. § 22–1907, now Ind.Code 16–15–1–3 (1971), governing commitment of "feeble-minded" persons. * * * If the judge determines that the individual is indeed "feeble-minded," he enters an order of commitment and directs the clerk of the court to apply for the person's admission "to the superintendent of the institution for feeble-minded persons located in the district in which said county is situated." A person committed under this section may be released "at any time," provided that "in the judgment of the superintendent, the mental and physical condition of the patient justifies it." The statutes do not define either "feeble-mindedness" or "insanity" as used in § 22–1907. But a statute establishing a special institution for care of such persons, refers to the duty of the State to provide care for its citizens who are "feeble-minded, and are therefore unable properly to care for themselves." These provisions evidently afford the State a vehicle for commitment of persons in need of custodial care who are "not insane" and therefore do not qualify as "mentally ill" under the State's general involuntary civil commitment scheme.

Scant attention was paid this general civil commitment law by the Indiana courts in the present case. An understanding of it, however, is essential to a full airing of the equal protection claims raised by petitioner. Section 22–1201(1) defines a "mentally ill person" as one who

> "is afflicted with a psychiatric disorder which substantially impairs his mental health; and, because of such psychiatric disorder, requires care, treatment, training or detention in the interest of the welfare of such person or the welfare of others of the community in which such person resides."

Section 22–1201(2) defines a "psychiatric disorder" to be any mental illness or disease, including any mental deficiency, epilepsy, alcoholism, or drug addiction. Other sections specify procedures for involuntary commitment of "mentally ill" persons that are substantially similar to those for commitment of the feeble-minded. * * * An individual adjudged mentally ill under these sections is remanded to the department of mental health for assignment to an appropriate institution. Discharge is in the discretion of the superintendent of the particular institution to which the person is assigned. The individual, however, remains within the court's custody, and release can therefore be revoked upon a hearing.

II. EQUAL PROTECTION

Because the evidence established little likelihood of improvement in petitioner's condition he argues that commitment under § 9–1706a in his case amounted to a commitment for life. This deprived him of equal protection, he contends, because, absent

_____

is intended to be synonymous with competence to
stand trial.

the criminal charges pending against him, the State would have had to proceed under other statutes generally applicable to all other citizens: either the commitment procedures for feeble-minded persons, or those for mentally ill persons. * * *

In *Baxstrom v. Herold,* 383 U.S. 107, 86 S.Ct. 760, 15 L.Ed.2d 620 (1966), the Court held that a state prisoner civilly committed at the end of his prison sentence on the finding of a surrogate was denied equal protection when he was deprived of a jury trial that the State made generally available to all other persons civilly committed. Rejecting the State's argument that Baxstrom's conviction and sentence constituted adequate justification for the difference in procedures, the Court said that "there is no conceivable basis for distinguishing the commitment of a person who is nearing the end of a penal term from all other civil commitments." * * *

If criminal conviction and imposition of sentence are insufficient to justify less procedural and substantive protection against indefinite commitment than that generally available to all others, the mere filing of criminal charges surely cannot suffice. * * *

Respondent argues, however, that because the record fails to establish affirmatively that Jackson will never improve, his commitment "until sane" is not really an indeterminate one. It is only temporary, pending possible change in his condition. Thus, presumably, it cannot be judged against commitments under other state statutes that are truly indeterminate. * * *

Were the State's factual premise that Jackson's commitment is only temporary a valid one, this might well be a different case. But the record does not support that premise. One of the doctors testified that in his view Jackson would be unable to acquire the substantially improved communication skills that would be necessary for him to participate in any defense. The prognosis for petitioner's developing such skills, he testified, appeared "rather dim." In answer to a question whether Jackson would ever be able to comprehend the charges or participate in his defense, even after commitment and treatment, the doctor said, "I doubt it, I don't believe so." The other psychiatrist testified that even if Jackson were able to develop such skills, he would *still* be unable to comprehend the proceedings or aid counsel due to his mental deficiency. * * * There is nothing in the record that even points to any possibility that Jackson's present condition can be remedied at any future time. * * *

We note also that neither the Indiana statute nor state practice makes the likelihood of the defendant's improvement a relevant factor. The State did not seek to make any such showing, and the record clearly establishes that the chances of Jackson's ever meeting the competency standards of § 9–1706a are at best minimal, if not nonexistent. The record also rebuts any contention that the commitment could contribute to Jackson's improvement. Jackson's § 9–1706a commitment is permanent in practical effect.

We therefore must turn to the question whether, because of the pendency of the criminal charges that triggered the State's invocation of § 9–1706a, Jackson was deprived of substantial rights to which he would have been entitled under either of the other two state commitment statutes. *Baxstrom* held that the State cannot withhold from a few the procedural protections or the substantive requirements for commitment that are available to all others. In this case commitment procedures under all three statutes appear substantially similar: notice, examination by two doctors, and a full judicial hearing at which the individual is represented by counsel and can cross-examine witnesses and introduce evidence. Under each of the three statutes, the commitment determination is made by the court alone, and appellate review is available.

In contrast, however, what the State must show to commit a defendant under § 9–1706a, and the circumstances under which an individual so committed may be released, are substantially different from the standards under the other two statutes.

Under § 9–1706a, the State needed to show only Jackson's inability to stand trial. We are unable to say that, on the record before us, Indiana could have civilly committed him as mentally ill under § 22–1209 or committed him as feeble-minded under § 22–1907. The former requires at least (1) a showing of mental illness and (2) a showing that the individual is in need of "care, treatment, training or detention." Whether Jackson's mental deficiency would meet the first test is unclear; neither examining physician addressed himself to this. Furthermore, it is problematical whether commitment for "treatment" or "training" would be appropriate since the record establishes that none is available for Jackson's condition at any state institution. The record also fails to establish that Jackson is in need of custodial care or "detention." He has been employed at times, and there is no evidence that the care he long received at home has become inadequate. The statute appears to require an independent showing of dangerousness ("requires * * * detention in the interest of the welfare of such person or * * * others * * * "). Insofar as it may require such a showing, the pending criminal charges are insufficient to establish it, and no other supporting evidence was introduced. For the same reasons, we cannot say that this record would support a feeble-mindedness commitment under § 22–1907 on the ground that Jackson is "unable properly to care for [himself]."

More important, an individual committed as feeble-minded is eligible for release when his condition "justifies it," and an individual civilly committed as mentally ill when the "superintendent or administrator shall discharge such person *or* [when] cured of such illness." Thus, in either case release is appropriate when the individual no longer requires the custodial care or treatment or detention that occasioned the commitment, or when the department of mental health believes release would be in his best interests. The evidence available concerning Jackson's past employment and home care strongly suggests that under these standards he might be eligible for release at almost any time, even if he did not improve. On the other hand, by the terms of his present § 9–1706a commitment, he will not be entitled to release at all, absent an unlikely substantial change for the better in his condition. * * *

As we noted above, we cannot conclude that pending criminal charges provide a greater justification for different treatment than conviction and sentence. Consequently, we hold that by subjecting Jackson to a more lenient commitment standard and to a more stringent standard of release than those generally applicable to all others not charged with offenses, and by thus condemning him in effect to permanent institutionalization without the showing required for commitment or the opportunity for release afforded by § 22–1209 or § 22–1907, Indiana deprived petitioner of equal protection of the laws under the Fourteenth Amendment.

III. Due Process

For reasons closely related to those discussed in Part II above, we also hold that Indiana's indefinite commitment of a criminal defendant solely on account of his incompetency to stand trial does not square with the Fourteenth Amendment's guarantee of due process.

A. *The Federal System.* In the federal criminal system, the constitutional issue posed here has not been encountered precisely because the federal statutes have been construed to require that a mentally incompetent defendant must also be found "dangerous" before he can be committed indefinitely. But the decisions have uniformly articulated the constitutional problems compelling this statutory interpretation. * * *

B. *The States*. Some States appear to commit indefinitely a defendant found incompetent to stand trial until he recovers competency. Other States require a finding of dangerousness to support such a commitment or provide forms of parole. New York has recently enacted legislation mandating release of incompetent defendants charged with misdemeanors after 90 days of commitment, and release and dismissal of charges against those accused of felonies after they have been committed for two-thirds of the maximum potential prison sentence. The practice of automatic commitment with release conditioned solely upon attainment of competence has been decried on both policy and constitutional grounds. Recommendations for changes made by commentators and study committees have included incorporation into pretrial commitment procedures of the equivalent of the federal "rule of reason," a requirement of a finding of dangerousness or of full-scale civil commitment, periodic review by court or mental health administrative personnel of the defendant's condition and progress, and provisions for ultimately dropping charges if the defendant does not improve. One source of this criticism is undoubtedly the empirical data available which tend to show that many defendants committed before trial are never tried, and that those defendants committed pursuant to ordinary civil proceedings are, on the average, released sooner than defendants automatically committed solely on account of their incapacity to stand trial. Related to these statistics are substantial doubts about whether the rationale for pretrial commitment—that care or treatment will aid the accused in attaining competency—is empirically valid given the state of most of our mental institutions. However, very few courts appear to have addressed the problem directly in the state context.

In *United States ex rel. von Wolfersdorf v. Johnston,* 317 F.Supp. 66 (S.D.N.Y.1970), an 86–year–old defendant committed for nearly 20 years as incompetent to stand trial on state murder and kidnapping charges applied for federal habeas corpus. He had been found "not dangerous," and suitable for civil commitment. The District Court granted relief. It held that petitioner's incarceration in an institution for the criminally insane constituted cruel and unusual punishment, and that the "shocking circumstances" of his commitment violated the Due Process Clause. The court quoted approvingly the language of *Cook v. Ciccone,* 312 F.Supp., at 824, concerning the "substantial injustice in keeping an unconvicted person in * * * custody to await trial where it is plainly evident his mental condition will not permit trial within a reasonable period of time."

In a 1970 case virtually indistinguishable from the one before us, the Illinois Supreme Court granted relief to an illiterate deaf mute who had been indicted for murder four years previously but found incompetent to stand trial on account of his inability to communicate, and committed. *People ex rel. Myers v. Briggs,* 46 Ill.2d 281, 263 N.E.2d 109 (1970). The institution where petitioner was confined had determined, "[I]t now appears that [petitioner] will never acquire the necessary communication skills needed to participate and cooperate in his trial." Petitioner, however, was found to be functioning at a "nearly normal level of performance in areas other than communication." The State contended petitioner should not be released until his competency was restored. The Illinois Supreme Court disagreed. It held:

> "This court is of the opinion that this defendant, handicapped as he is and facing an indefinite commitment because of the pending indictment against him, should be given an opportunity to obtain a trial to determine whether or not he is guilty as charged or should be released."

C. *This Case.* * * *

The States have traditionally exercised broad power to commit persons found to be mentally ill. The substantive limitations on the exercise of this power and the procedures for invoking it vary drastically among the States. The particular fashion in which the power is exercised—for instance, through various forms of civil commitment, defective delinquency laws, sexual psychopath laws, commitment of persons acquitted by reason of insanity—reflects different combinations of distinct bases for commitment sought to be vindicated. The bases that have been articulated include dangerousness to self, dangerousness to others, and the need for care or treatment or training. Considering the number of persons affected, it is perhaps remarkable that the substantive constitutional limitations on this power have not been more frequently litigated.

We need not address these broad questions here. It is clear that Jackson's commitment rests on proceedings that did not purport to bring into play, indeed did not even consider relevant, *any* of the articulated bases for exercise of Indiana's power of indefinite commitment. The state statutes contain at least two alternative methods for invoking this power. But Jackson was not afforded any "formal commitment proceedings addressed to [his] ability to function in society," or to society's interest in his restraint, or to the State's ability to aid him in attaining competency through custodial care of compulsory treatment, the ostensible purpose of the commitment. At the least, due process requires that the nature and duration of commitment bear some reasonable relation to the purpose for which the individual is committed.

We hold, consequently, that a person charged by a State with a criminal offense who is committed solely on account of his incapacity to proceed to trial cannot be held more than the reasonable period of time necessary to determine whether there is a substantial probability that he will attain that capacity in the foreseeable future. If it is determined that this is not the case, then the State must either institute the customary civil commitment proceeding that would be required to commit indefinitely any other citizen, or release the defendant. Furthermore, even if it is determined that the defendant probably soon will be able to stand trial, his continued commitment must be justified by progress toward that goal. In light of differing state facilities and procedures and a lack of evidence in this record, we do not think it appropriate for us to attempt to prescribe arbitrary time limits. We note, however, that petitioner Jackson has now been confined for three and one-half years on a record that sufficiently establishes the lack of a substantial probability that he will ever be able to participate fully in a trial. * * *

IV. DISPOSITION OF THE CHARGES

Petitioner also urges that fundamental fairness requires that the charges against him now be dismissed. The thrust of his argument is that the record amply establishes his lack of criminal responsibility at the time the crimes are alleged to have been committed. The Indiana court did not discuss this question. Apparently it believed that by reason of Jackson's incompetency commitment the State was entitled to hold the charges pending indefinitely. On this record, Jackson's claim is a substantial one. For a number of reasons, however, we believe the issue is not sufficiently ripe for ultimate decision by us at this time.

A. Petitioner argues that he has already made out a complete insanity defense. Jackson's criminal responsibility at the time of the alleged offenses, however, is a distinct issue from his competency to stand trial. The competency hearing below was not directed to criminal responsibility, and evidence relevant to it was presented only incidentally. Thus, in any event, we would have to remand for further consideration of Jackson's condition in the light of Indiana's law of criminal responsibility.

B. Dismissal of charges against an incompetent accused has usually been thought to be justified on grounds not squarely presented here: particularly, the Sixth–Fourteenth Amendment right to a speedy trial, or the denial of due process inherent in holding pending criminal charges indefinitely over the head of one who will never have a chance to prove his innocence. Jackson did not present the Sixth–Fourteenth Amendment issue to the state courts. Nor did the highest state court rule on the due process issue, if indeed it was presented to that court in precisely the above-described form. We think, in light of our holdings in Parts II and III, that the Indiana courts should have the first opportunity to determine these issues.

C. Both courts and commentators have noted the desirability of permitting some proceedings to go forward despite the defendant's incompetency. For instance, § 4.06(3) of the Model Penal Code would permit an incompetent accused's attorney to contest any issue "susceptible of fair determination prior to trial and without the personal participation of the defendant." An alternative draft of § 4.06(4) of the Model Penal Code would also permit an evidentiary hearing at which certain defenses, not including lack of criminal responsibility, could be raised by defense counsel on the basis of which the court might quash the indictment. Some States have statutory provisions permitting pretrial motions to be made or even allowing the incompetent defendant a trial at which to establish his innocence, without permitting a conviction. We do not read this Court's previous decisions to preclude the States from allowing at a minimum, an incompetent defendant to raise certain defenses such as insufficiency of the indictment, or make certain pretrial motions through counsel. Of course, if the Indiana courts conclude that Jackson was almost certainly not capable of criminal responsibility when the offenses were committed, dismissal of the charges might be warranted. But even if this is not the case, Jackson may have other good defenses that could sustain dismissal or acquittal and that might now be asserted. We do not know if Indiana would approve procedures such as those mentioned here, but these possibilities will be open on remand.

Reversed and remanded

Notes and Questions

1. "A review of legislation in the fifty states and the District of Columbia reveals that *Jackson* has been ignored or circumvented in a majority of jurisdictions. In California, for example, the legislature enacted a special conservatorship statute to permit civil commitment of permanently incompetent criminal defendants using different criteria than is used for other civilly committed patients. The California Supreme Court upheld the validity of that statute but imposed a requirement of proof beyond a reasonable doubt that the incompetent defendant presents a substantial danger of physical harm to others.

"An empirical study of patients in one of California's state mental hospitals led us to conclude that a majority of permanently incompetent criminal defendants confined there were not proven beyond a reasonable doubt to be dangerous either at the time the special conservatorship was established or at the time it was most recently renewed. In practice, the burden is often reversed—permanently incompetent criminal defendants must prove beyond a reasonable doubt that they are not dangerous. In some cases, defendants who have not acted violently for years are found to be dangerous simply because they exhibit symptoms of mental disorder. In essence, because they are out of their minds, they are kept out of sight.

"The alternative is simple; the alternative is *Jackson*. *Jackson* is not optional; it is the law. The Supreme Court interprets the Constitution for all fifty states, not just for some. Twenty-two states have accepted *Jackson* and accommodate permanently incompetent criminal defendants within their customary civil commitment process. The rest can—and must—do so. Permanently incompetent criminal defendants are not a special class to be separately categorized for commitment purposes. In truth, a decision to subject them to different commitment procedures and criteria inflicts punishment without a finding of guilt." Grant H. Morris & J. Reid Meloy, *Out of Mind? Out of Sight: The Uncivil Commitment of Permanently Incompetent Criminal Defendants*, 27 U.C.Davis L.Rev. 1, 77–78 (1993).

2. *United States v. DeBellis,* 649 F.2d 1 (1st Cir.1981), concludes: "No case that we have found has presented a factual setting in which commitment for competency determination alone has exceeded the maximum possible sentence, and we think our holding that it may not do so merely represents an inevitable application of the [*Jackson*] reasonableness limitation to that setting. Every court to have considered this specific question in dictum has reached the same conclusion."

3. Robert A. Burt & Norval Morris, *A Proposal for the Abolition of the Incompetency Plea,* 40 U.Chi.L.Rev. 66, 67 (1972): "States will likely be tempted, in the wake of *Jackson,* to resort to civil commitment proceedings rather than dismiss charges against and release permanently incompetent defendants. It is the thesis of this article, however, that the interests of both permanently incompetent defendants and the states would be better served by abandonment of the traditional rule against trying incompetent defendants. Incompetency should instead be grounds for obtaining a trial continuance during which the state must provide resources to assist the defendant toward greater trial competence. If trial competence is not achieved within six months, the state should be required to dismiss charges or proceed to a trial governed, where necessary, by procedures designed to compensate for the incompetent defendant's trial disabilities."

As for the compensating procedures, they suggest at 94–95: "(a) Prior to trial, the court shall review all the evidence that the prosecution intends to offer at trial and shall order pretrial disclosure of evidence that would materially assist the defendant in overcoming the disabilities under which he labors. Disclosure of evidence that may endanger the lives of witnesses, or in any way promote substantial injustice, shall not be ordered;

"(b) On motion for directed verdict, either before or after jury deliberation, the court shall demand from the prosecution a higher burden of proof than would obtain in an ordinary criminal prosecution, and the court shall insist on extensive corroboration of the prosecution's case with respect to issues on which the defendant is likely to be prevented by his disability from effective rebuttal;

"(c) If the trial is before a jury, the court shall instruct the jury that in weighing the evidence against the defendant, it should take into account, in the defendant's favor, the disabilities under which he went to trial. If trial is before the judge sitting alone, he shall take account of those disabilities."

4. Or, is the solution simply to allow the incompetent defendant to waive his *Robinson–Drope* rights, as proposed in Bruce J. Winick, *Restructuring Competency to Stand Trial,* 32 U.C.L.A.L.Rev. 921, 967–69 (1985): "A presumption should apply in favor of accepting the defendant's choice to stand trial or to plead guilty, if clearly expressed, notwithstanding his mental impairment, particularly when defense counsel concurs in his choice. Counsel's concurrence presumably eliminates instances in which the defendant's choice is based on irrelevant reasons ('I will plead guilty because I am an insect'), irrational beliefs ('I will stand trial and thereby become a movie star'), or outright delusions ('I am an extraterrestrial and will return to my planet'). Moreover, the concurrence of the defendant's attorney in his decision to stand trial or plead is strong evidence that the

risk/benefit ratio of his choice is acceptable compared to an adjudication of incompetency (*i.e.,* that the defendant's decision is not an unreasonable one). * * *

" * * * *Pate* does not hold that a defendant may not waive the right to be tried while incompetent, or that he may not waive the procedural due process right to a formal determination of competency."

5. Or, is it a matter of redefining incompetency in that context? Consider Christopher Slobogin & Amy Mashburn, *The Criminal Defense Lawyer's Fiduciary Duty to Clients With Mental Disability*, 68 Fordham L.Rev. 1581, 1641 (2000): "Suppose a person is unrestorably incompetent to make a decision about waiving the insanity defense, but is competent in the assistance sense. Because such an individual understands the trial process and can communicate relevant facts to the attorney, neither dignity interests nor reliability would be undermined by pursuing adjudication. Less obviously, even the autonomy preference would not be slighted by proceeding to trial. Unlike a policy which permits decisions to be made for the incompetent client who has not yet been treated (which this Article rejects), surrogate decision-making in this situation occurs only after society has made a good faith effort to restore the individual's decision-making capacity. In other words, autonomy has been given its due.

"When a client's decisional competence is not restorable, then, defense attorneys should act as the ultimate fiduciary, and be authorized to act as guardian. If the lawyer representing such a client believes a guilty plea is preferable to trial, the plea should be made and the court should accept it, regardless of the client's wishes. If instead the lawyer believes an insanity defense is the best defense after a sensitive appraisal of the counter-vailing factors described earlier, it should be raised, again regardless of the client's wishes. And presumably no waiver of counsel should ever be granted to such a client."

6. Incompetency to stand trial must be distinguished from incompetency to be executed, addressed in *Ford v. Wainwright*, 477 U.S. 399, 106 S.Ct. 2595, 91 L.Ed.2d 335 (1986): "Today, no State in the Union permits the execution of the insane. It is clear that the ancient and humane limitation upon the State's ability to execute its sentences has as firm a hold upon the jurisprudence of today as it had centuries ago in England. The various reasons put forth in support of the common-law restriction have no less logical, moral, and practical force than they did when first voiced. For today, no less than before, we may seriously question the retributive value of executing a person who has no comprehension of why he has been singled out and stripped of his fundamental right to life. See Note, *The Eighth Amendment and the Execution of the Presently Incompetent*, 32 Stan.L.Rev. 765, 777, n. 58 (1980). Similarly, the natural abhorrence civilized societies feel at killing one who has no capacity to come to grips with his own conscience or deity is still vivid today. And the intuition that such an execution simply offends humanity is evidently shared across this Nation. Faced with such widespread evidence of a restriction upon sovereign power, this Court is compelled to conclude that the Eighth Amendment prohibits a State from carrying out a sentence of death upon a prisoner who is insane. Whether its aim be to protect the condemned from fear and pain without comfort of understanding, or to protect the dignity of society itself from the barbarity of exacting mindless vengeance, the restriction finds enforcement in the Eighth Amendment."

In *Penry v. Lynaugh*, 492 U.S. 302, 109 S.Ct. 2934, 106 L.Ed.2d 256 (1989), *Ford* was deemed to cover one "unaware of the punishment they are about to suffer and why they are to suffer it," which was not the case as to the prisoner being considered, a mentally retarded person with the reasoning capacity of a 7–year-old child. As to him, the Court concluded "there is insufficient evidence of a national consensus against executing mentally retarded people convicted of capital offenses for us to conclude that it is categorically prohibited by the Eighth Amendment."

SECTION 2. TESTS FOR THE INSANITY "DEFENSE"

Introductory Notes

1. Although it is customary to speak of the insanity "defense," the actual consequence of a successful insanity defense is quite different than with respect to any other defense. In every other case, a successful defense results in acquittal and outright release of the defendant, but with the insanity defense the probable result is commitment of the defendant to a mental institution until he has recovered his sanity. Acceptance of the defendant's insanity defense is specially noted by a jury verdict (or, in a trial without jury, a judge's finding) of "not guilty by reason of insanity," after which he will (in some jurisdictions) be automatically committed or (in others) be subjected to proceedings which are most likely to result in commitment.

2. It is thus apparent that the insanity defense serves a unique purpose. Few efforts to articulate that purpose have been made, although the general assumption seems to be that the defense makes it possible to separate out for special treatment certain persons who would otherwise be subjected to the usual penal sanctions which may follow conviction: "The problem is the drawing of a line between the use of public agencies and force (1) to condemn the offender by conviction, with resulting sanctions in which the ingredient of reprobation is present no matter how constructive one may seek to make the sentence and the process of correction, and (2) modes of disposition in which the condemnatory element is absent, even though restraint may be involved. * * * Stating the matter differently, the problem is to etch a decent working line between the areas assigned to the authorities responsible for public health and those responsible for the correction of offenders."[a]

3. In examining the following materials, assess the relative merits of the following alternatives:

(a) adoption of the "right-wrong" or *M'Naghten* test (currently used in a majority of the states), set out in *Daniel M'Naghten's Case,* infra;

(b) adoption of *M'Naghten* with the unfortunately labeled "irresistible impulse" test (currently used in a very few of the jurisdictions following *M'Naghten*), discussed in *Parsons v. State,* infra;

(c) adoption of the "product" or *Durham* test, used in the District of Columbia until abandoned in *United States v. Brawner,* infra;

(d) adoption of the Model Penal Code "substantial capacity" test (currently used in a minority of the states), discussed in *Brawner,* infra;

(e) adoption of the "justice" approach of Judge Bazelon, dissenting in *Brawner,* infra; or

---

a. *Model Penal Code* § 4.01, Comment (1985).

Another view, however, is that the "real function" of the insanity defense "is to authorize the state to hold those 'who must be found not to possess the guilty mind *mens rea,*' even though the criminal law demands that no person be held criminally responsible if doubt is cast on any material element of the offense charged." Joseph Goldstein & Jay Katz, *Abolish the "Insanity Defense"—Why Not?,* 72 Yale L.J. 853, 864 (1963). That is, the defense is seen as a device whereby certain persons are singled out for commitment, not as an alternative to conviction and imprisonment, but rather as an alternative to outright acquittal. This characterization takes on greater force in those jurisdictions where, as discussed in Section 4 of this Chapter, the courts have declined to admit evidence of mental disease on the issue of whether the defendant had the mental state required for commission of the crime charged.

(f) abolition of the insanity defense, discussed in *Brawner,* infra.

DANIEL M'NAGHTEN'S CASE

House of Lords, 1843.

8 Eng.Rep. 718, 10 Cl. & Fin. 200.

[Daniel M'Naghten shot and killed Edward Drummond, private secretary to Sir Robert Peel. M'Naghten, believing that Peel was heading a conspiracy to kill him, had intended to take Peel's life, but he instead shot Drummond because he mistakenly believed him to be Peel. At the trial of his case, M'Naghten claimed that he was insane and could not be held responsible because it had been his delusions which caused him to act. The jury agreed, and M'Naghten was found not guilty by reason of insanity. Due to the importance of both the victim and the intended victim, the decision was not a popular one. The House of Lords debated the decision and posed five questions concerning the standards for acquitting a defendant due to his insanity to the justices of the Queen's Bench. The answers to these questions were appended to the report of the original case, and have come to be considered as if they were a part of that decision.]

Lord Chief Justice Tindal: * * *

The first question proposed by your Lordships is this: "What is the law respecting alleged crimes committed by persons afflicted with insane delusion in respect of one or more particular subjects or persons: as, for instance, where at the time of the commission of the alleged crime the accused knew he was acting contrary to law, but did the act complained of with a view, under the influence of insane delusion, of redressing or revenging some supposed grievance or injury, or of producing some supposed public benefit?"

In answer to which question, assuming that your Lordships' inquiries are confined to those persons who labour under such partial delusions only, and are not in other respects insane, we are of opinion that, notwithstanding the party accused did the act complained of with a view, under the influence of insane delusion, of redressing or revenging some supposed grievance or injury, or of producing some public benefit, he is nevertheless punishable according to the nature of the crime committed, if he knew at the time of committing such crime that he was acting contrary to law; by which expression we understand your Lordships to mean the law of the land.

Your Lordships are pleased to inquire of us, secondly, "What are the proper questions to be submitted to the jury, where a person alleged to be afflicted with insane delusion respecting one or more particular subjects or persons, is charged with the commission of a crime (murder, for example), and insanity is set up as a defence?" And, thirdly, "In what terms ought the question to be left to the jury as to the prisoner's state of mind at the time when the act was committed?" And as these two questions appear to us to be more conveniently answered together, we have to submit our opinion to be, that the jurors ought to be told in all cases that every man is to be presumed to be sane, and to possess a sufficient degree of reason to be responsible for his crimes, until the contrary be proved to their satisfaction; and that to establish a defence on the ground of insanity, it must be clearly proved that, at the time of the committing of the act, the party accused was labouring under such a defect of reason, from disease of the mind, as not to know the nature and quality of the act he was doing; or, if he did know it, that he did not know he was doing what was wrong. The mode of putting the latter part of the question to the jury on these occasions has generally been, whether the accused at the time of doing the act knew the difference between right and wrong: which mode, though rarely, if ever, leading to any mistake with the jury, is not, as we conceive, so accurate when put generally and in the abstract, as when put with reference to the party's knowledge of right and wrong in respect to the very act with which he is charged. If the question were to be put as to the knowledge of the accused solely and exclusively with reference to the law of the land, it might tend to confound the jury, by inducing them to believe that an actual knowledge of the law of the land was essential in order to lead to a conviction; whereas the law is administered upon the principle that every one must be taken conclusively to know it, without proof that he does know it. If the accused was conscious that the act was one which he ought not to do, and if that act was at the same time contrary to the law of the land, he is punishable; and the usual course therefore has been to leave the question to the jury, whether the party accused had a sufficient degree of reason to know that he was doing an act that was wrong: and this course we think is correct, accompanied with such observations and explanations as the circumstances of each particular case may require.

The fourth question which your Lordships have proposed to us is this:—"If a person under an insane delusion as to existing facts, commits an offence in consequence thereof, is he thereby excused?" To which question the answer must of course depend on the nature of the delusion: but, making the same assumption as we did before, namely, that he labours under such partial delusion only, and is not in other respects insane, we think he must be considered in the same situation as to responsibility as if the facts with respect to which the delusion exists were real. For example, if under the influence of his delusion he supposes another man to be in the act of attempting to take away his life, and he kills that man, as he supposes, in self-defense, he would be exempt from punishment. If his delusion was that the deceased had inflicted a serious injury to his character and fortune, and he killed him in revenge for such supposed injury, he would be liable to punishment.

The question lastly proposed by your Lordships is:—"Can a medical man conversant with the disease of insanity, who never saw the prisoner previously to the trial, but who was present during the whole trial and the examination of all the witnesses, be asked his opinion as to the state of the prisoner's mind at the time of the commission of the alleged crime, or his opinion whether the prisoner was conscious at the time of doing the act that he was acting contrary to law, or whether he was labouring under any and what delusion at the time?" In answer thereto, we state to your Lordships, that we think the medical man, under the circumstances supposed, cannot in strictness be asked his opinion in the terms above stated, because each of those questions involves the determination of the truth of the facts deposed to, which it is for the jury to decide, and the questions are not mere questions upon a matter of science, in which case such evidence is admissible. But where the facts are admitted or not disputed, and the question becomes substantially one of science only, it may be convenient to allow the question to be put in that general form, though the same cannot be insisted on as a matter of right.

Notes and Questions

1. In *State v. Coombs*, 18 Ohio St.3d 123, 480 N.E.2d 414 (1985), the trial court in a nonjury trial asked defendant's expert witness whether the defendant's disorder could be characterized as either a psychosis or a neurosis. The doctor answered in the negative. At the conclusion of the trial, the judge said a *M'Naghten*-type insanity defense had not been established, adding that the "defendant, whatever his emotional problems are, and were on that night, does not have a psychosis or even a neurosis by the testimony of his own expert witness." The supreme court responded that the "law of this state does not require such a showing," but concluded the trial judge had not actually utilized such a limited standard.

2. In *People v. Skinner*, 39 Cal.3d 765, 217 Cal.Rptr. 685, 704 P.2d 752 (1985), the court held that where the defendant murdered his wife believing that the marriage view

"till death do us part" bestowed on a marital partner a God-given right to kill the other partner if he or she was inclined to violate the marital vows, he could not distinguish right from wrong under the *M'Naghten* test: "Courts in a number of jurisdictions which have considered the question have come to the conclusion as we do, that a defendant who is incapable of understanding that his act is morally wrong is not criminally liable merely because he knows the act is unlawful. Justice Cardozo, in an opinion for the New York Court of Appeal, eloquently expressed the underlying philosophy: 'In the light of all these precedents, it is impossible, we think, to say that there is any decisive adjudication which limits the word "wrong" in the statutory definition to legal as opposed to moral wrong * * *. The interpretation placed upon the statute by the trial judge may be tested by its consequences. A mother kills her infant child to whom she has been devotedly attached. She knows the nature and quality of the act; she knows that the law condemns it; but she is inspired by an insane delusion that God has appeared to her and ordained the sacrifice. *It seems a mockery to say that, within the meaning of the statute, she knows that the act is wrong.* If the definition propounded by the trial judge is right, it would be the duty of a jury to hold her responsible for the crime. We find nothing either in the history of the rule, or in its reason or purpose, or in judicial exposition of its meaning, to justify a conclusion so abhorrent * * *. [¶] Knowledge that an act is forbidden by law will in most cases permit the inference of knowledge that, according to the accepted standards of mankind, it is also condemned as an offense against good morals. Obedience to the law is itself a moral duty. If, however, there is an insane delusion that God has appeared to the defendant and ordained the commission of a crime, we think it cannot be said of the offender that he knows the act to be wrong.' (*People v. Schmidt* (1915) 216 N.Y. 324, 338–340 [110 N.E. 945, 949–950], emphasis added.)[16]"

3. Compare *State v. Boan*, 235 Kan. 800, 686 P.2d 160 (1984), also a murder case, where defendant's experts testified that Boan had a feeling of being God or a representative of God, who was present at the Last Supper, and that he believed other persons were in his body trying to displace him, requiring him to defend himself in the fashion he did from "salvation level attacks." They said defendant was aware of the laws of the state and that it was wrong to shoot someone, but that because of his "religious delusion" he "modified the definition of what was right, according to his belief that he, as God, made the rights." In affirming Boan's murder conviction, the court upheld this instruction: "Right and wrong are used here in their legal sense, not the social or moral sense. 'Wrong' means that which is prohibited by law."

4. A seminal case adding the so-called "irresistible impulse" test to *M'Naghten* (as some jurisdictions have done) is *Parsons v. State*, 81 Ala. 577, 2 So. 854 (1887):

"We first consider what is *the proper legal rule of responsibility in criminal cases.* No one can deny that there must be two constituent elements of legal responsibility in the commission of every crime, and no rule can be just and reasonable which fails to recognize either of them: (1) Capacity of intellectual discrimination; and (2) freedom of will. Mr. Wharton, after recognizing this fundamental and obvious principle, observes: 'If there be either incapacity to distinguish between right and wrong as to the particular act, or

---

16. Justice Cardozo's opinion continued: "It is not enough, to relieve from criminal liability, that the prisoner is morally depraved [citation]. It is not enough that he has views of right and wrong at variance with those that find expression in the law. The variance must have its origin in some disease of the mind [citation]. The anarchist is not at liberty to break the law because he reasons that all government is wrong. The devotee of a religious cult that enjoins polygamy or human sacrifice as a duty is not thereby relieved from responsibility before the law [citations]. In such cases the belief, however false according to our own standards, is not the product of disease. Cases will doubtless arise where criminals will take shelter behind a professed belief that their crime was ordained by God, just as this defendant attempted to shelter himself behind that belief. We can safely leave such fabrications to the common sense of juries."

delusion as to the act, or inability to refrain from doing the act, there is no responsibility.' I Whart. *Crim.Law* (9th Ed.) § 33. Says Mr. Bishop, in discussing this subject: 'There cannot be, and there is not, in any locality, or age, a law punishing men for what they cannot avoid.' 1 Bish. *Crim.Law* (7th Ed.) § *383b.* If therefore, it be true, as matter of fact, that the disease of insanity can, in its action on the human brain through a shattered nervous organization, or in any other mode, so affect the mind as to subvert the freedom of the will, and thereby destroy the power of the victim *to choose* between the right and wrong, although he perceive it,—by which we mean the power of volition to adhere in action to the right and abstain from the wrong—is such a one criminally responsible for an act done under the influence of such controlling disease? We clearly think not, and such we believe to be the just, reasonable, and humane rule, towards which all the modern authorities in this country, legislation in England, and the laws of other civilized countries of the world, are gradually but surely tending, as we shall further on attempt more fully to show. * * *

"In the present state of our law, under the rule in *McNaghten's Case,* we are confronted with this practical difficulty, which itself demonstrates the defects of the rule. The courts, in effect charge the juries, as matter of law, that no such mental disease exists, as that often testified to by medical writers, superintendents of insane hospitals, and other experts; that there can be, as matter of scientific fact, no cerebral defect, congenital or acquired, which destroys the patient's power of self control,—his liberty of will and action,—provided only he retains a mental consciousness of right and wrong. The experts are immediately put under oath, and tell the juries just the contrary, as matter of evidence; asserting that no one of ordinary intelligence can spend an hour in the wards of an insane asylum without discovering such cases, and in fact that 'the whole management of such asylums presupposes a knowledge of right and wrong on the part of their inmates.' * * *

"In the learned treatise of Drs. Bucknill and Tuke on *Psychological Medicine,* 269, (4th Ed., London, 1879), the legal tests of responsibility are discussed, and the adherence of the courts to the right and wrong test is deplored as unfortunate, the true principle being stated to be 'whether, in consequence of congenital defect or acquired disease, *the power of self-control* is absent altogether, or is so far wanting as to render the individual irresponsible.' * * *

"It is no satisfactory objection to say that the rule above announced by us is of difficult application. The rule in *McNaghten's Case* is equally obnoxious to a like criticism. The difficulty does not lie in the rule, but is inherent in the subject of insanity itself. * * * We think we can safely rely in this matter upon the intelligence of our juries, guided by the testimony of men who have practically made a study of the disease of insanity; and enlightened by a conscientious desire, on the one hand, to enforce the criminal laws of the land, and, on the other, not to deal harshly with any unfortunate victim of a diseased mind, acting without the light of reason or the power of volition. * * *

"In conclusion of this branch of the subject, that we may not be misunderstood, we think it follows very clearly from what we have said that the inquiries to be submitted to the jury, then, in every criminal trial where the defense of insanity is interposed, are these: *First.* Was the defendant at the time of the commission of the alleged crime, as matter of fact, afflicted with a *disease of the mind,* so as to be either idiotic, or otherwise insane? *Second.* If such be the case, did he know right from wrong as applied to the particular act in question? If he did not have such knowledge, he is not legally responsible. *Third.* If he did have such knowledge, he may nevertheless not be legally responsible if the two following conditions concur: (1) If, by reason of the duress of such mental disease, he had so far lost the *power to choose* between the right and wrong, and to avoid doing the act in question, as that his free agency was at the time destroyed; (2) and if, at the same time, the alleged crime was so connected with such mental disease, in the relation of cause and effect, as to have been the product of it *solely*."

UNITED STATES v. BRAWNER

United States Court of Appeals, District of Columbia Circuit, 1972.

471 F.2d 969.

LEVENTHAL, CIRCUIT JUDGE:

The principal issues raised on this appeal from a conviction for second degree murder and carrying a dangerous weapon relate to appellant's defense of insanity. After the case was argued to a division of the court, the court *sua sponte* ordered rehearing en banc * * * to reconsider the appropriate standard for the insanity defense * * *.

We have stretched our canvas wide; and the focal point of the landscape before us is the formulation of the American Law Institute. The ALI's primary provision is stated thus in its Model Penal Code, see § 4.01(1).

Section 4.01 Mental Disease or Defect Excluding Responsibility.

(1) A person is not responsible for criminal conduct if at the time of such conduct as a result of mental disease or defect he lacks substantial capacity either to appreciate the criminality [wrongfulness] of his conduct or to conform his conduct to the requirements of the law.

We have decided to adopt the ALI rule as the doctrine excluding responsibility for mental disease or defect, for application prospectively to trials begun after this date. * * *

B. PRIOR DEVELOPMENTS OF THE INSANITY DEFENSE IN THIS JURISDICTION * * *

1. The landmark opinion was written by Judge Bazelon in *Durham v. United States,* 94 U.S.App.D.C. 228, 214 F.2d 862 (1954). Prior to *Durham* the law of the District of Columbia * * * stated a traditional test of insanity, in terms of right and wrong and irresistible impulse. *Durham* adopted the "product rule," pioneered in *State v. Pike,* 49 N.H. 399, 402 (1869–70), and exculpated from criminal responsibility those whose forbidden acts were the product of a mental disease or defect.

Few cases have evoked as much comment as *Durham*. It has sparked widespread interest in the legal-judicial community and focused attention on the profound problems involved in defining legal responsibility in case of mental illness. It has been hailed as a guide to the difficult and problem-laden intersection of law and psychiatry, ethics and science. It has been scored as an unwarranted loophole through which the cunning criminal might escape from the penalty of the law. We view it more modestly, as the court's effort, designed in the immemorial manner of the case method that has built the common law, to alleviate two serious problems with the previous rule.

The first of these was a problem of language which raised an important symbolic issue in the law. We felt that the language of the old right-wrong/irresistible impulse rule for insanity was antiquated, no longer reflecting the community's judgment as to who ought to be held criminally liable for socially destructive acts. We considered the rule as restated to have more fruitful, accurate and considered reflection of the sensibilities of the community as revised and expanded in the light of continued study of abnormal human behavior.

The second vexing problem that *Durham* was designed to reach related to the concern of the psychiatrists called as expert witnesses for their special knowledge of the problem of insanity, who often and typically felt that they were obliged to reach outside of their professional expertise when they were asked, under the traditional insanity rule established in 1843 by *M'Naghten's* Case, whether the defendant knew right from wrong. They further felt that the narrowness of the traditional test, which framed the issue of responsibility solely in terms of cognitive impairment, made it impossible to convey to the judge and jury the full range of information material to an assessment of defendant's responsibility.

2. Discerning scholarship now available asserts that the experts' fears and concerns reflected a misapprehension as to the impact of the traditional standard in terms of excluding relevant evidence.

> Wigmore states the rule to be that when insanity is in issue, "any and all conduct of the person is admissible in evidence." And the cases support Wigmore's view. The almost unvarying policy of the courts has been to admit *any* evidence of aberrational behavior so long as it is probative of the defendant's mental condition, without regard to the supposed restrictions of the test used to define insanity for the jury.[5]

Moreover if the term "know" in the traditional test of "know right from wrong" is taken as denoting affective knowledge, rather than merely cognitive knowledge, it yields a rule of greater flexibility than was widely supposed to exist. Livermore and Meehl, *The Virtues of M'Naghten,* 51 Minn.L.Rev. 789, 800–08 (1967).

We need not occupy ourselves here and now with the question whether, and to what extent, the *M'Naghten* rule, ameliorated by the irresistible impulse doctrine, is susceptible of application to include medical insights and information as justice requires. In any event, the experts felt hemmed in by the traditional test; they felt that they could not give the jury and judge the necessary information in response to the questions which the traditional test posed.

The rule as reformulated in *Durham* permitted medical experts to testify on medical matters properly put before the jury for its consideration, and to do so without the confusion that many, perhaps most, experts experienced from testimony structured under the *M'Naghten* rule. That was a positive contribution to jurisprudence—and one that was retained when the American Law Institute undertook to analyze the problem and proposed a different formulation.

3. A difficulty arose under the *Durham* rule in application [because] the court failed to explicate what abnormality of mind was an essential ingredient of these concepts. In the absence of a definition of "mental disease or defect," medical experts attached to them the meanings which would naturally occur to them—medical meanings—and gave testimony accordingly. The problem was dramatically highlighted by the weekend flip flop case, *In re Rosenfield,* 157 F.Supp. 18 (D.D.C.1957). The petitioner was described as a sociopath. A St. Elizabeths psychiatrist testified that a person with a sociopathic personality was not suffering from a mental disease. That was Friday afternoon. On Monday morning, through a policy change at St. Elizabeths Hospital, it was determined as an administrative matter that the state of a psychopathic or sociopathic personality did constitute a mental disease.

The concern that medical terminology not control legal outcomes culminated in *McDonald v. United States,* 114 U.S.App.D.C. 120, 312 F.2d 847, 851 (en banc, 1962), where this court recognized that the term, mental disease or defect, has various meanings, depending upon how and why it is used, and by whom. Mental disease means one thing to a physician bent on treatment, but something different, if somewhat overlapping, to a court of law. We provided a legal definition of mental disease or defect, and held that it included "any abnormal condition of the mind which substantially affects mental or

---

5.   A. Goldstein, *The Insanity Defense* 54 (1967).

emotional processes and substantially impairs behavior controls." "Thus the jury would consider testimony concerning the development, adaptation and functioning of these processes and controls."

While the *McDonald* standard of mental disease was not without an attribute of circularity, it was useful in the administration of justice because it made plain that clinical and legal definitions of mental disease were distinct, and it helped the jury to sort out its complex task and to focus on the matters given it to decide.

4. The *Durham* rule also required explication along other lines, notably the resolution of the ambiguity inherent in the formulation concerning actions that were the "product" of mental illness. It was supplemented in *Carter v. United States,* 102 U.S.App. D.C. 227 at 234, 235, 252 F.2d 608 at 615–616 (1957):

> The simple fact that a person has a mental disease or defect is not enough to relieve him of responsibility for a crime. There must be a relationship between the disease and the criminal act; and the relationship must be such as to justify a reasonable inference that the act would not have been committed if the person had not been suffering from the disease.

Thus *Carter* clarified that the mental illness must not merely have entered into the production of the act, but must have played a necessary role. *Carter* identified the "product" element of the rule with the "but for" variety of causation.

The pivotal "product" term continued to present problems, principally that it put expert testimony on a faulty footing. Assuming that a mental disease, in the legal sense, had been established, the fate of the defendant came to be determined by what came to be referred to by the legal jargon of "productivity." On the other hand, it was obviously sensible if not imperative that the experts having pertinent knowledge should speak to the crucial question whether the mental abnormality involved is one associated with aberrant behavior. But since "productivity" was so decisive a factor in the decisional equation, a ruling permitting experts to testify expressly in language of "product" raised in a different context the concern lest the ultimate issue be in fact turned over to the experts rather than retained for the jurors representing the community. * * *

It was in this context that the court came to the decision in *Washington v. United States,* 129 U.S.App.D.C. 29, 390 F.2d 444 (1967), which forbade experts from testifying as to productivity altogether. Chief Judge Bazelon's opinion illuminates the basis of the ruling, as one intended "to help the psychiatrists understand their role in court, and thus eliminate a fundamental cause of unsatisfactory expert testimony," namely, the tendency of the expert to use "concepts [which] can become slogans, hiding facts and representing nothing more than the witness's own conclusion about the defendant's criminal responsibility." * * *

C.   INSANITY RULE IN OTHER CIRCUITS * * *

The core rule of the ALI has been adopted, with variations, by all save one of the Federal circuit courts of appeals, and by all that have come to reconsider the doctrine providing exculpation for mental illness. * * *

D.   COMMENTS CONCERNING REASON FOR ADOPTION OF ALI RULE AND SCOPE OF RULE AS ADOPTED BY THIS COURT * * *

1. Need to depart from "product" formulation and undue dominance by experts.

A principal reason for our decision to depart from the *Durham* rule is the undesirable characteristic, surviving even the *McDonald* modification, of undue dominance by the experts giving testimony. * * *

The expert witnesses—psychiatrists and psychologists—are called to adduce relevant information concerning what may for convenience be referred to as the "medical" component of the responsibility issue. But the difficulty—as emphasized in *Washington*—is that the medical expert comes, by testimony given in terms of a non-medical construct ("product"), to express conclusions that in essence embody ethical and legal conclusions. There is, indeed, irony in a situation under which the *Durham* rule, which was adopted in large part to permit experts to testify in their own terms concerning matters within their domain which the jury should know, resulted in testimony by the experts in terms not their own to reflect unexpressed judgments in a domain that is properly not theirs but the jury's. The irony is heightened when the jurymen, instructed under the esoteric "product" standard, are influenced significantly by "product" testimony of expert witnesses really reflecting ethical and legal judgments rather than a conclusion within the witnesses' particular expertise.

It is easier to identify and spotlight the irony than to eradicate the mischief. The objective of *Durham* is still sound—to put before the jury the information that is within the expert's domain, to aid the jury in making a broad and comprehensive judgment. But when the instructions and appellate decisions define the "product" inquiry as the ultimate issue, it is like stopping the tides to try to halt the emergence of this term in the language of those with a central role in the trial—the lawyers who naturally seek to present testimony that will influence the jury who will be charged under the ultimate "product" standard, and the expert witnesses who have an awareness, gained from forensic psychiatry and related disciplines, of the ultimate "product" standard that dominates the proceeding.

The experts have meaningful information to impart, not only on the existence of mental illness or not, but also on its relationship to the incident charged as an offense. In the interest of justice this valued information should be available, and should not be lost or blocked by requirements that unnaturally restrict communication between the experts and the jury. The more we have pondered the problem the more convinced we have become that the sound solution lies not in further shaping of the *Durham* "product" approach in more refined molds, but in adopting the ALI's formulation as the linchpin of our jurisprudence.

The ALI's formulation retains the core requirement of a meaningful relationship between the mental illness and the incident charged. The language in the ALI rule is sufficiently in the common ken that its use in the courtroom, or in preparation for trial, permits a reasonable three-way communication—between (a) the law-trained, judges and lawyers; (b) the experts and (c) the jurymen—without insisting on a vocabulary that is either stilted or stultified, or conducive to a testimonial mystique permitting expert dominance and encroachment on the jury's function. There is no indication in the available literature that any such untoward development has attended the reasonably widespread adoption of the ALI rule in the Federal courts and a substantial number of state courts.

2. Retention of McDonald definition of "mental disease or defect."

Our ruling today includes our decision that in the ALI rule as adopted by this court the term "mental disease or defect" includes the definition of that term provided in our 1962 en banc *McDonald* opinion, as follows:

> [A] mental disease or defect includes any abnormal condition of the mind which substantially affects mental or emotional processes and substantially impairs behavior controls. * * *

The *McDonald* rule has helped accomplish the objective of securing expert testimony needed on the subject of mental illness, while guarding against the undue dominance of expert testimony or specialized labels. It has thus permitted the kind of communication without encroachment, as between experts and juries, that has prompted us to adopt the ALI rule, and hence will help us realize our objective. This advantage overrides the surface disadvantage of any clumsiness in the blending of the *McDonald* component, defining mental disease, with the rest of the ALI rule, a matter we discuss further below. * * *

4. Consideration and rejection of other suggestions.

a. Proposal to abolish insanity defense.

A number of proposals in the journals recommend that the insanity defense be abolished altogether. * * *

This proposal has been put forward by responsible judges for consideration, with the objective of reserving psychiatric overview for the phase of the criminal process concerned with disposition of the person determined to have been the actor. However, we are convinced that the proposal cannot properly be imposed by judicial fiat.

The courts have emphasized over the centuries that "free will" is the postulate of responsibility under our jurisprudence. 4 Blackstone's *Commentaries* 27. The concept of "belief in freedom of the human will and a consequent ability and duty of the normal individual to choose between good and evil" is a core concept that is "universal and persistent in mature systems of law." *Morissette v. United States,* 342 U.S. 246, 250, 72 S.Ct. 240, 243, 96 L.Ed. 288 (1952). Criminal responsibility is assessed when through "free will" a man elects to do evil. And while, as noted in *Morissette,* the legislature has dispensed with mental element in some statutory offenses, in furtherance of a paramount need of the community, these instances mark the exception and not the rule, and only in the most limited instances has the mental element been omitted by the legislature as a requisite for an offense that was a crime at common law.

The concept of lack of "free will" is both the root of origin of the insanity defense and the line of its growth. This cherished principle is not undercut by difficulties, or differences of view, as to how best to express the free will concept in the light of the expansion of medical knowledge. We do not concur in the view of the National District Attorneys Association that the insanity defense should be abandoned judicially, either because it is at too great a variance with popular conceptions of guilt or fails "to show proper respect for the personality of the criminal [who] is liable to resent pathology more than punishment."

These concepts may be measured along with other ingredients in a legislative reexamination of settled doctrines of criminal responsibility, root, stock and branch. Such a reassessment, one that seeks to probe and appraise the society's processes and values, is for the legislative branch, assuming no constitutional bar. The judicial role is limited, in Justice Holmes's figure, to action that is molecular, with the restraint inherent in taking relatively small steps, leaving to the other branches of government whatever progress must be made with seven-league leaps. Such judicial restraint is particularly necessary when a proposal requires, as a mandatory ingredient, the kind of devotion of resources, personnel and techniques that can be accomplished only through whole-hearted legislative commitment. * * *

b. Proposal for defense if mental disease impairs capacity to such an extent that the defendant cannot "justly be held responsible."

We have also pondered the suggestion that the jury be instructed that the defendant lacks criminal responsibility if the jury finds that the defendant's mental disease impairs his capacity or controls to such an extent that he cannot "justly be held responsible."

This was the view of a British commission,[23] adapted and proposed in 1955 by Professor Wechsler, the distinguished Reporter for the ALI's Model Penal Code, and sustained by some, albeit a minority, of the members of the ALI's Council.[24] In the ALI, the contrary view prevailed because of a concern over presenting to the jury questions put primarily in the form of "justice."

The proposal is not to be condemned out of hand as a suggestion that the jury be informed of an absolute prerogative that it can only exercise by flatly disregarding the applicable rule of law. It is rather a suggestion that the jury be informed of the matters the law contemplates it will take into account in arriving at the community judgment concerning a composite of factors.

However, there is a substantial concern that an instruction overtly cast in terms of "justice" cannot feasibly be restricted to the ambit of what may properly be taken into account but will splash with unconfinable and malign consequences. The Government cautions that "explicit appeals to 'justice' will result in litigation of extraneous issues and will encourage improper arguments to the jury phrased solely in terms of 'sympathy' and 'prejudice.' "

Nor is this solely a prosecutor's concern.

Mr. Flynn, counsel appointed to represent defendant, puts it that even though the jury is applying community concepts of blameworthiness "the jury should not be left at large, or asked to find out for itself what those concepts are."

The amicus submission of the Public Defender Service argues that it would be beneficial to focus the jury's attention on the moral and legal questions intertwined in the insanity defense. It expresses concern, however, over a blameworthiness instruction without more, saying "it may well be that the 'average' American condemns the mentally ill." It would apparently accept an approach not unlike that proposed by the ALI Reporter, under which the justice standard is coupled with a direction to consider the individual's capacity to control his behavior. Mr. Dempsey's recommendation is of like import, with some simplification.[27] But the problem remains, whether, assuming justice calls for the exculpation and treatment of the mentally ill, that is more likely to be gained from a jury, with "average" notions of mental illness, which is explicitly set at large to convict or acquit persons with impaired mental capacity according to its concept of justice.

The brief of the D.C. Bar Association as amicus submits that with a "justly responsible" formulation the test of insanity "would be largely swallowed up by this consideration." And it observes that the function of giving to the jury the law to be applied to the

---

23. In 1953 the British Royal Commission on Capital Punishment proposed:

[A person is not responsible for his unlawful act if] at the time of the act the accused was suffering from disease of the mind (or mental deficiency) *to such a degree that he ought not to be held responsible.*

24. The minority, together with the Reporter for the Model Penal Code (Professor Herbert Wechsler), proposed the following test of insanity:

A person is not responsible for criminal conduct if at the time of such conduct as a result of mental disease or defect his capacity either to appreciate the criminali-

ty of his conduct or to conform his conduct to the requirements of law is *so substantially impaired that he cannot justly be held responsible.*

This proposal appears as alternative (a) to paragraph (1) of *Model Penal Code* § 4.01 (Tent.Draft No. 4, 1955) (emphasis added).

27. He proposes an instruction with this crucial sentence: "It is up to you to decide whether defendant had such an abnormal mental condition, and if he did whether the impairment was substantial enough, and was so related to the commission of the crime, *that he ought not to be held responsible.*" (Emphasis added.)

facts is not only the duty of the court, but is also "a bedrock right of every citizen"—and, possibly, his "only protection."

We are impressed by the observation of Professor Abraham S. Goldstein, one of the most careful students of the problem:

[The] overly general standard may place too great a burden upon the jury. If the law provides no standard, members of the jury are placed in the difficult position of having to find a man responsible for no other reason than their personal feeling about him. Whether the psyches of individual jurors are strong enough to make that decision, or whether the "law" should put that obligation on them, is open to serious question. It is far easier for them to perform the role assigned to them by legislature and courts if they know—or are able to rationalize—that their verdicts are "required" by law.[28]

Professor Goldstein was referring to the broad "justice" standard recommended by the Royal Commission. But the problems remain acute even with the modifications in the proposal of the ALI Reporter, for that still leads to "justly responsible" as the ultimate and critical term. * * *

6. Elements of the ALI rule adopted by this court * * *.

a. Intermesh of components.

The first component of our rule, derived from *McDonald*, defines mental disease or defect as an abnormal condition of the mind, and a condition which substantially (a) affects mental or emotional processes and (b) impairs behavioral controls. The second component, derived from the Model Penal Code, tells which defendant with a mental disease lacks criminal responsibility for particular conduct: it is the defendant who, as a result of this mental condition, at the time of such conduct, either (i) lacks substantial capacity to appreciate that his conduct is wrongful, or (ii) lacks substantial capacity to conform his conduct to the law.

The first component establishes eligibility for an instruction concerning the defense for a defendant who presents evidence that his abnormal condition of the mind has substantially impaired behavioral controls. The second component completes the instruction and defines the ultimate issue, of exculpation, in terms of whether his behavioral controls were not only substantially impaired but impaired to such an extent that he lacked substantial capacity to conform his conduct to the law.[39]

b. The "result" of the mental disease.

The rule contains a requirement of causality, as is clear from the term "result." Exculpation is established not by mental disease alone but only if "as a result" defendant lacks the substantial capacity required for responsibility. Presumably the mental disease of a kleptomaniac does not entail as a "result" a lack of capacity to conform to the law prohibiting rape.

c. At the time of the conduct.

Under the ALI rule the issue is not whether defendant is so disoriented or void of controls that he is never able to conform to external demands, but whether he had that capacity at the time of the conduct. The question is not properly put in terms of whether he would have capacity to conform in some untypical restraining situation—as with an attendant or policeman at his elbow. The issue is whether he was able to conform in the

---

28. A. Goldstein, *The Insanity Defense* 81–82 (1967).

39. Defendant is also exculpated if he lacks substantial capacity to appreciate the conduct is wrongful.

unstructured condition of life in an open society, and whether the result of his abnormal mental condition was a lack of substantial internal controls. * * *

d. Capacity to appreciate wrongfulness of his conduct.

As to the option of terminology noted in the ALI code, we adopt the formulation that exculpates a defendant whose mental condition is such that he lacks substantial capacity to appreciate the wrongfulness of his conduct. We prefer this on pragmatic grounds to "appreciate the criminality of his conduct" since the resulting jury instruction is more like that conventionally given to and applied by the jury. While such an instruction is of course subject to the objection that it lacks complete precision, it serves the objective of calling on the jury to provide a community judgment on a combination of factors. And since the possibility of analytical differences between the two formulations is insubstantial in fact in view of the control capacity test, we are usefully guided by the pragmatic considerations pertinent to jury instructions.[40] * * *

e. Caveat paragraph.

Section 4.01 of the Model Penal Code as promulgated by ALI contains in subsection (2) what has come to be known as the "caveat paragraph":

> (2) The terms "mental disease or defect" do not include an abnormality manifested only by repeated criminal or otherwise anti-social conduct.

The purpose of this provision was to exclude a defense for the so-called "psychopathic personality."[41]

There has been a split in the Federal circuits concerning this provision. Some of the courts adopting the ALI rule refer to both subsections but without separate discussion of the caveat paragraph. As to the decisions considering the point, those of the Second and

---

40. In *M'Naghten's* case, 10 Cl. & F. 200, 211, 8 Eng.Rep. 718, 722 (H.L.1843), the majority opinion of Lord Chief Justice Tindal ruled that the jury should be instructed in terms of the ability of the accused "to know that he was doing an act that was wrong," adding: "If the question were to be put as to the knowledge of the accused solely and exclusively with reference to the law of the land, it might tend to confound the jury, by inducing them to believe that an actual knowledge of the law of the land was essential in order to lead to a conviction."

When the question arose as to whether "wrong" means moral or legal wrong, the American courts split. One group, following *M'Naghten,* held the offender sane if he knew the act was prohibited by law. A second group, following the lead of Judge Cardozo in *People v. Schmidt,* 216 N.Y. 324, 110 N.E. 945, 948–950 (1915) ruled that, e.g., the defense was available to a defendant who knew the killing was legally wrong but thought it morally right because he was so ordered by God. The issue is discussed and authorities collected in A. Goldstein, *The Insanity Defense,* and notes thereto. In *Sauer v. United States,* 241 F.2d 640, 649 (9th Cir.1957), Judge Barnes summed up the practicalities: "[The] practice has been to state merely the word 'wrong' and leave the decision for the jury. While not entirely condonable, such practice is explained in large measure by an awareness that the jury will eventually exercise a moral judgment as to the sanity of the accused."

This issue rarely arose under *M'Naghten,* and its substantiality was reduced if not removed by the control capacity test, since anyone under a delusion as to

God's mandate would presumably lack substantial capacity to conform his conduct to the requirements of the law.

We are not informed of any case where a mental illness left a person with capacity to appreciate wrongfulness but not a capacity to appreciate criminality. If such a case ever arises, supported by credible evidence, the court can then consider its correct disposition more meaningfully, in the light of a concrete record.

41. See Comments to Fourth Draft, p. 160:

6. Paragraph (2) of section 4.01 is designed to exclude from the concept of "mental disease or defect" the case of so-called "psychopathic personality." The reason for the exclusion is that, as the Royal Commission put it, psychopathy "is a statistical abnormality; that is to say, the psychopath differs from a normal person only quantitatively or in degree, not qualitatively; and the diagnosis of psychopathic personality does not carry with it any explanation of the causes of the abnormality." While it may not be feasible to formulate a definition of "disease," there is much to be said for excluding a condition that is manifested only by the behavior phenomena that must, by hypothesis, be the result of disease for irresponsibility to be established. Although British psychiatrists had agreed, on the whole, that psychopathy should not be called "disease," there is considerable difference of opinion on the point in the United States. Yet it does not seem useful to contemplate the litigation of what is essentially a matter of terminology; nor is it right to have the legal result rest upon the resolution of a dispute of this kind.

Third Circuits conclude the paragraph should be retained while the decisions, of the Sixth and Ninth Circuits, conclude it should be omitted. The Sixth Circuit's position is (404 F.2d at 727, fn. 8) that there is "great dispute over the psychiatric soundness" of the caveat paragraph. The *Wade* opinion considers the matter at great length and puts forward three grounds for rejecting the caveat paragraph: (1) As a practical matter, it would be ineffectual in keeping sociopaths out of the definition of insanity; it is always possible to introduce some evidence, other than past criminal behavior, to support a plea of insanity. (2) The criminal sanction ought not be sought for criminal psychopaths—constant recidivists—because such people should be taken off the streets indefinitely, and not merely for a set term of years. (3) Its third ground is stated thus (426 F.2d at 73):

> It is unclear whether [the caveat paragraph] would require that a defendant be considered legally sane if, although the only overt acts manifesting his disease or defect were "criminal or otherwise anti-social," there arises from his acts a reasonable inference of mental derangement either because of the nature of the acts or because of credible medical or other evidence.

Our own approach is influenced by the fact that our rule already includes a definition of mental disease (from *McDonald*). Under that definition, as we have pointed out, the mere existence of "a long criminal record does not excuse crime." We do not require the caveat paragraph as an insurance against exculpation of the deliberate and persistent offender.[42] Our *McDonald* rule guards against the danger of misunderstanding and injustice that might arise, say, from an expert's classification that reflects only a conception defining all criminality as reflective of mental illness. There must be testimony to show both that the defendant was suffering from an abnormal condition of the mind and that it substantially affected mental or emotional processes and substantially impaired behavioral controls.

In this context, our pragmatic approach is to adopt the caveat paragraph as a rule for application by the judge, to avoid miscarriage of justice, but not for inclusion in instructions to the jury.

The judge will be aware that the criminal and antisocial conduct of a person—on the street, in the home, in the ward—is necessarily material information for assessment by the psychiatrist. On the other hand, rarely if ever would a psychiatrist base a conclusion of mental disease solely on criminal and anti-social acts. Our pragmatic solution provides for reshaping the rule, for application by the court, as follows: The introduction or proffer of past criminal and anti-social actions is not admissible as evidence of mental disease unless accompanied by expert testimony, supported by a showing of the concordance of a responsible segment of professional opinion, that the particular characteristics of these actions constitute convincing evidence of an underlying mental disease that substantially impairs behavioral controls.

This formulation retains the paragraph as a "caveat" rather than an inexorable rule of law. It should serve to obviate distortions of the present state of knowledge that would constitute miscarriages of justice. Yet it leaves the door open—on shouldering the "convincing evidence" burden—to accommodate our general rule to developments that may lie ahead. It is the kind of imperfect, but not unfeasible, accommodation of the abstract and pragmatic that is often found to serve the administration of justice.

We do not think it desirable to use the caveat paragraph as a basis for instructions to the jury. It would be difficult for a juryman—or anyone else—to reconcile the caveat

---

42. We note that the Second Circuit adopted the caveat paragraph on the ground that a contrary holding would reduce to absurdity a test designed to encourage full analysis of all psychiatric data and would exculpate those who knowingly and deliberately seek a life of crime. (*Freeman*, 357 F.2d at 625).

paragraph and the basic (*McDonald*) definition of mental disease if a psychiatrist testified that he discerned from particular past criminal behavior a pattern that established defendant as suffering from an abnormal condition of the mind that substantially impaired behavioral controls. If there is no such testimony, then there would be no evidence that mere misconduct betokens mental illness, it would be impermissible for defense counsel to present such a hypothesis to the jury, and there would be very little likelihood that a jury would arrive at such a proposition on its own. On the other hand, an instruction along the lines of the caveat paragraph runs the risk of appearing to call for the rejection of testimony that is based materially, but only partially, on the history of criminal conduct.

f. Broad presentation to the jury.

Our adoption of the ALI rule does not depart from the doctrines this court has built up over the past twenty years to assure a broad presentation to the jury concerning the condition of defendant's mind and its consequences. Thus we adhere to our rulings admitting expert testimony of psychologists, as well as psychiatrists, and to our many decisions contemplating that expert testimony on this subject will be accompanied by presentation of the facts and premises underlying the opinions and conclusions of the experts, and that the Government and defense may present, in Judge Blackmun's words, "all possibly relevant evidence" bearing on cognition, volition and capacity. We agree with the amicus submission of the National District Attorneys Association that the law cannot "distinguish between physiological, emotional, social and cultural sources of the impairment"—assuming, of course, requisite testimony establishing exculpation under the pertinent standard—and all such causes may be both referred to by the expert and considered by the trier of fact.

Breadth of input under the insanity defense is not to be confused with breadth of the doctrines establishing the defense. As the National District Attorneys Association brief points out, the latitude for salient evidence of e.g., social and cultural factors pertinent to an abnormal condition of the mind significantly affecting capacity and controls, does not mean that such factors may be taken as establishing a separate defense for persons whose mental condition is such that blame can be imposed. We have rejected a broad "injustice" approach that would have opened the door to expositions of e.g., cultural deprivation, unrelated to any abnormal condition of the mind.

We have recognized that "Many criminologists point out that even normal human behavior is influenced by such factors as training, environment, poverty and the like, which may limit the understanding and options of the individual." Determinists may contend that every man's fate is ultimately sealed by his genes and environment, over which he has no control. Our jurisprudence, however, while not oblivious to deterministic components, ultimately rests on a premise of freedom of will. This is not to be viewed as an exercise in philosophic discourse, but as a governmental fusion of ethics and necessity, which takes into account that a system of rewards and punishments is itself part of the environment that influences and shapes human conduct. Our recognition of an insanity defense for those who lack the essential, threshold free will possessed by those in the normal range is not to be twisted, directly or indirectly, into a device for exculpation of those without an abnormal condition of the mind. * * *

BAZELON, CHIEF JUDGE, concurring in part and dissenting in part: * * *

Our instruction to the jury should provide that a defendant is not responsible *if at the time of his unlawful conduct his mental or emotional processes or behavior controls were impaired to such an extent that he cannot justly be held responsible for his act.* This test would ask the psychiatrist a single question: what is the nature of the impairment of the defendant's mental and emotional processes and behavior controls? It would leave for the jury the question whether that impairment is sufficient to relieve the defendant of responsibility for the particular act charged.

* * * The Court * * * rejects an instruction "overtly cast in terms of 'justice' "on the grounds that such an instruction "cannot feasibly be restricted to the ambit of what may properly be taken into account but will splash with unconfinable and malign consequences." That argument seems to present two separate justifications for pretending that the inquiry is confined to fact.

First, the argument apparently reflects a concern that adoption of the "justice" approach would permit the introduction at trial of extraneous information. But under the approach urged by a minority of the ALI Council, a defendant must still demonstrate that proffered evidence is relevant to an impairment of capacity. The test does not provide him with a license to introduce evidence merely for the purpose of engendering sympathy for him in the jury. Adoption of the "justice" approach would still leave standing all of the traditional obstacles to the introduction of irrelevant evidence.

The Court's second ground of objection is apparently that an instruction cast in terms of justice would permit the jury to convict or acquit without regard to legal standard. * * * I take it that in the Court's view the majority version of the ALI test offers the jury "legal rules that crystallize the requirements of justice as determined by the lawmakers of the community," and that the minority version sets the jury adrift without such crystallized rules. What, then, are these crystallized rules? I pointed out above that while the minority version asks the jury to measure the impairment in terms of its own sense of justice, the majority version requires acquittal if the incapacity is *substantial,* and requires conviction if the incapacity is *insubstantial.* Can we seriously maintain that the majority ALI instruction is preferable because its determination that the impairment must be "substantial" reflects a crystallization of the requirements of justice by the lawmakers of the community? Naturally, we would all prefer a rule that could, as a matter of law, draw a bright line between responsible and non-responsible defendants. But the ALI test adopted by this Court is plainly not such a rule. It offers the jury no real help in making the "intertwining moral, legal, and medical judgments" that all of us expect. In fact, because it describes the question as one of fact it may lull the jury into the mistaken assumption that the question of responsibility can best be resolved by experts, leaving the jury at the mercy of the witness who asserts most persuasively that, in his expert judgment, the defendant's capacity was or was not *substantially* impaired. * * *

Notes And Questions

1. Following the public outcry (not unlike that after M'Naghten's acquittal) when John Hinckley was found not guilty by reason of insanity as to his attempted assassination of President Reagan, Congress enacted the Insanity Defense Reform Act of 1984, which provides in 18 U.S.C.A. § 20(a): "It is an affirmative defense to a prosecution under any Federal statute that, at the time of the commission of the acts constituting the offense, the defendant, as a result of a severe mental disease or defect, was unable to appreciate the nature and quality or the wrongfulness of his acts. Mental disease or defect does not otherwise constitute a defense."

2. "The most recent legislative efforts to abolish the insanity defense followed public outcry over the verdict in the *Hinckley* case in 1981. In April 1982, Idaho became the first state in recent times to abolish the insanity defense. Its new law provides that '[m]ental condition shall not be a defense to any charge of criminal conduct' and states that 'nothing herein is intended to prevent the admission of expert evidence on the issues of mens rea or

any state of mind which is an element of the offense, subject to the rules of evidence.' The states of Montana and Utah have since followed suit."[a] Samuel J. Brakel, John Parry & Barbara A. Weiner, *The Mentally Disabled and the Law* 717 (3d ed. 1985). Is this constitutional? Is it wise?

3. In *State v. Korell,* 213 Mont. 316, 690 P.2d 992 (1984), the court rejected the defendant's contention that the insanity defense was so firmly established in the common law at the time our Constitution was adopted that it was a fundamental right protected by the Fourteenth Amendment due process clause. The court noted that the Supreme Court, in *Powell v. Texas,* p. 447 of this Book, characterized the defense as one of those doctrines which "have historically provided the tools for a constantly shifting adjustment of the tension between the evolving aims of the criminal law and changing religious, moral, philosophical, and medical views of the nature of man," a process always "thought to be the province of the States." Early court decisions holding abolition of the insanity defense unconstitutional were distinguished because the statutes there challenged, unlike their modern counterparts, did not even permit trial testimony on mental condition to cast doubt on whether a defendant had the requisite mental state. As for the contention that abolition of the insanity defense constitutes cruel and unusual punishment under the Eighth Amendment, the *Korell* court concluded this was not so because the Supreme Court's teaching in *Robinson v. California,* p. 448 of this Book, and *Powell* were merely that neither status nor illness could themselves be made criminal.

4. Norval Morris & Gordon Hawkins, *The Honest Politician's Guide to Crime Control* 184–85 (1970): "We find it impossible morally to distinguish the insane from others who may be convicted though suffering deficiencies of intelligence, adversities of social circumstances, indeed all the ills to which the flesh and life of man is prey. It seems to us that our approach better accords with the total role of the criminal law in society than does a system which makes a special exculpatory case out of one rare and unusual criminogenic process, while it determinedly denies exculpatory effects to other, more potent processes. In the long run we will better handle these problems, as well as the whole and more complex problem of criminality in the community, if we will recognize that within crime itself there lies the greatest disparity of human wickedness and the greatest range of human capacities for self-control.

"Our perennial perseverations about the defense of insanity impede recognition of this diversity, since they push us to a false dichotomy between the responsible and the irresponsible. They should be abandoned. One occupation for the energies thus released might be suggested, a task in which the psychiatrist has an important role to play: the defining of those categories of psychologically disturbed criminals who are serious threats to the community and to whom special treatment measures should therefore be applied."

5. Compare Brakel et al., supra, at 718–19: "It is unlikely that the United States Supreme Court will permit the insanity defense to be abolished or allow the concept to be so narrowed that the defendant's rational knowledge and understanding of the prohibited act are not considered essential to establishing the mens rea. * * *

"As one leading psychiatrist has pointed out in defending the insanity defense:

The contradiction between this experience of being without choice and the moral intuition of free will is one of the inescapable contradictions of human existence. That contradiction is expressed and denied by the insanity defense. The insanity defense is the exception that 'proves' the rule of law.... the insanity defense does more than test the law; it *demonstrates* that all other criminals had free will—the ability to choose

---

a. Kansas joined this group in 1996.

between good and evil—but that they choose evil and therefore deserve to be punished.[311]

"A just society must have the ability to express compassion and exercise moral judgment so as to excuse those rare individuals who could not comprehend the wrongfulness of their actions. This vision of law has led civilized societies for centuries and will likely continue to sustain resistance to demands to abolish the insanity defense in the future."

6. What, then, of partial abolition? Consider David B. Wexler, *An Offense–Victim Approach to Insanity Defense Reform*, 26 Ariz.L.Rev. 18, 21–23 (1984):

"We should, therefore, be able rather easily to dissipate public fear over and objection to the insanity defense if, through legislation, we render the defense *unassertable in the prosecution of specified crimes* (e.g., homicide, attempted homicide, and perhaps aggravated assault) *unless the victim of the offense is somehow 'related to' the defendant.*

" * * * In terms of the public protection interest, the distinction is particularly potent. Surely, the public at large will be less fearful of one who has killed a family member than of one who has killed a stranger. Moreover, although this is an area that can profit from empirical research, a person who has killed a non-relative seems in actuality to be more likely to pose a threat—particularly to the general public—than does a person who has killed a family member."

SECTION 3. THE INSANITY DEFENSE—PROCEDURAL ASPECTS

A. RAISING THE DEFENSE—WHY AND BY WHOM?

1. Arthur R. Matthews, *Mental Disability and the Criminal Law* 34, 36–37, 47 (1970): "Criminal responsibility cases are rare[a] because defendants, given the alternatives, choose not to plead insanity as a defense. The plea has drawbacks stemming both from the procedural difficulties it involves and from the consequences that follow if it is successful. This seems strange in view of the widespread belief—a belief that has colored procedural approaches to criminal responsibility in this century—that the defense is a great benefit to the defendant, who can readily purchase psychiatric testimony and thus have an easy way out of criminal liability. * * *

"How is it, then, that more defendants do not rely on this tactic if in a serious case in which trial may not occur for a year, or perhaps two, a defendant may have himself psychiatrically examined by experts of his own choosing and not raise the defense until the prosecution has put on its case at trial? In practice, this advantage belongs only to defendants who are well-off. The vast majority of persons charged with crime, including those who are mentally disabled, are indigent. Indigence means, as a practical matter, that

---

311. Stone, *The Insanity Defense on Trial*, 33 Hosp. & Community Psychiatry 636, 640 (1982).

a. He notes at 25–26 that his field research disclosed that the insanity defense was raised with the following frequency in the cities and during the interval indicated:

Place	Period of Observation	Number
Chicago	4 Months	1
San Francisco	4 months	1
New York City	3 months	1
Detroit	3 months	0
Miami	2 months	0

the accused typically cannot hire his own psychiatric experts freely as he could if he had money, but must depend for psychiatric evidence on 'impartial' experts appointed by the court. Indigence has other consequences which also adversely affect a defendant's chances of preparing and successfully presenting a defense of insanity in court (assuming that, in view of the consequences of success, he wants to do so). It is difficult for the defendant either to obtain, as a preliminary matter, expert advice on his chances for success should he raise the defense of insanity or to obtain psychiatric evidence that might be persuasive in court. * * *

"Furthermore, aside from capital cases, the defense of insanity in New York, Chicago, and Detroit seemed to many lawyers and psychiatrists an empty undertaking since the dispositional consequences of the successful insanity plea did not look any better than those which follow upon conviction. While there is no single explanation of this aspect of the 'last resort' quality of the insanity plea, the following were given to us: (1) the inevitability of indefinite commitment if the defense is successful and the defendant found 'insane'; (2) the belief that psychiatric treatment at the maximum-security hospital 'does not exist' or is likely to prove ineffective; (3) the reluctance of many defendants to label themselves 'maniacs' or even fit candidates for mental treatment; and (4) fear that the prospects of release are dim even if the mental health of the offender improves."

2. In *State v. Jones,* 99 Wash.2d 735, 664 P.2d 1216 (1983), holding the trial court committed prejudicial error by entering a not guilty by reason of insanity plea over defendant's objection, the court explained:

"Courts have taken two basic approaches to the particular question of whether a court may *sua sponte* impose an NGI plea on an unwilling defendant. The first is that taken by the District of Columbia Circuit (hereinafter D.C. Circuit) of the United States Court of Appeals. It recognizes a broad discretion in the trial court to enter an NGI plea sua sponte whenever necessary in the pursuit of justice. In exercising its discretion, the court is to weigh various factors, including the defendant's opposition to asserting an insanity defense, the quality of the defendant's reasoning, the viability of the defense, the court's personal observations of the defendant, and the reasonableness of the defendant's decision. *United States v. Wright,* 627 F.2d 1300 (D.C.Cir.1980).[b] The rationale for the rule is that society has '[an] obligation, through the insanity defense, to withhold punishment of someone not blameworthy.' This, the D.C. Circuit has concluded, distinguishes *Alford*[c] and *Faretta.*[d]

"In *Frendak v. United States,* 408 A.2d 364 (D.C.App.1979), in contrast, the District of Columbia Court of Appeals concluded that *Alford* and *Faretta* required reevaluation of the D.C. Circuit rule.

[T]he underlying philosophy of *Alford* and *Faretta* is inconsistent with *Whalem* as currently interpreted. *Whalem* and succeeding cases have laid substantially more emphasis on the strength of the evidence supporting an insanity defense than on the defendant's choice. In contrast, *Alford* and *Faretta* reason that respect for a defendant's freedom as a person mandates that he or she be permitted to make fundamental decisions about the course of the proceedings.

b. *Wright* was overruled in *United States v. Marble,* 940 F.2d 1543 (D.C.Cir.1991).

c. The reference is to *North Carolina v. Alford,* 400 U.S. 25, 91 S.Ct. 160, 27 L.Ed.2d 162 (1970), allowing a defendant asserting his innocence to plead guilty when a factual basis for such a plea is shown, and quoting in support from a case stating courts "should not 'force any defense on a defendant in a criminal case.'"

d. The reference is to *Faretta v. California,* 422 U.S. 806, 95 S.Ct. 2525, 45 L.Ed.2d 562 (1975), holding a defendant in a criminal case has a constitutional right to represent himself at his trial, which, as one court has asserted, embodies "the conviction that a defendant has the right to decide, within limits, the type of defense he wishes to mount." *United States v. Laura,* 607 F.2d 52 (3d Cir.1979).

Thus, the D.C. Court of Appeals concluded, any competent defendant has the absolute right to refuse an NGI plea, as long as he is competent to make and does make an intelligent and voluntary waiver.[e]

"The D.C. Circuit rejected the *Frendak* approach and questioned whether it would differ significantly in practice. Nonetheless, we believe that the approaches differ in two important respects. First, the focus in *Frendak* is solely on *present* mental condition while much, if not most, of the D.C. Circuit's focus is on the defendant's mental condition *at the time of the alleged offense.* Second, the two approaches differ in the standard by which they assess the defendant's mental condition. Under *Frendak,* the court focuses on competency to make decisions while, under the D.C. Circuit approach, the court focuses on legal insanity.

"We favor *Frendak* for several reasons. First, we find its reasoning more in accord with *Faretta* and *Alford.* The D.C. Circuit's attempt to distinguish cases involving an insanity defense is unpersuasive. A defendant who is not guilty because of insanity is no more blameless than a defendant who has a valid alibi defense or who acted in legitimate self-defense. Yet courts do not impose these other defenses on unwilling defendants.

"More generally we concur in the belief that basic respect for a defendant's individual freedom requires us to permit the defendant himself to determine his plea. As noted by the court in *Frendak,* there exist numerous reasons why a defendant might choose to forgo an NGI plea. Absent bifurcation, such a choice may be a wise tactical maneuver where the insanity defense conflicts with some other defense the defendant wishes to interpose. The defendant may find confinement in a mental institution more distasteful than confinement in prison. The stigma of insanity may in some cases be more damaging. Finally, a defendant may have legitimate philosophical reasons for opposing entry of an NGI plea. He may view such a plea as a tacit admission of guilt which he does not wish to make. Alternatively, he may admit the act but maintain its justifiability or intend it to symbolize his strong opposition to some policy of the State. The forced mental commitment of critics in other countries to discredit their dissent is well documented.

"The existence in this state of a right to plead guilty provides an independent rationale for adopting the *Frendak* approach. * * * In entering such a plea, a defendant necessarily waives both his right to plead not guilty and his right to plead not guilty by reason of insanity. To hold that a defendant has a right to waive both rights together but not to waive them separately strikes us as wholly absurd. * * *

"As with waiver of all rights, waiver of an NGI plea must satisfy certain conditions in order to be constitutionally valid. In particular, the defendant must be capable of making and must actually make an intelligent and voluntary decision. This requires the trial judge to 'conduct an inquiry designed to assure that the defendant has been fully informed of the alternatives available, comprehends the consequences of failing to assert the [insanity] defense, and freely chooses to raise or waive the defense.' In some instances, the defendant may not be competent to make an intelligent and voluntary decision.

"Among the courts adopting the *Frendak* approach, however, there is disagreement about the relationship between competency to waive the insanity defense and competency to stand trial. The split arises not from a difference of opinion regarding the level of competency necessary to waive the insanity defense but rather from differences regarding

---

e. Should this be so even if defense counsel objects? Consider *State v. Lowenfield,* 495 So.2d 1245 (La.1985): "It appears beyond argument that when a competent defendant wishes to plead not guilty rather than not guilty by reason of insanity, and clearly understands the consequences of his choice, then the counsel must acquiesce to the wishes of his competent client. The court had no choice but to allow the defendant to withdraw his pleas and in this we find no error."

the level of competency necessary to stand trial. In *Frendak* itself, the court concluded that a greater degree of competency was necessary to waive the insanity defense because the test for competency to stand trial 'is not intended to measure whether the defendant is also capable of making intelligent decisions on important matters relating to the defense.' In *State v. Khan*, 175 N.J.Super. 72, 417 A.2d 585 (1980), on the other hand, the court concluded that the test for competency to waive the insanity defense and the test for competency to stand trial were identical because in New Jersey the latter does require the ability to help plan the defense.

"*Frendak's* conclusion, that the competency standards for waiver of the insanity defense and standing trial do differ, rests upon a shaky foundation. It is premised in large part on decisions holding that the level of competency necessary to plead guilty is greater than that necessary to stand trial, because the former requires an 'ability to make a reasoned choice among the alternatives presented'. *Sieling v. Eyman*, 478 F.2d 211, 215 (9th Cir.1973). *Sieling* and its progeny have been severely criticized, however, and do not represent the majority view. We believe the better view is that both competency standards should require an ability to make necessary decisions at trial.

"In any event, the test for competency to stand trial in Washington does rise to the level of competency to waive the insanity defense. As in New Jersey, a Washington defendant must be capable of 'assist[ing] in his own defense'. *Compare Frendak* (quoting *Dusky v. United States*, 362 U.S. 402, 80 S.Ct. 788, 4 L.Ed.2d 824 (1960) (per curiam) (defendant need only have ability 'to consult with his lawyer with a reasonable degree of rational understanding')). We construe this to include the same ability to understand and choose among alternative defenses which is necessary to intelligently and voluntarily waive the insanity defense.

"Thus, the only permissible inquiries when a defendant seeks to waive his insanity defense are whether he is competent to stand trial and whether his decision is intelligent and voluntary.[3] If the court finds that the defendant is not competent to stand trial, trial must be stayed or dismissed. If the court finds that the defendant is competent to stand trial but that his decision to forgo an NGI plea is not intelligent and voluntary, it should provide him with whatever additional information or assurances are necessary to enable such a decision. In only the rarest of cases, if ever,[4] will it be impossible to make the decision intelligent and voluntary and hence be necessary to enter an NGI plea sua sponte."

3. In *Wright*, discussed in *Jones*, the court noted that in an earlier case involving the same defendant, 511 F.2d 1311 (D.C.Cir.1975), the court held that procedures for automatic commitment after a verdict of not guilty by reason of insanity "*do not* apply where the insanity defense is raised by the court over defendant's objection." Does this make the *Wright* position more palatable?

B. RAISING THE DEFENSE—WHEN AND HOW?

4. Arraignment (the time at which the defendant is called upon to enter his plea) is the earliest point at which the defendant is likely to be able to interpose the defense of insanity. In most jurisdictions, however, he is under no obligation to do so at that time. A minority of jurisdictions, in recognition of the fact that it is extremely important for the

---

3. We deal here only with waiver by defendants represented by counsel. Where a defendant represents himself, his decisions to waive various rights should be scrutinized more carefully and a higher competency standard applied.

4. For example, some courts have held that threats of a private party may render a plea involuntary. We need not decide that issue here.

prosecution to know in advance of trial whether an insanity defense will be raised, require the defendant to give advance notice. In some states, a special plea of not guilty by reason of insanity is a prerequisite to raising the defense at trial. Some other states require the defendant to file a written notice at a certain time prior to trial of his intention to defend on the ground of insanity.

5. In *Williams v. Florida,* 399 U.S. 78, 90 S.Ct. 1893, 26 L.Ed.2d 446 (1970), the Court held that the Florida requirement that a defendant give advance notice of an alibi defense (including the names and addresses of alibi witnesses) did not violate the privilege against self-incrimination. The Court stressed that the Florida rule only required the defendant to disclose evidence that he intended to produce subsequently at trial, and, if he changed his mind, the rule permitted the defendant to abandon the alibi defense without any harm to his case.

Courts have rather consistently rejected the claim that to require advance notice of an insanity defense violates the privilege against self-incrimination, *State ex rel. Sikora v. District Court,* 154 Mont. 241, 462 P.2d 897 (1969); the recent cases rely upon *Williams* as support, *Gilday v. Commonwealth,* 360 Mass. 170, 274 N.E.2d 589 (1971). But consider the dissent in *Sikora,* concluding that there "is a fundamental difference" between the defense of alibi and insanity or self-defense in this regard: "The defense of alibi denies that the defendant committed the crime with which he is charged, claiming that he was elsewhere at the time the crime was committed. Clearly no self-incrimination is involved here. Not so with the other two defenses. In pleading self-defense, the defendant admits committing the act constituting the crime but claims his act is legally justifiable. * * * Thus, under Montana law the defendant necessarily must admit he committed the act constituting the crime with which he is charged before self-defense applies. The same is true of the defense of insanity—defendant necessarily admits he did the killing but claims it to be legally excusable because of his lack of the requisite mental capacity."

6. *Wardius v. Oregon,* 412 U.S. 470, 93 S.Ct. 2208, 37 L.Ed.2d 82 (1973), established that any state rule providing for prosecution discovery must be reciprocal to meet due process requirements; the Court thus held invalid a notice-of-alibi provision that failed to require the prosecution to provide reciprocal disclosure of its rebuttal witnesses on the alibi issue. In *State v. Curtis,* 544 S.W.2d 580 (Mo.1976), the court relied on *Wardius* in holding due process was violated where the defendant was required to give advance notice of his insanity defense and of the expert witnesses he would call in support, but the state was not required to disclose the identity of a psychiatrist called as a rebuttal witness.

7. In both *Williams* and *Wardius,* the Supreme Court emphasized that "[w]hether and to what extent a State can enforce discovery rules against a defendant who fails to comply, by excluding relevant, probative evidence is a question raising Sixth Amendment issues which we have no occasion to explore." Lower courts have utilized the sanction; illustrative is *Government of Virgin Islands v. Knight,* 989 F.2d 619 (3d Cir.1993), upholding exclusion of an insanity defense because of defendant's unjustified[f] failure to give timely notice. But consider Note, 81 Yale L.J. 1342 (1972), arguing that the exclusion sanction violates defendant's Sixth Amendment right to compulsory process in light of the "less drastic means" available for enforcing pretrial discovery, such as: (i) granting the

f. Compare *Taylor v. District Court,* 182 Colo. 406, 514 P.2d 309 (1973) (where, prior to arraignment, counsel for defendant had discussed insanity defense with defendant who did not want to plead not guilty by reason of insanity, but on date of severance defendant disclosed new evidence to counsel leading to discovery of other evidence indicative of a foundation for insanity pleas, and defendant then stated he wanted to plead insanity defense, trial court acted arbitrarily in denying leave to so plead, as defendant showed good cause why the defense was not raised at arraignment).

prosecution a continuance when surprised by the defense; (ii) allowing court or prosecution comment on the failure; and (iii) holding defense counsel in contempt for the failure.

C. EXAMINATION AND DIAGNOSIS BEFORE TRIAL

8. Most jurisdictions have enacted statutes providing for examination of the defendant by a court-appointed psychiatrist. Appointment under these provisions may come because the defense, prosecutor, or court has asserted that the defendant is not competent to stand trial (in which case the examination will nonetheless probably result in the psychiatrist gaining information relating to the accused's condition at the time of the alleged crime), or it may be triggered by the defendant's action of pleading or giving notice of an insanity defense. Under the most common type of procedure, the court designates a specific psychiatrist who will thereafter examine the defendant in his office or in a court clinic or the jail. Elsewhere, the defendant is temporarily committed to a mental hospital for examination by a member of the staff. Under both procedures, the examination is usually by a government psychiatrist, either because he is the only one available or because the law so requires.

9. *Riles v. McCotter,* 799 F.2d 947 (5th Cir.1986): "Riles first argues that the rights guaranteed him under the Fifth and Sixth Amendments were abridged under the standards set forth in *Estelle v. Smith,* 451 U.S. 454, 101 S.Ct. 1866, 68 L.Ed.2d 359 (1981) because: (1) the state's medical experts interviewed him absent counsel; (2) he was not advised of his right to remain silent; and (3) he was not informed that the results of the interviews could be used against him. * * *

"[T]his case is distinguishable from *Smith,* where the prosecution introduced harmful psychiatric evidence during the punishment phase of the trial and the defendant had no clue, because he had never raised a defense of insanity, that such evidence would be introduced. The damaging testimony was based on an unrequested court-ordered psychiatric interview of the defendant conducted without the benefit of *Miranda* warnings. Because advance notice as to the purpose of the examination was not provided to the defendant's counsel, the Court in *Smith* held that the defendant was also denied assistance of counsel in making a decision of whether to submit to the examination. Here, the record reflects that Riles, represented by counsel, requested most (if not all) of the psychiatric examinations, the results of which he now finds objectionable. Moreover, unlike the defendant in *Smith,* Riles raised the insanity defense; the state, therefore, had every right to rebut that defense. By pursuing this avenue of defense, and by offering psychiatric evidence to support this defense, Riles opened the door to the state's evidence and waived his Fifth Amendment privilege against self-incrimination. Neither was Rile's Sixth Amendment right to assistance of counsel abridged. Finally, a defendant has 'no constitutional right to have his attorney present *during* the psychiatric examination.' "

Is this reasoning convincing? Compare *United States v. Byers,* 740 F.2d 1104 (D.C.Cir. 1984), asserting that it is "at best a fiction to say that when the defendant introduces his expert's testimony he 'waives' his Fifth Amendment rights," but that denial of a defendant's Fifth Amendment claim is nonetheless justified "because of the unreasonable and debilitating effect it would have upon society's conduct of a fair inquiry into the defendant's culpability."

10. But what should the consequences be if the defendant refuses to talk with the court-appointed psychiatrist? Consider *State v. Karstetter,* 110 Ariz. 539, 521 P.2d 626 (1974) (not a violation of defendant's privilege against self-incrimination to permit the psychiatrist to so testify at trial); and *State ex rel. Johnson v. Richardson,* 276 Or. 325, 555 P.2d 202 (1976) (trial court ordered "to order the defendant to answer questions asked by

the psychiatrist about matters 'other than acts or conduct immediately near the scene of the crime' and if he does not, to strike the defense of lack of responsibility due to mental defect"); *Motes v. State,* 256 Ga. 831, 353 S.E.2d 348 (1987) (trial judge's response, striking defendant's insanity defense, too severe; defendant is simply barred from relying on expert testimony, as "the state should have an equal opportunity to tell that story through the mouth of an expert" as is exercised by the defendant).

11. In *Ake v. Oklahoma,* 470 U.S. 68, 105 S.Ct. 1087, 84 L.Ed.2d 53 (1985), indigent defendant Ake was convicted of murder despite his attempted defense of insanity. Ake's request for a psychiatric evaluation at state expense was denied, and at trial defense counsel's inquiry of state psychiatrists who had examined Ake concerning his competency to stand trial was not fruitful, for they had not inquired into Ake's mental state at the time of the crime. Emphasizing that consequently "there was no expert testimony for either side on Ake's sanity at the time of the offense," the Supreme Court ruled Ake had been denied due process: "[W]ithout the assistance of a psychiatrist to conduct a professional examination on issues relevant to the defense, to help determine whether the insanity defense is viable, to present testimony, and to assist in preparing the cross-examination of a State's psychiatric witnesses, the risk of an inaccurate resolution of sanity issues is extremely high. With such assistance, the defendant is fairly able to present at least enough information to the jury, in a meaningful manner, as to permit it to make a sensible determination.

"A defendant's mental condition is not necessarily at issue in every criminal proceeding, however, and it is unlikely that psychiatric assistance of the kind we have described would be of probable value in cases where it is not. The risk of error from denial of such assistance, as well as its probable value, are most predictably at their height when the defendant's mental condition is seriously in question. When the defendant is able to make an *ex parte* threshold showing to the trial court that his sanity is likely to be a significant factor in his defense, the need for the assistance of a psychiatrist is readily apparent. It is in such cases that a defense may be devastated by the absence of a psychiatric examination and testimony; with such assistance, the defendant might have a reasonable chance of success. In such a circumstance, where the potential accuracy of the jury's determination is so dramatically enhanced, and where the interests of the individual and the State in an accurate proceeding are substantial, the State's interest in its fisc must yield.

"We therefore hold that when a defendant demonstrates to the trial judge that his sanity at the time of the offense is to be a significant factor at trial, the State must, at a minimum, assure the defendant access to a competent psychiatrist who will conduct an appropriate examination and assist in evaluation, preparation, and presentation of the defense. This is not to say, of course, that the indigent defendant has a constitutional right to choose a psychiatrist of his personal liking or to receive funds to hire his own. Our concern is that the indigent defendant have access to a competent psychiatrist for the purpose we have discussed, and as in the case of the provision of counsel we leave to the State the decision on how to implement this right."

12. In *State v. Gambrell,* 318 N.C. 249, 347 S.E.2d 390 (1986), the court concluded: "We reject defendant's contention that he is entitled to such an independent, privately employed psychiatrist. The appointment of state employed psychiatrists may fulfill the state's constitutional obligation. Their employment by the state, we are satisfied, creates no conflict of interest which would disable them from fulfilling the constitutional requirements." Is this a fair reading of *Ake* ? See Notes, 84 Mich.L.Rev. 1326 (1986); 61 N.Y.U.L.Rev. 703 (1986).

Is this a sensible result? Consider Arthur A. Matthews, *Mental Disability and the Criminal Law* 43 (1970): "The doctors in private practice, perhaps because they treat a variety of mentally ill persons, tend to have a broader notion of mental disease than their counterparts in state mental hospitals. Their patients may resemble the person charged with crime more closely than do patients in a state hospital, who are more likely to be the victims of obvious and disabling mental illnesses. Since doctors in private practice have no need to fit patients into diagnostic categories for administrative or statistical purposes, they are less concerned with the importance of psychiatric systems of classification than with the individual dynamics of each patient. Their objective being treatment, their diagnostic procedures tend to be more thorough, more deeply probing, and more time-consuming than the diagnostic procedures of a typical state hospital. Psychiatrists in private practice are well aware of the limitations of a forty-five-minute interview with a person in the local county jail. In contrast, many institutional psychiatrists affirm that forty-five-minute interviews qualify them to render an opinion on the accused's mental condition, perhaps because such interviews are their routine hospital mode."

D. BURDEN OF PROOF

13. The initial burden of going forward with evidence of insanity is everywhere placed upon the defendant. This proposition is often stated in terms of a presumption of sanity: most men are sane, and thus the defendant in this case is presumed to be sane until some amount of evidence to the contrary is produced. Were it otherwise, the prosecution would be confronted with the intolerable burden of establishing the defendant's sanity in every criminal case. As to what is required to discharge this burden, the prevailing rule is that the evidence must raise a reasonable doubt of defendant's mental responsibility, though a few jurisdictions use a lesser standard (sometimes stated as "some evidence" or a "scintilla" of evidence).

14. If the defendant meets his burden of going forward, the question then becomes which party has the burden of persuasion. Some states place this burden on the prosecution, but in most states, the burden of persuasion is on the defendant to convince the jury of his insanity, usually by the civil standard of a preponderance of the evidence. See *Commonwealth v. Keita*, 429 Mass. 843, 712 N.E.2d 65 (1999) (citing 32 state statutes and cases in 5 other states placing the burden on the defendant). In the federal system, by virtue of the Insanity Defense Reform Act of 1984, 18 U.S.C.A. § 20, the burden is on the defendant to establish the insanity defense by "clear and convincing evidence." Which view is preferable?

15. In *Leland v. Oregon*, 343 U.S. 790, 72 S.Ct. 1002, 96 L.Ed. 1302 (1952), the Court held a state could constitutionally require a defendant to prove insanity beyond a reasonable doubt. *Mullaney v. Wilbur*, p. 264 of this Book, and the *Winship* case relied upon therein created some doubt regarding the constitutionality of placing the burden of persuasion on the defendant, but the matter has now been resolved. In *Rivera v. Delaware*, 429 U.S. 877, 97 S.Ct. 226, 50 L.Ed.2d 160 (1976), the Court dismissed, as not presenting a substantial federal question, an appeal claiming a state statute burdening the defendant with proving insanity by a preponderance of the evidence was unconstitutional. As noted in *Patterson v. New York*, p. 270 of this Book, in so doing "the Court confirmed that it remained constitutional to burden the defendant with proving his insanity defense."

E. PRESENTATION OF EVIDENCE AT TRIAL

16. *United States v. Milne*, 487 F.2d 1232 (5th Cir.1973): "It has long been the rule in most jurisdictions that the lay opinion of a witness who is sufficiently acquainted with the

person involved and has observed his conduct is admissible as to the sanity of such individual. * * * While familiarity with such person and an opportunity to observe usual or normal human behavior may support a lay opinion as to sanity, additional or more substantial proof may be required to support a lay opinion as to insanity. Insanity is a variance from usual or normal conduct. For that reason a lay witness should be required to testify as to unusual, abnormal or bizarre conduct before being permitted to express an opinion as to insanity. As in other cases involving the qualification of a witness, the trial judge must exercise a sound discretion in concluding whether or not a particular witness is qualified."

17. *Jones v. State,* 289 So.2d 725 (Fla.1974): "Unless a person is a raving maniac or complete imbecile, a jury can hardly be deemed competent to reach a satisfactory decision on the question of his mental condition without the aid of expert witnesses.[g] It is accordingly well settled that the opinions of psychiatrists are admissible in evidence on an issue of sanity or insanity. Such opinions may be drawn (1) from the evidential facts placed before the expert witness in a hypothetical question or based upon the testimony given in the case to establish the sanity or insanity of the person in question, upon the hypothesis that such testimony is all true, even though he made no personal examinations and knew nothing of the actual facts; or (2) upon symptoms and circumstances observed by the witness and testimony in the case, if he has been in Court and heard it all; or (3) upon examination made of the person whose condition is in question. However, the expert cannot give an opinion as to sanity or insanity based upon the opinion or belief of others or based upon statements of third persons out of court."

18. Although it is generally agreed that the witness may not be asked the ultimate question of whether the defendant was responsible, the prevailing rule is that the witness may be asked to respond to a question phrased in the language of the applicable legal test of insanity. As to the latter, Abraham Goldstein, *The Insanity Defense* 103–04 (1967), objects: "The essential vice of allowing the test questions is that they tend to supplant the factual detail upon which the decision on responsibility should ideally be based. Too often, psychiatric testimony consists of little else, as the test questions convert the insanity issue into what seems to be a search for something the psychiatric witnesses can 'see'—like speed or weather, some seeing it one way and some another. The issue is treated as little more than a matter of credibility: which of the witnesses is to be believed? Which of them had a better vantage point, sharper eyes, less bias, etc.? The jury is left with the impression that it must choose between the experts, because it is not told enough about the defendant's mental life to enable it to make an intelligent judgment about *him,* rather than about the psychiatric witnesses."

19. The jury rejected defendant's insanity defense and convicted him of first degree murder. It later came to light that during the course of the trial state doctors were administering a drug to the defendant for the purpose of rendering him quiet and tractable. In *In re Pray,* 133 Vt. 253, 336 A.2d 174 (1975), the court reversed the conviction because "the jury never looked upon an unaltered, undrugged Gary Pray at any time during the trial. Yet his deportment, demeanor, and day-to-day behavior during that trial, before their eyes, was a part of the basis of their judgment with respect to the kind of person he really was, and the justifiability of his defense of insanity. At the very least, they

g. This is not to suggest that the jury must inevitably accept the expert's conclusions. As stated in *United States v. Shackelford,* 494 F.2d 67 (9th Cir.1974), the jury "may, of course, reject expert opinion if it finds that the opinion was based on an incorrect view of the facts." See also *Commonwealth v. Cullen,* 395 Mass. 225, 479 N.E.2d 179 (1985) (even though burden of proof on prosecution, trier of fact could reject defendant's insanity defense where defendant had two psychiatrists testify in his behalf and the prosecution produced no lay or expert testimony directly in point, as factfinder may take account of the circumstances of the crime and defendant's conduct before and after the crime).

should have been informed that he was under heavy, sedative medication, that his behavior in their presence was strongly conditioned by drugs administered to him at the direction of the State, and that his defense of insanity was to be applied to a basic behavior pattern that was not the one they were observing. In fact, it may well have been necessary, in view of the critical nature of the issue, to expose the jury to the undrugged, unsedated Gary Pray, at least, insofar as safety and trial progress might permit."[26]

F. THE BIFURCATED TRIAL

20. In a very few jurisdictions the defense of insanity is tried separately from the other issues in the case. The guilt-stage of the trial is first concluded without any reference to the insanity defense, after which (if defendant was found guilty) a separate proceeding takes place before the same or a different jury for purposes of trying the insanity defense. The reasoning underlying adoption of this bifurcated trial procedure was that it would eliminate from the basic trial on the issue of whether the defendant engaged in the conduct a great mass of evidence having no bearing on that question and which may confuse the jury or be made the basis of appeals to the sympathy or prejudice of the jury. However, in those jurisdictions where psychiatric testimony may be received on the question of whether the defendant had the requisite mental state (a matter discussed in the next Section), this objective has not been realized. David W. Louisell & Geoffrey C. Hazard, *Insanity as a Defense: The Bifurcated Trial*, 49 Cal.L.Rev. 805 (1961). In this regard, consider George Dix, *Mental Illness, Criminal Intent, and the Bifurcated Trial*, 1970 Law & Soc. Order 559, 575, suggesting that the solution is not to bar receipt of such evidence on the mental state issue, but rather to bifurcate the trial differently so that issues unrelated to mental illness are tried in the first portion and issues involving proof of such illness are tried in the second portion.

21. In jurisdictions where bifurcation is not required, the defendant may wish to seek such a trial. As noted in *State v. Helms,* 284 N.C. 508, 201 S.E.2d 850 (1974), this is a matter within the sound discretion of the judge, but bifurcation is called for only when "a defendant shows that he has a substantial insanity defense and a substantial defense on the merits to any element of the charge, either of which would be prejudiced by simultaneous presentation with the other."

22. Courts have not been receptive to the claim that a defendant has a constitutional right to a bifurcated trial merely because he will interpose a defense of insanity. See, e.g., *Vardas v. Estelle,* 715 F.2d 206 (5th Cir.1983). But bifurcation will sometimes be the best way to avoid a serious constitutional issue, as is illustrated by *United States v. Bennett,* 460 F.2d 872 (D.C.Cir.1972). An important part of the government's case in establishing sanity was the testimony of a psychiatrist as to the significance of the defendant's recall of his conduct and of the manner in which the defendant related it to the psychiatrist during his examination. The court noted that as between bifurcation and a jury instruction to consider that evidence only on the insanity issue, the latter was "an unsatisfactory solution" because even "the most conscientious juror will have enormous difficulty forgetting a confession when turning from the insanity issue to the case on the merits."

---

26. Compare *State v. Law,* 270 S.C. 664, 244 S.E.2d 302 (1978) (it sufficient that "both the fact of medication and its effect upon the appellant were fully imparted to the jury by the testimony of the medical witnesses"); with *Commonwealth v. Louraine,* 390 Mass. 28, 453 N.E.2d 437 (1983) (holding the "ability to present expert testimony describing the effect of medication on the defendant is not an adequate substitute" for defendant's "own demeanor in an unmedicated state").

G. INSTRUCTIONS AND VERDICT

23. In most jurisdictions, if the insanity issue reaches the jury then it will be given three alternative verdict forms: guilty; not guilty; and not guilty by reason of insanity. The jury will be instructed that their first order of business is to determine whether the defendant committed the acts charged and that they should reach the insanity question only if they make that initial determination in the affirmative.

24. At the conclusion of all the evidence, the jury will be told what the legal test for the insanity defense is and who has the burden of proving what. It is improper, however, to instruct the jury on the presumption of sanity. This is because, as explained in *United States v. Lawrance,* 480 F.2d 688 (5th Cir.1973), the presumption vanishes once the defendant has met his burden of going forward and has successfully injected the insanity issue into the case.

25. Note, 93 Colum.L.Rev. 1223, 1223–24, 1245–46 (1993): "Vigorous debate exists among the state courts about the propriety of instructing jurors about the consequences of a verdict of not guilty by reason of insanity (NGI). Some state courts require judges to give an instruction, on the theory that most jurors do not know what happens to the defendant after such a verdict, and that giving the instruction therefore prevents juror confusion. Others explicitly forbid judges to give the instruction, maintaining that information about the consequences of their verdicts distracts jurors from their proper function as the finders of fact. Still others hold that the instruction should be given only under particular circumstances.

" * * * Prior to 1984, almost all federal circuit courts agreed that trial judges should not instruct jurors as to the consequences of an acquittal based on insanity. The enactment of the Insanity Defense Reform Act (the 'Act') in 1984, however, has led several circuit courts to reexamine this issue. The resulting opinions set forth three different approaches—one approach states that the instruction should not be given, another states that it should be given, and a third states that the issue should be left to the discretion of the trial judge. * * *

"Courts should instead instruct the jury of the consequences of an NGI verdict, and at the same time take steps to address the traditional concern that such an instruction may pose a risk of a compromise verdict. This can be accomplished by coupling the instruction with an explicit admonition to the jury not to consider the information in deciding the facts of the case. Giving the instruction eliminates completely the risk of mistake. Even when jurors generally know that an NGI verdict results in commitment of the defendant, an explicit instruction may put to rest any lingering doubts or concerns about the possibility of the defendant's release.

"Although giving the instruction may increase the risk of compromise, procedural safeguards can minimize this danger. For example, immediately following the NGI instruction, the judge can explain that the purpose of the information is solely to put to rest any speculation on the part of the jury, and admonish the jury not to consider the information as a factor in determining the defendant's guilt. The instruction could take a form similar to the following:

> If you find [the defendant] not guilty by reason of insanity, the law requires that [he/she] be committed to a suitable facility until such time, if ever, that the Court finds [he/she] may safely be released back into the community.

> This information is given to you so that you will not speculate about what will happen to [the defendant] if found not guilty by reason of insanity. You are not to consider it in determining whether or not [the defendant] is guilty, not guilty, or not guilty by reason of insanity.

The traditional instruction informing the jury that issues of punishment are to be left to the court would further reinforce this warning."

26. In recent years, a substantial minority of states have enacted legislation requiring that in trials involving an insanity defense a fourth alternative verdict form be provided: "guilty but mentally ill." The jury is given both an insanity defense instruction and an instruction as to what lesser or different type of mental illness permits a GBMI verdict. If a GBMI verdict is returned, the defendant is then sentenced just as if an unqualified guilty verdict had been returned. The only significance of the GBMI verdict is that the defendant is examined by psychiatrists before beginning his prison term and, if he is found to be in need of treatment, is transferred to a mental health facility. If the defendant's mental illness persists, absent civil commitment he may be held only until his sentence expires; if the defendant regains his sanity he nonetheless serves the balance of his sentence.

Several commentators have questioned the constitutionality of these provisions. See, e.g., Linda Fentiman, *"Guilty But Mentally Ill": The Real Verdict is Guilty*, 26 B.C.L.Rev. 601 (1985). However, GBMI statutes have been upheld against claims that they deny equal protection, violate due process and impose cruel and unusual punishment, *Cooper v. State*, 253 Ga. 736, 325 S.E.2d 137 (1985), and also against the contention that the statutes are impermissibly vague in setting out two ambiguous and overlapping definitions of insanity, *People v. Ramsey*, 422 Mich. 500, 375 N.W.2d 297 (1985). If, as conceded in *Ramsey*, the GBMI alternative "complicates a trial and creates greater opportunity for confusion," then what of *Keener v. State*, 254 Ga. 699, 334 S.E.2d 175 (1985), simultaneously upholding the GBMI procedure and ruling that the jury is *not* to be told what disposition follows from such a verdict because it is "irrelevant to the jury's deliberations"?

On policy grounds, what do you think of the GBMI alternative? Is it undesirable because "decisions concerning the proper placement of incarcerated offenders should be made by correctional and mental health authorities, not by juries or trial judges"?[i] Because it weakens the insanity defense in that "it is possible, and indeed likely, for a trier of fact to resolve any doubts it may have about a defendant's sanity at the time of the offense in favor of a finding of 'mere' mental illness"?[j] Or, is it desirable because it "provides a workable middle ground for fact-finders who must face the vagaries of conflicting psychiatric opinion"?[k]

Consider in this regard Ira Mickenberg, *A Pleasant Surprise: The Guilty but Mentally Ill Verdict Has Both Succeeded in Its Own Right and Successfully Preserved the Traditional Role of the Insanity Defense*, 55 U.Cin.L.Rev. 943, 991–92 (1987): "Ironically, the fears of those who opposed GBMI and the hopes of those who supported it have both been proven wrong. Because GBMI is a supplement to the insanity defense and not a replacement for it, defendants who would have been acquitted by reason of insanity before GBMI was adopted should still be NGRI after the supplementary plea is in use. GBMI defendants should come exclusively from among those who would otherwise have been found guilty, and the rate of NGRI verdicts should be unchanged. In Michigan, this is exactly what has happened. Since the GBMI verdict was adopted in 1975, the percentage of defendants who successfully assert the insanity defense has remained constant. Aided by clear and thorough jury instructions, Michigan jurors have not become confused over the difference between mental illness and insanity, and have not used the GBMI verdict as an excuse to reach improper compromises. Defendants who should be acquitted by reason of insanity are still

---

i. Richard Bonnie, *The Moral Basis of the Insanity Defense*, 69 A.B.A.J. 194 (1983).

j. Fentiman, supra, at 652.

k. Comment, 85 Dick.L.Rev. 289, 290 (1981).

being acquitted, and those who are mentally ill but not legally insane are being found GBMI."

H. COMMITMENT AND RELEASE

27. Samuel J. Brakel, John Parry & Barbara A. Weiner, *The Mentally Disabled and the Law* 725–26 (3d ed. 1985): "State statutes dealing with the disposition of persons acquitted by reason of insanity are of four basic types. The first approach, formerly followed by the federal courts, has no special provisions: the insanity acquittee is treated like any other defendant found not guilty, and the court has no hold on him. The second type provides for automatic commitment of the acquittee for a period of evaluation to determine if he is a candidate for civil commitment, followed by a hearing to determine need for continued hospitalization. The third provides for automatic commitment, with no set procedure or date for determining the need for continued hospitalization. The fourth type provides for a hearing immediately after the verdict in which commitment must be predicated on an affirmative finding that the acquittee is mentally ill and/or dangerous.

"The statutes vary in their approach to the duration of commitment. In most states, to be discharged the acquittee must be found by hospital doctors or by the court to be no longer in need of mental treatment or no longer dangerous. In some states the acquittee is to be released when he no longer meets the civil commitment criteria. A number of states specify that the person cannot be held longer than the period for which he could be imprisoned had he been convicted and received the maximum sentence for the crime of which he was accused. If he is to be retained after that, it must be through regular civil commitment. Some states set limits on the amount of time the acquittee can be subject to court-supervised outpatient care.

"In a few states where commitment of a person acquitted by reason of insanity is mandatory, the commitment is indeterminate and is based on information gathered at the criminal trial, with no separate evidence or further hearing required. In other states, the automatic commitment is only for an evaluation period, usually lasting from 30 to 90 days, to be followed by a full commitment hearing."

28. At issue in *Jones v. United States*, 463 U.S. 354, 103 S.Ct. 3043, 77 L.Ed.2d 694 (1983), were provisions in the D.C.Code whereunder a defendant acquitted by reason of insanity (upon a showing of insanity by a preponderance of the evidence) is automatically committed to a mental hospital and within 50 days thereafter (and periodically subsequently) receives a judicial hearing regarding eligibility for release, at which he has the burden of proving by a preponderance of the evidence that he is no longer mentally ill or dangerous. Jones, who had he been convicted on the shoplifting charge could have received a jail term not exceeding one year, had been hospitalized for longer following his acquittal on insanity grounds.

"It is clear that 'commitment for any purpose constitutes a significant deprivation of liberty that requires due process protection.' *Addington v. Texas,* 441 U.S. 418, 425, 99 S.Ct. 1804, 1809, 60 L.Ed.2d 323 (1979).

"Petitioner's argument rests principally on *Addington v. Texas,* in which the Court held that the Due Process Clause requires the Government in a civil-commitment proceeding to demonstrate by clear and convincing evidence that the individual is mentally ill and dangerous. * * *

"We turn first to the question whether the finding of insanity at the criminal trial is sufficiently probative of mental illness and dangerousness to justify commitment. A verdict of not guilty by reason of insanity establishes two facts: (i) the defendant committed an act that constitutes a criminal offense, and (ii) he committed the act because of mental illness. Congress has determined that these findings constitute an adequate basis for hospitalizing the acquittee as a dangerous and mentally ill person. * * * We cannot say that it was unreasonable and therefore unconstitutional for Congress to make this determination.

"The fact that a person has been found, beyond a reasonable doubt, to have committed a criminal act certainly indicates dangerousness.[12] Indeed, this concrete evidence generally may be at least as persuasive as any predictions about dangerousness that might be made in a civil-commitment proceeding. We do not agree with petitioner's suggestion that the requisite dangerousness is not established by proof that a person committed a non-violent crime against property. This Court never has held that 'violence,' however that term might be defined, is a prerequisite for a constitutional commitment.

"Nor can we say that it was unreasonable for Congress to determine that the insanity acquittal supports an inference of continuing mental illness. It comports with common sense to conclude that someone whose mental illness was sufficient to lead him to commit a criminal act is likely to remain ill and in need of treatment. The precise evidentiary force of the insanity acquittal, of course, may vary from case to case, but the Due Process Clause does not require Congress to make classifications that fit every individual with the same degree of relevance. Because a hearing is provided within 50 days of the commitment, there is assurance that every acquittee has prompt opportunity to obtain release if he has recovered. * * *

"Petitioner next contends that his indefinite commitment is unconstitutional because the proof of his insanity was based only on a preponderance of the evidence, as compared to *Addington*'s civil-commitment requirement of proof by clear and convincing evidence. In equating these situations, petitioner ignores important differences between the class of potential civil-commitment candidates and the class of insanity acquittees that justify differing standards of proof. The *Addington* Court expressed particular concern that members of the public could be confined on the basis of 'some abnormal behavior which might be perceived by some as symptomatic of a mental or emotional disorder, but which is in fact within a range of conduct that is generally acceptable.' In view of this concern, the Court deemed it inappropriate to ask the individual 'to share equally with society the risk of error.' But since automatic commitment under § 24–301(d)(1) follows only if the *acquittee himself* advances insanity as a defense and proves that his criminal act was a product of his mental illness, there is good reason for diminished concern as to the risk of error. More important, the proof that he committed a criminal act as a result of mental illness eliminates the risk that he is being committed for mere 'idiosyncratic behavior.' A criminal act by definition is not 'within a range of conduct that is generally acceptable.' * * *

"The remaining question is whether petitioner nonetheless is entitled to his release because he has been hospitalized for a period longer than he could have been incarcerated if convicted. The Due Process Clause 'requires that the nature and duration of commitment bear some reasonable relation to the purpose for which the individual is committed.' *Jackson v. Indiana.* The purpose of commitment following an insanity acquittal, like that of civil commitment, is to treat the individual's mental illness and protect him and society from his potential dangerousness. The committed acquittee is entitled to release when he has recovered his sanity or is no longer dangerous. And because it is impossible to predict

---

12. The proof beyond a reasonable doubt that the acquittee committed a criminal act distinguishes this case from *Jackson v. Indiana,* in which the Court held that a person found incompetent to stand trial could not be committed indefinitely solely on the basis of the finding of incompetency. In *Jackson* there never was any affirmative proof that the accused had committed criminal acts or otherwise was dangerous.

how long it will take for any given individual to recover—or indeed whether he ever will recover—Congress has chosen, as it has with respect to civil commitment, to leave the length of commitment indeterminate, subject to periodic review of the patient's suitability for release.

"In light of the congressional purposes underlying commitment of insanity acquittees, we think petitioner clearly errs in contending that an acquittee's hypothetical maximum sentence provides the constitutional limit for his commitment. A particular sentence of incarceration is chosen to reflect society's view of the proper response to commission of a particular criminal offense, based on a variety of considerations such as retribution, deterrence, and rehabilitation. The State may punish a person convicted of a crime even if satisfied that he is unlikely to commit further crimes.

"Different considerations underlie commitment of an insanity acquittee. As he was not convicted, he may not be punished. His confinement rests on his continuing illness and dangerousness. Thus, under the District of Columbia statute, no matter how serious the act committed by the acquittee, he may be released within 50 days of his acquittal if he has recovered. In contrast, one who committed a less serious act may be confined for a longer period if he remains ill and dangerous. There simply is no necessary correlation between severity of the offense and length of time necessary for recovery. The length of the acquittee's hypothetical criminal sentence therefore is irrelevant to the purposes of his commitment."

29. What result, then, if the trial court rather than the defendant had intruded the insanity defense into the case? What if the burden of proof had been on the prosecution to establish beyond a reasonable doubt the absence of an insanity defense?

I. THE RIGHT TO TREATMENT

30. In *Rouse v. Cameron,* 373 F.2d 451 (D.C.Cir.1966), the habeas corpus petitioner (committed upon a finding he was not guilty by reason of insanity of carrying a dangerous weapon) objected to the district court's refusal to consider his allegation that he had received no psychiatric treatment. The court of appeals, per Bazelon, J., indicated that absence of treatment might render mandatory commitment unconstitutional under various theories: (i) commitment without an express finding of present insanity might violate due process if treatment were not promptly undertaken; (ii) confinement longer than would have been permissible upon conviction might violate due process if no treatment was provided; (iii) failure to provide treatment might constitute a denial of equal protection; and (iv) indefinite confinement without treatment may be so inhumane as to be cruel and unusual punishment. However, the right to treatment recognized by the court was based upon statutory language providing that a "person hospitalized in a public hospital for a mental illness shall, during his hospitalization, be entitled to medical and psychiatric care and treatment." The court declined "to detail the possible range of circumstances in which release would be the appropriate remedy."

31. Abraham Goldstein, *The Insanity Defense* 169 (1967): "One approach, which has been taken recently in *Rouse v. Cameron,* is to hold the state to its promise of treatment, upon which the indeterminate detention is ordinarily based, and to release patients if the promise is not fulfilled. That approach is so easily avoided, however, by legislative action to withdraw the promise of treatment and to base the detention instead on probable danger, that it is not likely to serve for long. Moreover, it would assign too great a role to litigation and to the judiciary to superintend treatment processes."

32. P. Browning Hoffman & Robert C. Dunn, *Beyond Rouse and Wyatt: An Administrative–Law Model for Expanding and Implementing the Mental Patient's Right to Treat-*

ment, 61 Va.L.Rev. 297, 302 (1975): "The final and most troublesome difficulty with the *Rouse* approach is the single remedy the court allowed—release upon a finding of inadequate treatment. The medical community views premature release of a patient who is proved to be within statutory commitment criteria as ultimately harmful to both the patient and society if the result is to leave the patient without further access to treatment which is medically necessary." What other remedies should the court have allowed?

SECTION 4. THE BORDERLAND OF RESPONSIBILITY

In recent times, imaginative defense attorneys have in a variety of circumstances claimed that their clients should be found to lack responsibility by virtue of something unique about their condition or background. On some occasions the effort has been to fit the situation within the insanity defense, in which case it must be determined whether the condition is in fact a mental disease or defect and, if so, whether it could produce the effects required under the applicable test for the insanity defense. On other occasions, however, it has been frankly admitted that the circumstances being relied upon are *not* a manifestation of a mental disease. Any reference to the insanity defense is merely by way of analogy; the contention typically is that the condition or background being relied upon is an equally deserving basis for holding the defendant not responsible for his actions.

1. *The XYY Syndrome.* In *People v. Yukl,* 83 Misc.2d 364, 372 N.Y.S.2d 313 (1975), in response to an indigent murder defendant's request for appointment of a cytogeneticist to conduct tests on defendant's blood for chromosomal abnormalities, for possible use in an insanity defense, the court reasoned:

"The existence of the XYY genetic phenomenon was firmly established in 1961. Early studies of chromosome imbalance focused almost exclusively on prison populations. The XYY male, in prison samples, appears to be a very tall, slightly retarded individual with a severely disordered personality characterized by violent, aggressive behavior. However, the sampling, thus far, has been inadequate and inconclusive. A built-in bias exists because samples comprised of institutionalized persons will, of course, contain more than a fair number of violent and aggressive types. The statistical significance to be attached to the results of these studies is in doubt until such time as adequate control group data can be compiled. Scientists and legal commentators appear to be in agreement that further study is required to confirm the initial findings and to concretely establish a causal connection between one's genetic complement and a predisposition toward violent criminal conduct.

"The courts have therefore been noticeably reluctant to admit evidence of genetic abnormality as a factor to negate criminal responsibility. In Maryland, Carl Millard sought to introduce evidence of his XYY condition in his trial for armed robbery. The court excluded the evidence and held that research into the relationship between genetics, criminality, and insanity did not yet 'meet reasonable medical certainty standards' necessary for its admission into evidence. The Appellate Court, affirming the order, did not find that a defense based on XYY was beyond the pale of proof, but that on the basis of the record the trial court acted properly in declining to permit the information to go to the jury (*Millard v. State,* 8 Md.App. 419, 261 A.2d 227 [1970]).

"In *People v. Tanner,* 13 Cal.App.3d 596, 91 Cal.Rptr. 656 (1970), the California intermediate appellate court upheld a lower court ruling barring admission of XYY testimony to support a defense of insanity, stating:

'the studies of the "47 XYY individuals" undertaken to this time are few, they are rudimentary in scope, and their results are at best inconclusive.'

"Moreover, the court indicated three specific objections that precluded admission of the testimony of genetic abnormality. First, the experts merely suggested that aggressive behavior may be one manifestation of the XYY syndrome. However, they could not confirm that all XYY individuals are involuntarily aggressive; in fact, some identified XYY individuals have not exhibited such tendencies. Second, the experts could not determine whether or not the defendant's aggressive behavior even resulted from chromosome imbalance. Third, the experts were unable to state that possession of the XYY anomaly resulted in mental disease which would constitute legal insanity under California law.

"The California Appellate Court considered the problem and found it an entirely proper use of discretion for the lower court to exclude evidence of an XYY condition because the evidence was 'not clear and convincing.' The court analogized to other scientific data—i.e., voice print analysis, lie detector testing—which had likewise been denied admission because they failed to reach the necessary standards of acceptance and reliability in their field.

"The objections raised in *People v. Tanner,* supra, appear to be equally valid in this jurisdiction. The Penal Law, section 30.05 states:

'1. A person is not criminally responsible for conduct if at the time of such conduct, as a result of mental disease or defect, he lacks substantial capacity to know or appreciate either:

'a. The nature and consequence of such conduct; or

'b. That such conduct was wrong.'

"Thus, in New York an insanity defense based on chromosome abnormality should be possible only if one establishes with a high degree of medical certainty an etiological relationship between the defendant's mental capacity and the genetic syndrome. Further, the genetic imbalance must have so affected the thought processes as to interfere substantially with the defendant's cognitive capacity or with his ability to understand or appreciate the basic moral code of his society.

"While there is strong evidence which indicates a relationship between genetic composition and deviant behavior, the exact biological mechanism has yet to be determined. Moreover, studies have failed to indicate why only some XYY individuals appear to have a propensity for violence and aggression and not others. The answers to these problems are currently being sought by scientists and their solution will assist immeasurably in providing a firmer footing for the incorporation of chromosome abnormality under the defense of insanity.

"However, in New York, Judge Farrell has taken a different approach and permitted, in *People v. Farley,* Supreme Court, Queens County, Indictment Number 1827 (April 30, 1969), evidence of an XYY condition to go to the jury. The defendant's insanity defense consisted of the testimony of two witnesses. A reputable psychiatrist rendered his opinion as to the defendant's mental state at the time of the commission of the crime without regard to the chromosome imbalance of the defendant. The other witness, a medical doctor engaged in genetics research, testified that, based on recent studies in the field, inmates in penal institutions have higher incidence of chromosome imbalance and in the expert's opinion, the defendant's chromosome abnormality affected his antisocial behavior. The jury rejected the insanity defense and found the defendant guilty of murder as charged.

"Judge Farrell, writing for St. John's Law Review, indicated that

'Its [the XYY syndrome] relevancy as part of an insanity defense should not be opened to serious dispute. At present, the law is geared to continuous expansion of the latitude of proof to be allowed to a defendant in such cases.'

In addition, a court in Australia has accepted the XYY syndrome as part of a valid insanity defense. Laurence E. Hannett was charged with murder and was acquitted after a psychiatrist testified that every cell in his body was abnormal. Likewise in France, Daniel Hugon presented the XYY abnormality as a defense and the court permitted its use in mitigation of sentence.

"Notwithstanding the comments of and the practices followed by Judge Farrell in the trial over which he presided and the acceptance by some foreign courts of the XYY syndrome, it appears on the whole that the genetic imbalance theory of crime causation has not been satisfactorily established and accepted in either the scientific or legal communities to warrant its admission in criminal trials.

"Accordingly, the motion for the appointment of a cytogeneticist is denied."

2. *Genetic Determinism.* Consider Marcia Johnson, *Genetic Technology and Its Impact on Culpability for Criminal Actions*, 46 Clev.St.L.Rev. 443, 469–70 (1998): "Technological advances in genetics is creating the probability of finding and identifying genes linked to violence. Once genes for behavior are identified, many geneticists believe a person's genetic predisposition to violent behavior can be shown. When that predisposition is so compelling that a person cannot overcome the compulsion to act in accordance with noncriminal behavior, then he or she is not responsible for his or her actions. A criminal defendant suffering such a genetic predisposition could be found not guilty by reason of genetic determinism.

"Once the burdens of proof are met, the justice system is faced with balancing its duties to remove unsafe persons from the public and its obligations to comply with the Eighth Amendment of the United States Constitution. The options are several, including:

1. Once found not guilty, the defendant could be released back into society.

2. The defendant could be found guilty but genetically impaired and confined in a penal institution.

3. The defendant can be committed to a genetic treatment center.

4. The defendant can be isolated in some sort of genetic compound.

5. Genetic therapy or genetic engineering and

6. Mitigation of punishment

"Of course, there are significant problems which the genetics industry poses for our society. * * * Determining which gene is good and which is bad is couched in social, economic, racial, and other biases. Genetic determination itself has social implications, including creating in a person the belief that they are limited by their genealogical map. These are all issues that a responsible society must address as the technology develops, because it will develop."

3. *Dissociative Identity Disorder.* In *State v. Greene*, 139 Wash.2d 64, 984 P.2d 1024 (1999), the defendant pled not guilty by reason of insanity to charges of indecent liberties and kidnaping. Defendant, who had previously been diagnosed as having dissociative identify disorder (commonly known as multiple personality) by virtue of manifesting no less than 24 separate personalities, "claimed that 'Tyrone,' one of his diagnosed alternate personalities, was the prime instigator of the incident," that " 'Tyrone' was manifesting as a 'child, clearly less than seven years of age, and incapable of understanding the nature

and quality of his acts or the fact that they were either right or wrong,' " and that "at least four other of his alternate personalities exchanged executive control of his body during the incident." The trial court granted state's motion to exclude any evidence of defendant's DID, and the jury convicted. On appeal, the state supreme court held that the proposed testimony was properly excluded:

"In our view, the helpfulness of the proffered expert testimony can be determined only in relation to a legal standard for culpability in the context of DID. [W]e are invited by the testifying experts, the parties, and amici to adopt a specific approach to determine whether an individual suffering from DID is legally insane at the time of committing an offense. The various approaches primarily differ on which personality (or personalities) any mental examination should focus. Thus, an approach may focus on the mental condition of the host personality at the time of the offense; or, conversely, on the mental condition of the alter in control at the time of the offense; or, possibly, on the mental condition of each and every alter personality at the time of the crime (under this approach, if any significant alter is not aware of or does not acquiesce in the commission of the crime, such innocent 'personlike' entities do not deserve to suffer punishment). According to the testimony and argument in this case, however, none of the various approaches have been accepted as producing results capable of reliably helping to resolve questions regarding sanity and/or mental capacity in a legal sense.* * *

"We recognize that ultimately the question of who should be held responsible for the commission of a crime is a legal one. In the present context, however, the answer largely depends on the ability of the scientific community to assist the courts in understanding how DID affects individuals suffering from it and how this may be related to a determination of legal culpability.

"We do not exclude the possibility that there may be a case in which the sanity of a defendant suffering from DID can be reliably evaluated. However, based upon the evidence and testimony presented here, we do not find this is such a case. Accordingly, we must agree with the trial court that the proposed expert testimony in this case was inadmissible * * * because it would not have been helpful to the trier of fact."

4. *Neurotoxic Exposure.* Consider Note, 14 Va.Envtl.L.J. 151, 151–53 (1994): "Greg rested his head on the garage workbench as the dizziness crested. He spent most of his free time building model ships in his tiny garage to sell to local antique shops and art galleries, and the fumes of paint, glue, and varnish sometimes overcame him. He was to be the featured craftsperson at a show the next weekend and was working feverishly to complete his replica of the H.M.S. Serapis.

"Greg had suffered from periodic spells of dizziness since he started building models twenty years ago. Recently, the spells had become more frequent and intense. His friends and family had also noticed uncharacteristic and increasing irritability over the past several weeks, but they attributed it to the tension of preparing for a major show.

"His wife, Roseanna, brought lunch to him in the garage, but he shouted at her to leave him alone. He did the same a few hours later when she tried to bring him dinner. Now it was 2:00 a.m. Once again, a tentative tap echoed throughout the garage. 'Greg, I reheated some spaghetti in case you're hungry now.'

"Roseanna gingerly opened the door with a nervous smile. Greg lifted his head from the bench and had a sudden flash of clarity. Roseanna had poisoned his food—she was planning to kill him because she was jealous about his featured position in the show. She wanted to deny him the recognition that he so richly deserved! Consumed by rage, he grabbed a chisel from the bench and leapt for his wife. The plate of spaghetti crashed to the floor and a bare garage lightbulb swung wildly, casting liquid shadows on Roseanna's lifeless body.

"Minutes later, Greg called 9–1–1. He was weeping over the body when the police and paramedics arrived. After Greg's arraignment, he and his attorney decided to argue that Greg was not responsible for the act because exposure to the model building materials had caused neurological damage which triggered his homicidal behavior.

"The preceding scenario may seem farfetched, but exposure to certain chemicals can cause disordered reasoning and violent behavior. The average American is exposed to thousands of different natural and synthesized toxic substances over his lifetime. The vast majority of those chemicals have not been tested, either alone or in combination, for their effects on human neurological systems. Researchers, however, have established some linkage between neurological damage and exposure to particular substances even within the small subset of tested chemicals. The resulting neuropathy can lead to behavioral or cognitive aberration. In a few criminal cases, defendants have argued that the behavioral/cognitive sequelae from neurotoxic exposure should excuse the offense.

"This strategy has had only limited success, but neurotoxic exposure may provide the basis for a legitimate defense. If a defendant can draw a causative physiological connection between exposure to a toxin, consequential neurological damage, and a correlative behavioral/cognitive deficit which is relevant to the offense, a valid claim of non-responsibility should lie. Such defendants should be permitted to present etiological evidence so that fact-finders will have a more informed basis for determining culpability.

"The philosophical and legal framework of Anglo–American criminal jurisprudence provides a niche of non-responsibility for behavior which is the product of endogenous or exogenous mental disease. Since punishment is predicated on the free will of the actor, we do not punish those who have not freely chosen to commit bad acts and may be undeterred by the prospect of punishment."

5. *Pathological Gambling Disorder.* In *United States v. Gould,* 741 F.2d 45 (4th Cir.1984), defendant was convicted of entry of a bank with intent to commit robbery and intent to commit larceny. On appeal, he challenged the trial judge's instruction to the jury "that as a matter of law pathological gambling disorder is not a disease or defect within the meaning of the American Law Institute test which would constitute a basis for the insanity defense." The court responded:

"Two other circuits, the Eighth and the Second, recently have held in closely analogous cases that, under the ALI test, evidence of a compulsive gambling disorder could not be considered as the basis for an insanity defense to charges of theft-type federal offenses. *See United States v. Torniero,* 735 F.2d 725 (2d Cir.1984) (interstate transportation of stolen property); *United States v. Lewellyn,* 723 F.2d 615 (8th Cir.1983) (embezzlement; false statement; mail fraud). In both cases, the courts reserved decision upon the general question whether the compulsive gambling disorder might under any circumstance and in respect of any offenses constitute a 'mental disease or defect' within the ALI substantive test. Each focused more narrowly upon whether the evidence sufficed under the appropriate procedural-evidentiary test to establish the requisite causal connection between the 'disorder' and the specific offenses in issue, a causal connection that is required by the 'as a result of' language in the ALI test. Both courts also concentrated only upon the 'volitional' prong of the ALI test since in both cases, as in the instant case, the defense was proffered only in that respect.

"The gist of the Eighth Circuit's rationale was that, applying the test of *Frye v. United States,* 293 F. 1013, 1014 (D.C.Cir.1923), the expert testimony offered to establish the requisite causal link between the gambling disorder and the defendant's volition in respect of the 'collateral' criminal offenses there charged did not sufficiently show that the underlying scientific principle had gained 'general acceptance' in the relevant discipline.

"The Second Circuit, analyzing the problem as one of foundational relevance of the proffered evidence, upheld a district court's exclusion of comparable expert testimony on the basis that it did not show that the 'hypothesis' of a causal link between this disorder and commission of the type offenses there charged commanded 'substantial acceptance' in the relevant discipline.

"While there are undoubtedly shadings of conceptual difference between us, we basically agree with the approaches which led both of these courts to reject compulsive gambling as the basis for an insanity defense to criminal offenses collateral to gambling."

6. *Premenstrual Syndrome.* In Elizabeth Holtzman, *Premenstrual Symptoms: No Legal Defense,* 60 St. John's L.Rev. 712, 712–14 (1986), the Kings County, New York, district attorney comments: "The first reported criminal case in the United States in which a defendant asserted premenstrual syndrome as a defense occurred in the jurisdiction where I serve. In that case a mother was accused of assaulting her four-year-old child with a stick. The defense raised the claim of premenstrual syndrome as one of several grounds for its motion to dismiss in the interests of justice.

"In 1982 my office did extensive research on the issue of premenstrual syndrome in preparing the case for trial. We reviewed some 3,000 medical periodicals published since 1971 in English and foreign languages and interviewed gynecologists, psychiatrists and endocrinologists. From this research we learned that there is no single well-defined medical condition which can be called 'premenstrual syndrome.'

"We also found that there is no scientific evidence for the proposition that the onset of the menstrual cycle provokes aggressive or violent behavior in women. The scientific evidence is confirmed by common sense experience—if women became violent each month our jails would be filled with women. But, as it is, the overwhelming number of jail inmates are men; no menstrual cycle caused their aggression.

"The scientific evidence does show, however, that women experience different symptoms in different degrees in connection with their menstrual cycle. The symptoms cited are myriad. Among them are anxiety, irritability and depression. Insanity is not a symptom of the menstrual cycle. And there *is* no syndrome—'a group of signs and symptoms that occur together and characterize a particular abnormality.'

"Moreover, research has shown that there is no diminution of the cognitive abilities of women in connection with the menstrual cycle. In a study of this question, fifty women between the ages of thirty and forty-five years old were placed in groups matched by age, education and numbers of their children. The two groups were tested for anxiety, depression and cognition, one group tested premenstrually and the other tested intermenstrually. As to depression and anxiety, the distress of the premenstrual women was comparable to that reported for freshmen college women during orientation and testing. But the study found that the 'mood change[s] had no effect on cognitive test performance.' These tests 'measured sensory-perceptive factors, memory, problem solving, induction, concept formation and creativity.' * * *

"In a recent Denver, Colorado bankruptcy case[12] a defendant sought to have a judgment debt she owed to plaintiff discharged under bankruptcy on the ground that the defendant was suffering from 'premenstrual syndrome' when she stabbed the plaintiff, her

---

12. *Lovato v. Irvin,* 31 Bankr. 251 (Bankr. D.Colo. 1983) (mem.).

roommate. In that case, the court decisively rejected the claim of premenstrual syndrome as a way to limit responsibility. The court observed that premenstrual syndrome was not established either medically or legally as an explanation for improper conduct. It further held, after hearing expert testimony on the issue of premenstrual syndrome, that the expert testimony demonstrated a lack of any general acceptance of premenstrual syndrome in the psychiatric community as an explanation for inappropriate behavior.''

7. *Post-Traumatic Stress Disorder.* As reported in Samuel J. Brakel, John Parry & Barbara A. Weiner, *The Mentally Disabled and the Law* 713 (3d ed. 1985): "Post-traumatic stress disorder (PTSD), since officially recognized as a mental illness by the psychiatric profession, strikes survivors of traumatic events, such as natural disasters, plane crashes, and wartime combat, who may reexperience elements of the trauma in dreams, uncontrollable and emotionally intrusive images, dissociative states of consciousness, and unconscious behavioral reenactments of the traumatic situation. PTSD has received the most attention in cases involving Vietnam veterans who raise the condition as the basis for an insanity defense, in which it is argued that the defendant engaged in criminal behavior as a result of a stressful event that caused him to revert to the behavior he exhibited under conditions of war in Vietnam.

"An insanity defense based on PTSD is most plausible and is most likely to be successful in cases in which the defendant exhibited behavior during the crime indicating that he was reliving his war experience. In cases where the defense is less plausible, it will still provide the attorney with an opportunity to present a wide range of evidence contrasting the defendant's behavior before and after the war, in the hopes of getting a conviction for a lesser offense or a lighter sentence. Because of its relatively recent recognition as an 'illness,' there are yet few reported cases involving PTSD as a defense. This situation may change, particularly given the concept's potential for extension to other kinds of cases, such as those involving women who have committed criminal acts after being raped."[a]

8. *Postpartem Psychosis.* Consider Note, 21 Rutgers L.J. 669, 669–70, 697 (1990): "Postpartum psychosis is receiving increased attention in current literature since it has appeared more frequently as a defense to criminal activity. In the past five years, the defense was pleaded in at least eighteen cases in which mothers have harmed or killed their babies while allegedly suffering from postpartum psychosis. About one-half of these cases resulted in verdicts of not guilty by reason of insanity, while the other half witnessed guilty verdicts resulting in sentences ranging from probation to eight to twenty years imprisonment. The diverse dispositions in these cases and the apparent inequities raise questions concerning the nature and causes of the illness in relation to its legitimacy as a mental illness sufficient to support a finding of legal insanity. * * *

"Postpartum psychosis as the basis of an insanity defense is characterized as a controversial defense. Disagreement among medical experts as to the cause of the condition and the peculiar manifestations of the syndromes have added to the controversy. However, postpartum psychosis as the basis of an insanity defense should not be so controversial. The more severe syndrome results in symptoms very similar to the symptoms associated with schizophrenia and affective disorders, which are disabilities that cause excusing conditions under a general insanity defense. Thus, if the symptoms of postpartum psychosis indicate a disability causing an excusing condition, courts should apply general insanity defense principles. However, a different problem arises when the mother is aware that she may suffer a recurrence of postpartum psychosis and she has the power to take precaution-

---

a. See also Erlinder, *Paying the Price for Vietnam: Post–Traumatic Stress Disorder and Criminal Behav-*   *ior,* 25 B.C.L.Rev. 305 (1984).

ary measures against the possibility of criminal conduct. In this instance, the jury should be permitted to consider the mother's culpability as to the ultimate offense at that time, and, if the circumstances so justify, hold her accountable."

9. *Homosexual Panic.* The term "homosexual panic" expresses "the idea that a latent homosexual—and manifest 'homophobe'—can be so upset by a homosexual's advances to him that he becomes temporarily insane." *Parisie v. Greer*, 705 F.2d 882 (7th Cir. 1983)(conc. op'n). The issue has not been squarely addressed in appellate decisions. Sometimes insanity defenses so grounded have been permitted to go to the jury, see, e.g., *People v. Parisie*, 5 Ill.App.3d 1009, 287 N.E.2d 310 (1972) (defense rejected by jury; defense psychiatrist testified homosexual panic not a mental disease but is a symptom of mental disease; prosecution psychiatrist testified it not a mental disease), and sometimes they have succeeded, Peter Finn, *Bias Crime: Difficult to Define, Difficult to Prosecute*, 3 Crim.Just. 19 (Summer 1998) (homosexual panic/temporary insanity claims have resulted in "acquittals for defendants charged with assaulting or murdering gay men in several communities in California"). Consider the argument, as stated in *Developments-Sexual Orientation and the Law*, 102 Harv.L.Rev. 1508, 1543–44 (1989), that "the acceptance of homosexual panic as a legitimate insanity defense encounters theoretical, evidentiary, and sociological problems.

"The classification of homosexual panic as a mental defect or form of insanity is theoretically problematic because it attributes a defendant's mental illness to his or her sexual orientation. Homophobia differs from recognized mental illnesses because it is a product of culturally imposed values rather than abnormal psychological traits. Homosexual panic should therefore not be accepted as a mental defect negating or reducing individual culpability. Moreover, given the American Psychiatric Association's declassification of homosexuality as a mental illness, it is unclear why someone who is latently gay or lesbian should be classified as mentally disturbed when someone who has openly chosen a gay lifestyle is not.

"Homosexual panic as a legal defense also encounters evidentiary problems of proof. The premise of homosexual panic—that latent homosexuality is provable—implicates fundamental assumptions about human sexuality that are themselves unproven. Many researchers depict sexual orientation as a continuum in which persons are neither entirely homosexual nor entirely heterosexual, but fall somewhere in between. Under this paradigm, all persons not acting on their homosexual impulses could be classified as 'latently homosexual'; thus, any person committing an act of anti-gay violence could assert a homosexual panic defense. Even if the judiciary does not adopt such an expansive view of sexual orientation, proof of latent homosexuality is highly manipulable by defendants.

"By relying upon a normative determination that fear and hatred of gay people as a group is determined by a person's mental state, rather than volitional choice, the defense also has adverse implications for controlling anti-gay violence. Recognizing homosexual panic as a mental disease or defect diminishes individual responsibility for the consequences of bias and prejudice, and accepts such behavior as unchangeable and unavoidable, thereby encouraging its reoccurrence."

10. *Cultural Defense.* In *State v. Kargar*, 679 A.2d 81 (Me.1996), Mohammad Kargar, an Afghani refugee, was charged with two felony counts of gross sexual assault, defined as a sexual act with another person under the age of 14. (The statute defines sexual act as, among other things, "direct physical contact between the genitals of one and the mouth * * * of the other"; the requirement of sexual gratification was removed from the statute some years earlier.) The charges arose out of a neighbor witnessing Kargar kissing his 18–month-old son's penis and discovery in a photo album of a picture of such activity. After

the trial phase of the case the court held a de minimis hearing pursuant to a state statute based on *Model Penal Code* § 2.12, at which "Kargar's witnesses, all relatively recent emigrants from Afghanistan, testified that kissing a son's penis is common in Afghanistan, that it is done to show love for the child, and that it is the same whether the penis is kissed or entirely put into the mouth because there are no sexual feelings involved." The court declined to dismiss under the de minimis statute, and Kargar was convicted. On appeal the court ruled the motion should have been granted and that the trial judge had "erred as a matter of law because it found culture, lack of harm, and his innocent state of mind irrelevant to its de minimis analysis." Considering that only a few states have adopted such a de minimis statute, does *Kargar* show the need for a "cultural defense," and, if so, of what dimensions? Consider:

(a) Note, 99 Harv.L.Rev. 1293, 1311 (1986): "The values of individuals who are raised in minority cultures may at times conflict with the values of the majority culture. To the extent that the values of the majority are embodied in the criminal law, these individuals may face the dilemma of having to violate either their cultural values or the criminal law. Two recent cases in the United States illustrate this conflict and the difficult issues it raises for American jurisprudence. In *People v. Kimura*, a Japanese–American woman's children died when she attempted to commit oyakoshinju—parent-child suicide—after learning of her husband's extramarital affair. According to the defense attorney and members of the Japanese community, in traditional Japanese culture, the death ritual was an accepted means for a woman to rid herself of the shame resulting from her husband's infidelity. A second example of cultural conflict arose in a case in which a member of the Hmong tribe from the mountains of Laos living in the United States exercised his right under Hmong culture to execute his adulterous wife. In both of these cases, the defendants were confronted with charges of felony homicide. Should cases like these proceed to trial, the defendants may attempt to raise an affirmative defense based on their cultural backgrounds—a 'cultural defense.' * * *

"Neither the current law nor discretionary procedures within the criminal justice system are adequate vehicles for dealing with cultural factors: what is needed is a formal cultural defense within the substantive law. It is often all too tempting for a society to betray its underlying values when confronted with overstated fears of violence and anarchy. In the case of American society, blanket repudiation of the cultural defense sacrifices two very important values—individualized justice and cultural pluralism. Perhaps more telling, the American legal system's rejection of the cultural defense reveals an underlying fear of beliefs that are different from ours. Immolating one's own children for the sake of honor, executing an adulterous wife, and lashing out at someone in order to break a voodoo spell may seem very bizarre—indeed barbaric and disturbing—to the majority. But this is no reason to attempt immediately to quash the values of foreign cultures. American society has thrived on tolerance, curiosity toward the unknown, and experimentation with new ideas. The legal system, however, recognizes that if tolerance, curiosity, and experimentation are carried too far, social disorder and disintegration of common values may result. The cultural defense would give courts an opportunity to strike the necessary balance among these competing interests."

(b) Stanislaw Pomorski, *On Multiculturism, Concepts of Crime, and the "De Minimis" Defense*, 1997 B.Y.U.L.Rev. 51, 64–65: "Evidence regarding defendants' cultural background is hardly a novelty in American courts; it has been used for over a century. By introducing this kind of evidence, defendants usually try to demonstrate that due to their distinct cultural upbringing, their perception of material facts as well as their mental attitudes are different from those alleged by the prosecution. This way, cultural evidence supports a theory that a defendant either did not entertain the requisite mens rea for the crime charged or qualified for one of the traditional affirmative defenses such as duress, self-defense, or even insanity. In other words, cultural evidence formally introduced at the trial level has always been translated into one of the specific rules of substantive criminal law with exonerating or mitigating potential. Cultural evidence has also been used in less formal settings such as plea negotiations and as a mitigating factor at the sentencing stage. On the other hand, cultural evidence has never been used in support of a freestanding 'cultural defense.' The reason for the conspicuous absence of such claims is clear and simple: * * *

> There is not and will not be a separate cultural defense because as a practical matter such a defense can be neither defined nor implemented. In short, debate over a new cultural defense is misguided because the use of cultural information is not new, a workable legal definition of culture is impossible to develop, and the information is not being offered in court to create a separate defense.

"Although the debate over a cultural defense is indeed conceptually misguided and the opponents struggle over a phantom created by themselves, nonetheless concerns animating the debate are not futile. Proponents of a cultural defense are motivated by a genuine problem created by the insufficient responsiveness of the legal actors to the plight of defendants of radically different cultural backgrounds. Critics of the defense, on the other hand, are concerned about the threat that overcommitment to normative pluralism could pose to the supremacy of law; the protection of victims, particularly against acts of violence; and the principle of legal equality. Others, primarily feminist writers, oppose a 'cultural defense,' sounding the alarm that excessive deference to foreign cultures could lead to condoning and perpetuating intrafamily violence or, generally, the violence against women which many of those cultures legitimize. All of these concerns are valid."

11. *Black Rage.* Consider Comment, 143 U.Pa.L.Rev. 2251, 2251–53, 2288 (1995): "Tragedy struck the Long Island Railroad on December 7, 1993, as the 5:33 to Hicksville left the New York City limits. Methodically, as if collecting train tickets, Colin Ferguson passed down the aisle of the third car of the train, steadily shooting to his right and then to his left, until he emptied two fifteen-bullet clips into twenty-five defenseless Long Island commuters. Handwritten notes in Ferguson's pockets explained his actions as a venting of the rage he—a black man—felt toward 'everyone from Gov[ernor] Mario M. Cuomo to the state Workers' Compensation Board to Asians, whites, and "Uncle Tom Negroes." ' Months later, the racial stress, anxiety, and anger evidenced in these notes would provide the foundation for Ferguson's legal defense: a new twist on the traditional insanity defense called the 'black rage' defense.

"According to Ferguson's former defense attorneys,[5] American society's pervasive and destructive racism gradually kindled and fueled a smoldering rage that operated as a catalyst to push their already mentally unstable client over the edge into insanity. * * * The seminal sociological and psychiatric study *Black Rage* also propounds this argument, devoting an entire chapter to mental conditions arising from the constant racial stress many black Americans experience. Drawing upon these and other sources, Ferguson's attorneys intended to persuade the jury that their client should not be held accountable for his actions on the ill-fated train car.

---

5. Criminal defense attorneys William M. Kunstler and Ronald L. Kuby represented Ferguson at the height of the case's publicity. * * *. Convinced that he was not insane and did not perpetrate any crime, Ferguson resisted the planned black rage insanity defense, fired Kunstler and Kuby, and represented himself. * * *

On February 17, 1995, after 10 hours of deliberation, a jury rejected Ferguson's mistaken identity defense and found him guilty of murder and of attempted murder. * * *

"As might be expected, the prospect of a black rage defense has drawn both criticism and praise. Many find the defense demeaning to blacks, exhuming 'ancient stereotypes of the "crazy nigger," child-like primitive, straight out of D.W. Griffith's *Birth of a Nation*, unable to control his hot-blooded tropical lusts.' [O]thers find the black rage defense 'compelling.' They celebrate the defense as a political legitimization of aggressive responses to racial oppression, noting that the appropriate flip side to black rage is white guilt and fear. * * *

"In light of the dearth of black rage cases, the viability of a black rage insanity defense * * * is far from certain. Applying the black rage psychiatric and sociological studies to the legal definitions of insanity reveals that black rage may, at least in some instances, pass even the strictest of insanity tests. The paranoid schizophrenia, the delusional disorder of the persecutory type, and the post-traumatic stress disorder analogies further point to this conclusion, implying that black rage is a form of legal insanity that the criminal law should recognize. * * *

"However, insofar as black rage insanity is the product of an actor's choice to pursue destructive rather than constructive coping mechanisms as a means of dealing with racial stress, the contraction of black rage represents a deterrable, blameworthy choice that is subject to criminal law punishment."

12. *Rotten Social Background.* Sanford H. Kadish, *Fifty Years of Criminal Law: An Opinionated Review*, 87 Calif.L.Rev. 943, 961–62 (1999): "The inelegantly named 'rotten social background' defense argues that the defendant should be excused because he or she was reared in the criminogenic circumstances of the inner city.[93] Though it has made no headway in the law, the controversy it engendered thrust into prominence the disquieting issue of the justice of punishing people whose actions we know were powerfully influenced by growing up in deplorable conditions of life for which society at large bears at least some measure of responsibility.

"As an excuse of non-responsibility the defense got nowhere.[95] True, children brought up in these circumstances are more likely when they grow up to commit certain crimes (street crimes especially) than children from the suburbs. That's a statistical fact. But it doesn't follow that the child once grown who commits a crime has been disabled from making a responsible choice. If it did, then it is hard to see who couldn't claim a comparable excuse. So the case for the excuse has to rest on the particular nature of this criminogenic influence, namely its roots in the historic injustice of American slavery and the failure to remedy its dire consequences. Even though growing up in criminogenic circumstances does not itself render the person irresponsible, may justice not require exculpation when the State itself is responsible for the perpetuation of those circumstances? The question is not unique to our period. Karl Marx, for example, believed that no capitalist society could justly punish offenders in view of the criminogenic influence of poverty that capitalism produces. But the perdurability of the fallout from slavery and the racism that followed it has made the problem acutely relevant to our times.

"Practically speaking it would be hopeless for society to exculpate a major class of offenders just because the deleterious environmental circumstances that influenced their behavior were products of that society. The hardest question is the moral one: What policies would the nation be obliged in good conscience to pursue toward ameliorating the criminogenic conditions of life for inner city offenders in order to make punishing them

---

93. See Richard Delgado, *"Rotten Social Background": Should the Criminal Law Recognize a Defense of Severe Environmental Deprivation?*, 3 Law & Ineq. J. 9 (1985).

95. See, e.g., *United States v. Alexander*, 471 F.2d 923, 959, 968 (D.C.Cir.1972) (upholding the trial judge's instruction to the jury precluding consideration of the rotten social background defense).

morally sustainable?[98] I fear we will not soon be relieved of the moral burden this question imposes."

SECTION 5. DIMINISHED CAPACITY

STATE v. McVEY

Supreme Court of Iowa, 1985.

376 N.W.2d 585.

McCORMICK, JUSTICE. * * *

Defendant Donald Lee McVey was charged in October 1983 with second-degree theft based on exercising control over a stolen motor vehicle under Code sections 714.1(4) and 714.2(2) and with attempting to elude a pursuing law enforcement vehicle in violation of Code section 321.279. The State's evidence was that defendant and a companion escaped from a prison farm and stole an automobile in Fort Madison. They were subsequently observed in the automobile in Urbandale and were apprehended and charged after a high speed chase.

Before trial defendant gave the State notice of a defense of diminished responsibility in accordance with Iowa Rule of Criminal Procedure 11(b)(1). The State moved to strike the defense on the ground it is unavailable as a defense to the charges involved. The trial court sustained the State's motion, and defendant was precluded at trial from offering the testimony of a psychologist on the issue of diminished responsibility. * * *

In relevant part, section 714.1(4) makes it theft for a person to "[exercise] control over stolen property, knowing such property to have been stolen, or having reasonable cause to believe that such property has been stolen, unless the person's purpose is to promptly restore it to the owner or to deliver it to an appropriate public officer." In *State v. Hutt*, 330 N.W.2d 788, 790 (Iowa 1983), we held that the mens rea of this offense requires proof that the accused actually believe the property is stolen. We have also held that the offense does not require proof of specific intent.

The offense is a general intent crime because it is complete without intent to do a further act or achieve a further consequence. General criminal intent exists when from the circumstances the prohibited result may reasonably be expected to flow from the voluntary act itself "irrespective of any subjective desire to have accomplished such result." Thus the crime of theft based on exercising control over stolen property does not require proof of any intent beyond the voluntary act of exercising the prohibited control over property the accused knows is stolen.

In contending the defense of diminished responsibility is available in this case, defendant recognizes that this court has previously held that the defense is not available to crimes that require only a general criminal intent. He argues nevertheless that the statutory requirement of proof of knowledge the property was stolen introduces a special mental element that should be subject to the defense. This argument necessitates review of the nature and scope of the diminished responsibility defense.

The diminished responsibility defense was first recognized by this court in *State v. Gramenz*, 256 Iowa 134, 126 N.W.2d 285 (1964). It is a common law doctrine that "permits proof of defendant's mental condition on the issue of [the defendant's] capacity to form a

---

98. See generally R. George Wright, *The Progressive Logic of Criminal Responsibility and the Circumstances of the Most Deprived*, 43 Cath. U. L. Rev. 459 (1994) (exploring the relationship between deprivation and moral responsibility).

specific intent in those instances in which the state must prove defendant's specific intent as an element of the crime charged." The court held that evidence of an accused's mental unsoundness may be received to negate specific intent, premeditation and deliberation on a charge of first degree murder, refusing, however, to allow the evidence on the elements of malice aforethought and general criminal intent. The court noted:

> While malice aforethought is the specific state of mind necessary to convict of murder, it is far different from the specific intent which is a necessary element of murder in the first degree. It may be express or implied from the acts and conduct of defendant.

> * * *

> It appears * * * that testimony sufficient to establish defendant's lack of mental capacity to have malice aforethought would also be sufficient to satisfy the requirements of the right and wrong test and entitle defendant to an acquittal on a plea of insanity rather than a reduction of the sentence to manslaughter.

Subsequently this court held that the defense is available to any crime in which specific intent is an element. The court has continued to recognize the defense even though it is not listed among the special defenses to crime delineated in Code chapter 701. The court has also continued to contrast the defense with the insanity defense, distinguishing diminished responsibility on the ground it allows evidence of mental unsoundness establishing lack of capacity to form a requisite criminal intent rather than requiring proof of the more aggravated kind of distortion of the thinking process required for the absolute defense of insanity.

As of January 1, 1978, the General Assembly codified the insanity defense. The statute incorporates the M'Naghten standard previously adopted by this court as a common law rule. * * * This is obviously a much more stringent standard than is involved in the diminished responsibility defense. Section 701.4 was recently amended to impose the burden on the defendant to prove an insanity defense by a preponderance of the evidence.

Both defenses nevertheless are absolute defenses to specific intent crimes. This was the situation when the M'Naghten rule was codified. The question is whether diminished responsibility should be extended, despite codification of the insanity defense, so that it is also an absolute defense to a general intent crime that requires proof of guilty knowledge. We conclude the defense should not be extended beyond specific intent crimes.

In formulating the insanity defense the legislature defined limits upon the effect of evidence of mental disease or defect relating to criminal culpability generally. This court earlier drew the same line at common law in the *Gramenz* case. It would undercut the legislative policy inherent in the insanity defense for this court to extend the defense of diminished responsibility.

Insanity and mens rea are legal concepts without psychiatric counterparts. As legal concepts they are used to establish limits to legal culpability. The extent to which evidence of mental impairment will be permitted to affect criminal responsibility is therefore a legal question. The argument that evidence of mental impairment should be received because it bears on the mens rea of an offense presupposes that the mens rea requirement has a legal meaning which makes the evidence from the psychological model relevant.

A prominent psychiatrist observed that, "When the law says that the absence of intent renders one incapable of committing a crime, it really means that the triers are incapable of attaching guilt upon the offender, i.e., of inflicting punishment on one who actually committed a harm which if done by a sane person would be punishable." P. Roche, *The Criminal Mind* 87 (1958). In practical terms a court's refusal to recognize the relevancy of evidence of mental impairment short of legal insanity results from the court's understanding of the legislative intention concerning the blameworthiness of the defendant's conduct. To the extent evidence of mental impairment that does not meet the legal insanity standard permits an accused to avoid responsibility for otherwise culpable conduct, the policy inherent in the insanity defense is undermined.

In view of the fact the Iowa common law recognized mental impairment other than legal insanity as a defense only to specific intent crimes at the time the insanity defense was codified, we believe the General Assembly drew the line at that point. The legislature thus established the applicable legal standard for deciding culpability upon evidence of mental impairment in cases requiring proof only of guilty knowledge or general criminal intent accompanying a prohibited act. The mens rea of those crimes is not affected by evidence of mental impairment that does not meet the insanity standard. Therefore we hold that the diminished responsibility defense is available only to specific intent crimes. A similar limitation appears to exist in most other jurisdictions that recognize the defense.

No reversible error has been established.

CARTER, JUSTICE (dissenting). * * *

There is a popular maxim among debaters that, if you allow your opponent to state the issue, your chances of success are indeed slight. The majority opinion utilizes this principle to support its result by treating the issue in the present case as if it were whether the "defense of diminished responsibility" should be further extended. In reality, the issue presented is whether a court in the trial of a criminal case may exclude relevant and material evidence concerning a basic element of the offense charged. Placing labels on similar concepts in order to foster accurate analysis and facilitate uniformity of treatment among like things is acceptable only as long as the concepts which are identically labeled are in fact similar. What something in fact is and how something in fact operates cannot be established by labels.

Commencing with the seminal decision in *State v. Gramenz,* our characterization of the use of expert testimony negating an essential element of a criminal charge has been inaccurate. Unfortunately, this error in description has produced error in application. The fundamental flaw in the analysis upon which these decisions are based is the acceptance of the premise that "diminished responsibility" is a partial defense which reduces responsibility in some types of crimes. Clearly, it is not and never has been.

An illuminating description of the use of expert testimony to negate an element of a criminal charge is contained in the following commentary:

> Mental illness commonly negates an element without amounting to insanity. As a failure of proof defense, at least in cases where the defendant is still guilty of a lesser included offense, it is often called "partial responsibility" or "diminished capacity." Its name highlights the fact that it is something short of insanity; but it is nonetheless an unfortunate choice of terms because there is nothing *partial* about the defense. The mental illness either negates a required element of an offense or it does not, thereby providing a complete defense *to that offense* or providing no defense. It is true that many offenses, especially homicide offenses, have lesser included offenses with less demanding culpability elements. Thus mental illness may negate the culpability element of the greater offense but not the lesser offense. When this occurs, the net effect of the mental illness is to reduce the defendant's liability from the greater to the lesser * * *. However, this ultimate reduction effect results from the different offenses, not from a special rule that, when faced with diminished responsibility due to mental illness, generates diminished liability. If there is no lesser included offense, or

if the mental illness also negates an element of any lesser included offense, the mental illness will prevent conviction altogether.

Robinson, *Criminal Law Defenses: A Systematic Analysis,* 82 Colum.L.Rev. 199, 206 (1982) (footnotes omitted) (emphasis in original).

The point which professor Robinson makes is fully applicable to the use of this type of evidence under Iowa law. The concept of partial defense exists only as an inaccurate label, spawned from the rhetoric of our decisions, but thoroughly, contradicted in the actual application of the doctrine. In the so-called specific intent crimes in which it has been allowed to operate, the doctrine of diminished responsibility in actual practice is a defense only in the respect that, in the common usage of language, any evidence presented by a defendant to negate the State's evidence is defensive in nature.

The majority seeks to show meaningful differences between specific intent crimes and general intent crimes through the use of definitions from our cases which have no bearing on the present problem. What difference does it make that a general intent crime has been said to be complete without intent to do a further act or achieve a further consequence? * * *

* * * No reason has been suggested by the majority why there is any less need, in the interest of a fair trial, for the accused to be allowed to defend himself when charged with general intent crimes than is the case with respect to specific intent crimes. * * *

Notes and Questions

1. The Insanity Defense Reform Act of 1984, 18 U.S.C. § 17, states in part: "It is an affirmative defense to a prosecution under any Federal statute that, at the time of the commission of the acts constituting the offense, the defendant, as a result of a severe mental disease or defect, was unable to appreciate the nature and quality or the wrongfulness of his acts. Mental disease or defect does not otherwise constitute a defense." In *United States v. Pohlot,* 827 F.2d 889 (3d Cir.1987), where the government claimed that this language "bars a defendant from using evidence of mental abnormality to negate mens rea," the court disagreed, stating: "Both the wording of the statute and the legislative history leave no doubt that Congress intended, as the Senate Report stated, to bar only alternative 'affirmative defenses' that 'excuse' misconduct not evidence that disproves an element of the crime itself.

"Pohlot essentially contends that 'mental disease or defect is admissible whenever it is relevant to prove that the defendant did or did not have a state of mind that is an element of the offense.' *Model Penal Code*, § 4.02(1) (1962). Although this principle has sometimes been phrased as a version of the 'diminished capacity defense,' it does not provide any grounds for acquittal not provided in the definition of the offense. Properly understood, it is therefore not a defense at all but merely a rule of evidence."

2. In *State v. Maas*, 242 Kan. 44, 744 P.2d 1222 (1987), the court determined there were other consequences that attended recognition of diminished capacity: (i) the matter can be argued to the jury in the defense closing argument; (ii) it may necessitate an instruction on some lesser-included offense which does not require the questioned mental state, and (iii) under the "better practice," the trial court will "give an instruction on diminished capacity when such instruction is reasonably necessary to inform the jury of the effect of defendant's diminished capacity on the specific intent required for the crime charged." The court in *Maas* added there was no legal requirement of such an instruction, but there is authority otherwise, e.g., *State v. Breakiron*, 108 N.J. 591, 532 A.2d 199 (1987).

3. "Since the purpose of the diminished-capacity doctrine is to establish the absence of an essential element of the crime, the state still has the burden of overcoming this effort by proof of all the essential elements beyond a reasonable doubt." *State v. Correra*, 430 A.2d 1251 (R.I.1981). But consider *Breakiron*, supra, where the defendant claimed that a state statute declaring "mental disease or defect is an affirmative defense which must be proved by a preponderance of the evidence" impermissibly shifted to him the burden of disproving an essential element of the crime. The court construed the statute as not having this effect: "The Legislature could not have intended that a mentally deficient defendant be more at a disadvantage than any other citizen. * * * Since its sole function is to establish the absence of an essential element of the crime, this defense cannot have the effect of shifting the burden of proof on that essential element to the defendant." But the court then went on to hold that the statute, literally construed, was valid, as it merely required the defendant to prove mental disease or defect, which "is not an essential element of the crime," and thereby "does nothing more than create an inference that the ordinary defendant is possessed of the capacity to reach the mental states required by the Code." The court in *Breakiron* went on to reject defendant's contention "that juries will be impossibly confused by an acrobatic effort to isolate the presence of mental disease or defect from the specific culpable mental state required." Are you convinced?

4. Note, 20 Am.J.Trial Advoc. 381, 387–88, 391–97 (1997): "Not all jurisdictions allow defendants to use diminished capacity evidence. Also, those jurisdictions that do allow the use of such evidence vary as to when and how the evidence may be used.

"Generally, American jurisdictions take one of four views of permitting or disallowing mental abnormality evidence. Depending on which view is taken, the jurisdiction will follow either the mens rea variant, the partial responsibility variant, or not allow the evidence at all. The four views found in the United States are: (1) to admit any evidence of a mental abnormality to negate the requisite state of mind required as an element of the offense charged, (2) to admit evidence of a mental abnormality only to negate a specific intent element of the offense charged, (3) to admit evidence of a mental abnormality only in homicide cases to negate malice or premeditation as required as an element of homicide, or (4) to disallow evidence of a mental abnormality unless the defendant's mental state rises to the level of insanity.

"Jurisdictions that admit any evidence of a mental abnormality to negate the required state of mind element of the offense charged, essentially do nothing more than recognize that relevant evidence is admissible. This view is merely a failure of proof defense which recognizes that because a defendant must possess a certain state of mind in order to be convicted of that crime, any evidence showing the absence of that state of mind is admissible. This view seems to have the most jurisdictional support of the four views. * * *

"Jurisdictions that admit evidence of a mental abnormality only to negate a specific intent element of the offense charged are numerous, making this the second most followed view of the four. This view is limited, however, meaning that, while the evidence is admissible, it is only admissible under the restrictions. Here, the restriction is admissibility of mental abnormality evidence only for specific intent crimes.

"Most specific intent crimes have a lesser included criminal offense not requiring specific intent. When mental abnormality evidence is presented under this view, the evidence may provide a complete defense to the specific intent crime, but it provides no defense to the lesser included crime. * * *

"A handful of jurisdictions admit evidence of mental abnormality only in homicide cases to negate malice or premeditation as required as an element of the offense of homicide. Under this view, the mental abnormality evidence is used either to negate the malice or premeditation required of murder or as a form of lesser insanity. When the mental abnormality evidence is used to negate malice or premeditation, the court is merely confirming that such evidence is relevant on the issue of a required state of mind for homicide. Such confirmation means that the court will recognize the use of such evidence as a failure of proof defense. * * *

"Jurisdictions that disallow evidence of mental abnormality follow an extreme hard line view. This view finds support in approximately twelve jurisdictions as well as federal military law. Under this view, any evidence of a mental abnormality that cannot show that the defendant was legally insane is inadmissible. * * *

"The last use of mental abnormality evidence is outside of and in addition to the four views already discussed. Ten jurisdictions and the Model Penal Code allow for the admission of mental abnormality evidence in sentence mitigation. When mental abnormality evidence is used in sentencing, it is usually used to decide between imposing death or life imprisonment.* * *

"If there is a trend among the jurisdictions, it would seem to be in allowing evidence of a mental abnormality to negate the required state of mind under the crime charged. Congress, state legislatures, and the courts are moving in this direction, although many states have recently explicitly held such evidence inadmissible."

Are any of these distinctions defensible, or must "diminished capacity" be an all or nothing proposition?

5. Constitutional challenges to states' refusal to utilize the "diminished capacity" doctrine have in the main failed. Illustrative is *Wong v. Money*, 142 F.3d 313 (6th Cir.1998), a federal habeas corpus review of petitioner's Ohio conviction on five counts of assaulting police officers and one count of assaulting her husband by firing a shotgun at the victims, following a trial at which the court refused "to allow * * * two psychologists to testify to establish the defense of diminished capacity":

"Ohio does not recognize the defense of diminished capacity, and a defendant may not offer expert psychiatric testimony, unrelated to the presentation of an insanity defense, to show that she lacked the mental capacity to form the specific mental state required for a particular crime or degree of crime. *Ohio v. Wilcox*, 70 Ohio St.2d 182, 436 N.E.2d 523, 533 (1982). In *Wilcox*, the Ohio Supreme Court stated that 'the diminished capacity theory forcefully challenges conventional concepts of culpability and "involve(s) a fundamental change in the common law theory of responsibility." ' The court undertook a comprehensive review of the diminished capacity defense, including the history of the defense and the purposes it was designed to serve. The court stated:

While some courts may have blind faith in all phases of psychiatry, this court does not. There is substantial doubt whether evidence such as was sought to be introduced here is scientifically sound, and there is substantial legal doubt that it is probative on the point for which it was asserted.

The state supreme court also noted:

In light of the linedrawing difficulties courts and juries face when assessing expert evidence to make the "bright line" insanity determination, we are not at all confident that similar evidence will enable juries, or the judges who must instruct them, to bring the blurred lines of diminished capacity into proper focus so as to facilitate principled and consistent decision-making in criminal cases. In short, the fact that psychiatric evidence is admissible to prove or disprove insanity does not necessarily dictate the conclusion that it is admissible for purposes unrelated to the insanity defense.

"On appeal, Petitioner posits two arguments: (1) that the exclusion of psychiatric testimony, unrelated to the insanity defense, to show the absence of the requisite mental capacity to form the specific mens rea for a particular crime, or to show a state of mind susceptible to provocation, violates a defendant's right to compulsory process and due process under the Sixth and Fourteenth Amendments; and (2) the wholesale exclusion of expert testimony on an issue that directly impacts the mens rea element of an offense (i.e. diminished capacity) is violative of due process as an arbitrary rule that excludes evidence which is material and relevant. Petitioner contends that

> expert medical testimony should have been received both to negate the mens rea element of felonious assault, and to support an argument in favor of the lesser included offenses. In particular, such evidence would have gone directly to the issue of whether Petitioner was sufficiently provoked [as] to be guilty of only the lesser included offense of aggravated assault.

Petitioner essentially asks us to impose, as a matter of federal constitutional law, an obligation upon the State of Ohio to recognize the defense of diminished capacity. This we are unwilling to do.

"In *Muench v. Israel*, 715 F.2d 1124 (7th Cir.1983), the Court of Appeals for the Seventh Circuit concluded that 'a state is not constitutionally compelled to recognize the doctrine of diminished capacity and hence a state may exclude expert testimony offered for the purpose of establishing that a criminal defendant lacked the capacity to form a specific intent.' As the basis for its constitutional holding, the *Muench* court relied primarily upon three Supreme Court cases involving the question of whether a criminal defendant has a constitutional right to present evidence of psychological abnormalities (that fall short of legal insanity) in order to establish lack of capacity to form an intent to kill.

"In *Coleman v. California*, 317 U.S. 596, 63 S.Ct. 162, 87 L.Ed. 487 (1942)(per curiam), and *Troche v. California*, 280 U.S. 524, 50 S.Ct. 87, 74 L.Ed. 592 (1929)(per curiam), the defendants had been convicted of first-degree murder in California state court after their requests to introduce evidence of mental abnormalities in the guilt phase of their bifurcated trials had been denied. The Supreme Court dismissed the appeals for want of a substantial federal question. *Muench* explained that these are decisions on the merits and constitute binding precedent unless and until subsequent Supreme Court decisions indicate otherwise. In *Fisher v. United States*, 328 U.S. 463, 66 S.Ct. 1318, 90 L.Ed. 1382 (1946), the defendant had been convicted of first degree murder in the District of Columbia, and he contended that the trial court erred in its refusal to instruct the jury to consider the defendant's abnormal personality in determining the issue of intent. The Supreme Court, which possesses supervisory powers over the District's courts, rejected the claim, stating:

> It may be that psychiatry has now reached a position of certainty in its diagnosis and prognosis which will induce Congress to enact the rule of responsibility for crime for which petitioner contends. For this Court to force the District of Columbia to adopt such a requirement for criminal trials would involve a fundamental change in the common law theory of responsibility.

"Following its review of this trilogy, the Seventh Circuit explained:

> In our view, *Troche*, *Coleman*, and *Fisher* are dispositive of the question presented in the instant case. *Troche* and *Coleman* deemed petitioners' due process arguments as insubstantial, and *Fisher* carefully considered the same arguments and did not even find them sufficiently compelling to justify an exercise of the Court's supervisory authority over the District of Columbia courts. A theory that the Supreme Court has

twice refused to impose upon the state of California, albeit in summary decisions, and has refused to impose upon the District of Columbia courts under its supervisory powers, is not one that this lower federal court will impose on the state of Wisconsin as a matter of federal constitutional due process.

We agree. Accordingly, we hold that the Constitution does not require Ohio to recognize the defense of diminished capacity.

"The Compulsory Process Clause grants a criminal defendant the right to call witnesses that are 'material and favorable to his defense.' However, '[a] defendant's right to present relevant evidence is not unlimited, but rather is subject to reasonable restrictions.' *United States v. Scheffer*, 523 U.S. 303, 118 S.Ct. 1261, 140 L.Ed.2d 413 (1998)* * *

"In *Scheffer*, the Court explained that evidentiary rules do not abridge the right of an accused to present a defense 'so long as they are not "arbitrary" or "disproportionate to the purposes they are designed to serve." ' In addition, the Court pointed out that it has 'found the exclusion of evidence to be unconstitutionally arbitrary or disproportionate only where it has infringed upon a weighty interest of the accused.'

"The application of the *Wilcox* rule has not 'significantly undermined fundamental elements of the accused's defense.' First, *Wilcox* did not preclude Petitioner from introducing any factual evidence; i.e. ' "facts" about the alleged crime at hand.' Rather, *Wilcox* precluded Petitioner from offering psychiatric testimony, unrelated to an insanity defense, to show that she lacked the necessary mental capacity to form the specific mental state required for the crime of felonious assault. Second, the *Wilcox* rule did not prohibit Petitioner from testifying in her own behalf; presumably, Petitioner freely chose not to do so in this case. Hence, we find that the requirements outlined in *Scheffer* are satisfied."

    6.   To what extent is the concern not merely about the value of psychiatric evidence, but about the use of such evidence when the possible result is different from that which obtains when there is a successful insanity defense? Consider *People v. Wetmore*, 22 Cal.3d 318, 149 Cal.Rptr. 265, 583 P.2d 1308 (1978): "The same danger may arise, however, when a diminished capacity defense does not result in the defendant's acquittal, but in his conviction for a lesser included offense. A defendant convicted of a lesser included misdemeanor, for example, will be confined for a relatively short period in a facility which probably lacks a suitable treatment program, and may later, having served his term, be released to become a public danger. The solution to this problem thus does not lie in barring the defense of diminished capacity when the charged crime lacks a lesser included offense, but in providing for the confinement and treatment of defendants with diminished capacity arising from mental disease or defect."

Chapter 7

ALCOHOLISM AND ADDICTION; INTOXICATION; IMMATURITY

SECTION 1. CHRONIC ALCOHOLISM AND DRUG ADDICTION

POWELL v. TEXAS

Supreme Court of the United States, 1968.
392 U.S. 514, 88 S.Ct. 2145, 20 L.Ed.2d 1254.

MR. JUSTICE MARSHALL announced the judgment of the Court and delivered an opinion in which THE CHIEF JUSTICE, MR. JUSTICE BLACK, and MR. JUSTICE HARLAN join.

In late December 1966, appellant was arrested and charged with being found in a state of intoxication in a public place, in violation of Vernon's Ann.Texas Penal Code, Art. 477 (1952), which reads as follows:

"Whoever shall get drunk or be found in a state of intoxication in any public place, or at any private house except his own, shall be fined not exceeding one hundred dollars." * * *

The trial judge in the county court, sitting without a jury, * * * found appellant guilty, and fined him $50. * * *

The principal testimony was that of Dr. David Wade, a Fellow of the American Medical Association, duly certificated in psychiatry. * * * Dr. Wade sketched the outlines of the "disease" concept of alcoholism; noted that there is no generally accepted definition of "alcoholism"; alluded to the ongoing debate within the medical profession over whether alcohol is actually physically "addicting" or merely psychologically "habituating"; and concluded that in either case a "chronic alcoholic" is an "involuntary drinker," who is "powerless not to drink," and who "loses his self-control over his drinking." He testified that he had examined appellant, and that appellant is a "chronic alcoholic," who "by the time he has reached [the state of intoxication] * * * is not able to control his behavior, and [who] * * * has reached this point because he has an uncontrollable compulsion to drink." Dr. Wade also responded in the negative to the question whether appellant has "the willpower to resist the constant excessive consumption of alcohol." He added that in his opinion jailing appellant without medical attention would operate neither to rehabilitate him nor to lessen his desire for alcohol.

On cross-examination, Dr. Wade admitted that when appellant was sober he knew the difference between right and wrong, and he responded affirmatively to the question whether appellant's act in taking the first drink in any given instance when he was sober was a "voluntary exercise of his will." Qualifying his answer, Dr. Wade stated that "these individuals have a compulsion, and this compulsion, while not completely overpowering, is a very strong influence, an exceedingly strong influence, and this compulsion coupled with the firm belief in their mind that they are going to be able to handle it from now on causes their judgment to be somewhat clouded."

Appellant testified concerning the history of his drinking problem. He reviewed his many arrests for drunkenness; testified that he was unable to stop drinking; stated that when he was intoxicated he had no control over his actions and could not remember them later, but that he did not become violent; and admitted that he did not remember his arrest on the occasion for which he was being tried. On cross-examination, appellant admitted that he had had one drink on the morning of the trial and had been able to discontinue drinking.

Evidence in the case then closed. [T]he State contented itself with a brief argument that appellant had no defense to the charge because he "is legally sane and knows the difference between right and wrong."

Following this abbreviated exposition of the problem before it, the trial court indicated its intention to disallow appellant's claimed defense of "chronic alcoholism." Thereupon defense counsel submitted, and the trial court entered, the following "findings of fact":

"(1) That chronic alcoholism is a disease which destroys the afflicted person's will power to resist the constant, excessive consumption of alcohol.

"(2) That a chronic alcoholic does not appear in public by his own volition but under a compulsion symptomatic of the disease of chronic alcoholism.

"(3) That Leroy Powell, defendant herein, is a chronic alcoholic who is afflicted with the disease of chronic alcoholism."

Whatever else may be said of them, those are not "findings of fact" in any recognizable, traditional sense in which that term has been used in a court of law; they are the premises of a syllogism transparently designed to bring this case within the scope of this Court's opinion in *Robinson v. California,* 370 U.S. 660, 82 S.Ct. 1417, 8 L.Ed.2d 758 (1962). Nonetheless, the dissent would have us adopt these "findings" without critical examination; it would use them as the basis for a constitutional holding that "a person may not be punished if the condition essential to constitute the defined crime is part of the pattern of his disease and is occasioned by a compulsion symptomatic of the disease."

The difficulty with that position, as we shall show, is that it goes much too far on the basis of too little knowledge. In the first place, the record in this case is utterly inadequate to permit the sort of informed and responsible adjudication which alone can support the announcement of an important and wide-ranging new constitutional principle. We know very little about the circumstances surrounding the drinking bout which resulted in this conviction, or about Leroy Powell's drinking problem, or indeed about alcoholism itself.
* * *

Furthermore, the inescapable fact is that there is no agreement among members of the medical profession about what it means to say that "alcoholism" is a "disease." One of the principal works in this field states that the major difficulty in articulating a "disease concept of alcoholism" is that "alcoholism has too many definitions and disease has practically none." This same author concludes that *"a disease is what the medical profession recognizes as such."* In other words, there is widespread agreement today that "alcoholism" is a "disease," for the simple reason that the medical profession has concluded that it should attempt to treat those who have drinking problems. There the agreement stops. Debate rages within the medical profession as to whether "alcoholism" is a separate "disease" in any meaningful biochemical, physiological or psychological sense, or whether it represents one peculiar manifestation in some individuals of underlying psychiatric disorders. * * *

The trial court's "finding" that Powell "is afflicted with the disease of chronic alcoholism," which "destroys the afflicted person's will power to resist the constant, excessive consumption of alcohol" covers a multitude of sins. Dr. Wade's testimony that appellant suffered from a compulsion which was an "exceedingly strong influence," but which was "not completely overpowering" is at least more carefully stated, if no less mystifying. [C]onceptual clarity can only be achieved by distinguishing carefully between "loss of control" once an individual has commenced to drink and "inability to abstain" from drinking in the first place. Presumably a person would have to display both characteristics in order to make out a constitutional defense, should one be recognized. Yet the "findings" of the trial court utterly fail to make this crucial distinction, and there is serious question whether the record can be read to support a finding of either loss of control or inability to abstain.

Dr. Wade did testify that once appellant began drinking he appeared to have no control over the amount of alcohol he finally ingested. Appellant's own testimony concerning his drinking on the day of the trial would certainly appear, however, to cast doubt upon the conclusion that he was without control over his consumption of alcohol when he had sufficiently important reasons to exercise such control. However that may be, there are more serious factual and conceptual difficulties with reading this record to show that appellant was unable to abstain from drinking. Dr. Wade testified that when appellant was sober, the act of taking the first drink was a "voluntary exercise of his will," but that this exercise of will was undertaken under the "exceedingly strong influence" of a "compulsion" which was "not completely overpowering." Such concepts, when juxtaposed in this fashion, have little meaning. * * *

It is one thing to say that if a man is deprived of alcohol his hands will begin to shake, he will suffer agonizing pains and ultimately he will have hallucinations; it is quite another to say that a man has a "compulsion" to take a drink, but that he also retains a certain amount of "free will" with which to resist. It is simply impossible, in the present state of our knowledge, to ascribe a useful meaning to the latter statement. This definitional confusion reflects, of course, not merely the undeveloped state of the psychiatric art but also the conceptual difficulties inevitably attendant upon the importation of scientific and medical models into a legal system generally predicated upon a different set of assumptions. * * *

There is as yet no known generally effective method for treating the vast number of alcoholics in our society. * * * Thus it is entirely possible that, even were the manpower and facilities available for a full-scale attack upon chronic alcoholism, we would find ourselves unable to help the vast bulk of our "visible"—let alone our "invisible"—alcoholic population.

However, facilities for the attempted treatment of indigent alcoholics are woefully lacking throughout the country. It would be tragic to return large numbers of helpless, sometimes dangerous and frequently unsanitary inebriates to the streets of our cities without even the opportunity to sober up adequately which a brief jail term provides. Presumably no State or city will tolerate such a state of affairs. Yet the medical profession cannot, and does not, tell us with any assurance that, even if the buildings, equipment and trained personnel were made available, it could provide anything more than slightly higher-class jails for our indigent habitual inebriates. Thus we run the grave risk that nothing will be accomplished beyond the hanging of a new sign—reading "hospital"—over one wing of the jailhouse.

One virtue of the criminal process is, at least, that the duration of penal incarceration typically has some outside statutory limit; this is universally true in the case of petty offenses, such as public drunkenness, where jail terms are quite short on the whole. "Therapeutic civil commitment" lacks this feature; one is typically committed until one is "cured." Thus, to do otherwise than affirm might subject indigent alcoholics to the risk that they may be locked up for an indefinite period of time under the same conditions as before, with no more hope than before of receiving effective treatment and no prospect of periodic "freedom."

Faced with this unpleasant reality, we are unable to assert that the use of the criminal process as a means of dealing with the public aspects of problem drinking can never be defended as rational. * * *

Ignorance likewise impedes our assessment of the deterrent effect of criminal sanctions for public drunkenness. The fact that a high percentage of American alcoholics conceal their drinking problems, not merely by avoiding public displays of intoxication but also by shunning all forms of treatment, is indicative that some powerful deterrent operates to inhibit the public revelation of the existence of alcoholism. Quite probably this deterrent effect can be largely attributed to the harsh moral attitude which our society has traditionally taken toward intoxication and the shame which we have associated with alcoholism. * * *

Obviously, chronic alcoholics have not been deterred from drinking to excess by the existence of criminal sanctions against public drunkenness. But all those who violate penal laws of any kind are by definition undeterred. The longstanding and still raging debate over the validity of the deterrence justification for penal sanctions has not reached any sufficiently clear conclusions to permit it to be said that such sanctions are ineffective in any particular context or for any particular group of people who are able to appreciate the consequences of their acts. Certainly no effort was made at the trial of this case, beyond a monosyllabic answer to a perfunctory one-line question, to determine the effectiveness of penal sanctions in deterring Leroy Powell in particular or chronic alcoholics in general from drinking at all or from getting drunk in particular places or at particular times. * * *

Appellant, however, seeks to come within the application of the Cruel and Unusual Punishment Clause announced in *Robinson v. California,* which involved a state statute making it a crime to "be addicted to the use of narcotics." This Court held there that "a state law which imprisons a person thus afflicted [with narcotic addiction] as a criminal, even though he has never touched any narcotic drug within the State or been guilty of any irregular behavior there, inflicts a cruel and unusual punishment * * *."

On its face the present case does not fall within that holding, since appellant was convicted, not for being a chronic alcoholic, but for being in public while drunk on a particular occasion. The State of Texas thus has not sought to punish a mere status, as California did in *Robinson;* nor has it attempted to regulate appellant's behavior in the privacy of his own home. Rather, it has imposed upon appellant a criminal sanction for public behavior which may create substantial health and safety hazards, both for appellant and for members of the general public, and which offends the moral and esthetic sensibilities of a large segment of the community. This seems a far cry from convicting one for being an addict, being a chronic alcoholic, being "mentally ill, or a leper * * *."

Robinson so viewed brings this Court but a very small way into the substantive criminal law. And unless *Robinson* is so viewed it is difficult to see any limiting principle that would serve to prevent this Court from becoming, under the aegis of the Cruel and Unusual Punishment Clause, the ultimate arbiter of the standards of criminal responsibility, in diverse areas of the criminal law, throughout the country.

It is suggested in dissent that *Robinson* stands for the "simple" but "subtle" principle that "[c]riminal penalties may not be inflicted upon a person for being in a condition he is powerless to change." In that view, appellant's "condition" of public intoxication was "occasioned by a compulsion symptomatic of the disease" of chronic alcoholism, and thus, apparently, his behavior lacked the critical element of *mens rea.* Whatever may be the merits of such a doctrine of criminal responsibility, it surely cannot be said to follow from *Robinson.* The entire thrust of *Robinson's* interpretation of the Cruel and Unusual Punishment Clause is that criminal penalties may be inflicted only if the accused has committed some act, has engaged in some behavior, which society has an interest in preventing, or perhaps in historical common law terms, has committed some *actus reus.* It thus does not deal with the question of whether certain conduct cannot constitutionally be punished because it is, in some sense, "involuntary" or "occasioned by a compulsion."

Likewise, as the dissent acknowledges, there is a substantial definitional distinction between a "status," as in *Robinson,* and a "condition," which is said to be involved in this case. Whatever may be the merits of an attempt to distinguish between behavior and a condition, it is perfectly clear that the crucial element in this case, so far as the dissent is concerned, is whether or not appellant can legally be held responsible for his appearance in public in a state of intoxication. The only relevance of *Robinson* to this issue is that because the Court interpreted the statute there involved as making a "status" criminal, it was able to suggest that the statute would cover even a situation in which addiction had been acquired involuntarily. That this factor was not determinative in the case is shown by the fact that there was no indication of how Robinson himself had become an addict.

Ultimately, then, the most troubling aspects of this case, were *Robinson* to be extended to meet it, would be the scope and content of what could only be a constitutional doctrine of criminal responsibility. In dissent it is urged that the decision could be limited to conduct which is "a characteristic and involuntary part of the pattern of the disease as it afflicts" the particular individual, and that "[i]t is not foreseeable" that it would be applied "in the case of offenses such as driving a car while intoxicated, assault, theft, or robbery." That is limitation by fiat. In the first place, nothing in the logic of the dissent would limit its application to chronic alcoholics. If Leroy Powell cannot be convicted of public intoxication, it is difficult to see how a State can convict an individual for murder, if that individual, while exhibiting normal behavior in all other respects, suffers from a "compulsion" to kill, which is an "exceedingly strong influence," but "not completely overpowering." Even if we limit our consideration to chronic alcoholics, it would seem impossible to confine the principle within the arbitrary bounds which the dissent seems to envision.
* * *

Traditional common-law concepts of personal accountability and essential considerations of federalism lead us to disagree with appellant. We are unable to conclude, on the state of this record or on the current state of medical knowledge, that chronic alcoholics in general, and Leroy Powell in particular, suffer from such an irresistible compulsion to drink and to get drunk in public that they are utterly unable to control their performance of either or both of these acts and thus cannot be deterred at all from public intoxication. And in any event this Court has never articulated a general constitutional doctrine of *mens rea.*

We cannot cast aside the centuries-long evolution of the collection of interlocking and overlapping concepts which the common law has utilized to assess the moral accountability of an individual for his antisocial deeds. The doctrines of *actus reus, mens rea,* insanity, mistake, justification, and duress have historically provided the tools for a constantly shifting adjustment of the tension between the evolving aims of the criminal law and changing religious, moral, philosophical, and medical views of the nature of man. This process of adjustment has always been thought to be the province of the States. * * *

Affirmed.

MR. JUSTICE BLACK, whom MR. JUSTICE HARLAN joins, concurring.

* * * The argument is made that appellant comes within the terms of our holding in *Robinson* because being drunk in public is a mere status or "condition." Despite this many-faceted use of the concept of "condition," this argument would require converting *Robinson* into a case protecting actual behavior, a step we explicitly refused to take in that decision. * * *

The rule of constitutional law urged upon us by appellant would have a revolutionary impact on the criminal law, and any possible limits proposed for the rule would be wholly illusory. If the original boundaries of *Robinson* are to be discarded, any new limits too would soon fall by the wayside and the Court would be forced to hold the States powerless to punish any conduct that could be shown to result from a "compulsion," in the complex, psychological meaning of that term. * * *

The real reach of any such decision, however, would be broader still, for the basic premise underlying the argument is that it is cruel and unusual to punish a person who is not morally blameworthy. I state the proposition in this sympathetic way because I feel there is much to be said for avoiding the use of criminal sanctions in many such situations. But the question here is one of constitutional law. The legislatures have always been allowed wide freedom to determine the extent to which moral culpability should be a prerequisite to conviction of a crime. The criminal law is a social tool that is employed in seeking a wide variety of goals, and I cannot say the Eighth Amendment's limits on the use of criminal sanctions extend as far as this viewpoint would inevitably carry them.

But even if we were to limit any holding in this field to "compulsions" that are "symptomatic" of a "disease," in the words of the findings of the trial court, the sweep of that holding would still be startling. Such a ruling would make it clear beyond any doubt that a narcotics addict could not be punished for "being" in possession of drugs or, for that matter, for "being" guilty of using them. A wide variety of sex offenders would be immune from punishment if they could show that their conduct was not voluntary but part of the pattern of a disease. More generally speaking, a form of the insanity defense would be made a constitutional requirement throughout the Nation, should the Court now hold it cruel and unusual to punish a person afflicted with any mental disease whenever his conduct was part of the pattern of his disease and occasioned by a compulsion symptomatic of the disease. * * *

MR. JUSTICE WHITE, concurring in the result.

If it cannot be a crime to have an irresistible compulsion to use narcotics, *Robinson v. California,* I do not see how it can constitutionally be a crime to yield to such a compulsion. Punishing an addict for using drugs convicts for addiction under a different name. Distinguishing between the two crimes is like forbidding criminal conviction for being sick with flu or epilepsy but permitting punishment for running a fever or having a convulsion. Unless *Robinson* is to be abandoned, the use of narcotics by an addict must be beyond the reach of the criminal law. Similarly, the chronic alcoholic with an irresistible urge to consume alcohol should not be punishable for drinking or for being drunk.

Powell's conviction was for the different crime of being drunk in a public place. Thus even if Powell was compelled to drink, and so could not constitutionally be convicted for drinking, his conviction in this case can be invalidated only if there is a constitutional basis for saying that he may not be punished for being in public while drunk. * * *

The trial court said that Powell was a chronic alcoholic with a compulsion not only to drink to excess but also to frequent public places when intoxicated. Nothing in the record before the trial court supports the latter conclusion, which is contrary to common sense and to common knowledge. The sober chronic alcoholic has no compulsion to be on the public streets; many chronic alcoholics drink at home and are never seen drunk in public. Before and after taking the first drink, and until he becomes so drunk that he loses the power to know where he is or to direct his movements, the chronic alcoholic with a home or financial resources is as capable as the nonchronic drinker of doing his drinking in private, of removing himself from public places and, since he knows or ought to know that he will become intoxicated, of making plans to avoid his being found drunk in public. For these reasons, I cannot say that the chronic alcoholic who proves his disease and a compulsion to drink is shielded from conviction when he has knowingly failed to take feasible precautions against committing a criminal act, here the act of going to or remaining in a public place. On such facts the alcoholic is like a person with smallpox, who could be convicted for being on the street but not for being ill, or, like the epileptic, who would be punished for driving a car but not for his disease.[2]

For the purposes of this case, it is necessary to say only that Powell showed nothing more than that he was to some degree compelled to drink and that he was drunk at the time of his arrest. He made no showing that he was unable to stay off the streets on the night in question.[5] * * *

Mr. Justice Fortas, with whom Mr. Justice Douglas, Mr. Justice Brennan, and Mr. Justice Stewart join, dissenting. * * *

The sole question presented is whether a criminal penalty may be imposed upon a person suffering the disease of "chronic alcoholism" for a condition—being "in a state of intoxication" in public—which is a characteristic part of the pattern of his disease and

2. Analysis of this difficult case is not advanced by preoccupation with the label "condition." In *Robinson* the Court dealt with "a statute which makes the 'status' of narcotic addiction a criminal offense * * *." By precluding criminal conviction for such a "status" the Court was dealing with a condition brought about by acts remote in time from the application of the criminal sanctions contemplated, a condition which was relatively permanent in duration, and a condition of great magnitude and significance in terms of human behavior and values. Although the same may be said for the "condition" of being a chronic alcoholic, it cannot be said for the mere transitory state of "being drunk in public." "Being" drunk in public is not far removed in time from the acts of "getting" drunk and "going" into public, and it is not necessarily a state of any great duration. And, an isolated instance of "being" drunk in public is of relatively slight importance in the life of an individual as compared with the condition of being a chronic alcoholic. If it were necessary to distinguish between "acts" and "conditions" for purposes of the Eighth Amendment, I would adhere to the concept of "condition" implicit in the opinion in *Robinson*; I would not trivialize that concept by drawing a nonexistent line between the man who appears in public drunk and that same man five minutes later who is then "being" drunk in public. The proper subject of inquiry is whether volitional acts brought about the "condition" and whether those acts are sufficiently proximate to the "condition" for it to be permissible to impose penal sanctions on the "condition."

5. I do not question the power of the State to remove a helplessly intoxicated person from a public street, although against his will, and to hold him until he has regained his powers. The person's own safety and the public interest require this much. A statute such as the one challenged in this case is constitutional insofar as it authorizes a police officer to arrest any seriously intoxicated person when he is encountered in a public place. Whether such a person may be charged and convicted for violating the statute will depend upon whether he is entitled to the protection of the Eighth Amendment.

which, the trial court found, was not the consequence of appellant's volition but of "a compulsion symptomatic of the disease of chronic alcoholism." We deal here with the mere *condition* of being intoxicated in public.[2]

As I shall discuss, consideration of the Eighth Amendment issue in this case requires an understanding of "the disease of chronic alcoholism" with which, as the trial court found, appellant is afflicted, which has destroyed his "will power to resist the constant, excessive consumption of alcohol," and which leads him to "appear in public [not] by his own volition but under a compulsion symptomatic of the disease of chronic alcoholism." * * * Although there is some problem in defining the concept, its core meaning, as agreed by authorities, is that alcoholism is caused and maintained by something other than the moral fault of the alcoholic, something that, to a greater or lesser extent depending upon the physiological or psychological makeup and history of the individual, cannot be controlled by him. * * *

Authorities have recognized that a number of factors may contribute to alcoholism. Some studies have pointed to physiological influences, such as vitamin deficiency, hormone imbalance, abnormal metabolism, and hereditary proclivity. Other researchers have found more convincing a psychological approach, emphasizing early environment and underlying conflicts and tensions. Numerous studies have indicated the influence of sociocultural factors. It has been shown, for example, that the incidence of alcoholism among certain ethnic groups is far higher than among others.

The manifestations of alcoholism are reasonably well identified. * * * It is well established that alcohol may be habituative and "can be physically addicting." It has been said that "the main point for the nonprofessional is that alcoholism is not within the control of the person involved. He is not willfully drinking." * * *

Robinson stands upon a principle which, despite its subtlety, must be simply stated and respectfully applied because it is the foundation of individual liberty and the cornerstone of the relations between a civilized state and its citizens: Criminal penalties may not be inflicted upon a person for being in a condition he is powerless to change. In all probability, Robinson at some time before his conviction elected to take narcotics. But the crime as defined did not punish this conduct. The statute imposed a penalty for the offense of "addiction"—a condition which Robinson could not control. Once Robinson had become an addict, he was utterly powerless to avoid criminal guilt. He was powerless to choose not to violate the law.

In the present case, appellant is charged with a crime composed of two elements—being intoxicated and being found in a public place while in that condition. The crime, so defined, differs from that in *Robinson*. The statute covers more than a mere status. But the essential constitutional defect here is the same as in *Robinson*, for in both cases the particular defendant was accused of being in a condition which he had no capacity to change or avoid. The trial judge sitting as trier of fact found upon the medical and other relevant testimony, that Powell is a "chronic alcoholic." He defined appellant's "chronic alcoholism" as "a disease which destroys the afflicted person's will power to resist the constant, excessive consumption of alcohol." He also found that "a chronic alcoholic does not appear in public by his own volition but under a compulsion symptomatic of the disease

2. It is not foreseeable that findings such as those which are decisive here—namely that the appellant's being intoxicated in public was a part of the pattern of his disease and due to a compulsion symptomatic of that disease—could or would be made in the case of offenses such as driving a car while intoxicated, assault, theft, or robbery. Such offenses require independent acts or conduct and do not typically flow from and are not part of the syndrome of the disease of chronic alcoholism. If an alcoholic should be convicted for criminal conduct which is not a characteristic and involuntary part of the pattern of the disease as it afflicts him, nothing herein would prevent his punishment.

of chronic alcoholism." I read these findings to mean that appellant was powerless to avoid drinking; that having taken his first drink, he had "an uncontrollable compulsion to drink" to the point of intoxication; and that, once intoxicated, he could not prevent himself from appearing in public places.

The findings in this case, read against the background of the medical and sociological data to which I have referred, compel the conclusion that the infliction upon appellant of a criminal penalty for being intoxicated in a public place would be "cruel and inhuman punishment" within the prohibition of the Eighth Amendment. This conclusion follows because appellant is a "chronic alcoholic" who, according to the trier of fact, cannot resist the "constant excessive consumption of alcohol" and does not appear in public by his own volition but under a "compulsion" which is part of his condition.

I would reverse the judgment below.

Notes and Questions

1. "*Powell* turned out to be the end of the Court's flirtation with the possibility of a constitutional criminal law doctrine. How should we now view this episode? As a missed opportunity or as a close call? Like many, I'm of two minds. One is naturally uncomfortable with nine appointed lawyers calling the moral shots for the rest of us in deciding which criminal law doctrine should pass muster. Yet they've been known to do just that in other areas and to do so here might have served to temper the promiscuous legislative passion for punishment." Sanford H. Kadish, *Fifty Years of Criminal Law: An Opinionated Review*, 87 Calif.L.Rev. 943, 966 (1999).

2. In *Robinson*, the opinion of the Court, by Stewart, J., asserted that a state "might impose criminal sanctions, for example, against the unauthorized manufacture, prescription, sale, purchase, or possession of narcotics within its borders." White, J., dissenting, noted: "It is significant that in purporting to reaffirm the power of the States to deal with the narcotics traffic, the Court does not include among the obvious powers of the State the power to punish for the use of narcotics. I cannot think that the omission was inadvertent."

In *People v. Davis*, 27 Ill.2d 57, 188 N.E.2d 225 (1963), a statute making it an offense to be "under the influence of * * * narcotic drugs" was held unconstitutional; the court stressed that the defendant could have used the drugs outside the state. But in *Salas v. State*, 365 S.W.2d 174 (Tex.Cr.App.1963), notwithstanding an offer of evidence that defendant was under the influence when he crossed the international bridge into Texas, the court upheld a conviction under a similar provision, reasoning that the defendant had not been convicted for his status but rather for "the 'act' of being under the influence."

What bearing does *Powell* have on this issue?

3. *State ex rel. Harper v. Zegeer*, 170 W.Va. 743, 296 S.E.2d 873 (1982): "Since *Powell*, no state court has held that alcoholics could not be punished criminally for public intoxication, except Minnesota. Minn.Stat. § 340.96 provided that 'every person who becomes intoxicated by *voluntarily drinking* intoxicating liquors is guilty of the crime of drunkenness.' (Emphasis added.) In *State v. Fearon*, 283 Minn. 90, 166 N.W.2d 720 (1969), that court determined 'voluntarily drinking' applied only to those who consumed liquor by choice, not to alcoholics:

> However, on the evidence presented in this case, defendant was no more able to make a free choice as to when or how much he would drink than a person would be who is forced to drink under threat of physical violence. To ignore such evidence or distort the meaning of words used by the legislature in order to avoid application of advances

in man's knowledge of himself and his environment to existing laws would, we think, be a disservice to the law.

"Although statutes and ordinances involved here do not use the word 'voluntary', we agree with the reasoning of the Minnesota court.

"Other courts, however, have held that alcoholism is not a defense to public drunkenness charges. They have emphasized one or more of these notions: drinking is a voluntary action; if alcoholism is allowed to be a defense to public intoxication charges it might become a defense to other crimes; fear that an alcoholism defense will be expanded to other crimes; jail benefits drunks; and there is a distinction between the status of being an alcoholic and the act of appearing drunk in public. We believe that none of these reasons justifies incarceration of alcoholics.

" * * * Relying on the protections mandated by the West Virginia Constitution, we hold that no chronic alcoholic can be criminally prosecuted for public drunkenness."

4. David Robinson, Jr., *Powell v. Texas: The Case of the Intoxicated Shoeshine Man– Some Reflections a Generation Later by a Participant*, 26 Am.J.Crim.L. 401, 439–45 (1999): "In the years following the litigation in *Powell*, many states decriminalized public intoxication by statute, rather than by judicial decision. One model was the Uniform Alcoholism and Intoxication Treatment Act. This rather loosely-drafted act defines 'alcoholic' broadly to include both a person 'who habitually lacks self-control as to the use of alcoholic beverages' and those who use alcohol to the extent that 'health is substantially impaired or endangered or [their] social or economic function is substantially disrupted.' The latter is designed, according to the Comment, to make as large a group as possible eligible for treatment. Much of the body of the Act is designed to facilitate treatment of alcoholics, including voluntary or involuntary civil commitment. The Act also invalidates local laws and ordinances criminalizing drinking and intoxication and encourages repeal of state laws of the same character. Thirteen states adopted the Act in part; two subsequently repealed it.

"A number of states and local governments have enacted similar statutes. Among the incentives for these reforms is that they create eligibility for federal grants under the Comprehensive Alcohol Abuse and Alcoholism Prevention, Treatment, and Rehabilitation Act of 1974. Among the declared purposes of this legislation was 'the development of methods for diverting problem drinkers from criminal justice systems into prevention and treatment programs.' In Los Angeles following legislative, judicial, and administrative rulings, arrests for public intoxication declined sixty percent, and prosecutions declined ninety-two percent. * * *

"Other statutes may of course be utilized to deal with public inebriation, such as those proscribing loitering, vagrancy, begging, public urination, camping, sleeping, jaywalking, and disorderly conduct. In view of the opportunities for coercive interventions provided by this galaxy of offenses, the practice of local police departments may be of more practical importance than whether a jurisdiction has adopted a theoretically more focused reform, such as the Uniform Alcoholism and Intoxication Treatment Act. * * *

" * * * While the 1967 President's Crime Commission Report stated that in 1965 there were two million public drunkenness arrests in America, for the year 1996, the number of reported arrests had fallen to less than 465,000 for people over eighteen.

"The assessment of noncriminal detoxification programs is a challenging process. If the group studied is ordered into the program by courts or deposited there by police, the recidivism rates are much higher than programs voluntarily sought-out by more stable individuals, particularly if the evaluation is limited to those who remain in the program for a long period of time. Many alcoholics have personality problems in addition to their drinking behaviors. There is also the possibility of spontaneous remission. Many inebriates enter detoxification programs at a low point in their functioning and might improve whatever the institutional stimulus. There are also difficulties of reliability in studies relying on reports of clients as to their former alcohol use and their degree of improvement under treatment programs. In addition, persons entering and continuing in treatment programs are likely to be more highly motivated to change their behaviors. Skepticism with respect to reports of the effectiveness of various treatment programs is supported by studies indicating similar results notwithstanding wide variation in methods and duration in programs. A recent national review concludes: 'While the general consensus is that some treatment is better than none . . ., there is little evidence that more intensive and costly care (such as hospital inpatient) is more effective than less intensive care (e.g., outpatient).'

"From the standpoint of those formerly arrested for being drunk in public, the change has not been a marked therapeutic success: * * *

Standard approaches to treatment for this group are not generally very successful. There was hope in the mid–1970s that decriminalization of public drunkenness would lead to engagement of CPIs [chronic public inebriates] in treatment, with a consequent reduction in their numbers. It soon became apparent that most CPIs had little interest in treatment. Instead of using detoxification services as the entry point into a continuum of care leading to abstinence, CPIs frequently used it as a sort of "wet" shelter, part of a cycle to and from the streets. For the most part, recidivism has not been reduced.

"The medical model may have other unintended consequences, as well. To the extent that criminal sanctions project a moral message that public intoxication is not simply a symptom of an illness, they may serve to reinforce important social norms. Going to jail for being drunk in public can deliver a message that being ordered or carried to a detoxication facility and released cannot. * * * The threat of loss of self-esteem and respect may be a more significant consequence of the criminal sanction than the threat of the formal penalty itself.

"An alternative is simply to tolerate the presence of intoxicated persons on our sidewalks and streets. This, too, is problematic in terms of its consequences for the quality of urban life and in the flight of those who can afford it to the suburbs, leaving the central cities largely to the poor."

5. If the law enforcement practices mentioned by Robinson are by their nature directed predominantly at the homeless, are they objectionable on that basis? In *Joyce v. City and County of San Francisco*, 846 F.Supp. 843 (N.D.Cal.1994), a class action by homeless persons seeking to enjoin such enforcement as would prohibit "life-sustaining activities such as sleeping, sitting or remaining in a public place," the court in denying a preliminary injunction stated:

"Depicting homelessness as 'status' is by no means self-evident * * *. That depiction, made upon serious analysis only in *Pottinger v. Miami*, 810 F.Supp. 1551 (S.D.Fla.1992), is a dubious extension of *Robinson* and *Powell*, and of questionable merit in light of concerns implicating federalism and the proper role of the Court in such adjudications.

"Insofar as *Pottinger* attempts to reason from applicable Supreme Court precedent that homelessness equals a 'status,' and that acts derivative of such status are constitutionally protected, the reasoning of that court cannot be said at this stage of the litigation to be sufficiently persuasive to indicate a likely possibility of success on the merits of the underlying suit. *Pottinger* explained that, [while a]n initial reading of *Powell* suggests that all conduct is outside the rule of *Robinson* ... [the] plurality was not confronted with a critical distinguishing factor that is unique to the plight of the homeless plaintiffs in this case: that they have no realistic choice but to live in public places.

Finding as a matter of fact that being homeless is only 'rarely' a choice, and that alternative shelter was unavailable, the court held that:

plaintiffs have no choice but to conduct involuntary, life-sustaining activities in public places. The harmless conduct for which they are arrested is inseparable from their involuntary condition of being homeless.

The Court concluded that the City of Miami was liable to a class of homeless plaintiffs for 'effectively punish[ing] them for something for which they may not be convicted under the eighth amendment.'

"This Court is unable to conclude at this time that the extension of the Eighth Amendment to the 'acts' at issue here is warranted by governing authorities. Plaintiffs argue that the failure of the City to provide sufficient housing compels the conclusion that homelessness on the streets of San Francisco is cognizable as a status. This argument is unavailing at least for the fundamental reason that status cannot be defined as a function of the discretionary acts of others.[9]

"On no occasion, moreover, has the Supreme Court invoked the Eighth Amendment in order to protect acts derivative of a person's status. *Robinson* prohibited penalizing a person based on their status as having been addicted, whereas the plurality in *Powell* approved a state's prosecution of the act of appearing intoxicated in public. What justified invocation of the Eighth Amendment in one case and not the other was not the difference between drug and alcohol addiction; such distinction is without analytical difference. Rather, the different results were reached because of the distinct targets of the challenged laws—one punished a status, the other an act. * * *

"Plaintiffs' argument that *Powell* would have been differently decided had the defendant been homeless does not reflect the holding of the case and is sheer speculation. While language in Justice White's concurrence can be argued to support that contention, such language was dicta. One can only hypothesize that Justice White would actually have cast his vote differently had the defendant been homeless. Nothing underscores this point more vividly than the fact that Justice White was one of two vigorous dissenters in *Robinson*.

"As an analytical matter, more fundamentally, homelessness is not readily classified as a 'status.' * * * While the concept of status might elude perfect definition, certain factors assist in its determination, such as the involuntariness of the acquisition of that quality (including the presence or not of that characteristic at birth), and the degree to which an individual has control over that characteristic.

"Examples of such 'status' characteristics might include age, race, gender, national origin and illness. The reasoning of the Court in including drug addiction as status involved the analogy of drug addiction to a disease or an illness which might be contracted involuntarily. While homelessness can be thrust upon an unwitting recipient, and while a person may be largely incapable of changing that condition, the distinction between the ability to eliminate one's drug addiction as compared to one's homelessness is a distinction in kind as much as in degree. To argue that homelessness is a status and not a condition,

---

9. As the Supreme Court has declined to find any "constitutional guarantee of access to dwellings of a particular quality," *Lindsey v. Normet,* 405 U.S. 56, 74, 92 S.Ct. 862, 874, 31 L.Ed.2d 36 (1972), the housing provided to the City's homeless is a matter for the discretion of the City and State.

moreover, is to deny the efficacy of acts of social intervention to change the condition of those currently homeless.

"In addition to the fact that homelessness does not analytically fit into a definition of a status under the contours of governing case law, the effects which would ensue from such a determination by this Court would be staggering. Courts seeking analytical consistency with such a holding would be required to provide constitutional protection to any condition over which a showing could be made that the defendant had no control."

UNITED STATES v. MOORE

United States Court of Appeals, District of Columbia Circuit, 1973.

486 F.2d 1139.

WILKEY, CIRCUIT JUDGE, with whom CIRCUIT JUDGES MacKINNON and ROBB join.

This is an appeal from a conviction under two federal statutes for possession of heroin. * * * Arguing that he has lost the power of self-control with regard to his addiction, appellant maintains that by applying "the broad principles of common law criminal responsibility" we must decide that he is entitled to dismissal of the indictment or a jury trial on this issue. The gist of appellant's argument here is that "the common law has long held that the capacity to control behavior is a prerequisite for criminal responsibility."

It is inescapable that the logic of appellant's argument, if valid, would carry over to all other illegal acts of any type whose purpose was to obtain narcotics for his own use, a fact which is admitted by Judge Wright in his opinion.

* * * Drug addiction of varying degrees may or may not result in loss of self-control, depending on the strength of character opposed to the drug craving. Under appellant's theory, adopted by the dissenters, only if there is a resulting loss of self-control can there be an absence of *free will* which, under the extension of the common law theory, would provide a valid defense to the addict. If there is a demonstrable absence of free will (loss of self-control), the illegal acts of possession and acquisition cannot be charged to the user of the drugs.

But if it is absence of free will which excuses the mere possessor-acquirer, the more desperate bank robber for drug money has an even more demonstrable lack of free will and derived from precisely the same factors as appellant argues should excuse the mere possessor.

* * * In fact, it seems clear that the addict who restrains himself from committing any other crimes except acquisition and possession, assuming he obtains his funds by lawful means, has demonstrated a greater degree of self-control than the addict who in desperation robs a bank to buy at retail. If the addict can restrain himself from committing any other illegal act except purchase and possession, then he is demonstrating a degree of self-control greater than that of the one who robs a pharmacy or a bank, and thus his defense of loss of control and accountability is even less valid than that of the addict who robs the pharmacy or the bank. * * *

All of this points up the wisdom of Justice Black's observations in *Powell,* where he reached the conclusion that questions of "voluntariness" or "compulsion" should not be "controlling on the question [of] whether a specific instance of human behavior should be immune from punishment as a constitutional matter" * * *.

Just as Justice Black turned away from the proposed constitutional rule, we spurn the proposed "common law" rule, not only because the recently created statutory scheme of dealing with narcotics addicts stands a reasonable chance of reaching the objectives of "deterrence, isolation, and treatment," but also because the particular nature of the problem of the heroin traffic makes certain policies necessary that should not be weakened by the creation of this defense. There is no compelling policy requiring us to intervene here. * * *

To evaluate the proposed defense in light of the Eighth Amendment we review the case law, in particular, *Robinson v. California* and *Powell v. Texas.* This review demonstrates that the case law simply does not support the position advanced by appellant. * * *

Standing alone, * * * *Robinson* is no authority for the proposition that the Eighth Amendment prevents punishment of an addict for acts he is "compelled" to do by his addiction, since *Robinson* recognizes no compulsion in addiction. *Robinson* simply illustrates repugnance at the prospect of punishing one for his status as an addict. * * *

Where the asserted analogy with *Powell* breaks down * * * is, first, that the acts in *Powell* were held to be punishable, as Justice White's separate opinion for the majority makes clear. Second, here the acquisition and possession of the addictive substance by Moore are *illegal* activities, whereas in *Powell* the "addict" induced his addictive state through *legal* means. Powell's violation was in actions taken later, which to four members of the Court were punishable without question, and which to Justice White were punishable so long as the acts had not been proved to be the product of an established irresistible compulsion. In *Moore,* however, the acquisition and possession of the addictive substance (narcotics) are themselves illegal, whether considered as initial acts *causing* addiction or acts *resulting* from addiction.

* * * Moore could never put the needle in his arm the first and many succeeding times without an exercise of will. His *illegal acquisition and possession* are thus the direct product of a *freely willed illegal act.*

According to the appellant's thesis, an addict only has a choice as to the manner in which he obtains the funds (or the drugs) to support his habit; this neglects the choice that each addict makes *at the start* as to whether or not he is going to take narcotics and run the risk of becoming addicted to them. Although the narcotics user may soon through continued use acquire a compulsion to have the drug, and thus be said to have lost his self-control (insofar as he must take the drug regularly) due to a "disease," it is a disease which he has induced himself through a violation of the law. In contrast to the alcoholic Powell, the drug addict Moore has contracted a disease which virtually always commences with an illegal act. * * *

LEVENTHAL, CIRCUIT JUDGE; with whom McGOWAN, CIRCUIT JUDGE, concurs. * * *

Appellant's key defense concepts are impairment of behavioral control and loss of self-control. These have been considered by this court most fully in discussion of the insanity defense, and the philosophy of those opinions is invoked, although appellant disclaims the insanity defense as such. * * *

Appellant's presentation rests, in essence, on the premise that the "mental disease or defect" requirement of [the cases defining the insanity defense] is superfluous. He discerns a broad principle that excuses from criminal responsibility when conduct results from a condition that impairs behavior control. * * * The broad assertion is that in general the mens rea element of criminal responsibility requires freedom of will, which is negatived by an impairment of behavioral control and loss of self-control.

If drug dependence really negatived mens rea, it would be a defense not only to the offense of possession or purchase of prohibited drugs but to other actions taken under the compulsion of the need to obtain the drug. If there is an impairment and lack of capacity to alter conduct, there is no way in which the line can be drawn in mens rea terms so as to exclude the very large percentage of addicts who must support their habit by engaging in retail sales, or, indeed, committing other crimes in order to satisfy their compulsion for drugs. * * *

Appellant's surface logic loses luster with analysis. It does not follow that because one condition (mental disease) yields an exculpatory defense if it results in impairment of and lack of behavioral controls the same result follows when some other condition impairs behavior controls. * * *

The legal conception of criminal capacity cannot be limited to those of unusual endowment or even average powers. A few may be recognized as so far from normal as to be entirely beyond the reach of criminal justice, but in general the criminal law is a means of social control that must be potentially capable of reaching the vast bulk of the population. Criminal responsibility is a concept that not only extends to the bulk of those below the median line of responsibility, but specifically extends to those who have a realistic problem of substantial impairment and lack of capacity due, say, to weakness of intellect that establishes susceptibility to suggestion; or to a loss of control of the mind as a result of passion, whether the passion is of an amorous nature or the result of hate, prejudice or vengeance; or to a depravity that blocks out conscience as an influence on conduct.

The criminal law cannot "vary legal norms with the individual's capacity to meet the standards they prescribe, absent a disability that is both gross and verifiable, such as the mental disease or defect that may establish irresponsibility. The most that it is feasible to do with lesser disabilities is to accord them proper weight in sentencing." * * *

In our view, the rule for drug addiction should not be modeled on the rule for mental disease because of crucial distinctions between conditions. The subject of mental disease, though subject to some indeterminacy, and difficulty of diagnosis when extended to volitional impairment as well as cognitive incapacity, has long been the subject of systematic study, and in that framework it is considered manageable to ask psychiatrists to address the distinction, all-important and crucial to the law, between incapacity and indisposition, between those who can't and those who won't, between the impulse irresistible and the impulse not resisted. These are matters as to which the court has accepted the analysis of medicine, medical conditions and symptoms, and on the premise that they can be considered on a verifiable basis, and with reasonable dispatch, the courts have recognized a defense even in conditions not as obvious and verifiable as those covered in the older and limited test of capacity to know right from wrong.

As to the subject of drug dependence and psychic incapacity to refrain from narcotics, even the 1970 Study Draft of the Staff of the National Commission on Reform of Federal Criminal Laws, which favors on balance a drug dependence defense to the crime of possession, for incapacity to refrain from use, candidly recognizes the problems involved. One is "the paradox of jail for the least dangerous possessors (non-addict experimenters and the like) while addicts go free." More important, for present purposes, is the Staff's caution first, that even physical symptoms might "be successfully feigned," and, more broadly, that there is considerable difficulty of verification of the claim of a drug user that he is unable to refrain from use. * * *

The difficulty of the verification problem of lack of capacity to refrain from use is sharpened on taking into account that the issue comprehends the addict's failure to participate in treatment programs. This raises problems of the addict's personal knowledge, disposition, motivation, as well as extent of community programs, that may usefully be assessed by someone considering what program to try now or next, but would irretrievably tangle a trial. * * *

The difficulty is sharpened by the appreciable number of narcotic "addicts" who do abandon their habits permanently, and much larger number who reflect their capacity to refrain by ceasing use for varying periods of time. The reasons are not clear but the phenomenon is indisputable. It is noted in the Staff Report, and reported by specialists voicing different approaches to addiction problems.

There is need for reasonable verifiability as a condition to opening a defense to criminal responsibility. The criminal law cannot gear its standards to the individual's capacity "absent a disability that is both gross and verifiable, such as the mental disease or defect that may establish irresponsibility."

* * * Not dissimilar considerations undergird the maxim, ignorance of the law is no excuse, which contradicts salient principles underlying mens rea, yet rejects the defense claim in the interest of society. "The plea would be universally made, and would lead to interminable questions incapable of solution." The needs of society require overriding the subjective good faith of the individual as a legal defense, remitting his position to mitigation of punishment and executive clemency.

Reliability and validity of a legal defense require that it can be tested by criteria external to the actions which it is invoked to excuse. And so the Model Penal Code's caveat paragraph rejects an insanity defense based on an abnormality manifested only by repeated criminal or otherwise anti-social conduct. * * *

WRIGHT, CIRCUIT JUDGE, with whom BAZELON, CHIEF JUDGE, and TAMM and ROBINSON, CIRCUIT JUDGES, join, dissenting:

* * * I suggest that the development of the common law of *mens rea* has reached the point where it should embrace a new principle: a drug addict who, by reason of his use of drugs, lacks substantial capacity to conform his conduct to the requirements of the law may not be held criminally responsible for mere possession of drugs for his own use. The trial judge refused appellant's request to give the jury an instruction based on this principle. I would, therefore, reverse this conviction and remand the case for a new trial. * * *

Although *Powell* left unsettled the precise relationship between criminal responsibility and the Constitution, no member of the Court expressed even the slightest disagreement with the basic proposition that the Eighth Amendment provides only the floor and not the ceiling for development of common law notions of criminal responsibility. Indeed, Mr. Justice Marshall, adopting a restrictive view of the constitutional issue, emphasized that the "doctrines of *actus reus, mens rea,* insanity, mistake, justification, and duress have historically provided the tools for a constantly shifting adjustment of the tension between the evolving aims of the criminal law and changing religious, moral, philosophical, and medical views of the nature of man. * * * "

Thus, no matter what interpretation of *Powell* eventually is adopted, the decision must "be read not as a bar, but as an exhortation toward further experiment with common-law doctrines of criminal responsibility."

The concept of criminal responsibility is, by its very nature, "an expression of the moral sense of the community." In western society, the concept has been shaped by two dominant value judgments—that punishment must be morally legitimate, and that it must not unduly threaten the liberties and dignity of the individual in his relationship to society. As a result, there has historically been a strong conviction in our jurisprudence that to hold a man criminally responsible his actions must have been the product of a "free will." * * *

Thus criminal responsibility is assessed only when through "free will" a man elects to do evil, and if he is not a free agent, or is unable to choose or to act voluntarily, or to avoid the conduct which constitutes the crime, he is outside the postulate of the law of punishment.

Despite this general principle, however, it is clear that our legal system does not exculpate all persons whose capacity for control is impaired, for whatever cause or reason. Rather, in determining responsibility for crime, the law assumes "free will" and then recognizes known deviations "where there is a broad consensus that free will does not exist" with respect to the particular condition at issue. The evolving nature of this process is amply demonstrated in the gradual development of such defenses as infancy, duress, insanity, somnambulism and other forms of automatism, epilepsy and unconsciousness, involuntary intoxication, delirium tremens, and chronic alcoholism.

A similar consensus exists today in the area of narcotics addiction. * * * Thus it can no longer seriously be questioned that for at least some addicts the "overpowering" psychological and physiological need to possess and inject narcotics cannot be overcome by mere exercise of "free will."

Moreover, recognition of a defense of "addiction" for crimes such as possession of narcotics is consistent not only with our historic common law notions of criminal responsibility and moral accountability, but also with the traditional goals of penology—retribution, deterrence, isolation and rehabilitation.

Unlike other goals of penology, the retributive theory of criminal justice looks solely to the past for justification, without regard to considerations of prevention or reformation. Although the primordial desire for vengeance is an understandable emotion, it is a testament to the constantly evolving nature of our social and moral consciousness that the law has, in recent decades, come to regard this "eye-for-an-eye" philosophy as an improper basis for punishment. But even if this barbaric notion of justice retained its validity, it clearly would be inapplicable to those persons who act under a compulsion. Revenge, if it is ever to be legitimate, must be premised on moral blameworthiness, and what segment of our society would feel its need for retribution satisfied when it wreaks vengeance upon those who are diseased because of their disease? * * *

The most widely employed argument in favor of punishing addicts for crimes such as possession of narcotics is that such punishment or threat of punishment has a substantial deterrent effect. Given our present knowledge, however, the merits of this argument appear doubtful. Deterrence presupposes rationality—it proceeds on the assumption that the detriments which would inure to the prospective criminal upon apprehension can be made so severe that he will be dissuaded from undertaking the criminal act. In the case of the narcotic addict, however, the normal sense of reason, which is so essential to effective functioning of deterrence, is overcome by the psychological and physiological compulsions of the disease. As a result, it is widely agreed that the threat of even harsh prison sentences cannot deter the addict from using and possessing the drug.

A similar situation prevails insofar as deterrence of *potential* addicts is concerned. * * * Since the nonaddict may still be punished for his possession of narcotics, the only consolation he might find in exculpation of addict possessors is that if he eventually attains the status of "addict" he must be treated rather than punished. But given what we now know about the pitiable life of an addict, this somewhat dubious consolation is hardly likely to "encourage" persons to use narcotics.

There is another side to the question of deterrence, however, which should not be ignored. The criminal law may serve as a deterrent not only through the fear of apprehension and prosecution, but also through the more general educative or moralizing effect the law may have upon society. Viewed in this manner, punishment as a concrete expression of society's disapproval of particular conduct helps to instill a desired moral code in the citizenry against commission of the proscribed acts.

* * * Since the addict's possession of narcotics is simply a symptom of his disease and not an act of "free will," however, this conduct cannot properly be deemed "culpable," and it would therefore seem inappropriate for society to utilize him as a mere vehicle through which to deter others. * * *

Shifting our focus now to the goal of isolating the offender, we arrive here at not only a justifiable basis for action but one which, in some cases at least, may be vital to the interests of society. * * *

This does not mean, however, that the goal of isolation justifies infliction of criminal punishment upon the addict. On the contrary, this interest may be fully vindicated through a program of civil commitment with treatment as well as by criminal incarceration. And since the addict is not a culpable offender, treatment is clearly a preferable alternative to mere imprisonment. * * *

This, then, brings us to the final and most important goal of modern penology—to rehabilitate the offender. In this age of enlightened correctional philosophy, we now recognize that society has a responsibility to both the individual and the community to treat the offender so that upon his release he may function as a productive, law-abiding citizen. And this is all the more true where, as with the non-trafficking addict possessor, the offender has acted under the compulsion of a disease. The task of rehabilitating the narcotic addict is not, as once was thought, a hopeless task. Great strides have been made in recent years toward development of effective and humane treatment techniques at both community-based and institutional levels, and the cure rate for addiction is now far higher than that of many other illnesses. Thus, with the possible exception of those addicts who remain incurable, society clearly cannot meet its responsibilities simply by confining the addict without treatment. Such an approach does nothing to cure the chronic relapsing aspects of the disease, and where confinement takes the form of imprisonment the addict is thrust inevitably into a "revolving door" of arrest, conviction, imprisonment, release and arrest, with the period of incarceration serving as but a temporary and futile stopping point in an otherwise interminable cycle. * * *

Perhaps the most troublesome question arising out of recognition of the addiction defense I suggest is whether it should be limited only to those acts—such as mere possession for use—which are inherent in the disease itself. It can hardly be doubted that, in at least some instances, an addict may in fact be "compelled" to engage in other types of criminal activity in order to obtain sufficient funds to purchase his necessary supply of narcotics. In such cases, common law principles of criminal responsibility would clearly be applicable. Indeed, it would seem intolerable that such addicts, who are "already crippled by an almost hopeless cycle of poverty, ignorance and drugs, should be further burdened by the moral stigma of guilt, *not* because they are morally blameworthy, but merely because we cannot afford to treat them as if they are not." Nevertheless, I am convinced that Congress has manifested a clear intent to preclude common law extension of the defense beyond those crimes which, like the act of possession, cause direct harm only to the addict himself. * * *[a]

a. In an omitted portion of Judge Wright's opinion, he observed (i) that in the 1956 amendments to the Jones–Miller and Harrison Acts, Congress stated unequivocally that addict traffickers should be treated no differently than nonaddict traffickers; and (ii) that in enacting Titles I and II of the Narcotics Addict Rehabilitation Act, "Congress expressly intended that addicts charged with specified crimes of violence or certain types of trafficking should be held criminally liable despite their addiction. For lesser crimes such as shop-

The basic question of criminal responsibility under the addiction defense is a legal, and not a purely medical, determination. Not all drug users are "addicts" and, as with any compulsion, the degree of dependence may vary among different individuals and, indeed, even in a given individual at different stages of his addiction. Thus what we are concerned with here is not an abstract medical or psychiatric definition of addiction which sets forth a clinical checklist of relevant symptoms but, rather, a behavioral model, based upon traditional legal and moral principles, which tests the ability of the defendant to control his behavior. The essential inquiry, then, is simply whether at the time of the offense, the defendant, as a result of his repeated use of narcotics, lacked substantial capacity to conform his conduct to the requirements of the law. * * *

BAZELON, CHIEF JUDGE (concurring in part and dissenting in part):

* * * I would also permit a jury to consider addiction as a defense to a charge of, for example, armed robbery or trafficking in drugs, to determine whether the defendant was under such duress or compulsion, because of his addiction, that he was unable to conform his conduct to the requirements of the law. * * *

Notes and Questions

1. In *People v. Davis,* 33 N.Y.2d 221, 351 N.Y.S.2d 663, 306 N.E.2d 787 (1973), the court offered yet another reason for the conclusion that an addict may be convicted of drug possession: "Moreover, while it may be that the policy of rehabilitation would be well-served by affording addicts a cruel and unusual punishment and drug dependence defense to possession for their own use, we should not lose sight of the utility of such penalties to law enforcement. For example, these possible penalties may, through the exercise of prosecutorial discretion, enable law enforcement to enlist addict-informers in ferreting out the wholesalers of illicit drugs, thereby facilitating the policy of elimination of the drug traffic. Then, too, punishment may persuade some addicts to undertake rehabilitation through various State or private programs. On the other hand, recognition of the defense might conceivably make the addict the witting or unwitting tool of the drug trafficker."

2. Herbert Fingarette, *Addiction and Criminal Responsibility,* 84 Yale L.J. 413, 443–44 (1975): "In spite of a vast literature, professionals in the field of drug addiction acknowledge that no satisfactory scientific understanding of drug addiction has been reached. Thus there is no medical foundation for adopting the general proposition at the crux of the exculpatory legal arguments, the proposition that addictive conduct is involuntary. On the other hand, massive descriptive evidence indicates that individuals often make choices to abandon addictive conduct or abstain from drug use permanently or temporarily. Moreover, authorities observe that narcotic addiction often involves little in the way of chemical or biological influences. Yet it may provide an important individual or group identity for many who lack socially approved skills or are socially alienated. Popular beliefs about the chemically-induced hell of withdrawal agony or the insatiable craving for ecstatic pleasures are profoundly at odds with the facts, though they have deeply colored the thinking of the courts. All this information forces abandonment of the argument that drug addiction—and acts associated with it—be regarded as legally involuntary. * * *

"Undoubtedly there are those who regard possible legal approaches to addiction in polar terms: Either we inflict harsh, punitive and degrading measures on the addict, or we declare the person sick and therefore not responsible for his conduct. What is needed here is the abandonment of such extreme and fixed positions. In the present antipunitive

lifting or fraud, civil commitment was made available *in lieu of prosecution or sentencing* and only *after* the addict offender had been brought into the criminal process."

atmosphere in many enlightened circles, it is appropriate to recall that the lawful and proper threat of sanctions may be not only a pragmatically effective approach, but also a morally humane approach. It regards the addict as an autonomous person, responsible for guiding his own life, and subject to law. The medical approach can also reflect a humane concern, a concern for the weak and ailing and for those who cannot, in some respects, handle their own lives. By now it is no news that both of these approaches, however inspired, can in practice disregard human dignity when ignorance, social prejudice, well-intentioned dogma, lack of funding, or routinization take over. We need to rethink the implications of both approaches against the background of the limited knowledge that we have. Coordinating the attack on the complex problem of drug abuse is preeminently a legislative responsibility. For the courts to assume that addictive drug use or addiction-related conduct is involuntary and to build such an unworthy assumption into constitutional and common law doctrine would be a grave error."

3. In Robinson, the court noted that "a state might establish a program of compulsory treatment for those addicted to narcotics." Is this the best solution? Consider Note, 60 Geo.L.J. 667, 670–72 (1972): "Efforts to provide treatment for drug addicts in a systematic way have concentrated primarily on the development of involuntary commitment procedures. Since 1961, several states and the federal government have enacted statutes authorizing the involuntary commitment of drug addicts convicted of a crime to an institution for a period of inpatient treatment, followed by compulsory aftercare. While such involuntary commitment procedures do provide an alternative to imprisonment, they have been found wanting for several reasons. First, it has been questioned whether involuntary commitment to an institution is in fact nonpunitive and significantly different from criminal incarceration. Distrust of these programs because of their punitive aspects has resulted in defendants often trying to avoid the 'treatment' alternative at any cost. Second, the rehabilitative successes of the programs have been small. This has led some to question whether the long period of confinement authorized in the statutes can be justified. Third, the requirement that a full adversary hearing be held to order certification, upon the demand of the defendant, has resulted in additional court congestion and consequent underutilization of this treatment route. There are ways to modify the involuntary commitment programs, but because the problems with these programs are so manifold, there is good reason to look in other directions for a response to the needs of the addict, the courts, and society."

4. In *Gorham v. United States,* 339 A.2d 401 (D.C.App.1975), following *Moore,* the court made much of the fact that a "pretrial diversion program for drug abusers" was available. Is this the best solution? How should such a program be structured? Consider Steven Belenko, *The Challenges of Integrating Drug Treatment Into the Criminal Justice Process,* 63 Alb.L.Rev. 833, 844–46 (2000):

"Formal diversion programs originated in the 1960s, and despite some concerns about 'net-widening' or 'net-tightening,' these programs still exist in many jurisdictions. In the typical treatment diversion model, recent arrestees are offered an opportunity to have their cases held in abeyance while they attend a court-monitored treatment program.

"In the pre-plea or deferred prosecution model, the offender is diverted into treatment prior to any adjudication. In the post-plea model the offender is required to plead guilty (and may be sentenced) prior to treatment diversion. Successful completion of the treatment program results in the dismissal of the original criminal charges (for pre-plea models), the withdrawal of the guilty plea and dismissal of the charges (for post-plea models), or a reduction in the sentence or resentencing from incarceration to probation (in the post-plea, post-sentencing model). Diversion programs are nearly always operated and controlled by the district attorney, who has overall responsibility for determining eligibility, screening the cases, and monitoring treatment progress.

"Despite their relatively long history, diversion programs continue to be relatively uncommon, and tend to serve a small percentage of the drug-involved offender population. There are several reasons for this. First, for political reasons, many prosecutors are hesitant to offer treatment to offenders, especially those charged with drug sale or other felonies. Second, diversion programs require additional screening, assessment, and monitoring resources that many prosecutors' offices or courts lack. Third, it can be difficult to locate a sufficient number of community-based treatment slots that can be set aside for offenders: treatment resource constraints or a reluctance by providers to accept criminal justice clients can impact on treatment availability for offenders. Finally, diversion programs have the potential to widen the restrictive net over defendants. These interventions often place additional restrictions and reporting requirements on defendants who, in the absence of such programs, might have been handled much more leniently. By placing release conditions on defendants that may be difficult to fully adhere to, such as abstention from any drugs for an addict or heavy user, there becomes a high probability of failure and the subsequent revocation of release, or imposition of additional sanctions that are unrelated to the original criminal event.

"With a few exceptions, * * * diversion programs tend to target low-level offenders such as misdemeanants or first offenders. This population is more politically acceptable for prosecutors, and more serious offenders may have restrictions placed on case processing alternatives by mandatory sentencing laws or legislated plea bargaining restrictions. However, diverting low-level offenders may have a more limited impact on crime. Although politically and legally more difficult to place in treatment alternatives, diverting more serious offenders may actually save more resources and have a greater impact on crime."

5. What then of methadone maintenance? Consider James Vorenberg & Irving F. Lukoff, *Addiction, Crime, and the Criminal Justice System*, 37 Fed.Prob. 3, 7 (Dec.1973): "The public's first exposure to methadone created high expectations. Some reports suggested the new drug had almost magical qualities—heroin hunger would in some mysterious way be blocked, patients would turn dramatically from crime to a constructive, happy life. What little we have learned to date shows that the early picture was too rosy. For the addicts in Bedford–Stuyvesant—who clearly are economically, socially and medically a more depressed group than those groups who were first the subjects of methadone treatment programs and experiments—the results have been far less dramatic. Our data suggest that different subgroups in the sample respond differently to the program with regard to such things as drug use, criminal activity, and even kinds of crimes whose incidence are reduced. Many addicts on methadone maintenance continue to use heroin and other drugs, although at lower levels than before entering treatment. The level of criminal charges for patients in the first year of treatment is actually *higher* than the average rate over the full period of the patients' addiction, but shows a drop as compared with the year immediately preceding entry to the program. What this suggests is that addicts may not come into such programs until they reach a point at which the level of drug use and required criminal activity to support that use has gotten uncomfortably high.

"What we have found to date suggests that it is unrealistic to expect radical changes in behavior from a methadone-based program. The rejection of a long-term life in deviance—aggravated by addiction[6]—is at best a slow process. Any effective results would appear to

---

6. They earlier noted "that for a substantial segment of the patient group criminal behavior *antedates*   the onset of heroin use."

be a function of a long tenure in treatment in which the administration of methadone is but one rehabilitative tool. Such a trend is indicated by the early figures we have on the criminal behavior of the patients who remained in the program for 2 years."

SECTION 2. VOLUNTARY AND INVOLUNTARY INTOXICATION

MONTANA v. EGELHOFF

Supreme Court of the United States, 1996.

518 U.S. 37, 116 S.Ct. 2013, 135 L.Ed.2d 361.

JUSTICE SCALIA announced the judgment of the Court and delivered an opinion, in which THE CHIEF JUSTICE, JUSTICE KENNEDY, and JUSTICE THOMAS join.

We consider in this case whether the Due Process Clause is violated by Montana Code Annotated § 45–2–203, which provides, in relevant part, that voluntary intoxication "may not be taken into consideration in determining the existence of a mental state which is an element of [a criminal] offense."

In July 1992, while camping out in the Yaak region of northwestern Montana to pick mushrooms, respondent made friends with Roberta Pavola and John Christenson, who were doing the same. On Sunday, July 12, the three sold the mushrooms they had collected and spent the rest of the day and evening drinking, in bars and at a private party in Troy, Montana. Some time after 9 p.m., they left the party in Christenson's 1974 Ford Galaxy station wagon. The drinking binge apparently continued, as respondent was seen buying beer at 9:20 p.m. and recalled "sitting on a hill or a bank passing a bottle of Black Velvet back and forth" with Christenson.

At about midnight that night, officers of the Lincoln County, Montana, sheriff's department, responding to reports of a possible drunk driver, discovered Christenson's station wagon stuck in a ditch along U.S. Highway 2. In the front seat were Pavola and Christenson, each dead from a single gunshot to the head. In the rear of the car lay respondent, alive and yelling obscenities. His blood-alcohol content measured .36 percent over one hour later. On the floor of the car, near the brake pedal, lay respondent's .38-caliber handgun, with four loaded rounds and two empty casings; respondent had gunshot residue on his hands.

Respondent was charged with two counts of deliberate homicide, a crime defined by Montana law as "purposely" or "knowingly" causing the death of another human being. A portion of the jury charge, uncontested here, instructed that "[a] person acts purposely when it is his conscious object to engage in conduct of that nature or to cause such a result," and that "[a] person acts knowingly when he is aware of his conduct or when he is aware under the circumstances his conduct constitutes a crime; or, when he is aware there exists the high probability that his conduct will cause a specific result." Respondent's defense at trial was that an unidentified fourth person must have committed the murders; his own extreme intoxication, he claimed, had rendered him physically incapable of committing the murders, and accounted for his inability to recall the events of the night of July 12. Although respondent was allowed to make this use of the evidence that he was intoxicated, the jury was instructed that it could not consider respondent's "intoxicated condition . . . in determining the existence of a mental state which is an element of the offense." The jury found respondent guilty on both counts, and the court sentenced him to 84 years' imprisonment.

The Supreme Court of Montana reversed. * * *

The cornerstone of the Montana Supreme Court's judgment was the proposition that the Due Process Clause guarantees a defendant the right to present and have considered by the jury *"all relevant evidence* to rebut the State's evidence on all elements of the offense charged." (emphasis added). Respondent does not defend this categorical rule; he acknowledges that the right to present relevant evidence "has not been viewed as absolute." That is a wise concession, since the proposition that the Due Process Clause guarantees the right to introduce all relevant evidence is simply indefensible. As we have said: "The accused does not have an unfettered right to offer [evidence] that is incompetent, privileged, or otherwise inadmissible under standard rules of evidence." * * * Of course, to say that the right to introduce relevant evidence is not absolute is not to say that the Due Process Clause places no limits upon restriction of that right. But it is to say that the defendant asserting such a limit must sustain the usual heavy burden that a due process claim entails * * *. Respondent's task, then, is to establish that a defendant's right to have a jury consider evidence of his voluntary intoxication in determining whether he possesses the requisite mental state is a "fundamental principle of justice."

Our primary guide in determining whether the principle in question is fundamental is, of course, historical practice. Here that gives respondent little support. By the laws of England, wrote Hale, the intoxicated defendant "shall have no privilege by this voluntary contracted madness, but shall have the same judgment as if he were in his right senses." According to Blackstone and Coke, the law's condemnation of those suffering from dementia affectata was harsher still: Blackstone, citing Coke, explained that the law viewed intoxication "as an aggravation of the offence, rather than as an excuse for any criminal misbehaviour." This stern rejection of inebriation as a defense became a fixture of early American law as well. * * *

The historical record does not leave room for the view that the common law's rejection of intoxication as an "excuse" or "justification" for crime would nonetheless permit the defendant to show that intoxication prevented the requisite mens rea. Hale, Coke, and Blackstone were familiar, to say the least, with the concept of mens rea, and acknowledged that drunkenness "deprive [s] men of the use of reason." It is inconceivable that they did not realize that an offender's drunkenness might impair his ability to form the requisite intent; and inconceivable that their failure to note this massive exception from the general rule of disregard of intoxication was an oversight. Hale's statement that a drunken offender shall have the same judgment "as if he were in his right senses" must be understood as precluding a defendant from arguing that, because of his intoxication, he could not have possessed the mens rea required to commit the crime. * * *

Against this extensive evidence of a lengthy common-law tradition decidedly against him, the best argument available to respondent is the one made by his amicus and conceded by the State: Over the course of the 19th century, courts carved out an exception to the common law's traditional across-the-board condemnation of the drunken offender, allowing a jury to consider a defendant's intoxication when assessing whether he possessed the mental state needed to commit the crime charged, where the crime was one requiring a "specific intent." The emergence of this new rule is often traced to an 1819 English case, in which Justice Holroyd is reported to have held that "though voluntary drunkenness cannot excuse from the commission of crime, yet where, as on a charge of murder, the material question is, whether an act was premeditated or done only with sudden heat and impulse, the fact of the party being intoxicated [is] a circumstance proper to be taken into consideration." * * * Eventually, however, the new view won out, and by the end of the 19th century, in most American jurisdictions, intoxication could be considered in determining whether a defendant was capable of forming the specific intent necessary to commit the crime charged.

On the basis of this historical record, respondent's amicus argues that "[t]he old common-law rule ... was no longer deeply rooted at the time the Fourteenth Amendment was ratified." That conclusion is questionable, but we need not pursue the point, since the argument of amicus mistakes the nature of our inquiry. It is not the State which bears the burden of demonstrating that its rule is "deeply rooted," but rather respondent who must show that the principle of procedure violated by the rule (and allegedly required by due process) is " 'so rooted in the traditions and conscience of our people as to be ranked as fundamental.' " Thus, even assuming that when the Fourteenth Amendment was adopted the rule Montana now defends was no longer generally applied, this only cuts off what might be called an a fortiori argument in favor of the State. The burden remains upon respondent to show that the "new common-law" rule—that intoxication may be considered on the question of intent—was so deeply rooted at the time of the Fourteenth Amendment (or perhaps has become so deeply rooted since) as to be a fundamental principle which that Amendment enshrined.

That showing has not been made. Instead of the uniform and continuing acceptance we would expect for a rule that enjoys "fundamental principle" status, we find that fully one-fifth of the States either never adopted the "new common-law" rule at issue here or have recently abandoned it.

It is not surprising that many States have held fast to or resurrected the common-law rule prohibiting consideration of voluntary intoxication in the determination of mens rea, because that rule has considerable justification—which alone casts doubt upon the proposition that the opposite rule is a "fundamental principle." A large number of crimes, especially violent crimes, are committed by intoxicated offenders; modern studies put the numbers as high as half of all homicides, for example. Disallowing consideration of voluntary intoxication has the effect of increasing the punishment for all unlawful acts committed in that state, and thereby deters drunkenness or irresponsible behavior while drunk. The rule also serves as a specific deterrent, ensuring that those who prove incapable of controlling violent impulses while voluntarily intoxicated go to prison. And finally, the rule comports with and implements society's moral perception that one who has voluntarily impaired his own faculties should be responsible for the consequences.[4]

There is, in modern times, even more justification for laws such as § 45–2–203 than there used to be. Some recent studies suggest that the connection between drunkenness and crime is as much cultural as pharmacological—that is, that drunks are violent not simply because alcohol makes them that way, but because they are behaving in accord with their learned belief that drunks are violent. This not only adds additional support to the traditional view that an intoxicated criminal is not deserving of exoneration, but it suggests that juries—who possess the same learned belief as the intoxicated offender—will be too quick to accept the claim that the defendant was biologically incapable of forming the requisite mens rea. Treating the matter as one of excluding misleading evidence therefore makes some sense.[5]

4. As appears from this analysis, we are in complete agreement with the concurrence that § 45–2–203 "embodies a legislative judgment regarding the circumstances under which individuals may be held criminally responsible for their actions." We also agree that the statute " 'extract[s] the entire subject of voluntary intoxication from the mens rea inquiry.' " We believe that this judgment may be implemented, and this effect achieved, with equal legitimacy by amending the substantive requirements for each crime, or by simply excluding intoxication evidence from the trial. We address this as an evidentiary statute simply because that is how the Supreme Court of Montana chose to analyze it.

5. These many valid policy reasons for excluding evidence of voluntary intoxication refute JUSTICE O'CONNOR's claim that § 45–2–203 has no purpose other than to improve the State's likelihood of winning a conviction.

In sum, not every widespread experiment with a procedural rule favorable to criminal defendants establishes a fundamental principle of justice. Although the rule allowing a jury to consider evidence of a defendant's voluntary intoxication where relevant to mens rea has gained considerable acceptance, it is of too recent vintage, and has not received sufficiently uniform and permanent allegiance, to qualify as fundamental, especially since it displaces a lengthy common-law tradition which remains supported by valid justifications today. * * *

"The doctrines of actus reus, mens rea, insanity, mistake, justification, and duress have historically provided the tools for a constantly shifting adjustment of the tension between the evolving aims of the criminal law and changing religious, moral, philosophical, and medical views of the nature of man. This process of adjustment has always been thought to be the province of the States." *Powell v. Texas*, [p. 447 of this Book]. The people of Montana have decided to resurrect the rule of an earlier era, disallowing consideration of voluntary intoxication when a defendant's state of mind is at issue. Nothing in the Due Process Clause prevents them from doing so, and the judgment of the Supreme Court of Montana to the contrary must be reversed.

It is so ordered.

JUSTICE GINSBURG, concurring in the judgment.

The Court divides in this case on a question of characterization. * * * If § 45–2–203 is simply a rule designed to keep out "relevant, exculpatory evidence," JUSTICE O'CONNOR maintains, Montana's law offends due process. If it is, instead, a redefinition of the mental-state element of the offense, on the other hand, JUSTICE O'CONNOR's due process concern "would not be at issue," for "[a] state legislature certainly has the authority to identify the elements of the offenses it wishes to punish," and to exclude evidence irrelevant to the crime it has defined.

Beneath the labels (rule excluding evidence or redefinition of the offense) lies the essential question: Can a State, without offense to the Federal Constitution, make the judgment that two people are equally culpable where one commits an act stone sober, and the other engages in the same conduct after his voluntary intoxication has reduced his capacity for self-control? For the reasons that follow, I resist categorizing § 45–2–203 as merely an evidentiary prescription, but join the Court's judgment refusing to condemn the Montana statute as an unconstitutional enactment.

Section 45–2–203 does not appear in the portion of Montana's Code containing evidentiary rules (Title 26), the expected placement of a provision regulating solely the admissibility of evidence at trial. Instead, Montana's intoxication statute appears in Title 45 ("Crimes"), as part of a chapter entitled "General Principles of Liability." No less than adjacent provisions governing duress and entrapment, § 45–2–203 embodies a legislative judgment regarding the circumstances under which individuals may be held criminally responsible for their actions. * * *

Comprehended as a measure redefining mens rea, § 45–2–203 encounters no constitutional shoal. States enjoy wide latitude in defining the elements of criminal offenses, particularly when determining "the extent to which moral culpability should be a prerequisite to conviction of a crime." * * *

Other state courts have upheld statutes similar to § 45–2–203, not simply as evidentiary rules, but as legislative redefinitions of the mental-state element. * * *

If, as the plurality, JUSTICE O'CONNOR, and JUSTICE SOUTER agree, it is within the legislature's province to instruct courts to treat a sober person and a voluntarily intoxicated person as equally responsible for conduct—to place a voluntarily intoxicated person on a level with a sober person—then the Montana law is no less tenable under the Federal

Constitution than are the laws, with no significant difference in wording, upheld in sister States. The Montana Supreme Court did not disagree with the courts of other States; it simply did not undertake an analysis in line with the principle that legislative enactments plainly capable of a constitutional construction ordinarily should be given that construction.

Justice O'Connor, with whom Justice Stevens, Justice Souter, and Justice Breyer join, dissenting.

* * * Due process demands that a criminal defendant be afforded a fair opportunity to defend against the State's accusations. Meaningful adversarial testing of the State's case requires that the defendant not be prevented from raising an effective defense, which must include the right to present relevant, probative evidence. To be sure, the right to present evidence is not limitless; for example, it does not permit the defendant to introduce any and all evidence he believes might work in his favor, nor does it generally invalidate the operation of testimonial privileges. Nevertheless, "an essential component of procedural fairness is an opportunity to be heard. That opportunity would be an empty one if the State were permitted to exclude competent, reliable evidence" that is essential to the accused's defense. Section 45–2–203 forestalls the defendant's ability to raise an effective defense by placing a blanket exclusion on the presentation of a type of evidence that directly negates an element of the crime, and by doing so, it lightens the prosecution's burden to prove that mental-state element beyond a reasonable doubt.

This latter effect is as important to the due process analysis as the former. A state legislature certainly has the authority to identify the elements of the offenses it wishes to punish, but once its laws are written, a defendant has the right to insist that the State prove beyond a reasonable doubt every element of an offense charged. Because the Montana Legislature has specified that a person commits "deliberate homicide" only if he "purposely or knowingly causes the death of another human being," the prosecution must prove the existence of such mental state in order to convict. That is, unless the defendant is shown to have acted purposely or knowingly, he is not guilty of the offense of deliberate homicide. The Montana Supreme Court found that it was inconsistent with the legislature's requirement of the mental state of "purposely" or "knowingly" to prevent the jury from considering evidence of voluntary intoxication, where that category of evidence was relevant to establishment of that mental-state element.

Where the defendant may introduce evidence to negate a subjective mental-state element, the prosecution must work to overcome whatever doubts the defense has raised about the existence of the required mental state. On the other hand, if the defendant may not introduce evidence that might create doubt in the factfinder's mind as to whether that element was met, the prosecution will find its job so much the easier. A subjective mental state is generally proved only circumstantially. If a jury may not consider the defendant's evidence of his mental state, the jury may impute to the defendant the culpability of a mental state he did not possess. * * *

The plurality brushes aside this Court's precedents as variously fact-bound, irrelevant, and dicta. I would afford more weight to principles enunciated in our case law than is accorded in the plurality's opinion today. It seems to me that a State may not first determine the elements of the crime it wishes to punish, and then thwart the accused's defense by categorically disallowing the very evidence that would prove him innocent.

The plurality does, however, raise an important argument for the statute's validity: the disallowance, at common law, of consideration of voluntary intoxication where a defendant's state of mind is at issue. Because this disallowance was permitted at common law, the plurality argues, its disallowance by Montana cannot amount to a violation of a "fundamental principle of justice."

[But] significant modification took place in the 19th century. Courts acknowledged the fundamental incompatibility of a particular mental-state requirement on the one hand, and the disallowance of consideration of evidence that might defeat establishment of that mental state on the other. In the slow progress typical of the common law, courts began to recognize that evidence of intoxication was properly admissible for the purpose of ascertaining whether a defendant had met the required mental-state element of the offense charged. * * *

Courts across the country agreed that where a subjective mental state was an element of the crime to be proved, the defense must be permitted to show, by reference to intoxication, the absence of that element. * * *

* * * The plurality argues that rejection of the historical rule in the 19th century simply does not establish that the " 'new common-law' "rule is a principle of procedure so "deeply rooted" as to be ranked "fundamental." But to determine whether a fundamental principle of justice has been violated here, we cannot consider only the historical disallowance of intoxication evidence, but must also consider the "fundamental principle" that a defendant has a right to a fair opportunity to put forward his defense, in adversarial testing where the State must prove the elements of the offense beyond a reasonable doubt. As concepts of mens rea and burden of proof developed, these principles came into conflict, as the shift in the common law in the 19th century reflects.

JUSTICE GINSBURG concurs in the Court's judgment based on her determination that § 45-2-203 amounts to a redefinition of the offense that renders evidence of voluntary intoxication irrelevant to proof of the requisite mental state. * * *

There is, however, no indication that such a "redefinition" occurred. JUSTICE GINSBURG's reading of Montana law is plainly inconsistent with that given by the Montana Supreme Court, and therefore cannot provide a valid basis to uphold § 45-2-203's operation. "We are, of course, bound to accept the interpretation of [state] law by the highest court of the State."

JUSTICE SOUTER, dissenting.

* * * Montana had at least one way to give effect to its judgment that defendants should not be permitted to use evidence of their voluntary intoxication to defeat proof of culpable mental state, and perhaps a second. First, it could have defined culpable mental state so as to give voluntary intoxication no exculpatory relevance. While the Due Process Clause requires the government to prove the existence of every element of the offense beyond a reasonable doubt, within fairly broad limits the definition of those elements is up to the State. * * *

While I therefore find no apparent constitutional reason why Montana could not render evidence of voluntary intoxication excludable as irrelevant by redefining "knowledge" and "purpose," as they apply to the mental state element of its substantive offenses, or by making some other provision for mental state, I do not believe that I am free to conclude that Montana has done so here. Our view of state law is limited by its interpretation in the State's highest court, and I am not able to square the State Supreme Court's opinion in this case with the position advanced by the State here (and supported by the United States as amicus curiae), that Montana's legislature changed the definition of culpable mental states when it enacted § 45–2–203.

A second possible (although by no means certain) option may also be open. Even under a definition of the mental state element that would treat evidence of voluntary intoxication as relevant and exculpatory, the exclusion of such evidence is typically permissible so long as a State presents a " 'valid' reason" to justify keeping it out. * * *

Hence, I do not rule out the possibility of justifying exclusion of relevant intoxication evidence in a case like this. At the least, there may be reasons beyond those actually advanced by Montana that might have induced a State to reject its prior law freely admitting intoxication evidence going to mental state.

A State (though not necessarily Montana) might, for example, argue that admitting intoxication evidence on the issue of culpable mental state but not on a defense of incapacity (as to which it is widely assumed to be excludable as generally irrelevant) would be irrational since both capacity to obey the law and purpose to accomplish a criminal result presuppose volitional ability. * * * And quite apart from any technical irrationality, a State might think that admitting the evidence in question on culpable mental state but not capacity (when each was a jury issue in a given case) would raise too high a risk of juror confusion. While Thomas Reed Powell reportedly suggested that "learning to think like a lawyer is when you learn to think about one thing that is connected to another without thinking about the other thing it is connected to," a State might argue that its law should be structured on the assumption that its jurors typically will not suffer from this facility.

Quite apart from the fact that Montana has made no such arguments for justification here, however, I am not at all sure why such arguments would go any further than justifying redefinition of mental states (the first option above). I do not understand why they would justify the State in cutting the conceptual corner by leaving the definitions of culpable mental states untouched but excluding evidence relevant to this proof. Absent a convincing argument for cutting that corner, [we should] hold the current Montana statute unconstitutional. I therefore respectfully dissent.

Justice Breyer, with whom Justice Stevens joins, dissenting.

* * * To have read the statute differently—to treat it as if it had redefined the mental element—would produce anomalous results. A statute that makes voluntary intoxication the legal equivalent of purpose or knowledge but only where external circumstances would establish purpose or knowledge in the absence of intoxication, is a statute that turns guilt or innocence not upon state of mind, but upon irrelevant external circumstances. An intoxicated driver stopped at an intersection who unknowingly accelerated into a pedestrian would likely be found guilty, for a jury unaware of intoxication would likely infer knowledge or purpose. An identically intoxicated driver racing along a highway who unknowingly sideswiped another car would likely be found innocent, for a jury unaware of intoxication would likely infer negligence. Why would a legislature want to write a statute that draws such a distinction, upon which a sentence of life imprisonment, or death, may turn? If the legislature wanted to equate voluntary intoxication, knowledge, and purpose, why would it not write a statute that plainly says so, instead of doing so in a roundabout manner that would affect, in dramatically different ways, those whose minds, deeds, and consequences seem identical? I would reserve the question of whether or not such a hypothetical statute might exceed constitutional limits.

Notes and Questions

1. Given that a majority of the Court believes that how the statute is characterized is determinative, what alternative interpretations of § 45–2–203 are possible and how would they differ in terms of how individual cases would come out? Consider Ronald J. Allen, *Montana v. Egelhoff-Reflections on the Limits of Legislative Imagination and Judicial*

Authority, 87 J.Crim.L. & Criminology 633, 637–38 (1997): "Under the substantive interpretation, a person who happens to be drunk, but still sufficiently in possession of her senses so that there is sufficient cognitive activity to permit willed bodily movements (voluntary act) and intent to commit, even if stupidly and later regretfully, the natural and probable consequences of those acts is simply out of luck. But so, too, apparently, is the person completely lacking even minimal cognitive activity. Like an irrebuttable presumption of negligence from the violation of a safety statute or the irrebuttable presumption of paternity when a child is born to a couple during wedlock, the finding of a death caused by a drunken individual would be murder. End of story. Thus, the state would not have to show any (other) evidence of any mental state. If the evidentiary exclusion interpretation is adopted, a much different situation is presented. Sufficient evidence of voluntariness and intentionality would have to be adduced to permit a finding of these elements beyond reasonable doubt, and the defendant would not be permitted to respond to that evidence with her own evidence of intoxication. * * *

"Both Scalia and Ginsburg gave a different interpretation to the statute from either of the ones I have advanced, although one that is very hard to comprehend:

> To obtain a conviction, the prosecution must prove only that (1) the defendant caused the death of another with actual knowledge or purpose, or (2) that the defendant killed "under circumstances that would otherwise establish knowledge or purpose 'but for' [the defendant's] voluntary intoxication."

"This formulation requires the resolution of a very strange counter factual. It requires the fact finder to ask whether the mental elements 'would have been' established had the defendant not been intoxicated, even though he was and even though he in fact may not have committed a voluntary act with the intent to bring out the forbidden consequence. What might that mean?"

2. Peter Westen, *Egelhoff Again*, 36 Am.Crim.L.Rev. 1203, 1276–77 (1999), claims the Supreme Court "foundered * * * because it failed to recognize the significance of the distinctive way in which James Egelhoff claimed to be too drunk to know what he was doing.

"James Egelhoff claimed that his intoxication induced a fugue state of automatism during which he was wholly unconscious of what he was doing. Unfortunately, the Court unwittingly confounded Egelhoff's claim with one he did not make—namely, that, though he was conscious at the time, his intoxication caused him to act accidentally or by mistake."

If that was in fact Egelhoff's claim, then how does this change the issue before the Court?

3. Consider Larry Alexander, *The Supreme Court, Dr. Jekyll, and the Due Process of Proof*, 1996 Sup.Ct.Rev. 191, 213–15: "If the real message of the Court in *Egelhoff* is that *Mullaney* [p. 264 of this Book] is dead and that the Constitution permits intoxicant-induced killings to be punished as severely as intentional ones, what should be our verdict on that message? * * *

"Of course, for overruling *Mullaney* to be a good thing, the Supreme Court will have to do a decent job in deciding what are the core elements of crimes that due process (or the Eighth Amendment) requires be proved beyond a reasonable doubt. And that leads to asking how well the Court did on the question of whether intoxication can be an alternative to intent in the most serious of all crimes, murder.

"Because the Justices overwhelmingly expressed support for allowing states to substitute voluntary intoxication for intent in murder statutes, it is instructive to look at the much more common practice among the states, namely, substituting voluntary intoxication for the mens rea of recklessness. The Model Penal Code's approach [in § 2.08(1),(2)] to voluntary intoxication is the prototype for this more common practice. * * *

"The Model Penal Code approach to intoxication can be viewed as one in which voluntary intoxication is treated like a culpable but nonpunishable act that enters the actor in a punishment lottery. If he is lucky and does not commit the actus reus of any crime, nothing happens. If, however, he is unlucky and commits the actus reus of some crime, he is punished for whatever crime he happens to commit at the level that he would have been punished had he committed the crime recklessly, including reckless homicide. The approach bears similarities to felony-murder statutes, where the underlying felony can be upgraded to murder if a death occurs even if the mens rea required for murder is otherwise absent.

"The Model Penal Code approach to voluntary intoxication can be contrasted with an alternative that is less lottery-like. A state could make voluntary intoxication itself a crime on the ground that it produces an unreasonable risk of uncontrollable harmful conduct. The seriousness of the crime and the severity of its punishment could be based on the average social harm voluntary intoxication leads to, or they could be based on the greatest social harm for which voluntary intoxication is a substantial and unjustifiable risk. In either case, the punishment for homicide committed by an intoxicated actor unaware of what he was doing would probably be much lower than the standard punishment for reckless homicide. On the other hand, the great majority of intoxicated actors who harm no one would all be criminally punishable at that level.

"Montana has taken the Model Penal Code's penal lottery approach to voluntary intoxication, but it has upped the stakes. Now if the actor kills someone while intoxicated and possesses neither the purpose to kill, the knowledge that he is killing, nor even an awareness that he is risking death, he can be convicted of a crime that is the equivalent of intentional homicide. * * * And the Justices of the Supreme Court appeared to have no difficulty, at least as a constitutional matter, with either the lottery nature of Montana's approach or the severity of the consequences that befall the losers in such a lottery, as Egelhoff himself could well have been."

4. The traditional view has been to distinguish between "specific intent," the category discussed in *Egelhoff*, and "general intent," and thus it has commonly been held that voluntary intoxication is no defense where the offense is of the general intent type, e.g., *State v. Sterling*, 235 Kan. 526, 680 P.2d 301 (1984) (crime of criminal damage to property), but that a "defense" of intoxication may be interposed where the crime is characterized as one requiring a specific intent, e.g., *United States v. Scott*, 529 F.2d 338 (D.C.Cir.1975) (crime of entering bank with intent to rob). In *People v. Langworthy*, 416 Mich. 630, 331 N.W.2d 171 (1982), the court asserted "the illogic and incongruity of the general intent-specific intent dichotomy," but then said "the remedy is not clear cut." Is either of those propositions correct?

5. As to the latter assertion, consider *United States v. Nix*, 501 F.2d 516 (7th Cir.1974), involving the convictions of Nix and Peterson under 18 U.S.C.A. § 751 for attempted escape and escape, respectively, from a federal institution. Nix was apprehended inside a locked truck a few hours after it had been driven out of the institution and parked adjacent thereto; Peterson was caught 8 miles away on the day following his disappearance. In both trials, the court instructed that the defendants' claimed intoxication was no defense, and on appeal the court, after noting Nix's claim that attempted escape, unlike escape, was a specific intent crime, concluded:

"The trouble with this approach is the impossibility of drawing a line between escape and attempted escape. Was the difference between Nix' act and Peterson's the eight miles Peterson traveled? Or an overnight absence versus the hours Nix was missing? * * * We believe the distinction between the two crimes is too flimsy to support a rule of law that would attach great importance to the prosecutor's choice between a charge of escape and one of attempted escape.

"This deficiency in the traditional analysis might be overcome by labeling both crimes as general-intent crimes, as the district judge did, or as specific-intent crimes, as Peterson urges. These labels are 'often used in the cases but seldom defined.' They were developed, at least with regard to intoxication, primarily to allow drunkenness as a defense to first-degree murder but not to lesser degrees of homicide. The attempt to apply the terms to nonviolent crimes such as escape has produced confused reasoning and disparate results.

> Categorizing all crimes as either having 'general' or 'specific' intent seems too mechanical and often forecloses evaluation by the court of the important consideration involved, i.e., what elements are involved in the crime and whether the prosecution has satisfactorily established them. *Intoxication as a Criminal Defense*, 55 Colum.L.Rev. 1210, 1217 (1955).

* * *

"Most courts, confronted with evidence that a defendant could not or did not form an intent to leave and not to return, have held such an intent essential to proof of the crime of escape. * * *

"These cases lead us to a definition of escape as a voluntary departure from custody with an intent to avoid confinement. Whatever label is placed on this intent, a defendant under § 751 is entitled to an instruction that includes this mental component as an element of the crime which the government must prove. If the defendant offers evidence that he was intoxicated at the time of the offense, the jury must be instructed to consider whether he was so intoxicated he could not form an intent to escape."

6. Given *Egelhoff*, what if a state takes the lesser step of placing the burden of proof re involuntary intoxication negating the mental state on the defendant? Consider that in *Egelhoff* the plurality opinion concludes that, "as the Montana court itself recognized, '[t]he burden is not shifted' under § 45–2–203," and compare these two pre-*Egelhoff* decisions:

(a) *State v. Schulz*, 102 Wis.2d 423, 307 N.W.2d 151 (1981): "When the defendant introduces evidence to demonstrate that, because of his intoxicated state, he did not intend to kill his victim, the accused seeks to negate a fact which the state must prove in order to convict the defendant of murder. This is the type of negative defense which was contemplated by the decisions in *Mullaney* [p. 264 of this Book] and *Patterson* [p. 270 of this Book]. When such a defense is asserted, the burden of persuasion cannot be placed upon the defendant without violating his right to due process of law."

(b) *United States ex rel. Goddard v. Vaughn*, 614 F.2d 929 (3d Cir.1980) ("since the Court has held that the defense may be required to establish insanity, it follows that a state may impose the burden of proof upon the accused when the effect upon rational behavior may be less severe. Indeed, in the case of voluntary intoxication, the state has displayed an even greater degree of leniency because the impaired intellectual functioning was caused by the defendant's own voluntary act, unlike deficiencies caused by forces beyond one's control").

7. Assuming a situation in which the defense is permitted to introduce evidence of voluntary intoxication to show an absence of the requisite mental state, precisely how severe must the intoxication have been? Typical of the expressions in the cases are these: *United States v. Navarrete,* 125 F.3d 559 (7th Cir.1997) ("the intoxication must be so severe as to suspend all reason"); *State v. McLaughlin,* 286 N.C. 597, 213 S.E.2d 238 (1975) ("intoxication to a degree precluding the ability to form a specific intent to kill"); *State v. Cameron,* 104 N.J. 42, 514 A.2d 1302 (1986) ("prostration of faculties such that defendant was rendered incapable of forming an intent"). *Cameron* adds that the factors pertinent to a determination of whether such circumstances were present are: "the quantity of intoxicant consumed, the period of time involved, the actor's conduct as perceived by others (what he said, how he said it, how he appeared, how he acted, how his coordination or lack thereof manifested itself), any odor of alcohol or other intoxicating substance, the results of any tests to determine blood-alcohol content, and the actor's ability to recall significant events."

But consider *State v. Mash,* 323 N.C. 339, 372 S.E.2d 532 (1988), where on a first-degree murder charge the jury was instructed that "the intoxication must be so great that his mind and reason were so completely overthrown so as to render him utterly incapable to form a deliberate and premeditated purpose to kill. Mere intoxication cannot serve as an excuse for the defendant. It must be intoxication to the extent that the defendant's mental processes were so overcome by the excessive use of liquor or other intoxicants that he had temporarily, at least, lost the capacity to think and plan." The court held those instructions erroneous because they "impose on the jury the standard applicable to defendant's burden of production at trial, a burden defendant must meet before being entitled to voluntary intoxication instructions at all. While meeting such a standard is a prerequisite to defendant's entitlement to voluntary intoxication instructions, the standard is inapplicable to the jury's consideration of the intoxication evidence. The jury must decide, in light of the intoxication evidence as well as other evidence in the case, whether there is a reasonable doubt that defendant formed a deliberate and premeditated intent to kill, not whether his intoxication was 'so great ... as to render him utterly incapable' of forming such an intent. In other words, to find for defendant on the intoxication issue, the jury does not have to conclude that his intoxication rendered defendant 'utterly incapable' of forming the necessary intent; it need only conclude that because of his intoxication either defendant did not form the requisite intent or there is at least a reasonable doubt about it."

8. *Parker v. State,* 7 Md.App. 167, 254 A.2d 381 (1969): "Regardless of what test is applicable to determining insanity, the majority [of courts] distinguish between (1) the mental effect of voluntary intoxication which is the immediate result of a particular alcoholic bout; and (2) an alcoholic psychosis resulting from long continued habits of excessive drinking. The first does not excuse responsibility for a criminal act; the second may. In other words, if a person drinks intoxicating liquor and is sane both prior to drinking and after the influences of the intoxicant has worn off, but is insane by the applicable test while under the influence of the intoxicant, he comes under the first category. If he is insane whether or not he is directly under the influence of an intoxicant, even though that insanity was caused by voluntary drinking, he comes under the second category. The cases usually refer to the first category as a 'temporary' insanity and the second category as a 'permanent', 'fixed' or 'settled' insanity. These terms may be an oversimplification. What 'permanent', 'fixed' or 'settled' means within the frame of reference is that the insanity not only existed while a person was under the influence of intoxicating spirits as an immediate result of imbibing, but existed independent of such influence, even though the insanity was caused by past imbibing. So if a person while in

the throes of delirium tremens which may meet the test for insanity, commits a crime, he is not responsible for his criminal conduct, although such defect, resulting remotely from excessive drinking is only a temporary toxic state. It would seem that the distinction, notwithstanding the language of the cases, is not so much between temporary and permanent insanity as it is one between the direct results of drinking, which are voluntarily sought after, and its remote and undesired consequences."

9. Monrad G. Paulsen, *Intoxication as a Defense to Crime*, 1961 U.Ill.L.F. 1, 21: "While alcoholism may not be a mental disease recognized clinically, heavy drinking is often a symptom of deep mental disturbance. If the evidence concerning the defendant's psychic disorientation is such as to satisfy the medical experts that the defendant suffers from some recognized mental disorder, he should not be treated by the law in a way different from others simply because his disorder brings him to an excessive use of alcohol. The appellate cases leave the writer with the impression that advocates have not been skillful in pressing this point. Defense lawyers tend to lay stress on the gross intoxication without attempting to probe carefully into the underlying psychic disorder which may be allied with the drunkenness. Perhaps the failure is explained simply by the lack of defense funds available in most cases of this sort. At any rate it is true, in today's law, that insanity will exculpate completely; drunkenness will not. Therefore, defense strategy should focus attention clearly on the former factor in the intoxication cases."

10. In *State v. Hall*, 214 N.W.2d 205 (Iowa 1974), defendant testified that before he shot and killed his companion he had taken a pill (apparently LSD) which induced hallucinations, and that he had fired at what appeared to him as a rabid dog. On appeal from his murder conviction, the court held the trial judge properly refused defendant's requested insanity instruction. Deeming the rule developed regarding insanity and use of alcohol (see *Parker,* supra) equally applicable in cases where drugs were ingested,[a] the court concluded defendant's evidence did not show "settled or established" insanity. The dissenters objected: "Our intoxication rationale as applied to alcohol simply does not fit the use of modern hallucinatory drugs; and it was never meant to. It was adopted before such drugs, as we now know them, were in common use. That is why I would say they *are* dissimilar and should be so regarded. There is no justifiable reason for equating the effects of so-called 'hard' drugs, particularly those classified as hallucinatory, with the use of alcohol."

11. What, if anything, does *Egelhoff* tell us about the constitutionality of not permitting the defendant to pursue a "diminished capacity" claim? Note that in *Wong v. Money*, p. 444 of this Book, *Egelhoff* was never mentioned. What does *Egelhoff* tell us about the constitutionality of not permitting the insanity defense, either generally or in cases of "settled" insanity? Consider Note, 78 B.U.L.Rev. 75, 102 (1998): "The Supreme Court has never directly decided whether the denial of either the insanity defense or the settled insanity defense violates the fourteenth amendment. Courts in almost every jurisdiction have treated settled insanity as a subset of insanity. Given the variance between the common law history, present acceptance, and policy justifications of the defenses, however, a due process analysis of each defense leads to a markedly different result.

a. In this regard, consider *Commonwealth v. Herd*, 413 Mass. 834, 604 N.E.2d 1294 (1992), where the state argued defendant's mental disease should not be so considered in light of the fact that it was "the natural and inevitable result" of *illegal* drug use, and the court responded: "The weight of authority in this country recognizes an insanity defense that is based on a mental disease or defect produced by long-term substance abuse. We see no logical reason for rejecting a drug-induced mental disease or defect * * * simply because the disease or defect is caused only by the drug ingestion. We are unwilling, in order to justify a homicide conviction, to permit the moral fault inherent in the unlawful consumption of drugs to substitute for the moral fault that is absent in one who lacks criminal responsibility."

"The insanity defense has a lengthy and widespread common law history, dating back to fourteenth century England. In contrast, American courts did not begin to recognize the settled insanity defense until the mid-nineteenth century. Moreover, many states have not yet recognized the settled insanity defense at all, while nearly all of the states continue to recognize insanity as a valid affirmative defense. In addition, although both defenses have valid policy justifications, settled insanity involves a substantial degree of voluntariness that is noticeably absent from the regular insanity defense.

"One can, by analogy to the plurality's rationale of voluntary intoxication in *Egelhoff*, make a strong argument that individuals have a constitutional right to present potentially exculpatory evidence of insanity. The defense is not of recent vintage, and it is sufficiently uniform and permanent. The insanity defense is also supported by valid policy justifications.

"Even if the Supreme Court decides that due process requires the availability of an insanity defense, the lower courts should refrain from extending fundamental right status to the settled insanity defense. Settled insanity necessarily implicates moral responsibility and the public policy of preventing drug abuse. Accordingly, the settled insanity defense, like the voluntary intoxication defense, is a recent defense and lacks sufficient and uniform permanence recognition by the state courts to qualify for fundamental right status."

CITY OF MINNEAPOLIS v. ALTIMUS

Supreme Court of Minnesota, 1976.

306 Minn. 462, 238 N.W.2d 851.

KELLY, JUSTICE.

Defendant, who was found guilty by a Hennepin County Municipal Court jury of careless driving and hit and run as to an attended vehicle, and not guilty of simple assault, was sentenced by the trial court to terms of 30 and 90 days in the workhouse, sentences to be served concurrently with revocation of parole from Federal prison. * * *

At 12:15 p.m. on September 28, 1973, defendant, driving south on Hiawatha Avenue, made an illegal left turn from the right-hand lane and crashed into a garbage truck proceeding northward on Hiawatha. Immediately after impact, defendant backed up and drove easterly on Lake Street at a slow speed. This slow speed resulted from the fact that the automobile defendant was driving had been badly damaged in the collision. Policemen who observed the accident followed defendant and stopped him about a block from the point of impact. Defendant, who appeared to one of the officers to be somewhat confused, told the officers that his head and shoulder hurt and asked to be taken to the hospital. In response to questions by the officers, defendant, who gave "William Jones" as his name, stated that he did not have his driver's license with him but showed the officers a paper purporting to be a transfer of title from Robert Altimus to William Jones.

Because of a gap in the evidence, we do not know for certain what happened next, but it appears that an ambulance took defendant to General Hospital and defendant ran away after police discovered his true identity. In any event, we have the testimony of an off-duty uniformed police officer that at about 1:30 p.m. he was on his way to the Minnesota Auto Body Shop at Seventh Street and Park Avenue when another officer told him to be on the lookout for a man fitting defendant's description and that when he got to the body shop he saw the defendant. He testified that defendant refused to identify himself and ran toward the General Hospital construction area, where an altercation occurred when the officer caught him; that defendant then ran to a church at Seventh Street and Chicago Avenue where he broke the officer's nose; and that finally he was apprehended at the St. Barnabas School of Nursing.

At trial, the defense did not dispute the evidence adduced by the state, but introduced evidence designed to show that defendant did not have the requisite state of mind to be guilty of either simple assault or the two remaining traffic charges. Defendant testified that on September 25, 1973, three days before the incident, he had seen a doctor at the Veterans Administration Hospital for treatment of a back problem and the flu and that the doctor had prescribed Valium, which he had taken as prescribed. He testified that on September 28 the Valium began to have a strange effect on him, making it impossible for him to control himself. He testified that he did not know who owned the automobile which he had driven, and that he remembered nothing about the accident or the events that followed.

The only other defense witness was Dr. Humberto Ortiz, the doctor who treated defendant at the Veterans Administration Hospital. He testified that he prescribed the Valium because it was a skeletal muscle relaxant and was the type of drug which would relieve the acute back pain defendant had been experiencing. He testified that he also prescribed empirin, bed rest, and heat. Dr. Ortiz listed drowsiness, fatigue, ataxia, and confusion as the normal side effects of Valium. He testified, however, that hyperexcitability, although more rare, was also a possible side effect. On cross-examination, he stated that he did not know if the drug might cause one to be confused as to his identity; but in response to a hypothetical question stating the facts of the case, he expressed the opinion that defendant might have been suffering from the effects of the drug.

After resting, the defense requested the trial court to instruct on the defense of involuntary intoxication and submitted proposed instructions to that effect,[2] but the trial court refused to instruct on the defense or to give these instructions. The trial judge did instruct the jury that defendant's alleged intoxication would be a defense to the charge of assault if it rendered him unable to formulate the specific intent to inflict bodily harm on the person of another which is an essential element of the crime of assault. We do not express an opinion as to the propriety of this voluntary intoxication instruction on the assault charge, but we note that we have not decided whether that defense applies to simple assault cases.

The general rule in Minnesota is that voluntary intoxication is a defense * * * only if a specific intent or purpose is an essential element of the crime charged and the trier of fact concluded that the defendant's intoxication deprived him of the specific intent or purpose requisite to the alleged offense.[4] Because [the] traffic offenses with which defendant was charged do not require a specific intent to do a prohibited act, the defense of voluntary intoxication cannot and does not apply to those offenses.

While general traffic offenses do not require that the wrongdoer specifically intend to commit the crime for which he is charged, we have held that before criminal liability can attach it is essential that the defendant intentionally or negligently do the act which

---

2. The defense submitted the following proposed instructions as to involuntary intoxication: "Intoxication is involuntary when it is produced in a person without his willing and knowing use of intoxicating liquor, drugs or other substance and without his willing assumption of the risk of possible intoxication.

"Proof of the involuntary intoxication of a defendant should be considered by the jury in determining whether the defendant had the capacity or ability to commit any of the four offenses with which he is charged or to

form a criminal intent at the time the offenses are alleged to have been committed."

4. Minn.St. 609.075 provides: "An act committed while in a state of voluntary intoxication is not less criminal by reason thereof, but when a particular intent or other state of mind is a necessary element to constitute a particular crime, the fact of intoxication may be taken into consideration in determining such intent or state of mind."

constitutes the crime. *State v. Kremer,* 262 Minn. 190, 114 N.W.2d 88 (1962). In *Kremer* we reversed the conviction of a defendant who unintentionally and non-negligently drove through a stop signal because his brakes failed. We acknowledged there that a defendant may be held criminally responsible for some activities, even though he does not criminally intend the harm caused by his acts, because he "usually is in a position to prevent it with no more care than society might reasonably expect and no more exertion than it might reasonably exact from one who assumed his responsibilities." When that duty of due care is breached, the driver may properly be found criminally responsible for a traffic offense. We reversed the defendant's conviction in *Kremer* because the above rationale did not apply when there was no negligence by the defendant and no intent to do the act which turned out to be criminal. The unusual issue presented on this appeal is whether the defendant is entitled to assert the defense of involuntary intoxication if due to such intoxication he unintentionally and non-negligently did the acts for which he is charged. In brief, we hold that defendant was entitled to an instruction on involuntary intoxication, that the trial court erred in refusing to grant such an instruction, and that a new trial is required.

We begin our analysis of the defense of involuntary intoxication by considering its origins and its relationship to the partial defense of voluntary intoxication. The common-law rule was that voluntary intoxication was never a defense to a criminal charge. * * * The common law distinguished involuntary from voluntary intoxication, however, and found the former to be a defense to criminal liability if it caused the defendant to become temporarily insane. * * *

Four different kinds of involuntary intoxication have been recognized: Coerced intoxication, pathological intoxication, intoxication by innocent mistake, and unexpected intoxication resulting from the ingestion of a medically prescribed drug. Coerced intoxication is intoxication involuntarily induced by reason of duress or coercion. Some courts have declared in general terms that coerced intoxication may be a complete defense to all criminal liability. See, e.g., *Burrows v. State,* 38 Ariz. 99, 297 P. 1029 (1931). In *Burrows,* the Arizona Supreme Court approved the trial court's instruction which stated that involuntary intoxication would be a complete defense if the defendant was compelled to drink against his will and "his reason was destroyed" so "that he did not understand and appreciate the consequences of his act." Courts have strictly construed the requirement of coercion, however, so that acquittal by reason of coerced intoxication is an exceedingly rare result.

Pathological intoxication has been defined as "intoxication grossly excessive in degree, given the amount of the intoxicant, to which the actor does not know he is susceptible." Pathologically intoxicated offenders have been held not criminally responsible for their acts when they ingested the intoxicant not knowing of their special susceptibility to its effects. The defense of pathological intoxication has been limited in some jurisdictions, however, by the requirement that the intoxicated defendant must be deprived of mental capacity to the degree necessary for an insanity defense.

Involuntary intoxication may also occur when intoxication results from an innocent mistake by the defendant about the character of the substance taken, as when another person has tricked him into taking the liquor or drugs. See, *People v. Penman,* 271 Ill. 82, 110 N.E. 894 (1915). In *Penman,* the defendant killed his victim after apparently taking cocaine tablets which, due to the deception of another, he believed to be breath purifiers. The Illinois Supreme Court held that this would constitute involuntary intoxication and a full defense to criminal liability if it caused the defendant to become temporarily insane.

The last kind of involuntary intoxication recognized in the case law arises when the defendant is unexpectedly intoxicated due to the ingestion of a medically prescribed drug.

Several courts have declared that such intoxication constitutes a valid defense to criminal liability if the prescribed drug is taken pursuant to medical advice and without defendant's knowledge of its potentially intoxicating effects.

Appellant asserts that due to the ingestion of a prescribed drug, Valium, he was unexpectedly intoxicated to the point of unconsciousness, incapable of controlling his actions, and thus not criminally responsible for his actions. To assess fully the merits of this claim, it is necessary to review carefully the circumstances in which a defense of involuntary intoxication due to ingestion of a prescribed drug is properly available.

The first requirement is that the defendant must not know, or have reason to know, that the prescribed drug is likely to have an intoxicating effect. If the defendant knows, or has reason to know, that the prescribed drug will have an intoxicating effect, then he is voluntarily intoxicated[8] and may plead his voluntary intoxication as a partial defense only as provided for in Minn.St. 609.075.

The second requirement is that the prescribed drug, and not some other intoxicant, is in fact the cause of defendant's intoxication at the time of his alleged criminal conduct.

The third requirement is that the defendant, due to involuntary intoxication, is temporarily insane. The numerous cases cited above in which the common-law defense of involuntary intoxication has been recognized are virtually unanimous in holding that this defense is available only when the defendant is legally insane at the time of the alleged criminal offense. We believe that the Minnesota Legislature has already prescribed in Minn.St. 611.026 the test applicable to the defense of involuntary intoxication. Section 611.026 states:

> "No person shall be tried, sentenced, or punished for any crime while mentally ill or mentally deficient so as to be incapable of understanding the proceedings or making a defense; but he shall not be excused from criminal liability except upon proof that at the time of committing the alleged criminal act he was laboring under such a defect of reason, from one of these causes, as not to know the nature of his act, or that it was wrong."

We hold that if the defendant is mentally deficient due to involuntary intoxication, then he may be excused from criminal responsibility only if temporarily insane as defined in § 611.026.

Mr. Justice Rogosheske in his special concurrence argues that the insanity test and § 611.026 are not applicable to the defense of involuntary intoxication. He asserts that the better test is that found in the *Model Penal Code,* § 2.08(4). * * * Several states in enacting statutes expressly defining the defense of involuntary intoxication have followed the above test proposed in the Model Penal Code. The Minnesota Legislature, however, has passed no statute expressly addressing the test to be applied when a defendant asserts the defense of involuntary intoxication. In the absence of such an express statute on involuntary intoxication, we adhere to the legislative policy articulated in Minn.St. 611.026. * * *

In the case of voluntary intoxication, the defendant must establish the defense by a fair preponderance of the evidence. Similarly, when insanity is a matter of defense we have held that the defendant must prove by the preponderance of the evidence that he was legally insane; it is not enough that he raise a reasonable doubt as to his sanity. In light of the above, we today hold that the defendant in the instant case bears the burden of

---

8. The *Model Penal Code,* § 2.08(5)(b) defines self-induced intoxication as "intoxication caused by substances which the actor knowingly introduces into his body, the tendency of which to cause intoxication he knows or ought to know * * *."

establishing by the preponderance of the evidence that he was temporarily insane due to involuntary intoxication.

Involuntary intoxication, we note in summary, is a most unusual condition. The circumstances in which an instruction on the defense of involuntary intoxication will be appropriate will accordingly be very rare. We hold, nevertheless, that in the instant case such an instruction was necessary because defendant introduced evidence sufficient to raise the defense of temporary insanity due to involuntary intoxication. Defendant's evidence indicated that at the time he committed the acts in question he was intoxicated and unaware of what he was doing due to an unusual and unexpected reaction to drugs prescribed by a physician. We further believe that failure to give an instruction on involuntary intoxication was prejudicial error in view of the finding of not guilty on the charge of simple assault, a finding which suggests very strongly that the jury believed defendant's evidence that the Valium was responsible for his behavior.

Reversed and remanded for a new trial.

ROGOSHESKE, JUSTICE (concurring specially). * * *

The premise underlying the defense of involuntary intoxication is that a person should not be held criminally liable in the absence of volitional fault, that is, conscious fault. * * * In recognition of the above principle, the authors of the Model Penal Code declared that involuntary intoxication is an affirmative defense if—

> " * * * by reason of such intoxication the actor at the time of his conduct lacks substantial capacity either to appreciate its criminality [wrongfulness] or to conform his conduct to the requirements of law." *Model Penal Code,* § 2.08(4).

I would apply the above principle to the case at bar by instructing the jury that defendant should be excused from criminal liability if defendant establishes by the preponderance of the evidence that due to the ingestion of Valium he was intoxicated to such an extent that he was incapable of exercising reasonable care in operating his automobile, and that he did not know or have reasonable grounds to foresee that in taking the Valium pursuant to his doctor's prescription his mental condition would become such as to render him incapable of exercising reasonable care in driving an automobile.

The majority opinion declares that involuntary intoxication is a defense only when it causes temporary insanity as insanity is defined in Minn.St. 611.026. In my view, § 611.026 has no application to the defense asserted because involuntary intoxication due to the ingestion of a medically prescribed drug is simply not a form of mental "illness" or "deficiency" as those terms are commonly used. To describe the asserted mental state of defendant in this case as one of insanity stretches that word far beyond its ordinary meaning and gives § 611.026 a construction it is doubtful was ever contemplated by the legislature.

In my opinion, the defense of involuntary intoxication does not rest upon so tenuous a statutory basis. Involuntary intoxication is a defense anchored firmly in the theory of mens rea, which has long been a part of Anglo–American common law. * * *

The majority opinion suggests that this court must defer to the legislative judgment expressed in § 611.026 and allow the defense of involuntary intoxication only when it creates temporary insanity. I do not agree because it has traditionally been the duty of the courts and not the legislature to define the defenses which necessarily follow from the doctrine of mens rea. * * *

Notes and Questions

1.   May it not be argued that the defense is too narrowly stated by both Justice Kelly and Justice Rogosheske? Specifically, if Altimus was not at fault in becoming intoxicated, then why shouldn't the question be whether he would have driven carelessly and hit and run if he had been sober?

2.   In *Altimus* the court holds that the defendant must establish the involuntary intoxication defense by a preponderance of the evidence. Is this a proper allocation of the burden of proof? Compare the cases in Note 6, p. 477 of this Book.

3.   The intoxication of a person who is an alcoholic, *See v. State,* 296 Ark. 498, 757 S.W.2d 947 (1988), or a drug addict, *State v. Bishop,* 632 S.W.2d 255 (Mo.1982), is not, because of that condition, deemed to be *in*voluntary so as to bring the case within the *Altimus* rule. Why should this be so?

4.   With respect to what should constitute intoxication by duress, consider Monrad G. Paulsen, *Intoxication as a Defense to Crime,* 1961 U.Ill.L.F. 1, 18–19: "The opinions that can be found take a hard line of defining 'voluntary.' A case summarized by Professor Hall makes the point.

> 'A college student under eighteen, who had never before tasted intoxicating liquor, was given a ride by the deceased in his automobile. The latter had been drinking heavily and insisted that the boy participate, became abusive and threatened to put him off in the Arizona desert if he refused. The court, noting that the "defendant, being alone, penniless, and fearing that he might be ejected and left on the desert did drink some beer and whiskey," nonetheless held that involuntary intoxication "must be induced by acts amounting in effect to duress." '

The Model Penal Code has taken a similarly tough stand. Section 2.08(4) makes intoxication a defense if it is not self-induced. In section 2.08(5) the definition of 'self-induced intoxication' excludes the case of one brought to drunkenness by 'such duress as would afford a defense to a charge of crime.' The definition of duress is found in section 2.09(1) of the Code. * * *

"In the case of the college boy crossing the desert it is hardly possible to assert that the driver used or threatened to use such force against the boy's person 'which a person of reasonable firmness in his situation would have been *unable* to resist.' The requirement of inability puts the test of voluntariness for this purpose too high. What may be needed in the Code is a separate definition of duress for purposes of the intoxication section. Reference could be made to a 'person of reasonable firmness' in the 'situation' of the actor but the test should ask whether that person *would have* resisted not whether he was *able* to do so. To do that would take into account the choice of evils facing the actor."

5.   With respect to what should constitute intoxication by innocent mistake, consider *State v. Hall,* 214 N.W.2d 205 (Iowa 1974). The defendant testified he killed his companion while hallucinating that the object of his attack was a rabid dog, and that prior to the killing he took a pill "that casual acquaintances in California gave him * * * and told him it was a 'little sunshine' and would make him feel 'groovy.' " The majority concludes this was not a case of involuntary intoxication, as "no one tricked him into taking it or forced him to do so." The dissenters objected:

"The testimony shows defendant took a pill which he knew to be a drug but which he did not know to be LSD and which he testified he thought to be harmless, although he had been told it would make him feel groovy. There is nothing to indicate he knew it could induce hallucinations or lead to the frightening debilitating effects of mind and body to which the doctors testified. The majority nevertheless holds the defendant's resulting drug intoxication was voluntary. I disagree. * * *

"In other words, does voluntary in this context refer to the *mechanical* act of ingesting the pill or does it refer to a willing and intelligent assumption of the possible harmful consequences of that act?

"I am convinced voluntary as here used should relate to a knowledgeable acceptance of the danger and risk involved. Applied to the instant case, that rule would demand submission of the issue to a jury."

6. In *State v. Gardner*, 230 Wis.2d 32, 601 N.W.2d 670 (App.1999), the court held it was error to exclude expert testimony "about his prescription medication's effect on his ability to distinguish right from wrong." The state argued the circumstances did not qualify as involuntary intoxication, for defendant made no claim of ignorance regarding the intoxicating effects of the medication. The court, citing *Altimus*, noted there was "ample case law" supporting the state's position, but then concluded it could "see no reason to so limit the defense. Even if forewarned of the intoxicating effect of a prescription drug, a person should have recourse to the defense if the drug renders him or her unable to distinguish between right and wrong. When faced with a medical condition requiring drug treatment, the patient hardly has a choice but to follow the doctor's orders."

7. In *People v. Walker*, 33 Ill.App.3d 681, 338 N.E.2d 449 (1975), the court noted that the "only basis for the idea of involuntarily produced intoxication was the defendant's testimony that a week or so previous to the shooting he had obtained some pills from his brother to alleviate a stomach ache; that he had taken these pills with beneficial effect, and that on the evening in question he had taken two more of these pills from the jar where they were kept in his brother's house. Afterwards, he had drunk some beer and some wine. The tenuous basis for the involuntariness of his intoxication was that his brother did not tell him—and probably did not know—that the pills in question contained Seconal, a tranquillizing drug which, mixed with alcohol, could have the effect of intensifying the defendant's intoxication and reducing his control over his impulses." The court held that the trial judge properly refused to give an instruction on involuntary intoxication because defendant's drunkenness was not "caused by trick, artifice or force."

Is *Walker* more like *Hall* than *Gardner*, or are the three cases different? How would each be decided under *Model Penal Code* § 2.08(4) and (5)?

SECTION 3. IMMATURITY

STATE v. Q.D.

Supreme Court of Washington, 1984.

102 Wash.2d 19, 685 P.2d 557.

DIMMICK, JUSTICE.

Two juveniles appeal from separate adjudications which found that they had committed offenses which if committed by an adult would be crimes. The Court of Appeals, in these consolidated appeals, certified to this court the questions whether the statutory presumption of infant incapacity, RCW 9A.04.050,[1] applies to juvenile adjudications, and if it does, what standard of proof is required to rebut the presumption. * * *

---

1. RCW 9A.04.050 provides in part: "Children under the age of eight years are incapable

Appellant Q.D. was found to have capacity per RCW 9A.04.050 in a pretrial hearing. He was 11½ years old at the time of the alleged offense. At trial a different judge determined he had committed trespass in the first degree. The evidence introduced to show capacity consisted of testimony from a case worker and a detective who had worked with him in connection with his plea of guilty to a burglary committed at age 10 years. The case worker testified that Q.D. was familiar with the justice system, was street wise, and that he used his age as a shield. The detective told the court that Q.D. was cooperative in the burglary investigation, and he appeared to know his rights. The evidence in the guilt phase consisted of testimony from the principal and a custodial engineer of the school in which Q.D. was charged with trespass. The engineer testified that he saw Q.D. sitting on the school grounds about 2 p.m. playing with some keys that looked like the set belonging to the night custodian. When the engineer checked his desk which was in an unlocked office, he found that the keys were missing as was the burglar alarm key. The engineer could not be certain that he had seen the keys since the morning. He called the principal and they brought Q.D. into the office. When Q.D. arose from the chair he had been sitting on in the office, the burglar alarm key was discovered on a radiator behind the chair.

Appellant M.S., in a single proceeding, was found to have capacity and to have committed indecent liberties on a 4½–year–old child for whom she was babysitting. Evidence included the testimony of the victim, the victim's mother, a physician who had examined the victim, and a social worker who had interviewed the victim. M.S. was less than 3 months from 12 years old at the time of the offense. The issue of capacity was first raised by the defendant in a motion to dismiss at the close of the State's evidence. The State argued that defendant's proximity to the age when capacity is assumed, the defendant's threats to the victim not to tell what had happened, and her secrecy in carrying out the act were ample proof of capacity. The trial judge, in his oral ruling finding capacity, stated that the responsibility entrusted to the defendant by the victim's mother and her own parents in permitting her to babysit showed a recognition of the defendant's maturity.

I

Counsel for both the State and the defendants urge us to hold that the infant incapacity defense in RCW 9A.04.050 applies to juvenile proceedings. We so hold.

At common law, children below the age of 7 were conclusively presumed to be incapable of committing crime, and children over the age of 14 were presumed capable and treated as adults. Children between these ages were rebuttably presumed incapable of committing crime. Washington codified these presumptions amending the age of conclusive incapacity to 7, and presumed capacity to 12 years of age. As recently as 1975, the Legislature again included the infancy defense in the criminal code. The purpose of the presumption is to protect from the criminal justice system those individuals of tender years who are less capable than adults of appreciating the wrongfulness of their behavior.

The infancy defense fell into disuse during the early part of the century with the advent of reforms intended to substitute treatment and rehabilitation for punishment of juvenile offenders. This parens patriae system, believed not to be a criminal one, had no need of the infancy defense.

The juvenile justice system in recent years has evolved from parens patriae scheme to one more akin to adult criminal proceedings. The United States Supreme Court has been

of committing crime. Children of eight and under twelve years of age are presumed to be incapable of committing crime, but this presumption may be re-

moved by proof that they have sufficient capacity to understand the act or neglect, and to know that it was wrong."

critical of the parens patriae scheme as failing to provide safeguards due an adult criminal defendant, while subjecting the juvenile defendant to similar stigma, and possible loss of liberty. *See In re Gault,* 387 U.S. 1, 87 S.Ct. 1428, 18 L.Ed.2d 527 (1967); and *In re Winship,* 397 U.S. 358, 90 S.Ct. 1068, 25 L.Ed.2d 368 (1970). This court has acknowledged Washington's departure from a strictly parens patriae scheme to a more criminal one, involving both rehabilitation and punishment. Being a criminal defense, RCW 9A.04.050 should be available to juvenile proceedings that are criminal in nature.

The principles of construction of criminal statutes, made necessary by our recognition of the criminal nature of juvenile court proceedings, also compel us to conclude that RCW 9A.04.050 applies to proceedings in juvenile courts.

A finding that RCW 9A.04.050 does not apply to juvenile courts would render that statute meaningless or superfluous contrary to rules of construction. Juvenile courts have exclusive jurisdiction over all individuals under the chronological age of 18 who have committed acts designated criminal if committed by an adult. Declination of jurisdiction and transfer to adult court is limited to instances where it is in the best interest of the juvenile or the public. Thus, all juveniles who can avail themselves of the infancy defense will come under the jurisdiction of the juvenile court, and most will remain there. Implied statutory repeals are found not to exist where two statutes can be reconciled and given effect. Goals of the Juvenile Justice Act of 1977 include accountability for criminal behavior and punishment commensurate with age and crime. A goal of the criminal code is to safeguard conduct that is not culpable. The infancy defense which excludes from criminal condemnation persons not capable of culpable, criminal acts, is consistent with the overlapping goals of the Juvenile Justice Act of 1977 and the Washington Criminal Code.

II

The State has the burden of rebutting the statutory presumption of incapacity of juveniles age 8 and less than 12 years. Capacity must be found to exist separate from the specific mental element of the crime charged. While capacity is similar to the mental element of a specific crime or offense, it is not an element of the offense, but is rather a general determination that the individual understood the act and its wrongfulness. Both defendants liken the incapacity presumption to a jurisdictional presumption. Were capacity an element of the crime, proof beyond a reasonable doubt would be required. *In re Winship, supra.* But capacity, not being an element of the crime, does not require as stringent a standard of proof.

Few jurisdictions have ruled on the appropriate standard of proof necessary to rebut the presumption of incapacity, and fewer still have discussed their reasoning for preferring one standard over another. It appears that other states have split between requiring proof beyond a reasonable doubt, and clear and convincing proof.

Our recent discussion of the standard of proof to be applied in involuntary commitment proceedings offers guidance. In *Dunner v. McLaughlin,* 100 Wash.2d 832, 676 P.2d 444 (1984), we held that the burden of proof should be by clear, cogent and convincing evidence. In so holding, we recognized that the preponderance of the evidence standard was inadequate, but the proof beyond a reasonable doubt standard imposed a burden which, as a practical matter, was unreasonably difficult, thus undercutting the State's legitimate interests.

The Legislature, by requiring the State to rebut the presumption of incapacity, has assumed a greater burden than the minimal proof imposed by the preponderance of the evidence standard. On the other hand, to require the State to prove capacity beyond a reasonable doubt when the State must also prove the specific mental element of the charged offense by the same standard, is unnecessarily duplicative. Frequently, the same facts required to prove mens rea will be probative of capacity, yet the overlap is not complete. Capacity to be culpable must exist in order to maintain the specific mental element of the charged offense. Once the generalized determination of capacity is found, the State must prove beyond a reasonable doubt that the juvenile defendant possessed the specific mental element. The clear and convincing standard reflects the State's assumption of a greater burden than does the preponderance of the evidence standard. At the same time, the liberty interest of the juvenile is fully protected by the requirement of proof beyond a reasonable doubt of the specific mental element. We therefore require the State to rebut the presumption of incapacity by clear and convincing evidence.

III

We do not need to reach the question of whether there was substantial evidence to show that Q.D. understood the act of trespass or understood it to be wrong, as we reverse on other grounds. Nevertheless, a discussion of capacity in this case may prove instructive to trial courts. Q.D. argues that the evidence showed only that he was familiar with the juvenile system through his previous plea of guilty to a burglary charge, but did not show he understood the act and wrongfulness of trespass. The language of RCW 9A.04.050 clearly indicates that a capacity determination must be made in reference to the specific act charged: "understand *the act* * * * and to know that *it* was wrong." (Italics ours.) If Q.D. is correct that the evidence showed no more than a general understanding of the justice system, he would be correct in concluding that the State did not show an understanding and knowing wrongfulness of trespass. In addition, an understanding of the wrongfulness of burglary does not alone establish capacity in regard to trespass. While both offenses include entry or unlawfully remaining in a building, burglary also requires an intent to commit a crime against a person or property therein. Defendant may well understand that it is wrong to enter a locked building with the intention of committing a crime, but not know that entering an unlocked school building is wrong.

The issue of capacity was first raised on M.S.'s motion to dismiss at the end of the trial. The judge stated in response to arguments of counsel that he was persuaded by the confidence in defendant's maturity held by the mother of the victim and her own parents in permitting her to assume the responsibility for babysitting. Contrary to defendant's arguments that the trial judge created a prima facie proof of capacity based solely on babysitting, there was other evidence to support his finding of capacity. The defendant waited until she and the victim were alone evidencing a desire for secrecy. The defendant later admonished the victim not to tell what happened, further supporting the finding that the defendant knew the act was wrong. Lastly, the defendant was less than 3 months from the age at which capacity is presumed to exist. There was clear and convincing circumstantial evidence that M.S. understood the act of indecent liberties and knew it to be wrong.
* * *

Notes and Questions

1.   Compare *In re Michael,* 423 A.2d 1180 (R.I.1981): "Once one accepts the principle that a finding of delinquency or waywardness in a juvenile proceeding is not the equivalent of a finding that the juvenile has committed a crime, there is no necessity of a finding that the juvenile had such maturity that he or she knew what he or she was doing was wrong. A juvenile is delinquent or wayward, not because the juvenile has committed a crime, but because the juvenile has committed an act that would be a crime if committed by a person not a juvenile and because the juvenile requires 'such care, guidance and control * * * as

will serve the child's welfare and the best interests of the state * * *.' General Laws 1956 (1969 Reenactment) § 14–1–2.''

2. The commentators are not in agreement as to whether the *Q.D.* or *Michael* approach is best. Consider: (a) Frederick J. Ludwig, *Rationale of Responsibility for Young Offenders,* 29 Neb.L.Rev. 521, 534 (1950), asserts that when "the purpose of treatment of immature offenders is solely rehabilitation, it is unnecessary to set limits of absolute irresponsibility. The same is true of conditional responsibility. Age lines and rebuttable presumptions of incapacity become superfluous in the light of this treatment purpose. Indeed if all offenders should be treated by the criminal law like patients by a physician, the concept of criminal responsibility would vanish * * *. The problem of responsibility can exist only in connection with treatment for the sake of deterrence.''

(b) Andrew Walkover, *The Infancy Defense in the New Juvenile Court,* 31 U.C.L.A.L.Rev. 503, 538 (1984): "Like its adult counterpart, the juvenile justice system operates as a screening device. It shares with and complements the adult system's functions of imposing social controls and attributing blame. Moreover, as a consequence of juvenile justice proceedings, convicted youth may suffer the social stigma and loss of liberty associated with the adult criminal process. It follows that the commitment to punishing only the culpable that animates adult criminal jurisprudence should also be applicable to the juvenile process.''

3. Couch, age 16 at the time of his conduct, was convicted in criminal court of murder, armed robbery and motor vehicle theft. On appeal, *Couch v. State,* 253 Ga. 764, 325 S.E.2d 366 (1985), the court stated: "Couch insists that the trial court erred in excluding evidence regarding the circumstances of his childhood, his emotional maturity and his mental capacity, maintaining that it would have shown that he had the *mental* age of a ten-year-old child. This evidence was proffered for the sole purpose of showing that Couch was incapable of forming the requisite intent under OCGA § 16–3–1, which provides that '[a] person shall not be considered or found guilty of a crime unless he has attained the age of 13 years at the time of the act. * * *'

"The age referred to in the code section is, of course, biological age. Nothing evidences a legislative intent to refer to 'mental age'—if, indeed, such a thing could ever be determined.''

Chapter 8

JUSTIFICATION AND EXCUSE

SECTION 1. INTRODUCTION

KENT GREENAWALT—DISTINGUISHING JUSTIFICATIONS FROM EXCUSES

49 Law & Contemp.Probs. 89, 91 (Summer 1986).

When something is fully justified, it is warranted. A justified belief is a belief based on good grounds; a justified action is a morally appropriate action. When something is fully excused, it is not warranted, but the person involved is not blameworthy. An excusable belief is one that a person cannot be blamed for holding;[6] an excusable action is one for which a person is not fully responsible. This is the central distinction between justification and excuse. Insofar as others are responsible and have the power of choice, they would do well to replicate a justified action but to avoid an act like that excused.

Occasionally commentators have suggested other distinguishing characteristics as central to the distinction. For example, it has been argued that justifications are general, applying to everyone in the same situation, and excuses are individual, relating to the characteristics of the particular actor. Although a substantial correlation of this type does exist, some legal excuses as well as some moral appraisals have objective components: their application depends on how ordinary people would react to difficult conditions. If, as this article claims, justifications depend partly on an actor's state of mind, then they do take account of an important individual characteristic.

Another proposed distinction concerns the rights of others. Generally, justified acts may be aided and not prevented, and excused acts may be prevented but not aided. These correlations, however, are imperfect. In the field of moral evaluation, one can speak of clashing courses of action as justified. A person may be morally justified in shielding a family member from the police, and the police may be morally justified in searching the person's apartment to find the family member. On occasion, the law may also privilege competing courses of action. And if excused action may be stopped, it may not always be stopped with the same tactics as unexcused action. Perhaps Richard is morally and legally justified in shooting an ordinary assailant who runs toward him with a knife in his apartment, even if he could retreat. He may not, however, be justified in shooting if he knows the assailant is crazy.

---

6. Someone might, for example, lack solid rational basis for a belief, but be "excused" because his parents powerfully instilled that belief during childhood.

MODEL PENAL CODE

Article 3, Introduction (1985).

The Model Code does not * * * attempt to draw a fine line between all those situations in which a defense might more precisely be labelled a justification and all those situations in which a defense might more precisely be labelled an excuse. Thus, it treats in justification sections those cases in which an actor mistakenly perceives the circumstances or the necessity for force; in some of the cases, at least, it might be said that the actor is really offering an excuse for his conduct rather than a full-fledged justification. The Code's approach is based on a skepticism that any fine line between excuse and justification can sensibly be drawn, and on the belief that any possible value of attempting such a line would be outweighed by the cost of complicating the content of relevant provisions.

To say that someone's conduct is "justified" ordinarily connotes that the conduct is thought to be right, or at least not undesirable; to say that someone's conduct is "excused" ordinarily connotes that the conduct is thought to be undesirable but that for some reason the actor is not to be blamed for it. Usually one can say whether a defense that is offered is justificatory or excusatory, but there are some troublesome borderline cases. Suppose an actor makes a mistake of fact that is not only reasonable but also consistent with the highest standards of perception and apprehension. For example, relying on the consistently prevailing wind, a person sets a fire that will destroy private property but will also stop the advance of a large forest fire that looks as if it will destroy much more property. A sudden unexpected shift in the wind renders the forest fire harmless, while the set fire does the expected amount of property damage. In retrospect it is regrettable that the second fire was set, and one might consider a defense of setting it an "excuse" for an unfortunate occurrence. But based on all available information, the act of setting the fire was appropriate, and society would hope that similar fires would be set by persons with similar available information; thus the conduct of setting the fire was justified. Whether in this circumstance, one speaks of "justification" or "excuse" is a question of vague linguistic boundary lines rather than of substantive judgment.

In other circumstances there may be genuine doubt as to how behavior should be judged. Self-defense serves as an acceptable reason for the use of deadly force both because it is often desirable that people defend their lives and because it is thought that people will "naturally" defend themselves if they believe their lives are in danger. For many cases of self-defense it would probably be generally agreed that the use of deadly force was actually desirable, but for others, e.g., resistance by one family member to attack by another, there would be disagreement whether the use of deadly force was actually desirable or should merely be accepted as a natural response to a grave threat.

There is little point in trying to "purify" justification provisions of all situations in which it might be said that the defense offered is really an excuse. The main aim of a criminal code is to differentiate conduct that warrants criminal sanctions from conduct that does not. If it is clear that conduct will not be subject to criminal sanctions, the effort to establish precisely in each case whether that conduct is actually justified or only excused does not seem worthwhile, especially since, in regard to the difficult cases, members of society may disagree over the appropriate characterization. Moreover, insofar as determinations of justification and excuse are made by juries and both sorts of defenses are offered in difficult cases, a general verdict of acquittal would conceal the precise defense accepted even if the criminal code drew a fine line between justification and excuse.

SECTION 2. DEFENSE OF SELF AND OTHERS

UNITED STATES v. PETERSON

United States Court of Appeals, District of Columbia Circuit, 1973.
483 F.2d 1222.

SPOTTSWOOD W. ROBINSON, III, CIRCUIT JUDGE: * * *

The events immediately preceding the homicide are not seriously in dispute. The version presented by the Government's evidence follows. Charles Keitt, the deceased, and two friends drove in Keitt's car to the alley in the rear of Peterson's house to remove the windshield wipers from the latter's wrecked car. While Keitt was doing so, Peterson came out of the house into the back yard to protest. After a verbal exchange, Peterson went back into the house, obtained a pistol, and returned to the yard. In the meantime, Keitt had reseated himself in his car, and he and his companions were about to leave.

Upon his reappearance in the yard, Peterson paused briefly to load the pistol. "If you move," he shouted to Keitt, "I will shoot." He walked to a point in the yard slightly inside a gate in the rear fence and, pistol in hand, said, "If you come in here I will kill you." Keitt alighted from his car, took a few steps toward Peterson and exclaimed, "What the hell do you think you are going to do with that?" Keitt then made an about-face, walked back to his car and got a lug wrench. With the wrench in a raised position, Keitt advanced toward Peterson, who stood with the pistol pointed toward him. Peterson warned Keitt not to "take another step" and, when Keitt continued onward shot him in the face from a distance of about ten feet. Death was apparently instantaneous. Shortly thereafter, Peterson left home and was apprehended 20–odd blocks away.

This description of the fatal episode was furnished at Peterson's trial by four witnesses for the Government. Peterson did not testify or offer any evidence, but the Government introduced a statement which he had given the police after his arrest, in which he related a somewhat different version. Keitt had removed objects from his car before, and on the day of the shooting he had told Keitt not to do so. After the initial verbal altercation, Keitt went to his car for the lug wrench, so he, Peterson, went into his house for his pistol. When Keitt was about ten feet away, he pointed the pistol "away of his right shoulder;" adding that Keitt was running toward him, Peterson said he "got scared and fired the gun. He ran right into the bullet." "I did not mean to shoot him," Peterson insisted, "I just wanted to scare him."

At trial [for murder], Peterson moved for a judgment of acquittal on the ground that as a matter of law the evidence was insufficient to support a conviction. The trial judge denied the motion. After receiving instructions which in two respects are challenged here, the jury returned a verdict finding Peterson guilty of manslaughter. Judgment was entered conformably with the verdict, and this appeal followed. * * *

More than two centuries ago, Blackstone, best known of the expositors of the English common law, taught that "all homicide is malicious, and of course, amounts to murder, unless * * * *justified* by the command or permission of the law; *excused* on the account of accident or self-preservation; or *alleviated* into manslaughter, by being either the involuntary consequence of some act not strictly lawful, or (if voluntary) occasioned by some sudden and sufficiently violent provocation."

Tucked within this greatly capsulized schema of the common law of homicide is the branch of law we are called upon to administer today. No issue of justifiable homicide, within Blackstone's definition is involved.[35] But Peterson's consistent position is that as a matter of law his conviction of manslaughter—alleviated homicide—was wrong, and that his act was one of self-preservation—excused homicide. The Government, on the other hand, has contended from the beginning that Keitt's slaying fell outside the bounds of lawful self-defense. The questions remaining for our decision inevitably track back to this basic dispute.

Self-defense, as a doctrine legally exonerating the taking of human life, is as viable now as it was in Blackstone's time, and in the case before us the doctrine is invoked in its purest form. But "[t]he law of self-defense is a law of necessity;" the right of self-defense arises only when the necessity begins, and equally ends with the necessity; and never must the necessity be greater than when the force employed defensively is deadly.[40] The "necessity must bear all semblance of reality, and appear to admit of no other alternative, before taking life will be justifiable as excusable." Hinged on the exigencies of self-preservation, the doctrine of homicidal self-defense emerges from the body of the criminal law as a limited though important exception to legal outlawry of the arena of self-help in the settlement of potentially fatal personal conflicts.

So it is that necessity is the pervasive theme of the well defined conditions which the law imposes on the right to kill or maim in self-defense. There must have been a threat, actual or apparent, of the use of deadly force against the defender. The threat must have been unlawful and immediate. The defender must have believed that he was in imminent peril of death or serious bodily harm, and that his response was necessary to save himself therefrom. These beliefs must not only have been honestly entertained, but also objectively reasonable in light of the surrounding circumstances. It is clear that no less than a concurrence of these elements will suffice.

Here the parties' opposing contentions focus on the roles of two further considerations. One is the provoking of the confrontation by the defender. The other is the defendant's failure to utilize a safe route for retreat from the confrontation. The essential inquiry, in final analysis, is whether and to what extent the rule of necessity may translate these considerations into additional factors in the equation. To these questions, in the context of the specific issues raised, we now proceed.

The trial judge's charge authorized the jury, as it might be persuaded, to convict Peterson of second-degree murder or manslaughter, or to acquit by reason of self-defense. On the latter phase of the case, the judge instructed that with evidence of self-defense present, the Government bore the burden of proving beyond a reasonable doubt that Peterson did not act in self-defense; and that if the jury had a reasonable doubt as to whether Peterson acted in self-defense, the verdict must be not guilty. The judge further instructed that the circumstances under which Peterson acted, however, must have been such as to produce a reasonable belief that Keitt was then about to kill him or do him serious bodily harm, and that deadly force was necessary to repel him. In determining whether Peterson used excessive force in defending himself, the judge said, the jury could consider all of the circumstances under which he acted.

---

35. By the early common law, justification for homicide extended only to acts done in execution of the law, such as homicides in effecting arrests and preventing forcible felonies, and homicides committed in self-defense were only excusable. The distinction between justifiable and excusable homicide was important because in the latter case the slayer, considered to be not wholly free from blame, suffered a forfeiture of his goods. However, with the passage of 24 Henry VIII, ch. 5 (1532), the basis of justification was enlarged, and the distinction has largely disappeared. More usually the terms are used interchangeably, each denoting a legally non-punishable act, entitling the accused to an acquittal.

40. When we speak of deadly force, we refer to force capable of inflicting death or serious bodily harm.

These features of the charge met Peterson's approval, and we are not summoned to pass on them. There were, however, two other aspects of the charge to which Peterson objected, and which are now the subject of vigorous controversy. The first of Peterson's complaints centers upon an instruction that the right to use deadly force in self-defense is not ordinarily available to one who provokes a conflict or is the aggressor in it. Mere words, the judge explained, do not constitute provocation or aggression; and if Peterson precipitated the altercation but thereafter withdrew from it in good faith and so informed Keitt by words or acts, he was justified in using deadly force to save himself from imminent danger or death or grave bodily harm. And, the judge added, even if Keitt was the aggressor and Peterson was justified in defending himself, he was not entitled to use any greater force than he had reasonable ground to believe and actually believed to be necessary for that purpose. Peterson contends that there was no evidence that he either caused or contributed to the conflict, and that the instructions on that topic could only mislead the jury.

It has long been accepted that one cannot support a claim of self-defense by a self-generated necessity to kill. The right of homicidal self-defense is granted only to those free from fault in the difficulty; it is denied to slayers who incite the fatal attack, encourage the fatal quarrel or otherwise promote the necessitous occasion for taking life. The fact that the deceased struck the first blow, fired the first shot or made the first menacing gesture does not legalize the self-defense claim if in fact the claimant was the actual provoker. In sum, one who is the aggressor in a conflict culminating in death cannot invoke the necessities of self-preservation. Only in the event that he communicates to his adversary his intent to withdraw and in good faith attempts to do so is he restored to his right of self-defense.

This body of doctrine traces its origin to the fundamental principle that a killing in self-defense is excusable only as a matter of genuine necessity. Quite obviously, a defensive killing is unnecessary if the occasion for it could have been averted, and the roots of that consideration run deep with us. A half-century ago, in *Laney v. United States*,[53] this court declared

> that, before a person can avail himself of the plea of self-defense against the charge of homicide, he must do everything in his power, consistent with his safety, to avoid the danger and avoid the necessity of taking life. If one has reason to believe that he will be attacked, in a manner which threatens him with bodily injury, he must avoid the attack if it is possible to do so, and the right of self-defense does not arise until he has done everything in his power to prevent its necessity.

And over the many years since *Laney,* the court has kept faith with its precept.

In the case at bar, the trial judge's charge fully comported with these governing principles. The remaining question, then, is whether there was evidence to make them applicable to the case. A recapitulation of the proofs shows beyond peradventure that there was.

It was not until Peterson fetched his pistol and returned to his back yard that his confrontation with Keitt took on a deadly cast. Prior to his trip into the house for the gun, there was, by the Government's evidence, no threat, no display of weapons, no combat. There was an exchange of verbal aspersions and a misdemeanor against Peterson's property was in progress but, at this juncture, nothing more. Even if Peterson's post-arrest version of the initial encounter were accepted—his claim that Keitt went for the lug

<hr>

53. 54 App.D.C. 56, 294 F. 412 (1923).

wrench before he armed himself—the events which followed bore heavily on the question as to who the real aggressor was.[60]

The evidence is uncontradicted that when Peterson reappeared in the yard with his pistol, Keitt was about to depart the scene. Richard Hilliard testified that after the first argument, Keitt reentered his car and said "Let's go." This statement was verified by Ricky Gray, who testified that Keitt "got in the car and * * * they were getting ready to go;" he, too, heard Keitt give the direction to start the car. The uncontroverted fact that Keitt was leaving shows plainly that so far as he was concerned the confrontation was ended. It demonstrates just as plainly that even if he had previously been the aggressor, he no longer was.

Not so with Peterson, however, as the undisputed evidence made clear. Emerging from the house with the pistol, he paused in the yard to load it, and to command Keitt not to move. He then walked through the yard to the rear gate and, displaying his pistol, dared Keitt to come in, and threatened to kill him if he did. While there appears to be no fixed rule on the subject, the cases hold, and we agree, that an affirmative unlawful act reasonably calculated to produce an affray foreboding injurious or fatal consequences is an aggression which, unless renounced, nullifies the right of homicidal self-defense. We cannot escape the abiding conviction that the jury could readily find Peterson's challenge to be a transgression of that character. * * *

The second aspect of the trial judge's charge as to which Peterson asserts error concerned the undisputed fact that at no time did Peterson endeavor to retreat from Keitt's approach with the lug wrench. The judge instructed the jury that if Peterson had reasonable grounds to believe and did believe that he was in imminent danger of death or serious injury, and that deadly force was necessary to repel the danger, he was required neither to retreat nor to consider whether he could safely retreat. Rather, said the judge, Peterson was entitled to stand his ground and use such force as was reasonably necessary under the circumstances to save his life and his person from pernicious bodily harm. But, the judge continued, if Peterson could have safely retreated but did not do so, that failure was a circumstance which the jury might consider, together with all others, in determining whether he went further in repelling the danger, real or apparent, than he was justified in going.

Peterson contends that this imputation of an obligation to retreat was error, even if he could safely have done so. He points out that at the time of the shooting he was standing in his own yard, and argues he was under no duty to move. We are persuaded to the conclusion that in the circumstances presented here, the trial judge did not err in giving the instruction challenged.

Within the common law of self-defense there developed the rule of "retreat to the wall," which ordinarily forbade the use of deadly force by one to whom an avenue for safe retreat was open. This doctrine was but an application of the requirement of strict necessity to excuse the taking of human life, and was designed to insure the existence of that necessity. Even the innocent victim of a vicious assault had to elect a safe retreat, if available, rather than resort to defensive force which might kill or seriously injure.

In a majority of American jurisdictions, contrarily to the common law rule, one may stand his ground and use deadly force whenever it seems reasonably necessary to save

---

60. Notwithstanding that the deceased provoked the original quarrel, the accused cannot, after that quarrel has ended or the deceased has withdrawn, invoke the right of self-defense in a subsequent difficulty which he himself causes or brings on.

himself. While the law of the District of Columbia on this point is not entirely clear, it seems allied with the strong minority adhering to the common law. * * *

That is not to say that the retreat rule is without exceptions. Even at common law it was recognized that it was not completely suited to all situations. Today it is the more so that its precept must be adjusted to modern conditions non-existent during the early development of the common law of self-defense.[86] One restriction on its operation comes to the fore when the circumstances apparently foreclose a withdrawal with safety. The doctrine of retreat was never intended to enhance the risk to the innocent; its proper application has never required a faultless victim to increase his assailant's safety at the expense of his own. On the contrary, he could stand his ground and use deadly force otherwise appropriate if the alternative were perilous, or if to him it reasonably appeared to be. A slight variant of the same consideration is the principle that there is no duty to retreat from an assault producing an imminent danger of death or grievous bodily harm. "Detached reflection cannot be demanded in the presence of an uplifted knife," nor is it "a condition of immunity that one in that situation should pause to consider whether a reasonable man might not think it possible to fly with safety or to disable his assailant rather than to kill him."

The trial judge's charge to the jury incorporated each of these limitations on the retreat rule. Peterson, however, invokes another—the so-called "castle" doctrine. It is well settled that one who through no fault of his own is attacked in his home is under no duty to retreat therefrom. The oft-repeated expression that "a man's home is his castle" reflected the belief in olden days that there were few if any safer sanctuaries than the home. The "castle" exception, moreover, has been extended by some courts to encompass the occupant's presence within the curtilage outside his dwelling. Peterson reminds us that when he shot to halt Keitt's advance, he was standing in his yard and so, he argues, he had no duty to endeavor to retreat.

Despite the practically universal acceptance of the "castle" doctrine in American jurisdictions wherein the point has been raised, its status in the District of Columbia has never been squarely decided. But whatever the fate of the doctrine in the District law of the future, it is clear that in absolute form it was inapplicable here. The right of self-defense, we have said, cannot be claimed by the aggressor in an affray so long as he retains that unmitigated role. It logically follows that any rule of no-retreat which may protect an innocent victim of the affray would, like other incidents of a forfeited right of self-defense, be unavailable to the party who provokes or stimulates the conflict. Accordingly, the law is well settled that the "castle" doctrine can be invoked only by one who is without fault in bringing the conflict on. That, we think, is the critical consideration here.

We need not repeat our previous discussion of Peterson's contribution to the altercation which culminated in Keitt's death. It suffices to point out that by no interpretation of the evidence could it be said that Peterson was blameless in the affair. And while, of course, it was for the jury to assess the degree of fault, the evidence well nigh dictated the conclusion that it was substantial.

---

86. "We are aware of the wide diversity of opinion as to the duty to retreat, but this difference arises from the circumstances of the particular case under consideration, rather than from any difference of conception as to the rule itself. Time, place, and conditions may create a situation which would clearly justify a modification of the rule. For example, the common-law rule, which required the assailed to retreat to the wall, had its origin before the general introduction of firearms. If a person is threatened with death or great bodily harm by an assailant, armed with a modern rifle, in open space, away from safety, it would be ridiculous to require him to retreat. Indeed, to retreat would be to invite almost certain death." *Laney v. United States,* supra.

The only reference in the trial judge's charge intimating an affirmative duty to retreat was the instruction that a failure to do so, when it could have been done safely, was a factor in the totality of the circumstances which the jury might consider in determining whether the force which he employed was excessive. We cannot believe that any jury was at all likely to view Peterson's conduct as irreproachable. We conclude that for one who, like Peterson, was hardly entitled to fall back on the "castle" doctrine of no retreat, that instruction cannot be just cause for complaint. * * *

The judgment of conviction appealed from is accordingly

Affirmed.

Notes and Questions

1. *The reasonable belief requirement.* In *Coleman v. State,* 320 A.2d 740 (Del.1974), the court held it was reversible error to instruct that the defendant must have had a reasonable belief the defensive force was necessary. Such a holding, the court noted, was required in light of the new state criminal code, which adopted the Model Penal Code position (a) that self defense only requires a subjective belief, and (b) that if the defendant is negligent or reckless in having such belief, the defense is unavailable in a prosecution for an offense for which negligence or recklessness, as the case may be, suffices to establish culpability. Most jurisdictions, however, still require a reasonable belief, although a modern trend is to treat death-causing conduct prompted by an unreasonable belief as an "imperfect" defense situation which downgrades the crime from murder to voluntary manslaughter.

As explained in *State v. Faulkner,* 301 Md. 482, 483 A.2d 759 (1984): "The doctrine of imperfect self defense gained a foothold in the United States in the late 1800's. The 'cornerstone' case for this defense is an 1882 decision by the Court of Criminal Appeals of Texas. *Reed v. State,* 11 Tex.Crim.App. 509 (1882). * * * Shortly after *Reed,* courts fashioned three variations of the doctrine.

"First, some courts indicated that the doctrine would apply where the homicide would fall within the perfect self defense doctrine but for the fault of the defendant in provoking or initiating the difficulty at the non-deadly force level. Second, courts noted that the doctrine would apply when the defendant committed a homicide because of a honest but unreasonable belief that he was about to suffer death or serious bodily harm. Third, other courts recognized the doctrine when the defendant used unreasonable force in defending himself and, as a result, killed his opponent.

"Since the acceptance of this doctrine by several jurisdictions during the late 1800's and early 1900's, comparatively few modern jurisdictions have analyzed the doctrine. Of those jurisdictions that have considered the doctrine in recent times, however, several have adopted the honest but unreasonable belief variation of the imperfect self defense doctrine. * * *

"Many states that recognize the doctrine on the basis of statutory law have adopted the subjectively honest but objectively unreasonable standard of the imperfect self defense doctrine. * * *

"We agree that this statement represents an analytically sound view, and reflects the position taken by a majority of those jurisdictions that have addressed and embraced this defense. Logically, a defendant who commits a homicide while honestly, though unreasonably, believing that he is threatened with death or serious bodily harm, does not act with malice. Absent malice he cannot be convicted of murder. Nevertheless, because the killing was committed without justification or excuse, the defendant is not entitled to full exoneration. Therefore, as we see it, when evidence is presented showing the defendant's subjective belief that the use of force was necessary to prevent imminent death or serious bodily harm, the defendant is entitled to a proper instruction on imperfect self defense.[7]"

To what extent might the *Coleman* and *Faulkner* approaches produce different results? See, e.g., *Richmond v. State*, 330 Md. 223, 623 A.2d 630 (1993). Which is to be preferred?

2. *Provokers and aggressors.* In *Peterson,* it is said that the "right of homicidal self-defense is granted only to those free from fault in the difficulty." In the context of this rule, what should suffice to make one a provoker or aggressor? Consider:

(a) *People v. Townes,* 391 Mich. 578, 218 N.W.2d 136 (1974): Townes entered Burnett's store and loudly accused employee McMillion of dating his wife. Burnett ordered Townes to leave, and when Townes refused to do so, Burnett obtained a pistol from his office and again ordered Townes to leave, which he did. The state's evidence is that once Burnett holstered his gun, Townes reentered and shot him. Townes' version is that he shot in self-defense when Burnett made a "sudden motion" toward his holster. The jury, instructed that Townes could not invoke the doctrine of self-defense if he were "the aggressor in the conflict," convicted Townes of murder. On appeal it was held the instruction was erroneous, in that it was based upon "the incorrect assumption that there had been some evidence introduced at trial from which the jury could reasonably infer that appellant was the 'aggressor' in the fatal confrontation with Burnett. * * * The only reasonable conclusion from the trial testimony is that appellant's actions created a potential threat to Burnett's property and it was to this threat that Burnett responded; but, a threat to property in such a situation, is not a legally sufficient provocation to render appellant an aggressor."

(b) *State v. Riley*, 137 Wash.2d 904, 976 P.2d 624 (1999): According to Riley's testimony, he approached Jaramillo and asked about buying a vehicle and a gun Jaramillo had stolen, departed and then returned and made comments about Jaramillo's gang and said Jaramillo was only a "wannabe," at which Jaramillo said he was going to shoot Riley, prompting Riley to draw his gun and then, when it appeared Jaramillo was reaching for a gun, to shoot Jaramillo. Riley was convicted of assault with a deadly weapon at a trial where the judge gave a self-defense instruction and also an instruction that self-defense is not available if "defendant's acts and conduct provoked or commenced the fight." On appeal, Riley claimed the latter instruction could not be based upon his remarks to Jaramillo; the court responded that the instruction was properly grounded in the "evidence that Riley drew his gun first and aimed it at Jaramillo," but then went on to say that "the giving of an aggressor instruction where words alone are the asserted provocation would be error." The court explained: "If words alone, and in particular insulting words alone, could justify the 'victim' in using force in response and preclude the speaker from self-defense, principles of self-defense would be distorted."

The concurring judge objected that the "majority's rule defies human nature": "Imagine a funeral ceremony with hundreds of mourners for a widely respected African–American civil rights leader. A white supremacist appears at the church and begins shouting nonthreatening, racial epithets. Enraged mourners rush the person, who pulls out a concealed gun and kills several of them. At his trial for murder, he argues self-defense. Under the majority's reasoning, because he used only words to provoke the attack, the

---

7. Because this case presents the sole issue of imperfect self defense, we express no opinion as to the applicability of other suggested forms of "imperfect" mitigation defenses, such as imperfect duress, imperfect defense of others, imperfect defense of property, imperfect right to prevent a felony, and imperfect necessity.

white supremacist was not an aggressor and the State is not entitled to an aggressor instruction."

(c) *McMahan v. State,* 617 P.2d 494 (Alaska 1980). Bill and Sheila lived together. When Bill moved out, Steve moved in. Steve told Bill not to return to Sheila's, saying: "I have a new rifle and I wouldn't want to use it—have to use it on you." Bill later went to Sheila's; he had a rifle with him because "I'd be foolish to go back up there if I wasn't able to defend myself." Bill claimed he shot and killed Steve because, when he entered Sheila's apartment Steve came at him with a knife. It was held on appeal of Bill's murder conviction that he was not entitled to a self-defense instruction, for "when a defendant has a prior grievance with the deceased and takes a deadly weapon to an encounter with the deceased, the defendant should be deemed to have provoked the violence which resulted in the death of the deceased."

3. *The retreat doctrine.* Does the retreat doctrine represent sound policy? If so, why is it, as noted in *Peterson,* that a majority of American jurisdictions have rejected it? If it is sound, should it be extended so that even nondeadly force may not be used defensively when retreat is possible, as apparently is now the law in England? See A. J. Ashworth, *Self-defence and the Right to Life,* 34 Camb.L.J. 282 (1975).

4. *Safe avenue of retreat.* Assuming the retreat doctrine is sound, precisely when should the victim of an attack be held criminally liable because he used deadly force instead of retreating? Consider *Commonwealth v. Palmer,* 467 Pa. 476, 359 A.2d 375 (1976), in which (a) the trial judge instructed that the defendant was obligated to retreat "unless he is excused from retreating by showing that retreat was not possible and would not have saved him from death or serious bodily harm"; (b) the defendant on appeal objected that the correct rule was that he "need not have retreated if he reasonably believed no avenue of retreat remained open to him"; but (c) the court concluded that the applicable statute instead provided that "the use of deadly force, otherwise allowable, is disallowed only where the defendant *knows* an avenue of retreat is available."

5. *The "castle" doctrine exception.* In *Peterson* it is noted that "one who through no fault of his own is attacked in his home is under no duty to retreat therefrom." Why should this be so? Compare *Commonwealth v. Shaffer,* 367 Mass. 508, 326 N.E.2d 880 (1975), rejecting the majority view and holding "that one assaulted in his own home does not have the unlimited right to react with deadly force without any attempt at retreat. However, the importance of the location of the assault and the surrounding circumstance should be stressed to the jury."[a]

6. *Dimensions of the exception.* It is noted in *Peterson* that some courts have extended the "castle" doctrine "to encompass the occupant's presence within the curtilage outside his dwelling." Compare *State v. Bonano,* 59 N.J. 515, 284 A.2d 345 (1971): "It may be seriously doubted whether a concept arising in the mediaeval land law furnishes an intelligent guide in determining whether the taking of a life is to be justified. What, also, of a disputed boundary line? Is the justification for a slaying to rest upon the resolution of a title issue? If a defendant can show good title to the ground upon which he stood when he fired the fatal shot, is he to be exonerated, whereas if the land is later determined to be that of his neighbor, is he to be found guilty? Might not the better rule be that a duty to retreat should exist except as to the dwelling house itself, defined, as stated above, to include a porch or other similar appurtenance?"

a. The *Shaffer* position was later superceded by a statute taking the traditional position. See *Common-* *wealth v. Gregory,* 17 Mass.App.Ct. 651, 461 N.E.2d 831 (1984).

Does the reasoning underlying the "castle" exception warrant its extension to places other than one's home, such as one's place of business? See Annots., 52 A.L.R.2d 1458 (1957); 41 A.L.R.3d 584 (1972).

7. *Attacker's status re the "castle".* In *State v. Thomas,* 77 Ohio St.3d 323, 673 N.E.2d 1339 (1997), Teresa was convicted of murder after she shot and killed her live-in boyfriend Jerry. Their relationship was marked by violence and intimidation. On the night of the killing, Jerry came home and started yelling; Teresa ran to the bathroom but could not get out of the tiny bathroom window and thus, afraid that Jerry was going to kill her, she ran to Jerry's closet and grabbed his gun and then ran back to the kitchen as Jerry continued to yell at her and threaten to kill her. She fired two warning shots and, when Jerry continued to threaten her, shot him in the arm twice. Jerry fell and then started to get up again, continuing to threaten Teresa, and she then shot Jerry two more times while he was bent over; the shots entered his back. On appeal, Teresa argued that the trial court erred by not instructing the jury that she had no duty to retreat from a cohabitant.

The majority reversed the conviction by adopting the view taken by the "majority of jurisdictions in the United States," namely, "that there is no duty to retreat when one is attacked in one's own home, regardless of whether or not the assailant has a right to be in the home equal to that of the one being assailed." The court explained that there "is no reason to make * * * a distinction" between those cases in which the assailant is an intruder and those where the assailant is a cohabitant, for in both instances "a person in her own home has already retreated 'to the wall,' [and so] there is no place to which she can further flee in safety."

On the thesis that the court should not "ignore the issues of domestic violence wrapped up in this case," the concurring opinion took a somewhat narrower approach. Because "research demonstrates that the battered woman's attempt to retreat often increases the immediate danger to herself," this was a case where the jury should have "been given instructions that properly allowed them to evaluate the battered woman syndrome with no duty to retreat." On the other hand, in "cases where there are no issues of domestic violence or battered woman syndrome," the "balancing of societal interests"— "for preserving the sanctity of life on one hand and, on the other hand, for allowing one to protect oneself from harm in one's own home"—is more complex, and thus the jury then should be free to "weigh all these competing interests" and judge whether the defendant "could have reasonably avoided the danger."

The two dissenters, contending that "the sanctity of human life must pervade the law," reasoned that the majority was wrong in asserting there was no rational reason for a distinction between intruder cases and cohabitant cases: "[T]here is at least one: the number of times the situation arises. While there are all too many instances of unknown people intruding into the homes of others, the number of such occurrences is negligible compared to the number of times cohabitants are in their home together. There are dramatically more opportunities for deadly violence in the domestic setting than in the intrusion setting. Thus, to hold that cohabitants do not have to retreat before resorting to lethal force is to invite violence."

Which view is correct? In those states not accepting the majority view, what then should be the situation where the attack comes from neither an intruder or a cohabitant, but rather one invited into the premises as a guest? See *State v. Walton,* 615 A.2d 469 (R.I.1992).

8. *Relationship of self-defense and crime prevention.* In *State v. Harris,* 222 N.W.2d 462 (Iowa 1974), the defendant "adduced proof that Frondle accosted her at the tavern, she left and went to her apartment, he followed and demanded sexual relations, she resisted,

and they wrestled. Defendant further contends that she got a shotgun from the corner of the room and told Frondle to leave, which he refused to do. She then got a shell out of a drawer, loaded the gun, pointed it at Frondle, and again told him to leave. When Frondle went to the door and put his hand on the knob, she shot him in the back. Frondle staggered from the building to the street and died shortly thereafter. Defendant contends she shot Frondle because she thought he was going to lock the door and rape her." The trial judge instructed that before a person may take another's life in self-defense, the person must believe he is in imminent danger of "death or great bodily harm," but refused defendant's request to add "or some felony about to be committed against the defendant." On appeal, this was held not to be reversible error because the requested charge was overbroad:

"Essentially, two situations are involved in this area of homicide. One situation involves the defense of one's own person from attack, self-defense. The law's respect for human life is such that the attacker's life may not be taken unless the victim reasonably and honestly believes he is in imminent danger of loss of life or great bodily injury, quite apart from the question of whether the conduct of the other person is felonious. * * *

"In the other situation, a person may kill if he observes an atrocious, violent felony about to be or being committed—whether upon such person himself or not. From earliest common law, the person may take the life of the offender if necessary to prevent such a crime. * * * The commentators generally treat this type of homicide separately from self-defense. * * * The law's rationale for allowing human life to be taken to prevent commission of atrocious, violent felonies is that such crimes themselves imperil human life or involve danger of great bodily harm. * * *

"From this it is clear that not every felony will permit the taking of human life. The elements of force and atrocity must exist. Blackstone lists those felonies as murder, robbery, burglary, arson, breaking a house with intent to rob, rape, and other forcible and detestable capital crimes. Adultery, as an example, is not within that class of felonies."

Consider also *Model Penal Code* §§ 3.04(2)(b), 3.07(5); and *State v. Havican*, 213 Conn. 593, 569 A.2d 1089 (1990) (although state's self-defense statute, otherwise based on Model Penal Code, fails to address use of force to prevent commission of certain offenses upon the defendant, trial court nonetheless erred in not instructing the jury that the defendant could use deadly physical force if reasonably necessary to repel a forcible homosexual assault, as such statutes "should be read in the light of their common law background" and thus are deemed to have "codified the common law rule that a person can justifiably use deadly force in self-defense of sodomy and rape").

9. *Injury to or death of third party.* In *Commonwealth v. Fowlin*, 551 Pa. 414, 710 A.2d 1130 (1998), "Fowlin was present in a nightclub in Easton, Pennsylvania. He was armed with a handgun. Three men, two of whom were also armed with handguns, accosted Fowlin in the club, and one of the three sprayed pepper gas in his eyes. At approximately the same time, a second man drew a handgun. Fearing that he was about to be killed, Fowlin drew his own handgun and fired repeatedly in the direction of the attackers. Although he was nearly blinded by the pepper spray, he killed the assailant who had drawn the gun and wounded one of the others. He also wounded a bystander. At the time of the shooting, approximately 200 people were present in the nightclub." Fowlin, charged with reckless endangerment and aggravated assault upon the bystander, sought to dismiss the charges, claiming that a person who lawfully employs self defense could not be criminally liable for unintentionally inflicting injury upon a bystander while employing self-defense. The trial court held that in order to avoid criminal liability, the person defending himself must not only be properly engaged in defending himself, but he must not act recklessly. An

evenly divided Superior Court affirmed; those in favor of affirmance relied on *Model Penal Code* § 3.09. On further appeal, the court held:

"Because the crimes with which Fowlin was charged require proof of recklessness, and because * * * a claim of self-defense, if believed, negates any element of recklessness, Fowlin, a fortiori, cannot be found to have been reckless, for the Commonwealth admits that his actions were justified. If he cannot be held to have been reckless, he cannot be convicted of aggravated assault or reckless endangerment. * * *

"[W]hen one is the victim of an attack, the assailant, not the victim, picks the time, the place, the manner, and the circumstances of the attack. Leisurely assessment of the circumstances and the danger to others is almost never a feature of such an assault, and most often, the best the victim can do is to mount a defense which hopefully will preserve his life. In many cases, the victim has only seconds to act in order to avoid injury or death. In this case, Fowlin was accosted by three men who assaulted him with pepper spray and simultaneously drew a handgun. Fowlin assumed, with reason, that they intended to kill or seriously injure him. He acted instinctively and within our law in defending himself."

A dissenting justice objected: "I do not believe that a successful claim of self-defense negates the element of recklessness with respect to persons other than the attacker. Accordingly, even though I agree that appellant was justified in defending himself against his attackers, the issue of whether or not he acted recklessly towards an innocent bystander was a question of fact that should have gone to the jury.

"[The majority's] reasoning would apply only if appellant were to be found liable under the doctrine of transferred intent. However, here the Commonwealth does not seek to transfer appellant's intent with respect to his attackers, but rather seeks to impose criminal liability because of appellant's intent with respect to a third party. I believe that Pennsylvania's statutory scheme and sound policy reasons allow the Commonwealth to seek to impose criminal liability in these circumstances."

Consider *People v. Adams*, 9 Ill.App.3d 61, 291 N.E.2d 54 (1972), reaching essentially the same result as *Fowlin*, but adding that "the above rule is not absolute and * * * it may be subject to modification depending on the circumstances involved." What circumstances would require modification?

As for more deliberate acts directed at a third party, consider *State v. Cooper*, 128 N.M. 428, 993 P.2d 745 (App.1999) (defendant who reasonably feels threatened by multiple assailants who appear to be acting in concert, and who forcibly uses one assailant as a shield against the other, is entitled to a self-defense instruction with regard to charges of assault of the person used as a shield, although there is no comparable right to use an innocent third party as a shield). Does it follow that shooting an accomplice is permissible? Consider *State v. Coffin*, 128 N.M. 192, 991 P.2d 477 (1999): "While it is true that a person may act in self-defense against multiple attackers acting in concert, this principle applies only to the extent that each accomplice poses an immediate danger of death or great bodily harm, thereby necessitating an act of self-defense. * * * Coffin's tendered instruction would have allowed a claim of self-defense against an accomplice to an attacker despite the fact that the accomplice posed no immediate danger of death or great bodily harm and despite a lack of necessity for the actions against the accomplice."

10. *Threatening deadly force.* In *Commonwealth v. Cataldo*, 423 Mass. 318, 668 N.E.2d 762 (1996), defendant, an auto repossessor licensed to carry a gun, was walking down the street with two friends when a scuffle broke out. Someone summoned two off-duty detectives from a nearby bar. One of them approached defendant with his revolver drawn and, when defendant drew his gun, shot him in the chest. Upon his recovery,

defendant was charged with assault with a deadly weapon upon the detective. Regarding defendant's self-defense claim, the trial judge only instructed upon the circumstances which would justify resort to deadly force by the defendant. The intermediate appellate court, on the other hand, ruled that instead the circumstances called for only an instruction on when nondeadly force is permissible. The matter, not directly addressed in the state's self-defense statute, is now before the state supreme court, which has tended to rely upon the Model Penal Code in the absence of settled state law. Should that court rule that the trial judge was correct, that the intermediate appellate court was correct, or that neither of them was correct? See *Model Penal Code* §§ 3.04, 3.11.

11. *Self-defense and weapon possession.* Minifie, a convicted felon, entered a crowded bar about midnight and was confronted by a large man on crutches, Tino, who disliked Minifie because he had killed Tino's friend Jackie Knight. When Tino knocked Minifie to the floor with a single punch and then reached for his crutches, Minifie drew a gun and shot Tino in the hand and then fled. Despite his self-defense claim, Minifie was convicted of (i) assault with a deadly weapon, and (ii) possession of a firearm by a convicted felon. On appeal, the court held that the trial judge had erred in rejecting Minifie's offered proof that he had received repeated threats from the Knight family, "the meanest, baddest family" in the county, reasoning that because "the law recognizes the justification of self-defense not because the victim 'deserved' what he or she got, but because the defendant acted reasonably under the circumstance," it follows that just as evidence of prior threats by a victim are admissible, the same is true of prior threats "by members of a group who in the defendant's mind are reasonably associated with the victim." *People v. Minifie*, 13 Cal.4th 1055, 56 Cal.Rptr.2d 133, 920 P.2d 1337 (1996). Should the court now reverse *both* convictions?

12. *Burden of proof.* A very few states place the burden on the defendant to prove the defense of self defense by a preponderance of the evidence. In *Martin v. Ohio,* 480 U.S. 228, 107 S.Ct. 1098, 94 L.Ed.2d 267 (1987), the Supreme Court, in a 5–4 decision, held that under the reasoning of *Patterson v. New York,* p. 270 of this Book, such allocation of the burden is constitutionally permissible:

"We agree with the State and its Supreme Court that this conviction did not violate the Due Process Clause. The State did not exceed its authority in defining the crime of murder as purposely causing the death of another with prior calculation or design. It did not seek to shift to Martin the burden of proving any of those elements, and the jury's verdict reflects that none of her self-defense evidence raised a reasonable doubt about the state's proof that she purposefully killed with prior calculation and design. She nevertheless had the opportunity under state law and the instructions given to justify the killing and show herself to be blameless by proving that she acted in self-defense. The jury thought she had failed to do so, and Ohio is as entitled to punish Martin as one guilty of murder as New York was to punish Patterson.

"It would be quite different if the jury had been instructed that self-defense evidence could not be considered in determining whether there was a reasonable doubt about the state's case, *i.e.,* that self-defense evidence must be put aside for all purposes unless it satisfied the preponderance standard. Such instruction would relieve the state of its burden and plainly run afoul of *Winship's* mandate. The instructions in this case could be clearer in this respect, but when read as a whole, we think they are adequate to convey to the jury that all of the evidence, including the evidence going to self-defense, must be considered in deciding whether there was a reasonable doubt about the sufficiency of the state's proof of the elements of the crime.

"We are thus not moved by assertions that the elements of aggravated murder and self-defense overlap in the sense that evidence to prove the latter will often tend to negate the former. It may be that most encounters in which self-defense is claimed arise suddenly and involve no prior plan or specific purpose to take life. In those cases, evidence offered to support the defense may negate a purposeful killing by prior calculation and design, but Ohio does not shift to the defendant the burden of disproving any element of the state's case. * * *

"Petitioner submits that there can be no conviction under Ohio law unless the defendant's conduct is unlawful and that because self-defense renders lawful what would otherwise be a crime, unlawfulness is an element of the offense that the state must prove by disproving self-defense. This argument founders on state law, for it has been rejected by the Ohio Supreme Court and by the Court of Appeals for the Sixth Circuit. It is true that unlawfulness is essential for conviction, but the Ohio courts hold that the unlawfulness in cases like this is the conduct satisfying the elements of aggravated murder—an interpretation of state law that we are not in a position to dispute."

The four dissenters, though later expressing a preference for the methodology of the *Patterson* dissent, argued that the instant case was wrongly decided even under the principles set forth in *Patterson,* especially the "clear implication * * * that when an affirmative defense *does* negate an element of the crime, the state may not shift the burden. In such a case, *In re Winship,* 397 U.S. 358, 90 S.Ct. 1068, 25 L.Ed.2d 368 (1970), requires the state to prove the nonexistence of the defense beyond a reasonable doubt.

"The reason for treating a defense that negates an element of the crime differently from other affirmative defenses is plain. If the jury is told that the prosecution has the burden of proving all the elements of a crime, but then also is instructed that the defendant has the burden of *dis*proving one of those same elements, there is a danger that the jurors will resolve the inconsistency in a way that lessens the presumption of innocence. For example, the jury might reasonably believe that by raising the defense, the accused has assumed the ultimate burden of proving that particular element. Or, it might reconcile the instructions simply by balancing the evidence that supports the prosecutor's case against the evidence supporting the affirmative defense, and conclude that the state has satisfied its burden if the prosecution's version is more persuasive. In either case, the jury is given the unmistakable but erroneous impression that the defendant shares the risk of nonpersuasion as to a fact necessary for conviction.[1] * * *

"The Court gives no explanation for this apparent rejection of *Patterson*. * * * The Court seems to conclude that as long as the jury is told that the state has the burden of proving all elements of the crime, the overlap between the offense and defense is immaterial.

"This reasoning is flawed in two respects. First, it simply ignores the problem that arises from inconsistent jury instructions in a criminal case. The Court's holding implicitly assumes that the jury in fact understands that the ultimate burden remains with the prosecutor at all times, despite a conflicting instruction that places the burden on the accused to disprove the same element. But as pointed out above, the *Patterson* distinction

---

1. Indeed, this type of instruction has an inherently illogical aspect. It makes no sense to say that the prosecution has the burden of proving an element beyond a reasonable doubt *and* that the defense has the burden of proving the contrary by a preponderance of the evidence. If the jury finds that the prosecutor has *not* met his burden, it of course will have no occasion to consider the affirmative defense. And if the jury finds that each element of the crime *has* been proved beyond a reasonable doubt, it necessarily has decided that the defendant has not disproved an element of the crime. In either situation the instructions on the affirmative defense are surplusage. Because a reasonable jury will attempt to ascribe some significance to the court's instructions, the likelihood that it will impermissibly shift the burden is increased. * * *

between defenses that negate an element of the crime and those that do not is based on the legitimate concern that the jury *will* mistakenly lower the state's burden. In short, the Court's rationale fails to explain why the overlap in this case does not create the risk that *Patterson* suggested was unacceptable.

"Second, the Court significantly, and without explanation, extends the deference granted to state legislatures in this area. Today's decision could be read to say that virtually all state attempts to shift the burden of proof for affirmative defenses will be upheld, regardless of the relationship between the elements of the defense and the elements of the crime. As I understand it, *Patterson* allowed burden-shifting because evidence of an extreme emotional disturbance did not negate the *mens rea* of the underlying offense. After today's decision, however, even if proof of the defense *does* negate an element of the offense, burden-shifting still may be permitted because the jury can consider the defendant's evidence when reaching its verdict."

BECHTEL v. STATE

Court of Criminal Appeals of Oklahoma, 1992.

840 P.2d 1.

JOHNSON, JUDGE:

[Donna Lee Bechtel, Appellant, was convicted of first degree murder of her husband Ken and sentenced to life imprisonment. They were married on August 25, 1982, and the first of approximately 23 incidents of violence perpetrated by the victim upon her was on July 4, 1982. The batterings consisted of the deceased grabbing Appellant by either her ears or hair and pounding her head on the ground, wall, door, cabinet or other available object. During all of the episodes, the deceased threatened or otherwise intimidated Appellant. On September 23, 1984, the day of his death, the deceased returned home at approximately 5:30 A.M. from a hunting trip highly intoxicated. He awakened Appellant and ordered her to get out of the bed so they could have a drink. * * * When she tried to leave, he pulled her by the hair and threw her back on the bed, and then they both fell onto the floor. He threatened to "kill your ass" and began pounding her head into the floor. He picked her up by the head and pulled her back on the bed and beat her head against the headboard. He then slumped on top of her.]

Appellant tried to get from under him, but he would mumble whenever she made an effort. Finally, she eased herself from under him. As she sat on her knees on the floor beside the bed, she lit a cigarette, held it in one hand and her head with the other hand. As she got ready to smoke the cigarette, she heard a gurgling sound, looked up and saw the contorted look and glazed eyes of the deceased with his arms raised. Appellant reached for the gun under the bed and shot the deceased as she tried to get up and run.

Appellant defended this case on the theory of self-defense.[a] * * *

On appeal, Appellant contends that the trial court erred in refusing to allow expert testimony on the battered woman syndrome as such testimony would aid the trier of fact in assessing how her experiences as a battered woman affected her state of mind at the time of the killing. This, she argues, goes to the reasonableness of her belief that she was in imminent danger. We agree.

---

a. The relevant statute says homicide is justifiable when "in the lawful defense of such person, * * * when there is a reasonable ground to apprehend a design to commit a felony, or to do some great personal injury, and imminent danger of such design being accomplished."

An offer of proof concerning the admissibility of testimony on the Battered Woman Syndrome was made in-camera where the trial judge heard testimony from Dr. Lenore Walker, a licensed, practicing psychologist and diplomate in clinical psychology who pioneered the research on the Battered Woman Syndrome, and the State's witness, Dr. Herbert C. Modlin, a licensed, practicing psychiatrist. Dr. Walker discussed the methodology used by her in diagnosing such syndrome and related that this is taught in the graduate schools and accepted in the entire scientific community of research. On refusing to allow the testimony, the trial judge offered the following three reasons:

1. The lack of general acceptance of the theory in the psychological community based on the fact that the syndrome is not listed in the Diagnostic and Statistical Manual of Mental Disorders–3–R (DMS–3R), a publication of the American Psychiatric Association.

2. The testimony did not appear to be necessary or helpful to the jury since the jury was capable of making a decision based on all of the evidence.

3. The lapse of time between the incident and the psychological testing, which "would certainly permit time for manufacturing of a defense or for the healing of whatever emotional and personality abnormalities or wounds had been caused by the relationship."

We find no support for the trial court's first reason. The relevant scientific community in this case is the psychological community and not the psychiatric community. Moreover, both experts acknowledged that the syndrome is considered a sub-category of Post-traumatic Stress Disorder, which is generally accepted and is listed in the DSM–3R. Based upon our independent review of the available sources on the subject, we believe that the syndrome is a mixture of both psychological and physiological symptoms but is not a mental disease in the context of insanity. Further, we believe that because psychologists see more battered women than psychiatrists, the psychological community has had the opportunity to be and, indeed, have been more responsive to the problems or symptoms experienced by those suffering from the syndrome.

Other courts have accepted the syndrome as a scientifically recognized theory. To date, thirty-one (31) states and the District of Columbia allow the use of expert testimony on the subject. Five (5) states acknowledged its validity, but held the testimony inadmissible based on the facts of the particular case. In addition, hundreds of books, articles and commentaries have been written and numerous studies have been done on the subject. Based on the aforesaid, we find that the Battered Woman Syndrome is a substantially scientifically accepted theory.

We next address the trial court's ruling that expert testimony does not appear to be necessary or helpful to the jury since Appellant's testimony concerning numerous drunken assaults and threats, including the vicious assault and threat to kill her on the night of the homicide, are, in the trial court's opinion, "easily within the common understanding of all the jurors and easily come[s] within the legal definition of self-defense. * * *

Appellant argues that expert testimony regarding the syndrome is admissible to help the jury understand the battered woman, and, why Appellant acted out of a reasonable belief that she was in imminent danger when considering the issue of self-defense. We agree.

While the Court does not, as a matter of law, adopt the definition of a "Battered Woman", it was first defined by Dr. Lenore Walker in her book, *The Battered Woman Syndrome* (1979), as follows:

The battered woman is a woman who is repeatedly subjected to any forceful, physical or psychological behavior by a man in order to coerce her to do something he wants her to do without any concern for her rights. Battered women include wives or women in any form of intimate relationship with men. Furthermore, in order to be classified as a battered woman, the couple must go through the battering cycle at least twice. Any woman may find herself in an abusive relationship with a man once. If it occurs a second time, and she remains in the situation, she is defined as a battered woman.

Misconceptions regarding battered women abound, making it more likely than not that the average juror will draw from his or her own experience or common myths, which may lead to a wholly incorrect conclusion. Thus, we believe that expert testimony on the syndrome is necessary to counter these misconceptions.[8]

We next address the trial court's third reason for not allowing the expert testimony, i.e., that the 3 ½ years lapse of time between the commission of the offense and the psychological examination would allow for the manufacturing of a defense. [W]e hold that the lapse of time between the commission of the offense and the examination of the accused is not per se grounds to exclude evidence by the expert. The Court may not allow the expert to testify to the ultimate fact and further, must determine the reasonableness of the testimony based upon the passage of time.

We believe that the Battered Woman Syndrome has gained substantial scientific acceptance and will aid the trier of fact in determining facts in issue, i.e., reasonableness and imminence (discussed below), when testimony on the same is offered in cases of self-defense. However, before such testimony may be admitted, this Court today sets forth the following guidelines:

1. The defendant must offer evidence which establishes herself as a "battered woman."

2. The expert must establish herself/himself as one who is qualified by knowledge, skill, experience, training or education to diagnose the defendant as suffering from the Battered Woman Syndrome.

3. The defendant, who has submitted herself to psychological or psychiatric examination and who intends to use or otherwise rely on testimony resulting from said examination, may be ordered, at the discretion of the trial court, to submit to an examination by the State's expert witness, upon application of the State. The defendant's expert is permitted to be present and observe the examination.

4. A report of the State's expert setting forth all relevant findings, opinions, conclusions and their factual bases shall be prepared and a copy provided to the defendant forthwith. Testimony of the State's witness shall be admitted only in rebuttal on matters covered by the expert for the defense and for the same purposes for which the defense expert's testimony was offered.

5. The expert may not give an opinion on whether the defendant acted reasonably in perceiving herself as being in imminent danger and whether the defendant acted in self defense.

---

8. Dr. Walker writes: "Expert testimony on the battered woman syndrome would help dispel the ordinary lay person's perception that a woman in a battering relationship is free to leave at anytime. The expert evidence would counter any 'common sense' conclusions by the jury that if the beatings were really that bad the woman would have left her husband much earlier. Popular misconceptions about battered women would be put to rest, including the beliefs that the women are masochistic and enjoy the beatings and that they intentionally provoke their husbands into fits of rage."

6. The trial court shall give in its charge to the jury the specific instruction on standard of reasonableness, which we adopt today (see below).

Thus, we conclude that the trial court erred in not allowing testimony on the syndrome. * * *

The key to the defense of self-defense is reasonableness. A defendant must show that she had a reasonable belief as to the imminence of great bodily harm or death and as to the force necessary to compel it. Several of the psychological symptoms that develop in one suffering from the syndrome are particularly relevant to the standard of reasonableness in self-defense. One such symptom is a greater sensitivity to danger which has come about because of the intimacy and history of the relationship. Dr. Walker, in her offer of proof below, explained that the abuse occurs in a cycle (The Cycle Theory), which consists of three phases. The first phase is the "tension-building" period. The second stage is the "acute-explosion" period, where the abuse takes place. The third stage is the "loving, contrition" period.

It is during the tension-building period that the battered woman develops a heightened sensitivity to any kinds of cues of distress. Thus, because of her intimate knowledge of her batterer, the battered woman perceives danger faster and more accurately as she is more acutely aware that a new or escalated violent episode is about to occur. * * *

During the loving, contrition period, the abuser makes amends by being loving, making promises to change and avowing that the abuse will never happen again. It is during this stage that the battered woman is being positively reinforced by her abuser. In most battering cases, this period is of the longest duration. The cultural characteristics of women influence the battered woman's belief that if she could only do something to help her abuser, then the bad part of him will go away. Thus, the battered woman learns to develop coping skills rather than escape skills and develops a "psychological paralysis" and "learned helplessness."

Thus, Dr. Walker's testimony as to how Appellant's particular experiences as a battered woman suffering from the Battered Woman Syndrome affected her perceptions of danger, its imminence, what actions were necessary to protect herself and the reasonableness of those perceptions are relevant and necessary to prove Appellant's defense of self-defense. However, it now becomes necessary to determine the standard of reasonableness against which the finder of fact must measure the accused's belief.

Standards of reasonableness have been traditionally characterized as either "objective" or "subjective." Under the objective standard of reasonableness, the trier of fact is required to view the circumstances, surrounding the accused at the time of the use of force, from the standpoint of hypothetical reasonable person. Under the subjective standard of reasonableness, the fact finder is required to determine whether the circumstances, surrounding the accused at the time of the use of force, are sufficient to induce in the accused an honest and reasonable belief that he/she must use force to defend himself/herself against imminent harm.

Oklahoma's standard of reasonableness may be gleaned from past decisions of this Court and is set forth in OUJI–CR 743, which reads as follows:

A person is justified in using deadly force in self-defense if that person reasonably believed that use of deadly force was necessary to protect herself from imminent danger of death or great bodily harm. Self-defense is a defense although the danger to life or personal security may not have been real, if a reasonable person, in the circumstances and from the viewpoint of the defendant, would reasonably have believed that she was in imminent danger of death or great bodily harm.

The aforesaid instruction was given in this case. While the instruction explicitly states that the fact finder should assume the viewpoint and circumstances of the defendant in assessing the reasonableness of his or her belief, i.e. subjective, it also requires the defendant's viewpoint to be that of a reasonable person, in similar circumstances and with the same perceptions, i.e., objective. Thus, Oklahoma's standard is a hybrid, combining both the objective and subjective standards. * * *

However, in light of * * * our decision today to allow testimony on the Battered Woman Syndrome in appropriate cases, we deem it necessary to modify OUJI–CR 743 by striking the words "reasonably" [in the first sentence] and "reasonable" [in the second sentence] from such instruction. * * *

In addition to the reasonableness standard, Oklahoma's law of self-defense also imposes the temporal requirement of imminence. The thinking is that it is unreasonable to be provoked to the point of killing well after the provocative or assertive conduct has occurred.

Furthermore, the syndrome has been analogized to the classic hostage situation in that the battered woman lives under long-term, life-threatening conditions in constant fear of another eruption of violence. [An] example [is] where the captor tells the hostage that he intends to kill him in three days. If on the first day, the hostage sees an opportunity to kill the captor and avoid the threat of his own death, a literal application of the requirement that the threat be "imminent" would prevent the hostage from using deadly force until the captor is standing over him with a knife. For the battered woman, if there is no escape or sense of safety, then the next attack, which could be fatal or cause serious bodily harm, is imminent. Based on the traditionally accepted definition of imminent and its functional derivatives, a battered woman, to whom the threat of serious bodily harm or death is always imminent, would be precluded from asserting the defense of self-defense.

Under our "hybrid" reasonableness standard, the meaning of imminent must necessarily envelope the battered woman's perceptions based on all the facts and circumstances of his or her relationship with the victim. In *Women's Self-defense Cases: Theory and Practice* (1981), Elizabeth Bochnak writes:

> The battered woman learns to recognize the small signs that precede periods of escalated violence. She learns to distinguish subtle changes in tone of voice, facial expression, and levels of danger. She is in a position to know, perhaps with greater certainty than someone attacked by a stranger, that the batterer's threat is real and will be acted upon.

Thus, according to the author, an abused woman may kill her mate during the period of threat that precedes a violent incident, right before the violence escalates to the more dangerous levels of an acute battering episode. Or, she may take action against him during a lull in an assaultive incident, or after it has culminated, in an effort to prevent a recurrence of the violence. And so, the issue is not whether the danger was in fact imminent, but whether, given the circumstances as she perceived them, the defendant's belief was reasonable that the danger was imminent. * * *

PARKS, JUDGE, concurring in results:

* * * While I conclude that the syndrome should have been presented to the jury in this case, I disagree with the majority's decision to radically overhaul the laws pertaining to self defense. The facts asserted by appellant, that the victim made a threatening movement and she shot him, constitute classic self defense and do not necessitate the sweeping changes imposed by the majority. * * *

Currently, the jury is asked to view the circumstances as they appeared to the defendant and then is asked to determine whether a reasonable person, caught in the dynamics of those identical circumstances, would respond as the defendant did. I find that the syndrome should have been admitted as it sheds light on the circumstances surrounding the altercation as they appeared to the appellant. The facts before us require us to decide nothing more.

I find the majority's position regarding reasonableness puzzling. After stating that "we deem it necessary to modify OUJI–CR 743 by striking the words 'reasonably' and 'reasonable' from such instruction," the majority nevertheless includes the reasonableness requirement in the modified instruction. Thus, to the extent that the majority has correctly identified a deficiency in the current instruction, the problem survives the majority's attempt at a cure. * * *

LUMPKIN, VICE–PRESIDING JUDGE, dissenting:

[W]hile I agree some revision regarding our application of self defense might be warranted, the facts of this case do not present the evidentiary predicate which is required to adopt the changes proposed by the Court. * * *

If and when a record on appeal is submitted to the Court which supports consideration of whether to adopt this type of concept as a part of the jurisprudence of this State, the Court should endeavor to adopt a rule of law which would apply equally to all citizens of the State, regardless of gender, who may be placed in a like situation. To do otherwise creates not only confusion as to its applicability but also question as to its validity if subjected to equal protection analysis. It is interesting to note the Court accurately identifies that the Diagnostic and Statistical Manual of Mental Disorders–3R (DSM–3R) recognizes the Post-traumatic Stress Disorder. See DSM-3R, 309.89 Post-traumatic Stress Disorder. However, rather than adopting a gender neutral diagnostic criteria accepted by the entire scientific community, the Court seeks to adopt a gender specific syndrome which has acceptance by only a subsection of the scientific community. If this disorder is such that it warrants this Court to review the reasonableness factor regarding action taken in self defense, then it should be considered in a gender neutral context. The information supplied to this Court reveals the Post-traumatic Stress Disorder, as does the proposed Battered Woman Syndrome, is a mixture of psychological and physiological symptoms which make it a medical issue. Psychologists do not have the medical training received by psychiatrists, therefore I cannot agree with the Court's unsupported statement that we should accept only the opinions of a sub-group of members of the psychological community as the gospel on this complex issue. This statement alone raises concern regarding the validity of the Court's determination and it creates a future problem for the Court when we are again required to determine if a proposed new "syndrome" of some type is generally accepted by the medical or scientific community. * * *

The fact that the Legislature has addressed the issue of self defense within our statutory framework restricts the ability of the Court to act beyond the context of the statute. [T]he statute requires "imminent danger" of the threat to the person, [and] therefore the Court cannot change that substantive element of the defense. In addition, the statute also allows the defense when there "is a reasonable ground to apprehend" the threat. It is within the Court's power and authority to interpret and determine the parameters of the application of a "reasonable ground to apprehend" and imminent threat to the person. * * *

Notes and Questions

1. Compare David L. Faigman & Amy J. Wright, *The Battered Woman Syndrome in the Age of Science*, 39 Ariz.L.Rev. 67, 114–15 (1997): "If a history of the law and science connection is written in a hundred years, the battered woman syndrome will serve as a particularly trenchant example of the law's inability to assess science at the close of the twentieth century. The syndrome, first proposed in the 1970's and based on the clinical observations of a single researcher, has yet to be corroborated by serious and rigorous empirical work. The syndrome, in fact, is a product of advocacy and not science, designed originally to support justification claims by battered women who have killed. However, the syndrome has been seriously misunderstood and misused by courts and it no longer serves the needs of its original constituency. Given the lack of a scientific basis and its failure to achieve specific political and policy goals, the battered woman syndrome can be expected to soon pass from the legal scene.

"The battered woman syndrome has been employed in a wide assortment of cases, ranging from the prototypical self-defense case to the more novel prosecutorial use of the syndrome. In the former set of cases, courts define the syndrome's relevance variously, from supporting the honesty of the woman's belief in the need to use deadly force to her mental incapacity to form the requisite mental intent. In the latter set of cases, in which prosecutors use the evidence, the evidence's relevance is ostensibly offered to explain why a battered woman might change her testimony (i.e., commit perjury) and testify that she was not a victim of battering; in fact, it is probably used to buttress the prosecution's case by showing prior violent acts by the defendant that would otherwise be excluded by the rules of evidence.

"The battered woman syndrome permits such broad interpretations because it is so little grounded in reality. Given the paucity of research that supports it, there are no empirical boundaries to contain it. As courts begin to apply tests of admissibility that query the scientific basis for expert testimony, they will see the serious lack of rigor in the tests used to study the syndrome hypothesis. Consequently, courts will begin to doubt the evidentiary relevance of this research.

"Advocates for battered women also should be expected to begin doubting the political value of syndrome testimony. Although so elastic that it can be shaped to fit any case, the syndrome has caused certain unintended consequences. In particular, syndrome evidence is interpreted by many courts as an indication that battered women suffer from mental deficiencies. Concepts such as learned helplessness contribute to this perception. The syndrome has transformed the pathology of domestic violence to the pathology of the battered woman. For instance, courts are increasingly ordering women claiming the defense to undergo state psychiatric examinations. Originally proposed as a theory entirely sympathetic to feminist ideals, the syndrome now reinforces some of the most archaic and destructive stereotypes historically attached to women."

2. Consider also Anne M. Coughlin, *Excusing Women*, 82 Calif.L.Rev. 1, 87–92 (1994): "If the community holds powerful feelings of sympathy for women who offend under the pressure of domestic violence (and the widespread recognition of the new defense certainly suggests that it does), then we must decide whether we can embody those feelings in a defense that does not effectively withhold from women the respect for their achievements and authority over their lives that the capacity for responsible conduct presently secures for men. * * * I am persuaded that the battered woman syndrome defense, at least as it is presently constituted, is profoundly anti-feminist. To invert a remark made by Joan

Williams about the work of Carol Gilligan, this defense reclaims for women all of the insults of the gender ideology of domesticity while endorsing none of its compliments. * * *

"As I suggested above, the facts reported in the battered woman cases are capable of generating multiple theoretical interpretations, each of which provides different experiences (or realities, if you will), both for the people who live in violent homes and for those who observe or assist the family members. For example, the widely cited work of Carol Gilligan offers an alternative explanation that we might draw upon if we were inclined to revise the battered woman syndrome defense. * * *

"Applied to the woman who lives in a violent home, Gilligan's findings suggest that the woman is not trapped there by a paralyzing mental disorder, but rather that she made a choice to remain in the relationship out of a conviction that she has a responsibility to care for her troubled spouse and to sustain the network of family life, especially to assure the welfare of her children. According to this argument, then, the woman who experiences battering at the hands of her husband should not be faulted for her failure to leave such a physically and psychologically damaging situation, but, on the contrary, applauded for her endurance, her perseverance, and self-sacrifice in order to nurture her violently explosive spouse and repair, if possible, their pathological interactions.

"Although the foregoing account seems to be both as plausible and less misogynist than that provided by the learned helplessness diagnosis, there are several reasons to doubt that the defense, if revised along these lines, would constitute much of an improvement over the battered woman syndrome theory. * * *

"In short, special excuses for women, in whatever form, reinforce incommensurable gender differences, in which the qualities characterized as male inevitably are privileged over those characterized as female; such excuses obscure feminist efforts to clarify our understanding of gender as a patriarchally constructed hierarchy of social differences and behavioral expectations. By the same token, our practice of excusing women reveals the inadequacy of the theory of responsibility presently endorsed by the criminal law. The theory is inadequate precisely because it is not capable of accommodating women's experiences without judging women to be deviant from and inferior to the model human actor the theory describes. Our practice of excusing women reveals that the ostensibly human traits and psychological processes privileged by the model of responsibility are those that culture construes as male. Therefore, the task we must undertake is to reconceive and revise the model of responsibility so that it values characteristics traditionally associated with women, as well as with men."

3. Compare the *Bechtel* view of "imminence" with that in *State v. Norman*, 324 N.C. 253, 378 S.E.2d 8 (1989), holding that defendant Judy Norman, a woman who had been physically and mentally abused by her husband over period of several years, and who had been diagnosed as suffering from battered woman's syndrome, was not acting in either perfect or imperfect self-defense when, out of alleged desire to prevent abuse in the future, she shot her husband while he slept.

"The defendant testified at trial that she was too afraid of her husband to press charges against him or to leave him. She said that she had temporarily left their home on several previous occasions, but he had always found her, brought her home and beaten her. Asked why she killed her husband, the defendant replied: 'Because I was scared of him and I knowed when he woke up, it was going to be the same thing, and I was scared when he took me to the truck stop that night it was going to be worse than he had ever been. I just couldn't take it no more. There ain't no way, even if it means going to prison. It's better than living in that. That's worse hell than anything.' * * *

"Based on the evidence that the defendant exhibited battered wife syndrome, that she believed she could not escape her husband nor expect help from others, that her husband had threatened her, and that her husband's abuse of her had worsened in the two days preceding his death, the Court of Appeals concluded that a jury reasonably could have found that her killing of her husband was justified as an act of perfect self-defense. The Court of Appeals reasoned that the nature of battered wife syndrome is such that a jury could not be precluded from finding the defendant killed her husband lawfully in perfect self-defense, even though he was asleep when she killed him. We disagree. * * *

"The defendant in the present case was not entitled to a jury instruction on either perfect or imperfect self-defense. The trial court was not required to instruct on either form of self-defense unless evidence was introduced tending to show that at the time of the killing the defendant reasonably believed herself to be confronted by circumstances which necessitated her killing her husband to save herself from imminent death or great bodily harm. No such evidence was introduced in this case, and it would have been error for the trial court to instruct the jury on either perfect or imperfect self-defense.

"The killing of another human being is the most extreme recourse to our inherent right of self-preservation and can be justified in law only by the utmost real or apparent necessity brought about by the decedent. For that reason, our law of self-defense has required that a defendant claiming that a homicide was justified and, as a result, inherently lawful by reason of perfect self-defense must establish that she reasonably believed at the time of the killing she otherwise would have immediately suffered death or great bodily harm. Only if defendants are required to show that they killed due to a reasonable belief that death or great bodily harm was imminent can the justification for homicide remain clearly and firmly rooted in necessity. The imminence requirement ensures that deadly force will be used only where it is necessary as a last resort in the exercise of the inherent right of self-preservation. * * *

"The term 'imminent,' as used to describe such perceived threats of death or great bodily harm as will justify a homicide by reason of perfect self-defense, has been defined as 'immediate danger, such as must be instantly met, such as cannot be guarded against by calling for the assistance of others or the protection of the law.' Our cases have sometimes used the phrase 'about to suffer' interchangeably with 'imminent' to describe the immediacy of threat that is required to justify killing in self-defense."

4. Compare *Norman* with Richard A. Rosen, *Self-Defense, Imminence, and Women Who Kill Their Batterers*, 71 N.C.L.Rev. 371, 410–11 (1993): "What this Article has attempted to do is to focus on the role of the imminence requirement and examine the possibility of lessening the law's reliance on it in order to further the values embodied in the doctrine of self-defense. If the premises of this Article are correct—that the imminence requirement works against these values in enough cases to warrant change, and that in appropriate cases the imminence requirement can be eliminated without undermining the basic fabric of the self-defense laws—then the time has come for legislatures and courts to begin to make these modifications.

"The continuing reports of jury nullifications in cases of women who kill those who batter them, as well as the recent spate of executive clemencies in such cases, may signal that the present law of self-defense has been outstripped by society's changing morality. It is no longer considered moral or legal for a man to beat his wife or girlfriend or to forcibly rape her. Perhaps society no longer considers it a moral imperative that a woman delay taking defensive action until a man who has already threatened to kill her begins to demonstrate again that he meant what he said.

"The development and acceptance of the 'battered women's syndrome' defense assuredly is one response to this evolution in society's values. This defense, however, seeks to solve the problem of women who kill their batterers by focusing on the psychological inadequacies of those who kill, and does nothing to help those who kill in non-confrontational situations. This Article suggests that if Judy Norman reasonably believed that she needed to kill her torturer in order to protect herself, it was not because she had acquired a psychological disability—although psychological scars would be an understandable product of the abuse she endured—but because her husband had created the conditions that made such a belief at least reasonable, if not absolutely correct."

5. Does *Bechtel* mean that under the prevailing objective approach any evidence bearing upon the defendant's personal characteristics and experiences is admissible? Compare:

(a) *People v. Goetz,* 68 N.Y.2d 96, 506 N.Y.S.2d 18, 497 N.E.2d 41 (1986). This is the widely-publicized and much-debated case of the New York City subway rider who was charged with attempted murder and assault. After Goetz boarded the subway and took a seat in a section of a car occupied by four youths, one of the four approached and said "give me five dollars." Goetz pulled a gun and shot at each of the four, wounding all but one. The lower court dismissed the charges on the ground that the prosecutor's instructions to the grand jury on self-defense were erroneously stated in terms of a "reasonable man in [Goetz's] situation." The court of appeals reversed, concluding that the statutory language that a person may use deadly force if he "reasonably believes that such other person is using or about to use deadly physical force" stated an objective test. But the court went on to emphasize that in support of Goetz's assertion that though "he was certain that none of the youths had a gun, he had a fear based on prior experience, of being 'maimed,'" he would be allowed to introduce into evidence "any prior experiences he had which could provide a reasonable basis for [such] belief," e.g., that a few years earlier he had been injured in a mugging. (Goetz was later tried and acquitted.)

(b) *Werner v. State,* 711 S.W.2d 639 (Tex.Crim.App.1986). "Appellant testified that he pursued the deceased's vehicle 'to hold whoever hit my friend's car for the police.' After he found the vehicle he stated he 'yelled at him to get up against the car,' and the deceased replied, 'You're just going to have to shoot me, you son of a bitch.' Appellant testified the deceased made a 'shrugging' motion with his shoulders and took a step towards him. With the flashlight he saw the deceased's face and the deceased 'looked crazy.' He couldn't see the deceased's hands and didn't know whether the deceased was armed. Appellant stated he was in fear of his life, and to protect himself he shot the deceased in the chest." Excluded from appellant's murder trial was testimony by a psychiatrist, who had examined appellant, concerning the "Holocaust syndrome," specifically, that appellant, as the child of a survivor of Nazi concentration camps and one who had often been told stories about the camps, by virtue of that background had a "state of mind to defend himself because he comes from a family that did not." In affirming the murder conviction, the court took note of the objective "reasonable belief" standard in the self-defense statute and concluded: "All that can be inferred from this evidence is that appellant may have been more susceptible to actions in self-defense. * * * The evidence excluded only tended to show that possibly appellant was not an ordinary and prudent man with respect to self-defense. This did not entitle appellant to an enlargement of the statutory defense on account of his psychological peculiarities."

NOTES AND QUESTIONS ON DEFENSE OF ANOTHER

1. In *State v. Cook*, 204 W.Va. 591, 515 S.E.2d 127 (1999), Brenda Cook was convicted of second degree murder of Homer Buckler. As part of an ongoing dispute between neighbors, the 6'4" and 300 lb. Buckler threw Brenda's husband to the ground and began beating him. Mr. Cook was defenseless and pleaded for mercy. Brenda tried to pull Buckler off her husband, but Buckler pushed her aside, so she aimed the shotgun she was carrying at his right arm and fired. Buckler was killed. In the course of holding that the state had failed to prove beyond a reasonable doubt that Brenda did not lawfully act in defense of her husband, the court noted:

"The basic premise underlying the doctrine of defense of another (also called defense of others) is that a person is justified in using force to protect a third party from unlawful force by an aggressor. (The defense of another doctrine closely parallels the common law doctrine of self-defense.). * * *

"Our cases have succinctly articulated the development and scope of the doctrine of self-defense and the use of deadly force under it. However, we have not had occasion to thoroughly discuss the defense of another doctrine. The facts of the instant case require that we fully explore this doctrine's principles.

"*1. Initial limitations on the doctrine of defense of another*. The application of the common law doctrine of defense of another was very limited in its earliest beginnings. The doctrine was imposed only as a defense when a homicide occurred in defense of a member of one's family.* * *

"The initial limitation of the doctrine to one's family eroded with time as courts began to extend the doctrine to allow for the defense of strangers. The expansion of the doctrine to include strangers brought with it a theory of potential liability. This theory was called the 'alter ego' rule. The alter ego rule held that a defendant using deadly force to defend a person who was not entitled to use deadly force would be held criminally liable. * * *

"*2. Development of reasonable belief standard*. The alter ego rule worked a considerable hardship upon defendants who unknowingly intervened to aid third parties who were not privileged to use self-defense. In such situations, the intervenor was criminally liable for any injury or death he or she caused .. Many jurisdictions began to reject the alter ego rule, to a large extent, because of the position taken by the American Law Institute's *Model Penal Code*, § 3.05 (1985). * * * Under this rule, a defendant may be legally justified in killing to defend another, even if the intervenor acted under a mistaken belief as to who was at fault, provided his or her belief was reasonable.[17]

"In this Court's review of its past decisions, decisions of other jurisdictions and commentaries, the doctrine of defense of another may be succinctly articulated. We therefore hold that to establish the doctrine of defense of another in a homicide prosecution, a defendant must show by sufficient evidence that he or she used reasonable force, including deadly force, in a situation where the defendant had a reasonable belief of the lawfulness of his or her intervention on behalf of another person who was in imminent danger of death or serious bodily harm from which such person could save himself/herself only by using force, including deadly force, against his or her assailant, but was unable to do so. We will now proceed to examine the key elements of the doctrine of defense of another.

"*1. Burden of proof*. The doctrine of defense of another is an affirmative defense[, which in this state means that] a defendant must introduce 'sufficient' evidence of the

---

17. The defense of another doctrine has been codified consistent with the Model Penal Code in [40] states.

defense in order to shift the burden to the State to prove beyond a reasonable doubt that the defendant did not act in defense of another.

"*2. Amount of Force.* A defendant asserting the defense of another must show that the force used was reasonable. This requirement is also known as the 'proportionality' rule. * * *

"*3. Reasonable belief that intervention was lawful.* The 'reasonable belief' standard of intervention emphasizes what the intervenor believes about the circumstances, as opposed to what are the actual circumstances. * * *

"The reasonableness of an intervenor's belief is determined by both a subjective and an objective inquiry. * * * In other words, the 'actor must actually believe that [another] is in danger and that belief must be a reasonable one.' * * *

"*4. Level of danger.* An intervenor is not obliged to use deadly force in defense of another, unless the third party is in imminent danger of death or serious bodily harm. This 'simply means that an intervenor cannot act until the party whom the intervenor is defending is immediately threatened.'"

2. In *Commonwealth v. Martin*, 369 Mass. 640, 341 N.E.2d 885 (1976), where the court adopted a defense-of-another defense essentially like that in *Cook*, the question was raised as to whether any defense-of-another defense, or at least one of such proportions, should be recognized with respect to the particular situation before the court, i.e., where a prison inmate who had assaulted a guard sought to defend on the ground that he did so in an effort to defend another inmate he believed was being illegally beaten by correctional officers. How should that question be resolved?

3. Steve Duckett and his wife spent the day at Mary's house with Mary and her boy friend Mylo drinking and music-making. "As time went on, the comradery deteriorated in conjunction with the sobriety of the participants"; Steve's wife and Mary became engaged in a physical altercation, while at the same time Steve and Mylo struggled on the floor. Steve heard his wife scream, "Help, she's killing me," and turned and saw Mary slamming his wife's head against the concrete floor. When he moved to help her, Mylo tackled him and held him down, but when Steve heard his wife's continued screams he pulled his knife and stabbed Mylo several times until he was able to push Mylo off him, but others then chased Steve from the scene. The proprietor of a nearby motel called 911 at Steve's request, and when Steve then saw his wife outside the two of them fled. Steve was charged with aggravated assault. Steve testified he never believed he was in danger and acted as he did only because he believed his wife was in imminent danger. The trial judge ruled the defense-of-others defense was inapplicable here because Steve used force against his own assailant rather than his wife's, and Steve was convicted. The conviction was reversed in *Duckett v. State*, 966 P.2d 941 (Wyo.1998):

"The State correctly notes that the cases addressing the use of force in situations other than the common three-person 'assailant/victim/rescuer' scenario contain facts indicating the additional assailant was in some way also directly threatening the victim .. However, we see no reasoned distinction between the justification to use force against an individual approaching the fray and the use of force against one knowingly standing guard to prevent rescue. In either case, the assailant's purpose, and the danger to the victim, is furthered by the actions of the assailant's confederate, and the danger to the victim may be alleviated only by the use of force against those acting in concert with the actual assailant. * * *

"We therefore hold that a person raising the 'defense of others' in justification for injury to a person other than the victim's actual assailant must show a reasonable belief that the person defended is in imminent danger of unlawful bodily harm, and a reasonable belief that another person is associated and participating with the actual assailant, and the force used against any aggressor is reasonable and necessary to prevent the harm."

What would/should the result be, then, if it was apparent to Steve that Mylo had his own score to settle with him and was indifferent to a totally separate fight between Mary and Steve's wife, but again Steve stabbed Mylo because that was the only way he might be able to intercede on his wife's behalf?

SECTION 3. DEFENSE OF PROPERTY

LAW v. STATE

Court of Special Appeals of Maryland, 1974.

21 Md.App. 13, 318 A.2d 859.

LOWE, JUDGE.

When James Cecil Law, Jr. purchased a thirty-nine dollar shotgun for "house protection," he could not possibly have conceived of the ordeal it would cause him to undergo.

Mr. Law, a 32 year old black man, had recently married and moved to a predominantly white middle-class neighborhood. Within two weeks his home was broken into and a substantial amount of clothing and personal property was taken. The investigating officer testified that Mr. Law was highly agitated following the burglary and indicated that he would take the matter in his own hands. The officer quoted Mr. Law as saying: " 'I will take care of the job. I know who it is.' "The officer went on to say that Law told him " * * * he knew somebody he could get a gun from in D.C. and he was going to kill the man and he was going take care of it." Two days later he purchased a 12 gauge shotgun and several "double ought" shells.

The intruder entered the Law's home between 6:30 and 9:00 in the evening by breaking a windowpane in the kitchen door which opened onto a screened back porch. The intruder then apparently reached in and unlocked the door. Law later installed "double locks" which required the use of a key both inside and outside. He replaced the glass in the door window in a temporary manner by holding it in place with a few pieces of molding, without using the customary glazing compound to seal it in.

One week after the break-in a well meaning neighbor saw a flickering light in the Law's otherwise darkened house and became suspicious. Aware of the previous burglary, he reported to the police that some one was breaking into the Laws' home. Although the hour was 8:00 p.m., Mr. Law and his bride had retired for the evening. When the police arrived, a fuse of circumstances ignited by fear exploded into a tragedy of errors.

The police did not report to or question the calling neighbor. Instead they went about routinely checking the house seeking the possible illegal point of entry. They raised storm windows where they could reach them and shook the inside windows to see if they were locked. They shined flashlights upon the windows out of reach, still seeking evidence of unlawful entry. Finding none, two officers entered the back screened porch to check the back door, whereupon they saw the windowpane which appeared to have been temporarily put in place with a few pieces of molding. These officers apparently had not known of the repair or the cause of damage.

Upstairs Mr. and Mrs. Law heard what sounded like attempts to enter their home. Keenly aware of the recent occurrence, Mr. Law went downstairs, obtained and loaded his newly acquired shotgun and, apparently facing the rear door of the house, listened for more sounds.

In the meantime, the uniformed officers found what they thought to be the point of entry of a burglar, and were examining the recently replaced glass. While Officer Adams held the flashlight on the recently replaced pane of glass, Officer Garrison removed the molding and the glass, laid them down and stated that he was going to reach in and unlock the door from the inside to see if entry could be gained. Officer Adams testified that they "were talking in a tone a little lower than normal at this point." Officer Adams stated that Officer Garrison then tested the inside lock, discovered it was a deadlock and decided no one could have gotten in the door without a key. A law enforcement student, riding with Officer Garrison that evening, testified that he then heard a rattling noise and someone saying "if there was somebody here, he's still in there." As Officer Garrison removed his hand from the window he was hit by a shotgun blast which Law fired through the door. Officer Garrison was dead on arrival at the hospital.

Officer Potts, the officer next to arrive at the scene, saw Officer Adams running to his car to call for reinforcements. He heard another shot and Officer Adams yell "they just shot at me."

The tragedy of errors had only begun. The officers, having obtained reinforcements and apparently believing they had cornered a burglar, subjected the house to a fussillade of gun fire evinced by over forty bullet holes in the bottom of the kitchen door and the police department transcription of a telephone conversation during the ensuing period of incomprehensible terror.

Mr. Law testified that while he stood listening to the sounds and voices at the door, fearful that someone was about to come in " * * * the gun went off, like that, and when it went off like that it scared me and I was so scared because I had never shot a shotgun before and then I heard a voice on the outside say that someone had been shot." Mr. Law was not able to hear who had been shot but he then " * * * hollered up to my wife, call a police officer, I think I shot a burglar." His wife called the police and most of her conversation was recorded. * * *

The appellant, James Cecil Law, Jr. was found guilty of murder in the second degree and of assault with intent to murder. He was convicted by a jury in the Circuit Court for Charles County following removal from Prince George's County. Judge James C. Mitchell sentenced him to concurrent ten year terms. * * *

The appellant's first question assigning error for failure to grant his motion for judgment of acquittal is a request for our review of the trial court's constitutional responsibility to pass upon the sufficiency of the evidence. In doing so we are not permitted to substitute our judgment of whether there was reasonable doubt of the defendant's guilt for that exercised by the jury. The limit of our review is to determine whether there was relevant and legally sufficient evidence, properly before the jury, to sustain a conviction.

The necessity of responding to this question is diminished by the result we reach here;[a] however, appellant's assertion of the defense of habitation requires that we do more than summarily declare the question moot.

There is a dearth of Maryland authority upon the question of what constitutes justifiable homicide in the defense of one's home. We hasten to note, however, that the single case directly meeting the question does so concisely and clearly. In 1962, the Court

---

a. This is a reference to the fact that the court, in a part of the opinion omitted here, reversed the convictions and remanded for a new trial because unconstitutionally obtained admissions by the defendant were received in evidence at trial.

of Appeals in *Crawford v. State,* 231 Md. 354, 190 A.2d 538, reversed a conviction of manslaughter against a 42 year old man, suffering from a nervous condition and ulcers, whose home was being broken into by a 23 year old man and a partner. The decedent had knocked out a piece of masonite replacing one of four glass panes in the door. Crawford fired a shotgun through the door killing the attacker before he was able to enter.

Certain of the circumstances of that case coincide remarkably with the case at bar. It is as remarkably distinguished, however, by the character and purpose of the decedent, who had previously beaten Crawford and was returning to rob and beat him again after threatening to do so. Without digression on tangential issues, Chief Judge Brune noted with little discussion, as we do here, the appropriateness of the holding of *Gunther v. State,* 228 Md. 404, 409, 179 A.2d 880, that one not seeking a fight may arm himself in anticipation of a violent attack. * * *

The regal aphorism that a man's home is his castle has obscured the limitations on the right to preserve one's home as a sanctuary from fear of force or violence.

Crawford articulates the rule well, distilling it from a review of cases in many jurisdictions:

> "Most American jurisdictions in which the question has been decided have taken the view that if an assault on a dwelling and an attempted forcible entry are made under circumstances which would create *a reasonable apprehension* that it is the design of the assailant *to commit a felony* or to inflict on the inhabitants injury which may result in loss of life or great bodily harm, and that the danger that the design will be carried into effect is imminent, a lawful occupant of the dwelling may prevent the entry even by the taking of the intruder's life." (Emphasis partially added.)

The felonies the prevention of which justifies the taking of a life "are such and only such as are committed by forcible means, violence, and surprise such as murder, robbery, burglary, rape or arson."

[I]t is "essential that killing is *necessary* to prevent the commission of the felony in question. If other methods would prevent its commission, a homicide is not justified; all other means of preventing the crime must first be exhausted."

The right thus rests upon real or apparent necessity. It is this need for caution in exercising the right that has been relegated to obscurity. The position espoused by appellant typifies the misunderstanding of the extent of the right to defend one's home against intrusion. He says:

> "The defendant is not required to act as a reasonable, prudent and cautious individual, nor was he required to limit his force to only that that was required under the circumstances—not when the defendant was in his own home, and believed he was being set upon, or about to be set upon by would be robbers or burglars who were in the act of breaking into his home at the time."

The judgment which must usually be made precipitously under frightening conditions nevertheless demands a certain presence of mind and reasonableness of judgment. Although one is "not obliged to retreat * * * but * * * may even pursue the assailant until he finds himself or his property out of danger * * *, this will not justify a person['s] firing upon everyone who forceably enters his house, even at night." * * *

Appellant points to a portion of the court's instructions which he feels indicates an erroneous shifting of the burden of proof. He contends this is tantamount to removing the presumptive cloak of innocence constitutionally enveloping a defendant. The judge issued a variant of the stock instruction that once an illegal homicide is established the law presumes it to be murder in the second degree. He then went on to say that:

> *"the burden rests upon the accused as part of his defense to prove by a fair preponderance of the evidence* circumstances of a deviation or mitigation, which would lower, reduce the crime to manslaughter or he may show, by way of defense, that the killing was justifiable or excusable and that therefore he should not be held criminally accountable for any crime and the State has the burden of proving not by merely a preponderance of the greater weight of the evidence, but proving beyond a reasonable doubt the element which will raise the crime from second degree murder to first degree." (Emphasis supplied by appellant.)

[handwritten margin note: Jury instruction →]

We are unable to see how the "trial judge illegally shifted the burden of proof to the defendant." Appellant points to cases that draw semantic distinctions between the shifting of the burden of proof and the burden of going forward with the evidence. Undoubtedly the judge chose to avoid confusing the jury with the fine academic distinctions of shifting burdens. His choice of words was not such as appear misleading or prejudicial. This court has itself used that very expression.

Any possibility of a misunderstanding was averted by emphatically placing upon the State the burden of proving guilt beyond a reasonable doubt. The judge elaborated upon that instruction as well as the presumption of innocence favoring the accused. * * *

The same authorities answer appellant's third assignment of error that answered his first. Appellant argues that in defense of his home he "is not subject to the standards of a reasonable, prudent and cautious person, nor is his degree of force limited only to that required under the circumstances to repel the intruder." Quite the contrary, we do not find the right to defend one's habitation to be so absolute as to sanction promiscuous shooting upon a baseless apprehension by an unreasonable person. The permissible degree of force used to repel an intruder must not be excessive. * * * The question of excessive force to resist the intrusion, in most instances, as in *Crawford*, supra, is the most difficult problem the jury has to cope with when death of the intruder was the result. Apropos of the appellant's question is the statement in *State v. Sorrentino*, 31 Wyo. 129, 224 P. 420, 423, that a defendant is not justified in taking a life "[i]f a cautious and prudent man, under the same circumstances, would not believe the danger to have been real * * *."[d]

Notes and Questions

1. What should Mr. Law have done? How significant is it that he failed to call out to the supposed burglar to desist? Consider in this regard the request to desist provision in *Model Penal Code* § 3.06(3)(a).

2. How would Mr. Law fare otherwise under *Model Penal Code* § 3.06? Assuming he could not prevail, should his crime be deemed murder or some lesser degree of criminal homicide? Consider *Model Penal Code* § 3.09.

3. Considering Mr. Law's plight, what do you think of Oklahoma's aptly-named "make my day" law, which provides: "Any occupant of a dwelling is justified in using any degree of physical force, including but not limited to deadly force, against another person who has made an unlawful entry into that dwelling, and when the occupant has a

---

d. Equally apropos are the circumstances in *Sorrentino* which created the reasonable belief of danger:

"The effect upon the human mind of darkness in the stillness of the night is a factor well known * * *. A sudden appearance from out the darkness is apt to give

at least a temporary nervous shock to the stoutest heart. Much more is that apt to be true when, roused from rest or slumber, on a dark night, footsteps and other sounds are heard which are calculated, as in this case, of giving the impression of boding no good."

reasonable belief that such other person might use any physical force no matter how slight, against any occupant of the dwelling." In *State v. Anderson*, 972 P.2d 32 (Okl.Cr.1998), rejecting the state's argument that the amount of force must be reasonable under the circumstances, the court declared that the intent of the statute "was to remove any 'reasonable under the circumstances' test and permit the force used against the intruder based solely upon the occupant's belief that the intruder might use any force against the occupant."

4. If Mr. Law had known that the person outside was a police officer but believed that the officer was making an illegal entry, should Law be able to engage in any sort of forcible resistance? Consider *State v. Brosnan*, 221 Conn. 788, 608 A.2d 49 (1992), ruling that "if, in the present case, the trier determines that the defendant was an overnight guest in the bedroom of another's home, that the police made an unlawful nighttime entry into that bedroom, and that the defendant's host was in the house and did not consent to that entry, his status was so comparable to that of his host that he had a privilege to resist such an illegal entry analogous to that of a householder. Thus, the defendant was entitled to an appropriate jury instruction that he had a 'privilege to offer reasonable resistance, not rising to the level of an assault, to an unlawful entry' into the bedroom, and that such a privilege was a defense to prosecution for interfering with a police officer."

5. Compare *State v. Haas*, 134 N.H. 480, 596 A.2d 127 (1991), where defendant, who used force against a police officer to prevent towing of his vehicle, relied upon a statute stating a "person is justified in using force upon another when and to the extent that he reasonably believes it necessary to prevent what is or reasonably appears to be an unlawful taking of his property, or criminal mischief, or to retake his property immediately following its taking." The court concluded: "To say that a statute designed to permit and condone self-help as a way of protecting oneself from the actions of tort-feasors, wrongdoers, and run-of-the-mill miscreants authorizes the use of force against a police officer discharging his duties in the removal of an automobile from disputed turf is to stretch the statute past the breaking point."

6. Regarding the matter at issue in *Haas*, use of force to prevent an illegal dispossession of personal property, should deadly force ever be permissible for that purpose? Consider *Model Penal Code* § 3.06(d) and Louisiana's "shoot the carjacker" law, which provides that a homicide is justifiable "when committed by a person lawfully inside a dwelling, a place of business, or a motor vehicle * * *, against a person who is attempting to make an unlawful entry into the dwelling, place of business, or motor vehicle, or who has made an unlawful entry into the dwelling, place of business, or motor vehicle, and the person committing the homicide reasonably believes that the use of deadly force is necessary to prevent the entry or to compel the intruder to leave the premises or motor vehicle. The homicide shall be justifiable even though the person committing the homicide does not retreat from the encounter." La.Rev.Stat.Ann. § 14:20(4), discussed in Stuart P. Green, *Castles and Carjackers: Proportionality and the Use of Deadly Force in Defense of Dwellings and Vehicles*, 1999 U.Ill.L.Rev. 1.

BISHOP v. STATE

Supreme Court of Georgia, 1987.
257 Ga. 136, 356 S.E.2d 503.

GREGORY, JUSTICE.

Robert C. Bishop was convicted of malice murder and sentenced to life imprisonment. We affirm.

Bishop lived in a trailer park in Coweta County. Because he was concerned about past break-ins to his trailer, he erected a spring gun or trap gun. He positioned a Mauser 8mm high-powered rifle on two chairs with the barrel pointed in the direction of the trailer's front door. A string attached to the door knob ran over the back of one of the chairs and was connected to the trigger.

Bishop went to work on the night of February 13, 1986 with the spring gun in place. Later, James Freeman, an acquaintance of Bishop, attempted to enter the front door of the trailer. The rifle discharged and hit the metal molding at the foot of the door. Freeman was hit by either a ricocheting bullet fragment or a piece of flying metal. Neighbors heard the shot and found Freeman lying wounded in Bishop's driveway. The neighbors said the house was dark, but that Bishop's car was in the driveway.

Freeman * * * died of a pulmonary embolism or blood clot.

Bishop was tried by a jury and found guilty of malice murder. * * *

Bishop * * * contends erecting the spring gun was not unlawful in his case because the killing of Freeman was justified. He cites OCGA § 16–3–23, which provides: "A person is justified in threatening or using force against another when and to the extent that he reasonably believes that such a threat or force is necessary to prevent or terminate such other's unlawful entry into or attack upon a habitation; however, he is justified in the use of force which is intended or likely to cause death or great bodily harm only if: * * * (2) He reasonably believes that the entry is made or attempted for the purpose of committing a felony therein and such force is necessary to prevent the commission of the felony."

Apparently Bishop's trailer had been broken into on several occasions. According to Bishop, the evidence indicates Freeman was burglarizing the trailer when he was shot, although the State disputes this. Bishop argues had he been at home in the darkened trailer and Freeman attempted to enter unannounced he could have reasonably believed a felony was being committed upon his habitation and been justified in using deadly force pursuant to § 16–3–23.

The weakness in Bishop's argument is that he was working and not at home when the spring gun activated. Bishop contends the traditional rule observed in other jurisdictions is that a person is not justified in taking a life indirectly with a mechanical device unless he would have been justified had he been personally present and taken the life with his own hand.

We decline Bishop's invitation to adopt such a rule in these circumstances. Section 16–3–23 justifies the use of deadly force to protect a habitation only when the inhabitant "reasonably believes" the entry is made for the purpose of committing a felony. We find that under these circumstances, however, it was impossible for Bishop to form a reasonable belief in light of his absence from the trailer. "Allowing persons, at their own risk, to employ deadly mechanical devices imperils the lives of children, firemen and policemen acting within the scope of their employment, and others. Where the actor is present, there is always a possibility he will realize that deadly force is not necessary, but deadly mechanical devices are without mercy or discretion. * * * It seems clear that the use of such devices should not be encouraged. Moreover, whatever may be thought in torts, the foregoing rule setting forth an exception to liability for death or injuries inflicted by such devices 'is inappropriate in penal law for it is obvious it does not prescribe a workable standard of conduct; liability depends upon fortuitous results.' " *People v. Ceballos,* 12 Cal.3d 470, 116 Cal.Rptr. 233, 526 P.2d 241, 244–245 (1974), quoting Model Penal Code (Tent. Draft No. 8), § 3.06, comment 15. * * *

SMITH, JUSTICE, dissenting.

"Every man's home is his castle." This statement all of us have heard since childhood. This case involves the extent to which a man may use deadly force to protect that "castle."

In the venerable case *Collins v. Rennison,* 1 Sayer 138 (K.B.1754), an English court described the allowable extent by employing the phrase "moliter manus imposuit." The use of this phrase indicated that a person should gently push a non-felonious intruder out the door. Blackstone, in advocating a tougher response to intrusions into the home, noted that all felonies were punishable by death. He advocated sanction of the use of deadly force to prevent an intruder from entering a home to commit a felony. 4 Blackstone's Commentaries 188.

In 1820, the first "spring gun" case came on the scene. In *Ilott v. Wilkes,* 3 Barn. & Ald. 304, 106 Eng.Rep. 674 (K.B.1820), the defendant set up a spring gun in some woods on his property. The gun worked as planned, injuring a trespasser. The Court of King's Bench entered a non-suit in favor of the defendant when evidence emerged showing that the plaintiff had notice of the spring gun.

In the case of *Bird v. Holbrook,* 4 Bing. 628, 130 Eng.Rep. 911 (C.P.1828), the Court of Common Pleas heard a case similar to *Ilott* in which the plaintiff was injured by a spring gun while searching a neighbor's garden for his fowl. In *Bird,* unlike *Ilott,* however, the plaintiff had no notice of the spring gun. In the opinion of Chief Justice Best, who had taken part in the *Ilott* decision, the lack of notice distinguished the two cases, and the plaintiff was entitled to a verdict. In these early cases, the spring gun owner was arguably not subject to civil damages, much less a murder or assault charge.

Around this time, Parliament became involved in the spring gun debate, passing a statute which criminalized the use of spring guns. 7 & 8 Geo. 4, c. 18 (1827). Parliament did, however, create an exception allowing the use of the guns between dusk and dawn in the home for the prevention of a felony. *Id.;* Bohlen & Burns, *The Privilege to Protect Property by Dangerous Barriers and Mechanical Devices,* 35 Yale L.J., 525, 541 n. 46 (1926).

The first spring gun case in the United States appeared in Kentucky in 1832. *Gray v. Combs,* 30 Ky. 478 (1832). The Kentucky court neither approved nor disapproved of the earlier English cases in holding use of a spring gun to protect property justified under the circumstances. In *Johnson v. Patterson,* 14 Conn. 1 (1840), the Supreme Court of Connecticut in dicta rejected the use of spring guns sanctioned in *Gray.*

Since the early cases, the courts and legislatures in this country have in the absence of complete prohibition, drawn a line between spring guns used in the home and spring guns used elsewhere. Some cases have stated that spring guns could be used to protect dwelling places when the owner could have used deadly force had he been present. See *Prosser on Torts,* p. 136 n. 40 (5th ed. 1984). Others like the majority opinion here, flatly forbid the use of spring guns.

From the broad range of standards dealing with spring guns and criminal law, I would select the rule that views as justified a homicide committed by spring gun at night in the home of the defendant when the defendant can establish under the totality of the circumstances that he possessed a reasonable expectation that someone would be breaking into his home to commit a felony and that the victim was, indeed, breaking into his home to commit a felony. To do this, we simply should look to the intent of the defendant at the time that he sets the spring gun, setting the chain of events leading to the death in motion, rather than to the time at which the victim is shot. Viewed in this manner, OCGA § 16–3–23 would justify a homicide such as the one involved in this case. I would reverse.

Notes and Questions

1. Should the case turn upon whether Freeman, as Bishop claims, "was burglarizing the trailer"? Even if he was, did Bishop utilize means which are inappropriate because of the danger to firefighters or others who might have occasion lawfully to enter the premises? If so, is the solution prosecution of Bishop for reckless endangerment instead of murder?

2. Is such a prosecution called for even if the spring gun is never discharged? Consider Leo Katz, *Blackmail and Other Forms of Arm–Twisting*, 141 U.Pa.L.Rev. 1567, 1614 (1993): "The installation of the spring gun or of a nuclear doomsday machine is not wrongful, even though it would be wrongful if they actually went off, because the successfully demanded, not the threatened contingency, determines the level of blameworthiness of the defendant's conduct. The successfully demanded behavior in this case is the non-attack of one's country and the non-intrusion onto one's property, neither of which is blameworthy by itself." If this is so, then isn't Bishop's criminal culpability left to a matter of chance (i.e., whether anyone trips the spring gun), or can it be said on the other hand that the *Ceballos-Bishop* doctrine has "decisively ruled out the ability for chance to determine liability" because "setting up a spring gun is wrong no matter who it happens to hit or what the circumstances are," as concluded in Comment, 142 U.Pa.L.Rev. 2183, 2196 (1994).

3. Is it relevant that Bishop was the victim of "past break-ins to his trailer"? Should such circumstances ever be relevant? Consider this account from *N.Y. Times*, Oct. 5, 1986, at L37, col. 1:

"After his small general merchandise store was robbed eight times since it opened a year ago, four times in two recent weeks, Prentice F. Rasheed decided to catch the thief himself.

"Last week he installed an electric booby trap in the ceiling of his shop, situated in an area where the police record many crimes. On Tuesday the trap electrocuted a man who managed to get into the store at night and was leaving with stolen goods.

"Mr. Rasheed was arrested the next day by the Miami police on a manslaughter charge. He was released on $6,500 bond paid by fellow merchants who sided with him, including members of the Edison Model City Merchants Association, of which William J. Calhoun is a director.

"Mr. Calhoun, owner of a tailor shop 50 yards from Mr. Rasheed's, called the death 'regrettable' but added:

" 'We are all in sympathy with Prentice. We understand his frustration. We have put iron bars on the windows and doors of our establishments, but that does not stop burglars because there is virtually no protection here.' * * *

"The man who died, Odell Hicks, 27 years old, lived a block from Mr. Rasheed's store. Mr. Hicks had a long record of criminal offenses, the police say. In 1976 he was found guilty of burglary and sexual battery and sentenced to eight years in prison on each charge. In 1981, several months after his release, he was arrested again and accused of breaking into a house.

"Mr. Rasheed, who is 43, said he regretted the incident. 'I can't be happy that a young man lost his life,' he said. He said that by rigging the booby trap and connecting it to a 110–volt outlet, he only wanted to scare would-be robbers.

"The police theorized that when Mr. Hicks entered the store he was protected from the current by his rubber-soled sneakers. But when he was leaving, he touched metal with sweaty hands and died."[a]

SECTION 4. LAW ENFORCEMENT AND RESPONSE THERETO

TENNESSEE v. GARNER

Supreme Court of the United States, 1985.

471 U.S. 1, 105 S.Ct. 1694, 85 L.Ed.2d 1.

JUSTICE WHITE delivered the opinion of the Court.

This case requires us to determine the constitutionality of the use of deadly force to prevent the escape of an apparently unarmed suspected felon. We conclude that such force may not be used unless it is necessary to prevent the escape and the officer has probable cause to believe that the suspect poses a significant threat of death or serious physical injury to the officer or others.

I

At about 10:45 p.m. on October 3, 1974, Memphis Police Officers Elton Hymon and Leslie Wright were dispatched to answer a "prowler inside call." Upon arriving at the scene they saw a woman standing on her porch and gesturing toward the adjacent house. She told them she had heard glass breaking and that "they" or "someone" was breaking in next door. While Wright radioed the dispatcher to say that they were on the scene, Hymon went behind the house. He heard a door slam and saw someone run across the back yard. The fleeing suspect, who was appellee-respondent's decedent, Edward Garner, stopped at a 6-feet-high chain link fence at the edge of the yard. With the aid of a flashlight, Hymon was able to see Garner's face and hands. He saw no sign of a weapon, and, though not certain, was "reasonably sure" and "figured" that Garner was unarmed. He thought Garner was 17 or 18 years old and about 5'5" or 5'7" tall. While Garner was crouched at the base of the fence, Hymon called out "police, halt" and took a few steps toward him. Garner then began to climb over the fence. Convinced that if Garner made it over the fence he would elude capture, Hymon shot him. The bullet hit Garner in the back of the head. Garner was taken by ambulance to a hospital, where he died on the operating table. Ten dollars and a purse taken from the house were found on his body.

In using deadly force to prevent the escape, Hymon was acting under the authority of a Tennessee statute and pursuant to Police Department policy. The statute provides that "[i]f, after notice of the intention to arrest the defendant, he either flee or forcibly resist, the officer may use all the necessary means to effect the arrest." The Department policy was slightly more restrictive than the statute, but still allowed the use of deadly force in cases of burglary. The incident was reviewed by the Memphis Police Firearm's Review Board and presented to a grand jury. Neither took any action.

Garner's father then brought this action in the Federal District Court for the Western District of Tennessee, seeking damages under 42 U.S.C. § 1983 for asserted violations of Garner's constitutional rights. * * *

The District Court * * * found that the statute, and Hymon's actions, were constitutional. * * *

---

a. A Miami attorney's website asserts that he "cleared" Rasheed. <http://www.ellisrubin.com/biography.html>.

The Court of Appeals reversed and remanded. * * *

The State of Tennessee, which had intervened to defend the statute, appealed to this Court.

II

Whenever an officer restrains the freedom of a person to walk away, he has seized that person. While it is not always clear just when minimal police interference becomes a seizure, there can be no question that apprehension by the use of deadly force is a seizure subject to the reasonableness requirement of the Fourth Amendment.

A

A police officer may arrest a person if he has probable cause to believe that person committed a crime. Petitioners and appellant argue that if this requirement is satisfied the Fourth Amendment has nothing to say about *how* that seizure is made. This submission ignores the many cases in which this Court, by balancing the extent of the intrusion against the need for it, has examined the reasonableness of the manner in which a search or seizure is conducted. * * * Because one of the factors is the extent of the intrusion, it is plain that reasonableness depends on not only when a seizure is made, but also how it is carried out. * * *

B

The same balancing process applied in the cases cited above demonstrates that, notwithstanding probable cause to seize a suspect, an officer may not always do so by killing him. The intrusiveness of a seizure by means of deadly force is unmatched. The suspect's fundamental interest in his own life need not be elaborated upon. The use of deadly force also frustrates the interest of the individual, and of society, in judicial determination of guilt and punishment. Against these interests are ranged governmental interests in effective law enforcement.[16] It is argued that overall violence will be reduced by encouraging the peaceful submission of suspects who know that they may be shot if they flee. Effectiveness in making arrests requires the resort to deadly force, or at least the meaningful threat thereof. "Being able to arrest such individuals is a condition precedent to the state's entire system of law enforcement."

Without in any way disparaging the importance of these goals, we are not convinced that the use of deadly force is a sufficiently productive means of accomplishing them to justify the killing of nonviolent suspects. The use of deadly force is a self-defeating way of apprehending a suspect and so setting the criminal justice mechanism in motion. If successful, it guarantees that that mechanism will not be set in motion. And while the

---

16. The dissent emphasizes that subsequent investigation cannot replace immediate apprehension. We recognize that this is so; indeed, that is the reason why there is any dispute. If subsequent arrest were assured, no one would argue that use of deadly force was justified. Thus, we proceed on the assumption that subsequent arrest is not likely. Nonetheless, it should be remembered that failure to apprehend at the scene does not necessarily mean that the suspect will never be caught.

In lamenting the inadequacy of later investigation, the dissent relies on the report of the President's Commission on Law Enforcement and Administration of Justice. It is worth noting that, notwithstanding its awareness of this problem, the Commission itself proposed a policy for use of deadly force arguably even more stringent than the formulation we adopt today. See President's Commission on Law Enforcement and Administration of Justice, Task Force Report: The Police 189 (1967). The Commission proposed that deadly force be used only to apprehend "perpetrators who, in the course of their crime threatened the use of deadly force, or if the officer believes there is a substantial risk that the person whose arrest is sought will cause death or serious bodily harm if his apprehension is delayed." In addition, the officer would have "to know, as a virtual certainty, that the suspect committed an offense for which the use of deadly force is permissible."

meaningful threat of deadly force might be thought to lead to the arrest of more live suspects by discouraging escape attempts, the presently available evidence does not support this thesis. The fact is that a majority of police departments in this country have forbidden the use of deadly force against nonviolent suspects. If those charged with the enforcement of the criminal law have abjured the use of deadly force in arresting nondangerous felons, there is a substantial basis for doubting that the use of such force is an essential attribute of the arrest power in all felony cases. Petitioners and appellant have not persuaded us that shooting nondangerous fleeing suspects is so vital as to outweigh the suspect's interest in his own life.

The use of deadly force to prevent the escape of all felony suspects, whatever the circumstances, is constitutionally unreasonable. It is not better that all felony suspects die than that they escape. Where the suspect poses no immediate threat to the officer and no threat to others, the harm resulting from failing to apprehend him does not justify the use of deadly force to do so. It is no doubt unfortunate when a suspect who is in sight escapes, but the fact that the police arrive a little late or are a little slower afoot does not always justify killing the suspect. A police officer may not seize an unarmed, nondangerous suspect by shooting him dead. The Tennessee statute is unconstitutional insofar as it authorizes the use of deadly force against such fleeing suspects.

It is not, however, unconstitutional on its face. Where the officer has probable cause to believe that the suspect poses a threat of serious physical harm, either to the officer or to others, it is not constitutionally unreasonable to prevent escape by using deadly force. Thus, if the suspect threatens the officer with a weapon or there is probable cause to believe that he has committed a crime involving the infliction or threatened infliction of serious physical harm, deadly force may be used if necessary to prevent escape, and if, where feasible, some warning has been given. As applied in such circumstances, the Tennessee statute would pass constitutional muster.

[handwritten marginalia: This part is unsettled about case: if he had done a violent crime, force would of been o.k. while escaping. → This is what the passage suggests, but it is unclear if that is the law.]

III

A

It is insisted that the Fourth Amendment must be construed in light of the common-law rule, which allowed the use of whatever force was necessary to effect the arrest of a fleeing felon, though not a misdemeanant. * * *

The State and city argue that because this was the prevailing rule at the time of the adoption of the Fourth Amendment and for some time thereafter, and is still in force in some States, use of deadly force against a fleeing felon must be "reasonable." It is true that this Court has often looked to the common law in evaluating the reasonableness, for Fourth Amendment purposes, of police activity. On the other hand, it "has not simply frozen into constitutional law those law enforcement practices that existed at the time of the Fourth Amendment's passage." Because of sweeping change in the legal and technological context, reliance on the common-law rule in this case would be a mistaken literalism that ignores the purposes of a historical inquiry.

B

It has been pointed out many times that the common-law rule is best understood in light of the fact that it arose at a time when virtually all felonies were punishable by death. * * * Courts have also justified the common-law rule by emphasizing the relative dangerousness of felons.

Neither of these justifications makes sense today. Almost all crimes formerly punishable by death no longer are or can be. And while in earlier times "the gulf between the felonies and the minor offences was broad and deep," today the distinction is minor and often arbitrary. Many crimes classified as misdemeanors, or nonexistent, at common law are now felonies. These changes have undermined the concept, which was questionable to begin with, that use of deadly force against a fleeing felon is merely a speedier execution of someone who has already forfeited his life. They have also made the assumption that a "felon" is more dangerous than a misdemeanant untenable. Indeed, numerous misdemeanors involve conduct more dangerous than many felonies.

There is an additional reason why the common-law rule cannot be directly translated to the present day. The common-law rule developed at a time when weapons were rudimentary. Deadly force could be inflicted almost solely in a hand-to-hand struggle during which, necessarily, the safety of the arresting officer was at risk. Handguns were not carried by police officers until the latter half of the last century. Only then did it become possible to use deadly force from a distance as a means of apprehension. As a practical matter, the use of deadly force under the standard articulation of the common-law rule has an altogether different meaning—and harsher consequences—now than in past centuries.

One other aspect of the common-law rule bears emphasis. It forbids the use of deadly force to apprehend a misdemeanant, condemning such action as disproportionately severe.

In short, though the common law pedigree of Tennessee's rule is pure on its face, changes in the legal and technological context mean the rule is distorted almost beyond recognition when literally applied.

C

In evaluating the reasonableness of police procedures under the Fourth Amendment, we have also looked to prevailing rules in individual jurisdictions. The rules in the States are varied. Some 19 States have codified the common-law rule, though in two of these the courts have significantly limited the statute. Four States, though without a relevant statute, apparently retain the common-law rule. Two States have adopted the Model Penal Code's provision [§ 3.07(2)(b)] verbatim. Eighteen others allow, in slightly varying language, the use of deadly force only if the suspect has committed a felony involving the use or threat of physical or deadly force, or is escaping with a deadly weapon, or is likely to endanger life or inflict serious physical injury if not arrested. Louisiana and Vermont, though without statutes or case law on point, do forbid the use of deadly force to prevent any but violent felonies. The remaining States either have no relevant statute or case-law, or have positions that are unclear.

It cannot be said that there is a constant or overwhelming trend away from the common-law rule. In recent years, some States have reviewed their laws and expressly rejected abandonment of the common-law rule. Nonetheless, the long-term movement has been away from the rule that deadly force may be used against any fleeing felon, and that remains the rule in less than half the States.

This trend is more evident and impressive when viewed in light of the policies adopted by the police departments themselves. Overwhelmingly, these are more restrictive than the common-law rule. * * * Overall, only 7.5% of departmental and municipal policies explicitly permit the use of deadly force against any felon; 86.8% explicitly do not. In light of the rules adopted by those who must actually administer them, the older and fading common-law view is a dubious indicium of the constitutionality of the Tennessee statute now before us.

D

Actual departmental policies are important for an additional reason. We would hesitate to declare a police practice of long standing "unreasonable" if doing so would severely hamper effective law enforcement. But the indications are to the contrary. There has been no suggestion that crime has worsened in any way in jurisdictions that have adopted, by legislation or departmental policy, rules similar to that announced today. * * *

Nor do we agree with petitioners and appellant that the rule we have adopted requires the police to make impossible, split-second evaluations of unknowable facts. We do not deny the practical difficulties of attempting to assess the suspect's dangerousness. However, similarly difficult judgments must be made by the police in equally uncertain circumstances. Nor is there any indication that in States that allow the use of deadly force only against dangerous suspects, the standard has been difficult to apply or has led to a rash of litigation involving inappropriate second-guessing of police officers' split-second decisions. Moreover, the highly technical felony/misdemeanor distinction is equally, if not more, difficult to apply in the field. An officer is in no position to know, for example, the precise value of property stolen, or whether the crime was a first or second offense. Finally, as noted above, this claim must be viewed with suspicion in light of the similar self-imposed limitations of so many police departments.

IV

* * * In reversing, the Court of Appeals accepted the District Court's factual conclusions and held that "the facts, as found, did not justify the use of deadly force." We agree. Officer Hymon could not reasonably have believed that Garner—young, slight, and unarmed—posed any threat. Indeed, Hymon never attempted to justify his actions on any basis other than the need to prevent an escape. * * *

The dissent argues that the shooting was justified by the fact that Officer Hymon had probable cause to believe that Garner had committed a nighttime burglary. While we agree that burglary is a serious crime, we cannot agree that it is so dangerous as automatically to justify the use of deadly force. The FBI classifies burglary as a "property" rather than a "violent" crime. Although the armed burglar would present a different situation, the fact that an unarmed suspect has broken into a dwelling at night does not automatically mean he is physically dangerous. This case demonstrates as much. In fact, the available statistics demonstrate that burglaries only rarely involve physical violence. During the 10–year period from 1973–1982, only 3.8% of all burglaries involved violent crime.[23]

V

* * *

The judgment of the Court of Appeals is affirmed * * *.

JUSTICE O'CONNOR, with whom THE CHIEF JUSTICE and JUSTICE REHNQUIST join, dissenting.
* * *

---

23. The dissent points out that three-fifths of all rapes in the home, three-fifths of all home robberies, and about a third of home assaults are committed by burglars. These figures mean only that if one knows that a suspect committed a rape in the home, there is a good chance that the suspect is also a burglar. That has nothing to do with the question here, which is whether the fact that someone has committed a burglary indicates that he has committed, or might commit, a violent crime.

The dissent also points out that this 3.8% adds up to 2.8 million violent crimes over a 10–year period, as if to imply that today's holding will let loose 2.8 million violent burglars. The relevant universe is, of course, far smaller. At issue is only that tiny fraction of cases where violence has taken place and an officer who has no other means of apprehending the suspect is unaware of its occurrence.

For purposes of Fourth Amendment analysis, I agree with the Court that Officer Hymon "seized" Garner by shooting him. Whether that seizure was reasonable and therefore permitted by the Fourth Amendment requires a careful balancing of the important public interest in crime prevention and detection and the nature and quality of the intrusion upon legitimate interests of the individual. * * *

The public interest involved in the use of deadly force as a last resort to apprehend a fleeing burglary suspect relates primarily to the serious nature of the crime. Household burglaries represent not only the illegal entry into a person's home, but also "pos[e] real risk of serious harm to others." According to recent Department of Justice statistics, "[t]hree-fifths of all rapes in the home, three-fifths of all home robberies, and about a third of home aggravated and simple assaults are committed by burglars." During the period 1973–1982, 2.8 million such violent crimes were committed in the course of burglaries. Victims of a forcible intrusion into their home by a nighttime prowler will find little consolation in the majority's confident assertion that "burglaries only rarely involve physical violence." Moreover, even if a particular burglary, when viewed in retrospect, does not involve physical harm to others, the "harsh potentialities for violence" inherent in the forced entry into a home preclude characterization of the crime as "innocuous, inconsequential, minor, or 'nonviolent.' "

Because burglary is a serious and dangerous felony, the public interest in the prevention and detection of the crime is of compelling importance. Where a police officer has probable cause to arrest a suspected burglar, the use of deadly force as a last resort might well be the only means of apprehending the suspect. With respect to a particular burglary, subsequent investigation simply cannot represent a substitute for immediate apprehension of the criminal suspect at the scene. Indeed, the Captain of the Memphis Police Department testified that in his city, if apprehension is not immediate, it is likely that the suspect will not be caught. Although some law enforcement agencies may choose to assume the risk that a criminal will remain at large, the Tennessee statute reflects a legislative determination that the use of deadly force in prescribed circumstances will serve generally to protect the public. Such statutes assist the police in apprehending suspected perpetrators of serious crimes and provide notice that a lawful police order to stop and submit to arrest may not be ignored with impunity. * * *

Against the strong public interests justifying the conduct at issue here must be weighed the individual interests implicated in the use of deadly force by police officers. The majority declares that "[t]he suspect's fundamental interest in his own life need not be elaborated upon." This blithe assertion hardly provides an adequate substitute for the majority's failure to acknowledge the distinctive manner in which the suspect's interest in his life is even exposed to risk. For purposes of this case, we must recall that the police officer, in the course of investigating a nighttime burglary, had reasonable cause to arrest the suspect and ordered him to halt. The officer's use of force resulted because the suspected burglar refused to heed this command and the officer reasonably believed that there was no means short of firing his weapon to apprehend the suspect. Without questioning the importance of a person's interest in his life, I do not think this interest encompasses a right to flee unimpeded from the scene of a burglary. * * *

A proper balancing of the interests involved suggests that use of deadly force as a last resort to apprehend a criminal suspect fleeing from the scene of a nighttime burglary is not unreasonable within the meaning of the Fourth Amendment. Admittedly, the events giving rise to this case are in retrospect deeply regrettable. No one can view the death of an unarmed and apparently nonviolent 15–year old without sorrow, much less disapproval. Nonetheless, the reasonableness of Officer Hymon's conduct for purposes of the Fourth

Amendment cannot be evaluated by what later appears to have been a preferable course of police action. The officer pursued a suspect in the darkened backyard of a house that from all indications had just been burglarized. The police officer was not certain whether the suspect was alone or unarmed; nor did he know what had transpired inside the house. He ordered the suspect to halt, and when the suspect refused to obey and attempted to flee into the night, the officer fired his weapon to prevent escape. The reasonableness of this action for purposes of the Fourth Amendment is not determined by the unfortunate nature of this particular case; instead, the question is whether it is constitutionally impermissible for police officers, as a last resort, to shoot a burglary suspect fleeing the scene of the crime. * * *

Even if I agreed that the Fourth Amendment was violated under the circumstances of this case, I would be unable to join the Court's opinion. The Court holds that deadly force may be used only if the suspect "threatens the officer with a weapon or there is probable cause to believe that he has committed a crime involving the infliction or threatened infliction of serious physical harm." The Court ignores the more general implications of its reasoning. Relying on the Fourth Amendment, the majority asserts that it is constitutionally unreasonable to *use* deadly force against fleeing criminal suspects who do not appear to pose a threat of serious physical harm to others. By declining to limit its holding to the use of firearms, the Court unnecessarily implies that the Fourth Amendment constrains the use of any police practice that is potentially lethal, no matter how remote the risk.

Although it is unclear from the language of the opinion, I assume that the majority intends the word "use" to include only those circumstances in which the suspect is actually apprehended. Absent apprehension of the suspect, there is no "seizure" for Fourth Amendment purposes. * * *

The Court's silence on critical factors in the decision to use deadly force simply invites second-guessing of difficult police decisions that must be made quickly in the most trying of circumstances. Police are given no guidance for determining which objects, among an array of potentially lethal weapons ranging from guns to knives to baseball bats to rope, will justify the use of deadly force. The Court also declines to outline the additional factors necessary to provide "probable cause" for believing that a suspect "poses a significant threat of death or serious physical injury," when the officer has probable cause to arrest and the suspect refuses to obey an order to halt. But even if it were appropriate in this case to limit the use of deadly force to that ambiguous class of suspects, I believe the class should include nighttime residential burglars who resist arrest by attempting to flee the scene of the crime. We can expect an escalating volume of litigation as the lower courts struggle to determine if a police officer's split-second decision to shoot was justified by the danger posed by a particular object and other facts related to the crime. Thus, the majority opinion portends a burgeoning area of Fourth Amendment doctrine concerning the circumstances in which police officers can reasonably employ deadly force. * * *

Notes and Questions

1. Does *Garner* give the police sufficient guidance as to just when they are permitted to use deadly force? Consider Richard Uviller, *Seizure by Gunshot: The Riddle of the Fleeing Felon*, 14 N.Y.U.Rev.L. & Soc.Chg. 705, 711–13 (1986): "Unfortunately, the category of a 'dangerous' or 'violent' suspect upon which deadly force may be used to foil escape is not a clearly described or readily recognized breed. Apart from the easy cases where the fleeing felon brandishes a firearm in attempting to evade capture or is in flight from a crime, just committed, that included an armed assault, the Court's view on this point is obscure. Indeed, it would not put the opinion under great strain to interpret it as

authorizing the use of deadly force in only these easy cases. But, proceeding on the assumption that the Court did not intend to compel the states to allow all other criminals to escape if they were swift enough, we must probe the decision a bit deeper.

"For our test, let us start with this cryptic message from the heart of the opinion: 'Where the suspect poses no immediate threat to the officer and no threat to others, the harm resulting from failing to apprehend him does not justify the use of deadly force to do so.' The nature of the 'threat' the Court has in mind is clear from the opening paragraph: 'a significant threat of death or serious physical injury.' Thus, as to his own person, the officer must have a well-grounded fear of immediate and mortal injury before he may fire. In the instance of the fleeing felon, these conditions, one would suppose, cannot be met except by the actual possession of firearms or explosives, coupled with a manifest, aggressive disposition. A knife or bat, for example, cannot pose a grave threat except at close quarters. And even the armed felon who keeps his gun in his belt and runs without looking back poses no real threat of imminent injury. Nor can the police officer use his gun to capture someone because he reasonably fears that otherwise he may be subjected to attack some appreciable time thereafter. The fourth amendment's tolerance for deadly force on this basis is limited, but it's fairly clear.

"Did Justice White deliberately omit the critical adjective 'immediate' when speaking of the threat to the safety of persons other than the pursuing officer? Unless reason be strained to the fracture point, conscious craft should be assumed. Justice White probably intended to offer a wide window for speculation on the types of harm to 'others' that a police officer may shoot to avoid. I think of the automobile speeding in an erratic path toward a town, pulling away from the pursuing patrol car. Shooting to kill a reckless, perhaps even intoxicated, driver may seem extreme, but the potential harm to others is clear. Does the constitutional litmus come up: 'reasonable'? Imagine a person wanted for a series of violent crimes, but showing no signs of being armed or violent at the moment; let him get away and he might well strike a future unknown victim in a harmful way. Does the fourth amendment allow the use of deadly force to capture that 'dangerous' person?

"About halfway into his opinion, Justice White, by way of example, indicates in the following language that the nature of the crime from which the felon flees has some bearing on the degree of force appropriate to apprehend him: 'Thus if ... there is probable cause to believe that he has committed a crime involving the infliction or threatened infliction of serious physical harm, deadly force may be used if necessary to prevent escape, and if, where feasible, some warning has been given.' Passing the odd insertion of a requirement of warning (found nowhere else in the decision), several other curiosities appear. The first may be the unstated assumption that only those crimes of substantial physical injury are socially serious enough to risk killing the perpetrator to halt him. One can think of a number of crimes such as sexual abuse of children, extortion, major drug trafficking, racketeering, or treason that on some scales are the equal in social harm to a knifepoint street robbery. Even some 'crimes against property' such as arson might qualify as serious. Or for that matter the nighttime flatburglary—Garner's crime—might seem to some so frightening, so volatile, so deeply invasive, that it should be regarded as very serious even if the burglar is unarmed (as most legislatures do when they set up punishment quotients), notwithstanding its FBI classification as a property crime or the statistics showing the relative infrequency of actual physical violence during the commission of the crime. (Both factors were cited by the Court in reaching a contrary conclusion.)

"Does the 'prevent escape' phrase suggest a requirement of immediacy? Is the use of deadly force reasonable only if the perpetrator is in actual flight from the crime, moments after its commission, when he might still be armed and dangerous? Or is it enough that the officer have probable cause to believe that the person he shoots committed such a violent crime and is trying to evade capture? May execution of a warrant of arrest for rape, for instance, be aided by a gun if the suspect takes off, regardless of when the rape occurred, or the present inclination of the suspect to resist arrest by dangerous aggression?''

2. Does *Garner* make it clear what constitutes deadly force? Consider Uviller, supra, at 709–10: "Even taking the decision at face value, the notion of 'deadly' force is far from self-defining, particularly in the context of less-than-lethal consequences. * * *

"More chased suspects probably die in high speed vehicle pursuits (not to count the innocent bystanders) than are brought down by police gunfire. Is the trooper, stepping on the gas and opening the siren behind a wayward car, using 'deadly' means to capture the fleeing driver? A hickory club brought down upon the head of a struggling suspect is quite capable of inflicting a mortal blow. Is the swing controlled by the fourth amendment? Some may even argue that not every gunshot amounts to 'deadly force'; an expert police marksman, drawing a clear and careful bead on his target's lower extremities, it could be said, incurs little risk of fatality.

"To compound the definitional uncertainty, Justice White in several places couples the phrase 'deadly force' with the alternative: 'or the threat of it.' This would seem to prohibit even the pointed pistol or the raised stick. 'Stop or I'll shoot' would offend the fourth amendment to the same extent as a bullet through the head. Can that be the Court's intended meaning?''

3. Regarding the meaning of the term "deadly force" in *Garner*, consider also *Vera Cruz v. City of Escondido*, 139 F.3d 659 (9th Cir.1997), where an officer acting solely to terminate a person's flight released his "K–9 companion," who bit the fleeing party on the arm and held him until the officer took away the arrestee's knife, resulting in wounds requiring surgery and eight days of hospitalization. In a § 1983 action, plaintiff argued for the Model Penal Code definition, "force that the actor uses with the purpose of causing or that he knows to create a substantial risk of causing death or serious bodily injury," but the court ruled that "deadly force is that force which is reasonably likely to cause death." Which is correct?

4. In *Graham v. Connor*, 490 U.S. 386, 109 S.Ct. 1865, 104 L.Ed.2d 443 (1989), the Court declared that the Fourth Amendment reasonableness standard (1) applies to "*all* claims that law enforcement officers have used excessive force—deadly or not—in the course of an arrest, investigatory stop, or other 'seizure' of a free citizen"; (2) "requires careful attention to the facts and circumstances of each particular case, including the severity of the crime at issue, whether the suspect poses an immediate threat to the safety of the officers or others, and whether he is actively resisting arrest or attempting to evade arrest by flight"; (3) "must embody allowance for the fact that police officers are often forced to make split-second judgments—in circumstances that are tense, uncertain, and rapidly evolving—about the amount of force that is necessary in a particular situation"; and (4) asks "whether the officers' actions are 'objectively reasonable' in light of the facts and circumstances confronting them, without regard to their underlying intent or motivation."

5. If the police conduct causing death or bodily harm was *not* a search or seizure, then the Fourteenth Amendment due process shocks-the-conscience test, rather than *Garner*'s Fourth Amendment reasonableness test, applies. Illustrative is *County of Sacramento v. Lewis*, 523 U.S. 833, 118 S.Ct. 1708, 140 L.Ed.2d 1043 (1998), where the Court decided "that no Fourth Amendment seizure would take place where a 'pursuing police car sought to stop the suspect only by the show of authority represented by flashing lights and continuing pursuit,' but accidentally stopped the suspect by crashing into him," because

for a Fourth Amendment seizure there must be "a governmental termination of freedom of movement *through means intentionally applied.*"

6.   In *Commonwealth v. Klein,* 372 Mass. 823, 363 N.E.2d 1313 (1977), defendant, a private citizen, saw two men break into a drug store across the street from his home during the early morning hours. He telephoned the police and then went outside with a pistol, where he intercepted the thieves and told them to stop or he would shoot. They did not stop, so he fired several shots at them, wounding both of them. Defendant was thereafter convicted on two counts of assault and battery by means of a deadly weapon. The court noted "that we have never clearly set the limits of the arresting citizen's right to use deadly force.

"Thus, we must consider in this context what rules of law will best serve the public interest in this Commonwealth. Our common law has long recognized a private citizen's right to arrest. Nevertheless, limits must be set, as to the use of deadly force, against the dangers of uncontrolled vigilantism and anarchistic actions and particularly against the danger of death or injury of innocent persons at the hands of untrained volunteers using firearms. In our view, for example, there would be no wisdom in approving the unqualified right of a private citizen to use deadly force to prevent the escape of one who has committed a crime against property only.

"Some jurisdictions have adopted such limiting rules. In *Commonwealth v. Chermansky,* 430 Pa. 170, 242 A.2d 237 (1968), for example, it was held that the prerequisites to justify the use of deadly force by a private person in order to effect the arrest or prevent the escape of a felon are that the person must be in fresh pursuit of the felon and that he must give notice of his purpose to make the arrest for the felony if the attendant circumstances are themselves insufficient to warn the felon of the intention of the pursuing party to arrest him; that such felony must actually have been committed by the person against whom the force is used; *and the felony must be one which normally causes or threatens death or great bodily harm.*

"We have examined comparable law elsewhere, and we think the relevant provisions of the Model Penal Code will best serve this Commonwealth. * * * Accordingly, we establish as the law of Massachusetts the rules (in so far as they are material to the instant case) as found in § 3.07 of the Model Penal Code * * *."

The court then decided it would be unfair to apply these new standards retroactively to the defendant's conduct, but asserted that he "met the standards for justification of his use of the firearm (as we now for the first time establish them) in all respects except that the felons were not themselves engaged in a crime which threatened death or great bodily harm." Is this so?

7.   Is *Garner* of any relevance regarding use of deadly force to arrest by private persons? Compare *People v. Couch,* 436 Mich. 414, 461 N.W.2d 683 (1990) (court concludes that common law privilege extends to *any* felony, that *Garner* does not mandate a different result because constitutional limitations apply only to "state action," and that policy question of whether a change in the law should be made is a matter for the legislature); with *State v. Johnson,* 124 N.M. 647, 954 P.2d 79 (App.1997) (though *Garner* not applicable, court, citing cases in accord from other states, answers in negative policy question of "whether private citizens are permitted to use lethal force when the police, despite their greater training and expertise, cannot").

STATE v. HOBSON

Supreme Court of Wisconsin, 1998.

218 Wis.2d 350, 577 N.W.2d 825.

JANINE P. GESKE, JUSTICE.

* * *. The defendant, Ms. Shonna Hobson was the mother of a five-year-old boy. On July 31, 1995, a member of the Beloit Police Department, Officer Nathan Shoate, went to a home address to interview a child suspected in a bike theft. Another juvenile had reported to Officer Shoate that he had seen Ms. Hobson's son riding the juvenile's sister's stolen bicycle. When Officer Shoate reached the address reported by the juvenile, he saw Ms. Hobson's son near a bicycle. When the officer got out of his car, he saw Ms. Hobson's son run upstairs.

The juvenile who had reported the theft was in Officer Shoate's car at the time. The juvenile pointed out Ms. Hobson's son as the person he had seen on the stolen bicycle. Officer Shoate met Ms. Hobson at her home, and told her that her son was suspected in a bike theft. Specifically, the officer told Ms. Hobson that her son was seen on a stolen bike and that the officer would need to talk to the boy about where the boy got the bike.

Ms. Hobson told her son to go in the house. She then told Officer Shoate that her son was not on a bicycle, and that he had his own bike. Ms. Hobson, according to the officer, became a bit irritated, and refused to allow Officer Shoate to speak with her son. She said that her son did not do anything, and had not stolen any bike. Officer Shoate then told Ms. Hobson that he would have to take her son to the police station to be interviewed about the stolen bicycle, and gave Ms. Hobson the opportunity to go along to the station. She replied that the officer was not taking her son anywhere.

At that point in the conversation, because of Ms. Hobson's resistance, Officer Shoate called for backup police officers to assist him. Shortly thereafter, Officers Eastlick, Anderson and Alisankus arrived at the Hobson address. According to Officer Eastlick's report, when the three backup officers arrived Ms. Hobson was standing with her son on the front steps of her residence yelling, swearing and saying "bullshit" in a very loud voice. Officer Shoate then repeated to Ms. Hobson that they had to take her son to the police station, to which Ms. Hobson again replied "You aren't taking my son anywhere." Officer Shoate then advised Ms. Hobson that she was under arrest for obstructing an officer.

Officers Eastlick and Alisankus proceeded to attempt to handcuff Ms. Hobson. When Officer Eastlick tried to take hold of Ms. Hobson's arm and advise her that she was under arrest, Ms. Hobson pushed the officer away. Ms. Hobson became combative and struck Officer Alisankus across the face. Ms. Hobson then was taken to the ground by other officers. Both Officers Shoate and Eastlick reported that once she was on the ground, Ms. Hobson continued to fight with Officer Alisankus and kicked at Officer Eastlick.

On August 1, 1995, Ms. Hobson was charged with obstructing an officer, disorderly conduct, and resisting an officer. In an amended complaint filed August 15, 1995, the prosecutor added a fourth count. The amended complaint also charged Ms. Hobson with the felony of causing intentional bodily harm (battery) to a peace officer. The amended complaint included a report by Officer Alisankus, stating that he assisted other officers in arresting Ms. Hobson for obstructing at her residence. He reported that Officer Shoate advised Ms. Hobson that she was under arrest for obstructing, and that Officer Eastlick then attempted to take Ms. Hobson into custody. Ms. Hobson then forcibly pulled her arm away from Officer Eastlick, stating "let me go." Officer Alisankus then took Ms. Hobson's right hand and wrist in an effort to apply a compliance hold. At that point Ms. Hobson began to struggle and tried to pull away from Officer Alisankus. Ms. Hobson successfully pulled away and then began to swing her fist and kick at Officer Alisankus. Ms. Hobson's fist struck Officer Alisankus on the left cheek. Ms. Hobson also kicked Officer Alisankus in the left leg and right forearm. Officer Alisankus was later treated at Beloit Memorial Hospital for injuries sustained during this incident. * * *

On January 2, 1996 the circuit court conducted an evidentiary hearing on the motions to dismiss and suppress. The court dismissed the obstructing and resisting counts, finding no probable cause for Ms. Hobson's arrest. The circuit court also concluded that [Ms. Hobson had a common law privilege to forcibly resist her arrest [and] then dismissed the entire complaint.] The State appealed only the dismissal of the battery charge.

This court is faced with two questions. First, we must ascertain whether a common law privilege to forcibly resist unlawful arrest, in the absence of unreasonable force, has existed in Wisconsin until now. Second, if that privilege exists, we must decide whether public policy is best served by continuing to recognize that privilege, or by abrogating it. * * *

American courts adopted the English common law rule that unlawful arrest was a justified provocation to resist with physical force. American common law broadly recognized a privilege to forcibly resist an unlawful arrest throughout the 19th and 20th centuries. * * *

Midway through the 20th century, the Supreme Court reaffirmed that "[o]ne has an undoubted right to resist an unlawful arrest, and courts will uphold the right of resistance in proper cases." *United States v. Di Re*, 332 U.S. 581, 594, 68 S.Ct. 222, 228, 92 L.Ed. 210 (1948).

We * * * conclude that Wisconsin has recognized this privilege since achieving statehood. * * *

Ms. Hobson urges that any change in the privilege to forcibly resist an unlawful arrest be left to the legislature. However, in other cases we have deemed it our responsibility to change a common law rule when we concluded that the change was necessary in the interest of justice. This was true even though the legislature had failed to make the change. * * *. The legal and societal developments since that right was first enunciated provide "compelling reasons" for us to conclude that it is now appropriate for this court to abolish that right, despite apparent legislative inaction.

Many other states have faced the question of whether to abrogate the right to forcibly resist an unlawful arrest, with varying results. The overall trend has been toward abrogation of the right.[19] Treatment of this issue by the American Law Institute represented a turning point in the evolution of this right. After significant debate, the A.L.I. in 1958 promulgated a version of the Model Penal Code abrogating the right, and declaring "[t]he use of force is not justifiable ... to resist an arrest which the actor knows is being made by a peace officer, although the arrest is unlawful." Model Penal Code § 3.04(2)(a)(i). * * *

The common law right to forcibly resist unlawful arrest * * * "developed when long imprisonment, often without the opportunity of bail, 'goal (sic) fever', physical torture, and other great dangers were to be apprehended from arrest, whether legal or illegal." With those dire possibilities, and no viable judicial or administrative redress, forcibly resisting an unlawful arrest was the only effective option a citizen had. But circumstances have

19. Eleven states have judicially abrogated the common law right to use physical force to resist an arrest which is unlawful but which does not utilize unreasonable force. Seventeen other states have signaled their agreement by legislatively abrogating the common law defense.

changed. Unhealthy conditions in jails have decreased, while the physical risks of resisting arrest have increased.

When the law of arrest developed, resistance to an arrest by a peace officer did not involve the serious dangers it does today. Constables and watchmen were armed only with staves and swords, and the person to be apprehended might successfully hold them off with his own weapon and thus escape. Today, every peace officer is armed with a pistol and has orders not to desist from making an arrest though there is forceful resistance. * * *

Not only is forcible resistance now a substantially less effective response to unlawful arrest, there are many safeguards and opportunities for redress. No longer must individuals languish for years in disease-ridden jails. Now, bail is available. No longer are individuals detained indefinitely on dubious charges. Now, prompt arraignment and determination of probable cause are mandated. No longer are individuals left to fend for themselves in the legal system. Now, there is a right to counsel. No longer must individuals violently resist to prevent the fruits of an unlawful arrest from being used to prosecute them. Now, the exclusionary rule is in operation. No longer must unlawful police action go undetected or undeterred. Now there are internal review and disciplinary procedures in police departments. No longer must patterns of police misconduct go unchecked. Now, civil remedies and injunctions are available.

The State Public Defender, in its amicus curiae brief, disputes the adequacy or efficacy of the safeguards described above. Some of the Public Defender's arguments, however, are broad generalizations that illustrate why a bright line prohibition of citizen resistance to an unlawful arrest is preferable. For example, the Public Defender characterizes Ms. Hobson's resistance as a "measured response." That characterization may be apt in this case. However, perpetuating the privilege to resist an unlawful arrest offers no guarantee that other resisting citizens will act in a measured fashion. The Public Defender acknowledges that a citizen may not resist with force "disproportionate to the effort made to take the individual into custody." But in arrest situations that are often ripe for rapid escalation, one's "measured" response may fast become excessive. Our ruling today, abrogating the privilege, is a step toward deescalation.[22]

Ms. Hobson disputes that the common law rule was founded because of "particular hazards of a primitive local jail," and instead suggests that the privilege emerged from a respect for personal liberty, and the idea that unlawful interference with such liberty was a provocation justifying reasonable resistance. * * *

This position is reminiscent of the position advocated, unsuccessfully, by petitioners in *Walker v. City of Birmingham*, 388 U.S. 307, 87 S.Ct. 1824, 18 L.Ed.2d 1210 (1967). There, individuals asserted that they were free to disobey an injunction against participating in a mass street parade without a permit, because the ordinance on which the injunction was based had been administered in an arbitrary fashion. The petitioners failed to challenge

---

22. At oral argument, Ms. Hobson's counsel also urged that we keep the privilege as modified by the circuit court. The circuit court concluded that the blanket common law privilege to forcibly resist an unlawful arrest should be modified "so as to not permit resistance to an unlawful arrest unless the health or safety of the individual or a member of his or her family is threatened in a way that is not susceptible of cure later in a court room." Ms. Hobson's counsel contended that adoption of the rule as modified by the circuit court would involve application of an "objectively reasonable standard." Specifically, the fact-finder would have to determine whether the arrestee was reasonable in judging, at the moment of attempted arrest, that the threat to health or safety was not susceptible to a later legal cure. That standard, as articulated by Ms. Hobson's counsel, would also apply in assessing whether the arrestee used "reasonable force" to resist what he or she perceived to be an unlawful arrest. We decline to maintain a modified privilege, because even in modified form the privilege runs counter to the public policy concerns identified herein.

the ordinance in court prior to disobeying it by publicly marching. Violence ensued during one of the marches. The petitioners were found in contempt. The United States Supreme Court declined to hold that an injunction issued by a court with jurisdiction over the defendants was constitutionally impermissible:

> The rule of law that Alabama followed in this case reflects a belief that in the fair administration of justice no man can be judge in his own case, however exalted his station, however righteous his motives, and irrespective of his race, color, politics, or religion. This Court cannot hold that the petitioners were constitutionally free to ignore all the procedures of the law and carry their battle to the streets. One may sympathize with the petitioners' impatient commitment to their cause. But respect for judicial process is a small price to pay for the civilizing hand of law, which alone can give abiding meaning to constitutional freedom.

Accordingly, an injunction arising under an arguably unlawful ordinance was not sufficient "provocation" to permit disregard of the injunction.

In sum, the majority of jurisdictions has concluded that violent self-help is antisocial and unacceptably dangerous. We agree that there should be no right to forcibly resist an unlawful arrest in the absence of unreasonable force. When persons resist arrest, they endanger themselves, the arresting officers, and bystanders. Although we are sympathetic to the temporary deprivation of liberty the individual may suffer, the law permits only a civilized form of recourse. * * *

Because we decide to abrogate the common law defense of resisting an unlawful arrest in the absence of unreasonable force, we next must determine how this abrogation affects Ms. Hobson's invocation of the defense. We conclude that the effect of our abrogation of the affirmative defense is prospective only [because the] Ex Post Facto clauses of both the United States and Wisconsin Constitutions prohibit the state from enacting any law which imposes punishment for acts not punishable at the time they were committed. This principle of due process applies also to law arising from judicial decisions. * * *

SHIRLEY S. ABRAHAMSON, CHIEF JUSTICE (concurring). * * *

Although I share the majority's concern about avoiding the escalation of violence between law enforcement officers and those who are unlawfully arrested, I conclude that the majority's decision to abrogate the common law privilege is not really a step toward "deescalation." [A] person unlawfully arrested may understandably act out of passion; in the heat of the moment a person does not, indeed cannot, carefully consider his or her alternatives. The mother in this case did not contemplate the state of the law before responding to the unlawful arrest of her child; nor would other persons facing her situation in the future.

The real question here is not about escalating violence; it is about whether a person ought to be prosecuted for resistance of the kind in this case. In contrast to Justice Geske's characterization in her concurrence of other possible fact situations, in this case Ms. Hobson did not fight with the police and she was not violent. The circuit court found that Ms. Hobson "clearly used only force sufficient to attempt to prevent her illegal arrest. She flailed her legs and arms about as the police officer had 'taken her to the ground.' She did not chase an officer down the street. There is a complete absence of an intent to assault an officer. Her only evident intent was to prevent her illegal arrest. She did not assault the police officer; the police officer assaulted her."

The common law right to resist unlawful arrest was designed for just the situation presented in this case. A person is unlawfully arrested and is provoked to anger and emotion to resist the unlawful arrest. Under such circumstances, according to the common law, the person wrongfully arrested should not be subject to criminal prosecution.

The majority opinion does not abrogate a person's common law right to use force when resisting an arrest in which a law enforcement officer uses unreasonable force. The reasoning of the majority opinion is thus internally inconsistent.

WILLIAM A. BABLITCH, JUSTICE (concurring).

The majority opinion completely abrogates the common law right to forcibly resist an unlawful arrest in the absence of unreasonable force. By so doing, the majority refuses to admit any exceptions for the future such as the one the facts so compellingly present here.

I would admit a very narrow exception to the general rule enunciated by the majority. Like the majority, I would not permit resistance to an unlawful arrest in the absence of unreasonable force; however, I would allow resistance if the individual reasonably believes that serious and substantial mental or physical health concerns of the individual or a member of his or her family are threatened in a way that are not susceptible of cure later in a court room. I would require an objective, reasonableness standard. This holding would be similar to, but not in complete accord with, the holding of the circuit court * * *.

Notes and Questions

1. Should the Supreme Court of Wisconsin minded its own business, or was this its business? Compare *State v. Wiegmann*, 350 Md. 585, 714 A.2d 841 (1998), where the court concluded that, while the state's arguments against the common law rule "have merit," "we decline to abolish the long-standing common law privilege permitting persons to resist an illegal warrantless arrest. We believe this change is best left to the Legislature and its primary power to, in the first instance, declare the public policy of the state."

2. Do the facts of *Hobson* demonstrate that there is good reason to retain the common law rule, as concluded in the Chief Justice's concurrence? If not, is there some sensible middle ground between retention and abolition? Consider Paul G. Chevigny, *The Right to Resist an Unlawful Arrest*, 78 Yale L.J. 1128, 1141 (1969): "The impairment of fourth amendment rights, however, is not enough to justify resistance to an unlawful arrest. The problem is to determine the circumstances under which such a seizure becomes so provocative as to make unfair the imposition of a criminal penalty for resisting it." If a part of the defense were to be retained, how should that part be described? Do you agree with the formulation of concurring Justice Bablitch? With Penn Lerblance, *Impeding Unlawful Arrest: A Question of Authority and Criminal Liability*, 61 Denver L.J. 655, 697 (1984), who would recognize a defense when "the resistance was reasonable in view of the totality of the circumstances of the encounter"?

3. The issue of whether self-help should be a defense also arises when the charge is escape. Compare:

(a) *People v. Alexander*, 39 Mich.App. 607, 197 N.W.2d 831 (1972): "On appeal, the defendant claims that his being detained after April 1, 1970, was illegal and, therefore, he was justified in escaping. The basis of defendant's argument is that under *Browning v. Michigan Department of Corrections*, 385 Mich. 179, 188 N.W.2d 552 (1971) which established the proper method of computing 'dead time', defendant's sentence should have ended on April 1, 1970. Defendant therefore argues that he was wrongfully kept in jail for more than ten months and had a right to escape.

"In the case of *People v. Hamaker*, 92 Mich. 11, 52 N.W. 82 (1892), the Supreme Court held that one could not be convicted of the crime of escape if his incarceration is unlawful.

Although it is not always clear just what circumstances will justify self-help on the part of a prisoner improperly detained, it is clear that personal liberty is given the utmost importance under the laws of this country:

> "The right to personal liberty, is accorded a pre-eminent position under our system of law and government, and the history of the last few decades has vividly demonstrated the danger of invasions of the right by governmental agents acting under color of law, so that there is something to be said for the view that the citizen improperly deprived of his liberty should be entitled to recover it by any means available to him, *ruat coelum,* and it seems hard that one improperly imprisoned should be subjected to further punishment for merely asserting the right to liberty guaranteed him by the Constitution.' 70 A.L.R.2d 1432.

"It is our opinion that defendant should not have been prosecuted for the crime of escape if at the time he left prison he was illegally incarcerated."

(b) *Johnson v. State,* 258 Ind. 515, 282 N.E.2d 802 (1972): "Counsel for both the defense and the State have dwelled at length on the proceedings leading up to the order of confinement, attempting to convince us of their illegality or legality, as supports their respective positions. We believe these labors to be lost, however, as such is not determinative of the issue herein. Although grave doubts appear with regard to the legality of the defendant's confinement upon the contempt charge, we do not meet that issue. True, the statute applies only to escapes from 'lawful' confinement, but that does not entitle all who may question the legality of the proceedings leading to their confinement to resort to self-help. Although numerous cases involving justification for escape have arisen in other jurisdictions, the question has not previously been passed upon by this Court. We find a substantial number of decisions from other states where, under circumstances obviously lacking due process, breaking jail was found not to be a criminal offense. We have made no attempt to analyze all these cases or to reconcile them with the majority view to the contrary, which is the view we believe to square with reason. Not necessarily inconsistent with the rule that escape is justifiable where the imprisonment is 'unlawful' are a number of cases holding that where the imprisonment is under color of law, the prisoner is not entitled to resort to self-help but must apply for his release through regular legal channels, even though he might be able to show such defects in the procedure by which he was arrested, tried, sentenced, committed, or imprisoned as to justify or require his release on appeal or habeas corpus. * * *

"As was said by the court in *State v. Palmer* (1950) 6 Terry 308, 45 Del. 308, 72 A.2d 442, this rather severe attitude on the part of the courts was founded upon sound public policy, since jailbreaks are extremely disruptive to prison routine, dangerous to guards, police and the public, and to make it the province of every prisoner in every jail to decide for himself whether conditions justified his escape would only serve to increase the number of attempts to break jail, so that a plea of justification for escape, if permissible at all, would be recognized only in the most extreme situations."

SECTION 5. DOMESTIC AUTHORITY

STATE v. WILDER

Supreme Judicial Court of Maine, 2000.

748 A.2d 444.

ALEXANDER, J.

This appeal requires identification of the border between a parent's justified use of physical force to control a child and a criminal assault. Lawrence Wilder appeals from a decision of the Superior Court, which affirmed a judgment of the District Court finding him guilty of three counts of assault on his nine-year-old son. * * *

At the time of trial, Lawrence Wilder and Bernice Landry had been divorced for eight years. They have a daughter and a son from their three-year marriage. Pursuant to the divorce, Wilder had responsibility for his son on many weekends and during some school vacations, a pattern that had continued for about a year. The events at issue in this case arose during the April 1998 school vacation when the son, then nine years old, stayed with his father for a week. Previous times when the father and son were together had apparently gone without significant incident.

The son was the only witness to the events who testified at trial. * * *

Regarding the first assault charge, the son testified: "We were playing a little board game and I was talking too much, so he turned around and grabbed me on the shoulder and told me to shut up." * * *

Describing this first incident in its brief, presumably in a way most favorable to its position, the State asserts that, "[The boy] was talking too much, although he was neither being fresh or saying anything bad to appellant, and appellant grabbed him on the shoulder and told him to shut up. Appellant squeezed [his son] hard enough to hurt him."

The second assault charge is based on * * * an event which occurred "a couple days later." The son testified: "We were still sitting in the living room, and we were playing a game again. And I was still talking too much, and he just grabbed me again.... [H]e grabbed me in the same shoulder." * * *

In its brief, the State describes the second assault charge as follows: "Once again, when [the boy] was talking too much, appellant grabbed him on the same shoulder. [The boy] was not mouthing off and was neither rude nor fresh. This time the pain was greater since appellant grabbed [him] in the same spot." * * *

Describing the third assault charge in its brief, the State asserts: "Appellant claimed that [his son] was exaggerating, then grabbed [the boy] on his mouth, squeezed and said[,] 'Shut up.'"

Thus, in each of the three incidents, when Wilder "grabbed" his son, he caused transient pain and minor, temporary bruises.

When the son returned home he was questioned by Bernice Landry, as was her regular practice, as to whether he had been hit by his father. She also asked him about a bruise on his face. Initially the boy gave his mother another explanation for the bruise because he was concerned that Landry would respond to the bruises by attempting to have Wilder jailed; "I thought my mom would put him in jail."

Responding to her observations, Landry called the Department of Human Services, went to Westbrook Hospital, contacted the Cumberland Police, and reported the events to a school counsellor. The incident was investigated by a Cumberland police officer, who took a report from the boy. The matter was then presented to the District Attorney's Office, and prosecution on three counts of assault was initiated.

The case was tried in the District Court in November 1998. At the close of the State's case, and again at the close of all of the evidence, the defense requested acquittal arguing that the justification for parents using physical force to prevent or punish misconduct by their children[2] prevented conviction by proof beyond a reasonable doubt on the available evidence.

---

2. 17–A M.R.S.A. § 106(1) states:

§ 106. Physical force by persons with special re-

In its findings at the close of trial, the court concluded that the elements of assault—intentionally, knowingly, or recklessly causing bodily injury—had been proven beyond a reasonable doubt for each of the three incidents. The court also ruled that the parental control justification "does not apply here." The court determined that:

> There is no evidence of misconduct in this record, or a reasonable inference that could be drawn from the evidence in this record as to misconduct. I don't find that excessive talking and exaggerating, in and of themselves, without some further evidence, would rise in any way to a level of misconduct as it's plainly defined.

The court found Wilder guilty on each charge. He was sentenced on one charge to 364 days in the county jail with all but 90 days suspended and a year's probation. On the other two charges he was given a consecutive sentence of 364 days, all suspended and a year's probation, for a total sentence of 728 days, all but 90 days suspended and 2 years probation. One of the conditions of probation, also a bail condition, was that Wilder have no contact with his son. The record indicates that the sentence was motivated, in part, by the court's concern that Wilder had been convicted of gross sexual assault against a daughter a number of years in the past. * * *

A parent has a fundamental liberty interest in maintaining a familial relationship with his or her child. This fundamental liberty interest includes the right of parents "to direct the upbringing and education of children," including the use of reasonable or moderate physical force to control behavior. "The parent may be subject to the criminal law when his punishment of the child exceeds the bounds of reason and moderation." A parental privilege to use moderate or reasonable physical force, without criminal liability, was recognized at common law: "battery is, in some cases, justifiable or lawful; as where one who hath authority, a parent or a master, gives moderate correction to his child, his scholar, or his apprentice."

Today a parent's privilege to exercise physical control over a child is recognized by Maine law in 17–A M.R.S.A. § 106(1). * * *

Since adoption of the Criminal Code, we have only had one occasion to address the parental discipline justification, and the facts in that case were not close. In *State v. Dodd*, 503 A.2d 1302 (Me.1986), we affirmed a conviction where a defendant spanked a three-year-old child to stop her from crying, taped her ankles and hands together, taped her mouth shut and hung her from a door knob by her ankles on two occasions for a total of over twenty minutes. We addressed the parental control justification in a footnote stating that: "[t]he trial justice had ample grounds to conclude that the defendant's conduct went far beyond being a 'reasonable degree of force' to discipline."

With this background, we must analyze the District Court's determination that the parental control justification "does not apply here." * * *

The evidence here is that the triggers for Wilder's exercise of parental control were talking too much or exaggerating. Taking this evidence most favorably to the parent, as we must, talking too much which can "annoy people sometimes" is a justifiable basis for a parent's exercising control over a child to prevent or punish misconduct. Likewise, exaggerating, which may be construed as misstating or lying, is a justifiable basis for a parent's exercising control to prevent or punish misconduct. Certainly we cannot rule, as a

sponsibilities

1. A parent, foster parent, guardian or other similar person responsible for the long term general care and welfare of a person is justified in using a reasonable degree of force against such person when and to the extent that he reasonably believes it necessary to prevent or punish such person's misconduct. A person to whom such parent, foster parent, guardian or other responsible person has expressly delegated permission to so prevent or punish misconduct is similarly justified in using a reasonable degree of force.

matter of law, that talking too much or exaggerating is not a basis for disciplining or controlling a child. But that is a ruling we would have to make to uphold the District Court's determination. The record contains sufficient evidence to place the parental control justification at issue for each of the three assault charges.

Once a justification is placed at issue as a result of evidence presented at trial, "the state must disprove its existence beyond a reasonable doubt."

The charge here was assault, which requires proof that a defendant caused bodily injury "intentionally, knowingly, or recklessly." Accordingly, proving beyond a reasonable doubt that the force that Wilder used and his belief that such force was necessary to control his child were unreasonable, is not enough. The Criminal Code in effect at the time of these events specified that:

> If a defense provided under this chapter is precluded solely because the requirement that the actor's belief be reasonable has not been met, he may be convicted only of a crime for which recklessness or criminal negligence suffices, depending on whether his holding the belief was reckless or criminally negligent.

Thus, to sustain a conviction for assault where the parental control justification is generated, the State had to prove, at a minimum, that (1) the force Wilder used was reckless; and (2) Wilder's belief that such force was necessary to control his son and prevent misconduct was reckless.

In 1999, by legislation not applicable to this case, [the above-quoted] section was amended to clarify the law by placing into the law the definitional prerequisites for conviction that had previously been incorporated by reference from the definition of recklessness. The law now specifies that, where recklessness is an element of a crime, as it is here, and the reasonableness of one's belief is at issue due to a justification defense, a person may be convicted "only if holding the belief, when viewed in light of the nature and purpose of the person's conduct and the circumstances known to the person, is grossly deviant from what a reasonable and prudent person would believe in the same situation." This clarifying language essentially incorporates existing law on the recklessness standard.

Accordingly, the District Court erred in (i) refusing to consider the parental control justification; and (ii) not requiring the State to prove beyond a reasonable doubt that the force Wilder used was reckless and that his belief that such force was necessary for parental control was reckless or "grossly deviant from what a reasonable and prudent person would believe in the same situation."

At this point we must determine whether to proceed to address the evidentiary issues raised on the appeal and remand for additional findings or a new trial or remand for a judgment of acquittal if, as a matter of law, the evidence presented was insufficient to support the convictions.

Determination of whether the State's evidence in this case is sufficient to disprove the parental control justification beyond a reasonable doubt necessarily requires some articulation of what conduct may be justified under section 106(1). * * *

The criminal liability threshold set out in section 106(1), "reasonable degree of force" that the actor "reasonably believes is necessary to prevent or punish such person's misconduct," is derived from the common law and is shared by at least five other states.

By way of comparison, the Model Penal Code [§ 3.08(1)] expressly rejects the "reasonableness" and "necessity" approach * * *.

The comment to the Model Penal Code supports this differing approach, stating:

The formulation also differs from the Restatement [of Torts] in not explicitly demand-ing that the force be reasonable. It was believed that so long as a parent uses moderate force for permissible purposes, the criminal law should not provide for review of the reasonableness of the parent's judgment. Of course, even if a statute includes language about necessity or reasonableness or both, it would be extraordinary for a parent using moderate force for a permissible purpose to be prosecuted because of misjudgment. Thus the less stringent language of the Model Code is unlikely to make a great practical difference, but it does more accurately reflect the latitude that is actually given to judgments of parents in disciplining their children. * * *

Cases from other states that have addressed close questions of sufficiency of the evidence in parental justification-assault cases lend support to a distinction between those acts that cause only transient pain and temporary marks or bruises, which the parental justification protects, and those acts that cause long-term pain, permanent marks, or disfigurement upon which criminal liability is assessed. * * *

In *State v. Ivey*, 98 Ohio App.3d 249, 648 N.E.2d 519 (1994), a ten-year-old boy was disciplined for not reporting a school detention by being whipped on the buttocks and legs with a belt, leaving bruises and welts observable the next day but causing no permanent damage. The Ohio Appeals Court, Eighth District, ruled that this evidence was insufficient to support a child endangerment conviction in the face of a parental justification defense because "the harm that resulted was temporary and slight, and did not require medical attention." Addressing the governing law and standards of review, the court stated:

Parents are responsible for the upbringing, education and discipline of their children, as parents have a fundamental liberty interest in the care, custody and management of a child. The state should intervene only when a serious risk of physical or mental harm to the child is clear from the evidence. Parents have to be given reasonable latitude to impose discipline as the best interests of the child dictate. Some children need more discipline than others. Some respond without ever being struck—a sharp word suffices. It is the parent who in the first instance is the best judge of what works with each child.

Two cases from the Fifth District Court of Appeal of Florida illustrate distinctions that may become important at the boundary between permissible parental control and viola-tions of criminal law. See *Lowery v. State*, 641 So.2d 489 (Fla.Dist.Ct.App.1994); *Moakley v. State*, 547 So.2d 1246 (Fla.Dist.Ct.App.1989). Both addressed a child abuse statute impos-ing criminal liability on one who "maliciously punishes a child." *Moakley* involved a conviction for striking an eight-year-old girl on the buttocks and hip with a leather belt, leaving bruise marks. The court ruled that the evidence was insufficient to support the conviction, noting there was no evidence of great bodily harm, permanent disability, or permanent disfigurement. *Lowery* involved a conviction for striking a seven-year-old boy many times with an electric cord, leaving bruises, lesions, and scabs. The court affirmed the conviction, distinguishing *Moakley* on the basis that the evidence in *Lowery* indicated that the defendant's actions had drawn blood and left some permanent marks or "disfig-urement." * * *

This analysis of statutes, the common law, precedent, a scholarly survey of the law of the 50 states, and the efforts of the drafters of the Model Penal Code and the Restatement of Torts leads to the following conclusions:

1. All American jurisdictions allow parents to use at least moderate or reasonable physical force when they reasonably believe that such force is necessary to control their children;

2. To trigger criminal liability:

(a) the physical harm caused by the parent's use of force must be greater than transient pain and minor, temporary marks or bruises; and

(b) the parent's belief that such physical contact is necessary must be more than unreasonable; it must be a gross deviation from what a reasonable and prudent parent would believe in the same situation; and

3. Once a parental control justification is placed in issue, the triggers for criminal liability must be proven by the State, beyond a reasonable doubt.

Section 106(1) must be interpreted with this background. * * *

The evidence in this record must be examined against the above criteria. * * *

In the first assault incident in which the boy was "talking too much," the State characterizes Wilder as having "grabbed him on the shoulder and told him to shut up" and having squeezed the boy "hard enough to hurt him." If such acts, as characterized by the State, and with no apparent evidence of any aggravating factors, are sufficient to support an assault charge, then any physical contact by a parent with a child that hurts the child may support an assault conviction if the State elects to prosecute. But while neither the State nor this Court may necessarily condone or agree with Wilder's approach to control of his son, we can say, as a matter of law, that (1) the physical harm caused was not, beyond a reasonable doubt, greater than transient pain and temporary marks; and (2) grabbing his son hard to get his attention and stop him from talking too much was not, beyond a reasonable doubt, an action grossly deviant from what a reasonable and prudent parent would believe necessary in the same situation.

The same may be said of the second incident involving grabbing the shoulder in the same spot and for the same reason. In neither case was the child squeezed firmly enough to make him cry, and in both cases, father and son apparently continued the games they had been playing before the incidents.

The third incident involving "exaggerating" resulted in Wilder grabbing his son on the mouth, squeezing firmly enough to leave bruises, and saying "shut up." Again, while this is not an action to control or reprimand a child that the State or this Court might take or condone, we can say as a matter of law that the evidence is insufficient to support a finding, beyond a reasonable doubt, that (1) Wilder's beliefs that he needed to use force to control his son were grossly deviant from what a reasonable and prudent parent would believe necessary in the same situation; and (2) the force used caused harm greater than transient pain and temporary marks.

At oral argument, the State asserted that even in the face of 17–A M.R.S.A. § 106(1), any physical action by a parent to control a child which causes the child pain and which is brought to the State's attention, may subject the parent to criminal prosecution for assault, depending upon how the State exercises its prosecutorial discretion. * * *

Certainly, the State should and does frequently inject itself into family situations to protect children from assaults and other abuse. But the standards for such involvement must respect the standards specified in section 106(1).* * * While there are individuals who legitimately and firmly believe that any discipline which causes a child physical pain is inappropriate,[13] any change in the parental control justification presently set by the Maine

---

13. Many people believe that parents should not use physical force to control their children. At least nine countries ban corporal punishment of children. However, in the United States, "greater than ninety percent of American parents use physical force to punish their children." * * *

Criminal Code is an issue of policy properly subject to action by the Legislature, not the courts. * * *

Notes and Questions

1. If *Wilder* had been a jury case, exactly what should the jury have been told about the dimensions of the applicable defense? Consider *State v. Thorpe,* 429 A.2d 785 (R.I. 1981), upholding, re a charge of assault upon defendant's 4–month–old daughter, an instruction that "no one has the right to inflict excessive corporal punishment upon a child." The court reasoned that there "is no inflexible rule that defines what, under all circumstances, is unreasonable or excessive force," and that the word "excessive" is "sufficient to convey the meaning that a parent may inflict corporal punishment to discipline and correct the child but may not do so to vent his/her own anger or frustration on the child."

2. In *Ingraham v. Wright,* 430 U.S. 651, 97 S.Ct. 1401, 51 L.Ed.2d 711 (1977), the Court held that the Eighth Amendment prohibition on "cruel and unusual punishment" was "designed to protect those convicted of crimes" and thus "does not apply to the paddling of children as a means of maintaining discipline in public schools." The Court added that "[t]he schoolchild has little need for the protection of the Eighth Amendment," in that "[p]ublic school teachers and administrators are privileged at common law to inflict only such corporal punishment as is reasonably necessary for the proper education and discipline of the child; any punishment going beyond the privilege may result in both civil and criminal liability."

3. Should use of force by school teachers be subject to the same standard applicable to parents? Consider *People v. Ball*, 15 Ill.App.3d 143, 303 N.E.2d 516 (1973), where, after a student disrupted a class, the teacher "had the boy bend down with his hands on his knees and he then struck him 10 times on the buttocks with a wooden paddle about 20 inches long, one-fourth inch thick and three inches wide. * * * The paddling occurred at approximately 2:30 in the afternoon. When school dismissed at 3:15 the boy walked to his home and reported the paddling to his parents. His father took him to the police station and then to the home of their family doctor where they were directed to the emergency room of a local hospital. There the boy was treated by a doctor who applied a surface anesthesia and gauze bandage. The condition as described by the doctor was that the boy had severe burn-type bruises of both buttocks, the right side being worse than the left. The skin temperature was hot to the touch, there was marked discoloration and redness requiring treatment. There may have been minute abrasions in the bruised area but the main effect was one of swelling, redness, heat and a thickening of the area above the surface surrounding the skin. The redness and swelling disappeared in due course with no after effects, except that the mother testified that the boy had some lingering emotional problems stemming from the paddling." The teacher's conviction for batter was overturned on appeal.

A dissenting justice in *Ball* objected that "the majority grants teachers more power in disciplining school children than possessed by their parents" by use of the "outmoded" malice test, whereunder "the teacher is the sole arbiter of the right to punish as well as the degree of punishment to be administered, subject only to the limitation as to punishment maliciously inflicted or punishment which results in disfigurement or permanent injury." The dissent then described the prevailing reasonableness test in the following language (which should be compared with the description in *Wilder*): "The reasonableness test is clearly the rule in the majority of American courts. Its philosophical basis is that the right or privilege of a parent or teacher to discipline a child is grounded not in the adult's liberty of action, but in the child's welfare. Therefore, this discipline must not exceed what is reasonable and moderate under the circumstances, considering the age, sex, physical and mental condition of the child, the nature of his offense and his apparent motive, and whether the punishment is disproportionate to the offense, unnecessarily degrading, or likely to cause serious or permanent harm. If the punishment is unreasonable the adult is criminally liable."

The dissent then concluded: "Because the punishment in the present case was unreasonable, I feel that it constituted the criminal offense of battery. Had the punishment been reasonable it might have been legal, but I would still question its wisdom. Although beyond the scope of this opinion, the following sources cast light on the problem. In Aron and Katz, 'Corporal Punishment in the Public Schools,' 6 Harvard Civil Rights—Civil Liberties Law Review 583 (1971), the authors conclude at 584–585:

'Corporal punishment in the public schools is ineffective and harmful. If mildly and irregularly applied, it is useless in controlling behavior. In order to prevent the recurrence of unwanted behavior, corporal punishment must either be applied continually or its exemplary application must have a "terrifying and traumatic" effect. Not surprisingly, the National Education Association has concluded that corporal punishment is ineffective in reducing behavioral problems. Furthermore, an English study found that a deterioration of behavior and an increase in delinquency accompany increased use of corporal punishment.

'Corporal punishment has further deleterious effects on children. Insofar as it relies on fear, it disrupts the learning process by repressing the natural tendency of children to explore. This fear may be channeled into aggression against the teacher, against the school, or against society. At the extreme, juvenile delinquency may result. Finally, and perhaps most seriously, the use of corporal punishment may inhibit the development of self-criticism and self-direction in the child. Corporal punishment may drive students to concentrate their energies on conflict with the teacher instead of encouraging them to adjust to their classroom situation.

'While theoretically corporal punishment need not be brutal, there is no assurance that it will be inflicted moderately or responsibly. In the heat of anger, especially if provoked by personal abuse, some teachers are likely to exceed legal bounds. Moreover, if limited corporal punishment were permitted, controls would be unlikely to prevent the "really unmistakable kind of satisfaction which some teachers feel in applying the rattan." A total ban of this punishment would provide far more effective control.

'Finally, corporal punishment undermines human dignity. Students are placed at the mercy of teachers who have the power to beat them without explanation or justification. In an institution which purports to inculcate the value of reason in human affairs and the worth of each individual in society, it is antithetical to educate by brutality and unreason.' "

4. What other relationships permit resort to reasonable corporal punishment? Consider State v. Pittard, 45 N.C.App. 701, 263 S.E.2d 809 (1980) (day care center employee not in loco parentis re child placed in the temporary care of the center, as such "relationship is established only when the person with whom the child is placed intends to assume the status of a parent—by taking on the obligations incidental to the parental relationship, particularly that of support and maintenance"; and was not a teacher, as her "employment at the center carried with it none of the attributes of teaching nor did the evidence show that she possessed any of the credentials of a teacher").

SECTION 6. DURESS, NECESSITY AND CHOICE OF EVILS

STATE v. WARSHOW

Supreme Court of Vermont, 1979.

138 Vt. 22, 410 A.2d 1000.

BARNEY, CHIEF JUSTICE.

The defendants were part of a group of demonstrators that travelled to Vernon, Vermont, to protest at the main gate of a nuclear power plant known as Vermont Yankee. The plant had been shut down for repairs and refueling, and these protestors had joined a rally designed to prevent workers from gaining access to the plant and placing it on-line.

They were requested to leave the private premises of the power plant by representatives of Vermont Yankee and officers of the law. The defendants were among those who refused, and they were arrested and charged with unlawful trespass.

The issue with which this appeal of their convictions is concerned relates to a doctrine referred to as the defense of necessity. At trial the defendants sought to present evidence relating to the hazards of nuclear power plant operation which, they argued, would establish that defense. After hearing the defendants' offer of proof the trial court excluded the proffered evidence and refused to grant compulsory process for the witnesses required to present the defense. The jury instruction requested on the issue of necessity was also refused, and properly preserved for appellate review.

In ruling below, the trial court determined that the defense was not available. It is on this basis that we must test the issue.

The defense of necessity is one that partakes of the classic defense of "confession and avoidance." It admits the criminal act, but claims justification. * * *

The doctrine is one of specific application insofar as it is a defense to criminal behavior. This is clear because if the qualifications for the defense of necessity are not closely delineated, the definition of criminal activity becomes uncertain and even whimsical. The difficulty arises when words of general and broad qualification are used to describe the special scope of this defense.

In the various definitions and examples recited as incorporating the concept of necessity, certain fundamental requirements stand out:

(1) there must be a situation of emergency arising without fault on the part of the actor concerned;

(2) this emergency must be so imminent and compelling as to raise a reasonable expectation of harm, either directly to the actor or upon those he was protecting;

(3) this emergency must present no reasonable opportunity to avoid the injury without doing the criminal act; and

(4) the injury impending from the emergency must be of sufficient seriousness to outmeasure the criminal wrong.

It is the defendants' position that they made a sufficient offer of proof to establish the elements of the necessity defense to raise a jury question. The trial court rejected this contention on the ground, among others, that the offer did not sufficiently demonstrate the existence of an emergency or imminent danger.

This ruling was sound, considering the offer. The defendants wished to subpoena witnesses to testify to the dangers of nuclear accidents and the effect of low-level radiation. It was conceded that there had been no serious accident at Vermont Yankee, but defendants contended that the consequences could be so serious that the mere possibility should suffice. This is not the law.

There is no doubt that the defendants wished to call attention to the dangers of low-level radiation, nuclear waste, and nuclear accident. But low-level radiation and nuclear waste are not the types of imminent danger classified as an emergency sufficient to justify criminal activity. To be imminent, a danger must be, or must reasonably appear to be, threatening to occur immediately, near at hand, and impending. We do not understand the defendants to have taken the position in their offer of proof that the hazards of low-level radiation and nuclear waste buildup are immediate in nature. On the contrary, they cite long-range risks and dangers that do not presently threaten health and safety. Where the hazards are long term, the danger is not imminent, because the defendants have time to exercise options other than breaking the law.

Nor does the specter of nuclear accident as presented by these defendants fulfill the imminent and compelling harm element of the defense. The offer does not take the position that they acted to prevent an impending accident. Rather, they claimed that they acted to foreclose the "chance" or "possibility" of accident. This defense cannot lightly be allowed to justify acts taken to foreclose speculative and uncertain dangers. Its application must be limited to acts directed to the prevention of harm that is reasonably certain to occur. Therefore the offer fails to satisfy the imminent danger element. The facts offered would not have established the defense.

These acts may be a method of making public statements about nuclear power and its dangers, but they are not a legal basis for invoking the defense of necessity. Nor can the defendants' sincerity of purpose excuse the criminal nature of their acts. * * *

Judgment affirmed.

HILL, JUSTICE, concurring.

While I agree with the result reached by the majority, I am unable to agree with their reasoning. * * *

The defense of necessity proceeds from the appreciation that, as a matter of public policy, there are circumstances where the value protected by the law is eclipsed by a superseding value, and that it would be inappropriate and unjust to apply the usual criminal rule. The balancing of competing values cannot, of course, be committed to the private judgment of the actor, but must, in most cases, be determined at trial with due regard being given for the crime charged and the higher value sought to be achieved.

Determination of the issue of competing values and, therefore, the availability of the defense of necessity is precluded, however, when there has been a deliberate legislative choice as to the values at issue. The common law defense of necessity deals with imminent dangers from obvious and generally recognized harms. It does not deal with non-imminent or debatable harms, nor does it deal with activities that the legislative branch has expressly sanctioned and found not to be harms.

Both the state of Vermont and the federal government have given their imprimatur to the development and normal operation of nuclear energy and have established mechanisms for the regulation of nuclear power. Implicit within these statutory enactments is the policy choice that the benefits of nuclear energy outweigh its dangers.

If we were to allow defendants to present the necessity defense in this case we would, in effect, be allowing a jury to redetermine questions of policy already decided by the legislative branches of the federal and state governments. This is not how our system of government was meant to operate. * * *

In my opinion the majority puts the cart before the horse. It measures the offer made against the requisite elements of the defense of necessity and concludes that the defendants failed to show a likelihood of imminent danger; yet it reserves judgment on the legislative policy exception to the defense. It is illogical to consider whether the necessary elements of a defense have been shown before determining whether the defense is even available in the particular situation.

The dissent, on the other hand, assumes that defendants' offer was sufficient to show not only imminent danger but also a failure of the regulatory scheme. I cannot agree with this assumption because the offer failed to show a danger not contemplated by the legislative scheme. The legislative framework was set up to deal with the very situation defendants offered to prove "might" happen. But because neither the state legislature nor Congress acted to shut down the power plant based on speculative possibilities does not, in my opinion, give rise to the questionable inference that there was an emergency which the regulatory scheme failed to avert. * * *

BILLINGS, JUSTICE, dissenting. * * *

The defendants offered evidence on all the requisite elements of the defense of necessity. They stated as follows:

> [They had] a feeling that there was a situation of an emergency or imminent danger that would have occurred with the start up of the reactor on October 8th the time of [their] alleged crime * * * the chance * * * of the nuclear power plant having a serious accident which would cause * * * great untold damage to property and lives and health for many generations.

The defendants also stated that "there was reasonable belief that it would have been an emergency had they started that reactor up * * * there was a very good chance of an accident there for which there is no insurance coverage or very little." Specifically, the defendants offered to show by expert testimony that there were defects in the cooling system and other aspects of the power plant which they believed could and would result in a meltdown within seven seconds of failure on the start up of the plant. In addition, the defendants went to great lengths to base their defense on the imminent danger that would result from the hazardous radiation emitted from the plant and its wastes when the plant resumed operations.

While the offer made by the defendants was laced with statements about the dangers they saw in nuclear power generally, it is clear that they offered to show that the Vermont Yankee facility at which they were arrested was an imminent danger to the community on the day of the arrests; that, if it commenced operation, there was a danger of meltdown and severe radiation damage to persons and property. In support of this contention, the defendants stated that they would call experts familiar with the Vermont Yankee facility and the dangerous manner of its construction, as well as other experts who would testify on the effects of meltdown and radiation leakage, on the results of governmental testing, and on the regulation of the Vermont Yankee facility. These witnesses were highly qualified to testify about the dangers at the Vermont Yankee facility based either on personal knowledge or on conditions the defendants offered to show existed at the time of the trespass.

Furthermore, the defendants offered to show that, in light of the imminent danger of an accident, they had exhausted all alternative means of preventing the start up of the plant and the immediate catastrophe it would bring. Under the circumstances of imminent danger arising from the start up of the plant, coupled with the resistance of Vermont Yankee and government officials, which the defendants offered to prove, nothing short of preventing the workers access to start up the plant would have averted the accident that the defendants expected.

Through this offer, it cannot be said, without prejudgment, that the defendants failed to set forth specific and concrete evidence, which, if proven, would establish the existence of an imminent danger of serious proportions through no fault of the defendants which could not be averted without the trespass. Whether the defendants' expectations and opportunities were reasonable under the circumstances of this case is not for the trial court to decide without hearing the evidence. From a review of the record, I am of the opinion that the offer here measured up to the standard required and that the trial court struck too soon in excluding the offered evidence.

I would also dissent from the concurring opinion in so far as it attempts to hide behind inferences that the legislature precluded the courts from hearing the defense of necessity in the instant case. Even assuming that such inferences can be drawn from the regulatory schemes cited, they have no bearing on this case. We were asked to infer under the facts, which the defendants offered to prove (that they were acting to avert an imminent nuclear disaster), that the legislative branch of government would not permit the courts of this state to entertain the defense of necessity because it had legislatively determined nuclear power to be safe. Were the defense raised without any offer to show an imminent danger of serious accident, it might fail both because defendants did not offer evidence on imminent danger and on the basis of legislative preclusion. But, where, as here, the defendants offer to prove an emergency which the regulatory scheme failed to avert, the inference of preclusion is unwarranted. The defendants are entitled to show that although there is a comprehensive regulatory scheme, it had failed to such an extent as to raise for them the choice between criminal trespass and the nuclear disaster which the regulatory scheme was created to prevent. * * *

Notes and Questions

1. In *United States v. Schoon*, 971 F.2d 193 (9th Cir.1991), the defendants gained admittance to the IRS office in Tucson, where they chanted "keep America's tax dollars out of El Salvador," splashed simulated blood on the counters, walls, and carpeting, and generally obstructed the office's operation. After a federal police officer ordered the group, on several occasions, to disperse or face arrest, appellants were arrested. They were charged with obstructing activities of an IRS office and failing to comply with order of a federal police officer, and, after the trial court precluded a necessity defense based on the defendants' claim that their acts in protest of American involvement in El Salvador were necessary to avoid further bloodshed in that country, were convicted. On appeal, the court noted that it "could affirm substantially on [the] grounds relied upon by the district court," i.e., that in this particular case the elements of a necessity defense were not shown, but the court found "a deeper, systemic reason for the complete absence of federal case law recognizing a necessity defense in an indirect civil disobedience case" (i.e., where the defendants are charged with "violating a law or interfering with a government policy that is not, itself, the object of protest"), and thus reached "the conclusion that necessity can never be proved in a case of indirect civil disobedience."

As the court in *Schoon* explained: "Indirect civil disobedience seeks first and foremost to bring about the repeal of a law or a change of governmental policy, attempting to mobilize public opinion through typically symbolic action. These protestors violate a law, not because it is unconstitutional or otherwise improper, but because doing so calls public attention to their objectives. Thus, the most immediate 'harm' this form of protest targets is the existence of the law or policy. However, the mere existence of a constitutional law or governmental policy cannot constitute a legally cognizable harm. * * *

"A final reason the necessity defense does not apply to these indirect civil disobedience cases is that legal alternatives will never be deemed exhausted when the harm can be mitigated by congressional action. As noted above, the harm indirect civil disobedience aims to prevent is the continued existence of a law or policy. Because congressional action can always mitigate this 'harm,' lawful political activity to spur such action will always be a legal alternative. * * *

"As have courts before us, we could assume, as a threshold matter, that the necessity defense is conceivably available in these cases, but find the elements never satisfied. Such a decision, however, does not come without significant costs. First, the failure of the federal courts to hold explicitly that the necessity defense is unavailable in these cases results in district courts expending unnecessary time and energy trying to square defendants' claims with the strict requirements of the doctrine. Second, such an inquiry oftentimes requires the courts to tread into areas constitutionally committed to other branches of government. For example, in [a case] which involved trespass on a naval base to protest American nuclear weapons policy, we noted that, '[t]o consider defendants' argument [that trespassing was justified by the nefariousness of the Trident missile] would put us in the position of usurping the functions that the Constitution has given to the Congress and to the President.' * * * Third, holding out the possibility of the defense's applicability sets a trap for the unwary civil disobedient, rather than permitting the individual to undertake a more realistic cost-benefit analysis before deciding whether to break the law in political protest. Fourth, assuming the applicability of the defense in this context may risk its distortion in traditional cases. Finally, some commentators have suggested that the courts have sabotaged the usually low threshold for getting a defense theory before the jury as a means of keeping the necessity defense from the jury."[a]

2. The defendants in *United States v. Montgomery,* 772 F.2d 733 (11th Cir.1985), were convicted of depredation of United States Army property because they broke into a defense plant and hammered and poured blood onto nuclear missile launchers and components belonging to the Army. On appeal, the court first rejected the defendants' claim they were entitled to a necessity defense because, inter alia, the defendants "could not hold a reasonable belief that a direct consequence of their actions would be nuclear disarmament," and then turned to the defendant's other contention, that they were entitled to a "Nuremberg defense":

"Defendants here misperceive the persons for whom such a Nuremberg 'defense' is appropriate. There the German defendants were in positions which required them to participate in sentencing dissidents to death or in utilizing slave labor because domestic law or superior authority ordered them to do so. The question is whether what they were required to do by domestic law could escape international criminal proscription. The War Crimes Tribunal ruled, however, that in certain circumstances those defendants were charged with a duty not to act in accordance with domestic law to avoid liability under international law. Defendants in the case before us stand this doctrine on its head in arguing that a person charged with no duty or responsibility by domestic law may voluntarily violate a criminal law and claim that violation was required to avoid liability

a. For more on the necessity defense and civil disobedience, see Comment, 54 U.Chi.L.Rev. 1070 (1987); Notes, 64 N.Y.U.L.Rev. 79 (1989); 39 Stan.L.Rev. 1173 (1987).

under international law. The domestic law simply did not require defendants to do anything that could even arguably be criminal under international law. The attempt to transfer the Nuremberg defense out of context to the case before us was properly rejected by the district court."

3.   Consider the fact situations set out in the notes following with a view to determining what the boundaries of the necessity defense ought to be. In that connection, compare the defense as defined in *Warshow* with *Model Penal Code* § 3.02 (concerning choice of evils) and with the proposal in Comment, 29 U.C.L.A.L.Rev. 409, 435 (1981), that the defense be reformulated to consist of these three elements: (i) "the result of the criminal act must be the socially desirable outcome" (thus excluding "those fact situations where the alternative outcomes cannot be comparatively measured"); (ii) "the benefit of the criminal act must outweigh the social cost associated with it"; and (iii) "the criminal act need not be the only alternative," just "the least costly alternative."

4.   Debra Braun has been charged with trespass because of her participation with others in a demonstration within the reception area of a health clinic which offers a variety of health care services, including first trimester abortions. Braun has explained that she engaged in this conduct because she wished both "to save the life of unborn fetuses" and "to protect the health and well-being of the women who were going into the Clinic that day for abortions."[b]

5.   An American ship left Liverpool for Philadelphia with a crew of 17 and 65 passengers. The vessel struck an iceberg and began sinking rapidly. The captain, the second mate, 7 crew members and one passenger got into a lowered jolly-boat. The first mate, 8 seamen and 32 passengers got into a long-boat. The remaining 31 passengers went down with the ship. The next morning, the long-boat began to leak, and that night the situation worsened because of wind and rain. Because it appeared the overloaded boat might sink, the crew threw 14 male passengers overboard in response to the first mate's directions that man and wife should not be parted and that women should be spared. The next morning everyone yet on the long-boat was rescued by a passing ship. A member of the crew who participated in these acts was charged with manslaughter.[c]

6.   On Monday, Michel challenged Lindsey to a fight and, when Lindsey declined, charged him with a knife. Lindsey fended Michel off and escaped and then filed a complaint with the police. On Tuesday, Lindsey was told by fellow employees that Michel said he would "get" Lindsey. When Lindsey left for work on Wednesday, he carried a firearm although he was not licensed to do so. Michel approached Lindsey on the street and pulled a knife, and when Michel was six feet away and still advancing, Lindsey drew his gun and fired at Michel. Lindsey has now been charged with unlawfully carrying a firearm.[d]

b. *Sigma Reproductive Health Center v. State,* 297 Md. 660, 467 A.2d 483 (1983), holding the defense of necessity was not available on such facts. See Note, 48 U.Cin.L.Rev. 501 (1979).

c. See *United States v. Holmes,* 26 F.Cas. 360 (No. 15,383) (C.C.E.D.Pa.1842), where the seaman was convicted and sentenced to six months at hard labor and a fine of $20. A petition to Pres. Tyler for a pardon, joined in by the convicting jury, was denied because not joined in by the presiding judges. The seaman served his sentence of imprisonment, but the fine was remitted. See Frederick Hicks, *Human Jettison* 275–76 (1927).

d. *Commonwealth v. Lindsey,* 396 Mass. 840, 489 N.E.2d 666 (1986) (affirming defendant's conviction and mandatory one-year sentence; though it "is possi-

ble that the defendant is alive today only because he carried the gun that day for protection," necessity instruction properly refused, for were the court "to establish an exception * * * for an unlicensed person to carry a firearm in public if he reasonably believed he was likely to be threatened with serious bodily harm," this "would exonerate every unlicensed person who wants to carry a gun. Such a person wants to carry a gun precisely because he fears that at some time he might be threatened with serious bodily injury"). Compare *State v. Crawford,* 308 Md. 683, 521 A.2d 1193 (1987) (necessity instruction required re charge of unlawful possession of handgun where defendant testified that after being attacked and shot in his apartment he wrestled the gun away and in doing so fell out the window onto the street and then, upon hearing foot-

7.   Theodore Patrick, charged with kidnapping, "was contacted by a group of parents who believed their daughters were members of a 'dangerous religious cult,' and, at a meeting with the parents on July 16, 1973, defendant agreed to 'deprogram' the women. Later defendant came to Denver and, as a result of arrangements made by the parents previously, on August 23, 1973, drove one of the parents' cars to the parking lot of a medical center in Denver, where Dena Thomas (age 21) worked. While Dena Thomas and Kathy Markis (age 23) were attempting to drive out of the parking lot in their automobile, defendant effectively blocked their exit with the car he was driving. This made it possible for Dena's father, (who had been chasing the women's car on foot) to unlock the door of the women's car, and, together with Kathy's father, to push their way into the car and drive the women away without their consent. The young women were driven to Eldorado Springs, Colorado, where they were detained for two days, while defendant undertook his 'deprogramming' procedure."[e]

8.   Joseph Hutchins, charged with of possession or cultivation of marijuana, is "a forty-seven year old man who has been diagnosed as having scleroderma accompanied by Raynaud's phenomenon, related to his service in the Navy. Scleroderma is a chronic disease that results in the buildup of scar tissue throughout the body. The cause of scleroderma is not known and no effective treatment or cure has been discovered. In the most severe cases, scleroderma may result in death. The defendant's medical history includes episodes of fatigue, hypertension, loss of appetite, weight loss of up to twenty-five pounds, diarrhea, nausea, vomiting, reflux of food and stomach acid into the mouth, reduced motility and constriction of the esophagus, extreme difficulty and pain in swallowing, and swollen, painful joints and extreme sensitivity to the cold in his hands and feet. * * * The defendant has informed his treating physicians that since 1975, with some success, he has used marihuana, in lieu of antidepressants and surgery, to alleviate certain symptoms of his illness including nausea, loss of appetite, difficulty in eating, drinking or swallowing, loss of motility of the esophagus, spasticity, hypertension, and anxiety. Two of his treating physicians state that, although they are unable to 'confirm [the defendant's] claim that his use of mari[h]uana has caused his remarkable remission, . . . it does appear that his use of mari[h]uana does alleviate the previously mentioned symptoms.' * * * The Massachusetts Legislature has considered a bill providing for the use of marihuana in therapeutic research on more than one occasion, but no such statute has been enacted in the Commonwealth."[f]

9.   Harry Leno has been charged with sixty-five counts of unauthorized possession of hypodermic needles and fifty-two counts of unauthorized possession of syringes. He "is a fifty-five year old grandfather, who * * * learned of needle exchange programs from a National AIDS Brigade lecturer. Leno worked for needle exchange programs in Boston, in New Haven, Connecticut, and in New York City. Leno started a needle exchange program in Lynn in September, 1990, after realizing that 'in my own back yard . . . people were dying of AIDS . . . and this particular service was not offered to them.' [He] offered expert

steps approaching picked up the gun to defend himself).

e.   *People v. Patrick,* 541 P.2d 320 (Colo.App.1975), holding the trial court properly refused to instruct on a choice of evils defense. Compare *United States v. Patrick,* 532 F.2d 142 (9th Cir.1976) (trial judge found defendant not guilty on ground parents had reasonable belief their daughter in danger and that they not able to recapture her alone, so their necessity defense could be claimed by their agent Patrick). See Note, 80 Mich. L.Rev. 271 (1981).

f.   *Commonwealth v. Hutchins,* 410 Mass. 726, 575 N.E.2d 741 (1991), where the court, in upholding the trial court's refusal to instruct on medical necessity, explained that "the alleviation of the defendant's medical symptoms, the importance to the defendant of which we do not underestimate, would not clearly and significantly outweigh the potential harm to the public were we to declare that the defendant's cultivation of marihuana and its use for his medicinal purposes may not be punishable." Compare *State v. Diana,* 24 Wash. App. 908, 604 P.2d 1312 (1979), and see Note, 46 Geo.Wash.L.Rev. 273 (1978).

testimony on AIDS and needle exchange programs [to the effect] that: the sharing of needles by infected drug users transmits the AIDS virus; the mortality rate of persons diagnosed with human immunodeficiency virus (HIV) ten years ago is very high, in that fewer than five per cent still are alive; there is no cure for AIDS; studies of needle exchange programs revealed no evidence that such programs cause people who are not drug addicts to become addicts, but that evidence indicates that needle exchange programs bring some addicts into drug and AIDS treatment programs who would not otherwise be there."[g]

10. Ronald Cooley escaped with others from the District of Columbia jail by crawling through a window from which a bar had been removed and then sliding down a knotted bedsheet. He later explained that he escaped because of prison conditions. "Construed in the light most favorable to [him], this evidence demonstrated that the inmates of Northeast One, and on occasion the guards in that unit, set fire to trash, bedding, and other objects thrown from the cells. According to the inmates, the guards simply allowed the fires to burn until they went out. Although the fires apparently were confined to small areas and posed no substantial threat of spreading through the complex, poor ventilation caused smoke to collect and linger in the cellblock." Cooley was apprehended a month after his escape. He "testified that his 'people' had tried to contact the authorities, but 'never got in touch with anybody,' "and suggested his sister had been told the FBI would kill him when he was apprehended.[h]

UNITED STATES v. LAFLEUR

United States Court of Appeals, Ninth Circuit, 1991.

971 F.2d 200.

WIGGINS, CIRCUIT JUDGE. * * *

On January 10, 1989, Otto Bloomquist, an eighty-two-year-old man, drove with his wife to a shopping mall in Carlsbad, California, to have lunch. Bloomquist, who had approximately $300 in cash in his possession, waited in his car while his wife entered the mall to shop before lunch. The appellants, Larry LaFleur and Nick Holm, approached Bloomquist's car and, each displaying the gun he was carrying, forced Bloomquist to relinquish control of the vehicle. With LaFleur driving and Holm keeping Bloomquist at gun point, the car left the parking lot.

LaFleur drove the car to a remote area known as De Luz Canyon, which is part of the Camp Pendleton military base. After exiting the car, the three men walked down a deserted path and LaFleur and Holm killed Bloomquist by shooting him several times. It is undisputed that both men shot Bloomquist. LaFleur fired the first several shots, and then Holm shot Bloomquist in the back and head. However, there was conflicting testimony regarding the specific circumstances surrounding the shooting of Bloomquist. Each appellant claims both that the other initiated the killing, and that he committed the crime only under duress, alleging that the other forced him at gunpoint to shoot Bloomquist.

g. *Commonwealth v. Leno*, 415 Mass. 835, 616 N.E.2d 453 (1993), where court, in upholding the trial judge's denial of a necessity instruction, explained: "The prevention of possible future harm does not excuse a current systematic violation of the law in anticipation of the eventual over-all benefit to the public. * * * That some States prohibit the distribution of hypodermic needles without a prescription, and others do not, merely indicates that the best course to

take to address the long-term hazard of the spread of AIDS remains a matter of debate."

h. *United States v. Bailey*, 444 U.S. 394, 100 S.Ct. 624, 62 L.Ed.2d 575 (1980), holding such evidence insufficient to require an instruction on the necessity defense. See George Fletcher, *Should Intolerable Prison Conditions Generate a Justification or an Excuse for Escape?*, 26 U.C.L.A.L.Rev. 1355 (1979).

LaFleur and Holm were indicted on January 26, 1989 for a host of counts encompassing the murder, kidnapping, and robbery of Bloomquist. The district court granted a defense motion to have the trials of LaFleur and Holm severed. LaFleur's trial began on June 20, 1989. The next day, Holm entered a guilty plea to premeditated murder, and the remaining charges against him were dropped. LaFleur's trial ended on July 7, 1989 when the jury returned a guilty verdict on all counts. He was convicted of premeditated murder, felony murder, conspiracy to kidnap, kidnapping, robbery, use of a firearm during murder, use of a firearm during kidnapping, and use of a firearm during robbery. Both men were sentenced pursuant to 18 U.S.C. § 1111(b) to life in prison for the murder of Bloomquist. In addition, LaFleur received sentences for his other crimes. * * *

Appellant LaFleur contends that the district court erred by refusing to instruct the jury on voluntary manslaughter. LaFleur argued at trial that he participated in the murder only as a result of duress inflicted by Holm, who allegedly held LaFleur at gunpoint and forced him to shoot Bloomquist. LaFleur contends that such duress legally mitigates murder to voluntary manslaughter, and that he was therefore entitled to a voluntary manslaughter instruction. * * * We are, therefore, confronted with a legal question: whether or not duress is a valid defense to murder under 18 U.S.C. § 1111(a) such that it mitigates murder to voluntary manslaughter. This is an issue of first impression * * *.

When a defendant commits a criminal act under the direct threat of another person, he commits the crime under duress. The duress defense, which provides the defendant a legal excuse for the commission of the criminal act, is based on the rationale that a person, when confronted with two evils, should not be punished for engaging in the lesser of the evils.[3] LaFave and Scott aptly describe the defense as follows:

> One who, under the pressure of an unlawful threat from another human being to harm him ... , commits what would otherwise be a crime may, under some circumstances, be justified in doing what he did and thus not be guilty of the crime in question.... The rationale of the defense is not that the defendant, faced with the unnerving threat of harm unless he does an act which violates the literal language of the criminal law, somehow loses his mental capacity to commit the crime in question. Nor is it that the defendant has not engaged in a voluntary act. Rather it is that, even though he has done the act the crime requires and has the mental state which the crime requires, his conduct which violates the literal language of the criminal law is justified because he has thereby avoided a harm of greater magnitude.

The "choice of evils" rationale for the duress defense is strained when a defendant is confronted with taking the life of an innocent third person in the face of a threat on his own life. The choice of evils rationale necessarily presumes that the threatened harm to the defendant is greater than the resulting harm from the defendant's commission of the crime. When the defendant commits murder under duress, the resulting harm—i.e. the death of an innocent person—is at least as great as the threatened harm—i.e. the death of the defendant. For this reason, the common law rejected duress as a defense to murder.

Our review of state law indicates that the majority of states considering the issue have adopted the common law rule.

---

3. The duress defense consists of three elements: 1) an immediate threat of death or serious bodily injury; 2) a well-founded fear that the threat will be carried out; and 3) no reasonable opportunity to escape the threatened harm. A fourth element is sometimes required, namely, that the defendant submit to the authorities after the threat dissipates.

The duress defense is related to the necessity defense (necessity defense traditionally involves natural physical forces beyond the actor's control whereas duress defense involves coercion from another human being).

We are persuaded that duress is not a valid defense to § 1111(a) first degree murder. We believe that, consistent with the common law rule, a defendant should not be excused from taking the life of an innocent third person because of the threat of harm to himself. This, however, does not directly answer the question before us. LaFleur argues essentially that, even if duress is not a complete defense to § 1111(a) murder, it can act to mitigate murder to voluntary manslaughter.[5] We have found no compelling authority for LaFleur's proposition, and, after careful consideration, we reject it. We hold that duress cannot legally mitigate murder to manslaughter. The same rationale which dictates that duress is not a complete defense to murder demands that duress not be used by a defendant to mitigate the intentional killing of an innocent third person. Therefore, the district court did not err in denying LaFleur's request for a manslaughter instruction. * * *

Notes and Questions

1. Consider Alan Reed, *Duress and Provocation as Excuses to Murder: Salutary Lessons from Recent Anglo–American Jurisprudence*, 6 J.Trans.L. & Pol'y 51, 59–61 (1996): "The most significant difference between the common law and the Model Penal Code is that the Model Penal Code allows duress as a defense, even for murder.[58] Additionally, the Model Penal Code vastly enhances the jury's role in the determination of the excuse. Under the Model Penal Code, the jury must consider 'whether the hypothetical "person of reasonable firmness" would have resisted the threat.' * * * The material part of the Model Penal Code [test has] unfortunately [been] adopted by only a minority of states * * *.

"Unfortunately, the majority of American jurisdictions still apply the common law, which is predicated on the presence of a deadly threat, an objective standard, and an intolerance for the defense of duress in cases involving any form of homicide or attempted murder. In Oklahoma, however, the case of *Tully v. State*[66] provides a rare exception. Therein, an appellate court allowed duress as a defense in a felony-murder case. This decision and its rationale demand closer attention, especially considering the extremely limited number of cases accepting duress as a defense to felony-murder before *Tully*.

"In *Tully*, the duressor coerced the defendant by threatening him with a baseball bat if he did not participate in the robbery of a stricken victim. The defendant contended that he had initially refused this demand and that his eventual participation had occurred because he had no valid choice to do otherwise. On appeal, the defendant claimed that the trial court's lacuna in failing to give the jury any instruction about duress constituted a reversible error. The appellate court categorically agreed and refuted the common law principle that a defendant should die rather than kill a wholly innocent victim in the case of felony murder."

Can *LaFleur* be squared with *Tully*?

2. Consider next Joshua Dressler, *Exegesis of the Law of Duress: Justifying the Excuse and Searching for its Proper Limits*, 62 So.Cal.L.Rev. 1331, 1370–74 (1989): "Stemming from antiquity, the nearly 'unbroken tradition' of Anglo–American common law is that duress never excuses murder, that the person threatened with his own demise 'ought rather to die himself, than escape by the murder of an innocent.' Indeed, one recent English judicial venture from this traditional path[208] in which the House of Lords permitted

---

5. LaFleur points us to three states, Arizona, Minnesota, and Wisconsin, which have, in some form, adopted the proposition that duress can mitigate murder to something less than murder. See Ariz.Rev.Stat. Ann. § 13–1103; Minn.Stat.Ann. § 609.20; Wis.Stat. Ann. 940.05.

58. Model Penal Code § 2.09(1) (1985).

66. 730 P.2d 1206 (Okla.Crim.App.1986).

208. D.P.P. v. Lynch, 1975 App. Cas. 653.

the defense to be pled by an accomplice to a murder was recently overruled.[209] And, although the MPC would abrogate the common law rule, most statutory authority in this country runs contrary to reform.

"We ought to be respectful of such common law tradition and not assume that centuries of nearly consistent rejection of the duress defense in murder cases is self-evidently wrong, 'obsolescent or inhumane or unjust.' The burden is placed correctly on those who would allow the defense to murder. Nonetheless, and despite my earlier published reservations on the subject, I am now satisfied that the American Law Institute was correct in rejecting the common law no-homicide rule.

"Utilitarian reasoning, although not without dissenters, probably supports the excuse. But, in this context, as with excuses in general, the argument of utility 'smells of the lamp.' The question is more properly framed as an issue of just deserts: Does a person always deserve to be punished as murderer if he kills another innocent individual as the result of coercion? While the common law punishes in these instances, the underlying basis for this position almost certainly is the Kanitan moral principle that 'a human being can never be manipulated merely as a means to the purposes of someone else.... His innate personality that is, his right as a person protects him against such treatment....'

"The moral imperative against killing innocent persons was evident in the recent House of Lords opinion reaffirming the common law rule. In the most significant opinion, Lord Hailsham described the common law rule as 'good morals' and categorically rejected the conclusion 'that the law must "move with the times" in order to keep pace with the immense political and social changes since what are alleged to have been the bad old days of Blackstone and Hale.' At least for this Lord, the question of excusing a coerced killer should not be determined by juries deciding moral deserts on a case-by-case basis. As he put it, 'the question is not one of the reliability of juries. It is one of principle.'

"The difficulty with Hailsham's reasoning is not with the moral principle he reveres, but with its relevance to the question at hand. His essential point is that Kant's imperative against killing innocents is (or should be) as powerful today as it was in the past. But this position only demonstrates that such homicides are as wrong, as unjustifiable, today as in earlier times. By this he has only 'proven' that those who accept the categorical imperative should reject modern departures from the imperative, such as the MPC's version of the necessity justification defense,[218] as well as its apparent justification of self-defense against morally innocent aggressors.[219]

"But, since duress is an excuse rather than a justification, the real issue (it bears repeating with some additional emphasis) is whether a coerced person who unjustifiably violates the moral principle necessarily, unalterably, and unfailingly deserves to be punished as a murderer, as the common law insists. If a murderer were insane, involuntarily intoxicated, or especially young, society would not necessarily, unalterably, and unfailingly demand punishment. These excuses affirm the moral imperative, but render the actor blameless who violates it. Why treat duress differently?

"Admittedly, duress is unlike these other excuses because it is a normative defense. A reasoned advocate of the common law rule can, therefore, assert that as a matter of principle there always is a fair opportunity to avoid killing another person, regardless of the coercive circumstances. Although there is no way to disclaim the plausibility of this

209. Regina v. Howe, [1987] 2 W.L.R. 568.

218. Model Penal Code § 3.02 (1985). * * *

219. See Model Penal Code §§ 3.04(1) (general self-defense provision, justifying the use of force as is immediately necessary to repel unlawful force), 3.11(1) (defining 'unlawful force' to include force which would constitute a tort of criminal offense except for a defense, such as insanity or infancy) (1985). * * *

position, I reject it. I am afraid that such a rule, like Lord Hailsham's opinion, has the imprint of self-righteousness, which the law should avoid. The rule asks us to be virtuous; more accurately, it demands our virtual saintliness, which the law has no right to require. It is precisely in the case of kill-or-be-killed threats that the criminal law ought to be prepared in some cases to attempt to assuage the guilt feelings of the homicidal wrongdoer by excusing him—by reminding him that he acted no less valiantly than any person of reasonable moral strength would have done.

"I am not suggesting that all coerced homicides should be excused. The desirability of the MPC approach is that the excusing decision is made by the jury on a contextual basis. It is realistic to believe that juries will not excuse all coerced killers. It is not inherently implausible to contend that persons of reasonable moral strength will accede to some, but not all, homicides.

"For example, juries would probably excuse many coerced accomplices to murders, especially those whose participation in the crime was relatively minor, while usually punishing triggermen. Society also has a right to expect a person to demonstrate a higher level of moral strength when ordered to kill a hundred innocent children than when commanded to kill one. A jury might also rightly expect people to manifest the utmost moral strength—even, at some point, to chose death—when they have reason to known that they are playing a part, even a minor role, in an especially barbaric scenario, such as the Holocaust. But there is a far more compelling reason to support the MPC. Once one realizes, as Lord Hailsham may not, that the issue with duress is desert of punishment and not justification of the act, the jury is an especially suitable institution to determine whether and when coercion excuses."

3. As Reed, supra Note 1, observes at 66, "English courts have never expressly recognized a general defense of necessity, where an individual commits an offense to avoid the greater evil to himself or another that would occur from the dangerous circumstances in which he or the other person is placed." In the *Lynch* case, cited in the previous Reed excerpt, Lord Simon reasoned:

"[The concept of] *necessity* came to be used, most misleadingly, to denote a situation where circumstances faced a person, not with no choice at all, but with the choice between two evils; so that he could hardly be blamed if he chose the lesser. The classic case was the pulling down of another man's house to prevent a fire spreading. * * * But it has been decisively rejected in the criminal law generally. It is certainly not the law that what would otherwise be the theft of a loaf ceases to be criminal if the taker is starving.[a] Morally, there is a world of difference between a man who steals to satisfy his children's hunger and a man who steals to satisfy his own cupidity; but the moral distinction is marked, not by the provision of some eccentric defence in the positive law, but by the discretion of the court in its sentence. And Bacon's 'necessity of conservation of life,' with his example of the 'necessity' of pushing a shipwrecked man off a boat's side in order to secure his place, was

---

a. In *State v. Moe*, 174 Wash. 303, 24 P.2d 638 (1933), the unemployed defendants were convicted of grand larceny and riot for taking groceries from a store. They were not allowed to prove the conditions of poverty under which they were living. The court affirmed, noting:

"Economic necessity has never been accepted as a defense to a criminal charge. The reason is that, were it ever countenanced, it would leave to the individual the right to take the law into his own hands. In larceny cases economic necessity is frequently invoked in mitigation of punishment, but has never been recognized as a defense. Nor is it available as a defense to the charge of riot. The fact that a riot is spontaneous makes it none the less premeditated. Premeditation may and frequently does, arise on the instant. A lawful assembly may turn into a riotous one in a moment of time over trivial incident or substantial provocation. When it does, those participating are guilty of riot, and neither the cause of the riot nor their reason for participation in it can be interposed as a defense. The causes, great or small, are available to the participants only in mitigation of punishment. The court did not err in rejecting the offer of proof."

called in aid on behalf of the appellants in the famous and terrible case of *Reg. v. Dudley and Stephens,* 14 Q.B.D. 273. The two accused were in a ship's boat without food or water; they killed and ate the ship's boy, who was with them. The accused would otherwise probably have died before they were picked up, and the boy would probably have died before them. At the time of the homicide there was no appreciable chance of saving life except by killing someone for the others to eat. Their conviction for murder was upheld on appeal,[b] though the sentence was respited.

"Attempts have been made to explain this case away; but the appellants' argument rested on Bacon's 'necessity of conservation of life'; and the rejection of any such doctrine was, in my view, the ratio decidendi. Unless some distinction can be drawn in principle between 'necessity' and duress as defences to a charge of murder, the instant appellant can, I think, only succeed if *Reg. v. Dudley and Stephens* is overruled—unless, indeed, a distinction is to be drawn in these regards between principals in the first and second degrees."

Is this to say that consistency requires the same result in *LaFleur* and in *Dudley and Stephens*? If not, who is the better candidate for either leniency or exoneration, Mr. LaFleur or the sailors?

4. American case law generally states the defense of duress in narrow terms, so that it "does not excuse taking the life of an innocent person"[c] and excuses lesser crimes only if the coercion is "present, imminent, and impending and of such a nature as to induce a well grounded apprehension of death or serious bodily injury if the act is not done" and if in addition the actor had no "reasonable opportunity to avoid doing the act without undue exposure to death or serious bodily injury." *State v. St. Clair,* 262 S.W.2d 25 (Mo.1953). In *State v. Dissicini,* 126 N.J.Super. 565, 316 A.2d 12 (1974), the contention that the defense should be available to one who aided and abetted a killing was summarily dismissed "because the argument has little merit."

Model Penal Code § 2.09 states the defense somewhat more broadly, and comparable provisions are to be found in some of the modern codes. Even where such provisions are lacking, courts have sometimes been influenced by the Model Penal Code approach. Illustrative is *State v. Toscano,* 74 N.J. 421, 378 A.2d 755 (1977), where the defendant, charged with conspiracy to obtain money by false pretenses, testified that he prepared a fraudulent insurance claim after being directed to do so by one Leonardo, who threatened him several times over the telephone. The trial judge refused to charge the jury on the defense of duress because there had been no showing of a "present, imminent and impending" threat of harm. Reversing, the court concluded that "a per se rule based on immediate injury may exclude valid claims of duress by persons for whom resistance to threats or resort to official protection was not realistic," and ruled that henceforth "duress shall be a defense to a crime other than murder if the defendant engaged in conduct because he was coerced to do so by the use of, or threat to use, unlawful force against his person or the person of another, which a person of reasonable firmness in his situation would have been unable to resist."

---

b. In that case, Lord Coleridge, C.J., stated:

"It must not be supposed that in refusing to admit temptation to be an excuse for crime it is forgotten how terrible the temptation was; how awful the suffering; how hard in such trials to keep the judgment straight and the conduct pure. We are often compelled to set up standards we cannot reach ourselves, and to lay down rules which we could not ourselves satisfy. But a man

has no right to declare temptation to be an excuse, though he might himself have yielded to it, nor allow compassion for the criminal to change or weaken in any manner the legal definition of the crime."

c. From this perspective, consider again the ducking-shielding distinction drawn in the material quoted in Note 6 at p. 220 of this Book.

Consider the fact situations set out in notes 5 through 9 below with a view to determining what the boundaries any defense grounded in the coercion of another ought to be.

5. Knapp was riding with Stratton and Thompson in Stratton's car. Stratton assaulted the driver of another car, and the victim's car was then taken to a remote area. Stratton sent Knapp in his car to a nearby town to obtain tools to aid in stripping the car. When Knapp returned, the stripping was nearly completed. The items were then loaded into Stratton's car; Stratton later dropped Knapp off at home with the stolen car stereo. Knapp, charged with larceny, testified that he participated in the larceny "because he feared what Stratton would do to him if he refused," a fear which "even extended to the moment when Stratton dropped the defendant off at home with the stolen car stereo."[d]

6. Unger, who was serving a term of 1 to 3 years in the state penitentiary, was charged with the crime of escape. At trial, he "testified that at some time during the first two months of his imprisonment, while he was working in the clothing room, he was threatened by an inmate who possessed a 6–inch knife and defendant was told he would be required to engage in homosexual activity with the inmate. Defendant requested and received a transfer to the minimum security honor farm where, one week later, on March 2, 1972, he was beaten and forcibly sexually assaulted by a gang of prisoners. In his testimony he named three of the assailants. He stated that he did not tell the authorities about the incident because he was told he would be killed if he did so and was afraid he would be killed. Several days following the attack, on March 7, 1972, he received a phone call in the evening while working at the dairy farm. The caller (whose voice he did not recognize) informed him that he would be killed that evening as the caller had heard that defendant had gone to the authorities about the sexual assault and the beating. After receiving the call, Unger walked off the dairy farm. He was apprehended two days later in a motel room in St. Charles, Illinois. He was still wearing his prison clothes. He stated in his testimony that he left the honor farm in fear of his life and intended to return to the institution."[e]

7. Francese and Tripodi, engaged in illegal gambling activities, have been charged with bribery of members of the city gambling squad. They "testified that they were fearful of legal reprisals from the police should they fail to pay them. Francese testified that one of the [officers] threatened to plant incriminating evidence on him if he stopped paying. When he did cease his payments, the police raided his establishment five times in succession, sometimes without a warrant. He testified that he was also beaten by the police for having stopped the payments. Once, when Tripodi would not pay off on a bet allegedly placed by Detective Court (but denied by Tripodi), the gambling squad parked its van in front of Tripodi's store, obviously to deter any gambling operations thereat, until he relented and paid Detective Court $1,000. This Tripodi believed, was the kind of occurrence which he was paying to prevent. Once, when he was raided, he approached Detectives Bradford and Weber to ascertain the reason therefor—as he had been making his payments. He was informed that the gambling squad had not initiated the raid. All of the gamblers involved herein recognized that if they did not pay they would be harassed and put out of business by the police."[f]

d. *State v. Knapp*, 147 Vt. 56, 509 A.2d 1010 (1986), holding defendant was not entitled to a duress instruction.

e. In *People v. Unger*, 33 Ill.App.3d 770, 338 N.E.2d 442 (1975), aff'd 66 Ill.2d 333, 5 Ill.Dec. 848, 362 N.E.2d 319 (1977), the defendant's conviction was reversed. The court held it was error for the trial judge to instruct that the reasons given for the escape were immaterial and not to be considered as justifying or excusing the escape.

f. Cf. *People v. Court*, 52 A.D.2d 891, 383 N.Y.S.2d 66 (1976), where the defendants were the police, charged with receiving the bribes. The court ruled that the situation "reeks with coercion" and that conse-

8. "On August 10, 1971 defendant, then 19 years-of-age, while at the Green Isle Bar in the company of his brother, witnessed a murder. Notwithstanding the fact that there were 30 other patrons in the bar at the time of the shooting, defendant emerged as the sole eyewitness. All the other patrons claimed they had not witnessed the incident.

"Defendant appeared before the Grand Jury on September 8, 1971 and testified that a man known to him as Ricciardi (alias Tony Long) took out a pistol, shot one Reda, and then left the tavern.

"From the time of his Grand Jury testimony and continuing up to February, 1973, defendant intermittently received threats against his own life and well-being as well as against his family. He relayed the threats to the office of the District Attorney, advised the District Attorney that he was unwilling to identify Ricciardi as the killer and voiced his intention of leaving the jurisdiction.

"Forthwith, the District Attorney had him arrested as a material witness and confined to jail on high bail. Defendant remained in jail for approximately one month, unable to furnish the bail set. During his confinement he changed his mind and indicated his willingness to cooperate with the prosecution and to testify in accordance with his testimony before the Grand Jury. Thereupon his bail was reduced and, by the posting of $2,000 cash, his father effected his release.

"On April 18, 1973 defendant importuned both the District Attorney and the Trial Judge that he not be forced to testify against Ricciardi as he feared for his life. Notwithstanding such request, defendant was sworn. In essence he recanted his Grand Jury testimony. Thereupon the trial court granted an order of dismissal and released Ricciardi. Based on defendant's trial testimony, he was indicted for perjury."[g]

9. "Mrs. Stevison (appellant) was cashier of the Bank of Sesser, in Sesser, Illinois, for more than 25 years. In the period from May 12 to October 10, 1970, her daughter wrote 48 checks—ranging in amounts from $100 to $20,000—drawn on the Sesser Bank against her account. The account had insufficient funds to cover the checks. Her daughter drew three other checks against an account of the fictitious Indiana and Kentucky Health Care Development, an account maintained at another bank, payable to herself which the appellant cashed at the Sesser Bank when the account of the Health Care Development had insufficient funds to cover the checks. All of the checks drawn on the Sesser Bank account, amounting to $52,800, were paid by appellant from the Sesser Bank's cash items and deducted by her from undivided profits. * * * She asserts that her daughter 'coerced' her into covering the overdrafts by threatening to commit suicide."[h]

10. Under the common law doctrine of "coverture," when a married woman engaged in criminal conduct in her husband's presence, there arose a rebuttable presumption that the wife had been coerced by her husband. Most jurisdictions now reject this doctrine as "outdated and inapplicable to modern society." *Commonwealth v. Santiago*, 462 Pa. 216,

---

quently the gamblers were not accomplices of the police, so that an indictment based upon the gamblers' testimony alone was valid.

g. In *People v. Colgan*, 50 A.D.2d 932, 377 N.Y.S.2d 602 (1975), the conviction was reversed because defendant had not been allowed to introduce evidence bearing upon the defense of duress. Compare *People v. Carradine*, 52 Ill.2d 231, 287 N.E.2d 670 (1972), affirming a contempt citation against a woman who refused to testify about a homicide she had witnessed because she feared retaliation by members of the Blackstone Rangers, a youth gang. As for the prosecutor's offer of protection, she testified: "Well, look, Judge, I am going

to tell you, I live in the middle of the slums, down in the slums. Where I live the police don't even come in there even if we call. I called the police one night about a fight. You'd think they were going to kill one another. But the police don't even come up in there where I live. So how are they going to protect me and my family when they don't even come up in the building where we live?"

h. *United States v. Stevison*, 471 F.2d 143 (7th Cir.1972), holding the trial court did not unduly limit development of the coercion defense.

340 A.2d 440 (1975). Compare *Goodwin v. State,* 506 P.2d 571 (Okl.Cr.1973), retaining the coverture doctrine but concluding that "the presumption is slight and may be rebutted by slight circumstances."

11. The battered woman syndrome, evidence of which has often been received as relevant to a claim of self-defense (see the *Bechtel* case, p. 506 of this Book, and notes following), has not fared as well with respect to the defense of duress. Rather typical is *United States v. Willis*, 38 F.3d 170 (5th Cir.1994), holding "that such evidence is not relevant. This is because in order for a duress defense to criminal liability to succeed, the coercive force of the threat must be sufficient such that a person of ordinary firmness would succumb. *Model Penal Code* § 2.09. Additionally, there must be no reasonable legal alternative to violating the law. These requirements set out an objective test. To consider battered woman's syndrome evidence in applying that test, however, would be to turn the objective inquiry that duress has always required into a subjective one. The question would no longer be whether a person of ordinary firmness could have resisted. Instead, the question would change to whether this individual woman, in light of the psychological condition from which she suffers, could have resisted. In addition to being contrary to settled duress law, we conclude that such a change would be unwise. Accordingly, while evidence that a defendant is suffering from the battered woman's syndrome provokes our sympathy, it is not relevant, for purposes of determining criminal responsibility, to whether the defendant acted under duress."

One of the cases relied upon in *Willis* is *United States v. Johnson*, 956 F.2d 894 (9th Cir.1992), which, upon closer inspection does not appear to support the result in *Willis*. The fact of the matter is that in *Johnson* battered woman syndrome evidence *was* admitted by the trial court, and the appellate court does not say that was in error, but instead notes that the jury's failure nonetheless to accept defendant's duress defense might have been grounded in doubts about the credibility of defendant's testimony. The court in *Johnson* then proceeds to address another point, which is that even if in such a case the duress defense did not prevail with the jury, the federal sentencing guidelines provide for the possibility of downward departure if the defendant "committed the offense because of serious coercion, blackmail or duress, under circumstances not amounting to a complete defense" (U.S.S.G. § 5K2.12). Perhaps more significant, however, is the observation in *Johnson* that battered woman syndrome evidence is accepted in self-defense cases, immediately followed with this:

"The defense has a particular relation to the defense of duress as it has been expanded by the commentary to the Model Penal Code. The Model Penal Code itself, as has already been remarked, uses a person of ordinary firmness as the measure of duress but its commentary expands the defense to encompass a case where 'by the continued use of unlawful force, persons effectively break down the personality of the actor, rendering him [or her] submissive to whatever suggestions they make. They then, using neither force nor threat of force on that occasion suggest that he [or she] perform a criminal act; and the actor does what they suggest.' Id. § 2.09, comment 3. A leading authority on the common law has added that the defense applies when the defendant is so far 'in thrall to some power' that a legal sanction would be ineffective in controlling any choice that may be made. Glanville Williams, *Criminal Law: The General Part*, 755–62 (2nd ed. 1961). The commentary to the Model Penal Code repeats Williams' language without disapproval. *Model Penal Code* § 2.09 n. 40. This substantial expansion of the defense may go too far if not linked to gross and identifiable classes of circumstances. Battered women are in circumstances forming such a class."[i]

---

i. See also Comment, 85 Calif.L.Rev. 993 (1997) (noting that while duress used a purely objective approach to reasonableness while self-defense uses a hybrid objective/subjective approach to reasonableness,

SECTION 7. CONSENT AND CONDONATION

WASHINGTON v. GLUCKSBERG

Supreme Court of the United States, 1997.

521 U.S. 702, 117 S.Ct. 2258, 138 L.Ed.2d 772.

CHIEF JUSTICE REHNQUIST delivered the opinion of the Court.

The question presented in this case is whether Washington's prohibition against "caus[ing]" or "aid[ing]" a suicide offends the Fourteenth Amendment to the United States Constitution. We hold that it does not.

* * * Washington law provides: "A person is guilty of promoting a suicide attempt when he knowingly causes or aids another person to attempt suicide." "Promoting a suicide attempt" is a felony, punishable by up to five years' imprisonment and up to a $10,000 fine. At the same time, Washington's Natural Death Act, enacted in 1979, states that the "withholding or withdrawal of life-sustaining treatment" at a patient's direction "shall not, for any purpose, constitute a suicide."

[The respondents, physicians who practice in Washington and who occasionally treat terminally ill, sued in the United States District Court, seeking a declaration that the above-quoted statute is, on its face, unconstitutional. They asserted "the existence of a liberty interest protected by the Fourteenth Amendment which extends to a personal choice by a mentally competent, terminally ill adult to commit physician-assisted suicide." The District Court agreed, and the Ninth Circuit affirmed.]

We begin, as we do in all due process cases, by examining our Nation's history, legal traditions, and practices. In almost every State—indeed, in almost every western democracy—it is a crime to assist a suicide.[g] The States' assisted-suicide bans are not innovations. Rather, they are longstanding expressions of the States' commitment to the protection and preservation of all human life. Indeed, opposition to and condemnation of suicide—and, therefore, of assisting suicide—are consistent and enduring themes of our philosophical, legal, and cultural heritages.

More specifically, for over 700 years, the Anglo–American common-law tradition has punished or otherwise disapproved of both suicide and assisting suicide. * * *.

That suicide remained a grievous, though nonfelonious, wrong is confirmed by the fact that colonial and early state legislatures and courts did not retreat from prohibiting assisting suicide. * * * And the prohibitions against assisting suicide never contained exceptions for those who were near death. * * *

The earliest American statute explicitly to outlaw assisting suicide was enacted in New York in 1828, and many of the new States and Territories followed New York's example. * * * By the time the Fourteenth Amendment was ratified, it was a crime in most States to assist a suicide. * * * In this century, the Model Penal Code [§ 210.5] also prohibited "aiding" suicide, prompting many States to enact or revise their assisted-suicide bans. The

and concluding that there is no logical basis for applying different standards of reasonableness to these doctrines and that therefore duress should adopt a hybrid approach as well, thus ensuring admission of battered woman syndrome evidence); Comment, 70 Temple L.Rev. 699 (1997); Note, 1994 U.Ill.L.Rev. 955.

g. See *Compassion in Dying v. Washington*, 79 F.3d 790, 847, and nn. 10–13 (C.A.9 1996) (Beezer, J., dissenting) ("In total, forty-four states, the District of Columbia and two territories prohibit or condemn assisted suicide") * * *.

code's drafters observed that "the interests in the sanctity of life that are represented by the criminal homicide laws are threatened by one who expresses a willingness to participate in taking the life of another, even though the act may be accomplished with the consent, or at the request, of the suicide victim."

Though deeply rooted, the States' assisted-suicide bans have in recent years been reexamined and, generally, reaffirmed. Because of advances in medicine and technology, Americans today are increasingly likely to die in institutions, from chronic illnesses. Public concern and democratic action are therefore sharply focused on how best to protect dignity and independence at the end of life, with the result that there have been many significant changes in state laws and in the attitudes these laws reflect. Many States, for example, now permit "living wills," surrogate health-care decisionmaking, and the withdrawal or refusal of life-sustaining medical treatment. At the same time, however, voters and legislators continue for the most part to reaffirm their States' prohibitions on assisting suicide. * * *

Attitudes toward suicide itself have changed since Bracton, but our laws have consistently condemned, and continue to prohibit, assisting suicide. Despite changes in medical technology and notwithstanding an increased emphasis on the importance of end-of-life decisionmaking, we have not retreated from this prohibition. Against this backdrop of history, tradition, and practice, we now turn to respondents' constitutional claim.

The Due Process Clause guarantees more than fair process, and the "liberty" it protects includes more than the absence of physical restraint. The Clause also provides heightened protection against government interference with certain fundamental rights and liberty interests. In a long line of cases, we have held that, in addition to the specific freedoms protected by the Bill of Rights, the "liberty" specially protected by the Due Process Clause includes the rights to marry, to have children, to direct the education and upbringing of one's children; to marital privacy, to use contraception, to bodily integrity, and to abortion. We have also assumed, and strongly suggested, that the Due Process Clause protects the traditional right to refuse unwanted lifesaving medical treatment.

But we "ha[ve] always been reluctant to expand the concept of substantive due process because guideposts for responsible decisionmaking in this unchartered area are scarce and open-ended." By extending constitutional protection to an asserted right or liberty interest, we, to a great extent, place the matter outside the arena of public debate and legislative action. We must therefore "exercise the utmost care whenever we are asked to break new ground in this field," lest the liberty protected by the Due Process Clause be subtly transformed into the policy preferences of the Members of this Court.

Our established method of substantive-due-process analysis has two primary features: First, we have regularly observed that the Due Process Clause specially protects those fundamental rights and liberties which are, objectively, "deeply rooted in this Nation's history and tradition," and "implicit in the concept of ordered liberty," such that "neither liberty nor justice would exist if they were sacrificed." Second, we have required in substantive-due-process cases a "careful description" of the asserted fundamental liberty interest. * * *

Turning to the claim at issue here, * * * the question before us is whether the "liberty" specially protected by the Due Process Clause includes a right to commit suicide which itself includes a right to assistance in doing so.

We now inquire whether this asserted right has any place in our Nation's traditions. Here, as discussed supra, we are confronted with a consistent and almost universal tradition that has long rejected the asserted right, and continues explicitly to reject it today, even for terminally ill, mentally competent adults. To hold for respondents, we would have to reverse centuries of legal doctrine and practice, and strike down the considered policy choice of almost every State.

Respondents contend, however, that the liberty interest they assert is consistent with this Court's substantive-due-process line of cases, if not with this Nation's history and practice. Pointing to *Casey* and *Cruzan*,[a] respondents read our jurisprudence in this area as reflecting a general tradition of "self-sovereignty," and as teaching that the "liberty" protected by the Due Process Clause includes "basic and intimate exercises of personal autonomy."

In *Cruzan*, we considered whether Nancy Beth Cruzan, who had been severely injured in an automobile accident and was in a persistive vegetative state, "ha[d] a right under the United States Constitution which would require the hospital to withdraw life-sustaining treatment" at her parents' request. We began with the observation that "[a]t common law, even the touching of one person by another without consent and without legal justification was a battery." We then discussed the related rule that "informed consent is generally required for medical treatment." After reviewing a long line of relevant state cases, we concluded that "the common-law doctrine of informed consent is viewed as generally encompassing the right of a competent individual to refuse medical treatment." Next, we reviewed our own cases on the subject, and stated that "[t]he principle that a competent person has a constitutionally protected liberty interest in refusing unwanted medical treatment may be inferred from our prior decisions." * * *

The right assumed in *Cruzan*, however, was not simply deduced from abstract concepts of personal autonomy. Given the common-law rule that forced medication was a battery, and the long legal tradition protecting the decision to refuse unwanted medical treatment, our assumption was entirely consistent with this Nation's history and constitutional traditions. The decision to commit suicide with the assistance of another may be just as personal and profound as the decision to refuse unwanted medical treatment, but it has never enjoyed similar legal protection. Indeed, the two acts are widely and reasonably regarded as quite distinct. In *Cruzan* itself, we recognized that most States outlawed assisted suicide—and even more do today—and we certainly gave no intimation that the right to refuse unwanted medical treatment could be some-how transmuted into a right to assistance in committing suicide.

Respondents also rely on *Casey*. There, the Court's opinion concluded that "the essential holding of *Roe v. Wade*[, 410 U.S. 113, 93 S.Ct. 705, 35 L.Ed.2d 147 (1973),] should be retained and once again reaffirmed." We held, first, that a woman has a right, before her fetus is viable, to an abortion "without undue interference from the State"; second, that States may restrict post viability abortions, so long as exceptions are made to protect a woman's life and health; and third, that the State has legitimate interests throughout a pregnancy in protecting the health of the woman and the life of the unborn child ... In reaching this conclusion, the opinion discussed in some detail this Court's substantive-due-process tradition of interpreting the Due Process Clause to protect certain fundamental rights and "personal decisions relating to marriage, procreation, contraception, family relationships, child rearing, and education," and noted that many of those rights and liberties "involv[e] the most intimate and personal choices a person may make in a lifetime."

* * * That many of the rights and liberties protected by the Due Process Clause sound in personal autonomy does not warrant the sweeping conclusion that any and all impor-

---

a. The references here are to *Planned Parenthood of Southeastern Pa. v. Casey*, 505 U.S. 833, 112 S.Ct. 2791, 120 L.Ed.2d 674 (1992); and *Cruzan v. Director,* *Mo. Dept. of Health*, 497 U.S. 261, 110 S.Ct. 2841, 111 L.Ed.2d 224 (1990).

tant, intimate, and personal decisions are so protected, and *Casey* did not suggest otherwise.

The history of the law's treatment of assisted suicide in this country has been and continues to be one of the rejection of nearly all efforts to permit it. That being the case, our decisions lead us to conclude that the asserted "right" to assistance in committing suicide is not a fundamental liberty interest protected by the Due Process Clause. The Constitution also requires, however, that Washington's assisted-suicide ban be rationally related to legitimate government interests. This requirement is unquestionably met here. As the court below recognized, Washington's assisted-suicide ban implicates a number of state interests.

First, Washington has an "unqualified interest in the preservation of human life." The State's prohibition on assisted suicide, like all homicide laws, both reflects and advances its commitment to this interest. See *Model Penal Code* § 210.5, Comment 5, at 100 ("[T]he interests in the sanctity of life that are represented by the criminal homicide laws are threatened by one who expresses a willingness to participate in taking the life of another").

Relatedly, all admit that suicide is a serious public-health problem, especially among persons in otherwise vulnerable groups. * * *

Those who attempt suicide—terminally ill or not—often suffer from depression or other mental disorders. Research indicates, however, that many people who request physician-assisted suicide withdraw that request if their depression and pain are treated .. Thus, legal physician-assisted suicide could make it more difficult for the State to protect depressed or mentally ill persons, or those who are suffering from untreated pain, from suicidal impulses.

The State also has an interest in protecting the integrity and ethics of the medical profession. [T]he American Medical Association, like many other medical and physicians' groups, has concluded that "[p]hysician-assisted suicide is fundamentally incompatible with the physician's role as healer." And physician-assisted suicide could, it is argued, undermine the trust that is essential to the doctor-patient relationship by blurring the time-honored line between healing and harming.

Next, the State has an interest in protecting vulnerable groups—including the poor, the elderly, and disabled persons—from abuse, neglect, and mistakes. We have recognized * * * the real risk of subtle coercion and undue influence in end-of-life situations.

The State's interest here goes beyond protecting the vulnerable from coercion; it extends to protecting disabled and terminally ill people from prejudice, negative and inaccurate stereotypes, and "societal indifference." The State's assisted-suicide ban reflects and reinforces its policy that the lives of terminally ill, disabled, and elderly people must be no less valued than the lives of the young and healthy, and that a seriously disabled person's suicidal impulses should be interpreted and treated the same way as anyone else's.

Finally, the State may fear that permitting assisted suicide will start it down the path to voluntary and perhaps even involuntary euthanasia. * * * The Court of Appeals' decision, and its expansive reasoning, provide ample support for the State's concerns. The court noted, for example, that the "decision of a duly appointed surrogate decision maker is for all legal purposes the decision of the patient himself," that "in some instances, the patient may be unable to self-administer the drugs and ... administration by the physician ... may be the only way the patient may be able to receive them," and that not only physicians, but also family members and loved ones, will inevitably participate in assisting suicide. Thus, it turns out that what is couched as a limited right to "physician-assisted suicide" is likely, in effect, a much broader license, which could prove extremely difficult to police and contain. Washington's ban on assisting suicide prevents such erosion. * * *

We need not weigh exactingly the relative strengths of these various interests. They are unquestionably important and legitimate, and Washington's ban on assisted suicide is at least reasonably related to their promotion and protection. * * *

Throughout the Nation, Americans are engaged in an earnest and profound debate about the morality, legality, and practicality of physician-assisted suicide. Our holding permits this debate to continue, as it should in a democratic society. The decision of the en banc Court of Appeals is reversed, and the case is remanded for further proceedings consistent with this opinion.

It is so ordered.

JUSTICE SOUTER, concurring in the judgment.

* * * [T]he lines proposed here (particularly the requirement of a knowing and voluntary decision by the patient) would be more difficult to draw than the lines that have limited other recently recognized due process rights. Limiting a State from prosecuting use of artificial contraceptives by married couples posed no practical threat to the State's capacity to regulate contraceptives in other ways * * *; the trimester measurements of *Roe* and the viability determination of *Casey* were easy to make with a real degree of certainty. But the knowing and responsible mind is harder to assess. Second, this difficulty could become the greater by combining with another fact within the realm of plausibility, that physicians simply would not be assiduous to preserve the line. They have compassion, and those who would be willing to assist in suicide at all might be the most susceptible to the wishes of a patient, whether the patient was technically quite responsible or not. Physicians, and their hospitals, have their own financial incentives, too, in this new age of managed care. Whether acting from compassion or under some other influence, a physician who would provide a drug for a patient to administer might well go the further step of administering the drug himself; so, the barrier between assisted suicide and euthanasia could become porous, and the line between voluntary and involuntary euthanasia as well. The case for the slippery slope is fairly made out here, not because recognizing one due process right would leave a court with no principled basis to avoid recognizing another, but because there is a plausible case that the right claimed would not be readily containable by reference to facts about the mind that are matters of difficult judgment, or by gatekeepers who are subject to temptation, noble or not. * * *

JUSTICE O'CONNOR, concurring.*

* * * I join the Court's opinions because I agree that there is no generalized right to "commit suicide." But respondents urge us to address the narrower question whether a mentally competent person who is experiencing great suffering has a constitutionally cognizable interest in controlling the circumstances of his or her imminent death. I see no need to reach that question in the context of the facial challenges to the New York and Washington laws at issue here. The parties and amici agree that * * * a patient who is suffering from a terminal illness and who is experiencing great pain has no legal barriers to obtaining medication, from qualified physicians, to alleviate that suffering, even to the point of causing unconsciousness and hastening death. In this light, even assuming that we would recognize such an interest, I agree that the State's interests in protecting those who are not truly competent or facing imminent death, or those whose decisions to hasten

* JUSTICE GINSBURG concurs in the Court's judgments substantially for the reasons stated in this opinion. JUSTICE BREYER joins this opinion except insofar as it joins the opinions of the Court.

death would not truly be voluntary, are sufficiently weighty to justify a prohibition against physician-assisted suicide. * * *

Justice Stevens, concurring in the judgments. * * *

History and tradition provide ample support for refusing to recognize an open-ended constitutional right to commit suicide. Much more than the State's paternalistic interest in protecting the individual from the irrevocable consequences of an ill-advised decision motivated by temporary concerns is at stake. There is truth in John Donne's observation that "No man is an island." The State has an interest in preserving and fostering the benefits that every human being may provide to the community—a community that thrives on the exchange of ideas, expressions of affection, shared memories, and humorous incidents, as well as on the material contributions that its members create and support. The value to others of a person's life is far too precious to allow the individual to claim a constitutional entitlement to complete autonomy in making a decision to end that life. Thus, I fully agree with the Court that the "liberty" protected by the Due Process Clause does not include a categorical "right to commit suicide which itself includes a right to assistance in doing so."

But just as our conclusion that capital punishment is not always unconstitutional did not preclude later decisions holding that it is sometimes impermissibly cruel, so is it equally clear that a decision upholding a general statutory prohibition of assisted suicide does not mean that every possible application of the statute would be valid. A State, like Washington, that has authorized the death penalty, and thereby has concluded that the sanctity of human life does not require that it always be preserved, must acknowledge that there are situations in which an interest in hastening death is legitimate. Indeed, not only is that interest sometimes legitimate, I am also convinced that there are times when it is entitled to constitutional protection. * * *

Notes and Questions

1. In the companion case of *Vacco v. Quill*, 521 U.S. 793, 117 S.Ct. 2293, 138 L.Ed.2d 834 (1997), the Court rejected the claim that a legal prohibition on suicide assistance violated the equal protection clause because persons on life-support machinery can hasten their death by ending treatment, whereas other terminally ill persons cannot:

"The distinction comports with fundamental legal principles of causation and intent. First, when a patient refuses life-sustaining medical treatment, he dies from an underlying fatal disease or pathology; but if a patient ingests lethal medication prescribed by a physician, he is killed by that medication.

"Furthermore, a physician who withdraws, or honors a patient's refusal to begin, life-sustaining medical treatment purposefully intends, or may so intend, only to respect his patient's wishes and 'to cease doing useless and futile or degrading things to the patient when [the patient] no longer stands to benefit from them.' The same is true when a doctor provides aggressive palliative care; in some cases, painkilling drugs may hasten a patient's death, but the physician's purpose and intent is, or may be, only to ease his patient's pain. A doctor who assists a suicide, however, 'must, necessarily and indubitably, intend primarily that the patient be made dead.' Similarly, a patient who commits suicide with a doctor's aid necessarily has the specific intent to end his or her own life, while a patient who refuses or discontinues treatment might not.

"The law has long used actors' intent or purpose to distinguish between two acts that may have the same result. Put differently, the law distinguishes actions taken 'because of' a given end from actions taken 'in spite of' their unintended but foreseen consequences."

2. How do the issues in *Glucksberg* and *Vacco* relate to the broader question of when, if ever, a homicide victim's consent should be a defense in a criminal prosecution? Consider:

(a) David Orentlicher, *The Alleged Distinction Between Euthanasia and the Withdrawal of Life–Sustaining Treatment: Conceptually Incoherent and Impossible to Maintain*, 1998 U.Ill.Rev. 837, 849–51: "We can derive an explanation for the law's bright-line approach by considering Epstein's response to an important argument against euthanasia/assisted suicide. As Daniel Callahan has observed, ordinarily the law does not allow a person's consent to authorize the killing of that person by another individual. In his response to Callahan, Epstein discusses why consent is rejected as a defense to homicide in a society in which the law normally gives great weight to a person's consent. He points out that, when the law decides whether there is consent to a particular agreement, it can rely on 'observation in the individual case' or 'inference from background knowledge about general patterns and motivations of human behavior.' For some transactions, we assume that people act in their self-interest and that, if they agreed to a deal, they must have done so because it made them better off. In such cases, the only issue for the state is to ensure that the person did not act out of incompetence, fraud, or duress. For other transactions, however, it is highly unlikely that a competent person would make the alleged deal in the absence of fraud and duress. If such transactions occur, it is much more likely that they reflect undetected incompetence, fraud, or duress than that they reflect a genuine expression of autonomy by the person who appears to be disadvantaged by the agreement. Thus, for example, when a person is killed, and the killer claims consent on behalf of the victim, we believe it is highly unlikely that the victim actually consented. Moreover, Bayesian analysis tells us that efforts to ascertain whether genuine consent was given are going to be unhelpful. Because our methods of ascertainment are necessarily imperfect, and the likelihood of genuine consent is very low, most cases in which we think there was genuine consent will in fact be cases in which we falsely conclude that there was genuine consent. In a case of a killing, we might be fooled by the killer into believing that consent was given, and we cannot turn to the victim for the other side of the story. Accordingly, we reject consent as a defense to a killing. We assume that all killings are involuntary and therefore unlawful.

"How does this point help us with the distinction between treatment withdrawal and euthanasia/assisted suicide? When a patient refuses life-sustaining treatment, we recognize that there are good reasons for a patient to do so. The patient may find the side effects of the treatment intolerable, may feel that the benefits of continued life are outweighed by its burdens, or may have religious objections to the treatment. Given these reasons why patients may refuse treatment, we allow a right to refuse treatment as long as we are comfortable that the withdrawal is consistent with the patient's wishes or best interests. In other words, we can rely on 'observation in the individual case.'

"With euthanasia or assisted suicide, on the other hand, we have good reason to suspect that the person's choice is not a genuine expression of autonomy. Treatable depression is a common reason for patients to attempt, or seek help with, suicide. We worry that the same would be true for euthanasia. Because we will make mistakes in deciding whether a person is choosing euthanasia/assisted suicide genuinely or not, we choose to prohibit the practices entirely. In other words, we rely on 'inference from background knowledge about general patterns and motivations of human behavior.'"

(b) Richard A. Epstein, *Living Dangerously: A Defense of Mortal Peril*, 1998 U.Ill. L.Rev 909, 944–45: "The reason why we do not allow consent as a defense to murder is that we are quite convinced that most individuals wish to preserve their own lives. In the basic case, the background presumption is so strong that we think that we will make far more mistakes if we allow (dubious) evidence of prior consent is to killings when the victim cannot protest the outcome. But how strong is that background presumption when individuals are terminally ill? It has to be far weaker. The impulse to end one's own life is likely to be far greater, so here it is defensible to create institutions that allow for physician-assisted suicide or active euthanasia. My disagreement with Orentlicher is not that the change in background condition should lead to a change in legal response. It is with his new-found conviction that the distinction between withdrawing treatment and physician-assisted suicide, or active euthanasia, is a serviceable proxy for any of the relevant issues. It is not. The key variable is that of terminal illness, which is operative in both cases of withdrawing treatment and active euthanasia or physician-assisted suicide. But the choice of ending one's own life depends on all sorts of judgments about how long a person is likely to linger if life supports are removed, the emotional support from one's family, and religious beliefs about the relevance of the killing/letting die distinction. Likewise, a patient's wishes can be disregarded in withdrawal cases just as they are in cases of physician-assisted suicide and active euthanasia. The key relevant background fact is terminal illness. For the rest we have to rely on individual determinations, and a set of social mechanisms that control against the prospect of abuse or overreaching."

3. After *Glucksberg* and *Vacco*, what legislation, if any, should be enacted? Consider Yale Kamisar, *Physician Assisted Suicide: The Problems Presented by the Compelling, Heartwrenching Case,* 88 J.Crim.L. & Criminology1121, 1144–46 (1998): "Now that the U.S. Supreme Court has upheld New York and Washington state laws prohibiting the aiding of another to commit suicide, the spotlight will shift to the state courts, the state legislatures and state referenda. And once again proponents of physician-assisted suicide (PAS) will point to a heartwrenching case, perhaps the relatively rare case where a dying person is experiencing unavoidable pain (i.e., pain that not even the most skilled palliative care experts are able to mitigate), and ask: What would you want done to you if you were in this person's shoes?

"That is a hard question for opponents of PAS to answer, but, as I shall try to spell out in this article, I think it is the wrong question to ask. To put it another way, I think it is a very different question than one which asks: Should we enact a law allowing PAS under certain circumstances? * * *

"I do not deny it is hard to defend an absolute prohibition when you not only expect the prohibition to be violated in certain situations, but you can visualize circumstances where you would understand and forgive the person who did so. The best analogy I can think of is the absolute prohibition against torture. There, too, if we thought about it for a while, we could envisage some dramatic individual cases where there would be tremendous pressure to violate the prohibition, e.g., the 'ticking bomb' case. * * *

"For purposes of the present discussion, I need not answer the hard question of whether it should ever be permissible for law enforcement officials to resort to torture, e.g., to elicit information that would prevent a large explosion or some other calamity. I need only maintain that it is a very different question than whether we should enact a law formally sanctioning the use of torture in certain situations. It is much easier for the government to resort to torture in less-than-compelling situations when such methods are already formally permitted in some circumstances. On the other hand, by refusing to make any formal or official exceptions to the prohibition against torture, or by refusing to acknowledge that we should balance the costs and benefits of torture as a general matter, we strengthen the presumption against torture and maximize the likelihood that it will only be resorted to in the rarest and most compelling circumstances.

"Here, as elsewhere, it is very hard to maintain absolute prohibitions. But here, as elsewhere, problems arise when one starts carving out exceptions. I venture to say that, however great the care with which one formulates the exceptions, 'hard' cases are bound to emerge on the other side of the line and with it the pressure to extend the outer boundaries of the exceptions to embrace these new 'hard' cases."

STATE v. HIOTT

Court of Appeals of Washington, 1999.

97 Wash.App. 825, 987 P.2d 135.

ARMSTRONG, A.C.J.

Richard Hiott appeals his conviction in juvenile court of assault in the third degree. The assault occurred during a game in which Hiott and his friend, Jose, were shooting at each other with BB guns. Jose was hit in the eye and lost his eye as a result. Hiott was charged with assault in the third degree; the trial court found him guilty, ruling that: "[a]t no time did either consent to be injured by the other, but both boys were engaged in a very reckless form of play ... [and] this mutual play has lead [sic] to a crime." * * *

The trial court orally ruled that "[a]t no time did either consent to be injured by the other." Hiott contends that the court applied the wrong legal standard. He argues that the question is not whether Jose consented to the injury, but to the game activity. We need not address this, however, because we hold that consent is not available as a defense where the game is shooting at another with a BB gun.

Consent can be a defense to a criminal assault charge .. Most recently, in *State v. Shelley*, 85 Wash.App. 24, 929 P.2d 489 (1997), Division One held that consent can be a defense to an assault occurring during an athletic contest. During a game of "pickup" basketball, Shelley punched another player, breaking his jaw. Division One reviewed the use of consent as a defense and extended its use beyond that of sexual assault, adopting the approach of the Model Penal Code.[1] Under *Shelley*, consent can be a defense if "the conduct of defendant constituted foreseeable behavior in the play of the game" and the injury "occurred as a by-product of the game itself." In addition, consent is a defense only if the game is a lawful athletic contest, competitive sport, or other concerted activity not forbidden by law. Cf. *State v. Dejarlais*, 136 Wash.2d 939, 969 P.2d 90 (1998) (consent not a defense to charge of violating a domestic violence protection order).

Hiott argues that Jose consented to the game, Hiott's conduct was foreseeable behavior in the game, and the injury resulted from the game itself. Further, according to Hiott, the game they were playing "is within the limits of games for which society permits consent." Hiott compares the boys' shooting of BB guns at each other to dodgeball, football, rugby, hockey, boxing, wrestling, "ultimate fighting," fencing, and "paint-ball." We disagree.

The games Hiott uses for comparison, although capable of producing injuries, have been generally accepted by society as lawful athletic contests, competitive sports, or concerted activities not forbidden by law. And these games carry with them generally accepted rules, at least some of which are intended to prevent or minimize injuries. In addition, such games commonly prescribe the use of protective devices or clothing to prevent injuries. Shooting BB guns at each other is not a generally accepted game or

---

1. The court in *Shelley* adopted the approach of the Model Penal Code, which provides [in § 2.11] that: "the conduct and the injury are reasonably foreseeable hazards of joint participation in a lawful athletic contest or competitive sport or other concerted activity not forbidden by law."

athletic contest; the activity has no generally accepted rules; and the activity is not characterized by the common use of protective devices or clothing. * * *

Moreover, consent is not a valid defense if the activity consented to is against public policy. Thus, a child cannot consent to hazing, a gang member cannot consent to an initiation beating, and an individual cannot consent to being shot with a pistol. *People v. Lenti*, 44 Misc.2d 118, 253 N.Y.S.2d 9, 15 (1964); *Helton* [*v. State*, 624 N.E.2d 499 (Ind.Ct.App.1993)]; *State v. Fransua*, 85 N.M. 173, 510 P.2d 106, 58 A.L.R.3d 656 (1973). In *Fransua*, the New Mexico court held that consent was not a defense to aggravated battery, recognizing that criminal statutes are enacted to protect citizens and to prevent breaches of the public peace. Assaults in general are breaches of the public peace. And we consider shooting at another person with a BB gun a breach of the public peace and therefore, against public policy. We conclude that the trial court did not err in refusing to consider Jose's consent as a defense.

Notes and Questions

1. *Consent and sports violence.* (a) "The incident occurred on April 17, 1998, in the first period of the fourth game during the Guelph Storm's sweep of the [Plymouth] Whalers in the OHL semifinals at the Compuware Sports Arena in Plymouth, Michigan. Storm forward Andrew Long checked [Jesse] Boulerice, [the Whaler's left wing], into the boards. After a shoving match, Long skated off to rejoin the play. Then, according to the police report, Boulerice 'grabbed his hockey stick at the end of the handle with both hands and swung his hockey stick, in a baseball-type swing, at Long,' and struck him across the bridge of the nose. Long was knocked unconscious and went into convulsions on the ice. He suffered a contusion of the brain, fractures to his nose, nasal cavity, and cheekbone, a Grade III concussion accompanied by a seizure, and a gash from the tip of his nose to his lip that required twenty stitches to close."[a] Boulerice was charged with assault to do great bodily harm, a felony that carries a maximum penalty of ten years in prison and a $5,000 fine.

(b) If the case were to go to trial,[b] what should the jury be told about the matter of consent, and what should the result be? Consider Daniel R. Karon, *Winning Isn't Everything, It's the Only Thing: Violence in Profession Sports: The Need for Federal Regulation and Criminal Sanctions*, 25 Ind.L.Rev. 147,153–54 (1991): "With respect to the Model Penal Code, the difficult issue is distinguishing between reasonably foreseeable hazards that are consented to as part of the sport and hazards for which there is no consent.

"One approach to distinguishing between behavior that is consented to and behavior for which there is no consent concerns conduct that is customarily part of a particular sport. Under this approach, a player will be deemed to consent to conduct that is normally associated with the particular sport in which the player participates. This approach, however, is too broad. Fisticuffs and stick fighting, for example, are customary activities in professional hockey. Under this approach, a player will be understood to consent to these violent activities.

"An alternative approach is the 'rules-of-the-game' test. Under this test, a player will not be deemed to consent to acts that are illegal under the rules of the sport. This approach is too narrow in scope. This test considers all technical violations of a sport to be conduct

---

a. Note, 31 Rutgers L.J. 833, 841 (2000).

b. Note, supra, at 872, reports that Boulerice entered a no-contest plea to a reduced charge of aggravat-

ed assault, meaning that if Boulerice stayed out of trouble for a ninety-day probationary period the incident would be expunged from his record.

to which the player did not consent. For example, intentional fouls in basketball, committed for strategic purposes, will be considered conduct to which there is no consent and criminal liability could result.

"A third approach looks to the seriousness of the injury. Under this approach, a victim is deemed not to have consented to behavior that causes grave injury. The problem with this final approach is that a player does not know beforehand whether contact with the victim will result in serious injury. The most innocent hit, if the recipient lands poorly, for example, could result in grave injury. Consequently, this test does not establish an adequate means by which a player can gauge his conduct.

"No useful American authority exists that clarifies the consent issue. Canadian cases, however, provide some guidance, and when coupled with the Model Penal Code's 'reasonably foreseeable' approach, one can derive the following standard: 'An athlete will not be deemed to have consented to intentional or reckless acts that are not reasonably related to the conduct of the sport in question.' This standard, however, raises the amorphous issue of 'reasonableness' and from whose standpoint it is to be considered.

"Consent then, is an evasive concept with respect to the prosecution of a professional athlete. This concept's unstable character, however, does not mean that consent is not readily used as a defense. Consent is a valid and occasionally successful defense for an athlete."

2. *Consent and unperceived risks.* A university student seeking employment was told by the university employment office that there were no jobs available but that he could earn $50 by being the subject of a test at the university hospital. The student then spoke to the doctor who would conduct the test, who explained that he was testing a new drug by a "perfectly safe" procedure which involved putting electrodes on the subject's arms, legs and head and inserting a catheter into the vein of his left arm. The student agreed to undergo the test and signed a consent form so indicating. The test involved a new anaesthetic agent which the doctor had not previously used or tested in any way, and the procedures were as had been described to the student, except that the catheter was advanced through the various heart chambers out into the pulmonary artery. When the student began coughing, indicating he was on the verge of waking up, the concentration of anaesthesia was increased, resulting in the student suffering a complete cardiac arrest. The doctor took appropriate medical steps to get the heart functioning again, but the student remained unconscious for four days. He was discharged from the hospital 10 days later, at which time he was paid the $50. It is undisputed that the use of any anaesthetic agent involves a certain amount of risk and that in general medical practice the risk involved is balanced against the threat to life presented by the ailment to be treated.[c] If criminal charges are brought against the doctor, does he have a valid consent defense?

3. *Consent and the masochist.* "Defendant Dr. Samuels, a self-confessed sadist, released his desire to inflict physical pain on others by producing and acting in motion pictures depicting sado-masochistic behavior. One of these films—showing defendant whipping a naked man gagged and suspended from the ceiling—was voluntarily turned over to the police by the developer, Eastman Kodak. The victim was never located or formally identified, but the defendant testified that the victim was a masochist who consented to the physical abuse depicted in the film."[d] Dr. Samuels has been charged with

c. These facts are essentially those in *Halushka v. University of Saskatchewan*, 53 D.L.R.2d 436 (1965), holding the doctor liable in tort. For a discussion of possible criminal liability in cases of this sort, see P. D. G. Skegg, *'Informed Consent' to Medical Procedures*, 15 Med.Sci.Law 125 (1975).

d. Recent Case, 81 Harv.L.Rev. 1339 (1968), commenting on *People v. Samuels*, 250 Cal.App.2d 501, 58 Cal.Rptr. 439 (1967), upholding the defendant's convicaggravated assault. Does he have a consent defense? Consider L.H. Leigh, *Sado–Masochism, Consent, and the Reform of the Criminal Law,* 39 Mod.L.Rev. 130 (1976), concluding that if the victim consents to sado-masochistic activities there should be no criminal liability unless the conduct results in "mutilation," "disfigurement, either permanently or for an extended period," or "serious impairment of mental or physical powers either permanently or for a protracted period." Does this go too far, or not far enough? Compare:

(a) Meir Dan–Cohen, *Basic Values and the Victim's State of Mind,* 88 Calif.L.Rev. 759, 776–77 (2000): "One close analogy [to *Samuels*] that comes naturally to mind is to boxing. In both cases violence is used within an established and familiar practice, marked by the participants' consent and consistent with their welfare. No disrespect attaches to the use of violence within either practice. [T]hese facts shield the acts of violence in either case from the meaning that would ordinarily attach to an act of violence as such. On this view of the matter, to recognize a violent action as an instance of sadomasochism is ipso facto to exempt it from its ordinary nefarious meaning. * * * The judges ought to take account of the fact that a sadomasochistic community exists, and that within it the violence depicted in the incriminating film carries a distinct and well-understood meaning. Acquitting Samuels could, accordingly, be an expression of the court's deference to a community other than its own and to a meaning the court does not share."

(b) Kent Greenawalt, *Dignity and Victimhood,* 88 Calif.L.Rev. 779, 783 (2000): "Dan–Cohen treats the sadomasochist community as one in which the meaning of certain acts of physical violence differs from that in the more general community. I believe that matters are more complicated than he develops. One reason why (many) masochists find the infliction of pain to be sexually stimulating is that they have a desire to be humiliated; (many) sadists like to inflict pain because they want to treat partners in an abusive way. The sexual power of sadomasochist acts is intertwined with desires for dominance and humiliation. These acts are not typically expressions of equal worth; feelings of equality are suspended for the duration."

STATE v. GAROUTTE

Supreme Court of Arizona, 1964.

95 Ariz. 234, 388 P.2d 809.

BERNSTEIN, JUSTICE.

The defendant, Wayne Garoutte, was charged by direct information in the Superior Court of Maricopa County, Arizona, with the crime of manslaughter in the driving of a motor vehicle, a misdemeanor, said crime happening on or about May 21, 1961. The defendant filed a motion to dismiss on the basis of A.R.S. § 13–1591[1] which was granted. The order of the trial judge dismissing the charge was as follows:

tion on the ground that the consent was legally ineffective because "[i]t is a matter of common knowledge that a normal person in full possession of his mental faculties does not freely consent to the use, upon himself, of force likely to produce great bodily injury."

1. "A. When a defendant is accused of a misdemeanor for which the person injured by the act constituting the offense has a remedy by a civil action, the offense may be compromised as provided in this section, except when the offense is committed by or upon any officer of justice while in the execution of the duties of his office, or when the offense is committed riotously, or with intent to commit a felony.

"B. If the party injured appears before the court in which the action is pending at any time before trial, and acknowledges that he has received satisfaction for the injury, the court may, on payment of the costs incurred, order the prosecution dismissed, and the defendant discharged. The reasons for the order shall be set forth and entered of record on the minutes and the order shall be a bar to another prosecution for the same offense.

"C. No public offense shall be compromised or the prosecution or punishment upon a compromise dismissed or stayed except as provided by law.

"The misdemeanor with which defendant herein is charged arises as an alleged law violation based upon defendant's negligence and which negligence is defined under the manslaughter statute (13–456ARS) as a necessary element of the offense charged. In such respect, therefore, and unlike the usual criminal charge where criminal intent is a necessary element of the crime, the elements of negligence under civil and common law principals [sic] appear to enter into a determination of this particular type of offense.

"The statute in question (13–1591ARS) can not be considered as an isolated fragment of our legal system. The manslaughter statute involving operation of motor vehicles (13–456ARS) passed by the legislature in 1957 must necessarily be considered and construed in the light of the whole body of the law on this subject matter as it existed when that 1957 act was enacted into law, and the legislature is presumed to know of long established laws and procedures when passing new legislation. This is in accordance with well established rules of statutory construction.

"The statute in question (13–1591ARS), which has been in effect since 1901 and applied by the courts for sixty years, specifically recognizes civil satisfaction in a misdemeanor charge based upon compromise of the civil rights and causes of action growing out of the same alleged negligent act of the defendant which forms the basis for the criminal charge. If such satisfaction is accomplished according to the provisions of this statute, then the action appropriately may be dismissed.

"The Court, upon the evidence and stipulation of facts entered into between the County Attorney and counsel for defendant, FINDS:

"That the widow and legal representative of the minor children of the decedent appeared before the court and acknowledged receipt of financial satisfaction and payment of damages for the injuries sustained and in compromise and settlement of all civil causes of action arising from the act in question; that the satisfaction and damages paid, as aforesaid, were fair and substantial in amount; that there was no criminal intent on the part of defendant in committing the act in question; that the death in question resulted solely from negligence on the part of defendant; and that the widow and said decedent requested that defendant not be prosecuted under the pending charge.

"IT IS ORDERED, therefore, that for the foregoing reasons the complaint against defendant herein be and the same is hereby dismissed, pursuant to defendant's motion.

"DONE IN OPEN COURT this 10 day of August, 1961."

The state appealed. * * *

In principle, civil suits and criminal prosecutions should be kept separate. The law should treat rich and poor alike, and the fact that a man might be able to pay for damages due to his negligence should not save him from criminal prosecution. But in practice, this principle is not always applied in misdemeanors, and some states, Arizona among them, have adopted statutes similar to A.R.S. § 13–1591, supra, authorizing the dismissal of misdemeanor cases where the injured party has been compensated. Miller, *"The Compromise of Criminal Cases,"* 1 Southern California L.Rev. 1.

New York was among the first states to adopt this policy. * * *

In 1849, the New York Commissioners on Practice and Pleading, in explaining the policy of the statute, said:

" 'There are many cases, which are technically public offences, but which are in reality rather of a private than a public nature, and where the public interests are better promoted by checking than by encouraging criminal prosecutions. Of this class are libels, and simple assaults and batteries; or those which are not committed by or upon an officer of justice, while in the execution of the duties of his office, or riotously, or with an intent to commit a felony. With these exceptions, cases of this nature have by the policy of our statutes, always been considered fit subjects of compromise. * * * ' ''

The California Act from which the Arizona statute was derived, was first adopted in 1850. The Arizona compromise statute was adopted in 1864. Other states with similar legislation include Alaska, Georgia, Louisiana, Montana, Oregon, Pennsylvania, Virginia and Wisconsin.

Until modern traffic problems arose, manslaughter, as the lowest degree of homicide, was a felony in Arizona. It was never thought that the taking of a human life could be paid for and forgotten.

"Misdemeanor Manslaughter" made its appearance in Arizona law with the adoption of A.R.S. § 28–691 in 1950. * * * On both occasions where the statute was before this court, the crime created was described as a "high misdemeanor".

In the light of this history the problem presented to us here is whether the compromise statute includes "high misdemeanors". The statute, A.R.S. § 13–103, divides crimes only into felonies and misdemeanors, and bases its classification on the term and place of imprisonment. The classification of misdemeanors as "high misdemeanors" or "misdemeanors" is a common law judicial classification. It is based on the seriousness of the crime and has nothing to do with the term or place of confinement or judgment. Arizona statutes make no distinction between high misdemeanors and mere misdemeanors. The legislature is presumed to have known of the compromise statute when it created misdemeanor manslaughter.

After the adoption of the Arizona compromise statute, courts in other states warned against the public evils of extending the compromise statute to all crimes which might be classed by statute as misdemeanors. See e.g. *Commonwealth v. Heckman*, 113 Pa.Super. 70, 172 A. 28 (1934).

The situation calls for clarification by the legislature. A bill which would specifically exclude misdemeanor manslaughter from the compromise statute is now pending before it. The present state of the law has this incongruous result. If a drunk or reckless driver does not hit anyone, he may go to jail. If guilty, he cannot escape punishment. There is no "injured person" or "injured party" or possible "remedy by civil action," and the compromise statute may not be invoked. But if he damages property, hits someone, or even kills them, under the compromise statute he may completely escape criminal punishment by paying civil damages. * * *

Notes and Questions

1. The compromise statute in *Garoutte* (now § 13–3981) has since been amended by adding: "If a defendant is accused of an act involving assault, threatening or intimidating or a misdemeanor offense of domestic violence as defined in § 13–3601, the offense shall not be compromised except on recommendation of the prosecuting attorney." In *State v. Larson*, 159 Ariz. 14, 764 P.2d 749 (1988), the trial judge dismissed a domestic assault charge upon a showing that the offense had been compromised albeit absent the prosecutor's recommendation, which the judge concluded could not be required without "an unconstitutional invasion of the powers of the judiciary." On appeal, the court reversed, noting that a violation of the separation of powers doctrine involves "a usurpation by one department of the powers of another department," which had not occurred here because

the amendment of the compromise statute had simply restored a part of the prosecutor's traditional power, "the discretion to proceed or not to proceed once an action has been commenced unless the legislature has restricted that authority."

2.   In *State v. Nelles*, 713 P.2d 806 (Alaska App.1986), Bruce was charged with misdemeanor assault after he struck his girl friend, Mary, on the mouth with his fist, necessitating four stitches. At the bail hearing, Bruce's attorney submitted a "compromise of criminal action" form signed by Mary, and Mary testified she and Bruce were planning to be married. The trial judge dismissed the charges, explaining that the state's compromise statute "recognizes that the court system and the police, and the prosecutor should not be some type of a buffer zone and have their time taken up with boy-girl relations." The prosecutor appealed, arguing "that the district court's order of dismissal amounts to 'a usurpation of the executive power court residing in the state district attorney's office to bring charges and determine their disposition,'" but the appellate court found "his argument to be without merit. * * *

"In the present case, there was no judicial interference with the prosecution's initial decision to charge Nelles. Judge Crutchfield did subsequently exercise his discretion to dismiss the case. Yet this dismissal was expressly authorized by the legislature. There is no suggestion in the civil compromise statutes that the court's power to dismiss is conditioned upon the agreement of the prosecutor. In fact, the contrary appears to be the case. The state has cited no case purporting to hold that prosecutorial consent to a civil compromise is necessary as a matter of constitutional law, and we are aware of none. Because the court's authority to compromise misdemeanors has been expressly conferred by the legislature, we * * * conclude that there is no separation of powers violation made out here.

"The state's next argument is that crimes arising from domestic disputes should not be amenable to civil compromise. Certainly, the state has a valid concern: that domestic assaults not go unpunished merely because the victims wish to withdraw their complaints in the hope that no further abuse will occur. However, the state cites no support for the argument that public policy mandates a judicially created exception to the civil compromise statute. The statute, in its current form, does not exempt domestic disputes. Amendment to create additional exceptions is clearly a matter of legislative, rather than judicial, concern."

3.   J. Cross Creason, *Eliminating the Use of Civil Compromise in Cases of Domestic Violence, Elder Abuse, and Child Abuse*, 29 McGeorge L.Rev. 641, 647–48 (1998), discussing California legislation eliminating the availability of civil compromise in misdemeanor cases of domestic violence, elder abuse, and child abuse, summarizes the pros and cons:

"Opponents of civil compromise in domestic violence cases argue that abusers may take advantage of the reconciliation pattern that follows a battering incident. For example, victims of domestic violence often regret their decision to participate in civil compromise because the cycle of abuse frequently continues—despite assurances from the batterer. Opponents of civil compromise also believe that civil compromise sends the message to abusers and their victims that society does not take abuse among people living together seriously when it allows the abuser to escape without serious outside intervention.

"Proponents of Chapter 243 believe that these concerns relating to civil compromise will play a part in coercing or pressuring the victim into compromising with the abuser when prosecution is more appropriate. Moreover, supporters of Chapter 243 assert that in cases of child and elder abuse, where the law is, in part, designed to protect victims who are unable to make informed decisions, the victim is often not truly capable of condoning crimes committed upon them. And if it appears to the abuser that the victim does not have the option to prevent the prosecution from continuing by compromising, then the victim may be shielded from blame and coercive pressure by the abuser to compromise.

"Opponents of Chapter 243 point out that eliminating civil compromise in domestic violence cases limits the court's options in fashioning a solution appropriate to the particular case. Civil compromise is an especially important option in hard to prove cases because without it abuse victims may be left with no remedy at all.

"Eliminating civil compromise in abuse cases is subject to the same criticism laid upon 'no-drop' policies that argue such policies are paternalistic. A practical effect of taking this discretion away from victims could be that they will be more reluctant to call the police in the first place if they believe that arrest will automatically lead to prosecution."

Chapter 9

RAPE: THE DILEMMAS OF LAW REFORM

SECTION 1. INTRODUCTION AND OVERVIEW

1. *Reasons for Studying Rape*. In this Book, the principal emphasis is rightly upon general principles; examination of specific categories of crime is the exception rather than the rule. The "crime against nature" was explored in Chapter 2 to reveal the sources and limits of the criminal law, while homicide was covered in Chapter 5 in order to assess how a broad range of criminal conduct producing the same serious consequences might best be further subdivided. As for rape, it is an appropriate subject for close examination because the crime has been and continues to be the focal point of law reform efforts, a process raising bedeviling questions about the legitimate scope of the criminal law and, for that matter, about several of the general principles heretofore examined.

As stated in Susan Estrich, *Teaching Rape Law*, 102 Yale L.J. 509, 516 (1992): "I can think of no subject of substantive criminal law in greater ferment, no area where the concepts that are at the core of the 'general course' come alive so vividly, and none that demonstrates some of the dilemmas of criminalization and just punishment so clearly as the law of rape. The line between what is criminal and what is noncriminal has been shifting, and not painlessly, for the last [several] years * * *. Could there be a better case study of the complexities of defining what is reasonable? One that more keenly tests students' understanding of mens rea? Or that more successfully shows mistake of fact as something other than a series of improbable hypotheticals? Consider the possibilities: He met her in a bar, got her to take him home, showed her around, pushed her down on the beach or the bed. Is that how a reasonable man behaves? If he's wrong, is his mistake reasonable? Should he be guilty for being stupid? What if he didn't care what she thought: is that recklessness or just plain churlishness? Is it enough that she said no, and then took her stockings off, and performed oral sex? Is that how a reasonable woman behaves? Do you really take your victim as you find her?"

2. *The Attendant Risks.* The teaching of rape is not without its risks, as is attested by the fact there exists a body of literature on that very point. Among the risks are that some members of the class may find themselves extremely uncomfortable discussing the subject, that emotion may sometimes overwhelm reason, that there may be reluctance to express anything other than presumably "acceptable" viewpoints, and/or that charges of sexism running both directions may polarize the class. The point is mentioned here only to suggest that with a bit of additional effort by all concerned, such difficulties can be largely avoided. It is useful to reflect at the outset upon these comments by Prof. Estrich:

"I know there's some pressure in classrooms these days to be politically correct * * *. Still, [it is necessary] to create an atmosphere where both sides of the argument are heard. * * *. I have always believed that you need to understand the other side's approach as well as they do before you can formulate your own. So I expect the feminists to articulate the defendant's strongest arguments, and those most skeptical of the feminist position to be able prosecutors. I know it's difficult, but that's not an excuse. * * *

"Of course some students, the ones who are victims or perhaps the ones who have been accused, may still find these classes painful. But no one would ever suggest that we should skip homicide in those years when we have students who have been touched by it, or skip insanity because some of our students have fought mental illness, or never mention drunk driving because we're all probably too familiar with that. Why should rape be different? Besides, I think the majority would find it even more painful to learn nothing about rape in law school. * * *

"I know many students, and even a few professors, who believe that the women are always right and the men are always wrong; that if she didn't consent fully and voluntarily, it is rape, no matter what she said or did, or what he did or did not realize. Everything about his past should be admitted, and nothing about hers. And that's what they want to hear in class.

"This kind of orthodoxy is not only bad educationally but, in the case of rape, it also misses the point. Society is not so orthodox in its views. There is a debate going on in courthouses and prosecutors' offices, and around coffee machines and dinner tables * * * about when women should be believed, and what counts as consent. There's a debate going on in America as to what is reasonable when it comes to sex. Turn on the radio and you will hear it. To silence that debate in the classroom is to remove the classroom from reality, and to make ourselves irrelevant. It may be hard for some students, but ultimately the only way to change things—and that's usually the goal of those who find the discussions most difficult—is to confront the issues squarely, not to pretend that they don't exist. Besides, the purpose of education * * * is to prepare our students to participate in the controversies that animate the law, not to provide them with a shelter from reality." Estrich, supra, at 514–15.

3. *Rape at Common Law.* The crime of rape was defined at common law as "the carnal knowledge of a woman forcibly and against her will."[a] This definition suggests that the elements of the crime of rape are (i) a specified act, i.e., "carnal knowledge," (ii) brought about by a specified means of imposition, i.e., "forcibly," and (iii) in circumstances where the woman had a particular state of mind concerning the perpetration of that act by those means, i.e., "against her will." However, as the common law crime of rape came to be utilized in this country, including as a basis for many early rape statutes, some uncertainty developed about a definition so expressed. Two noteworthy questions which arose were: (a) whether the *defendant's* state of mind is at all relevant, considering that some mental state is required for most other serious offenses; and (b) whether force and nonconsent are separate and distinct elements of the crime of rape, or whether on the other hand force merely plays an evidentiary role with regard to the nonconsent element.

4. *The Traditional Approach.* Most states ultimately defined the crime of rape by statute; these statutes often followed the common law, although some variations in definition developed as a consequence of this legislation. However, a fair generalization of the "traditional approach" to the crime of rape in the United States (that is, the approach that prevailed prior to the reforms undertaken in relatively recent years) would be that it had the following noteworthy features: (1) The physical act necessary for rape, usually

---

a. 4 William. Blackstone, *Commentaries* *210.

referred to as "carnal knowledge," was penetration of the female sex organ by the male organ. (2) With rare exception, the necessary manner of commission of this act was "forcibly," which ordinarily required resort to force or threat of force above and beyond that inherent in the penetration. (3) Limited alternatives to force were recognized, namely, resort to fraud so extreme that the woman either did not know she was engaging in intercourse or did not know the intercourse was not with her husband, or to administration of drugs or intoxicants depriving the woman of the ability to resist. (4) The penetration also had to be against the will of the victim, and the need to establish such nonconsent often necessitated proof of the victim's continued physical resistance to the man's advances or a showing of force or threats to such a degree as to make such resistance unavailing. (5) Consent was conclusively presumed when a man engaged in intercourse with his wife. (6) No manifestation of refusal of consent was necessary when the female was under ten years of age and thus deemed incapable of consent as a matter of law, or when she was so incapacitated as to be unable to give consent. (7) The defendant's mental state at the time of the intercourse was generally deemed irrelevant, so that inquiry into whether he mistakenly believed the woman consented and on that basis should be exonerated was typically foreclosed. (8) Absence of a prompt complaint about an alleged rape was admissible as evidence that the later complaint was not genuine. (9) Some jurisdictions required that the victim's testimony be corroborated by other evidence. (10) Prior sexual conduct of the complainant was admissible in a rape prosecution as evidence of consent and to impeach the complainant's credibility. (11) Many jurisdictions used cautionary jury instructions warning that the offense was easily charged but hard to disprove and that consequently the victim's testimony required especially close scrutiny. (12) The crime of rape was at one time punishable by death in about half the states, and by extended prison terms in the others, but the number authorizing capital punishment ultimately dropped to just a few, and later the Supreme Court held such punishment unconstitutional in rape cases.

5. *The Impetus for Reform.* One of the most frequently encountered quotations on the subject of rape, indeed, "one of the most oft-quoted passages in our jurisprudence"[b] on any subject, originated with Lord Chief Justice Matthew Hale of England back in the seventeenth century: "rape * * * is an accusation easily to be made and hard to be proved, and harder to be defended by the party accused, tho never so innocent."[c] The longstanding prevalence of that attitude doubtless accounts not only for the narrow and curious fashion in which the crime of rape came to be defined, but also for the array of procedural and evidentiary rules that are both unique to and inimical to rape prosecutions. This concern with false accusations is manifested in a variety of ways, including the usual requirement that force or threat of force must be shown, that nonconsent must ordinarily be manifested by physical resistance, that the victim's testimony must be corroborated, and that the prior sexual conduct of the complainant may be inquired into fully.

In more recent times, many have seen the aforementioned requirements in a quite different light, as a result of which "rape has increasingly become a topic of controversy * * * captur[ing] the public imagination."[d] Those seeking redefinition of the crime of rape and reform of evidentiary and procedural impediments have frequently and vigorously put forward another proposition sharply contradictory to Hale's assertion: "In a rape case it is the victim, not the defendant, who is on trial."[e] Critics of the status quo "argued that this focus on the victim was unique to rape law," and

---

b. *United States v. Wiley,* 492 F.2d 547 (D.C.Cir. 1973).

c. 1 Matthew Hale, *Pleas of the Crown* 635 (1680).

d. *Model Penal Code,* art. 213, Introductory Note at 281 (1980).

e. Cassia C. Spohn, *The Rape Reform Movement: The Traditional Common Law and Rape Law Reforms,* 39 Jurimetrics J. 119 (1999).

contended that traditional rape law negatively affected both victims of rape and the outcome of rape cases. They charged that the rules of evidence unique to rape caused pervasive skepticism of rape victims' claims and allowed criminal justice officials to use legally irrelevant assessments of the victim's character, behavior, and relationship with the defendant in processing and disposing of rape cases. Critics further suggested that traditional rape law was at least partially responsible for the unwillingness of victims to report rape, as well as low rates of arrest, prosecution, and conviction for rape. They argued, in short, that traditional rape law made it "easy to commit rape and get away with it."[f]

Those pragmatic concerns were the primary motivation of victims' rights and "law and order" groups, while some feminist groups instead saw the consequences of rape law reform as being "largely symbolic and ideological—to educate the public about the seriousness of all forms of sexual assault, to reduce the stigma experienced by victims of rape, and to neutralize rape myth stereotypes."[g]

6. *The Modern Approach.* As a consequence of reforms undertaken in recent years, what might be called the modern approach to the crime of rape looks considerably different from the traditional approach of years past. This is not to suggest that all needed reforms have been accomplished in all jurisdictions, for this is not the case. Nor is it to suggest that in those many states where a full range of reform legislation has been adopted that all of the problems previously identified have been fully solved. In part this is attributable to the fact that the problem has never been entirely "the words of the statutes," but has also involved the general understanding in our society regarding such concepts and "consent," "will" and "force,"[h] which doubtless is changing, albeit at a somewhat slower pace.

The modern approach to rape has these features: (1) The newer statutes are often drawn in gender-neutral terms and cover not only genital copulation but also anal and oral copulation and, sometimes, digital and mechanical penetration as well. (2) There is a trend toward recognition of a broader range of impositions as a basis for finding coercive conduct by the defendant, including other types of fraud and also certain nonphysical coercion. (3) The requirements regarding physical resistance manifesting nonconsent have been lessened in some jurisdictions, while elsewhere there is movement toward more ready recognition that verbal resistance (if not absence of affirmative consent) should suffice. (4) The marital exemption has been removed in most states and substantially limited in the others. (5) Protection of younger females has been extended by raising the age for so-called "statutory rape," where no showing of nonconsent is necessary. (6) There is somewhat greater recognition that the defendant's mental state is not always irrelevant, and that some mistaken beliefs in consent are a basis for exoneration. (7) The concept of a "prompt" complaint has been considerably broadened, and the fact of such a complaint is now admissible in support of the prosecution's case. (8) Most jurisdictions have abolished any requirement that the victim's testimony be corroborated. (9) So-called rape shield laws have been enacted everywhere and bar admission of the complainant's prior sexual conduct in most instances. (10) Cautionary instructions calling upon the jury to give special scrutiny to the victim's testimony have been largely abandoned. (11) The great majority of states now divide the offense into degrees, taking into account the severity of the injury and the seriousness of the imposition employed.

---

f. Id. at 120.

g. Ronet Backman & Raymond Paternoster, *A Contemporary Look at the Effects of Rape Law Reform: How Far Have We Really Come?*, 84 J.Crim.L. & Criminology 554, 555 (1993).

h. Susan Estrich, *Rape*, 95 Yale L.J. 1087, 1093 (1986).

7. *Focus of this Chapter.* As is evident from a comparison of the traditional and modern approaches, the subject of rape encompasses many provocative substantive and procedural issues, which is doubtless why two extraordinary books on the subject have been published in recent years: Susan Estrich, *Real Rape* (1987); and Stephen J. Schulhofer, *Unwanted Sex: The Culture of Intimidation and the Failure of Law* (1998). Rather than attempt a survey of all these issues, the focus in this Chapter is upon three substantive law problem areas which have been and doubtless *will continue to be*[i] particularly troublesome to the law reformers.

These three areas are: (i) imposition; (ii) consent; and (iii) mental state. With regard to *imposition*, read the materials in Section 2 with a view to deciding whether a model rape statute should include a specification of the kind and degree of impositions which are a predicate to criminal liability and, if so, what impositions should suffice, either within the traditional "force or threat of force" category or in terms of other coercion or of fraud. With regard to *consent*, read the materials in Section 3 with a view to deciding whether a model rape statute should contain either a nonconsent element or a consent defense and, if either, whether resistance, verbal refusal or the mere absence of an affirmative expression by the victim is a sufficient manifestation of nonconsent, and, further, whether there are circumstances in which either consent or nonconsent should be conclusively presumed. With regard to *mental state,* read the materials in Section 4 with a view to deciding whether a model rape statute should impose strict liability or should instead require some mental state and, if the later, what mental state is most appropriate.

SECTION 2. NATURE AND DEGREE OF IMPOSITION

A. FORCE OR THREAT OF FORCE

STATE v. ALSTON

Supreme Court of North Carolina, 1984.

310 N.C. 399, 312 S.E.2d 470.

MITCHELL, JUSTICE.

The defendant raises on appeal the question whether the evidence of his guilt of kidnaping and second degree rape was sufficient to support his convictions of those crimes. For reasons discussed herein, we conclude the evidence was insufficient to support his conviction of either crime.

The State's evidence tended to show that at the time the incident occurred the defendant and the prosecuting witness in this case, Cottie Brown, had been involved for approximately six months in a consensual sexual relationship. During the six months the two had conflicts at times and Brown would leave the apartment she shared with the defendant to stay with her mother. She testified that she would return to the defendant and the apartment they shared when he called to tell her to return. Brown testified that she and the defendant had sexual relations throughout their relationship. Although she sometimes enjoyed their sexual relations, she often had sex with the defendant just to accommodate him. On those occasions, she would stand still and remain entirely passive while the defendant undressed her and had intercourse with her.

---

i. This may be the point to recall Justice Arthur   for the short-winded."
Vanderbilt's famous quip that "law reform is no sport

Brown testified that at times their consensual sexual relations involved some violence. The defendant had struck her several times throughout the relationship when she refused to give him money or refused to do what he wanted. Around May 15, 1981, the defendant struck her after asking her for money that she refused to give him. Brown left the apartment she shared with the defendant and moved in with her mother. She did not have intercourse with the defendant after May 15 until the alleged rape on June 15. After Brown left the defendant, he called her several times and visited her at Durham Technical Institute where she was enrolled in classes. When he visited her they talked about their relationship. Brown testified that she did not tell him she wanted to break off their relationship because she was afraid he would be angry.

On June 15, 1981, Brown arrived at Durham Technical Institute by taxicab to find the defendant standing close to the school door. The defendant blocked her path as she walked toward the door and asked her where she had moved. Brown refused to tell him, and the defendant grabbed her arm, saying that she was going with him. Brown testified that it would have taken some effort to pull away. The two walked toward the parking lot and Brown told the defendant she would walk with him if he let her go. The defendant then released her. She testified that she did not run away from him because she was afraid of him. She stated that other students were nearby.

Brown stated that she and the defendant then began a casually paced walk in the neighborhood around the school. They walked, sometimes side by side, sometimes with Brown slightly behind the defendant. As they walked they talked about their relationship. Brown said the defendant did not hold her or help her along in any way as they walked. The defendant talked about Brown's "dogging" him and making him seem a fool and about Brown's mother's interference in the relationship. When the defendant and Brown left the parking lot, the defendant threatened to "fix" her face so that her mother could see he was not playing. While they were walking out of the parking lot, Brown told the defendant she wanted to go to class. He replied that she was going to miss class that day.

The two continued to walk away from the school. Brown testified that the defendant continually talked about their relationship as they walked, but that she paid little attention to what he said because she was preoccupied with her own thoughts. They passed several people. They walked along several streets and went down a path close to a wooded area where they stopped to talk. The defendant asked again where Brown had moved. She asked him whether he would let her go if she told him her address. The defendant then asked whether the relationship was over and Brown told him it was. He then said that since everyone could see her but him he had a right to make love to her again. Brown said nothing.

The two turned around at that point and began walking towards a street they had walked down previously. Changing directions, they walked in the same fashion they had walked before—side by side with Brown sometimes slightly behind. The defendant did not hold or touch Brown as they walked. Brown testified that the defendant did not say where they were going but that, when he said he wanted to make love, she knew he was going to the house of a friend. She said they had gone to the house on prior occasions to have sex. The defendant and Brown passed the same group of men they had passed previously. Brown did not ask for assistance because some of the men were friends of the defendant, and she assumed they would not help. The defendant and Brown continued to walk to the house of one of the defendant's friends, Lawrence Taylor.

When they entered the house, Taylor was inside. Brown sat in the living room while the defendant and Taylor went to the back of the house and talked. When asked why she did not try to leave when the defendant and Taylor were in the back of the house, Brown replied, "It was nowhere to go. I don't know. I just didn't." The defendant returned to the living room area and turned on the television. He attempted to fix a broken fan. Brown asked Taylor for a cigarette, and he gave her one.

The defendant began talking to Brown about another man she had been seeing. By that time Taylor had gone out of the room and perhaps the house. The defendant asked if Brown was "ready." The evidence tended to show that she told him "no, that I wasn't going to bed with him." She testified that she did not want to have sex with the defendant and did not consent to do so at any time on June 15.

After Brown finished her cigarette, the defendant began kissing her neck. He pulled her up from the chair in which she had been sitting and started undressing her. He noticed that she was having her menstrual period, and she sat down pulling her pants back up. The defendant again took off her pants and blouse. He told her to lay down on a bed which was in the living room. She complied and the defendant pushed apart her legs and had sexual intercourse with her. Brown testified that she did not try to push him away. She cried during the intercourse. Afterwards they talked. The defendant told her he wanted to make sure she was not lying about where she lived and that he would not let her up unless she told him.

After they dressed they talked again about the man Brown had been seeing. They left the house and went to the defendant's mother's house. After talking with the defendant's mother, Brown took a bus home. She talked with her mother about taking out a complaint against the defendant but did not tell her mother she and the defendant had had sex. Brown made a complaint to the police the same day.

The defendant continued to call Brown after June 15, but she refused to see him. One evening he called from a telephone booth and told her he had to talk. When he got to her apartment he threatened to kick her door down and Brown let him inside. Once inside he said he had intended merely to talk to her but that he wanted to make love again after seeing her. Brown said she sat and looked at him, and that he began kissing her. She pulled away and he picked her up and carried her to the bedroom. He performed oral sex on her and she testified that she did not try to fight him off because she found she enjoyed it. The two stayed together until morning and had sexual intercourse several times that night. Brown did not disclose the incident to the police immediately because she said she was embarrassed.

The defendant put on no evidence and moved at the close of the State's evidence for dismissal of both charges based on insufficiency of evidence. The trial court denied the motions and the majority in the Court of Appeals affirmed the trial court.

Upon the defendant's motion to dismiss, the question for the court is whether substantial evidence was introduced of each element of the offense charged and that the defendant was the perpetrator. Substantial evidence is "such relevant evidence as a reasonable mind might accept as adequate to support a conclusion." The issue of substantiality is a question of law for the court. If the evidence is sufficient only to raise a suspicion or conjecture as to either the commission of the offense or the identity of the perpetrator, the motion to dismiss should be allowed. This is true even though the suspicion is strong.

The court is to consider the evidence in the light most favorable to the State in ruling on a motion to dismiss. The State is entitled to every reasonable intendment and inference to be drawn from the evidence; contradictions and discrepancies do not warrant dismissal—they are for the jury to resolve.

[In an omitted part of the opinion dealing with the kidnaping charge, the court concluded: "Since there was no substantial evidence of forcible confinement, restraint or removal for the purpose of committing rape, the State failed to present substantial evidence of every element of the offense."]

In his second assignment of error the defendant contends there was no substantial evidence that the sexual intercourse between Brown and him was by force and against her will. He argues that the evidence was insufficient to allow the trial court to submit the issue of his guilt of second degree rape to the jury. After a review of the evidence, we find this argument to have merit.

Second degree rape involves vaginal intercourse with the victim both by force and against the victim's will. Consent by the victim is a complete defense, but consent which is induced by fear of violence is void and is no legal consent.

A defendant can be guilty of raping even his mistress or a "common strumpet." This is so because consent to sexual intercourse freely given can be withdrawn at any time prior to penetration. If the particular act of intercourse for which the defendant is charged was both by force and against the victim's will, the offense is rape without regard to the victim's consent given to the defendant for prior acts of intercourse.

Where as here the victim has engaged in a prior continuing consensual sexual relationship with the defendant, however, determining the victim's state of mind at the time of the alleged rape obviously is made more difficult. Although inquiry in such cases still must be made into the victim's state of mind at the time of the alleged rape, the State ordinarily will be able to show the victim's lack of consent to the specific act charged only by evidence of statements or actions by the victim which were clearly communicated to the defendant and which expressly and unequivocally indicated the victim's withdrawal of any prior consent and lack of consent to the particular act of intercourse.

In the present case the State introduced such evidence. It is true, of course, that Brown gave no physical resistance to the defendant. Evidence of physical resistance is not necessary to prove lack of consent in a rape case in this jurisdiction. Brown testified unequivocally that she did not consent to sexual intercourse with the defendant on June 15. She was equally unequivocal in testifying that she submitted to sexual intercourse with the defendant only because she was afraid of him. During their walk, she told the defendant that their relationship was at an end. When the defendant asked her if she was "ready" immediately prior to having sexual intercourse with her, she told him "no, that I wasn't going to bed with him." Even in the absence of physical resistance by Brown, such testimony by her provided substantial evidence that the act of sexual intercourse was against her will.

The State did not offer substantial evidence, however, of the element of force. As we have stated, actual physical force need not be shown in order to establish force sufficient to constitute an element of the crime of rape. Threats of serious bodily harm which reasonably induce fear thereof are sufficient. In the present case there was no substantial evidence of either actual or constructive force.

The evidence in the present case tended to show that, shortly after the defendant met Brown at the school, they walked out of the parking lot with the defendant in front. He stopped and told Brown he was going to "fix" her face so that her mother could see he was not "playing." This threat by the defendant and his act of grabbing Brown by the arm at the school, although they may have induced fear, appeared to have been unrelated to the act of sexual intercourse between Brown and the defendant. More important, the record is devoid of evidence that Brown was in any way intimidated into having sexual intercourse with the defendant by that threat or any other act of the defendant on June 15. Brown said she did not pay a lot of attention to what the defendant said because she was thinking about other things. She specifically stated that her fear of the defendant was based on an experience with him prior to June 15 and that on June 15 he did not hold her down or threaten her with what would happen if she refused to submit to him. The State failed to offer substantial evidence of force used or threatened by the defendant on June 15 which related to his desire to have sexual intercourse on that date and was sufficient to overcome the will of the victim.

We note that the absence of an explicit threat is not determinative in considering whether there was sufficient force in whatever form to overcome the will of the victim. It is enough if the totality of the circumstances gives rise to a reasonable inference that the unspoken purpose of the threat was to force the victim to submit to unwanted sexual intercourse. The evidence introduced in the present case, however, gave rise to no such inference. Under the peculiar facts of this case, there was no substantial evidence that threats or force by the defendant on June 15 were sufficiently related to sexual conduct to cause Brown to believe that she had to submit to sexual intercourse with him or suffer harm. Although Brown's general fear of the defendant may have been justified by his conduct on prior occasions, absent evidence that the defendant used force or threats to overcome the will of the victim to resist the sexual intercourse alleged to have been rape, such general fear was not sufficient to show that the defendant used the force required to support a conviction of rape.

In summary, we think that the State's evidence was sufficient to show that the act of sexual intercourse in question was against Brown's will. It was not sufficient, however, to show that the act was accomplished by actual force or by a threat to use force unless she submitted to sexual intercourse. Since the State did not introduce substantial evidence of the element of force required to sustain a conviction of rape, the trial court erred in denying the defendant's motion to dismiss the case against the defendant for second degree rape. * * *

Notes and Questions

1. "Decisions such as * * * *Alston* are vulnerable to attack on traditional doctrinal grounds. The courts' unwillingness to credit the victim's past experience of violence at the hands of the defendant stands in sharp contrast to the black letter law that a defendant's knowledge of his attacker's reputation for violence or ownership of a gun is relevant to the reasonableness of his use of deadly force in self-defense. * * *

"To say that there is no 'force' in such a situation is to create a gulf between power and force, and to define the latter solely in schoolboy terms. Mr. Alston did not beat his victim—at least not with his fists. He didn't have to. She had been beaten—physically and emotionally—long before. But that beating was one that the court was willing to go to great lengths to avoid recognizing.

"That the law prohibiting forced sex understands force in such narrow terms is frustrating enough for its women victims. Worse, however, is the fact that the conclusion that no force is present may emerge as a judgment not that the man did not act unreasonably, but as a judgment that the woman victim did." Susan Estrich, *Rape*, 95 Yale L.J. 1087, 1111–12 (1986).

2. "The court dissected the sequence of events into discrete time bits, isolated the segments, and then disregarded any relationship between the victim's fear of the defendant at earlier times and the occurrence of the rape. Although her attacker threatened her, and

used fear as a means of intimidation during their relationship, the court viewed these facts as too far removed from the rape to be relevant. The court treated each arbitrarily defined block as independent from the others, and this compartmentalization effectively blocked out the significant contextual fear and violence in which this relationship was embedded. This imbalanced power relationship gave the attacker a 'silent' force. His past violence and threats were equivalent to any kind of force he could have used at the time of the rape. When the court refused to acknowledge the context in which this rape occurred, it ignored the fact that continuous fear and threats are critical components of the final result—rape. The court in *Alston* aligned itself with a social structure that systematically disregards the institutionalized and normalized nature of violence against women." Mustafa Kasubhai, *Destabilizing Power in Rape: Why Consent Theory in Rape Law is Turned on Its Head*, 11 Wis. Women's L.J. 37, 56–57 (1996).

3.   "It is striking that the *Alston* court, on the one hand, rejected a 'general fear' rationale insofar as it related to the defendant's use of force, finding that a violent history between victim and defendant was irrelevant to the defendant's ability to coerce the victim. Yet at the same time, the court found this history highly probative to the extent that it normalized any violence that might have occurred between victim and defendant. Hence, the court found not only that the prior relationship did not contribute to a context of fear and violence sufficient to create 'force' under the law, but that it actually normalized any fear and violence that might have continued to occur, making the victim's passivity 'while the defendant ... engaged in some violence [during] sexual intercourse' amount to consent. Thus, the defendant had 'no reason to think' that such 'consensual' relations would not continue." Heidi Kitrosser, *Meaningful Consent: Toward a New Generation of Statutory Rape Laws*, 4 Va.J.Soc.Pol'y & L. 287, 302 (1997).

4.   "Although the prior beatings should not nullify the victim's apparent consent, they should satisfy the force requirement. Like an explicit threat, a history of violence (in sufficiently analogous circumstances) can create a reasonable ground for fear that physical resistance would be dangerous. The prior beatings are, therefore, the functional equivalent of a threat, though not of nonconsent.

"Thus, in a case like *Alston*, where nonconsent is clear, Estrich is right that the conviction should be affirmed despite the victim's failure to resist. But if the woman seems to desire sex, the encounter should not be treated as rape merely because of the defendant's violence on other occasions." David P. Bryden, *Redefining Rape*, 3 Buff.Crim. L.Rev. 317, 354–55 (2000).

5.   "Catharine MacKinnon and Andrea Dworkin have argued that women do not have real choices in heterosexual sex because of the systemic presence of male dominance in relationships between men and women and because our male-dominated society eroticizes dominance. Although acknowledging male dominance in heterosexual relationships does not lead to the conclusion that all heterosexual sex should be criminalized, it demands that the criminal law recognize the impossibility of consent in egregious circumstances where a man exercises control over a woman through physical and mental intimidation. The dominance branch of the confidential relationship doctrine is the means by which the courts could acknowledge the impossibility of a victim's consent. If the state shows that the defendant had a history of physically abusing the victim within the definitions used for domestic abuse prosecutions, the defense that the victim consented to the sexual contact with positive words or positive conduct would be unavailable." Beverly Balos & Mary Louise Fellows, *Guilty of the Crime of Trust: Nonstranger Rape*, 75 Minn.L.Rev. 599, 609 (1991).

6. "In response to Estrich's outrage over *Alston*, I wrote that I considered 'rape' at least arguably a misnomer for what had happened to the woman: 'Her stated "no," while not a "yes," bore greater resemblance to a mental reservation or a "do what you will" than to a firm and clear rejection, when viewed against the totality of the couple's ongoing interactions.' This analysis now seems to me wrong in the sense that I found ambiguity regarding the nonconsent element, which even the court had failed to find—when, simply put, it did not exist. * * *

"With 20–20 hindsight * * *, I feel I relied on the wrong case as a springboard for what I still consider a point worth making: Women should not be overprotected. I feared then, and still do, that a global portrayal, reflected in rape law, of females as weak, subordinate creatures, incapable of withstanding pressure of any sort, invites nullification and backlash and, on a philosophical level, cheapens rather than celebrates 'the rights to self-determination, sexual autonomy, and self- and societal respect of women.' Thus, for example, I reject, as wrongheaded, the proposal by Professors Balos and Fellows that a history of physical abuse of the woman (as in *Alston*) should vitiate even positive consent to sexual relations, thereby imposing 'a mandatory divorce' on the parties. A legal rule of 'yes means no' would effectively turn adult sex into statutory rape—women into children—and only limit the life options of victims who have far too few choices already." Vivian Berger, *Rape Law Reform at the Millennium*, 3 Buff.Crim.L.Rev. 513, 521–22 (2000).

7. "Substantive rape law has changed, much of it for the good * * *. And, in perhaps the most significant change in judicial attitudes, courts are becoming more realistic in their conception of force.

"Consider here *State v. Rusk*.[53] The victim agreed to drive Rusk, whom she had met that evening in a bar, to his rooming house. When they arrived, at night, he tried to convince her to come up to his place. When she refused, he took the keys out of the ignition, and asked 'Now will you come up?' She acceded because, as she testified, she was scared being in an unfamiliar area. When they entered his room, he went to the bathroom for a few minutes, but she did not leave or seek help. When he returned, he sat down on the bed, while she sat in a chair. He turned off the lights and began to remove her blouse. She took off her slacks because 'her [sic] asked me to do it.' She begged him to let her leave, and she testified that she was scared because of a 'look in his eyes.' At one point, she apparently asked him, 'If I do what you want, will you let me go without killing me?' He said yes. She also testified that at one point 'he put his hands on my throat and started lightly to choke me.' She did not physically resist Rusk.

"Now, how do these facts compare to *Alston*? Which presents a stronger case of forcible rape? One substantial fact supports the argument that *Rusk* is the more compelling case of rape. In *Rusk*, we have the light choking, whereas no actual force was used during the commission of the sexual act in *Alston*.

"Virtually everything else strikes me as supporting the claim that *Alston* is the better case for conviction. First, in *Rusk*, the Court of Special Appeals inferentially disparaged the victim when it noted the irrelevant fact that she was 'a twenty-one year old mother of a two-year-old son ... separated from her husband but not yet divorced' who had left her son with her mother to go 'bar hopping.' The implicit message is that the victim was 'asking for trouble,' a precursor to an unfriendly judicial outcome. Second, there is the history of physical abuse in *Alston*, absent in *Rusk*, that should have counted in measuring the victim's reasonable fear of Alston.

53. 43 Md.App. 476, 406 A.2d 624 (Md.1979), rev'd, 289 Md. 230, 424 A.2d 720 (1981).

"Third, the physical force in *Rusk* (the 'light choke') could easily have been characterized by an unfriendly court or jury as ambiguous evidence: one person's light choke is another person's inartful caress. Fourth, Rusk's victim had the opportunity to leave the apartment; Alston's victim could not get away. Fifth, in *Alston*, there was an explicit threat of physical harm ('fixing' the victim's face), whereas *Rusk* involved only an implicit threat (his yes to her question whether he would let her go and not kill her if she acceded). Even this 'threat' was ambiguous. It is unclear that his 'yes' was intended as a response to a plea not to be killed; it may have been that he was affirming that he would let her go after the sex.

"It is hard for me to imagine that the *Alston* court would have upheld a forcible rape conviction in *Rusk*. But, the Court of Appeals in Maryland affirmed the rape conviction. It agreed with the dissent below that a jury could reasonably have found that Rusk's conduct was calculated to create in the victim's mind 'a real apprehension, due to fear, of imminent bodily harm, serious enough to overcome her will to resist.' Thus, the resistance requirement was mooted because the court applied a less strict—a far more realistic—understanding of physical force.

"The *Alston/Rusk* dichotomy cannot be explained on the basis of a trend in rape law. We are dealing here with two different state courts, and the *Rusk* decision actually preceded *Alston* by three years. But, what we see, I think, is emblematic of something like the start of a trend in *Rusk*, and the beginning of the end of the 'bad old days' in *Alston*. Indeed, the North Carolina Supreme Court has virtually repudiated its decision in *Alston*.[65] It has since characterized the facts in *Alston* as 'unique,' 'peculiar,' and perhaps 'sui generis,' and it has since affirmed forcible rape convictions in more ambiguous circumstances." Joshua Dressler, *Where We Have Been, and Where We Might be Going: Some Cautionary Reflections on Rape Law Reform*, 46 Clev.St.L.Rev. 409, 418–21 (1998).

8. Not everyone has taken such a kindly view toward *Rusk*, given the nature of the court of appeals' decision: "The court of appeals majority ultimately affirmed the conviction on the narrowest possible ground. The court stated that 'generally, . . . the correct standard' is that the victim's fear must 'be reasonably grounded in order to obviate the need for either proof of actual force on the part of the assailant or physical resistance on the part of the victim.' Was this victim's fear reasonable? The court strove to avoid the question. The fundamental error of the intermediate court was its violation of the principle of appellate restraint; the question of reasonableness was a question of fact to be left to the jury. Still, the court of appeals could not avoid entirely the obligation to review the sufficiency of the evidence. Thus, 'considering all of the evidence in the case, with particular focus upon the actual force applied by Rusk to Pat's neck, we conclude that the jury could rationally find that the essential elements of second degree rape had been established.'

"The emphasis on the light choking/heavy caresses is, perhaps, understandable: It is the only 'objective' (as the supreme court dissent put it) force in the victim's testimony; it is certainly the only 'force' that a schoolboy might recognize. As it happens, however, that force was not applied until the two were already undressed and in bed. Whatever it was— choking or caressing—was a response to the woman's crying as the moment of intercourse approached. It was not, it seems fairly clear, the only force that produced that moment.

---

65. In *State v. Brown*, 332 N.C. 262, 420 S.E.2d 147 (N.C. 1992), the state supreme court signaled its wish to bury the decision entirely by citing and quoting from Susan Estrich [Note 1 supra], characterizing it as a "thoughtful article" "which makes strong arguments that the law should treat such conduct [as occurred in *Alston*] as 'force' . . . or should abandon the element of force."

"Unable to understand force as the power one need not use (at least physically), courts are left either to emphasize the 'light choking' or to look for threats of force. Technically, these threats of force may be implicit as well as explicit. But implicit to whom? That a woman feels genuinely afraid, that a man has created the situation that she finds frightening, even that he has done it intentionally in order to secure sexual satisfaction, may not be enough to constitute the necessary force or even implicit threat of force which earns bodily integrity any protection under the law of rape." Estrich, supra, at 1114–15.

9.   How, then, should the matter of force/threat of force be assessed? Consider, e.g., *Model Penal Code* § 213.1, Comment (1980): "It seems clear, however, that one who takes advantage of a woman's unreasonable fears of violence should not escape punishment any more than a swindler who cheats gullible people by false statements which they should have found incredible. Neither the blameworthiness of the actor nor the gravity of the insult to the victim is ameliorated by a finding that the threat was implausible * * *. The Model Code approach, therefore, is to reject the 'reasonable person' * * * limitation[ ], although it is important to this judgment that the Model Code has also reduced the penalty for rape in circumstances * * * where the actor's overreaching is not objectively corroborated by the infliction of serious bodily injury or his prior relationship to the victim."

10.   When the *Model Penal Code* was drafted, "the law provided little guidance as to the kind of threat that could lead to a rape conviction, other than a threat of physical injury to the female herself. It was even doubtful whether rape was committed where, for example, the offender compelled a mother to submit by threatening to shoot her child or where a girl submitted to save her escort's life." *Model Penal Code*, § 213.1, Comment (1980). Code § 213.1(1)(a) provides language to resolve this point, and several jurisdictions have now adopted that or similar language. See, e.g., *Fitzpatrick v. State*, 93 Nev. 21, 558 P.2d 630 (1977) (defendant's threat that otherwise victim's incarcerated fiancé would be killed sufficient).

B. OTHER COERCION

STATE v. THOMPSON

Supreme Court of Montana, 1990.

243 Mont. 28, 792 P.2d 1103.

SHEEHY, JUSTICE.

On May 25, 1989, the defendant Gerald Roy Thompson was charged with two counts of sexual intercourse without consent and one count of sexual assault. Subsequently, Thompson moved to dismiss Counts I and II of the information, those counts charging defendant with sexual intercourse without consent. Thompson moved to dismiss Counts I and II of the information on the specific ground that the probable cause affidavit was insufficient. On September 1, 1989, the District Court, Tenth Judicial District, Judith Basin County, granted Thompson's motion and dismissed Counts I and II of the information for lack of probable cause in the supporting affidavit. The State now appeals the District Court. We affirm.

The State raised the following issue on appeal: Did the District Court err when it granted defendant's motion to dismiss Counts I and II of the information charging defendant with sexual intercourse without consent for failure to state offenses?

The defendant, Gerald Roy Thompson, the principal and boys basketball coach at Hobson High School, was accused of two counts of sexual intercourse without consent, and one count of sexual assault. This appeal only concerns the two counts of sexual intercourse without consent. The information, filed with the District Court, alleged the defendant committed the crime of sexual intercourse without consent, and stated [that on two occasions between Sept. '86 and June '87] the defendant knowingly had sexual intercourse without consent with a person of the opposite sex; namely Jane Doe, by threatening Jane Doe that she would not graduate from high school * * *.

The affidavits filed in support of this information contained facts and allegations supporting the two counts of sexual intercourse without consent. In essence, they alleged that the threats "caused Jane Doe great psychological pain and fear."

The State contended that fear of the power of Thompson and his authority to keep her from graduating forced Jane Doe into silence until after she graduated from high school in June of 1987. On November 25, 1988, Jane Doe filed a letter with the Hobson School Board describing the activities against her by Thompson. After investigations by both the school board and the Judith Basin County prosecutor's office, the prosecutor filed an information on May 25, 1989. * * *

Thompson was charged with two counts of alleged sexual intercourse without consent under § 45–5–503, MCA. Section 45–5–503, MCA, states the following:

A person who knowingly has sexual intercourse without consent with a person of the opposite sex commits the offense of sexual intercourse without consent ...

The phrase "without consent"—the key element of the crime—has a very specific definition in Montana's criminal code. This phrase is defined in § 45–5–501, MCA, which states in pertinent part:

As used in 45–5–503 and 45–5–505, the term "without consent" means:

(i) the victim is compelled to submit by force or by threat of imminent death, bodily injury, or kidnaping to be inflicted on anyone; ...

Section 45–5–501, MCA, makes it clear that the element of "without consent" is satisfied if submission of the victim is obtained either by force or by threat of imminent death, bodily injury, or kidnaping. No other circumstances relating to force or threat eliminate consent under the statute.

Thompson challenged the probable cause affidavit in the District Court, contending it failed to state any fact or circumstance showing that Jane Doe's submission to an alleged act of sexual intercourse was obtained by force or by any of the threats listed in § 45–5–501, MCA. In contrast, the State argues that Thompson's actions constitute sexual intercourse through force or threats. The District Court, in its opinion and order, agreed with Thompson's contentions, and found that the facts in the affidavit supporting the information failed to show the element of "without consent." In reaching this conclusion, the District Court first considered whether or not there were facts or circumstances in the probable cause affidavit to indicate that submission to the alleged act of sexual intercourse without consent was obtained "by force." In order to determine whether Thompson forced Jane Doe to submit to the sexual act, the District Court had to define the phrase "by force" since there is no definition contained in the Montana Criminal Code. The District Court in its order defined force as follows:

The word "force" is used in its ordinary and normal connotation: physical compulsion, the use or immediate threat of bodily harm, injury.

Next, the District Court examined the information and probable cause affidavit to determine if there were any facts or circumstances constituting force. The District Court found that "force was not alleged in the information nor in the affidavit in support of it."

In contrast, the State argues the District Court's definition of force is too limited. The State, relying on *Raines v. State* (1989), 191 Ga.App. 743, 382 S.E.2d 738, 739, argues that intimidation and fear may constitute force.[a] The State also contends that Thompson, in his position of authority as the principal, intimidated Jane Doe into the alleged acts. Furthermore, the State argues the fear and apprehension of Jane Doe show Thompson used force against her. We agree with the State that Thompson intimidated Jane Doe; however, we cannot stretch the definition of force to include intimidation, fear, or apprehension. Rather, we adopt the District Court's definition of force.

Other jurisdictions, such as California, have expanded the definition of force, beyond its physical connotation. *People v. Cicero* (1984), 157 Cal.App.3d 465, 204 Cal.Rptr. 582. The California Supreme Court adopted the following reasoning to expand the word force:

> ... the fundamental wrong at which the law of rape is aimed is not the application of physical force that causes physical harm. Rather, the law of rape primarily guards the integrity of a women's will and the privacy of her sexuality from an act of intercourse undertaken without her consent. Because the fundamental wrong is the violation of a woman's will and sexuality, the law of rape does not require that "force" cause physical harm. Rather, in this scenario, "force" plays merely a supporting evidentiary role, as necessary only to ensure an act of intercourse has been undertaken against a victim's will.

The California Supreme Court's definition of the word force is too broad under Montana's definition of the crime. Until the legislature adopts a definition for the word "force", we must adopt the ordinary and normal definition of the word "force" as set forth by the District Court.

The State in its information and accompanying affidavit complain that Thompson deprived Jane Doe of consent to the sexual act by threatening that he would prevent her from graduating from high school. The threat required in § 45–5–501, MCA, is "a threat of imminent death, bodily injury, or kidnaping to be inflicted on anyone ... " The District Court found that something more than a threat is necessary to satisfy the statutory

---

a. *Raines* states: "As to the rape charge, the trial court's denial of appellant's motion for a directed verdict of acquittal is enumerated as error. The contention is that 'there was no evidence that the sexual acts were induced by any acts of force or threats of force on the part of appellant.'

"The evidence, construed most strongly against appellant and in favor of the guilty verdict, showed the following: The fourteen-year-old victim accepted appellant's offer of a ride home. However, appellant drove her to a secluded location and parked. There, she repeatedly rejected appellant's persistent requests for sex. She asked to be driven home or to be allowed to walk home. Appellant refused to drive her home or to allow her to leave the car unless she had sex with him. Finally realizing that appellant 'wasn't going to take [her] home' and concluding that she had no other choice, the victim gave in to his sexual demands. Over appellant's objection, the victim was allowed to testify that she had not offered any physical resistance to appellant because she had been raped previously and had been counseled against such resistance. When appellant did return the victim to her home, she made an immediate outcry.

" 'The rape statute reads in pertinent part as follows: "A person commits [the offense of] rape when he has carnal knowledge of a female, forcibly and against

her will." True consent to the act, of course, negates the element of force; but it is both entirely logical and legally certain that apparent "consent" induced by fear is not the free consent required to prevent he act's constituting a crime, but is the mere product of force within the meaning of the statute. Intimidation may substitute for force. Whether the victim consented is a fact question. 'The present case does not show the degree of force frequently found in crimes of rape, or the violent threats often made. However, there was evidence of force [or intimidation], and the circumstances provided ample ground for fear on [the victim's] part. She repeatedly testified in regard to her fears. The jury apparently believed that it was the force exercised, and the fears which their actions produced in her mind, that caused her to yield to them, and that her consent was not of the kind to prevent the intercourse from constituting rape. The jury was authorized under the evidence to find [appellant] guilty of the crimes charged, and it was not error ... to deny the motion for [directed verdict] of acquittal.' After a review of the record, we find that a rational trier of fact could reasonably have found from the evidence adduced at trial proof of appellant's guilt beyond a reasonable doubt."

requirement. A threat one will not graduate from high school is not one of the threats listed under § 45–5–501, MCA. The State argues that the definition "threat of bodily injury" includes psychological impairment. Unfortunately, the statute sets forth bodily injury, not psychological impairment. A threat that eventually leads to psychological impairment is not sufficient under the statute. The statute only addresses the results of three specific kinds of threats, and psychological impairment is not one of them.

The State urges this Court to adopt the definitions of threat set forth in § 45–2–101(68), MCA.[b] Section 45–2–101(68), MCA, has no application in regard to the crime of sexual intercourse without consent. Section 45–5–501, MCA, plainly and succinctly lays out the types of threats necessary to make the victim act "without consent."

Under § 45–5–501, MCA, the threat also must be of "imminent death, bodily injury, or kidnaping." Thompson's threats cannot be considered imminent. The alleged sexual act and threat occurred in December of 1986. Jane Doe graduated from Hobson High School in June of 1987. Clearly, Thompson's alleged threats were not imminent.

Peppered throughout the State's brief is the contention that "under Montana law the issue of consent is a fact question, and therefore a question for the jury to decide." The State is correct, the jury is the proper trier of facts in regard to issues such as consent. However, in this case, the State's information and probable cause affidavit have failed to set forth any facts or circumstances to show that the alleged act of sexual intercourse were within the statute defining the elements of the crime. So, the issue in this case is not whether the jury was denied its role as trier of the facts, but whether the State sufficiently set forth facts or circumstances to show the element of "without consent." The court properly granted defendant's motion to dismiss for lack of probable cause.

This case is one of considerable difficulty for us, as indeed it must have been for the District Court judge. The alleged facts, if true, show disgusting acts of taking advantage of a young person by an adult who occupied a position of authority over the young person. If we could rewrite the statutes to define the alleged acts here as sexual intercourse without consent, we would willingly do so. The business of courts, however, is to interpret statutes, not to rewrite them, nor to insert words not put there by the legislature. With a good deal of reluctance, and with strong condemnation of the alleged acts, we affirm the District Court.

Notes and Questions

1. Was the court in *Thompson* unduly timid in not opting for the *Cicero* approach? What then of *Commonwealth v. Mlinarich*, 518 Pa. 247, 542 A.2d 1335 (1988), where "the defendant guardian threatened a fourteen-year-old girl in his care with return to a juvenile detention facility if she did not accede to his sexual demands. The question that the court had to address was whether such threat constituted 'forcible compulsion' or the 'threat of forcible compulsion that would prevent resistance by a person of reasonable resolution' within the meaning of Pennsylvania's rape law. The court answered the question in the

---

b. This statute, which contains the "general definitions" for use in interpreting provisions in the state's criminal code, reads in part: "Unless otherwise specified in the statute, all words will be taken in the objective standard rather than in the subjective, and unless a different meaning plainly is required, the following definitions apply in this title: * * *

"(75) 'Threat' means a menace, however communicated, to:

"(a) inflict physical harm on the person threatened or any other person or on property;

"(b) subject any person to physical confinement or restraint;

"(c) commit a criminal offense;

"(d) accuse a person of a criminal offense;

"(e) expose a person to hatred, contempt, or ridicule."

negative. It noted that forcible compulsion includes both physical force and psychological duress, but the latter must be of sufficient intensity to overpower the will to resist and here it did not. The court stated: 'Notwithstanding, she was left with a choice and therefore the submission was a result of a deliberate choice and was not an involuntary act.' One dissenter characterized this fact pattern as clearly involving psychological coercion. Another dissenting judge wrote: 'The question is not whether she could make a choice to yield or be confined, but whether the law should allow such a choice at all.' In a subsequent Pennsylvania case involving sexual acts by a male therapist with his adolescent male patient,[227] the court found the forcible element of rape was satisfied by the therapist's position of authority.[228]" Patricia J. Falk, *Rape by Fraud and Rape by Coercion*, 64 Brook.L.Rev. 39, 81 (1998).

2. The judges in *Thompson* assert that if they were a legislature rather than a court they would "rewrite the statute to define the alleged acts here as sexual intercourse without consent," so that conduct such as defendant's would be rape. Would you do likewise? If so, in what way would you rewrite the statute? Would your amendment deal specifically with teachers and others in a position of authority, or would it deal more broadly with the problem by merely requiring nonconsent rather than any imposition (as the *Thompson* judges seem to suggest) or by describing some other forms of impermissible imposition?

Before answering that question, consider a few variations on *Thompson*. For one thing, should the prohibited "pressures" be limited to threatening bad consequences if sexual intercourse is not allowed, or should honest promises of good consequences if sexual intercourse is forthcoming also be covered? For example, what if Jane Doe was rightly on the verge of flunking out of high school but Thompson offered to prevent that from happening in exchange for intercourse? Or, what if Jane was near the top of her class and Thompson threatened to change her A in his course to a B unless she had intercourse with him? Or, promised to change her B to an A if she did? What if Thompson threatened that absent intercourse he would not write any letters of recommendation for her? Or promised that in exchange for intercourse he would write favorable letters of recommendation? Or, what if the "pressures" came instead from Jane's supervisor at McDonald's, who threatened to fire her unless she engage in intercourse? Who promised to give her a raise if she engaged in intercourse? Or, what if the "pressures" came from her 19–year-old boy friend, who said that unless she engaged in sex with him he would tell Thompson about her cheating on an exam? Would tell her classmates they were sleeping together regularly? Would distribute about town nude photos of her? Or would break up with her? As for all the prior instances involving a promised exchange of a benefit, should it make any difference whether the bargaining was commenced by Jane?

3. Does this array of hypotheticals lend support to the conclusion that extending the law of rape beyond force/threat of force situations is not possible because there is no way to articulate the distinction between those pressures that should be prohibited and those that should not? Indeed, is such extension a bad idea in any event because: (1) "One potential cost of expanding rape law to include fraud and coercion is the possibility of undercutting rape reform"; (2) "A second potential cost of expanding rape law to encompass * * * coercion cases is the trivialization of violent rape by comparison"; and (3) "Some theorists worry that juries will not convict defendants if the evidence fails to disclose the use of force

---

227. *Commonwealth v. Frank*, 577 A.2d 609 (Pa. 1990).

228. The *Frank* court wrote: "Appellant occupied a position of authority such that it may be reasonably inferred that the victim would feel coerced to submit to appellant's demands out of a sense of duty to obey not only the appellant, but also the wishes of his then adoptive mother."

because this does not correspond to jurors' intuitive notions of rape." Falk, supra, at 142–45 (summarizing views of others).

4. Is the solution here a broader concept of what constitutes force? Consider Stephen J. Schulhofer, *The Feminist Challenge in Criminal Law*, 143 U.Pa.L.Rev. 2151, 2176–77 (1995): "The other strand in current reform proposals is to tackle the problem by expanding the conception of force. Many rape reformers stress that force can take the form of strength that a man does not need to use. Force can involve not only physical violence but also other kinds of power. This approach reflects the theories of male dominance developed by Catharine MacKinnon that are now supported by many moderate feminists and by several courts. * * *

"The move to expand the conception of force thus has much truth to it but no stopping point. In that sense, it is too radical. That is a common reaction to Professor MacKinnon's approach. But the dominance approach is also too conservative because it remains linked to notions of force. In actual administration, it is almost certain to be held back by the cultural preconceptions that determine what force means to the many police, prosecutors, judges, and jurors who are not feminists. Efforts to expand accepted conceptions of force can offer interest and excitement to conversations within feminist circles, but as these approaches rest upon accordion-like notions of power or pressure, they inevitably lead the discussion into an area where boundaries will be unclear and social consensus will be elusive."

5. What then of eliminating any reference to any particular kind of imposition and simply defining rape in terms of unconsented sex? Consider Joshua Dressler, *Where We Have Been, and Where We Might Be Going: Some Cautionary Reflections on Rape Law Reform*, 46 Clev.St.L.Rev. 409, 429–30 (1998): "If we are going to punish nonconsensual sexual contact, even when there is no physical force or threatened force intimated, then we must look with more care than in the past at what constitutes 'voluntary' consent * * *. It is easy to determine that permission or consent is coerced if the man has a knife, uses his fists, or threatens physical injury, but what now? * * *

"There are no easy answers to what constitutes duress. Although courts sometimes suggest otherwise, the law does not really treat coercion as an empirical matter: we do not really seek to determine what is undeterminable, namely, whether a particular person's 'free will' (whatever that is) was overborne. The real issue is normative: What degree of fortitude do we have a right to expect from ordinary human beings when they are confronted—as we all are in our daily lives—by hard decisions, by great temptations, and by lawful and unlawful pressures?"

6. The best answer to that question, Dressler goes on to say, is that provided by *Model Penal Code* § 213.1(2)(a). Others are not so sure. Consider David P. Bryden, *Redefining Rape*, 3 Buff.Crim.L.Rev. 317, 440–42 (2000): "The most obvious limitation of this new crime is the objective test implicit in the concept of a 'woman of ordinary resolution.' Plainly, this language, unlike the language concerning threats of force, excludes protection of an 'unreasonably' neurotic victim, even if the actor deliberately takes advantage of her weakness.* * *

"The phrase 'woman of ordinary resolution' is open to various interpretations. The MPC Commentaries indicate that a 'threat to cause her to lose her job or to deprive her of a valued possession' might be criminal under this section, while a threat to withhold an expensive present would not. * * * Generalizing, the Code's Commentaries offer a murky distinction:

The threat must be such that submission by the female results from coercion rather than bargain. This inquiry into the essential character of the threat is distinct from, though complementary to, the requirement that it achieve a gravity sufficient to 'prevent resistance by a woman of ordinary resolution.' Thus, if a wealthy man were to threaten to withdraw financial support from his unemployed girlfriend, it is at least arguable under the circumstances that he is making a threat 'that would prevent resistance by a woman of ordinary resolution.' The reason why this case is excluded from liability ... is not the gravity of the harm threatened—it may be quite substantial—but its essential character as part of a process of bargain. He is not guilty of compulsion overwhelming the will of his victim but only of offering her an unattractive choice to avoid some unwanted alternative.

"The distinction in this passage between 'coercion' and 'bargain' is unhelpful. Lawful bargains are often preceded by pressure that could be described as 'coercive.' Conversely, extortionate threats can be thought of as 'part of a process of bargain.' "

7. What then of the proposal in Susan Estrich, *Rape*, 95 Yale L.J. 1087, 1120–21, 1182 (1986): "To the argument that it is either impossible or unwise for the law to regulate sexual 'bargains' short of physical force, the law of extortion stands as a sharp rebuke: It has long listed prohibited threats in fairly inclusive terms.[a] While extortion may be a lesser offense than robbery, it is nonetheless prohibited.

"It is almost certainly impossible to expect that the law could address all of the techniques of power and coercion which men use against women in sexual relations. I am not suggesting that we try.[96] Rather, I am suggesting that we do something that is actually quite easy—* * * prohibit extortion to secure sex to the same extent[b] we prohibit extortion to secure money. Many states already have criminal coercion * * * provisions that are worded with sufficient breadth * * * to be applied to prohibit such coerced sex. But cases enforcing such prohibitions are relatively rare, and the results have been divided. The broad reach of such statutes not only invites overbreadth challenges and claims of lack of warning, but fails to make clear that loss of bodily integrity is a different and greater

---

a. "Perhaps the most interesting and potentially important sexual extortion case is *Lovely v. Cunningham*[, 796 F.2d 1 (1st Cir.1986).] Lovely, a liquor store manager, befriended a young drifter, gave him a job involving little work, spent $1000 on him, paid $60 as restitution for a theft he had committed, paid his rent, and invited him to live in Lovely's home. Demanding sexual relations, Lovely threatened to withdraw various benefits he had conferred on Cunningham and to sue him for the $60, and thereby have him imprisoned. Lovely was found guilty in New Hampshire courts of aggravated sexual assault, statutorily defined as coercing the victim to submit 'by threatening to retaliate' against him. In a habeas suit, Lovely argued that the New Hampshire statutes, and traditional extortion law, did not give him fair warning that his conduct was criminal. The First Circuit disagreed, and upheld the conviction. The court conceded that if Lovely had merely threatened to terminate free housing, this would only have been 'the withholding of an expensive present' and not a crime. But Lovely's threats to deprive the victim of his job, and to make trouble for him with the police, were deemed extortionate.

"[Extortion statutes] vary in their descriptions of the prohibited threats. They commonly include threats to publicize a secret that will subject the victim to public ridicule or disgrace. Virtually all statutes cover threats

to accuse the victim of a crime as well as threats to cause bodily harm, or to injure property. But most threats to cause economic harm are lawful. For example, a rich uncle is free to say, 'Unless you take care of me, I'll cut you out of my will.' " Bryden, supra, at 436–37, 439.

96. Nor am I arguing that these cases must of necessity be considered in the same category as first degree, armed and brutal rape. I am more than willing to treat them as a lesser degree of "rape" and to impose lighter punishment in the same way that the unarmed robber, or the blackmailer, is treated as a less serious offender than the one who uses a deadly weapon in a robbery.

b. Compare Bryden, supra, at 452: "On the other hand, there are some contexts in which one can plausibly argue that the law of extortion should forbid sexual conduct that would be permissible in superficially analogous nonsexual cases. Consider, for example, a woman who can't afford to rent a decent apartment. The landlord is entitled to request that she give him her precious antique furniture in lieu of rent. But it does not follow that he should be entitled to request sexual services instead of rent. Hard-core libertarians aside, most people don't want sex to be treated as an ordinary item of commerce, especially not in return for a necessity like housing."

injury than loss of money and thus merits greater punishment. Criminal coercion statutes are, at best, poor substitutes for an expanded understanding of the 'force' that makes sex rape.[c]

" * * * The powerlessness of women and the value of bodily integrity are great enough to argue that women deserve more comprehensive protection for their bodies than the laws of extortion or fraud provide for money. But if going so far seems too complicated and fraught with difficulty, as it does to many, then we need not. For the present, it would be a significant improvement if the law of rape in any state prohibited exactly the same threats as that state's law of extortion * * *.[334]"

8. Compare Schulhofer, supra, at 2179: "This seems a sensible way to begin thinking about factors that taint consent. But Estrich unfortunately does not spell out her notion of * * * extortion * * *. Without further detail, the approach seems either plausible but vague, or clear but far too broad." Schulhofer himself, in what one commentator has characterized as "the broadest, most well-developed categorization of coercive pressures * * *, without resort to concepts that are hopelessly open-ended," Falk, supra, at 176, would focus on women's autonomy, "the right to protection from those interferences that our culture and our legal system already consider impermissible." Schulhofer, supra, at 2180. He further identifies three illegitimate pressures of the coercive type: (i) extortionate behavior, which is "already understood to be unprivileged and illegitimate"; (ii) coercion arising out of institutional and professional relationships; and (iii) coercion via economic pressure, the latter two of which involve situations where "coercion results from altering the [person's] ordinary range of options in a legally impermissible way." Stephen J. Schulhofer, *Taking Sexual Autonomy Seriously: Rape Law and Beyond*, 11 Law & Phil. 35, 79, 85 (1992).

9. As for just how far legislative reforms have encompassed coercive impositions beyond the traditional force requirement, Falk, supra (summarizing these developments at 177–78, and discussing them in more detail at 89–132), notes that state legislatures have adopted three general approaches to the line-drawing problem in cases of rape by coercion: (1) Some states have criminalized sexual intercourse between victims and persons holding positions of trust or authority, as by making it a crime to use that position to cause submission, altering or removing the consent requirement with regard to certain relationships (e.g., psychotherapist-patient), or by prohibiting sexual extortion in employment. (2) Several states have more generally made certain nonphysical coercion to accomplish sexual intercourse criminal, either by enactment of statutes like or similar to the Model Penal Code provision quoted above, or by specifying certain impermissible means of coercion, such as threats to retaliate (including extortion) or to expose the victim to public humiliation and disgrace. (3) A few other jurisdictions have enacted special provisions regarding sexual extortion, sometimes specifying such threats as exposing secrets or harming another in health, business or reputation.

---

c. Compare Donald A. Dripps, *Beyond Rape: An Essay on the Difference Between the Presence of Force and the Absence of Consent*, 92 Colum. L. Rev. 1780, 1802 (1992): "Professor Estrich has a point when she argues that one who obtains sex by extortionate or fraudulent means acts as culpably as one who obtains money by the same means. Extortion can be covered simply by amending the extortion statutes to include sex among the things it is criminal to obtain by unlawful threat."

334. To the difficult hypothetical, there is thus an easy answer: resolve it as if money were involved, and I will gladly apply that resolution in the context of rape. Drawing lines between bargains and threats is not always easy. Deciding which misstatements are material is not always automatic. But I have never heard either problem offered as a reason for the repeal of the laws against blackmail, extortion, deception or false pretenses. And in practice, there are likely to be more than enough easy cases for victims, prosecutors and judges who are so inclined.

C. FRAUD

PEOPLE v. EVANS

Supreme Court, New York County, New York, 1975.
85 Misc.2d 1088, 379 N.Y.S.2d 912.

EDWARD J. GREENFIELD, JUSTICE:

The question presented in this case is whether the sexual conquest by a predatory male of a resisting female constitutes rape or seduction.

In making the distinction, we must deal with patterns of behavior which have been exhibited by aggressive males towards gentle or timid or submissive females, the broad outlines of which have been similar for hundreds or maybe thousands of years, but the particulars of which vary markedly in individual cases.

It is a fact, I suppose, that since before the dawn of history men with clubs have grabbed women, willing or unwilling, by the hair, to have their way with them. Techniques have become more varied and more subtle with the years.

As we have become more civilized, we have come to condemn the more overt, aggressive and outrageous behavior of some men towards women and we have labeled it "rape." We have attempted to control or deter it by providing for extremely heavy sentences, second to and, in some jurisdictions, equaled by the penalties set by the law for murder.

At the same time we have recognized that there are some patterns of aggression or aggressive male sexual behavior toward females which do not deserve such extreme penalties, in which the male objective may be achieved through charm or guile or protestations of love, promises or deceit.

Where force is not employed to overcome reluctance, and where consent, however reluctant initially, can be spelled out, this we label "seduction," which society may condone, even as it disapproves.

There is some conduct which comes close to the line between rape and seduction. This is such a case.

Since a jury has been waived, this Court is called upon to scrutinize the conduct involved and to draw the line between the legally permissible and the impermissible and to determine on which side of the line this conduct falls.

Rape is defined in our Penal Law, Section 130.35, subdivision 1, as follows: "A male is guilty of rape in the first degree when he engages in sexual intercourse with a female: 1. By forcible compulsion."

Rape can also be premised upon other conditions which would indicate the incapacity of a female to give consent either in actuality or as a matter of law. We are concerned here with the first subdivision, sexual intercourse by forcible compulsion. That is the essence of the crime.

Forcible compulsion is defined in Section 130.00 subdivision 8, of the Penal Law as "physical force that overcomes earnest resistance; or a threat, express or implied, that places a person in fear of immediate death or serious physical injury to himself or another person, or in fear that he or another person will immediately be kidnaped."

Rape, though it sometimes may be abetted by other females, appears to be exclusively a proscribed activity for males.

Seduction, on the other hand, may be freely indulged in by both sexes. It involves allurement, enticement, or persuasion, to overcome initial unwillingness or resistance. Its ends may be achieved by fair means or foul, but seduction eschews the crudities of force and threats. In which category does defendant's conduct fall?

In answering that inquiry, and based upon the testimony in this case, the Court first makes the following findings of fact:

The defendant, a bachelor of approximately thirty-seven years of age, aptly described in the testimony as "glib," on July 15, 1974 met an incoming plane at LaGuardia Airport, from which disembarked Lucy Elizabeth Peterson, of Charlotte, North Carolina, a twenty-year-old petite, attractive second-year student at Wellesley College, an unworldly girl, evidently unacquainted with New York City and the sophisticated city ways, a girl who proved to be, as indicated by the testimony, incredibly gullible, trusting and naive.

The testimony indicates that the defendant struck up a conversation with her, posing as a psychologist doing a magazine article and using a name that was not his, inducing Miss Peterson to answer questions for an interview.

The evidence further shows that the defendant invited Miss Peterson to accompany him by automobile to Manhattan, her destination being Grand Central Station. They were accompanied in the automobile by other persons, some of whom were introduced by the defendant as colleagues on a professional basis. But it appears that a funny thing happened on the way to the station. There were numerous detours before Beth Peterson ever found her way to Grand Central Station. First, they were taken to an apartment on the east side. Some of the party were left there.

Then the evidence indicates that this defendant and a girl named Bridget took Miss Peterson to an establishment called Maxwell's Plum, which the defendant explained was for the purpose of conducting a sociological experiment in which he would observe her reactions and the reactions of males towards her in the setting of a singles bar. After several hours there, in which Miss Peterson evidently was still under the belief that her stopping for a drink at Maxwell's Plum was part of this psychological and sociological experiment, she was persuaded to accompany the defendant to the west side, upon the defendant's explanation that he was there going to pick up his automobile and drive her to Grand Central Station.

Instead of going to the automobile, she was induced to come up to an apartment on the fourteenth floor, which the defendant explained was used as one of his five offices or apartments throughout the city; and Miss Peterson, still believing that the defendant was in fact what he purported to be, went up and accompanied him there. That apartment, Apartment 14—D, at 1 Lincoln Plaza, was in truth and in fact the apartment of one Heinz Patzak, who ran the Austrian National Tourist Bureau and who at that time was in Austria. Mr. Patzak has testified that he never had given approval or permission for the defendant to enter, use or occupy that apartment.

Miss Peterson came to the apartment and her questions as to the existence of photographs of children, a crib, stuffed animals and toys, were readily explained away by the defendant as being connected with his treatment of patients as a psychologist, the explanation of the crib and the toys being that there were used for the purposes of primal therapy to enable his patients to associate with their childhood years more readily. In the apartment the psychological interviewing continued, the defendant having explained to Miss Peterson that he was searching for the missing link between the "girl-woman" and the "woman-girl." Miss Peterson, who was then working in a psychiatric branch of New York Hospital, Cornell Medical School, in White Plains, and who had some training in psychology, believed that all of this legitimately related to a psychological research project which the defendant was conducting.

During the course of the interview in the apartment the defendant probed Miss Peterson's life and she had, during the course of their conversation together, made a revelation of her prior intimacies and her feelings, and her experiences with respect to various people. In the apartment she was asked to participate in an adjective word game, applying five adjectives to certain designated persons, including herself and the defendant.

She had been there for one to two hours when the defendant made his move and pulled her on to the opened sofa-bed in the living room of that apartment and attempted to disrobe her. She resisted that, and she claims that as articles of clothing were attempted to be removed she would pull them back on and ultimately she was able to ward off these advances and to get herself dressed again. At that point, the defendant's tactics, according to her testimony, appeared to have changed.

First, he informed her of his disappointment that she had failed the test, that this was all part of his psychological experiment, that, in fact, this was a way in which he was trying to reach her innermost consciousness, one of the ways in which that could be done. Then, after expressing disappointment in the failure of this psychological experiment, he took steps to cause doubt and fear to arise in the mind of Miss Peterson. He said, "Look where you are. You are in the apartment of a strange man. How do you know that I am really who I say I am? How do you know that I am really a psychologist?" Then, he went on and said, "I could kill you. I could rape you. I could hurt you physically."

Miss Peterson testified that at that point she became extremely frightened, that she realized, indeed, how vulnerable she was. The defendant did not strike her, did not beat her, he exhibited no weapons at the time, but he made the statement, "I could kill you; I could rape you." Then there was yelling and screaming, further to intimidate the defendant, and then an abrupt switch in which the defendant attempted to play on the sympathy of Miss Peterson by telling her a story about his lost love, how Miss Peterson had reminded him of her, and the hurt that he had sustained when she had driven her car off a cliff. Obviously, Miss Peterson's sympathy was engaged, and at that time acting instinctively, she took a step forward and reached out for him and put her hand on his shoulders, and then he grabbed her and said, "You're mine, you are mine." There thereupon followed an act of sexual intercourse, an act of oral-genital contact; a half-hour later a second act of sexual intercourse, and then, before she left, about seven o'clock that morning, an additional act.

The sexual intercourse appears to be corroborated by the findings of the laboratory confirmation of seminal fluid on the underclothing which she had worn at the time.

The testimony indicates that during these various sexual acts Miss Peterson, in fact, offered little resistance. She said that she was pinned down by the defendant's body weight, but in some manner all her clothing was removed, all his clothing was removed, and the acts took place. There was no torn clothing, there were no scratches, there were no bruises. Finally, at approximately seven a.m. Miss Peterson dressed and left the apartment. She says that the defendant acknowledged to her that he was aware that it had been against her will, but he nevertheless gave her three telephone numbers. Miss Peterson then returned to White Plains, where later that day she recited some of the events to a fellow-worker, and then to a roommate. Ultimately she reported the facts to the New York City Police and to the Westchester County Sheriff's office, resulting in her being taken to New York City by personnel from the Westchester County Sheriff's office where, at the Gulf & Western Building at Columbus Circle they saw the defendant emerging from an elevator. Despite her identification of him at that time the defendant initially denied that his name was Marty, that he knew Miss Peterson, or that he had had any involvement with her in any way.

After he had been placed under arrest in a coffee shop of the Mayflower Hotel, and they had proceeded to the building at No. 1 Lincoln Plaza, the defendant began to make partial admissions as to his identity, his occupation of Apartment 14—D at No. 1 Lincoln Plaza, his knowledge of Miss Peterson and ultimately the fact that he had had sexual intercourse with her, which he claimed was consensual and a matter of mutual enjoyment. He further told the police officers that the whole psychology bit was a "game that he played with girls' heads."

The testimony further indicates that after he had been placed under arrest, and while he was in custody, he escaped from the police car in which he had been placed, and that Detective Kelleher chased him in and around the streets and up 15 flights of a building, where he ultimately located Evans on a water tower. The explanation given to Detective Magnusson was that he was looking for a lawyer.

Those being the facts, the Court arrives at the following conclusions:

The Court finds that the testimony of Beth Peterson was essentially credible testimony. The Court finds from the story which she has narrated that the defendant was a person who was crafty, scheming, manipulative, and ever ready with explanations.

From the testimony which has been given there are some factors which tend to point toward guilt and some towards innocence. As factors indicating guilt are the assumption of the false identity by the defendant, his not giving his true name, his denial to the police when first confronted of what his name was, and his denial of any knowledge of Miss Peterson, which denials he ultimately retracted. Then, of course, there is the evidence about flight which is always evidence that can be considered as evincing some consciousness of guilt. On the other hand, there are some factors pointing to innocence on the part of the defendant, and a lack of criminal culpability on his part. The fact that Miss Peterson had no bruises or scratches, no torn clothing, that she had been allowed to proceed from the apartment without any further threats or concealment as to location. The fact that she was given phone numbers by the defendant which made it relatively easy to trace his location and whereabouts; the fact that he attempted to call her on several occasions after she had left the apartment; and the fact that he had continued in his prior haunts at the Gulf & Western Building and at No. 1 Lincoln Plaza. From all this, the Court concludes that the defendant inveigled Miss Peterson, deceived her, put her on, and took advantage of her.

The question is whether having had sexual intercourse by the same means described constitutes rape in the first degree. The essential element of rape in the first degree is forcible compulsion. The prevailing view in this country is that there can be no rape which is achieved by fraud, or trick, or stratagem. Provided there is actual consent, the nature of the act being understood, it is not rape, absent a statute, no matter how despicable the fraud, even if a woman has intercourse with a man impersonating her husband (*Lewis v. Alabama*, 30 Ala. 54); or if a fraudulent ceremony leads her to believe she is legally married to a man (*Alabama v. Murphy*, 6 Ala. 765), or even if a doctor persuades her that sexual intercourse is necessary for her treatment and return to good health. *Don Moran v. People*, 25 Mich. 356. "Fraud cannot be allowed to supply the place of the force which the statute makes mandatory."

It should be noted that seduction, while not considered to be a criminal act at common law, has been made a criminal offense by statute in some jurisdictions. In seduction, unlike rape, the consent of the woman, implied or explicit, has been procured, by artifice, deception, flattery, fraud or promise.

The declared public policy of this state looks with disfavor on actions for seduction since the civil action was abolished more than forty years ago. The statute did not repeal any Penal Law provisions, but there are no presently existing penal sanctions against seduction. The law recognizes that there are some crimes where trickery and deceit do constitute the basis for a criminal charge. Since the common law, we have recognized the existence of larceny by trick. But of course, for a larceny there has to be a taking of property of value. I do not mean to imply that a woman's right to her body is not a thing of value, but it is not property in the sense which is defined by the law.

It is clear from the evidence in this case that Beth Peterson was intimidated; that she was confused; that she had been drowned in a torrent of words and perhaps was terrified. But it is likewise clear from the evidence that the defendant did not resort to actual physical force. There was " 'no act of violence, no struggle, no outcry, and no attempt to restrain or confine the person ... which constitute the usual ... and essential evidence' of rape." The restraint which was imposed upon Miss Peterson was a restraint imposed by his body weight, which would be the normal situation in which any sexual contact would be achieved. Miss Peterson manifested little or no resistance. She indicated at some point she kicked. I asked her what she was doing with her arms and hands at the time. The answers indicated that it was not very much. Now, that can be understandable. A woman is not obligated to resist to the uttermost under all circumstances, when her will to resist has been paralyzed by fear and by threats. That is why the law recognizes the existence of a threat as being the equivalent of the use of actual force. As stated in *People v. Connor*, 126 N.Y. 278, 281, 27 N.E. 252, 253, an ancient but still followed case, in the Court of Appeals:

> "The extent of the resistance required of an assaulted female is governed by the circumstances of the case, and the grounds which she has for apprehending the infliction of great bodily harm.

> "When an assault is committed by the sudden and unexpected exercise of overpowering force upon a timid and inexperienced girl, under circumstances indicating the power and the will of the aggressor to effect his object, and an intention to use any means necessary to accomplish it, it would seem to present a case for a jury to say whether the fear naturally inspired by such circumstances had not taken away or impaired the ability of the assaulted party to make effectual resistance to the assault."

Whether resistance was useless under the prevailing circumstances is a always a question for the trier of facts.

So the question here is not so much the use of force, but whether threats uttered by the defendant had paralyzed her capacity to resist and had, in fact, undermined her will. Now, what was it the defendant said? He said, "Look where you are. You are in the apartment of a strong man. How do you know that I really am who I say I am? How do you know that I am really a psychologist? I could kill you. I could rape you. I could hurt you physically." Those words, as uttered, are susceptible to two possible and diverse interpretations. The first would be in essence that—you had better do what I say, for you are helpless and I have the power to use ultimate force should you resist. That clearly would be a threat which would induce fear and overcome resistance. The second possible meaning of those words is, in effect, that—you are a foolish girl. You are in the apartment of a strange man. You put yourself in the hands of a stranger, and you are vulnerable and defenseless. The possibility would exist of physical harm to you were you being confronted by someone other than the person who uttered this statement.

Of course, it is entirely possible that Miss Peterson, who heard the statements, construed that as a threat, even though it may not have been intended as such by the person who uttered those words. The question arises as to which is the controlling state of mind—that of a person who hears the words and interprets them as a threat, or the state of mind of the person who utters such words. It appears to the Court that the controlling state of mind must be that of the speaker.* * * * And so, if he utters words which are taken as a threat by the person who hears them, but are not intended as a threat by the person who utters them, there would be no basis for finding the necessary criminal intent to establish culpability under the law.

So where a statement is ambiguous, where the words and the acts which purport to constitute force or threats are susceptible of diverse interpretations, which may be consistent with either guilt or innocence, the Court, as the trier of the facts, cannot say beyond a reasonable doubt that the guilt of the defendant has been established with respect to the crime of rape. The words which were uttered both as to what the defendant could do, "I could kill you. I could rape you." and subsequent words that he was going to do to the complainant what his lost love had done to him—the Court finds are ambiguous. They were not accompanied by violence. They were not accompanied by a demonstration of the intention to carry out the threats. There was no beating. There was no weapon displayed. There was a statement as to a possibility, a statement of vulnerability. The Court finds it cannot conclude that there was the utterance of a threat of such a nature as to enable the Court to find the defendant guilty of the crime of rape in the first degree beyond a reasonable doubt. Since the Court, therefore, can find neither forcible compulsion nor threat beyond a reasonable doubt, the defendant is found not guilty on the charges of rape, sodomy and unlawful imprisonment.

Now, acquittal on these charges does not imply that the Court condones the conduct of the defendant. The testimony in the case reveals that the defendant was a predator, and that naive and gullible girls like Beth Peterson were his natural prey. He posed. He lied. He pretended and he deceived. He used confidences which were innocently bestowed as leverage to effect his will. He used psychological techniques to achieve vulnerability and sympathy, and the erosion of resistance. A young and inexperienced girl like Beth Peterson was then unable to withstand the practiced onslaught of the defendant. The defendant apparently got his kicks through the exercise of these techniques. He apparently spurned the readily available women, the acquiescent women, like Bridget, who was living in the same apartment. To him, the game was worth more than the prize. He boasted to the police that this was a game he played with girls' heads. The Court finds his conduct, if not criminal, to be reprehensible. It was conquest by con job. Truly, therefore, this defendant may be called "The Abominable Snowman."

So bachelors, and other men on the make, fear not. It is still not illegal to feed a girl a line, to continue the attempt, not to take no for a final answer, at least not the first time. But there comes a point at which one must desist. It is not criminal conduct for a male to make promises that will not be kept, to indulge in exaggeration and hyperbole, or to assure any trusting female that, as in the ancient fairy tale, the ugly frog is really the handsome prince. Every man is free, under the law, to be a gentleman or a cad. But take heed.

---

* On the same date as this decision the press reported a decision by the British House of Lords, holding that there could be no conviction of rape if the accused really believed that there was consent, despite the vociferous protest of the woman, when he had been told beforehand that she preferred intercourse to be accomplished over her vehement protests. The principle, of course, is that the subjective state of mind of the defendant controls in determining criminal intent.

[The court's reference is to the *Morgan* case, p. 630 of this Book, where the mental state issue will be considered in more detail.]

Violence, force and threats are totally out of bounds. Their employment will transform a heel into a criminal.

While the Court must conclude that the defendant's conduct towards Miss Peterson cannot be adjudged criminal so as to subject him to the penalty of imprisonment for up to twenty-five years, the Court finds, on the undisputed facts, that defendant did enter Apartment 14—D, at No. 1 Lincoln Plaza, the dwelling of Heinz Patzak and his family, illegally and without permission or authority. There being no proof that the illegal entry was for the purpose of committing a crime, the defendant is found not guilty of the charge of burglary in the second degree. But he is found guilty of the lesser included offense of criminal trespass in the second degree, pursuant to Section 140.15 of the Penal Law, under Indictment No. 3861 of 1974.

Further, the evidence clearly establishes that the defendant, after having been arrested for a felony, escaped from the custody of the police officers, and he is found guilty of the crime of escape in the second degree, under Section 205.10 of the Penal Law.

It may be ironic that the defendant, having been acquitted of the charges for which he was arrested, is found guilty of attempting to flee from the possibilities of having to face up to the charge. But the facts are clear, and whatever consequences flow from that fact will flow. The defendant fancied himself to be terribly clever, but, as frequently happens with terribly clever men, he made a rather stupid mistake.

Notes and Questions

1. *Evans* is a case that understandably evokes strong reactions, especially because there is no denying that "the judge's language is often flip and insensitive."[a] Some view the case as virtually a how-to set of instructions of the worst kind, whereby "male law students are taught [that] by being insensitive they can rape with impunity, as *Evans* indicates."[b] Yet even those who take such a harsh view of the case acknowledge that it "can be a valuable teaching tool."[c] That *Evans* appears here reflects the fact that the editor shares the latter conclusion, albeit not the qualifying assertion that the case needs to be "edited well"[d] before being exposed to law students. The case does not lend itself to much editing, and in any event it does not appear that the pedagogical value of the case, in terms of exploring the kinds of questions raised in the notes following, would be enhanced by making the decision (or, for that matter, the judge) look better.

2. While the main purpose of *Evans* is to serve as a springboard for exploring whether intercourse by fraud is (or should be) rape, the case is also usefully viewed in terms of the force/threat of force variety of imposition discussed earlier. The question here is simply this: Without regard to whether the various misrepresentations in Evans' elaborate subterfuge could serve as a basis for convicting him, is not the totality of his conduct a sufficient manifestation of a threat to resort to force that, on that ground alone, Judge Greenfield should have found Evans guilty of rape? Consider: (a) "The judge ignored the realities of women's lives. The differences between women and men that make women feel afraid or intimidated by men include size difference, weight difference, women's relative lack of upper body strength, women's lack of training in self-defense, and their conditioning to be afraid of men." Erickson, supra fn. b, at 112. (b) "The male judge, who

a. Nancy S. Erickson, *Final Report: "Sex Bias in the Teaching of Criminal Law,"* 42 Rutgers L.Rev. 309, 348 (1990).

b. Nancy S. Erickson, *Sex Bias in Law School Courses: Some Common Issues*, 38 J.Legal Ed. 101, 112 (1988).

c. Erickson, supra note a, at 348.

d. Ibid.

was sitting as a trier of the facts, stated that Evans's words were 'ambiguous.' To a woman in the victim's situation those words are not ambiguous but threatening." Erickson, supra fn. a, at 348.

3. Assuming there was not a sufficient threat of force to constitute rape on that score alone, is the deception in Evans' elaborate scheme itself a basis upon which a rape conviction could be grounded? No, the court says in *Evans*, because "there can be no rape which is achieved by fraud, or trick, or stratagem," and on this count *Evans* hardly stands alone. Other courts have likewise taken that position with respect to a great variety of misrepresentations. Among the better known cases of this genre, in addition to those cited in *Evans*, are: *Commonwealth v. Goldenberg*, 338 Mass. 377, 155 N.E.2d 187 (1959), where a physiotherapist had intercourse with his patient on the misrepresentation that it would be helpful in the abortion procedures she sought; *Boro v. Superior Court*, 163 Cal.App.3d 1224, 210 Cal.Rptr. 122 (1985), where a doctor later dubbed "Dr. Feelgood" by the press tricked women into intercourse by telling them it was necessary to cure their fatal blood disease; *People v. Hough*, 159 Misc.2d 997, 607 N.Y.S.2d 884 (1994), where the defendant impersonated his twin brother in order to have sexual intercourse with the brother's girlfriend; and *Goldberg v. State*, 41 Md.App. 58, 395 A.2d 1213 (1979), where defendant induced his victim to engage in intercourse after misrepresenting himself as a free-lance agent and telling her she would be a good model.

4. The statement in *Evans* quoted in the preceding Note is not entirely correct, however, for rape law has long drawn a distinction between different kinds of fraud. As explained in Joshua Dressler, *Where We Have Been, and Where We Might Be Going: Some Cautionary Reflections on Rape Law Reform*, 46 Clev.St.L.Rev. 409, 439–40 (1998): "The traditional rule is that consent obtained by fraud-in-the-factum—when the defrauded party does not know that she has consented to intercourse—is a nullity, whereas fraud-in-the-inducement—when the defrauded party knows that she has consented to intercourse, but was induced to do so by deceit—does not vitiate the consent. Thus, a female who agrees to insertion of a surgical instrument in her vagina by her male doctor, is the victim of rape if the doctor has intercourse with her instead, but a female who agrees to intercourse on the fraudulently induced belief that it will cure her of a disease has not been raped.

"I have purposely juxtaposed the medical examples to show how odd the traditional rule seems to be. Why should one form of fraud negate consent, but not the other?" Is there an answer, or should the distinction between the two, as Dressler concludes, not serve as the line between rape and noncriminal conduct, but rather as the line between rapes of different seriousness? In either event, do *Lewis* (in *Evans*) and *Hough* place the mistaken identity cases in the wrong category? Compare *United States v. Booker*, 25 M.J. 114 (C.M.A.1987): "The better view is that the 'factum' involves both the nature of the act and some knowledge of the identity of the participant."

5. Should rape statutes be amended to expressly state that even intercourse-inducing fraud outside the fraud in the factum category suffices, and, if so, just how broadly should this new rape-by-deception principle be stated? Do you agree that *Evans* and all the cases mentioned in *Evans* and the preceding Notes should be encompassed within the law of rape? Does it follow that *all* intercourse-inducing fraud should be criminal? Consider:

(a) Susan Estrich, *Rape*, 95 Yale L.J. 1087, 1119–20 (1986): "As for Mr. Evans, had he sought money rather than sex as part of his 'sociological test,' he too could have been found guilty of theft.* * * Evans could [not] have escaped liability on the ground that a 'reasonable person' would not have been deceived, any more than a victim's leaving his front door unlocked or his keys in the automobile ignition serves as a defense to burglary or larceny.* * *

"Lying to secure money is unlawful theft by deception or false pretenses, a lesser crime than robbery, but a crime nonetheless. Yet lying to secure sex is old-fashioned seduction—not first-degree rape, not even third-degree rape. * * * I am suggesting that we do something that is actually quite easy—prohibit fraud to secure sex to the same extent we prohibit fraud to secure money."

(b) Dressler, supra, at 441–42, though "tentatively persuaded that the fraud-in-the-inducement cases ought to constitute a crime," appears nervous about the cases lying at the periphery, for he expresses the "hope that prosecutors would use their substantial discretion to pick and choose only the worst cases of deception for prosecution." Moreover, he sees a necessity for legislative grading within that broad category:

"I would assert that a male who exploits a female's naivete in order to secure sexual relations is acting in a manner wrongful enough to justify the community's sanction. But, once one agrees that fraud-in-the-inducement vitiates consent in rape cases, we are left with a line-drawing issue. If all cases of such fraud vitiate consent, then rape occurs in such disparate cases as the doctor who falsely convinces his patient that she has a disease that is best treated by intercourse with him, to the male who falsely claims to be a Hollywood producer and promises to get Actress an audition for a major role in a movie if she sleeps with him,[e] to the male who falsely claims to Greedy Monica, the object of his sexual desires, that he is a millionaire, and thereby induces her to believe that her sexual compliance will result in marriage and a wealthy future.

"In each of these examples, the male has acted wrongly. He has exploited the victim for his own sexual purposes. But, the wrongdoing here is not as serious as forcible rape, in which bodily integrity is also at stake, or of fraud-in-the-factum rape, in which the victim has made no decision to have intercourse. Indeed, we would be guilty of seriously trivializing the harm suffered in those other rape cases if we were to characterize Actress and Greedy Monica as 'rape' victims.

"Depending on the facts, Actress and Greedy Monica may justly be held partially responsible for their own plight. They evinced false interest in the men in order to further their own interests. Each party was manipulating the other. What do we do, for example, if Actress, through no fault of the male, believed the man was a producer, feigned sexual interest in him, only after which the man took the opportunity to play Producer to the hilt? The cases of Actress and Greedy Monica strike me as petty criminal conduct, at most. They do not deserve to be equated to forcible intercourse, intercourse coerced by serious economic threats, fraud-in-the-factum rape, or intercourse induced by a promise to cure a serious disease. In short, not only does fraud-in-the-inducement justify less punishment than the other forms of sexual misconduct, but fraudulently induced intercourse varies in seriousness on a case-by-case basis."

(c) David P. Bryden, *Redefining Rape*, 3 Buff.Crim.L.Rev. 317, 460–69 (2000), notes that the Estrich proposal "has several plausible justifications," particularly that "deception impairs autonomous choice," but then proceeds to note that "there are powerful arguments against comprehensive criminal liability for sexual deception. Posner, Wechsler, and Schulhofer dispute the analogy to acquiring property by false pretenses. They emphasize the difficulty of ascertaining the materiality of sexual deception. In commercial transactions, the exchange is usually merely a means to an end such as acquiring land or making

e. Compare Bryden, infra, at 467: "In *United States v. Condolon*, [600 F.2d 7 (4th Cir.1979),] a federal court found the operator of a bogus talent agency guilty of wire fraud, for having falsely represented that he could obtain acting and modeling opportunities for women who had sex with him. Professor Berger is surely right to wonder whether 'the law should protect, via criminal sanctions, the cheated expectations of women who sought to sleep their way to the top but discovered, too late, that they were dealing with swindlers.'"

money. Fraud usually deprives the victim of much or all of the benefit he sought from the transaction. Then too, the market value of the property often provides strong evidence of the causal role of the deception. Motivations for sex are more complicated. It is desired partly, at times, as an episode in a larger enterprise, such as marriage, but unlike commercial transactions sex is typically pleasurable in itself. Consequently, it usually is less clear whether the sexual encounter would have occurred without the deception and also whether the deception destroyed the value of the encounter to the victim."

"Sometimes the deception may have been a 'but for' cause of a particular sexual encounter, but not of the long-term sexual relationship. For example, suppose that Ted and Sally are lovers. Ted is unfaithful, lies about it, and has sex the next day with Sally. In this hypothetical, the lie may well have been essential to obtain sex so quickly after the infidelity, but the underlying relationship antedated the lie, and might eventually have resumed even if Ted had promptly confessed to Sally. Perhaps we should trust prosecutors and juries to reach commonsensical results in such cases, but a general principle of criminal liability for sexual deception would raise many similar problems.

"[I]t is also true that the need for government intervention is less clear in the social-emotional context. Notwithstanding the anonymity of modern life, the most common techniques of sexual deception are obvious to potential victims. It is much more reasonable to require victims to protect themselves against such lies as, 'I'm talking to a lawyer about a divorce from my wife,' than it would be to leave them at the mercies of commercial swindlers, whose ruses are on average less notorious.

"[T]he practical impact of line-drawing in this area is not proportionate to the difficulty of the task. Nearly all of the most common types of deception by suitors—particularly professions of love and commitment—will fall within the exemptions that courts and legislatures will surely create for emotional declarations, immaterial lies, lies about infidelity, and, perhaps, mere promises.

"This reality has two major implications. First, as Schulhofer recognizes, statutory reform should take the form of a list of relatively specific classes of forbidden deceptions, rather than a misleading general prohibition. And second, we should not expect criminal liability for sexual deception to have much effect on the age-old problem of the lying lover. Unless we criminalize infidelity, or false declarations of love and commitment, the main deceptions will still be lawful. If, on the other hand, we were to criminalize those deceptions, we would authorize a massive governmental intrusion into our romantic lives."

6.   If, as Bryden says, what we need is a statutory list of "forbidden deceptions," what should be on the list? For example, what is your view of these four hypotheticals put by Bryden? (1) Bob is an important executive in the corporation where Sally is a new secretary. He falsely informs her that the company is going to "downsize" and that many employees will be laid off, although the company will retain senior employees with superior long-term performance records, as well as secretaries chosen by executives like himself. Subsequently, Sally has sex with Bob. She would not have done so except that his lie made her feel economically insecure; as he intended, this made her receptive to his advances. (2) Bob is a famous acting coach; Sally was one of his paying pupils. He informed her that she had the potential to be a star, but needed to "loosen up" and in particular become more comfortable in romantic scenes. He offered to give her some free, extra lessons in his apartment. At one of those sessions he urged her to disrobe and perform sexual acts on him in order to become a better actress. After initial hesitation, she complied. She subsequently learned that he had done the same thing with several other attractive aspiring actresses. In fact, his intentions were sexual, not educational. Had she realized this, she would not have had sex with him. (3) Bob pretends to be single but is married and not contemplating

divorce. He dates Sally, a single woman, and they have an affair. Sally would not have consented to sex with Bob if she had known that he was married. (4) Bob and Sally have sex after Bob asks Sally whether she is using birth control and she lies, saying that she is. Bob would not have had intercourse if he had known the truth.[f]

7. Several jurisdictions have moved beyond the traditional common law position with respect to fraudulent conduct as a basis for a rape prosecution, and thus have at least made an attempt at drawing some lines. One exhaustive study[g] has identified four different approaches to the problem: (1) Some states have outlawed fraud in the context of certain professional relationships, so that in such a setting even a fraud in the inducement, utilized by one in a position of trust or authority against a person likely to be vulnerable, can support a rape prosecution. (2) Some states specify a few very precise varieties of fraud under which victim consent is not a defense, as when sexual activity is obtained by misrepresentations regarding necessity or authority. (3) At least one state revised its rape statute to encompass, without limitation, sexual penetration "accomplished by fraud," which has been treated as abolishing the traditional factum-inducement distinction but provides no other basis for distinguishing effective and ineffective consent in the fraud context. (4) Some states have adopted a global consent definition in the criminal code declaring consent to be ineffective if obtained by "deception," which is also likely to be interpreted as superceding the factum-inducement distinction, again without other guidance to the courts.

8. A quite different form of deception, commonly included within the crime of rape, is where the defendant has surreptitiously administered drugs or intoxicants to the victim; see *Model Penal Code* § 213.1(1)(b). Consider the Comment thereto, stating that while "it might be possible to condemn as rape intercourse with any female who lacks substantial capacity to appraise or control her conduct," which on "a wholly conceptual level * * * would accord with the underlying premises that the law of rape * * * should protect against nonconsensual intimacy," such a rule of law "would be unsatisfactory[, as] it fails to take into account the social context of romance and seduction. Liquor and drugs may be potent agents of incapacitation, but they are also common ingredients of the ritual of courtship. The traditional routine of soft music and wine or the modern variant of loud music and marijuana implies some relaxation of inhibition. With continued consumption, relation blurs into intoxication and insensibility. Where this progression occurs in a course of mutual and voluntary behavior, it would be unrealistic and unfair to assign to the male total responsibility for the end result."

SECTION 3. CONSENT/NONCONSENT

A. MANIFESTATION OF NONCONSENT

JONES v. STATE

Supreme Court of Indiana, 1992.
589 N.E.2d 241.

SHEPARD, CHIEF JUSTICE.

---

f. These four hypotheticals are part of a series of 18 used in a survey of public attitudes about sexual deception, carried out by polling of 165 professors, 148 staff and 206 students at 13 law schools. The percentage of males and females, respectively, favoring criminal liability with respect to the above four hypotheticals was:

(1) 43%, 53%; (2) 31%, 46%; (3) 6%, 19%; (4) 12%, 16%. Bryden, supra, at 507, 510, 512.

g. Patricia J. Falk, *Rape by Fraud and Rape by Coercion*, 64 Brook.L.Rev. 39 (1998). This legislation is discussed in detail at pp. 89–132, and is summarized at pp. 169–71.

After a bench trial, Jerry L. Jones was convicted of rape, a class B felony. He was sentenced to twenty years in prison. * * *

Jones contends that there was insufficient evidence to support his rape conviction. Specifically, he argues there was insufficient evidence to prove he compelled C.L. to have sexual intercourse by force or imminent threat of force.

When reviewing a claim of insufficient evidence, we do not reweigh the evidence or judge the credibility of the witnesses. We affirm the conviction if, looking to the evidence and reasonable inferences therefrom which support the verdict, there is substantial evidence of probative value to support the conclusion reached by the trier of fact.

The evidence most favorable to the verdict follows. The victim, twenty-six year old C.L., lived in the same home with Jones, Jones' wife and child, and C.L.'s foster mother. One night in July 1989 when Jones had been drinking, he came into C.L.'s bedroom and asked her to have sex with him. She said no, and asked him why he did not have intercourse with his wife. He again asked her to have intercourse, and again she refused because it would not be fair to his wife and child. He asked her a third time and C.L. testified she "just let him have it, you know." She was laying on her side, and he turned her over and had sexual intercourse with her. She testified he told her not to tell anyone, particularly not to tell his wife. She said she did not give him permission to have sexual intercourse with her. She did not yell out or cry for help because she was afraid. She testified on cross-examination that she was afraid of Jones, his wife and her own foster mother. She stated it was difficult to tell her foster mother. She testified Jones did not have a weapon, and she did not think to hit him.

Jones was charged with rape pursuant to Indiana Code § 35–42–4–1(1) which states, "A person who knowingly or intentionally has sexual intercourse with a member of the opposite sex when the other person is compelled by force or imminent threat of force commits rape, a Class B felony." The force necessary to sustain a rape conviction need not be physical; it may be constructive or implied from the circumstances. "Force or threat of force may be shown even without evidence of the attacker's oral statement of intent or willingness to use a weapon and cause injury, if from the circumstances it is reasonable to infer the attacker was willing to do so."

We conclude that the evidence recited above does not constitute substantial evidence of probative value showing that Jones had sexual intercourse with C.L. by force or imminent threat of force. There was no evidence that Jones used any force or threats to encourage C.L. to engage in sexual intercourse. He asked her three times, and on the third time she "just let him have it." There was no evidence of any previous threats or force against C.L. from which the trier of fact could infer a fear of force or threats on this occasion. The circumstances do not lead to an inference of constructive or implied force. C.L. stated she was afraid to yell for help, but there was no evidence she was afraid because Jones had forced her to do anything or threatened her. There are reasons a person might be afraid to attract attention other than fear of forced activity.

We have upheld rape convictions where the force or threat was conveyed through something other than menacing words. See, e.g., Ives v. State (1981), 275 Ind. 535, 418 N.E.2d 220 (sufficient evidence of force when rape victim told defendant to stop, he pinned her down, she cried and screamed and tried to prevent him from removing her clothing); Jenkins v. State (1978), 267 Ind. 543, 372 N.E.2d 166 (sufficient evidence of force when defendant broke into rape victim's home, demanded her money, and pushed her onto the bed); Lewis, 440 N.E.2d 1125 (sufficient evidence of force when rape victim honked horn to attract attention and told defendant to stop; he pointed a pocketknife at her). In all of these cases, however, there was some evidence of force or threats, either actual or implied from the surrounding circumstances. In this case, there is no evidence that Jones forced or threatened force against C.L. to induce her to have sexual intercourse with him. By her own testimony, C.L. "just let him have it" after he had made three requests for sexual intercourse.

Because there is insufficient evidence to prove force or imminent threat of force, we reverse Jones' rape conviction.

Notes and Questions

1. The English common law rule was that for there to be rape it was necessary that the carnal knowledge of the woman be done not only "by force," but also "against her will." This also came to be the accepted rule in the United States. Contemporary statutes in most jurisdictions either list absence of consent as one of the elements of the crime or else indicate that consent is a defense.[h] Even when, as in *Jones*, the applicable statute makes no specific mention of nonconsent, it cannot be said "that consent by the victim is irrelevant or that inquiry into the level of resistance by the victim cannot or should not be made."[i] That is, the requirement of force "triggers an inquiry identical to that which informs the understanding of consent," so that even in these circumstances the "prohibition is defined in terms of a woman's resistance."[j]

2. At one time, many courts insisted upon proof of the "utmost resistance" by the victim, which was a very demanding test. Thus, as one court put it, the victim must manifest her nonconsent by showing she "did everything she could under the circumstances to prevent defendant from accomplishing his purpose," and "resistance must have continued from the inception of the case to the close."[k] Later on, most courts became somewhat less demanding, requiring only that women exert "earnest resistance" or "reasonable resistance." Further reforms were thereafter undertaken, and it is now the case that over 30 states "do not mention resistance in the statutory language describing rape," while 6 more "explicitly note in their criminal codes that physical resistance is not required to substantiate a rape charge."[l] The former step, at least, appears to have produced a difference only in degree: "Even in the absence of a formal resistance requirement, many courts continue to define force and nonconsent in terms of the woman's resistance, and often, resistance is still required."[m] Even when that proposition is not stated directly, it may be apparent from the nature of a court's discussion of evidence sufficiency—as in *Jones*, where the court distinguishes the instant case from prior cases (e.g., *Ives*) where the victim did offer physical resistance.

3. David P. Bryden, *Redefining Rape*, 3 Buff.Crim.L.Rev. 317, 360 (2000), notes that "most rape-law scholars have sharply criticized" this state of affairs. Given the facts and result in *Jones,* are you inclined to agree? Apart from *Jones*, what *exactly* is wrong with such a focus upon whether or not the victim offered physical resistance? If you prefer multiple choice, consider these common complaints (listed and discussed in Bryden, supra, at 360–73): (i) it prompts findings of insufficient evidence "even though the woman plainly did not desire sex and the man's behavior was threatening"; (ii) it is "a remnant of more patriarchal times" that "still serves men's interests"; (iii) it was brought about by men "obsessed with the irrational male fear of false rape accusations, and determined to

h. See Michelle J. Anderson, *Reviving Resistance in Rape Law*, 1998 U.Ill.L.Rev. 953, 1000–01 (citing statutes in each category).

i. *Model Penal Code* § 213.1, Comment (1980).

j. Susan Estrich, *Rape*, 95 Yale L.J. 1087, 1107–08 (1986).

k. *People v. Murphy*, 145 Mich. 524, 108 N.W. 1009 (1906).

l. Anderson, supra, at 964–65.

m. Id. at 968.

preserve respectable males' sexual access to women"; (iv) it "places an unfair and potentially fatal burden on women," as "resistance to a rapist may be dangerous"; (v) it causes the factfinders to "focus too much" on the woman's behavior when they "should instead focus on the man's"; (vi) the requirements are "administered inconsistently," as reversals for lack of resistance occur as to defendants who were acquaintances of the victim but not as to defendants who were strangers; (vii) it makes rape law "uniquely pro-defendant," as "there is no resistance requirement in other fields of law where the victim's nonconsent is an element of the crime: for example, nonsexual assault, theft, and trespass."

If some of these or other concerns have a measure of validity, are there countervailing considerations? Bryden—who, it must be emphasized, goes no farther than to contend that the problem under consideration here "is considerably more complex than most critics * * * have recognized," id. at 386–87—finds several "legitimate functions" served by the above-described situation. Two will be mentioned here:

(a) *The bright line function*: "Citizens need to know, approximately, the boundary between lawful and unlawful conduct. This is especially true of a serious crime like rape. Physical force marks the well-known bright line between seduction and rape. That purpose would be defeated if the only force required by the courts were the 'force' that is inherent in intercourse. It would also be defeated by a wholly subjective definition of nonconsent. Courts could say, of course, that the man is guilty if the woman did not consent *and he knew it*. This would create a bright line of sorts, but the question would remain: When is he supposed to know it? Without an answer to that question, the line between lawful and unlawful behavior would be obscure and subject to the vagaries of aberrant juries." Id. at 375–76.

(b) *The Rubicon function*: "In legal discourse, one either consents or doesn't consent; equivocation is not a legal category. But consent, as a legal construct, is not synonymous with subjective desire, which is often equivocal. One may desire something in one sense but not in another. For example, one with no physical desire for sex may nevertheless accede to a companion's wishes in order to preserve a relationship, to make a loved one happy, to avoid a scene, or because one is weary of the ordeal of refusal and recrimination. On any given occasion, some combination of these ulterior motives may or may not outweigh one's purely sexual feelings, which of course may also be mixed. Conversely, one's affirmative sexual feelings may be outweighed by negative, ulterior feelings ('he's married,' 'it's too soon,' etc.). Frequently, the affirmative and negative feelings are, for a time, in equipoise, or in flux.

"Given the many possible combinations of mixed desires, the law's yes/no answer to the question, 'Did she consent to have sex?' is, as a description of subjective desire, grossly simplistic: Yes/no answers do not take account of mixed or half-conscious feelings. No purely subjective approach to consent can solve this problem[, and hence] the fact finder must rely on some sort of external standard." Id. at 382–84.

4. In the final analysis, the ultimate conclusion concerning the problem raised in the preceding Note may depend upon whether there is an alternative, superior approach. Two are worth exploring here; to return to *Jones*, the first is suggested by the recited fact that when Jones "came into C.L.'s bedroom and asked her to have sex with him," she "said no." Should such "verbal resistance" be enough to make the intercourse that followed rape, as some courts have concluded?[n] Consider:

---

n. See, e.g., *Fletcher v. State*, 698 So.2d 579 (Fla. App.1997) (where no physical resistance but defendant admitted victim said "no" three times before the intercourse, and despite defendant's claim about such pro-

(a) "I am arguing that 'consent' should be defined so that 'no means no.' * * * As for mens rea, unreasonableness as to consent, understood to mean ignoring a woman's words, should be sufficient for liability: Reasonable men should be held to know that no means no, and unreasonable mistakes, no matter how honestly claimed, should not exculpate. * * * The crime I have described would be a lesser offense than the aggravated rape in which life is threatened or bodily injury inflicted, but it is, in my judgment, 'rape.' One could, I suppose, claim that as we move from such violent rapes to 'just' coerced or nonconsensual sex, we are moving away from a crime of violence toward something else. But what makes the violent rape different—and more serious—than an aggravated assault is the injury to personal integrity involved in forced sex. That same injury is the reason that forced sex should be a crime even when there is no weapon or no beating. In a very real sense, what does make rape different from other crimes, at every level of the offense, is that rape is about sex and sexual violation." Susan Estrich, *Rape*, 95 Yale L.J. 1087, 1182–83 (1986).

(b) " 'No means no' is an excellent rule to teach men (and women) in our culture. And, it is an excellent starting point—initial premise—in rape trials. But, bright-line rules such as this can only result, at best, in the correct outcome most of the time. Such rules do not assure justice to the individual whose case might not fit the bright-line assumptions. As troubling as it is to acknowledge, no does not always—in one hundred percent of the cases—mean no in sexual relations, even today.[119] If no does not always mean no, there can surely be cases in which a reasonable person could believe that no does not mean no in the specific incident, even when it does. Such cases will be relatively few in number, but it is improper to convict a person on the basis of the law of averages. It is wrong to use the bludgeon of the criminal law to impose rules intended to change cultural attitudes when this means punishing an individual for rape who made a mistake that the community, represented by the jurors, would characterize as reasonable. If the mistake was, indeed, unreasonable—or if the jurors don't believe the defendant's claim that he was mistaken—they can convict on the facts. The jury should not be deprived of the issue of mens rea through bright-line rules. Each case should be considered on its own merits." Joshua Dressler, *Where We Have Been, And Where We Might Be Going: Some Cautionary Reflections in Rape Law Reform*, 46 Clev.St.L.Rev. 409, 433–34 (1998).

(c) "[M]uch of this debate results from misunderstanding the significance of empirical data for what is ultimately not an empirical issue. For law, the relevant question is the effect that should be attributed to a woman's use of the word 'no.'

"Although not decisive, the empirical landscape is obviously relevant here, because in an inquiry about what people mean when they speak, no one would want to give a word a meaning for legal purposes that is utterly at odds with ordinary usage. But the matter becomes a legal issue precisely because the usage of the word is not uniform throughout the culture. It can hardly be fatal to the feminist position, therefore, to discover that women who say 'no' do not always mean the same thing. Because they do not, mistakes are possible. And so long as neither law nor culture develops rules to permit uniform appraisal of such mistakes, some of them can plausibly be described (although this will pain many feminists) as reasonable. The proposition that, for legal purposes, 'no' means no is,

---

testations "really meaning something other than 'no,' " sufficient evidence to affirm conviction).

119. [Footnote refers back to fn. 90, which reads:] Women, as well as men, need to learn this message. According to some studies, a significant number of females sometimes say "no" when, in fact, they do not want the male to desist from his efforts to obtain intercourse. E.g., Charlene L. Muehlenhard & Lisa C. Hollabaugh, *Do Women Sometimes Say No When They Mean Yes? The Prevalence and Correlates of Token Resistance To Sex*, 54 J. Person & Soc. Psychol. 872, 874 (1988) (39% of female undergraduates at Texas A & M University reported saying no to intercourse although they "had every intention to and were willing to engage in sexual intercourse."). Any mixed message arising in such circumstances can lend credence to a male's claim of reasonable belief, which can trigger a mens rea claim on his part.

therefore, primarily a normative claim about how the word should be understood in the face of ambiguity about its actual meaning in any given context.

"The objection that taking 'no' to mean no will make it 'harder for some women to get what they want' therefore misses the point of such a proposal. As with any default rule, the legal proposition that 'no' means no does not claim infallible accuracy; to the contrary, the absence of empirical consensus is its raison d'etre. It presupposes ambiguity and seeks to allocate the risk of the inevitable misunderstandings.

" * * *Although the 'no'-means-no claim should not be controversial, the more serious difficulty is that this proposition offers surprisingly little help. In real cases, the 'no' is often followed by some form of equivocal acquiescence, or even a 'yes.' How should the 'no'-means-no rule apply in cases like that?

" * * * Suppose a woman says 'no' to her lover before dinner and then changes her mind after several hours of intimate conversation? Would the consent have to be considered invalid? That cannot be the right result. The only way to sort out these problems is to focus on the conduct that leads to a 'yes'—in other words, whether the persuasions are improper. 'No' means no just does not help sort out whether the things that happen after the 'no' are legitimate or abusive." Stephen J. Schulhofer, *The Feminist Challenge in Criminal Law*, 143 U.Pa.L.Rev. 2151, 2173–75 (1995).

(d) As to certain other positions that have been taken on the subject of rape law reform (e.g., as seen earlier, declaring a much broader range of deceptions as prohibited impositions, or, as will be seen later, making negligence as to absence of consent a sufficient mental state), it is often said that the "new" criminal liability should exist with respect to an offense–whether called a lesser form of rape or something else–carrying lower penalties. May this even be said as to adoption of a no-means-no rule? Consider Dan M. Kahan, *Gentle Nudges vs. Hard Shoves: Solving the Sticky Norms Problem*, 67 U.Chi. L.Rev. 607 (2000), presenting the thesis that the solution to the "sticky norms problem," i.e., the reluctance of decisionmakers–police, prosecutors, jurors–to carry out a law intended to change social norms, is for the law to condemn the behavior only slightly more than does the typical decisionmaker, that is, by changing the law by "gentle nudges" rather than "hard shoves."

A case in point, Kahan says at 623–24, is where "lawmakers have modified aspects of rape law that accommodate this 'no sometimes means yes' norm," for "such reforms have proven famously ineffective. In jurisdictions that have adopted them, prosecutors are no more likely to charge men who disregard a woman's verbal protestations, and juries no more likely to convict them, than are prosecutors and juries in other states," for the reason that there "is genuine societal ambivalence about the 'no sometimes means yes' norm." The problem becomes compounded, he adds, because "the conspicuous failure of prosecutors to charge and juries to convict reinforces the public perception that men who follow the 'no sometimes means yes' norm aren't engaged in rape after all–at which point jurors become even less likely to convict and prosecutors to charge." The solution, Kahan suggests, is that adopted in some states, where "nonconsensual but nonforcible sex is styled 'indecent contact' or 'indecent assault'" and is "punished less severely." This approach, he opines, would produce more consistent enforcement of the law which in turn "would, over time, make members of the public revise upward their assessment of the gravity of such conduct, thereby enabling the enforcement of laws treating it as a form of 'rape.'"

Do you agree, and, if so, precisely what strategies are needed to accomplish such a result? Consider these further words of caution by Kahan at 624–25: "But it is also possible that 'indecent assault' statutes, too, will end up reinforcing the 'no sometimes means yes' norm. Critics argue that these statutes, precisely because they grade nonforcible, nonconsensual sex so much less severely than rape, are likely to corroborate the conviction that such behavior is not really worthy of criminal punishment at all.

"This anxiety points up a general implementation problem for the 'gentle nudges' strategy. That strategy implies that lawmakers should favor less condemnatory policies over more condemnatory ones in order to avoid triggering the 'hard shove' dynamic. But policies that are only weakly condemnatory can be seen as signaling that the underlying conduct isn't genuinely worthy of condemnation, an inference that is likely to reinforce itself insofar as moral appraisals are shaped by social influence. Fines and community service penalties, for example, are thought to have this effect.

"What was intended as a 'gentle nudge' at this point becomes a 'sly wink.' To avoid this pernicious transmutation, policymakers must identify strategies that strike citizens as genuinely albeit moderately condemnatory."

5. Consider now another alternative, namely, a requirement that there be affirmatively expressed consent by the woman. In *Jones*, for example, it may be asked whether, even if the facts did not show that C.L. "said no," Jones should be subject to conviction merely because, as the court says, "she did not give him permission to have sexual intercourse with her." Should affirmative consent be required, and, if so, should the consent be verbal or could it be manifested in other ways, should it apply in all or only certain types cases, and should the absence of such affirmative expression be conclusive or only give rise to a presumption? Consider:

(a) "[T]his Comment proposes a rape law based on a norm of affirmative verbal consent. Under this standard, 'no' would mean 'no,' 'yes' would mean 'yes,' and the lack of any verbal communication as to consent would be presumed to mean 'no.' In more specific terms, a 'no' or its verbal equivalent would be dispositive of the issue of consent, as would a freely-given 'yes' or its verbal equivalent. The lack of a 'yes' or its verbal equivalent would raise a presumption of nonconsent. * * *

"Although there are other crimes for which nonconsent is an element or consent is a defense, only in rape is proof of a lack of consent insufficient to prove nonconsent. A common defense to a charge of auto theft, for example, is that the car's owner consented to the defendant's use of the vehicle. A mere showing that the owner never gave the defendant permission to take the car is enough to defeat this defense; no showing that the owner actually told the defendant not to take the car is necessary. In rape law, however, the 'default' position is consent. * * *

"Requiring a woman to do anything at all as a prerequisite to protection under the rape laws implies that her freedom from nonconsensual sex is a privilege rather than a right. Furthermore, it suggests that a woman who fails to take such actions has caused her own rape." Comment, 141 U. Pa. L. Rev. 1103, 1105, 1111–12 (1993).

(b) "If the civil doctrine of confidential relationship were transported to the criminal arena, proof of a preexisting relationship would create a presumption that the parties reposed trust in each other and, based on that presumption, the law would require each party to exercise a heightened duty of care. The civil law presumes trust from the fact that one party made a promise to the other. Analogously, the criminal law should presume trust from the fact of familiarity between the parties. * * *

"The heightened duty of care imposes an obligation on the defendant to meet a stricter standard of conduct than mere reasonable belief. This duty requires the defendant to inquire as to the victim's desire for sexual contact and the form of contact desired. The defendant's subjective belief that the victim's words or acts constituted consent is not relevant because under the heightened duty of care the defendant has no right to rely on his own belief, but rather has the obligation to listen to the victim." Beverly Balos & Mary Louise Fellows, *Guilty of the Crime of Trust: Nonstranger Rape*, 75 Minn.L.Rev. 599, 605–08 (1991).

(c) "I now view a 'no means no' standard as insufficient to safeguard legitimate interests of women in the setting of sexual assault. Schulhofer writes: '[W]e seldom think it "patronizing" to insist on permission, not just silence, when the interests affected are ones that men can easily recognize as important.' He claims, persuasively, that non-verbalization may denote 'confusion, ambivalence, or fright,' often complicated by intoxication, as opposed to willingness to have sex. If autonomy is the central value that modern rape law ought to vindicate (and I, like Schulhofer, think it is), Schulhofer makes a powerful case for reversing the present presumption of consent." Vivian Berger, *Rape Law Reform at the Millennium*, 3 Buff.Crim.L.Rev. 513, 523 (2000).

(d) "The affirmative-consent proposal seeks to overcome traditional attitudes about how one manifests consent or nonconsent to sex. If juries are left free to define 'consent' for themselves they may in effect create a force requirement—or at least a verbal protest requirement—even if force (or verbal protest) is not a nominal element of the crime. To avert this result, Schulhofer's model act defines consent as 'actual words or conduct indicating affirmative, freely-given permission to the act of sexual penetration.' Subjective nonconsent would not be an element of the crime; therefore, a mistake about subjective consent—even one that a jury thought reasonable—would be immaterial. To nullify an element of the crime, the mistake would have to be about whether the consent had been affirmatively expressed. Strictly speaking, not even actual subjective consent would be a defense unless it had been manifested affirmatively.

"Obviously, this proposal is a bold effort to steer men—and juries—in the right direction. It raises one of the perennial questions of criminal jurisprudence: To what extent should or must the law follow the folkways rather than trying to change them? A gap between custom and law creates two potential problems: unfairness to those who don't know the law and nullification of the law by those charged with enforcing it—victims, police, prosecutors, juries, and judges. In a sense, these potential problems are mutually exclusive. But not completely: Any unfairness of a law is compounded if it is almost never enforced." David P. Bryden, *Redefining Rape*, 3 Buff.Crim.L.Rev. 317, 405–06 (2000).

(e) "Although much ink has been spilt over issues of sexual communication, I suspect that there are very few cases in which the token of consent is actually ambiguous. Some commentators have argued that we should insist that B tokens consent only when she gives explicit verbal permission to intercourse. Schulhofer thinks that a verbal-permission rule would impose an excessive degree of formality and artificiality on a dimension of life in which spontaneity is important. While verbal permission will certainly do, so will cheerfully following someone into a bedroom and taking off one's clothes. Nonetheless, Schulhofer insists that 'by requiring affirmative permission, through words or conduct, we can insist that any person who engages in intercourse show full respect for the other person's autonomy—by pausing, before he acts, to be sure that he has a clear indication of her actual consent.' By contrast, silence should not be understood as tacit consent. Some affirmative consent token is required.

"I believe that this is much ado about very little. Nothing problematic will follow from construing any behavior or act of omission as a token of consent so long as its meaning is clear and so long as B can indicate to the contrary if it is not. As a general proposition, silence is an acceptable token of morally transformative consent in those contexts in which silence can be safely understood to be a token of consent and the background conditions are such as to render the silence-token morally transformative. If, for example, B really did not intend to consent to sexual relations after silently allowing her clothing to be removed and says, 'I'm sorry, I didn't know that you meant that, I think I better go,' then there should be little confusion as to whether she has consented to sex." Alan Wertheimer, *What is Consent? And is It Important?*, 3 Buff.Crim.L.Rev. 557, 573–74 (2000).

(f) "The burden of asking permission can be placed on the man, or the burden of expressing refusal can be placed on the woman. Granting that gender prejudice is implicated by either choice, I think the second alternative is superior, because sexual encounters ought not to be lived or analyzed as sequences of particular touchings. In practice couples do not discuss in advance each specific sex act that one or another might initiate, and there is no strong reason why the law should attempt to compel them to do so. * * * If uncertainty and spontaneity can enhance the pleasures of love-making, people of either sex might prefer not being asked—so long as they can be sure that behavior they don't like will be stopped on demand. The interest in freedom from wrong guesses by one's bedmates is not so great as to call the criminal law into play." Donald A. Dripps, *Beyond Rape: An Essay on the Difference Between the Presence of Force and the Absence of Consent*, 92 Colum.L.Rev. 1780, 1792 n.41 (1992).

(g) The case most often cited as an illustration of the affirmative consent requirement is *State in Interest of M.T.S.*, 129 N.J. 422, 609 A.2d 1266 (1992), upholding the trial judge's determination of delinquency based upon his finding beyond a reasonable doubt that M.T.S. had raped C.G. The trial judge found that 15–year-old C.G. "had consented to a session of kissing and heavy petting" with 17–year-old M.T.S., who was temporarily living with C.G. and her mother. C.G. testified that at approximately 1:30 she awoke to use the bathroom and saw M.T.S. standing in her doorway, and she claimed she walked past him, used the bathroom and then returned to bed and fell into a heavy sleep from which she awoke to find M.T.S on top of her engaging in sexual intercourse. The court disbelieved C.G.'s claim she was asleep at the time of penetration, before which she said nothing, and further found that M.T.S. had not used "any unusual or extra force or threats." Starting with a statute which required physical force but not a showing of nonconsent, the court concluded the force was proved by the victim's failure to provide "affirmative and freely-given permission" to penetration, thus seemingly turning the statute into one where force was not required but nonconsent was and then finding the nonconsent from the victim's failure to verbalize consent!

6. *Retroactive consent?* Mr. *A* enticed Ms. *B* to his apartment and attempted to entice her to have sexual intercourse with him. *B* refused to consent and asked to leave, but *A* proceeded with his intentions nonetheless, to which *B* manifested her consent only after penetration had occurred. *A* has now been charged with rape. This is essentially the fact situation assumed in 2 William L. Burdick, *The Law of Crime* 236 (1946), concluding: "If penetration alone completes the act, it is illogical and unsound to say that consent may follow the penetration." Why?

7. *Consent by mistake?* "The complainant, a young girl of eighteen, went to bed at her mother's home after she had spent the evening with her boyfriend. The bed was very near the window of her room which was wide open. It was her habit to sleep without wearing night attire. The defendant, a young man who was walking down the street, looked in through the window and decided to enter it. He took off his clothes before pulling himself on to the window sill. While he crouched there she became aware of him and thought that he was her boy-friend with whom she had been on terms of intimacy. She sat up in bed and held out her arms to him. After they had relations there was something that

made her think that he was not her boy-friend. She turned on the bedside light and slapped his face.''[i] Assume that the defendant has been charged with rape.

B. CONCLUSIVELY PRESUMED CONSENT—THE MARITAL EXCEPTION

PEOPLE v. LIBERTA

Court of Appeals of New York, 1984.

64 N.Y.2d 152, 485 N.Y.S.2d 207, 474 N.E.2d 567.

WACHTLER, JUDGE.

The defendant, while living apart from his wife pursuant to a Family Court order, forcibly raped and sodomized her in the presence of their 2 ½ year old son. * * * On July 15, 1981 the defendant was indicted for rape in the first degree and sodomy in the first degree.

Section 130.35 of the Penal Law provides in relevant part that "A male is guilty of rape in the first degree when he engages in sexual intercourse with a female * * * by forcible compulsion". "Female", for purposes of the rape statute, is defined as "any female person who is not married to the actor". Section 130.50 of the Penal Law provides in relevant part that "a person is guilty of sodomy in the first degree when he engages in deviate sexual intercourse with another person * * * by forcible compulsion". "Deviate sexual intercourse" is defined as "sexual conduct between persons not married to each other consisting of contact between the penis and the anus, the mouth and penis, or the mouth and the vulva". Thus, due to the "not married" language in the definitions of "female" and "deviate sexual intercourse", there is a "marital exemption" for both forcible rape and forcible sodomy. The marital exemption itself, however, has certain exceptions. For purposes of the rape and sodomy statutes, a husband and wife are considered to be "not married" if at the time of the sexual assault they "are living apart * * * pursuant to a valid and effective: (i) order issued by a court of competent jurisdiction which by its terms or in its effect requires such living apart, or (ii) decree or judgment of separation, or (iii) written agreement of separation". * * *

The defendant was then convicted of rape in the first degree and sodomy in the first degree and the conviction was affirmed by the Appellate Division. Defendant asserts on this appeal that the temporary order of protection is not the type of order which enables a court to treat him and Denise as "not married" and that thus he is within the marital exemption. Defendant next asserts, assuming that because of the Family Court order he is treated just as any unmarried male would be, that he cannot be convicted of either rape in the first degree or sodomy in the first degree because both statutes are unconstitutional. Specifically, he contends that both statutes violate equal protection because they burden some, but not all males (all but those within the "marital exemption") * * *. The lower courts rejected the defendant's constitutional arguments, finding that neither statute violated the equal protection clause in the Fourteenth Amendment. Although we affirm the conviction of the defendant, we do not agree with the constitutional analysis of the lower courts * * *.

We first address the defendant's argument that, despite the order of protection, he was within the "marital exemption" to rape and sodomy and thus could not be prosecuted for

i. 88 L.Q.Rev. 458 (1972), commenting on *Regina v. Collins,* [1972] 3 W.L.R. 243, [1972] 2 All E.R. 1105. The charge in *Collins* was burglary rather than rape, and the court held the defendant could not be convict-ed if his entry was based on the belief he had been invited to enter. See Scutt, *Fraudulent Impersonation and Consent in Rape,* 9 U.Queens.L.J. 59 (1975).

either crime. Until 1978, the marital exemption applied as long as the marriage still legally existed. In 1978, the Legislature expanded the definition of "not married" to include those cases where the husband and wife were living apart pursuant to either a court order "which by its terms or in its effect requires such living apart" or a decree, judgment, or written agreement of separation. We agree with the Appellate Division that the order of protection in the present case falls squarely within the first of these situations. * * *

The defendant's constitutional challenges to the rape and sodomy statutes are premised on his being considered "not married" to Denise and are the same challenges as could be made by any unmarried male convicted under these statutes. The defendant's claim is that both statutes violate equal protection because they are underinclusive classifications which burden him, but not others similarly situated. A litigant has standing to raise this claim even though he does not contend that under no circumstances could the burden of the statute be imposed upon him. This rule of standing applies as well to a defendant in a criminal prosecution who, while conceding that it is within the power of a State to make criminal the behavior covered by a statute, asserts that the statute he is prosecuted under violates equal protection because it burdens him but not others. Thus, defendant's constitutional claims are properly before this court.

As noted above, under the Penal Law a married man ordinarily cannot be convicted of forcibly raping or sodomizing his wife. This is the so-called marital exemption for rape. Although a marital exemption was not explicit in earlier rape statutes, an 1852 treatise stated that a man could not be guilty of raping his wife. The assumption, even before the marital exemption was codified, that a man could not be guilty of raping his wife, is traceable to a statement made by the 17th century English jurist Lord Hale, who wrote: "[T]he husband cannot be guilty of a rape committed by himself upon his lawful wife, for by their mutual matrimonial consent and contract the wife hath given up herself in this kind unto her husband, which she cannot retract". Although Hale cited no authority for his statement it was relied on by State Legislatures which enacted rape statutes with a marital exemption and by courts which established a common-law exemption for husbands.

The first American case to recognize the marital exemption was decided in 1857 by the Supreme Judicial Court of Massachusetts, which stated in dictum that it would always be a defense to rape to show marriage to the victim. Decisions to the same effect by other courts followed, usually with no rationale or authority cited other than Hale's implied consent view. In New York, a 1922 decision noted the marital exemption in the Penal Law and stated that it existed "on account of the matrimonial consent which [the wife] has given, and which she cannot retract".

Presently, over 40 States still retain some form of marital exemption for rape.[6] While the marital exemption is subject to an equal protection challenge, because it classifies unmarried men differently than married men, the equal protection clause does not prohibit a State from making classifications, provided the statute does not arbitrarily burden a particular group of individuals. Where a statute draws a distinction based upon marital status, the classification must be reasonable and must be based upon "some ground of difference that rationally explains the different treatment".

We find that there is no rational basis for distinguishing between marital rape and nonmarital rape. The various rationales which have been asserted in defense of the

---

6. Statutes in nine States provide a complete exemption to rape as long as there is a valid marriage. In 26 other States, statutes provide for a marital exemption but with certain exceptions, most typically where the spouses are living apart pursuant to either a court order or a separation agreement. In three other States and the District of Columbia the exemption appears to still exist as a common-law doctrine * * *. Finally, in [4 other states] there is a marital exemption for some, but not all degrees of forcible rape.

exemption are either based upon archaic notions about the consent and property rights incident to marriage or are simply unable to withstand even the slightest scrutiny. We therefore declare the marital exemption for rape in the New York statute to be unconstitutional.

Lord Hale's notion of an irrevocable implied consent by a married woman to sexual intercourse has been cited most frequently in support of the marital exemption. Any argument based on a supposed consent, however, is untenable. Rape is not simply a sexual act to which one party does not consent. Rather, it is a degrading, violent act which violates the bodily integrity of the victim and frequently causes severe, long-lasting physical and psychic harm. To ever imply consent to such an act is irrational and absurd. Other than in the context of rape statutes, marriage has never been viewed as giving a husband the right to coerced intercourse on demand. Certainly, then, a marriage license should not be viewed as a license for a husband to forcibly rape his wife with impunity. A married woman has the same right to control her own body as does an unmarried woman. If a husband feels "aggrieved" by his wife's refusal to engage in sexual intercourse, he should seek relief in the courts governing domestic relations, not in "violent or forceful self-help".

The other traditional justifications for the marital exemption were the common-law doctrines that a woman was the property of her husband and that the legal existence of the woman was "incorporated and consolidated into that of the husband". Both these doctrines, of course, have long been rejected in this State. Indeed, "[n]owhere in the common-law world—[or] in any modern society—is a woman regarded as chattel or demeaned by denial of a separate legal identity and the dignity associated with recognition as a whole human being".

Because the traditional justifications for the marital exemption no longer have any validity, other arguments have been advanced in its defense. The first of these recent rationales, which is stressed by the People in this case, is that the marital exemption protects against governmental intrusion into marital privacy and promotes reconciliation of the spouses, and thus that elimination of the exemption would be disruptive to marriages. While protecting marital privacy and encouraging reconciliation are legitimate State interests, there is no rational relation between allowing a husband to forcibly rape his wife and these interests. The marital exemption simply does not further marital privacy because this right of privacy protects consensual acts, not violent sexual assaults. Just as a husband cannot invoke a right of marital privacy to escape liability for beating his wife, he cannot justifiably rape his wife under the guise of a right to privacy.

Similarly, it is not tenable to argue that elimination of the marital exemption would disrupt marriages because it would discourage reconciliation. Clearly, it is the violent act of rape and not the subsequent attempt of the wife to seek protection through the criminal justice system which "disrupts" a marriage. Moreover, if the marriage has already reached the point where intercourse is accomplished by violent assault it is doubtful that there is anything left to reconcile. This, of course, is particularly true if the wife is willing to bring criminal charges against her husband which could result in a lengthy jail sentence.

Another rationale sometimes advanced in support of the marital exemption is that marital rape would be a difficult crime to prove. A related argument is that allowing such prosecutions could lead to fabricated complaints by "vindictive" wives. The difficulty of proof argument is based on the problem of showing lack of consent. Proving lack of consent, however, is often the most difficult part of any rape prosecution, particularly where the rapist and the victim had a prior relationship. Similarly, the possibility that married women will fabricate complaints would seem to be no greater than the possibility of unmarried women doing so.[8] The criminal justice system, with all of its built-in safeguards, is presumed to be capable of handling any false complaints. Indeed, if the possibility of fabricated complaints were a basis for not criminalizing behavior which would otherwise be sanctioned, virtually all crimes other than homicides would go unpunished.

The final argument in defense of the marital exemption is that marital rape is not as serious an offense as other rape and is thus adequately dealt with by the possibility of prosecution under criminal statutes, such as assault statutes, which provide for less severe punishment. The fact that rape statutes exist, however, is a recognition that the harm caused by a forcible rape is different, and more severe, than the harm caused by an ordinary assault. "Short of homicide, [rape] is the 'ultimate violation of self' ". Under the Penal Law, assault is generally a misdemeanor unless either the victim suffers "serious physical injury" or a deadly weapon or dangerous instrument is used. Thus, if the defendant had been living with Denise at the time he forcibly raped and sodomized her he probably could not have been charged with a felony, let alone a felony with punishment equal to that for rape in the first degree.

Moreover, there is no evidence to support the argument that marital rape has less severe consequences than other rape. On the contrary, numerous studies have shown that marital rape is frequently quite violent and generally has more severe, traumatic effects on the victim than other rape.

Among the recent decisions in this country addressing the marital exemption, only one court has concluded that there is a rational basis for it (see *People v. Brown*, 632 P.2d 1025 [Col.]).[10] We agree with the other courts which have analyzed the exemption, which have been unable to find any present justification for it. Justice Holmes wrote: "It is revolting to have no better reason for a rule of law than that so it was laid down in the time of Henry IV. It is still more revolting if the grounds upon which it was laid down have vanished long since, and the rule simply persists from blind imitation of the past". This statement is an apt characterization of the marital exemption; it lacks a rational basis, and therefore violates the equal protection clauses of both the Federal and State Constitutions.

Accordingly, the order of the Appellate Division should be affirmed.

Notes and Questions

1. Law reform regarding the marital exemption has continued apace since *Liberta*; it has more recently been noted that "no state retains an absolute version of the common law rule that barred the prosecution of a husband for raping his wife." Comment, 61 Alb.L.Rev. 237 (1997). Sometimes this has been accomplished by court decision, as in *Liberta*, but more often it has come about as a result of legislative action.

2. As elaborated in Notes, 18 Am.J.Trial Adv. 657 (1995); 43 Clev.-St.L.Rev. 351 (1995); 48 Stan.L.Rev. 677 (1996), legislatures have responded in a variety of ways, including making spousal rape a separate crime, removing the words "not his spouse" or "unlawful" from an existing rape statute, passing a separate statute expressly excluding marriage as a defense to rape, or replacing the rape statute with a gender-neutral sexual battery statute. In a small number of jurisdictions, the changes have been modest, limited

---

8. The stigma and other difficulties associated with a woman reporting a rape and pressing charges probably deter most attempts to fabricate an incident; rape remains a grossly under-reported crime.

10. The Colorado Supreme Court, relying on a 1954 Law Review comment, stated that the marital exemp-

tion "may remove a substantial obstacle to the resumption of normal marital relations" and "averts difficult emotional issues and problems of proof inherent in this sensitive area. We have considered, and rejected, both of these arguments.

to declaring the marital exemption inapplicable in certain circumstances, such as where the couple is living apart. But about half of the states have eliminated the exemption except where there is no force or threat of force (often adding as well a prompt reporting requirement for the spouse), while a slightly smaller number have abolished the exemption entirely (as has England; see Note, 27 Ga.J. Int'l & Comp.L. 139 (1998)). A relatively small number of the states that have criminalized spousal rape make it a lesser offense than other varieties of rape. Many of the jurisdictions that have generally abolished the marital exception have retained it with respect to statutory rape.

3. Which of these legislative changes do you favor? Before deciding, consider these points from *Model Penal Code* § 213.1, Comment (1980):

"First, marriage or equivalent relationship, while not amounting to a legal waiver of the woman's right to say 'no,' does imply a kind of generalized consent that distinguishes some versions of the crime of rape from parallel behavior by a husband. The relationship itself creates a presumption of consent, valid until revoked. At a minimum, therefore, husbands must be exempt from those categories of liability based not on force or coercion but on a presumed incapacity of the woman to consent. For example, a man who has intercourse with his unconscious wife should scarcely be condemned to felony liability on the ground that the woman in such circumstances is incapable of consenting to sex with her own husband, at least unless there are aggravating circumstances. The same holds true for intercourse with a wife who for some reason other than unconsciousness is not aware that a sexual act is committed upon her. Plainly there must also be some form of spousal exclusion applicable to the crime of statutory rape. Given the age limit for effective consent to sexual relations set in some states, the possibility of marriage exists, and without a spousal exclusion every act of sex between the husband and wife would be a literal violation of the statute.

"The major context of which those who would abandon the spousal exclusion are thinking, however, is the situation of rape by force or threat. The problem with abandoning the immunity in many such situations is that the law of rape, if applied to spouses, would thrust the prospect of criminal sanctions into the ongoing process of adjustment in the marital relationship. Section 213.1, for example, defines as gross sexual imposition intercourse coerced 'by any threat that would prevent resistance by a woman of ordinary resolution.' It may well be that a woman of ordinary resolution would be prevented from resisting by her husband's threat to expose a secret to her mother, for example. Behavior of this sort within the marital relationship is no doubt unattractive, but it is a risky business for the law to intervene by threatening criminal sanctions. Retaining the spousal exclusion avoids this unwarranted intrusion of the penal law into the life of the family.

"Finally, there is the case of intercourse coerced by force or threat of physical harm. Here the law already authorizes a penalty for assault. If the actor causes serious bodily injury, the punishment is quite severe. The issue is whether the still more drastic sanctions of rape should apply. The answer depends on whether the injury caused by forcible intercourse by a husband is equivalent to that inflicted by someone else. The gravity of the crime of forcible rape derives not merely from its violent character but also from its achievement of a particularly degrading kind of unwanted intimacy. Where the attacker stands in an ongoing relation of sexual intimacy, that evil, as distinct from the force used to compel submission, may well be thought qualitatively different. The character of the voluntary association of husband and wife, in other words, may be thought to affect the nature of the harm involved in unwanted intercourse. That, in any event, is the conclusion long endorsed by the law of rape and carried forward in the Model Code provisions."

4. Assuming retention of the marital exemption, especially if limited as in the statute at issue in *Liberta*, does it follow that the exemption should extend to a cohabiting couple that is not married? Consider *Model Penal Code* § 213.6(2), and the Commentary thereto stating: "This aspect of the provision does not bring within the exemption all actors who have previously enjoyed sexual relations, even on a regular basis. It is intended, rather, to reach persons living in a relationship of common-law marriage, regardless of whether such unions are recognized in a particular jurisdiction, and persons who have purported to contract a marriage that is for some reason invalid."

5. Even where the marital exemption prevails, a husband may be convicted of rape as an accomplice, that is, where he assists, aids, or procures another to commit the act. See, e.g., *Davis v. State*, 611 So.2d 906 (Miss.1992).

C. CONCLUSIVELY PRESUMED NONCONSENT— IMMATURITY AND INCAPACITY

OWENS v. STATE

Court of Appeals of Maryland, 1999.

352 Md. 663, 724 A.2d 43.

CHASANOW, JUDGE. * * *

The facts in this case are not in dispute. According to the agreed statement of facts, on April 11, 1997, a police officer conducting a routine nighttime patrol discovered Timothy Owens and Ariel Correta Johnson in the rear seat of a parked car, dressing. When asked, Johnson told the police officer that she was 16 years old. After calling Johnson's residence, he discovered that her correct date of birth was October 16, 1983, making her 13 years old at the time of the incident. Owens was born April 27, 1978, making him 18 years old at the time. After compiling evidence that the two had just engaged in sexual intercourse, Owens was charged with second degree rape in violation of § 463(a), which states in pertinent part: "A person is guilty of rape in the second degree if the person engages in vaginal intercourse with another person: * * * (3) Who is under 14 years of age and the person performing the act is at least four years older than the victim." Owens elected to proceed by way of a not guilty agreed statement of facts, which the prosecutor recited into the record. It was not disputed that "[t]he victim, if asked, would also testify that she had told the Defendant that she was 16 years of age."

Owens' counsel made a motion to dismiss the charges, arguing that the statute was unconstitutional in that it violated Owens' due process rights under the United States Constitution and the Maryland Declaration of Rights. * * *[a]

Appellant contends that § 463(a)(3) unconstitutionally creates an irrebuttable presumption that the victim's mental state is irrelevant and that children under age 14 are incapable of consenting to sexual intercourse. We disagree.

First, we note that § 463(a)(3) simply prohibits sexual intercourse with one who is "under 14 years of age" when the person "performing the act is at least four years older than the victim." Intent is simply not relevant to the charges. As the Iowa Supreme Court has concluded, "[h]ere we are not dealing with a presumption (or, more correctly, inference) at all. The statute is not concerned with presumptions or inferences. Rather it

---

a. In an omitted portion of this opinion, the court rejected the argument that the statute was an unconstitutional strict liability crime because the defendant was not allowed, under the statute, to present a de- fense that he reasonably believed the girl's statement as to her age. This issue is explored later herein; see Note 5 on p. 643 of this Book.

flatly prohibits the act defendant committed." [T]he legislature may constitutionally prohibit sexual intercourse with a child below age 14 in order to protect the child's physical and mental health and welfare. Since Maryland's statutory rape statute directly prohibits vaginal intercourse with children below age 14 without regard to the minor's ability to consent, it does not utilize any presumption that unconstitutionally burdens the criminal defendant.

Second and relatedly, under the statutory scheme of § 463(a)(3), age is not used to determine any element of the crime beyond the age itself. Thus, it is distinguishable from the Supreme Court's decisions in *LaFleur, Vlandis,* and *Stanley,* as well as our decision in *Mahoney.*[b] In each of these cases, the provision held to violate due process took one fact and used it to justify a separate, factual conclusion, and, moreover, the fact presumed bore little or no relation to the objective of the law. In *LaFleur,* the public school policies took the fact of pregnancy and presumed that pregnancy made women physically unfit for classroom teaching. The statute in question in *Vlandis* presumed that one who applied to a state school while living out-of-state was a non-resident regardless of facts suggesting otherwise, for as long as that individual remained a student. In *Stanley,* the statute conclusively presumed that all unmarried fathers are unqualified to raise their children. In *Mahoney,* the regulation invalidated specifically stated that presence of drugs in saliva or urine "shall be conclusive evidence" that the trainer had knowledge or was careless in allowing the horse to be drugged.

In sharp contrast, § 463(a)(3) does not presume that anyone engaging in sexual intercourse with one under the age of 14 intended to do so, or that the victim is incapable of consenting; rather, the statute protects children from sexual conduct, regardless of whether the defendant intended to engage in the prohibited conduct with one under age 14 and whether the victim purported to consent. Unlike the statutes stricken down as unconstitutional, § 463(a)(3) does not take as one fact (pregnancy, an application for admission when living out-of-state, the unmarried father, or a positive drug test) and use that fact to arrive at a separate conclusion (fitness for classroom teaching, resident status, fitness for raising children, or the administering of drugs to horses with knowledge or carelessness). In other words, § 463(a)(3) does not require intent to engage in intercourse with one under 14 years old and then presume that intent simply because of the victim's age; nor does it prohibit sexual intercourse without consent and then presume that children under age 14 are incapable of consenting. As a result, the irrebuttable presumption doctrine does not apply.

Finally, even if we were to agree that the statute creates an irrebuttable presumption that children age 13 and under are incapable of making an informed decision about whether to consent to sexual intercourse, the nexus between the presumption and the state's interest in protecting children is sufficient enough to ameliorate any due process concerns.[16] See Rita Eidson, *The Constitutionality of Statutory Rape Laws,* 27 U.C.L.A.

---

b. The references here are to *Cleveland Board of Education v. LaFleur,* 414 U.S. 632, 94 S.Ct. 791, 39 L.Ed.2d 52 (1974); *Vlandis v. Kline,* 412 U.S. 441, 93 S.Ct. 2230, 37 L.Ed.2d 63 (1973); *Stanley v. Illinois,* 405 U.S. 645, 92 S.Ct. 1208, 31 L.Ed.2d 551 (1972); *Mahoney v. Byers,* 187 Md. 81, 48 A.2d 600 (1946).

16. New York's statutory rape law explicitly incorporates an irrebuttable presumption, which was nevertheless upheld in *People v. Gonzales,* 148 Misc.2d 973, 561 N.Y.S.2d 358 (Co.Ct.1990). The statute declared that it "is an element ... that the sexual act was committed without consent of the victim," and it fur-

ther provided that "[a] person is deemed incapable of consent when he is: (a) less than seventeen years old." The defendant argued that the irrebuttable presumption that children under age 17 cannot consent "unconstitutionally presumes an element of the crime which the People would otherwise be under an obligation to prove by proof beyond a reasonable doubt." The court determined that the presumption created by the statute "is equivalent to a substantive rule of law expressed in terms of rules of evidence.... Lack of true consent of those under seventeen is not an element of the substantive crime."

L.Rev. 757, 811 (1980) (concluding that the irrebuttable presumption doctrine may apply only to statutory rape laws "with a high age of consent," i.e., age 16). Basing one's ability to consent to sexual intercourse on the individual's meeting the age of 14 is not "wholly unrelated" to the state's objective of protecting minor children, and it is hard to imagine when the presumption would not "operate to effectuate the State's asserted interest" in protecting children from sexual abuse, exploitation and early pregnancy. Therefore, even if the irrebuttable presumption doctrine would apply, we could not conclude that § 463(a)(3) is "so arbitrary as to constitute a denial of due process of law." * * *

Notes and Questions

1. Compare the opinion of Sears–Collins, J., dissenting in part in *In the Interest of B.L.S.*, 264 Ga. 643, 449 S.E.2d 823 (1994), a case upholding a finding of delinquency for a 13–year-old boy's statutory rape of a girl under 14: "Additionally, I believe that the statutory rape statute violates due process by including among the potential offenders young boys involved in consensual sexual relations with girls in their age group. The effect of Georgia's statutory rape law is to create an irrebuttable presumption that a female under the age of 14 is incapable of consenting to sex. Such a presumption is reasonable when applied to a relationship between a young girl and an adult male, especially an adult male in a position of authority or control. However, for the following reasons, I do not think that the application of such a presumption is either reasonable or just when applied to relationships between consenting peers.

"An irrebuttable presumption precludes any opportunity for the production of contrary evidence, depriving the accused of a hearing on the matter presumed. Because of this conclusiveness, the United States Supreme Court has held that the imposition of an irrebuttable presumption which is not 'necessarily or universally true in fact' violates the Due Process Clause of the Fourteenth Amendment. *Vlandis v. Kline*. I do not believe that we can fairly and legitimately say that today it is 'necessarily and universally true in fact' that girls under 14 are incapable of consenting to sex with partners who are their own age. To find that to be true is to be blind to the unfortunate phenomenon of teenage sex.

"At some time in this state's history it may well have been 'necessarily and universally' true that females under 14 were too innocent and naive to understand the implications and nature of their acts and, therefore, could not give genuine consent to sexual intercourse. However, I do not believe that the same can still be said given that sexual activity has increased drastically among young people in recent years, so few children are being prosecuted for their behavior, and exposure to sex and sex education at an early age, like it or not, has become a way of life.

"In a recent study administered at 32 Georgia high schools, fully 46% of the freshman girls (generally aged 14 to 15) surveyed reported that they were sexually active. Furthermore, one in seven of all of the students polled said they had started having sex before age 13! The statistics make it clear that the behavior is becoming more common: one in ten seniors said they had sex before age 13, while one in six freshmen said they had become sexually active before that age. A study of child welfare recipients indicated that 35% of the children in foster care, and 22% of those living at home, had had sexual intercourse before their thirteenth birthday. Another recent study shows that 20% of this country's young people who attend church had participated in some form of sexual experimentation by age 13. Even as early as 1982, in a survey of 160,000 teenagers regarding their feelings and experiences with sexual matters, 31% of the 13 to 15 year olds surveyed reported that they had had sexual intercourse.

"The foregoing shocking statistics and reports indicate the following: consensual sexual relations between young girls and young boys, or peer relationships, while not necessarily condoned, are pervasive, generally ignored, and arbitrarily and rarely prosecuted."

2. Is the solution that the defendant should have an opportunity, at least under some circumstances and in some way, to show that his underage sex partner was capable of consenting? If so, under what circumstances and in what way? Consider Comment, 65 U.Chi.L.Rev. 1251, 1258 (1998): "Where the defendant admits the sexual encounter, some courts have allowed evidence of the victim's sexual experience and sophistication to override or nullify the statutorily defined age of consent. In effect, previous sexual experience renders the victim capable of consenting in fact. The rationale underlying these decisions is that sexually experienced girls understand the benefits and risks associated with sexual activity and can make rational, informed decisions. Furthermore, courts explain that the state's goal is to protect the innocent and the naive, because they are the victims least likely to recognize the consequences of premature sexual activity. Accordingly, the courts reason that the legislature did not intend to protect sexually experienced adolescents. These courts engage in the questionable practice of turning an irrebuttable presumption into one that can be rebutted." Cf. the "promiscuity defense" in *Model Penal Code* § 213.6(3), and consider Kitrosser, infra, at 336, asserting "that any reforms in the area of age-based rape and sexual assault law should eliminate such vestiges of the past. Such provisions hearken back to the notion of young girls' 'sexual treasures,' with protection from sexual imposition based not on bodily autonomy, but on the worth, or lack thereof, of a young woman's 'treasure,' or, alternatively, of her soiled sexuality."

3. What then of the proposal in Heidi Kitrosser, *Meaningful Consent: Toward New Generation of Statutory Rape Laws*, 4 Va. J.Soc.Pol'y & L. 287, 287–91 (1997): "The law of statutory rape has undergone dramatic changes in most jurisdictions over the last two decades. While traditional statutory rape law generally criminalized participation by any male in sexual intercourse with a female below a prescribed age, the vast majority of modern day statutes are gender neutral and define statutory rape based on more complex 'age span' provisions. Such provisions provide, for example, that a person is guilty of an offense for engaging in sex with a minor only if he or she is a specified number of years older than the minor.

"These changes have touched off a debate in the feminist community. Some feminists applaud the changes, and even suggest that statutory rape laws should be further reformed or abolished. These arguments are based largely on the notion that statutory rape laws violate female autonomy and thus deny young women the right to choose when and with whom they will engage in sexual activity. Feminist opponents of such changes, however, argue that these changes serve primarily to grant men sexual access to minor females. Specifically, they argue that, given social norms that make sex less than a free choice for many women, given forcible rape laws that tend to recognize only the most violent forms of sexual coercion, and given that underage females may face greater sexual pressures and be less equipped to handle such pressures than adults, decriminalizing strict liability age-based sexual offenses makes underage girls 'fair game' for boys and men.

"[T]he solution to substantive inequality in sexual relations between boys and girls and men and women is no longer the per se criminalization of sexual activity with young girls. There are two primary reasons for this conclusion—one philosophical and one practical. Philosophically, simple per se age restrictions obfuscate any meaningful inquiry into consent. This enables us to avoid asking difficult questions about consent, coercion, and the relevance of age-and gender-based dynamics to determine why, when, and how age-

and gender-based power imbalances combine with a coercive context to make sex lack meaningful consent. [I]t is far too simplistic to suggest that adolescent girls are incapable of making consensual sexual choices in all instances. As such, to place all sexual activity in certain age-based categories under the statutory umbrella of 'assault' or 'rape' misses the real issue, because it fails to isolate, name, and target those instances of sex that are coercive and that should, for that reason, be subject to criminal punishment.

"The primary counter-argument is, of course, that because the law of rape generally fails sufficiently to isolate and punish many instances of coercive sex, without statutory rape laws underage girls would be left largely unprotected from such coercion. This counterpoint fails, however, to account for some current phenomena that undermine the practical appeal of traditional statutory rape laws: the failure of at least some prosecutors' offices to seek statutory rape prosecutions for underage sex that they deem 'consensual,' dicta indicating judicial reluctance to uphold statutory rape convictions for consensual sex, and the refusal of at least two courts to uphold statutory rape convictions for consensual sex despite clear statutory mandates. These factors, combined with the overwhelming prevalence of adolescent sexual activity, suggest not only that per se age restrictions muddle meaningful inquiries into consent as a philosophical matter, but that, in practice, the growing acceptance of underage sex has made statutory rape laws antiquated 'jokes,' with increasingly diminished effectiveness.

"In response to these problems, and with an eye toward developing a more progressive understanding of consent and female autonomy in the law of rape, this Article proposes further reform and modification of age-based provisions, combined with fundamental changes to legal conceptions of 'consent' and 'coercive' sex. While ideally the latter changes would also permeate the general law of rape, at a minimum they should be implemented in the context of age-based rape law. This Article proposes a scheme under which consent would serve as an affirmative defense within particular age spans. There would, however, be a rebuttable presumption of nonconsent as to this affirmative defense, with rebuttal dependent upon a more meaningful inquiry into coercion and consent than is generally provided by current rape law. Furthermore, certain combinations of age and relationship status would create categories of per se illegality based on the inherent power relations in a given status relationship; for example, that between a father and his sixteen-year-old daughter."

4. Or, on the other hand, is voluntary consent in statutory rape cases irrelevant in any event under the "new" justification for such statutes relied upon in *Michael M. v. Superior Court*, 450 U.S. 464, 101 S.Ct. 1200, 67 L.Ed.2d 437 (1981)? In that case, the petitioner, then a 17 ½-year-old male, who was charged with violating California's statutory rape law—which defines unlawful sexual intercourse as "an act of sexual intercourse accomplished with a female not the wife of the perpetrator, where the female is under the age of 18 years"—claimed that the statute unlawfully discriminated on the basis of gender since men alone were criminally liable thereunder. In rejecting that contention, the plurality opinion in *Michael M.* stated:

"We are satisfied not only that the prevention of illegitimate pregnancy is at least one of the 'purposes' of the statute, but also that the State has a strong interest in preventing such pregnancy. At the risk of stating the obvious, teenage pregnancies, which have increased dramatically over the last two decades, have significant social, medical, and economic consequences for both the mother and her child, and the State. Of particular concern to the State is that approximately half of all teenage pregnancies end in abortion. And of those children who are born, their illegitimacy makes them likely candidates to become wards of the State.

"We need not be medical doctors to discern that young men and young women are not similarly situated with respect to the problems and the risks of sexual intercourse. Only women may become pregnant, and they suffer disproportionately the profound physical, emotional and psychological consequences of sexual activity. The statute at issue here protects women from sexual intercourse at an age when those consequences are particularly severe.

"The question thus boils down to whether a State may attack the problem of sexual intercourse and teenage pregnancy directly by prohibiting a male from having sexual intercourse with a minor female. We hold that such a statute is sufficiently related to the State's objectives to pass constitutional muster.

"Because virtually all of the significant harmful and inescapably identifiable consequences of teenage pregnancy fall on the young female, a legislature acts well within its authority when it elects to punish only the participant who, by nature, suffers few of the consequences of his conduct. It is hardly unreasonable for a legislature acting to protect minor females to exclude them from punishment. Moreover, the risk of pregnancy itself constitutes a substantial deterrence to young females. No similar natural sanctions deter males. A criminal sanction imposed solely on males thus serves to roughly 'equalize' the deterrents on the sexes."

5. Statutory rape is not the only situation in which it has been customary to presume conclusively that consent was lacking. Under English common law, the established rule was "that unlawful and forcible connection with a woman in a state of unconsciousness at the time, whether that state has been produced by the act of the prisoner or not, is presumed to be without her consent, and is rape." *Commonwealth v. Burke*, 105 Mass. 376 (1870). American courts reached the same conclusion, and in more recent times the point has often been covered by a specific provision in the applicable rape statute. There is considerable variation in the current statutes as to what condition or conditions are covered, and the broader term of "physically helpless" is sometimes used. These statutes do not require that the defendant have brought about the victim's condition; the theory underlying these provisions is that "the actor may be held liable for rape even where he did nothing to cause her incapacity but merely took advantage of her helpless state." *Model Penal Code* § 213.1, Comment (1980).

Under English common law, the situation was considered no different where the intercourse was with a mentally incompetent female, and here again the point is often covered in contemporary rape statutes. There is considerable variation in the statutory language, but in terms of defining the degree of mental disease that suffices to make noncoercive intercourse a crime, many fall short of *Model Penal Code* § 213.1(2)(b).

SECTION 4. MENTAL STATE; MISTAKE OF FACT

DIRECTOR OF PUBLIC PROSECUTIONS v. MORGAN

House of Lords, 1975.

[1976] A.C. 182, [1975] 2 W.L.R. 913, [1975] 2 All E.R. 347.

Appeal by the defendants from an order of the Court of Appeal (Criminal Division) dismissing their appeals against conviction.

The appellants were convicted at Stafford Crown Court on January 24, 1974; Morgan of aiding and abetting rape, Parker of aiding and abetting rape and of rape; McLarty of aiding and abetting rape and of rape; McDonald of rape and of aiding and abetting rape.

They were sentenced by Kenneth Jones J.: Parker, McLarty and McDonald to concurrent terms of four years' imprisonment and Morgan to concurrent terms of 10 years' imprisonment. * * *

Morgan was a senior N.C.O. in the Royal Air Force. He was 37 years old, his wife 34, and they had been married for about 13 years and had boys of 11 and 12. For some time husband and wife had been on poor terms, and she had engaged in two love affairs, at least one of them being (as Mrs. Morgan alleged) at her husband's instigation. Of the other three accused, one was nearly 20, the other two were in their twenties, all three of them serving in the Royal Air Force and having arrived at the R.A.F. Depot at Cosford on August 15, 1973. It was common ground that Morgan invited the other three accused, all complete strangers to him, that night to go back to his house and have intercourse with his wife and that as he drove them from Wolverhampton to his home at Cosford he supplied each of them with a contraceptive. The only issue between the various accused relating to this part of the case was that Morgan denied the assertion of the others that during the car journey he told them that his wife might put up a show of struggling, but that this would only be a charade stimulating her sexual excitement, as in reality she would welcome intercourse with them. They claimed that, although they were at first incredulous, Morgan finally persuaded them that he was serious and that their behavior thereafter was throughout based on their belief that Mrs. Morgan was indeed only play-acting. Certainly she could have done nothing more than she did to resist the attacks made upon her, and before the House of Lords counsel for the appellants accepted that in fact she never did consent to what transpired from the moment the four men reached Morgan's home. She was awakened from sleep in a bedroom which she shared with her 11–year-old son and her evidence was that all four accused in part dragged and in part carried her into another room which contained a double bed. She claimed that she struggled violently and shouted "Police!" several times until a hand was placed over her mouth, that both children were awakened and that thereafter each of the four accused had sexual intercourse with her. It was established that, as soon as the three strangers had departed and Morgan had gone to bed, Mrs. Morgan drove off to Cosford Hospital and complained of having been raped, her case being that she did all she could to resist but that she was throughout held down on the bed by three men while the fourth had intercourse with her. * * *

LORD CROSS OF CHELSEA: * * * The question of law which is raised by the appeal is whether the judge was right in telling the jury that, if they came to the conclusion that Mrs. Morgan had not consented to the intercourse in question but that the defendants believed or may have believed that she was consenting to it, they must nevertheless find the defendants guilty of rape if they were satisfied that they had no reasonable grounds for so believing. * * * The Sexual Offences Act 1956, which provides by section 1(1) that it is an offence "for a man to rape a woman," contains no definition of the word "rape." No one suggests that rape is an "absolute" offence to the commission of which the state of mind of the defendant with regard to the woman's consent is wholly irrelevant. The point in dispute is as to the quality of belief which entitles the defendant to be acquitted and as to the "evidential" burden of proof with regard to it.

* * * Rape is not a word in the use of which lawyers have a monopoly and the question to be answered in this case, as I see it, is whether according to the ordinary use of the English language a man can be said to have committed rape if he believed that the woman was consenting to the intercourse and would not have attempted to have it but for his belief, whatever his grounds for so believing. I do not think that he can. * * *

LORD HAILSHAM OF ST. MARYLEBONE: * * * Bridge J., in giving the judgment of the Court of Appeal, attempted to do so by three propositions which, again, I quote in extenso. He said: "The relevant principles can perhaps be restated in the following propositions:

1. In all crimes the Crown has both the evidential and the probative burden of showing that the accused did the prohibited act * * * .

2. Wherever the definition of a crime includes as one of its express ingredients a specific mental element both the evidential and the probative burden lie upon the Crown with respect to that element. * * * In seeking to rebut the Crown's case against him in reference to his state of mind the accused may and frequently does assert his mistaken belief in non-existent facts. Of course it is right that in this context the question whether there were reasonable grounds for the belief is only a factor for the jury's consideration in deciding whether the Crown has established the necessary mental element of the crime. This is because the issue is already before the jury and no evidential burden rests upon the accused. * * *

3. But where the definition of the crime includes no specific mental element beyond the intention to do the prohibited act, the accused may show that though he did the prohibited act intentionally he lacked *mens rea* because he mistakenly but honestly and reasonably, believed facts which, if true, would have made his act innocent. Here the evidential burden lies upon the accused but once evidence sufficient to raise the issue is before the jury the probative burden lies upon the Crown to negative the mistaken belief. The rationale of requiring reasonable grounds for the mistaken belief must lie in the law's consideration that a bald assertion of belief for which the accused can indicate no reasonable ground is evidence of insufficient substance to raise any issue requiring the jury's consideration. Thus, for example, a person charged with assault upon a victim shown to have been entirely passive throughout who said he had believed himself to be under imminent threat of attack by the victim but could indicate no circumstance giving cause for such a belief would not discharge the evidential burden of showing a mistaken belief that he was acting lawfully in self-defence."

In the event Bridge J. then went on to subsume rape under the third and not the second heading and so to reach the conclusion: "The correct view, we think, is that, on proof of the fact of absence of consent from circumstances which in the nature of the case must have come to the notice of the defendant, he may be presumed to have appreciated their significance, and it is this presumption which casts upon the defendant the evidential burden of showing an honest and reasonable belief in consent before any issue as to his state of mind can arise for the jury's consideration." He goes on to say that, once the "evidential" burden is discharged the "probative burden" is cast once more on the Crown.

With due respect * * * I do not believe the conclusion follows. * * * I can see no reason why the class of case to which his second proposition applies should be limited to cases where the mental ingredient is limited to a "specific mental element" * * * .

I believe the law on this point to have been correctly stated by Lord Goddard C.J. in *Steane* (1947) 32 Cr.App.R. 61, 66; [1947] K.B. 997, 1004, when he said: "if on the totality of the evidence there is room for more than one view as to the intent of the prisoner, the jury should be directed that it is for the prosecution to prove the intent to the jury's satisfaction, and if, on review of the whole evidence, they either think the intent did not exist or they are left in doubt as to the intent, the prisoner is entitled to be acquitted." * * *

Once one has accepted, what seems to me abundantly clear, that the prohibited act in rape is non-consensual sexual intercourse, and that the guilty state of mind is an intention to commit it, it seems to me to follow as a matter of inexorable logic that there is no room either for a "defence" of honest belief or mistake, or of a defence of honest and reasonable belief and mistake. Either the prosecution proves that the accused had the requisite intent, or it does not. In the former case it succeeds, and in the latter it fails. Since honest belief clearly negatives intent, the reasonableness or otherwise of that belief can only be evidence for or against the view that the belief and therefore the intent was actually held, and it matters not whether, to quote Bridge J. in the passage cited above: "the definition of a crime includes no specific element beyond the prohibited act." If the mental element be primarily an intention and not a state of belief it comes within his second proposition and not his third. Any other view, as for insertion of the word "reasonable" can only have the effect of saying that a man intends something which he does not. * * *

LORD SIMON OF GLAISDALE. * * * [A]greeing as I do with the judgment of Bridge J. in the Court of Appeal, I feel no reluctance in coming to this conclusion, which seems to me to accord with legal principle and with good sense. * * *

The common law seems to be the same in the U.S.A.; see specifically as regards rape *U.S. v. Short* (1954) 4 U.S.C.M.A. 437; 16 C.M.R. 11.[a] * * *

It remains to consider why the law requires, in such circumstances, that the belief in a state of affairs whereby the *actus* would not be *reus* should be held on reasonable grounds. One reason was given by Bridge J. in the Court of Appeal: "The rationale of requiring reasonable grounds for the mistaken belief must lie in the law's consideration that a bald assertion of belief for which the accused can indicate no reasonable ground is evidence of insufficient substance to raise any issue requiring the jury's consideration." I agree; but I think there is also another reason. The policy of the law in this regard could well derive from its concern to hold a fair balance between victim and accused. It would hardly seem just to fob off a victim of a savage assault with such comfort as he could derive from knowing that his injury was caused by a belief, however absurd, that he was about to attack the accused. A respectable woman who has been ravished would hardly feel that she was vindicated by being told that her assailant must go unpunished because he believed, quite unreasonably, that she was consenting to sexual intercourse with him. * * *

LORD EDMUND DAVIES: * * * The parties to these appeals are at one in regarding the offence of rape as falling within the third of Bridge J.'s propositions, but they differ widely in relation to what is involved in "the intention to do the prohibited act." Before this House, learned prosecuting counsel submitted that rape consists simply in having sexual intercourse with a woman who does not in fact consent, and that more than this the Crown need not establish in order to secure a conviction. This simplistic approach is reminiscent of the minority judgments in *Tolson* (1889) 23 Q.B.D. 168, of which more hereafter, that a man commits bigamy if he goes through a marriage ceremony while his wife is alive, even though he honestly and reasonably believes she is dead. Indeed, it would mean that rape involved no mental element save the intention to have intercourse * * *.

It was rightly submitted for the appellants that such an approach involves a fundamentally wrong conception of what constitutes rape. The offence lacks statutory definition,

---

a. In *Short*, the defendant was court-martialed for assault with intent to commit rape. At trial, he claimed he thought the girl was a consenting prostitute. His request for an instruction that "the accused must think victim is not consenting" was refused. In affirming the conviction, Quinn, C. J., held the instruction was properly refused because it "fails to qualify the accused's belief by requiring that it be reasonable and honest." Brosman, J., dissenting argued that rape "has ordinarily been treated as requiring only a general criminal intent," while assault with intent to rape requires "a specific intent," so that an unreasonable belief would negative the prerequisites for finding guilt of the latter offense but not the former. He added: "It may be regarded as anomalous to conclude that an accused may be exonerated for guilt of assault with intent to commit rape because of an unreasonable mistake, whereas he could have been convicted lawfully of rape had penetration been effected under the same misapprehension."

the Sexual Offences Act 1956, s. 1(1) merely declaring it an offence for a man to rape a woman. [But all the definitions in the treatises] indicate that knowledge by the accused of the woman's unwillingness to have intercourse is essential to the crime of rape. * * *

In the absence of contrary evidence, the accused may be presumed to have appreciated the significance of circumstances which must have come to his notice. But it does not follow inexorably that he in fact did so * * *. The presumption is not conclusive and, unless it emerges that there is a weight of authority compelling a different conclusion, I should have considered that the honest belief of an accused charged with rape that the woman was willing, being wholly inconsistent with the criminal intention necessary to constitute the crime, would call for his acquittal. * * *

In this country a long line of authorities and numerous dicta indicate that, when an accused challenges that he had the necessary *mens rea* involved in the offence charged by asserting that he committed the *actus reus* under a mistake of fact, his belief must have been based on reasonable grounds. Of these cases, the best known are those arising from charges of bigamy. * * *

Such an approach has been criticised. In America, for example, Professor Jerome Hall observed ((1957) 33 *Indiana Law Journal*), "Anglo–American law restricts the scope of *ignorantia facti* in ways which constitute serious limitations. * * * An honest mistake is not sufficient. [It] must be bona fide and reasonable * * * The plain consequences of this application of objective liability to *ignorantia facti* is that persons who commit harms solely because they are mistaken regarding the material facts are nonetheless criminally liable, i.e. despite the complete lack of criminal intent. * * * The elimination of 'reasonableness' as a substantive restriction of the doctrine of *ignorantia facti* would clarify the public mind regarding the nature of criminal conduct. It would facilitate analysis of the criminal law and stimulate a sounder administration of it." In this country, *Russell on Crime* (12th ed. Vol. 1, p. 76), in the course of a discussion of *mens rea*, refers to "the ancient doctrine that the mistake must be reasonable" and adds: "It is hardly necessary to point out that such a doctrine, based purely on an objective test, is out of keeping with the modern principle that the *mens rea* required by the common law is a subjective element." And Professor Glanville Williams has commented (*Criminal Law*, 2nd ed. (1961) p. 177): " * * * it is not true to say that the general run of crimes can be committed by inattention. * * * It is submitted that this is not the law. In the absence of words in the statute dispensing with proof of *mens rea*, it should be held that the crime can be committed only intentionally or recklessly. If a person charged with bigamy believed that he was legally free to marry again, it cannot be said that the crime was committed either intentionally or recklessly, and the question whether the belief was unreasonable is irrelevant." And, after a discussion of reported cases, he concluded: "Even if, as a result of decisions like this, it must now be conceded that unreasonable mistake is no defence in bigamy, this only means that bigamy can be committed negligently. It does not prove that other crimes can be committed negligently."

For myself, I am greatly impressed by these forceful passages * * *. But regard must be had to the uniformity of approach over a wide area and for a long time—*Tolson*[b], it

---

b. 23 Q.B.D. 168 (1889), described by Lord Cross in *Morgan* as follows: "The statute [Offences against the Person Act 1861, s. 57] there provided that 'whoever being married shall marry any other person during the life of the former husband or wife shall be guilty of felony' with a proviso that: 'nothing in this section contained shall extend * * * to any person marrying a second time whose husband or wife shall have been continually absent from such person for the space of seven years then last past, and shall not have been known by such person to be living within that time. * * *' The defendant who was found by the jury to have had reasonable grounds for believing that her husband was then dead—though in fact he was not—went through a ceremony of marriage with another man within seven years of the time when she last knew should be remembered, was decided nearly 90 years ago. Paying such regard, the conclusion I have come to is that the necessary course is to uphold, as being in accordance with established law, the direction given in this case by the learned trial judge as to the necessity for the mistake of fact urged to be based on reasonable grounds. The approach which I should have preferred must, I think, wait until the legislature reforms this part of the law * * *.

LORD FRASER OF TULLYBELTON: * * * All the definitions of rape quoted to us which made any reference to the state of mind required of the rapist included a statement to the effect that: "One of the elements of the crime of rape is an intention on the part of an accused person to have intercourse without consent." * * * If that is so, then the logical difficulty of requiring a belief in the woman's consent to be based on reasonable grounds arises sharply. If the effect of the evidence as a whole is that the defendant believed, or may have believed, that the woman was consenting, then the Crown has not discharged the onus of proving commission of the offence as fully defined and, as it seems to me, no question can arise as to whether the belief was reasonable or not. Of course, the reasonableness or otherwise of the belief will be important as evidence tending to show whether it was truly held by the defendant, but that is all.

The argument for the Crown in support of an affirmative answer to the question in this case was not supported by any English decision on rape. It was supported by reference to English decisions in relation to other offences which are more or less analogous to rape, and to Australian decisions on rape, some of which I have already referred to. The English case upon which most reliance was placed was *Tolson,* supra, which was concerned with bigamy, and which decided that a bona fide belief *on reasonable grounds* in the death of the husband at the time of the second marriage afforded a good defence to the indictment for bigamy. The main argument in the case concerned with the question whether a mistaken belief could be a defence to a charge of bigamy at all, and comparatively little attention was given to the subsidiary point of whether the belief had to be based upon reasonable grounds. The case seems to me therefore of only limited assistance for the present purpose. We were invited to overrule *Tolson* but, as it has stood for over 80 years, and has been followed in many later cases, I would not favour that course. But in my opinion the case is distinguishable from the present. Bigamy was a statutory offence under the Offences against the Person Act 1861, s. 57. So far as appears from the words of the section, bigamy was an absolute offence, except for one defence set out in a proviso, and it is clear that the mental element in bigamy is quite different from that in rape. In particular, bigamy does not involve any intention except the intention to go through a marriage ceremony, unlike rape in which I have already considered the mental element. So, if a defendant charged with bigamy believes that his spouse is dead, his belief does not involve the absence of any intent which forms an essential ingredient in the offence, and it is thus not comparable to the belief of a defendant charged with rape that the woman consents. The difficulty of arguing by analogy from one offence to another is strikingly illustrated by reference to the case of *Prince* (1875) 13 Cox C.C. 138. That case dealt with abduction of a girl under the age of 16, an offence created by section 55 of the Act of 1861. Lord Bramwell, with whom

of his being alive. She therefore fell within the very words of the statute. Nevertheless, the majority of the Court of Crown Cases Reserved held that she was entitled to be acquitted because on general principles of criminal liability, having no particular relation to the crime of bigamy, a mistaken belief based on reasonable grounds in the existence of facts, which, if true, would have made the act charged against her innocent, afforded her a defence since it was not to be supposed that Parliament intended bigamy to be an 'absolute' offence to the commission of which the state of mind of the defendant was wholly irrelevant. The minority of the judges, on the other hand, thought that the existence of the proviso which gave an express exemption from liability in certain circumstances made it impossible to imply an exemption from liability in other circumstances not covered by it."

five other judges concurred, held that a mistaken and reasonable belief by the defendant that the abducted girl was aged 16 or more was no excuse, because abduction of a young girl was immoral as well as illegal, although a mistaken and reasonable belief by the defendant that he had the consent of the girl's father would have been an excuse. If such differences can exist about mistaken beliefs of different facts in one offence, it is surely dangerous to argue from one offence to another. No doubt a rapist, who mistakenly believes that the woman is consenting to intercourse, must be behaving immorally, by committing fornication or adultery. But those forms of immoral conduct are not intended to be struck at by the law against rape; indeed, they are not now considered appropriate to be visited with penalties of the criminal law at all. There seems therefore to be no reason why they should affect the consequences of the mistaken belief. * * *c

Notes and Questions

1. *Morgan*, as with each of the other principal cases in this Book, is included here because of the editor's view of its pedagogical value. Such an observation would be unnecessary but for the doubts on that score occasionally expressed in the past. Thus, one commentator says that "there seems to be * * * an almost prurient interest in toying with farfetched rape problems. For example, criminal law professors cannot seem to let go of the *Morgan* case. * * * The persistent interest in discussing *Morgan* may stem at least in part from the sexual stimulation derived from picturing a woman who would desire sex in the form of rape. Though the victim in *Morgan* did not possess this desire and though the jury and the court did not believe that the men believed (reasonably or not) that she did, the class will debate whether men could honestly (or even reasonably) believe that a resisting woman was actually consenting."a Other concerns are that the result reached in *Morgan* finds stronger support in other cases "with more sympathetic defendants making more believable claims,"b and that *Morgan* produces a one-sided discussion because students "refrain from defending it" even though the legal doctrine relied upon to reach the result in that case "is plainly defensible."c

How, then, is *Morgan*—followed in some American jurisdictionsd and later codified in Englande—best defended? Consider this bit of advice to a professor confronted with student

---

c. Although a majority of the House of Lords concluded the instruction was incorrect, the appeal was dismissed on the ground, as stated by Lord Davies, that "no reasonable jury could have failed to convict all four accused even had they been directed as counsel for the appellants urges they should."

Consider Comment, 39 J.Crim.L. 264, 267 (1975): "At first sight, this may seem rather remarkable, in that there is nothing inherently unlikely in a group of very young soldiers being convinced by an older and senior N.C.O. that his wife was 'kinky' and enjoyed sexual intercourse only when she was stimulated by feigning resistance. If a jury had been properly directed that such a belief honestly held was a defence, is it inevitable that they would have convicted? The view taken by the House of Lords appears to have depended on the fact that, at their trial, the defendants changed their story and asserted that the woman had actively participated in an orgy. If this were really the ground upon which the proviso was applied, four years' imprisonment seems to be a severe penalty for lying, however grossly."

a. Ann Althouse, *The Lying Woman, the Devious Prostitute, and Other Stories From the Evidence Casebook,* 88 Nw.U.L.Rev. 914, 994 n.198 (1994).

b. Susan Estrich, *Teaching Rape Law,* 102 Yale L.J. 509, 510 (1992), adding in n.7 that she teaches "a case in which three men were convicted of raping a woman who had left a party with them and smoked marijuana with them before each man, in turn, had sex with her. She testified to having said no, but did not physically resist the men. Numerous appeals followed the initial convictions. See, e.g., *Commonwealth v. Sherry,* 386 Mass. 682, 437 N.E.2d 224 (Mass.1982); *Commonwealth v. Lefkowitz,* 20 Mass.App.Ct. 513, 481 N.E.2d 227 (Mass.App.Ct.1985)." For a similar but more recent Massachusetts case, see Note 3(a) infra.

c. James J. Tomkovicz, *On Teaching Rape: Reasons, Risks, and Rewards,* 102 Yale L.J. 481, 494 n.37 (1992).

d. E.g., *Reynolds v. State,* 664 P.2d 621 (Alaska App.1983) (prosecution must have proved defendant "knowingly engaged in sexual intercourse and recklessly disregarded his victim's lack of consent")

e. "(1) A man commits rape if (a) he has unlawful sexual intercourse with a woman who at the time does not consent to it; and (b) at the time he knows that she does not consent to the intercourse or he is reckless as to whether she consent to it * * *". (2) It is hereby silence on this question: "Referring students back to homicide law's preference for subjective culpability and the rationales for that preference and asking them to reconcile rejection of subjective culpability in rape with homicide's reliance on its gives the professor a means of getting students to confront the arguments in favor of subjective culpability without having to advance those arguments explicitly herself."[f]

Is this analogy useful? What then of the contention that the problem with *Morgan* is that it illustrates "how the law values the male voice over the female voice * * * because it is the male's view of whether the woman consented that is determinative,"[g] so that instead "the standard for the determination of intent in rape should center on the perceptions of both the accused and the victim, as well as the objective evidence presented."[h]

2.　Does the strength of the above defense of *Morgan* depend upon which of the "reforms" discussed earlier have been made in the definition of rape? Compare Jennifer Temkin, *The Limits of Reckless Rape*, 1983 Crim.L.Rev. 5, 14–15 (concluding defendant's mistaken belief in the woman's consent should not be "a sufficient answer to a charge of rape" "where the defendant has been told a tale by a third party or where he is drunk" or where he "did not believe her when she said 'no' "); with Joshua Dressler, *Where We Have Been, And Where We Might Be Going: Some Cautionary Reflections on Rape Law Reform*, 46 Clev.St.L.Rev. 409, 430–32 (1998):

"It is a fundamental principle of the criminal law—'no provincial or transient notion'—that we do not send people to prison and stigmatize them as serious wrongdoers in the absence of culpability for their actions. No matter how serious the harm caused, the general rule is that a person is not guilty of a criminal offense in the absence of mens rea. Imagine for a moment that you are driving safely on the highway, under an overpass, when a piece of the bridge crumbles, strikes your windshield, and causes you to lose control of your car. As a consequence, your car strikes and kills another. You are likely to feel awful about what happened, and in criminal law terms, you have committed the *actus reus* of criminal homicide. That is, you have caused precisely the type of harm that the criminal law wishes to prevent, the death of another human being. But, of course, you are guilty of no crime. You did not kill the pedestrian intentionally, or even recklessly or negligently.

"Increasingly, we are forgetting—or, at least, at risk of forgetting—this basic culpability principle in the context of rape. In one sense, this is understandable. The female who is the victim of undesired sexual contact is initially apt to feel just as violated, whether the male knew he was acting against her will or, at the other extreme, was understandably clueless. The harm to her, after all, is the same. But, of course, the harm to the dead person on the highway in the imagined overpass accident is the same whether you killed him purposely or innocently—nonetheless, the law will exculpate you for the death assuming non-culpability in causing the harm. Unfortunately, as obvious as this seems, some people find the notion of a *mens rea* requirement in the rape context silly. The principle that a male should not be convicted of rape if he reasonably (but incorrectly) believed that the female consented has been trivialized (or distorted) to mean that 'a woman [[was] raped but not by a rapist'?

declared that if at trial for a rape offense the jury has to consider whether a man believed that a woman was consenting to sexual intercourse, the presence or absence of reasonable grounds for such a belief is a matter to which the jury is to have regard, in conjunction with any other relevant matters, in considering whether he so believed." Ch. 82, § 1.

f.　Kevin C. McMunigal, *Reducing the Risk to Realizing the Rewards: An Approach to Teaching Rape Law*, 34 San Diego L.Rev. 519, 528–29 (1997).

g.　Cheryl M. Herden, *Women in Legal Education: A Feminist Analysis of Law School*, 63 Rev.Jur.U.P.R. 551, 571 n.69 (1994).

h.　Comment, 7 Pace. Int'l L.Rev. 207, 209 (1995).

"Before rape law reform, the issue of *mens rea* rarely arose in rape trials. As a practical matter, the *actus reus* proved the *mens rea*. If a male used or threatened force to obtain intercourse, then it was evident that he purposely or knowingly had nonconsensual sexual relations. If his conduct was not forcible, the female had to resist, and this gave the male reasonable warning of her lack of consent: if he proceeded against her resistance, a jury could reasonably assume that he knew she did not want sexual relations. At a minimum, the resistance meant that the male acted recklessly or negligently in regard to her wishes. Thus, there was always some form of culpability proven.

"With the abandonment or softening of the resistance requirement and the increased willingness of lawmakers to permit prosecutions for nonforcible forms of nonconsensual intercourse—an appropriate change, as I have suggested—the risk of conviction in the absence of *mens rea* is enhanced."

3.   A full assessment of the *Morgan* position, of course, requires identification and evaluation of alternative positions, one of which is a strict liability form of rape. Consider:

(a) In *Commonwealth v. Simcock*, 31 Mass.App.184, 575 N.E.2d 1137 (1991), Richard and Matthew had a phone conversation with the complainant in which it was decided they would visit her. They arrived with Matthew's brother Patrick, who had been her high school classmate. They rented a movie, and later Steven arrived with a case of beer. The complainant drank one beer and a part of another. As to the events which followed, the complainant's testimony differed from that of the men. She said that the beer caused her to become overheated, so she went into her bedroom and changed into shorts and tank top, upon which Steven walked in, forced her onto the bed, removed her clothes and had sexual intercourse with her, despite her protests of "not yet" and "please stop." When Steven was finished, she said, the others entered in turn and forced her to have sexual intercourse. The defendants, on the other hand, characterized the complainant as an initiator and enthusiastic participant in sexual intercourse after dancing provocatively in the living room to the film's soundtrack. The next day the complainant reported the incident to a family friend, stating (so the friend testified) that she had done "something very bad" and was "ashamed." A day following, the complainant spoke to her mother about the incident; several days later, she first spoke to the police. At the rape trial, it was brought out that the complainant had suffered a severe head injury three years earlier. One doctor testified that a possible effect of such a head injury was lack of impulse control and sexually inappropriate behavior and that such disinhibitive tendencies could be amplified by drinking alcohol. Another doctor stated complainant's injuries probably were not of the kind which would produce disinhibition, but on cross-examination stated that her medical records indicated she had engaged in inappropriate behavior while hospitalized and thus treatment with Tegretol for three years was prescribed but had ended after one year. The trial judge refused to give the defendants' requested instruction that the Commonwealth had to prove that the sexual intercourse was committed without a reasonable and honest belief that the complaining witness freely consented, and instead told the jury: "Even a good faith belief on the part of the defendants that the alleged victim consented is not a defense. The focus of the offense in rape is lack of consent on the part of the victim and not the subjective intent of the defendant while performing the act." The appellate court concluded that denial of the requested instruction and the giving of the other instruction were both consistent with extant state law on the subject, as expressed in *Commonwealth v. Ascolillo*, 405 Mass. 456, 541 N.E.2d 570 (1989).

(b) May *Simcock* be supported and *Morgan* rightly criticized by analogy to the *Prince* case, discussed in *Morgan* by Lord Fraser? That is, may it not be concluded, as stated in *White v. State,* 44 Ohio App. 331, 185 N.E. 64 (1933), that the "sound doctrine underlying the rule that guilty knowledge is not required to accomplish the crime of rape with consent is that the act of the accused is at best an immoral one, and that he cannot enter upon the accomplishment of an admittedly immoral act except at his peril, and if in law his act is in fact felony he must suffer the consequences thereof although so far as his actual knowledge was concerned he may not have known the enormity of the offense of which he is guilty"?

(c) Or, what of an argument "that even if strict liability is generally disfavored in the criminal law, it is appropriate in this particular situation because those who fail to perceive the absence of consent even when the requisite force or threat of force has been utilized are sufficiently dangerous to justify their incapacitation, and in any event the situations in which such a mistake of fact would be even arguably justifiable are so rare that trying to identify them is not worth the candle, especially since the efforts to do so would have unfortunate side effects, not the least of which is the biased, inconsistent and unpredictable verdicts that would occur in light of the fact that men and women have such divergent views on the matters at issue"?[g]

(d) Consider Susan Estrich, *Rape*, 95 Yale L.J. 1087, 1097–99 (1986): "In defining the crime of rape, most American courts have omitted *mens rea* altogether. In Maine, for example, the Supreme Judicial Court has held that there is no *mens rea* requirement at all for rape. In Pennsylvania, the Superior Court held in 1982 that even a reasonable belief as to the victim's consent would not exculpate a defendant charged with rape. In 1982 the Supreme Judicial Court of Massachusetts left open the question whether it would recognize a defense of reasonable mistake of fact as to consent, but it rejected the defendant's suggestion that any mistake, reasonable or unreasonable, would be sufficient to negate the required intent to rape; such a claim was treated by the court as bordering on the ridiculous. The following year the court went on to hold that a specific intent that intercourse be without consent was not an element of the crime of rape; that decision has since been construed to mean that there is no intent requirement at all as to consent in rape cases.

"To treat what the defendant intended or knew or even should have known about the victim's consent as irrelevant to his liability sounds like a result favorable to both prosecution and women as victims. But experience makes all too clear that it is not. To refuse to inquire into *mens rea* leaves two possibilities: turning rape into a strict liability offense where, in the absence of consent, the man is guilty of rape regardless of whether he (or anyone) would have recognized nonconsent in the circumstances; or defining the crime of rape in a fashion that is so limited that it would be virtually impossible for any man to be convicted where he was truly unaware or mistaken as to nonconsent. In fact, it is the latter approach which has characterized all of the older, and many of the newer, American cases. In practice, abandoning *mens rea* produces the worst of all possible worlds: The trial emerges not as an inquiry into the guilt of the defendant (is he a rapist?) but of the victim (was she really raped? did she consent?). The perspective that governs is therefore not that of the woman, nor even of the particular man, but of a judicial system intent upon protecting against unjust conviction, regardless of the dangers of injustice to the woman in the particular case. * * *

" * * * Rather than inquire whether the man believed (reasonably or unreasonably) that his victim was consenting, the courts have demanded that the victim demonstrate her nonconsent by engaging in resistance that will leave no doubt as to nonconsent. The definition of nonconsent as resistance—in the older cases, as utmost resistance, while in

g. Wayne R. LaFave, *Criminal Law* § 7.18(e) (3d ed.2000), summarizing Brian Kennan, *Evolutionary Biology and Strict Liability for Rape*, 22 Law & Psych. Rev. 131, 161–77 (1998).

some more recent ones, as 'reasonable' physical resistance—functions as a substitute for *mens rea* to ensure that the man has notice of the woman's nonconsent."

4. Yet another alternative to the *Morgan* approach is that of barring conviction of rape only where the defendant had a *reasonable* belief that the woman had consented. Consider:

(a) *People v. Mayberry,* 15 Cal.3d 143, 125 Cal.Rptr. 745, 542 P.2d 1337 (1975), a well-known American contemporary of *Morgan*, where the defendant, on trial for rape (defined by statute as "an act of sexual intercourse, accomplished with a female not the wife of the perpetrator, under either of the following circumstances: * * * 2. Where she resists, but her resistance is overcome by force or violence; 3. Where she is prevented from resisting by threats of great and immediate bodily harm, accompanied by apparent power of execution"), was refused his requested instruction that he should be acquitted if the jury had a reasonable doubt as to whether he "reasonably and genuinely believed" that the woman consented. The court reversed: "If a defendant entertains a reasonable and bona fide belief that a prosecutrix voluntarily consented to accompany him and to engage in sexual intercourse, it is apparent he does not possess the wrongful intent that is a prerequisite * * * to a conviction of * * * rape by means of force or threat. * * *

"The Attorney General further argues that a defense based on mistake of fact as to the prosecutrix' consent in prosecutions for * * * rape should not be permitted because it will promote greater resistance by the victim to assure there is no misunderstanding as to consent and that such resistance could result in harm to the victim. The Attorney General notes that utmost resistance by the female to establish lack of consent to intercourse is not required. Such an argument, in our view, invokes a policy consideration for the Legislature * * *."

(b) Does *Mayberry* represent what should have been done in *Morgan*? Consider the views of a leading English criminal law scholar, Glanville Williams ("People ought not be punished for negligence except in some minor offenses established by statute. Rape carries a possible sentence of imprisonment for life, and it would be wrong to have a law of negligent rape")[h]; and one of this country's leading authority on rape, Estrich, *supra*, at 1101–03 ("such a 'negligent rapist' should be punished, albeit—as in murder—less severely than the man who acts with purpose or knowledge, or even knowledge of the risk").

(c) Or, can it be said in response, considering that most of the traditional defenses to crime are stated as to require a reasonable belief by the defendant, that "some of these rules are at least roughly analogous to liability for negligent rape; others may pose distinguishable issues but nonetheless help to demonstrate that serious criminal liability based on negligence is not anomalous, though it may be unwise.

"Two concerns seem to underlie the frequent willingness of courts and legislatures to convict defendants who were 'merely negligent.' First, certain types of conduct are extremely dangerous even if unintentional. In such situations, the need for deterrence or incapacitation of the defendant is sometimes thought to outweigh considerations of moral culpability. Second, and probably more important, subjective tests lend themselves to abuse because in some contexts it is difficult for jurors to appraise the defendant's state of mind. Thus, an objective standard can be thought of as a judicial device for preventing excessive jury leniency.

"Of course, one may reject these justifications. But whatever validity they have is greater in the context of rape than in the context of, say, theft, the classic example of an intentional crime. Negligent theft is not a serious social problem, because those who

h. Quoted in David P. Bryden, *Redefining Rape,* 3 Buff.Crim.L.Rev. 317, 331 (2000).

negligently take another's valuable property usually return it, voluntarily or not, without serious harm. Thus, the MPC's Commentary defends the claim of right defense to theft on the ground that, 'Persons who take only property to which they believe themselves entitled constitute no significant threat to the property system and manifest no character trait worse than ignorance.' This rationale is inapplicable to a negligent rape: Men who rape cannot undo the harm; they are dangerous even if they made a mistake; and they manifest, in most realistic scenarios, a callous indifference to the victim's interests." David P. Bryden, *Redefining Rape*, 3 Buff.Crim.L.Rev. 317, 335–36 (2000).

(d) If an objective negligence/reasonableness standard is employed either in defining a defense to a rape charge or in describing a required mental state, just what should the standard mean in this context? "Estrich argues that reasonableness in rape should be judged from the viewpoint of a non-sexist reasonable man 'who understands that a woman's word is deserving of respect.'[70] But a defendant in a rape case might claim that he should be judged by what appears 'reasonable' from an admittedly sexist viewpoint, especially if many others, perhaps a majority, in his community share such sexist attitudes towards norms of sexual interaction and sexual mores are in transition.[71] [T]he issue of whether the reasonable man standard should be tailored in rape to incorporate a non-sexist or sexist viewpoint [parallels] the issue raised in *Dudley & Stephens* [p. 561 of this Book] of whether criminal law should reflect or shape community standards." Kevin C. McMunigal, *Reducing the Risk to Realizing the Rewards: An Approach to Teaching Rape Law*, 34 San Diego L.Rev. 519, 538–39 (1997).

(e) "Indeed, just how workable the *Mayberry* objective standard would be if more widely utilized is itself a significant question, especially in light of the arguments stated earlier for the strict liability alternative, for the prospect of rape prosecutions generally being confounded by bogus claims of reasonably mistaken belief in consent is a troublesome one. Courts have shown concern for this problem, as is reflected in those cases not rejecting the objective negligence test but yet finding the instant case not to be one justifying a jury instruction about defendant's possible mistaken belief in consent. The hard question is just when juries should be permitted to consider the possibility of a reasonably mistaken belief in consent, as to which some courts and commentators have offered answers. One approach, severely criticized by some, is the so-called rule of equivocality, which means that the defense of mistake as to consent is unavailable as a matter of law unless there is 'substantial evidence of equivocal conduct that would have led a defendant to reasonably and in good faith believe consent existed where it did not.'[112] In

---

70. *Real Rape*, at 97.

71. On the prevalence of sexist attitudes in society, Estrich notes:

Women as well as men have viewed male aggressiveness as desirable and forced sex as an expression of love. Women as well as men have been taught and come to believe that if a woman "encourages" a man, he is entitled to sexual satisfaction. Or, as Ann Landers put it in 1985, "the someone who 'repairs to some private place for a few drinks and a little shared affection' has, by her acceptance of such a cozy invitation, given the man reason to believe she is a candidate for whatever he might have in mind." From sociological surveys to prime-time television, one can find ample support in our society and culture for even the broadest notions of seduction enforced by the most traditional judges.

But the evidence is not entirely one-sided. College men and women may think that the typical male is

forward and primarily interested in sex, but they no longer conclude that he is the desirable man. Older sex manuals may have lauded male sexual responses as automatic and uncontrollable, but some of the newer ones no longer see men as machines and even advocate sensitivity as seductive. Date rape is beginning to be thought of as just that, by its women victims and by those in positions of authority on college campuses.

We live in a time of changing sexual mores, and we are likely to for some time to come.

Id. at 100–01.

112. *People v. Williams*, 4 Cal.4th 354, 14 Cal. Rptr.2d 441, 841 P.2d 961 (1992). *Williams* is the leading case on the rule, but similar rulings are to be found elsewhere. * * *

other words, if at trial the defendant testified to a set of facts which, if accepted by the jury, would support a finding of actual consent, and the alleged victim testified to a different set of facts which, if believed, would preclude any reasonable belief of consent, there remains 'no middle ground'[113] which could serve as a basis for sending the reasonable belief issue to the jury. Another feature of this equivocality test is that there is only one recognized permissible source of the defendant's confusion: 'the victim's equivocal conduct.'[114] In a similar fashion, some other courts, without specifically mentioning equivocality, have likewise held that defendant's mistaken belief must be grounded in the complainant's conduct." Wayne R. LaFave, *Criminal Law* § 7.18(e) (3d ed.2000).

(f) Does the equivocality approach make the negligence alternative more or less attractive? Consider Dressler, supra, at 438–39: "The real issue should be whether the defendant's belief is reasonable. That is, if *Williams* is rightly decided, it is because we believe that there is no way a reasonable jury could find that Williams's subjective belief was objectively reasonable. But, this point needs to be placed in perspective. A defendant has a constitutional right to trial by jury; when a judge decides that there is no way that a jury could find a particular fact to exist based on the evidence introduced and, therefore, refuses to instruct the jury on that issue, the judge substitutes herself for the jury as factfinder. In order to avoid a constitutional violation, courts have set a very low evidentiary standard in regard to criminal law defenses. For example, when a self-defense theory is raised, even minimally, by the evidence, a defendant is entitled to have the jury instructed on that theory 'regardless of whether such evidence is strong or weak, unimpeached or contradicted.' *Williams* seems in conflict with this principle.

"But, the problem with *Williams* is more serious than the prior example suggests. Self-defense—my example above—is an affirmative defense. That is, a defendant who seeks to prove self-defense does not, by making such a claim, deny the fact that he possessed the mens rea of the offense, e.g., the intent to kill or cause bodily injury. He seeks to justify that intent on self-protection grounds. In contrast, a rape defendant who claims that he believed that the victim consented to intercourse is arguing that he lacks the mens rea of the offense. That is, a mistake-of-fact claim in a rape prosecution constitutes a failure-of-proof claim—a claim that the prosecution has not, in fact, proven beyond a reasonable doubt one of the essential elements of the offense, the defendant's culpability.

"Why should this distinction matter? The reason is that the Constitution requires the prosecutor to prove every element of an offense beyond a reasonable doubt, but the Constitution does not compel the State to carry the burden of persuasion regarding defenses to crimes. As a result of this distinction, a trial judge does not need to instruct the jury on a defense unless the defendant produces 'more than a scintilla' of evidence, 'slight evidence,' 'some credible evidence' or 'evidence sufficient to raise a reasonable doubt' in regard to the defense.

"But, no matter how compelling and even uncontradicted the prosecutor's case is in regard to the elements of the crime, a trial judge may not direct a verdict for conviction, but must let the jury determine for itself whether the prosecution has satisfied its constitutional burden of proof. I would argue from this that, as a matter of fair play, although apparently not constitutional edict, courts should hesitate long and hard before they ease the Government's constitutional burden of proof regarding the element of mens rea by refusing to instruct the jury in regard to a defendant's 'reasonable belief' claim. Let

---

113. *People v. Williams*, 4 Cal.4th 354, 14 Cal. Rptr.2d 441, 841 P.2d 961 (1992).

114. *People v. Williams*, 4 Cal.4th 354, 14 Cal. Rptr.2d 441, 841 P.2d 961 (1992). This feature of the test has sometimes been criticized because it continues

the focus upon the victim's conduct and permits a reasonable belief to be grounded on defendant's failure to resist or submission after initial resistance. Note, 100 Yale L.J. 2687, 2698 (1991).

juries convict men who claim mistake in implausible cases; but be very, very slow to deny defendants the opportunity to have their theory of the case heard by juries. And, surely, the standard for determining when a 'reasonable belief' (or 'mistake') instruction is required should be no harsher in rape cases than in other criminal prosecutions."

Are the problems raised by Dressler best obviated by resort to the no-means-no or silence-means-no approaches discussed earlier? In that regard, just how should the no-means-no approach be tied in with the *mens rea* determination? Compare Note, 100 Yale L.J. 2687, 2704 (1991) ("verbal resistance during the encounter" should merely give rise to "a rebuttable presumption" that a reasonable belief in consent is lacking); with Donald A. Dripps, *Beyond Rape: An Essay on the Difference Between the Presence of Force and the Absence of Consent*, 92 Colum.L.Rev. 1780, 1804 (1992) ("Specific intent should remain the standard, but the intent that matters should be the intent to engage in sex with a person who says she refuses").

5. In *Simcock*, supra, the court gave as added justification for its result the fact that it "is also in harmony with the analogous rule that a defendant in a statutory rape case is not entitled to an instruction that a reasonable mistake as to the victim's age is a defense." Is the *Simcock* analogy convincing? And, in any event, is the latter rule sound? Consider the conflicting views in the *Owens* case, p. 625 of this Book, on this issue. The majority concluded:

"The state's compelling interest in promoting the welfare of children provides a powerful justification for disallowing a mistake-of-age defense to statutory rape. 'The prevention of sexual exploitation and abuse of children constitutes a government objective of surpassing importance.' The case law testing the constitutionality of strict liability statutory rape laws is unanimous in recognizing the significance of the potential harm caused by sexual activity involving children, even with their consent. These risks involve potential physical harm, including the risk of venereal diseases, especially the HIV virus, trauma, and even permanent damage to a child's organs. Statutory rape laws may help prevent pregnancies, which carry 'significant social, medical, and economic consequences for both the mother and her child, and the State.'

"Perhaps most significantly, an adult who engages in sexual activity with a child may cause the child serious psychological damage, regardless of the child's maturity or lack of chastity. Since the adult will almost always be more physically mature and experienced in sexual matters, the risk of sexual exploitation is significant. Moreover, the effects on children of sexual exploitation often follow the child into adulthood, with societal consequences as well. * * *

"The legislature's decision to disallow a mistake-of-age defense to statutory rape furthers its interest in protecting children in ways that may not be accomplished if the law were to allow such a defense. Precisely because § 463(a)(1) eliminates the need for the state to prove that the potential offender knew or was unreasonable in the failure to recognize that the victim was under age 14, the statute 'may reasonably be expected to have some deterrent effect.'

"Deterrence is accomplished by placing the risk of an error in judgment as to a potential sex partner's age with the potential offender. Moreover, even though a criminal statute that dispenses with any mens rea requirement could unconstitutionally infringe upon innocent conduct, we believe that the statute in question here does not intrude upon innocent conduct to the extent of outweighing the state's interest.[15] Where doubt exists as

---

15. Maryland's statutory rape law is less likely than a number of other state statutes to reach non-criminal sexual conduct since the victim in Maryland must be under 14 years of age, while other states have to a potential sexual partner's age, abstention from intercourse is a readily available solution:

> 'The defendant in a statutory rape case does not lack the ability to comply with the law; he must simply abstain from sexual intercourse when there is even the remotest possibility that his partner is below the statutory age. Moreover, unlike the defendant who reasonably believes his wife to be dead, remarries, and is convicted of bigamy, the man who contemplates intercourse with a partner of indeterminate age can resolve doubts in favor of compliance with the law without sacrificing behavior that society considers desirable.... [T]he maximization of deterrence for socially undesirable behavior may sometimes require the deterrence of socially neutral conduct as well.'

"[T]he statutory rape statute effectively furthers a significant state interest. Aside from deterring sexual activity with children, by disallowing a mistake-of-age defense, the state avoids the risk that the inevitably emotional statutory rape trial will focus unjustifiably on the child's appearance and level of maturity. 'The obvious problem is that because early adolescents tend to grow at a rapid rate, by the time of trial a relatively undeveloped young girl or boy may have transformed into a young woman or man.' Defendant's assertion that he had made a reasonable mistake regarding the victim's age is best considered as a mitigating circumstance at sentencing, which is what occurred in this case."

To this, the dissenters in *Owens* responded: "In this case, the majority concludes the mandates of procedural due process were satisfied, because the appellant was given sufficient notice of what actions constitute statutory rape. The majority ignores the real issue. Even if the appellant were on notice that having sexual relations with someone below the consensual age constitutes statutory rape, this does not mean, and there is no evidence to suggest, that the appellant knew that the particular female with whom he was having sexual relations was underage. [N]otice means more than simply cursory knowledge of the law.* * *

"Here, the interest the appellant seeks to vindicate is his fundamental due process right to present a defense, a right guaranteed to every criminal defendant. * * *

"The majority lists the state's interests as: promoting the physical and mental health of children, preventing the sexual exploitation and abuse of children, and preventing venereal disease and pregnancy. To be sure, these interests are compelling. * * *

"Aside from the fact that, rather than an exploitation or abuse of one of the parties, the facts of this case reveal only two teenagers engaged in a fully consensual act, Maryland's statutory rape law, as currently formulated is not the most narrowly tailored method for addressing those concerns.

"[T]he State cannot demonstrate, nor has it even attempted to show, that Maryland's statutory rape law is the most narrowly tailored means to achieve the state's interest in protecting children, while infringing upon as few due process rights as possible. And, when the state has open to it less drastic ways of satisfying its legitimate interests, it may not choose a legislative scheme that broadly stifles fundamental liberties. While some children may require the protection of strict liability, many others do not. There are reasonable options available to the State. Recognizing 'the increased maturity and independence of

adopted older ages of consent. These other statutes have withstood constitutional challenges despite their greater potential to affect noncriminal sexual conduct.

today's teenagers ...,' the Model Penal Code [§ 213.6(1)] has developed an approach that limits strict liability to those cases of sexual relations involving children under ten years of age. There are, in addition, other options utilized by other States, such as allowing the defendant to present a defense whenever the 'victim' lies about his or her age.[c]

"Maryland's sexual offense statutes protect some, but by no means all, children and punish only a few alleged perpetrators. Maryland Code Art. 27, §§ 463 and 464A punish the defendant who is 17 years old or older and engages in sexual activity with a 13–year-old. Likewise, §§ 464B and 464C punish defendants who engage in sexual relations with a 14 or 15–year-old, when the defendant is four or more years older than his partner. These are the only statutes the Legislature has enacted to punish persons who engage in consensual sexual acts with underage partners. This statutory scheme demonstrates the following. First, the State is not as concerned about the sexual exploits of all children as it is those who are considered so immature that there can be little doubt that they are too young to give consent. In those cases, strict liability may well be appropriate. Second, the State has made arbitrary distinctions between persons engaging in sexual intercourse. The 18–year-old who has consensual sexual relations with a 14–year-old, reasonably believing him or her to be older, faces 20 years in prison, while the person who is 17 3/4 years of age, who engages in the exact same conduct is guilty of no crime and, therefore, will face no punishment. The protection of those truly in need of strict liability protection certainly can be achieved short of putting at risk a defendant's right to a fair trial.

"The fact that a majority of the States[11] hold that a defendant's due process rights may be ignored when the charge is statutory rape, is not a compelling reason for this Court to do likewise; whatever other courts may do does not provide a justification for us to sanction the infringement upon a defendant's due process right to a fair trial."

6. As for the remaining presumed nonconsent situation described earlier, i.e., where the woman is physically or mentally incapacitated through no fault of the defendant, does it represent a stronger or weaker case for strict liability? That is, what do you think of *State v. Dombroski,* 145 Minn. 278, 176 N.W. 985 (1920), where defendant was convicted of rape in that he had intercourse without force or threat with a woman of unsound mind. The trial judge instructed the jury that it was not necessary for the prosecution to prove the defendant knew the woman was of unsound mind. On appeal, affirmed:

"Subdivision 1 of section 8655, upon which the prosecution rests, declares in plain and unambiguous language, that whoever has carnal intercourse with a female so devoid of mental powers, as to be incapable of rational consent thereto shall be guilty of rape; it is positive in its terms and unqualifiedly prohibits an act of the kind. It does not make knowledge by the accused of the defective mental condition of the female an element of the crime, and, construed in the light of subdivisions 4 and 5 of the same section, it is clear that the legislature did not intend to make that a necessary ingredient thereof. Subdivision 4 treats of such an act with a female while under stupor from liquor or narcotics

c. Consider in this regard the earlier stated facts in *Owens* and the assertion in another case with similar facts, *State v. Elton,* 680 P.2d 727 (Utah 1984), that it "is fundamentally unfair to allow the victim in such a crime—who necessarily has also violated the law—to mislead the defendant as to an element of the crime and then place the blame for the mistake on the defendant rather than the person who created the deceit and entrapped the defendant into committing a crime he or she attempted to avoid."

11. Justice Flanders of the Rhode Island Supreme Court reports that, "[w]ith [*People v.*] *Hernandez* [, 61 Cal.2d 529, 39 Cal.Rptr. 361, 393 P.2d 673 (Cal.1964)] and [the Model Penal Code of 1962] taking the lead, twenty three American jurisdictions, nearly half, now explicitly recognize some form of mistake of age defense."

administered to her by or with the privity of the accused; subdivision 5 expressly makes knowledge by the accused of the unconsciousness of the female an essential to a conviction. By thus making knowledge and intent necessary elements as to those subdivisions, and omitting it from subdivision 1, the legislature must be deemed to have deliberately made the distinction, and for reasons deemed by it satisfactory. We need not go into that field in inquiry.''

Chapter 10

ATTEMPTS

SECTION 1. MENTAL STATE

PEOPLE v. HARRIS

Supreme Court of Illinois, 1978.

72 Ill.2d 16, 17 Ill.Dec. 838, 377 N.E.2d 28.

WARD, CHIEF JUSTICE.

[T]he defendant was convicted on a charge, made by information, of the attempted murder of Joyce Baker on the night of November 18, 1975, in a country area east of Champaign. In a separate count the defendant was charged with aggravated kidnapping.

The alleged murder attempt took place while Miss Baker was sitting inside her car and the defendant was standing behind the car with a pistol in his hand. The defendant and Miss Baker had been keeping company. For much of the evening they had been engaged in an argument in which the defendant accused the victim of infidelity. As the argument became more heated, the defendant, who was driving, reached down and picked up a revolver from the floor of the car and placed it in his lap with the barrel pointed toward Miss Baker. He made several remarks which Miss Baker interpreted as threats to kill her.

Alarmed, she opened the door on her side of the car, got out and began to run away, but ran into a barbed wire fence, injuring her leg. The defendant also got out of the car. He did not pursue her, but remained standing by the car. After her collision with the fence, Miss Baker returned to the car, and made an unsuccessful attempt to capture the gun, which the defendant was holding in his hand and pointing in her general direction. Miss Baker then got into the car on the driver's side, and drove off toward a nearby farmhouse. She testified that as she drove off she looked in the rear vision mirror and saw the defendant standing behind the car. He was holding the gun with both hands, and pointing it at her. Then she heard something strike the rear window, and the broken pane of glass in the rear window fell out of its frame. There were no other witnesses, but following this episode the police were summoned, and they found the defendant walking down the road near the scene of the episode just described. When the car was located, the police officers testified, the rear glass was broken, and a bullet fragment was found on the left side of the rear seat.

The jury returned a verdict of guilty on the charge of attempted murder and a verdict of not guilty on the aggravated kidnapping charge. The defendant was sentenced to serve a term of not less than 4 years and not more than 12 years. * * *

The following instructions to the jury were tendered by the State and were given, over the objection of the defendant:

"A person commits the crime of attempt who, with intent to commit the crime of murder, does any act which constitutes a substantial step toward the commission of the crime of murder. The crime attempted need not have been committed."

"To sustain the charge of attempt, the State must prove the following propositions:

First: That the defendant performed an act which constituted a substantial step toward the commission of the crime of murder; and

Second: That the defendant did so with intent to commit the crime of murder. * * *

"A person commits the crime of murder who kills an individual if, in performing the acts which cause the death, he intends to kill or do great bodily harm to that individual."

The defendant objected to the last of the instructions on the ground that it told the jury it could find him guilty of attempted murder if the jury found that he had acted only with the intent to do great bodily harm and did not have the intent to cause death. * * *

The central difficulty * * * arises out of the difference between the elements of the offense of attempt and those of the specific offense attempted, murder. The definition of attempt, contained in section 8–4(a) of the Criminal Code of 1961, is:

"A person commits an attempt when, with intent to commit a specific offense, he does any act which constitutes a substantial step toward the commission of that offense."

The statutory definition of murder is found in section 9–1(a) of the Code, and reads:

"A person who kills an individual without lawful justification commits murder if, in performing the acts which caused the death:

(1) He either intends to kill or do great bodily harm to that individual or another, or knows that such acts will cause death to that individual or another; or

(2) He knows that such acts create a strong probability of death or great bodily harm to that individual or another; or

(3) He is attempting or committing a forcible felony other than voluntary manslaughter."

The crime of murder is thus committed not only when a person intends to kill another individual, but also when he intends to do great bodily harm (par. 9–1(a)(1)), or when he knows that his acts create a strong probability of death or great bodily harm (par. 9–1(a)(2)), or when he is attempting or committing a forcible felony (par. 9–1(a)(3)).

This court held in *People v. Koshiol* (1970), 45 Ill.2d 573, 262 N.E.2d 446, that in a trial for attempted murder it is not error to give an instruction defining the elements of murder. As was stated there, "[I]t would seem utterly meaningless to instruct a jury on attempt to commit a 'specific offense' without defining the specific offense * * *." Since an attempted murder requires an intent to kill, however, it is obvious that the "specific offense" referred to in section 8–4(a) cannot be construed as incorporating the alternative definitions of murder contained in section 9–1(a) in their entirety.

The point is illustrated by *People v. Viser* (1975), 62 Ill.2d 568, 343 N.E.2d 903, in which the indictment in a prosecution for attempted murder charged that the defendants' acts were committed while they were engaged in a forcible felony. With respect to the indictment in *Viser,* it was observed: "[T]he offense of attempt requires 'an intent to commit a specific offense' * * * while the distinctive characteristic of felony murder is that it does not involve an intention to kill. There is no such criminal offense as an attempt to achieve an unintended result."

This court in *People v. Muir* (1977), 67 Ill.2d 86, 8 Ill.Dec. 94, 365 N.E.2d 332, and *People v. Trinkle* (1977), 68 Ill.2d 198, 12 Ill.Dec. 181, 369 N.E.2d 888, considered, among other questions, whether it was proper in prosecutions for attempted murder to include in instructions to the jury the definition of murder under section 9–1(a)(2), that is, that one commits murder if he knows that his acts "create a strong probability of death or great bodily harm."

In *Muir* the evidence was that the defendant was being approached by a police officer who was investigating a reported burglary at a nearby building. When the officer was about 30 feet away, the defendant pointed a pistol at him and pulled the trigger, but the gun failed to discharge. The defendant then began to run away. While running he pointed his gun at the officer for a second time, and pulled the trigger. Again the pistol failed to go off. It was subsequently ascertained that the barrel of the pistol contained two cartridges which were jammed in the barrel.

The indictment charged that the defendant " * * * did with the intent to commit the offense of Murder in violation of Section 9–1a2 of Chapter 38, Illinois Revised Statutes take a substantial step towards the commission of said offense in that he did without lawful justification point a loaded gun at [name of officer] and pull the trigger knowing such acts created a strong probability of death or great bodily harm * * *."

The appellate court had reversed the conviction on the ground that the necessary ingredient of specific intent was lacking in the indictment. This court in turn reversed the decision of the appellate court. It approved those parts of the appellate court opinion which held that it was necessary in a charge of attempted murder to allege a specific intent to commit murder, and that such intent could be inferred from the character of the defendant's actions. It was held, however, that since the indictment did charge that the defendant intended to commit murder, the additional charge that the defendant had acted with the knowledge that his acts created a strong probability of death or great bodily harm did not invalidate the indictment.

In *Muir* the court also rejected a contention by the defendant that it was error for the court to have given at the request of the prosecution an instruction that "[a] person commits the crime of murder who kills an individual if, in performing the acts which cause the death, he knows that such acts create a strong probability of death or great bodily harm to that individual."

The circumstances in *Trinkle* were these: The defendant had been refused further service at a tavern after the bartender concluded that he was already intoxicated. The defendant, after threatening to "shoot or blow up the bar," left the premises, purchased a gun, returned to the vicinity of the tavern and fired a shot at the front door of the building. The shot struck a patron who, without the defendant's knowing of it, was standing behind the door.

The indictment in *Trinkle* charged in part:

"David Francis Trinkle committed the offense of ATTEMPT (MURDER) in that said defendant did perform a substantial step toward the commission of that offense in that he did without lawful justification shoot Gayle Lane with a gun knowing that such act created a strong probability of death or great bodily harm to Gayle Lane or another * * *."

The following instructions were given to the jury:

"A person commits the crime of attempt who, with intent to commit the crime of murder, does any act which constitutes a substantial step toward the commission of the crime of murder.

The crime attempted need not have been committed."

"A person commits the crime of murder who kills an individual if, in performing the acts which cause the death he knows that such acts create a strong possibility of death or great bodily harm to that individual or another."

"To sustain the charge of attempted murder, the State must prove the following propositions:

FIRST: That the defendant performed the acts which caused the injury of Gayle E. Lane;

SECOND: That when the defendant did so, he knew that his act created a strong probability of causing death or great bodily harm to Gayle E. Lane, or another; * * *."

This court correctly held that both the indictment and the instructions were defective in that they permitted the jury to find the defendant guilty of attempted murder if it concluded that the defendant knew that his acts created a strong probability of great bodily harm to another person even if the evidence did not show that the defendant had acted with an intent to kill.

Although [the instruction in this case] follows the language of section 9–1(a)(1) rather than that of section 9–1(a)(2), as in *Trinkle,* it is subject to the same objection that it permits the jury to return a verdict of guilty upon evidence that the defendant intended only to cause great bodily harm short of death. An instruction must make it clear that to convict for attempted murder nothing less than a criminal intent to kill must be shown.

The part of the holding in *Muir* that an instruction was not erroneous which charged that proof only that a defendant knowingly and intentionally created a strong probability of death or great bodily harm to another person satisfies the intent element required for attempted murder was error and is hereby overruled. Erroneous also was that part of the holding that an indictment for attempted murder was not defective which alleged that the defendant's acts to his knowledge created a strong probability of death or great bodily harm to another person. That part too of the holding in *Muir* is overruled. Observations of LaFave and Scott (*Criminal Law* sec. 59, at 428–29 (1972)) are representative of authority that it is not sufficient to prove attempted murder to show that the accused intended to cause serious bodily harm:

"Some crimes, such as murder, are defined in terms of acts causing a particular result plus some mental state which need not be an intent to bring about that result. Thus, if A, B, and C have each taken the life of another, A acting with intent to kill, B with an intent to do serious bodily injury, and C with a reckless disregard of human life, all three are guilty of murder because the crime of murder is defined in such a way that any one of these mental states will suffice. However, if the victims do not die from their injuries, then only A is guilty of attempted murder; on a charge of attempted murder it is not sufficient to show that the defendant intended to do serious bodily harm or that he acted in reckless disregard for human life. Again, this is because intent is needed for the crime of attempt, so that attempted murder requires an intent to bring about that result described by the crime of murder (*i.e.*, the death of another)." * * *

Reversed and remanded. * * *

Notes and Questions

1, 2, 3 = wrongly decided

1. Compare with *Harris* the case of *People v. Castro*, 657 P.2d 932 (Colo.1983), holding there *is* such a crime as attempted extreme indifference murder. A statute says one commits an attempt "if, acting with the kind of culpability otherwise required for commission of an offense, he intentionally engages in conduct constituting a substantial step toward the commission of the offense." The crime of extreme indifference murder then consisted of these elements: (1) under circumstances manifesting extreme indifference to the value of human life; (2) "intentionally" engaging in conduct that creates a grave risk of death to another; and (3) thereby causing the death of another. The court reasoned:

"It is quite obvious that the statutory ingredients of attempted extreme indifference murder do not postulate a logical or legal inconsistency by requiring an intent to engage in an unintentional act. The crime of extreme indifference murder requires an intentional state of mind with respect to proscribed conduct. The actor must be aware of his conduct and have a conscious object to engage in it. This form of consciously directed action is the antithesis of the unintentional conduct which the defendant erroneously ascribes to the crime of extreme indifference murder. Because the underlying offense of extreme indifference murder entails intentional rather than unintentional conduct, the defendant's assertion that the crime of attempted extreme indifference murder requires an intent to commit an unintentional act is without legal foundation."

incorrect ← *intent is not required*

2. Compare with *Viser*, discussed in *Harris*, the case of *Amlotte v. State*, 456 So.2d 448 (Fla.1984): "We find that whenever an individual perpetrates or attempts to perpetrate an enumerated felony, and during the commission of the felony the individual commits, aids, or abets a specific overt act which could, but does not, cause the death of another, that individual will have committed the crime of attempted felony murder. Because the attempt occurs during the commission of a felony, the law, as under the felony murder doctrine, presumes the existence of the specific intent required to prove attempt."

Wrong Attempt for Felony murder is not allowed

3. In *People v. Weeks*, 86 Ill.App.2d 480, 230 N.E.2d 12 (1967), defendant was convicted of attempting to commit voluntary manslaughter,[a] on a charge which alleged that "he, acting under a sudden and intense passion, resulting from serious provocation by Omar Joel, attempted to shoot Omar Joel with intent to kill or do great bodily harm." The court reversed: "We have previously held that the 'intent' required for conviction of the offense of Attempt must be a 'specific intent'. The act that constitutes the attempt must result from some calculation on the part of the accused. Voluntary Manslaughter, on the other hand, precludes any calculation but can only result from 'a sudden and intense passion' that is itself triggered by a 'serious provocation'. The passion engendered by the provocation must be sufficiently intense to vitiate the normal, self-imposed controls against the criminal act. An act cannot be both the result of a 'sudden and intense passion' and a calculated goal of prior deliberation. It is either one or the other but it cannot be both.

---

a. The Illinois voluntary manslaughter statute provided: "A person who kills an individual without lawful justification commits voluntary manslaughter if at the time of the killing he is acting under a sudden and intense passion resulting from serious provocation by:

"(1) The individual killed, or

"(2) Another whom the offender endeavors to kill, but he negligently or accidentally causes the death of the individual killed.

"Serious provocation is conduct sufficient to excite an intense passion in a reasonable person."

Wrong. Hof Manslaughter is an intentional Killing + Attempt is allowed.

Consequently, we agree that there can be no such crime as an Attempt to commit a Voluntary Manslaughter."

Joshua Sachs, *Is Attempt to Commit Voluntary Manslaughter a Possible Crime?*, 71 Ill.B.J. 166, 167 (1982), asserts that the "rule of *Weeks*," which "has been rejected in most other states," "is not logically or legally persuasive." Is this so? Why? May the same be said for *Harris*?

4. *Weeks* relied upon *People v. Brown*, 21 A.D.2d 738, 249 N.Y.S.2d 922 (1964), holding that there is no crime of attempted manslaughter with respect to a manslaughter statute which defined that crime as a killing "committed without a design to effect death." (See, with regard to the current New York code, *People v. Zimmerman*, 46 A.D.2d 725, 360 N.Y.S.2d 127 (1974), holding there is no crime of attempted manslaughter when manslaughter is defined as causing death "by a reckless act." Citing *Brown*, the court concluded one "may not intentionally attempt to cause the death of another human being by a reckless act.") Was the reliance upon *Brown* in *Weeks* justified?

5. Yet another variety of manslaughter recognized in several jurisdictions is that in which the defendant's defense of self defense to a charge of murder is "imperfect" because the defendant's belief in the need for the force used was unreasonable. *State v. Grant*, 418 A.2d 154 (Me.1980), holds there can be no such thing as an attempt to commit this kind of manslaughter, as it is "a logical impossibility." Is this so?

6. Do not such cases as *Castro* and *Amlotte* represent the better view, i.e., that the mens rea requirement for an attempt should be not greater than for the completed crime? Arnold N. Enker, *Mens Rea and Criminal Attempt*, 1977 A.B.F.Res.J. 845, 848, states the argument in favor of such a rule: "The protection of society by incapacitating and correcting the socially dangerous is thought to be best achieved by subjecting them to the correctional process before they do harm. If the lesser forms of mens rea are a sufficient predicate for criminal liability for harm done, arguably they should equally be so for harm risked. For it is the mens rea that is the true indicium of the defendant's dangerousness. The actor's guilt ought not to depend on the fortuitous chance that the harm risked did not ensue."

7. But Enker ultimately decides, at 859, that the *Harris–Viser* approach is best because "attempt differs from substantive crime in that it combines mens rea of intent with an undefined actus reus. While this risks violation of the principle that punishment should be based on previously defined criminal conduct, it is made necessary and is justified by the fact that the actor's harmful intent is not merely the basis for ascribing to him culpability but is itself the source of potential harm. The extreme tendency of attempt to reach purely subjective guilt is controlled to a degree by notions of mere preparation and impossibility.

"Situations in which the actor did not intend to cause harm do not call for the use of this technique. Recklessly dangerous conduct should indeed be penalized, but as a substantive crime in which the actus reus is defined as precisely as the circumstances permit while the actor's mens rea determines his personal guilt. The ordinary requirements of harm and of conduct, in conjunction with the principle of legality, will determine just how broadly the actus reus should be defined."

8. Consider *Model Penal Code* § 5.01, Comment (1985): "The requirement of purpose extends to the conduct of the actor and to the results that his conduct causes, but his purpose need not encompass all of the circumstances included in the formal definition of the substantive offense. As to them, it is sufficient that he acts with the culpability that is required for commission of the completed crime.

"Several illustrations may serve to clarify the point. Assume, for example, a statute that provides that sexual intercourse with a female under a prescribed age is an offense, and that a mistake as to age will not afford a defense no matter how reasonable its foundation. The policy of the substantive offense as to age, therefore, is one of strict liability, and if the actor has sexual intercourse with a female, he is guilty or not, depending upon her age and irrespective of his views as to her age. Suppose, however, that he is arrested before he engages in the proscribed conduct, and that the charge is an attempt to commit the offense. Should he then be entitled to rely on a mistake as to age as a defense? Or should the policy of the substantive crime on this issue carry over to the attempt as well? Or, assume a statute that makes it a federal offense to murder an FBI agent and treats the agent's status as a member of the FBI as a jurisdictional ingredient, with no culpability required in respect to that element. The question again is whether the policy of the substantive crime should control the same issue when it arises on a charge of attempt, or whether there is a special policy that the law of attempt should embrace to change the result on this point.

"Under the formulation in Subsection (1)(c), the proffered defense would not succeed in either case. In the statutory rape example, the actor must have a purpose to engage in sexual intercourse with a female in order to be charged with the attempt, and must engage in a substantial step in a course of conduct planned to culminate in his commission of that act. With respect to the age of the victim, however, it is sufficient if he acts 'with the kind of culpability otherwise required for the commission of the crime,' which in the case supposed is none at all. Since, therefore, mistake as to age is irrelevant with respect to the substantive offense, it is likewise irrelevant with respect to the attempt. The same result would obtain in the murder illustration. The actor must, in the case supposed, engage in a substantial step in a course of conduct planned to culminate in the death of his victim. But with respect to his awareness of the status of his victim as an FBI agent, a mistake would not be relevant since the policy of the substantive offense controls on such matters and that policy is one of strict liability.

"The judgment is thus that if the defendant manifests a purpose to engage in the type of conduct or to cause the type of result that is forbidden by the criminal law, he has sufficiently exhibited his dangerousness to justify the imposition of criminal sanctions, so long as he otherwise acts with the kind of culpability that is sufficient for the completed offense. The objective is to select out those elements of the completed crime that, if the defendant desires to bring them about, indicate with clarity that he poses the type of danger to society that the substantive offense is designed to prevent. This objective is well served by the Code's approach, followed in a number of recently enacted and proposed revisions, of allowing the policy of the substantive offense to control with respect to circumstance elements. * * *

"Subsection (1)(b) provides that when causing a particular result is an element of the crime, as in homicide offenses or criminally obtaining property, an actor commits an attempt when he does or omits to do anything with the purpose of causing 'or with the belief that it will cause' such result without further conduct on his part. Thus, a belief that death will ensue from the actor's conduct, or that property will be obtained, will suffice, as well as would a purpose to bring about those results. If, for example, the actor's purpose were to demolish a building and, knowing that persons were in the building and that they would be killed by the explosion, he nevertheless detonated a bomb that turned out to be defective, he could be prosecuted for attempted murder even though it was no part of his purpose that the inhabitants of the building would be killed.

"It is difficult to say what the decision would be under prevailing attempt principles in a case of this kind. It might be held that the actor did not specifically intend to kill the inhabitants of the building; on the other hand, the concept of 'intent' has always been an ambiguous one and might be thought to include results that the actor believed to be the inevitable consequence of his conduct. In any event, the inclusion of such conduct as the basis for liability under Subsection (1)(b) is based on the conclusion that the manifestation of the actor's dangerousness is just as great—or very nearly as great—as in the case of purposive conduct. In both instances a deliberate choice is made to bring about the consequence forbidden by the criminal laws, and the actor has done all within his power to cause this result to occur. The absence of any desire that the result occur is not, under these circumstances, a sufficient basis for differentiating between the two types of conduct involved. Only a minority of recent revisions have explicitly followed the Model Code on this point."

9. In *Gardner v. Akeroyd*, [1952] 2 Q.B. 743, a butcher was acquitted of attempting to violate a regulation prohibiting the sale of meat above a certain price. Inspectors visited his shop and found 33 parcels of meat, prepared by the butcher's assistant, ready for delivery and bearing name tickets and excessive prices. Had the parcels been sold, clearly the butcher would have been guilty of violating the regulation, for it had previously been interpreted as imposing strict and vicarious liability. But the court held the butcher was rightly acquitted, for the charge of attempting a strict liability offense requires proof of mens rea.

Is this result sound? Consider John C. Smith and Brian Hogan, *Criminal Law* 149 (1965): "If there is a valid policy underlying the imposition of liability for negligence and strict liability in the substantive offence, it is difficult to see why it does not apply equally to the attempt. The only difference between the man who attempts and fails and another who attempts and succeeds may be chance. There is, *ex hypothesi*, no difference in moral blameworthiness between them and the one may be as dangerous as the other."

IN RE SMITH

Supreme Court of California, 1970.

3 Cal.3d 192, 90 Cal.Rptr. 1, 474 P.2d 969.

Mosk, Justice.

Petitioner, John Alexander Smith, is presently incarcerated at San Quentin under sentence imposed in 1967 after he was convicted of two counts of kidnaping, one count of rape, and one count of attempted kidnaping. We issued an order to show cause in response to his petition in propria persona for a writ of habeas corpus to consider the contention that he was deprived of his right to the effective assistance of counsel on appeal. This is a case of first impression on the subject of incompetency of appellate counsel.

The crimes of which petitioner was convicted occurred between November 1, 1966, and February 1, 1967, in Los Angeles. On November 1, Miss Audrey George, while waiting for a bus, was accosted from behind by a man. He pressed a file to her neck and compelled her to walk about a block and a half to a vacant house, where he forcibly committed an act of sexual intercourse upon her. He then walked with her back to the vicinity of the bus stop and permitted her to call a friend to pick her up. At the lineup in February 1967, Miss George identified petitioner as her assailant. At the trial, she again identified petitioner and confirmed her lineup identification.

On January 21, 1967, Mrs. Carla Braswell was approached by a man on the sidewalk after she had parked and locked her car near her home. After asking directions, the man grabbed her arm and brandished a screwdriver. He ordered her to unlock the door on the driver's side of her automobile and told her "that we were going in my car." Mrs. Braswell indicated that she was too frightened to unlock the door and she gave her purse to her assailant, telling him to do it. While he searched for the keys, another car pulled alongside and during the confusion Mrs. Braswell was able to escape to her home. At the February lineup Mrs. Braswell did not unequivocally identify petitioner as her assailant, but she was positive at the trial.

At 11 p.m. on February 1, Miss Delores Burton was grabbed from behind by a man and threatened with a screwdriver held to her neck. She was forced to walk to an alley about two blocks away, where she was told to take off her clothes. She removed her coat, but when an automobile light at the end of the alley prompted the attacker to retrieve the screwdriver he had put down, Miss Burton was able to escape. She ran to a nearby market with the attacker in pursuit, but he did not enter the market. John Wesley saw Miss Burton being chased and described her assailant to the police. Miss Burton identified petitioner at a lineup and in court as the man who attacked her. Wesley could not make a positive identification.

Petitioner was arrested on February 1, about a half hour after the Burton incident. He was walking near the market where Miss Burton had fled and he was wearing a blue shirt, dark pants, and a hat, with a dark coat under his arm. He was perspiring. Miss Burton was brought to the police station to identify him that night.

In April 1967, petitioner was tried by the court and was convicted of the kidnaping and rape of Miss George, the attempted kidnaping of Mrs. Braswell, and the kidnaping of Miss Burton. His defense was alibi on the occasions of all three offenses. The convictions were affirmed on appeal and no petition for hearing was filed.

Petitioner contends that he was denied the effective assistance of counsel in his appeal because his court-appointed appellate counsel was incompetent and failed to raise substantial allegations of error which arguably might have resulted in reversal of his convictions. * * *

Petitioner's conviction of attempted kidnaping in the episode involving Mrs. Braswell was likewise subject to plausible assignments of error. It is well settled that "[t]o constitute an attempt, there must be (a) the specific intent to commit a particular crime, and (b) a direct ineffectual act done towards its commission. * * * To amount to an attempt the act or acts must go further than mere *preparation;* they must be such as would ordinarily result in the crime except for the interruption."

It is at least arguable that petitioner's conduct in regard to Mrs. Braswell exhibited neither the intent nor the action requisite to attempted kidnaping. The only direct evidence of his intention was his statement, paraphrased by Mrs. Braswell, as follows: "Then he told me to unlock my car door, that we were going in my car." Certainly, it could be maintained that this statement is not an unequivocal expression of an intention to abduct Mrs. Braswell, unless moving her from the sidewalk to the inside of the car was sufficient to constitute kidnaping. Also plausible was the inference that petitioner intended to rape his victim inside her car without driving it away, or that he intended to steal from her person or her car. Furthermore, petitioner's actions to effectuate his criminal purpose arguably did not reach that stage of development beyond mere preparation. His search for the keys might as logically have been for the purpose of robbing or sexually assaulting his victim, rather than kidnaping her. * * *

In the instant action we hold that the inexcusable failure of petitioner's appellate counsel to raise crucial assignments of error, which arguably might have resulted in a reversal, deprived petitioner of the effective assistance of appellate counsel to which he was entitled under the Constitution. * * *

Notes and Questions

1. The court directed the court of appeals to "vacate its decision, reinstate the appeal, and appoint other counsel for appellant." If on the new appeal it is argued that the evidence is not sufficient to show the defendant's intent to kidnap, what should the result be?

2. Did the prosecutor err in the charge he brought against Smith regarding the Braswell incident? Would he have been any better off if he had charged attempted robbery? Or, attempted rape?

SECTION 2. ACTS

Introductory Notes

1. Consider Richard Buxton, *Incitement and Attempt,* 1973 Crim.L.Rev. 656, 660:

"The law of Attempt has over the years proved more confused, and therefore more controversial, than almost any other part of the criminal law; primarily because of a reluctance to recognise that the social reasons for punishing attempts, and therefore the proper analysis of Attempt as a crime, are generically different from the considerations that control the analysis of substantive crimes. In the latter, certain forms of conduct, or the production of certain effects in the physical world, are deemed to be socially undesirable, and are therefore prohibited, the persons who produce those effects being however protected from the morally or socially undesirable exercise of state power against them by the (usual) requirement that they should not be punished unless they acted consciously or intentionally in producing those forbidden results. The crime of Attempt, on the other hand, looks not to the accused's past conduct but to his threatened future conduct, and the analytical roles of *actus reus* and *mens rea* are thus, as it were, reversed. We have a law of Attempt because persons who threaten to commit acts forbidden by the substantive criminal law should be open to social prevention and deterrence, since such persons are, by reason of their intentions, socially dangerous. The *primary* justification for punishing a man for Attempt is thus not his *actus reus* but his *mens rea*. At the same time, however, quite as many threats to liberty seem to be presented by the possibility of punishing a man for *mens rea,* without more, as are presented, in the case of substantive crime, by the possibility of punishing him for *actus reus* alone. The law of Attempt therefore limits its deterrent and preventive role in the interests of freedom by requiring action, of some sort, as well as intention, on the part of the accused; in the same way as in substantive crime the deterrent and preventive role of the law is to some degree limited by the requirement of *mens rea*."

2. What test should be used in determining whether a defendant, charged with attempting some crime, has engaged in sufficient acts? Consider the reasoning and results in the following six cases, which illustrate these approaches:

(a) the "last act" test, whereunder the defendant must have done everything that he believes necessary to bring about the criminal result (*Regina v. Eagleton*);

(b) the "dangerous proximity" test, which focuses upon what the defendant has done and how close he thereby came to succeeding in his criminal objective (*People v. Rizzo*);

(c) the "indispensible element" test, which focuses instead upon what remains to be done in order to accomplish the criminal objective (*People v. Orndorff*);

(d) the "probable desistance" test, under which a judgment must be made as to whether the defendant had reached a point where it was unlikely he would thereafter abandon his efforts to achieve the criminal objective (*Commonwealth v. Skipper*);

(e) the "equivocality" test, whereunder the question is whether the defendant's actions manifest the intent to achieve the criminal objective (*People v. Bowen*); and

(f) the "substantial step" test (see *Model Penal Code* § 5.01), whereunder the defendant's acts must be strongly corroborative of his criminal purpose (*United States v. Mandujano*).

REGINA v. EAGLETON

Court of Criminal Law, England, 1855.

6 Cox C.C. 559.

[The defendant, a baker, contracted with the guardians of the poor of the parish of Great Yarmouth to supply the poor with loaves of bread, each loaf to weigh three and a half pounds, to be paid for at sevenpence a loaf. Under the contract, each poor person who presented defendant with a "ticket" was to receive such a loaf. The defendant would then turn in the tickets, together with a statement of the number of loaves supplied, to the relieving officer, who would credit the defendant in his books for the amount owed him. The money was to be paid to the defendant at a future time as stipulated in the contract, but before such payment was made it was discovered that the defendant had intentionally furnished loaves deficient in weight and that he had returned the tickets intending to represent that he had delivered loaves of the weight provided for in the contract. Defendant, convicted of attempting to obtain money by false pretenses, appealed.]

PARKE, B., now delivered the judgment of the court. * * * On the part of the defendant, his learned counsel contended—1st. That the attempt to obtain credit in account for a sum of money by delivering up the tickets as vouchers, was not in itself an attempt to obtain money within the meaning of the statute, for that credit in account was not equivalent to money; and no doubt the credit in the relieving officer's book was not equivalent to money, and the defendant could not have been convicted of the offence of actually obtaining money by false presences. * * * But our doubt has been whether the obtaining that credit, though undoubtedly a necessary step towards obtaining the money, can be deemed an attempt to do so. The mere intention to commit a misdemeanor is not criminal, some act is required; and we do not think that all acts towards committing a misdemeanor are indictable. Acts remotely leading towards the commission of the offence are not to be considered as attempts to commit it; but acts immediately connected with it are; and if in this case, after the credit with the relieving officer for the fraudulent overcharge, any further step on the part of the defendant had been necessary to obtain payment, as the making out a further account, or producing the vouchers to the board, we should have thought that the obtaining credit in account with the relieving officer would not have been sufficiently proximate to the obtaining of the money.

But on the statement in this case no other act on the part of the defendant would have been required. It was the last act depending on himself towards the payment of the money, and therefore it ought to be considered as an attempt. The receipt of the money appears to have been prevented by a discovery of the fraud, by the relieving officer, and it is very much the same case as if, supposing rendering an account to the guardians at their office with the vouchers annexed were a preliminary necessary step to receiving the money, the defendant had gone to the office, rendered the account and vouchers, and then been discovered, and the money consequently refused.

Notes and Questions

1. The "last act" test did not long survive. See *Regina v. Roberts,* 7 Cox C.C. 39 (1855).

2. Should the test have been retained? Consider *Rex v. White,* [1910] 2 K.B. 124. Defendant's mother died of heart failure; on a nearby table was a glass of wine with two grains of cyanide in it, and there was evidence showing that defendant had put the cyanide in the wine glass. However, there was no evidence that his mother had consumed any of the liquid, and it was also shown that the quantity of cyanide in the drink would not suffice to cause death. On appeal of his conviction for attempted murder, the defendant objected "that the jury must have acted upon a suggestion of the learned judge in his summing up that this was one, the first or some later, of a series of doses which he intended to administer and so cause her death by slow poisoning; and that if they did act on that suggestion there was no attempted murder." The court affirmed, holding that "the completion or attempted completion of one of a series of acts intended by a man to result in killing is an attempt to murder even although this completed act would not, unless followed by the others acts, result in killing. It might be the beginning of the attempt, but would none the less be an attempt."

3. Also consider Larry Alexander & Kimberly D. Kessler, *Mens Rea and Inchoate Crimes*, 87 J.Crim.L. & Criminology 1138, 1169 (1997), where the authors propose elimination of what they call "incomplete attempts": "If the actus reus of an incomplete attempt is not itself dangerous, then defendant's committing the actus reus cannot be considered a culpable act. The reason is that for an act to be culpable, the act must appear to defendant to increase risks to others in a way that is not dependent on defendant's further choices. In other words, defendant cannot view his own future choices as matters subject to his prediction. Indeed, so long as defendant views himself as having control over any future choices to create risks that will then be beyond his control, it is doubtful that even he, much less the law, can clearly distinguish in terms of risks already present between what he intends on the one hand and his mere wishes or fantasies on the other. Thus, even though an incomplete attempt requires an act as well as purpose, the act required is not a culpable act because, from defendant's point of view, the act does not increase others' risks. It does not increase others' risks because, from defendant's point of view, those risks cannot materialize without a further choice or choices by defendant, a matter over which he believes himself to have total control."

PEOPLE v. RIZZO

Court of Appeals of New York, 1927.

246 N.Y. 334, 158 N.E. 888.

CRANE, J. The police of the city of New York did excellent work in this case by preventing the commission of a serious crime. It is a great satisfaction to realize that we have such wide-awake guardians of our peace. Whether or not the steps which the defendant had taken up to the time of his arrest amounted to the commission of a crime, as defined by our law, is, however, another matter. He has been convicted of an attempt to commit the crime of robbery in the first degree, and sentenced to state's prison. There is no doubt that he had the intention to commit robbery, if he got the chance. An examination, however, of the facts is necessary to determine whether his acts were in preparation to commit the crime if the opportunity offered, or constituted a crime in itself, known to our law as an attempt to commit robbery in the first degree. Charles Rizzo, the defendant, appellant, with three others, Anthony J. Dorio, Thomas Milo, and John Thomasello, on January 14th planned to rob one Charles Rao of a pay roll valued at about $1,200 which he was to carry from the bank for the United Lathing Company. These defendants, two of whom had firearms, started out in an automobile, looking for Rao or the man who had the pay roll on that day. Rizzo claimed to be able to identify the man, and was to point him out to the others, who were to do the actual holding up. The four rode about in their car looking for Rao. They went to the bank from which he was supposed to get the money and to various buildings being constructed by the United Lathing Company. At last they came to One Hundred and Eightieth street and Morris Park avenue. By this time they were watched and followed by two police officers. As Rizzo jumped out of the car and ran into the building, all four were arrested. The defendant was taken out from the building in which he was hiding. Neither Rao nor a man named Previti, who was also supposed to carry a pay roll, were at the place at the time of the arrest. The defendants had not found or seen the man they intended to rob. No person with a pay roll was at any of the places where they had stopped, and no one had been pointed out or identified by Rizzo. The four men intended to rob the pay roll man, whoever he was. They were looking for him, but they had not seen or discovered him up to the time they were arrested.

Does this constitute the crime of an attempt to commit robbery in the first degree? The Penal Law, § 2, prescribes:

"An act, done with intent to commit a crime, and tending but failing to effect its commission, is 'an attempt to commit that crime.' "

The word "tending" is very indefinite. It is perfectly evident that there will arise differences of opinion as to whether an act in a given case is one *tending* to commit a crime. "Tending" means to exert activity in a particular direction. Any act in preparation to commit a crime may be said to have a tendency towards its accomplishment. The procuring of the automobile, searching the streets looking for the desired victim, were in reality acts tending toward the commission of the proposed crime. The law, however, has recognized that many acts in the way of preparation are too remote to constitute the crime of attempt. The line has been drawn between those acts which are remote and those which are proximate and near to the consummation. The law must be practical, and therefore considers those acts only as tending to the commission of the crime which are so near to its accomplishment that in all reasonable probability the crime itself would have been committed, but for timely interference. The cases which have been before the courts express this idea in different language, but the idea remains the same. The act or acts must come or advance very near to the accomplishment of the intended crime. * * *

How shall we apply this rule of immediate nearness to this case? The defendants were looking for the pay roll man to rob him of his money. This is the charge in the indictment. Robbery is defined in section 2120 of the Penal Law as "the unlawful taking of personal property from the person or in the presence of another, against his will, by means of force, or violence, or fear of injury, immediate or future, to his person;" and it is made robbery in the first degree by section 2124 when committed by a person aided by accomplices actually present. To constitute the crime of robbery, the money must have been taken from Rao by means of force or violence, or through fear. The crime of attempt to commit robbery was committed, if these defendants did an act tending to the commission of this robbery. Did the acts above described come dangerously near to the taking of Rao's property? Did the acts come so near the commission of robbery that there was reasonable likelihood of its accomplishment but for the interference? Rao was not found; the defendants were still looking for him; no attempt to rob him could be made, at least until he came in sight; he was not in the building at One Hundred and Eightieth street and Morris Park avenue. There was no man there with the pay roll for the United Lathing Company whom these defendants could rob. Apparently no money had been drawn from the bank for the pay roll by anybody at the time of the arrest. In a word, these defendants had planned to commit a crime, and were looking around the city for an opportunity to commit it, but the opportunity fortunately never came. Men would not be guilty of an attempt at burglary if they had planned to break into a building and were arrested while they were hunting about the streets for the building not knowing where it was. Neither would a man be guilty of an attempt to commit murder if he armed himself and started out to find the person whom he had planned to kill but could not find him. So here these defendants were not guilty of an attempt to commit robbery in the first degree when they had not found or reached the presence of the person they intended to rob.

For these reasons, the judgment of conviction of this defendant appellant must be reversed and a new trial granted. * * *

PEOPLE v. ORNDORFF

Court of Appeal, Second District, 1968.
261 Cal.App.2d 212, 67 Cal.Rptr. 824.

KINGSLEY, ASSOCIATE JUSTICE.

Defendant was charged with attempted grand theft. The case was submitted on the transcript of the preliminary examination, together with testimony by defendant. He was found guilty as charged, probation was denied and he was sentenced to state prison. He has appealed. We reverse the judgment.

The victim, Juniper Griffis, testified that he was accosted on a street in Long Beach by a Negro sailor, who asked him concerning a hotel. In the conversation that followed, the sailor displayed a roll of bills and told Griffis that he had been given it by his ship's captain as the proceeds of insurance on the life of the sailor's brother. Griffis advised the sailor to put the money (allegedly $19,000) in a bank but the sailor demurred, saying that he understood that if a Negro deposited money in a bank, the bank would not let him withdraw it. At this stage, defendant appeared, walked by the two men and was accosted by Griffis, who asked defendant to help "straighten out" the sailor. After further conversation, the three men drove, in defendant's car, to Griffis' home to procure his bank book so that Griffis, by making a withdrawal from his account, could satisfy the sailor that the sailor could safely make a deposit. They then drove to the vicinity of Griffis' bank. The sailor remained in the car, Griffis and defendant walked toward the bank but, before reaching it, defendant stopped, telling Griffis to go to the bank alone, as defendant wanted to watch the sailor. Griffis went to the bank where he met his wife; after Griffis and his wife talked to the assistant manager they left the bank to find that defendant, the sailor and the car had disappeared.

Thereafter police officers went to defendant's home, advised him of his constitutional rights, secured permission to search the apartment, discovered a roll of "play money" and arrested defendant. The roll of play money was introduced into evidence. During conversations that took place, then and later, defendant admitted his participation in the affair, but claimed that he recognized that the sailor was attempting a scheme known as the "Jamaica Switch," did not want to get involved because he was on parole, and dropped out of the proceedings as he and Griffis approached the bank.

A police officer, properly qualified as an expert on "bunco" schemes, described the so-called "Jamaica Switch," as follows:

"A The No. 1 Negro I will refer to as the sailor, stops an elderly white man and gives a conversation similar or in scale to what Mr. Griffin [sic] described, in which he will talk about how he is a poor old Negro. He says he is from Jamaica or Martinique or one of the islands down there. He has been left this amount of money, that the captain keeps the money and he is interested in keeping the money in the captain's safe; the night before the girl had tried to take him, getting the victim's sympathy. He then talks about the girl and the hotel, bringing in the sex angle. The third subject will come along, the No. 2 Negro comes by, a man that looks prosperous, has a fine fitting suit, probably wearing a hat and as Mr. Griffis stated, the sailor will constantly refer to himself as a nigger.

" * * *

"A Yes sir. There is a discussion about finding a hotel, they then go around and get the victim's bank book. Usually a roll of 100 and 500 dollars is shown to the victim by the sailor, after showing him that he can get his money in and out of the bank. They will take the victim to the bank, he gets his money out and shows it to the sailor. The sailor will then grab the money and get the victim's money in his hand and tell the victim what a wonderful man he is, and he will have a handkerchief or a bag or a container he can put the money in. So he will take the victim's money, put it in the handkerchief and tell him what a wonderful man he is. He also will take the award money and put the money in the sack and hand it back to the victim. At that time the victim has his own money and then the money the suspect had carried. The victim will start to put it into his pocket, coat pocket, inside pocket or even in his hand. The sailor grabs the package back and says, 'Oh no, man, like my momma used to tell me,' and he will open the victim's shirt and put the package back into there in between the flesh and the shirt, then button it back up. As he grabs the shirt, the No. 2 suspect will turn the victim's attention by saying something to him just after the sailor has taken the money back. At that time the switch is made and the package is inserted and when the victim gets back to deposit his money he finds he has newspapers or worthless articles and his money has gone south with the sailor."

It is the prosecution's theory that defendant and the sailor (who is not involved in the present case) attempted to practice a Jamaica Switch on Griffis but were prevented from success. On appeal, defendant urges, among other contentions, that the evidence shows, at the most, mere preparation not going far enough to constitute an attempt. Since we agree with that contention, it is not necessary to discuss the objections made in the trial court and here to the introduction of certain evidence.

Both parties cite and rely on *People v. Fulton* (1961) 188 Cal.App.2d 105, 10 Cal.Rptr. 319. We conclude that that case supports the defendant rather than the prosecution. *Fulton* also involved an alleged Jamaica Switch, practiced on two alleged intended victims. The schemes failed, on one instance because a bank officer told the intended victim that it was a bunco scheme, in the other because the intended victim became suspicious and refused to enter his bank and make the proposed withdrawal. In *Fulton*, the court unanimously held that the first instance was a punishable attempt; by a divided court, the second instance was also held to have reached the status of attempt. All three judges lay stress on the element of the procuring cause of failure, saying that it must be "by extraneous circumstances," or "by circumstances independent of any actions on their [defendants'] part." But while, in *Fulton*, the schemes failed because the victim withdrew, here the only evidence is that it failed because defendant abandoned the scheme before it reached the first significant step. It is, of course, possible that Griffis' wife and the bank manager had (as in the first count in *Fulton*) warned Griffis that he was involved in a classic bunco scheme and that he had abandoned the scheme. But there is no evidence to that effect. We do not know what either the wife or the bank officer told Griffis or what he told them. The Attorney General suggests that "inferably" defendant had seen Mrs. Griffis at the bank and had been frightened off by that fact; but there is no evidence that he saw her or knew that she was to intervene in the events.

Looking at the expert's description of the classic scheme, it is to be noticed that not one, but many steps still remained to be performed: the victim must withdraw his money, deliver it to the thief, the thief must perform his slight-of-hand "switch" of the victim's money for the substitute play money or newspaper, and the thief must leave the scene before the victim opens the substituted package. None of these had taken place. Only the first two steps had been accomplished: the victim had procured his bank book and had gone to his bank. Too many potential slips remained before the cup of success would reach the defendant's lip for us to say that there was here anything more than preparation.

The judgment is reversed.

COMMONWEALTH v. SKIPPER

Superior Court of Pennsylvania, 1972.

222 Pa.Super. 242, 294 A.2d 780.

HOFFMAN, JUDGE:

In this *pro se* appeal appellant contends that the evidence was insufficient to sustain his conviction as the principal perpetrator of an attempted prison breach.

At appellant's trial a Commonwealth witness testified that appellant had approached him in prison, asking that he procure some hacksaw blades for the sum of $150.00, which was to be paid by William Schaeffer, a fellow inmate. The witness was a day release prisoner employed at a nearby bakery which made bread for prison use. The plan, allegedly, was that the witness would conceal the blades in loaves of bread to be retrieved inside the prison by appellant, who worked in the kitchen. The witness testified that he placed the blades in the bread at the bakery, and that at a later time the appellant indicated that he had received the blades. Appellant then told the witness to talk to Schaeffer. Schaeffer gave the witness a note to obtain the $150.00. Prison officials intercepted another note, this one written by the witness to Schaeffer, when the witness attempted to illicitly transfer the note to Schaeffer. This note contained a reference to blades.

One June 2, 1970, prison officials caught Schaeffer while he was attempting to go over the prison wall, and they found a hacksaw blade on his person. The officials then conducted a "shake-down" of the prison and discovered two hacksaw blades and a small file in a bread wrapper inside the radiator of appellant's cell.

On the basis of this evidence, the trial judge instructed the jury as to the law of attempts. * * * The jury returned a verdict of guilty.

In *Commonwealth v. Eagan*, 190 Pa. 10, 21–22, 42 A. 374, 377 (1899), our Supreme Court defined an attempt as being " * * * an overt act done in pursuance of an intent to do a specific thing, tending to the end but falling short of complete accomplishment of it. In law, the definition must have this further qualification, that the overt act must be sufficiently proximate to the intended crime to form one of the natural series of acts which the intent requires for its full execution. So long as the acts are confined *to preparation* *only,* and can be abandoned before any transgression of the law or of others' rights, they are within the sphere of intent and do not amount to attempts."

The trial judge charged the jury in conformity with the definition of attempt accepted in Pennsylvania. Under this definition, however, appellant could not have been found guilty * * *. The discovery of the hacksaw blades in appellant's cell did no more than interrupt appellant's alleged plan in a preparatory stage. If the hacksaw blades were in fact procured by the appellant for use in an intended prison breach, appellant would have had sufficient time to withdraw before the commission of the offense. * * *

Notes and Questions

1. If the question is whether the defendant still "had sufficient time to withdraw before the commission of the offense," then isn't this essentially the same as asking whether the last act has occurred?

2. Consider the somewhat different formulation proposed in Robert H. Skilton, *The Requisite Act in a Criminal Attempt,* 3 U.Pitt.L.Rev. 308, 309–10 (1937), namely, "that the defendant's conduct must pass that point where most men, holding such an intention as the defendant holds, would think better of their conduct and desist. All of us, or most of us, at some time or other harbor what may be described as a criminal intent to effect unlawful consequences. Many of us take some steps—often slight enough in character—to bring the consequences about; but most of us, when we reach a certain point, desist, and return to our roles as law-abiding citizens. The few who do not and pass beyond that point are, if the object of their conduct is not achieved, guilty of a criminal attempt." Had Skipper reached that point?

PEOPLE v. BOWEN

Court of Appeal of Michigan, 1968.

10 Mich.App. 1, 158 N.W.2d 794.

Levin, Judge.

Defendants, Sherrel Bowen and William Rouse, appeal their convictions of attempted larceny in a building.

On January 19, 1965, at approximately eight o'clock p.m., the defendants and two female companions were admitted to the home of one Matilda Gatzmeyer, an 80 year old woman. The defendants' car was observed parked in front of Miss Gatzmeyer's residence and a neighbor, believing the defendants to have designs upon her property, called the police. Two police officers arrived and entered the home along with the neighbor. The defendants were found in the rear of the house near or on the basement steps. The two female companions were seated on either side of Miss Gatzmeyer, apparently engaged with her in conversation. The bedroom of the house was in a state of disarray.

The police ordered defendants to come to the front of the house and sit in the living room. Defendant Rouse seated himself within a foot of the TV, and some time thereafter one of the police officers spotted under the TV set two rings belonging to Miss Gatzmeyer. The neighbor testified she found a necklace on the staircase near where defendant Bowen had been standing when he was first sighted by the police. When the neighbor's discovery was called to the attention of one of the police officers, he and Miss Gatzmeyer went to the staircase and found the necklace in that location.

After interrogation, the defendants were arrested and charged with larceny of "rings and a necklace" in a building.

Bowen had been to the Gatzmeyer home on a number of prior occasions, ostensibly as a handy man, the same reason he gave Miss Gatzmeyer for appearing on the night in question. Miss Gatzmeyer testified that on this occasion the defendants sought to hire themselves out to clean and to do some masonry work on the chimney. She complained about the high prices charged by Bowen and his failure to do work as agreed, and that Bowen's helper (the role allegedly filled by Rouse at the time of the incident) generally helped himself to things that belonged to her.

The neighbor testified that she had met Bowen on three occasions prior to the one in question and that on one occasion Bowen had induced Miss Gatzmeyer to go with him to the bank, but it was not clear whether the visit to the bank was to withdraw money to pay Bowen that which was due him or unlawfully to separate Miss Gatzmeyer from her money.

The neighbor testified that she visited with Miss Gatzmeyer daily and assisted her in various chores and generally in getting around. She stated that when she and the police officers arrived on the night in question the dresser drawers in the bedroom were all pulled out and everything thrown all over the bed. This was not the way Miss Gatzmeyer generally kept the house according to the neighbor: "she has a very neat house, everything is in its place." The neighbor further testified that "after Miss Gatzmeyer cleaned up (presumably after the police left) she found more jewelry back of the pillows" on the couch Bowen sat on during his interrogation by the police.

Miss Gatzmeyer testified that the defendants removed the jewelry from her bedroom without her consent.

At the beginning of his charge to the jury, the trial judge stated that because he doubted whether the case properly could be submitted to the jury on the original charge of larceny in a building he had decided to submit it to the jury solely on the included offense of attempt to commit larceny in a building. * * *

We do find error in the judge's failure properly to charge the jury on the necessity of finding an overt act. It has been said that the overt act "is the essence of the offense" or the "gravamen of the offense." Not only did the trial judge fail to charge the jury at all concerning the necessity of finding an overt act, but he also incorrectly charged that the jury could convict if it found that the defendants came to or entered Miss Gatzmeyer's house with the intention of committing larceny. * * *

There was ample evidence from which the jury could have found felonious intent. * * *

In the absence of a request, the trial judge's failure to charge the jury on the necessity of finding commission of an overt act, as a separate ingredient or element, might not be error if he were correct in charging the jury that if it found defendants "came" to or "entered" Miss Gatzmeyer's house with intent to commit larceny it could bring in a verdict of guilty. If defendants' coming to, or entering, Miss Gatzmeyer's house with felonious intent was an "overt act", the jury verdict of guilty could be viewed as a finding of the requisite overt act.

Thus, the narrow question before us is whether the defendants when they came to or entered Miss Gatzmeyer's house with the intent to commit larceny committed an overt act that would support their conviction of attempted larceny. In our opinion, their mere coming to or entry of Miss Gatzmeyer's house was not an overt act, under the circumstances that Mr. Bowen and other helpers had rightfully been in the house on prior occasions and were admitted to the house by Miss Gatzmeyer on the night in question.

Whether the defendants came to or entered Miss Gatzmeyer's house with a felonious intent is, of course, a question of fact to be decided by the jury. However, whether the facts found by the jury constitute an overt act, or whether the jury from particular circumstances could find that an overt act had been committed, is a question of law to be decided by the court.

In *People v. Coleman,* 350 Mich. 268, 86 N.W.2d 281 (1957), the Supreme Court stated that a defendant may not be convicted of an attempt unless he has "gone beyond acts of an ambiguous nature" or those that are "equivocal", and that a "thoughtful test for the resolution of the equivocal act has been phrased by Turner in his article, *'Attempts to Commit Crimes'* in 5 Camb.L.J., 230, 237 [238,] in these words:

> 'If the acts of the accused, taken by themselves, are unambiguous, and cannot, in reason, be regarded as pointing to any other end than the commission of the specific crime in question, then they constitute a sufficient *actus reus.* In other words, his acts must be *unequivocally referable* to the commission of the specific crime. They must, as the late Sir John Salmond said, "speak for themselves." If the example may be permitted, it is as though a cinematograph film, which has so far depicted merely the accused person's acts without stating what was his intention, had been suddenly stopped, and the audience were asked to say to what end those acts were directed. If there is only one reasonable answer to this question then the accused has done what amounts to an "attempt" to attain that end. If there is more than one reasonably possible answer, then the accused has not yet done enough.' * * *

It has been suggested that the basic function of the overt act is corroboration of the felonious intent. However, that analysis can become somewhat circular if we permit intent to be gleaned from the overt act itself.

The testimony in this case was that defendant Bowen had, on a number of prior occasions, been in Miss Gatzmeyer's house with helpers. With that in mind and even if it be assumed (on the basis of the jury finding) that the defendants entered her house with a felonious intent, their mere presence there did not indicate, let alone "corroborate", that intention. The defendants did not break into Miss Gatzmeyer's house—they were voluntarily admitted by her. At the time of defendants' admission to Miss Gatzmeyer's house their *acts* were entirely "ambiguous" and "equivocal". It is the acts thereafter allegedly committed (but as to which we have no finding from the jury) that were neither ambiguous nor equivocal.

Our analysis of the authorities convinces us that the function of the overt act is not to "corroborate", but rather to demonstrate that the defendant has converted resolution into action. Man being what he is, evil thoughts and intentions are easily formed. Fortunately, for society, most felonious thoughts are not fulfilled. The law does not punish evil intent or even every act done with the intent to commit a crime. The requirement that the jury find an overt act proceeds on the assumption that the devil may lose the contest, albeit late in the hour.

The overt act is not any act. In this connection "overt" is used in the sense of "manifest" or symbolic. The act must manifest, or be symbolic of, the crime. Considering that Bowen and helpers had been in Miss Gatzmeyer's house on previous occasions (and, whatever her differences with Bowen may have been, she nevertheless again admitted him on the night in question), the fact that the defendants came to and entered Miss Gatzmeyer's house would not manifest or symbolize the crime of which they were convicted of attempting to commit. * * *

Reversed and remanded for a new trial.

Notes and Questions

1. Does the *Bowen* court mean that Bowen and Rouse could not be convicted of the attempt even if, following their arrest, they had given a voluntary confession admitting that it had been their intention to steal Miss Gatzmeyer's jewelry?

2. Consider *Campbell and Bradley v. Ward*, [1955] N.Z.L.R. 471. Upon approaching his parked car at about 11 p.m., Eastwick saw McCallion emerging from the front seat. There was no evidence that he had taken anything from the car or that he had done anything beyond entering and leaving the car. McCallion fled, but Eastwick pursued him and pulled him from a moving car just as it was driving off. At 3 a.m., Bradley was arrested at his home and taken to the police station. In a signed statement, he said that he, McCallion and Campbell agreed it would be "a good idea" to get a battery and that McCallion tried to get into several cars for that purpose and for the subsidiary purpose of getting a radio. Bradley also described the events previously related by Eastwick. Campbell was brought to the station at 4:30 a.m., and he gave a statement which generally accorded with Bradley's.

The court deemed it settled, pursuant to *Rex v. Barker*, [1924] N.Z.L.R. 865, "that there can be a conviction for attempt to commit a crime if, and only if, the act done with intent to commit it is in itself sufficient evidence of the intent: it must be a case of *res ipsa loquitor,* in the sense that, with no other evidence before it, a jury could properly infer the intent. * * *

"In these circumstances, though the Court knows full well as against both appellants that it was theft that was contemplated, it is impossible to convict them of attempted theft. Accordingly, the convictions for the attempt cannot stand. If this be regarded as unsatisfactory, the remedying of it seems to rest with the Legislature."

3. The legislature did ultimately remedy the situation. N.Z. Crimes Act of 1961, § 72(3) provides: "An act done or omitted with intent to commit an offense may constitute an attempt if it is immediately or proximately connected with the intended offense, whether or not there was any act unequivocally showing the intent to commit that offense." Was this a change for the better? Consider Donald Stuart, *The Actus Reus in Attempts*, 1970 Crim.L.Rev. 505, 507: "The main criticism of the 'equivocality' test is that, in requiring the act to show unequivocal purpose on its face without reference to evidence *aliunde,* it places the *actus reus* in too watertight a compartment. Any rule that the *actus reus* must be established independently of what is known about the *mens rea* is undesirable and likely to lead to the capricious results reached in New Zealand. If a locksmith is found next to a bank safe with his tools of trade it would be ludicrous to exclude a confession or other evidence that his intention had been to steal. It has also been pointed out that an act in itself will rarely reveal an unequivocal purpose and that it therefore seems unwise to use equivocality as the basis for non-liability in attempts. Even if the purpose is unequivocal from the face of the act the act may still be so remote that policy would be against a conviction."

4. In *Bowen*, the court says that the requisite "overt act is not any act." But why not? Consider Glanville Williams, *Criminal Law: The General Part* 632 (2d ed. 1961): "Another way of supporting the proximity rule is to say that it results from the notion of crime as a punishable wrong. Society has not thought it desirable to extend the scope of punishment too widely. So long as the law was purely deterrent or retributive in its aim, this circumscription of the offence of attempt was perhaps justified. At the present day, when courts have wide powers of probation, there is much to be said for a broader measure

of responsibility. Any act done with the fixed intention of committing a crime, and by way of preparation for it, however remote it may be from the crime, might well be treated as criminal. The rational course would be to catch intending offenders as soon as possible, and set about curing them of their evil tendencies: not leave them alone on the ground that their acts are mere preparation. It must be said, however, that this opinion is not generally held in the legal profession.

"A particularly unfortunate effect of the present law is that it often puts the police into a most awkward position. If they apprehend the suspect too soon, he may be acquitted; if they delay, they may be criticised for allowing a crime to be committed that they could have prevented."

UNITED STATES v. MANDUJANO

United States Court of Appeals, Fifth Circuit, 1974.

499 F.2d 370.

RIVES, CIRCUIT JUDGE:

Mandujano appeals from the judgment of conviction and fifteen-year sentence imposed by the district court, based upon the jury's verdict finding him guilty of attempted distribution of heroin in violation of 21 U.S.C. § 846. We affirm.

The government's case rested almost entirely upon the testimony of Alfonso H. Cavalier, Jr., a San Antonio police officer assigned to the Office of Drug Abuse Law Enforcement. Agent Cavalier testified that, at the time the case arose, he was working in an undercover capacity and represented himself as a narcotics trafficker. At about 1:30 P.M. on the afternoon of March 29, 1973, pursuant to information Cavalier had received, he and a government informer went to the Tally–Ho Lounge, a bar located on Guadalupe Street in San Antonio. Once inside the bar, the informant introduced Cavalier to Roy Mandujano. After some general conversation, Mandujano asked the informant if he was looking for "stuff." Cavalier said, "Yes." Mandujano then questioned Cavalier about his involvement in narcotics. Cavalier answered Mandujano's questions, and told Mandujano he was looking for an ounce sample of heroin to determine the quality of the material. Mandujano replied that he had good brown Mexican heroin for $650.00 an ounce, but that if Cavalier wanted any of it he would have to wait until later in the afternoon when the regular man made his deliveries. Cavalier said that he was from out of town and did not want to wait that long. Mandujano offered to locate another source, and made four telephone calls in an apparent effort to do so. The phone calls appeared to be unsuccessful, for Mandujano told Cavalier he wasn't having any luck contacting anybody. Cavalier stated that he could not wait any longer. Then Mandujano said he had a good contact, a man who kept narcotics around his home, but that if he went to see this man, he would need the money "out front." To reassure Cavalier that he would not simply abscond with the money, Mandujano stated, "[Y]ou are in my place of business. My wife is here. You can sit with my wife. I am not going to jeopardize her or my business for $650.00." Cavalier counted out $650.00 to Mandujano, and Mandujano left the premises of the Tally–Ho Lounge at about 3:30 P.M. About an hour later, he returned and explained that he had been unable to locate his contact. He gave back the $650.00 and told Cavalier he could still wait until the regular man came around. Cavalier left, but arranged to call back at 6:00 P.M. When Cavalier called at 6:00 and again at 6:30, he was told that Mandujano was not available. Cavalier testified that he did not later attempt to contact Mandujano, because, "Based on the information that I had received, it would be unsafe for either my informant or myself to return to this area."

The only other government witness was Gerald Courtney, a Special Agent for the Drug Enforcement Administration. Agent Courtney testified that, as part of a surveillance team in the vicinity of the Tally–Ho Lounge on March 29, 1973, he had observed Mandujano leave the bar around 3:15 or 3:30 P.M. and drive off in his automobile. The surveillance team followed Mandujano but lost him almost immediately in heavy traffic. Courtney testified that Mandujano returned to the bar at about 4:30 P.M. * * *

Mandujano urges that his conduct as described by agent Cavalier did not rise to the level of an attempt to distribute heroin under section 846. He claims that at most he was attempting to acquire a controlled substance, not to distribute it; that it is impossible for a person to attempt to distribute heroin which he does not possess or control; that his acts were only preparation, as distinguished from an attempt; and that the evidence was insufficient to support the jury's verdict. * * *

Although the * * * cases give somewhat varying verbal formulations, careful examination reveals fundamental agreement about what conduct will constitute a criminal attempt. First, the defendant must have been acting with the kind of culpability otherwise required for the commission of the crime which he is charged with attempting. * * *

Second, the defendant must have engaged in conduct which constitutes a substantial step toward commission of the crime. A substantial step must be conduct strongly corroborative of the firmness of the defendant's criminal intent. * * * The use of the word "conduct" indicates that omission or possession, as well as positive acts, may in certain cases provide a basis for liability. The phrase "substantial step," rather than "overt act," is suggested by *Gregg v. United States,* 113 F.2d 687 (8th Cir.1940) ("a step in the direct movement toward the commission of the crime"); *United States v. Coplon,* 185 F.2d 629 (2d Cir.1950) ("before he has taken the last of his intended steps") and *People v. Buffum,* 40 Cal.2d 709, 256 P.2d 317 (1953) ("some *appreciable fragment* of the crime") and indicates that the conduct must be more than remote preparation. The requirement that the conduct be strongly corroborative of the firmness of the defendant's criminal intent also relates to the requirement that the conduct be more than "mere preparation," and is suggested by the Supreme Court's emphasis upon ascertaining the intent of the defendant, *United States v. Quincy,* 31 U.S. 445, 8 L.Ed. 458 (1832), and by the approach taken in *United States v. Coplon,* supra ("* * * some preparation may amount to an attempt. It is a question of degree").[6] * * *

After the jury brought in a verdict of guilty, the trial court propounded a series of four questions to the jury:

"(1) Do you find beyond a reasonable doubt that on the 29th day of March, 1973, Roy Mandujano, the defendant herein, knowingly, wilfully and intentionally placed several telephone calls in order to obtain a source of heroin in accordance with his negotiations with Officer Cavalier which were to result in the distribution of approximately one ounce of heroin from the defendant Roy Mandujano to Officer Cavalier?"

"(2) Do you find beyond a reasonable doubt that the telephone calls inquired about in question no. (1) constituted overt acts in furtherance of the offense alleged in the indictment?"

"(3) Do you find beyond a reasonable doubt that on the 29th day of March, 1973, Roy Mandujano, the defendant herein, knowingly, wilfully and intentionally requested and received prior payment in the amount of $650.00 for approximately one ounce of

6. Our definition is generally consistent with and our language is in fact close to the definitions proposed by the National Commission on Reform of Federal Criminal Laws and the American Law Institute's Model Penal Code.

heroin that was to be distributed by the defendant Roy Mandujano to Officer Cavalier?"

"(4) Do you find beyond a reasonable doubt that the request and receipt of a prior payment inquired about in question no. (3) constituted an overt act in furtherance of the offense alleged in the indictment?"

Neither the government nor the defendant objected to this novel procedure. After deliberating, the jury answered "No" to question (1) and "Yes" to questions (3) and (4). The jury's answers indicate that its thinking was consistent with the charge of the trial court.

The evidence was sufficient to support a verdict of guilty under section 846. Agent Cavalier testified that at Mandujano's request, he gave him $650.00 for one ounce of heroin, which Mandujano said he could get from a "good contact." From this, plus Mandujano's comments and conduct before and after the transfer of the $650.00 the jury could have found that Mandujano was acting knowingly and intentionally and that he engaged in conduct—the request for and the receipt of the $650.00—which in fact constituted a substantial step toward distribution of heroin. From interrogatory (4), it is clear that the jury considered Mandujano's request and receipt of the prior payment a substantial step toward the commission of the offense. Certainly, in the circumstances of this case, the jury could have found the transfer of money strongly corroborative of the firmness of Mandujano's intent to complete the crime. Of course, proof that Mandujano's "good contact" actually existed, and had heroin for sale, would have further strengthened the government's case; however, such proof was not essential. * * *

Notes and Questions

1. Is the "substantial step" test of *Model Penal Code* § 5.01 the best solution? Consider Donald Stuart, *The Actus Reus in Attempts,* 1970 Crim.L.Rev. 505, 522–23: "It is also questionable whether it is really necessary to have a requirement of corroboration. It might well revive some of the absurdities experienced with the 'equivocality' theory. The normal caution in approaching an uncorroborated confession seems to be a sufficient safeguard against induced or false confessions. * * * In fact, the problem of the proximity rule is retained in a different guise together with * * * 'the element of imprecision found in most other approaches to the preparation-attempt problem.' One cannot help a feeling of scepticism as to the value of the suggested switch in emphasis 'from what remains to be done, the chief concern of the proximity tests, to what the actor has already done.' The unfortunate truth is that there is no definable quality that will distinguish a 'substantial step,' 'a step,' 'an act of preparation' and 'an act of perpetration.' "

2. Would Mandujano's conviction have been affirmed under any of the other tests? Does the answer to this question affect your judgment as to the adequacy of the "substantial step" test?

3. In support of the Model Penal Code formulation, it is said that "apprehension of dangerous persons will be facilitated and law enforcement officials and others will be able to stop the criminal effort at an earlier stage, thereby minimizing the risk of substantive harm, but without providing immunity for the offender." Model Penal Code § 5.01, Comment (1985). Compare Robert Misner, *The New Attempt Laws: Unsuspected Threat to the Fourth Amendment,* 33 Stan.L.Rev. 201, 201–02 (1981):

"Commentators and jurists have expressed legitimate concern about recent *judicial* erosion of the fourth amendment protection against unreasonable search and seizure. Unrecognized, however, is the equally serious threat created by *legislatures* which, following the lead of the Model Penal Code, have adopted broad, expansive definitions of inchoate crimes such as attempt. Because the Supreme Court has upheld the right of police to conduct a full search of an individual incident to *any* arrest, broader attempt laws narrow the procedural protection of the fourth amendment. Conduct that formerly warranted no more than a brief detention for questioning or a patdown search for weapons (a 'frisk') may now justify an attempt arrest and therefore a full search.''

In *Terry v. Ohio,* 392 U.S. 1, 88 S.Ct. 1868, 20 L.Ed.2d 889 (1968), where a police officer saw several men repeatedly look into a store as if they were "casing" it for a holdup, the Supreme Court held that such reasonable suspicion short of probable cause to arrest authorized the police to make a brief stop of the suspects and to frisk them for weapons.

"Under most common law tests, Terry's conduct falls short of attempted robbery. Because Terry and his confederates did not brandish their weapons or enter the store they were casing, their actions were neither 'unequivocal' nor 'dangerously proximate' to completion of the crime. And they never committed the 'last proximate act' prior to the robbery. While their conduct came closest to an attempt under the 'probable desistance' test, it is arguable that the defendants left the front of the store, indicating desistance, *before* the police confronted them.

"But in a jurisdiction that follows the Model Penal Code approach, the case for attempt is clear. Because the police could reasonably conclude that Terry's behavior amounted to 'reconnoitering,' they would have probable cause to arrest him for attempted robbery and conduct a full search incident to the arrest." Misner, supra, at 216.

4. Finally, consider also Lawrence Crocker, *Justice in Criminal Liability: Decriminalizing Harmless Attempts*, 53 Ohio St.L.J. 1057, 1109 (1992), who argues that many of the actions which would constitute attempts under the Model Penal Code or even several of the other tests, "because they impose no immediate objective risk, ought not be subject to criminal liability.

"There may sometimes be crime control advantages to punishing interrupted and impossible attempts. We should, however, forego those advantages for reasons that go deep into the conception of a just and free society. Most fundamentally, society lacks any moral license to impose a criminal sanction upon anyone who has not herself imposed by violating the rights of some other person or persons. Second, a society with proper respect for liberty and autonomy will not bring the heavy hand of the criminal law down at any earlier stage than necessary in the chain of steps leading towards the final harm.

"It is at this point that commentators have tried to work a balance of security and liberty interests by compromising between the pure subjective and pure imposition theories. This Article argues that any such compromise is intellectually unstable. In the end, one must either embrace the imposition theory or be prepared, in principle, to embrace the findings of a machine that measures mental depravity or predicts future dangerousness."

NOTES AND QUESTIONS ON ATTEMPTING ATTEMPTS

1. *Attempting to Attempt a Crime.* Because the cases previously considered in this section are all concerned with identifying that point in a person's efforts to bring about a substantive crime (e.g., murder) when the law can legitimately intervene with an attempt prosecution, it would seem apparent that a prosecutor cannot circumvent this body of law by charging the defendant with an attempt to attempt a murder. As stated in Ira P. Robbins, *Double Inchoate Crimes*, 26 Harv.J.Legis. 1, 37 (1989): "Viewed as an abstract principle, the construction of attempt to attempt presents the possibility of regression *ad infinitum*, with the concomitant distortion of the attempt concept's protections against punishment for equivocal behavior. An indictment for the attempt to attempt a substantive

crime would ask a court to punish the defendant for acts that would not qualify under the jurisdiction's definition of attempt."

2. *Varieties of Inchoate Offenses.* The problem becomes more complicated, however, once it is appreciated that there are two varieties of what, from one perspective, can fairly be called inchoate crimes. As explained in Comment, 20 No.Ill.U.L.Rev. 219, 222–23 (2000): "Crimes that are punished before the harm that is the ultimate concern of society occurs are called inchoate crimes. Historically, there has been confusion surrounding the question of what exactly constitutes an inchoate crime. Clearly, attempt, solicitation, and conspiracy are the three major crimes expressly recognized as inchoate. However, there is some question about whether there are other inchoate crimes (besides attempt, solicitation, and conspiracy). * * *

"Thankfully, scholars have cleared up some of the confusion surrounding inchoate crimes by classifying inchoate crimes into two categories. First, attempt, solicitation, and conspiracy are categorized as 'complex' inchoate crimes—complex because they become a crime only when used in conjunction with another crime (an object or target offense), and are not crimes in and of themselves. A second category of inchoate crimes are called 'simple' inchoate crime—simple because they are their own offense, they do not need a target or object offense such as the complex inchoate crimes need. There is no statutory combination needed to create these crimes. A brief examination of both complex inchoate crimes and simple inchoate crimes provides a useful foundation for understanding what category an offense falls into and why combining two inchoate crimes is so troublesome."

And thus the question has naturally arisen as to whether a charge of attempting to commit an inchoate crime of the second type[a] is permissible.

3. *Attempted Assault.* Consider:

(a) In the case of *In re James M.*, 9 Cal.3d 517, 108 Cal.Rptr. 89, 510 P.2d 33 (1973), James M. was found by the juvenile court to be a ward of the court for committing the crime of attempting to commit an assault with a deadly weapon on a peace officer. The evidence was that the 13–year-old boy had thrown a rock which dented the fender of a patrol car a few feet away from the officer. On appeal, the court reversed:

"At common law an assault was defined as an attempted battery. It was said that one cannot attempt to commit an attempt, and, therefore, attempted assault was a deductive impossibility. A century ago one court described the matter thus: 'As an assault is itself an attempt to commit a crime, an attempt to make an assault can only be an attempt to attempt to do it * * *. This is simply absurd.' (*Wilson v. State* (1874) 53 Ga. 205, 206.) Yet esoteric theories have been advanced to demonstrate that the concept of an attempted assault is not wholly illogical.

"One such theory is based on the concept of 'proximity,' i.e., that a greater degree of proximity is required to commit an assault than to commit a general criminal attempt. Hence, it is reasoned, conduct which goes further than preparation, but falls short of assault, may be punished as a general criminal attempt. A second theory, apparently relied on by the trial court herein, suggests that inasmuch as an assault is defined in California as an attempt to commit battery coupled with the present ability to do so, an attempted assault means, in substance, an attempt to commit a battery *without* such present ability.

"Whether or not the foregoing theories are entirely tenable, it is apparent that the abstract concept of an attempted assault is not necessarily a logical absurdity. Yet to

a. There is also a question of whether one can be charged with an attempt to commit either of the other two kinds of inchoate offenses of the first type, solicita- tion and conspiracy. This matter will be explored in the next Chapter.

concede, in an academic sense, the possibility that there can be an attempted assault is not the equivalent of declaring it to be a punishable offense under the laws of this state.

"Section 6 of the Penal Code declares that 'No act or omission * * * is criminal or punishable, except as prescribed or authorized by this Code' or by other statutes or ordinances. Since its first session, our Legislature has defined criminal assault as an attempt to commit a battery by one *having present ability* to do so and no offense known as attempt to assault was recognized in California at the time that statutory definition of assault was adopted. Under the doctrine of manifested legislative intent, an omission from a penal provision evinces a legislative purpose not to punish the omitted act. Hence, there is a clear manifestation of legislative intent under this doctrine for an attempt to commit a battery without present ability to go unpunished.

"It is also an established rule of statutory construction that particular provisions will prevail over general provisions. Therefore, the legislative intent not to punish batteries attempted without present ability prevails over the general criminal attempt provisions of section 664. It follows that to judicially find a crime in California in an attempt to commit a battery where the actor lacks the present ability to consummate the battery would be to invade the province of the Legislature by redefining the elements of the underlying crime.

"In addition, we foresee serious pragmatic difficulties if attempted assault were judicially established as a punishable crime. Trial courts must instruct on lesser included offenses if the evidence raises questions as to whether all the elements of the charged crime are present. If it were a crime trial courts would be required to instruct on attempted assault in every prosecution for a crime involving any type of assault, whether simple or aggravated, when the proof of one of the elements of the underlying crime is unclear or contested. The injection of an additional issue into such trials, with attendant likelihood of confusion of the jury and unwarranted reversals, does not seem justified, particularly since the lack of seriousness of a mere attempted assault has been evidenced by consistent legislative omission since 1850 to provide for any such crime. Juries should not be required to engage in fruitless metaphysical speculation as to differing degrees of proximity between an assault and a general attempt, nor as to the logical possibility of attempting to commit any crime of assault, either simple or aggravated, the basic nature of which is an attempt in itself."

(b) Compare *State v. Wilson*, 218 Or. 575, 346 P.2d 115 (1959), affirming defendant's conviction for attempted assault with a dangerous weapon. (The defendant, with the intention of shooting his wife, came to her place of employment with a shotgun, but did not find her because she was hiding; it was thus assumed that the "present ability to inflict corporal injury" needed to convict of assault was lacking.) The court reasoned:

"If we should regard assault as an attempted battery, is it reasonable to recognize the crime of attempted assault? It has been categorically asserted that there can be no attempt to commit a crime which is itself merely an attempt. Upon the basis of this premise it is said that there can be no such offense as an attempted assault. * * * In none of these sources is it explained why this conclusion is inevitable. It appears to be assumed that logic permits no other conclusion. But is that so? Thurman Arnold, in an article in 40 Yale L.J. 53, 65 (1930) answers as follows:

'* * * [It is said that] there can be no attempt at a direct attempt. But the query immediately arises, Why not? We do not punish attempts at ordinary assaults which carry light penalties. But suppose the accused is guilty of conduct tending toward an aggravated assault but which does not seem to require the heavier penalty. The court is confronted with the alternative of either discharging the accused or modifying the penalty to make it more nearly fit his conduct. An easy way to accomplish this is by making attempts at aggravated assaults punishable, and this is frequently done. It is academic to call such cases "wrong" because assault is in the nature of an attempt and hence cannot be attempted, particularly when a common sense result is reached. In short the generalization that there can be no attempt at a crime in the nature of an attempt tells us nothing and tends merely to divert the court's mind from the real issue.'

"We agree with the foregoing analysis. The mere fact that assault is viewed as preceding a battery should not preclude us from drawing a line on one side of which we require the present ability to inflict corporal injury, denominating this an assault, and on the other side conduct which falls short of a present ability, yet so advanced toward the assault that it is more than mere preparation and which we denominate an attempt."

4. *Attempted Burglary*. Consider:

(a) *Model Penal Code* § 221.1, Comment (1980): "The common-law concept of burglary encompassed breaking and entering the dwelling house of another at night with the intent to commit a felony therein. The scope of the offense had been enlarged by judicial interpretation and legislation, however, with the result that, at least under the most comprehensive of the statutes in force at the time the Model Penal Code was drafted, the offense could be committed by entry alone, in the daytime as well as at night, in any building, structure, or vehicle, with the intent to commit any criminal offense. Enlargement of the offense in this manner was accompanied by the adoption of various grading distinctions. Generally, the most serious penalties were reserved for situations involving actual or potential danger to persons, and misdemeanor or lesser felony sanctions were provided for less aggravated conduct.

"The initial development of the offense of burglary, as well as much of the later expansion of the offense, probably resulted from an effort to compensate for defects of the traditional law of attempt. The common law of attempt ordinarily did not reach a person who embarked on a course of criminal behavior unless he came very close to his goal. * * * Moreover, even when the actor's conduct reached the stage where an attempt was committed, penalties for attempt were disproportionately low as compared to the penalties for the completed offense.

"The development and expansion of the offense of burglary provided a partial solution to these problems."

(b) In *DeGidio v. State*, 289 N.W.2d 135 (Minn.1980), the defendant claimed on appeal that the offense of which he had been convicted, attempted burglary, was not a valid crime. The court disagreed, reasoning that "while burglary is in a sense an inchoate crime, the legislature clearly has determined that the conduct covered by the burglary statute merits separate treatment as a substantive offense. Because the legislature in enacting the attempt statute gave no indication that some substantive crimes could not serve as a foundation for attempt convictions and because burglary is a separate substantive offense, it seems clear to us that the legislature intended to permit prosecutions and convictions for attempted burglary."

(c) Consider John E. Nowak's suggestion, 1970 U.Ill.L.F. 391, 400–01: "The best way to deal with the offense of burglary would be to abolish it. The offense lacks any theoretical or historical justification, and modern laws of attempt would better serve in punishing such conduct. This would establish a punishment rationally connected to the seriousness of the offense which was being attempted. An attempted petty theft would no longer be punished as severely as attempted murder, and the moving of the situs of the offense a few feet would no longer determine the degree of punishment."

(d) What about a preparation-for-burglary crime, such as possession of burglary tools"? Consider Robbins, supra, at 96–97: "Criminal sanctions for possession of burglary tools exemplify the proscription-of-means approach. Like criminal trespass, such sanctions punish the commission of an essential element of the parent crime. Possession of burglary tools, however, is an act that is clearly more preparatory than is illegal entry, which at least constitutes an element of the offense of burglary. Viewed as the gathering of the means to effect an illegal entry to commit another crime, possession of burglary tools can be conceived as representing an attempt to attempt to attempt to commit larceny, robbery, murder, or some ultimate offense.

"Nevertheless, the rationale behind treating both criminal trespass and possession of burglary tools as separate substantive offenses is sound. In either case, it is highly probable that the actor intends to commit a burglary. This conclusion reflects judicial and other observation of human behavior; it is so commonly held as to merit the description 'common sense.'

"Thus, the basis for liability is experiential rather than merely positivist. Illegal entry and possession of burglary tools are crimes not only because the state has made them crimes, but also because common experience has indicated that they are preparatory acts that frequently lead to burglaries. Thus, they fulfill a major purpose of the criminal law— the prevention of social harm. The prohibited acts are sufficiently dangerous to justify intervention and to shift the burden to the actor to justify his behavior as legally permissible. Any perceived unfairness in the imposition of liability can be addressed by adjusting the sentence within the range of punishment prescribed for the crime."

(e) What about reaching even farther back by charging an attempt to possess burglary tools? Consider *State v. Thomas*, 362 So.2d 1348 (Fla.1978), where the court stated that while it is generally the case that under Florida law the trial court must grant a defense request for an instruction on the lesser included offense of attempt to commit the crime charged, the instant case was different:

"A different question is presented where a trial court concludes that, regardless of the evidence presented in the case, an instruction on an attempt to commit the major offense charged is not warranted because an attempt to commit that offense does not constitute a crime under the laws of this state. Usually, such a situation will arise when the major offense charged includes the attempt to commit that act. For example, this court has held that the crime of uttering a forged instrument includes the attempt to pass a forged check as well as the actual negotiating of the forged instrument. *King v. State*, 339 So.2d 172 (Fla.1976).

"The answer is much more difficult with regard to crimes which do not themselves include an attempt. Although it may be possible for a person to be convicted of an attempt to possess items which are contraband per se, burglary tools are not contraband per se, and it is only the actual possession of burglary tools along with a criminal intent or usage that constitutes a punishable offense. Possession of otherwise 'innocent' items, coupled with a use or intended use of such tools in a burglary, is unlawful. No crime is committed until the items are in the actual or constructive possession of a person who is using or attempting to use the objects as burglary tools."

5. *Attempted Stalking.* Consider:

(a) Comment, supra, at 230: "The antistalking laws vary significantly from state to state. Generally, stalking is defined as 'willful, malicious, and repeated following and harassing of another person.' Most state stalking statutes require the alleged stalker to engage in a course of threatening behavior and through that behavior, the alleged stalker must intend to cause his or her victim fear. The crime of stalking is a new creation. In fact, prior to 1990 the crime did not exist. However, between 1990 and 1994 all fifty states and Washington D.C. created antistalking laws.''

(b) In *State v. Rooks*, 266 Ga. 528, 468 S.E.2d 354 (1996), the court, in overturning the intermediate appellate court's reversal of defendant's conviction for attempted stalking, explained: ''In reversing Rooks' conviction, the court of appeals reasoned that stalking is in essence an assault. Because there is no such crime as an attempted assault, the court of appeals reasoned that attempted stalking is likewise a legal impossibility. While we agree that there is no such crime as an attempted assault, we disagree that stalking is merely an assault crime. In recent years states have begun to enact stalking laws in response to the increase in stalking behavior and the ineffectiveness of traditional criminal statutes in preventing and curtailing this behavior. Georgia's stalking law mirrors this trend by proscribing intentional actions not covered by the assault statutes. * * *

''While assault and stalking may overlap in some circumstances, the rationale for not punishing an attempted assault does not apply to an attempted stalking. In refusing to recognize the crime of attempted assault, this court stated that to attempt an assault is 'to do any act towards doing an act towards the commission of the offense' and noted the absurdity and impracticality of criminalizing such behavior. To attempt to stalk, however, is to attempt to follow, place under surveillance or contact another person. It is neither absurd nor impractical to subject to criminal sanction such actions when they are done with the requisite specific intent to cause emotional distress by inducing a reasonable fear of death or bodily injury.''

(c) Compare Comment, supra, at 242–43: ''However, the logical absurdity argument is applicable to crimes other than attempts and assaults. The logical absurdity argument is applicable to all double inchoate constructions and is therefore applicable to attempted stalking. In fact, attempted stalking seems to beckon the use of the logical absurdity argument more than other double inchoate constructions because stalking is further from a substantive crime than is an attempt. The main argument against an attempt-to-attempt crime is that it would give courts unlimited discretion to punish acts further removed from a contemplated offense than an attempt statute does. Attempted stalking does just this. As it is, the stalking statutes proscribe acts that are innocuous, and sometimes the legal is indistinguishable from the illegal. Attempted stalking gives courts unlimited discretion to punish acts even further removed from an ultimate harm than an attempt-to-attempt would. An ideal stalking conviction would involve a person who would have killed, raped, or caused some other ultimate harm to another, but was stopped from doing so, or failed in the process. If they are stopped from creating the ultimate harm, they should only be stopped after their conduct reaches the level of stalking. If the police can step in any sooner, then they have the power to arbitrarily step in at anytime, whether they have a prima facie case of stalking or not.''

SECTION 3. IMPOSSIBILITY

UNITED STATES v. THOMAS

United States Court of Military Appeals, 1962.

13 U.S.C.M.A. 278, 32 C.M.R. 278.

KILDAY, JUDGE:

The accused herein, Thomas and McClellan, were tried in common by general court-martial. Separate charges against the pair alleged the offense of conspiracy to commit rape,

rape, and lewd and lascivious conduct, in violation of Articles 81, 120, and 134, Uniform Code of Military Justice, respectively. Upon arraignment, both men entered pleas of not guilty. Each was acquitted of rape, but the court-martial found them guilty of attempted rape, contrary to Article 80 of the Uniform Code, and likewise convicted them of the other two charges upon which they were brought to trial. Both received identical sentences to dishonorable discharge, confinement at hard labor for three years, forfeiture of all pay and allowances for a like period, and reduction to the grade of airman recruit.

Thereafter, the findings and sentences adjudged by the trial court were approved by the officer exercising general court-martial jurisdiction. The board of review, however, set aside the findings of guilty of attempted rape and conspiracy as to both accused. It approved a modified finding of lewd and lascivious conduct as to each and reassessed the punishment, reducing the sentences of the pair to bad-conduct discharge, confinement at hard labor for five months, total forfeitures, and reduction. * * *

The evidence adduced at the trial presents a sordid and revolting picture which need not be discussed in detail other than as necessary to decide the certified issues. In brief, both these young accused—Thomas being twenty years of age, and McClellan only nineteen, at the time of the instant offenses—started their fateful evening on a "bar hopping" spree. They were accompanied by an eighteen-year-old companion, Abruzzese, who, like both accused, held the grade of airman in the Navy. The latter was a co-actor in these offenses, but was granted immunity from prosecution for his criminality in the incidents, and testified as a witness for the Government.

After several stops the trio entered a tavern known as "Taylor's Place" where McClellan began dancing with a girl. Almost at once she collapsed in McClellan's arms. Thereafter, he, with his two companions, volunteered to take her home. They placed the apparently unconscious female in McClellan's car and left. Abruzzese was seated beside McClellan, who drove; Thomas was in the left rear seat next to the girl. Before they had proceeded very far McClellan, in frank, expressive language, suggested that this was a good chance for sexual intercourse as apparently this woman was just drunk and would never know the difference. Each of the three subsequently did or attempted to consummate this act and then started their return to town. The three became concerned as the woman had not regained consciousness.

In the meantime they dropped Abruzzese off at the USO. The accused, unable to find the female's home and becoming more concerned about her condition, stopped at a service station seeking help. The attendant called the police who, upon arriving at the service station, examined the girl and determined she was dead. An ambulance was called and she was taken to a hospital for further examination. An autopsy, later performed, revealed that she apparently died of "acute interstitial myocarditis." In general terms this is a weakening of the heart muscles with edema and inflammation which occurs more in young people without its presence being suspected. It was the general undisputed opinion that her death probably occurred at the time she collapsed on the dance floor at Taylor's Place or very shortly thereafter. Apparently, in deaths of this type, rigor mortis does not usually begin for some time and as a result the accused were unaware of the fact she was dead. * * *

Despite the fact that defense counsel at trial vigorously urged to the law officer that the offenses of attempt and conspiracy could not be found validly if the victim's death occurred prior to the commission of the alleged acts, the law officer ruled otherwise. * * *

Before the board of review, appellate defense counsel contended that the law officer erred in his instructions to the court on the attempt and conspiracy offenses. In support of that position, the defense argued that where circumstances beyond the accused's control make it legally impossible to commit a crime, as distinguished from factual impossibility to do so, there can be no attempt nor can there be a conspiracy to commit the substantive offense. * * * The board of review held that an attempt to commit a crime must be directed to an object on which it is possible to commit the crime. Reasoning that a corpse is not a person, the board of review determined that the law officer erred in his instruction that there was no requirement that the victim be alive before the accused could be convicted of attempted rape. * * * Similarly, it was found that the accused could not be found guilty of conspiring to do that which if effected or consummated would not be an offense. Accordingly, the board of review set aside both accused's convictions for attempt to commit rape and for conspiracy to commit rape. * * *

Practically all writers on this subject, whether in law journal articles, texts, or judicial opinions, cite and discuss the same relatively limited number of decisions. These decisions are generally placed in the two following categories:

1. "Legal impossibility" in which attempt convictions have been set aside on the ground that it was legally impossible for the accused to have committed the crime contemplated. These are as follows:

(a) A person accepting goods which he believed to have been stolen, but which were not then "stolen" goods, was not guilty of an attempt to receive stolen goods. *People v. Jaffe,* 185 N.Y. 497, 78 N.E. 169 (1906).

(b) An accused who offered a bribe to a person believed to be a juror, but who was not a juror, could not be said to have attempted to bribe a juror. *State v. Taylor,* 345 Mo. 325, 133 S.W.2d 336 (1939).

(c) An official who contracted a debt which was unauthorized and a nullity, but which he believed to be valid, could not be convicted of an attempt to illegally contract a valid debt. *Marley v. State,* 58 N.J.L. 207, 33 Atl. 208 (1895).

(d) A hunter who shot a stuffed deer believing it to be alive had not attempted to take a deer out of season. *State v. Guffey,* 262 S.W.2d 152 (Mo.1953).

(e) It is not an attempt to commit subornation of perjury where the false testimony solicited, if given, would have been immaterial to the case at hand and hence not perjurious. *People v. Teal,* 196 N.Y. 372, 89 N.E. 1086 (1909).

2. Instances in which a claim of impossibility has been rejected and convictions sustained, are included below. Apparently these can all be classified as "impossibility in fact." These decisions are:

(a) It is now uniformly held that one is guilty if he attempts to steal from an empty pocket. *Commonwealth v. McDonald,* 5 Cushing 365 (Mass.1850). The same is true as to an empty receptacle, *Clark v. State,* 86 Tenn. 511, 8 S.W. 145 (1888); and an empty house, *State v. Utley,* 82 N.C. 556 (1880). * * *

(b) One can attempt to possess narcotics, even though accused obtained possession of talcum believing it to be narcotics. *People v. Siu,* 126 Cal.App.2d 41, 271 P.2d 575 (1954). * * *

(c) An accused may be guilty of attempted murder who, suspecting that a policeman on the roof was spying upon him through a hole, but ignorant that the policeman was then upon another part of the roof, fired at the hole with intent to kill. *People v. Lee Kong,* 95 Cal. 666, 30 Pac. 800 (1892). It is attempted murder to shoot into the intended victim's bed believing he is there asleep when in fact he is some place else. *United States v. Cruz–Gerena,* C.M. 228955, 49 B.R. 245 (1943); *State v. Mitchell,* 170 Mo. 633, 71 S.W. 175 (1902). An accused is not absolved from the charge of attempted murder when he points an unloaded gun at his wife's head and pulls the trigger, if he actually thought at the time that it was loaded. *State v. Damms,* 9 Wis.2d 183, 100 N.W.2d 592 (1960).

(d) In attempted abortion cases an accused may be guilty in the absence of proof that the woman was pregnant. *Commonwealth v. Tibbetts,* 157 Mass. 519, 32 N.E. 910 (1893) * * *.

It must be noted, however, that efforts to arrange these various authorities into some sort of classification have met with little real or satisfactory success. * * *

" * * * There are no degrees of impossibility and no sound basis for distinguishing among the conditions necessary for commission of the intended harm." [Hall, *General Principles of Criminal Law,* 2d ed., page 589 (1960).]

"The distinctions * * * are ingenious, but * * * they lead us either to absurd results or else to no results. * * * "[40 Yale Law Journal, supra, at page 71.]

So, too, Professor Sayre indicates that regardless of artificial classifications, one stabbing a corpse thinking it a live person should be liable for attempted murder. Thus he states in a footnote, at 41 Harvard Law Review, supra, page 853:

" * * * [W]here one comes upon his enemy lying apparently asleep and stabs him to the heart, and it is later shown that the victim was dead before the defendant stabbed him, although the defendant could not of course be convicted for murder, he should be held liable for an attempt to kill if his belief that the victim was still living was under all the circumstances a natural and reasonable one."

The lack of logic between some of the holdings, supra; the inherent difficulty in assigning a given set of facts to a proper classification; the criticism of existing positions in this area; and, most importantly, the denial of true and substantial justice by these artificial holdings have led, quite naturally, to proposals for reform in the civilian legal concepts of criminal attempts.

In addition to a progressive and modern view now evident in some judicial decisions and writings, The American Law Institute in its proposal of a "Model Penal Code" defines Criminal Attempts, in Article 5.01 * * *. The import of that suggested statute is made clear in Tentative Draft No. 10 of the Model Penal Code of The American Law Institute, supra, at page 25, where it is stated:

" * * * It should suffice, therefore, to indicate at this stage what we deem to be the major results of the draft. They are:

(a) to extend the criminality of attempts by sweeping aside the defense of impossibility (including the distinction between so-called factual and legal impossibility) and by drawing the line between attempt and non-criminal preparation further away from the final act; the crime becomes essentially one of criminal purpose implemented by an overt act strongly corroborative of such purpose; * * *."

After having given this entire question a great deal more than casual attention and study, we are forced to the conclusion that the law of attempts in military jurisprudence has tended toward the advanced and modern position, which position will be achieved for civilian jurisprudence if The American Law Institute is completely successful in its advocacy of this portion of the Model Penal Code. * * *

We hold, therefore, in accordance with the foregoing authorities, that in this instance the fact that the female, upon whom these detestable acts were performed, was already dead at the time of their commission, is no bar to conviction for attempted rape.

However, for purposes of clarity, we should make mention of that portion of paragraph 159, Manual for Courts–Martial, supra, which reads:

"It is not an attempt when every act intended by the accused could be completed without committing an offense, even though the accused may at the time believe he is committing an offense."

That provision has no reference to questions we have here discussed. Such language says no more than that if what an accused believed to be a substantive crime was actually no crime at all, he cannot be guilty of an attempt to commit such crime. That is, when the intended action, even if completed, is not an offense despite the fact accused believed otherwise, he cannot be held for a criminal attempt. Under those circumstances a substantive offense is nonexistent, and an accused's acts, whether carried to fruition or not, constitute wholly lawful conduct. It is interesting to observe that the same situation will exist under the Model Penal Code. See Tentative Draft No. 10, supra, page 31, which states, in the commentary:

"Of course, it is still necessary that the result desired or intended by the actor constitute a crime. If, according to his beliefs as to facts and legal relationships, the result desired or intended is not a crime, the actor will not be guilty of an attempt even though he firmly believes that his goal is criminal." * * *

FERGUSON, JUDGE (concurring in part and dissenting in part):

Professor Jerome Hall traces the difficulty in analyzing the defense of impossibility in criminal attempts to Baron Bramwell's original use of illustrative fact situations "from Never–Never Land" in *Regina v. Collins*, 9 Cox.C.C. 497, 169 Eng.Rep. 1477 (1864). Hall, *General Principles of Criminal Law*, 2d ed., page 593. I am inclined to attribute it to a growing tendency on the part of legal theoreticians to attach more importance to the evilness of a man's intent than to his acts—a belief, if you will, that the law should punish sinful thoughts if accompanied by any sort of antisocial conduct which evidences the design to execute forbidden acts. When certain courts adopt such broad penal theories and others reject them, the result is the legal morass to which my brothers refer. * * *

Impossibility cases have generally involved homicide, larceny and related crimes, rape, and what might be classified as a hodgepodge of statutory offenses, ranging from abortion to corruption of jurors.

The homicide cases have usually involved the absence of the victim. In *State v. Mitchell*, 170 Mo. 633, 71 S.W. 175 (1902), it was established that the defendant fired two shots into his intended victim's bedroom for the purpose of slaying him. The victim, however, was elsewhere in the house, and the attack went for nought. Rejecting the contention that accused should not have been convicted of attempted murder, the court stated, at page 177:

" * * * So in this case the intent evidenced by the firing into the bedroom with a deadly weapon, accompanied by a present capacity in defendant to murder Warren if he were in the room, and the failure to do so only because Warren happily retired upstairs instead of in the bed into which defendant fired, made out a perfect case of an attempt within the meaning of the statute. * * * " * * *

In *State v. Damms*, 9 Wis.2d 183, 100 N.W.2d 592 (1960), a different situation was presented. Accused, with intent to kill, held a pistol to his wife's head, and pulled the trigger twice. The weapon did not fire, as it did not contain any cartridges. The evidence indicated that accused in fact thought it was fully loaded.

Relying on a great number of decisions involving similar facts, the Wisconsin Supreme Court held that the defendant was properly convicted of attempted murder. It said, at page 596:

"Sound public policy would seem to support the majority view that impossibility not apparent to the actor should not absolve him from the offense of attempt to commit the crime he intended. An unequivocal act accompanied by intent should be sufficient to constitute a criminal attempt. Insofar as the actor knows, he has done everything necessary to insure the commission of the crime intended, and he should not escape punishment because of the fortuitous circumstance that by reason of some fact unknown to him it was impossible to effectuate the intended result." * * *

In *People v. Jaffe,* 185 N.Y. 497, 78 N.E. 169 (1906), it was concluded that the defendant could not be guilty of an attempt to receive stolen property when the cloth which he received was in fact not stolen. In the *Jaffe* case, the court noted, at page 169:

" * * * In passing upon the question here presented for our determination, it is important to bear in mind precisely what it was that the defendant attempted to do. He simply made an effort to purchase certain specific pieces of cloth. He believed the cloth to be stolen property, but it was not such in fact. The purchase, therefore, if it had been completely effected, could not constitute the crime of receiving stolen property, knowing it to be stolen, since there could be no such thing as knowledge on the part of the defendant of a nonexistent fact, although there might be a belief on his part that the fact existed. As Mr. Bishop well says, it is a mere truism that there can be no receiving of stolen goods which have not been stolen. 2 Bishop's New Crim.Law, § 1140. It is equally difficult to perceive how there can be an attempt to receive stolen goods, knowing them to have been stolen, when they have not been stolen in fact.

"The crucial distinction between the case before us and the pickpocket cases, and others involving the same principle, lies not in the possibility or impossibility [factual?] *of the commission of the crime, but in the fact that, in the present case, the act, which it was doubtless the intent of the defendant to commit would not have been a crime if it had been consummated."* [Emphasis supplied.]

Some jurisdictions have concluded that attempts to commit larceny by false pretenses occur where the victim knows the defendant's representations are false but parts with his money or property without reliance thereon. Thus, in *State v. Peterson,* 109 Wash. 25, 186 Pac. 264 (1919), the appellant called a department store and sought to obtain delivery of merchandise by falsely representing herself as another credit customer. The store was not deceived by her pretense and notified police officers. Appellant was apprehended when she called for the merchandise. In concluding that attempted larceny had been made out, the Washington Supreme Court stated:

" * * * Had the ruse succeeded in its entirety, there would have been a consummated offense, and it does not follow from the fact that the employes of the merchandise house were not deceived there is taken away from the transaction the element of attempt to deceive." * * *

In *Marley v. State,* 58 N.J.L. 207, 33 Atl. 208 (1895), the defendants were indicted for incurring a debt on behalf of their county in excess of the limit permitted by law. It was shown in defense that the debt which the defendants contracted was void in law. In upsetting a conviction of attempt to incur a debt beyond the permissible limit, the court pointed out that, as the debt was a nullity from the standpoint of the body politic, it was legally impossible for it to have been incurred. Hence, the conviction of attempt would not lie.

In like manner, it has been held that one does not commit the crime of attempted embracery when the individual whom he sought to corrupt was in fact not a juror, having been previously excused from attendance upon the trial. *State v. Taylor,* 345 Mo. 325, 133 S.W.2d 336 (1939); *State v. Porter,* 125 Mont. 503, 242 P.2d 984 (1952). And where defendants intended to sell pears in violation of a pricing order and did in fact sell them, it was concluded that there could be no conviction of an attempt to violate the order upon a showing that the actual sale was within the order's terms. *Rex v. Dalton,* 33 Crim.App.R. 102 (1949). Nor could there be a conviction of an attempt to pursue and take a deer out of season upon proof that the defendant shot a stuffed deer. *State v. Guffey,* 262 S.W.2d 152 (1953) (Missouri). In the last cited case, the court remarked, at page 156:

" * * * The State's evidence shows that one of the defendants did shoot the dummy but did they pursue, chase or follow a *deer* by shooting this stuffed defunct doe hide? It was not a deer. If the dummy had been actually taken, (it could not be pursued) defendants would not have committed any offense. It is no offense to attempt to do that which is not illegal. Neither is it a crime to attempt to do that which it is legally impossible to do. For instance, it is no crime to attempt to murder a corpse because it cannot be murdered." * * *

Charges of attempted rape seem uniformly to have allowed legal impossibility as a defense when a juridical impediment was found to prevent the consummation of the crime. Thus, in *Frazier v. State,* 48 Tex.Crim. 142, 86 S.W. 754 (1905), it was concluded to be legally impossible for a husband to be convicted of the attempted criminal violation of his wife's person. And in *Foster v. Commonwealth,* 96 Va. 306, 31 S.E. 503 (1898), a jurisdiction applying the common-law's conclusive presumption of legal incapacity of a boy under the age of fourteen to commit rape determined that, because of such presumption, he could not be convicted of attempted rape. The court said:

"The accused being under 14 years of age, and conclusively presumed to be incapable of committing the crime of rape, it logically follows, as a plain legal deduction, that he was also incapable in law of an attempt to commit it. He could not be held to be guilty of an attempt to commit an offense which he was physically impotent to perpetrate."

Where, however, a jurisdiction holds to the view that a boy's age as less than fourteen years creates only a *rebuttable factual* presumption of noncapacity, it also is concluded that there may be a conviction of attempted rape by such an individual. *Davidson v. Commonwealth,* 20 Ky.Law.Rep. 540, 47 S.W. 213 (1898). So, also, is the defense of legal impossibility unavailable in the case of individuals above the common-law age of legal capacity who, for physical reasons, are impotent and thus unable to consummate the crime of rape. *Preddy v. Commonwealth,* 184 Va. 765, 36 S.E.2d 549 (1946).

It seems to me that, from the foregoing authorities—representative as they are of the welter of decisions in this field—definite principles may be derived which, when applied to the facts depicted in the record before us, lead inevitably to the conclusion that accused's conviction of attempted rape must be vitiated on the basis of legal impossibility. In the homicide cases, we find in every instance a victim in being upon whom the crime could have been committed * * *.

In the false pretense cases, again we find victims in being and defendants who have done everything necessary to the commission of the consummated crime except to convince their quarry of the validity of the confidence game. Their crimes were unsuccessful not because of legal considerations but only because of the fact that, in each instance, the actors underestimated the acumen of their human targets. * * *

In contrast to these cases upholding convictions of attempts wherein, but for the fact of absence, disbelief, poor aim, and physical inability to accomplish the result sought, are those in which there is, so to speak, no "victim in being." Thus, we find that one cannot attempt to influence a juror who is not a juror. *State v. Taylor,* supra; *State v. Porter,* supra. One cannot attempt to pursue a deer which is nothing more than a stuffed hide. *State v. Guffey,* supra. One cannot attempt to kill by firing into a corpse or commit rape upon a mannequin. Nor can one attempt to receive stolen goods which are not in fact stolen, *People v. Jaffe,* supra, or attempt rape where he legally has no capacity so to act, *Foster v. Commonwealth,* supra.

In each of these instances, there is simply no "victim" or thing which the particular law intended to be broken is designed to protect. Thus, embracery statutes are designed to protect jurors rather than those whom an accused believes to be jurors. Only *stolen* goods are within the proscription against attempts to receive. Only a deer can be the subject of an attempt to hunt deer. In short, the subject matter of accused's acts must be one within the prohibition of the particular statute which he is alleged to have violated, no matter what his personal belief may be, so that he could have been convicted of the consummated crime had he been entirely successful.

No series of cases more clearly portray this distinction than those which deal with the legal incapacity of a boy under fourteen years of age to attempt rape as compared to those which hold simple physical impotency to be no such bar to conviction. In the one instance, the actor, because of a pure rule of law, is incapable of violating a woman, regardless of his actual precocity. In the other, there is no legal bar, the inability being a fact resulting from some disease, disability, or infirmity of which the law refuses to take notice.

In like manner, the barrier to consummation of the crime charged here is not factual but legal. Indeed, accused did everything they set out to do, but they admittedly could not commit the actual crime of rape because their victim was dead and thus outside the protection of the law appertaining to that offense. Because the objective of their loathsome attentions was no longer subject to being raped, it seems to me that there cannot be any liability for an attempt, for, just as in the case of the lad under the age of fourteen, the stuffed "deer," and the nonjuror, a legal rather than a factual impediment existed to the offense's consummation. In brief, this is not the case of an empty pocket but one in which there was no pocket to pick. And, as is succinctly stated in the Manual, supra:

> "It is not an attempt when every act intended by the accused [sexual intercourse with a woman in fact dead] could be completed without committing an offense [rape], even though the accused may at the time believe he is committing an offense [rape]."

Finally, I believe that the position which my brothers take unnecessarily emphasizes the accused's mental frame of reference at the expense of what they actually did. The common-law concept that danger to society lay chiefly in action rather than in thought has much to commend it, based as it is upon centuries of experiential development. Particularly, however, is this true in the armed services, furnished as they are with general articles of the Code within whose scope conduct potentially invasive of any important social interest easily falls. Indeed, such is the course which was wisely followed here, for accused's reprehensible behavior was charged as—and so sustained by the board of review—lewd and lascivious conduct in violation of Code, supra, Article 134. With the propriety of that conclusion, I am certain that none of us argue. When, however, it is found that such acts, albeit legally incapable of consummation, are also punishable as attempted rape, I believe we so widen the thrust of Code, supra, Article 80, that we permit punishment to be predicated upon one's plans quite without regard to whether they may legally be completed. The door, therefore, is left open for the protection of logs against homicidal attack and of the supposed honor of dressmaker's dummies. And to those who, as does Professor Hall, believe that these are hypotheses from Never–Never Land, I recommend the reading of the transcript before us. * * *

Notes and Questions

1. Compare *United States v. Berrigan,* 482 F.2d 171 (3d Cir.1973), the appeal by Fr. Philip Berrigan and Sister Elizabeth McAlister from their convictions for attempting to send seven letters into and out of Lewisburg Federal Penitentiary "without the knowledge and consent of the warden." The court reversed: "Applying the principles of the law of attempt to the instant case, the writing of the letters, and their copying and transmittal by the courier, Boyd Douglas, constituted the *Act.* This much the government proved. What the government did not prove—and could not prove because it was a legal impossibility— was the 'external, objective situation which the substantive law may require to be present,' to-wit, absence of knowledge and consent of the warden. Thus, the government failed to prove the *'Circumstances or attendant circumstances'* vital to the offense. Without such proof, the *Consequence* or *Result* did not constitute an offense that violated the federal statute. The warden and the government were aware of the existence of the letters. The courier acted with the consent of the warden. Although there was no entrapment, the public authorities were privy to the *Act* which gave rise to these charges."

In *United States v. Hsu,* 155 F.3d 189 (3d Cir.1998), the court reaffirmed *Berrigan,* despite being "the only circuit which continues to recognize a common law defense of legal impossibility," and notwithstanding the fact "that the distinction between factual and legal impossibility is essentially a matter of semantics." While "legal impossibility occurs when *A* shoots a corpse believing it to be alive and intended to commit murder, the attempt does not amount to murder even if completed," while "factual impossibility occurs when *A* fires a gun at a bed intending to kill *V*, and *V* is not on the bed; the crime cannot be completed because of extraneous factors beyond *A*'s control." But "every case of legal impossibility can reasonably be characterized as a factual impossibility. For instance, the fact that *A* shoots a corpse, rather than a person, is also a product of circumstances beyond *A*'s control."

The court in *Hsu* then held that the defendant there, charged with attempted theft of trade secrets under the Economic Espionage Act, could *not* rely on the legal impossibility defense, for in the instance case, unlike *Berrigan,* the statute under which the prosecution was brought (I) sought a "comprehensive" solution to the problem of illegal industrial espionage at odds with recognition of such a defense, and (ii) was drafted in 1996, after "abolition of legal impossibility was already 'the overwhelming modern position.' "

2. The *Jaffe* case, discussed in *Thomas,* is one of the most famous and most commented upon impossibility cases. Does it present an easier or more difficult problem than *Thomas?* Consider the views on *Jaffe* in notes 3 through 8 following.

3. *Model Penal Code* § 5.01, Comment (1985), concludes that the *Jaffe* approach "is unsound in that it seeks to evaluate a mental attitude—'intent' or 'purpose'—not by looking to the actor's mental frame of reference, but to a situation wholly at variance with the actor's beliefs. In so doing, the courts exonerate defendants in situations where attempt liability most certainly should be imposed. In all of these cases the actor's criminal purpose has been clearly demonstrated; he went as far as he could in implementing that purpose; and as a result, his 'dangerousness' is plainly manifested."

4. Edwin R. Keedy, *Criminal Attempts at Common Law,* 102 U.Pa.L.Rev. 464, 477 (1954), says that *Jaffe* is "easily explainable, without reference to any conception of 'legal impossibility.' In the *Jaffe* case the necessary intent * * * was lacking."

5. Arnold N. Enker, *Impossibility in Criminal Attempts—Legality and the Legal Process,* 53 Minn.L.Rev. 665, 679–80, 682 (1969): "Those who would eliminate the defense of legal impossibility from the legal lexicon and would convict Jaffe of attempted possession of stolen goods because he thought they were stolen presumably would convict any other defendant of the same crime with respect to goods that had never been stolen if it could be proved that the defendant thought they were stolen. Having dispensed with the need for establishing the circumstance that the goods are stolen, they must permit this result if there is evidence of guilty belief. Assume two cases in which the sole direct evidence of the defendant's alleged belief that the goods are stolen is a confession or the testimony of an informer or an accomplice. In one case the goods possessed are in fact stolen; in the other they are not. It is reasonably clear that most of us would rest easier with a conviction in the first case than in the second although we might have a difficult time articulating reasons for this distinction. [This may be because] possession of stolen goods furnishes some evidence of belief that they are stolen while, clearly, possession of goods not in fact stolen furnishes no reason to believe that the defendant thought they were stolen.

"This requires some elaboration. Concededly, the probative relationship between the fact that the goods are stolen and the possessor's knowledge that they are stolen differs from the probative relationship between, say, the fact that certain goods are machine guns or narcotics and the possessor's knowledge of their nature. Ordinarily, knowledge that goods are within one's possession carries with it knowledge of their physical nature. Where the defendant is proved to have had in his possession certain objects, say, narcotics, it seems reasonable to conclude that he knew the physical nature of those objects and to cast on him the risk of conviction if he does not adduce some evidence to dispel this normal inference. It is clear, then, that to convict someone of attempted possession of narcotics for possessing nonnarcotic goods which he allegedly believed were narcotics would be to redefine the crime of possession of narcotics to eliminate an objective element that had major evidentiary significance and to increase the risk of mistaken conclusions that the defendant believed the goods were narcotics.

" * * * The point is, however, that by eliminating these objective elements we create newly defined crimes in which we replace the statutorily defined fixed reference points for judging the defendant's mens rea with an open-ended sufficiency-of-the-evidence test which may include the less reliable forms of evidence such as questionable admissions, the testimony of informers and accomplices, and proof of prior convictions."

6. Similar analysis is found in *United States v. Oviedo,* 525 F.2d 881 (5th Cir.1976). Oviedo was contacted by an undercover agent who desired to purchase narcotics, and thereafter sold to the agent what he said was one pound of heroin. Though a field test of the substance was positive, later chemical analysis revealed it was in fact procaine hydrochloride, an uncontrolled substance. Oviedo was charged with attempt to distribute heroin. At trial, he testified he knew the substance was not heroin and that he had been trying to "rip off" the agent. In reversing his conviction, the court reasoned:

"When the defendant sells a substance which is actually heroin, it is reasonable to infer that he knew the physical nature of the substance, and to place on him the burden of dispelling that inference. However, if we convict the defendant of attempting to sell heroin for the sale of a non-narcotic substance, we eliminate an objective element that has major evidentiary significance and we increase the risk of mistaken conclusions that the defendant believed the goods were narcotics.

"Thus, we demand that in order for a defendant to be guilty of a criminal attempt, the objective acts performed, without any reliance on the accompanying *mens rea,* mark the defendant's conduct as criminal in nature. The acts should be unique rather than so commonplace that they are engaged in by persons not in violation of the law."

7. Thomas Weigand, *Why Lady Eldon Should be Acquitted: The Social Harm in Attempting the Impossible,* 27 DePaul L.Rev. 231, 268–69 (1977), proposes this test: "An attempt which cannot succeed is punishable if the offender's conduct, seen in the light of his statements accompanying the acts he deemed necessary for achieving his purpose, would cause alarm or apprehension to an average observer." He continues at 271: "Under the standards here suggested, Oviedo's attorney would face a most difficult task. Too much evidence speaks against his client. Not only had Oviedo promised heroin to the government agent, but he had also stored a large amount of the procaine hydrochloride in his television set—certainly an odd place to keep substances which one regards as innocent. Both elements, taken together, would strongly suggest to our hypothetical observer that Oviedo intended to sell a controlled substance, particularly since the hiding of the powder is not consistent with the possible alternative purpose of 'ripping off' the supposed customer. Inasmuch as the observer feels threatened by persons dealing in drugs, he would be alarmed by Oviedo's conduct. The original conviction, which was overturned by the Fifth Circuit, therefore was probably the correct decision of the case."

8. Enker, supra, at 685–87: "[I]n drafting the substantive statute involved in *Jaffe,* nothing prevented the legislature from defining the crime as the possession of goods in the belief that they are stolen without also requiring that they be in fact stolen. As earlier suggested, a crucial factor justifying legislative delegation of the power to define the act element of attempts in the preparation-attempt cases was the inability of the legislature to provide for the infinitely varying acts in advance. In the case of the circumstantial elements of the crimes here considered—whether the goods are in fact dutiable, are stolen, or are narcotics—the legislature is perfectly capable of deciding in advance whether or not to require the particular element. There is no need to delegate that power to the courts under the attempt rubric. * * *

"We may, therefore, characterize the issue presented by legal impossibility thus: the legislature has defined the substantive crime to require the presence of a particular circumstance; there is no reason why—for cases in which that circumstance is absent but the defendant allegedly thinks it is present—the legislature should delegate to the courts the power or the duty to decide whether that circumstance may be dispensed with; if the legislature were to delegate the issue to the courts—or the courts were to assume it—the courts would have no analytic tools for deciding the issue; delegation to the court of the power to define the elements of a crime after the act raises serious issues of legality, particularly when such analytic tools are lacking; and there are in any event good policy reasons favoring retention of the circumstance as an element of the crime."

9. In *Damms,* the unloaded gun case discussed in *Thomas,* the applicable statute defined an attempt in terms of an act demonstrating that the defendant "would commit the crime except for the intervention of another person or some extraneous factor." Was the dissent in that case correct in saying that the cause of failure was not extraneous because it was defendant's own conduct in omitting to load the gun? Compare Note, 70 Yale L.J. 160, 165 (1960): "Neither opinion adequately utilizes the 'extraneous factor' criterion to examine the potential dangerousness of the offender. The dissent, by ignoring defendant's state of mind, failed to consider the possibility that the act of omission, although directly traceable to the actor, may have been caused by a factor other than the exercise of internal control. Likewise, the majority's definition, by focusing solely upon defendant's awareness at the conscious level of the omission, did not consider the

possibility that failure to load the gun might have resulted from internal control at the unconscious level."

10. Consider the case put by Maxey, J., dissenting in *Commonwealth v. Johnson*, 312 Pa. 140, 167 A. 344 (1933): "Even though a 'voodoo doctor' just arrived here from Haiti actually believed that his malediction would surely bring death to the person on whom he was invoking it, I cannot conceive of an American court upholding a conviction of such a maledicting 'doctor' for attempted murder or even attempted assault and battery. Murderous maledictions might have to be punished by the law as disorderly conduct, but they could not be classed as attempted crimes unless the courts so far departed from the law of criminal attempts as to engage in legislation. A malediction arising out of a murderous intent is not such a substantial overt act that it would support a charge of attempted murder."

Compare *State v. Smith*, 262 N.J.Super. 487, 621 A.2d 493 (1993), affirming defendant's conviction for attempted murder on evidence that inmate Smith, knowing he was HIV-positive, bit a corrections officer with intent to kill him: "[D]efendant contends 'plain error' in the charge in barring the jury from considering the unlikelihood that the AIDS virus could be spread by a bite. * * *

"Defendant invokes the following excerpt from the commentary to the Model Penal Code as authority for his theory: 'if the means selected were absurd, there is good ground for doubting that the actor really planned to commit a crime.' Defendant equates his biting Waddington with a 'voodoo incantation' which is medically incapable of causing death, regardless of whether a person believed to the contrary.

"Again, defendant's theory founders on its premise. There was no proof at trial that biting could not possibly transmit HIV. Rather, the evidence was equivocal, with even defendant's expert conceding that there was at least a 'remote' possibility of transmission. In any event, the objective likelihood of transmission is irrelevant * * *. It is sufficient that defendant believed his attack would infect Waddington. Such a belief would not necessarily be 'absurd' in the same way that a belief in the efficacy of a voodoo curse is unfounded.

"Moreover, even if the voodoo analogy is apt, defendant could still be found guilty if the circumstances showed that defendant was 'dangerous':

Cases can be imagined in which it might well be accurate to say that the nature of the means selected, say black magic, substantially negates dangerousness of character. On the other hand, there are many cases as well where one who tries to commit a crime by what he later learns to be inadequate methods will recognize the futility of his course of action and seek more efficacious means. There are, in other words, many instances of dangerous character revealed by 'impossible' attempts, and to develop a theory around highly exceptional situations ignores the propriety of convictions in these. [*Model Penal Code*, supra, § 5.01, commentary at 316 n. 88.]

"In the present case defendant's violent assaults and venomous harangues before, during and after biting Waddington, all justified an inference that he bore the requisite criminal state of mind * * *. The judge did not err in failing to charge that the jury should consider the probable efficacy of a bite in spreading HIV."

11. Consider *Wilson v. State,* 85 Miss. 687, 38 So. 46 (1905): "Wilson was convicted of an attempt to commit forgery, the court below properly charging the jury that it could not convict of the crime itself. The instrument of which attempt to commit forgery is predicated is a draft for 'two and $^{50}/_{100}$ dollars,' as written out in the body of it, having in the upper right-hand corner the figures '$2.$^{50}/_{100}$,' as is customary in checks, drafts, and notes,

and having plainly printed and stamped on the face of the instrument the words 'Ten Dollars or Less.' Wilson, with a pen, put the figure '1' before the figure '2' in the upper right-hand corner, making these immaterial figures appear '$12.50' instead of '$2.50,' and undertook to negotiate it as $12.50. This was not forgery, because it was an immaterial part of the paper, and because it could not possibly have injured anybody. In order to constitute the crime, there must not only be the intent to commit it, but also an act of alteration done to a material part, so that injury might result. [I]t is enough to say * * * that an instrument void on its face is not the subject of forgery, and in order to be so subject, it must have been capable of working injury if it had been genuine, and that the marginal numbers and figures are not part of the instrument, and their alteration is not forgery.

"This being true, can the conviction of an attempt to commit forgery be sustained in the case before us? We think not. No purpose appears to change anything on the paper except the figures in the margin, and this could not have done any hurt. Our statute confines the crime of forgery to instances where 'any person may be affected, bound, or in any way injured in his person or property.' This is not such a case, and section 974 forbids convicting of an attempt 'when it shall appear that the crime intended or the offense attempted was perpetrated.' In this record the innocuous prefix of the figure '1' on the margin was fully accomplished, and no other effort appears, and, if genuine, could have done no harm; and so the appellant is guiltless, in law, of the crime of which he was convicted."

12. Some have asserted that the *Jaffe* rule is wrong but that nonetheless *Wilson* is correct because, were *Wilson* decided otherwise, "the law of attempt would be used to manufacture a new crime, when the legislature has left the situation outside of the ambit of the law." Glanville Williams, *Criminal Law: The General Part* 634 (2d ed. 1961). Is this consistent? Such persons, complains Mark Kelman, *Interpretive Construction in the Substantive Criminal Law,* 33 Stan.L.Rev. 591, 622 (1981), "simply interpret, without rationale, Wilson's intent narrowly and Jaffe's intent broadly. They view Wilson as intending the most precise deed imaginable—altering the numbers on the check—rather than as intending a broader category of acts—intending to receive money from a bank by aptly altering an instrument. They view Jaffe as intending a broader category of acts—receiving stolen property—rather than intending a precise act—receiving the particular goods that were actually delivered to him. Viewed narrowly, Jaffe 'thought he was committing a crime' but was not because the criminal law does not prohibit receiving unstolen goods. Similarly, viewed broadly, Wilson intended to violate the law of forgery; had he *correctly* altered the instrument (so as to make a bank pay him money), he would have been guilty of the completed crime."

SECTION 4. ABANDONMENT

PEOPLE v. STAPLES

Court of Appeal, Second District, 1970.
6 Cal.App.3d 61, 85 Cal.Rptr. 589.

REPPY, ASSOCIATE JUSTICE.

Defendant was charged in an information with attempted burglary. Trial by jury was waived, and the matter submitted on the testimony contained in the transcript of the preliminary hearing together with exhibits. Defendant was found guilty. Proceedings were suspended before pronouncement of sentence, and an order was made granting defendant probation. The appeal is from the order which is deemed a final judgment.

In October 1967, while his wife was away on a trip, defendant, a mathematician, under an assumed name, rented an office on the second floor of a building in Hollywood which was over the mezzanine of a bank. Directly below the mezzanine was the vault of the bank. Defendant was aware of the layout of the building, specifically of the relation of the office he rented to the bank vault. Defendant paid rent for the period from October 23 to November 23. The landlord had 10 days before commencement of the rental period within which to finish some interior repairs and painting. During this prerental period defendant brought into the office certain equipment. This included drilling tools, two acetylene gas tanks, a blow torch, a blanket, and a linoleum rug. The landlord observed these items when he came in from time to time to see how the repair work was progressing. Defendant learned from a custodian that no one was in the building on Saturdays. On Saturday, October 14, defendant drilled two groups of holes into the floor of the office above the mezzanine room. He stopped drilling before the holes went through the floor. He came back to the office several times thinking he might slowly drill down, covering the holes with the linoleum rug. At some point in time he installed a hasp lock on a closet, and planned to, or did, place his tools in it. However, he left the closet keys on the premises. Around the end of November, apparently after November 23, the landlord notified the police and turned the tools and equipment over to them. Defendant did not pay any more rent. It is not clear when he last entered the office, but it could have been after November 23, and even after the landlord had removed the equipment. On February 22, 1968, the police arrested defendant. After receiving advice as to his constitutional rights, defendant voluntarily made an oral statement which he reduced to writing.

Among other things which defendant wrote down were these:

"Saturday, the 14th * * * I drilled some small holes in the floor of the room. Because of tiredness, fear, and the implications of what I was doing, I stopped and went to sleep.

"At this point I think my motives began to change. The actutal [sic] commencement of my plan made me begin to realize that even if I were to succeed a fugitive life of living off of stolen money would not give the enjoyment of the life of a mathematician however humble a job I might have.

"I still had not given up my plan however. I felt I had made a certain investment of time, money, effort and a certain pschological [sic] commitment to the concept.

"I came back several times thinking I might store the tools in the closet and slowly drill down (covering the hole with a rug of linoleum square. As time went on (after two weeks or so). My wife came back and my life as bank robber seemed more and more absurd."

Defendant's position in this appeal is that, as a matter of law, there was insufficient evidence upon which to convict him of a criminal attempt under Penal Code section 664. Defendant claims that his actions were all preparatory in nature and never reached a stage of advancement in relation to the substantive crime which he concededly intended to commit (burglary of the bank vault) so that criminal responsibility might attach.

In order for the prosecution to prove that defendant committed an attempt to burglarize as proscribed by Penal Code section 664, it was required to establish that he had the specific intent to commit a burglary of the bank and that his acts toward that goal went beyond mere preparation.

The required specific intent was clearly established in the instant case. Defendant admitted in his written confession that he rented the office fully intending to burglarize the bank, that he brought in tools and equipment to accomplish this purpose, and that he began drilling into the floor with the intent of making an entry into the bank.

The question of whether defendant's conduct went beyond "mere preparation" raises some provocative problems. The briefs and the oral argument of counsel in this case point up a degree of ambiguity and uncertainty that permeates the law of attempts in this state. Each side has cited us to a different so-called "test" to determine whether this defendant's conduct went beyond the preparatory stage. Predictably each respective test in the eyes of its proponents yielded an opposite result.

Defendant relies heavily on the following language: "Preparation alone is not enough [to convict for an attempt], there must be some appreciable fragment of the crime committed, *it must be in such progress that it will be consummated unless interrupted by circumstances independent of the will of the attempter,* and the act must not be equivocal in nature." Defendant argues that while the facts show that he did do a series of acts directed at the commission of a burglary—renting the office, bringing in elaborate equipment and actually starting drilling—the facts do not show that he was interrupted by any outside circumstances. Without such interruption and a voluntary desistence on his part, defendant concludes that under the above stated test, he has not legally committed an attempt. The attorney general has replied that even if the above test is appropriate, the trial judge, obviously drawing reasonable inferences, found that defendant was interrupted by outside circumstances—the landlord's acts of discovering the burglary equipment, resuming control over the premises, and calling the police.

However, the attorney general suggests that another test is more appropriate: " * * * Whenever the design of a person to commit crime is clearly shown, slight acts in furtherance of the design will constitute an attempt." (Note absence of reference to interruption.) The People argue that defendant's felonious intent was clearly set out in his written confession; that the proven overt acts in furtherance of the design, although only needing to be slight, were, in fact, substantial; that this combination warrants the affirmance of the attempt conviction.

We suggest that the confusion in this area is a result of the broad statutory language of section 664, which reads in part: "Every person who attempts to commit any crime, but fails, or is prevented or intercepted in the perpetration thereof, is punishable * * *."

An examination of the decisional law reveals *at least two* general categories of attempts, both of which have been held to fall within the ambit of the statute.

In the first category are those situations where the actor does all acts necessary (including the last proximate act) to commit the substantive crime, but nonetheless he somehow is unsuccessful. This lack of success is either a "failure" or a "prevention" brought about because of some extraneous circumstance, e.g., a malfunction of equipment, a miscalculation of operations by the actor or a situation wherein circumstances were at variance with what the actor believed them to be. Certain convictions for attempted murder illustrate the first category. Some turn on situations wherein the actor fires a weapon at a person but misses; takes aim at an intended victim and pulls the trigger, but the firing mechanism malfunctions; plants on an aircraft a homemade bomb which sputters but does not explode. * * *

In the above situations application of the rule * * * which defendant herein seeks to have applied, would appear to be quite appropriate. After a defendant has done all acts necessary under normal conditions to commit a crime, he is culpable for an attempt if he is unsuccessful *because* of an extraneous or fortuitous circumstance.

However, it is quite clear that under California law an overt act, which, when added to the requisite intent, is sufficient to bring about a criminal attempt, need not be the last proximate or ultimate step towards commission of the substantive crime. "It is not necessary that the overt act proved should have been the ultimate step toward the consummation of the design. It is sufficient if it was 'the first or some subsequent step in a direct movement towards the commission of the offense after the preparations are made.' " * * *

This rule makes for a second category of "attempts." * * *

* * * There was definitely substantial evidence entitling the trial judge to find that defendant's acts had gone beyond the preparation stage. Without specifically deciding where defendant's preparations left off and where his activities became a completed criminal attempt, we can say that his "drilling" activity clearly was an unequivocal and direct step toward the completion of the burglary. It was a fragment of the substantive crime contemplated i.e., the beginning of the "breaking" element. Further, defendant himself characterized his activity as the *actual commencement of his plan.* The drilling by defendant was obviously one of a series of acts which logic and ordinary experience indicate would result in the proscribed act of burglary.

The instant case provides an out-of-the-ordinary factual situation within the second category. Usually the actors in cases falling within that category of attempts are intercepted or caught in the act. Here, there was no direct proof of any actual interception. But it was clearly inferable by the trial judge that defendant became aware that the landlord had resumed control over the office and had turned defendant's equipment and tools over to the police. This was the equivalent of interception.

The inference of this nonvoluntary character of defendant's abandonment was a proper one for the trial judge to draw. However, it would seem that the character of the abandonment in situations of this type, whether it be voluntary (prompted by pangs of conscience or a change of heart) or nonvoluntary (established by inference in the instant case), is not controlling. The relevant factor is the determination of whether the acts of the perpetrator have reached such a stage of advancement that they can be classified as an attempt. Once that attempt is found there can be no exculpatory abandonment. "One of the purposes of the criminal law is to protect society from those who intend to injure it. When it is established that the defendant intended to commit a specific crime and that in carrying out this intention he committed an act that caused harm or sufficient danger of harm, it is immaterial that for some collateral reason he could not complete the intended crime."

The order is affirmed.

Notes and Questions

1.   Daniel G. Moriarty, *Extending the Defense of Renunciation,* 62 Temple L.Rev. 1, 9–10 (1989), notes that because of the influence of the Model Penal Code "renunciation has been made a defense by statute in twenty-six states," while "courts in two states, without a legislative provision concerning renunciation, have recognized the defense." Should abandonment be a defense? If so, under what circumstances? Compare *Model Penal Code* § 5.01(4) with *People v. Von Hecht,* 133 Cal.App.2d 25, 283 P.2d 764 (1955) ("Abandonment is a defense if the attempt to commit a crime is freely and voluntarily abandoned before the act is put in process of final execution and where there is no outside cause prompting such abandonment"), and consider also Moriarty, supra, at 31 ("We would do better to return to statutes in line with the original draft of the Model Code, which

required only a 'renunciation of [the actor's] criminal purpose' "). In deciding upon the answers to these questions, consider the fact situations set out in notes 2 through 5 following.

2. "At the time of the alleged offense, appellant was serving a one-to three-year sentence for larceny in the Luzerne County Prison. At about 12:15 a.m., on December 26, 1972, James Larson, a Guard Supervisor at the prison, heard an alarm go off that indicated that someone was attempting an escape in the recreation area of the prison. The alarm was designed so that it could be heard in the prison office, but not in the courtyard. Larson immediately contacted Guards Szmulo and Banik. Initially, the guards checked the prison population, but found no one missing. The three men then conducted a search of the area where the alarm had been 'tripped'. Near the recreation yard between two wings of the prison, they found one piece of barbed wire that had been cut. In addition, Guard Szmulo found a laundry bag filled with civilian clothing. The bags are issued by the prison and are marked with a different number for each prisoner. A check revealed that the bag belonged to appellant.

"At approximately 5:15 a.m., on December 26, the appellant voluntarily approached Larson. Appellant had spent that night on the nine p.m. to five a.m. shift at work in the boiler room, situated near the point where the alarm had been triggered. Appellant explained to Larson 'I was gonna make a break last night, but I changed my mind because I thought of my family, and I got scared of the consequences.' Appellant testified at trial that he had become depressed prior to his decision to escape because he had been denied a Christmas furlough on December 24, 1972. His testimony at trial was consistent with Larson's version of the episode: ' * * * in the yard, I realized that I had shamed my family enough, and I did not want to shame them any more * * *. So I went back to the boiler room and continued working.' "[a]

3. "In the fall of 1980 McDowell purchased two kilograms of cocaine from Fernando Dalmau. Dalmau was arrested later for an unrelated offense and agreed to act as an undercover agent for the Drug Enforcement Administration (DEA).

"In the summer of 1981 Dalmau and McDowell began negotiating another cocaine deal. They discussed the deal in a series of telephone conversations that DEA recorded. McDowell, a resident of Knoxville, Tennessee, agreed to travel to Atlanta, Georgia to make the purchase.

"McDowell, Dalmau and Crane, an undercover DEA agent, met in McDowell's motel room in Atlanta and negotiated the sale of one kilo of cocaine for $58,500. Crane told McDowell that he wanted to see the money before bringing the cocaine into the room. McDowell insisted on examining the cocaine first. Crane and Dalmau left the motel. A few minutes later they returned with two packages of sham cocaine and advised McDowell that he could examine the packages but not test the cocaine until Crane had seen the money. McDowell examined the packages closely and stated: 'This does not look like anything I ever done before. I don't want to buy it.'

"Crane later arrested McDowell in his motel room."

McDowell was charged with attempt to possess cocaine with intent to distribute same.[b]

---

a. *Commonwealth v. McCloskey,* 234 Pa.Super. 577, 341 A.2d 500 (1975). Defendant's conviction for attempted prison breach was reversed on the ground he had never engaged in sufficient acts for such an attempt. Cercone, J., concurring, "would have found little difficulty, for instance, in affirming appellant's conviction had he been apprehended by the guards immediately after he had snipped the barbed wire and crossed the inner fence," but concluded that "appellant's abandonment of his plan is a sufficient defense to the crime of attempted prison breach and should be recognized as such."

b. *United States v. McDowell,* 705 F.2d 426 (11th Cir.1983), affirming defendant's conviction because

4. "The only evidence at trial was the testimony of the complainant, Scott Kodanko. The complainant testified that he was waiting for a bus at about 4:30 P.M. on a Saturday, after leaving work. He was alone in a three-sided plexiglass bus shelter open to the street in downtown Milwaukee. Two men, Mr. Moore and the defendant, entered the bus shelter while a third man, Mr. Levy, remained outside.

"Moore and the defendant stood one to two feet from the complainant. The complainant was in a corner of the shelter, his exit to the street blocked by the two men. Moore asked the complainant if he wanted to buy some cigarettes. The complainant responded that he did not. Moore then said, 'Give us some change.' When the complainant refused, the defendant said 'Give us some change, man.' The defendant repeated this demand in an increasingly loud voice three to four times. The complainant still refused to give the two men change. The defendant then reached into his coat with his right hand at about the waist level, whereupon Moore stated something to the effect of 'put that gun away.' At that point Levy, who had been waiting outside the bus shelter, entered and said to the defendant and Moore 'Come on, let's go.' Levy showed the complainant some money, stating, 'I don't want your money, I got lots of money.'

"The three men left the bus shelter together and entered a restaurant across the street. A few minutes later Moore returned and made 'small talk' with the complainant. The three men were arrested a short while later. It appears from the record that the complainant did not report the incident to the police. The record does not reveal who called the police.

"The complainant testified that he felt threatened throughout the encounter, which lasted less than three minutes. None of the men ever touched him or raised a hand to him, and at no time did he attempt to leave the shelter."[c]

5. "On March 3, 1965 at 6:55 p.m., the complaining witness, Jodean Randen, a housewife, was walking home across a fairly well-traveled railroad bridge in Eau Claire. She is a slight woman whose normal weight is 95 to 100 pounds. As she approached the opposite side of the bridge she passed a man who was walking in the opposite direction. The man turned and followed her, grabbed her arm and demanded her purse. She surrendered her purse and at the command of the man began walking away as fast as she could. Upon discovering that the purse was empty, he caught up with her again, grabbed her arm and told her that if she did not scream he would not hurt her. He then led her— willingly, she testified, so as to avoid being hurt by him—to the end of the bridge. While walking he shoved her head down and warned her not to look up or do anything and he would not hurt her.

"On the other side of the bridge along the railroad tracks there is a coal shack. As they approached the coal shack he grabbed her, put one hand over her mouth, and an arm around her shoulder and told her not to scream or he would kill her. At this time Mrs. Randen thought he had a knife in his hand. He then forced her into the shack and up against the wall. As she struggled for her breath he said, 'You know what else I want,' unzipped his pants and started pulling up her skirt. She finally succeeded in removing his hand from her mouth, and after reassuring him that she would not scream, told him she was pregnant and pleaded with him to desist or he would hurt her baby. He then felt of her

"McDowell spurned the deal not to renounce his criminal intent but because he doubted either the genuineness or quality of the cocaine."

c. *State v. Stewart*, 143 Wis.2d 28, 420 N.W.2d 44 (1988), affirming defendant's conviction for attempted robbery because the attempt statute "does not express-

ly make voluntary abandonment a defense," and the court deemed it inappropriate to "distort the statutory language to incorporate the defense," as the "public policy arguments in favor of the defense are better addressed to the legislature than to the court."

stomach and took her over to the door of the shack, where in the better light he was able to ascertain that, under her coat, she was wearing maternity clothes. He thereafter let her alone and left after warning her not to scream or call the police, or he would kill her."[d]

6.   When abandonment is a defense, the abandonment, to be effective, need not inevitably come before the time the defendant has otherwise done everything necessary to be guilty of attempting a crime. But, is there a point short of actually committing the attempted crime when it is too late? Consider Moriarty, supra, at 51–53:

"In [*State v.*] *Smith*, [409 N.E.2d 1199 (Ind.App.1980)], the defendant quarreled with his uncle Melvin while both were intoxicated. After Smith stabbed his uncle twice in the chest, the uncle fled, pursued for a block by an agitated, knife-wielding Smith, who caught up with his uncle when Melvin had collapsed from loss of blood. Smith then suddenly suffered a change of heart, became remorseful and broke into tears, threw down his knife and rushed his uncle to the hospital where emergency surgery saved his life. Smith was charged both with battery and attempted murder. The trial court directed a verdict for defendant as to the attempted murder charge upon the ground of abandonment. The State appealed solely on the issue of whether the trial court had erred in ruling that Smith 'had abandoned the crime of attempted murder after he had inflicted serious knife wounds upon his intended victim.' The battery charge was not reviewed. The court held against Smith, stating that ' "[a]ttempted murder cannot be purged after the victim has been wounded, no matter what may cause the plan to be abandoned" ' and that ' "[o]bviously ... it would hardly do to excuse the defendant from attempted murder after he had wounded the intended victim." ' The court went on to note that where an actor 'has put in motion forces which he is powerless to stop, then the attempt has been completed and cannot be abandoned' and ruled that '[h]ere, abandonment came too late.'

" * * * Insofar as the incentive to desist rationale is emphasized, [a contrary] rule seems superior. Uncle Melvin, although stabbed, has not yet been killed * * *. If the promise of legal rewards may be thought to have some influence on conduct, we have reason to offer impunity to the assailant. The fact that many who have considered the renunciation defense are reluctant to do so underscores the inability of the incentive to desist argument to serve as a complete rationale for the defense.

"Insofar as the proof of dangerousness rationale is emphasized it is not entirely clear which rule is superior. It can be argued that the actor's renunciation once, for example, he has assaulted his victim does not rebut the prima facie proof of dangerousness provided by his attempt. He has shown that he can muster up the fortitude necessary to carry our a criminal aggression, hence, we have sufficient reason to fear his future conduct. Contrarily, it can be argued that the actor has proved by his renunciation that he could not carry his plan through. He has not shown himself as a man to be feared for he could not let the harm occur while he had the power to stop it. Both arguments seem plausible and the choice between them may be settled by the 'Uncle Melvin' test: at the next Smith family gathering, does Uncle Melvin have reason to feel apprehensive when his nephew takes up the carving knife to slice the roast turkey? One's conclusion on the alternative arguments under the proof of dangerousness rationale is apt to depend upon one's judgment as to the feelings a reasonable Uncle Melvin is likely to have.

---

d. *Le Barron v. State,* 32 Wis.2d 294, 145 N.W.2d 79 (1966), affirming defendant's conviction of attempted rape. The defendant on appeal did not claim that he should have a defense of abandonment. Rather, he unsuccessfully claimed (i) that the evidence did not show beyond a reasonable doubt an intent to rape, and (ii) that the woman's pregnancy was not an "extraneous factor" under the Wisconsin attempt statute, which defines an attempt as conduct demonstrating the defendant "would commit the crime except for the intervention of another person or some other extraneous factor."

"Another argument that may be raised at this point is the retributive claim that the actor, in justice, ought to pay for the harm he has wrongfully caused. A reply to the claim is available: the actor may be punished for those wicked deeds he has committed without denying him the defense of renunciation as to those harms he has wrongfully avoided causing. It appears that the battery charges were so clearly established in *Smith*, for example, that they were not even brought before an appellate court. It seems no affront to justice to convict such actors of battery, or of whatever other crimes are appropriate depending upon the harms they in fact have caused, and yet to extend to them a defense of renunciation as to those harms they have averted. Smith did act voluntarily, both to injure his uncle and to prevent the more serious harm of homicide. To make a renunciation defense available to the charge of attempted murder only, and not to battery, seems entirely consistent with conceptions of retributive justice."

7. Consider Mark Kelman, *Interpretive Construction in the Substantive Criminal Law,* 33 Stan.L.Rev. 591, 628–30 (1981): "Suppose a defendant sets out to shoplift from a department store. He has taken steps sufficient to constitute an attempt, were he to be interrupted by external forces. However, he stops of his own accord because: (a) he decides that stealing is bad; (b) he decides that stealing is too risky; (c) he spots a warning that 'Shoplifters will be apprehended and prosecuted'; or (d) he spots the store detective watching him. Many jurisdictions would exculpate the defendant in any of the first three situations. But none would allow a voluntary abandonment defense in the last case. They would find the defendant guilty of attempt if he decided that unpredicted legal consequences would befall him and so decided 'to postpone the criminal conduct until a more advantageous time or to transfer the criminal effort to another but similar objective or victim.' In other words, using interpretive construction language, if the defendant abandons because of fear of legal consequences on the particular occasion, he has still demonstrated an intent to commit the categorical crime of theft, but has simply shifted the instance of the category. * * *

"This particular interpretive construction seems defensible, at least at first blush. The person who reads the sign has not discovered anything unique to the particular situation. There appears to be no reason *not* to equate the abandonment of this larceny with the abandonment of larcenies in general, because other larcenies appear to pose the same threats. But imagine that one defendant decides not to crack a safe because he discovers there is an alarm system he cannot crack, while another desists when he discovers there are alarm systems in general, none of which he *ever* can hope to crack. The first safecracker is looking for an easier safe system to break, the second for an object of his larcenous desires that is unprotected. Both could be seen as simply looking for safer targets. Yet it is implausible that a defendant who abandoned his attempted crime because he read a sign, 'This Safe Protected by Alarms' could be convicted while one who read a sign, 'Safe-crackers will be Apprehended and Prosecuted' would be acquitted. Both are simply being informed of the riskiness of their activity. It is simply unwarranted assertive construction to treat these defendants as renouncing larceny because they renounce *this* larceny. It is not clear how we would ever know that someone is moving on to a more advantageous time and place for his mischief, rather than abandoning a life of crime because he has at least understood the social signals about the costs of crime. It is quite plain we cannot *know* that, because the social signals concerning the propriety of cost-benefit calculation are ambivalent and uninterpretable. We suppress the recognition of this ambivalence by asserting clear cases of total acceptable renunciation and by blocking the knowledge that in a world where selfish calculation is acceptable, all renunciations are in significant senses partial."

SECTION 5. PROSECUTION AND PUNISHMENT

1. *Charge of completed crime, conviction of attempt.* Assume that *A* has been charged with and is on trial for the offense of burglary, but during the course of the trial the evidence develops in such a way that it appears *A* may have only attempted the offense of burglary. May *A* be convicted of attempted burglary? At one time the answer was no, for while it was generally recognized that when a charge of an offense included within it a lesser offense the defendant could be convicted of that lesser crime, this rule was subject to one important qualification: upon an indictment for a felony, the defendant could not be convicted of a misdemeanor. Thus a conviction for the common law misdemeanor of attempt could not be had upon an indictment charging the felony of burglary.

Insofar as can be determined, that exception was based upon the fact that under early English criminal procedure a defendant in a felony trial had fewer rights than a defendant on trial for a misdemeanor. That quite clearly is not the case in the United States, and thus there has been no reason to honor this exception in this country. The courts are in general agreement that an attempt conviction may be had on a charge of the completed crime, and statutes to this effect are not uncommon.

This is not to say, however, that upon any charge of a completed crime the trier of fact will inevitably be confronted with the possibility of returning a verdict or finding of only an attempt. The judge may give an instruction on the attempt alternative only if the evidence would support such a verdict. For example, if on *A's* trial for burglary *A* merely interposes an alibi defense or admits to being within the dwelling but claims to have been acting with an innocent intent, then the only logical alternatives are guilty of burglary or not guilty. On the other hand, if *A* asserts that he had not yet entered at the time of his apprehension, then the third alternative of guilt of attempted burglary exists. In such a case the attempt alternative may go to the jury even over the defendant's objection.

2. *Charge of attempt, proof of completed crime.* Quite obviously, a defendant charged only with an attempt may not be convicted of the completed crime. That is, if *A* had been on trial only for attempted burglary but it was shown at trial that he had actually entered the dwelling, clearly *A* may not be convicted of the greater uncharged offense of burglary. But, under those facts may he even be convicted of attempted burglary? As we have seen, the crime of attempt is often defined as if failure were an essential element, and on this basis it has sometimes been held that proof of the completed crime requires reversal of an attempt to commit it. The assumption that failure is required may be derived from the old common law rule of merger, whereby if an act resulted in both a felony and a misdemeanor the misdemeanor was said to be absorbed into the felony. (Taking that as the basis of the rule, then the problem would not arise if the completed crime would also be only a misdemeanor or, in the alternative, if the completed crime would be a felony but an attempt to commit it had by statute also been made a felony.)

The English merger rule was laid to rest by statute in 1851, and there seems no reason to follow it in this country. As one court observed, a defendant can hardly complain "where the determination of his case was more favorable to him than the evidence warranted." *People v. Vanderbilt*, 199 Cal. 461, 249 P. 867 (1926). Thus, many recent cases have held that a defendant may be convicted of the attempt even if the completed crime is proved, and many jurisdictions expressly so provide by statute.

3. *Punishment.* Considerable variation is to be found across the country concerning the authorized penalties for attempt. As to statutory provisions concerning the sentences which may be imposed for all or a broad class of attempts, the most common permits a penalty up to one-half the maximum penalty for the completed crime, except that a specific

maximum is set for attempts to commit crimes punishable by death or life imprisonment. Another common provision establishes categories according to the severity of the penalty for the completed crime and specifies a range of penalties for attempts to commit crimes within each category, while some states have a combination of these two patterns. A few jurisdictions have set a maximum penalty for all attempts encompassed by the general attempt statute, and a few others merely provide that the penalty for attempt may be as great as for the completed crime. As to statutes dealing with attempts to commit particular crimes, the authorized punishment is usually lower than for the completed crime, but in some instances the same or even a higher punishment is possible.

Taking into account the rationale of the crime of attempt, what kind of penalty provisions would be most sensible?

Chapter 11

CONSPIRACY AND SOLICITATION

SECTION 1. CONSPIRACY: INTRODUCTION

The definition of conspiracy which persists in those jurisdictions retaining common law crimes is: a combination between two or more persons formed for the purpose of doing either an unlawful act or a lawful act by unlawful means. (Where conspiracy is defined by statute, the common law definition is sometimes followed, elsewhere other language is used which makes it apparent that some noncriminal objectives are also covered, while some states have now limited conspiracy to criminal objectives.) Although a more precise definition of conspiracy may be difficult, it is useful to keep in mind that conspiracy, like most other offenses, requires both an act and an accompanying mental state. The agreement constitutes the act, while the intention to achieve the objective is the mental state.

Some years ago, Judge Learned Hand called conspiracy "the darling of the modern prosecutor's nursery,"[a] and this characterization certainly is not without justification. It is clear that a conspiracy charge gives the prosecution certain unique advantages and that one who must defend against such a charge bears a particularly heavy burden.

1. *Vagueness.* The criticism which commentators have voiced most often and most strongly is that there is an inherent vagueness in the crime of conspiracy. "In the long category of crimes there is none," wrote Dean Harno, "not excepting criminal attempt, more difficult to confine within the boundaries of definitive statement than conspiracy."[b] Professor Sayre, in his classic article on the subject, noted: "A doctrine so vague in its outlines and uncertain in its fundamental nature as criminal conspiracy lends no strength or glory to the law; it is a veritable quicksand of shifting opinion and ill-considered thought."[c] And Justice Jackson, in his oft-quoted concurring opinion in *Krulewitch v. United States,*[d] referred to conspiracy as an "elastic, sprawling and pervasive offense, * * * so vague that it almost defies definition [and also] chameleon-like [because it] takes on a special coloration from each of the many independent offenses on which it may be overlaid."

2. *Venue.* The Sixth Amendment provides that in "all criminal prosecutions, the accused shall enjoy the right to a speedy and public trial, by an impartial jury of the State

a. *Harrison v. United States,* 7 F.2d 259, 263 (2d Cir.1925).

b. Albert J. Harno, *Intent in Criminal Conspiracy,* 89 U.Pa.L.Rev. 624 (1941).

c. Francis B. Sayre, *Criminal Conspiracy,* 35 Harv. L.Rev. 393 (1922).

d. 336 U.S. 440, 69 S.Ct. 716, 93 L.Ed. 790 (1949).

and district wherein the crime shall have been committed." Similarly, most state constitutions also provide that a defendant in a criminal case is entitled to be tried in the county, parish, or district where the crime occurred. These venue provisions constitute an important constitutional guarantee, for they "safeguard against the unfairness and hardship involved when an accused is prosecuted in a remote place."[e]

Given the common reference to the agreement in conspiracy as the "gist" of the offense, it might be thought that the place of trial for conspiracy prosecutions must be the place where the agreement was made. But, while it has long been settled that a conspiracy prosecution may be brought at the place of agreement, it is clear that the prosecution may also elect to have the trial in any locale where any overt act by any of the conspirators took place. Although it is argued in support of this rule that if it were otherwise conspiracy prosecutions would often be impossible because of the frequent difficulty of proving the place of agreement, the rule makes it possible for the prosecution to select a district inconvenient to the defendant or one in which a jury may be more disposed to convict.

3. *Hearsay exception.* The general rule that hearsay is not admissible in a criminal prosecution is marked by many exceptions. One of these is the co-conspirator exception: any act or declaration by one co-conspirator committed during and in furtherance of the conspiracy is admissible against each co-conspirator. The rationale most often given for this exception is that each of the conspirators is the agent of all the others.

However, the co-conspirator hearsay exception as applied often extends beyond that rationale. The requirement that the act or statement be in furtherance of the conspiracy is often applied broadly, with the result that any evidence somehow relating to the conspiracy comes in. Sometimes statements are admitted into evidence notwithstanding the fact that they were made prior to the formation of the conspiracy or after its termination. And on the ground that the addition of a new member does not create a new conspiracy, statements by one conspirator are held admissible against others who joined the group after they were made.

Another requirement of the co-conspirator hearsay exception is that a statement by one conspirator is not admissible against the others unless the existence of the conspiracy has been independently established. However, courts have been sympathetic to the problems of the prosecution in presenting evidence in a vast conspiracy case, and thus have admitted evidence falling under the exception, subject to an instruction to the jury that such evidence is not to be considered against the other defendants if independent proof of the conspiracy is not thereafter presented. As Justice Jackson saw it, "In other words, a conspiracy often is proved by evidence that is admissible only upon assumption that conspiracy existed. The naive assumption that prejudicial effects can be overcome by instructions to the jury * * * all practicing lawyers know to be unmitigated fiction."

4. *Circumstantial evidence.* Most conspiracy convictions are based upon circumstantial evidence, and this evidence is often admitted under rather loose standards of relevance. As one court put it, "Wide latitude is allowed [the prosecution] in presenting evidence, and it is within the discretion of the trial court to admit evidence which even remotely tends to establish the conspiracy charged."[f]

5. *Joint trial.* When several defendants have been charged as participants in a single conspiracy, they may be required to defend against the charges in a single trial, which may present added disadvantages for the several defendants. For one thing, what would otherwise be rights individual to each defendant may become, in effect, group rights which

---

e. *United States v. Cores,* 356 U.S. 405, 407, 78 S.Ct. 875, 877, 2 L.Ed.2d 873, 876 (1958).

f. *Nye & Nissen v. United States,* 168 F.2d 846, 857 (9th Cir.1948).

must be exercised jointly by all of the defendants. The greatest danger, however, is that the probability of an individual defendant being convicted may be greatly enhanced by his association through joinder with the others. This is particularly true when there is a long, complicated trial involving many defendants, where the jury may have great difficulty in keeping the evidence and jury instructions straight as they apply to particular defendants.[g]

6. *Rationale.* However, even those who have voiced such criticisms have acknowledged that "the basic conspiracy principle has some place in modern criminal law."[h] The crime of conspiracy is said to serve two important but different functions: (1) as with solicitation and attempt, it is a means for preventive intervention against persons who manifest a disposition to criminality; and (2) it is also a means of striking against the special danger incident to group activity.

SECTION 2. THE AGREEMENT

UNITED STATES v. JAMES

United States Court of Appeals, Fifth Circuit, 1976.
528 F.2d 999.

Brewster, District Judge:

[The seven appellants were convicted of conspiracy to commit the offenses of (i) assault on federal officers engaged in the performance of their duties, (ii) using firearms to commit the assault, and (iii) possessing unregistered firearms. The conspiracy was claimed to have begun about July 15 and to have continued to August 18, when it culminated in a shoot-out between FBI agents and local police, on the one hand, and the appellants, on the other, at the "capitol" of the Republic of New Africa (RNA) in Jackson, Miss. The RNA claims to be an independent foreign nation composed of "citizens" descended from Africans who were at one time slaves in this country. The officers lived and worked in the "capitol," a residential building; some "citizens" and potential "citizens" stayed there for periods of time. The substantial part of a three-day meeting at the "capitol" in mid-July was devoted to discussion of security measures for RNA officials and the "capitol." Drills with weapons were held periodically during the two months following, and "citizens" participating were taught that, upon the command "jump," they should go to certain vantage points where they could fire upon persons trying to intrude. The FBI was kept posted on these developments by an informer posing as a "citizen." A reliable informant told the FBI that one Steiner, for whom they had an arrest warrant for unlawful flight to avoid prosecution, was present in the "capitol," so 15 FBI agents and 12 local police planned a raid on those premises. They took positions around the building and then, using a bullhorn, advised the occupants of their authority and purpose and that the occupants should leave the building. When no response was forthcoming, tear gas cannisters were fired into the building, and

g. Paul Marcus, *Criminal Conspiracy Law: Time to Turn Back from an Ever Expanding, Ever More Troubling Area,* 1 Wm. & Mary Bill Rts.J. 1, 10–11 (1992): notes: "Perhaps the most striking change in the conspiracy area during the past two decades has been the enormous number of cases involving many defendants, complex evidentiary issues, and dozens and dozens of complicated charges. While it was not highly unusual twenty years ago to see such big and cumbersome cases, today it is absolutely commonplace * * *

"It is difficult to imagine how a jury goes about sorting the testimony of hundreds of witnesses, or

considering evidence it heard more than a year earlier. Indeed, how does a jury begin to apply the reasonable doubt standard when there are more than fifty counts charging more than a dozen different individuals? In today's world of conspiracy prosecution, however, such a situation—while perhaps not the norm—occurs with great frequency. And the impact on individual defendants can be quite severe."

h. *Krulewitch v. United States,* 336 U.S. 440, 448, 69 S.Ct. 716, 721, 93 L.Ed. 790, 797 (1949) (Jackson, J., concurring).

simultaneously a heavy barrage of gunfire came from the "capitol." One police officer was killed; one officer and one FBI agent were wounded. About 20 minutes later, several persons exited the building. After *Miranda* warnings were given to them, Norman, Shillingford, James and Jackson (not one of the appellants) admitted firing from the building. Stalling said he did not fire because he was engaged in getting the two females (Austin and Lockhart) into a fortified bunker. The two women denied firing any weapons. After it was determined that Steiner was not in the building, the authorities turned their attention to another building to which the RNA was in the process of moving. A similar announcement by bullhorn was made, and four persons (including Henry) exited. Henry had a fully loaded ammunition clip in his pocket. Various weapons were found in plain view in both premises.]

All of the appellants contend that the evidence is insufficient to support any conviction under the conspiracy count. The principal grounds urged in support of this contention are: (1) the evidence did not show (a) any *agreement* to assault, intimidate or interfere with anyone, or (b) any "knowledge that federal officers would come in conflict with the essentially defensive precautions"; or (2) any connection of any individual defendant with the conspiracy. * * *

The discussion of appellants in support of their contention would be more fitting for a jury argument. They take a view of the evidence most favorable to themselves; and, when evidence supporting the government's theory stands in their way, they insist that it is not credible. Other shortcomings in their contentions are that they assume that a conspiracy must be based on an express agreement; that it must be full and complete from the beginning; that it is not subject to change; and that each participant must have full knowledge of all its details. * * *

The facts above stated, along with others included in the statement of the case at the beginning of the opinion, are adequate to establish a common plan among the appellants alleged as the basis of the conspiracy. The actions of the defendants themselves are always important circumstances from which to draw inferences of a conspiracy. The manner in which the appellants acted during the shoot-out on the morning of August 18 was strong evidence of a common plan and certainly showed concerted action. They did not go about things haphazardly in trying to carry out what some of the RNA "citizens" had called their "combat-win procedures". The evidence of a common plan or unlawful combination is much stronger in this case than it was in many of the cases cited under this heading, where the evidence was held to be sufficient. There is no doubt that there was a common plan to defy, intimidate and shoot it out with any law enforcement officers when the opportunity presented itself.

The following legal principles support the Court's holding that the evidence is sufficient to show the existence of the agreement or common design which formed the basis for the conspiracy alleged in the indictment. To establish the common plan element of a conspiracy, it is not necessary for the government to prove an express agreement between the alleged conspirators to go forth and violate the law. The "common purpose and plan may be inferred from a 'development and collocation of circumstances'." *Glasser v. United States,* 1942, 315 U.S. 60, 80, 62 S.Ct. 457, 469, 86 L.Ed. 680, 704. "A conspiracy is seldom born of 'open covenants openly arrived at.'" "The proof, by the very nature of the crime, must be circumstantial and therefore inferential to an extent varying with the conditions under which the crime may be committed." *Direct Sales Co. v. United States,* 1943, 319 U.S. 703, 714, 63 S.Ct. 1265, 1270, 87 L.Ed. 1674, 1683. Knowledge by a defendant of all details or phases of a conspiracy is not required. It is enough that he knows the essential nature of it. *Blumenthal v. United States,* 1947, 332 U.S. 539, 68 S.Ct. 248, 92 L.Ed. 154.

"And, it is black letter law that all participants in a conspiracy need not know each other; all that is necessary is that each know that it has a 'scope' and that for its success it requires an organization wider than may be disclosed by his personal participation." * * *

The claims of each of the appellants that the evidence is insufficient to connect him or her with the conspiracy, if it was established, must be judged in the light of the legal principles that follow in this paragraph. Once the existence of a common scheme of a conspiracy is shown, slight evidence is all that is required to connect a particular defendant with the conspiracy. The connection may be shown by circumstantial evidence. "A person may be held as a conspirator although he joins the criminal concert at a point in time far beyond the initial act of the conspirators. If he joins later, knowing of the criminal design, and acts in concert with the original conspirators, he may be held responsible, not only for everything which may be done thereafter, but also for everything which has been done prior to his adherence to the criminal design * * *". The fact that a conspirator is not present at, or does not participate in, the commission of any of the overt acts does not, by itself, exonerate him.

A few conclusory comments based on the facts already set out will suffice in the discussion of the question of the sufficiency of the evidence to show the connection, or lack of it, of each defendant with the conspiracy. It would unduly lengthen this opinion to do otherwise.

Henry. He was the President of RNA. All of the "security" measures and "combat-win procedures" were planned and practiced under his direct supervision. He had made public threats of violence against law enforcement officers who might come to the "capitol". Within less than a month of the shoot-out, he held a meeting wherein instructions were given RNA "citizens" to shoot people, especially police officers and FBI Agents, who might try to intrude the "capitol". The shoot-out went according to the plan and procedure he had helped set up. While he was at the Lynch Street house to which the "capitol" was being moved, instead of the Lewis Street "capitol", at the time of the shoot-out, his presence and participation in the shoot-out were not necessary to support his conviction under the conspiracy count. * * * The overwhelming evidence shows that this tragedy would not have taken place except for the work of Henry.

Norman. He was Vice–President of RNA, and had been actively involved in RNA in Jackson for some time. He and President Henry designated the chain of command for the security forces. He assisted Henry in the RNA meeting in July when instructions were given to shoot intruders attempting to enter the "capitol", especially police and FBI Agents. He admitted just after the shoot-out that he was a participant in it. He said he was firing a British 303 gun from inside the house.

James. He held the title of Interior Minister of the RNA. He lived at the Lewis Street "capitol" for most of six weeks before August 18. He was a participant in the "combat-win procedure" drills. He was in charge of the arsenal of some 30 weapons and ammunition to be used in carrying out the common plan. It was his job to assign the weapons to members of the crack security guard. He discussed the bomb and the Molotov cocktails with such members and told them how to use them. He told the officers shortly after the shoot-out that he had shot at any white man he saw. His fingerprints were on the automatic rifle found under the house beside a pile of spent rounds after the shoot-out. He was one of the main actors in the conspiracy.

Toni Rene Austin. As Minister of Finance of the RNA, she was in charge of the treasury. She lived with her husband, appellant James, in the room in the back part of the "capitol" where the arsenal and ammunition for the security guard were kept. She did guard duty at the "capitol", and participated in the "jump" drills. On July 27, she wrote out a list of ammunition to be bought for use by the security guard. The ammunition was not purchased until the night before the shoot-out.[17] She was in the "capitol" when the officers made their announcements on the morning of August 18, but did not come out until forced by tear gas to do so after the shootout.

Shillingford. He was a "citizen" of the RNA. He had come to Jackson a few days before the shoot-out to participate in the RNA activities at the "capitol". He stayed at the "capitol" and was an active "citizen" there. He was the one who went on the night of August 17 and got the ammunition which was on the list prepared by appellant Toni Austin on July 27. He was a member of the crack security guard, and fired an M–1 rifle from his station inside the west part of the "capitol" during the shoot-out.

Stalling. He was an active "citizen" of the RNA. He lived in the Lewis Street "capitol". He helped dig the escape tunnel which was to figure importantly in the security procedures when it was finished. He did active guard duty at the "capitol" and participated in the "jump" drills. He took the female defendants to the escape tunnel during the shooting.

Under the circumstances, a reasonably-minded jury could well conclude beyond a reasonable doubt that the conspiracy alleged actually existed, and that the appellants, Henry, Norman, James, Austin, Shillingford and Stalling, were each members of it. That leaves the question of the sufficiency of the evidence to connect Ann Lockhart with it.

Lockhart. Her residence was in Wisconsin. She was not a "citizen" of RNA, but she obviously sympathized with its objectives. Her husband was appellant Norman, the Vice-President of RNA. She had spent over a month of the summer in Africa, and was not in Jackson for the People's Center Council in July. She arrived at the Lewis Street "capitol" on August 16, and stayed with her husband until after the shoot-out. On August 16 and 17, she purchased groceries and prepared meals for the occupants of the "capitol". Her stopover there was intended to be very short, as her plans were to leave for North Carolina on the morning of August 18. The evidence is insufficient to show that she had any knowledge of the conspiracy or participation in it. There is nothing in the record to justify making her responsible for her husband's unlawful conduct. Mere presence at the scene of a crime or mere association with the members of a conspiracy is not enough to prove participation in it.

Notes and Questions

1. Jack Rude entered a guilty plea to first-degree murder and conspiracy to commit first-degree murder, which the court may accept if a "factual basis" for the plea is established. After Rude recited facts showing he had shot and killed his daughter-in-law with premeditation and deliberation, the court proceeded to inquire about the second count. Rude said that by virtue of statements made to him by his son "many times over the previous * * * two months," he knew from those statements that his son "wanted her [i.e., his wife] dead." Thereafter, "based on [the] son's statements," Rude took a commercial flight from Ohio to Cheyenne, bringing a disassembled pistol in his checked luggage. He reassembled and loaded the gun and used it in shooting his daughter-in-law three times,

---

17. On the night of August 17, some 30 officers made plans to go to the "capitol" the next morning to serve arrest warrants. The following events also occurred on that night: (1) The fugitive, Steiner, left town unexpectedly around 11:00 o'clock. (2) A purchase order for ammunition for the security guard which had lain around for almost three weeks was executed. (3) President Henry did not stay at the Lewis Street "capitol" on that night. Whether the "citizens" of RNA had got wind of the plans for the officers' visit to the Lewis Street "capitol" on the early morning of August 18 does not appear; but the possibility that the three occurrences above described were just coincidences seems somewhat remote.

causing her death.[a] Should the judge accept the plea?

2. "Officer Grimball was the Government's principal witness. He testified that early in the evening of October 9, 1984, he approached Gregory Valentine on the corner of 115th Street and Eighth Avenue and asked him for a joint of 'D'. Valentine asked Grimball whom he knew around the street. Grimball asked if Valentine knew Scott. He did not. Brown 'came up' and Valentine said, 'He wants a joint, but I don't know him.' Brown looked at Grimball and said, 'He looks okay to me.' Valentine then said, 'Okay. But I am going to leave it somewhere and you [meaning Officer Grimball] can pick it up.' Brown interjected, 'You don't have to do that. Just go and get it for him. He looks all right to me.' After looking again at Grimball, Brown said, 'He looks all right to me' and 'I will wait right here.'

"Valentine then said, 'Okay. Come on with me around to the hotel.' Grimball followed him to 300 West 116th Street, where Valentine instructed him, 'Sit on the black car and give me a few minutes to go up and get it.' Valentine requested and received $40, which had been prerecorded, and then said, 'You are going to take care of me for doing this for you, throw some dollars my way?,' to which Grimball responded, 'Yeah.'

"Valentine then entered the hotel and shortly returned. The two went back to 115th Street and Eighth Avenue, where Valentine placed a cigarette box on the hood of a blue car. Grimball picked up the cigarette box and found a glassine envelope containing white powder, stipulated to be heroin. Grimball placed $5 of prerecorded buy money in the cigarette box, which he replaced on the hood. Valentine picked up the box and removed the $5. Grimball returned to his car and made a radio transmission to the backup field team that 'the buy had went down' and informed them of the locations of the persons involved. Brown and Valentine were arrested. Valentine was found to possess two glassine envelopes of heroin and the $5 of prerecorded money. Brown was in possession of $31 of his own money; no drugs or contraband were found on him. The $40 of marked buy money was not recovered, and no arrests were made at the hotel."[b] What result on Brown's appeal of his conviction for conspiracy to distribute heroin?

3. "On the evening of April 4, 1966, a man and woman entered a pharmacy on West Colfax Avenue in Denver, Colorado. The man remained in the front portion of the store and the woman proceeded to the rear and presented a prescription for Dilaudid to the druggist in charge, requesting that it be filled. The druggist described Dilaudid as 'an unusual drug in not too much use today.' Because of the nature of the drug and the handwriting which he suspected not to be genuine, the druggist called the doctor whose name appeared on the prescription blank. As he commenced this telephone inquiry, the woman and man proceeded rapidly from the store. The doctor advised that the prescription was false and the druggist immediately notified the police. Investigating officers presented photographs to the druggist and to a clerk, who each identified the man and the woman, respectively, as Ronald Arthur Ziatz and Lorraine Irene Valdez. Both Valdez and Ziatz were thereafter apprehended and placed under arrest. Miss Valdez was charged jointly with Ziatz in this case, but was tried separately and is not a party to this writ of error.

"The People's evidence showed that the handwriting on the prescription was that of Ziatz. He did not testify and presented only one witness, whose testimony related to his employment prior to the time of the transaction under consideration."[c] What result on his appeal from his conviction for conspiracy to forge a prescription?

a. *Rude v. State*, 851 P.2d 15 (Wyo.1993), overturning defendant's plea.

b. *United States v. Brown*, 776 F.2d 397 (2d Cir. 1985), a 3–1 affirmance of the conviction.

c. *Ziatz v. People*, 171 Colo. 58, 465 P.2d 406 (1970), reversing the conviction.

4. If a defendant is sufficiently involved in a crime to be an accomplice in its commission, does it necessarily follow that he is a member of a conspiracy to commit that crime? Consider *Commonwealth v. Cook*, 10 Mass.App.Ct. 668, 411 N.E.2d 1326 (1980), where a 17–year-old girl stopped on the street to chat with the Cook brothers, Maurice and Dennis. Because she had not met them before and had trouble remembering their names, each of the brothers displayed identification to her and indicated where they were employed. After about 45 minutes, Maurice suggested they walk to a nearby store so he could purchase cigarettes, and he directed the group along a path through a wooded area toward the store. The girl tripped and fell and sat on the ground laughing; Maurice then jumped on her, scratched her with a stick and said, "No blood, no blood." Dennis laughed and said, "The bitch doesn't want to bleed, we'll make her bleed." Maurice then raped the girl; she lost consciousness, awoke later and went home. When Dennis appealed his conviction of conspiracy to rape, claiming insufficient evidence, the prosecution countered that it sufficed the evidence showed Dennis to be an accomplice in the rape under the rule (as stated by the appellate court) that "accomplice liability is based on the defendant's desire to make the crime succeed and is usually established by proof that the defendant was present at the scene, that he assented to the crime occurring, and that he put himself in a position where he could render aid to the perpetrator if it should become necessary." Is this so? Is the evidence sufficient without relying upon that theory?

5. Although courts have found there is no agreement where essential terms have been rejected, *United States v. Melchor–Lopez*, 627 F.2d 886 (9th Cir.1980), or are still a matter of negotiation, *United States v. Iennaco*, 893 F.2d 394 (D.C.Cir.1990), there is no "general rule that as a matter of law there can be no conspiracy without proof of an agreement not merely to carry out an illegal objective but also on such terms as price, quantity, and time, place and manner of delivery." *United States v. Sharif*, 817 F.2d 1375 (9th Cir.1987).

6. The assertion in *James* that only "slight evidence" is needed to connect a particular defendant with a proven conspiracy is commonly found in conspiracy decisions. Given the due process requirement that a particular defendant's guilt be proved beyond a reasonable doubt, how can this be so? Consider *United States v. Alvarez*, 548 F.2d 542 (5th Cir.1977), where defendant appealed his conviction of conspiracy to possess marijuana. Customs agents intervened when a boat which had crossed the Rio Grande was being unloaded. Villareal was arrested, but the others (including a short, stocky man) escaped in the darkness. At Alvarez' trial, Villareal denied having said that Alvarez had been involved, but this testimony was impeached by testimony of the arresting agents that Villareal had told them Alvarez was the stocky man who fled. Said the appellate court: "We note first that the existence of a conspiracy has certainly been established—that the presence of seven men working under cover of darkness on the banks of the Rio Grande to unload 1,600 pounds of marijuana which was floated across the river 'is sufficient to show a concert of action, all parties working together understandingly, with a single design.' Thus, at first blush, it might appear that in reviewing Alvarez' conviction on the conspiracy count we should concern ourselves only with searching for the 'slight evidence' required on appellate review to connect a person with an existing conspiracy, including, at the least, some showing of Alvarez' knowledge of the conspiracy's purpose and some action in his participation therein. Mature reflection has convinced us, however, that the 'slight evidence' rule is of doubtful application to the state of facts presented here, where the issue for review is whether Alvarez was connected with the demonstrated conspiracy *at all*. It being of the nature of a conspiracy to conceal itself, the 'slight evidence' rule finds its proper application where persons are clearly connected to the conspiring group or are found acting in such a manner as unmistakably to forward its purposes. In such instances,

given the clandestine character of such projects, slight additional evidence suffices to base an inference that one who had been shown beyond reasonable doubt to be a participant was as well a *knowing* participant. But where, as here, the question is whether a defendant was connected with the conspiracy at all, to apply such a rule is to risk convicting him of the crime itself upon 'slight evidence.' We conclude that Alvarez' presence at the river must be established by evidence which a jury could conclude rules out any reasonable hypothesis of innocence. Once presence is so established as to his knowing participation, the 'slight evidence' rule may have its day."[d]

Is the distinction convincing?

7. Consider Brent E. Newton, *The Antiquated "Slight Evidence Rule" in Federal Conspiracy Cases*, 1 J.App.Prac. & Process 49, 51–54 (1999): "With respect to the quantum of proof necessary to link a defendant to a criminal conspiracy, virtually every United States Court of Appeals, at one time or the other during the past several decades, has applied the 'slight evidence rule.' That rule provides that, where there is evidence establishing the existence of a conspiracy between at least two other people, the prosecution need only offer 'slight evidence' of a defendant's 'knowing participation' or 'intentional involvement' in the existing conspiracy—that is, the defendant's mens rea—to secure the defendant's conviction. The 'slight evidence rule' was created out of thin air by the Fifth Circuit in 1930 * * *. Other circuits adopted it in the following decades. * * *

"The slight evidence rule was applied only sporadically from 1930 until 1970, when the use of the rule in the lower federal courts 'increased dramatically.' However, by the mid- to late-1970s, the Fifth and Ninth Circuits—the leading proponents of the rule up until that point—stemmed the tide by 'banish[ing]' the slight evidence rule in favor of the requirement that the prosecution must offer 'substantial evidence' that proves 'beyond a reasonable doubt' that a defendant knowingly participated in a conspiracy with others. Such a proof requirement was consistent with the Supreme Court's repeated holding in the 1970s that the Due Process Clause requires proof of every element of an offense 'beyond a reasonable doubt' to uphold a conviction.

"The First, Third, Fourth, Seventh, and Eleventh Circuits followed suit in the next two decades by rejecting the traditional slight evidence rule. Rather than outright abolishing the rule, some courts have purported to reformulate the slight evidence rule by requiring 'substantial evidence' of a defendant's knowing participation in the conspiracy but upholding convictions based on evidence of a defendant's 'slight involvement' in the conspiracy. However, such a reformulation effectively abolished the traditional slight evidence rule insofar as the reformulated rule requires substantial proof of a defendant's mens rea, even if the defendant's relative role in the conspiracy—his actus reus—was extremely minor. Because the gravamen of a criminal conspiracy is a 'meeting of the minds' to break the law, a defendant's degree of participation in furtherance of the conspiracy is not particularly important.

"The Second, Sixth, Eighth, and Tenth Circuits have never abolished or reformulated, and regularly continue to apply, the traditional slight evidence rule in conspiracy cases. Curiously, these circuits have never even addressed the frequently-voiced criticisms of the rule. The Eighth Circuit has taken the lead in applying the slight evidence rule in dozens of conspiracy cases decided in the last few years.

d. The conviction was affirmed. The court relied upon this collection of circumstantial evidence regarding Alvarez' presence: (1) a van found at the scene belonged to him and his 7 brothers; (2) he used the truck more than his brothers; (3) the stocky man fled toward the house of Alvarez' father; (4) Alvarez was the only one of the brothers who was short and stocky; (5) he lied about his identity when arrested; (6) his alibi testimony was somewhat dubious; and (7) Villareal worked at a truck stop owned by one of Alvarez' relatives.

"Perhaps more troubling than these four circuits' failure to abolish the antiquated slight evidence rule is the inexplicable reappearance of the traditional rule by other circuits that had previously claimed to have abolished the rule. During the last decade, panels of the First, Fifth and Ninth Circuits have seemingly ignored their circuits' prior decisions abolishing the slight evidence rule and have continued to apply the traditional rule in conspiracy cases."

STATE v. ST. CHRISTOPHER

Supreme Court of Minnesota, 1975.

305 Minn. 226, 232 N.W.2d 798.

ROGOSHESKE, JUSTICE.

Defendant was found guilty by the court, sitting without a jury, of conspiracy to commit murder, and attempted first-degree murder, and sentenced under the conspiracy conviction to a maximum indeterminate term of 20 years' imprisonment. He contends upon this appeal from the judgment (1) that he was improperly convicted of conspiracy because the evidence shows that the only party with whom he conspired never intended to aid defendant but merely feigned agreement while cooperating with police; (2) that the trial court erred in finding him guilty of attempted murder because the information did not charge him with that crime and attempted murder is not, a lesser included offense of the charge of conspiracy to commit murder * * *. We affirm the conviction of conspiracy and reverse the conviction of attempted first-degree murder.

The facts in this case are relatively simple. On March 16, 1974, defendant (who formerly was named Marlin Peter Olson but legally changed his name to Daniel St. Christopher) stated to his cousin, Roger Zobel, that he wanted to kill his mother, Mrs. Marlin Olson, and that he wanted Zobel's help. He would pay him $125,000 over the years, money defendant would get from his father after his mother was dead. Zobel, the key witness against defendant at his trial on the charge of conspiracy, testified that at no time did he ever intend to participate in the murder but that he discussed the matter with defendant on that and subsequent occasions and acted as if he intended to participate in the plan. On March 18, Zobel contacted the police and told them of defendant's plan and they later told him to continue to cooperate with defendant. The plan, which became definite in some detail as early as March 20, was for Zobel to go to the Olson farmhouse on Saturday, March 23, when defendant's father was at the weekly livestock auction. Since defendant's mother was Zobel's aunt, Zobel could gain entrance readily. The idea was for Zobel to break her neck, hide her body in his automobile trunk, and then attach bricks to it and throw it in a nearby river after dark. Later it developed that defendant's father might not go to the sale on Saturday, so a plan was developed whereby defendant would feign car trouble, call his father for help, then signal Zobel when the father was on his way. Police followed defendant on Saturday when he left his apartment and observed him make a number of telephone calls. In one of these he called his father and told him he was having car trouble and asked him to come and help him pay the bill. In a call to Zobel, which was taped, defendant told Zobel that his father was coming and that Zobel should proceed with the plan. Shortly thereafter, police arrested defendant. * * *

We have not found any Minnesota cases in point on the issue of the validity of the conspiracy conviction. However, in two criminal conspiracy cases this court has stated, or at least implied, that a person cannot be guilty of conspiracy where the only person with whom he has conspired or agreed has feigned agreement. The first of these cases is *State v. Burns,* 215 Minn. 182, 186, 9 N.W.2d 518, 520 (1943), where this court stated that "[t]o constitute a conspiracy to cheat and defraud, there must be not only a combination, but a common object to cheat and defraud, which each member of the combination intends shall be accomplished by the concerted action of all."[2]

The more recent Minnesota case is *State v. Willman,* 296 Minn. 322, 208 N.W.2d 300 (1973). In that case, there was a true meeting of the minds by both defendant and one Toles followed by an overt act in furtherance of the conspiracy to commit murder in the first degree. Subsequently, Toles changed his mind and contacted the police. In holding that there was sufficient evidence that defendant was guilty of conspiracy, this court arguably implied (but did not hold or even say) that this might not be the case if there had not been a true meeting of the minds or if an overt act had not occurred until after Toles contacted the police.

There is extensive authority from other jurisdictions which supports defendant's contention. The reasoning employed in these cases was summarized in Fridman, *Mens Rea in Conspiracy,* 19 Modern L.Rev. 276, as follows:

" * * * Conspiracy is the agreement of two or more to effect an unlawful purpose. Two people cannot agree unless they both intend to carry out the purpose which is stated to be the object of their combination. Therefore there is no agreement, and consequently no conspiracy, where one of the two never intends to carry out the unlawful purpose."[a]

If there had been some evidence to suggest that, contrary to his testimony, Zobel in fact had intended to participate in the conspiracy and had not feigned agreement from the start, then the court as factfinder could have found defendant guilty of conspiracy without rejecting the rule followed in the cited cases. However, the only evidence that the state produced was that Zobel did not intend at any time to participate in the conspiracy and that his agreement was feigned, and the trial court believed this evidence. Therefore, if we accept the rule followed in these cases, we would have to reverse defendant's conviction.

We are persuaded not to accept this rule and base our decision on (a) our belief that the rule is unsound, and (b) our belief that the present conspiracy statute authorizes a conviction in this situation.

(a) One criticism by a number of commentators of the rule followed in the cited cases is that the courts have reached their conclusion by using as a starting point the definition of conspiracy as an agreement between two or more persons, a definition which was framed in cases not involving the issue. As one commentator put it, "if a conspiracy is arbitrarily defined as 'an agreement of intentions and not merely of language (the intentions being unlawful)' the answer to the problem is undoubtedly that where there is no such agreement of intentions then there is no conspiracy." Fridman, *Mens Rea in Conspiracy,* 19 Modern L.Rev. 276, 278. In other words, the basis for the rule is a strict doctrinal approach toward the conception of conspiracy as an agreement in which two or more parties not only objectively indicate their agreement but actually have a meeting of the minds.

Addressing the rule to be applied as a policy issue, a number of commentators have come to the conclusion that there should be no requirement of a meeting of the minds.

2. Actually, this dictum does not accurately state the rule which courts have followed. The fact that A's agreement is feigned does not prevent a conspiracy conviction of B where C is also involved and has not feigned agreement. Note, 72 Harv.L.Rev. 920, 925 note 35.

a. But if there are more than two persons involved, then the fact that one is an undercover agent only feigning agreement is irrelevant, and this is so even if that person served as a link between genuine conspirators who had no direct dealings with one another. See, e.g., *United States v. Fincher,* 723 F.2d 862 (11th Cir.1984).

Thus, Fridman points to cases holding that factual impossibility is no defense to a charge of attempt to commit a crime and argues that, because of close connections between the origins and purposes of the law of conspiracy and of attempt, a similar rule should obtain in conspiracy. Specifically, he argues that "[t]he fact that, unknown to a man who wishes to enter a conspiracy to commit some criminal purpose, the other person has no intention of fulfilling that purpose ought to be irrelevant as long as the first man does intend to fulfill it if he can" because "a man who believes he is conspiring to commit a crime and wishes to conspire to commit a crime has a guilty mind and has done all in his power to plot the commission of an unlawful purpose."

Professor Glanville Williams makes a somewhat similar argument, basing his opinion on the fact that conspiracy, like attempt, is an inchoate crime and that it is the act of conspiring by a defendant which is the decisive element of criminality, for it makes no difference in logic or public policy that the person with whom the defendant conspires is not himself subject to prosecution. Williams, *Criminal Law—The General Part,* § 157(a).

The draftsmen of the Model Penal Code take a slightly different approach. They recognize that conspiracy is not just an inchoate crime complementing the law of attempt and solicitation but that it is also a means of striking at the special dangers incident to group activity. *Model Penal Code* (Tent.Draft No. 10, 1960) § 5.03, Comment. In view of that recognition, it is probably not quite as easy to reject the approach taken by the cases cited, yet this is what the draftsmen have done. The provision which accomplishes this, § 5.03(1), reads as follows:

"A person is guilty of conspiracy with another person or persons to commit a crime if with the purpose of promoting or facilitating its commission he:

"(a) agrees with such other person or persons that they or one or more of them will engage in conduct which constitutes such crime or an attempt or solicitation to commit such crime; or

"(b) Agrees to aid such other person or persons in the planning or commission of such crime or of an attempt or solicitation to commit such crime."

In comments explaining this provision, the reporters state as follows:

"2. *The Conspiratorial Relationship.*

"*Unilateral Approach of the Draft.* The definition of the Draft departs from the traditional view of conspiracy as an entirely bilateral or multilateral relationship, the view inherent in the standard formulation cast in terms of 'two or more persons' agreeing or combining to commit a crime. Attention is directed instead to each individual's culpability by framing the definition in terms of the conduct which suffices to establish the liability of any given actor, rather than the conduct of a group of which he is charged to be a part—an approach which in this comment we have designated 'unilateral.' * * *

"*Second:* Where the person with whom the defendant conspired secretly intends not to go through with the plan. In these cases it is generally held that neither party can be convicted because there was no 'agreement' between two persons. Under the unilateral approach of the Draft, the culpable party's guilt would not be affected by the fact that the other party's agreement was feigned. He has conspired, within the meaning of the definition, in the belief that the other party was with him; apart from the issue of entrapment often presented in such cases, his culpability is not decreased by the other's secret intention. True enough, the project's chances of success have not been increased by the agreement; indeed, its doom may have been sealed by this turn of events. But the major basis of conspiratorial liability—the unequivocal evidence of a firm purpose to commit a crime—remains the same. The result would be the same under the Draft if the only co-conspirator established a defense of renunciation under Section 5.03(6). While both the Advisory Committee and the Council support the Draft upon this point, it should be noted that the Council vote was 14–11, the dissenting members deeming mutual agreement on the part of two or more essential to the concept of conspiracy."[6]

(b) We find the scholarly literature persuasive on this subject.[7] The question is whether this court can take the recommended approach. We think the answer lies in the wording of our statute. The Minnesota statute formerly dealing with the crime of conspiracy read as follows (Minn.St.1961, § 613.70):

"When two or more persons shall conspire:

(1) To commit a crime; * * *

"Every such person shall be guilty of a misdemeanor."

This is the most common type of conspiracy statute, and it is understandable that this type of statute lends itself easily to the result reached by the cases because the statute starts with the phrase, "When two or more persons shall conspire."

However, the Minnesota statute as it presently reads omits this phrase and is now phrased in unilateral terms similar to those used in the Model Penal Code. The provision, Minn.St. 609.175, subd. 2, reads in part:

"Whoever conspires with another to commit a crime and in furtherance of the conspiracy one or more of the parties does some overt act in furtherance of such conspiracy may be sentenced as follows:"

Because of this wording, we hold that the trial court was free to convict defendant of conspiracy under the facts of this case.

The second issue raised by defendant is whether he was properly convicted of attempted murder. We hold that he was not and reverse this part of the judgment.

Because defendant was charged only with conspiracy to commit murder, the trial court could not find him guilty of attempted murder unless attempted murder is an included offense of conspiracy to commit murder. We believe that attempted murder is not, as the state contends, necessarily proved by proof of conspiracy to commit murder. * * *

Notes and Questions

1. Note, 75 Colum.L.Rev. 1122, 1135–37 (1975): "Nearly all jurisdictions [with recent recodifications] have elected to follow the [Model Penal Code] recommendation that conspiracy be redefined as a unilateral, rather than a bilateral (or multilateral), crime. Statutory descriptions of the conspiracy offense have been carefully reworded to focus on the behavior of a single malefactor rather than the collaboration of several wrongdoers.

---

6. The proposed Federal Criminal Code takes a similar approach. The full text of the conspiracy section, § 1–2A5, is reproduced and discussed in Note, 47 Tulane L.Rev. 1017. See, also, Final Report of the National Commission on Reform of Federal Criminal Laws (1971) § 1004.

7. An alternative approach would be to say that in cases of this sort the factfinder may find the defendant guilty of attempted conspiracy. This is the approach recommended in Note, 72 Harv.L.Rev. 920, 926, note

35. The approach is undesirable because it would result in disparate sentences for defendants whose conduct was the same, the length of sentence turning on a fortuity. Thus, if A agreed with B (a policeman who merely feigns agreement) to commit murder, A would be guilty of attempted conspiracy and could receive a maximum of 10 years' imprisonment, whereas if A agreed with C (who does not feign agreement), A could be guilty of conspiracy and could receive a maximum of 20 years' imprisonment. See, Minn.St. 609.17, subd. 4(2), and 609.175, subd. 2(2).

Under a unilateral formulation, the crime of conspiracy is committed *when a person agrees* to proceed in a prohibited manner; under a bilateral formulation, the crime of conspiracy is committed *when two or more persons* agree to proceed in such manner.

"While the basic elements of the offense are identical under either formulation, the unilateral approach is preferred because it solves a number of problems which arise in cases where, for one reason or another, co-conspirators are differently situated with respect to the legal system. By concentrating on individual, rather than group, liability, the guilt of a particular actor is made independent of that of his co-conspirator(s). Such treatment is important when, for example, defendant's only co-conspirator * * * has feigned agreement, usually as part of some law enforcement scheme * * *."

2.   Compare Dierdre A. Burgman, *Unilateral Conspiracy: Three Critical Perspectives*, 29 DePaul L.Rev. 75, 77–78 (1979): "This [unilateral] approach ignores the historical rationale of the common law crime of conspiracy: the threat to society of two or more persons pursuing crime. When one of two conspirators has no intention of pursuing the criminal objective, the rationale for increased punishment is absent. Therefore, although this latest extension of the law appears logical when viewed alongside its judicial precursors, it actually defies its own reason. While the move may be heralded as a step toward more effective law enforcement, it is not justified because society's interest in punishing such conduct is already met by the charges of solicitation and attempt.

"Moreover, because the crime of unilateral conspiracy inevitably punishes predisposition to commit crime, without the safeguards incorporated in bilateral conspiracy, it opens the door to entrapment. Unfortunately, recent judicial treatment of the entrapment defense has curtailed its effectiveness. Courts that have considered the entrapment issue in the context of unilateral conspiracy cases have dismissed it summarily or, after discussion, have deemed it inapplicable."

3.   Is the *St. Christopher* rejection in fn. 7 of the attempted conspiracy alternative sound? Consider Burgman, supra, at 95–96: "With this tour de force, the court constructed what is tantamount to an equal protection rationale for the unilateral doctrine. What it patently ignored was the fact that the two situations differ considerably: in the first, *none* of the justifications for penalizing conspiracy applies; in the second, *all* the rationales apply. The argument simply makes too much of the idea of 'fortuity.' If X shoots at Y and misses, while Z shoots Y and kills Y, the criminal jurisprudence does not seek to punish both X and Z equally, even though it is clear that both X and Z have exhibited a dangerous predisposition. The punishment is commensurate with the harm sustained; this principle is true for both the crime of attempt and the crime of conspiracy."

4.   Is the attempted conspiracy alternative a rational theory when the applicable conspiracy statute does not follow the unilateral approach? See *Hutchinson v. State*, 315 So.2d 546 (Fla.App.1975), concluding that "there is no case law in Florida or other jurisdictions which proscribes or defines attempted conspiracy. * * * To concede in the academic sense the possibility that there can be an attempted conspiracy is not the equivalent of declaring it to be reasonable and a punishable statutory offense. Moreover, the judicial creation of attempted conspiracy to punish solicitation is not needed here to fill a gap in the definition of a crime or to extend the reach of the conspiracy statute. Appellant's conduct could have been reached * * * as common law solicitation, which as of July 1, 1975, will also be a statutory crime."

Query, would or should a court reach a different result if there is no applicable solicitation crime or if that crime is not applicable to the defendant because he attempted to agree with an undercover agent who first solicited him? See *State v. Sexton*, 232 Kan. 539, 657 P.2d 43 (1983) (though defendant's murder solicitation of undercover agent who feigned agreement is "behavior of a type ordinarily prohibited by the criminal statutes," such conduct occurring prior to recent enactment of solicitation statute cannot be prosecuted as attempted conspiracy, for "it is not our function to create a crime where the legislature has not done so").

5.   May a defendant who was not a party to the conspiratorial agreement nonetheless be convicted of conspiracy on the theory that he aided and abetted the conspiracy and thus was an accomplice in the conspiracy? An instruction to that effect was upheld in *United States v. Kasvin,* 757 F.2d 887 (7th Cir.1985), where the defendant claimed to have been nothing more than a customer of an ongoing marijuana distribution conspiracy. The court stated: "The decision in the case of Kasvin's co-defendant, *United States v. Galiffa,* 734 F.2d 306 (7th Cir.1984), established the following principles of law which apply with equal force in this case:

"1. A defendant can be convicted of aiding and abetting a conspiracy for deeds other than acting as a liaison for the parties to the conspiratorial agreement provided the defendant has knowledge of the conspiracy's existence at the time of his act.

"2. One can aid and abet a conspiracy without necessarily participating in the original agreement.

"3. The charge of aiding and abetting under 18 U.S.C. § 2(a) 'need not be specifically pleaded and a defendant indicted for a substantive offense can be convicted as an aider and abettor' upon a proper demonstration of proof so long as no unfair surprise results.

"4. No fatal amendment to an indictment occurs where a defendant may have been convicted as a principal in a conspiracy by aiding and abetting it even though he was not charged with aiding and abetting in the original indictment.

" * * * [I]f the jury simply regarded Kasvin as a major customer of the ring, it was fully justified in finding that he associated himself with the criminal venture, participated in it as something he wished to bring about and sought by his actions to make it succeed. It is difficult to imagine what greater contribution Kasvin could have made to the financial success of the venture than by becoming its largest regular customer. In short, if he was not a member of the conspiracy, he was clearly an aider and abettor of it."

Swygert, J., dissenting, objected: "There is some authority that the only manner in which a defendant may aid and abet a conspiracy is by bringing two other persons together to conspire. There is some merit to this argument because the crime of conspiracy always requires the act of agreement. But it must be that certain other 'extraneous acts' might also aid and abet a conspiracy if they facilitate agreement by keeping the group of conspirators together and the conspiracy going. Thus, liability for aiding and abetting a conspiracy might be imposed on a defendant who brings two parties together with the intention and knowledge that they will conspire, or warns drug conspirators of undercover police activity, or permits one's home to be used as a rendezvous for drug trafficking, or provides police protection to drug dealers, or acts as a paid bodyguard to the principal of an illegal scheme to distribute stolen securities. In these cases, the clear theoretical and practical difference between aiding and abetting a conspiracy and aiding and abetting the substantive offense that is the object of the conspiracy simply was not and could not be merged. * * *

"In this case, the Government insisted at trial that a customer who frequently purchases large amounts of illegal goods from a conspiracy may under certain circumstances be found guilty as a coconspirator. But, as I note in Part III of this dissent, the trial judge found there was insufficient evidence to create an issue as to whether the defendant was a member of the conspiracy, and, even if it was questionable whether the judge was warranted in granting the directed verdict in favor of the defendant, this court may not engage in *de novo* decisionmaking at this juncture by second-guessing the trial judge.

"Under this state of affairs the only charge that remained was that of aiding and abetting, and the only evidence to support this theory of liability was that the defendant was a frequent customer of the organization who bought large amounts of marijuana on credit and who was apparently a friend of the conspirators. But these distributions to the defendant were overt acts and objectives of the conspiracy. They were not extraneous to it; they are analogous to plunging the knife into the murder victim, not to providing the murderer with the knife. * * * Thus, in applying the analysis of what aiding and abetting a conspiracy means, the defendant's conduct did not come within that meaning."

SECTION 3. MENTAL STATE

MITCHELL v. STATE

Court of Special Appeals of Maryland, 1999.

132 Md.App. 312, 752 A.2d 653.

HOLLANDER, JUDGE.

Antoine Markee Mitchell, appellant, was charged with numerous offenses in connection with the assault and shooting of Eddy Arias. Following a jury trial in the Circuit Court for Prince George's County, appellant was convicted of attempted second degree murder, first degree assault, use of a handgun in the commission of a felony, conspiracy to commit second degree murder, and conspiracy to commit first degree assault. At the close of the State's case, the circuit court granted appellant's motion for judgment of acquittal as to the charges of attempted first degree murder, conspiracy to commit first degree murder, and possession of a firearm by a convicted felon. The jury subsequently acquitted appellant of second degree assault. * * *

Sometime between noon and 1:15 p.m. on September 5, 1997, Eddy Arias was shot from behind by two men wearing stocking masks. The bullet entered the victim's right hip area, just above his buttocks, and exited through the other side. The attack occurred in the interior stairwell of the apartment building at which Mr. Arias resided, located at 8805 Barnsley Court in Laurel. [Mitchell and Ellis were later identified as the perpetrators.]

On appeal, Mitchell asserts for the first time that conspiracy to commit second degree murder is not a crime, and therefore his conviction for that offense must be reversed. The indictment charged, inter alia, conspiracy to commit second degree murder, alleging that appellant "did conspire with Gregory Ellis, to feloniously with malice aforethought, kill and murder Eddy Arias in violation of the Common Law of Maryland." * * *

The premise of Mitchell's appellate argument is that the circuit court lacked subject matter jurisdiction with respect to the charge, because any conspiracy to commit murder is necessarily a conspiracy to commit first degree murder, and the court acquitted him of that charge. Thus, appellant contends that when he was convicted of conspiracy to commit second degree murder, he was convicted of an illusory offense. Because appellant's argument is based on the "jurisdictional sufficiency" of the count alleging conspiracy to commit second degree murder, it may be raised on appeal, notwithstanding his failure to raise the issue below. We turn to consider the merits of appellant's contention.

Murder remains a common law crime in Maryland. Common law "murder" is defined as "a killing with 'malice aforethought.' " * * *

The term "malice" includes the presence of the required malevolent state of mind as well as the absence of justification, excuse, or mitigating circumstances. There are four mental states that qualify as "malevolent," and are consequently associated with four kinds of murder: (1) intent-to-kill murder; (2) intent to commit grievous harm murder; (3) felony murder; and (4) depraved heart murder. * * *

A homicide that satisfies the common law definition of murder is then categorized by statute as either murder in the first or second degree. * * *

Murder in the second degree is defined in Md.Code Art. 27, § 411 as those kinds of murder not enumerated in Md.Code, Art. 27, §§ 407 through 410. The aggravating factors that raise a common law/second degree murder to murder in the first degree have been codified in Md.Code, Art. 27, §§ 407 through 410. Sections 408 through 410 provide that a killing committed during the perpetration, or attempted perpetration, of certain felonies qualifies as first degree murder. Murder in the first degree also includes a killing "perpetrated by means of poison, or lying in wait" under section 407. In addition, that section includes a "wilful, deliberate and premeditated killing" as first degree murder.

Although a common law intent-to-kill murder is initially regarded as a second degree murder, the presence of wilfulness, deliberation, and premeditation elevates the offense to murder in the first degree. The Court of Appeals explained in *Tichnell v. State*, 287 Md. 695, 717–18, 415 A.2d 830 (1980):

> For a killing to be "wilful" there must be a specific purpose and intent to kill; to be "deliberate" there must be a full and conscious knowledge of the purpose to kill; and to be "premeditated" the design to kill must have preceded the killing by an appreciable length of time, that is, time enough to be deliberate. It is unnecessary that the deliberation or premeditation shall have existed for any particular length of time. * * *

In order to convict a defendant of conspiracy to commit murder, the State must establish (1) that the defendant entered into an agreement to commit murder (the "agreement element") and (2) that he or she did so with the specific intent to commit the murder (the "intent element"). In connection with the intent element, appellant urges that, without regard to the particular degree of murder, proof of a conspiracy to commit murder requires a showing that the conspirators had the specific intent to kill. We agree.

[O]f the four kinds of common law murder, i.e., intent-to-kill, intent to commit grievous harm, felony, and depraved heart, only intent-to-kill murder is an intended murder. The others are unintended murders. "Intended murder, by definition, comprehends, inter alia, an intended killing, to wit, an intent to kill." Accordingly, when a defendant conspires to commit murder, he or she intends to kill. Stated differently, the specific intent to kill is the only mens rea sufficient to support a conviction for conspiracy to commit murder. It contravenes logic to suggest that a defendant charged with conspiracy to commit murder conspired to commit an unintended murder.

Appellant also argues that if the State proves the intent and agreement elements of a conspiracy to commit murder charge, then it has necessarily established that the defendant intended a "wilful, deliberate and premeditated killing," thereby rendering any charge of conspiracy to commit murder as a conspiracy to commit first degree murder. Mitchell's argument is appealing on the surface. As we discussed above, a specific intent to kill is a prerequisite to a conviction for conspiracy to commit murder. It follows that if the intent to kill is established, it was wilful. What is less clear is whether satisfaction of the "dual" conspiracy elements necessarily evidences deliberation and premeditation. * * *

In urging us to declare that conspiracy to commit second degree murder is not a criminal offense, appellant also directs us to cases from two jurisdictions that have so held. We turn to consider those cases.

In *People v. Hammond*, 187 Mich.App. 105, 466 N.W.2d 335, 337 (1991), the Michigan Court of Appeals held "that conspiracy to commit second-degree murder is not a criminal offense because such a conspiracy is logically inconsistent." * * *

Quoting its [prior] decisions, the *Hammond* Court stated:

"Criminal conspiracy is a specific intent crime which arises from a mutual agreement between two or more parties to do or accomplish a crime or unlawful act. The gist of a criminal conspiracy is the specific, mutual agreement to perform the crime in question; the conspiracy statute provides punishment for the actual advance planning and agreement to perform the substantive criminal acts. However, second-degree murder is distinguishable from first-degree murder in that it does not require premeditation and in fact may not require a specific intent to kill." * * *

"Since prior 'planning' and 'agreement' are necessary, mandatory requisite elements of the crime of conspiracy, we find it analytically consistent to 'plan' to commit first-degree murder but logically inconsistent to 'plan' to commit second-degree murder. To prove a conspiracy to commit murder, it must be established that each of the conspirators have [sic] the intent required for murder and, to establish that intent, there must be foreknowledge of that intent. Foreknowledge and plan are compatible with the substantive crime of first-degree murder as both the crime of conspiracy and the crime of first-degree murder share elements of deliberation and premeditation. Prior planning denotes premeditation and deliberation. The elements of conspiracy, conversely, are incompatible and inconsistent with second-degree murder. One does not 'plan' to commit an 'unplanned' substantive crime. It is not 'absence' of the elements but the 'inconsistency' of the elements which lead [sic] us to conclude that one conspires to commit first-degree murder but not second-degree murder."

Although the issue was framed somewhat differently in *People v. Cortez*, 18 Cal.4th 1223, 77 Cal.Rptr.2d 733, 960 P.2d 537 (1998), the California Supreme Court reached a similar conclusion. * * * The court reasoned:

[C]onspiracy is a specific intent crime requiring both an intent to agree or conspire and a further intent to commit the target crime or object of the conspiracy. Murder that is premeditated and deliberated is murder of the first degree. " '[P]remeditated' means 'considered beforehand,' and 'deliberate' means 'formed or arrived at or determined upon as a result of careful thought and weighing of considerations for and against the proposed course of action.' The process of premeditation and deliberation does not require any extended period of time. 'The true test is not the duration of time as much as it is the extent of the reflection. Thoughts may follow each other with great rapidity and cold, calculated judgment may be arrived at quickly.... ' "

Consequently, it logically follows that where two or more persons conspire to commit murder—i.e., intend to agree or conspire, further intend to commit the target offense of murder, and perform one or more overt acts in furtherance of the planned murder—each has acted with a state of mind "functionally indistinguishable from the mental state of premeditating the target offense of murder." The mental state required for conviction of conspiracy to commit murder necessarily establishes premeditation and deliberation of the target offense of murder—hence all murder conspiracies are conspiracies to commit first degree murder, so to speak. More accurately stated, conspiracy to commit murder is a unitary offense punishable in every instance in the same manner as is first degree murder under the provisions of [Cal.Penal Code §] 182.

The discussion did not end there. The California Supreme Court explained that, in granting Cortez's request for review, it asked the parties to address any error that may have arisen from the trial judge's failure to instruct the jury on premeditation and deliberation. The court opined that, in light of its holding, "it follows logically that there was no occasion or requirement for the jury to determine the 'degree' of the underlying target offense of murder, and thus no need for specific instruction on premeditation and deliberation respecting the conspiracy count." Thus, in the court's view, the trial judge was only required to instruct the jury on the dual intents of conspiracy and the "basic elements of murder" (murder is the unlawful killing of a human being with malice aforethought, i.e., the intent to kill).

Justice Joyce L. Kennard dissented in *Cortez*, criticizing what she framed as the majority's "conclu[sion] that conspiracy to murder is a unitary crime requiring proof of only intent to kill, the mental state of second degree murder, but subject to the punishment for first degree murder." Justice Kennard expounded upon this point in a footnote:

> The majority contends that it does no such thing but that it "merely recogniz[es] that the mental state required for conviction of conspiracy to commit express malice murder necessarily equates with and establishes the mental state of deliberate and premeditated first degree murder." Despite its protestations, however, the majority nevertheless refuses to require the jury to find the existence of the elemental facts of premeditation and deliberation, as a jury must find before convicting a defendant of first degree murder. Instead, it holds that intent to kill (the mental state of second degree murder) is the only mental state the jury need find to convict the defendant of conspiracy to murder, the punishment for which is that of first degree murder. Judicial presumption of premeditation and deliberation, however, is no substitute for jury fact-finding on those issues.

We find persuasive Justice Kennard's view that it is, indeed, factually possible for two or more individuals to conspire without premeditation and deliberation. She reasoned:

> By creating the separate crimes of (1) first degree murder for killings in which the killer acts not only with the intent to kill but with premeditation and deliberation, and (2) second degree murder for killings in which the killer acts with the intent to kill but without premeditation and deliberation, the Legislature has recognized that the intent to kill can exist without premeditation and deliberation. Contrary to the majority, there is no logical reason why a sudden intent to kill that is neither "considered beforehand" nor "formed or arrived at or determined upon as a result of careful thought and weighing of considerations for and against the proposed course of action," "cannot arise in two persons just as it can arise in one."

> Conspiracies do not require formal expressions of agreement or advance planning. For example, with a shout of "let's get him," two friends who have been drinking all night in a bar can, without premeditation and deliberation, impulsively form and share the intent to kill when their sworn enemy walks in. Similarly, a sudden and unexpected encounter on disputed turf between groups from two different gangs can similarly lead to a spontaneous and unreflective agreement to kill. Juries are capable of distinguishing between first degree murder conspiracies requiring premeditation and deliberation and second degree murder conspiracies requiring only intent to kill.

Justice Kennard is not alone in her view. As she points out, the Fifth and Ninth Circuits have also recognized varying degrees of murder as the object offense of criminal conspiracy. See *United States v. Croft*, 124 F.3d 1109 (9th Cir.1997); *United States v. Chagra*, 807 F.2d 398 (5th Cir.1986). * * *

To be sure, an agreement is a necessary predicate to a conspiracy, but the agreement "need not be spoken or formal so long as there is a meeting of the minds reflecting a unity of purpose and design." On the other hand, there is no requirement that the conspirators reach an agreement to commit the offense well in advance of its actual commission. In other words, an agreement to commit a crime could be arrived at virtually instantaneously with the commission (or attempt) of that crime. Justice Kennard recognized this phenomenon when she hypothesized about an encounter between rival gangs. Similarly, in *Chagra*, the Fifth Circuit contemplated an impulsive decision to kill a judge. Indeed, we can conceive of numerous examples of a spontaneous agreement to kill.

In sum, we are not persuaded that the dual elements of conspiracy necessarily establish premeditation and deliberation. Admittedly, unreflective agreements to kill between conspirators will be few and far between; the vast majority of conspiracies to murder will most certainly involve premeditation and deliberation and, thus, qualify as conspiracy to commit first degree murder. Statistical unlikeliness is not a sufficient ground, however, to invalidate a legally cognizable crime. We are unwilling to remove from the province of the jury the determination of whether the aggravating factors of premeditation and deliberation are present in a given case. It is properly left to the jury to ascertain whether the State has proven the aggravating elements of conspiracy to commit first degree murder, or if it has, instead, only established the elements sufficient to convict a defendant of the lesser included offense of conspiracy to commit second degree/common law murder. * * *

Our conclusion unmasks the flaw in appellant's argument, and reveals the windfall that would result from a holding in his favor. Under appellant's reasoning, assuming the State proved that he was one of the persons who attacked Mr. Arias, the State necessarily proved conspiracy to commit first degree murder. Because the trial judge granted appellant's motion for judgment of acquittal as to the conspiracy to commit first degree murder, appellant contends that the court necessarily acquitted him of conspiracy to commit second degree murder, and thus rendered conviction on any conspiracy to murder charge impossible.

A verdict of guilty with respect to a lesser included offense ordinarily results from the State's failure to prove an aggravating element. Appellant overlooks that when a defendant is charged with first degree murder, regardless of the quantum of proof, a jury may nonetheless opt to convict for the lesser included offense of second degree murder. In this case, it makes no sense to dismiss a lesser included offense merely because, as appellant argues, the State actually proved more. * * *

MURPHY, CHIEF JUDGE, dissenting. * * *

Deliberation and premeditation are essential elements of an agreement to participate in an intentional killing. In this case, the jurors were instructed that, to convict appellant of conspiracy to commit murder in the second degree, "the State must prove that [appellant] ... entered into the agreement with the intent that murder in the second degree ... be committed." In accordance with those instructions, the jurors convicted appellant of a charge that the court had already resolved in his favor. I would therefore reverse (only) appellant's conviction for conspiracy to commit second degree murder.

Notes and Questions

1. Consider also *State v. Baca*, 124 N.M. 333, 950 P.2d 776 (1997), where, in concluding there was no such crime as conspiracy to commit depraved-heart murder (called depraved-mind murder in that state), the court commented: "We are not convinced that the crime of conspiracy to commit depraved-mind murder is logically impossible. Nevertheless, we are convinced that, as presently written, Section 30–28–2 does not encompass the crime of depraved-mind murder. Conspiracy in New Mexico requires both an intent to agree and an intent to commit the offense which is the object of the conspiracy. As depraved-mind murder is presently defined by statute and case law, the charge of conspiracy to commit depraved-mind murder was not valid.

"The California Supreme Court recently reached a similar result in connection with conspiracy to commit that form of second-degree murder under California law known as 'implied malice murder.' See *People v. Swain*, 12 Cal.4th 593, 49 Cal.Rptr.2d 390, 394–97, 909 P.2d 994, 998–1001 (1996) (describing 'implied malice murder' under California law). For 'implied malice murder,' under California law, the required mens rea is 'implied from the specific intent to do some act other than an intentional killing and the resulting circumstance: a killing that has in fact occurred as "the direct result of such an act." ' The California Supreme Court reasoned the 'nature' of implied malice murder is inconsistent with the 'nature of the crime of conspiracy.' In conspiracy, culpability is fixed at an earlier point in time than even the crime of attempt. Because implied malice murder requires a particular result and depends on that result to support an inference of intent, the two crimes have been considered incompatible. Conspiracy cannot be based on this theory because a defendant cannot agree to kill and simultaneously disregard the risk of death. In *State v. Beccia*, 199 Conn. 1, 505 A.2d 683, 684–85 (1986), the Connecticut Supreme Court similarly described the crime of conspiracy to commit arson in the third degree as not 'cognizable' under Connecticut law. The Court explained that 'conspirators can agree to start a fire intentionally or to cause an explosion or even agree to act recklessly, [but] they cannot agree to accomplish a required specific result unintentionally.'

"We construe Section 30–28–2 to limit conspiracy as provided in the Model Penal Code and applied in California and Connecticut. Therefore, we hold that Section 30–28–2 does not encompass conspiracy to commit depraved-mind murder. Baca might have been charged with conspiracy to shoot at or from a vehicle. Cf. Model Penal Code § 5.03 cmt. 2(c)(i), at 408 (distinguishing 'a crime defined in terms of conduct that creates a risk of harm, such as reckless driving or driving above certain speed limit,' from crime defined in terms of a result)."

2. In *Beccia*, supra, what if the proof was that the sole objective of the defendants was to destroy the building by firebombing, though they knew that persons in the building would in all likelihood be killed by the firebombing? Should this be treated as a conspiracy to murder? *Model Penal Code* § 5.03, Comment (1985), puts this case and says that under the Code "they are nevertheless guilty only of a conspiracy to destroy the building and not of a conspiracy to kill the inhabitants. While this result may seem unduly restrictive from the viewpoint of the completed crime, it is necessitated by the extremely preparatory behavior that may be involved in conspiracy."

3. Compare *United States v. United States Gypsum Co.*, 438 U.S. 422, 98 S.Ct. 2864, 57 L.Ed.2d 854 (1978), involving a conviction for violating § 1 of the Sherman Act by conspiracy to fix the prices of gypsum board. The Court, per Burger, C.J., first concluded that "the Sherman Act should be construed as including intent as an element," but then concluded "that action undertaken with knowledge of its probable consequences and

having the requisite anticompetitive effects can be a sufficient predicate for a finding of criminal liability under the antitrust laws. * * *"

"Nothing in our analysis of the Sherman Act persuades us that this general understanding of intent should not be applied to criminal antitrust violations such as charged here. The business behavior which is likely to give rise to criminal antitrust charges is conscious behavior normally undertaken only after a full consideration of the desired results and a weighing of the costs, benefits, and risks. A requirement of proof not only of this knowledge of likely effects, but also of a conscious desire to bring them to fruition or to violate the law would seem, particularly in such a context, both unnecessarily cumulative and unduly burdensome. Where carefully planned and calculated conduct is being scrutinized in the context of a criminal prosecution, the perpetrator's knowledge of the anticipated consequences is a sufficient predicate for a finding of criminal intent."

PEOPLE v. LAURIA

Court of Appeal, Second District, 1967.
251 Cal.App.2d 471, 59 Cal.Rptr. 628.

FLEMING, ASSOCIATE JUSTICE.

In an investigation of call-girl activity the police focused their attention on three prostitutes actively plying their trade on call, each of whom was using Lauria's telephone answering service, presumably for business purposes. * * *

Lauria and the three prostitutes were indicted for conspiracy to commit prostitution, and nine overt acts were specified. Subsequently the trial court set aside the indictment as having been brought without reasonable or probable cause. The People have appealed, claiming that a sufficient showing of an unlawful agreement to further prostitution was made.

To establish agreement, the People need show no more than a tacit, mutual understanding between coconspirators to accomplish an unlawful act. Here the People attempted to establish a conspiracy by showing that Lauria, well aware that his codefendants were prostitutes who received business calls from customers through his telephone answering service, continued to furnish them with such service. This approach attempts to equate knowledge of another's criminal activity with conspiracy to further such criminal activity, and poses the question of the criminal responsibility of a furnisher of goods or services who knows his product is being used to assist the operation of an illegal business. Under what circumstances does a supplier become a part of a conspiracy to further an illegal enterprise by furnishing goods or services which he knows are to be used by the buyer for criminal purposes?

The two leading cases on this point face in opposite directions. In *United States v. Falcone*, 311 U.S. 205, 61 S.Ct. 204, 85 L.Ed. 128, the sellers of large quantities of sugar, yeast, and cans were absolved from participation in a moonshining conspiracy among distillers who bought from them, while in *Direct Sales Co. v. United States*, 319 U.S. 703, 63 S.Ct. 1265, 87 L.Ed. 1674, a wholesaler of drugs was convicted of conspiracy to violate the federal narcotic laws by selling drugs in quantity to a codefendant physician who was supplying them to addicts. The distinction between these two cases appears primarily based on the proposition that distributors of such dangerous products as drugs are required to exercise greater discrimination in the conduct of their business than are distributors of innocuous substances like sugar and yeast.

In the earlier case, *Falcone,* the sellers' knowledge of the illegal use of the goods was insufficient by itself to make the sellers participants in a conspiracy with the distillers who bought from them. Such knowledge fell short of proof of a conspiracy, and evidence on the volume of sales was too vague to support a jury finding that respondents knew of the conspiracy from the size of the sales alone.

In the later case of *Direct Sales,* the conviction of a drug wholesaler for conspiracy to violate federal narcotic laws was affirmed on a showing that it had actively promoted the sale of morphine sulphate in quantity and had sold codefendant physician, who practiced in a small town in South Carolina, more than 300 times his normal requirements of the drug, even though it had been repeatedly warned of the dangers of unrestricted sales of the drug. The court contrasted the restricted goods involved in *Direct Sales* with the articles of free commerce involved in *Falcone:* "All articles of commerce may be put to illegal ends," said the court. "But all do not have inherently the same susceptibility to harmful and illegal use. * * * This difference is important for two purposes. One is for making certain that the seller knows the buyer's intended illegal use. The other is to show that by the sale he intends to further, promote and cooperate in it. This intent, when given effect by overt act, is the gist of conspiracy. While it is not identical with mere knowledge that another purposes unlawful action, it is not unrelated to such knowledge. * * * The step from knowledge to intent and agreement may be taken. There is more than suspicion, more than knowledge, acquiescence, carelessness, indifference, lack of concern. There is informed and interested cooperation, stimulation, instigation. And there is also a 'stake in the venture' which, even if it may not be essential, is not irrelevant to the question of conspiracy."

While *Falcone* and *Direct Sales* may not be entirely consistent with each other in their full implications, they do provide us with a framework for the criminal liability of a supplier of lawful goods or services put to unlawful use. Both the element of *knowledge* of the illegal use of the goods or services and the element of *intent* to further that use must be present in order to make the supplier a participant in a criminal conspiracy.

Proof of *knowledge* is ordinarily a question of fact and requires no extended discussion in the present case. The knowledge of the supplier was sufficiently established when Lauria admitted he knew some of his customers were prostitutes and admitted he knew that Terry, an active subscriber to his service, was a prostitute. In the face of these admissions he could scarcely claim to have relied on the normal assumption an operator of a business or service is entitled to make, that his customers are behaving themselves in the eyes of the law. Because Lauria knew in fact that some of his customers were prostitutes, it is a legitimate inference he knew they were subscribing to his answering service for illegal business purposes and were using his service to make assignations for prostitution. On this record we think the prosecution is entitled to claim positive knowledge by Lauria of the use of his service to facilitate the business of prostitution.

The more perplexing issue in the case is the sufficiency of proof of *intent* to further the criminal enterprise. The element of intent may be proved either by direct evidence, or by evidence of circumstances from which an intent to further a criminal enterprise by supplying lawful goods or services may be inferred. Direct evidence of participation, such as advice from the supplier of legal goods or services to the user of those goods or services on their use for illegal purposes, such evidence as appeared in a companion case we decide today, *People v. Roy,* 59 Cal.Rptr. 636, provides the simplest case.[a] When the intent to

---

a. In *Roy,* the defendant (also the operator of a telephone answering service) advised a supposed prostitute of precautions she should take in conducting business as a prostitute and also undertook to arrange the sharing of customers between prostitutes using her answering service. Said the court: "By no stretch of the imagination does the making of arrangements for the referral of overflow business from one prostitute to further and promote the criminal enterprise comes from the lips of the supplier himself, ambiguities of inference from circumstance need not trouble us. But in cases where direct proof of complicity is lacking, intent to further the conspiracy must be derived from the sale itself and its surrounding circumstances in order to establish the supplier's express or tacit agreement to join the conspiracy.

In the case at bench the prosecution argues that since Lauria knew his customers were using his service for illegal purposes but nevertheless continued to furnish it to them, he must have intended to assist them in carrying out their illegal activities. Thus through a union of knowledge and intent he became a participant in a criminal conspiracy. Essentially, the People argue that knowledge alone of the continuing use of his telephone facilities for criminal purposes provided a sufficient basis from which his intent to participate in those criminal activities could be inferred.

In examining precedents in this field we find that sometimes, but not always, the criminal intent of the supplier may be inferred from his knowledge of the unlawful use made of the product he supplies. Some consideration of characteristic patterns may be helpful.

1. Intent may be inferred from knowledge, when the purveyor of legal goods for illegal use has acquired a stake in the venture. (*United States v. Falcone*, 2 Cir., 109 F.2d 579, 581.) For example, in *Regina v. Thomas* (1957), 2 All.E.R. 181, 342, a prosecution for living off the earnings of prostitution, the evidence showed that the accused, knowing the woman to be a convicted prostitute, agreed to let her have the use of his room between the hours of 9 p.m. and 2 a.m. for a charge of £3 a night. The Court of Criminal Appeal refused an appeal from the conviction, holding that when the accused rented a room at a grossly inflated rent to a prostitute for the purpose of carrying on her trade, a jury could find he was living on the earnings of prostitution.

In the present case, no proof was offered of inflated charges for the telephone answering services furnished the codefendants.

2. Intent may be inferred from knowledge, when no legitimate use for the goods or services exists. The leading California case is *People v. McLaughlin*, 111 Cal.App.2d 781, 245 P.2d 1076, in which the court upheld a conviction of the suppliers of horse-racing information by wire for conspiracy to promote bookmaking, when it had been established that wire-service information had no other use than to supply information needed by bookmakers to conduct illegal gambling operations. * * *

Other services of a comparable nature come to mind: the manufacturer of crooked dice and marked cards who sells his product to gambling casinos; the tipster who furnishes information on the movement of law enforcement officers to known lawbreakers. (Cf. *Jackson v. State of Texas*, 164 Tex.Cr.R. 276, 298 S.W.2d 837 (1957), where the furnisher of signaling equipment used to warn gamblers of the police was convicted of aiding the equipping of a gambling place.) In such cases the supplier must necessarily have an intent to further the illegal enterprise since there is no known honest use for his goods.

another have anything to do with the legitimate operation of a telephone answering service. The mischief for which Mrs. Roy was indicted had thus been divorced from the operation of the telephone answering service and become a separate venture of its own, even though some of its acts were derived from and dependent upon the use of facilities of the legitimate business. * * *

"Introducing one prostitute to another to facilitate the sharing of customers can have no legitimate function or purpose. The case thus falls within the rule of *People v. McLaughlin*, 111 Cal.App.2d 781, 245 P.2d 1076, where the furnishing of wire service information having no other use than to service the illegal operations of bookmakers, made the defendants knowing and intentional participants in a criminal conspiracy to further bookmaking."

However, there is nothing in the furnishing of telephone answering service which would necessarily imply assistance in the performance of illegal activities. Nor is any inference to be derived from the use of an answering service by women, either in any particular volume of calls, or outside normal working hours. Night-club entertainers, registered nurses, faith healers, public stenographers, photographic models, and free lance substitute employees, provide examples of women in legitimate occupations whose employment might cause them to receive a volume of telephone calls at irregular hours.

3. Intent may be inferred from knowledge, when the volume of business with the buyer is grossly disproportionate to any legitimate demand, or when sales for illegal use amount to a high proportion of the seller's total business. In such cases an intent to participate in the illegal enterprise may be inferred from the quantity of the business done. For example, in *Direct Sales,* supra, the sale of narcotics to a rural physician in quantities 300 times greater than he would have normal use for provided potent evidence of an intent to further the illegal activity. In the same case the court also found significant the fact that the wholesaler had attracted as customers a disproportionately large group of physicians who had been convicted of violating the Harrison Act. * * *

No evidence of any unusual volume of business with prostitutes was presented by the prosecution against Lauria.

Inflated charges, the sale of goods with no legitimate use, sales in inflated amounts, each may provide a fact of sufficient moment from which the intent of the seller to participate in the criminal enterprise may be inferred. In such instances participation by the supplier of legal goods to the illegal enterprise may be inferred because in one way or another the supplier has acquired a special interest in the operation of the illegal enterprise. His intent to participate in the crime of which he has knowledge may be inferred from the existence of his special interest.

Yet there are cases in which it cannot reasonably be said that the supplier has a stake in the venture or has acquired a special interest in the enterprise, but in which he has been held liable as a participant on the basis of knowledge alone. Some suggestion of this appears in *Direct Sales,* supra, where both the knowledge of the illegal use of the drugs and the intent of the supplier to aid that use were inferred. In *Regina v. Bainbridge* (1959), 3 W.L.R. 656 (CCA 6), a supplier of oxygen-cutting equipment to one known to intend to use it to break into a bank was convicted as an accessory to the crime. In *Sykes v. Director of Public Prosecutions* [1962] A.C. 528, one having knowledge of the theft of 100 pistols, 4 submachine guns, and 1960 rounds of ammunition was convicted of misprision of felony for failure to disclose the theft to the public authorities. It seems apparent from these cases that a supplier who furnishes equipment which he *knows* will be used to commit a serious crime may be deemed from that knowledge alone to have intended to produce the result. Such proof may justify an inference that the furnisher intended to aid the execution of the crime and that he thereby became a participant. For instance, we think the operator of a telephone answering service with positive knowledge that his service was being used to facilitate the extortion of ransom, the distribution of heroin, or the passing of counterfeit money who continued to furnish the service with knowledge of its use, might be chargeable on knowledge alone with participation in a scheme to extort money, to distribute narcotics, or to pass counterfeit money. The same result would follow the seller of gasoline who knew the buyer was using his product to make Molotov cocktails for terroristic use.

Logically, the same reasoning could be extended to crimes of every description. Yet we do not believe an inference of intent drawn from knowledge of criminal use properly applies to the less serious crimes classified as misdemeanors. The duty to take positive action to dissociate oneself from activities helpful to violations of the criminal law is far

stronger and more compelling for felonies than it is for misdemeanors or petty offenses. In this respect, as in others, the distinction between felonies and misdemeanors, between more serious and less serious crime, retains continuing vitality. In historically the most serious felony, treason, an individual with knowledge of the treason can be prosecuted for concealing and failing to disclose it. In other felonies, both at common law and under the criminal laws of the United States, an individual knowing of the commission of a felony is criminally liable for concealing it and failing to make it known to proper authority. But this crime, known as misprision of felony, has always been limited to knowledge and concealment of felony and has never extended to misdemeanor. A similar limitation is found in the criminal liability of an accessory, which is restricted to aid in the escape of a principal who has committed or been charged with a *felony*. We believe the distinction between the obligations arising from knowledge of a felony and those arising from knowledge of a misdemeanor continues to reflect basic human feelings about the duties owed by individuals to society. Heinous crime must be stamped out, and its suppression is the responsibility of all. Venial crime and crime not evil in itself present less of a danger to society, and perhaps the benefits of their suppression through the modern equivalent of the posse, the hue and cry, the informant, and the citizen's arrest, are outweighed by the disruption to everyday life brought about by amateur law enforcement and private officiousness in relatively inconsequential delicts which do not threaten our basic security.
* * *

With respect to misdemeanors, we conclude that positive knowledge of the supplier that his products or services are being used for criminal purposes does not, without more, establish an intent of the supplier to participate in the misdemeanors. With respect to felonies, we do not decide the converse, viz. that in all cases of felony knowledge of criminal use alone may justify an inference of the supplier's intent to participate in the crime. The implications of *Falcone* make the matter uncertain with respect to those felonies which are merely prohibited wrongs. But decision on this point is not compelled, and we leave the matter open.

From this analysis of precedent we deduce the following rule: the intent of a supplier who knows of the criminal use to which his supplies are put to participate in the criminal activity connected with the use of his supplies may be established by (1) direct evidence that he intends to participate, or (2) through an inference that he intends to participate based on, (a) his special interest in the activity, or (b) the aggravated nature of the crime itself.

When we review Lauria's activities in the light of this analysis, we find no proof that Lauria took any direct action to further, encourage, or direct the call-girl activities of his codefendants and we find an absence of circumstances from which his special interest in their activities could be inferred. Neither excessive charges for standardized services, nor the furnishing of services without a legitimate use, nor an unusual quantity of business with call girls, are present. The offense which he is charged with furthering is a misdemeanor, a category of crime which has never been made a required subject of positive disclosure to public authority. Under these circumstances, although proof of Lauria's knowledge of the criminal activities of his patrons was sufficient to charge him with that fact, there was insufficient evidence that he intended to further their criminal activities, and hence insufficient proof of his participation in a criminal conspiracy with his codefendants to further prostitution. Since the conspiracy centered around the activities of Lauria's telephone answering service, the charges against his codefendants likewise fail for want of proof.

In absolving Lauria of complicity in a criminal conspiracy we do not wish to imply that the public authorities are without remedies to combat modern manifestations of the world's oldest profession. Licensing of telephone answering services under the police power, together with the revocation of licenses for the toleration of prostitution, is a possible civil remedy. The furnishing of telephone answering service in aid of prostitution could be made a crime. (Cf. Pen.Code, § 316, which makes it a misdemeanor to let an apartment with knowledge of its use for prostitution.) Other solutions will doubtless occur to vigilant public authorities if the problem of call-girl activity needs further suppression.

The order is affirmed.

Notes and Questions

1. Consider Paul Marcus, *Criminal Conspiracy: The State of Mind Crime—Intent, Proving Intent, and Anti–Federal Intent*, 1976 U.Ill.L.F. 627, 643–44: "The conclusion of the *Lauria* court is remarkable. Why can a factfinder infer intent if the object crime is a felony, but cannot if the crime is a misdemeanor? The distinction is difficult to understand. The nature of the defendant's conduct and state of mind rather than the category of the ultimate or object crime should determine if a court may infer intent. Whether the object crime is a felony or a misdemeanor is irrelevant in deciding if a defendant is a criminal conspirator."

2. Rush was charged with conspiracy to import marijuana into the United States with intent to distribute it. He loaned $25,000 to others, knowing they would use the money to finance purchases of marijuana from sources in the Bahamas, and was later repaid the principal and $15,000 interest. On appeal from his conviction, Rush emphasized he did not receive a percentage share of the proceeds of the marijuana sales and that his loan had been fully secured. He argued (relying on *Falcone*) that consequently he was not guilty of conspiracy because his only intent was "to profit from a loan transaction." In affirming the conviction, the court of appeals stressed that Rush "was a podiatrist" and "not a money lender" and that he made "an exorbitant and usurious profit." *United States v. Rush*, 666 F.2d 10 (2d Cir.1981). What if Rush *had* been a money lender? Or, what if he had charged the usual rate for a secured loan?

3. Gallishaw, who supplied a machine gun which others used in robbing a bank, was charged with bank robbery and conspiracy to rob a bank. The jury failed to agree except on the conspiracy count, for which Gallishaw was convicted. During its deliberations, the jury sent this note to the judge: "Does the supplying or renting of a gun, which is subsequently used in a bank robbery, constitute grounds for a conspiracy if the person who rents the gun doesn't know how or where the gun will be used?" The judge answered: "Well, I charge you that it isn't necessary for the Government to prove that the one who rented the gun knew precisely what was intended or all the objectives of the conspiracy or the specific objectives of the conspiracy, or how the gun was to be used. But if you find that the defendant rented the gun and understood and knew that there was a conspiracy to do something wrong and to use the gun to violate the law, you may find that he willfully entered the conspiracy.

"Now, of course, that element must be proved beyond a reasonable doubt. If that is all the evidence that the Government has established, you must be satisfied that by that evidence the Government has proved beyond a reasonable doubt that he entered the conspiracy willfully and knowingly. And willfully and knowingly, as I charged you, means that he entered it intentionally and with the specific knowingly [*sic*] and with the specific intent to do something which the law forbids. That means to violate some law."

In *United States v. Gallishaw*, 428 F.2d 760 (2d Cir.1970), the court reversed:

"On appeal, we are thus faced with the following situation. The Government's witness, Carballo, testified that when Gallishaw handed over the machine gun, Thomas said he would either 'pull the bank job' or 'pull something else' with it. This imprecision about both Thomas's intentions and Gallishaw's knowledge of them apparently bothered the jury and led it to inquire about the possibility of participation in a conspiracy 'if the person who rents the gun doesn't know how or where the gun will be used.' It may be that the jury was asking only whether a conspirator had to know about specific places and times. However, it is at least as likely that this jury, which failed to convict Gallishaw on the substantive offense counts, was asking whether a weapon supplier who knew in a general way that a machine gun was to be used to 'pull something' could be said to have joined a conspiracy to rob a bank. The judge answered, in the press of the moment, that the jury could convict if Gallishaw rented the gun with the knowledge 'that there was a conspiracy to do something wrong and to use the gun to violate the law.' The jury was thus told, in a singularly pointed way, that it could convict on the conspiracy count without deciding whether to believe Carballo's testimony that Thomas has specifically mentioned a possible bank robbery to Gallishaw along with his generalized statement about pulling something.

"Under this instruction, the jury may simply have drawn the perfectly reasonable inference that one who rents a machine gun knows it is likely to be used 'to do something wrong' or 'to violate the law,' and therefore convicted Gallishaw, totally without regard to anything Thomas said, of the conspiracy charged in the indictment. A verdict on such a basis would have been improper. In *Ingram v. United States*, 360 U.S. 672, 678, 79 S.Ct. 1314, 1319, 3 L.Ed.2d 1503 (1959), the Supreme Court stated:

"C]onspiracy to commit a particular substantive offense cannot exist without at least the degree of criminal intent necessary for the substantive offense itself.' [Footnote omitted.]

"On this record, to convict Gallishaw for the substantive crime of aiding and abetting a violation of 18 U.S.C. § 2113(a), the Government would have had to show at a minimum that he knew that a bank was to be robbed. To convict him of conspiracy, at the very least no less was required."

UNITED STATES v. FEOLA

Supreme Court of the United States, 1975.

420 U.S. 671, 95 S.Ct. 1255, 43 L.Ed.2d 541.

Mr. Justice Blackmun delivered the opinion of the Court.

This case presents the issue whether knowledge that the intended victim is a federal officer is a requisite for the crime of conspiracy, under 18 U.S.C. § 371, to commit an offense violative of 18 U.S.C. § 111,[1] that is, an assault upon a federal officer while engaged in the performance of his official duties.

Respondent Feola and three others (Alsondo, Rosa, and Farr) were indicted for violations of §§ 371 and 111. A jury found all four defendants guilty of both charges. * * *

---

1. "§ 111. **Assaulting, Resisting, or Impeding Certain Officers or Employees.**

"Whoever forcibly assaults, resists, opposes, impedes, intimidates, or interferes with any person designated in section 1114 of this title while engaged in or on account of the performance of his official duties, shall be fined not more than $5,000 or imprisoned not more than three years, or both.

"Whoever, in the commission of any such acts uses a deadly or dangerous weapon, shall be fined not more than $10,000 or imprisoned not more than ten years, or both."

Among the persons "designated in section 1114" of 18 U.S.C. is "any officer or employee * * * of the Bureau of Narcotics and Dangerous Drugs."

The facts reveal a classic narcotics "rip-off." The details are not particularly important for our present purposes. We need note only that the evidence shows that Feola and his confederates arranged for a sale of heroin to buyers who turned out to be undercover agents for the Bureau of Narcotics and Dangerous Drugs. The group planned to palm off on the purchasers, for a substantial sum, a form of sugar in place of heroin and, should that ruse fail, simply to surprise their unwitting buyers and relieve them of the cash they had brought along for payment. The plan failed when one agent, his suspicions being aroused, drew his revolver in time to counter an assault upon another agent from the rear. Instead of enjoying the rich benefits of a successful swindle, Feola and his associates found themselves charged, to their undoubted surprise, with conspiring to assault, and with assaulting, federal officers.

At the trial, the District Court, without objection from the defense, charged the jurors that, in order to find any of the defendants guilty on either the conspiracy count or the substantive one, they were not required to conclude that the defendants were aware that their quarry were federal officers.

The Court of Appeals reversed the conspiracy convictions on a ground not advanced by any of the defendants. Although it approved the trial court's instructions to the jury on the substantive charge of assaulting a federal officer, it nonetheless concluded that the failure to charge that knowledge of the victim's official identity must be proved in order to convict on the conspiracy charge amounted to plain error. * * *

The Government's plea is for symmetry. It urges that since criminal liability for the offense described in 18 U.S.C. § 111 does not depend on whether the assailant harbored the specific intent to assault a federal officer, no greater scienter requirement can be engrafted upon the conspiracy offense, which is merely an agreement to commit the act proscribed by § 111. Consideration of the Government's contention requires us preliminarily to pass upon its premise, the proposition that responsibility for assault upon a federal officer does not depend upon whether the assailant was aware of the official identity of his victim at the time he acted. * * *

Section 111 has its origin in § 2 of the Act of May 18, 1934, c. 299, 48 Stat. 781. Section 1 of that Act, in which the present 18 U.S.C. § 1114 has its roots, made it a federal crime to kill certain federal law enforcement personnel while engaged in, or on account of, the performance of official duties, and § 2 forbade forcible resistance or interference with, or assault upon, any officer designated in § 1 while so engaged. The history of the 1934 Act, though scanty, offers insight into its multiple purposes. The pertinent committee reports consist, almost in their entirety, of a letter dated January 3, 1934, from Attorney General Cummings urging the passage of the legislation. * * *

Attorney General Cummings, in his letter, emphasized the importance of providing a federal forum in which attacks upon named federal officers could be prosecuted. This, standing alone, would not indicate a congressional conclusion to dispense with a requirement of specific intent to assault a federal officer, for the locus of the forum does not of itself define the reach of the substantive offense. But the view that § 111 requires knowledge of the victim's office rests on the proposition that the reference to the federal forum was merely a shorthand expression of the need for a statute to fill a gap in the substantive law of the States. In that view § 111 is seen merely as a federal aggravated assault statute, necessary solely because some state laws mandate increased punishment only for assaults on state peace officers; assaults on federal personnel would be punishable, under state law, only for simple assault. As a federal aggravated assault statute, § 111 would be read as requiring the same degree of knowledge as its state-law counterparts. The argument fails, however, because it is fairly certain that Congress was not enacting § 111 as a federal counterpart to state proscriptions of aggravated assault.

The Attorney General's call for a federal forum in which to prosecute an attacker of a federal officer was directed at both sections of the proposed bill that became the 1934 Act. The letter concerned not only the section prohibiting assaults but also the section prohibiting killings. The latter, § 1, was not needed to fill a gap in existing substantive state law. The States proscribed murder, and, until recently, with the enactment of certain statutes in response to the successful attack on capital punishment, murder of a peace officer has not been deemed an aggravated form of murder, for all States usually have punished murderers with the most severe sanction the law allows. Clearly, then, Congress understood that it was not only filling one gap in state substantive law but in large part was duplicating state proscriptions in order to insure a federal forum for the trial of offenses involving federal officers. Fulfillment of the congressional goal to protect federal officers required then, as it does now, the highest possible degree of certainty that those who killed or assaulted federal officers were brought to justice. In the congressional mind, with the reliance upon the Attorney General's letter, certainty required that these cases be tried in the federal courts, for no matter how "respectable and well disposed," it would not be unreasonable to suppose that state officials would not always or necessarily share congressional feelings of urgency as to the necessity of prompt and vigorous prosecutions of those who violate the safety of the federal officer. From the days of prohibition to the days of the modern civil rights movement, the statutes federal agents have sworn to uphold and enforce have not always been popular in every corner of the Nation. Congress may well have concluded that § 111 was necessary in order to insure uniformly vigorous protection of federal personnel, including those engaged in locally unpopular activity.

We conclude, from all this, that in order to effectuate the congressional purpose of according maximum protection to federal officers by making prosecution for assaults upon them cognizable in the federal courts, § 111 cannot be construed as embodying an unexpressed requirement that an assailant be aware that his victim is a federal officer. All the statute requires is an intent to assault, not an intent to assault a federal officer. A contrary conclusion would give insufficient protection to the agent enforcing an unpopular law, and none to the agent acting under cover. * * *

We hold, therefore, that in order to incur criminal liability under § 111 an actor must entertain merely the criminal intent to do the acts therein specified. We now consider whether the rule should be different where persons conspire to commit those acts.

Our decisions establish that in order to sustain a judgment of conviction on a charge of conspiracy to violate a federal statute, the Government must prove at least the degree of criminal intent necessary for the substantive offense itself. Respondent Feola urges upon us the proposition that the Government must show a degree of criminal intent in the conspiracy count greater than is necessary to convict for the substantive offense; he urges that even though it is not necessary to show that he was aware of the official identity of his assaulted victims in order to find him guilty of assaulting federal officers, in violation of 18 U.S.C. § 111, the Government nonetheless must show that he was aware that his intended victims were undercover agents, if it is successfully to prosecute him for conspiring to assault federal agents. And the Court of Appeals held that the trial court's failure to charge the jury to this effect constituted plain error.

The general conspiracy statute, 18 U.S.C. § 371, offers no textual support for the proposition that to be guilty of conspiracy a defendant in effect must have known that his conduct violated federal law. The statute makes it unlawful simply to "conspire * * * to commit any offense against the United States." A natural reading of these words would be that since one can violate a criminal statute simply by engaging in the forbidden conduct, a conspiracy to commit that offense is nothing more than an agreement to engage in the prohibited conduct. Then where, as here, the substantive statute does not require that an assailant know the official status of his victim, there is nothing on the face of the conspiracy statute that would seem to require that those agreeing to the assault have a greater degree of knowledge.

We have been unable to find any decision of this Court that lends support to the respondent. On the contrary, at least two of our cases implicitly repudiate his position. The appellants in *In re Coy,* 127 U.S. 731, 8 S.Ct. 1263, 32 L.Ed. 274 (1888), were convicted of conspiring to induce state election officials to neglect their duty to safeguard ballots and election results. The offense occurred with respect to an election at which Indiana voters, in accordance with state law, voted for both local officials and members of Congress. Much like Feola here, those appellants asserted that they could not be punished for conspiring to violate federal law because they had intended only to affect the outcome of state races. In short, it was urged that the conspiracy statute embodied a requirement of specific intent to violate federal law. The Court rejected this contention and held that the statute required only that the conspirators agree to participate in the prohibited conduct.

Similarly, in *United States v. Freed,* 401 U.S. 601, 91 S.Ct. 1112, 28 L.Ed.2d 356 (1971), we reversed the dismissal of an indictment charging defendants with possession of, and with conspiracy to possess, hand grenades that had not been registered, as required by 26 U.S.C. § 5861(d). The trial court dismissed the indictment for failure to allege that the defendants knew that the hand grenades in fact were unregistered. We held that actual knowledge that the grenades were unregistered was not an element of the substantive offense created by Congress and therefore upheld the indictment both as to the substantive offense and as to the charge of conspiracy. Again, we declined to require a greater degree of intent for conspiratorial responsibility than for responsibility for the underlying substantive offense.

With no support on the face of the general conspiracy statute or in this Court's decisions, respondent relies solely on the line of cases commencing with *United States v. Crimmins,* 123 F.2d 271 (C.A.2 1941), for the principle that the Government must prove "antifederal" intent in order to establish liability under § 371. In *Crimmins,* the defendant had been found guilty of conspiring to receive stolen bonds that had been transported in interstate commerce. Upon review, the Court of Appeals pointed out that the evidence failed to establish that Crimmins actually knew the stolen bonds had moved into the State. Accepting for the sake of argument the assumption that such knowledge was not necessary to sustain a conviction on the substantive offense, Judge Learned Hand nevertheless concluded that to permit conspiratorial liability where the conspirators were ignorant of the federal implications of their acts would be to enlarge their agreement beyond its terms as they understood them. He capsulized the distinction in what has become well known as his "traffic light" analogy:

> "While one may, for instance, be guilty of running past a traffic light of whose existence one is ignorant, one cannot be guilty of conspiring to run past such a light, for one cannot agree to run past a light unless one supposes that there is a light to run past."

Judge Hand's attractive, but perhaps seductive, analogy has received a mixed reception in the Courts of Appeals. The Second Circuit, of course, has followed it; others have rejected it. It appears that most have avoided it by the simple expedient of inferring the requisite knowledge from the scope of the conspiratorial venture. We conclude that the analogy, though effective prose, is, as applied to the facts before us, bad law.[24]

The question posed by the traffic light analogy is not before us, just as it was not before the Second Circuit in *Crimmins.* Criminal liability, of course, may be imposed on one who runs a traffic light regardless of whether he harbored the "evil intent" of disobeying the light's command; whether he drove so recklessly as to be unable to perceive the light; whether, thinking he was observing all traffic rules, he simply failed to notice the light; or whether, having been reared elsewhere, he thought that the light was only an ornament. Traffic violations generally fall into that category of offenses that dispense with a *mens rea* requirement. These laws embody the social judgment that it is fair to punish one who intentionally engages in conduct that creates a risk to others, even though no risk is intended or the actor, through no fault of his own, is completely unaware of the existence of any risk. The traffic light analogy poses the question whether it is fair to punish parties to an agreement to engage intentionally in apparently innocent conduct where the unintended result of engaging in that conduct is the violation of a criminal statute.

But this case does not call upon us to answer this question, and we decline to do so, just as we have once before. *United States v. Freed,* 401 U.S., at 609 n. 14, 91 S.Ct. at 1118. We note in passing, however, that the analogy comes close to stating what has been known as the "*Powell* doctrine," originating in *People v. Powell,* 63 N.Y. 88 (1875), to the effect that a conspiracy, to be criminal, must be animated by a corrupt motive or a motive to do wrong. Under this principle, such a motive could be easily demonstrated if the underlying offense involved an act clearly wrongful in itself; but it had to be independently demonstrated if the acts agreed to were wrongful solely because of statutory proscription. Interestingly, Judge Hand himself was one of the more severe critics of the *Powell* doctrine.[25]

That Judge Hand should reject the *Powell* doctrine and then create the *Crimmins* doctrine seems curious enough. Fatal to the latter, however, is the fact that it was announced in a case to which it could not have been meant to apply. In *Crimmins,* the substantive offense, namely, the receipt of stolen securities that had been in interstate commerce, proscribed clearly wrongful conduct. Such conduct could not be engaged in without an intent to accomplish the forbidden result. So, too, it is with assault, the conduct forbidden by the substantive statute, § 111, presently before us. One may run a traffic light "of whose existence one is ignorant," but assaulting another "of whose existence one is ignorant," probably would require unearthly intervention. Thus, the traffic light analogy, even if it were a correct statement of the law, is inapt, for the conduct proscribed by the substantive offense, here assault, is not of the type outlawed without regard to the intent of the actor to accomplish the result that is made criminal. If the analogy has any vitality at all, it is to conduct of the latter variety; that, however, is a question we save for another day. We hold here only that where a substantive offense embodies only a requirement of *mens rea* as to each of its elements, the general federal conspiracy statute requires no more.

---

24. The Government rather effectively exposes the fallacy of the *Crimmins* traffic light analogy by recasting it in terms of a jurisdictional element. The suggested example is a traffic light on an Indian reservation. Surely, one may conspire with others to disobey the light but be ignorant of the fact that it is on the reservation. As applied to a jurisdictional element of this kind the formulation makes little sense.

25. "Starting with *People v. Powell* * * * the anomalous doctrine has indeed gained some footing in the circuit courts of appeals that for conspiracy there must be a 'corrupt motive * * *.' Yet it is hard to see any reason for this, or why more proof should be necessary than that the parties had in contemplation all the elements of the crime they are charged with conspiracy to commit." *United States v. Mack,* 112 F.2d 290, 292 (2d Cir.1940).

The *Crimmins* rule rests upon another foundation: that it is improper to find conspiratorial liability where the parties to the illicit agreement were not aware of the fact giving rise to federal jurisdiction, because the essence of conspiracy is agreement and persons cannot be punished for acts beyond the scope of their agreement. This "reason" states little more than a conclusion, for it is clear that one may be guilty as a conspirator for acts the precise details of which one does not know at the time of the agreement. See *Blumenthal v. United States,* 332 U.S. 539, 557, 68 S.Ct. 248, 256, 92 L.Ed. 154 (1947). The question is not merely whether the official status of an assaulted victim was known to the parties at the time of their agreement, but whether the acts contemplated by the conspirators are to be deemed legally different from those actually performed solely because of the official identity of the victim. Put another way, does the identity of the proposed victim alter the legal character of the acts agreed to, or is it no more germane to the nature of those acts than the color of the victim's hair?

Our analysis of the substantive offense is sufficient to convince us that for the purpose of individual guilt or innocence, awareness of the official identity of the assault victim is irrelevant. We would expect the same to obtain with respect to the conspiracy offense unless one of the policies behind the imposition of conspiratorial liability is not served where the parties to the agreement are unaware that the intended target is a federal law enforcement official.

It is well settled that the law of conspiracy serves ends different from, and complementary to, those served by criminal prohibitions of the substantive offense. Because of this, consecutive sentences may be imposed for the conspiracy and for the underlying crime. Our decisions have identified two independent values served by the law of conspiracy. The first is protection of society from the dangers of concerted criminal activity. That individuals know that their planned joint venture violates federal as well as state law seems totally irrelevant to that purpose of conspiracy law which seeks to protect society from the dangers of concerted criminal activity. Given the level of criminal intent necessary to sustain conviction for the substantive offense, the act of agreement to commit the crime is no less opprobrious and no less dangerous because of the absence of knowledge of a fact unnecessary to the formation of criminal intent. Indeed, unless imposition of an "anti-federal" knowledge requirement serves social purposes external to the law of conspiracy of which we are unaware, its imposition here would serve only to make it more difficult to obtain convictions on charges of conspiracy, a policy with no apparent purpose.

The second aspect is that conspiracy is an inchoate crime. This is to say, that, although the law generally makes criminal only antisocial conduct, at some point in the continuum between preparation and consummation, the likelihood of a commission of an act is sufficiently great and the criminal intent sufficiently well formed to justify the intervention of the criminal law. The law of conspiracy identifies the agreement to engage in a criminal venture as an event of sufficient threat to social order to permit the imposition of criminal sanctions for the agreement alone, plus an overt act in pursuit of it, regardless of whether the crime agreed upon actually is committed. Criminal intent has crystallized, and the likelihood of actual, fulfilled commission warrants preventive action.

Again, we do not see how imposition of a strict "anti-federal" scienter requirement would relate to this purpose of conspiracy law. Given the level of intent needed to carry out the substantive offense, we fail to see how the agreement is any less blameworthy or constitutes less of a danger to society solely because the participants are unaware which body of law they intend to violate. Therefore, we again conclude that imposition of a requirement of knowledge of those facts that serve only to establish federal jurisdiction would render it more difficult to serve the policy behind the law of conspiracy without serving any other apparent social policy. * * *

The judgment of the Court of Appeals with respect to the respondent's conspiracy conviction is reversed. * * *

MR. JUSTICE STEWART, with whom MR. JUSTICE DOUGLAS joins, dissenting. * * *

The history of § 111 permits no doubt that this is an aggravated assault statute, requiring proof of scienter. The provision derives from a 1934 statute, 18 U.S.C. § 254 (1940 ed.). * * *

Rummaging through the sparse legislative history of the 1934 law, the Court manages to persuade itself that Congress intended to reach unknowing assaults on federal officers. But if that was the congressional intention, which I seriously doubt, it found no expression in the legislative product. *The fact is that the 1934 statute expressly required scienter for an assault conviction.* An assault on a federal officer was proscribed only if perpetrated *"on account of* the performance of his official duties." That is, it was necessary not only that the assailant have notice that his victim possessed official status or duties but also that the assailant's *motive* be retaliation against the exercise of those duties.

It was not until the *1948 recodification* that the proscription was expanded to cover assaults on federal officers "while engaged in," as well as "on account of," the performance of official duties. This was, as the Reviser observed, a technical alteration; it produced no instructive legislative history. As presently written, the statute does clearly reach knowing assaults regardless of motive. But to suggest that it also reaches wholly unknowing assaults is to convert the 1948 alteration into one of major substantive importance, which it concededly was not.

The Court has also managed to convince itself that § 254 was not an aggravated assault statute. The surest evidence that § 254 *was* an aggravated assault statute may be found in its penalty provision. A single unarmed assault was made, and remains, punishable by a sentence of three years' imprisonment and a $5,000 fine. One need not make an exhaustive survey of state law to appreciate that this is a harsher penalty than is typically imposed for an unarmed assault on a private citizen. * * *

* * * So far as the scienter requirement is concerned, it makes no difference whether the statute aims to protect individuals, or functions, or both. The Court appears to think that extending § 111 to unknowing assaults will deter such assaults—will "give * * * protection * * * to the agent acting under cover." This, of course, is nonsense. The federal statute "protects" an officer from assault only when the assailant knows that the victim is an officer. Absent such knowledge, the only "protection" is that provided by the *general* law of assault, for that is the only law which the potential assailant reasonably, if erroneously, believes applicable in the circumstances.

The Court also suggests that implication of a scienter requirement "would give insufficient protection to the agent enforcing an unpopular law." This is to repeat the same error. Whatever the "popularity" of the laws he is executing, and whatever the construction placed on § 111, a federal officer is "protected" from assault by that statute only where the assailant has some indication from the circumstances that his victim is other than a private citizen. * * *

Turning from the history of the statute to its structure, the propriety of implying a scienter requirement becomes manifest. The statute proscribes not only assault but also a whole series of related acts. It applies to any person who "forcibly assaults, *resists, opposes, impedes, intimidates,* or *interferes* with [a federal officer] * * * while engaged in or on account of the performance of his official duties." (Emphasis added.) It can hardly be denied that the emphasized words imply a scienter requirement. Generally speaking, these acts are legal and moral wrongs only if the actor knows that his "victim" enjoys a moral or legal privilege to detain him or order him about. * * *

For the reasons stated, I believe that before there can be a violation of 18 U.S.C. § 111, an assailant must know or have reason to know that the person he assaults is an officer. It follows *a fortiori* that there can be no criminal conspiracy to violate the statute in the absence of at least equivalent knowledge. Accordingly, I respectfully dissent from the opinion and judgment of the Court.

Notes and Questions

1. Compare *United States v. Prince,* 529 F.2d 1108 (6th Cir.1976), reversing Prince's conviction of violating and conspiring to violate 18 U.S.C.A. § 1952,[a] the Interstate Travel Act. Prince was a madam in a West Virginia house of prostitution; there was no evidence that she used interstate facilities in carrying on that activity or that she was aware any of the women working for her had been transported from another state. "Prince relies primarily on this court's decision in *United States v. Barnes,* 383 F.2d 287 (6th Cir.1967), for the proposition that one who is shown to have violated a local law may not be convicted of violating the Travel Act, or conspiring to do so, without proof of direct agreement to illegal interstate transportation or proof of an indirect agreement evidenced by substantial participation in an unlawful scheme with actual knowledge of illegal interstate transportation.

"The Government argues that the decision of the Supreme Court in *United States v. Feola,* requires that we reexamine and overrule *Barnes.* * * *

"We are not persuaded, however, that *Feola* requires us to overrule *Barnes.* The Travel Act does not make it a federal offense to engage in prostitution, an activity which is illegal under State law. It provides an additional string to the law enforcement bow, however, by providing that '[w]hoever travels in interstate or foreign commerce or uses any facility in interstate or foreign commerce * * * *with intent* * * * 'to engage in enumerated types of unlawful activity including prostitution may be punished thereunder. * * * In *Feola* the Supreme Court was construing a statute which made the performance of an act a federal offense without any requirement of intent separate from that which led to the act itself (the assault of another person). Its federal character depended upon the identity of the victim, whether known or unknown to the assailant. On the other hand, the Travel Act only reaches those who engage in interstate activities *with intent* to perform other illegal acts. Thus there is a requirement of a separate intent related to the use of interstate facilities which is different from the intent required to commit the underlying State offense. So far as this record shows the defendant Prince was nothing more than the

---

a. § 1952. Interstate and Foreign Travel or Transportation in Aid of Racketeering Enterprises.

(a) Whoever travels in interstate or foreign commerce or uses any facility in interstate or foreign commerce, including the mail, with intent to—

(1) distribute the proceeds of any unlawful activity; or

(2) commit any crime of violence to further any unlawful activity; or

(3) otherwise promote, manage, establish, carry on, or facilitate the promotion, management, establishment, or carrying on, of any unlawful activity.

and thereafter performs or attempts to perform any of the acts specified in subparagraphs (1), (2), and (3), shall be fined not more than $10,000 or imprisoned for not more than five years, or both.

(b) As used in this section "unlawful activity" means (1) any business enterprise involving gambling, liquor on which the Federal excise tax has not been paid, narcotics, or controlled substances (as defined in section 102(6) of the Controlled Substances Act), or prostitution offenses in violation of the laws of the State in which they are committed or of the United States, or (2) extortion, bribery, or arson in violation of the laws of the State in which committed or of the United States.

madam of a house of prostitution in West Virginia. The Travel Act is not written so broadly as to subject such a person to federal prosecution.

"Since Pandelli was shown to have actually caused a woman to travel from Ohio to West Virginia for the purpose of engaging in prostitution, it was immaterial whether or not he had actual knowledge of the jurisdictional element. The act coupled with the intent was sufficient. However, since Prince was not shown either to have traveled interstate or used interstate facilities, her strictly intrastate activities could not be held to constitute a violation of the Travel Act in the absence of a showing that she knew or reasonably should have known of Pandelli's interstate activities.

"In *Feola* the defendant urged that the Government was required to 'show a degree of criminal intent in the conspiracy count greater than is necessary to convict for the substantive offense; * * *.' This argument was rejected, but the rule was reaffirmed that 'in order to sustain a judgment of conviction on a charge of conspiracy to violate a federal statute, the Government must prove at least the degree of criminal intent necessary for the substantive offense itself.' Since that degree of criminal intent necessary for the substantive offense was not proven, the convictions of Prince both for violating the Travel Act and conspiring to do so must be reversed."[b]

2. *Model Penal Code* § 5.03, Comment (1985): "A doctrine that has had a somewhat confusing effect on the mens rea requirements of conspiracy was first formulated in the New York case of *People v. Powell*.[111] The defendants in the *Powell* case were prosecuted for conspiracy to violate a statute requiring municipal officials to advertise for bids before buying supplies for the city. The defendants urged as a defense that they had acted in good faith since they did not know of the existence of the statute. The court accepted this argument, holding that a confederation to do an act 'innocent in itself' is not criminal unless it is 'corrupt.' The agreement must have been entered into with an evil purpose, as distinguished from a purpose simply 'to do the act prohibited in ignorance of the prohibition. This is implied in the meaning of the word conspiracy.'

"The decision is subject to and has been given a number of interpretations. Some courts have read it literally as requiring knowledge by the conspirators that their object is prohibited by law, while others have rejected this interpretation but required a 'corrupt motive' of uncertain and varying content. The fact that the offense in the *Powell* case was 'innocent in itself' is often emphasized and a number of decisions have imported into the doctrine the distinction between offenses malum prohibitum and malum in se. Despite the considerable amount of attention and deference that the *Powell* doctrine has received, its actual effect upon the decisions and its vitality prior to the Model Code were probably smaller than was generally believed. Although no cases in New York questioned its authority, its status in most of the other jurisdictions that considered it was uncertain. * * *

"The *Powell* rule, and many of the decisions that rely upon it, may be viewed as a judicial endeavor to import fair mens rea requirements into statutes creating regulatory offenses that do not rest on traditional concepts of personal fault and culpability. This should, however, be the function of the statutes defining such offenses. * * * There is no good reason why the fortuity of concert should be used as the device for limiting

---

b. Although this distinction remains valid *if* the court is correct about the mental state required by the Travel Act, there is considerable doubt about that. More recently the court has noted that all of the other circuits that have considered the question "have determined that the Travel Act's interstate requirement is purely jurisdictional and carries with it no scienter requirement," so that "although *Prince* has not been explicitly overruled, its reasoning is questionable." *United States v. Winters*, 33 F.3d 720 (6th Cir.1994).

111. 63 N.Y. 88 (1875).

criminality in this area, just as there is no good reason for using it as the device to expand liability through imprecise formulations of objectives that include activity not otherwise criminal.''

3. Churchill was a bookkeeper employed by a company which, with an associated company, sold a quantity of diesel oil for use in vehicles. The oil bears a tax of 2s. 9d. a gallon, but a rebate of 2s. 7d. is allowed if the oil is used for home heating. Churchill was tried with others on a two-count indictment charging: (i) conspiracy to cheat and defraud the government of the rebate allowed on oil which was actually used in vehicles; and (ii) conspiracy to violate a statute which says that diesel oil on which the home use rebate has been allowed shall not be used in vehicles unless an amount equal to that rebate has been paid to the proper government official. This latter statute is a strict liability offense and thus one may be convicted under it for so using the oil even absent knowledge that the necessary repayment has not been made. Apparently because of that fact, the judge instructed the jury that they could convict Churchill on the second count if he was a party to an arrangement to use the fuel in vehicles, notwithstanding his lack of knowledge that a rebate had been allowed and not repaid with respect to the fuel so used. Churchill was acquitted on the first count, but was convicted on the second. The Court of Criminal Appeal dismissed the appeal but certified to the House of Lords this point of law: ''Whether mens rea is an essential ingredient in conspiracy to commit the absolute offence charged in count 2 of the indictment and, if so, what knowledge of the facts and/or law on the part of the defendant must be established to prove the charge.'' In *Churchill v. Walton*, [1967] 2 A.C. 224, [1967] 2 W.L.R. 682, [1967] 1 All E.R. 497, the House allowed the appeal, reasoning:

''In answer to the question posed by the Court of Criminal Appeal in this case, I would say that mens rea is only an essential ingredient in conspiracy in so far as there must be an intention to be a party to an agreement to do an unlawful act; that knowledge of the law on the part of the accused is immaterial and that knowledge of the facts is only material in so far as such knowledge throws a light on what was agreed.

''In cases of this kind, it is desirable to avoid the use of the phrase 'mens rea,' which is capable of different meanings, and to concentrate on the terms or effect of the agreement made by the alleged conspirators. The question is, 'What did they agree to do?' If what they agreed to do was, on the facts known to them, an unlawful act, they are guilty of conspiracy and cannot excuse themselves by saying that, owing to their ignorance of the law, they did not realise that such an act was a crime. If, on the facts known to them, what they agreed to do was lawful, they are not rendered artificially guilty by the existence of other facts, not known to them, giving a different and criminal quality to the act agreed upon.

''For the reasons I have given, I think that the direction given by the judge in relation to the second count was erroneous in point of law. The guilt of the accused did not depend on whether prohibited fuel was used in road vehicles but on whether he was a party to an agreement to use such fuel in road vehicles.''

Is this a sound result? Is it simply another application of the *Powell* rule, or what?

SECTION 4. THE OBJECTIVE

SHAW v. DIRECTOR OF PUBLIC PROSECUTIONS

House of Lords, 1961.

[1962]   A.C. 220, [1961] 2 W.L.R. 897, [1961] 2 All E.R. 446.

VISCOUNT SIMONDS: My Lords, the appellant, Frederick Charles Shaw, was, on Sept. 21, 1960, convicted at the Central Criminal Court on an indictment containing three counts which alleged the following offences:—(i) conspiracy to corrupt public morals; (ii) living on the earnings of prostitution contrary to s. 30 of the Sexual Offences Act, 1956; and (iii) publishing an obscene publication contrary to s. 2 of the Obscene Publications Act, 1959. He appealed against conviction to the Court of Criminal Appeal on all three counts. His appeal was dismissed * * *.

* * * When the Street Offences Act, 1959, came into operation, it was no longer possible for prostitutes to ply their trade by soliciting in the streets and it became necessary for them to find some other means of advertising the services that they were prepared to render. It occurred to the appellant that he could with advantage to himself assist them to this end. The device that he adopted was to publish on divers days between the dates mentioned in the particulars of offences a magazine or booklet which was called "Ladies Directory". It contained the names, addresses and telephone numbers of prostitutes with photographs of nude female figures, and in some cases details which conveyed to initiates willingness to indulge not only in ordinary sexual intercourse but also in various perverse practices. * * *

My Lords, as I have already said, the first count in the indictment is "Conspiracy to corrupt public morals", and the particulars of offence will have sufficiently appeared. I am concerned only to assert what was vigorously denied by counsel for the appellant, that such an offence is known to the common law and that it was open to the jury to find on the facts of this case that the appellant was guilty of such an offence. I must say categorically that, if it were not so, Her Majesty's courts would strangely have failed in their duty as servants and guardians of the common law. Need I say, my Lords, that I am no advocate of the right of the judges to create new criminal offences? * * * But I am at a loss to understand how it can be said either that the law does not recognise a conspiracy to corrupt public morals or that, though there may not be an exact precedent for such a conspiracy as this case reveals, it does not fall fairly within the general words by which it is described. * * * The fallacy in the argument that was addressed to us lay in the attempt to exclude from the scope of general words acts well calculated to corrupt public morals just because they had not been committed or had not been brought to the notice of the court before. It is not thus that the common law has developed. * * * In the sphere of criminal law, I entertain no doubt that there remains in the courts of law a residual power to enforce the supreme and fundamental purpose of the law, to conserve not only the safety and order but also the moral welfare of the state, and that it is their duty to guard it against attacks which may be the more insidious because they are novel and unprepared for. That is the broad head (call it public policy if you wish) within which the present indictment falls. It matters little what label is given to the offending act. To one of your Lordships it may appear an affront to public decency, to another, considering that it may succeed in its obvious intention of provoking libidinous desires, it will seem a corruption of public morals. Yet others may deem it aptly described as the creation of a public mischief or the undermining of moral conduct. The same act will not in all ages be regarded in the same way. The law must be related to the changing standards of life, not yielding to every shifting impulse of the popular will but having regard to fundamental assessments of human values and the purposes of society. [There is] a residual power, where no statute has yet intervened to supersede the common law, to superintend those offences which are prejudicial to the public welfare. Such occasions will be rare, for Parliament has not been slow to legislate when attention has been sufficiently aroused. But gaps remain and will always remain since no one can foresee every way in which the wickedness of man may disrupt the order of society. Let me take a single instance to which my noble and learned friend, Lord Tucker, refers. Let it be supposed that, at some future, perhaps, early, date homosexual practices between adult consenting males are no longer a crime. Would it not be an offence if, even without obscenity, such practices were publicly advocated and encouraged by pamphlet and advertisement? Or must we wait until Parliament finds time to deal with such conduct? I say, my Lords, that, if the common law is powerless in such an event, then we should no longer do her reverence. * * *

The appeal on both counts should, in my opinion, be dismissed.

LORD REID: * * * In my opinion, there is no such general offence known to the law as conspiracy to corrupt public morals. Undoubtedly there is an offence of criminal conspiracy and undoubtedly it is of fairly wide scope. * * * I think that Lord Goddard, C.J., was repeating the generally accepted view when he said: "A conspiracy consists of agreeing or acting in concert to achieve an unlawful act or to do a lawful act by unlawful means." But what is an "unlawful act"? * * *

There are two competing views. One is that conspiring to corrupt public morals is only one facet of a still more general offence, conspiracy to effect public mischief; and that, like the categories of negligence, the categories of public mischief are never closed. The other is that, whatever may have been done two or three centuries ago, we ought not now to extend the doctrine further than it has already been carried by the common law courts. Of course I do not mean that it should only be applied in circumstances precisely similar to those in some decided case. Decisions are always authority for other cases which are reasonably analogous and are not properly distinguishable. But we ought not to extend the doctrine to new fields. * * * Every argument against creating new offences by an individual appears to me to be equally valid against creating new offences by a combination of individuals. But there is this historical difference. The judges appear to have continued to extend the law of conspiracy after they had ceased to extend offences by individuals. * * * Even if there is still a vestigial power of this kind, it ought not, in my view, to be used unless there appears to be general agreement that the offence to which it is applied ought to be criminal if committed by an individual. Notoriously there are wide differences of opinion today how far the law ought to punish immoral acts which are not done in the face of the public. Some think that the law already goes too far, some that it does not go far enough. Parliament is the proper place, and I am firmly of opinion the only proper place, to settle that. When there is sufficient support from public opinion, Parliament does not hesitate to intervene. Where Parliament fears to tread it is not for the courts to rush in.

* * * It may, perhaps, be said that there is no question here of creating a new offence because there is only one offence of conspiracy—agreeing or acting in concert to do an unlawful act. In a technical sense, that is true. But, in order to extend this offence to a new field, the court would have to create a new unlawful act; it would have to hold that conduct of a kind which has not hitherto been unlawful in this sense must now be held to be unlawful. It appears to me that the objections to that are just as powerful as the objections to creating a new offence. The difference is a matter of words; the essence of the matter is that a type of conduct for the punishment of which there is no previous authority now for the first time becomes punishable solely by a decision of a court. * * *

LORD MORRIS OF BORTH-Y-GEST: * * *

It is said that there is a measure of vagueness in a charge of conspiracy to corrupt public morals, and also that there might be peril of the launching of prosecutions in order to suppress unpopular or unorthodox views. My Lords, I entertain no anxiety on those lines. Even if accepted public standards may to some extent vary from generation to generation, current standards are in the keeping of juries who can be trusted to maintain the corporate good sense of the community and to discern attacks on values that must be preserved. If there were prosecutions which were not genuinely and fairly warranted, juries would be quick to perceive this. There could be no conviction unless twelve jurors were unanimous in thinking that the accused person or persons had combined to do acts which were calculated to corrupt public morals. My Lords, as time proceeds, our criminal law is more and more being codified. Though it may be that the occasions for presenting a charge such as that in count 1 will be infrequent, I concur in the view that such a charge is contained within the armour of the law and that the jury were in the present case fully entitled to decide the case as they did.

I would dismiss the appeal.[a]

Notes and Questions

1. In *Commonwealth v. Bessette,* 351 Mass. 148, 217 N.E.2d 893 (1966), defendant, head of the Division of Waterways of the state Department of Public Works, appealed his conviction of conspiring with officers of two dredging companies to violate a Division regulation which prohibited assignment of contracts without the written consent of the Department. The court reversed:

"In *Commonwealth v. Dyer,* 243 Mass. 472, 485, 138 N.E. 296, 303, it was said, 'It is the consensus of opinion that conspiracy as a criminal offence is established when the object of the combination is either a crime, or if not a crime, is unlawful, or when the means contemplated are either criminal, or if not criminal, are illegal, provided that, where no crime is contemplated either as the end or the means, the illegal but noncriminal element involves prejudice to the general welfare or oppression of the individual of sufficient gravity to be injurious to the public interest.' Bessette argues that these general principles have not been broadly applied in Massachusetts in recent years. He in effect would have us interpret the term 'unlawful' as meaning 'criminal.' * * *

"The recent decisions undoubtedly have tended to apply the principles of criminal conspiracy primarily to group arrangements which have a criminal purpose or contemplate the use of criminal methods. Nevertheless, in view of the *Dyer* case, we are not prepared to say that criminal conspiracy has been completely restricted to this extent. The later discussion in the *Dyer* case (conspiracy for a monopoly) shows that the term 'unlawful,' in relation to a conspiracy, was thought to include situations where the purpose of a group plan or the proposed means of accomplishing that plan, even if not criminal, involve 'an

---

a. But see *Regina v. Withers,* [1974] 3 W.L.R. 751, where the defendants, in the course of their business as private investigators, obtained for clients confidential information about the financial standing of third parties. They did this by misrepresenting to banks and government departments that they were persons authorized to receive such information. They appealed to the House of Lords their convictions of conspiracy to effect public mischief, and their convictions were quashed. Viscount Dilhorne, after discussing *Shaw* and other cases, stated:

"What conclusions are to be drawn from the cases to which I have referred? I think they are these:

"1. There is no separate and distinct class of criminal conspiracy called conspiracy to effect a public mischief.

"2. That description has in the past been applied to a number of cases which might have been regarded as coming within well-known heads of conspiracy, e.g. conspiracy to defraud, to pervert the course of justice, etc.

"3. It is far too late to hold that a conspiracy of the kind that occurred in those cases was not criminal * * *.

"4. The judges have no power to create new offences.

"5. Where a charge of conspiracy to effect a public mischief has been preferred, the question to be considered is whether the objects or means of the conspiracy are in substance of such a quality or kind as has already been recognised by the law as criminal.

"6. If there are, then one has to go on to consider, on an appeal, whether the course the trial took in consequence of the reference to public mischief was such as to vitiate the conviction."

The Law Commission, *Working Paper No. 50* (June 1973), setting out the tentative views of the Commission regarding codification of the criminal law with respect to inchoate offenses, states at p. 10: "A law of conspiracy extending beyond the ambit of conspiracy to commit crimes has, in our view, no place in a comprehensively planned criminal code."

evil intent to oppress and injure the public' (or, perhaps, third persons) by activity, which is 'illegal, void and against public policy.'

"In view of the conclusion which we reach, it is not now necessary to determine precisely when, in situations comparable to that presented in the *Dyer* case, joint action may create additional dangers and risks sufficient to make criminal as a conspiracy an agreement upon a plan for unlawful acts which would not be criminal when done by individuals separately. We think it plain, however, that the term 'unlawful,' as used in the criminal conspiracy cases (where neither a criminal object nor criminal means are in contemplation), is limited in any event to a narrow range of situations, (a) where there is strong probability (as in the monopolistic plans involved in the *Dyer* case) that the execution of the plan by group action will cause such significant harm to an individual or to the general public, as to be seriously contrary to the public interest, and (b) where the unlawfulness of objective or contemplated means is substantial and clear. There is sound reason for such limitation. As Perkins, *Criminal Law*, 544, points out, a more inclusive definition of 'unlawful' might 'be held void for vagueness under the Due Process Clause [of the Federal and Massachusetts Constitutions] unless what is * * * proscribed is spelled out with sufficient clearness to guide those who would be law-abiding and to advise defendants of the offense with which they are charged.' Even as limited by this opinion, the rule of the *Dyer* case is necessarily indefinite and its application in a particular instance may present serious problems. This circumstance suggests strongly that certainty of statement of the criminal law would be greatly promoted by legislative definition of the types of unlawful, but not criminal, objectives and proposed means which may constitute elements of criminal conspiracy. * * *

"From the very general allegations it could be inferred that Bessette knowingly violated, by agreement with others, whatever department policy lay behind the use of art. 65 in the contracts. No allegations, however, tend to show the significance of that policy or that its violation by combined action (a) would cause loss to the Commonwealth, or any material interference with, or obstruction of, departmental operations, or (b) would be 'particularly dangerous to the public interests'."

2. In *State v. Bowling*, 5 Ariz.App. 436, 427 P.2d 928 (1967), the court held unconstitutional a statute providing that it "is unlawful for two or more persons to conspire to: * * * Commit any act injurious to the public health or public morals," reasoning:

"In considering a Utah statute with similar wording, the Supreme Court of the United States said:

'Standing by itself, it would seem to be warrant for conviction for agreement to do almost any act which a judge and jury might find at the moment contrary to his or its notions of what was good for health, morals, trade, commerce, justice or order.'

"*Musser v. State of Utah*, 333 U.S. 95, 68 S.Ct. 397, 398, 92 L.Ed. 562 (1948).

"The Supreme Court of the United States remanded the *Musser* case to the Utah Supreme Court to consider whether the language of this statute was unconstitutionally vague. The United States Supreme Court suggested that there was a possibility that under Utah statutory or case law the broad language of the statute might have been limited so as to give the required degree of specificity thereto.

"The Supreme Court of Utah, however, was unable to point to any limitations upon the subject language and came to the conclusion that this statute, making it a crime to conspire to commit an act ' * * * injurious * * * to public morals * * * ' was unconstitutional:

'No language in this or any other statute of this state or other law thereof or any historical fact or surrounding circumstance connected with the enactment of this statute has been pointed to as indicating that the legislature intended any limitation thereon other than that expressed on the face of the words used. We are therefore unable to place a construction on these words which limits their meaning beyond their general meaning. The conviction of the defendants thereunder cannot be upheld. This part of the statute is therefore void for vagueness and uncertainty under the Fourteenth Amendment to the Federal Constitution.'

"*State v. Musser,* 118 Utah 537, 223 P.2d 193, 194 (1950).

"Likewise, we know of no statutory or case law in this state which limits the broad sweep of that which is encompassed within the words ' * * * injurious to * * * public morals * * * '. Common-law crimes have not survived in this state, and unless certain conduct is singled out by criminal statute, conduct is not a crime no matter how reprehensible."

3.   The general conspiracy statute in the federal code, 18 U.S.C.A. § 371, makes it an offense to conspire "to commit any offense against the United States," and also to conspire "to defraud the United States, or any agency thereof in any manner or for any purpose." The meaning of the latter language has been considered by the Supreme Court, most recently in *Tanner v. United States,* 483 U.S. 107, 107 S.Ct. 2739, 97 L.Ed.2d 90 (1987):

"Section 371 is the descendent of and bears a strong resemblance to conspiracy laws that have been in the federal statute books since 1867. Neither the original 1867 provision nor its subsequent reincarnations were accompanied by any particularly illuminating legislative history. This case has been preceded, however, by decisions of this Court interpreting the scope of the phrase 'to defraud ... in any manner or for any purpose.' In those cases we have stated repeatedly that the fraud covered by the statute 'reaches "any conspiracy for the purpose of impairing, obstructing or defeating the lawful function of any department of Government." ' We do not reconsider that aspect of the scope of § 371 in this case. Therefore, if petitioners' actions constituted a conspiracy to impair the functioning of the REA, no other form of injury to the Federal Government need be established for the conspiracy to fall under § 371.

"The indictment against petitioners charged them with having conspired 'to defraud the United States by impeding, impairing, obstructing and defeating the lawful functions of the Rural Electrification Administration in its administration and enforcement of its guaranteed loan program.' Petitioners argue that if the evidence adduced at trial established a conspiracy to defraud, then the target of that conspiracy was Seminole Electric, and a conspiracy to defraud a private corporation receiving financial assistance from the Federal Government does not constitute a conspiracy to defraud the United States.

"The Government sets out two arguments in response to petitioners' challenge to the § 371 convictions. The first, which we accept, is that a conspiracy to defraud the United States may be effected by the use of third parties. The Government's second argument asserts that Seminole, as the recipient of federal financial assistance and the subject of federal supervision, may itself be treated as 'the United States' for purposes of § 371. This second argument must be rejected.

"The Government observes, correctly, that under the common law a fraud may be established when the defendant has made use of a third party to reach the target of the fraud. The Government also correctly observes that the broad language of § 371, covering conspiracies to defraud 'in any manner for any purpose,' puts no limits based on the method used to defraud the United States. A method that makes uses of innocent individuals or businesses to reach and defraud the United States is not for that reason beyond the scope of § 371. * * *

"The Government's principal argument for affirmance of petitioners' § 371 convictions, however, is a great deal broader than the proposition stated above. The Government argues that, because Seminole received financial assistance and some supervision from the United States, a conspiracy to defraud Seminole is itself a conspiracy 'to defraud the United States.'

"The conspiracies criminalized by § 371 are defined not only by the nature of the injury intended by the conspiracy, and the method used to effectuate the conspiracy, but also—and most importantly—by the target of the conspiracy. Section 371 covers conspiracies to defraud 'the United States or any agency thereof,' a phrase that the Government concedes fails to describe Seminole Electric. * * * The Government suggests, however, that Seminole served as an intermediary performing official functions on behalf of the Federal Government, and on this basis a conspiracy to defraud Seminole may constitute a conspiracy to defraud the United States under § 371. * * *

"[T]he interpretation of § 371 proposed by the Government in this case has not even an arguable basis in the plain language of § 371. * * * Rather than seeking a particular interpretation of ambiguous statutory language, the Government, in arguing that § 371 covers conspiracies to defraud those acting on behalf of the United States, asks this Court to expand the reach of a criminal provision by reading new language into it. This we cannot do.

"Moreover, even if the Government's interpretation of § 371 could be pegged to some language in that section, the Government has presented us with nothing to overcome our rule that 'ambiguity concerning the ambit of criminal statutes should be resolved in favor of lenity.' The Government has wrested no aid from § 371's stingy legislative history. Neither has the Government suggested much to commend its interpretation in terms of clarity of application. Petitioners assert that the Government's logic would require any conspiracy to defraud someone who receives federal assistance to fall within § 371. The Government replies that 'there must be substantial ongoing federal supervision of the defrauded intermediary or delegation of a distinctly federal function to that intermediary to render a fraud upon the intermediary a fraud upon the "United States."' Yet the facts of this case demonstrate the difficulty of ascertaining how much federal supervision should be considered 'substantial' The Government emphasizes the supervisory powers granted the REA in the loan agreement; petitioners argue that the restrictions placed by the REA on Seminole were comparable to those 'that a bank places on any borrower in connection with a secured transaction.' Given the immense variety of ways the Federal Government provides financial assistance, and the fact that such assistance is always accompanied by restrictions on its use, the inability of the 'substantial supervision' test to provide any real guidance is apparent. 'A criminal statute, after if not before it is judicially construed, should have a discernable meaning.'

"Although the Government's sweeping interpretation of § 371—which would have, in effect, substituted 'anyone receiving federal financial assistance and supervision' for the phrase 'the United States or any agency thereof' in § 371—must fail, the Government also charged petitioners with conspiring to manipulate Seminole in order to cause misrepresentations to be made to the REA, an agency of the United States. The indictment against petitioners stated that:

'It was further a part of the conspiracy that the defendants would and did cause Seminole Electric to falsely state and represent to the Rural Electrification Administration that an REA-approved competitive bidding procedure had been followed in awarding the access road construction contracts.'

"If the evidence presented at trial was sufficient to establish that petitioners conspired to cause Seminole to make misrepresentations to the REA, then petitioners' convictions may stand. Because the sufficiency of the evidence on this particular charge in the indictment was not passed on below, we remand this case to the Court of Appeals for further proceedings on this question."

4. Consider Abraham S. Goldstein, *Conspiracy to Defraud the United States,* 68 Yale L.J. 405, 461–62 (1959): " 'Conspiracy to defraud the United States' has evolved in several stages. First, it was a crime reaching only agreements to use falsehood to induce action by the Government which would cause it a loss of money or property. It expanded to include an agreed-upon falsehood which might disadvantage the Government in any way whatever, and ultimately covered virtually any impairment of the Government's operating efficiency. The end to be gained having thus been obscured, it remained only for the means to be made equally shadowy. This was accomplished in the cases which viewed any dishonest act, including concealment, as the measure of an interference with the Government. Suspiciously unethical conduct, the failure to disclose even that which Congress had never required to be disclosed, became the raw material from which criminal liability was fashioned.

"As a result of these interpretations, the federal conspiracy statute has become another governmental weapon in the eternal conflict between authority and the individual. By making unclear the line between what is permitted and what is prohibited, by conceiving the statute's reach to be as broad as that of an expanding government, present doctrine places within the power of police and prosecutor an instrument for intruding upon Everyman. The instrument is all the more dangerous because it wears the garb of conspiracy, with all the tactical and evidentiary benefits that that doctrine implies. Imprecise definition and procedural advantages combine to make it virtually certain that a charge of conspiracy to defraud the United States will get to the jury—where a showing of suspicious behavior by the sort of people who ought to know better and who least appeal to that body's occasional empathy for those who commit crimes of passion and violence, is very likely to produce conviction."

5. Most jurisdictions which have adopted new codes in recent years have followed *Model Penal Code* § 5.03, which requires that the object of a conspiracy be the commission of a crime.[a]

Does the Model Penal Code go far enough? Consider Note, 75 Colum.L.Rev. 1122, 1130–31 (1975): "A number of states have gone even further. For an agreement to be criminal in Oregon, either a felony or a class A misdemeanor must be included among its objectives. The laws of New Mexico, Texas, and Virginia do not prohibit conspiracies to commit any sort of misdemeanor; they subject agreements to criminal sanctions only where the goal sought constitutes a felony. Ohio has chosen the most drastic approach of all, making criminal only conspiracies designed to achieve one or more of certain enumerated criminal ends, including murder, kidnapping, compelling or promoting prostitution, arson, robbery, burglary, and felonious unauthorized use of a vehicle. Such limitation of the range

---

a. This is not to suggest that the sole objective or the primary objective must be criminal. In *Anderson v. United States,* 417 U.S. 211, 94 S.Ct. 2253, 41 L.Ed.2d 20 (1974), the Court held:

"In our view, petitioners err in seeking to attach significance to the fact that the primary motive behind their conspiracy was to affect the result in the local rather than the federal election. A single conspiracy may have several purposes, but if one of them—whether primary or secondary—be the violation of a federal law, the conspiracy is unlawful under federal law."

of possible conspiratorial objectives to a set of offenses narrower than the set of all crimes probably reflects a degree of legislative uneasiness with the basic notion of conspiracy as an independent crime. To the extent that certain crimes are rejected as potential bases for making agreements to commit them criminal, a judgment has been made that the societal benefits, measured in terms of prevention of substantive offenses and protection against group criminal endeavor, to be derived from early law enforcement action (and the other procedural advantages offered by conspiracy) are insufficient to counterbalance the likelihood of invasion of individual liberties inherent in a more far-reaching conspiracy statute.[b] Of course, such considerations go to the very heart of the justification for denominating conspiracy criminal. Widespread acceptance of the recently enacted Ohio statutory pattern would spell the end of conspiracy as a general inchoate crime."

SECTION 5. IMPOSSIBILITY

VENTIMIGLIA v. UNITED STATES

United States Court of Appeals, Fourth Circuit, 1957.

242 F.2d 620.

SOBELOFF, CIRCUIT JUDGE.

The Taft–Hartley Act forbids the payment of money by an employer subject to its provisions to "any representative of any of his employees." 29 U.S.C.A. § 186(a). The defendants were indicted for three substantive violations of this law and for conspiracy to violate it. At a trial before the District Judge, sitting without a jury, the defendants were acquitted of the substantive offenses, but convicted of the conspiracy. The sufficiency of the evidence to sustain the conviction is the question raised by this appeal.

Weather–Mastic, Inc., is a non-unionized contractor engaged in the insulating and weather-proofing business. Parran is its general manager and Ventimiglia its labor relations adviser. In the prevailing industry practice, workers are required to have in their possession some evidence of union membership, if in fact affiliated with a union, or "working cards," which the union customarily issues to a limited number of non-union men seeking work on union jobs. Having been accepted as a sub-contractor for a job in Alexandria on which Stone and Webster, a unionized company, was general contractor, Weather–Mastic faced the need of obtaining working cards for its men. Joseph Martin, business agent of Local No. 80 of United Slate, Tile and Composition Roofers, Damp and Water Proof Workers, complained to Weather–Mastic that its workmen were carrying

---

b. See Comment, 47 Tulane L.Rev. 1017, 1036 (1973), contending, with respect to conspiracy in the proposed federal code, that "the inchoate crime rationale and the group danger rationale should be adequately satisfied by prohibiting conspiratorial agreements to commit crimes involving potential violence to persons or property, or involving serious danger to the nation. No attempt will be made here to specify which offenses should be classified as involving potential violence to persons or property, or serious danger to the nation, but it is easily seen that conspiracy to commit murder should be included while conspiracy to disseminate obscene material should not. Those involved in the latter conspiracy could be liable for the offense itself, for attempt or for their complicity."

See also David B. Filvaroff, *Conspiracy and the First Amendment*, 121 U.Pa.L.Rev. 189, 234–35 (1972):

"The justification for intervening through the criminal process in the case of unexecuted conspiracy to murder, for example, is that should the conspirators carry out their plans immediate and irreparable harm is likely to result to the victim. The case of conspiracy to commit a speech crime is hardly comparable. Prosecution for conspiracy to incite to violence must be justified on remoter grounds. Just as conspiracy itself is an inchoate crime, so too is incitement, like most other speech crimes. Thus, to charge a speech conspiracy is to load one inchoate offense upon another. Even if the conspirators act, the immediate result is not violence but the impact on others of the assertedly inciting words. These may or may not prove effective in achieving the conspirators' ends. Another stage must be reached before the harm—here violence—befalls; the listeners must themselves move to do that which the conspirators seek to induce."

"working cards" issued, not by him, but by Ventimiglia, who was then in the service of Weather–Mastic, Inc., but had earlier been the business agent of the union. After discussion, Martin was persuaded by the defendants to issue working cards to Weather–Mastic's employees, for which the defendants agreed to pay Martin One Hundred Dollars each month.

Martin's duties as business agent for Local No. 80 are said to be of the usual type: negotiating wage contracts and working conditions, representing the union members and acting as peacemaker between employers and union members in respect to disputes or grievances. Martin never represented any of Weather–Mastic's employees in any of these respects. He did issue working cards signed by him, which he delivered to Ventimiglia. For this he received several monthly payments from the defendants.

An additional duty of union business agents is to check on the union credentials of men engaged on a union job who are not members of his union. The evidence is that if another business agent was skeptical of an employee's working card, the usual procedure would be to make inquiry of the agent who had issued the card, and if he verified its validity, that ordinarily would be enough to satisfy the inquirer. While Weather–Mastic's men were never asked to show their cards, except by the Federal Bureau of Investigation (to whom Martin had reported his agreement with the defendants), the significance sought to be attached to this fact is that Martin, it is said, was prepared to stand behind and vouch for Weather–Mastic's employees if questions as to their status should ever arise.

It is, of course, beyond dispute that a punishable conspiracy may exist independent of the actual commission of the substantive offense which was the object of the conspiracy. This need not be labored. However, there can be no conviction for conspiracy to commit an offense against the United States if the act that the alleged conspirators agree to do has not been made unlawful, and is not planned to be accomplished in an unlawful manner.

According to the court's findings, the testimony affirmatively established that the corporate defendant's employees were not at any time members of Martin's union, and that there is no evidence that they authorized or subsequently ratified Martin's representing them; and the court added—correctly, we think—that there is here no representation by operation of law. If Martin was no representative of the employees, section 186(a) did not apply to him. The court concluded, as we think was required in these circumstances, that the section was not violated, and he entered the not guilty verdict as to the three substantive counts.

In considering the conspiracy count, however, the Court predicated a verdict of guilty upon the theory that while the defendants did not desire Martin to represent the employees in *all* respects, they did intend to deal with him as their employees' representative in issuing cards evidencing the union's willingness to permit them to work on union jobs. The opinion says: "He [Martin] was to furnish the necessary indicia of union membership, and if questions arose, handle the matter so that there would be no interruption to work. * * * He was not to organize them, or to negotiate on their behalf with the employer as to wages. But there can be no doubt that the defendants intended Martin to do acts which a representative of employees would be expected to do—insure the availability and continuity of work. Likewise, Martin could have become the formal representative of the employees had they initiated the issuance of cards, or accepted or used them knowing the reasons for which, and the circumstances under which the cards were issued."

Thereupon, the Court concluded that, for a period at least, defendants intended to deal with and dealt with Martin as a representative of their employees. He added that "the defendants cannot avoid the natural consequences of their conduct by a simple denial that

Martin was such a representative when the evidence is that they intended him to be and dealt with him in that capacity; nor does the fact that they did not want him to be (and indeed forbade him to be) the employees' representative in certain respects, prevent him from being such representative in the limited field in which he was to, and did, act."

In analyzing the evidence in connection with the conspiracy count, the District Judge, we think fell into error. The testimony, it seems to us, does not lend itself to the treatment given it. Plainly enough, the defendants did not deal with Martin as their employees' representative, and never intended to deal with him as such. They did not want him to approach their employees or organize them, or represent them, and he did not do so. As the Court declared in a subsidiary finding of fact, the defendants induced Martin *not* to organize or represent the employees. The cards he issued were not "indicia of union membership;" on the contrary, they were working cards such as are customarily issued to non-members, to workers *not* represented by the union. Employees represented by the union or by its business agent require no such cards. The purpose of the cards is to sanction work by *non*-union men, who are unrepresented. So, far from treating them as union members and thus under representation by Martin, he treated them as the only class of workers who could carry such cards, namely, persons not in the union or represented by it or by its officers. * * *

The Government contends that a conspiracy may be punished even if the objective of the conspirators cannot be achieved, but the conspirators mistakenly think it can be. Even assuming that the defendants intended to treat Martin as their employees' representative, though in fact he was not, such a theory cannot avail to sustain the prosecution. The Government has referred us to cases in which conviction for conspiracy has been upheld despite the fact that, unknown to the conspirators, the object of the conspiracy was impossible of accomplishment, as where pickpockets conspired to rob an intended victim, but were frustrated by the fact that his pocket was empty. Such unexpected physical impossibility would not prevent successful prosecution for conspiracy.

But the present case is not comparable to the attempt to pick an empty pocket. The analogy to the present case would be closer if we assumed an attempt or conspiracy to pick the pocket of what is merely a wooden dummy. Criminal liability in such a case would seem highly implausible, and it would not save the prosecution to prove that the defendants thought that the object of their design and effort was human. A like distinction is that between an unsuccessful murder attempt due to a faulty gun or a blank cartridge, and a failure due to the fact that the intended victim was merely a block of wood, or a shadow. In the former, there would be a criminal attempt, while in the latter there would not. The distinction in these pairs of cases is readily discernible. It lies in the difference between, on the one hand, a physical impediment to completion of the crime due merely to miscalculation or to the choice of ineffective means which would normally be effective, and, on the other hand, a failure due to an inherent impossibility of completing the crime.

A legal impossibility might also, in many cases, be termed an inherent impossibility, in that the act, though consummated, would not be criminal, and consequently an attempt or agreement to commit it would also not be. * * *

* * * See also *O'Kelley v. U.S.,* 8 Cir., 116 F.2d 966, where it was held that there could be no conspiracy to commit larceny of an interstate shipment, because there could be no substantive violation inasmuch as the goods had lost their interstate character. Similarly, if one thinks that a uniformed doorman is a police officer and bribes him not to tag his car, it is no crime, and neither the attempt nor the conspiracy can be, for there is an inherent or legal impossibility of consummating the offense, although the act itself was completed. Likewise, where one mistakenly believes a certain individual is the union representative of

his employees, the misconception cannot sufficiently negative the impossibility of committing the substantive offense so as to provide the basis for a conspiracy conviction. But where the object of a bribe is a draft board official of the United States who, but for the defendant's mistake of registering with the wrong board, would have had no jurisdiction over the defendant, the impossibility was not inherent but was due simply to a prior mistaken course of action. See *United States v. Schanerman,* 3 Cir., 150 F.2d 941. * * *

Even were we to doubt the foregoing propositions and their application here, the present case is on the facts of an even more extreme variety, for it is said merely that the defendants *intended* to deal with Martin as their employees' representative. The previous example of the doorman will suffice to show the fallacy of basing a conviction on such a fact. Had the defendant in that hypothetical case, knowing that the doorman was not a police officer, nevertheless intended to deal with him as such, it could certainly not be said that he attempted to bribe a police officer. * * *

We conclude, therefore, that there could be no conviction under this indictment even if the defendants mistakenly thought that Martin was a representative of Weather–Mastic's employees. Even less can a conviction be sustained when it is clear beyond dispute, not only that he was not the employees' representative, but that no one concerned thought or pretended that he was.

Reversed.[a]

Notes and Questions

1.   In *United States v. Ho,* 155 F.3d 189 (3d Cir.1998), the court, notwithstanding its adherence to the principle that impossibility is a defense on an attempt charge, agreed with other federal decisions holding impossibility is *not* a defense on a conspiracy charge. *Ventimiglia* was dismissed on the ground that there "the court's comments regarding legal impossibility were entirely dicta." Is this correct?

2.   Also compare *United States v. Thomas,* p. 675 of this Book, where the majority went on to conclude that its holding that impossibility was no defense on the attempt charge was likewise applicable to the conspiracy charge. Significantly, Ferguson, J., who vigorously dissented from the affirmance of the attempt conviction, stated:

"Despite my position with respect to the charge of attempted rape, I would affirm the conviction of conspiracy to commit rape. Unlike criminal attempts, legal impossibility is not recognized as a defense to a charge of conspiracy. Although both crimes are, in a sense, inchoate offenses, their development has been somewhat different. At common law, conspiracy consisted only of the agreement to do an unlawful act or a lawful act in an unlawful manner. Although Code, supra, Article 81, 10 USC § 881, requires proof of an overt act in addition to the agreement to commit an offense under the Code, we have held that the heart of the crime remains the corrupt meeting of the minds. Here, the accused agreed to have intercourse with an unconscious girl against her will and while she was unable to resist. The averred overt act was also made out. As what these two men thus subjectively agreed to be their objective constitutes in law the offense of rape, in violation of Code, supra, Article 120, 10 USC § 920, and as thereafter one of them performed an overt act, guilt of conspiracy is made out. My objection is simply to the action of my brothers in transferring the subjective approach in conspiracy to the objective questions involved in attempts."

a. When Congress thereafter amended the labor laws, *Ventimiglia* served "as an example of a loophole that the amendments were designed to close." *United States v. Pecora,* 798 F.2d 614 (3d Cir.1986).

3. Is the Ferguson position inconsistent? Consider *State v. Moretti,* 52 N.J. 182, 244 A.2d 499 (1968), affirming convictions of conspiracy to commit an illegal abortion upon a woman who in fact was a nonpregnant police agent: "The case has been argued as though, for purposes of the defense of impossibility, a conspiracy charge is the same as a charge of attempting to commit a crime. It seems that such an equation could not be sustained, however, because, as discussed above, a conspiracy charge focuses primarily on the *intent* of the defendants, while in an attempt case the primary inquiry centers on the defendants' *conduct* tending toward the commission of the substantive crime. The crime of conspiracy is complete once the conspirators, having formed the intent to commit a crime, take any step in preparation; mere preparation, however, is an inadequate basis for an attempt conviction regardless of the intent. Thus, the impossibility that the defendants' conduct will result in the consummation of the contemplated crime is not as pertinent in a conspiracy case as it might be in an attempt prosecution."

4. Might it be argued that there is *more,* rather than less, reason to recognize impossibility as a defense when the charge is conspiracy? Consider *People v. Tinskey,* 394 Mich. 108, 228 N.W.2d 782 (1975), involving facts similar to those in *Moretti:* "It is possible, although we need not decide, that defendants could not have been convicted of attempted abortion; at common law the general rule is that while factual impossibility is not a defense, legal impossibility is a defense.

"The somewhat indeterminate common-law definition of conspiracy, as a combination to accomplish some criminal or unlawful purpose or end or to accomplish a lawful purpose or end by criminal or unlawful means, was replaced by 1966 P.A. 296, which defines the object of the conspiracy as the 'commit[ting of] an offense prohibited by law' or of 'a legal act in an illegal manner.'

"While the crime of conspiracy is distinct from the substantive offense, the Legislature has indicated that in Michigan the penalty for an attempt to commit an offense shall be significantly less than the penalty for the substantive offense. We note, without resting decision on this ground, that to charge a person with conspiracy—which may subject the offender to the same jail or prison sentence as the substantive offense—as a substitute for charging attempt to commit the offense tends to circumvent that legislative policy.

"There are two statutory patterns prevalent in this country: one requiring that the woman be pregnant (Michigan and other states), the other requiring only that the person to be aborted be a woman. The Legislature, having elected the pattern requiring that the person to be aborted be pregnant, has rejected prosecutions where the person is not pregnant. It has indicated that an attempted abortion which does not or cannot succeed because the person is not pregnant is not a crime. The Legislature has not, as to most other offenses, so similarly indicated that impossibility is not a defense.

"In this statutory pattern, the crime of conspiracy to commit abortion cannot be committed with respect to a person who is not pregnant."

SECTION 6. THE OVERT ACT REQUIREMENT

DEVELOPMENTS IN THE LAW—CRIMINAL CONSPIRACY

72 Harv.L.Rev. 920, 945–48 (1959).

At common law the crime of conspiracy was indictable upon the formation of the agreement. In enacting conspiracy statutes, several jurisdictions, including the federal government, have required that an overt act in furtherance of the conspiracy be proved. Such a provision has seldom materially increased the difficulty of securing convictions for conspiracy. A noncriminal and relatively minor act is held to satisfy the requirement if it is in furtherance of the conspiracy. An act committed by any one of the conspirators is sufficient both as to all present members of the conspiracy and as to persons subsequently joining the agreement. The act, however, cannot be part of the formation of the agreement, nor can it take place after termination of the conspiracy. But it may be the step which accomplishes the conspiracy's objective. There need not be an affirmative act, since nonfeasance may in some circumstances satisfy the requirement.

The inclusion of the overt-act requirement in the federal general conspiracy statute was unaccompanied by any indication of the function it was to serve. It may have represented merely a legislative interpretation of what was necessary to prove a conspiracy at common law. The secrecy normally surrounding formulation of criminal plans makes proof of the agreement by direct evidence improbable and usually forces the prosecution to rely upon conduct of the conspirators from which an inference of an agreement can be drawn. Thus, since most conspiracy prosecutions involved proof of an overt act, there emerged a practice of alleging such acts in the indictment. The courts, however, have pragmatically used other rationales of the requirement to justify results which seemed desirable.

In *United States v. Donau*[178] the defendant sought to quash an indictment on the ground that the overt acts alleged were not reasonably calculated to effect the specific object of the conspiracy. In overruling the motion, the court held that the statutory offense consisted of the agreement alone, the overt act merely affording a *"locus poenitentiae"* so that before the commission of the act a conspirator might withdraw from the scheme without incurring guilt. * * *

In *Hyde v. United States*,[180] the Court viewed the overt act as an element of the offense in order to hold that venue could be laid in any district in which such an act had been committed. Mr. Justice Holmes, dissenting, reasoned that the act itself was no more a part of the offense than was the fact that the statute of limitations had not run. That the rationale employed in *Hyde* was not the exclusive means of reaching the result of the case is indicated by the similar venue decisions in jurisdictions not requiring an overt act. * * *

The overt-act requirement may also be interpreted as a legislative determination that a mere agreement does not usually represent a sufficient threat of the specific offense or sufficient evidence of a general danger to warrant criminal prosecution. This rationale seems particularly apparent in the few instances in which legislatures have, for conspiracies to commit certain serious crimes, made specific exceptions to a general rule which requires allegation and proof of an overt act.

Notes and Questions

1. In *United States v. Shabani*, 513 U.S. 10, 115 S.Ct. 382, 130 L.Ed.2d 225 (1994), the Court found "it instructive that the general conspiracy statute, 18 U.S.C. § 371, contains an explicit requirement that a conspirator 'do any act to effect the object of the conspiracy,'" for that was deemed to support the Court's conclusion that special conspiracy provisions, such as 21 U.S.C. § 846 concerning drug conspiracies, which did not contain such or similar language, thus did *not* require proof of an overt act. As for Shabani's claim "that conspiracy without an overt act requirement violates [the] principle" "that the law does not punish criminal thoughts" because then "the offense is predominantly mental in composition," the Court responded that the conspiracy prohibition "does not punish mere thought; the criminal agreement itself is the *actus reus*."

178. 25 Fed.Cas. 890 (No. 14983) (S.D.N.Y.1873).   **180.** 225 U.S. 347 (1912).

2.   Note, 49 Stan.L.Rev. 111, 113–14 (1996), "argues that there is a more compelling explanation of the overt act requirement, one that the *Shabani* Court overlooked entirely: namely, that the overt act requirement protects a defendant's constitutional right not to be convicted 'except upon proof beyond a reasonable doubt of every fact necessary to constitute the crime with which he is charged.' The standard of proof beyond a reasonable doubt is central to American criminal law; as the Supreme Court observed in *In re Winship*, '[i]t is a prime instrument for reducing the risk of convictions resting on factual error.' * * * *Shabani*'s elimination of the overt act requirement is fundamentally irreconcilable with the *Winship* standard—the government cannot prove that a defendant is guilty of conspiracy beyond a reasonable doubt unless it can prove, through circumstantial evidence, that she committed at least one overt act in furtherance of the conspiracy.

" * * * *Shabani*'s primary evidentiary effect is to encourage the government to take drug conspiracy cases to trial in which it can connect the defendant to the conspiracy only through direct evidence. [D]irect evidence is not reliable enough to sustain a conspiracy conviction absent corroborating circumstantial evidence that the defendant committed an overt act in furtherance of the conspiracy. [A] conspiracy prosecution based solely on direct evidence violates the basic evidentiary assumption of conspiracy doctrine: that the secret nature of the crime requires the government to use circumstantial evidence to prove that the conspiracy exists. [U]nless corroborated by circumstantial evidence of an overt act, coconspirator testimony is not reliable enough to sustain a conspiracy conviction. [A]n overt act requirement is necessary to prevent juries from improperly convicting defendants through guilt by association. * * * *Shabani*'s elimination of the overt act requirement also effectively insulates unjust convictions from meaningful appellate review."

3.   Does the overt act requirement serve a useful purpose? Does it make sense to require an overt act for some types of conspiracies but not for others? Should more than a "mere" overt act be required? In assessing these questions, consider the variety of approaches taken in recent codifications, as reported in Note, 75 Colum.L.Rev. 1122, 1153–54 (1975):

"Some dispute exists among the states over whether an overt act in pursuance of an agreement to commit a crime should be a prerequisite for a conspiracy conviction. Though such an act was not necessary at common law, two-thirds of the jurisdictions which have revised or are considering revision of their conspiracy statutes have elected to impose such an additional requirement before an agreement to commit any offense will be proscribed. Another five states, choosing to follow the [Model Penal Code] pattern, insist on an overt act in all cases other than those involving agreements to commit a first or second degree felony (or one of a similar list of serious crimes). Maine, Ohio, Washington, and Vermont, all members of the former group, set even stricter standards than the rest of the majority. Statutes in these states permit conspiracy convictions only where a *'substantial step'* has been taken in furtherance of the conspiracy. Under the laws recently adopted in Ohio and proposed in Vermont, an act, to qualify as 'substantial,' must be 'of such character as to manifest a purpose on the part of the actor that the object of the conspiracy should be completed.' Maine's new conspiracy provision further narrows the definition of 'substantial step,' demanding 'conduct which, under the circumstances in which it occurs, is *strongly corroborative* of the firmness of the actor's intent to complete commission of the crime,' and adding that 'speech alone may not constitute a substantial step.' This language greatly resembles that found in Maine's attempt section, and indicates that Maine may be tending toward the elimination of all conspiracy liability where a substantive offense has not been at least attempted. Such a development may also be favored by Washington, which uses the phrase 'substantial step' without definition in both its conspiracy and its attempt provisions. At the opposite extreme, eight states have decided, for one reason or another, to preserve the common law scheme on this issue, and so require no overt act whatever. Under such statutes, the crime of conspiracy is complete when the agreement is formed."

4.   Under a statute requiring proof of an overt act, should proof of an omission of a legal duty suffice? Consider *People v. Abedi*, 156 Misc.2d 904, 595 N.Y.S.2d 1011 (1993): "There would seem to be no reason why an omission in the appropriate circumstances could not be an overt act. Filing a form with crucial information omitted might be such an overt act. But in general simply not doing something would not seem to qualify as an overt act. Certainly, since the purpose of requiring pleading and proof of overt acts is to show that a conspiracy has moved beyond the talk stage and is being carried out, alleging failure to act as an overt act seems to be a contradiction in terms. The overt acts alleged in the instant indictment consist of failing to inform an allied attorney over a period of five years of the means by which CCAH stock was purchased; failure by two of the defendants to inform their law partners over the same period of the means by which the stock was purchased; and, when informing an auditor of loans, failing to mention their non-recourse nature. None of these omissions seem to this court to be overt acts.

"[In] *Gerson v. United States*, 25 F.2d 49 [(8th Cir.1928)], the overt act in question consisted of failing to list assets on a bankruptcy petition. Here there was not so much an omission, but an act, namely, filing an incomplete petition. This is quite different from the supposed overt acts in the instant case."

SECTION 7. SCOPE: THE OBJECT DIMENSION

BRAVERMAN v. UNITED STATES

Supreme Court of the United States, 1942.

317 U.S. 49, 63 S.Ct. 99, 87 L.Ed. 23.

Mr. Chief Justice Stone delivered the opinion of the Court.

[The question is:] Whether a conviction upon the several counts of an indictment, each charging conspiracy to violate a different provision of the Internal Revenue laws, where the jury's verdict is supported by evidence of but a single conspiracy, will sustain a sentence of more than two years' imprisonment, the maximum penalty for a single violation of the conspiracy statute * * *.

Petitioners were indicted, with others, on seven counts, each charging a conspiracy to violate a separate and distinct internal revenue law of the United States.[1] On the trial there was evidence from which the jury could have found that for a considerable period of time petitioners, with others, collaborated in the illicit manufacture, transportation, and distribution of distilled spirits involving the violations of statute mentioned in the several counts of the indictment. At the close of the trial petitioners renewed a motion which they

---

1.   The seven counts respectively charged them with conspiracy, in violation of § 37 of the Criminal Code, unlawfully (1) to carry on the business of wholesale and retail liquor dealers without having the special occupational tax stamps required by statute, 26 U.S.C. § 3253, 26 U.S.C.A. Int.Rev.Code § 3253; (2) to possess distilled spirits, the immediate containers of which did not have stamps affixed denoting the quantity of the distilled spirits which they contained and evidencing payment of all Internal Revenue taxes imposed on such spirits, 26 U.S.C. § 2803, 26 U.S.C.A. Int.Rev.Code § 2803; (3) to transport quantities of distilled spirits, the immediate containers of which did not have affixed the required stamps, 26 U.S.C. § 2803, 26 U.S.C.A. Int.Rev.Code § 2803; (4) to carry on the business of distillers without having given bond as required by law, 26 U.S.C. § 2833, 26 U.S.C.A. Int.Rev.Code, § 2833; (5) to remove, deposit and conceal distilled spirits in respect whereof a tax is imposed by law, with intent to defraud the United States of such tax, 26 U.S.C. § 3321, 26 U.S.C.A. Int.Rev.Code § 3321; (6) to possess unregistered stills and distilling apparatus, 26 U.S.C. § 2810, 26 U.S.C.A. Int.Rev.Code § 2810; and (7) to make and ferment mash, fit for distillation, on unauthorized premises, 26 U.S.C. § 2834, 26 U.S.C.A. Int. Rev.Code § 2834.

had made at its beginning to require the Government to elect one of the seven counts of the indictment upon which to proceed, contending that the proof could not and did not establish more than one agreement. In response the Government's attorney took the position that the seven counts of the indictment charged as distinct offenses the several illegal objects of one continuing conspiracy, that if the jury found such a conspiracy it might find the defendants guilty of as many offenses as it had illegal objects, and that for each such offense the two-year statutory penalty could be imposed.

The trial judge submitted the case to the jury on that theory. The jury returned a general verdict finding petitioners "guilty as charged", and the court sentenced each to eight years' imprisonment. On appeal the Court of Appeals for the Sixth Circuit affirmed * * *.

Both courts below recognized that a single agreement to commit an offense does not become several conspiracies because it continues over a period of time, and that there may be such a single continuing agreement to commit several offenses. But they thought that in the latter case each contemplated offense renders the agreement punishable as a separate conspiracy.

The question whether a single agreement to commit acts in violation of several penal statutes is to be punished as one or several conspiracies is raised on the present record, not by the construction of the indictment, but by the Government's concession at the trial and here, reflected in the charge to the jury, that only a single agreement to commit the offenses alleged was proven. Where each of the counts of an indictment alleges a conspiracy to violate a different penal statute it may be proper to conclude, in the absence of a bill of exceptions bringing up the evidence, that several conspiracies are charged rather than one, and that the conviction is for each. But it is a different matter to hold, as the court below appears to have done in this case, that even though a single agreement is entered into, the conspirators are guilty of as many offenses as the agreement has criminal objects. * * *

[W]hen a single agreement to commit one or more substantive crimes is evidenced by an overt act, as the statute requires, the precise nature and extent of the conspiracy must be determined by reference to the agreement which embraces and defines its objects. Whether the object of a single agreement is to commit one or many crimes, it is in either case that agreement which constitutes the conspiracy which the statute punishes. The one agreement cannot be taken to be several agreements and hence several conspiracies because it envisages the violation of several statutes rather than one.

The allegation in a single count of a conspiracy to commit several crimes is not duplicitous, for "The conspiracy is the crime, and that is one, however diverse its objects". A conspiracy is not the commission of the crime which it contemplates, and neither violates nor "arises under" the statute whose violation is its object. Since the single continuing agreement, which is the conspiracy here, thus embraces its criminal objects, it differs from successive acts which violate a single penal statute and from a single act which violates two statutes. The single agreement is the prohibited conspiracy, and however diverse its objects it violates but a single statute, § 37 of the Criminal Code. For such a violation only the single penalty prescribed by the statute can be imposed. * * *

Reversed.

Notes and Questions

1. Compare *Lievers v. State,* 3 Md.App. 597, 241 A.2d 147 (1968), where the defendants were convicted of several conspiracies. The evidence was that their scheme involved the obtaining of a counterfeit chauffeur's license which was used in trying to utter (i.e., pass) a check they had forged, by which they would have obtained $104.87:

"As indicated, appellants were convicted of (a) conspiracy to forge a designated check in the amount of $104.87, (b) conspiracy to utter said forged check, (c) conspiracy to obtain $104.87 from a designated corporation by a 'certain' false pretense, and (d) conspiracy to hold and use a designated forged and counterfeited Maryland chauffeur's license. In *Tender v. State*, 2 Md.App. 692, 237 A.2d 65, we held that a person should not be twice punished for the same acts whether the offenses charged by reason of such acts be deemed to be inconsistent, duplicitous, or to have merged. The true test of merger of offenses is whether one crime necessarily involves the other. Thus in *Sutton v. State*, 2 Md.App. 639, 236 A.2d 301, we held, on the facts of that case, that the substantive offense of uttering merged into the offense of false pretenses where the false representation consisted only of the uttering. It appears to us from the evidence in this case that the conspiracy to utter merged into the conspiracy to obtain money by false pretenses since no false representation independent of the uttering of the forged check itself is shown by the evidence.

"Holding and using a forged Maryland chauffeur's license with fraudulent intent is a felony. We think it clear that appellant's conviction for conspiring to hold and use such a document clearly charges an act separate and distinct from any of the [other] conspiracies charged * * * and is indeed broader in scope than the other conspiracies since it is not limited to an agreement to hold and use such forged license solely in connection with an illegal effort to negotiate a forged check made payable to Steven Thompson in the amount of $104.87, dated March 18, 1965."

2. Compare the approach taken in *Braverman, Lievers,* and *Model Penal Code* § 5.03(3) in assessing whether there is more than one conspiracy in each of the following situations:

(a) *A, B* and *C* meet together and conceive a plan which they agree to use in robbing the First National Bank on June 1st and the Second National Bank on August 1st; equipment used for each robbery is thereafter acquired.

(b) *A, B* and *C* meet together and conceive a plan which they agree to use in robbing the First National Bank on June 1st. On May 30th, while working out the last minute details, it occurs to them that the plan is so good that they should also use it in robbing the Second National Bank on August 1st, which they agree to do. They continue meeting after the First National robbery for this latter purpose.

(c) *A, B* and *C* meet together and conceive a plan which they agree to use in robbing the First National Bank on June 1st. They carry out the robbery, distribute the proceeds, and disperse without any plan to meet again. On July 1st, *A* contacts *B* and *C* and proposes that they use the same plan to rob the Second National Bank on August 1st. *B* and *C* agree with *A*, and they thereafter meet to work out the details.

3. What then of the following facts, deemed in *People v. Burleson*, 50 Ill.App.3d 629, 8 Ill.Dec. 776, 365 N.E.2d 1162 (1977), to amount to two conspiracies? "On September 11, 1975, the defendant and Brown, having the necessary intent, agreed to rob the bank on September 13, 1975. In furtherance of this agreement, they committed the overt acts of 'casing' the bank, procuring a weapon and disguises, and going to the bank on September 13, 1975, to commit the crime. This first conspiracy was abandoned when the conspirators observed a large number of persons in and around the bank. Thereafter, the same conspirators, with the necessary intent, agreed to rob the bank on September 16, 1975, after which they committed the overt acts of preserving the disguises, participating in a practice escape from the bank and in approaching the bank on September 16, 1975."

4. Consider Note, 75 Colum.L.Rev. 1122, 1163–64 (1975): "The basic rule concerning the object dimension of conspiracy is that multiple criminal objectives do not imply

multiple conspiracies, 'so long as such multiple crimes are the object of the same agreement or continuous conspiratorial relationship.' Nearly two-thirds of the jurisdictions surveyed, including the federal, have devoted no statutory attention whatever to this issue, presumably in the belief that the controlling decisions dictate the same result. Fifteen states have included provisions similar or identical to the [Model Penal Code] subsection quoted above, and three more have drafted proposed sections in all likelihood intended to emulate the MPC. The efficacy of these latter sections in completely achieving their probable goal is cast in some doubt by their unexplained omission of the final phrase of MPC § 5.03(3): 'or continuous conspiratorial relationship.' That language was framed to dispose of logical problems encountered in the attempt to reconcile the agreement concept with the idea that a single conspiracy could be directed toward criminal objectives conceived at different times. The fundamental query under the MPC is a highly realistic one, namely, 'whether there was a single and continuous association for criminal purposes.' The statutory sections which fail to incorporate the notion of an ongoing conspiratorial relationship may nevertheless have been formulated with the MPC treatment in mind. The comments to the proposed Missouri provision evidence this fact. They state unequivocally that, 'If various offenses are the product of a continuous relationship they should be considered part of one conspiracy.'"

5. In *Albernaz v. United States,* 450 U.S. 333, 101 S.Ct. 1137, 67 L.Ed.2d 275 (1981), the Court held that notwithstanding a single agreement the defendants could be convicted and consecutively sentenced for violating 21 U.S.C.A. § 963, which proscribes conspiracy to commit any offense defined in Subchapter II of the Comprehensive Drug Abuse Prevention and Control Act of 1970, including importation of marijuana; and 21 U.S.C.A. § 846, which proscribes conspiracy to commit any offense defined in Subchapter I of the Act, including distribution of marijuana. The Court concluded this result conformed to the *Blockburger* rule of statutory construction—that where each provision requires proof of a fact the other does not, this indicates Congress intended to allow such cumulative conviction and punishment. *Braverman* was distinguished because the conspiracy there "violated but a single statute," while here two separate conspiracy statutes were involved.[a]

In *Mason v. State,* 302 Md. 434, 488 A.2d 955 (1985), where again it was conceded there was but a single agreement, the defendants were charged with two conspiracies: to distribute heroin; and to distribute cocaine. The state, noting that these were common law conspiracy charges because there is no conspiracy statute and noting further that cocaine distribution and heroin distribution are proscribed in separate sections of the Controlled Dangerous Substances Act, relied on *Albernaz.* The defendant relied on *Braverman.* What result?

6. In *United States v. Ervasti,* 201 F.3d 1029 (8th Cir.2000), the defendants were charged, inter alia, with conspiracy to commit mail fraud in violation of 18 U.S.C. § 371 for defrauding their corporation's clients of money and property, and with conspiracy to impede or injure the IRS in collection of taxes, also in violation of § 371. The defendants claimed that because there was but one agreement the charges violated *Braverman,* but the court disagreed. The court reasoned that § 371 "plainly establishes two offenses" because

a. In *Rutledge v. United States,* 517 U.S. 292, 116 S.Ct. 1241, 134 L.Ed.2d 419 (1996), by contrast, the Court applied *Blockburger* to hold that a defendant could not be convicted of both a conspiracy to distribute controlled substances under 21 U.S.C. § 846 and a continuing criminal enterprise "in concert" with others in violation of 21 U.S.C. § 848 where the "in concert" element of the latter was the same agreement as the § 846 conspiracy. Distinguishing *Albernaz,* the Court noted that "the proximity of §§ 846 and 848 indicates that Congress understood them to be directed to similar, rather than separate, evils."

On the other hand, the *Blockburger* rule presents no barrier to prosecution of the defendant for the conspiracy and also the attained criminal objective. *United States v. Felix,* 503 U.S. 378, 112 S.Ct. 1377, 118 L.Ed.2d 25 (1992).

of its reference to conspiracy "either to commit any offense against the United States or to defraud the United States," and thus concluded that because in the instant case there was a charge of both an "offense" type of conspiracy and a "defraud" type *Braverman* was not violated, for *Braverman* dealt only with multiple charges under the "offense" provision.

Do you agree? Does *Albernaz* support the conclusion in *Ervasti*? Compare *United States v. Smith*, 891 F.2d 703 (9th Cir.1989) ("the two clauses of [§ 371] should be interpreted to establish alternate means of commission, not separate offenses" as "[i]t would be strange to infer that Congress intended to punish twice a conspiracy that violates both clauses. Where a single criminal statute prohibits alternative acts, courts should not infer the legislature's intent to impose multiple punishment").

SECTION 8. SCOPE: THE PARTY DIMENSION

Introductory Notes

1. *Model Penal Code* § 5.03, Comment (1985): "Much of the most perplexing litigation in conspiracy has been concerned less with the essential elements of the offense than with the scope to be accorded to a combination i.e., the singleness or multiplicity of the conspiratorial relationships typical in a large, complex and sprawling network of crime. * * *

"The inquiry may be crucial for a number of purposes. These include not only defining each defendant's liability but also the propriety of joint prosecution, admissibility against a defendant of the hearsay acts and declarations of others, questions of multiple prosecution or conviction and double jeopardy, satisfaction of the overt act requirement or statutes of limitation or rules of jurisdiction and venue, and possibly liability for substantive crimes executed pursuant to the conspiracy. The scope problem is thus central to the present concern of courts and commentators about the use of conspiracy, a concern based on the conflict between the need for effective means of prosecuting large criminal organizations, and the dangers of prejudice to individual defendants."

2. Phillip E. Johnson, *The Unnecessary Crime of Conspiracy*, 61 Calif.L.Rev. 1137, 1168–71 (1973): "Most cases in which joinder by conspiracy is disputed reflect a variation or combination of two familiar models, the 'wheel' and the 'chain.' In a wheel conspiracy, various defendants accused of individual criminal transactions are linked together by the fact that one defendant or one group of defendants participated in every transaction. For graphic purposes, the defendant or defendants implicated in every charge are described as the hub of the wheel and those charged with individual crimes as the spokes. The United States Supreme Court discovered such a wheel in unusually pure form in *Kotteakos v. United States*. * * *

" * * * As the name indicates, a chain conspiracy involves the chain of distribution of some commodity, such as narcotics, from the initial manufacture or smuggling to the ultimate consumer. A chain conspiracy is similar to a wheel conspiracy in that the participants at opposite ends of the chain may not know or have any dealings with each other, but the two are different in that the participants in a chain conspiracy all deal with the same goods. A chain may, and frequently does, incorporate one or more subsidiary wheels. Thus in *United States v. Bruno*, the most famous chain case, the conspiracy consisted of smugglers who brought narcotics into New York, middlemen who purchased from the smugglers and resold to retailers, and two groups of retailers, one operating in New York and the other in Texas and Louisiana."

KOTTEAKOS v. UNITED STATES

Supreme Court of the United States, 1946.

328 U.S. 750, 66 S.Ct. 1239, 90 L.Ed. 1557.

Mr. Justice Rutledge delivered the opinion of the Court.

The only question is whether petitioners have suffered substantial prejudice from being convicted of a single general conspiracy by evidence which the Government admits proved not one conspiracy but some eight or more different ones of the same sort executed through a common key figure, Simon Brown. Petitioners were convicted of conspiring to violate the provisions of the National Housing Act. * * *

The indictment named thirty-two defendants, including the petitioners. The gist of the conspiracy, as alleged, was that the defendants had sought to induce various financial institutions to grant credit, with the intent that the loans or advances would then be offered to the Federal Housing Administration for insurance upon applications containing false and fraudulent information.

Of the thirty-two persons named in the indictment nineteen were brought to trial and the names of thirteen were submitted to the jury. Two were acquitted; the jury disagreed as to four; and the remaining seven, including petitioners, were found guilty.

The Government's evidence may be summarized briefly, for the petitioners have not contended that it was insufficient, if considered apart from the alleged errors relating to the proof and the instructions at the trial.

Simon Brown, who pleaded guilty, was the common and key figure in all of the transactions proven. He was president of the Brownie Lumber Company. Having had experience in obtaining loans under the National Housing Act, he undertook to act as broker in placing for others loans for modernization and renovation, charging a five per cent commission for his services. Brown knew, when he obtained the loans, that the proceeds were not to be used for the purposes stated in the applications.

In May, 1939, petitioner Lekacos told Brown that he wished to secure a loan in order to finance opening a law office, to say the least a hardly auspicious professional launching. Brown made out the application, as directed by Lekacos, to state that the purpose of the loan was to modernize a house belonging to the estate of Lekacos' father. Lekacos obtained the money. Later in the same year Lekacos secured another loan through Brown, the application being in the names of his brother and sister-in-law. Lekacos also received part of the proceeds of a loan for which one Gerakeris, a defendant who pleaded guilty, had applied.

In June, 1939, Lekacos sent Brown an application for a loan signed by petitioner Kotteakos. It contained false statements. Brown placed the loan, and Kotteakos thereafter sent Brown applications on behalf of other persons. Two were made out in the names of fictitious persons. The proceeds were received by Kotteakos and petitioner Regenbogen, his partner in the cigarette and pinball machine business. Regenbogen, together with Kotteakos, had indorsed one of the applications. Kotteakos also sent to Brown an application for a loan in Regenbogen's name. This was for modernization of property not owned by Regenbogen. The latter, however, repaid the money in about three months after he received it.

The evidence against the other defendants whose cases were submitted to the jury was similar in character. They too had transacted business with Brown relating to National Housing Act loans. But no connection was shown between them and petitioners, other than that Brown had been the instrument in each instance for obtaining the loans. In many cases the other defendants did not have any relationship with one another, other than Brown's connection with each transaction. * * *

The proof therefore admittedly made out a case, not of a single conspiracy, but of several, notwithstanding only one was charged in the indictment. The Court of Appeals aptly drew analogy in the comment, "Thieves who dispose of their loot to a single receiver—a single 'fence'—do not by that fact alone become confederates: they may, but it takes more than knowledge that he is a 'fence' to make them such." It stated that the trial judge "was plainly wrong in supposing that upon the evidence there could be a single conspiracy; and in the view he took of the law, he should have dismissed the indictment." Nevertheless the appellate court held the error not prejudicial, saying among other things that "especially since guilt was so manifest, it was 'proper' to join the conspiracies," and "to reverse the conviction would be a miscarriage of justice." * * *

The Government's theory seems to be, in ultimate logical reach, that the error presented by the variance is insubstantial and harmless, if the evidence offered specifically and properly to convict each defendant would be sufficient to sustain his conviction, if submitted in a separate trial. [I]n apparent support of its view the Government argues that there was no prejudice here because the results show that the jury exercised discrimination as among the defendants whose cases were submitted to it. As it points out, the jury acquitted some, disagreed as to others, and found still others guilty. From this it concludes that the jury was not confused and, apparently, reached the same result as would have been reached or would be likely, if the convicted defendants had been or now should be tried separately.

One difficulty with this is that the trial court itself was confused in the charge which it gave to guide the jury in deliberation. The court instructed: "The indictment charges but one conspiracy, and to convict each of the defendants of a conspiracy, the Government would have to prove, and you would have to find, that each of the defendants was a member of that conspiracy. You cannot divide it up. It is one conspiracy, and the question is whether or not each of the defendants or which of the defendants, are members of that conspiracy." * * *

This view, specifically embodied throughout the instructions, obviously confuses the common purpose of a single enterprise with the several, though similar, purposes of numerous separate adventures of like character. It may be that, notwithstanding the misdirection, the jury actually understood correctly the purport of the evidence, as the Government now concedes it to have been; and came to the conclusion that the petitioners were guilty only of the separate conspiracies in which the proof shows they respectively participated. But, in the face of the misdirection and in the circumstances of this case, we cannot assume that the lay triers of fact were so well informed upon the law or that they disregarded the permission expressly given to ignore that vital difference. * * *

On those instructions it was competent not only for the jury to find that all of the defendants were parties to a single common plan, design and scheme, where none was shown by the proof, but also for them to impute to each defendant the acts and statements of the others without reference to whether they related to one of the schemes proven or another, and to find an overt act affecting all in conduct which admittedly could only have affected some. True, the Court of Appeals painstakingly examined the evidence directly relating to each petitioner and concluded he had not been prejudiced in this manner. That judgment was founded largely in the fact that each was clearly shown to have shared in the fraudulent phase of the conspiracy in which he participated. Even so, we do not understand how it can be concluded, in the face of the instruction, that the jury considered and was influenced by nothing else. * * *

Reversed.

Notes and Questions

1. A year later, *Kotteakos* was distinguished by its author in *Blumenthal v. United States,* 332 U.S. 539, 68 S.Ct. 248, 92 L.Ed. 154 (1947). Francisco Distributing Co., operated by Weiss and Goldsmith, obtained two carloads of whiskey from an unidentified source. Feigenbaum (operator of a drugstore), Blumenthal (operator of a pawn shop) and Abel (operator of a jewelry store) acted as "salesmen" in selling this liquor to tavern owners at inflated prices. Weiss and Goldsmith later admitted to a federal agent that they were merely acting for their supplier, who they declined to name. The salesmen had no dealings with one another, and it was not shown that they knew of the unknown owner's existence or part in the scheme. The aforementioned persons were convicted of conspiring with one another and the unidentified owner to sell the whiskey at a price above the maximum permitted under wartime price control regulations. The Supreme Court affirmed:

"We think that in the special circumstances of this case the two agreements were merely steps in the formation of the larger and ultimate more general conspiracy. In that view it would be a perversion of justice to regard the salesmen's ignorance of the unknown owner's participation as furnishing adequate ground for reversal of their convictions. Nor does anything in the *Kotteakos* decision require this. The scheme was in fact the same scheme; the salesmen knew or must have known that others unknown to them were sharing in so large a project; and it hardly can be sufficient to relieve them that they did not know, when they joined the scheme, who those people were or exactly the parts they were playing in carrying out the common design and object of all. By their separate agreements, if such they were, they became parties to the larger common plan, joined together by their knowledge of its essential features and broad scope, though not of its exact limits, and by their common single goal.

"The case therefore is very different from the facts admitted to exist in the *Kotteakos* case. Apart from the much larger number of agreements there involved, no two of those agreements were tied together as stages in the formation of a larger all-inclusive combination, all directed to achieving a single unlawful end or result. On the contrary each separate agreement had its own distinct, illegal end. Each loan was an end in itself, separate from all others, although all were alike in having similar illegal objects. Except for Brown, the common figure, no conspirator was interested in whether any loan except his own went through. And none aided in any way, by agreement or otherwise, in procuring another's loan. The conspiracies therefore were distinct and disconnected, not parts of a larger general scheme, both in the phase of agreement with Brown and also in the absence of any aid given to others as well as in specific object and result. There was no drawing of all together in a single, overall, comprehensive plan.

"Here the contrary is true. All knew of and joined in the overriding scheme. All intended to aid the owner, whether Francisco or another, to sell the whiskey unlawfully, though the two groups of defendants differed on the proof in knowledge and belief concerning the owner's ability. All by reason of their knowledge of the plan's general scope, if not its exact limits, sought a common end, to aid in disposing of the whiskey. True, each salesman aided in selling only his part. But he knew the lot to be sold was larger and thus that he was aiding in a larger plan. He thus became a party to it and not merely to the integrating agreement with Weiss and Goldsmith.

"We think therefore that in every practical sense the unique facts of this case reveal a single conspiracy of which the several agreements were essential and integral steps, and accordingly that the judgments should be affirmed."

2. Stern was engaged in the business of performing illegal abortions. Many persons referred women desiring abortions to Stern, for which they were paid a fee. One of these individuals was Anderson, who referred several women to Stern. Anderson was later charged with conspiracy to commit abortions with Stern and the others who had made referrals. Anderson did not know the identity of the others, but did know that Stern was engaged in the performance of abortions on a regular basis and that thus he would be receiving referrals from others.[a] Is this one conspiracy or several?

3. "Appellants [Cole, Hawkins, Hensley, and Holley], along with Kenneth Hart and Jerry Owens, were active members of the Tampa (Florida) Chapter of the Outlaw Motorcycle Club. To join the Outlaws one must be male, own a Harley–Davidson motorcycle, and embrace the Outlaw lifestyle.

"The Tampa Outlaws are an insular group with members living at or near their clubhouse, occupying themselves primarily with their motorcycles, touring, and 'partying'. Gainful employment among the Outlaws is rare.

"Women closely associated with the Outlaws are termed 'patched old ladies' and sport insignia, sometimes tattoos, proclaiming them 'Property of Outlaws.' These women are treated as 'property' by the Outlaws. At a given time an individual woman is typically associated with a particular Outlaw. But she may be sold, traded, or given to another. Unlike the males, the women are expected to work—sometimes as waitresses, dancers, barmaids—often as prostitutes. An 'old lady's' duties to the man with whom she is associated include giving him her money and following orders without question. Mostly the women are compliant in all this; if not, compliance may be enforced with physical violence.

"In the spring of 1979, Mary Carley was living at the Outlaw clubhouse in Tampa with Kenneth Hart as his 'old lady' and supplying Hart's income by working locally as a prostitute. But local work became difficult. She was out on bond from a firearms charge, and the local police were cracking down on prostitution. Through Lori, another 'old lady,' she and Hart learned of the Club Caprice, a brothel in Meridian, Mississippi. Lori, Carley and Hart telephoned the club owner and arranged jobs there for Carley and Lori.

"The two women went to Meridian and began work at the club. Lori was fired soon after for misconduct. Carley continued to work there but didn't like working alone. She called Hart and asked him to send some other 'old ladies' to join her. Soon afterwards two more Outlaw women arrived from Tampa. Carley worked intermittently at the Club Caprice for more than a year, joined at different times by various Outlaw women including those associated with Hawkins, Cole, Hensley, and Owens. During that year she was traded by Hart and became Holley's 'old lady.' At times some of the men came to Meridian to see the women, and phone calls were exchanged between the women in Meridian and the men in Florida.

"At times Carley and the other women would return to Tampa. When this occurred Carley would personally deliver her prostitution proceeds to her 'old man.' Other times Hart, and later Holley, would telephone Carley asking for money, and she would wire the money via Western Union. She also instructed other Outlaw women on how to send money back to the men and on occasions accompanied them to the Meridian Western Union

---

a. *Anderson v. Superior Court,* 78 Cal.App.2d 22,   such facts.
177 P.2d 315 (1947), denying a writ of prohibition on

office."[b] Is this a single conspiracy to violate the Travel Act, proscribing use of the mails to "distribute the proceeds of any unlawful activity"?

4. Meyrick and Ribuffi are both operators of night clubs located with other clubs in the entertainment area of the community. Each of them individually approached the policeman responsible for enforcement in that area, Sgt. Goddard, and gave him a bribe in exchange for his promise to overlook violations of the laws regarding the sale of intoxicating liquors in their respective premises.[c] Does this alone establish the existence of a single conspiracy to corrupt the police involving those three individuals? What if Meyrick and Ribuffi each knew that Goddard was tolerating liquor law violations throughout the entertainment area? That Goddard was receiving bribes from one or more other club owners? That their bribery of Goddard was known by the other, who was also bribing Goddard?

UNITED STATES v. BRUNO

United States Court of Appeals, Second Circuit, 1939.

105 F.2d 921, rev'd on other grounds, 308 U.S. 287, 60 S.Ct. 198, 84 L.Ed. 257 (1939).

PER CURIAM.

Bruno and Iacono were indicted along with 86 others for a conspiracy to import, sell and possess narcotics; some were acquitted; others, besides these two, were convicted, but they alone appealed. They complain, (1), that if the evidence proved anything, it proved a series of separate conspiracies, and not a single one, as alleged in the indictment; * * *

The first point was made at the conclusion of the prosecution's case: the defendants then moved to dismiss the indictment on the ground that several conspiracies had been proved, and not the one alleged. The evidence allowed the jury to find that there had existed over a substantial period of time a conspiracy embracing a great number of persons, whose object was to smuggle narcotics into the Port of New York and distribute them to addicts both in this city and in Texas and Louisiana. This required the cooperation of four groups of persons; the smugglers who imported the drugs; the middlemen who paid the smugglers and distributed to retailers; and two groups of retailers—one in New York and one in Texas and Louisiana—who supplied the addicts. The defendants assert that there were, therefore, at least three separate conspiracies; one between the smugglers and the middlemen, and one between the middlemen and each group of retailers. The evidence did not disclose any coöperation or communication between the smugglers and either group of retailers, or between the two groups of retailers themselves; however, the smugglers knew that the middlemen must sell to retailers, and the retailers knew that the middlemen must buy of importers of one sort or another. Thus the conspirators at one end of the chain knew that the unlawful business would not, and could not, stop with their buyers; and those at the other end knew that it had not begun with their sellers. That being true, a jury might have found that all the accused were embarked upon a venture, in all parts of which each was a participant, and an abettor in the sense that the success of that part with which he was immediately concerned, was dependent upon the success of the whole. That distinguishes the situation from that in *United States v. Peoni*, 2 Cir., 100 F.2d 401, where Peoni, the accused, did not know that Regno, his buyer, was to sell the counterfeit bills to Dorsey, and had no interest in whether he did, since Regno might equally well have passed

---

b. *United States v. Cole*, 704 F.2d 554 (11th Cir. 1983), concluding "there was sufficient evidence of one overall conspiracy that each appellant joined."

c. *Rex v. Meyrick and Ribuffi*, 21 Crim.App. 94 (1929), rejecting the contention of separate conspiracies. But see *Regina v. Griffiths*, 49 Crim.App. 279 (1965).

them to innocent persons himself. It might still be argued that there were two conspiracies; one including the smugglers, the middlemen and the New York group, and the other, the smugglers, the middlemen and the Texas & Louisiana group, for there was apparently no privity between the two groups of retailers. That too would be fallacious. Clearly, quoad the smugglers, there was but one conspiracy, for it was of no moment to them whether the middlemen sold to one or more groups of retailers, provided they had a market somewhere. So too of any retailer; he knew that he was a necessary link in a scheme of distribution, and the others, whom he knew to be convenient to its execution, were as much parts of a single undertaking or enterprise as two salesmen in the same shop. We think therefore that there was only one conspiracy * * *.

UNITED STATES v. MICHELENA–OROVIO

United States Court of Appeals, Fifth Circuit, 1983.

719 F.2d 738.

Before CLARK, CHIEF JUDGE, BROWN, WISDOM, GEE, RUBIN, REAVLEY, POLITZ, RANDALL, TATE, JOHNSON, WILLIAMS, GARWOOD, JOLLY and HIGGINBOTHAM, CIRCUIT JUDGES.

RANDALL, CIRCUIT JUDGE:

[Undercover agents met with persons representing themselves as engaged in smuggling marijuana from Columbia. The agents were hired to provide ships to meet at sea other ships carrying marijuana and to transfer the cargo and then store it. When the smugglers said the mother ship had left Columbia, the agents alerted the Coast Guard. The described vessel, the Alex Luz, was boarded, and 363 bales of marijuana were found in the hold. The defendant, found aboard the Alex Luz, was charged with others with conspiracy to import marijuana into the United States and conspiracy to possess marijuana with intent to distribute it, and was convicted on both counts. A panel of the court of appeals held the evidence sufficient on the first count but not on the second count, 702 F.2d 496 (5th Cir.1983), and the court then agreed to rehear the case en banc.]

A. CONSPIRACY TO IMPORT.

Relying on the factors set forth in *United States v. Alfrey,* 620 F.2d 551, 556 (5th Cir.1980) (the length of the voyage, the quantity of contraband on board, and the relationship between captain and crew), the panel upheld Michelena–Orovio's conviction of conspiracy to import marijuana. We agree with the panel's conclusion that the government established more than the defendant's mere presence on board the ALEX LUZ, and that there was ample evidence to support the defendant's conviction on the importation count.

In particular, we note that Michelena–Orovio was arrested on board a small vessel that had just completed a relatively lengthy voyage from Colombia. The boat was laden with twelve tons of marijuana and reeked of its illicit cargo. Although the boat was a shrimping vessel, there was no fishing equipment aboard and no cargo other than the contraband. The marijuana was found in the ship's cargo hold. The cargo hatch was neither locked nor fastened, and there was open access to the cargo hold from the engine room of the vessel.

The ship's crew, including Michelena–Orovio, engaged in a concerted endeavor to elude capture and protect each other. When the Coast Guard first spotted the vessel, it had its lights reversed so that it appeared to be going in the direction opposite to its actual course, apparently in the hope that it would escape detection. The boat changed direction as soon as its crew became aware of the Coast Guard's presence. When the agents came on board, all eight crew members were waiting on deck with their bags packed, and all eight insisted that there was no captain aboard the vessel.

We are satisfied that a reasonable jury could have found Michelena–Orovio guilty beyond a reasonable doubt of conspiracy to import marijuana on the basis of this evidence. We turn then to our consideration of whether the evidence was also sufficient to support his conviction of conspiracy to possess the marijuana with intent to distribute it.

B. THE CONSPIRACY TO POSSESS WITH INTENT TO DISTRIBUTE.

1. Conflict In the Circuit.

In setting aside Michelena–Orovio's conviction of conspiracy to possess marijuana with intent to distribute it, the panel majority chose to follow *United States v. Cadena*, 585 F.2d 1252 (5th Cir.1978). In *Cadena,* we reversed the conviction of the captain of a mother ship that had transferred a large quantity of marijuana to a smaller craft 200 miles south of the Florida coast. We noted:

> Unlike the situation presented by an ongoing enterprise, Cadena had no interest in or awareness of what plans, if any, had been reached to dispose of the marijuana once he reached these shores. Although a conspiracy to import facilitates a conspiracy to distribute, one cannot joint [sic] a conspiracy, whether by conduct or verbal accord, unless one knows that it has in fact been concocted * * *. [F]rom Cadena's perspective, it was not apparent that any accord had yet been reached, either tacitly or otherwise. * * *

Relying on a long line of Fifth Circuit cases that had held that the jury may infer intent to distribute the contraband from the size of the cache, the panel dissent argued that Michelena–Orovio's conviction on the second count should be affirmed. * * *

2. Narcotics Conspiracies: Has the Chain Been Broken?

Conspiracies to distribute narcotics have generally been considered to be prime examples of chain, or interconnected, conspiracies, in which a participant in a segment of the conspiracy may be convicted of participation in the whole.

* * * The question in this case is whether Michelena–Orovio's knowledge of and participation in this distribution scheme may be inferred from his participation in the scheme to supply twelve tons of marijuana from Colombia. * * *

The panel majority * * * reasoned that where there is prolonged cooperation, the seller may have a "stake" in the successful outcome of the entire scheme, but where there is nothing more than a "single or casual transaction," the supplier may be indifferent to the buyer's illicit purpose. The panel majority failed to recognize that Michelena–Orovio was not just a supplier of goods to the conspirators; he was himself a member of a segment of an extensive conspiracy to obtain marijuana and to distribute it in the United States.

* * * The absence of any legal market provides an additional link that supports the inference of the illegal importer's involvement in the conspiracy to possess his cargo with intent to distribute it. Michelena–Orovio would have had no job if there had been no plan made for the distribution of his cargo, and the twelve tons of marijuana would have been virtually worthless if there had been no conspiracy to distribute. * * * [C]ommon sense leads to the conclusion that an importer of that much marijuana knows perfectly well, and indeed relies on the fact, that there is a plan for the distribution of his cargo. * * *

Where a single act itself is one from which knowledge and participation may be inferred, the courts have not hesitated in upholding a defendant's conviction. * * * Michelena–Orovio's attempted importation of a huge quantity of marijuana is such an act. The importation of twelve tons of marijuana with an approximate street value of between four to six million dollars is not readily characterized as a "casual" transaction, even if the transaction is planned for one time only.

Contrasting Captain Cadena's situation with the "situation presented by an ongoing enterprise," the *Cadena* court surmised that the captain "had no interest in or awareness of what plans, if any, had been reached to dispose of the marijuana once he reached these shores." The facts of the case before us demonstrate the fallacy in this reasoning. According to Agent Donald's testimony, the conspiracy to distribute the marijuana came into existence long before Michelena–Orovio's boat left Colombia; indeed, the ALEX LUZ apparently set sail under orders from the United States detailing the size of the cargo and the point of rendevous with the boats that were to take the cargo into the United States. The ALEX LUZ would never have left Colombia, and therefore Michelena–Orovio would have had no opportunity to earn his wages as a crew member, had there been no distributors in the United States placing orders for the contraband.

In summary, the fact that the defendant is involved in importing a huge quantity of marijuana into the United States may establish both the defendant's knowledge of and his joinder in the conspiracy to possess with intent to distribute. Since twelve tons of marijuana is more than mere mortals could personally consume in a lifetime, someone must have an intent to distribute the contraband. The defendant's awareness of the existence of the conspiracy flows from his participation in the conspiracy to import such a large quantity, for in the absence of any legal market in which to dispose of his wares, there is no reason to import the goods if there has been no plan made for their distribution. Similarly, the defendant's joinder or interest in the conspiracy to distribute may be inferred from his involvement in the importation scheme, for he would have no importing job if there was no conspiracy to distribute. Finally, the act of importation itself is an act in furtherance of the conspiracy to possess with intent to distribute, for there would be no distribution scheme if there were no marijuana to distribute.

3. The Mere Colombian Seaman.

Michelena–Orovio argues further that the absence of actual contact with the United States and his status as a "lowly non-English speaking seaman" further weakens the case against him. Michelena–Orovio's first argument concerns the fact that he, a Colombian national, was discovered on a foreign vessel on the high seas. He maintains that the evidence proved only that he was on a vessel loaded with marijuana headed for the United States, but that plans never actually called for his entry into this country. While the evidence might be sufficient to demonstrate that he knew that the vessel contained contraband and that he had joined in the conspiracy to bring it close enough to the United States for someone else to import it, he maintains that there is no evidence that he knew of or cared about the contraband's fate once it reached American shores.

The location and nationality of the vessel and its crew has no bearing on the issues in this case: knowledge of and participation in the conspiracy to possess marijuana with intent to distribute it. * * * Michelena–Orovio has never disputed the fact that the cargo's ultimate destination was the United States, a fact evidenced by Agent Donald's testimony about the Louisiana-based portion of the conspiracy.

Michelena–Orovio's nationality does not weaken the inference of his knowledge that a conspiracy to distribute the contraband must exist or of his knowing facilitation of that conspiracy. While a foreign national may not have the same detailed knowledge of our laws as a United States citizen might have, it would hardly be irrational for a jury to infer that Michelena–Orovio knew that the possession and distribution of marijuana in the United States is illegal. After all, both are also illegal in Colombia, and indeed, in most parts of the world. Therefore, to the extent that participation in the conspiracy to distribute may normally be inferred from participation in the conspiracy to import a large quantity of contraband, in light of the absence of a legal market for the imported goods, Michelena–Orovio's knowledge of and dependence on the existence of the distribution scheme are the same as those of his American counterpart.

We note further that a defendant's distribution of the contraband need not be made to the ultimate consumer in order to convict him of conspiracy to possess with intent to distribute; it may, in appropriate circumstances, be made to a coconspirator. * * *

Michelena–Orovio's final argument is that the inference of participation in the distribution scheme should not be applied to him because * * * he was simply a lowly member of the crew. * * *

Michelena–Orovio's lowly employee argument is in essence no more than a variation on the "mere presence" argument rejected in our discussion of the importation count. As was discussed in our disposition of the defendant's argument with regard to the importation count, more than mere presence was established in this case. The jury determined that the evidence demonstrated beyond a reasonable doubt that Michelena–Orovio was aware of and participated in the conspiracy to import a large quantity of marijuana. He was not a mere employee, but an employee aware of the nature of his business. It is well settled in this circuit that a conviction will not be reversed for lack of evidence merely because the defendant played only a minor role in the overall scheme. While the trial court might wish to take Michelena–Orovio's status as an employee into account in sentencing the defendant, his status as an employee does not weaken the inference of his knowledge of or complicity in the distribution scheme. * * *

The defendant's conviction on both counts is AFFIRMED.

Wisdom, Circuit Judge, with whom Rubin, Politz and Tate, Circuit Judges, join, dissenting: * * *

The en banc opinion rests not on the evidence, but on a figure of speech: a conspiracy is a single chain and each conspirator is a link. This premise is a deceptively appealing shortcut to evidence overcoming the presumption of innocence. The notion that the conspiracy in this case is a chain begs the question. If one accepts the premise, of course each person performing a function relating to handling the contraband—from the grower in Colombia, to the first purchaser, to the middleman, to the crewmen on a ship transporting the contraband, down to the retailer—is guilty of conspiring to import and to "possess with intent to distribute" the contraband. No doubt there are some conspiracies that may aptly be described as a chain in which an individual conspirator is an essential link, although he may not have any idea of details of the scheme and may be unknown to some other conspirators. That is not this case. Here the United States did not charge a single massive venture to import, sell, and distribute, as it did in *United States v. Bruno.* The indictment has two separate counts, one for importation and another for distribution, because the facts point to two separate conspiracies, at least with respect to some of the participants, the most conspicuous of whom was seaman Michelena–Orovio.

In dealing with the difficult problem of narcotics control, Congress chose to distinguish between the crime of conspiring to import controlled drugs in violation of 21 U.S.C. § 963 (1976) and the crime of conspiring to possess such drugs with intent to distribute them in violation of 21 U.S.C. § 846 (1976). This is not to say that the same defendant can never be guilty of both offenses. But the effect of the majority decision is that a violation of section 963 now automatically entails a violation of section 846—whenever the principal basis for conviction under section 963 rests on the inference that the large amount of contraband seized necessarily shows intent to import on the part of seamen on the vessel carrying the contraband. Such an inference is a non sequitur as to distribution, however, because it fails to take into account the element of *intent* necessary for proof of the crime.

In this case, one may reasonably infer from the size of the cargo knowledge and intent on the part of the defendant to participate in the conspiracy to import the contraband. But that inference cannot do double duty and show as well intent to distribute when the defendant had no role to play in distribution. With deference, I suggest that in the circumstances of this case, considering especially that Michelena–Orovio's role was to terminate on delivery of the marijuana to another vessel on the high seas, 150 to 200 miles from our shores, the only rational inference that can be drawn is that the defendant did *not* intend to play any part in any ongoing conspiracy to distribute the marijuana. The distribution in the United States, assuming that it was to take place in the United States, was to be handled by others. * * *

The position I advocate is not contrary to congressional objectives in enacting drug control legislation. The real culprits in this case, as in many similar cases, are the American ringleaders who made arrangements with the grower or broker in Colombia and unquestionably arranged for the purchase, transportation, and distribution in this country. They are guilty of conspiracy to import and conspiracy to distribute and perhaps other conspiracies as well. But Michelena–Orovio, the lowly Colombian seaman on the edge of the conspiracy to import, should not be punished twice by expediently adding a tenuous inference to an attenuated inference. The majority has succumbed to an alluring figure of speech as a substitute for facts and reason.

Notes and Questions

1. In *United States v. Manbeck*, 744 F.2d 360 (4th Cir.1984), the court, in declining to follow *Michelena-Orovio*, stated: "A close examination of the Court's reasoning reveals a fundamental flaw. The Court has simply established that a person importing a large quantity of marijuana should be aware that the marijuana will be distributed once it reaches the United States. Unless awareness of this fact is equivalent to joining the conspiracy to distribute, there is still no evidence indicating the extent of the agreement entered into by the defendant crew member. Evidence that 'someone must have an intent to distribute the marijuana' is a far cry from identifying the defendant as that someone.

"Recognizing this problem, the Fifth Circuit invoked a long line of cases adhering to the proposition that intent to distribute may be inferred from the possession of a large quantity of marijuana. The soundness of *Michelena-Orovio*, relied upon by the government in this case, thus rests on the validity of this inference. The inference that a person possessed of a large quantity of marijuana intends to distribute said marijuana is widely adhered to and well-recognized, but it is imperative to understand the context from which this inference originates. Invariably, every vessel case that cites this principle relies on cases which trace back to the situation where courts were distinguishing the mere possession of contraband from possession with intent to distribute. It makes perfect sense to infer that persons possessed of a suitcase full of marijuana intend to distribute that marijuana rather than keep it to themselves because there is more marijuana than those persons could consume. This conclusion does not follow so surely when applied to infer that a crew member of a vessel conspired to distribute as well as import the marijuana. In the former context, the inference is relied upon to distinguish two choices where quantity is a relevant factor: mere possession from possession with intent to distribute. Whereas, in the latter context, the inference is relied upon to distinguish two choices where quantity is not a relevant factor: mere importation from importation and distribution. Assuming that joining a conspiracy to import is distinct from joining a conspiracy to distribute, and assuming that in any given case a defendant may have conspired to participate in one or the other or both, the quantity of marijuana smuggled provides no basis for identifying which of the foregoing conspiracies were joined unless it is presumed that one who conspires to import a large quantity of marijuana also conspires to distribute it. In other words, through circular reasoning, the presumption used to find the ultimate fact in question—whether one who conspires to import a large quantity of marijuana also conspires to distribute it—is the ultimate fact itself. This latter presumption is entirely different from the inference that one possessed of a large quantity of marijuana intends to distribute it, and the facts do not support its adoption.''

2. Consider *United States v. MacDougall*, 790 F.2d 1135 (4th Cir.1986): ''The jury in this case heard testimony that 584 grams of hashish were found in Gunn's bag when he was arrested at the Savannah airport following the 'Caroline C' venture. This court in *Manbeck* held that where a crew member possesses his own cache, a fair inference would be the intent to both import and distribute. We did not need, however, to decide what amount would be necessary to distinguish between possession and possession with intent to distribute. In our view, given the facts of this case, particularly the size of the 'Caroline C' cargo, 584 grams or approximately one-half kilogram of hashish, is insufficient. Campbell also testified that Gunn participated in meetings with organizers of the conspiracy, including Leslie Riley and Leon Harvey. The subject of the meetings concerned arrangements for importation. The government argues that Campbell's testimony that Gunn deposited a bale of hashish on-shore after the unloading of the 'Second Life' establishes his involvement in the conspiracy to distribute. Campbell's testimony, however, indicated that Gunn, who was drunk at the time, dropped the bale on-shore to remove it from the vessel so that the vessel could clear customs. There is no indication that this act was part of any distribution plan but was rather a concluding act of the importation.

''Similarly, Gunn's participation in the off-loading of the hashish from the 'Caroline C' at a dock in North Carolina was insufficient to establish his connection to the conspiracy to distribute. In sum, we cannot infer Gunn's participation in the conspiracy to distribute marijuana and hashish solely from his involvement in the conspiracy to import them. There is practically no other evidence of his participation in the distribution conspiracy so we must reverse his conviction as to that count.''

SECTION 9. DURATION OF THE CONSPIRACY

GRUNEWALD v. UNITED STATES

Supreme Court of the United States, 1957.

353 U.S. 391, 77 S.Ct. 963, 1 L.Ed.2d 931.

MR. JUSTICE HARLAN delivered the opinion of the Court.

The three petitioners were convicted on Count 1 of an indictment brought under 18 U.S.C. § 371, 18 U.S.C.A. § 371 for conspiracy to defraud the United States with reference to certain tax matters. * * *

In 1947 and 1948 two New York business firms, Patullo Modes and Gotham Beef Co., were under investigation by the Bureau of Internal Revenue for suspected fraudulent tax evasion. Through intermediaries, both firms established contact with Halperin, a New York attorney, and his associates in law practice. Halperin in turn conducted negotiations on behalf of these firms with Grunewald, an ''influential'' friend in Washington, and reported that Grunewald, for a large cash fee, would undertake to prevent criminal prosecution of the taxpayers. Grunewald then used his influence with Bolich, an official in the Bureau, to obtain "no prosecution" rulings[5] in the two tax cases. These rulings were handed down in 1948 and 1949. Grunewald, through Halperin, was subsequently paid $60,000 by Gotham and $100,000 by Patullo.

Subsequent activities of the conspirators were directed at concealing the irregularities in the disposition of the Patullo and Gotham cases. Bolich attempted to have the Bureau of Internal Revenue report on the Patullo case "doctored," and careful steps were taken to cover up the traces of the cash fees paid to Grunewald. In 1951 a congressional investigation was started by the King Committee of the House of Representatives; the conspirators felt themselves threatened and took steps to hide their traces. Thus Bolich caused the disappearance of certain records linking him to Grunewald, and the taxpayers were repeatedly warned to keep quiet. In 1952 the taxpayers and the conspirators were called before a Brooklyn grand jury. Halperin attempted to induce the taxpayers not to reveal the conspiracy, and Grunewald asked his secretary not to talk to the grand jury. These attempts at concealment were, however, in vain. The taxpayers and some of Halperin's associates revealed the entire scheme, and petitioners' indictment and conviction followed.

The first question before us is whether the prosecution of these petitioners on Count 1 of the indictment was barred by the applicable three-year statute of limitations.

The indictment in these cases was returned on October 25, 1954. It was therefore incumbent on the Government to prove that the conspiracy, as contemplated in the agreement as finally formulated, was still in existence on October 25, 1951, and that at least one overt act in furtherance of the conspiracy was performed after that date. For where substantiation of a conspiracy charge requires proof of an overt act, it must be shown both that the conspiracy still subsisted within the three years prior to the return of the indictment, and that at least one overt act in furtherance of the conspiratorial agreement was performed within that period. Hence, in both of these aspects, the crucial question in determining whether the statute of limitations has run is the scope of the conspiratorial agreement, for it is that which determines both the duration of the conspiracy, and whether the act relied on as an overt act may properly be regarded as in furtherance of the conspiracy.

Petitioners, in contending that this prosecution was barred by limitations, state that the object of the conspiratorial agreement was a narrow one: to obtain "no prosecution" rulings in the two tax cases. When these rulings were obtained, in October 1948 in the case of Gotham Beef, and in January 1949 in the case of Patullo Modes, the criminal object of the conspiracy, petitioners say, was attained and the conspirators' function ended. They argue, therefore, that the statute of limitations started running no later than January 1949, and that the prosecution was therefore barred by 1954, when the indictment was returned.

The Government counters with two principal contentions: First, it urges that even if the main object of the conspiracy was to obtain decisions from the Bureau of Internal Revenue not to institute criminal tax prosecutions—decisions obtained in 1948 and 1949— the indictment alleged, and the proofs showed, that the conspiracy also included as a subsidiary element an agreement to conceal the conspiracy to "fix" these tax cases, to the end that the conspirators would escape detection and punishment for their crime. Says the Government, "from the very nature of the conspiracy * * * there had to be, and was, from the outset a conscious, deliberate, agreement to conceal * * * each and every aspect of the conspiracy * * *." It is then argued that since the alleged conspiracy to conceal clearly

---

5. A "no prosecution" ruling is an internal decision by the investigative branch of the Bureau of Internal Revenue not to press criminal charges against a taxpayer.

continued long after the main criminal purpose of the conspiracy was accomplished, and since overt acts in furtherance of the agreement to conceal were performed well within the indictment period, the prosecution was timely.

Second, and alternatively, the Government contends that the central aim of the conspiracy was to obtain for these taxpayers, not merely a "no prosecution" ruling, but absolute immunity from tax prosecution; in other words, that the objectives of the conspiracy were not attained until 1952, when the statute of limitations ran on the tax cases which these petitioners undertook to "fix." The argument then is that since the conspiracy did not end until 1952, and since the 1949–1952 acts of concealment may be regarded as, at least in part, in furtherance of the objective of the conspirators to immunize the taxpayers from tax prosecution, the indictment was timely.

For reasons hereafter given, we hold that the Government's first contention must be rejected, and that as to its second, which the Court of Appeals accepted, a new trial must be ordered.

We think that the Government's first theory—that an agreement to conceal a conspiracy can, on facts such as these, be deemed part of the conspiracy and can extend its duration for the purposes of the statute of limitations—has already been rejected by this Court in *Krulewitch v. United States,* 336 U.S. 440, 69 S.Ct. 716, 718, 93 L.Ed. 790, and in *Lutwak v. United States,* 344 U.S. 604, 73 S.Ct. 481, 97 L.Ed. 593. * * *

The crucial teaching of *Krulewitch* and *Lutwak* is that after the central criminal purposes of a conspiracy have been attained, a subsidiary conspiracy to conceal may not be implied from circumstantial evidence showing merely that the conspiracy was kept a secret and that the conspirators took care to cover up their crime in order to escape detection and punishment. As was there stated, allowing such a conspiracy to conceal to be inferred or implied from mere overt acts of concealment would result in a great widening of the scope of conspiracy prosecutions, since it would extend the life of a conspiracy indefinitely. Acts of covering up, even though done in the context of a mutually understood need for secrecy, cannot themselves constitute proof that concealment of the crime after its commission was part of the initial agreement among the conspirators. For every conspiracy is by its very nature secret; a case can hardly be supposed where men concert together for crime and advertise their purpose to the world. And again, every conspiracy will inevitably be followed by actions taken to cover the conspirators' traces. Sanctioning the Government's theory would for all practical purposes wipe out the statute of limitations in conspiracy cases, as well as extend indefinitely the time within which hearsay declarations will bind co-conspirators.

A reading of the record before us reveals that on the facts of this case the distinction between "actual" and "implied" conspiracies to conceal, as urged upon us by the Government, is no more than a verbal tour de force. True, in both *Krulewitch* and *Lutwak* there is language in the opinions stressing the fact that only an *implied* agreement to conceal was relied on. Yet when we look to the facts of the present cases, we see that the evidence from which the Government here asks us to deduce an "actual" agreement to conceal reveals nothing beyond that adduced in prior cases. What is this evidence? First, we have the fact that from the beginning the conspirators insisted on secrecy. Thus the identities of Grunewald and Bolich were sedulously kept from the taxpayers; careful steps were taken to hide the conspiracy from an independent law firm which was also working on Patullo's tax problems; and the taxpayers were told to make sure that their books did not reflect the large cash payments made to Grunewald. Secondly, after the "no prosecution" rulings were obtained, we have facts showing that this secrecy was still maintained. Thus, a deliberate attempt was made to make the above-mentioned independent law firm believe that it was *its* (quite legitimate) efforts which produced the successful ruling. Finally, we have the fact that great efforts were made to conceal the conspiracy when the danger of exposure appeared. For example, Bolich got rid of certain records showing that he had used Grunewald's hotel suite in Washington; Patullo's accountant was persuaded to lie to the grand jury concerning a check made out to an associate of the conspirators; Grunewald attempted to persuade his secretary not to talk to the grand jury; and the taxpayers were repeatedly told by Halperin and his associates to keep quiet.

We find in all this nothing more than what was involved in *Krulewitch,* that is, (1) a criminal conspiracy which is carried out in secrecy; (2) a continuation of the secrecy after the accomplishment of the crime; and (3) desperate attempts to cover up after the crime begins to come to light; and so we cannot agree that this case does not fall within the ban of those prior opinions. * * *

By no means does this mean that acts of concealment can never have significance in furthering a criminal conspiracy. But a vital distinction must be made between acts of concealment done in furtherance of the *main* criminal objectives of the conspiracy, and acts of concealment done after these central objectives have been attained, for the purpose only of covering up after the crime. Thus the Government argues in its brief that "in the crime of kidnapping, the acts of conspirators in hiding while waiting for ransom would clearly be planned acts of concealment which would be in aid of the conspiracy to kidnap. So here, there can be no doubt that * * * all acts of concealment, whether to hide the identity of the conspirators or the action theretofore taken, were unquestionably in furtherance of the initial conspiracy * * *." We do not think the analogy is valid. Kidnapers in hiding, waiting for ransom, commit acts of concealment in furtherance of the objectives of the conspiracy itself, just as repainting a stolen car would be in furtherance of a conspiracy to steal; in both cases the successful accomplishment of the crime necessitates concealment. More closely analogous to our case would be conspiring kidnapers who cover their traces after the main conspiracy is finally ended—i.e., after they have abandoned the kidnaped person and then take care to escape detection. In the latter case, as here, the acts of covering up can by themselves indicate nothing more than that the conspirators do not wish to be apprehended—a concomitant, certainly, of every crime since Cain attempted to conceal the murder of Abel from the Lord. * * *

In view of how the case was submitted to the jury, we are also unable to accept the Government's second theory for avoiding the statute of limitations. * * *

The Court of Appeals accepted this theory of the case in affirming these convictions. * * *

We find the legal theory of the Court of Appeals unexceptionable. * * *

If, therefore, the jury could have found that the aim of the conspiratorial agreement was to protect the taxpayers from tax prosecution, and that the overt acts occurring in the indictment period were in furtherance of that aim, we would affirm. We do not think, however, that we may safely assume that the jury so found, for we cannot agree with the Court of Appeals' holding that this theory of the case was adequately submitted to the jury. * * *

Notes and Questions

1. Comment, 17 Ga.L.Rev. 539, 556 (1983), observes: "The Court gave no rationale for requiring direct evidence under the 'express original agreement' theory other than the repetition of its reasoning in *Krulewitch* and *Lutwak.* Without the benefit of clear reasoning, federal courts have subsequently misapplied and even ignored the direct

evidence requirement in situations that by analogy to *Grunewald* would appear to require direct evidence."

2. In *United States v. Girard,* 744 F.2d 1170 (5th Cir.1984), Girard was charged with conspiracy to defraud the United States. The indictment stated that Girard, who contracted with the Housing Authority of New Orleans to replace space heaters in a housing complex, funds for which were provided by the U.S. Department of Housing and Urban Development, conspired with Housing Authority employees to rig the bidding process. The contract was signed on March 16, 1977; the work was accepted as complete on Nov. 22, 1977; a check to Girard as final payment was received March 13, 1978, but a June 7, 1978 check for $620 later arrived with an invoice identifying it as an adjustment to the March 13 payment. Girard's last payment to a co-conspirator was May 21, 1978. On the issue of whether the 5–year statute of limitations had run by June 3, 1983, the court concluded:

"Girard's contention that the purpose of the conspiracy ended with the award of the contract represents an overly narrow construction of the alleged agreement. His interest lay not in securing the contract itself, but in obtaining the money thereunder. The payments to his initial coconspirators were not made until after Girard Plumbing had received its first payment under the contract. Thus the conspiracy continued at least until Girard had received the full monetary benefits under the contract, including the $620 payment on June 7, 1978.

"Our earlier decision, *United States v. Davis,* 533 F.2d 921 (5th Cir.1976), does not affect the validity of this conclusion. In *Davis,* we held that a conspiracy to make false statements to a government agency ended with the last false statement, not when the government acted on the false statements to award the desired contract. According to the *Davis* indictment, the sole object of the conspiracy was to make false statements in violation of 18 U.S.C. § 1001. Given the narrow scope of the particular indictment, we could not say that the obtaining of the contract was an objective of the conspiracy as charged. We specifically noted, however, that the indictment could not be read as charging the defendants with a conspiracy to defraud the United States under 18 U.S.C. § 371. In the present case, the broader scope of the indictment allows us to accept the government's allegations that the purposes of the conspiracy included the receipt of the funds.

"Our determination that the conspiracy continued until Girard had realized fully his anticipated economic benefits is consistent with the law of other circuits. The Second Circuit, in *United States v. Mennuti,* 679 F.2d 1032 (2d Cir.1982), a prosecution under 18 U.S.C. § 371 for conspiracy to commit mail fraud, ruled that a conspiracy to fraudulently obtain insurance funds by burning a house did not end when the insurance check was issued. Instead it continued until each participant had received his agreed-upon payoff. Mennuti's compensation was the right to purchase the property after the fire at a reduced price. Accordingly, the conspiracy continued after the receipt of the insurance check and the execution of the contract giving Mennuti the right to purchase the land until the sale actually closed six months later. This closing was the only event within the statutory time period. * * *

"In deciding *Mennuti,* the Second Circuit relied heavily on *United States v. Walker,* 653 F.2d at 1343. Walker was convicted under 18 U.S.C. § 371 for bid-rigging in connection with a federal timber sale. On appeal, he argued that the charge was time-barred because the only purpose of the conspiracy was to secure the contract, which had been awarded more than five years before his indictment. The Ninth Circuit rejected this contention, holding that the conspiracy continued after the completion of the central objective, the securing of the contract, because it encompassed an additional objective, the continued acquisition and division of profits obtained by defrauding the United States.

"The defendant in *United States v. Helmich,* 704 F.2d 547 (11th Cir.1983), the defendant was indicted for conspiracy to commit espionage. He contended that his 1981 indictment was untimely because it did not charge him with transmitting information after 1964. The indictment, however, also alleged that the conspiracy included an agreement for the Soviet Union to pay Helmich and that he had travelled to Canada in 1980 to collect outstanding compensation. Therefore, the conspiracy continued until Helmich received his anticipated economic benefits in 1980. The payoff, which was the last overt act under the conspiracy, triggered the limitations period.

"Under the terms of the agreement alleged here, each of Girard's coconspirators was to receive a set payoff on specified dates between March 30, 1977 and March 21, 1978. The economic benefit for Girard was to be the funds obtained under the illegally secured contract. He did not receive this benefit on March 16, 1977, when the contract was awarded, but as the Housing Authority issued partial payments between March 30, 1977 and June 7, 1978. Girard's contention that the June 7 check was not a payment but an account adjustment is irrelevant. The accounting terminology used by the Housing Authority on its invoices is not controlling. Girard received these funds after signing an undated form certifying that the $620 was the balance due under the contract. Therefore, the money was part of the economic benefit which Girard sought and received under the alleged terms of the conspiracy.

"It is true, as the district court noted, that there was no plan to divide the $620 between the coconspirators after its receipt. The fact that Girard was to retain the entire sum himself, however, does not mean that obtaining the funds was not an objective of the conspiracy. As discussed above, according to the indictment, each coconspirator received a payment after payments on the contract had begun and Girard received the rest of the funds. The mere fact that the alleged agreement defined the payoff terms in this manner, instead of providing each coconspirator with a percentage of each Housing Authority payment, does not defeat our determination that one of the purposes of the conspiracy alleged here was to obtain all funds possible under the contract. The conspiracy continued until June 7, 1978 when the last $620 was paid."

3. 18 U.S.C.A. § 2312 makes it an offense to transport in interstate commerce a vehicle known to be stolen; 18 U.S.C.A. § 2313 makes it an offense to receive, conceal, store, barter, sell or dispose of a motor vehicle which has moved in interstate commerce and which is known to be stolen. Yow and Strand have been charged with conspiracy to violate those statutes. The government wishes to offer as part of its case the testimony of two witnesses: (i) Strand's brother, who will testify that Strand told him, a few days after receiving the vehicle at his Nebraska shop and before the car was dismantled, that Yow had delivered it from California; (ii) Scott, who will testify that several months after Strand received the car and at a time when only a few parts of the auto remained to be disposed of, Strand told him Yow had delivered the car from California.[a] What result upon Yow's objection that such hearsay testimony is not admissible against him because these declarations of his alleged co-conspirator Strand were not made "during and in furtherance of the conspiracy"?

4. Garcia, Pain and Yslas burglarized an elderly woman's home at about 2 a.m. They put a sewing machine, clock, radio, TV and other items into Garcia's car and later dropped them off at Garcia's house, but at about 7 a.m. Garcia and Pain dropped Yslas off at his house and gave him the TV to sell for himself so that it could be determined whether that would provide him with his fair "share" of the spoils. Later that day, Garcia's sister confronted him with a newspaper account of the burglary and death by skull fracture of

a. A variation on *United States v. Yow,* 465 F.2d 1328 (8th Cir.1972).

the victim, to which Garcia responded he was involved only in the burglary. Garcia and Pain then went to Yslas' house; Garcia said he wanted to get rid of the stolen property, and Yslas said he would take it. Garcia and Pain returned to Garcia's house to get the property, and while they were there Garcia's sister confronted Pain, who said Yslas had hit the woman with a tool. Yslas was not home when Garcia and Pain brought the stolen property to his residence, so they discarded it in the desert. Yslas tried to sell the TV to some friends without success. At Yslas' trial for murder, the prosecution offers against him Pain's statement to Garcia's sister on the theory that it is admissible under the evidence rule which says statements by a co-conspirator "during the course of and in furtherance of the conspiracy" may be received in evidence. What should the judge rule?[b]

5. After Clyde purchased an auto repair shop, he encountered serious financial problems. In January of 1968, Lauria and Smith loaned him $2,000, to be paid back over a 40–week period and with a "vig" (vigorish or excessive interest) of $4,000. Carvelli was to serve as collector. On April 10, 1968, Lauria, Smith and Carvelli visited Clyde's shop and threatened to burn it down if he didn't pay. On May 8, Lauria and Smith came to Clyde's home and told his wife something might happen to their children if the payments were not made. None of this violated federal law, for it was not until May 29, 1968, that the Consumer Credit Protection Act became effective. Clyde made payments to Carvelli in May, June and July, but in late July the Clydes fled their home in the middle of the night to escape further payments. Lauria and Smith were convicted of conspiracy to violate the CCPA, which prohibits knowing participation in the use of any extortionate means to collect any extension of credit. On appeal, they point out that there is no evidence of any threats to the person or property of the Clydes occurring after the effective date of the statute.[c] What result?

6. Note, 75 Colum.L.Rev. 1122, 1164–67 (1975): "The duration of a criminal agreement is important primarily for statute of limitations purposes. The [Model Penal Code] essentially codifies existing case law on the subject. According to MPC § 5.03(7)(a), 'conspiracy is a continuing course of conduct which terminates when the crime or crimes which are its object are committed or the agreement that they be committed is abandoned by the defendant and by those with whom he conspired.' Perhaps because prior decisions have left the key issues reasonably well settled, most state statutes say nothing about conspiracy's time dimension. Eleven states include provisions which track the MPC language, while Maine, North Dakota, Massachusetts, Vermont, and H.R. 333 add 'frustration' to 'success' and 'abandonment' in the catalog of means by which a conspiracy may reach its conclusion. This latter modification seems reasonable, unless frustration is too broadly defined. Where circumstances simply make the criminal object slightly more difficult to achieve, a conspiracy should not be regarded as terminated. On the other hand, when an intended victim permanently relocates in a distant land or when new security procedures are instituted which make effective implementation of a criminal plan virtually impossible, a permissible inference might be drawn that a conspiracy no longer continues. Of course, evidence would be required to the effect that the conspirators were aware of the relevant developments and that they had not transferred their criminal purpose to another object. In point of fact, the leading case cited in support of the 'frustration' alternative involved parties to a criminal agreement already in custody, and thus left little doubt that the participants would proceed no further.[242] * * *

---

b. *State v. Yslas,* 139 Ariz. 60, 676 P.2d 1118 (1984), holding the statement inadmissible.

c. Based on *United States v. Smith,* 464 F.2d 1129 (2d Cir.1972), affirming the conviction.

242. *Fiswick v. United States,* 329 U.S. 211, 215–17 (1946). For illustrations of the fact that claims of frustration will not be readily sustained, see *United States v. Franzese,* 392 F.2d 954, 963–64 (2d Cir.1968) (conspiracy to rob bank continued despite arrest of

"The MPC contains a further pronouncement on the duration of conspiracy. Section 5.03(7)(b) states the 'generally accepted' rule that 'abandonment is presumed if neither the defendant nor anyone with whom he conspired does any overt act in pursuance of the conspiracy during the applicable period of limitation.' Though like provisions characterize conspiracy statutes in but few jurisdictions, no implication should be drawn that the rule does not enjoy more widespread acceptance. The comment to Missouri's proposed statute clearly demonstrates that the draftsmen expected the 'presumed abandonment' rule to prevail, despite their omission of the MPC language. While closely akin to their MPC counterpart, corresponding sections in H.R. 333, North Dakota law, and pending Vermont legislation may impose a greater rigidity than the ALI reporters thought desirable. Rather than establishing a presumption of abandonment in the absence of an overt act during a given time period, these statutes provide that, '[a] conspiracy *shall be deemed* to have been abandoned if no overt act to effect its objectives has been committed by any conspirator during the applicable period of limitations.' If such legislation is construed to create an irrebuttable presumption, then lack of a sufficiently recent overt act would be fatal to a conspiracy prosecution, despite the possible availability of other evidence of the criminal agreement's continuing vitality. Such an outcome would not be endorsed by the MPC framers."

SECTION 10. WITHDRAWAL

NOTE, CONSPIRACY: STATUTORY REFORM SINCE THE MODEL PENAL CODE

75 Colum.L.Rev. 1122, 1168–72 (1975).

The rationale normally advanced for statutory inclusion of a renunciation defense involves two complementary ideas. First, repudiation of criminal purpose is said to indicate lack of firm antisocial intent, and hence the absence of any real public danger. Secondly, the theory runs, "the law should provide a means for encouraging persons to abandon courses of criminal activity which they have already undertaken." As a criminal plan nears fruition, the former notion diminishes in persuasive power, while the latter gains. * * *

Whatever the proper underlying justification, [*Model Penal Code*] § 5.03(6) provides a defense to a conspiracy indictment if "the actor, after conspiring to commit a crime, thwarted the success of the conspiracy, under circumstances manifesting a complete and voluntary renunciation of his criminal purpose." Twenty state statutes and both versions of the proposed Federal Criminal Code contain similar provisions. Under the language just quoted, the individual claiming the defense must have prevented commission of the object offense. Failure of the criminal scheme due to fortuitous natural causes or efficient, independent police work will not protect a defendant who contends he renounced. Pending New Jersey legislation would make the requirements of renunciation even more stringent. To sustain the defense under prospective New Jersey law, an actor would need to block not only his co-conspirators' consummation of the *object* offense(s), but also their commission of *any* substantive offense in furtherance of the conspiracy. Furthermore, the proposed New Jersey statute would insist on notification of a law enforcement officer, irrespective of any demonstration of a particular individual's effectiveness in defusing a criminal agreement through independent action. These additional burdens seem unduly onerous. If a person otherwise guilty of conspiracy should recant and foil the agreement of which he was

some participants), vacated on other grounds as to defendant Franzese only sub nom. *Giordano v. United States,* 394 U.S. 310 (1969); and *United States v. Gold-* *stein,* 135 F.2d 359, 361 (2d Cir.1943) (conspiracy to defraud government of liquor taxes continued despite seizure of still).

once a part, the method by which he accomplishes this task should be immaterial to his criminal liability. Moreover, availability of the renunciation defense should not be premised on prevention of all instrumental substantive offenses, no matter how minor in comparison with the conspiracy's object crime(s). To so limit the potential applicability of the defense is to greatly reduce renunciation's utility, especially with respect to large, complex criminal enterprises, which often entail a series of relatively insignificant, but nevertheless criminal, steps before attainment of the ultimate illegal objective. New Jersey's proposed provision would remove the primary incentive for renunciation, immediately upon commission of any substantive offense by a co-conspirator, regardless of how distant the larger goals of the criminal scheme might remain.

An attractive alternative to the MPC outline of renunciation has been endorsed by eight states. With slight variations of phrasing, the relevant statutory sections would allow a defense to conspiracy where an actor "gave a timely warning to law enforcement authorities or made a substantial effort to prevent the performance of the criminal conduct contemplated" by the agreement. Admittedly, difficult issues of fact might be raised by such a formula. Hawaii has tried to anticipate some of these problems by enacting more detailed specifications for determining whether the renunciation prerequisites have been met.[274] A more serious theoretical objection to this minority modification of the MPC is also possible. If the renunciation defense is regarded as essentially a form of statutory grace conferred on deserving transgressors, then the more limited applicability of the MPC definition may be justified. To put it another way, since renunciation by its very nature comprehends absolution for an already-completed conspiracy offense, the defense may legitimately be restricted to those occasions when an actor succeeds in protecting society from the consequences of his prior criminal agreement. Where prevention efforts are unavailing, even a reformed conspirator will not be heard, under this line of reasoning, to gainsay his part in the illegal scheme. In defense of the minority position, on the other hand, one might maintain that the law should not demand more than can reasonably be expected. In particular, criminal liability should not be imposed because of police ineptitude or other happenstance factors which deprive an actor's attempts to defuse a conspiracy of their ordinary effectiveness. The Hawaii comments expand on this argument.

> It would not be reasonable to hold the defendant strictly liable for his inchoate activities by imposing liability where unforeseeable circumstances thwart prevention of the substantive offense. If the defendant's renunciation is effective but for circumstances not reasonably foreseeable, that is all that may be asked. Moreover, to impose strict liability in such situations would be to ignore the rationales for allowing the defense of renunciation. If the defendant's renunciation is effective under all foreseeable circumstances, he has evidenced a sufficient lack of firmness in his criminal purpose, and the law has succeeded as far as is rationally possible in encouraging him to abandon such purpose.

Finally, fifteen states have adhered to the common law wisdom that the conspiracy offense is completed on agreement (with the performance of an overt act, if necessary), and that no subsequent events should serve to erase a previously committed crime. In embracing this view, these jurisdictions may have demonstrated their conception of conspiracy as a weapon against group criminal activity rather than as inchoate crime. Conceding the desirability of aiding public prosecutors in their struggle with large-scale corruption and organized crime, this end should not be achieved by the elimination of a

---

274. Under Hawaii § 530(5), warning is not "timely" unless "the authorities, reasonably acting upon the warning, would have the opportunity to prevent the conduct or result." Similarly, an effort is not "reasonable" (Hawaii substitutes this term for "substantial") unless "the defendant, under reasonably foreseeable circumstances, would have prevented the conduct or result." * * *

renunciation defense for the extremely preparatory behavior governed by conspiracy statutes.

Notes and Questions

1. Comparing the Model Penal Code, New Jersey, Hawaii and common law positions, which is preferable? Consider in this regard these comments to the Maryland Code reported in the Note at 1168: "The arguments utilized by the [Model Penal] Code framers seem somewhat divorced from reality. Availability or unavailability of the defense would seem to have little impact on conduct. The judgment should turn on whether the desirability of maintaining intellectual consistency by exonerating a relatively small number of persons where renunciation may be taken as evidence of reduced dangerousness of acts or persons is outweighed by the desirability of simplifying the Code provisions and the issues at trial." What then of the Georgia approach, discussed in *Sak v. State,* 129 Ga.App. 301, 199 S.E.2d 628 (1973), of permitting the defense only if the withdrawal occurs before any conspirator performs an overt act?

2. Even if withdrawal is not recognized as a defense to the conspiracy charge, it may be important for other purposes, namely: (i) preventing the admission into evidence against the withdrawn conspirator of acts and statements of his co-conspirators occurring after his withdrawal; (ii) starting the running of the statute of limitations as to the participation in the conspiracy by the withdrawn conspirator; and (iii) in those jurisdictions following the rule of *Pinkerton v. United States,* p. 822 of this Book, that conspirators are accountable for *all* crimes committed by their co-conspirators in furtherance of the conspiracy, preventing post-withdrawal crimes from being so attributed.

3. Should the test for effective withdrawal be different for these purposes? In *United States v. United States Gypsum Co.,* 438 U.S. 422, 98 S.Ct. 2864, 57 L.Ed.2d 854 (1978), where the issue was whether abandonment presented a statute of limitations bar, the trial judge instructed: "To withdraw, a defendant must have affirmatively notified each other member of the conspiracy he will no longer participate in the undertaking so they understand they can no longer expect his participation or acquiescence, or he must make disclosures of the illegal scheme to law enforcement officials." The Supreme Court concluded the instruction was "unnecessarily confining": "Nothing that we have been able to find in the case law suggests, much less commands, that such confining blinders be placed on the jury's freedom to consider evidence regarding the continuing participation of alleged conspirators in the charged conspiracy. Affirmative acts inconsistent with the object of the conspiracy and communicated in a manner reasonably calculated to reach co-conspirators have generally been regarded as sufficient to establish withdrawal or abandonment."

SECTION 11. THE PLURALITY REQUIREMENT

IANNELLI v. UNITED STATES

Supreme Court of the United States, 1975.
420 U.S. 770, 95 S.Ct. 1284, 43 L.Ed.2d 616.

Mr. Justice Powell delivered the opinion of the Court. * * *

Petitioners were tried under a six-count indictment alleging a variety of federal gambling offenses. Each of the eight petitioners, along with seven unindicted coconspirators and six codefendants, was charged, *inter alia,* with conspiring to violate and violating 18 U.S.C. § 1955, a federal gambling statute making it a crime for five or more persons to conduct, finance, manage, supervise, direct, or own a gambling business prohibited by state law. Each petitioner was convicted of both offenses and each was sentenced under both the substantive and conspiracy counts. The Court of Appeals for the Third Circuit affirmed, finding that a recognized exception to Wharton's Rule permitted prosecution and punishment for both offenses. * * *

Wharton's Rule owes its name to Francis Wharton, whose treatise on criminal law identified the doctrine and its fundamental rationale:

> "When to the idea of an offense plurality of agents is logically necessary, conspiracy, which assumes the voluntary accession of a person to a crime of such a character that it is aggravated by a plurality of agents, cannot be maintained. * * * In other words, when the law says, 'a combination between two persons to effect a particular end shall be called, if the end be effected, by a certain name,' it is not lawful for the prosecution to call it by some other name; and when the law says, such an offense—e.g., adultery—shall have a certain punishment, it is not lawful for the prosecution to evade this limitation by indicting the offense as conspiracy." 2 F. Wharton, *Criminal Law* § 1604, p. 1862 (12th ed. 1932).

The Rule has been applied by numerous courts, state and federal alike. * * *

The classic formulation of Wharton's Rule requires that the conspiracy indictment be dismissed before trial. * * * Federal courts earlier adhered to this literal interpretation and thus sustained demurrers to conspiracy indictments. More recently, however, some federal courts have * * * held that the Rule's purposes can be served equally effectively by permitting the prosecution to charge both offenses and instructing the jury that a conviction for the substantive offense necessarily precludes conviction for the conspiracy.

Federal courts likewise have disagreed as to the proper application of the recognized "third-party exception," which renders Wharton's Rule inapplicable when the conspiracy involves the cooperation of a greater number of persons than is required for commission of the substantive offense. In the present case, the Third Circuit concluded that the third-party exception permitted prosecution because the conspiracy involved more than the five persons required to commit the substantive offense. The Seventh Circuit reached the opposite result, however, reasoning that since § 1955 also covers gambling activities involving more than five persons, the third-party exception is inapplicable.

The Courts of Appeals are at odds even over the fundamental question whether Wharton's Rule ever applies to a charge for conspiracy to violate § 1955. * * *

Traditionally the law has considered conspiracy and the completed substantive offense to be separate crimes. * * * Thus, it is well recognized that in most cases separate sentences can be imposed for the conspiracy to do an act and for the subsequent accomplishment of that end. Indeed, the Court has even held that the conspiracy can be punished more harshly than the accomplishment of its purpose.

The consistent rationale of this long line of decisions rests on the very nature of the crime of conspiracy. This Court repeatedly has recognized that a conspiracy poses distinct dangers quite apart from those of the substantive offense.

> "This settled principle derives from the reason of things in dealing with socially reprehensible conduct: collective criminal agreement—partnership in crime—presents a greater potential threat to the public than individual delicts. Concerted action both increases the likelihood that the criminal object will be successfully attained and decreases the probability that the individuals involved will depart from their path of criminality. Group association for criminal purposes often, if not normally, makes possible the attainment of ends more complex than those which one criminal could

accomplish. Nor is the danger of a conspiratorial group limited to the particular end toward which it has embarked. Combination in crime makes more likely the commission of crimes unrelated to the original purpose for which the group was formed. In sum, the danger which a conspiracy generates is not confined to the substantive offense which is the immediate aim of the enterprise." * * *

The historical difference between the conspiracy and its end has led this Court consistently to attribute to Congress "a tacit purpose—in the absence of any inconsistent expression—to maintain a long-established distinction between offenses essentially different,—a distinction whose practical importance in the criminal law is not easily overestimated." Wharton's Rule announces an exception to this general principle. * * *

This Court's previous discussions of Wharton's Rule have not elaborated upon its precise role in federal law. In most instances, the Court simply has identified the Rule and described it in terms similar to those used in Wharton's treatise. But in *United States v. Holte,* 236 U.S. 140, 35 S.Ct. 271, 59 L.Ed. 504 (1915), the sole case in which the Court felt compelled specifically to consider the applicability of Wharton's Rule, it declined to adopt an expansive definition of its scope. In that case, Wharton's Rule was advanced as a bar to prosecution of a female for conspiracy to violate the Mann Act. Rejecting that contention, the Court adopted a narrow construction of the Rule that focuses on the statutory requirements of the substantive offense rather than the evidence offered to prove those elements at trial:

> "The substantive offence might be committed without the woman's consent; for instance, if she were drugged or taken by force. Therefore the decisions that it is impossible to turn the concurrence necessary to effect certain crimes such as bigamy or duelling into a conspiracy to commit them do not apply." * * *

This Court's prior decisions indicate that the broadly formulated Wharton's Rule does not rest on principles of double jeopardy. Instead, it has current vitality only as a judicial presumption, to be applied in the absence of legislative intent to the contrary. The classic Wharton's Rule offenses—adultery, incest, bigamy, duelling—are crimes that are characterized by the general congruence of the agreement and the completed substantive offense. The parties to the agreement are the only persons who participate in commission of the substantive offense,[15] and the immediate consequences of the crime rest on the parties themselves rather than on society at large. Finally, the agreement that attends the substantive offense does not appear likely to pose the distinct kinds of threats to society that the law of conspiracy seeks to avert. It cannot, for example, readily be assumed that an agreement to commit an offense of this nature will produce agreements to engage in a more general pattern of criminal conduct.

---

15. An exception to the Rule generally is thought to apply in the case in which the conspiracy involves more persons than are required for commission of the substantive offense. For example, while the two persons who commit adultery cannot normally be prosecuted both for that offense and for conspiracy to commit it, the third-party exception would permit the conspiracy charge where a "matchmaker"—the third party—had conspired with the principals to encourage commission of the substantive offense. The rationale supporting this exception appears to be that the addition of a third party enhances the dangers presented by the crime. Thus, it is thought that the legislature would not have intended to preclude punishment for a combination of greater dimension than that required to commit the substantive offense.

Our determination that Congress authorized prosecution and conviction for both offenses in all cases makes it unnecessary to decide whether the exception to Wharton's Rule could properly be applied to conspiracies to violate § 1955 involving more than five persons. We note, however, that the statute and its legislative history seem to suggest that it could not. By its terms, § 1955 reaches gambling activities involving "five or more persons." Moreover, the legislative history of the statute indicates that Congress assumed that it would generally be applied in cases in which more than the statutory minimum number were involved. It thus would seem anomalous to conclude that Congress intended the substantive offense to subsume the conspiracy in one case but not in the other.

The conduct proscribed by § 1955 is significantly different from the offenses to which the Rule traditionally has been applied. Unlike the consequences of the classic Wharton's Rule offenses, the harm attendant upon the commission of the substantive offense is not restricted to the parties to the agreement. Large-scale gambling activities seek to elicit the participation of additional persons—the bettors—who are parties neither to the conspiracy nor to the substantive offense that results from it. Moreover, the parties prosecuted for the conspiracy need not be the same persons who are prosecuted for commission of the substantive offense. An endeavor as complex as a large-scale gambling enterprise might involve persons who have played appreciably different roles, and whose level of culpability varies significantly. It might, therefore, be appropriate to prosecute the owners and organizers of large-scale gambling operations both for the conspiracy and for the substantive offense but to prosecute the lesser participants only for the substantive offense. Nor can it fairly be maintained that agreements to enter into large-scale gambling activities are not likely to generate additional agreements to engage in other criminal endeavors. The legislative history of § 1955 provides documented testimony to the contrary.

Wharton's Rule applies only to offenses that *require* concerted criminal activity, a plurality of criminal agents. In such cases, a closer relationship exists between the conspiracy and the substantive offense because *both* require collective criminal activity. The substantive offense therefore presents some of the same threats that the law of conspiracy normally is thought to guard against, and it cannot automatically be assumed that the Legislature intended the conspiracy and the substantive offense to remain as discrete crimes upon consummation of the latter. Thus, absent legislative intent to the contrary, the Rule supports a presumption that the two merge when the substantive offense is proved.[18]

But a legal principle commands less respect when extended beyond the logic that supports it. In this case, the significant differences in characteristics and consequences of the kinds of offenses that gave rise to Wharton's Rule and the activities proscribed by § 1955 counsel against attributing significant weight to the presumption the Rule erects. More important, as the Rule is essentially an aid to the determination of legislative intent, it must defer to a discernible legislative judgment. We turn now to that inquiry. * * *

In drafting the Organized Crime Control Act of 1970, Congress manifested its clear awareness of the distinct nature of a conspiracy and the substantive offenses that might constitute its immediate end. The identification of "special offenders" in Title X speaks both to persons who commit specific felonies during the course of a pattern of criminal activity and to those who enter into conspiracies to engage in patterns of criminal conduct. And Congress specifically utilized the law of conspiracy to discourage organized crime's corruption of state and local officials for the purpose of facilitating gambling enterprises.

But the § 1955 definition of "gambling activities" pointedly avoids reference to conspiracy or to agreement, the essential element of conspiracy. Moreover, the limited § 1955 definition is repeated in identifying the reach of § 1511, a provision that specifically prohibits conspiracies. Viewed in this context, and in light of the numerous references to conspiracies throughout the extensive consideration of the Organized Crime Control Act, we think that the limited congressional definition of "gambling activities" in § 1955 is significant. The Act is a carefully crafted piece of legislation. Had Congress intended to foreclose the possibility of prosecuting conspiracy offenses under § 371 by merging them

---

18. We do not consider initial dismissal of the conspiracy charge to be required in such a case. When both charges are considered at a single trial, the real problem is the avoidance of dual punishment. This problem is analogous to that presented by the threat of conviction for a greater and a lesser included offense, and should be treated in a similar manner.

into prosecutions under § 1955, we think it would have so indicated explicitly. It chose instead to define the substantive offense punished by § 1955 in a manner that fails specifically to invoke the concerns which underlie the law of conspiracy.

Nor do we find merit to the argument that the congressional requirement of participation of "five or more persons" as an element of the substantive offense under § 1955 represents a legislative attempt to merge the conspiracy and the substantive offense into a single crime. The history of the Act instead reveals that this requirement was designed to restrict federal intervention to cases in which federal interests are substantially implicated. * * * Recognizing that gambling activities normally are matters of state concern, Congress indicated a desire to extend federal criminal jurisdiction to reach only "those who are engaged in an illicit gambling business of major proportions." * * *

In expressing these conclusions we do not imply that the distinct nature of the crimes of conspiracy to violate and violation of § 1955 should prompt prosecutors to seek separate convictions in every case, or judges necessarily to sentence in a manner that imposes an additional sanction for conspiracy to violate § 1955 and the consummation of that end. Those decisions fall within the sound discretion of each, and should be rendered in accordance with the facts and circumstances of a particular case. We conclude only that Congress intended to retain these traditional options. Neither Wharton's Rule nor the history and structure of the Organized Crime Control Act of 1970 persuade us to the contrary.

Affirmed.

Mr. Justice Douglas, dissenting. * * *

In my view the Double Jeopardy Clause forbids simultaneous prosecution under §§ 1955 and 371. * * *

* * * The very same evidence was relied upon to establish the conspiracy—a conspiracy, apparently, enduring as long as the substantive offense continued, and provable by the same acts that established the violation of § 1955. Thus the very same transactions among the defendants gave rise to criminal liability under both statutes.

Under these circumstances, I would require the prosecutor to choose between § 371 and § 1955 as the instrument for criminal punishment. * * *

Apart from my views of the Double Jeopardy Clause, I would reverse on the additional ground that Congress did not intend to permit simultaneous convictions under §§ 371 and 1955 for the same acts. * * *

Conviction under § 1955 satisfies, in my view, the social concerns that punishment for conspiracy is supposed to address. The provision was aimed not at the single unlawful wager but at "syndicated gambling." Congress viewed this activity as harmful because on such a scale it was thought to facilitate other forms of illicit activity, one of the reasons traditionally advanced for the separate prosecution of conspiracies. Where § 1955 has been violated, the elements of conspiracy will almost invariably be found. The enterprises to which Congress was referring in § 1955 cannot, as a practical matter, be created and perpetuated without the agreement and coordination that characterize conspiracy. Section 1955 is thus most sensibly viewed as a statute directed at conspiracy in a particular context.

All this the majority seems to concede when it acknowledges a "presumption that the two [crimes] merge when the substantive offense is proved." But the majority concludes that simultaneous conviction is authorized because it is not "explicitly excluded." The majority thus implicitly concedes that the statute is silent on the matter of simultaneous conviction. To infer from silence an intention to permit multiple punishment is, I think, a departure from the "presupposition of our law to resolve doubts in the enforcement of a penal code against the imposition of a harsher punishment," *Bell v. United States,* 349 U.S. 81, 83, 75 S.Ct. 620, 622, 99 L.Ed. 905 (1955) * * *.

Mr. Justice Stewart and Mr. Justice Marshall join this opinion [except as to the double jeopardy contention].

Mr. Justice Brennan, dissenting.

* * * I would invoke *Bell's* rule of lenity. I therefore dissent.

Notes and Questions

1. *Iannelli* was distinguished in *Jeffers v. United States,* 432 U.S. 137, 97 S.Ct. 2207, 53 L.Ed.2d 168 (1977), where defendant was convicted in separate trials of violating 21 U.S.C.A. § 846, proscribing conspiracy to distribute heroin and cocaine, and 21 U.S.C.A. § 848, proscribing engaging in a continuing criminal enterprise "in concert with five or more other persons" to violate the drug laws. Noting that in *Iannelli* "the Court felt constrained to construe the statute to permit the possibility that the five persons 'involved' in the gambling operation might not be acting together," the Court in *Jeffers* concluded the "same flexibility does not exist with respect to the continuing-criminal-enterprise statute" because as to it "a conviction would be impossible unless concerted activity were present. * * * In the absence of any indication from the legislative history or elsewhere to the contrary, the far more likely explanation is that Congress intended the word 'concert' to have its common meaning of agreement in a design or plan." The Court thus concluded that § 846 was a lesser included offense of § 848; that this meant defendant was entitled to a joint trial at which a lesser included offense instruction was given; that defendant nonetheless could not complain because he opposed the government's joinder-for-trial motion; but that defendant was entitled to a sentence reduction because Congress had not authorized cumulative sentences for these two crimes. "[T]he reason for separate penalties for conspiracies lies in the additional dangers posed by concerted activity. Section 848, however, already expressly prohibits this kind of conduct. Thus, there is little legislative need to further this admittedly important interest by authorizing consecutive penalties from the conspiracy statute."

2. In which of the following situations should the defendant prevail by reliance on Wharton's rule? (a) Lupino gave Crippen a .38 caliber revolver which had been manufactured in Germany and transported to New York and then Minnesota. Lupino has been charged with conspiring with Crippen to violate 18 U.S.C.App. § 1202(a) (proscribing, in the part here applicable, receiving a firearm which had travelled in interstate commerce).[a]

(b) Helmich transmitted secret defense information to a known Soviet agent. Helmich has been charged with conspiring with that agent to violate 18 U.S.C.A. § 794 (covering one who, "with intent or reason to believe that it is to be used to the injury of the United States or to the advantage of a foreign nation, communicates, delivers, or transmits" to an agent of a foreign government "information relating to the national defense").[b]

(c) A power company employee gave Kimble money when Kimble gave her a note indicating that otherwise her sons would be harmed. When Kimble was arrested, he said Carter wrote the note and shared in the proceeds. Carter was charged (i) under the conspiracy statute with conspiring with Kimble to commit extortion, and (ii) under the aiding and abetting statute (intended "to ensure that any person who participates in a

---

a. A variation on *United States v. Lupino,* 480 F.2d 720 (8th Cir.1973).

b. A variation on *United States v. Helmich,* 704 F.2d 547 (11th Cir.1983).

substantive offense is held liable as if he had directly committed the offense") with aiding and abetting extortion.[c]

(d) Jacobson was the trustee of a condominium trust set up by his elderly aunt for several beneficiaries. After the aunt became incompetent, Jacobson sold the condo to Mangini notwithstanding a temporary restraining order against such sale obtained by the aunt's guardian and withstanding the fact that the trustee, although technically the owner of the property, could lawfully sell it only with the consent of all beneficiaries, which he did not obtain. Convicted of theft and conspiracy with Mangini to commit theft, Jacobson now appeals.[d]

(e) At Grandison's trial for first-degree murder and conspiracy to murder Scott, scheduled to testify at Grandison's narcotics trial, it was shown that Grandison promised to pay Evans $9,000 for the killing and that Evans carried it out. The jury found Grandison guilty of both offenses and at the sentencing proceeding returned a sentence of death based on the prosecution's showing of a requisite aggravating circumstance, i.e., that the homicide was a "murder for hire." Grandison appeals.[e]

3. Consider Note, 52 Wash.L.Rev. 142, 162–64 (1976): "Where one offense consists only of preparation to commit another offense, the former is not punishable if there is conviction for the latter. This principle is generally recognized for the crime of attempt but has not been embraced by the United States Supreme Court in regard to conspiracy. It has been adopted, however, by several state statutes[86] and the Model Penal Code[87] in order to limit conspiracy convictions.

"Application of the preparatory offense test to actions under section 1955 would serve to prevent unjustified conspiracy convictions. As previously discussed, a conspiracy charge should only be maintained when it serves one of the recognized functions of conspiracy law. Once the substantive offense has been consummated, additional punishment for conspiracy can only be justified by the existence of a clearly identifiable social threat greater than that posed by the consummated crime. Therefore, where the substantive offense encompasses and protects the same concerns that are threatened by the conspiracy, a conviction for the latter has no purpose other than increasing punishment beyond that prescribed by the legislature. This reasoning illustrates that the addition of a conspiracy charge to a section 1955 conviction is an example of unjustified multiple punishment.

"In order to accommodate the argument that a conspiracy with an objective broader than the commission of a specific offense presents an additional danger, the Model Penal Code does not provide for an absolute prohibition of a conspiracy conviction in the event the crime is consummated:[91]

[T]he limitation of the draft is confined to the situation where the completed offense was the sole criminal objective of the conspiracy. Therefore, there may be conviction of both a conspiracy and a completed offense committed pursuant to that conspiracy if the prosecution shows that the objective of the conspiracy was the commission of additional offenses.

c. See *People v. Carter*, 415 Mich. 558, 330 N.W.2d 314 (1982).

d. A variation on *State v. Jacobson*, 74 Wash.App. 715, 876 P.2d 916 (1994).

e. A variation on *Grandison v. State*, 341 Md. 175, 670 A.2d 398 (1995).

86. * * * These statutes prohibit all multiple convictions for conspiracy and the substantive offense, *irrespective of the conspiracy's scope.* * * *

87. The *Model Penal Code* § 1.07(1)(b) (Proposed Official Draft, 1962), states that a defendant may not "be convicted of more than one offense if: One offense consists only of a conspiracy or other form of preparation to commit the other." * * *

91. *Model Penal Code* § 1.08. Comment at 32 (Tent.Draft No. 5, 1956).

The Court in *Iannelli,* drawing from conclusions of the Senate Report on the Act, found that '[l]arge-scale gambling enterprises were seen to be both a substantive evil and a source of funds for other criminal conduct.' This finding may be true as a general proposition, but it is insufficient to prove that the objectives of any particular conspiracy include the commission of additional offenses. Thus, in the absence of other evidence to show such an objective, a conspiracy charge should be dismissed upon conviction for violation of section 1955."

4. Under the Model Penal Code approach, what should the result be on these facts? Morgan, in Cornman's presence, accepted Carney's offer of $5,000 to kill Sims. Cornman and Morgan then stole a rifle, and Cornman made inquiries revealing that Sims would not be at work that day. Morgan shot Haas, a neighbor of Sims, in the mistaken belief he was Sims. Haas survived. Cornman was convicted of first degree assault and conspiracy to murder, and was sentenced to consecutive terms of 30 and 10 years. Cornman appeals.[f]

5. In *Iannelli,* it is noted that the Court "has even held that the conspiracy can be punished more harshly than the accomplishment of its purpose." Is this a sensible sentencing scheme? Consider Note, 75 Colum.L.Rev. 1122, 1183–86 (1975):

"The job of grading the conspiracy offense demands an evaluation of the proper relationship between an inchoate and a substantive crime. The [Model Penal Code] has enjoyed considerable success in pressing the view that the degree of a criminal agreement should depend on the gravity of the substantive offense which is its object. Several pre-reform statutes classify all conspiracies as misdemeanors, regardless of their purpose. * * * Since the promulgation of the MPC, nearly all jurisdictions concerned with criminal law revision have endorsed conspiracy penalties more closely resembling those assigned to the particular substantive crime intended.

"For sentencing purposes, the MPC would treat conspiracy and its object offense identically, unless the latter were a first-degree felony. In that case, conspiracy would be labeled a felony of the second degree.[360] The justification for such a grading procedure rests on a conception of conspiracy as inchoate crime, and an accompanying conviction regarding the punishment appropriate for that sort of offense. Apart from retribution, the legitimate ends of punishment as commonly enumerated, are deterrence, reformation, and protection of society through incapacitation of the offender. By definition, a conspirator is one who agrees to commit a crime with the purpose of promoting or facilitating the commission of that crime. Theoretically, then, his criminal intent is established. He is as much in need of correction or reformation as a person successful in committing the crime. On the other hand, sanctions attached to the object offense have not dissuaded the conspirator from aligning himself with others in a plan to violate the law. From this perspective, the potential deterrent efficacy of any conspiracy penalty seems slight. The MPC framers believed that, given this lack of significant deterrent function, the harshest of the law's sanctions could safely be removed from inchoate crimes. Hence, the treatment of conspiracy to commit a first-degree felony. * * *

"A * * * prevalent alternative to the MPC pattern is the automatic downgrading of the inchoate offense, without regard to indications of the stage which the criminal project reached. Sixteen states have chosen to reduce conspiracy one degree from its object crime, and five other jurisdictions have favored even further reductions."

---

f. *State v. Cornman,* 695 S.W.2d 443 (Mo.1985), affirming where the statute said a person may not be convicted "on the basis of the same course of conduct of both the actual commission of an offense and a conspiracy to commit that offense."

360. MPC § 5.05(1) * * *.

6. Wharton's rule should not be confused with the doctrine utilized in *Gebardi v. United States,* 287 U.S. 112, 53 S.Ct. 35, 77 L.Ed. 206 (1932). The petitioners, a man and a woman, were convicted of conspiracy to violate the Mann Act, which makes it an offense to "knowingly transport or cause to be transported, or aid or assist in obtaining transportation for, or in transporting in interstate or foreign commerce * * * any woman or girl for the purpose of prostitution or debauchery or for any other immoral purpose." The evidence was that the man purchased rail tickets for both of them to travel interstate, as the woman had previously consented to do, for immoral purposes, and that they had done so. The Court, per Stone, J., after concluding that the "penalties of the statute are too clearly directed against the acts of the transporter as distinguished from the consent of the subject of the transportation" to warrant the conclusion that on these facts the woman could herself be convicted of violating the Act, then came "to the main question in the case," namely, "whether her concurrence, which was not criminal before the Mann Act, nor punished by it, may without more, support a conviction under the conspiracy section, enacted many years before.

"As was said in the *Holte* Case, an agreement to commit an offense may be criminal, though its purpose is to do what some of the conspirators may be free to do alone. Incapacity of one to commit the substantive offense does not necessarily imply that he may with impunity conspire with others who are able to commit it.[5] For it is the collective planning of criminal conduct at which the statute aims. The plan is itself a wrong which, if any act be done to effect its object, the state has elected to treat as criminal. And one may plan that others shall do what he cannot do himself.

"But in this case we are concerned with something more than an agreement between two persons for one of them to commit an offense which the other cannot commit. There is the added element that the offense planned, the criminal object of the conspiracy, involves the agreement of the woman to her transportation by the man, which is the very conspiracy charged.

"Congress set out in the Mann Act to deal with cases which frequently, if not normally, involve consent and agreement on the part of the woman to the forbidden transportation. In every case in which she is not intimidated or forced into the transportation, the statute necessarily contemplates her acquiescence. Yet this acquiescence, though an incident of a type of transportation specifically dealt with by the statute, was not made a crime under the Mann Act itself. * * * We do not rest our decision upon the theory of those cases [applying Wharton's rule]. We place it rather upon the ground that we perceive in the failure of the Mann Act to condemn the woman's participation in those transportations which are effected with her mere consent, evidence of an affirmative legislative policy to leave her acquiescence unpunished. We think it a necessary implication of that policy that when the Mann Act and the conspiracy statute came to be construed together, as they necessarily would be, the same participation which the former contemplates as an inseparable incident of all cases in which the woman is a voluntary agent at all, but does not punish, was not automatically to be made punishable under the latter. It would contravene that policy to hold that the very passage of the Mann Act effected a withdrawal by the conspiracy statute of that immunity which the Mann Act itself confers.

"It is not to be supposed that the consent of an unmarried person to adultery with a married person, where the latter alone is guilty of the substantive offense, would render

---

5. So it has been held repeatedly that one not a bankrupt may be held guilty under section 37 of conspiring that a bankrupt shall conceal property from his trustee * * *.

In like manner *Chadwick v. United States,* 141 F. 225 (6th Cir.1905) sustained the conviction of one not an officer of a national bank for conspiring with an officer to commit a crime which only he could commit.

the former an abettor or a conspirator, compare *In re Cooper,* 162 Cal. 81, 85, 121 P. 318, or that the acquiescence of a woman under the age of consent would make her a co-conspirator with the man to commit statutory rape upon herself. Compare *Queen v. Tyrrell,* [1894] 1 Q.B. 710. The principle, determinative of this case, is the same.

"On the evidence before us the woman petitioner has not violated the Mann Act and, we hold, is not guilty of a conspiracy to do so. As there is no proof that the man conspired with anyone else to bring about the transportation, the convictions of both petitioners must be

"Reversed."

But, why should the *man's* conviction also be reversed? Compare *Model Penal Code* § 5.04(1).

7. Note, 75 Colum.L.Rev. 1122, 1135–37 (1975): "Nearly all jurisdictions [with modern codes] have elected to follow the [Model Penal Code] recommendation that conspiracy be redefined as a unilateral, rather than a bilateral (or multilateral), crime. * * * By concentrating on individual, rather than group, liability, the guilt of a particular actor is made independent of that of his co-conspirator(s). Such treatment is important when, for example, defendant's only co-conspirator (a) is legally irresponsible or immune or incapable of committing a particular offense, (b) has feigned agreement, usually as part of some law enforcement scheme, or (c) is unknown, unapprehended, unindicted, unconvicted, or acquitted. A unilateral definition of conspiracy means that none of these circumstances will preclude defendant's conviction where the evidence is otherwise sufficient. Each of the possibilities mentioned in (c) above, especially the possibility of an acquitted co-conspirator, raises questions of consistency of disposition if the defendant is convicted. The framers of the MPC were cognizant of possible objections of this character, but they regarded disparate outcomes as preferable to the discharge of an offender whose own culpability was clearly established. '[T]he Code * * * recognizes that inequalities in the administration of the law are, to some extent, inevitable, that they may reflect unavoidable differences in proof, and that, in any event, they are a lesser evil than granting immunity to one criminal because justice may have miscarried in dealing with another.' "

8. Consider Paul Marcus, *Criminal Conspiracy Law: Time to Turn Back From an Ever Expanding, Ever More Troubling Area*, 1 Wm. & Mary Bill Rts. J. 1, 23–25 (1992): "The unilateral approach, I concede, well may have engendered more expressions of anguish and concern than now appear justified. In those jurisdictions embracing the bilateral approach to conspiracy, however, an analogous and more serious change has taken place over the past decade. For a long time the Rule of Consistency stood as a major obstacle to those who would lessen the requirement of a true multiparty agreement and instead emphasize individual culpability. Under this Rule, a conviction of one charged conspirator could not stand where the only other charged conspirator was acquitted of conspiracy. The Rule adopts the fundamental view that 'at least two persons are required to constitute a conspiracy.'

"The Rule has its critics, those who believe that it overemphasizes joint criminality and underemphasizes proof of individual intent. The Rule also has a considerable number of exceptions and limitations. The co-conspirator must actually be acquitted, a hung jury is not enough, nor will a plea suffice. The acquittal must occur at the joint trial with the remaining conspirator, and the Rule does not apply if an agreement is actually shown, even if the other conspirators are not named in the indictment. Even with these substantial limitations, the Rule has stood as a strong affirmation of the group danger base for the crime of conspiracy.

"Two Supreme Court decisions cast doubts on the continued viability of the Rule, in the minds of a number of judges. In *Standefer v. United States*, [p. 842 of this Book] the Court held that a person could be convicted of aiding a principal, even though the principal had been acquitted of the substantive offense.[128] The Court in *United States v. Powell*[129] went further when it held that a jury could reach inconsistent verdicts as to a single defendant in a trial.[130] These cases, it is argued, demonstrate that the Rule of Consistency would no longer be embraced by the Supreme Court. The leading opinion is *United States v. Bucuvalas*,[131] where the court wrote that 'the acquittal of all conspirators but one does not ... necessarily indicate that the jury found no agreement to act.' The court concluded that the Supreme Court's decisions now hold 'that inconsistent verdicts, whether the result of leniency, compromise, or mistake, "should not be reviewable." '

"I do not share the broad reading given to the Supreme Court's two decisions, nor do I view them as necessarily applicable to the conspiracy charge. On the former point, I note that *Standefer* involved separate trials for the parties, a situation which itself is excluded from the consistency principle. Moreover, *Powell* involved a very different fact pattern with multiple charges against a single person. On the latter point, the forceful dissent of Judge Clark in *United States v. Andrews*[134] is persuasive. He looked to the unique aspects of the crime of conspiracy and the violence this broad treatment does to the concept. Quoting an earlier court decision, he wrote:

> A conspiracy cannot be committed by a single individual acting alone; he must act in concert with at least one other person. The acquittal of one conspirator would thus be immaterial where there are several other named conspirators, or other conspirators charged but unknown to the jury. But where all but one of the charged conspirators are acquitted, the verdict against the one will not stand.

"It is inconceivable that the Supreme Court meant to say that a jury could convict one of only two alleged conspirators while finding the other charged individual not guilty. Could the Court genuinely have meant that it was willing to discard the fundamental basis for the crime of conspiracy, a basis which it has repeatedly cited over the past seventy years? Whatever else may be found in these cases, surely it is not a conspiracy which looks to the notions of group danger, multiple parties, and joint endeavors."

Do you agree?

9. Although it is clear that a corporation may be indicted as a conspirator, problems may arise in determining the existence of the plurality necessary for a conspiracy. No

128. The principal in the case was actually acquitted at a separate, earlier trial. Moreover, the jury in the later case was instructed that it could not find for the government unless it concluded, beyond a reasonable doubt, that the principal had committed the offense and that the defendant had aided in its commission.

129. 469 U.S. 57 (1984).

130. The defendant in *Powell* was convicted of facilitating felonies but was acquitted of the same underlying offenses. Though finding that the verdicts were inconsistent, the Supreme Court allowed the convictions because "[one cannot] necessarily assume[] that the acquittal ... was proper—the one the jury 'really meant.' "

131. 909 F.2d 593 (1st Cir.1990).

134. 850 F.2d 1557 (11th Cir.) (1988). [In *Andrews*, the majority concluded: "Consistent verdicts are unrequired in joint trials for conspiracy: where all but one of the charged conspirators are acquitted, the verdict

against the one can stand. * * * Andrews urges us to view the jury's verdict in favor of Ford as a finding that no conspiracy existed between Andrews and Ford. There are, however, explanations for this inconsistency that have nothing to do with whether Andrews actually conspired with Ford to commit a crime. It is just as likely that the admittedly inconsistent verdicts in this case are 'the result of mistake, or lenity * * *.' Under the circumstances, 'the best course to take is simply to insulate jury verdicts from review on this ground.'

"Our holding today leaves criminal defendants with substantial protection. As the Supreme Court noted in *Powell*, 'a criminal defendant already is afforded protection against jury irrationality or error by the independent review of the sufficiency of the evidence undertaken by the trial and appellate courts. This review should not be confused with the problems caused by inconsistent verdicts.' "]

problem exists when two corporations and an officer of each are indicted,[g] or when a corporation is indicted with one of its officers and a third party,[h] for in such situations it is clear (without regard to whether the corporation and its agent are one) that there are at least two distinct participants in the conspiracy. However, plurality has been found to be lacking when the corporate entity and a single agent are the only parties,[i] and also when two corporations and one person acting as the agent of both were the only alleged conspirators.[j]

Consider the soundness of those results and also that reached in *United States v. Hartley*, 678 F.2d 961 (11th Cir.1982), namely, that the necessary plurality for a conspiracy is present when the alleged co-conspirators are the corporation and two or more of that corporation's agents. The *Hartley* court explained that "the fiction of corporate personification * * * originated to broaden the scope of corporate responsibility; we will not use it to shield individuals or corporations from criminal responsibility."

Is *Hartley* consistent with the theory underlying criminal conspiracy? Consider Shaun P. Martin, *Intracorporate Conspiracies*, 50 Stan.L.Rev. 399, 455–57 (1998): "Although the judiciary's shield metaphor undoubtedly has a substantial persuasive effect, it is wholly misleading. The doctrine of corporate unity does not shield lawbreakers from punishment. Rather, it simply demarks the inherent limits of the fiction of corporate personality. The relevant inquiry in criminal intracorporate conspiracy cases is not the one currently posed by the judiciary: whether corporate defendants can permissibly articulate a 'creative' use of agency principles and thereby avoid a criminal conviction. The proper inquiry is instead whether the fiction of corporate personality—the same fiction that is necessarily employed to justify corporate liability in the first place—goes so far as to permit the imposition of vicarious corporate criminal liability for the wholly internal agreements of its agents.

"This analytical defect substantially undercuts the persuasive significance of the shield metaphor. Moreover, this analogy is not only inapplicable to the transmogrification of corporate agency principles into a fictional shield against criminal prosecution, but is also irrelevant to the validity of vicarious corporate liability for such conduct. The assertion that corporate unity principles should not preclude criminal prosecution is founded upon the view that wrongdoing should not be immunized simply because the wrongdoers have taken the time to incorporate. However, this argument is applicable, if at all, only to the criminal liability of the individual conspirators themselves. Incorporation does not limit corporate liability; indeed, it is its prerequisite, for without incorporation, there would be no corporate defendant in the first place. At least as applied to corporate, as opposed to individual, liability, the view of corporate unity as a shield is thus misplaced. * * *

"Only if corporate conduct necessarily results in actionable group danger can corporate unity principles arguably constitute an improper shield against the prosecutorial consequences of criminal behavior. When actionable group danger occurs, then the use of any principle, including the doctrine of corporate unity, might indeed unwisely shield such illegal conduct from prosecution. This argument, however, flounders upon the invalidity of its predicate. Not every corporate action involves group danger. Although corporations generally employ multiple actors and may occasionally have substantial economic powers, these general characteristics are not uniform. Corporate conduct may be undertaken by a single actor or may involve a small or relatively powerless corporate entity. In either case,

---

g. *United States v. MacAndrews & Forbes Co.*, 149 Fed. 823 (S.D.N.Y.1906).

h. *People v. Dunbar Contracting Co.*, 165 App.Div. 59, 151 N.Y.S. 164 (1914).

i. *Union Pac. Coal Co. v. United States*, 173 Fed. 737 (8th Cir.1909).

j. *United States v. Santa Rita Store Co.*, 16 N.M. 3, 113 P. 620 (1911).

corporate activities lack the qualities associated with group danger sufficient to create an actionable criminal conspiracy.

"The argument that every corporate action involves inherent group danger also proves too much. If the mere involvement of a corporate defendant creates actionable group danger, then even a single corporate officer acting alone could be found guilty of conspiracy. * * *

"In short, the mere involvement of a corporation, even if it acts through multiple employees, neither results in actionable group danger nor satisfies the plurality requirement of conspiracy law."

Given the penultimate sentence in that excerpt and the continued vitality of *Hartley*,[k] does the two-corporation, one-agent situation deserve a closer look? Consider the hypothetical in Kathleen F. Brickey, *Conspiracy, Group Danger and the Corporate Defendant*, 52 U.Cin.L.Rev. 431, 443–44 (1983): "Suppose, for example, that Deegan planned the following: Using false invoices from the Santa Rita Store Company, he intends to bill the Mining Company through the mail for goods that were never delivered. The Store Company will divert the payments from the Mining Company into a slush fund to be maintained in a secret foreign financial account for the purpose of bribing domestic and foreign governmental officials. Deegan will be able to conceal these transactions by keeping two false sets of corporate books. The Mining Company books will reflect that the goods that have been paid for actually have been ordered and received, and the Store Company books will reflect neither the issuance of phony invoices nor the receipt of the payments from the Mining Company."

10. Because of the old notion that husband and wife became one person by marriage, the early common law view was that an agreement between husband and wife only could not be a conspiracy. Typical of the modern response to this position is *United States v. Dege*, 364 U.S. 51, 80 S.Ct. 1589, 4 L.Ed.2d 1563 (1960), where the majority, per Frankfurter, J., stated:

"None of the considerations of policy touching the law's encouragement or discouragement of domestic felicities on the basis of which this Court determined appropriate rules for testimonial compulsion as between spouses * * * are relevant to yielding to the claim that an unqualified interdiction by Congress against a conspiracy between two persons precludes a husband and wife from being two persons. Such an immunity to husband and wife as a pair of conspirators would have to attribute to Congress one of two assumptions: either that responsibility of husband and wife for joint participation in a criminal enterprise would make for marital disharmony, or that a wife must be presumed to act under the coercive influence of her husband and, therefore, cannot be a willing participant. The former assumption is unnourished by sense; the latter implies a view of American womanhood offensive to the ethos of our society."

But the three dissenters in *Dege* thought otherwise: "It is not necessary to be wedded to fictions to approve the husband-wife conspiracy doctrine, for one of the dangers which that doctrine averts is the prosecution and conviction of persons for 'conspiracies' which Congress never meant to be included within the statute. A wife, simply by virtue of the intimate life she shares with her husband, might easily perform acts that would technically be sufficient to involve her in a criminal conspiracy with him, but which might be far removed from the arm's-length agreement typical of that crime. It is not a medieval mental quirk or an attitude 'unnourished by sense' to believe that husbands and wives should not

k. As noted in Martin, supra, at 412, "every federal appellate court that has squarely addressed the issue had affirmed the validity of intracorporate conspiracy prosecutions in which multiple agents were involved."

be subjected to such a risk, or that such a possibility should not be permitted to endanger the confidentiality of the marriage relationship. While it is easy enough to ridicule Hawkins' pronouncement in Pleas of the Crown from a metaphysical point of view, the concept of the 'oneness' of a married couple may reflect an abiding belief that the communion between husband and wife is such that their actions are not always to be regarded by the criminal law as if there were no marriage."

SECTION 12. CONSPIRACY: A FINAL LOOK

PHILLIP E. JOHNSON—THE UNNECESSARY CRIME OF CONSPIRACY

61 Calif.L.Rev. 1137, 1162–64 (1973).

Against the background of a law of attempt dominated by the proximity approach, an independent inchoate crime of conspiracy made sense. Although the defendants in the New York and California cases described previously[a] could not be convicted under traditional attempt law, they could each have been convicted of conspiracy because they worked with confederates and performed an "overt act" in furtherance of the criminal design. Each of these defendants, however, could also be convicted of attempt under the Model Penal Code * * *.

Under the conspiracy sections of the Model Penal Code and proposed Federal Criminal Code, however, the act of agreement *is* the forbidden conduct whether or not it strongly corroborates the existence of a criminal purpose. In justifying this per se rule, the Model Penal Code commentary relied heavily on the argument, quoted previously, that the act of agreeing is so decisive and concrete a step towards the commission of a crime that it ought always to be regarded as a "substantial step." Whether this point is sense or nonsense depends upon how restrictively one defines the term "agreement." Hiring a professional killer to commit murder is an agreement, and surely few would doubt that it is a substantial step toward accomplishing the killing. But the language of the conspiracy sections of both the Model Penal Code and proposed Federal Criminal Code is broad enough to reach conduct far less dangerous or deserving of punishment than letting a contract for murder. As the Model Penal Code commentary concedes, one may be liable for agreeing with another that *he* should commit a particular crime, although this agreement might be insufficient to establish complicity in the completed offense. Furthermore, neither code would change the well-established rule that the agreement may be tacit or implied as well as express, and that it may be proved by circumstantial evidence. In short, the term "agreement" may connote anything from firm commitment to engage in criminal activity oneself to reluctant approval of a criminal plot to be carried out entirely by others. To be sure, the Model Penal Code also requires that one enter into the agreement with the purpose of promoting or facilitating the crime, but the existence of that purpose need not be substantiated by any conduct beyond the express or implied agreement and performance in some cases of a single overt act by any party to it. This point is of particular importance in conspiracy cases involving political activity or agitation. Members of radical societies may be likely to discuss or even to begin to plan criminal activities that they have no serious intention of carrying through.

In summary, insofar as conspiracy adds anything to the attempt provisions of the reform codes under discussion, it adds only overly broad criminal liability. Like its use in

---

a. The cases referred to are *People v. Rizzo*, p. 658 of this Book, and *People v. Orndorff*, p. 660 of this Book.

every other area of the substantive criminal law, the use of an independent crime of conspiracy to punish inchoate crimes turns out to be unnecessary.

SECTION 13. SOLICITATION

PEOPLE v. LUBOW

Court of Appeals of New York, 1971.

29 N.Y.2d 58, 323 N.Y.S.2d 829, 272 N.E.2d 331.

BERGAN, JUDGE.

The revised Penal Law creates a new kind of offense, simpler in structure than an attempt or a conspiracy, and resting solely on communication without need for any resulting action (art. 100, Criminal Solicitation * * *).

The basic statutory definition of criminal solicitation is that with intent that another person shall "engage in conduct constituting a crime" the accused "solicits, requests, commands, importunes or otherwise attempts to cause such other person to engage in such conduct". This basic definitory language is continued through three grades of solicitation, the gravity depending on what crime the conduct sought to be induced would effectuate. * * *

As it has been noted, nothing need be done under the statute in furtherance of the communication ("solicits, commands, importunes") to constitute the offense. The communication itself with intent the other person engage in the unlawful conduct is enough. It needs no corroboration.

And an attempt at communication which fails to reach the other person may also constitute the offense for the concluding clause "or otherwise attempts to cause such other person to engage in such conduct" would seem literally to embrace as an attempt an undelivered letter or message initiated with the necessary intent.

Appellants have been convicted after a trial by a three-Judge panel in the Criminal Court of the City of New York of violation of section 100.05 which describes solicitation to commit a felony. The information on which the prosecution is based is made by complainant Max Silverman. It describes the charge as criminal solicitation and states that "defendants attempted to cause deponent to commit the crime of grand larceny" in that they "attempted to induce the deponent to obtain precious stones on partial credit with a view towards appropriating the property to their own use and not paying the creditors, said conduct constituting the crime of larceny by false promise". * * *

The evidence showed that complainant Silverman and both defendants were engaged in the jewelry business. It could be found that defendant Lubow owed Silverman $30,000 for diamonds on notes which were unpaid; that Lubow had told Silverman he was associated with a big operator interested in buying diamonds and introduced him to defendant Gissinger.

It could also be found that in October, 1967, Silverman met the two defendants together at their office, demanded his money, and said that because of the amount owed him he was being forced into bankruptcy.

Silverman testified in response to this Lubow said "Well, let's make it a big one, a big bankruptcy", and Gissinger said this was a good idea. When Silverman asked "how it is done" he testified that Lubow, with Gissinger participating, outlined a method by which diamonds would be purchased partly on credit, sold for less than cost, with the proceeds pyramided to boost Silverman's credit rating until very substantial amounts came in, when there was to be a bankruptcy with Silverman explaining that he had lost the cash gambling in Puerto Rico and Las Vegas. The cash would be divided among the three men. The gambling explanation for the disappearance of cash would be made to seem believable by producing credit cards for Puerto Rico and Las Vegas. Silverman testified that Lubow said "we would eventually wind up with a quarter of a million dollars each" and that Gissinger said "maybe millions".

Silverman reported this proposal to the District Attorney in October, 1967 and the following month a police detective equipped Silverman with a tape recorder concealed on his person which was in operation during conversations with defendants on November 16 and which tends to substantiate the charge. The reel was received in evidence on concession that it was taken from the machine Silverman wore November 16.

A police detective testified as an expert that a "bust out operation" is a "pyramiding of credit by rapid purchasing of merchandise, and the rapid selling of the same merchandise sometimes 10 and 20 per cent the cost of the merchandise itself, and they keep selling and buying until they establish such a credit rating that they are able to purchase a large order at the end of their operation, and at this time they go into bankruptcy or they just leave".

There thus seems sufficient evidence in the record to find that defendants intended Silverman to engage in conduct constituting a felony by defrauding creditors of amounts making out grand larceny and that they importuned Silverman to engage in such conduct. Thus the proof meets the actual terms of the statute.

The statute itself is a valid exercise of legislative power. Commentators closely associated with the drafting of the Model Penal Code of the American Law Institute, from which the New York solicitation statute stems, have observed: "Purposeful solicitation presents dangers calling for preventive intervention and is sufficiently indicative of a disposition towards criminal activity to call for liability. Moreover, the fortuity that the person solicited does not agree to commit or attempt to commit the incited crime plainly should not relieve the solicitor of liability, when otherwise he would be a conspirator or an accomplice."

Solicitation to commit a felony was a misdemeanor at common law. Summarizing this historical fact Judge Cardozo observed: "So at common law, incitement to a felony, when it did not reach the stage of an attempt, was itself a separate crime, and like conspiracy, which it resembled, was a misdemeanor, not a felony." * * *

Although this Penal Law provision is the first statutory enactment in New York, there have been statutes aimed at criminal solicitation in some other States, notably California.

In commenting on the criminal solicitation enactment of article 100, two lawyers who were active in the work of the State Commission on Revision of the Penal Law and Criminal Code which prepared the present statute observed that article 100 "closes that gap" for those who believe, as apparently the commission and the American Law Institute did, that "solicitation to commit a crime involves sufficient culpability to warrant criminal sanctions".

There are, however, potential difficulties inherent in this penal provision which should be looked at, even though all of them are not decisive in this present case. One, of course, is the absence of any need for corroboration. The tape recording here tends to give some independent support to the testimony of Silverman, but there are types of criminal conduct which might be solicited where there would be a heavy thrust placed on the credibility of a single witness testifying to a conversation. Extraordinary care might be required in deciding when to prosecute; in determining the truth; and in appellate review of the factual decision.

One example would be the suggestion of one person to another that he commit a sexual offense; another is the suggestion that he commit perjury. The Model Penal Code did not require corroboration; but aside from the need for corroboration which is traditional in some sexual offenses, there are dangers in the misinterpretation of innuendos or remarks which could be taken as invitations to commit sexual offenses. * * *

In two opinions for the California Supreme Court, Justice Traynor has analyzed that State's criminal solicitations statute (Penal Code, § 653f; *Benson v. Superior Ct. of Los Angeles County,* 57 Cal.2d 240, 18 Cal.Rptr. 516; 368 P.2d 116 [1962], and *People v. Burt,* 45 Cal.2d 311, 288 P.2d 503 [1955]).

The first case was for solicitation to commit perjury and the second for solicitation to commit extortion.

The California statute is based on a specific list of serious crimes to which criminal solicitation expressly applies; but as to all of them the statute requires that the offense "must be proved by the testimony of two witnesses, or of one witness and corroborating circumstances".

The basic public justification for legislative enactment is, however, very similar to New York's and was developed in the *Burt* opinion: "Legislative concern with the proscribed soliciting is demonstrated not only by the gravity of the crimes specified but by the fact that the crime, unlike conspiracy, does not require the commission of any overt act. It is complete when the solicitation is made, and it is immaterial that the object of the solicitation is never consummated, or that no steps are taken toward its consummation." The California Legislature was concerned "not only with the prevention of the harm that would result should the inducements prove successful, but with protecting inhabitants of this state from being exposed to inducements to commit or join in the commission of the crimes specified."

Another potential problem with the statute is that it includes an attempt to commit unlawful solicitation, i.e., solicits, etc., "or otherwise attempts to cause" the conduct. This has the same effect as the Model Penal Code, but the language there is different. The code spells the purpose out more specifically that: "It is immaterial * * * that the actor fails to communicate with the person he solicits to commit a crime if his conduct was designed to effect such communication" (*Model Penal Code,* § 5.02, subd. [2], Tent. Draft No. 10 * * *). This could be an attempt in the classic sense and might be committed by a telephone message initiated but never delivered. The present Penal Law, stated in different language, has the same effect. * * *

Notes and Questions

1. *Need.* Are you convinced, given the availability of the crimes of attempt and conspiracy to deal with inchoate criminality, that there is also a need for the crime of solicitation? What of the contention that a mere solicitation need not be made criminal because the "force set in motion is neither continuous nor mechanical, and its operation may be broken before the stage of attempt has been attained by the withdrawal or repentance" of the person solicited? *People v. Werblow,* 241 N.Y. 55, 148 N.E. 786 (1925).

2. *Risks.* Is whatever need exists outweighed by the risk of false charges arising out of misunderstanding or harassment? Consider:

(a) *Smith v. Commonwealth,* 54 Pa. 209 (1867), where, in holding there was no common law crime of soliciting fornication, the court commented: "It is observable that no assault or overt act is charged—no writing, or picture, or indecent exposure of person is alleged, nothing indeed is suggested but mere solicitation. And the manner of this is not even hinted. It may have been by direct request, by innuendo, by argument, founded, as has sometimes happened, upon scriptural texts and analogies, or it may have been by gay and frivolous anecdote or appeal. Possibly nothing was *said,* but only impure thoughts insinuated by looks or gestures. What evidence shall be sufficient to sustain such a charge?''

(b) *Kelly v. United States,* 194 F.2d 150 (D.C.Cir.1952), where, with respect to the charge against the defendant that he solicited sodomy from an undercover policeman (who had made six arrests upon such a charge the same evening), the court said: ''The public has a peculiar interest in the problem before us. The alleged offense, consisting of a few spoken words, may be alleged to have occurred in any public place, where any citizen is likely to be. They may be alleged to have been whispered, or to have occurred in the course of a most casual conversation. Any citizen who answers a stranger's inquiry as to direction, or time, or a request for a dime or a match is liable to be threatened with an accusation of this sort. There is virtually no protection, except one's reputation and appearance of credibility, against an uncorroborated charge of this sort. At the same time, the results of the accusation itself are devastating to the accused. The gratuitous solicitation of a total stranger for a perverted act is a phenomenon on the outer fringes of behavior. While technically this offense is a minor misdemeanor and in the catalog of crimes is graded as less serious than reckless driving, in the practical world of everyday living it is a major accusation.

''It follows that threatened accusation of this offense is the easiest of blackmail methods. The horror of the ordinary citizen at the thought of such an accusation may impel him to comply with a demand for money under such a threat. The public has a great interest in the prevention of any such criminal operation.''

3. *Minimizing the risks.* What can be done about these risks? Consider (a) the California corroboration rule discussed in *Lubow;* (b) the requirement in Wis.Stat.Ann. § 939.30 that the solicitation take place ''under circumstances which indicate unequivocally'' the defendant's intent that a crime be committed; and (c) the proposal in National Comm'n on Reform of Federal Criminal laws, *Final Report* § 1003 (1971), that an overt act by the person solicited be required.

4. *Acts.* (a) Does the New York statute specify sufficiently what acts will suffice for the crime? Would a broader statement be desirable? Compare the statute discussed in *State v. Ryan,* 48 Conn.App. 148, 709 A.2d 21 (1998), which uses the words ''advocates, encourages, justifies, praises, incites or solicits.''

(b) Must the solicitation be directed toward a particular person? See *State v. Schleifer,* 99 Conn. 432, 121 A. 805 (Dist.Ct.1923) holding sufficient an information charging the defendant with soliciting from a public platform a number of persons to commit the crimes of murder and robbery. Is it correct to say that ''solicitations of this type are more dangerous than solicitations of a special kind, for here solicitation is to a greater number''? James B. Blackburn, *Solicitation to Crimes,* 40 W.Va.L.Rev. 135, 146 (1934).

What result, then, on these facts: The defendants have been charged under the New York solicitation statute with soliciting the illegal possession of DMT, a psychedelic agent. The evidence is that they circulated a pamphlet highly critical of contemporary American life which included the assertion: ''What's needed is a generation of people who are freaky, crazy, irrational, sexy, angry, irreligious, childish and mad: people who burn draft cards, burn high school and college degrees: people who say: 'To hell with your goals'; people who lure youth with music, pot and acid.'' This was followed by a paragraph entitled ''How to make a fire bomb,'' and a recipe for producing DMT, which concluded: ''This cannot be drunk or injected, but may be smoked by sprinkling on mint or cannabis leaves and letting the solution evaporate."[a]

(c) In *State v. Lee*, 105 Or.App. 329, 804 P.2d 1208 (1991), Lee, while in jail, wrote letters to an acquaintance in a juvenile detention center soliciting participation in a robbery. The letters were intercepted by center personnel and never reached the intended recipient. Lee, convicted of solicitation of robbery under a statute stating one "commits the crime of solicitation if with the intent of causing another to engage in specific conduct constituting a crime * * * the person commands or solicits such other person to engage in that conduct," now appeals. What should the result be? What should the result be under the New York statute? See *State v. Cotton*, 109 N.M. 769, 790 P.2d 1050 (1990), involving similar facts and a comparable statute.

(d) In *State v. Yee*, 160 Wis.2d 15, 465 N.W.2d 260 (1990), Yee asked Conti to find someone to kill Li, but Conti instead informed the police. The state now appeals the granting of Yee's motion to dismiss the charge of solicitation of murder, under a statute stating that "whoever, with intent that a felony be committed, advises another to commit that crime under circumstances which indicate unequivocally that he or she has such intent is guilty of a * * * felony." What should the result be? Is *Yee* the same as *Lee*?

5. *Objectives.* May a statute prohibit the solicitation of conduct which is itself not criminal? In *City of Columbus v. Scott,* 47 Ohio App.2d 287, 353 N.E.2d 858 (1975), the court affirmed the dismissal of a complaint charging violation of an ordinance providing: "No person shall solicit a person to engage in sexual activity with the offender, when the offender knows such solicitation is offensive to the other person, or is reckless in that regard." In holding that "the ordinance makes a criminal offense of the social interrelationships and protected free speech rights of otherwise consenting adults," the court emphasized, as the trial court concluded, that "sexual activity is illegal only under specific circumstances" and that "the ordinance is not limited to *illegal* sexual activity." Consider also *Cherry v. State*, 18 Md.App. 252, 306 A.2d 634 (1973), upholding defendant's conviction of solicitation for purposes of prostitution on the theory that "if consummated crimes themselves are constitutional in terms of their criminality * * *, then constitutionality follows as to their incipient or inchoate phases."

But does this mean that on either policy or constitutional grounds particular solicitation-type statutes should be confined to objectives which are and constitutionally may be made criminal? Consider *United States v. Carson*, 319 A.2d 329 (D.C.App.1974), reversing the dismissal of several charges of soliciting for lewd and immoral purposes:

"In holding that this soliciting statute amounts to a violation of a right of privacy, the trial court used as its major premise 'the fundamental principle that the Constitution protects the right of an individual to control *the use and function* of his or her body without unreasonable interference from the state.' (Emphasis supplied.) The trial court's ruling thus appears to have been based on the assumption that an act of sodomy between consenting adults in privacy (i.e., 'use and function') may not constitutionally be proscribed. Irrespective of the validity of a criminal sanction against a private and consensual sodomitic act, the overbreadth doctrine may not properly be applied to the soliciting statute. The acts charged were public solicitations of strangers for sodomy. That any of the accused ultimately may have contemplated a private and consensual act is of no legal significance. Any such hope or expectation by an accused may not in contemplation of law

---

a. *People v. Quentin,* 58 Misc.2d 601, 296 N.Y.S.2d 443 (1968), concluding the statute was not "designed to cover a situation where the defendant makes a   general solicitation (however reprehensible) to a large undefinable group to commit a crime."

project him into a posture in which he can assert a right of privacy which arguably might arise from such a projected position.''

6. *Impossibility.* In *Benson,* cited in *Lubow,* an undercover investigator visited defendant, an attorney, and told him she was pregnant, that she wanted to have the child adopted, and that the child's father was unknown because she had been living with her husband and another man. Defendant told her there were ways of getting around the statutory requirement of obtaining her husband's consent to the adoption. At defendant's suggestion, the woman arranged for a friend (actually, another investigator) to meet with the defendant, and he instructed her as to the perjured testimony she should give at the custody proceedings. Defendant, charged with solicitation of perjured testimony, objected that he had not committed that crime because the investigator was not actually pregnant and thus the anticipated custody proceedings would never occur. Held: "If the solicitor believes that the act can be committed 'it is immaterial that the crime urged is not possible of fulfilment at the time when the words are spoken' or becomes impossible at a later time.''

7. *Abandonment.* In *Moran v. Schwarz,* 108 Nev. 200, 826 P.2d 952 (1992), two witnesses testified to a grand jury that Schwarz had solicited them to kill Susman. Schwarz challenged his indictment for solicitation of murder on the ground that the prosecutor had violated his statutory duty to present exculpatory evidence to the grand jury, in that the prosecutor failed to play for them a tape recording in his possession of defendant's renunciation of the scheme to one of the witnesses a few days later. The court responded "that a subsequent renunciation or withdrawal is not a defense to the crime of solicitation. * * * One of the purposes of the statute making solicitation a crime is 'to avoid citizen exposure to inducements to commit crime.' Unlike other criminal offenses, in the crime of solicitation, 'the harm is the asking—nothing more need be proven.' Because renunciation or withdrawal cannot undo that which has already been done, it 'has no effect on the elements of solicitation.' " Compare *Model Penal Code* § 5.02(3).

8. *Nonliability for offense solicited.* In *Leffel v. Municipal Court,* 54 Cal.App.3d 569, 126 Cal.Rptr. 773 (1976), it was held that a statute providing that "[e]very person * * * [w]ho solicits * * * an act of prostitution" is guilty of disorderly conduct, is applicable to a potential customer of a prostitute who solicits her. Is this a fair construction of the statute? A desirable result? Is it a proper result if the defendant would not have been an accomplice to the act of prostitution had it occurred? See *Model Penal Code* § 5.04(2); and compare *People v. Allen,* 92 N.Y.2d 378, 681 N.Y.S.2d 216, 703 N.E.2d 1229 (1998) (persons who attempted to purchase marijuana from undercover police participating in reverse sting operation cannot be convicted of soliciting sale of marijuana).

9. *Punishment.* As noted in *Lubow,* New York has three grades of solicitation. Each grade authorizes punishment which is not as great as that provided for the crimes specified as the object of that grade of solicitation. Compare *Model Penal Code* § 5.05. Which penalty scheme is most rational?

10. *Solicitation as an attempt.* "While a few of the courts have treated solicitation to commit a crime as an attempt, the great weight of authority warrants the assertion that mere solicitation, unaccompanied by an act moving directly toward the commission of the intended crime, is not an overt act constituting an element of the crime of attempt." *State v. Davis,* 319 Mo. 1222, 6 S.W.2d 609 (1928). What additional acts should suffice? Compare *State v. Otto,* 102 Idaho 250, 629 P.2d 646 (1981) (defendant not guilty of attempted murder where he told person referred to him as a "hit-man" who he wanted killed, negotiated fee of $1,000, paid $250 as an advance, and discussed type of weapon to be utilized and manner in which hit to be made); with *State v. Kilgus,* 128 N.H. 577, 519 A.2d

231 (1986) (defendant's conviction of attempted murder affirmed where he solicited killing of specified person, paid fee of $1,000 and stressed that body must be found out of state).

11. *The innocent solicitee.* In *State v. Bush*, 195 Mont. 475, 636 P.2d 849 (1981), defendant appealed his conviction of soliciting the possession of dangerous drugs. The evidence at trial was that defendant had hired a Ms. Kohse as a photographer of animals and sent her to Lima, Peru to take pictures at the zoo, during which time an accomplice placed cocaine into the lining of her camera case, which she transported into the United States.

"Appellant's final contention is that the crime of solicitation is not complete unless the person solicited is aware of the solicitor's criminal purpose and scheme. Since Kohse was unaware that she was to do anything but work for a movie company and since she was unaware of the drugs, appellant maintains she was not solicited.

"At common law the use of an innocent agent to accomplish a crime was considered an attempt but not a solicitation. The common law has been affirmatively changed in some jurisdictions by statutes which provide that it is no defense to a charge of solicitation that the solicitee is unaware of the criminal nature of the conduct solicited or of the defendant's purpose. The theory behind the change is that one is no less guilty of a crime because he employs an innocent agent.

"The Montana statute is not explicit in this regard. The language 'facilitates the commission of that offense' does not imply that the person solicited must be aware of the criminal purpose. As above noted, the Montana legislature has changed the common law, as is its prerogative, and has not required that the solicitee be aware of the criminal purpose of the solicitor or of the criminal nature of the conduct solicited. To do so would defeat the purpose of the statute which is to protect the citizens of this state from victimization and from exposure to inducements to commit or join in the commission of crime. The gravamen of the offense of solicitation is the intent of the solicitor and not the knowledge of the victim."

Consider also *State v. Rossi*, 520 A.2d 582 (R.I.1987) (rejecting defendant's claim his conviction of soliciting an 8–year–old girl to commit perjury cannot stand because the girl, as a minor, could not be convicted of perjury, and noting that a "similar view" is taken in *Model Penal Code* § 5.04(1)(b)).

12. *The cautious solicitor.* Persons seeking "customers" for some criminal activity, fearful of being discovered by undercover police, often phrase their solicitations in the most ambiguous terms possible. It is not uncommon, therefore, for courts to be confronted with the question of whether the events proved will support a solicitation conviction. Consider, for example, whether a conviction of soliciting for lewd and immoral purposes could be had on these facts:

"On November 7, 1972, Officer Keeton of the Vice Squad, Metropolitan Police Department, was driving his private car south in the 1000 block of 14th Street, N.W., when he was waived to the curb by two persons standing with others at a corner. Both persons, attired as women, approached the passenger side of the car and one of them (appellant) asked the officer who was in civilian clothes, 'You want to go out for a while?' The other person, identified as one Walter Modin, asked, 'How much money you spending?' When Officer Keeton replied that he had 'about $75', appellant's companion asked where he was staying to which Officer Keeton replied '[T]he Hilton.' Mr. Modin said, 'We can't get in there, so we'll have to find another place.' He left the car to speak to other persons attired also as women who were gathered on the corner. Appellant, while standing at the side of the car, was asked by Officer Keeton what he was going to get for his money, to which appellant replied, 'I'll do anything at all.' According to Officer Keeton's testimony the following then transpired:

> At that time I asked if he would [submit to rectal sodomy], and he [appellant] said, 'I'll do anything at all.' So, I asked him what he was best at, and * * * in the meantime, while this conversation was going on, Mr. Modin approached the auto again, and Mr. Shannon then said he would [participate in natural and perverted sexual acts] * * *. 'I'm good at everything, baby.'

"Both appellant and Mr. Modin then got into the car and Officer Keeton drove for a short distance to the 1000 block of Vermont Avenue, N.W., where he placed both men under arrest with the assistance of his partner, Officer Martin, who had followed Keeton's vehicle after observing the two approach it, engaged in apparent conversation, and then enter the vehicle."[b]

b. *Shannon v. United States,* 311 A.2d 501 (D.C.App.1973), modified, 319 A.2d 135 (1974), reversing the conviction.

Chapter 12

PARTIES; LIABILITY FOR CONDUCT OF ANOTHER

SECTION 1. THE COMMON LAW CLASSIFICATION

In the commission of each criminal offense there may be several persons or groups which play distinct roles before, during, and after the offense. Collectively these persons or groups are termed the parties to the crime.

The common law classification of parties to a felony consisted of four categories: (1) principal in the first degree; (2) principal in the second degree; (3) accessory before the fact; and (4) accessory after the fact. This classification scheme gave rise to many procedural difficulties, but if they were overcome a person in any one of the four categories could be convicted and subjected to the penalties authorized for commission of the felony. It was later recognized that the accessory after the fact, by virtue of his involvement only after the felony was completed, was not truly an accomplice in the felony. This category has thus remained distinct from the others, and today the accessory after the fact is not deemed a participant in the felony but rather one who has obstructed justice, subjecting him to different and lesser penalties.[a] The distinctions between the other three categories, however, have now been largely abrogated, although statutes frequently resort to the common law terminology in defining the scope of complicity. It thus remains important to understand what is collectively encompassed within these three categories.

The common law classification scheme described above existed only as to felonies. When treason was committed, those who would be included within any of the four felony categories were all classified as principals. As to misdemeanors, all parties were again held to be principals, although conduct which would constitute one an accessory after the fact to a felony was not criminal when the post-crime aid was to a misdemeanant.

1. *Principal in the First Degree.* A principal in the first degree may simply be defined as the criminal actor. He is the one who, with the requisite mental state, engages in the act or omission concurring with the mental state which causes the criminal result.

There can be more than one principal in the first degree. This occurs when more than one actor participates in the actual commission of the offense. Thus, when one man beats a victim and another shoots him, both may be principals in first degree to murder. And when

---

a. See Section 11 of this Chapter.

794

two persons forge separate parts of the same instrument, they are both principals in the first degree to the forgery.

Although it has been said that a principal in the first degree must be present at the commission of the offense, this is not literally so. He may be "constructively" present when some instrument which he left or guided caused the criminal result. Thus, when an actor leaves poison for another who later drinks it, he is a first degree principal, as is the person whose unwitting agent acts for him in his absence.

While there may be more than one principal in the first degree, there must always be at least one for a crime to have taken place.

2. *Principal in the Second Degree.* To be a principal in the second degree, one must be present at the commission of a criminal offense and aid, counsel, command, or encourage the principal in the first degree in the commission of that offense. This requirement of presence may be fulfilled by constructive presence. A person is constructively present when he is physically absent from the situs of the crime but aids and abets the principal in the first degree at the time of the offense from some distance. This may happen when one stands watch for the primary actor, signals to the principal from a distance that the victim is coming, or stands ready (though out of sight) to render aid to the principal if needed. However, one must be close enough to render aid if needed.

3. *Accessory Before the Fact.* An accessory before the fact is one who orders, counsels, encourages, or otherwise aids and abets another to commit a felony and who is not present at the commission of the offense. The primary distinction between the accessory before the fact and the principal in the second degree is presence. If a person was actually or constructively present at the offense, due to his participation he is a principal in the second degree; if he was not present, he is an accessory before the fact. Through prior counseling followed by appearance at the scene of the crime to aid the primary actor, one may become both an accessory before the fact and also a principal in the second degree.

Although the accessory before the fact is often the originator of the offense, this need not be the case. Indeed, if one is enlisted by another to lend aid toward the commission of the offense and the aid is given, the person giving the assistance may thereby become an accessory before the fact.

4. *Legislative Reform.* Virtually all states have now expressly abrogated the distinction between principals and accessories before the fact.[b] The most common form of legislation declares that accessories before the fact are now principals, although substantially the same result has been reached by providing that those who would have been accessories before the fact may be prosecuted, tried and punished as if they were principals.

A much more modern approach to the entire subject of parties to crime is to abandon completely the old common law terminology and simply provide that a person is legally accountable for the conduct of another when he is an accomplice of the other person in the commission of the crime. Such is the view taken in the Model Penal Code,[c] which provides that a person is an accomplice of another person in the commission of an offense if, with the purpose of promoting or facilitating the commission of the offense, he solicits the other person to commit it, or aids or agrees or attempts to aid the other person in planning or

b. In *State v. Sowell*, 353 Md. 713, 728 A.2d 712 (1999), the court concluded that "although Maryland apparently is the only jurisdiction that has not rejected the common law distinctions between principals and accessories, the majority of the other jurisdictions rejecting the distinctions have done so legislatively. Given the relative importance in completely abrogating an ancient and historic common law doctrine such as accessoryship, we believe such a task is generally better left to the legislative body of this State."

c. § 2.06(2)(c).

committing it, or (having a legal duty to prevent the crime) fails to make proper effort to prevent it. A similar approach has been taken in many of the recent recodifications.

SECTION 2. ACTS OR OMISSIONS

HICKS v. UNITED STATES

Supreme Court of the United States, 1893.

150 U.S. 442, 14 S.Ct. 144, 37 L.Ed. 1137.

MR. JUSTICE SHIRAS delivered the opinion of the court.

In the circuit court of the United States for the western district of Arkansas, John Hicks, an Indian, was jointly indicted with Stand Rowe, also an Indian, for the murder of Andrew J. Colvard, a white man, by shooting him with a gun on the 13th of February, 1892. Rowe was killed by the officers in the attempt to arrest him, and Hicks was tried separately, and found guilty, in March, 1893. * * *

At the trial the government's evidence clearly disclosed that John Hicks, the accused, did not, as charged in the indictment, shoot the deceased, nor take any part in the physical struggle. To secure a conviction it hence became necessary to claim that the evidence showed such participation in the felonious shooting of the deceased as to make the accused an accessory, or that he so acted in aiding and abetting Rowe as to make him guilty as a principal. The prosecution relied on evidence tending to show that Rowe and Hicks co-operated in inducing Colvard to leave the house, where they and a number of others had passed the night in a drunken dance, and to accompany them up the road to the spot where the shooting took place. Evidence was likewise given by two or three men, who, from a house about 100 yards distant, were eyewitnesses of the occurrence, that the three men were seated on their horses a few feet apart; that Rowe twice raised his gun and aimed at Colvard; that Hicks was heard to laugh on both occasions; that Rowe thereupon withdrew his gun; that Hicks pulled off his hat, and, striking his horse with it, said to Colvard, "Pull off your hat, and die like a man;" that thereupon Rowe raised his gun a third time, and fired at Colvard, whose horse then ran some distance before Colvard fell. As the horse ran, Rowe fired a second time. When Colvard's body was subsequently examined, it was found that the first bullet had passed through his chest, inflicting a fatal wound, and that the second had not taken effect.

The language attributed to Hicks, and which he denied having used, cannot be said to have been entirely free from ambiguity. It was addressed, not to Rowe, but to Colvard. Hicks testified that Rowe was in a dangerous mood, and that he did not know whether he would shoot Colvard or Hicks. The remark made,—if made,—accompanied with the gesture of taking off his own hat, may have been an utterance of desperation, occasioned by his belief that Rowe would shoot one or both of them. That Hicks and Rowe rode off together after seeing Colvard fall was used as a fact against Hicks, pointing to a conspiracy between them. Hicks testified that he did it in fear of his life; that Rowe had demanded that he should show him the road which he wished to travel. Hicks further testified—and in this he was not contradicted—that he separated from Rowe a few minutes afterwards, on the first opportunity, and that he never afterwards had any intercourse with him, nor had he been in the company of Rowe for several weeks before the night of the fatal occurrence. * * *

Another error is contained in that portion of the charge now under review, and that is the statement "that, if Hicks was actually present at that place at the time of the firing by Stand Rowe, and he was there for the purpose of either aiding, abetting, advising, or encouraging the shooting of Andrew J. Colvard by Stand Rowe, and that, as a matter of fact, he did not do it, but was present for the purpose of aiding or abetting or advising or encouraging his shooting, but he did not do it because it was not necessary, it was done without his assistance, the law says there is a third condition where guilt is fastened to his act in that regard."

We understand this language to mean that where an accomplice is present for the purpose of aiding and abetting in a murder but refrains from so aiding and abetting because it turned out not to be necessary for the accomplishment of the common purpose, he is equally guilty as if he had actively participated by words or acts of encouragement. Thus understood, the statement might, in some instances, be a correct instruction. Thus, if there had been evidence sufficient to show that there had been a previous conspiracy between Rowe and Hicks to waylay and kill Colvard, Hicks, if present at the time of the killing, would be guilty, even if it was found unnecessary for him to act. But the error of such an instruction, in the present case, is in the fact that there was no evidence on which to base it. The evidence, so far as we are permitted to notice it, as contained in the bills of exception and set forth in the charge, shows no facts from which the jury could have properly found that the rencounter was the result of any previous conspiracy or arrangement. The jury might well, therefore, have thought that they were following the court's instructions in finding the accused guilty because he was present at the time and place of the murder, although he contributed neither by word nor action to the crime, and although there was no substantial evidence of any conspiracy or prior arrangement between him and Rowe. * * *

The judgment of the court below is reversed, and the cause remanded, with directions to set aside the verdict and award a new trial. * * *

Notes and Questions

1. Should Hicks be deemed an accomplice because he failed to intervene or even manifest his disapproval? Consider *Pace v. State,* 248 Ind. 146, 224 N.E.2d 312 (1967), an appeal from a conviction for being an accessory to a robbery:

"Viewing the evidence most favorable to the State, the record shows the following: appellant, his wife and two infant children were in a car driving from South Bend to LaPorte. Eugene Rootes was riding with them. The appellant was driving with his wife and one child in the front seat. Rootes and appellant's other child were in the back seat. While in South Bend, appellant after asking his wife for permission stopped to pick up a hitchhiker, Mr. Reppert, who sat next to Rootes in the back seat with one of appellant's infant children. Later Rootes pulled a knife and took Reppert's wallet. After driving further, Reppert got out of the car, Rootes then took his watch. The appellant said nothing during the entire period and they continued driving to LaPorte. This is all of the evidence presented by the record which would have any bearing on the crime charged, i.e., accessory before the fact of robbery by placing in fear.

"The main question presented in the facts at bar is what evidence beyond the mere presence of a person at the scene of a crime is sufficient to sustain a connection as an accessory before the fact? This court has previously stated that negative acquiescence is not enough to constitute a person guilty of aiding and abetting the commission of a crime. * * * However, it has been further stated by this court in *Mobley v. State* (1949), 227 Ind. 335, 344, 85 N.E.2d 489, 492:

' * * * in the absence of anything in his conduct showing a design to encourage, incite, aid, abet or assist in the crime, the trier of the facts may consider failure of such person to oppose the commission of the crime in connection with other circumstances and conclude therefrom that he assented to the commission of the crime, lent his countenance and approval thereto and thereby aided and abetted it * * * '

It should be noted that the court in *Mobley,* supra, in stating that a failure to oppose the commission of a crime may be considered as aiding and abetting, impliedly qualified this statement wherein the Court stated:

'This, it seems to us, is particularly true when the person who fails to interfere owes a duty to protect as a parent owes to a child.'

In other cases relying on *Mobley,* supra, there has normally been some course of conduct of an affirmative nature to connect the defendant with the crime.

"In the facts at bar we have found no evidence or reasonable inferences therefrom which might demonstrate that the appellant aided and abetted in the alleged crime. While he was driving the car, nothing was said nor did he act in any manner to indicate his approval or countenance of the robbery. While there is evidence from which a jury might reasonably infer that he knew the crime was being committed, his situation was not one which would demonstrate a duty to oppose it. We do not intend to draw any hard and fast rules in this area of the law. Each case must be reviewed on its own facts; in so doing we hold that the verdict is not sustained by substantial evidence of probative value and is therefore contrary to law."

2. Compare *State v. Walden,* 306 N.C. 466, 293 S.E.2d 780 (1982), where defendant was convicted of aiding and abetting an assault by one Hoskins upon defendant's one-year-old son. The evidence was that the assault occurred in defendant's presence without her objection or intervention. On appeal, she challenged a jury instruction that one's mere presence is insufficient but that it is sufficient if one "is present with the reasonable opportunity and duty to prevent the crime and fails to take reasonable steps to do so." In affirming the conviction, the court reasoned:

"Parents in this State have an affirmative legal duty to protect and provide for their minor children. * * *

"We find no case from any jurisdiction directly in point on the precise question before us, i.e., whether a mother may be found guilty of assault on a theory of aiding and abetting solely on the ground that she was present when her child was attacked and had a reasonable opportunity to prevent or attempt to prevent the attack but failed to do so. * * *

"[W]e believe that to require a parent as a matter of law to take affirmative action to prevent harm to his or her child or be held criminally liable imposes a reasonable duty upon the parent. Further, we believe this duty is and has always been inherent in the duty of parents to provide for the safety and welfare of their children, which duty has long been recognized by the common law and by statute. This is not to say that parents have the legal duty to place themselves in danger of death or great bodily harm in coming to the aid of their children. To require such, would require every parent to exhibit courage and heroism which, although commendable in the extreme, cannot realistically be expected or required of all people. But parents do have the duty to take every step reasonably possible under the circumstances of a given situation to prevent harm to their children.

"In some cases, depending upon the size and vitality of the parties involved, it might be reasonable to expect a parent to physically intervene and restrain the person attempting to injure the child. In other circumstances, it will be reasonable for a parent to go for help or to merely verbally protest an attack upon the child. What is reasonable in any given case will be a question for the jury after proper instructions from the trial court.

"We think that the rule we announce today is compelled by our statutes and prior cases establishing the duty of parents to provide for the safety and welfare of their children. Further, we find our holding today to be consistent with our prior cases regarding the law of aiding and abetting. It remains the law that one may not be found to be an aider and abettor, and thus guilty as a principal, solely because he is present when a crime is committed. It will still be necessary, in order to have that effect, that it be shown that the defendant said or did something showing his consent to the criminal purpose and contribution to its execution. But we hold that the failure of a parent who is present to take all steps reasonably possible to protect the parent's child from an attack by another person constitutes an act of omission by the parent showing the parent's consent and contribution to the crime being committed. *Cf. State v. Haywood,* 295 N.C. 709, 249 S.E.2d 429 (1978) (When a bystander is a friend of the perpetrator and knows his presence will be regarded as encouragement, presence alone may be regarded as aiding and abetting.)."

Compare the following two cases, each also involving a defendant convicted as an accomplice because of failure to perform a parent's duty: *State v. Jackson,* 137 Wash.2d 712, 976 P.2d 1229 (1999) (reversed, as state's accomplice statute generally follows Model Penal Code but lacks subsection recognizing accomplice liability may be grounded in a failure to perform a legal duty, manifesting legislative "intent to reject the concept of extending accessory liability for omissions to act"); *State v. Rundle,* 176 Wis.2d 985, 500 N.W.2d 916 (1993) (where defendant charged with being accomplice to physical abuse of child by another, only affirmative aiding will suffice though person abused was defendant's child, as another subsection of statute specifically deals with failure to act to prevent abuse and carries a lesser penalty). Is the policy reflected in either *Jackson* or *Rundle* sound?

3. In *State v. Tazwell,* 30 La.Ann. 884 (1878), defendant was convicted as an accessory before the fact to the burglary of a barn, in that he had provided the burglar with an instrument to be used in committing the crime. On appeal, the defendant objected that the judge had refused to give the following requested charge: "That if there be no evidence to show that an instrument furnished by one accused as accessory before the fact was used for the purpose for which it was made, but another and different one is used to commit the offense, that it has not been sufficiently proved to justify a verdict of guilty as accessory before the fact. That the instrument said in the indictment to have been furnished for the purpose of committing an offense must be proved to have been used for that purpose."

The court affirmed, concluding that the requested charge "is manifestly wrong. It would be strange, indeed, if one who had so far counseled, aided, and abetted a burglary as to provide and furnish implements to effect it, could escape because when the burglar reached the place of his crime he found more convenient tools, and did not actually use those furnished him for the purpose by his confederate."

4. *Hicks* indicates that "words or acts of encouragement" can suffice as a basis for accomplice liability. What result then on the facts in *State v. Ulvinen,* 313 N.W.2d 425 (Minn.1981)? Helen told her son David that she was moving out of David's home because David's wife Carol "had been so nasty to me." David then said that he was going to kill Carol, and Helen responded "it will be for the best." Later that day David told Helen that "Tonight's got to be the night," and Helen answered that "it would be the best for the kids." That night, while Helen was sleeping, David strangled Carol. David later dismembered the body; while this was occurring, Helen remained upstairs to intercept the children should they awaken. Helen then helped David clean up the bathroom, where the dismemberment took place.

While in *Tally,* Note 5 infra, the court held an accomplice's assistance need not have a "but for" relationship to the results, should the same be true of encouragement? Consider

State v. Davis, 319 N.C. 620, 356 S.E.2d 340 (1987), where *A* encouraged *B* to kill *C*, *A*'s husband; thereafter *D*, *A*'s daughter and *B*'s lover, pleaded with *B* to kill *C* because of *C*'s sexual abuse of *D*; *B* later killed *C* and then gave conflicting statement as to whether he acted at the behest of *A* or of *D*. At *A*'s murder trial, is it sufficient that the jury was instructed they could convict upon a finding beyond a reasonable doubt that (i) *B* murdered *C*; and (ii) *A* encouraged *B* to murder *C*? If not, what needs to be added?

5.   *State ex rel. Martin v. Tally,* 102 Ala. 25, 15 So. 722 (1894), involved an appeal by Judge Tally from his impeachment for his complicity in a murder. At the impeachment proceedings it was shown that Ross had seduced the judge's sister-in-law and that consequently her brothers (the Skeltons) followed him to the nearby town of Stevenson for the purpose of killing Ross. While at the telegraph office in Scottsboro, the judge learned that a relative of Ross had just sent Ross a telegram reading: "Four men on horseback with guns following. Look out." The judge then sent a telegram to the telegraph operator in Stevenson, an acquaintance by the name of Huddleston, reading: "Do not let the party warned get away." Huddleston received both messages, but failed to deliver the one addressed to Ross. The Skeltons caught up with Ross and killed him. The court concluded that these facts sufficed to make Judge Tally an accomplice:

"We are therefore clear to the conclusion that, before Judge Tally can be found guilty of aiding and abetting the Skeltons to kill Ross, it must appear that his vigil at Scottsboro to prevent Ross from being warned of his danger was by preconcert with them, or at least known to them, whereby they would naturally be incited, encouraged, and emboldened— 'given confidence'—to the deed, or that he aided them to kill Ross, contributed to Ross' death, in point of physical fact, by means of the telegram he sent to Huddleston. The assistance given, however, need not contribute to the criminal result in the sense that but for it the result would not have ensued. It is quite sufficient if it facilitated a result that would have transpired without it. It is quite enough if the aid merely rendered it easier for the principal actor to accomplish the end intended by him and the aider and abettor, though in all human probability the end would have been attained without it. If the aid in homicide can be shown to have put the deceased at a disadvantage, to have deprived him of a single chance of life which but for it he would have had, he who furnishes such aid is guilty, though it cannot be known or shown that the dead man, in the absence thereof, would have availed himself of that chance; as, where one counsels murder, he is guilty as an accessory before the fact, though it appears to be probable that murder would have been done without his counsel; and as, where one being present by concert to aid if necessary is guilty as a principal in the second degree, though, had he been absent murder would have been committed, so, where he who facilitates murder even by so much as destroying a single chance of life the assailed might otherwise have had, he thereby supplements the efforts of the perpetrator, and he is guilty as principal in the second degree at common law, and is principal in the first degree under our statute, notwithstanding it may be found that in all human probability the chance would not have been availed of, and death would have resulted anyway."

6.   Compare Note, 61 So.Cal.L.Rev. 2169, 2171 (1988): "If *A* is determined to rob a liquor store and approaches *B* for help, in what sense does *B*'s cooperation in telling *A* when the store is the least crowded, or even *B*'s supplying a toy gun for the purpose of frightening the cashier, cause the holdup? *B*'s refusal to aid *A* would not have prevented the robbery; it merely would have changed the form of the robbery. While this aid may satisfy the 'but for' requirement, it does not satisfy the proximate cause element. If *A* was committed to the robbery before approaching *B*, and *B* could not have convinced *A* otherwise, then any resulting harm bears no relation to the aid that *B* rendered."

7. What if in *Tally* Huddleston had not acted on the judge's instructions but had instead delivered the warning telegram to Ross? If the Skeltons had nonetheless caught up with Ross and killed him, would the judge be an accomplice to murder? Consider *Model Penal Code* § 2.06(3)(a)(ii), which includes "attempts to aid" as a basis for accomplice liability.[a] The draftsmen explain: "The inclusion of attempts to aid may go in part beyond present law, but attempted complicity ought to be criminal, and to distinguish it from effective complicity appears unnecessary where the crime has been committed. Where complicity is based upon agreement or solicitation, one does not ask for evidence that they were actually operative psychologically on the person who committed the offense; there ought to be no difference in the case of aid." *Model Penal Code* § 2.06, Comment (1985).

What, then, should be the result if Ross escapes because Huddleston warns him notwithstanding the judge's instructions? Under *Model Penal Code* § 5.01(3) the judge is guilty of attempted murder. The draftsmen note: "If the judge had been unsuccessful in his effort to prevent Ross from being warned and Ross had escaped, or if, notwithstanding the effective suppression of the warning, Ross had not been killed, the judge would have engaged in conduct designed to aid the others to murder Ross and liability would be established under subsection (3)." *Model Penal Code* § 5.01, Comment (1985).

8. Can one by a single act become an accomplice to multiple crimes, or, for that matter, crimes by more than one principal? Yes, concluded the court in *Watts v. Bonneville*, 879 F.2d 685 (9th Cir.1989): "Watts first contends that the California courts should not have imposed two sentences for rape in concert. Although Watts admits that Simmons and Montgomery each raped Kathy B., he adamantly asserts that California can punish him only once for his single act of guarding her parents. To support his position, Watts attempts to rely on both state and federal law. He bases his state law argument on Cal.Penal Code § 654 (West 1982), which provides: 'An act or omission which is made punishable in different ways by different provisions of this code may be punished under either of such provisions, but in no case can it be punished under more than one.... ' Although it seems highly unlikely that the California courts violated this provision in sentencing Watts, we cannot review the contention as a matter of state law because 28 U.S.C. § 2254(a) authorizes the federal courts to grant habeas corpus relief only for violations of federal law.

"We must consider, however, Watts' alternative argument that imposing the two sentences for a single act violates the Fourteenth Amendment's due process clause. Watts reads the Supreme Court's decision in *Ball v. United States*, 470 U.S. 856, 865, 105 S.Ct. 1668, 1673, 84 L.Ed.2d 740 (1985), which prohibited sentencing a defendant for both receiving a firearm and possessing a firearm under a federal statute, to mean that the Constitution prohibits punishing a defendant for multiple offenses if the offenses stem essentially from the same act. He cites, as further support, *United States v. Arbelaez*, 812 F.2d 530, 533 (9th Cir.1987) (per curiam), which in a 'single act' event prohibited the imposition of separate sentences for (1) aiding and abetting the possession of cocaine and (2) aiding and abetting the distribution of cocaine. The court in *Arbelaez* stated: 'The applicable rule is that where the same act or transaction constitutes a violation of two distinct statutory provisions, the test to be applied to determine whether there are two

---

a. Several modern codes have adopted this innovation. Illustrative of its impact is *State v. Gelb*, 212 N.J.Super. 582, 515 A.2d 1246 (1986) (defendant convicted of being homicide accomplice to Wade, who pulled switch causing train to leave main track and hit brick wall, killing engineer; testimony was that one Held yelled "Throw the switch," and that Wade then began pulling the switch, after which he heard Gelb yell "to wait until the train passed Morlot Avenue so the engineer doesn't know the switch is pulled"; because of "attempt to aid" language in statute, defendant not entitled to jury instruction that he must be acquitted if his actions were "subsequent to the actual and irreversible lifting of the switch").

offenses or only one is whether each provision requires proof of an additional fact which the other does not.'

"We hold that no violation of due process has occurred in this case. The *Ball* and *Arbelaez* cases do not apply because California punished Watts for two separate criminal acts, not twice for a single act. The ancient and universally accepted principle of accomplice liability holds a defendant legally responsible for the unlawful conduct of others that he aids and abets. California, applying this principle as embodied in its law, quite properly punished Watts for each of the two acts of rape in concert that he aided and abetted when he guarded the parents. Nothing in the Constitution prohibits this; indeed, in applying federal law, this court routinely has upheld convictions for multiple crimes aided and abetted by a single course of conduct. See, e.g., *United States v. Rubier*, 651 F.2d 628, 629, 631 n. 4 (9th Cir.1981) (per curiam) (upholding convictions for bank robbery and assault when the defendant aided and abetted the actual perpetrator of the two crimes by driving a getaway car). Although Watts stood guard only once, he enabled his accomplices to commit two rapes in concert. This is more culpable than enabling them to commit only one. Each rape was a separate wrongful act."

9. To convict the perpetrator of a crime defined in terms of results (e.g., homicide), we saw in Chapter 5, Section 5, that the prosecution must establish that the defendant was the cause of death. By contrast, as the material in the present Section illustrates, one can become an accomplice to a murder even if one's acts did not, in a but-for sense, cause the perpetrator to do the killing. Is this (to use Professor Dressler's words[b]) "simplistic uniform treatment of all accomplices alike regardless of participation in the crime" inappropriate? Is the solution, as he suggests, a lesser offense of Noncausal Assistance where the accomplice's "assistance or influence did not cause the harm specified by the other offense to be committed"?

BAILEY v. UNITED STATES

United States Court of Appeals, District of Columbia Circuit, 1969.

416 F.2d 1110.

SPOTTSWOOD W. ROBINSON, III, CIRCUIT JUDGE:

Appellant was tried in the District Court on a single-count indictment charging robbery of an employee of the Center Market Provision Company. The prosecutive theory was that he aided and abetted the principal assailant, who remains unknown, in the commission of the crime. At the close of the Government's case in chief, appellant moved unsuccessfully for a judgment of acquittal on the ground that the proof did not establish a prima facie case against him. This motion he renewed, and the court again denied, after all the evidence was in. The jury returned a verdict finding appellant guilty as charged, and from the conviction this appeal was taken. * * *

Appellant spent some of the afternoon of September 26, 1966, the date of the robbery, in the vicinity of the Center Market Provision Company, a wholesale meat distributor. He was first seen across the street from the company's place of business "shooting craps" with a short, stocky man—the "other man" in the case, who was to become the actual robber. At one point appellant left the other man but returned minutes later. Appellant subsequently left him again to join several men in a game of "five-and-ten-cent crap" on a

b. Joshua Dressler, *Reassessing the Theoretical Underpinnings of Accomplice Liability: New Solutions to* an Old Problem, 37 Hastings L.J. 91, 121 (1985).

parking lot in front of the Center Market building. When the game terminated, appellant rejoined the other man, who in the meanwhile had remained across the street, and somewhat later they walked over to the parking lot and stood by a truck owned by Center Market. The offense for which appellant was prosecuted took place shortly thereafter.

Wilson C. Lawson, Jr., a part-time bookkeeper for Center Market, was the victim of the robbery. Each day he checked in the cash receipts of Center Market's drivers and prepared the company's bank deposit. His regular routine was to take the deposit with him when he left and to deliver it to a bank, at which he was employed full-time, on the following day.

As Lawson left Center Market on September 26, he carried a paper bag containing a deposit of approximately $4,200. He noticed appellant and the other man by the truck, but attached no significance to that circumstance. While Lawson stood on a loading platform locking the door, a driver whom he recognized came out of another building and conversed with him briefly. A second truck driver was sitting in a car parked facing the platform.

Lawson walked down the platform steps toward his car, which was parked next to the truck where appellant and the other man were. When Lawson reached his car, the other man took the bag with the deposit at gunpoint. Appellant, just prior to the holdup, had walked away from the gunman toward the curb of the street, and was then about ten feet away. The man who had conversed with Lawson yelled "Look, they're robbing him," and both appellant and the other man ran away in the same direction. The two truck drivers attempted to follow but lost them. Appellant was subsequently apprehended, but the other man was never identified or caught.

Appellant's conviction must stand, if at all, on the premise that he aided and abetted the unknown robber, for the record is barren of proof that appellant was an active perpetrator of the offense. * * *

Appellant's conduct, as portrayed in the view most favorable to the Government, amounted to presence at the scene of the crime, slight prior association with the actual perpetrator, and subsequent flight. A *sine qua non* of aiding and abetting, however, is guilty participation by the accused. "In order to aid and abet another to commit a crime it is necessary that a defendant 'in some sort associate himself with the venture, that he participate in it as in something that he wishes to bring about, that he seek by his action to make it succeed.'" The crucial inquiries in this case relate to the legal capabilities of the evidence to sustain a jury determination that appellant collaborated to that degree in the robbery.

An inference of criminal participation cannot be drawn merely from presence; a culpable purpose is essential. * * * Presence is thus equated to aiding and abetting when it is shown that it designedly encourages the perpetrator, facilitates the unlawful deed—as when the accused acts as a lookout—or where it stimulates others to render assistance to the criminal act. But presence without these or similar attributes is insufficient to identify the accused as a party to the criminality. And this case is devoid of evidence, beyond what the previous associative acts and the subsequent flight might themselves reflect, that appellant's presence on the scene was designed to in any way sanction or promote the robbery.

The Government urges the efficacy of appellant's presence when it is coupled with his association with the perpetrator on the date of and shortly prior to the robbery. But an accused's prior association with one who is to become a criminal offender, even when coupled with the accused's later presence at the scene of the offense, does not warrant an inference of guilty collaboration. Moreover, here the uncontradicted evidence shows that each of appellant's several brief meetings with the eventual robber occurred on the street or the parking lot in the open view of others, including the men with whom appellant fraternized for some time in a dice game—evidence becoming even more eloquent when scrutinized in the light of what was not shown at trial. The Government's proof did not expose appellant as a planner of the robbery, or as an aide or lookout in its consummation,[28] or as one who shared in its proceeds, or even as one who knew the unidentified robber. In these circumstances, we cannot say that reasonable jurors could find a taint of criminality in appellant's limited association with him.

The Government contends finally that the strength of its case against appellant was enhanced by the fact that appellant fled the scene after the crime was committed. The evidentiary value of flight, however, has depreciated substantially in the face of Supreme Court decisions delineating the dangers inherent in unperceptive reliance upon flight as an indicium of guilt. We no longer hold tenable the notion that "the wicked flee when no man pursueth, but the righteous are as bold as a lion." The proposition that "one who flees shortly after a criminal act is committed or when he is accused of committing it does so because he feels some guilt concerning that act" is not absolute as a legal doctrine "since it is a matter of common knowledge that men who are entirely innocent do sometimes fly from the scene of a crime through fear of being apprehended as the guilty parties, or from an unwillingness to appear as witnesses."

With cautious application in appreciation of its innate shortcomings, flight may under particular conditions be the basis for an inference of consciousness of guilt. But guilt, as a factual deduction, must be predicated upon a firmer foundation than a combination of unelucidated presence and unelucidated flight. Here there was no evidentiary manifestation that the appellant was prompted by subjective considerations related in any wise to the crime.[34] Moreover, as the evidence disclosed, appellant had several convictions prior to the affair in suit, and these might well have dictated what seemed to him to be best. Absent anything more, there was no more basis for attributing his flight to complicity in the robbery than to a purpose consistent with innocence.

If we consider presence, association and flight separately, the Government's case quite obviously did not qualify for submission to the jury. And while "the jury must take the Government's case as a whole and determine whether as a whole it proves guilt beyond a reasonable doubt," any effort to repair the Government's fragmented case still leaves a prosecution constructed from evidence which is pregnant with the probability that appellant was an innocent bystander. After all, it shows only that he openly gambled with the eventual robber, talked to him, and stood with him beside the truck at intermittent periods during the afternoon. Suddenly when the robbery victim appeared on the scene with the bag of money, it was the unidentified man who pointed a gun at him and grabbed the bag. Appellant, prompted by reasons which only random speculation could summon, ran away in the midst of shouts that "they" had committed a robbery.[35] The admonition that

28. The Government's aiding and abetting theory, as argued to the jury, was that appellant either planned the robbery or functioned as a lookout. But the record is devoid of evidence disclosing circumstances that could give that sort of color to appellant's conduct. There is no trustworthy indication that appellant was a party to the scheme to rob, and the Government did not ask any of its eyewitnesses to try to elucidate appellant's behavior as he walked away from the unidentified robber immediately before the crime took place.

34. There was no evidence of such things as manifest cooperation, division of the spoils, or the like, activities which have been factors in decisions reaching the contrary conclusion under their particular circumstances.

35. Our dissenting colleague emphasizes the word "they" in the shout but we are unable to attach particular significance to it. The witness who made that outcry testified that appellant had walked away from the gunman prior to the holdup and explained appellant's role thusly:

"innocent people caught in a web of circumstances frequently become terror-stricken" carries its usual force here.

In the annals of the case law we find well reasoned decisions exonerating from conviction persons accused in circumstances not significantly divergent from those appearing here. We hold concordantly that the Government's ambiguous evidence against appellant left too much room for the jury to engage in speculation, with the result that the motion for judgment of acquittal was erroneously denied. The totality of that evidence could only conjecturally support a finding that appellant "associate[d] himself with the [criminal] venture, that he participate[d] in it as in something that he wish[ed] to bring about, [and] that he [sought] by his action to make it succeed." The circumstances may arouse suspicions but, as we have counseled, even "grave suspicion is not enough."

We reverse the judgment of appellant's conviction and remand the case to the District Court with direction that a judgment of acquittal be entered.

Reversed and remanded.

Bastian, Senior Circuit Judge (dissenting): * * *

In this case, prior to the commission of the crime, appellant was closely associated with the actual perpetrator and was with him immediately before the robbery. Furthermore, appellant was present at the scene of the crime. Finally, he ran away together with the other man after the robbery. Yet, my colleagues decide that only by impermissible conjecture could the evidence support a finding that appellant "in some sort associate himself with the venture, that he participate in it as in something that he wishes to bring about, that he seek by his action to make it succeed."

I, on the other hand, state forcefully that the totality of this evidence, when considered in the light most favorable to the prosecution, is surely adequate, yea, more than adequate, to meet the governing standard, " * * * [that] a reasonable mind might fairly conclude guilt beyond a reasonable doubt * * * [and if the trial judge] concludes that either of the two results, a reasonable doubt or no reasonable doubt, is fairly possible, he must let the jury decide the matter." * * *

Notes and Questions

Consider in which of the following cases the evidence should be deemed sufficient to support defendant's conviction as an accomplice.

1. At 4:15 p.m. Settles and Whitley approached Ms. Smith from behind as she was walking with her 3–year-old son. Settles put his hand over Smith's mouth and shoved her and her son into the basement of a nearby apartment building. As she was being pushed, she turned and saw Whitley, and told Settles she knew Whitley. Settles hit her and said, "Shut up; Whitley is not with me." Smith saw Whitley standing "right outside of the door" to the basement. Inside the basement, Settles struck Ms. Smith several times, and her son then began to cry. Settles raped Ms. Smith and then left the basement. She looked out and saw "Settles and Whitely running away together, side by side." Whitely appeals his

Q. Did Mr. Bailey at any time ever go over to Mr. Lawson?

A. Not as I knows of. Only thing I seen was both running down the street.

Q. You ever see Mr. Bailey do anything to Mr. Lawson?

A. No, sir.

Q. You ever see Mr. Bailey anytime snatch anything out of Mr. Lawson's hands?

A. No, sir.

Q. The only thing you saw Mr. Bailey do was run up the street?

A. That is all.

This coincides with all else said at trial. * * *

conviction as an accessory to rape, arguing "that the evidence against him in the case was no stronger than the evidence in *Bailey*—'presence at the scene of the crime, slight prior association with the actual perpetrator, and subsequent flight.' "[a]

2. "The defendant was convicted of armed robberies of three stores which occurred on December 25 and 26, 1974. There was evidence that she rode to the scene of each robbery in a car with her brother and one Cote; that in each instance the car was parked in a street on which the store to be robbed either fronted or sided; that during each robbery she remained in the car while her brother and Cote entered the store and stole money, groceries and cigarettes at gunpoint; that she knew beforehand of their purpose in entering each store; and that she was present at the division of the proceeds, but received no share other than some cigarettes in unspecified amounts. There was no evidence that she drove (or did not drive) the car or that she knew (or did not know) how to drive. Except for what may be inferred from the foregoing, the evidence is silent as to her ability from her vantage point in the parked car to act as lookout or otherwise assist in any of the robberies."[b]

3. "Shortly before 5 a.m. on January 4, 1970, the burglar alarm sounded at Smith's Country Store in Cave City. Cave City Police Officer Shaw was notified and came to the scene quickly. He stated that a hole had been made in a side wall of the store building and that he observed James Orville Moore emerging from the building through that hole. Moore ran from the scene, up a hill back of the building. Officer Shaw fired at Moore but missed him. Moore left the scene and was not apprehended until five hours later. Shaw 'stayed at the hole until the sheriff got there' because he thought 'there was still maybe some more inside.' However, no one else was found inside, and Moore was the only person seen at or near the premises. There was a pick-up truck (which had been stolen in Hart County) parked near the hole. A tape recorder and perhaps one or two country hams which had been taken from the store were found in the truck. About thirty hams, averaging between twelve and fifteen pounds each, were found lying near the hole in the store. Apparently these hams had been carried from a rack on the opposite side of the storeroom. There was no testimony linking Moore or Hodges with the stolen truck.

"A substantial posse of peace officers was quickly assembled. An airplane was obtained which circled the area in the effort to thwart an escape from the area by the culprit or culprits.

"About 10 a.m. (some five hours after Officer Shaw observed Moore leaving the store building) he came upon Moore and Hodges [the defendant here] who were hiding under a log in a field at a point variously estimated as two or three-and-a-half miles from Smith's Country Store. The actual apprehension was thus described by Officer Shaw:

'Q 32. What did they do when they saw you?

'A. Well, I hollered at them and threw my gun on them, and they started to run, and I shot over them, and they stopped.' "[c]

4. At about 8:30 p.m. Mrs. Jackson was confronted by two men, one of whom was armed with a pistol. They wrenched a purse from her arms while striking a blow to her head. She saw a vehicle drive away, but could not describe the car or its occupants. A speeding vehicle was stopped five blocks away and the driver, McCall, was issued a traffic ticket at 8:40; the officer noted that there were 4 or 5 men in the car and that 1 or 2 of them left the vehicle immediately thereafter. The car was out of sight only seconds when

---

a. *Settles v. United States*, 522 A.2d 348 (D.C.App. 1987), affirming the conviction.

b. *Commonwealth v. Drew*, 4 Mass.App.Ct. 30, 340 N.E.2d 524 (1976), affirming the convictions.

c. *Hodges v. Commonwealth*, 473 S.W.2d 811 (Ky. App.1971), reversing the conviction.

the officer received a call regarding the robbery; he and other police then stopped the car. In addition to McCall, the occupants were Cephas (in the front seat) and Bonham (in the back seat). Mrs. Jackson's purse was seen on the right rear floor, and a loaded sawed-off shotgun was protruding from under the right front seat. McCall had a 4-inch blade knife on his person, but no pistol was found. Mrs. Jackson was unable to identify either Cephas or McCall, but they have been charged with armed robbery.[d]

SECTION 3. MENTAL STATE

BOGDANOV v. PEOPLE

Supreme Court of Colorado, 1997.

941 P.2d 247, amended by 955 P.2d 997.

JUSTICE KOURLIS delivered the Opinion of the Court.

The defendant, Branko Bogdanov (Bogdanov), was convicted under a complicity theory of second degree burglary of a warehouse and theft; and of criminal conspiracy to commit theft [on evidence that he accompanied three women to a warehouse clothing store and, while two women distracted the sales clerks at one end of the store, held up a large pair of pants while the third woman slipped behind him into the office and took from the safe bank bags containing $2200 in cash and $1100 in checks]. On appeal, Bogdanov argued, among other things, that the standard jury instruction on complicity violated his right to due process of law. * * *

The questions raised by this case require us to review and clarify the state of mind required of an accomplice. [W]e begin our analysis with the Colorado complicity statute, which states:

> Complicity. A person is legally accountable as principal for the behavior of another constituting a criminal offense if, with the intent to promote or facilitate the commission of the offense, he aids, abets, or advises the other person in planning or committing the offense.

[T]here is * * * a dual mental state requirement of the complicitor that must be proven before he or she can be legally accountable for the offense of another. Complicity liability exists when (1) the complicitor has the culpable mental state required for the underlying crime committed by the principal; and (2) the complicitor assists or encourages the commission of the crime committed by the principal "with the intent to promote or facilitate" such commission.* * *

Complicity is not a theory of strict liability. It is not sufficient that the defendant intentionally engaged in acts which ultimately assisted or encouraged the principal. Rather, the complicitor must intend that his conduct have the effect of assisting or encouraging the principal in committing or planning the crime committed by the principal. * * *

In this case, the trial court gave the jury the pattern complicity instruction, which states:

> A person is guilty of an offense committed by another person if he is a complicitor. To be guilty as a complicitor, the following must be established beyond a reasonable doubt:
>
> 1. A crime must have been committed.
>
> 2. Another person must have committed all or part of the crime.

d. *United States v. McCall,* 460 F.2d 952 (D.C.Cir. 1972), affirming both convictions.

3. The defendant must have had knowledge that the other person intended to commit (all or part of) the crime.

4. The defendant did intentionally aid, abet, advise, or encourage the other person in the commission or planning of the crime. * * *

We hold that * * * the plain language of the pattern complicity instruction sufficiently reflects the complicitor's two mental state requirements under the complicity statute: (1) the defendant had the requisite mens rea for the underlying crime committed by the principal; and (2) the defendant intended that his own conduct would promote or facilitate the commission of the crime committed by the principal. Therefore, the jury necessarily made a determination as to Bogdanov's mental state, and no structural error occurred. * * *

The fourth paragraph * * * adequately directs the jury to determine whether the defendant had the requisite mens rea of the crime, because the defendant could not have intended his participation to further the crime unless he also intended the crime to occur. For him to intend that the crime occur, he would necessarily share the principal's mental state. If the defendant did not intend that his actions would assist or encourage the other principal(s) in the commission or planning of the underlying crime, the defendant cannot be criminally liable for the commission of that crime. * * *[10] * * *

Notes and Questions

1. Can one have the "intent to promote and facilitate" a certain offense, as required by *Bogdanov*, without knowing of all the facts and circumstances which must be present for that offense to occur? Consider:

(a) *State v. Davis*, 101 Wash.2d 654, 682 P.2d 883 (1984), upholding defendant's conviction for being an accomplice to armed robbery by standing lookout, notwithstanding a jury instruction that it sufficed to elevate defendant's complicity to the armed robbery level that the principal "in fact had a gun." The court took note of *State v. McKim*, 98 Wash.2d 111, 653 P.2d 1040 (1982), where "we held that the deadly weapon statute requires that the State prove the defendant was either actually or constructively armed with a deadly weapon. Constructive possession exists if the defendant knew his coparticipant was armed.

"Our conclusion in *McKim* rested in part upon our recognition of the differences between accomplice liability for a substantive crime and accomplice liability for enhancement statutes. We reasoned that the new complicity statute, unlike the old one, made an

---

10. While we have concluded that the standard complicity instruction does not amount to structural error that would affect the entire trial from beginning to end or that would deny the defendant a basic protection, we nevertheless acknowledge that the pattern instruction should more properly mirror the applicable statutory language as follows:

A person is guilty of an offense committed by another person if he is a complicitor. To be guilty as a complicitor, the following must be established beyond a reasonable doubt:

1. A crime must have been committed.

2. Another person must have committed [all or part of] the crime.

3. The defendant must have had knowledge that the other person intended to commit [all or part of] the crime.

4. The defendant must have had the intent to promote or facilitate the commission of the crime.

5. The defendant must have aided, abetted, advised, or encouraged the other person in the commission or planning of the crime.

The language contained in brackets should be included in the complicity jury instruction only in those cases where one or more persons, possibly including the defendant, together committed the essential elements of the underlying crime. If only one person alone committed all essential elements of the crime with which the defendant is charged under a complicity theory, the language in brackets should be omitted from the jury instruction as given.

accomplice equally liable only for the substantive crime. We reaffirm this distinction. As to the substantive crime, the law has long recognized that an accomplice, having agreed to participate in a criminal act, runs the risk of having the primary actor exceed the scope of the preplanned illegality. * * *

"Furthermore, this distinction recognizes that the Legislature has a valid interest in discouraging the use of deadly weapons by imposing strict liability on all those involved in robbery which, by its very nature, generally requires use of weapons to facilitate the act of illegally obtaining money from another by force."

A dissent objected: "We have held, in *McKim*, that it is improper to enhance a defendant's sentence under the deadly weapon statute absent a showing that the defendant either had a weapon or knew that a coparticipant had a weapon. I see no reason why a different rule should apply to substantive offenses. The majority's rule allows the State to do indirectly what *McKim* says it may not do directly, namely, impose upon a defendant an enhanced sentence (by convicting the defendant of first degree robbery instead of second degree robbery) because of a deadly weapon which the defendant knew nothing about."

(b) *United States v. Gregg*, 612 F.2d 43 (2d Cir.1979), where Bates and other officers of REA Express in New York formulated a scheme to steal REA funds. Bates contacted a Florida acquaintance, Gregg, who agreed to and did "wash" some REA checks for 10% of the proceeds. Gregg was charged as an accomplice to violation of 18 U.S.C.A. § 660, which covers misappropriation by "a president, director, officer, or manager of any firm, association, or corporation engaged in commerce as a common carrier" of that organization's funds or assets. In upholding a jury instruction that Gregg could be convicted even if he did not know Bates was the manager of REA, the court concluded "that the requirement that the principal violator under the statute hold the position of president, director, officer, or manager of the interstate carrier is jurisdictional only. Upon the authority of *Feola*, [p. 724 of this Book] therefore, it was not essential that the court charge the jury that they must find that appellant knew of the status of the principal. As the Court stated in *Feola:*

> 'This interpretation poses no risk of unfairness to defendants. It is no snare for the unsuspecting. * * * The situation is not one where legitimate conduct becomes unlawful solely because of the identity of the individual or agency affected. * * * The concept. of criminal intent does not extend so far as to require that the actor understand not only the nature of his act but also its consequence for the choice of a judicial forum.'

Similarly, we note that appellant here was not engaged in legitimate conduct that was rendered unlawful 'solely because of the identity of the individual' with whom he conspired. Hence, there is no element of unfairness in holding appellant liable for conduct which he knew to be illegal."

2. Sometimes the question is whether the two mental states referred to in *Bogdanov* have been proved. Consider *State v. Meyers*, 683 So.2d 1378 (La.App.1996), where Meyers, Davis and Delmore were convicted of second-degree murder. The evidence was that one George was selling drugs on a street corner when an Olds Cutlass stopped nearby. Meyers was the driver, Delmore was the front seat passenger, and Davis was the rear seat passenger. A witness testified that Davis "stuck his head to the window" and "asked George 'did he have anything,'" at which George walked toward the vehicle, when Delmore fired three shots into George and the Cutlass then "pulled off like they ain't never did nothing." Bystanders identified the vehicle occupants to the police. In response to the claim of Meyers and Davis that their mental state was not proved, the appellate court responded:

"In the present case, neither Meyers nor Davis tried to assist the victim, George, after the shooting. They did not call the police to report the shooting or give any statement regarding the murder to anyone. Meyers drove the Cutlass to the scene and Davis watched the incident thru the car window. Although there was no direct evidence presented that either Meyers or Davis knew Delmore was armed, it can easily be assumed that the jury believed that all three knew exactly what their purpose was in confronting George on the street that night. This was a drive-by shooting quite common in the lives of drug dealers and the participants here all knew that Delmore intended to shoot Samuel George. They were definitely not an innocent driver and passenger in the car."

Do you agree?

3.   During an evening of drinking, Wilson accused Pierce of having stolen his watch, but Pierce denied it. They then discussed feats of crime, and decided to burglarize a certain drug store. Wilson boosted Pierce through a transom and then, while Pierce was inside, telephoned the police. After Pierce had handed several bottles of whiskey out to Wilson, the police arrived. Wilson told them Pierce was inside, and after Pierce escaped Wilson led the police to him and identified him. Wilson told the police that his purpose was to get even with Pierce for taking his watch. Wilson was convicted of aiding and abetting Pierce in the commission of burglary (breaking and entering the premises with intent to commit larceny) and larceny (trespassory taking and carrying away of the personal property of another with intent to deprive the owner of it permanently). On appeal, he objected to a jury instruction that one "who attempts to detect the commission of crime in others must himself stop short of lending assistance, or participation in the commission of the crime." In *Wilson v. People*, 103 Colo. 441, 87 P.2d 5 (1939), the court agreed and reversed.

Didn't Wilson, in the language of *Bogdanov*, "intend that his conduct have the effect of assisting or encouraging" Pierce? Why, then, should his conviction be reversed?

4.   If the mental states of the principal and the accomplice are not the same, another possible result is that they will be found guilty of different offenses. For example, it has been held that one is not an accomplice to the crime of assault with intent to kill (as compared to mere assault) if the accomplice did not share that intent.[a] But disparity in mental states has been a matter of greatest significance in the homicide area, where the precise state of mind of the defendant has great significance in determining the degree of the offense. To determine the kind of homicide of which the accomplice is guilty, it is necessary to look to his state of mind; it may have been different from the state of mind of the principal and they thus may be guilty of different offenses.[b] Thus, because first degree murder requires a deliberate and premeditated killing, an accomplice is not guilty of this degree of murder unless he acted with premeditation and deliberation.[c] And, because a killing in a heat of passion is manslaughter and not murder, an accomplice who aids while in such a state is guilty only of manslaughter even though the killer is himself guilty of murder.[d] Likewise, it is equally possible that the killer is guilty only of manslaughter because of his heat of passion but that the accomplice, aiding in a state of cool blood, is guilty of murder.[e]

a.   *State v. Taylor*, 70 Vt. 1, 39 A. 447 (1898).

b.   Some difficulty in this regard was experienced under the old common law view of parties, for an accessory before the fact could not be convicted of a higher crime than his principal. 4 Blackstone, *Commentaries on the Laws of England* 36 (1765).

c.   *State v. Clemons*, 946 S.W.2d 206 (Mo.1997).

d.   *Dorsey v. Commonwealth*, 13 Ky.L.R. 359, 17 S.W. 183 (1891); *Moore v. Lowe*, 116 W.Va. 165, 180 S.E. 1 (1935).

e.   *State v. McAllister*, 366 So.2d 1340 (La.1978).

STATE v. GLADSTONE

Supreme Court of Washington, 1970.

78 Wash.2d 306, 474 P.2d 274.

HALE, JUSTICE.

A jury found defendant Bruce Gladstone guilty of aiding and abetting one Robert Kent in the unlawful sale of marijuana. Deferring imposition of sentence, the court placed defendant on probation. He appeals the order deferring sentencing contending that the evidence as a matter of law was insufficient to sustain a verdict of guilty. His point, we think, is well taken. * * *

Gladstone's guilt as an aider and abettor in this case rests solely on evidence of a conversation between him and one Douglas MacArthur Thompson concerning the possible purchase of marijuana from one Robert Kent. There is no other evidence to connect the accused with Kent who ultimately sold some marijuana to Thompson. * * *

The conversation between defendant and Thompson occurred at defendant's residence. Douglas MacArthur Thompson, a 25–year-old student at the University of Puget Sound in Tacoma and an employee of the Internal Revenue Service of the United States, had done some investigative work for the government. From time to time, the Tacoma Police Department engaged him to investigate the use, possession and sale of narcotics, principally marijuana, among college students. When working for the Tacoma Police Department, he operated under the control and direction of the department's narcotics detail.

Thompson testified that Lieutenant Seymour and Detective Gallwas of the narcotics detail asked him to attempt a purchase of marijuana from Gladstone. During the evening of April 10, 1967—between 10 and 11 o'clock—the two officers and Thompson drove in a police car to the vicinity of defendant's apartment. Thompson went to Gladstone's door alone, beyond the hearing and out of the sight of the two officers. He knocked at the door and Gladstone responded. Thompson asked Gladstone if he would sell him some marijuana. Describing this incident, Thompson testified as follows:

> Well, I asked—at the time Gladstone told me that he was—he did not have enough marijuana on hand to sell me any, but he did know an individual who had quite a sufficient quantity and that was very willing to sell and he named the individual as Robert Kent, or Bob Kent as he put it, and he gave me directions to the residence and he—due to the directions I asked him if, you know, if he could draw me a map and he did.

When Thompson said he asked Gladstone to draw the map for him, he added, "I'm not sure whether he did give me the exact address or not, he told me where the residence was." He said that Gladstone then with pencil and paper sketched the location of Kent's place of residence. Thompson had no prior knowledge of where Kent lived, and did not know if he might have marijuana or that he had ever possessed it.

The two officers then took Thompson to Kent's residence where marijuana was purchased. The actual purchase was made by Thompson directly from Kent while Officer Gallwas and Lieutenant Seymour stayed in the police car. Kent was subsequently arrested and convicted of selling Thompson approximately 8 ounces of marijuana—the very sale which defendant here was convicted of aiding and abetting.

That ended the prosecution's case. Even if it were accorded all favorable inferences, there appears at this point a gap in the evidence which we feel as a matter of law is fatal to the prosecution's cause. Neither on direct examination nor under cross-examination did Thompson testify that he knew of any prior conduct, arrangements or communications between Gladstone and Kent from which it could be even remotely inferred that the defendant had any understanding, agreement, purpose, intention or design to participate or engage in or aid or abet any sale of marijuana by Kent. Other than to obtain a simple map from Gladstone and to say that Gladstone told him Kent might have some marijuana available, Thompson did not even establish that Kent and the defendant were acquainted with each other. Testimony of the brief conversation and Gladstone's very crude drawing consisting of 8 penciled lines indicating where Kent lived constitute the whole proof of the aiding and abetting presented. * * *

[E]ven without prior agreement, arrangement or understanding, a bystander to a robbery could be guilty of aiding and abetting its commission if he came to the aid of a robber and knowingly assisted him in perpetrating the crime. But regardless of the modus operandi and with or without a conspiracy or agreement to commit the crime and whether present or away from the scene of it, there is no aiding and abetting unless one " 'in some sort associate himself with the venture, that he participate in it as in something that he wishes to bring about, that he seek by his action to make it succeed.' " *Nye & Nissen v. United States,* 336 U.S. 613, 619, 69 S.Ct. 766, 769, 93 L.Ed. 919 (1949). * * *

Gladstone's culpability, if at all, must be brought within RCW 9.01.030, which makes a principal of one who aids and abets another in the commission of the crime. Although an aider and abettor need not be physically present at the commission of the crime to be held guilty as a principal, his conviction depends on proof that he did something in association or connection with the principal to accomplish the crime. Learned Hand, J., we think, hit the nail squarely when, in *United States v. Peoni,* 100 F.2d 401, 402 (2d Cir.1938), he wrote that, in order to aid and abet another to commit a crime, it is necessary that a defendant

in some sort associate himself with the venture, that he participate in it as in something that he wishes to bring about, that he seek by his action to make it succeed. All the words used—even the most colorless, "abet"—carry an implication of purposive attitude towards it. * * *

This court has recognized the necessity of proof of a nexus between aider and abettor and other principals to sustain a conviction. In *State v. Hinkley,* 52 Wash.2d 415, at 418, 325 P.2d 889 (1958), amplifying the term *abet,* we said:

Although the word "aid" does not imply guilty knowledge or felonious intent, the word "abet" includes *knowledge* of the wrongful purpose of the perpetrator, as well as counsel and encouragement in the crime.

and approved the instruction that:

To abet another in the commission of a crime implies a consciousness of guilt in instigating, encouraging, promoting or aiding in the commission of such criminal offense.

It would be a dangerous precedent indeed to hold that mere communications to the effect that another might or probably would commit a criminal offense amount to an aiding and abetting of the offense should it ultimately be committed.

There being no evidence whatever that the defendant ever communicated to Kent the idea that he would in any way aid him in the sale of any marijuana, or said anything to Kent to encourage or induce him or direct him to do so, or counseled Kent in the sale of marijuana, or did anything more than describe Kent to another person as an individual who might sell some marijuana, or would derive any benefit, consideration or reward from such a sale, there was no proof of an aiding and abetting, and the conviction should, therefore, be reversed as a matter of law. Remanded with directions to dismiss. * * *

HAMILTON, JUSTICE (dissenting).

* * * The statutory language and the overt action it contemplates does, however, give rise to the requirement that the aider or abettor entertain a conscious intent, i.e., knowledge and intent that his action will instigate, induce, procure or encourage perpetration of the primary crime.

The question to be resolved, then, in the instant case is whether the evidence sustains the jury's conclusion that the appellant entertained the requisite intent to render him culpable as an aider or abettor. In the resolution of this question, it is to be borne in mind that appellant's challenge to the sufficiency of the evidence requires that the evidence, and all reasonable inferences to be drawn therefrom, be interpreted in a light most favorable to the state. Furthermore, this court has held that an aider's or abettor's culpability may be established by circumstantial evidence.

Although the evidence in the case is conflicting, the jury was entitled to believe that on April 10, 1967, one Robert Kent sold marijuana to Douglas Thompson, who at the time was acting as an undercover agent for and in concert with officers of the Tacoma Police Department; that appellant Gladstone, Kent, and Thompson were students at the same school in Tacoma; that prior to the evening of April 10, 1967, when Thompson talked to appellant, *Thompson and the Tacoma Police Department were unaware of Kent or his association with marijuana;* that appellant knew Kent, whom he met and associated with on the campus of the school they respectively attended; that both appellant and Kent lived off campus; that appellant knew where Kent lived and on at least one occasion had driven him home; that at the time in question the Tacoma Police Department had information that appellant was supposed to be holding a supply of marijuana for sale; that Thompson, who was but slightly acquainted with appellant, approached appellant at his residence about 10:50 p.m. on April 10, 1967, and asked appellant to sell him some marijuana; that appellant then stated that he did not have enough marijuana on hand to sell but that he knew an individual who did have an ample supply and who was willing to sell some and named the individual as Robert Kent; that upon request appellant orally gave Thompson directions to Kent's apartment and drew a map to aid Thompson in finding the address, utilizing as a reference point a building known to appellant to be a student rendezvous where drugs had been sold; that by using the map and oral directions Thompson and the police went to Kent's residence; *that Thompson approached Kent and told him "Gladstone had sent me" whereupon Kent invited him to a room and sold him some marijuana for $30;* and that Thompson and one of the police officers later returned to the Kent residence, after again visiting appellant, and made a second purchase of marijuana at which time Kent was arrested.

Based upon the foregoing circumstances and the inferences reasonably derivable therefrom, I am satisfied that the jury was fully warranted in concluding that appellant, when he affirmatively recommended Kent as a source and purveyor of marijuana, entertained the requisite conscious design and intent that his action would instigate, induce, procure or encourage perpetration of Kent's subsequent crime of selling marijuana to Thompson. Furthermore, insofar as an element of preconcert be concerned, certainly the readiness with which the passwords, "Gladstone had sent me," gained a stranger's late evening entree to Kent's domain and produced two illegal sales strongly suggests, if not conclusively establishes, the missing communal nexus which the majority belabors. * * *

Notes and Questions

1. *Peoni*, relied upon in *Gladstone*, is a well-known case on this subject. Peoni sold counterfeit bills to Regno in the Bronx; Regno sold the same bills to Dorsey in the Bronx; and Dorsey was arrested while trying to pass them in Brooklyn. Peoni was convicted as an

accessory to the crime of possessing counterfeit money in Brooklyn. The court of appeals concluded that "Peoni was not an accessory to Dorsey's possession; his connection with the business ended when he got his money from Regno, who might dispose of the bills as he chose; it was of no moment to him whether Regno passed them himself, and so ended the possibility of further guilty possession, or whether he sold them to a second possible passer. His utterance of the bills was indeed a step in the causal chain which ended in Dorsey's possession, but that was all. Perhaps he was Regno's accessory. * * * Be that as it may nobody, so far as we can find, has ever held that a contract is criminal, because the seller has reason to know, not that the buyer will use the goods unlawfully, but that some one further down the line may do so. Nor is it at all desirable that the seller should be held indefinitely. The real gravamen of the charge against him is his utterance of the bills; and he ought not to be tried for that wherever the prosecution may pick up any guilty possessor—perhaps thousands of miles away."

2.   Compare *Backun v. United States*, 112 F.2d 635 (4th Cir.1940). Backun sold Zucker stolen silverware in New York, knowing that the goods were not saleable in New York and that Zucker intended to take the silverware with him to the South and dispose of it there. Backun's conviction of being an accessory to the interstate transportation of property known to have been stolen was affirmed:

"Whether one who sells property to another knowing that the buyer intends to use it for the commission of a felony renders himself criminally liable as aiding and abetting in its commission, is a question as to which there is some conflict of authority. It must be remembered, however, that guilt as accessory before the fact has application only in cases of felony; and since it is elementary that every citizen is under moral obligation to prevent the commission of felony, if possible, and has the legal right to use force to prevent its commission and to arrest the perpetrator without warrant, it is difficult to see why, in selling goods which he knows will make its perpetration possible with knowledge that they are to be used for that purpose, he is not aiding and abetting in its commission within any fair meaning of those terms. Undoubtedly he would be guilty, were he to give to the felon the goods which make the perpetration of the felony possible with knowledge that they would be used for that purpose; and we cannot see that his guilt is purged or his breach of social duty excused because he receives a price for them. In either case, he knowingly aids and assists in the perpetration of the felony.

"Guilt as an accessory depends, not on 'having a stake' in the outcome of crime, but on aiding and assisting the perpetrators; and those who make a profit by furnishing to criminals, whether by sale or otherwise, the means to carry on their nefarious undertakings aid them just as truly as if they were actual partners with them, having a stake in the fruits of their enterprise. To say that the sale of goods is a normally lawful transaction is beside the point. The seller may not ignore the purpose for which the purchase is made if he is advised of that purpose, or wash his hands of the aid that he has given the perpetrator of a felony by the plea that he has merely made a sale of merchandise. One who sells a gun to another knowing that he is buying it to commit a murder, would hardly escape conviction as an accessory to the murder by showing that he received full price for the gun; and no difference in principle can be drawn between such a case and any other case of a seller who knows that the purchaser intends to use the goods which he is purchasing in the commission of felony. In any such case, not only does the act of the seller assist in the commission of the felony, but his will assents to its commission, since he could refuse to give the assistance by refusing to make the sale. This is the view taken of the matter in a number of well considered cases in the federal courts. * * *

"But even if the view be taken that aiding and abetting is not to be predicated on an ordinary sale made with knowledge that the purchaser intends to use the goods purchased in the commission of felony, we think that the circumstances relied on by the government here are sufficient to establish the guilt of Backun. The sale here was not of a mere instrumentality to be used in the commission of felony, but of the very goods which were to be feloniously transported. Backun knew not only that the commission of felony was contemplated by Zucker with respect to such goods, but also that the felony could not be committed by Zucker unless the sale were made to him. The sale thus made possible the commission of the felony by Zucker; and, if Zucker is to be believed, the commission of the felony was one of the purposes which Backun had in mind in making the sale. After testifying that he had told Backun that he wished to go on the road with the silverware (i.e. transport it in interstate commerce), he says 'He (Backun) knew that. That is the reason he wanted to sell it to me.' There can be no question, therefore, but that the evidence sustains the view that the felony committed by Zucker flowed from the will of Backun as well as from his own will, and that Backun aided its commission by making the sale. There was thus evidence of direct participation of Backun in the criminal purpose of Zucker; and whatever view be taken as to the case of a mere sale, certainly such evidence is sufficient to establish guilt."

3. Does it follow that even "willful blindness" can suffice for accomplice liability? Reconsider *United States v. Giovannetti*, p. 149 of this Book, where the court went on to say:

"Although we think it was an error to give the ostrich instruction in this case, we do not agree with the further suggestion that such an instruction has no possible place in an aider and abettor case. It is true that to be guilty the alleged aider and abettor must want to make the principal's venture succeed, which may seem to imply that he must know what that venture is. But we think not, for the reasons stated in *United States v. Kehm*, [799 F.2d 354 (7th Cir.1986)], in rejecting the parallel argument that the ostrich instruction should never be given in a conspiracy case. We have already given an example, based on the facts of this case, of how an aider and abettor can be an ostrich. If Janis strongly suspected that his house was being used as a wireroom, and to avoid confirming his suspicions he expended resources on avoiding a confrontation with the facts (as by taking a circuitous route to work), then his actions, far from showing that he was not an aider and abettor under Judge Hand's formulation, would show that he was—would show that he wanted the gambling enterprise to succeed so badly that he expended time and effort to avoid acquiring proof of the enterprise's character and with it indisputably guilty knowledge that might compel him to withdraw for fear of being prosecuted with no chance of avoiding conviction by pleading ignorance of what the enterprise was up to."

4. The draftsmen of the Model Penal Code proposed a provision which would make a person an accomplice not only when he aided with the purpose of facilitating the crime, but also if "acting with knowledge that such other person was committing or had the purpose of committing the crime, he knowingly, substantially facilitated its commission." They explained that the "substantially facilitated" qualification "provides a basis for discrimination that should satisfy the common sense of justice. A vendor who supplies materials readily available upon the market arguably does not make substantial contribution to commission of the crime since the materials could have as easily been gotten elsewhere. The minor employee may win exemption on this ground, though he minded his own business to preserve his job. What is required is to give the courts and juries a criterion for drawing lines that must be drawn. The formula proposed accomplishes this purpose by a standard that is relevant, it is submitted, to all the legal ends involved. There will, of course, be arguable cases; they should, we think, be argued in these terms." *Model Penal Code* § 2.04, Comments (Tent. Draft No. 1, 1953). But that language was omitted from the

Code pursuant to a vote of the American Law Institute; the revised provision was renumbered as § 2.06(3).

5. Does the knowing aid approach of *Backun* have more appeal when the crime is a most serious one? Reconsider *People v. Lauria,* p. 718 of this Book, where the court argued "that a supplier who furnishes equipment which he *knows* will be used to commit a serious crime may be deemed from that knowledge alone to have intended to produce the result. Such proof may justify an inference that the furnisher intended to aid the execution of the crime and that he thereby became a participant. For instance, we think the operator of a telephone answering service with positive knowledge that his service was being used to facilitate the extortion of ransom, the distribution of heroin, or the passing of counterfeit money who continued to furnish the service with knowledge of its use, might be chargeable on knowledge alone with participation in a scheme to extort money, to distribute narcotics, or to pass counterfeit money. The same result would follow the seller of gasoline who knew the buyer was using his product to make Molotov cocktails for terroristic use."

6. Should mere knowing aid be dealt with as a lesser offense than the crime aided? This is the solution in the New York Penal Law:

"§ 115.00 Criminal facilitation in the second degree.

"A person is guilty of criminal facilitation in the second degree when, believing it probable that he is rendering aid to a person who intends to commit a crime, he engages in conduct which provides such person with means or opportunity for the commission thereof and which in fact aids such person to commit a felony.

"Criminal facilitation in the second degree is a class A misdemeanor [punishable by up to one-year imprisonment].

"§ 115.05 Criminal facilitation in the first degree.

"A person is guilty of criminal facilitation in the first degree when, believing it probable that he is rendering aid to a person who intends to commit murder or kidnapping in the first degree, he engages in conduct which provides such person with means or opportunity for the commission thereof and which in fact aids such person to commit murder or kidnapping in the first degree.

"Criminal facilitation in the first degree is a class C felony [punishable by up to 15 years imprisonment].

"§ 115.10 Criminal facilitation; no defense.

"It is no defense to a prosecution for criminal facilitation that: * * *

"3. The defendant is not guilty of the felony which he facilitated because he did not act with the intent or other culpable mental state required for the commission thereof."

7. What if the defendant in *Gladstone,* upon being approached by Thompson, acted for Thompson in getting the marijuana from Kent to Thompson and the purchase money from Thompson to Kent, and as a consequence was charged with having made (rather than aided in) the sale? Consider *Commonwealth v. Simione,* 447 Pa. 473, 291 A.2d 764 (1972):

"In *Commonwealth v. Harvard,* 356 Mass. 452, 253 N.E.2d 346 (1969), the Supreme Court of Massachusetts was recently faced with a case whose facts were virtually identical with those of the case before us. In *Harvard* an undercover agent named Martin had persuaded the defendant to obtain some marihuana for him. The defendant introduced the agent to a third individual named Zacharo. The transfer of marihuana took place with the defendant standing between the agent's car and Zacharo's car. '[D]efendant persuaded Zacharo to sell marihuana to Martin. Zacharo thereupon handed a plastic bag of marihuana to the defendant who passed it to Martin in Martin's car. Martin then gave $15 to the defendant who passed it to Zacharo. There was no evidence that the defendant received any of the proceeds of the sale.'

"On these facts the Massachusetts Supreme Court concluded that the evidence was insufficient to warrant a conviction on an indictment charging a 'sale' of marihuana. That court reasoned: 'The record shows that the defendant facilitated an illegal sale by introducing a willing buyer and seller and by aiding in the physical transfer of drug and money. There is nothing to show that the defendant had any financial interest in the transaction, or was employed by the seller to promote sales.'

"Under similar facts many other jurisdictions have held the prosecution's evidence insufficient to establish a 'sale.' * * *

"We agree with those jurisdictions which have held that one who acts solely as the agent of the buyer cannot be convicted of a 'sale' of an unlawful drug. Though Pennsylvania's Drug, Device and Cosmetic Act sets forth no definition of the term 'sale,' it should be noted that our Legislature has singled out the 'sale' of narcotic drugs as deserving of especially severe punishment. The minimum penalty for the 'sale' of drugs is five years imprisonment as compared to a minimum penalty of two years imprisonment for the 'possession' of narcotic drugs. Webster's New International Dictionary of the English Language (2d ed. 1954) defines 'sale' as 'a contract whereby the * * * ownership of property is transferred from one person to another for a price, or sum of money, or loosely, for any consideration * * *.' This Court is obligated to construe words employed in the laws of this Commonwealth 'according to their common and approved usage.' Where as here there is no evidence that the defendant received any of the proceeds of the sale or was employed by the seller to promote sales, we do not believe it can be fairly said that defendant is guilty of a 'sale,' and we hold that as a matter of law defendant cannot be included in the category of 'sellers' of narcotic drugs that the Legislature singled out for especially severe punishment."

8. Compare *State v. Hecht,* 116 Wis.2d 605, 342 N.W.2d 721 (1984), where the defendant was charged with being an accomplice to possession of a controlled substance with intent to deliver, based upon his efforts on behalf of the intended purchaser. The court concluded "that all circuits which have addressed the issue have concluded that the 'procuring agent' theory is no longer a valid defense under the federal law.

" * * * Wisconsin's statutes dealing with controlled substances are based upon the Uniform Controlled Substances Act. * * * When we review the decisions of those states which have adopted the act, we find that a majority of the jurisdictions have held that the procuring agent theory is no longer a valid defense.

"Based upon the similarity of the Wisconsin and federal statutes and the fact that this state has adopted in part the Uniform Controlled Substances Act, we hold that the procuring agent theory is not a valid defense in this state. Our statutes, like the federal statutes, no longer distinguish between buying and selling as separate offenses. Rather, the statute instead addresses the act of possession with the intent to deliver, with no mention of the terms buying and selling. The transfer itself has become the prohibited act, and participation in this transfer may amount to an offense. This is evidenced by the language of section 161.01(6), defining 'delivery' in terms of the 'actual, constructive or attempted transfer' of a controlled substance. There is no mention of the requirement of buying or selling. Accordingly, we hold that the procuring agent defense will not be recognized by this court."

9. As between *Simione* and *Hecht,* which represents better policy? What considerations bear upon making this judgment? What, for example, of this observation in Note, 22 Kan.L.Rev. 272, 280 (1974): "Conviction of a drug seller may depend entirely on a procuring agent's testimony. An agent's incentive to testify against a seller in exchange for a plea bargain may be diminished because he can now be charged with only possession. If the procuring agent does not wish to bargain for dismissal of the possession charge, the seller may have to be approached directly by undercover agents. This direct approach may be the only method to obtain sufficient evidence upon which to convict sellers who are insulated from buyers."

PEOPLE v. MARSHALL

Supreme Court of Michigan, 1961.

362 Mich. 170, 106 N.W.2d 842.

SMITH, JUSTICE.

At approximately 3:00 a.m. on the morning of February 4, 1958, a car driven by Neal McClary, traveling in the wrong direction on the Edsel Ford Expressway, crashed head-on into another vehicle driven by James Coldiron. The drivers of both cars were killed. Defendant William Marshall has been found guilty of involuntary manslaughter of Coldiron. At the time that the fatal accident took place, he, the defendant William Marshall, was in bed at his place of residence. His connection with it was that he owned the car driven by McClary, and as the evidence tended to prove, he voluntarily gave his keys to the car to McClary, with knowledge that McClary was drunk.

The principal issue in the case is whether, upon these facts, the defendant may be found guilty of involuntary manslaughter. It is axiomatic that "criminal guilt under our law is personal fault." As Sayre[b] puts the doctrine "it is of the very essence of our deep-rooted notions of criminal liability that guilt be personal and individual." This was not always true in our law, nor is it universally true in all countries even today, but for us it is settled doctrine.

The State relies on a case, *Story v. United States,*[c] in which the owner, driving with a drunk, permitted him to take the wheel, and was held liable for aiding and abetting him "in his criminal negligence." The owner, said the court, sat by his side and permitted him "without protest so recklessly and negligently to operate the car as to cause the death of another." If defendant Marshall had been by McClary's side an entirely different case would be presented, but on the facts before us Marshall, as we noted, was at home in bed. The State also points out that although it is only a misdemeanor to drive while drunk, yet convictions for manslaughter arising out of drunk driving have often been sustained. It argues from these cases that although it was only a misdemeanor for an owner to turn his keys over to a drunk driver, nevertheless a conviction for manslaughter may be sustained if such driver kills another. This does not follow from such cases as *Story,* supra. In the case before us death resulted from the misconduct of driver. The accountability of the owner must rest as a matter of general principle, upon his complicity in such misconduct. In turning his keys over, he was guilty of a specific offense, for which he incurred a specific penalty. Upon these facts he cannot be held a principal with respect to the fatal accident: the killing of Coldiron was not counselled by him, accomplished by another acting jointly with him, nor did it occur in the attempted achievement of some common enterprise.

b. Sayre, *Criminal Responsibility for the Acts of Another,* 43 Harv.L.Rev. 689, 717.

c. 57 App.D.C. 3, 16 F.2d 342, 344, 53 A.L.R. 246.

This is not to say that defendant is guilty of nothing. He was properly found guilty of violation of paragraph (b) of section 625 of the Michigan vehicle code which makes it punishable for the owner of an automobile knowingly to permit it to be driven by a person "who is under the influence of intoxicating liquor." The State urges that this is not enough, that its manslaughter theory, above outlined, "was born of necessity," and that the urgency of the drunk-driver problem "has made it incumbent upon responsible and concerned law enforcement officials to seek new approaches to a new problem within the limits of our law." What the State actually seeks from us is an interpretation that the manslaughter statute imposes an open-end criminal liability. That is to say, whether the owner may ultimately go to prison for manslaughter or some lesser offense will depend upon whatever unlawful act the driver commits while in the car. Such a theory may be defensible as a matter of civil liability but Gellhorn's[j] language in another criminal context is equally applicable here: "It is a basic proposition in a constitutional society that crimes should be defined in advance, and not after action has been taken." We are not unaware of the magnitude of the problem presented, but the new approaches demanded for its solution rest with the legislature, not the courts. * * *

Notes and Questions

1. Compare with *Marshall* the case of *State v. Foster*, 202 Conn. 520, 522 A.2d 277 (1987). Defendant beat up Bill, a man he thought had raped his girl friend, and then gave his friend Otha a knife and told him to prevent Bill from leaving while defendant summoned his girl friend to make identification. After defendant left, Otha became apprehensive and stabbed Bill, who died. Defendant was convicted of being an accessory to criminally negligent homicide. Noting that the accomplice statute "merely requires that a defendant have the mental state required for the commission of a crime while intentionally aiding another," the court affirmed, reasoning that accordingly "an accessory may be liable in aiding another if he acts intentionally, knowingly, recklessly or with criminal negligence toward the result, depending on the mental state required by the substantive crime. When a crime requires that a person act with criminal negligence, an accessory is liable if he acts 'with respect to a result or to a circumstance described by a statute defining an offense when he fails to perceive a substantial and unjustifiable risk that such result will occur or that such circumstance exists.' * * *

"[B]ecause accessorial liability is not a distinct crime, but only an alternative means by which a substantive crime may be committed, it would be illogical to impose liability on the perpetrator of the crime, while precluding liability for an accessory, even though both possess the mental state required for the commission of the crime. Connecticut 'long ago adopted the rule that there is no practical significance in being labeled an "accessory" or a "principal" for the purpose of determining criminal responsibility. The modern approach "is to abandon completely the old common law terminology and simply provide that a person is legally accountable for the conduct of another when he is an accomplice of the other person in the commission of the crime. * * * " ' '

"From the evidence presented, the jury could reasonably have found that the defendant intentionally had aided Cannon by giving him the knife. Additionally, the jury could reasonably have inferred that the defendant had failed to perceive a substantial and unjustifiable risk that death would occur by handing Cannon the knife to prevent Middleton from escaping."

2. In *State v. Garza*, 259 Kan. 826, 916 P.2d 9 (1996), Garza encountered Vaca outside a store, each obtained a gun and began firing at the other, and Jennifer Minton,

j. Gellhorn, *American Rights*, 85, 86.

who was standing behind Garza, was struck by a bullet fired by Vaca. Garza was charged with the aggravated battery of Minton. After the district court dismissed the charges, the state appealed. The appellate court concluded:

"Although the defendant and Vaca were certainly acting at cross-purposes in shooting at each other, * * * because the probable consequences were reasonably foreseeable, they were acting in concert as to bystanders. Giving assistance or encouragement to one who it is known will thereby engage in conduct dangerous to life is sufficient for accomplice liability as an aider or abettor as to crimes defined in terms of recklessness or negligence. * * *. The trial court erred in dismissing the charge against the defendant."

3. In *State v. Etzweiler,* 125 N.H. 57, 480 A.2d 870 (1984), on facts very similar to those in *Marshall,* the driver was indicted in the alternative with (i) having committed negligent homicide, and (ii) having acted as an accomplice to the intoxicated driver's negligent homicide. Was the appellate court correct in upholding the dismissal of both indictments?

4. In *People v. Turner,* 125 Mich.App. 8, 336 N.W.2d 217 (1983), defendant was convicted of being an accomplice to involuntary manslaughter. He furnished loaded firearms to two women with whom he lived and directed that a "trial by battle" be held. The trial court found that one of the women, Tomkins, intentionally pointed her gun at the other, Smith, at which point it accidentally discharged, killing Smith. The applicable statute says that death from a firearm "pointed or aimed, intentionally but without malice," is involuntary manslaughter. Was the court correct in concluding that notwithstanding *Marshall* the "extent of defendant's complicity in the instant case is clearly sufficient to render her liable as an accomplice to involuntary manslaughter"?

5. A builder offered a house for sale, and obtained from the purchaser an agreement to pay more for the house than was allowed by law. After the amount in excess was paid to the builder in advance, he instructed a firm of solicitors to act for him in the sale. He concealed from them the fact that he had received the additional amount. Two of the partners in the firm never learned otherwise at any material time, but the third partner received a letter from the purchaser's solicitors stating they had not proceeded because the builder was in breach. This partner sought an explanation from the builder, who said that the amount paid in advance was for work to be done on the house in the future. The solicitor accepted that explanation, formed the opinion that such payment was lawful, and called on the purchaser to complete. The builder was charged with offering to sell the house for a greater price than permitted by law, and the three solicitors were charged with aiding and abetting him. The builder was convicted, but the charges against the three solicitors were dismissed on the ground that mens rea was required. The prosecutor appealed, arguing: "Mens rea is not an essential ingredient of the offence of aiding and abetting the commission of a substantive offence of which mens rea is not a necessary ingredient." In *Johnson v. Youden,* [1950] 1 K.B. 544, the court ruled:

"Before a person can be convicted of aiding and abetting the commission of an offence he must at least know the essential matters which constitute that offence. He need not actually know that an offence has been committed, because he may not know that the facts constitute an offence and ignorance of the law is not a defence. If a person knows all the facts and is assisting another person to do certain things, and it turns out that the doing of those things constitutes an offence, the person who is assisting is guilty of aiding and abetting that offence, because to allow him to say, 'I knew of all those facts but I did not know that an offence was committed,' would be allowing him to set up ignorance of the law as a defence.

"The reason why, in our opinion, the justices were right in dismissing the informations against the first two defendants is that they found, and found on good grounds, that they did not know of the matters which in fact constituted the offence; and, as they did not know of those matters, it follows that they cannot be guilty of aiding and abetting the commission of the offence.

"With regard to their partner, the third defendant, a different state of affairs arises. His client, the builder, told him a story which, even if it were true, was on the face of it obviously a colourable evasion of the Act. The builder told him that he had received another 250*l*., that he had placed the sum in a separate deposit account, 'and that it was to be spent on payment for work as and when he, the builder, would be lawfully able to execute it in the future on the house on behalf of the said purchaser.' It seems impossible to imagine that anyone could believe such a story. Who has ever heard of a purchaser putting money into the hands of the builder when he bought a house from him because he might want some work done thereafter? Surely, if the builder did not think that the purchaser could pay for the work, he would say: 'Will you pay something on account?' A story of that kind, on the face of it, is a mere colourable evasion of the Act.

"It is more than likely, I think, that, in reading the Act, the third defendant did not read as carefully as he might have done sub-s. 5, of s. 7. If he had read that subsection carefully, I cannot believe that he—or indeed any solicitor, or even a layman,—would not have understood that the arrangement which the builder said that he had made was just the kind of thing which that sub-section prohibited.

"How could anybody say that the story which the builder told the third defendant was not a story with regard to a transaction with which the sale was associated? If that subsection had been read by the third defendant and appreciated by him, he would have seen at once that the extra 250*l*. which the builder was obtaining was an unlawful payment; but unfortunately he did not realize it, but either misread the Act or did not read it carefully; and the next day he called on the purchaser to complete. Therefore he was clearly aiding and abetting the builder in the offence which the latter was committing.

"The result is that, as far as the first two defendants are concerned, the appeal fails and must be dismissed; but as far as the third defendant is concerned, the case must go back to the justices with an intimation that an offence has been committed, and that he must be convicted."

6.   Consider Sanford H. Kadish, *Reckless Complicity*, 87 J.Crim.L. & Criminology 369, 385–86 (1997): "S lends P and P's underage girlfriend the keys to his apartment, which they use to have sex. S is liable for statutory rape if he gave them the keys in order for them to have sex, but not if he was just aware of a substantial risk that they would do so. This is the traditional position. Explanation? We don't want to make it too risky for people to do ordinarily lawful things because of what some other person might do. But suppose that though he did give them the keys in order that they might have sex he was unaware that the girl was underage. He would be liable anyway, because no mens rea is required of him beyond that required of P. But why? Lending keys to a friend for a sexual encounter is ordinarily a lawful action. It is here unlawful only because the girl is underage. But S did not know that—perhaps he was reckless, or negligent, but no more. Isn't the upshot just the same as making recklessness enough for helping or encouraging P's action, namely to burden ordinary lawful actions with the risk of guessing right as to the crimes others may commit as a consequence of your action? I am not suggesting that S should not be liable. Statutory rape does not require knowledge of the age of the girl; recklessness, negligence, even strict liability suffices. So it makes sense to require no greater mens rea for S than is required for P. But that is just the argument I am making concerning the mens rea as to

the action—if the crime of P requires no more than recklessness, then it makes the same sense to hold S liable for recklessly helping or encouraging him to do the action."

SECTION 4. THE CONSPIRACY–COMPLICITY RELATIONSHIP

STATE v. DIAZ

Supreme Court of Connecticut, 1996.

237 Conn. 518, 679 A.2d 902.

PALMER, ASSOCIATE JUSTICE.

[The defendant and four others retrieved guns from a nearby automobile and then fired about thirty-five to forty shots at a passing Bronco, approximately ten of which actually struck the vehicle; an 8–year-old boy was fatally injured . The defendant was thereafter convicted of murder, attempted murder, conspiracy to commit murder and carrying a pistol without a permit.]

The defendant first claims that the trial court's jury instruction under the *Pinkerton* doctrine was improper * * *.

In *Pinkerton v. United States*, 328 U.S. 640, 66 S.Ct. 1180, 90 L.Ed. 1489 (1946), the United States Supreme Court concluded that under the federal common law, a conspirator may be held liable for criminal offenses committed by a coconspirator if those offenses are within the scope of the conspiracy, are in furtherance of it, and are reasonably foreseeable as a necessary or natural consequence of the conspiracy. In *State v. Walton*, 227 Conn. 32, 630 A.2d 990 (1993), we were required to decide whether to recognize the *Pinkerton* doctrine for purposes of our state criminal law. We concluded, first, that *Pinkerton* liability is not inconsistent with our penal code and, therefore, that we were not prohibited from recognizing that theory of criminal liability as a matter of state common law. Without foreclosing the use of the *Pinkerton* doctrine in other circumstances, we then concluded that application of the doctrine was appropriate in that case, in which the defendant was a leader of the conspiracy, the offense for which vicarious liability was sought to be imposed was an object of the conspiracy and the offense was proved by one or more of the overt acts alleged in support of the conspiracy charge. We now must decide whether to extend the principle of vicarious liability that we adopted in *Walton* to a case in which not all of these conditions have been met, a question that we expressly reserved in *Walton*. Subject to the limitations set forth hereinafter, we conclude that *Pinkerton* liability may be imposed even if none of the three *Walton* conditions is present.

In adopting the principle of vicarious liability set forth in *Pinkerton*, we noted in *Walton* that "*Pinkerton* liability is now a recognized part of federal criminal conspiracy jurisprudence."; and that the *Pinkerton* doctrine has been adopted by the majority of state jurisdictions that have considered the issue. In so doing, we rejected the defendant's claim that the doctrine necessarily casts too wide a net of vicarious criminal liability. "Though it is sometimes mischaracterized, *Pinkerton* [liability] is not a broad principle of vicarious liability that imposes criminal responsibility upon every co-conspirator for whatever substantive offenses any of their confederates commit. On the contrary, in the very decision in which the principle was articulated, co-conspirator liability was carefully confined to offenses that are (a) committed in furtherance of the conspiracy, and (b) reasonably foresee[able] by the co-conspirator sought to be held responsible as a necessary or natural consequence of the unlawful agreement."

Thus, "the rationale of *Pinkerton* liability ... is essentially that, because the conspirator played a necessary part in setting in motion a discrete course of criminal conduct, he should be held responsible, within appropriate limits, for the crimes committed as a natural and probable result of that course of conduct. 'A conspiracy is a partnership in crime.' Each such partner 'instigated the commission of the crime,' and '[t]he unlawful agreement contemplated precisely what was done. It was formed for the purpose. The act was done in execution of the enterprise. The rule which holds responsible one who counsels, procures, or commands another to commit a crime is founded on the same principle. That principle is recognized in the law of conspiracy when the overt act of one partner in crime is attributable to all. An overt act is an essential ingredient of the crime of conspiracy.... If that can be supplied by the act of one conspirator, we fail to see why the same or other acts in furtherance of the conspiracy are likewise not attributable to the others for the purpose of holding them responsible for the substantive offense.' " *State v. Walton.* * * *

Under the facts of this case, we see no reason why it was improper for the trial court to have instructed the jury regarding the principle of vicarious liability enunciated in *Pinkerton*. Although the state did not prove that the defendant was the leader of the conspiracy to ambush the Gonzalez vehicle and its occupants, the evidence reasonably established that the defendant was a fully engaged member of the conspiracy who had actively participated in the shooting and that he, along with his coconspirators, intended to kill one or more of the vehicle's passengers. Thus, in circumstances where, as here, the defendant was a full partner in the illicit venture and the coconspirator conduct for which the state has sought to hold him responsible was integral to the achievement of the conspiracy's objectives, the defendant cannot reasonably complain that it is unfair to hold him vicariously liable, under the *Pinkerton* doctrine, for such criminal conduct.

As we acknowledged in *Walton*, however, the *Pinkerton* doctrine has been criticized, principally on the basis that the criminal "law would lose all sense of just proportion if one might, by virtue of his one crime of conspiracy, be held accountable for thousands of additional offenses of which ... he did not influence at all." Thus, as we also indicated in *Walton*, there may be occasions when it would be unreasonable to hold a defendant criminally liable for offenses committed by his coconspirators even though the state has demonstrated technical compliance with the *Pinkerton* rule. For example, a factual scenario may be envisioned in which the nexus between the defendant's role in the conspiracy and the illegal conduct of a coconspirator is so attenuated or remote, notwithstanding the fact that the latter's actions were a natural consequence of the unlawful agreement, that it would be unjust to hold the defendant responsible for the criminal conduct of his coconspirator. In such a case, a *Pinkerton* charge would not be appropriate. As we have explained, however, we are not presented with such a situation in this case. Because we continue to believe that the *Pinkerton* doctrine, when properly applied, is consistent with our penal code, we reiterate our approval of the doctrine for those cases in which the state can establish that its use would be fair and reasonable in light of the nature of the conspiracy, the defendant's participation therein, and the relationship between the defendant's role in the conspiracy and the coconspirators' conduct for which the state seeks to hold the defendant accountable. Accordingly, we reject the defendant's claim that the trial court improperly instructed the jury on *Pinkerton* liability.

The defendant next claims that *Pinkerton* liability is inconsistent with our penal code because it allows a jury to convict a defendant of murder even though the defendant did not himself have the specific intent to cause the death of another as required under § 53a–54a(a). He asserts that our felony murder statute sets forth an exclusive list of conduct for which a defendant may be convicted of murder without having the intent to kill as required under § 53a–54a(a). We disagree. The defendant's argument fails to account for an important distinction between felony murder liability and *Pinkerton* liability. A defendant may be convicted of felony murder for a death caused by himself or another when the death occurs during the commission of one of a number of specified felonies, even if neither the defendant nor his confederate had any intent to kill. Under the *Pinkerton* doctrine, however, a defendant may not be convicted of murder unless one of his criminal associates, acting foreseeably and in furtherance of the conspiracy, caused the victim's death with the intent to do so. Accordingly, the principle of vicarious liability articulated in *Pinkerton* does not impermissibly intrude upon the province of the felony murder statute.

Notes and Questions

1. Consider *Model Penal Code* § 2.06, Comment (1985): "The most important point at which the Model Penal Code formulation diverges from the language of many courts is that it does not make 'conspiracy' as such a basis of complicity in substantive offenses committed in furtherance of its aims. It asks, instead, more specific questions about the behavior charged to constitute complicity, such as whether the defendant solicited commission of the particular offense or whether he aided, or agreed or attempted to aid, in its commission.

"The reason for this treatment is that there appears to be no better way to confine within reasonable limits the scope of liability to which conspiracy may theoretically give rise. In *People v. Luciano*,[25] for example, Luciano and others were convicted of sixty-two counts of compulsory prostitution, each count involving a specific instance of placing a girl in a house of prostitution, receiving money for so doing or receiving money from the earnings of a prostitute—acts proved to have been committed pursuant to a combination to control commercialized vice in New York City.

"Liability was properly imposed with respect to these defendants, who directed and controlled the combination. They solicited and aided the commission of numberless specific crimes, including the ones for which they were held. But would so extensive a liability be just for each of the prostitutes or runners involved in the plan? They have, of course, committed their own crimes; they may actually have assisted in others but they exerted no substantial influence on the behavior of a hundred other prostitutes or runners, each pursuing his own ends within the shelter of the combination. A court would and should hold that they are parties to a conspiracy; this is itself a crime, under this Code as well as most others. And they should also be held for those crimes they actually committed, or within the principle of this section for those to which they were accomplices. However, law would lose all sense of just proportion if simply because of the conspiracy itself each were held accountable for thousands of additional offenses of which he was completely unaware and which he did not influence at all.

"Again, in *United States v. Bruno*, [p. 757 of this Book,] eighty-eight defendants were indicted for conspiracy to import, sell and possess narcotics. The evidence showed a large combination composed of four groups of persons: the smugglers who imported the drugs; the middlemen who paid the smugglers and distributed to retailers; and two groups of retailers, one in Texas and Louisiana and the other in New York. The Court held that this evidence sustained a verdict that there was one large conspiracy in which the members of each group were criminal participants. That judgment commands support in a prosecution for conspiracy, and is one that would follow from the application of the standards of Section 5.03 of this Code. But should it follow that each retailer in Texas commits the offenses of each retailer in New York, though he has not promoted or facilitated their commission and has no interest in them? Yet if the conspiracy involved one combination,

---

25. 277 N.Y. 348, 14 N.E.2d 433 (1938).

the commission of those crimes was certainly included in its objects, and a traditionally worded inquiry might lead to liability for them all.

"No decision has been found in which the liability of co-conspirators for acts of one another has been pressed to limits such as these, though the limits have been approached.[30] The cases that declare the doctrine normally involve defendants who have had a hand in planning, directing, or executing the crimes charged. When that is so, the other principles of accessorial liability establish guilt, and under this section the defendant has 'solicited,' 'aided,' 'agreed to aid,' or 'attempted to aid' in planning or committing the crime. Indeed, when that is not so, courts may be expected to seek ways to avoid the conclusion of complicity, though traditional doctrine hardly points the way. The right way, it is submitted, is to measure liability by the criteria of this section. Conspiracy may prove solicitation, aid or agreement to aid, etc.; it is evidentially important and may be sufficient for that purpose. But whether it suffices ought to be decided by the jurors; they should not be told that it establishes complicity as a matter of law. However proper it may be to draw the necessary inference from proof of the conspiracy, the jury ought to face in concrete cases whether or not, on the evidence, the inference is one that should be drawn.

"Virtually all recently enacted and proposed revisions adopt the principle of the Code that the liability of co-conspirators for substantive offenses should be controlled by the same limits that are otherwise the measure of liability for complicity."

2. Anderberg was convicted of assault on LaRoche with intent to inflict great bodily harm, in that he aided the person who broke a pool cue over LaRoche's head. In affirming the conviction, the court in *State v. Anderberg*, 89 S.D. 75, 228 N.W.2d 631 (1975), said: "On behalf of the defendant it is asserted that he can not be held as an aider and abettor in the assault on LaRoche without a showing that he and the others involved acted in furtherance of a conspiracy. The short answer to this is that one may aid and abet without having previously entered into a conspiracy to commit a crime. Being involved as an aider and abettor in the commission of a crime and being involved as a conspirator to commit the same crime are separate and distinct offenses."

SECTION 5. FORESEEABLE OR RELATED CRIMES

UNITED STATES v. CARTER

United States Court of Appeals, District of Columbia Circuit, 1971.

445 F.2d 669.

WILKEY, CIRCUIT JUDGE:

This is the sorry story of a brutal, senseless and unprofitable crime so characteristic of life and death in our urban centers such as Washington, D.C. Since the principal question in this appeal is the sufficiency of the evidence against appellant, and since he received a sentence of imprisonment from 20 years to life, we have examined the evidence with some care. Finding it sufficient, and appellant's other points of error not persuasive, we affirm.

The appellant and one Whiteside were charged with three offenses: robbery, premeditated murder, and felony murder. On premeditated murder the District Court directed an acquittal; the jury convicted of robbery and felony murder.

---

30. *See, e.g., Anderson v. Superior Court,* 78 Cal. App.2d 22, 177 P.2d 315 (1947). The defendant referred several women to an abortionist, receiving part of his fee. This evidence was held sufficient to support an indictment charging the defendant, the abortionist and sixteen others with a conspiracy to perform abortions and twenty-six substantive counts based on individual abortions. It was deemed immaterial that this defendant had no contact with any other co-defendant and had no part in any substantive offenses other than those involving the women whom she herself had referred.

On 29 December 1967 John Pointer, a part-time cab driver, made the mistake of picking up appellant and Whiteside at Fourteenth Street and Park Road, N.W., Washington, D.C. On the trip to the Southeast section of the city Whiteside rode in the back while appellant sat in front beside the cab driver. According to appellant's own story, in the Southeast section Whiteside called on the cab driver to stop, and when he did not do so immediately, Whiteside took out a .22 caliber pistol and shot Pointer twice. One bullet entered the right side of the victim's neck just under the right ear, the other to the rear of the right ear.

At approximately 10:00 p.m. Whiteside and appellant were seen by a witness leaving the cab; Whiteside had blood all over one side of his trench coat. Around midnight other witnesses noticed the cab with the driver slumped over and called the police. The homicide squad examination found a pack of Pall Malls, later determined as belonging to appellant, on the right side of the dashboard. A large amount of blood was on both the front and back seats; the inside of the right front door and the outside of the left rear door were smeared with blood. The victim's right-hand jacket pocket was turned inside out. The driver's record of fares for the day totalled $24.60, but only a one-dollar bill was discovered—that being in his wallet. His change carrier was missing.

Shortly after ten o'clock appellant Carter and Whiteside entered a house about two blocks away from the scene of the crime. Six people were present at a small party, three of whom later testified. One of these was James Makel, the credibility of whose testimony assumed some importance in the trial. At the time they entered the house appellant's coat had a little blood on the sleeve, and Whiteside still wore the trench coat with the blood-spattered front. Whiteside washed his coat in the bathtub. Both gentlemen felt the need to wash their hands. Appellant also washed blood from four one-dollar bills.

After an interval appellant Carter asked James Makel to drive them uptown. As the three left, appellant carried the two outer coats and put them in the back seat of Makel's car. On the way toward town Makel stopped for gas. Whiteside paid for the gas with six quarters which he took from a silver change carrier. Appellant Carter had four one-dollar bills lying in his lap, but explained they could not be used because they were still wet from his having washed off the blood.

According to Makel's testimony, as they drove toward town appellant kept reiterating that Whiteside did not have to kill the cab driver; he said that he had the cab driver "up tight" and that Whiteside didn't have to shoot him. Appellant demonstrated what he meant by "up tight" by putting his arm around Makel's neck and shoulders to show that he (appellant) had grabbed the cab driver by the shoulder and neck and yoked him. He further explained, "That's how I got blood on my arm." Makel demonstrated this yoking at the trial in the same manner he testified appellant Carter had demonstrated to him. As they drove along, appellant kept repeating that Whiteside did not have to kill the man, saying "He killed him for some junk change."

When they arrived in the Northwest section near the house of Makel's brother-in-law, the appellant and Whiteside asked Makel if he would dispose of the two coats. When Makel declined, Whiteside put the coats into a trash can behind Makel's brother-in-law's house. Makel later put the coats on the back porch of the house, where they were found by the police on 2 January 1968, the day Whiteside was apprehended. In a search of Whiteside's apartment pursuant to his arrest, a .22 caliber derringer pistol, identified as the one Whiteside carried on the evening of 29 December 1967, was found in his closet, and the cab driver's silver change carrier in a trash can in his kitchen.

After appellant Carter was arrested two days later, he made a voluntary statement in which he admitted being in the cab with Whiteside when Whiteside killed the driver. He described going with Whiteside to the house where they encountered Makel and the drive uptown with Makel. He claimed that after the shooting Whiteside had given him four one-dollar bills with blood on them and recalled that Whiteside had a silver change carrier with him when they were in Makel's car. The appellant denied that he had participated in any plan to rob or kill the driver, and denied he had actually seen Whiteside commit robbery, although he confirmed Whiteside's act of murder. * * *

Appellant argues strenuously that from the verbal descriptions of the various witnesses it was impossible for Whiteside to have shot the cab driver as described by both Makel and appellant, and for appellant to have yoked the cab driver at the same time as described and demonstrated by Makel. But it was for the jury and the trial judge, who had the opportunity of seeing Makel's demonstration in the courtroom, to determine if there was any inconsistency, and apparently there was not.

Appellant also inveighs heavily against the interpretation put by Makel on the words "up tight" used by appellant. But whatever appellant meant by saying he had the cab driver "up tight," those words could only mean that appellant was participating in some fashion in the robbery. If appellant had him "up tight," and he was participating in the attack on or in the robbery of the cab driver, appellant was participating in a felony. It may be true that the ultimate tragedy of the cab driver's senseless murder was far from appellant's mind, but under our statutory law, his participation in the robbery resulting in a killing made him guilty of murder in the first degree, of which he was duly convicted.[8]

This testimony of Makel was completely sufficient to implicate appellant Carter in the robbery of the cab driver. We cannot ascribe to the witness Makel an intimate knowledge of the intricacies of the felony murder doctrine, i.e., we cannot impugn Makel's testimony by attributing to him a scheme to put appellant's neck in the noose for murder by implicating appellant in the robbery, and having sufficient legal knowledge to rest confident that the felony murder doctrine would do the rest. * * *

Appellant's convictions for robbery and felony murder are therefore

Affirmed.

FAHY, SENIOR CIRCUIT JUDGE (concurring in part, dissenting in part):

I concur in the affirmance of appellant's conviction of robbery. As to his conviction of felony-murder based on the killing by appellant's co-felon of the victim of the robbery, during the course of its commission, I would reverse. The instruction to the jury on that phase of the case, insofar as the instruction applied to appellant who did not himself kill the victim, did not require the jury to find, as I believe to be essential to his conviction of first degree felony-murder, that the killing was committed in furtherance of a design or purpose which appellant held in common with the one who actually killed the victim.

22 D.C.Code § 2401 provides that "[w]hoever * * * in perpetrating or attempting to perpetrate any offense punishable by imprisonment in the penitentiary * * * kills another * * * is guilty of murder in the first degree." Under this provision only the person who actually kills another is guilty of first degree murder. To hold a co-felon such as appellant guilty of first degree murder more must be shown, namely, an aiding and abetting in the commission of the crime of murder defined by Section 2401. That section does not provide that one who aids and abets the commission of a robbery during which another commits a homicide is sufficient for conviction of the former of first degree murder.

---

8. This is so even though appellant was the accomplice of Whiteside, who did the actual shooting. 22 D.C.Code § 105. In pertinent part, 22 D.C.Code § 2401, defining first degree murder, reads:

Whoever, being of sound memory and discretion, * * * without purpose so to do, kills another in perpetrating or attempting to perpetrate any * * * robbery * * * is guilty of murder in the first degree.

The instruction to the jury, nevertheless, was as follows:

If two or more persons acting together and jointly are perpetrating a robbery or are attempting to perpetrate a robbery, and one or more of them, in the course of the robbery or attempted robbery, kills another person, then all the persons involved in the robbery or attempted robbery are guilty of murder in the first degree.

If one person is perpetrating or attempting to perpetrate a robbery and one or more other persons aids and abets him in so doing, and the first of these persons in the course of the robbery or attempted robbery kills a human being, then the person or persons who aided and abetted him in the robbery or attempted robbery and the person who committed the killing are both equally guilty of murder in the first degree.

Under the circumstances of this case, the elements of the offense of murder in the first degree which the Government must prove * * * are as follows:

* * *

(4) That the killing was within the scope of the robbery or attempted robbery which Whiteside and [appellant] undertook to commit, if you find they so undertook to do so.

Appellant did not himself kill the deceased cab driver, and indeed he seemed to repudiate the shooting. Possibly the homicide was the independent act of appellant's co-felon, committed to the dismay of appellant. This is not to say that appellant could not be found guilty of murder. The problem is that his guilt of that offense was not submitted to the jury in terms which would allow, but not require, the jury to find that he aided and abetted commission of the homicide. The proper test in such a case in my opinion should be, not whether the homicide was within the scope of the robbery, but whether it was in furtherance of a common design or purpose.[3]

For the foregoing reason I would reverse appellant's conviction of first degree murder and grant him a new trial of that charge with an instruction conformably with the views above expressed.

I concur in affirmance of the conviction of robbery.

Notes and Questions

1. The issue resurfaced in *Prophet v. United States*, 602 A.2d 1087 (D.C.App.1992). Merriweather walked past Allen and Prophet carrying a "boom box"; Allen asked Prophet if he wanted it and Prophet answered in the affirmative; the two then followed Merriweather, who resisted Allen's attempt to seize the radio, at which Allen shot him twice, killing him. Allen then took the radio and he and Prophet fled the area together. On appeal of Prophet's conviction of felony-murder, the court stated:

"Appellant asks us to adopt the reasoning of a panel of the United States Court of Appeals for the Ninth Circuit in *United States v. Jones*, 678 F.2d 102 (9th Cir.1982). In that case, the appellant was one of four participants in a bank robbery in which another of the participants shot and killed a bank security guard. The court held that it was not enough for the jury to find that the appellant had aided and abetted a bank robbery in which a killing occurred; the trial court should have instructed the jury to determine

---

3. This is not to say that the jury must find that appellant and Whiteside planned specifically to use the force of shooting the victim, but only that as a minimum they planned to use such force if necessary to consummate the robbery. This concert between co-felons, of course, could be shown by circumstantial evidence. The point, however, is that the determination should be left to the jury under instructions properly framing the issue.

whether the appellant had aided and abetted the killing itself. Without such an instruction here, appellant argues, the trial court failed to instruct on every essential element of the crime * * *.

"In the context of imposing accomplice liability for armed robbery, we recently held in *Ingram v. United States*, 592 A.2d 992, 1003–04 (D.C.1991), that the accomplice is liable for the 'while armed' element when he or she could 'reasonably foresee' that a weapon would be required to perpetrate the robbery. In *Ingram*, we were interpreting the 'natural and probable consequences' language of our accomplice liability cases * * *.

"We are bound, however, by this court's opinion in *Waller v. United States*, 389 A.2d 801 (D.C.1978), which clearly enunciates the requirements in this jurisdiction for a felony murder conviction:

> First, the defendant or an accomplice must have inflicted injury on the decedent from which he [or she] died. Second, the injury must have been inflicted in perpetration of a specified felony. No distinction [is] made between principals and aiders and abettors for purposes of felony murder liability. Only intent to commit the underlying felony need be proved.

All accomplices are culpable for the resulting death. This is so because the intent requirement for murder, in the case against an aider and abettor, is satisfied solely by the aider and abettor's participation in the felony that resulted in the killing."

2. What if instead Allen and Prophet had not conversed earlier and Prophet only became involved by helping Allen carry off the "boom box" after Allen had shot Merriweather twice? Consider *People v. Pulido*, 15 Cal.4th 713, 63 Cal.Rptr.2d 625, 936 P.2d 1235 (1997): "If one person, acting alone, kills in the perpetration of a robbery, and another person thereafter aids and abets the robber in the asportation and securing of the property taken, is the second person guilty of first degree murder under section 189? We conclude the answer is no. Although the second person is an accomplice to robbery, such participation in the robbery does not subject the accomplice to murder liability under section 189, because the killer and accomplice were not 'jointly engaged at the time of such killing' in a robbery; the killer, in other words, was not acting, at the time of the killing, in furtherance of a 'common' design to rob." But cf. the *Higginbotham* case, p. 335 of this Book.

3. Jenkins, Hilliard and Watkins conspired to rob Whittington. Watkins served as a lookout while Jenkins and Hilliard entered Whittington's motel room to commit the robbery. When a struggle ensued between Whittington and Jenkins, Jenkins shot Whittington and then shot Hilliard so as to leave no witnesses; both died. Watkins and Jenkins fled the scene together. On Watkins' appeal from his conviction for the felony-murder of cofelon Hilliard, the court in *Watkins v. State*, 357 Md. 258, 744 A.2d 1 (2000), stated: "[I]f several persons join together in a felonious enterprise and co-felon A, for a wholly independent purpose of his own, not part of, or in furtherance of, the common scheme and not reasonably anticipated by the remaining co-felons, kills co-felon B, the other co-felons are not liable, under the felony-murder doctrine, for that murder. * * *

" * * * If A, B, and C undertake to rob X and, in the process, B accidentally kills either X or C, A is guilty of felony-murder. If, however, B, angry at C's inept manner of assisting in the robbery of X, intentionally shoots C, 'B's intentional shooting of C is so far removed from the common plan as not to make A responsible for B's intent-to-kill murder.' The reason is that 'B's conduct had nothing to do with furthering the robbery, the only connection between the robbery and the shooting being a mere coincidence of time and place.' * * *

"Acceptance of the view that there must be some connection, beyond mere coincidence of time and place, between the joint undertaking and the killing does not assist Watkins in this case. As we have indicated, apart from the exceedingly tenuous evidence that Hillard was, indeed, a co-felon, the uncontradicted evidence, from Watkins's own lips, was that Hilliard, whether or not a co-felon, was killed because he was a witness. The killing of a witness, for the purpose of eliminating the person as a witness, is necessarily in further-ance of the common enterprise, whether the victim is the victim of the underlying felony, an innocent bystander, or a co-felon whom the actor desires to eliminate as a potential witness. Actual foreseeability is not the test; there is a range of conduct that the law regards as implicitly foreseeable, whether or not the prospect of that conduct was ever actually anticipated. An accidental killing may not be actually anticipated by all of the co-felons; resistance by the victim or by others and the killing of a person who resists may not be actually anticipated by all of the co-felons. Yet those are consequences that 'naturally or necessarily flow' from the felonious enterprise, and vicarious liability has long existed in those situations, whether or not the particular co-felon actually anticipated what occurred. The same is true with respect to the killing of witnesses, as witnesses."

4.   One jurisdiction has attempted to mitigate the harshness of the felony-murder rule with respect to accomplice liability. N.Y. Penal Law § 125.25(3) provides:

"A person is guilty of murder in the second degree when: * * *

"3. Acting either alone or with one or more other persons, he commits or attempts to commit robbery, burglary, kidnapping, arson, rape in the first degree, sodomy in the first degree, sexual abuse in the first degree, escape in the first degree, or escape in the second degree, and, in the course of and in furtherance of such crime or of immediate flight therefrom, he, or another participant, if there be any, causes the death of a person other than one of the participants; except that in any prosecution under this subdivision, in which the defendant was not the only participant in the underlying crime, it is an affirmative defense that the defendant:

"(a) Did not commit the homicidal act or in any way solicit, request, command, importune, cause or aid the commission thereof; and

"(b) Was not armed with a deadly weapon, or any instrument, article or substance readily capable of causing death or serious physical injury and of a sort not ordinarily carried in public places by law-abiding persons; and

"(c) Had no reasonable ground to believe that any other participant was armed with such a weapon, instrument, article or substance; and

"(d) Had no reasonable ground to believe that any other participant intended to engage in conduct likely to result in death or serious physical injury."

PEOPLE v. KESSLER

Supreme Court of Illinois, 1974.

57 Ill.2d 493, 315 N.E.2d 29.

DAVIS, JUSTICE.

In a jury trial in the circuit court of Winnebago County, defendant, Rudolph Louis Kessler, was convicted on one count of burglary and two counts of attempted murder. The appellate court affirmed the burglary conviction and reversed the attempted-murder convictions, and we allowed the People's petition for leave to appeal. The facts are stated in the opinion of the appellate court and will be restated here only to the extent necessary to more fully delineate the issues. Defendant waited in an automobile outside a tavern while his two unarmed companions entered the building to commit the burglary. While inside the tavern, they were surprised by the owner, and one of the burglars shot and wounded him with a gun taken during the burglary. Later, while defendant's companions were fleeing on foot, one of them fired a shot at a pursuing police officer. At that time defendant was sitting in the automobile. * * *

In reversing the attempted-murder convictions, the appellate court held that "The application of the 'common design' principle is not justified by the language of section 5—2 to hold a defendant accountable for crimes committed by an accomplice which the defendant was not shown to have intended." * * *

The People argue "that a person is responsible for all criminal violations actually committed by another if he assists another in the commission of a single criminal violation," and that "if the legislature had intended to limit accomplice liability only to further criminal acts which were specifically intended the word 'conduct' would not have been included in the language of section 5—2."

Sections 5—1 and 5—2 of the Criminal Code provide in pertinent part:

"Sec. 5—1. Accountability for *Conduct* of Another.

"A person is responsible for *conduct* which is an element of an offense if the conduct is either that of the person himself, or that of another and he is legally accountable for such *conduct* as provided in Section 5—2 or both." (Emphasis added.)

"Sec. 5—2. When Accountability Exists.

"A person is legally accountable for the conduct of another when:

* * *

(b) The statute defining the offense makes him so accountable; or

(c) Either before or during the commission of *an offense* and with the intent to promote or facilitate such commission, he solicits, aids, abets, agrees or attempts to aid, such other person in the planning or commission of the offense. * * *" (Emphasis added.)

"Conduct" is defined as:

" * * * an act or a series of acts, and the accompanying mental state." Ill.Rev. Stat.1971, ch. 38, par. 2–4. * * *

We believe the statute, as it reads, means that where one aids another in the planning or commission of an offense, he is legally accountable for the conduct of the person he aids; and that the word "conduct" encompasses any criminal act done in furtherance of the planned and intended act.

An early application of this rule is found in *Hamilton v. People* (1885), 113 Ill. 34. The defendant and two companions invaded a watermelon patch intending to steal some melons. The owner discovered them and a scuffle or fight ensued during which the owner pinned one of the three to the ground, and when in this position another of the three fired a gun at the owner, but the shot missed the owner and struck the potential watermelon thief, who the owner had thrown to the ground. During this occurrence, the third potential watermelon thief stood by. All three of the putative watermelon thieves were charged and convicted of assault with intent to commit murder. This court stated:

"The fact is undisputed that the three defendants, one of whom was armed with a pistol, invaded the premises of the prosecuting witness with a criminal purpose. The business upon which the parties had deliberately entered was a hazardous one. They had a right to expect that in the event they were detected in stealing the melons, it would result in violence endangering life or limb,—as it actually turned out afterwards. That they were all co-conspirators in a dangerous criminal enterprise, is an undisputed fact. Such being the case, whatever was done by one, in contemplation of law was done by all, and all are therefore equally responsible.''

In the case at bar, the record shows a common design to commit a robbery or burglary. Kessler, Mass and Abney sat in on the plan, and Kessler led Mass and Abney to the Anchor Tap where he stated the days' receipts were kept.

In *People v. Cole* (1964), 30 Ill.2d 375, 196 N.E.2d 691, the court stated:

"While it is true that mere presence or negative acquiescence is not enough to constitute a person a principal, one may aid and abet without actively participating in the overt act and if the proof shows that a person was present at the commission of the crime without disapproving or opposing it, it is competent for the trier of fact to consider this conduct in connection with other circumstances and thereby reach a conclusion that such person assented to the commission of the crime, lent to it his countenance and approval and was thereby aiding and abetting the crime. Stated differently, circumstances may show there is a common design to do an unlawful act to which all assent, and whatever is done in furtherance of the design is the act of all, making each person guilty of the crime."

A similar conclusion was reached in *People v. Hubbard* (1973), 55 Ill.2d 142, 302 N.E.2d 609, where in considering the problem at issue, we referred to *People v. Armstrong* (1968), 41 Ill.2d 390, 243 N.E.2d 825, wherein the court stated as follows:

"The next contention of defendants involves a request to depart from the long established common-design rule, i.e., that where defendants have a common design to do an unlawful act, then whatever act any one of them does in furtherance of the common design is the act of all and all are equally guilty of whatever crime is committed. * * * We have fully reiterated our support of this rule in recent cases, and we continue to do so in this case. Nor do we accept defendants' argument that the statutorily defined rules on accountability in any way modify or abrogate the common-design rule. This section provides that a person is legally accountable for the conduct of another when '(c) Either before or during the commission * * * he solicits, aids, abets, or agrees or attempts to aid, such other person in the planning or commission of the offense.' Applying this section to this case the attempted robbery was the offense which the defendants were jointly committing and each was legally accountable for the conduct of the other. The result was murder, the killing of an individual without lawful justification while attempting or committing a forcible felony other than voluntary manslaughter."

In applying the rationale of *Armstrong* to the case at bar, the burglary was the offense which the defendant, Mass, and Abney had jointly planned and were jointly committing, and each was legally accountable for the conduct of the other in connection therewith. The result was the offense of attempted murder of Louis Cotti, the tap owner, and of State Trooper Max L. Clevenger, who answered a report of the incident and who tried to apprehend the fleeing parties.

For the foregoing reasons, we affirm the part of the appellate court decision which affirmed the burglary conviction of the defendant, and we reverse the part of its decision which reversed the conviction of the defendant for attempted murder, and we affirm the judgment of the circuit court.

Appellate court affirmed in part and reversed in part; circuit court affirmed.

GOLDENHERSH, JUSTICE (dissenting): * * *

It is clear that defendant's accountability cannot stem from section 5—2(b) for the simple reason that the statute defining the offense of attempt murder does not make him so accountable. In support of its position the majority cites *People v. Armstrong,* and quotes at length from *People v. Hubbard.* These cases are clearly not in point. They involved defendants charged with murder and fall under section 5—2(b) for the reason that section 9—1(3) of the Criminal Code creates the "felony murder" classification and obviates the need of proof of intent. It should be further noted that [the cases] cited in and relied upon in *Armstrong* were also murder cases and are not relevant here.

The majority also quotes from *Hamilton v. People,* and *People v. Cole.* In *Hamilton* there was a common design to burglarize a watermelon patch, one of the co-defendants was armed, all were present and took part in the fight which followed their being accosted by the farmer whose melons they were stealing and the court applied a common design theory. The rationale of *Cole* is the basis on which the appellate court affirmed, correctly, defendant's conviction on the burglary charge but neither *Cole* nor *Hamilton* can be read so as to stretch the statute to cover the facts of this case.

The Committee Comments to section 5—2(c) *inter alia* state:

> "Subsection 5—2(c) is a comprehensive statement of liability based on counseling, aiding and abetting and the like, which includes those situations that, at common law, involve the liability of principals in the second degree and accessories before the fact. It will be observed that liability under this subsection requires proof of an 'intent to promote or facilitate * * * commission' of the substantive offense. Moreover, 'conspiracy' between the actor and defendant is not of itself made the basis of accountability for the actor's conduct, although the acts of conspiring may in many cases satisfy the particular requirements of this subsection."

It should be noted that emphasis is placed on the requirement of proof of an "intent to promote or facilitate * * * commission of the substantive offense" and the Criminal Code provides:

> "A person intends, or acts intentionally or with intent, to accomplish a result or engage in conduct described by the statute defining the offense, when his conscious objective or purpose is to accomplish that result or engage in that conduct." Ill.Rev. Stat.1971, ch. 38, par. 4—4.

The substantive offense involved is attempt murder and section 8—4(a) of the Code provides that the requisite elements of the offense of attempt are the intent to commit a specific criminal offense and the doing of an act which constitutes a substantial step toward the commission of that offense. * * * As pointed out by the appellate court, had either of the intended victims died, the provisions of section 9—1(3) of the Criminal Code would have served to make the defendant accountable, but the attempt statute contains no such provision. * * *

I submit that on this record the defendant was not proved guilty of attempt murder. The evidence is uncontradicted that when his companions embarked on the burglary they were unarmed and that he was not inside the tavern when the shot was fired. Again, when the shot was fired at the pursuing officer, defendant was in the automobile, and under the circumstances neither occurrence is shown to be a consequence of any action of the defendant from which the requisite specific intent could be inferred. * * *

Notes and Questions

1. *United States v. Andrews*, 75 F.3d 552 (9th Cir.1996), involved these facts: When Ivan heard that his sister Paula and Collins had been in a fight with Lowery, he became angry and grabbed a rifle. Paula then asked her father for guns, which he provided both to Paula and Ivan. Meanwhile, Collins and Bushyhead went across the street to Collins' house to get crowbars. The four of them got back into Collins' truck and returned to the area of the altercation to "get" Lowery and "trash" the car. When they reencountered Lowery's Geo, both vehicles came to a complete stop. Ivan stepped out of the truck carrying a shotgun, then Lowery stepped out of the Geo and Ivan approached Lowery and shot him. Paula then approached the car and—despite seeing something moving in the back of the car that she later admitted was obviously a person—began firing into it. Williams was killed, and John and Thomas were injured. A jury found Ivan guilty of second degree murder of Lowery (Count One), aiding and abetting in the second degree murder of Steven Williams (Count Two), aiding and abetting in the attempted voluntary manslaughter of the two injured individuals in the Geo (Counts Three and Four), and using a firearm in relation to a crime of violence, in violation of 18 U.S.C. § 924(c)(1) for each of the previous four predicate offenses (Counts Nine through Twelve). Ivan challenged all but his murder conviction (Count One) on the ground that there was insufficient evidence to support the conclusion that he aided and abetted in the other crimes. The appellate court agreed, noting there was "no evidence that Ivan shared Paula's intent to hurt anyone other than Lowery. The testimony as to what was discussed among Ivan and the others shows that any agreement or understanding between Paula and Ivan involved only 'getting' Lowery and 'trashing' his car.

"Neither are we convinced that a rational jury could infer Ivan's intent under the 'natural and probable consequences' doctrine. The jury may infer that Ivan intended the natural and probable consequences of his actions. Paula's actions, however, went beyond that scope. Paula did not shoot the victims in the car in the course of getting Lowery; she acted impulsively and on her own. Her actions were thus akin to those of a robber who, as part of an agreed scheme to steal a safe, robs the watchman in the building on his own. See LaFave & Scott § 6.8, at 158 (asserting that those stealing the safe are not accomplices to the robbery of the watchman under the natural and probable consequences doctrine). Allowing the jury to infer that Paula's actions here were the natural and probable consequence of Ivan's knowing actions would take the natural and probable consequences doctrine to an extreme, 'inconsistent with more fundamental principles of our system of criminal law.' Id. (noting that viewing the 'natural and probable consequence' doctrine in broad terms 'would permit liability to be predicated upon negligence even when the crime involved requires a different state of mind. Such is not possible as to one who has personally committed a crime, and should likewise not be the case as to those who have given aid or counsel.'); see also Joshua Dressler, *Understanding Criminal Law* § 30.05, at 426 (1987) (remarking that in the context of aiding and abetting, '[t]he natural-and-probable-consequences doctrine has been subjected to substantial criticism').[4]"

2. In *United States v. Powell*, 929 F.2d 724 (D.C.Cir.1991), Powell offered to sell an undercover officer cocaine and then led him to a basement where three men, one holding a gun, were waiting. The officer held Powell as a shield until his back-up team arrived. Powell was convicted of possessing cocaine with intent to distribute in violation of 21

---

4. The jury could reasonably conclude that Paula's shooting at the car was a natural and probable consequence of their agreement to "trash" the car. But this reasoning does not support an inference that Ivan had the requisite intent to commit murder.

U.S.C. §§ 841(a), (b)(1)(C) and of using or carrying a firearm in the commission of a drug offense in violation of 18 U.S.C. § 924(c)(1), or (as to each) aiding and abetting the crime, see 18 U.S.C. § 2(a). For the firearms charge, the trial judge added five years to Powell's sentence, as § 924(c) requires. On appeal, the court found the evidence insufficient to support the firearms charge and accordingly reversed that conviction.

"It is common to state that liability as an accomplice encompasses acts of the principal that are a ' "natural and probable consequence" ' of the criminal scheme the accomplice encouraged or aided.' The phrase 'natural and probable consequences' by no means communicates just how likely the forbidden act must have appeared to the accomplice. It could signify any position within a broad range: for example, all acts with a substantial probability of occurrence (e.g., one chance in five); acts that are more probable than not to occur; acts of very high probability (e.g., 90%); and acts so likely that their occurrence is a practical certainty. Given the imperfection of human knowledge, the latter is the equivalent of knowledge; an accomplice 'knows' an act will happen if he is 'practically certain' it will. See *Model Penal Code* § 2.02, at 236–37 n. 13 (1985). Our review of the cases suggests that no court uses one of these degrees of probability for all contexts; each varies the requirement with the circumstances.'

"For provisions such as the current version of § 924(c), enhancing a sentence simply because a defendant had a firearm with him for possible use in an independent crime, the courts appear generally to have drawn the line at the upper end of the spectrum, insisting that the accomplice 'knew' (or, perhaps, should have known) that the principal would carry a gun. Thus in *United States v. Hamblin*, 911 F.2d 551, 558 (11th Cir.1990), the court required actual knowledge, rejecting the idea that, as 'it would be difficult to rob a bank without a weapon,' the jury could infer from that truism that the accomplice 'had to know about the gun beforehand.' See also *State v. White*, 98 N.J. 122, 484 A.2d 691, 694–95 (1984) (accomplice guilty of robbery with firearms only if he knew or had reason to know that principal would possess or use the weapon); *State v. Ivy*, 119 Wis.2d 591, 350 N.W.2d 622, 629–30 (1984) (to be guilty of armed robbery as accomplice, defendant must have 'known or believed' that principal would carry weapon); cf. *Davies v. Director of Pub. Prosecutions*, 1954 A.C. 378, 401 (where one crew of boys fights another and one boy pulls a knife and makes a fatal stab, others would be guilty of murder only if they intended 'or at least contemplated an attack with a knife'). But see *State v. Davis*, 101 Wash.2d 654, 682 P.2d 883, 885–86 (1984) (law imposes 'strict liability on all those involved in robbery which, by its very nature, generally requires use of weapons').

"We have found two cases involving the scope of knowledge required for accomplice liability under § 924(c) where the main crime was a drug violation; they split. In *United States v. Morrow*, 923 F.2d 427 (6th Cir.1991), the majority overturned the conviction for want of evidence that the accomplice encouraged the principal's carrying of a gun, and even the dissent appeared to require that the accomplice clearly knew at the outset of the crime that his confederate was carrying a gun. In *United States v. Johnson*, 886 F.2d 1120, 1124 (9th Cir.1989), on the other hand, the court appeared to rest liability on the common understanding that the 'drug industry . . . is a dangerous, violent business,' with guilt sustainable so long as the accomplice 'could have reasonably foreseen' that the principal would carry a weapon. We see no reason why the test for ancillary gun liability should be laxer in drug trafficking cases than in bank robberies; possession of a gun is at most common in the former but is virtually essential in the latter.

"A number of cases in our circuit—none of them involving the issue of ancillary gun possession—appear to employ a rather sweeping use of the 'natural and probable consequences' tag. * * * We find the standard of our fellow circuits more suitable, insisting that an accomplice at least know that a gun would be carried (or 'used', in the broad sense of § 924(c)) before he can be said to aid and abet that crime. This standard puts the accomplice on a level with the principal, requiring the same knowledge for both.

"We pause to note an intermediate class of cases, where the extra charge is not the carrying of a gun in the course of a bank robbery, but its active use—to put another's life in jeopardy. See 18 U.S.C. § 2113(d). [W]e would expect the courts to insist on knowledge that someone would bring a gun, but not that the holder would use it actively—a matter likely to depend on how the scene unfolded. * * * In any event, the cases are quite consistent with our requirement that for § 924(c) liability the accomplice must have known to a practical certainty that the principal would be carrying a gun (using 'carry' as a stand-in for all variants of guilt under § 924(c)).

"The record here fails to show that knowledge. The government points to the testimony of its expert witness, who said that he (personally) had 'frequently' 'come across' the use of guns in connection with drug distribution. This * * * falls considerably short of showing that someone in Powell's position would know that Williams would be carrying a gun."

3. In *Roy v. United States*, 652 A.2d 1098 (D.C.App.1995), police informant Miller agreed with Roy to return with $400 to purchase a weapon and two ammunition clips. When he returned, Roy told him to await the arrival of Ross. When Ross arrived, Miller counted out the money and Ross handed him a gun, only to take it back and use it to rob Miller of the money. At Roy's trial as an accomplice to the armed robbery, the jury, given a natural and probable consequences instruction, convicted. On appeal, the court stated:

"By invoking the 'natural and probable consequences' theory, the government insists that we sustain Roy's convictions of armed robbery * * * without requiring a showing that Roy intended to participate in the robbery of Miller or in any other crime of violence. Armed robbery is a felony punishable by life imprisonment; selling a handgun, on the other hand, constitutes * * * a misdemeanor of which Roy has been independently convicted. The government's application of the 'natural and probable consequences' doctrine would thus dramatically expand Roy's exposure even where * * * he did not intend that a crime of violence be committed.

"This court has stated that 'an accessory is liable for any criminal act which *in the ordinary course of things was the natural and probable* consequence of the crime that he advised or commanded, although such consequence may not have been intended by him.' The italicized words place a number of obvious restrictions on the reach of [the doctrine]. The phrase 'in the ordinary course of things' refers to what may reasonably ensue from the planned events, not to what might conceivably happen, and in particular suggests the absence of intervening factors. 'Natural' has many meanings, but the most apposite dictionary definition is 'in accordance with or determined by nature.' A natural consequence is thus one which is within the normal range of outcomes that may be expected to occur if nothing unusual has intervened. We need not define 'probable,' except to note that, even standing alone, this adjective sets a significantly more exacting standard than the word 'possible.' Accordingly, if we accord to the words of our cases their ordinary everyday meaning, it is not enough for the prosecution to show that the accomplice knew or should have known that the principal might conceivably commit the offense which the accomplice is charged with aiding and abetting. Without inserting additional phrases or adjectives into the calculus, we think that our precedents require the government to prove a good deal more than that a 'natural and probable' consequence in the 'ordinary course of things' presupposes an outcome within a reasonably predictable range.

"The government contends that the armed robbery of Miller was in furtherance of the common purpose because it resulted in the defendants' obtaining Miller's money—an achievement which, according to the government, was the defendant's prime design and plan in the first place. In our view, however, an exchange of a handgun for $400 is qualitatively different from an armed robbery in which Ross stole $600 and retained for himself the object which, in Roy's contemplation, was supposed to be sold. Not the least of the differences is that violence directed to the intended buyer may ricochet against the seller-turned-assailant. To suggest that a sale and an armed robbery have a common purpose is to exaggerate their similarities and to understate their differences.

"The government argues that Peppi Miller was a logical target of a robbery because, 'given the illegal nature of the activity in which he was involved, [he] was unlikely to file a complaint with the police about the robbery.' This reasoning, however, recognizes no apparent limiting principle. If we were to accept the government's position, then the robbery of any buyer or seller in a drug or unlicensed pistol sale would be viewed as the 'natural and probable consequence' of that transaction, for a participant in any illegal project may well be reluctant to invoke the aid of the constabulary. Moreover, as Roy points out, the buyer may be as likely to rob the seller as the seller is to rob the buyer; the government's reasoning would arguably sustain prosecution of Roy as an aider and abettor of armed robbery even if Miller had robbed Ross, rather than the other way around.

"In this case, in our view, no impartial jury could rationally conclude, beyond a reasonable doubt, that Roy 'cross[ed] a moral divide by setting out on a project involving either the certain or contingent' commission of a robbery. Viewed in the light most favorable to the prosecution, the evidence would perhaps support a finding that Roy should have known that it was conceivable that Ross might rob Miller. The evidence was insufficient, however, to show that a robbery would follow in the 'ordinary course of events,' or that it was a 'natural and probable consequence' of the activities in which Roy was shown to have engaged. We must therefore reverse for evidentiary insufficiency Roy's conviction for armed robbery."

4. John C. Smith, *Case and Comment*, 1991 Crim.L.Rev. 134–35: "The law * * * is criticised on the ground that it leaves the accessory liable to conviction for murder although he is only reckless whereas, in the case of the principle offender, intention must be proved. But there is a difference between (i) recklessness whether death be caused (which is sufficient for manslaughter but not for murder) and (ii) recklessness whether murder be committed. The accessory's recklessness must extend to the principal's mens rea of murder. The person who embarks on a joint enterprise knowing that his confederate may intentionally kill is taking a deliberate risk of assisting or encouraging not merely killing but murder. * * * The principle applied in these cases is not confined to murder but extends to accessory liability generally. It is not unreasonable that one who is reckless whether he assists or encourages the commission of a crime should be held liable for it when it is committed."

5. Compare *Model Penal Code* § 2.06, Comment (1985): "Stephen thought the common law to be that if 'a person instigates another to commit a crime, and the person so instigated commits a crime different from the one he was instigated to commit, but likely to be caused by such instigation, the instigator is an accessory before the fact.' * * *.

"There is, on the other hand, impressive indication that, apart from the case of homicide, a liability based upon probability alone is not sustained. * * * Many decisions so hold.

"Whatever may have been the law on the point, in any event, it is submitted that the liability of an accomplice ought not to be extended beyond the purposes that he shares.

Probabilities have an important evidential bearing on these issues; to make them independently sufficient is to predicate the liability on negligence when, for good reason, more is normally required before liability is found. More extensive liability for consequences may be defensible in special situations; if so, the liability should be created by the section dealing with the special situation, not comprehended in a principle designed for application throughout the Code. Most modern revisions share this approach."[a]

SECTION 6. MUST THE PRINCIPAL BE GUILTY?

PEOPLE v. TAYLOR

Supreme Court of California, 1974.

12 Cal.3d 686, 117 Cal.Rptr. 70, 527 P.2d 622.

WRIGHT, CHIEF JUSTICE.

Defendant Alvin Taylor appeals from a judgment upon jury convictions of the murder of John H. Smith, one of the individuals who, with defendant, perpetrated a robbery of Jack West and of the robbery of said Jack West. * * *

While *Taylor I*[b] was pending in this court Daniels was separately tried and convicted of the robbery but was acquitted of the murder charge. Since defendant was sitting in the getaway car outside the store at the time of the shooting, his subsequent conviction for murder could result only upon a finding that one of his confederates, Daniels or Smith, harbored malice which the trier of fact then attributed to defendant because of his role as an aider and abettor. At Daniels' trial the People already have sought and have failed to establish that either Daniels or Smith entertained the requisite malice aforethought. Defendant thus argues that the doctrine of collateral estoppel should have precluded the People from relitigating this identical issue at his later trial.[5] We agree.

Collateral estoppel has been held to bar relitigation of an issue decided at a previous trial if (1) the issue necessarily decided at the previous trial is identical to the one which is sought to be relitigated; if (2) the previous trial resulted in a final judgment on the merits; and if (3) the party against whom collateral estoppel is assessed was a party or in privity with a party at the prior trial. The first two of these requirements are fully satisfied in the instant case. The question of whether the conduct of Daniels or Smith was sufficiently provocative to support a finding of implied malice was resolved adversely to the People in Daniels' trial, and the People have sought to relitigate the identical issue in these proceedings. Daniels' acquittal was a final judgment on the merits. * * *

In criminal cases the bar of collateral estoppel is constitutionally compelled when the same defendant was involved in both trials. (*Ashe v. Swenson* (1970) 397 U.S. 436, 443–447, 90 S.Ct. 1189, 25 L.Ed.2d 469.) However, courts have sometimes declined to apply the doctrine in behalf of a criminal defendant who was not involved in the prior trial. * * *

a. Some clearly do not, but their provisions have withstood constitutional challenge. See, e.g., *State v. Linscott*, 520 A.2d 1067 (Me.1987), upholding an accomplice liability statutory provision stating: "A person is an accomplice under this subsection to any crime the commission of which was a reasonably foreseeable consequence of his conduct."

b. The reference is to *Taylor v. Superior Court*, 3 Cal.3d 578, 91 Cal.Rptr. 275, 477 P.2d 131 (1970), holding that the felony-murder rule was inapplicable but that defendant might be found guilty on a theory of accomplice liability if his confederates entertained malice aforethought.

5. Although defendant did not raise the plea of collateral estoppel at trial, he should not be faulted for failing to do so since it does not appear that there were then any controlling precedents in California on the issue raised by such a plea.

We have failed to discover any controlling precedents on this issue. Although some cases contain dicta unfavorable to defendant's position, they are readily distinguishable. These cases (1) involved situations in which the basic requirements of collateral estoppel were not satisfied because identity of the issue was lacking[6] or because there was no prior final judgment on the merits as to the alleged perpetrators,[7] or (2) involved joint trials which failed to raise the issue of collateral estoppel;[8] or (3) did not involve the question of an accused's vicarious liability for the acts of a previously acquitted perpetrator.

The reported cases in other jurisdictions are divided on the question of whether an accused may be convicted by holding him vicariously responsible for the acts of a previously acquitted accomplice.

Some jurisdictions apply the defense of collateral estoppel in these circumstances, primarily to avoid the inconsistency and apparent unfairness of holding the accused liable for a crime which a previous adjudication has determined was not committed. Such distaste for inconsistent verdicts has caused the conviction of an aider and abettor to be vacated when the perpetrator is subsequently acquitted in a separate trial or is later convicted of a lesser offense than the aider and abettor.[10]

Although as stated there are no controlling cases on point there are nevertheless persuasive related cases which favor the application of collateral estoppel to foreclose the conviction of an accused based on his vicarious responsibility for the acts of a previously acquitted confederate.

It is settled that a defense judgment in a tort action will bar the plaintiff from relitigating the issue of the defendant's negligence in a subsequent suit against the defendant's employer based solely on a *respondeat superior* theory. * * *

An application of the doctrine of collateral estoppel similar to that in civil tort cases involving vicarious liability also has been made in criminal conspiracy cases which, like the instant case, involve criminal responsibility for other than purely unilateral conduct. Since a criminal conspiracy requires the participation of two or more conspirators, a conviction necessarily involves a finding that another person conspired with the accused. The courts also have applied the doctrine to preclude the conviction of an alleged conspirator when all other alleged coconspirators have been acquitted or the charges against all the other coconspirators have been dismissed because of insufficient evidence. The courts have thus refused to uphold the conviction of a sole remaining conspirator as he could be convicted only through a finding that at least one of the previously acquitted coconspirators had, in fact, engaged in a conspiracy.

There are strong policy considerations which, in addition to the holdings in related cases, favor application of the doctrine in the instant circumstances. We deem the purposes of an application of the doctrine to be: (1) to promote judicial economy by minimizing

6. In these cases, the accused's conviction was not based solely on the acts of his acquitted confederate because (1) the accused himself was on the scene of the crime and actively engaged in its commission or (2) the accomplice was acquitted because of the lack of a culpable mental state for reasons personal only to the accomplice (—lack of criminal intent by reason of deception practiced by the accused;—duress induced by the accused;—lack of criminal intent because of intoxication).

7. In these cases there was no final judgment of acquittal on the merits as to the alleged perpetrators because (1) at least one of the alleged perpetrators was convicted of the same crime for which the accused was

later prosecuted or (2) the perpetrator pleaded guilty to a lesser related offense than that with which the accused was charged.

8. One of these cases held that an accused could not be convicted as an aider and abettor when the perpetrator was acquitted in the same trial, although there is dicta that such a result would not be sanctioned if the two had been tried separately. * * *

10. Other jurisdictions have rejected the defense of collateral estoppel in a situation similar to the instant case thereby permitting conviction of an aider and abettor based solely on the acts of a previously acquitted accomplice * * *.

repetitive litigation; (2) to prevent inconsistent judgments which undermine the integrity of the judicial system; and (3) to provide repose by preventing a person from being harassed by vexatious litigation. In deciding whether the doctrine is applicable in a particular situation a court must balance the need to limit litigation against the right of a fair adversary proceeding in which a party may fully present his case.

The need for judicial economy by minimizing repetitive litigation is even more important in criminal than in civil trials. Crowded court dockets inevitably will impose a heavy burden on criminal defendants as substantial periods of incarceration may result while they await trial, and long delays between arrest and sentencing will decrease the effectiveness of the punishment which is ultimately meted out. Although the saving of the resources of the court system may be somewhat reduced when, in addition to the crime against which a plea of collateral estoppel is urged, other crimes must also be litigated, the other goals of an application of the doctrine can nevertheless be achieved.

Perhaps the most compelling reason for an application of collateral estoppel where vicarious liability is at issue is to prevent the compromising of the integrity of the judicial system caused by the rendering of inconsistent verdicts. Criminal trials generally receive more publicity than civil ones, and the public's view of the judicial system in general is often shaped by the impression of the fairness of the criminal justice system in particular. Few things undermine the layman's faith in the integrity of our legal institutions more than the spector of a system which results in a person being punished for the acts of another, when the actor himself under identical charges had been previously exonerated from responsibility for those very acts. This is particularly so under the facts of the instant case when the People seek to punish defendant, who was not even present on the immediate scene, for the death of an accomplice caused by the acts of another confederate who himself has been exonerated.

Although the third purpose of collateral estoppel, preventing harassment through vexatious litigation, does not appear to be fulfilled if the doctrine is applied when different defendants are tried but once in separate trials, the other general purposes of an application of the doctrine are as readily achievable in criminal as in civil trials and, as will be seen, the reasons for its greater limitation in criminal proceedings fail to justify the refusal to apply it in the instant circumstances.

In the past some courts have refused to dispense with identity of parties as a requirement for application of the doctrine of collateral estoppel, because of (1) difficulty of identifying the issues resolved against the People in the prior trial; (2) unfairness of binding the state when the defendant is not also bound by the first trial; or (3) undesirability of multiplying the results of a possibly erroneous verdict of acquittal.[12] None of these considerations, however, is applicable in the instant situation.

Where, as here, the accused's guilt is predicated only on vicarious liability, identity of issues is clear. Since defendant was outside the store in the getaway car at the time of the shooting, defendant's murder conviction can be based only on his being held responsible for Daniels' or Smith's conduct which must be vicariously attributed to defendant. There is no

12. The high burden of proof required for a criminal conviction has influenced some courts to hesitate to relax the identity-of-parties requirement for collateral estoppel in criminal cases. Such courts assert that the prior judgment of acquittal merely means that the crime was not proved beyond a reasonable doubt, not that the alleged perpetrator and therefore the accused are innocent. Such reasoning is not convincing. As is the case in civil litigation where identity of parties is not a prerequisite to the invocation of collateral estoppel, the burden of proof in a subsequent criminal trial is the same as the burden of proof in the previous criminal trial upon which the plea of collateral estoppel is based. Moreover, the previous acquittal of the perpetrator should create a reasonable doubt about his guilt thereby raising a reasonable doubt about the guilt of an alleged aider and abettor when his guilt is based solely on acts of the alleged perpetrator.

indication that Daniels' acquittal is based on anything other than a final determination that his and Smith's acts were not sufficiently provocative to support a finding of implied malice.[13]

As to the second of the reasons for reluctance to retreat from the requirement of identity of parties, it does not appear that the defense of collateral estoppel in defendant's case would result in any unfairness to the prosecution. At Daniels' murder trial the People had both the incentive and opportunity to litigate fully the issue of the provocativeness of the conduct of Daniels and Smith as Daniels appeared to be the leader in the robbery which resulted in the shootout. Furthermore, defendant appears to have played a minor role in the events leading to the death of Smith and there is no evidence that defendant directed or instigated the holdup of the liquor store.[14]

There is little support for the People's contention that relaxing the identity-of-parties requirement is unfair as it gives defendant two chances for exoneration, either through the prior acquittal of the perpetrator or through his own acquittal if the perpetrator should be convicted. We have rejected similar arguments in civil cases where we held that there is little real inequity in permitting strangers to take advantage of prior judgments where the party adversely affected had every motive and opportunity to litigate the matter fully in the prior trial. We note further that Daniels' acquittal affects only the case against defendant and therefore this is not a situation in which collateral estoppel may affect many potential defendants.[15]

It is unlikely that the application of the doctrine of collateral estoppel to the case at bar will result in spreading the effects of a possibly erroneous acquittal, the third of the reasons urged for not relaxing the identity-of-parties requirement. Contrary to the contention of the People the inconsistency in the results of Daniels' trial and defendant's trial cannot be explained by differences in evidence[16] or jury instructions.[17] The description of Daniels' conduct given by the prosecution witnesses was substantially the same in both trials. Although Daniels disputed the People's version of the events in the store while defendant did not,[18] Daniels' conviction of robbery reveals that the jury did not believe his account of the occurrences in the liquor store. Although defendant was exposed in a fabrication in his testimony and was forced to admit that he lied during some of his pretrial statements, Daniels likewise was caught in a falsehood during his trial and was also compelled to reveal that he had lied to investigators. Similarly, there is no significant difference in the instructions on malice given in the two trials. Both set out the standard that a finding of implied malice must be supported by a determination that the conduct in question involved a high risk of death and must be done with a conscious disregard for life.

---

13. We note that Daniels did not offer a defense such as insanity, intoxication, or duress based on his personal lack of culpability irrespective of the criminality of his acts.

14. We do not reach the question of whether the doctrine of collateral estoppel should be applied to bar the prosecution of a person who directed, instigated or participated in a crime for which the perpetrators were acquitted.

15. We thus do not reach the question of whether the doctrine should be applied where the issue decided in the previous trial may affect many persons whose criminal liability is not based solely on the acts of the previously acquitted defendant.

16. This case therefore does not present the issue of whether and under what circumstances the prosecution's discovery of new evidence after the first trial will

preclude a plea of collateral estoppel which otherwise may have been valid.

17. As the prosecution does not contend there were legal errors concerning matters other than jury instructions committed at Daniels' trial, we do not reach the question of whether the bar of collateral estoppel is applicable when the People allege that the prior verdict of acquittal was based on erroneous rulings which they were unable to correct through appellate review.

18. Daniels claimed he was an innocent bystander, did not participate in the robbery, and did not make the remarks attributed to him by the prosecution witnesses. Defendant, relying on alibi, denied any knowledge of the transactions in the store, and therefore did not dispute the Wests' description of Daniels' conduct.

We conclude that the lack of identity of parties defendant does not preclude the application of the doctrine of collateral estoppel; we limit today's holding to the particular circumstances of the instant case where an accused's guilt must be predicated on his vicarious liability for the acts of a previously acquitted confederate.

The judgment is reversed as to the conviction of murder and affirmed as to the conviction of robbery.

———

Compare *Standefer v. United States*, 447 U.S. 10, 100 S.Ct. 1999, 64 L.Ed.2d 689 (1980), where the Court declined to apply this doctrine of nonmutual collateral estoppel, used in federal *civil* cases, to criminal cases:

"This, however, is a criminal case, presenting considerations different from those in [civil cases]. First, in a criminal case, the Government is often without the kind of 'full and fair opportunity to litigate' that is a prerequisite of estoppel. Several aspects of our criminal law make this so: the prosecution's discovery rights in criminal cases are limited, both by rules of court and constitutional privileges; it is prohibited from being granted a directed verdict or from obtaining a judgment notwithstanding the verdict no matter how clear the evidence in support of guilt; it cannot secure a new trial on the ground that an acquittal was plainly contrary to the weight of the evidence; and it cannot secure appellate review where a defendant has been acquitted.

"The absence of these remedial procedures in criminal cases permits juries to acquit out of compassion or compromise or because of ' "their assumption of a power which they had no right to exercise, but to which they were disposed through lenity." ' It is of course true that verdicts induced by passion and prejudice are not unknown in civil suits. But in civil cases, post-trial motions and appellate review provide an aggrieved litigant a remedy; in a criminal case the Government has no similar avenue to correct errors. Under contemporary principles of collateral estoppel, this factor strongly militates against giving an acquittal preclusive effect.

"The application of nonmutual estoppel in criminal cases is also complicated by the existence of rules of evidence and exclusion unique to our criminal law. It is frequently true in criminal cases that evidence inadmissible against one defendant is admissible against another. The exclusionary rule, for example, may bar the Government from introducing evidence against one defendant because that evidence was obtained in violation of his constitutional rights. And the suppression of that evidence may result in an acquittal. The same evidence, however, may be admissible against other parties to the crime 'whose rights were [not] violated.' In such circumstances, where evidentiary rules prevent the Government from presenting all its proof in the first case, application of nonmutual estoppel would be plainly unwarranted."

UNITED STATES v. BRYAN

United States Court of Appeals, Third Circuit, 1973.

483 F.2d 88.

Present SEITZ, CHIEF JUDGE, and VAN DUSEN, ALDISERT, ADAMS, GIBBONS, ROSENN and HUNTER, CIRCUIT JUDGES.

OPINION OF THE COURT

ROSENN, CIRCUIT JUDGE.

[Bryan and Echols were jointly indicted and tried; Echols was charged with having stolen 950 cases of scotch from a pier, and Bryan was charged with having aided and abetted him. In a nonjury trial, the judge found Echols not guilty because the evidence created at least a reasonable doubt whether he was anything more than an innocent dupe; Echols was the truck driver who picked up the whiskey upon presentation of what he apparently did not know were false documents. But the judge concluded that the scotch had been stolen and that Bryan had aided and abetted that crime by supplying certain documents, and thus Bryan was convicted.]

Two permissible interpretations of the indictment and of the proof offered by the Government at trial would sustain the conviction: (1) that Bryan aided and abetted Echols in the commission of the offense; or (2) that Bryan was in fact the principal, but the discrepancy between indictment as an aider and abettor, and proof as a principal, was a non-prejudicial variance. On either interpretation, we find the conviction should be affirmed.

Appellant's argument suggests that Bryan could not have aided and abetted Echols because Echols was found innocent by the trial court and there is no aiding and abetting offense unless the Government first proves the principal committed the crime. *United States v. Jones*, 425 F.2d 1048, 1056–1057 (9th Cir.1970); *United States v. Rodgers*, 419 F.2d 1315 (10th Cir.1969). To the extent that there is dictum in *Jones* indicating that the Government cannot convict an aider and abettor without proving that the principal had committed the crime, the later opinion of the Ninth Circuit in *United States v. Azadian*, 436 F.2d 81 (9th Cir.1971), suggests re-examination of that dictum. The court permitted conviction of an aider and abettor even though the principal had been acquitted because of entrapment. The dissenter suggested that the court had wholly disregarded the *Jones* case.

In *Rodgers*, a number of prison inmates were each charged and convicted of aiding and abetting each other in instigating a riot, in violation of 18 U.S.C. § 1792. Because the statute makes instigation of a riot illegal, but does not prohibit mere participation therein, and because no principal was shown to have instigated the riot, the court reversed the convictions for aiding and abetting. This holding is consistent with the general criminal law principles that one cannot be convicted of aiding and abetting unless the proof establishes that the substantive crime was committed by someone.

The facts in the present case, however, are significantly different from those in *Rodgers*. The commission of the substantive offense was established. The whiskey was stolen. Echols played a significant role in perpetrating the offense. Although he was found not guilty, because the trial judge had a reasonable doubt as to Echols' criminal intent, there is no doubt that he removed the goods with false documents. Although Echols may have been an innocent dupe, it was he who at least physically removed the whiskey.

Appellant would seem to argue that the aider and abettor is guilty only if the principal is also *convicted*. The criminal law has no such requirement. * * *

We turn now to the remaining issue as to whether Bryan's conviction on Count II was so inconsistent with the terms of the indictment as to contravene the fifth amendment requirement of indictment by grand jury. We believe the proof adequately demonstrated that Bryan aided and abetted Echols in the commission of the crime, exactly as is charged in the indictment. Black's Law Dictionary (Revised 4th Ed. 1968), defines "abet," as "to encourage, incite or set another on to commit a crime." To term Bryan's actions as abetting Echols, therefore, is to describe them precisely. We therefore have difficulty with appellant's assertion that the proof at trial demonstrated that Bryan was the principal, and not the aider and abettor, in the crime charged. Nonetheless, even if the evidence at trial is so viewed and a discrepancy between indictment and proof therefore recognized, we still believe the conviction must stand.

We note first that the distinction between aiders and abettors and principals in cases such as this is to a great extent semantic. Is the driver of the truck the principal because of his physical contact with the stolen goods? Or, should he be viewed as the aider and abettor because the plan for taking the goods was conceived by another person? Conversely, is the man who engineered the theft the principal, or rather the aider and abettor? Such semantic difficulties were largely eliminated from the federal criminal code by passage of 18 U.S.C. § 2,[18] which makes aiders and abettors punishable as principals. At least for purposes of sentencing, therefore, the federal criminal code makes no distinctions between aiders and abettors and principals.

We further note that courts have had no difficulty sustaining convictions when defendants have been charged as principals and proven to have been aiders and abettors, * * *. Nor have courts had difficulty sustaining convictions when the indictment did not specify whether the defendant was the aider and abettor or the principal.

18 U.S.C. § 2 has eliminated the archaic common law distinctions between principals and accessories before and after the fact, and makes them all principals, whether the offense is a felony or a misdemeanor, and subject to the same liability. Thus, in *United States v. Bell*, 457 F.2d 1231, 1235 (5th Cir.1972), the court sustained the proposition that one charged as an aider and abettor could be found guilty as a principal. It rejected the contention that the defendant could not be convicted as a principal under a count charging him solely as an aider and abettor, holding: "While the better practice would have been to frame the charge in the alternative, the contention is without merit. Under 18 U.S.C.A. § 2 (1969) an aider and abettor is a principal and can be punished as such." * * *

The general rule that the Government may not amend an indictment, either explicitly by motion, or implicitly by presenting proof of a crime different from that charged, has its roots in the fifth amendment requirement of indictment by grand jury and Supreme Court interpretation as early as *Ex parte Bain*, 121 U.S. 1, 7 S.Ct. 781, 30 L.Ed. 849 (1887). The doctrine that a discrepancy between proof and indictment may be deemed an amendment, reversible *per se*, however, has been recognized and adjudicated extensively only in recent years. The Supreme Court's discussion of indictment and proof discrepancies in *Stirone v. United States*, 361 U.S. 212, 80 S.Ct. 270, 4 L.Ed.2d 252 (1960), has since been interpreted to distinguish between amendments, reversible *per se*, and variances, reversible only if prejudicial to the defendant. Prior to *Stirone*, most courts adjudged discrepancies between indictment and proof only by the prejudice standards of *Berger v. United States*, 295 U.S. 78, 82, 55 S.Ct. 629, 630, 79 L.Ed. 1314 (1935):

> The general rule that allegations and proof must correspond is based upon the obvious requirements (1) that the accused shall be definitely informed as to the charges against him, so that he may be enabled to present his defense and not be taken by surprise by the evidence offered at the trial; and (2) that he may be protected against another prosecution for the same offense.

Were we to find the discrepancy between indictment of Bryan as an aider and abettor, and proof as the principal in the theft of the scotch whiskey from the U.S. Lines dock, to be a variance judged by *Berger* standards, it would seem clear there was no prejudicial error. Acquittal in the trial would have protected Bryan from trial again for the theft of the

---

18. 18 U.S.C. § 2 provides:

(a) Whoever commits an offense against the United States or aids, abets, counsels, commands, induces or procures its commission, is punishable as a principal.

(b) Whoever wilfully causes an act to be done which if directly performed by him or another would be an offense against the United States, is punishable as a principal.

scotch whiskey. The indictment fully informed him of the crime for which he was to be tried. By explicitly stating that he would be tried for aiding and abetting a man named Echols in the taking of 950 cases of scotch whiskey from Pier 80 in Philadelphia on May 1, 1970, the indictment could not have been more specific in giving notice to Bryan. The proof conformed to the charge; Echols did take the 950 cases of whiskey from Pier 80 in Philadelphia on the date alleged by means of false documents supplied by Bryan. The trial revealed that Bryan not only aided Echols but was in fact the mastermind.

The question, therefore, is only whether the proof here varied from the indictment in such a manner that the indictment was constructively amended and, thus, the conviction was reversible *per se*, regardless of whether Bryan was actually prejudiced. * * * The focus of our inquiry is whether an element of the offense for which Bryan was convicted was different from an element of the offense for which it appears from the face of the indictment he was charged.

We find no difference between the elements of the crime charged and the crime proven. We are unable to see how the crime Bryan committed was any different whether he be labeled the aider and abettor of Echols or the principal who used Echols as his dupe. In either case, Bryan's actions, as presented first to the grand jury, and then to the judge at trial, would have been exactly the same; only the legal nomenclature would be changed. Under the federal statute, moreover, the common law nomenclature no longer has any significance.

We therefore hold (1) that a felonious taking was proven; (2) that this taking was a criminal act despite failure to prove Echols' criminal intent beyond a reasonable doubt; and (3) that Bryan was guilty as charged.

The judgment of the district court will be affirmed.

GIBBONS, CIRCUIT JUDGE, dissenting.

* * * If the grand jury had indicted Bryan as a principal, proof that he aided and abetted would suffice to convict. If, without naming a specific principal, an indictment charged him as an aider and abettor, proof that he aided and abetted anyone who may have committed the substantive offense would suffice to convict. But where the grand jury has charged that a specific person committed the substantive offense and that the defendant aided and abetted that specific person, a different problem is presented.

* * * The complicating factor is that clause of the Fifth Amendment requiring indictment by a grand jury for infamous crimes. The crime with which Bryan is charged falls within that clause, and if the grand jury charges one offense, the trial court may not try another. The grand jury did not indict Bryan as a principal. It did not indict him as an aider and abettor of persons unknown. It indicted him as an aider and abettor of a specific named principal. The Government in response to a motion for a bill of particulars reiterated that Echols was the thief who stole the whiskey with an intent to convert it to his own use and that Bryan aided and abetted Echols by supplying the means by which Echols converted the whiskey to Echols' own use. Bryan has been convicted, however, on evidence which does not establish beyond a reasonable doubt that the specific principal named in the indictment and in the bill of particulars committed the offense. The district court may not convict him of being an aider and abettor on the basis of evidence relevant only to a charge of being a principal; a charge for which he was not indicted.

Keeping in mind the language of both the indictment and the bill of particulars, and putting myself in the position of Bryan's trial attorney, the tactical decision not to offer Bryan's testimony seems eminently sound. Bryan did not have the burden of persuading the court that he hadn't committed a theft. The Government had the burden of proving beyond a reasonable doubt the one offense with which he was charged in the indictment. The Government attempted to prove not that persons unknown committed a theft, or that Bryan committed a theft, but that Echols committed a theft to which Bryan was an aider and abettor. The Government's proof on Echols' theft was insufficient to withstand a motion. Now, after the case is closed, and after Bryan has lost the opportunity to testify in his own behalf, the majority sustains the conviction on a theory that the grand jury did not consider, that the Government's case did not present, and of which neither before nor during the trial was Bryan given notice. * * *

CHIEF JUDGE SEITZ and JUDGE ALDISERT concur in this dissent.

Notes and Questions

1. Although the traditional view is to require acquittal of the alleged accomplice if the principal was acquitted in the same trial, *People v. Allsip*, 268 Cal.App.2d 830, 74 Cal.Rptr. 550 (1969), at least some jurisdictions have moved to the contrary position; see, e.g., *People v. Brown*, 120 Mich.App. 765, 328 N.W.2d 380 (1982) ("juries are not held accountable to rules of logic," and thus "a jury's decision to acquit the apparent principal while convicting the accessory is not grounds for reversal of the accomplice's conviction"). In any event, it is now generally accepted that an accomplice may be convicted notwithstanding the fact that the principal in the first degree has not yet been tried or has been acquitted in a separate trial. *State v. Kaplan*, 128 N.H. 562, 517 A.2d 1162 (1986). Often this is as the result of a statutory provision along the lines of *Model Penal Code* § 2.06(7).

2. In *Azadian*, cited in *Bryan*, appellant was convicted of aiding and abetting the bribery of a public official. On appeal, he urged that his conviction could not stand because the principal in the case was found not guilty by reason of entrapment. The court of appeals affirmed, relying upon *Carbajal–Portillo v. United States*, 396 F.2d 944 (9th Cir.1968), where it was emphasized that the entrapment defense "is made available not because inducement negatives criminal intent and thus establishes the fact of innocence; but because Government agents should not be permitted to act in such a fashion. The defense does not so much establish innocence as grant immunity from prosecution for criminal acts concededly committed." Ely, J., dissenting, noted that in *Carbajal* the entrapped principal had solicited the aider's help on his own, while in *Azadian* government agents solicited both the principal and the aider from the beginning. He concluded: "I deplore the prospect that my Brother's opinion could encourage an eager Government agent to engage in reprehensible conduct in order to lure others, as aiders and abettors, into a web of criminality, even while knowing that his principal entrapee would escape conviction."

See also *People v. Jones*, 184 Colo. 96, 518 P.2d 819 (1974); and *Babcock v. State*, 485 S.W.2d 85 (Mo.1972), both holding that an accomplice may be convicted notwithstanding the fact the principal has been found not guilty by reason of insanity; and *Springer v. Commonwealth*, 998 S.W.2d 439 (Ky.1999), holding that where the victim's wife and wife's sister were jointly charged with his murder on alternative theories as to who was the principal and who the accomplice, because the wife but not the sister was suffering from "battered woman syndrome," even if the wife had a defense of self-defense in killing her sleeping husband, it does not follow that her sister has a defense of protection of another.

3. Hayes proposed to Hill that he join in the burglary of a store. Hill, actually a relative of one of the owners, feigned agreement. On the night in question, they arrived at the store together; Hayes raised the window and boosted Hill in, after which Hill handed a side of bacon out to Hayes. Hayes was convicted of burglary and larceny upon an instruction that he was guilty of burglary if he, with felonious intent, assisted Hill to enter,

even if Hill had no intent to steal. In *State v. Hayes*, 105 Mo. 76, 16 S.W. 514 (1891), the court reversed:

"We may assume, then, for the sake of the argument, that Hill committed no crime in entering the wareroom. The act of Hill, however, was by the instruction of the court imputed to defendant. This act, according to the theory of the instructions, so far as Hill was concerned, was not a criminal act, but when it was imputed to defendant it became criminal because of the latter's felonious intent. This would probably be true if Hill had acted under the control and compulsion of defendant, and as his passive and submissive agent. But he was not a passive agent in this transaction. He was an active one. He acted of his own volition. He did not raise the window and enter the building with intent to commit crime, but simply to entrap defendant in the commission of crime, and have him captured. * * * [W]e find that defendant did not commit every overt act that went to make up the crime. He did not enter the warehouse, either actually or constructively, and hence he did not commit the crime of burglary, no matter what his intent was, it clearly appearing that Hill was guilty of no crime. To make defendant responsible for the acts of Hill, they must have had a common motive and common design. The design and the motives of the two men were not only distinct, but dissimilar, even antagonistic. * * * The court should instruct the jury that if Hill broke into and entered the wareroom with a felonious intent, and defendant was present, aiding him with the same intent, then he is guilty; but if Hill entered the room with no design to steal, but simply to entrap defendant, and capture him in the commission of crime, and defendant did not enter the room himself, then he is not guilty of burglary and larceny as charged. He may be found guilty, however, of petit larceny, in taking and removing the bacon after it was handed to him. This overt act he did in fact commit."

Is this a desirable result? Compare *Model Penal Code* § 5.01(3).

4. Of what, if anything, may the defendant be convicted on the facts of *Bailey v. Commonwealth*, 229 Va. 258, 329 S.E.2d 37 (1985): "Bailey and Murdock lived about two miles apart in the Roanoke area. On the evening in question, each was intoxicated. Bailey had consumed a 'twelve-pack' of beer and a 'fifth of liquor' since mid-afternoon; a test of Murdock's blood made during an autopsy showed alcoholic content of '.271% * * * by weight.' Murdock was also 'legally blind,' with vision of only $\frac{3}{200}$ in the right eye and $\frac{2}{200}$ in the left. Bailey knew that Murdock had 'a problem with vision' and that he was intoxicated on the night in question.

"Bailey also knew that Murdock owned a handgun and had boasted 'about how he would use it and shoot it and scare people off with it.' Bailey knew further that Murdock was easily agitated and that he became especially angry if anyone disparaged his war hero, General George S. Patton. During the conversation in question, Bailey implied that General Patton and Murdock himself were homosexuals.

"Also during the conversation, Bailey persistently demanded that Murdock arm himself with his handgun and wait on his front porch for Bailey to come and injure or kill him. Murdock responded by saying he would be waiting on his front porch, and he told Bailey to 'kiss [his] mother or [his] wife and children good-bye because [he would] never go back home.'

"Bailey then made two anonymous telephone calls to the Roanoke City Police Department. In the first, Bailey reported 'a man ... out on the porch [at Murdock's address] waving a gun around.' A police car was dispatched to the address, but the officers reported they did not 'see anything.'

"Bailey called Murdock back on the radio and chided him for not 'going out on the porch.' More epithets and threats were exchanged. Bailey told Murdock he was 'going to come up there in a blue and white car'[1] and demanded that Murdock 'step out there on the . . . porch' with his gun 'in [his] hands' because he, Bailey, would 'be there in just a minute.'

"Bailey telephoned the police again. This time, Bailey identified Murdock by name and told the dispatcher that Murdock had 'a gun on the porch,' had 'threatened to shoot up the neighborhood,' and was 'talking about shooting anything that moves.' Bailey insisted that the police 'come out here and straighten this man out.' Bailey refused to identify himself, explaining that he was 'right next to [Murdock] out here' and feared revealing his identity.

"Three uniformed police officers, Chambers, Beavers, and Turner, were dispatched to Murdock's home. None of the officers knew that Murdock was intoxicated or that he was in an agitated state of mind. Only Officer Beavers knew that Murdock's eyesight was bad, and he did not know 'exactly how bad it was.' Beavers also knew that Murdock would get 'a little 10–96 (mental subject) occasionally' and would 'curse and carry on' when he was drinking.

"When the officers arrived on the scene, they found that Murdock's 'porch light was on' but observed no one on the porch. After several minutes had elapsed, the officers observed Murdock come out of his house with 'something shiny in his hand.' Murdock sat down on the top step of the porch and placed the shiny object beside him.

"Officer Chambers approached Murdock from the side of the porch and told him to '[l]eave the gun alone and walk down the stairs away from it.' Murdock 'just sat there.' When Chambers repeated his command, Murdock cursed him. Murdock then reached for the gun, stood up, advanced in Chambers' direction, and opened fire. Chambers retreated and was not struck.

"All three officers returned fire, and Murdock was struck. Lying wounded on the porch, he said several times, 'I didn't know you was the police.' He died from 'a gunshot wound of the left side of the chest.' In the investigation which followed, Bailey stated that he was 'the hoss that caused the loss.'"

5.   Reconsider the facts of *Director of Public Prosecutions v. Morgan*, p. 630 of this Book. Assuming that Parker, McDonald and McLarty had been found not guilty of rape because of their belief in Mrs. Morgan's consent, then of what—if anything—would Morgan be guilty?[a]

Consider also whether the defendant may be convicted of rape on these facts from *Dusenbery v. Commonwealth*, 220 Va. 770, 263 S.E.2d 392 (1980): "At approximately 10:30 p.m. on September 16, 1978, T* * * M* * * and J* * * G* * *, both 16 years of age, parked their car in a secluded area and partially undressed in preparation for sexual intercourse. Defendant, a part-time security guard wearing a uniform, badge, handcuffs, and a holstered pistol, appeared at the window with a flashlight, ordered the couple to get out, and demanded identification. Defendant told them that he would take them to the authorities or report their conduct to their parents unless they finished what they had started and allowed him to watch. The couple entered the back seat of the car, discussed the options, and agreed to attempt to perform the act in defendant's presence. Defendant watched as the couple undressed and the boy assumed the superior position. Complaining

1.   Bailey owned a blue and white vehicle; the police vehicles were also blue and white.

a.   Consider Comment, 1975 Crim.L.Rev. 584, 585, contending that in such a case Morgan is guilty of rape "but that the correct theoretical basis of [his] liability was that of an aider and abettor rather than that of a principal in the first degree."

that the boy had not penetrated the girl, defendant thrust his head and shoulders through the open window, seized the boy's penis, and forced it 'partially in' the girl's vagina.''

6. Consider Douglas N. Husak, *Justifications and the Criminal Liability of Accessories*, 80 J.Crim.L. & Criminology 491, 494–95 (1989): "Supposed that *V* threatens to bloody the nose of one of *D1*'s children unless *D1* burglarizes *X*'s house. Unable to accomplish this result alone, *D1* explains his predicament to *D2*, his sympathetic friend. *D2* proposed to lend a ladder to *D1*, so that he can enter the house through a second story window. *D1*'s conduct falls under the defense of duress, but can *D2* benefit from *D1*'s defense? *D2* did not act under duress; *he* was not 'coerced' by a 'threat,' as most formulations of duress require. *D2*'s motives for assisting *D1* were friendship and sympathy. The commentators cited above would determine whether *D2* has a defense by first identifying what kind of defense *D1* possesses. Duress is almost always construed as an excuse rather than as a justification; thus *D1*'s conduct is 'objectively wrong,' and *D2*'s assistance is legally prohibited. According to this school of thought, if *D2*'s assistance is to be allowed, an argument would have to be established that *D1*'s conduct is 'objectively right,' and therefore justified.

"A number of problems lurk behind this deceptively simply approach. * * * In sum, the application of the distinction between justification and excuse to the problem of accessorial liability is more problematic than has been supposed."

SECTION 7. WITHDRAWAL

STATE v. ADAMS

Supreme Court of Connecticut, 1993.
225 Conn. 270, 623 A.2d 42.

NORCOTT, ASSOCIATE JUSTICE.

The defendant, Shelton Adams, Jr., was charged in a substitute information with the crimes of felony murder, conspiracy to commit robbery, first degree robbery and carrying a pistol without a permit in violation of General Statutes §§ 53a–54c, 53a–48, 53a–134(a)(2) and 29–35, respectively. After a jury trial, the defendant was convicted of felony murder, first degree robbery and carrying a pistol without a permit and was acquitted on the conspiracy count. The trial court sentenced the defendant to a total effective term of fifty-five years imprisonment. The defendant appealed to this court from the judgment of conviction pursuant to General Statutes § 51–199(b). We affirm the judgment of the trial court.

The jury could reasonably have found the following facts. During the month of April, 1990, the defendant resided with his father, Shelton Adams, Sr., and his aunt in a first floor apartment of a three-family house located at 58–60 Warren Place, New Haven. On the evening of April 15, 1990, the defendant and Sherman Sims approached Nathan Roberts, who lived on the second floor of the same house, and asked him for a gun. Roberts gave the defendant a .38 caliber handgun.

At approximately 2:48 a.m. on April 16, Sims and the defendant called for a taxicab to pick them up at 1561 Chapel Street and to take them to 230 Blatchley Avenue. The Metro Taxi Company dispatched a cab operated by the victim, Allen Hansen, to respond to the call.

When the cab arrived at the Chapel Street location, both the defendant and Sims sat in the back seat with Sims seated behind the victim. As the victim drove down Blatchley Avenue, Sims ordered him to pull over behind the Columbus School. The victim complied.

Sims then pulled out a gun, placed it to the victim's neck and fired the gun. Sims had been holding the victim with his left hand when he fired the gun, and consequently he suffered a bullet wound to his left pinkie finger.

Sims and the defendant exited the cab from the left, or driver's, side and pulled the victim from the vehicle onto the ground to allow easier access to his pockets. They then took both of the victim's wallets. The victim died almost immediately after the shooting. Powder burns found around the entry wound indicated that the gun had been held against the victim's skin when fired.

Sims and the defendant then walked back to the defendant's apartment. The defendant's father let the two men in and a few minutes later noticed that the defendant was wrapping Sims' bleeding hand. A short while later, Sims and the defendant called for another cab to take them to 28 Ellsworth Avenue, where a friend resided.

At 7:15 a.m., Roberts encountered Sims and the defendant walking toward the defendant's apartment. Roberts had heard about the shooting and asked the defendant if he knew anything about it. Neither the defendant nor Sims responded. Roberts then asked about the handgun that he had given to the defendant the previous night. The defendant first denied knowledge of the whereabouts of the gun, and then claimed that he had thrown it away. Roberts then noticed Sims' bleeding hand and asked the defendant whether he had shot the victim. In response, the defendant pointed at Sims.

Later that morning, the defendant asked his father to dispose of the handgun. The defendant, his father, and Sims were driven by a friend to the bank of the Mill River near East Rock Road. The defendant's father then threw the gun into the river.

With the assistance of the defendant's father, the New Haven police later retrieved the gun from the river. Ballistic tests performed on the gun established that it had fired the shot that had killed the victim. The police also conducted a search of the defendant's apartment in which they found a jacket identified as the one worn by the defendant on the night of the shooting. The left sleeve of the jacket was encrusted with blood that later tested to be of the same type as that of the victim.

The defendant's theory of defense focused on his lack of criminal intent. Through the testimony of New Haven police detective Anthony DiLullo during the state's case-in-chief, the defendant's version of the shooting was elicited. DiLullo testified that he had met with the defendant the day after the shooting at which time the defendant had given DiLullo a voluntary statement. The defendant admitted being with Sims on the night of the homicide and being in the victim's cab with Sims before the shooting. The defendant was seated on the right, or passenger's, side of the back seat of the cab. When the cab stopped at the traffic light at the intersection of Blatchley and Grand Avenues, Sims pulled out a silver colored handgun. The defendant told DiLullo that at this point he had left the cab through the right rear door and had run away. The defendant claimed that he had never seen the gun before and that he had had no idea that Sims was planning to rob the cab driver. He also stated that he had heard a gunshot when he was approximately one and one-half blocks away from the cab. * * *

The defendant next claims that the trial court improperly denied his request to instruct the jury on the defense of renunciation pursuant to General Statutes § 53a–10. He claims that the denial of this instruction violated his federal and state constitutional rights to due process and to present a defense pursuant to § 53a–10.[8] We disagree.

---

8. General Statutes § 53a–10 provides in relevant part: "(a) In any prosecution in which the criminal liability of the defendant is based upon the conduct of another person under section 53a–8, it shall be a defense that the defendant terminated his complicity prior to the commission of the offense under circum-

The defendant's theory of defense was that he fled the cab before Sims shot the victim and that he had no prior knowledge of Sims' criminal intentions when the two men entered the victim's cab. The state requested that the jury be charged on felony murder, which included a charge on accessorial liability under General Statutes § 53a–8. The defendant subsequently requested that the jury be charged on the defense of renunciation under § 53a–10, a defense which is only available in prosecutions based upon the conduct of another person under the provisions of § 53a–8.

The trial court granted the state's request to charge on felony murder, including accessorial liability, but denied the defendant's request to charge on the defense of renunciation. The defendant claims that the jury should have been instructed on renunciation because evidence had been introduced that he renounced any complicity by fleeing the cab when Sims pulled out the gun. The defendant's understanding of the defense of renunciation, however, is misplaced.

"A fundamental element of due process is the right of a defendant charged with a crime to establish a defense. . . ." We have said that a defendant is entitled to have the court present instructions to the jury relating to any theory of the defense for which there is any foundation in the evidence, even if weak or incredible. We must consider the evidence presented at trial in the light most favorable to supporting the defendant's request to charge. An instruction on a legally recognized theory of defense, however, is warranted only if the evidence indicates the availability of that defense. The trial court should not submit an issue to the jury that is unsupported by the facts in evidence.

The defendant was entitled to have the court instruct the jury on the defense of renunciation if there was any evidence to raise a reasonable doubt concerning the existence of the defense. The question on appeal is whether, viewing the evidence most favorable to the defendant's request for charge, we perceive any evidence supporting a defense of renunciation presented at trial. Having undertaken the appropriate review, we conclude that there was no evidentiary basis to support a defense of renunciation and consequently that the court correctly refused to instruct the jury on that defense.

At the outset, we note that the defense of renunciation is extremely narrow. " 'Renunciation' generally requires not only desistance, but more active rejection, and usually contains specific subjective requirements, such as a complete and voluntary renunciation." Connecticut has patterned its criminal code after the Model Penal Code, which permits the defense only if the defendant terminates his complicity by, inter alia, wholly depriving his complicity of its effectiveness in the commission of the offense. A mere change of heart or flight from the crime scene does not establish the defense of renunciation. Rather, it is necessary that the defendant accomplice both repudiate his prior aid and deprive that aid of effectiveness.

"If the prior aid consisted of supplying materials to be used in commission of the offense, effective withdrawal may require that these materials be reacquired so as to prevent their use by the principal." The action needed to deprive a prior action of its effectiveness will vary from case to case. Indeed, it is conceivable that some actions that serve as the basis for accessorial liability are impossible to renounce given the practical constraints involved in depriving some actions of their effectiveness. Under Connecticut law, for a charge on the defense of renunciation to be warranted, there must be evidence not only that the defendant completely and voluntarily renounced his participation in the crime, but also that he did so in such a way as to wholly deprive or neutralize his participation of its effectiveness.

stances: (1) Wholly depriving it of effectiveness in the commission of the offense, and (2) manifesting a com- plete and voluntary renunciation of his criminal purpose."

There is no evidence in the record before us that the defendant took any steps, beyond abandoning the cab, to deprive his complicity of its effectiveness. The sole theory of accessorial liability relied upon by the state was its claim that the defendant had, with the requisite intent, supplied the gun to Sims. The defendant's participation in the offense prior to its completion was established through the evidence indicating that he had procured the murder weapon and that he had been present when Sims held it to the victim, permitting an inference that the defendant had supplied Sims with the gun. When the act of complicity consists of providing arms, "a statement of withdrawal ought not to be sufficient; what is important is that he get back the arms, and thus wholly deprive [the] aid of its effectiveness in the commission of the offense." Depriving this act of its effectiveness would have required a further step, such as taking back the weapon, disposing of it so that it could play no role in the robbery, or warning the police so as to thwart the use of the weapon in the crime.[11] * * *

The defendant also claims that the court's failure to charge on the defense of renunciation under § 53a–10 violated his statutory rights. The defendant argues that the failure of the trial court to apply a clearly relevant statute to the case before it constituted plain error. The defendant's claim suggests that § 53a–10 provides a defendant with a right to have the jury charged on the defense of renunciation whenever a defendant is charged with liability for the acts of another person pursuant to General Statutes § 53a–8. Although § 53a–10 affords a defense when a defendant is charged with liability for the acts of another, it in no way absolves the defendant of the responsibility of providing an evidentiary foundation for any defense on which the jury is to be instructed. The defendant failed to provide such an evidentiary foundation. We conclude, therefore, that the trial court properly refused to charge the jury on the defense of renunciation.

Notes and Questions

1. What result on the following facts?

(a) In *Commonwealth v. Huber,* 15 Pa. D. & C.2d 726 (1959), the defendant was convicted of being an accessory before the fact to a robbery. On appeal, he claimed he was not proved guilty beyond a reasonable doubt. The evidence was that defendant loaned his rifle to Goodwin, who explained, "I am going to rob somebody," and that when Goodwin asked defendant to go along the defendant answered, "No, I ain't going to get involved in anything like that."

(b) In *State v. Thomas,* 140 N.J.Super. 429, 356 A.2d 433 (1976), after a police officer had struck and rendered unconscious a 13–year–old girl, Thomas accompanied Jennette to the roof of the building upon Jennette's invitation to go up on the roof "to shoot the police." Once on the room, and after he saw Jennette take out his gun, Thomas merely left the scene. A few minutes later, Jennette shot and killed a police officer from the roof. Is Thomas entitled to a withdrawal-of-accomplice instruction?

(c) In *People v. Brown,* 26 Ill.2d 308, 186 N.E.2d 321 (1962), Brown, McGarry, Washington and Gunn traveled together to an unlicensed tavern where gambling was occurring. Either before or upon arrival at the scene, it was decided to rob the people present. According to the prosecution's chief witness, Gunn walked in first and went to the bar, Washington remained at the door and McGarry and Brown walked to the middle of the room. When McGarry said there were too many people, Brown responded, "Yes, forget it, let's go," though Brown then asked McGarry to wait while he went to the rest room.

---

11. We note, however, that we do not set forth in this opinion an exclusive set of possibilities for renouncing the defendant's aid; rather, we conclude that under these facts the defendant's claimed act of renunciation was legally insufficient to permit the jury to be charged on the defense.

Washington then pulled his gun and started shouting, and when people began running McGarry pulled his gun, fired into the ceiling, and announced it was a stickup. Brown then came out of the rest room "looking surprised," and when several patrons attempted to seize him Brown ran out the door, after which Hunter was fatally shot while grappling with McGarry. Does Brown have a withdrawal defense to the charge of felony-murder?

2.   In contrast to *Model Penal Code* § 2.06(6)(c), some recent recodifications impose an additional requirement, namely, that the withdrawal occur "under circumstances manifesting a voluntary and complete renunciation of his criminal purpose," e.g., N.Y.Penal Law § 35.45. Is this desirable?

SECTION 8. EXCEPTIONS TO ACCOMPLICE LIABILITY

STATE v. COTA

Supreme Court of Arizona, 1998.

191 Ariz. 380, 956 P.2d 507.

MARTONE, JUSTICE. * * *

This is a drug case. Police saw Santiago Cota and Kevin Loomer talking on a street corner in Tucson. Cota walked across the street into De Anza Park while Loomer waited behind. Police watched as Cota approached Ronda Shulark. Cota handed Shulark two dollars. In return, Shulark placed a small amount of marijuana, the equivalent of two to three cigarettes, into Cota's bandana. Cota then walked back across the street to where Loomer stood. Shulark, Cota, and Loomer were each indicted for one count of unlawful sale of marijuana, and one count of unlawful transfer of marijuana—both class three felonies.

The state argued that Cota bought the marijuana from Shulark in order to sell it to Loomer. At the close of all the evidence, however, the trial court directed a verdict in favor of Loomer on both counts. The court concluded that no evidence linked Loomer to a transfer and that Loomer did not have the requisite mental state to establish a sale. The court also directed a verdict in favor of Cota on the sale count. It concluded that no evidence established the elements of a sale or the requisite mental state.

Thus, while Cota could have been a transferor to Loomer, the dismissal of Loomer from the case forced the state to shift its theory. Left only with the transfer from Shulark to Cota, the state now argued that Cota was an accomplice of Shulark in the transfer of the marijuana to himself. The court gave an accomplice instruction. The jury found him guilty and the court sentenced Cota to a mitigated term of 3.5 years. Cota appealed. * * *

Under A.R.S. § 13–3405(A)(4) it is unlawful to knowingly transfer marijuana. A.R.S. § 13–3401(31) defines "transfer" to mean "furnish, deliver or give away." To "deliver" is the "actual, constructive or attempted exchange from one person to another...." A.R.S. § 13–3401(7) (Supp.1997).

Transfer by its nature implies movement from one person to another. As a matter of logic, a transferee who receives something simply does not furnish, deliver or give away the item at the same time it is received. To suggest that one could be one's own transferor ignores the plain meaning of section 13–3405(A)(4). Had the legislature wanted to include a recipient, it could have expressly included such conduct. Because the offense is defined as a "transfer" it would distort its plain meaning to impose liability on the recipient. * * *

Nor can a recipient be an accomplice to a transferor of marijuana to himself or herself. * * * Whether a recipient is an accomplice depends upon whether the recipient could have been "informed against or indicted for the same offense" of which the transferor is accused. In order for one to be an accomplice, "[t]he aider or abettor must stand in the same relation to the crime as the criminal, approach it from the same angle, touch it at the same point." *Baumgartner v. State*, 20 Ariz. 157, 161, 178 P. 30, 32 (1919)(holding that a purchaser is not an accomplice to the seller in an unlawful sale of intoxicating liquor); see also *State v. Martin*, 74 Ariz. 145, 151, 245 P.2d 411, 415 (1952)(person giving a bribe cannot be accomplice to crime of receiving a bribe from oneself); *State v. Chitwood*, 73 Ariz. 161, 167, 239 P.2d 353, 357 (1951), modified on other grounds, 73 Ariz. 314, 240 P.2d 1202 (1952) (gambler could not be accomplice to one who operates the gambling house); *State v. Kuhnley*, 74 Ariz. 10, 19–20, 242 P.2d 843, 849 (1952) (thief cannot be accomplice to offense of knowingly receiving stolen goods); *State v. Miller*, 71 Ariz. 140, 146, 224 P.2d 205, 209 (1950) (minor could not be an accomplice to one contributing to his own delinquency); *State v. Green*, 60 Ariz. 63, 68, 131 P.2d 411, 413 (1942)(prostitute could not have been tried for receiving the earnings of a prostitute from herself); *Reser v. State*, 27 Ariz. 43, 45, 229 P. 936, 936 (1924) (one guilty of larceny cannot also be adjudged guilty of the offense of receiving the property stolen, "for the simple reason that he cannot receive it from himself"). * * *

These and other cases establish an exception to the general law of complicity. One who would otherwise be guilty as an accomplice because of assistance or encouragement, is not guilty

where the crime is so defined that participation by another is inevitably incident to its commission. It is justified on the ground that the legislature, by specifying the kind of individual who was guilty when involved in a transaction necessarily involving two or more parties, must have intended to leave the participation by the others unpunished.* * *

Notes and Questions

1. Given the liability of accessories in most circumstances, on what basis would the legislature want to exempt the types of accomplices involved in *Cota* and the cases cited therein? And, what basis is there for assuming that, e.g., failure to mention the purchaser in a drug sale statute means the legislature wanted the purchaser exempted? Consider *Model Penal Code* § 2.06, Comment (1985): "Should a woman be deemed an accomplice when a criminal abortion is performed upon her? Should the man who has intercourse with a prostitute be viewed as an accomplice in the act of prostitution, the purchaser an accomplice in the unlawful sale, the unmarried party to a bigamous marriage an accomplice of the bigamist, the bribe-giver an accomplice of the taker?

"These are typical situations where conflicting policies and strategies, or both, are involved in determining whether the normal principles of accessorial accountability ought to apply. One factor that has weighed with some state courts is that affirming liability makes applicable the requirement that testimony be corroborated; the consequence may be to diminish rather than enhance the law's effectiveness by making any convictions unduly difficult. More than this, however, is involved. In situations like prostitution, prohibition, even late abortion, there is an ambivalence in public attitudes that makes enforcement very difficult at best; if liability is pressed to its logical extent, public support may be wholly lost. Yet to trust only to the discretion of prosecutors makes for anarchical diversity and enlists sympathy for those against whom prosecution may be launched.

"To seek a systematic legislative resolution of these issues seems a hopeless effort; the problem must be faced and weighed as it arises in each situation. What is common to these cases, however, is that the question is before the legislature when it defines the individual offense involved. No one can draft a prohibition of adultery without awareness that two parties to the conduct necessarily will be involved. The provision, therefore, is that the general section on complicity is inapplicable, leaving to the definition of the crime itself the selective judgment that must be made. If legislators know that buyers will not be viewed as accomplices in sales unless the statute indicates that this behavior is included in the prohibition, they will focus on the problem as they frame the definition of the crime. And since the exception is confined to behavior 'inevitably incident to' the commission of the crime, the problem inescapably presents itself in defining the crime.

"This method of treatment might be unacceptable in legislating on accomplices for an established system, where the legislature may or may not have dealt with the issue in particular definitions and will not have been consistent in its practice. But in a model code or general revision, former legislative practice appears immaterial; the problem may be faced as each branch of the work proceeds."

2. In *State v. Duffy*, 8 S.W.3d 197 (Mo.App.1999), Duffy hired Pannell to work for Duffy Construction Co. Pannell injured his foot in a work-related accident on July 17, and a physician advised him to refrain from working until August 26. Pannell submitted a claim for temporary total disability benefits to the company's workers' compensation insurance carrier. On August 14, 1996, Duffy told Pannell he needed him to return to work and assured Pannell that he would not tell the insurance company Pannell was working while collecting workers' compensation benefits. Pannell returned to work the next day and continued to work until August 26, 1996, when he suffered another injury. When it was discovered Pannell had been working while collecting temporary total disability benefits, he was charged with workers' compensation fraud under a statute making it a crime to "knowingly make or cause to be made any false or fraudulent material statement or material representation for the purpose of obtaining or denying any benefit." He pled guilty, and Duffy was then charged as an accomplice. On appeal of his conviction, he relied on a statute (similar to *Model Penal Code* § 2.06(6)) stating a defendant is without accomplice liability if the "offense is so defined that his conduct was necessarily incident to the commission or attempt to commit the offense." What should the result be?

3. Although the quotation in *Cota* from the *Baumgartner* case might suggest otherwise, it is generally accepted that a person who cannot alone commit a particular crime can, by aiding and abetting another against whose class the statute is directed, become criminally liable under the statute. See e.g., *Rozell v. State*, 502 S.W.2d 16 (Tex.Cr.App. 1973) (holding "that a husband cannot be guilty of rape of his wife where he by himself forcibly has an act of intercourse with her, but if he acts as a co-principal with another man who ravishes his wife, he may be convicted of the rape as a principal"); *State v. Tronca*, 84 Wis.2d 68, 267 N.W.2d 216 (1978) (rejecting defendant's argument "that he could not be convicted as a party to a crime on the charge of misconduct in office, because he is not a public officer"). Aren't these cases inconsistent with *Cota* and the Model Penal Code approach?

SECTION 9. VICARIOUS LIABILITY

STATE v. BEAUDRY

Supreme Court of Wisconsin, 1985.

123 Wis.2d 40, 365 N.W.2d 593.

Abrahamson, Justice. * * *

The facts are undisputed. The defendant, Janet Beaudry, and her husband, Wallace Beaudry, are the sole shareholders of Sohn Manufacturing Company, a corporation which has a license to sell alcoholic beverages at the Village Green Tavern in the village of Elkhart Lake, Sheboygan county. Janet Beaudry is the designated agent for the corporate licensee pursuant to sec. 125.04(6)(a), Stats. 1981–82.

Janet Beaudry's conviction grew out of events occurring during the early morning hours of February 9, 1983. At approximately 3:45 a.m., a deputy sheriff for the Sheboygan County Sheriff's Department drove past the Village Green Tavern. He stopped to investigate after noticing more lights than usual inside the building and also seeing two individuals seated inside. As he approached the tavern, he heard music, saw an individual standing behind the bar, and saw glasses on the bar. Upon finding the tavern door locked, the deputy sheriff knocked and was admitted by Mark Witkowski, the tavern manager. The tavern manager and two men were the only persons inside the bar. All three were drinking. The deputy sheriff reported the incident to the Sheboygan county district attorney's office for a formal complaint.

At about noon on February 9, the tavern manager reported to Wallace Beaudry about the deputy's stop earlier that morning. After further investigation Wallace Beaudry discharged the tavern manager on February 11.

On March 2, 1983, the Sheboygan County Sheriff's Department served the defendant with a summons and a complaint charging her with the crime of keeping the tavern open after hours contrary to sec. 125.68(4)(c), Stats., and sec. 125.11(1), Stats. The tavern manager was not arrested or charged with an offense arising out of this incident.

The case was tried before a jury on May 20, 1983. At trial Janet Beaudry testified that she was not present at the tavern the morning of February 9. Wallace Beaudry testified that Janet Beaudry had delegated to him, as president of Sohn Manufacturing, the responsibilities of business administration associated with the Village Green Tavern; that he had hired Mark Witkowski as manager; that he had informed Witkowski that it was his duty to abide by the liquor laws; and that he never authorized Witkowski to remain open after 1:00 a.m., to throw a private party for his friends, or to give away liquor to friends.

Witkowski testified that he had served drinks after hours to two men. During cross-examination Witkowski confirmed that Wallace Beaudry had never authorized him to stay open after hours; that he had been instructed to close the tavern promptly at the legal closing time; that he knew it was illegal to serve liquor after 1:00 a.m. to anyone, including friends; that his two friends drank at the bar before 1:00 a.m. and had paid for those drinks; that he was having a good time with his friends before closing hours and wanted to continue partying and conversing with them after 1 a.m.; that after closing hours he was simply using the tavern to have a private party for two friends; that he did not charge his friends for any of the liquor they drank after 1:00 a.m.; and that by staying open he was trying to benefit not Wallace Beaudry but himself.

At the close of evidence, the jury was instructed that the law required the premises to be closed for all purposes between 1:00 a.m. and 8:00 a.m. and that if the jury found that there were patrons or customers on the premises after 1:00 a.m., it must find the premises open contrary to statute.

The jury was also instructed regarding Janet Beaudry's liability for the conduct of the tavern manager: As designated agent of the corporation, the defendant had full authority over the business and would be liable for the tavern manager's violation of the closing hour statute if he was acting within the scope of his employment. The instructions, which are pattern instructions Wis.J.I.Cr. 440 (1966), describe what activities are within the scope of employment and what are outside the scope of employment. Specifically, the jury was instructed as follows regarding the defendant's liability for the conduct of the tavern manager:

"It is also the law of the State of Wisconsin that violations of statutes regulating the sale of liquor do not require a showing of a willful or intentional act.

"It is a law that when a corporation is a licensee, the corporation vests in its agent, in this case Janet Beaudry, full control and authority over the premises and of the conduct of all business on the premises relative to alcohol beverages that the licensee could have exercised if it were a natural person.

"Under Wisconsin law if a person employs another to act for him [sic] in the conduct of his [sic] business, and such servant or agent violates the law, as in this case relating to open after hours, then the employer is guilty of that violation as if he [sic] had been present or had done the act himself [sic], if such act was within the scope of the employment of the servant or agent. It is no defense to prosecution under the statute that the employer was not upon the premises, did not know of the acts of his [sic] servant or agent, had not consented thereto, or even had expressly forbidden such act.

"A servant or agent is within the scope of his employment when he is performing work or rendering services he was hired to perform and render within the time and space limits of his authority and is actuated by a purpose in serving his employer in doing what he is doing. He is within the scope of his employment when he is performing work or rendering services in obedience to the express orders or directions of his master of doing that which is warranted within the terms of his express or implied authority, considering the nature of the services required, the instructions which he has received, and the circumstances under which his work is being done or the services are being rendered.

"A servant or agent is outside the scope of his employment when he deviates or steps aside from the prosecution of his master's business for the purpose of doing an act or rendering a service intended to accomplish an independent purpose of his own, or for some other reason or purpose not related to the business of his employer.

"Such deviation or stepping aside from his employer's business may be momentary and slight, measured in terms of time and space, but if it involves a change of mental attitude in serving his personal interests, or the interests of another instead of his employer's, then his conduct falls outside the scope of his employment.

"If you are satisfied beyond a reasonable doubt from the evidence in this case that Mark Witkowski, the employee of the registered agent, committed the acts charged in the complaint, that Mark Witkowski was the servant or agent of the defendant, and that the acts charged in the complaint were committed by him in the scope of his employment, then you should find the defendant guilty.

"If, however, you are not so satisfied, then you must find the defendant not guilty."

Having been so instructed, the jury returned a verdict of guilty.

In light of the facts and these instructions, we consider first the question of whether the statutes impose vicarious criminal liability on a designated agent for the illegal conduct of the tavern manager in this case, i.e., remaining open after 1:00 a.m.

The state's prosecution of the defendant under the criminal laws rests on a theory of vicarious liability, that is respondeat superior. Under this theory of liability, the master (here the designated agent) is liable for the illegal conduct of the servant (here the tavern manager). The defendant asserts, contrary to the position of the state, that the statutes do not impose vicarious criminal liability on her as designated agent of the corporation for the tavern manager's illegal conduct.

While the focus in this case is on the defendant's vicarious criminal liability, it is helpful to an understanding of vicarious liability to compare it with the doctrine of strict liability. Strict liability allows for criminal liability absent the element of *mens rea* found in the definition of most crimes. Thus under strict liability the accused has engaged in the act or omission; the requirement of mental fault, *mens rea,* is eliminated.

This court has construed violations of several statutes regulating the sale of alcoholic beverages which command that an act be done or omitted and which do not include words signifying scienter as imposing strict liability on the actor. As early as 1869, this court explained that the legislature imposed strict liability for the sale of spiritous liquors to a minor because protection of the public interest warrants the imposition of liability unhindered by examination of the subjective intent of each accused.[6] * * *

Vicarious liability, in contrast to strict liability, dispenses with the requirement of the *actus reus* and imputes the criminal act of one person to another.

Whether the defendant in this case is vicariously liable for the tavern manager's violation of sec. 125.68(4)(c), Stats.1981–82, depends on whether the specific statutes in question impose vicarious liability. We look first at the language of the statutes themselves.

The principal statutory provisions are secs. 125.68(4)(c)1., 125.11(1)(a), and 125.02(14). Sec. 125.68(4)(c), Stats.1981–82, provides that "no premises for which a 'Class B' license or permit has been issued may remain open between the hours of 1 a.m. and 8 a.m. * * * " Sec. 125.11(1)(a), provides that "[a]ny person who violates any provision of this chapter for which a specific penalty is not provided, shall be fined not more than $500 or imprisoned for not more than 90 days or both." Sec. 125.02(14), states that " '[p]erson' means a natural person, sole proprietorship, partnership, corporation or association."

It is apparent that no statute expressly imposes criminal liability upon the designated agent for the illegal conduct of the tavern manager. None of the statutes states, for example, that "whoever by herself or by an employee of the corporation for which she is the designated agent keeps the premises open shall be punished by * * * "or "whoever keeps the premises open is punishable by * * * and any act by a corporate employee shall be deemed the act of the designated agent as well as the act of the employee."

The state contends that the defendant's liability as designated agent for the illegal conduct of the tavern manager is predicated on sec. 125.04(6)(a), which requires a corporate licensee selling alcoholic beverages to designate an agent to whom the corporation delegates full authority and control of the premises and of the conduct of the business. Sec. 125.04(6)(a) equates the power and authority of the corporation's designated agent with that of a natural person who is a licensee or permittee. * * *

The state has not cited a statute expressly making the natural person licensee vicariously criminally liable for the conduct of an employee who illegally sells alcoholic beverages, and we have found none. Nevertheless, as the state correctly points out, over a long period the court has interpreted several statutes regulating the sale of alcoholic

---

6. Whether or not remaining open after hours is a strict liability offense is not squarely before the court. The jury was instructed that "violations of statutes regulating the sale of liquor do not require a showing of a willful or intentional act." The parties do not dispute the illegality of the bar manager's conduct in this case. We discuss the strict liability nature of the several alcoholic beverage sale statutes in order to distinguish strict liability from vicarious liability and to delineate the nature of the offense for which the defendant is determined to be vicariously liable.

beverages as imposing on the natural person licensee vicarious criminal liability for the illegal conduct of an employee. * * *

[S]ince [those] decisions the legislature has had the opportunity to adopt or to preclude vicarious liability for violations of laws regarding sale of alcoholic beverages. The legislature took neither course of action. Instead the legislature left the statutes in question substantially the same. We read this legislative history to mean that in enacting the current laws the legislature intended to retain the * * * decisional law interpreting the statutes as imposing vicarious liability on the natural person licensee for the conduct of the employee who illegally sells alcoholic beverages.

In addition to the legislative history, another consideration persuades us that the legislature intended the statutes in question to impose vicarious criminal liability on the natural person licensee for an employee's violation of the closing hour law. The purpose of the statute is promoted if the doctrine of vicarious liability is applied.

Several factors influence this court to conclude that the purpose of the statute is promoted by the imposition of vicarious liability. First, the state has imposed numerous restrictions on the sale of alcoholic beverages to protect the public health and safety. The state has been particularly concerned with when and to whom alcoholic beverages may be sold. Statutes regulating the sale of alcoholic beverages have been recognized as creating strict liability "public welfare offenses." Second, violation of the closing hours law is a misdemeanor; the penalty is a monetary fine and a relatively short period of imprisonment. Third, in many cases it may be difficult for the state to prove that the natural person licensee or corporate agent was negligent in hiring or supervising the employee, or knew about or authorized the employee's violation of the statute. Lastly, the number of prosecutions may be large so that the legislature would want to relieve the prosecution of the task of proving that the employer knew of or authorized the violation or was negligent. * * *

After reviewing the language of the current statutes, the legislative history of the current statutes, the cases interpreting the statutes, and the purpose of the statutes regulating the sale of alcoholic beverages, we conclude that the line of cases interpreting alcoholic beverage statutes as imposing vicarious criminal liability on the natural person licensee for an employee's violation of an alcoholic beverage sale law have continuing validity under the statutes in question in this case.

Inasmuch as the natural person licensee is subject to vicarious criminal liability for the conduct of her or his employee who illegally sells alcoholic beverages, it logically follows that a corporation licensee should be similarly liable for the illegal conduct of its employee. But in this case the defendant is not the corporation licensee; the defendant is the designated agent of the corporation. The question for the present case, therefore, is whether a designated corporate agent is subject to vicarious criminal liability for the illegal conduct, *i.e.*, remaining open after closing hours, of the tavern manager who is an employee of the corporation.

We agree with the court of appeals that the legislature intended to impose such liability on the designated agent. The court of appeals correctly noted that unless vicarious criminal liability was imposed on the designated agent, a natural person licensee could avoid criminal liability by simply incorporating the business. The legislative intent in vesting the designated agent with full authority and responsibility for conduct of the business was to treat the designated agent as a natural person licensee for all purposes, including criminal liability. The legislature could not have intended to allow a natural person licensee to avoid criminal liability by incorporating the business.

While legislative purpose and public policy support our holding that a designated agent is vicariously liable for the conduct of the corporate employee who violates the closing hours law, the defendant's final argument is that due process requires blameworthy conduct on the part of the defendant as a prerequisite to criminal liability. Although the imposition of criminal liability for faultless conduct does not comport with the generally accepted premise of Anglo–American criminal justice that criminal liability is based on personal fault, this court and the United States Supreme Court have upheld statutes imposing criminal liability for some types of offenses without proof that the conduct was knowing or wilful or negligent.

The defendant's chief challenge to the constitutionality of the statute in issue in this case appears to be that the defendant could have received a jail sentence of up to 90 days for the violation. As the state points out, the defendant was fined $200, and the due process issue the defendant raises, whatever its validity, is not presented by the facts in this case. A decision by this court on the constitutionality of a jail term where the statute imposes vicarious liability would not affect the judgment of conviction in this case or the sentence imposed on this defendant. We therefore do not consider this issue.

We turn now to the question of whether the evidence supports the verdict that the tavern manager was acting within the scope of his employment. * * *

The "scope of employment" standard as applied to alcoholic beverage regulation in this state can be traced to *Doscher v. State,* 194 Wis. 67, 214 N.W. 359 (1927). In *Doscher,* the defendant was licensed to conduct a business selling non-intoxicating beverages. Contrary to instructions, an employee brought intoxicating liquor on the premises. The defendant, a natural person licensee, was convicted of unlawfully having intoxicating liquor on his premises. The state urged the court to uphold the conviction on the ground that the conscious possession of contraband liquor by the defendant's employee who was in charge of the licensed premises must be held to be the conscious possession of the defendant. The court reversed the conviction. * * *

"In the [other] cases ... the agent was employed to have possession of and dispose of liquor for the defendant. The very employment, therefore, contemplated and covered the field of possession, disposal, and sale of the articles, so that the respective violations by the agents of the specific regulations as to the manner of carrying on such employment could properly be charged against the defendant employers who knowingly furnished the agents with the means and opportunity of violating the law. Here the defendant as employer did not confer upon the one left in charge of the premises any power, authority, or means for any such violation. The act of the employee in going outside of the premises and obtaining the forbidden alcohol was a stepping outside of any express or implied authority given him by defendant. For such an act, entirely independent of and beyond the purpose of the employment, the defendant ought not to stand charged merely because of an existing relationship of master and servant for an entirely different and lawful purpose."

The application of the standard of scope of employment limits liability to illegal conduct which occurred while the offending employee was engaged in some job-related activity and thus limits the accused's vicarious liability to conduct with which the accused has a factual connection and with which the accused has some responsible relation to the public danger envisaged by the legislature. * * *

We agree with the conclusion reached by the court of appeals. The credibility of the bar manager's testimony was a matter for the jury. The bar manager's testimony which supports the defendant's position that the manager was acting outside the scope of employment was based on a statement the bar manager gave defendant's counsel the night before trial. The jury may not have believed this testimony which was favorable to the defendant. Considering that the conduct occurred on the employer's premises and began immediately after "closing time"; that the employee had access to the tavern after hours only by virtue of his role as an employee of the corporate licensee, which role vested him with the means to keep the tavern open; and that the defendant may anticipate that employees may be tempted to engage in such conduct; the jury could conclude that the tavern manager's conduct was sufficiently similar to the conduct authorized as to be within the scope of employment. The jury could view the tavern manager's conduct as more similar to that of an employee to whom the operation of the business had been entrusted and for whose conduct the defendant should be held criminally liable than to that of an interloper for whose conduct the defendant should not be held liable. * * *

CECI, JUSTICE (dissenting).

I respectfully dissent from the majority's conclusion that there is sufficient evidence to support the verdict in this case finding that Mark Witkowski, the tavern manager, was acting within the scope of his employment. In reviewing the evidence in the light most favorable to sustaining Janet Beaudry's conviction, I believe that the record is devoid of evidence to sustain the verdict. I would reverse the decision of the court of appeals which affirmed the defendant's conviction because I am convinced that, as a matter of law, no trier of fact, acting reasonably, could conclude beyond a reasonable doubt that Mark Witkowski was acting within the scope of his employment when he kept the Village Green tavern open after 1:00 a.m. in violation of section 125.68(4)(c), Stats.

We have previously held that a servant is *not* within the scope of his employment if (a) his acts were different in kind than those authorized by the master, (b) his acts were far beyond the authorized time or space limits, or (c) his acts were too little actuated by a purpose to serve the master. It is important to note that this test is set out in the disjunctive and not the conjunctive, and, thus, not all three elements must be satisfied before there can be a finding that the servant was outside the scope of his authority.

* * * Unfortunately, the majority fails to evaluate the uncontroverted facts in this case with respect to these three criteria. In doing so, I conclude that Mark Witkowski was not within the scope of employment when he kept the tavern open after 1:00 a.m. * * *

Notes and Questions

1. On the matter of statutory construction, compare *People v. Byrne*, 77 N.Y.2d 460, 568 N.Y.S.2d 717, 570 N.E.2d 1066 (1991), involving sale of liquor to a minor in a tavern owned by brothers Thomas and James Byrne. The sale was made by Thomas, and there was no proof that James was present during, or had any other connection with, the illicit sales, so the question before the court re James' liability was whether the applicable statutes imposed vicarious liability. The court reasoned: (1) that the specific sections of the Alcoholic Beverage Control Law which define and criminalize the conduct in question refers to acts by "a person," and thus do not extend "the legislatively imposed duty beyond the actor who actually engages in the prohibited conduct"; (2) definition of "person" elsewhere in the Act to include corporations and other business entities likewise "does not support the inference that the Legislature intended to effect a much broader rule of general vicarious liability for all criminal prosecutions" under the Act, for holding a corporation for its own acts via its employees is "a far cry" from holding one individual for the crimes of another; (3) the fact the statute is of the strict liability variety is not determinative, as the strict and vicarious liability "concepts are distinct"; and (4) "where the Legislature has not clearly directed otherwise, we should be most reluctant to embrace the doctrine of vicarious liability for use in the criminal sphere," for the "doctrine runs

counter to the generally accepted premise in the criminal law that individuals 'must * * * answer for their own acts, and stand or fall by theirs own behavior'."

2. Also compare *Vachon v. New Hampshire,* 414 U.S. 478, 94 S.Ct. 664, 38 L.Ed.2d 666 (1974), where the operator of a store was sentenced to 30 days in jail and fined $100 after conviction under a statute applicable to "anyone * * * who shall knowingly or wilfully encourage, aid, cause or abet or connive at, or who has knowingly or wilfully done any act to produce, promote or contribute to the delinquency of [a] child." The conviction was based on the fact that a 14-year-old girl had purchased a button inscribed "Copulation Not Masturbation" at defendant's store. The Supreme Court reversed the conviction on the due process ground that it was "based on a record lacking any relevant evidence as to a crucial element," in that "there is no evidence whatever that the defendant sold the button, that he knew it had been sold to a minor, that he authorized such sales to minors, or that he was even in the store at the time of the sale." The three dissenters objected that the "entire thrust" of the state supreme court decision affirming the conviction "is that appellant need not *personally* have sold the button to the minor nor *personally* have authorized its sale to a minor in order to be guilty of the statutory offense. The only fair reading of the * * * language from the Supreme Court of New Hampshire is that the word 'wilfully' in the statute does *not* mean 'personally,' and the facts that the appellant controlled and operated the shop, that the same type of pin had been previously purchased at the shop, and that the pins were prominently offered for sale were sufficient evidence on the issue of wilfullness."

3. In *Beaudry,* the court carefully distinguished between strict and vicarious liability. But, are not the two related, in that the latter naturally follows from the former? Compare *People v. Travers,* 52 Cal.App.3d 111, 124 Cal.Rptr. 728 (1975) (employer vicariously liable for employee's sale of misbranded oil, as while it "is a settled rule of law that a principal is not criminally liable for the criminal act of his agent unless he authorized, consented to, advised, aided or encouraged the specific act," an "exception to this rule is the doctrine of criminal liability without fault which has been applied to criminal statutes enacted for the public morals, health, peace and safety. In general, such statutes deal with offenses of a regulatory nature and are enforceable irrespective of criminal intent or criminal negligence"); with *People v. Wilcox,* 83 Mich.App. 654, 269 N.W.2d 256 (1978) (employer not vicariously liable for employee's sale of second hand merchandise without keeping proper record of same, and this so even though "the statute does not require scienter or intent, but rather imposes strict liability for violations").

4. On the constitutional issue, consider *Lady J. Lingerie, Inc. v. City of Jacksonville,* 176 F.3d 1358 (11th Cir.1999), where individual and corporate plaintiffs, operators of various lingerie shops permitting nude dancing, challenged a city ordinance regulating such businesses, including a provision that "makes owners of adult entertainment establishments criminally liable for acts committed by their servants, agents and employees":

"*Respondeat superior* is a familiar concept in the context of 'public welfare' crimes. These offenses are not crimes in the traditional sense; instead, they are a means of regulating activities that pose a special risk to the public health or safety. * * *

"Commentators distinguish public welfare offenses from offenses for which the penalty involves imprisonment, and argue that respondeat superior is inappropriate for these 'true crimes.' We agree and hold that due process prohibits the state from imprisoning a person without proof of some form of personal blameworthiness more than a 'responsible relation.'[a] * * *

a. That is, where the defendant had the power to   prevent violations from occurring, deemed sufficient by

"Personal blameworthiness can take two forms: unlawful act and unlawful intent. It is common to convict and imprison defendants for the acts of others—witness conspiracy law. But conspiracy still requires individualized proof of unlawful intent. The converse is strict liability, which requires proof of act but not intent. We decline to consider whether *mens rea* is an indispensable constitutional requirement for sending someone to prison. Instead, we hold that due process at least requires individualized proof of intent or act. The owner liability provision requires neither, so the City may not use it to incarcerate owners."

5. Some state courts have reached a similar conclusion; see, e.g., *Davis v. Peachtree City,* 251 Ga. 219, 304 S.E.2d 701 (1983) (employer was convicted for employee's sale of liquor to minor and was sentenced to $200 fine and 60 days imprisonment, latter suspended upon payment of fine and so long as employer did not again violate the law; because defendant "faces a possible restraint of his liberty, particularly if another employee fails to exercise good judgment; damage will be done to his good name by having a criminal record; and his future will be imperiled because of possible disabilities or legal disadvantages arising from the conviction," this violates due process, especially "when, as here, there are other, less onerous alternatives which sufficiently promote these interests. * * * The Model Penal Code recommends that civil violations providing civil penalties such as fines or revocation of licenses be used for offenses for which the individual was not morally blameworthy and does not deserve the social condemnation 'implicit in the concept "crime"'"); *State v. Guminga,* 395 N.W.2d 344 (Minn.1986) (employer charged for employee's act of selling liquor to minor; charge dismissed on due process grounds: "Not only could Guminga be given a prison sentence or a suspended sentence, but, in the more likely event that he receives only a fine, his liberty could be affected by a longer presumptive sentence in a possible future felony conviction. Such an intrusion on personal liberty is not justified by the public interest protected, especially when there are alternative means by which to achieve the same end, such as civil fines or license suspension, which do not entail the legal and social ramifications of a criminal conviction").

STATE v. AKERS

Supreme Court of New Hampshire, 1979.
119 N.H. 161, 400 A.2d 38.

GRIMES, JUSTICE.

The case before us presents an issue of first impression. We are called upon to determine whether, under New Hampshire's Constitution and criminal code, parents of minors can be held criminally responsible for their children's offenses solely on the basis of their parental status. We hold that parents cannot be held criminally responsibly for the offenses of the child.

The defendants are fathers whose minor sons were found guilty of driving snowmobiles in violation of RSA 269–C:6–a II (operating on public way) and III (reasonable speed) (Supp.1977).

RSA 269–C:24 IV, which pertains to the operation and licensing of off Highway Recreational Vehicles (OHRV), provides that "(t)he parents or guardians or persons assuming responsibility will be responsible for any damage incurred or for any violations of this chapter by any person under the age of 18." * * *

The language of RSA 269–C:24 IV, "parents ... will be responsible ... for any violations of this chapter by any person under the age of 18," clearly indicates the

the Supreme Court in *United States v. Park,* p. 877 of this Book, in a case where the only punishment was a fine.

legislature's intention to hold the parents criminally responsible for the OHRV violations of their minor children.

It is a general principle of this State's Criminal Code that "(a) person is not guilty of an offense unless his criminal liability is based on conduct that includes a voluntary *act* or the voluntary omission to perform an act of which he is physically capable." RSA 626:1 I. (Emphasis added.). RSA 269–C:24 IV seeks to impose criminal liability on parents for the acts of their children without basing liability on any voluntary act or omission on the part of the parent. Because the statute makes no reference at all to parental conduct or acts it seeks to impose criminal responsibility solely because of their parental status contrary to the provisions of RSA 626:1 I.

The legislature has not specified any voluntary acts or omissions for which parents are sought to be made criminally responsible and it is not a judicial function to supply them. It is fundamental to the rule of law and due process that acts or omissions which are to be the basis of criminal liability must be specified in advance * * *.

It is argued that liability may be imposed on parents under the provisions of RSA 626:8 II(b), which authorizes imposing criminal liability for conduct of another when "he is made accountable for the conduct of such other person by the law defining the offense." This provision comes from the Model Penal Code § 2.04(2)(b). The illustrations of this type of liability in the comments to the Code all relate to situations involving employees and agents, and no suggestion is made that it was intended to authorize imposing vicarious criminal liability on one merely because of his status as a parent.

Without passing upon the validity of statutes that might seek to impose vicarious criminal liability on the part of an employer for acts of his employees, we have no hesitancy in holding that any attempt to impose such liability on parents simply because they occupy the status of parents, without more, offends the due process clause of our State constitution.

Parenthood lies at the very foundation of our civilization. The continuance of the human race is entirely dependent upon it. It was firmly entrenched in the Judeo–Christian ethic when "in the beginning" man was commanded to "be fruitful and multiply." Genesis I. Considering the nature of parenthood, we are convinced that the status of parenthood cannot be made a crime. This, however, is the effect of RSA 269–C:24 IV. Even if the parent has been as careful as anyone could be, even if the parent has forbidden the conduct, and even if the parent is justifiably unaware of the activities of the child, criminal liability is still imposed under the wording of the present statute. There is no other basis for criminal responsibility other than the fact that a person is the parent of one who violates the law.

* * * Because the net effect of the statute is to punish parenthood, the result is forbidden by substantive due process requirements of N.H.Const. pt. 1, art. 15.

BOIS, JUSTICE, dissenting: * * *

Even if I were to accept the majority's conclusion that the vicarious imposition of criminal liability on parents of children who have committed an OHRV violation under RSA ch. 269–C is constitutionally impermissible, I would still uphold the validity of RSA 269–C:24 IV. A closer reading of this State's Criminal Code belies the majority's reasoning that RSA 269–C:24 IV holds parents of minor offenders criminally responsible for their children's offenses solely on the basis of their parental status. RSA 626:1 I, enunciating the fundamental principle of the Criminal Code, states that all criminal liability must be based on a "voluntary act" or "voluntary omission." When RSA 269–C:24 IV is read in conjunction with RSA 626:1 I, a parental conviction can result only when the State shows beyond a reasonable doubt that a minor child has committed a violation under a provision of chapter 269–C, and that his parent voluntarily performed or omitted to perform an act such as participating in the minor's conduct, or entrusting, or negligently allowing his minor child to operate an OHRV.

When RSA 269–C:24 IV is construed to require a voluntary act or voluntary omission in accordance with RSA 626:1 I, there are no due process infirmities * * *. Culpable intent is not required to impose criminal penalties for minor infractions. * * *

When the legislature imposes criminal responsibility without requiring intent, we will override it only when such imposition violates concepts of fundamental fairness. In the present case, there is a demonstrable public interest to assure the safe operation of OHRVs, and the minor penalties imposed upon violators of RSA 269–C:24 IV are insubstantial. In such circumstances, we will not second guess the wisdom of the legislature. * * *

Notes and Questions

1. Naomi R. Cahn, *Pragmatic Questions About Parental Liability Statutes*, 1996 Wis.L.Rev. 399, 405–11: "States have been enacting laws holding parents criminally liable for the delinquent acts of their children for almost a century. Indeed, these laws, which are generally amendments to a state's juvenile court act, build upon prior traditions of blaming parents for their children's crimes. The early laws, many of which are still in effect, held parents liable for contributing to the delinquency of a minor and provided a method for the courts to assert jurisdiction over the child's family. The following 1936 New York statute is typical:

> The children's court shall have jurisdiction, whenever the issues involving a delinquent or neglected child are before the court summarily to try, hear and determine any charge or offense ... against any parent ... involving an act or omission in respect to such child in violation of any law of the state ... or which has or is alleged to have contributed to the delinquency, neglect or dependency of any such child.

This section only applied once the child had already been adjudicated delinquent. Although there are relatively few reported cases, parents were frequently prosecuted under these laws, at least during the first half of the century. In one case, a mother was sentenced to a year in prison for failing to provide a home for her son and for failing to make him attend school. The laws were extremely far-reaching, and criminalized behavior associated with poverty as well as with delinquency.

"In the middle part of the Twentieth Century, coinciding with a perception of increased youth crime, these laws experienced a revival when cities began to pass parental liability ordinances that echoed state laws. Simultaneously, the public demanded that states enforce parental liability laws more vigorously.

"More modern versions of these statutes take two approaches: they continue to impose liability for contributing to the delinquency of a minor, or they impose liability for endangering the welfare of a child. They differ as to whether they apply only to parents, or to any adult who encourages the minor's behavior. The statutes generally do not require an *actus rea*.

"Over the past decade, prompted by fears of increasing juvenile delinquency, there has been a renewed interest in these laws, with a strong public outcry for statutes which criminalize the actions of parents when their child commit a crime. While only a few jurisdictions have enacted new statutes, these laws provide a politically effective rhetorical tool. California was the first state to enact new legislation in this area, when it passed the Street Terrorism Enforcement and Prevention Act of 1988. Although this legislation was enacted largely to combat gang violence, it imposes criminal liability on a 'parent or legal guardian' who does not exercise the statutorily defined duty of 'reasonable care, supervision, protection, and control over the minor child.' Violations may result in a misdemeanor, a fine, imprisonment of a year, or five years probation. In one town, Silverton, Oregon, a similar law is credited with a fifty-three percent decrease in juvenile crime.

"Generally, the legislators' goals include involving parents in their child's life, affixing personal responsibility for criminal behavior, and attempting to decrease escalating rates of juvenile crime. By holding parents responsible for their child's actions, these laws seek improved parental control over their child. * * *

"Parental liability laws occupy an uneasy position in the criminal law because of their relation to notions of imputed liability and because of their overlap with child abuse and neglect laws. As a general matter, the criminal law assumes free will and assigns responsibility based only on intentional action. Indeed, there are a limited number of crimes for which the culpability level is strict negligence; apart from the felony murder rule, these are generally based on offenses against the public welfare or morality. The parental liability statutes, however, depend on vicarious or imputed liability. The parents have committed no criminal act of their own. The standard for conviction is generally negligence, although some legislation appears to be based on strict liability. * * *

"These laws are also problematic in that they are similar to and yet different from child abuse and neglect laws. Child abuse laws impose liability when the parent takes some action which physically or emotionally harms the child, while child neglect laws hold parents criminally liable for inaction which causes some form of harm to their child. Like the child abuse and neglect laws, the parental liability laws hold parents responsible for their child. But unlike them, the parents' action or inaction need not result in physical or emotional harm to the child; instead, the parents are responsible for their child's actions. The parental liability statutes establish vicarious liability, so that regardless of the parent's actions, they are culpable. Somewhat predictably, liability appears to be based on a presumption that the parents acted negligently in failing to supervise their child. In the child abuse area, it is the parent's conduct which is punished; the parental liability statutes punish the parent because of her status as 'parent.'"

2. Note, 27 Stetson L.Rev. 655, 677–78 (1997), has this to say about *Akers*: "This decision implies that if a parental responsibility statute provides a specific act or omission upon which to base parental liability for the criminal acts of their children, the statute would withstand constitutional scrutiny. Most courts addressing parental responsibility statutes have found that 'a duty to act can be created with liability resulting from nonperformance.... The state imposes an affirmative duty on the parent to provide guidance, which if ignored leads to criminal sanctions. The source of this duty is based on the relationship of the parent to the child.'

"Therefore, properly written parental responsibility statutes are constitutional and will withstand judicial scrutiny."

3. But, as a practical matter just how different are such laws from that held unconstitutional in *Akers*? Consider Note, 66 Fordham L.Rev. 1029, 1029–31 (1997): "Alex Provenzino is a suburban Detroit teenager who started getting into trouble shortly after he began associating with an older group of friends. He was first arrested in May 1995 for robbing his family's church. A month later, he was arrested for assaulting his father. His parents twice asked the police to keep Alex in jail. Three months later, in September, he was again in custody, this time for a string of house burglaries. This last arrest occurred

after police searched Alex's bedroom and found a stolen handgun and marijuana lying on his nightstand.

"A year after Alex's first arrest, his parents, Anthony and Susan Provenzino, were branded as criminals. They were found guilty of a misdemeanor for failing to prevent their son from committing the burglaries. This case was the first to be tried under the St. Clair Shores' new parental responsibility law, which requires parents 'to exercise reasonable control to prevent the minor from committing any delinquent act.' The St. Clair Shores ordinance exists:

> for the preservation of the public peace, health, safety and welfare of the people of the City of St. Clair Shores, and is intended to address situations where parents have failed to act responsibly and reasonably in the supervision of their minor children to the detriment of the general public.

The ordinance also defines the duties of 'reasonable parental control' as: ensuring a home free of illegal firearms and drugs, staying informed of the curfew ordinance, requiring that the child go to school, arranging supervision if the parent is absent, taking precautions to keep the child from committing property destruction, forbidding the child to keep stolen property, and seeking help from the government to control the child if necessary.

"The Provenzino parents were ordered to pay $2200 in fines and court costs, and to pay $13,000 a year for Alex's care in a youth detention home. While this verdict may appear extreme, the jury found otherwise. Elaborating on the reasons behind the guilty verdict, jurors said the Provenzinos' inability to get Alex into counseling was 'pivotal in their decision.' The Provenzinos claim that they tried to get Alex to attend counseling, but could not force him to go. The Provenzino parents also maintain that they discouraged Alex from associating with the older group of friends whom, it appears, he was trying to impress. Despite what the Provenzinos believed to be their best efforts, they could not stop him from breaking the law. They added, 'we know in our hearts we did everything we could.' The parents appealed the fines, which were later overturned by the Macomb County court because St. Clair Shores failed to show that the Provenzinos did not attempt to bring Alex to counseling. * * *

"Some people firmly believed that the Provenzinos were properly punished for their lack of control of Alex. Due to the increasing problem of juvenile crime, they believed that any measure that would help reduce youth offenses should be utilized. Others who endorsed the verdict indicated that the parents were better suited to pay for the juvenile's crimes than taxpayers.

"Other[s] argued that the verdict against the Provenzinos was 'unfair.' Some thought the ordinance invaded the privacy of parenting decisions by requiring certain parenting styles. Others noted that the ordinance could force parents to resort to desperate means, including physical abuse or emancipation. Some people even wrote that they would rather abstain from having children than be subjected to the statute. Other parents, who felt they could sympathize with the Provenzinos, related similar stories of delinquent children whom they could not control. One parent, whose child refused to attend counseling, stated that 'for a court to convict me of failing to control my kid would be the ultimate insult!' "

4. How might such parental responsibility laws be improved? Consider Comment, 139 U.Pa.L.Rev. 1123, 1161 (1991): "The duty of parenthood no doubt includes a responsibility to guide the child's personal development. The parent's ability to supervise is by no means uniform throughout the child's life, however, as maturity and competing social forces pull the youngster farther from the parent's command. The most glaring shortcoming of

parental responsibility laws has been their unwarranted assumption of parental omnipotence. Not only do they often fail to recognize varying levels of parental authority as the age of the child changes, they also assume the same degree of control no matter the nature of the child's actions or in what forum they occur. This has resulted in parents being punished not for their own acts or omissions, but for those of their children.

"The problem of unconcerned parents can not be disregarded when evaluating social issues such as juvenile delinquency. The public's anger at parents who are ambivalent to their children's criminal activity or abuse is justified. The response of lawmakers to constituent demands that parents who fail in their duty to care for their children be punished is understandable. These facts, however, are not sufficient justification to write legislation that bears little relation to the parent's capacity to supervise, is overly vague, and ignores principles of criminal causation. Parental responsibility laws should be tailored to correspond with narrowly conceived duties that reflect the parent's abilities."

5.   Another area as to which vicarious liability or some approximation thereof has been utilized concerns statutes and ordinances dealing with the parking of vehicles. *City of Missoula v. Shea*, 202 Mont. 286, 661 P.2d 410 (1983), reflects what one court concluded was constitutionally permissible in this area. At issue in *Shea* was a section in a parking ordinance declaring that proof a particular vehicle was illegally parked, together with proof defendant was the registered owner at the time, "shall constitute in evidence a prima facie presumption that the registered owner of such vehicle was the person who parked" the vehicle. The effect of this presumption, per the state's rules of evidence, was that absent a preponderance of evidence to the contrary, the trier of fact must find the assumed fact in accordance with the presumption. Consequently, the court concluded, this provision was unconstitutional under *Sandstrom v. Montana*, p. 135 of this Book. But the court then went on to overturn a prior holding invalidating an ordinance provision to the effect that the registered owner is responsible for all parking violations and that it is no defense that the vehicle was parked by another person unless it is shown that at such time the vehicle was being used without consent of the registered owner. The court in *Shea* now held "that vicarious criminal responsibility can be imposed, without breaching due process restrictions, in the regulation of traffic and the parking of motor vehicles."

SECTION 10. LIABILITY OF ORGANIZATIONS, THEIR OFFICERS AND AGENTS

COMMONWEALTH v. BENEFICIAL FINANCE CO.

Supreme Court of Massachusetts, 1971.

360 Mass. 188, 275 N.E.2d 33.

Spiegel, Justice. [Various individual and corporate defendants were convicted of conspiracy to engage in bribery, in that three finance companies (Household Finance, Beneficial Finance, and Liberty Loan) sought favorable treatment from state agencies. Household was held criminally responsible for the criminal conduct of Barber and Pratt, employees but neither directors nor officers; Liberty was held liable for the criminal acts of Woodstock, a director and executive vice-president; and Beneficial was held criminally responsible for the conduct of Farrell and Glynn, who were neither directors, officers nor employees of that corporation, but who were vice-president and an employee, respectively, of Beneficial Management, a wholly-owned subsidiary.]

The defendants and the Commonwealth have proposed differing standards upon which the criminal responsibility of a corporation should be predicated. The defendants argue that a corporation should not be held criminally liable for the conduct of its servants or agents unless such conduct was performed, authorized, ratified, adopted or tolerated by the corporations' directors, officers or other "high managerial agents" who are sufficiently high in the corporate hierarchy to warrant the assumption that their acts in some substantial sense reflect corporate policy. This standard is that adopted by the American Law Institute Model Penal Code, approved in May, 1962.[a] * * *

The Commonwealth, on the other hand, argues that the standard applied by the judge in his instructions to the jury was correct. These instructions, which prescribe a somewhat more flexible standard than that delineated in the Model Penal Code, state in part, as follows: "[T]he Commonwealth must prove beyond a reasonable doubt that there existed between the guilty individual or individuals and the corporation which is being charged with the conduct of the individuals, such *a relationship that the acts and the intent of the individuals were the acts and intent of the corporation.* * * *

"How is that to be shown? How is the jury to determine whether the Commonwealth has proved that? First let me say that the Commonwealth does not have to prove that the individual who acted criminally was expressly requested or authorized in advance by the corporation to do so, nor must the Commonwealth prove that the corporation expressly ratified or adopted that criminal conduct on the part of that individual or those individuals. *It does not mean that the Commonwealth must prove that the individual who acted criminally was a member of the corporation's board of directors, or that he was a high officer in the corporation, or that he held any office at all.* If the Commonwealth did prove that an individual for whose act it seeks to hold a corporation criminally liable was an officer of the corporation, the jury should consider that. *But more important than that, it should consider what the authority of that person was as such officer in relation to the corporation.* The mere fact that he has a title is not enough to make the corporation liable for his criminal conduct. The Commonwealth must prove that the individual for whose conduct it seeks to charge *the corporation criminally was placed in a position by the corporation where he had enough power, duty, responsibility and authority to act for and in behalf of the corporation to handle the particular business or operation or project of the corporation in which he was engaged at the time that he committed the criminal act, with power of decision as to what he would or would not do while acting for the corporation, and that he was acting for and in behalf of the corporation in the accomplishment of that particular business or operation or project, and that he committed a criminal act while so acting.* * * *"

The difference between the judge's instructions to the jury and the Model Penal Code lies largely in the latter's reference to a "high managerial agent" and in the Code requirement that to impose corporate criminal liability, it at least must appear that its directors or high managerial agent "authorized * * * or recklessly tolerated" the allegedly criminal acts. The judge's instructions focus on the authority of the corporate agent in relation to the *particular* corporate business in which the agent was engaged. The Code seems to require that there be authorization or reckless inaction by a corporate representative having some relation to framing corporate policy, or one "having duties of such responsibility that his conduct may fairly be assumed to represent the policy of the corporation." Close examination of the judge's instructions reveals that they preserve the underlying "corporate policy" rationale of the Code by allowing the jury to infer "corporate policy" from the *position* in which the corporation placed the agent in commissioning him to handle the particular corporate affairs in which he was engaged at the time of the criminal act. * * *

a. See § 2.07.

It may also be observed that the judge's standard is somewhat similar to the traditional common law rule of respondeat superior. However, in applying this rule to a criminal case, the judge added certain requirements not generally associated with that common law doctrine. He further qualified the rule of respondeat superior by requiring that the conduct for which the corporation is being held accountable be performed *on behalf of the corporation.* This factor is noted as important in the commentary to § 2.07(1) of the Model Penal Code. It may well be that there is often little distinction between an act done *on behalf of a principal* and an act done *within the scope of employment,* which is the traditional requirement of the doctrine of respondeat superior. Nevertheless, in the circumstances of this case it might reasonably be concluded that the explicit instruction of the judge that the jury look to the authority vested in the agent by the corporation to act within the particular sphere of corporate affairs relating to the criminal act, together with the explicit instruction that such act be performed on behalf of the corporation, required, in effect, the type of evidence which would support an inference that the criminal act was done as a matter of corporate policy. We deem this to be a valid conclusion, especially in view of the quantum of proof required in a criminal case in order to prove guilt beyond a reasonable doubt. * * *

The thrust of [earlier Mass. cases] involving a human principal is that it is fundamental to our criminal jurisprudence that for more serious offences guilt is personal and not vicarious. "One is punished for his own blameworthy conduct, not that of others." Professor Sayre's article[b] is heavily relied on by Beneficial for the proposition that the considerations proposed by Sayre apply with equal weight to corporations. However, we do not think that the Sayre article, or the rule in the master-servant cases, is helpful to these corporations. The essence of Sayre's discussion is that, as to certain crimes, a theory of vicarious liability is an inadequate basis for imposing criminal liability on a natural person who can suffer imprisonment or ignominy for the acts of his agents. * * *

As alluded to by Professor Sayre, and pointed out by the Commonwealth in its brief, the very nature of a corporation as a "person" before the law renders it impossible to equate the imposition of vicarious liability on a human principal with the imposition of vicarious liability on a corporate principal. "A corporation can act only through its agents. * * * [C]orporate criminal liability is necessarily vicarious." Since a corporation is a legal fiction, comprised only of individuals, it has no existence separate and distinct from those whom it has clothed with authority and commissioned to act for it whether such individuals are directors, officers, shareholders or employees. Thus, the issue is not whether vicarious liability should be imposed on a corporation under the "direct participation and assent rule" of the master-servant cases cited above, but rather, whether the acts and intent of natural persons, be they officers, directors or employees, can be treated as the acts and intent of the corporation itself. For the foregoing reasons, despite the strenuous urging of the defendants, we are unconvinced that the standard for imposing criminal responsibility on a human principal adequately deals with the evidentiary problems which are inherent in ascribing the acts of individuals to a corporate entity.

Since we have exhausted our review of Massachusetts cases in point, we turn to cases in other jurisdictions discussing the problem of corporate criminal responsibility. We note, however, that in view of the fact that the crimes alleged here, namely, conspiracy and the substantive offences of bribery, are mala in se, we necessarily exclude discussion of those cases which *clearly* involve "public welfare" offences by a corporation, unless such cases cast some insight into the question before us. Generally, these cases concern public

b. Francis Bowes Sayre, *Criminal Responsibility for the Acts of Another,* 43 Harv.L.Rev. 689 (1930).

nuisances resulting from the nonperformance of a nondelegable duty, rather than the rule of respondeat superior.

We first treat with the case of *New York Cent. & H.R.R. Co. v. United States,* 212 U.S. 481, 29 S.Ct. 304, 53 L.Ed. 613, a case relied upon by both the judge and the Commonwealth. There, the Supreme Court of the United States upheld the constitutionality of a statute which specifically made corporations liable for the acts of their officers, agents or employees acting within the scope of their employment. The statute in question prohibited shippers from receiving rebates from common carriers and specifically provided as follows: "In construing and enforcing the provisions of this section the act, omission, or failure of any officer, agent, or other person acting for or employed by any common carrier acting within the scope of his employment shall in every case be also deemed to be the act, omission, or failure of such carrier as well as that of the person." [T]he court made a number of pertinent observations and rulings from which we quote at some length: "A corporation is held responsible for acts not within the agent's corporate powers strictly construed, but which the agent has assumed to perform for the corporation when employing the corporate powers actually authorized, and in such cases there need be no written authority under seal or vote of the corporation in order to constitute the agency or to authorize the act. * * * We see no valid objection in law, and every reason in public policy, why the corporation, which profits by the transaction, and can only act through its agents and officers, shall be held punishable by fine because of the knowledge and intent of its agents to whom it has intrusted authority to act in the subject-matter of making and fixing rates of transportation, and whose knowledge and purposes may well be attributed to the corporation for which the agents act. While the law should have regard to the rights of all, and to those of corporations no less than to those of individuals, it cannot shut its eyes to the fact that the great majority of business transactions in modern times are conducted through these bodies, and particularly that interstate commerce is almost entirely in their hands, and to give them immunity from all punishment because of the old and exploded doctrine that a corporation cannot commit a crime would virtually take away the only means of effectually controlling the subject-matter and correcting the abuses aimed at." * * *

Household argues that the *New York Central* case is one in which Congress clearly dispensed with the necessity of proving corporate intent and is therefore distinguishable from the case before us. While we agree that the thrust of the opinion in that case is addressed to the constitutionality of the statutory imputation of the agent's acts to the corporation, we think that the case falls outside the class of offences generally denominated as "public welfare" offences and serves as precedent for the proposition that a corporation may be held criminally responsible for the acts of one who is neither a director, officer nor "high managerial agent" of the corporation. In this regard, the case illustrates the public policy rationale for imposing vicarious liability upon a corporation and thus warranting the treatment of corporations in a manner different from that of individuals for the acts of their agents. This rationale was subsequently developed and applied in lower Federal court cases which dealt with crimes requiring specific intent. * * *

Household, Beneficial and Liberty all vigorously attack these cases in an attempt to distinguish them from the cases before us. The thrust of their argument is that all of these cases fall into 1 of 2 categories; either they involve public welfare and regulatory statute crimes in which intent was not an element, or if the crimes did include intent as a necessary element, then they assert that the corporations were only held liable if one high in the corporate hierarchy directed, approved or acquiesced in the agent's criminal act. * * *

We think that the answer to these contentions is twofold. First, the defendants' attempted categorization of the above cases into two neat little groups greatly oversimplifies the complex and multifaceted issues which confronted the various courts in the cases we have cited. The principal cases all entail prosecutions for the crimes of conspiracy, a crime requiring specific intent. In addition, the object of the conspiracies in those cases involved a wide scope of serious criminal activity, usually in matters tending to be of benefit to the corporation, extending from violations of the Espionage Act through the making of illegal political contributions, various types of fraudulent acquisitive crimes, and conspiracy to violate the Sherman Act through price fixing. * * * Secondly, the argument that only high corporate officers were involved has no basis in fact. In [one] case, a minor branch manager was involved, and in [another] case, a salesman. * * *

It may be that the theoretical principles underlying this standard are, in general, the same as embodied in the rule of respondeat superior. Nevertheless, as we observed at the outset, the judge's instructions, as a whole and in context, required a greater quantum of proof in the practical application of this standard than is required in a civil case. In focusing on the "kinship" between the authority of an individual and the act he committed, the judge emphasized that the jury must be satisfied "beyond a reasonable doubt" that the act of the individual "*constituted*" the act of the corporation. Juxtaposition of the traditional criminal law requirement of ascertaining guilt beyond a reasonable doubt (as opposed to the civil law standard of the preponderance of the evidence), with the rule of respondeat superior, fully justifies application of the standard enunciated by the judge to a criminal prosecution against a corporation for a crime requiring specific intent.

The foregoing is especially true in view of the particular circumstances of this case. In order to commit the crimes charged in these indictments, the defendant corporations either had to offer to pay money to a public official or conspire to do so. The disbursal of funds is an act peculiarly within the ambit of corporate activity. These corporations by the very nature of their business are constantly dealing with the expenditure and collection of moneys. It could hardly be expected that any of the individual defendants would conspire to pay, or would pay, the substantial amount of money here involved, namely $25,000, out of his own pocket. The jury would be warranted in finding that the disbursal of such an amount of money would come from the corporate treasury. A reasonable inference could therefore be drawn that the payment of such money by the corporations was done as a matter of corporate policy and as a reflection of corporate intent, thus comporting with the underlying rationale of the Model Penal Code, and probably with its specific requirements.

Moreover, we do not think that the Model Penal Code standard really purports to deal with the evidentiary problems which are inherent in establishing the quantum of proof necessary to show that the directors or officers of a corporation authorize, ratify, tolerate, or participate in the criminal acts of an agent when such acts are apparently performed on behalf of the corporation. Evidence of such authorization or ratification is too easily susceptible of concealment. As is so trenchantly stated by the judge: "Criminal acts are not usually made the subject of votes of authorization or ratification by corporate Boards of Directors; and the lack of such votes does not prevent the act from being the act of the corporation."

It is obvious that criminal conspiratorial acts are not performed within the glare of publicity, nor would we expect a board of directors to meet officially and record on the corporate records a delegation of authority to initiate, conduct or conclude proceedings for the purpose of bribing a public official. Of necessity, the proof [of] authority to so act must rest on all the circumstances and conduct in a given situation and the reasonable inferences to be drawn therefrom.

Additional factors of importance are the size and complexity of many large modern corporations which necessitate the delegation of more authority to lesser corporate agents and employees. As the judge pointed out: "There are not enough seats on the Board of Directors, nor enough offices in a corporation, to permit the corporation engaged in widespread operations to give such a title or office to every person in whom it places the power, authority, and responsibility for decision and action." This latter consideration lends credence to the view that the title or position of an individual in a corporation should not be conclusively determinative in ascribing criminal responsibility. In a large corporation, with many numerous and distinct departments, a high ranking corporate officer or agent may have no authority or involvement in a particular sphere of corporate activity, whereas a lower ranking corporate executive might have much broader power in dealing with a matter peculiarly within the scope of his authority. Employees who are in the lower echelon of the corporate hierarchy often exercise more responsibility in the *everyday operations* of the corporation than the directors or officers. Assuredly, the title or office that the person holds may be considered, but it should not be the decisive criterion upon which to predicate corporate responsibility. * * *

To permit corporations to conceal the nefarious acts of their underlings by using the shield of corporate armor to deflect corporate responsibility, and to separate the subordinate from the executive, would be to permit "endocratic" corporations to inflict widespread public harm without hope of redress. It would merely serve to ignore the scramble and realities of the market place.[58] This we decline to do. We believe that stringent standards must be adopted to discourage any attempt by "endocratic" corporations' executives to place the sole responsibility for criminal acts on the shoulders of their subordinates. * * *

Considering everything we have said above, we are of opinion that the quantum of proof necessary to sustain the conviction of a corporation for the acts of its agents is sufficiently met if it is shown that the corporation has placed the agent in a position where he has enough authority and responsibility to act for and in behalf of the corporation in handling the *particular* corporate business, operation or project in which he was engaged at the time he committed the criminal act. The judge properly instructed the jury to this effect and correctly stated that this standard does not depend upon the responsibility or authority which the agent has with respect to the entire corporate business, but only to his position with relation to the particular business in which he was serving the corporation. Some of the factors that the jury were entitled to consider in applying the above test, although perhaps not in themselves decisive, are the following: (1) the extent of control and authority exercised by the individual over and within the corporation; (2) the extent and manner to which corporate funds were used in the crime; (3) a repeated pattern of criminal conduct tending to indicate corporate toleration or ratification of the agent's acts.[c]

---

58. The term "endocratic" was coined by Dean Rostow and means a "large, publicly-held corporation, whose stock is scattered in small fractions among thousands of stockholders." Note, *Increasing Community Control Over Corporate Crime—A Problem in the Law of Sanctions,* 71 Yale L.J. 280, 281, n. 3.

c. The court then went on to conclude:

(1) that there was sufficient evidence that Barber, divisional director of public relations, and Pratt, a subordinate of the vice-president in charge of public relations, acted "within the authority conferred on them" by Household in conspiring to bribe public officials, as the public relations men were responsible for

dealings between the corporation and persons in "public life";

(2) that there was sufficient evidence that Woodstock, in light of his position, had authority to act for Liberty; and

(3) that Farnell and Glynn possessed sufficient authority to act for Beneficial Management, the wholly-owned subsidiary of Beneficial Finance, and that the former was the agent of the latter under the test of *My Bread Baking Co. v. Cumberland Farms, Inc.,* 353 Mass. 614, 233 N.E.2d 748 (1968):

"Although common ownership of the stock of two or more corporations together with common management, standing alone, will not give rise to liability on the part

Notes and Questions

1. Does corporate criminal liability, under either the Model Penal Code or *Beneficial Finance* approach, represent sound policy? Evaluate the following objections: (1) that the imposition of a criminal fine on the corporation is often ineffective as a profit-diminishing sanction, in that the economic cost of the fine may be "passed on" to the consumer by means of higher prices or rates;[a] (2) that in the "endocratic" corporation (the large publicly-held corporation whose stock is scattered in small fractions among thousands of stockholders) the stockholders simply cannot control the management, and thus should not be penalized for their failure to do so;[b] (3) that the availability of the corporation as a defendant provides a convenient "scapegoat" whereby corporate agents engaged in the wrongdoing escape the personal criminal liability which would be a greater deterrent;[c] (4) that depriving wrongdoers of their ill-gotten gains is not a function of the criminal law,[d] and that in any event fines are usually unrelated to the gains and may penalize stockholders other than those who profited from the illegal activity;[e] and (5) that the criminal prosecutions of corporations are not adequately reported to the public to result in damage to the "corporate image."[f]

2. Under the traditional respondeat superior approach, "the prosecution must show that the illegal act was committed within the agent's scope of employment. The traditional agency definition limits scope of employment to conduct that is authorized, explicitly or implicitly, by the principal or that is similar or incidental to authorized conduct. However, courts generally find conduct to fall within the scope of employment even if it was specifically forbidden by a superior and occurred despite good faith efforts on the part of the corporation to prevent the crime. Thus, scope of employment in practice means little more than that the act occurred while the offending employee was carrying out a job-related activity." *Developments in the Law—Corporate Crime*, 92 Harv.L.Rev. 1227, 1249–50 (1979). Is this unduly harsh?

3. Where a corporation is prosecuted for a strict liability offense, such as the sale of alcoholic beverages to a person under age, the corporation may thus be convicted notwithstanding the absence of any bad state of mind by any corporate agent or employee, and notwithstanding the fact that the act was by a low-level employee such as a store clerk acting directly contrary to the corporation's instructions. Courts have typically held, as in *State v. Hy Vee Food Stores, Inc.*, 533 N.W.2d 147 (S.D.1995), that conviction in such circumstances does not violate the substantive due process rights of the corporation. As the court reasoned in *Hy Vee*, while the "law disfavors statutes which impose criminal liability without fault, much less those enactments which impose such liability vicariously," it is nonetheless well settled "that criminal liability for certain offenses may be imputed to corporate defendants for the unlawful acts of its employees, provided that the conduct is within the scope of the employee's authority, whether actual or apparent," just as it is

of one corporation for the acts of another corporation or its employees, additional facts may be such as to permit the conclusion that an agency or similar relationship exists between the entities. Particularly is this true (a) when there is active and direct participation by the representatives of one corporation, apparently exercising some form of pervasive control, in the activities of another and there is some fraudulent or injurious consequence of the intercorporate relationship, or (b) when there is a confused intermingling of activity of two or more corporations engaged in a common enterprise with substantial disregard of the separate nature of the corporate entities, or serious ambiguity about the manner and capacity in which the various corporations and their respective representatives are acting."

a. Glanville Williams, *Criminal Law: The General Part* § 283 (2d ed. 1961).

b. Note, 71 Yale L.J. 280, 281 (1961).

c. Id. at 292 n. 50.

d. Williams, supra note a, at § 186.

e. Id. at § 283.

f. Note, supra note b, at 287 n. 35.

clear that "merely stating or promulgating policies will not insulate a corporation from liability," and the claim that this is not so of an enactment that "goes beyond being a mere regulatory measure with minor consequences," which the statute at issue is because it provides for a potential of imprisonment, cannot be raised by the corporate defendant because of the simple fact that "corporations cannot be imprisoned."

4. Is the solution to give the corporation an affirmative defense along the lines of *Model Penal Code* § 2.07(5)? Consider:

(a) Samuel Miller, *Corporate Criminal Liability: A Principle Extended to Its Limits,* 38 Fed.B.J. 49, 66 (1979): "One of the principal justifications for the imposition of corporate criminal liability is that the corporate fine will encourage diligent supervision of corporate employees by managerial personnel. This goal is obviously furthered by encouraging corporate management to engage in self-policing functions. If corporate managers know that the company faces criminal sanctions despite their best efforts to insure compliance with the law, their motivation to undertake such efforts would be chilled. As Professor Mueller has pointed out: 'The imposition of punishment despite the exercise of due care, when the efforts were unsuccessful, creates frustration. If punishment followed as a matter of course upon every *discovered* technical breach of the law, no matter whether due care has been exercised or not, the managerial agents may well conclude that it is far more simple to let things take their own course, than it is to exercise care.' "

(b) John C. Coffee, Jr., *Corporate Criminal Responsibility,* 1 Encyclopedia of Crime & Justice 253, 262 (1983): "Without such a defense, the corporation would still have an incentive to monitor and police its employees since, as a practical matter, it will probably be held strictly liable for any offense committed by employees in the course of their work. But by recognizing the defense, one raises the possibility of feigned compliance and thus encourages cosmetic attempts at monitoring. Worse yet, there is the danger that honest efforts at monitoring and compliance will be mistaken by middle-level management as only a cynical attempt to prepare a due-diligence defense in advance.

"On a more theoretical level, once such a defense is recognized, the corporation might invest less funds in monitoring and detecting illegal and potentially illegal behavior since, once the minimal standard of diligence is met, the corporation becomes legally immune and has no remaining incentive to prevent criminal acts by its agents, even though further investment might prevent such crime. In theory, the ideal position for the corporation would be to invest just enough to establish the defense but not to prevent those crimes profitable to the corporation. Yet without the defense, the rational corporation would invest in crime prevention by any means (including research or experimentation with new techniques) up to the level at which such expenditures equaled the expected penalty—that is, the likely fine discounted by the likelihood of apprehension and conviction. In short, the absence of the defense creates an incentive to seek new methods of prevention not yet established or required by a due-diligence standard. Ironically, the more diligence is made a defense, the less it is encouraged."

5. In *United States v. Ladish Malting Co.,* 135 F.3d 484 (7th Cir.1998), remanding for retrial the prosecution of the corporation for a fatal injury to an employee caused by a knowing violation of an OSHA regulation, the corporation asked that the trial court be directed to instruct that only knowledge by a supervisory employee would suffice. The court responded: "As for the argument that only supervisors' knowledge counts: why? Corporations 'know' what their employees who are responsible for an aspect of the business know. Doubtless the knowledge of a worker who trips over a safety hazard but does not understand or report what he has found does not count. Most federal statutes that make anything of corporate knowledge also require the knowledge to be possessed by

persons authorized to do something about what they know. But what's so special, for this purpose, about supervisors? The magistrate judge told the jury to consider the knowledge of Ladish's 'officers, directors, and authorized agents' provided 'that supervisor or employee has some duty to communicate that knowledge to someone higher up in the corporation.' This definition, which asks whether a particular person has been given responsibility over safety (perhaps by being placed on an inspection team), makes more sense than asking whether someone is a supervisor—a status that refers to the power to hire and fire others but that may be unrelated to workplace safety. Following the ordinary law of agency, the instructions told the jury that employers may decide for themselves who is 'authorized' to inspect the plant for safety hazards, who is to receive and respond to safety complaints, and who is to report to the persons with authority to make decisions. If 'authorized agents' with reporting duties acquire actual knowledge, it is entirely sensible to say that the corporation has acquired knowledge. Ladish could not, by delegating all safety inspection and reporting functions to non-supervisors, shield itself from knowledge of the hazards."

6. In *Granite Construction Co. v. Superior Court*, 149 Cal.App.3d 465, 197 Cal.Rptr. 3 (1983), denying a writ of prohibition re a grand jury indictment of the corporation for manslaughter after seven workers were killed in an accident at a power plant construction site, the petitioner asserted "that a corporation may be charged with crimes against 'property,' but 'not against the person.' This attempt to distinguish crimes against property from crimes against the person relies on the corporation's nature as an economically motivated entity. While a corporation may directly benefit from a crime against property, crimes against persons are not as directly linked to the profit motive. This argument is unsuccessful. It overlooks the substantial *indirect* economic benefits that may accrue to the corporation through crimes against the person. To get these economic benefits, corporate management may shortcut expensive safety precautions, respond forcibly to strikes, or engage in criminal anticompetitive behavior. If any such risk-taking is a corporate action, the corporation becomes a proper criminal defendant."

7. Recall that in *Beneficial Finance* the court found the cases "involving a human principal" not controlling. Does this mean that if the organizations had been partnerships rather than corporations and if the defendants had been the partners, the court would have taken a different approach?

Consider, in this regard, *Gordon v. United States*, 203 F.2d 248 (10th Cir.1953), where the defendants, partners in an appliance business, were convicted of "willfully" violating regulations concerning the selling of sewing machines on credit. The case was submitted to the jury on the theory that the knowledge of one partner was imputable to the other and that the knowledge and acts of the salesmen employed by the partnership were imputable to the partners. The court affirmed on the ground it was proper "to charge the employer with knowledge of records he is required to keep and acts he is required or forbidden to do, and which he necessarily keeps, does or omits to do by and through his agents and employees." The Supreme Court granted certiorari and reversed per curiam, 347 U.S. 909, 74 S.Ct. 473, 98 L.Ed. 1067 (1954): "The jury was instructed that the knowledge of petitioners' employees was chargeable to petitioners in determining petitioners' wilfulness. Because of the instruction, the Government has confessed error. We agree, and accordingly reverse the judgment and remand the case to the District Court for retrial."

8. What, then, of a prosecution of the partnership rather than the partners? In *United States v. A & P Trucking Co.*, 358 U.S. 121, 79 S.Ct. 203, 3 L.Ed.2d 165 (1958), the government appealed the dismissal of criminal charges against two partnerships. As for charges brought under 49 U.S.C.A. § 322(a), a part of the Motor Carrier Act, which provided a penalty for "any person knowingly and willfully violating" certain provisions,

the government pointed out that the Act defined person to mean "any individual, firm, copartnership, corporation, company, association or joint-stock association." As for charges brought under 18 U.S.C.A. § 835, dealing with "whoever knowingly violates" ICC regulations on the transport of dangerous articles, the government relied on 1 U.S.C.A. § 1, which provides that "in determining the meaning of any Act of Congress, unless the context indicates otherwise * * * the words 'person' and 'whoever' include corporations, companies, firms, partnerships, societies, and joint stock companies, as well as individuals." The Court reversed:

"We think that partnerships as entities may be proceeded against under both § 322(a) and § 835. The purpose of both statutes is clear: to ensure compliance by motor carriers, among others, with safety and other requirements laid down by the Interstate Commerce Commission in the exercise of its statutory duty to regulate the operations of interstate carriers for hire. In the effectuation of this policy it certainly makes no difference whether the carrier which commits the infraction is organized as a corporation, a joint stock company, a partnership, or an individual proprietorship. The mischief is the same, and we think that Congress intended to make the consequences of infraction the same.

"True, the common law made a distinction between a corporation and a partnership, deeming the latter not a separate entity for purposes of suit. But the power of Congress to change the common-law rule is not to be doubted. We think it beyond dispute that it has done so in § 322(a) for, as we have seen, 'person' in that section is expressly defined in the Motor Carrier Act to include partnerships. We think it likewise has done so in § 835, since we find nothing in that section which would justify us not applying to the word 'whoever' the definition given it in 1 U.S.C.A. § 1, which includes partnerships. Section 835 makes regulations promulgated by the ICC for the transportation of dangerous articles binding on 'all common carriers.' In view of the fact that many motor carriers are organized as partnerships rather than as corporations, the conclusion is not lightly to be reached that Congress intended that some carriers should not be subject to the full gamut of sanctions provided for infractions of ICC regulations merely because of the form under which they were organized to do business. More particularly, we perceive no reason why Congress should have intended to make partnership motor carriers criminally liable for infractions of § 322(a), but not for violations of § 835."

Four members of the Court dissented in part: "If the rule of strict construction of a criminal statute is to obtain, 18 U.S.C. § 835 must be read narrowly to reflect the prevailing view of partnership law. If the entity theory is to be applied for the purpose of imposing criminal penalties on partnership assets, where the partners are wholly innocent of any wrongful act, it should be done only on the unequivocal command of Congress, as is the case under the Motor Carrier Act."

UNITED STATES v. PARK

Supreme Court of the United States, 1975.

421 U.S. 658, 95 S.Ct. 1903, 44 L.Ed.2d 489.

Mr. Chief Justice Burger delivered the opinion of the Court. * * *

Acme Markets, Inc., is a national retail food chain with approximately 36,000 employees, 874 retail outlets, 12 general warehouses, and four special warehouses. Its headquarters, including the office of the president, respondent Park, who is chief executive officer of the corporation, are located in Philadelphia, Pennsylvania. In a five-count information filed in the United States District Court for the District of Maryland, the Government charged Acme and respondent with violations of the Federal Food, Drug and Cosmetic Act. Each count of the information alleged that the defendants had received food that had been shipped in interstate commerce and that, while the food was being held for sale in Acme's Baltimore warehouse following shipment in interstate commerce, they caused it to be held in a building accessible to rodents and to be exposed to contamination by rodents. These acts were alleged to have resulted in the food being adulterated within the meaning of 21 U.S.C. §§ 342(a)(3) and (4),[1] in violation of 21 U.S.C. § 331(k).[2]

Acme pleaded guilty to each count of the information. Respondent pleaded not guilty. The evidence at trial demonstrated that in April 1970 the Food and Drug Administration (FDA) advised respondent by letter of insanitary conditions in Acme's Philadelphia warehouse. In 1971 FDA found that similar conditions existed in the firm's Baltimore warehouse. An FDA consumer safety officer testified concerning evidence of rodent infestation and other insanitary conditions discovered during a 12–day inspection of the Baltimore warehouse in November and December 1971. He also related that a second inspection of the warehouse had been conducted in March 1972.[5] On that occasion the inspectors found that there had been improvement in the sanitary conditions, but that "there was still evidence of rodent activity in the building and in the warehouse and we found some rodent-contaminated lots of food items."

The Government also presented testimony by the Chief of Compliance of FDA's Baltimore office, who informed respondent by letter of the conditions at the Baltimore warehouse after the first inspection. There was testimony by Acme's Baltimore division vice president, who had responded to the letter on behalf of Acme and respondent and who described the steps taken to remedy the insanitary conditions discovered by both inspections. The Government's final witness, Acme's vice president for legal affairs and assistant secretary, identified respondent as the president and chief executive officer of the company and read a bylaw prescribing the duties of the chief executive officer.[7] He testified that respondent functioned by delegating "normal operating duties," including sanitation, but that he retained "certain things, which are the big, broad principles of the operation of the company," and had "the responsibility of seeing that they all work together." * * *

Respondent was the only defense witness. He testified that, although all of Acme's employees were in a sense under his general direction, the company had an "organizational structure for responsibilities for certain functions" according to which different phases of

1. Section 402 of the Act, 21 U.S.C. § 342, provides in pertinent part:

"A food shall be deemed to be adulterated—(a) * * * (3) if it consists in whole or in part of any filthy, putrid, or decomposed substance, or if it is otherwise unfit for food; or (4) if it has been prepared, packed, or held under insanitary conditions whereby it may have become contaminated with filth, or whereby it may have been rendered injurious to health * * *."

2. Section 301(k) of the Act, 21 U.S.C. § 331(k), provides:

"The following acts and the causing thereof are prohibited:

* * *

"(k) The alteration, mutilation, destruction, obliteration, or removal of the whole or any part of the labeling of, or the doing of any other act with respect to, a food, drug, device, or cosmetic, if such act is done while such article is held for sale (whether or not the first sale) after shipment in interstate commerce and results in such article being adulterated or misbranded."

5. The first four counts of the information alleged violations corresponding to the observations of the inspectors during the November and December 1971 inspection. The fifth count alleged violations corresponding to observations during the March 1972 inspection.

7. The bylaw provided in pertinent part:

"The Chairman of the board of directors or the president shall be the chief executive officer of the company as the board of directors may from time to time determine. He shall, subject to the board of directors, have general and active supervision of the affairs, business, offices and employees of the company * * *.

"He shall, from time to time, in his discretion or at the order of the board, report the operations and affairs of the company. He shall also perform such other duties and have such other powers as may be assigned to him from time to time by the board of directors."

its operation were "assigned to individuals who, in turn, have staff and departments under them." He identified those individuals responsible for sanitation and related that upon receipt of the January 1972 FDA letter, he had conferred with the vice president for legal affairs, who informed him that the Baltimore division vice president "was investigating the situation immediately and would be preparing a summary of the corrective action to reply to the letter." Respondent stated that he did not "believe there was anything [he] could have done more constructively than what [he] found was being done."

On cross-examination, respondent conceded that providing sanitary conditions for food offered for sale to the public was something that he was "responsible for in the entire operation of the company," and he stated that it was one of many phases of the company that he assigned to "dependable subordinates." Respondent was asked about and, over the objections of his counsel, admitted receiving, the April 1970 letter addressed to him from FDA regarding insanitary conditions at Acme's Philadelphia warehouse. He acknowledged that, with the exception of the division vice president, the same individuals had responsibility for sanitation in both Baltimore and Philadelphia. Finally, in response to questions concerning the Philadelphia and Baltimore incidents, respondent admitted that the Baltimore problem indicated the system for handling sanitation "wasn't working perfectly" and that as Acme's chief executive officer he was responsible for "any result which occurs in our company."

At the close of the evidence, respondent's renewed motion for a judgment of acquittal was denied. The relevant portion of the trial judge's instructions to the jury challenged by respondent is set out in the margin.[9] Respondent's counsel objected to the instructions on the ground that they failed fairly to reflect our decision in *United States v. Dotterweich,* 320 U.S. 277, 64 S.Ct. 134, 88 L.Ed. 48, and to define " 'Responsible relationship.' " The trial judge overruled the objection. The jury found respondent guilty on all counts of the information, and he was subsequently sentenced to pay a fine of $50 on each count.

The Court of Appeals reversed the conviction and remanded for a new trial. That court viewed the Government as arguing "that the conviction may be predicated solely upon a showing that * * * [respondent] was the President of the offending corporation," and it stated that as "a general proposition, some act of commission or omission is an essential element of every crime." * * *

The question presented by the Government's petition for certiorari in *United States v. Dotterweich,* supra, and the focus of this Court's opinion, was whether "the manager of a corporation, as well as the corporation itself, may be prosecuted under the Federal Food, Drug, and Cosmetic Act of 1938 for the introduction of misbranded and adulterated articles

9. "In order to find the Defendant guilty on any count of the Information, you must find beyond a reasonable doubt on each count * * *.

* * *

"Thirdly, that John R. Park held a position of authority in the operation of the business of Acme Markets, Incorporated.

"However, you need not concern yourselves with the first two elements of the case. The main issue for your determination is only with the third element, whether the Defendant held a position of authority and responsibility in the business of Acme Markets.

* * *

"The statute makes individuals, as well as corporations, liable for violations. An individual is liable if it is clear, beyond a reasonable doubt, that the elements of the adulteration of the food as to travel in interstate commerce are present. As I have instructed you in this case, they are, and that the individual had a responsible relation to the situation, even though he may not have participated personally.

"The individual is or could be liable under the statute, even if he did not consciously do wrong. However, the fact that the Defendant is pres[id]ent and is a chief executive officer of the Acme Markets does not require a finding of guilt. Though, he need not have personally participated in the situation, he must have had a responsible relationship to the issue. The issue is, in this case, whether the Defendant, John R. Park, by virtue of his position in the company, had a position of authority and responsibility in the situation out of which these charges arose."

into interstate commerce." In *Dotterweich,* a jury had disagreed as to the corporation, a jobber purchasing drugs from manufacturers and shipping them in interstate commerce under its own label, but had convicted Dotterweich, the corporation's president and general manager. The Court of Appeals reversed the conviction on the ground that only the drug dealer, whether corporation or individual, was subject to the criminal provisions of the Act, and that where the dealer was a corporation, an individual connected therewith might be held personally only if he was operating the corporation "as his 'alter ego.' "

In reversing the judgment of the Court of Appeals and reinstating Dotterweich's conviction, this Court looked to the purposes of the Act and noted that they "touch phases of the lives and health of the people which, in the circumstances of modern industrialism, are largely beyond self-protection." It observed that the Act is of "a now familiar type" which "dispenses with the conventional requirement for criminal conduct—awareness of some wrongdoing. In the interest of the larger good it puts the burden of acting at hazard upon a person otherwise innocent but standing in responsible relation to a public danger."

Central to the Court's conclusion that individuals other than proprietors are subject to the criminal provisions of the Act was the reality that "the only way in which a corporation can act is through the individuals who act on its behalf." The Court also noted that corporate officers had been subject to criminal liability under the Federal Food and Drugs Act of 1906, and it observed that a contrary result under the 1938 legislation would be incompatible with the expressed intent of Congress to "enlarge and stiffen the penal net" and to discourage a view of the Act's criminal penalties as a " 'license fee for the conduct of an illegitimate business.' "

At the same time, however, the Court was aware of the concern which was the motivating factor in the Court of Appeals' decision, that literal enforcement "might operate too harshly by sweeping within its condemnation any person however remotely entangled in the proscribed shipment." A limiting principle, in the form of "settled doctrines of criminal law" defining those who "are responsible for the commission of a misdemeanor", was available. In this context, the Court concluded, those doctrines dictated that the offense was committed "by all who have * * * a responsible share in the furtherance of the transaction which the statute outlaws".

The Court recognized that, because the Act dispenses with the need to prove "consciousness of wrongdoing", it may result in hardship even as applied to those who share "[a] responsibility in the business process resulting in" a violation. It regarded as "too treacherous" an attempt "to define or even to indicate by way of illustration the class of employees which stands in such a responsible relation." The question of responsibility, the Court said, depends "on the evidence produced at the trial and its submission—assuming the evidence warrants it—to the jury under appropriate guidance." The Court added: "In such matters the good sense of prosecutors, the wise guidance of trial judges, and the ultimate judgment of juries must be trusted."

The rule that corporate employees who have "a responsible share in the furtherance of the transaction which the statute outlaws" are subject to the criminal provisions of the Act was not formulated in a vacuum. Cases under the Federal Food and Drugs Act of 1906 reflected the view both that knowledge or intent were not required to be proved in prosecutions under its criminal provisions, and that responsible corporate agents could be subjected to the liability thereby imposed. Moreover, the principle had been recognized that a corporate agent, through whose act, default, or omission the corporation committed a crime, was himself guilty individually of that crime. The principle had been applied whether or not the crime required "consciousness of wrongdoing", and it had been applied not only to those corporate agents who themselves committed the criminal act, but also to those who by virtue of their managerial positions or other similar relation to the actor could be deemed responsible for its commission.

In the latter class of cases, the liability of managerial officers did not depend on their knowledge of, or personal participation in, the act made criminal by the statute. Rather, where the statute under which they were prosecuted dispensed with "consciousness of wrongdoing", and omission or failure to act was deemed a sufficient basis for a responsible corporate agent's liability. It was enough in such cases that, by virtue of the relationship he bore to the corporation, the agent had the power to have prevented the act complained of. * * *

Thus *Dotterweich* and the cases which have followed reveal that in providing sanctions which reach and touch the individuals who execute the corporate mission—and this is by no means necessarily confined to a single corporate agent or employee—the Act imposes not only a positive duty to seek out and remedy violations when they occur but also, and primarily, a duty to implement measures that will insure that violations will not occur. The requirements of foresight and vigilance imposed on responsible corporate agents are beyond question demanding, and perhaps onerous, but they are no more stringent than the public has a right to expect of those who voluntarily assume positions of authority in business enterprises whose services and products affect the health and well-being of the public that supports them.

The Act does not, as we observed in *Dotterweich,* make criminal liability turn on "awareness of some wrongdoing" or "conscious fraud". The duty imposed by Congress on responsible corporate agents is, we emphasize, one that requires the highest standard of foresight and vigilance, but the Act, in its criminal aspect, does not require that which is objectively impossible. The theory upon which responsible corporate agents are held criminally accountable for "causing" violations of the Act permits a claim that a defendant was "powerless" to prevent or correct the violation to "be raised defensively at a trial on the merits." If such a claim is made, the defendant has the burden of coming forward with evidence, but this does not alter the Government's ultimate burden of proving beyond a reasonable doubt the defendant's guilt, including his power, in light of the duty imposed by the Act, to prevent or correct the prohibited condition. Congress has seen fit to enforce the accountability of responsible corporate agents dealing with products which may affect the health of consumers by penal sanctions cast in rigorous terms, and the obligation of the courts is to give them effect so long as they do not violate the Constitution.

We cannot agree with the Court of Appeals that it was incumbent upon the District Court to instruct the jury that the Government had the burden of establishing "wrongful action" in the sense in which the Court of Appeals used that phrase. The concept of a "responsible relationship" to, or a "responsible share" in, a violation of the Act indeed imports some measure of blameworthiness; but it is equally clear that the Government establishes a prima facie case when it introduces evidence sufficient to warrant a finding by the trier of the facts that the defendant had, by reason of his position in the corporation, responsibility and authority either to prevent in the first instance, or promptly to correct, the violation complained of, and that he failed to do so. The failure thus to fulfill the duty imposed by the interaction of the corporate agent's authority and the statute furnishes a sufficient causal link. The considerations which prompted the imposition of this duty, and the scope of the duty, provide the measure of culpability. * * *

Reading the entire charge satisfies us that the jury's attention was adequately focused on the issue of respondent's authority with respect to the conditions that formed the basis of the alleged violations. Viewed as a whole, the charge did not permit the jury to find guilt solely on the basis of respondent's position in the corporation; rather, it fairly advised the jury that to find guilt it must find respondent "had a responsible relation to the situation," and "by virtue of his position * * * had authority and responsibility" to deal with the situation. The situation referred to could only be "food * * * held in unsanitary conditions in a warehouse with the result that it consisted, in part, of filth or * * * may have been contaminated with filth." * * *

We conclude that, viewed as a whole and in the context of the trial, the charge was not misleading and contained an adequate statement of the law to guide the jury's determination. Although it would have been better to give an instruction more precisely relating the legal issue to the facts of the case, we cannot say that the failure to provide the amplification requested by respondent was an abuse of discretion. Finally, we note that there was no request for an instruction that the Government was required to prove beyond a reasonable doubt that respondent was not without the power or capacity to affect the conditions which founded the charges in the information.[17] In light of the evidence adduced at trial, we find no basis to conclude that the failure of the trial court to give such an instruction *sua sponte* was plain error or a defect affecting substantial rights. * * *

Respondent testified in his defense that he had employed a system in which he relied upon his subordinates, and that he was ultimately responsible for this system. He testified further that he had found these subordinates to be "dependable" and had "great confidence" in them. By this and other testimony respondent evidently sought to persuade the jury that, as the president of a large corporation, he had no choice but to delegate duties to those in whom he reposed confidence, that he had no reason to suspect his subordinates were failing to insure compliance with the Act, and that, once violations were unearthed, acting through those subordinates he did everything possible to correct them.

Although we need not decide whether this testimony would have entitled respondent to an instruction as to his lack of power had he requested it,[19] the testimony clearly created the "need" for rebuttal evidence. [Thus, it was not error, as the Court of Appeals had believed, to admit into evidence the fact that the respondent had been advised in 1970 of insanitary conditions in the *Philadelphia* warehouse.]

Reversed.

Mr. Justice Stewart, with whom Mr. Justice Marshall and Mr. Justice Powell join, dissenting.

The trial judge instructed the jury to find Park guilty if it found beyond a reasonable doubt that Park "had a responsible relation to the situation * * *. The issue is, in this case, whether the Defendant, John R. Park, by virtue of his position in the company, had a position of authority and responsibility in the situation out of which these charges arose." Requiring, as it did, a verdict of guilty upon a finding of "responsibility," this instruction standing alone could have been construed as a direction to convict if the jury found Park "responsible" for the condition in the sense that his position as chief executive officer gave him formal responsibility within the structure of the corporation. But the trial judge went on specifically to caution the jury not to attach such a meaning to his instruction, saying that "the fact that the Defendant is present [*sic*] and is a chief executive officer of the

---

17. Counsel for respondent submitted only two requests for charge: (1) "Statutes such as the ones the Government seeks to apply here are criminal statutes and should be strictly construed," and (2) "The fact that John Park is President and Chief Executive Officer of Acme Markets, Inc. does not of itself justify a finding of guilty under Counts I through V of the Information."

19. Assuming, *arguendo*, that it would be objectively impossible for a senior corporate agent to control fully day-to-day conditions in 874 retail outlets, it does not follow that such a corporate agent could not prevent or remedy promptly violations of elementary sanitary conditions in 16 regional warehouses.

Acme Markets does not require a finding of guilt." "Responsibility" as used by the trial judge therefore had whatever meaning the jury in its unguided discretion chose to give it.

The instructions, therefore, expressed nothing more than a tautology. They told the jury: "You must find the defendant guilty if you find that he is to be held accountable for this adulterated food." In other words: "You must find the defendant guilty if you conclude that he is guilty." * * *

We deal here with a criminal conviction, not a civil forfeiture. It is true that the crime was but a misdemeanor and the penalty in this case light. But under the statute even a first conviction can result in imprisonment for a year, and a subsequent offense is a felony carrying a punishment of up to three years in prison. So the standardless conviction approved today can serve in another case tomorrow to support a felony conviction and a substantial prison sentence. However highly the Court may regard the social objectives of the Food, Drug, and Cosmetic Act, that regard cannot serve to justify a criminal conviction so wholly alien to fundamental principles of our law.

The *Dotterweich* case stands for two propositions, and I accept them both. First, "any person" within the meaning of 21 U.S.C. § 333 may include any corporate officer or employee "standing in responsible relation" to a condition or transaction forbidden by the Act. Second, a person may be convicted of a criminal offense under the Act even in the absence of "the conventional requirement for criminal conduct—awareness of some wrongdoing."

But before a person can be convicted of a criminal violation of this Act, a jury must find—and must be clearly instructed that it must find—evidence beyond a reasonable doubt that he engaged in wrongful conduct amounting at least to common-law negligence. There were no such instructions, and clearly, therefore, no such finding in this case.

For these reasons, I cannot join the Court in affirming Park's criminal conviction.

Notes and Questions

1. Would the Court have reached the same result if Park had received the more serious penalties allowed under the Act? Consider in this regard a survey of the reported decisions in the 32–year period between *Dotterweich* and *Park*, David F. O'Keefe & Marc H. Shapiro, *Personal Criminal Liability Under the Federal Food, Drug, and Cosmetic Act*, 30 Food Drug Cosm.L.J. 5, 18–19 (1975), noting: "Jail sentences, terms of probation, and criminal fines have been imposed, all without the necessity of proof of *scienter*, and in situations where persons other than the convicted defendant performed the violative acts. In one case, a jail sentence was imposed although the offense charged related to economic misbranding, without risk to public health or safety. In another case, the court ruled that intent was not a necessary element, even for conviction of a felony under the Act."

In *Lady J. Lingerie, Inc. v. City of Jacksonville*, 176 F.3d 1358 (11th Cir.1999), the court concluded: "Park's only punishment was a fine; incarceration is a different matter. Commentators distinguish public welfare offenses from offenses for which the penalty involves imprisonment, and argue that respondeat superior is inappropriate for these 'true crimes.'. We agree and hold that due process prohibits the state from imprisoning a person without proof of some form of personal blameworthiness more than a 'responsible relation.' "

2. Is the availability of criminal sanctions for corporate officers an essential part of the enforcement machinery under the Act, or would criminal liability on the corporation suffice? Compare:

(a) Marsha Cohen, *Enforcement Under the Food, Drug and Cosmetic Act—The Park Case in Perspective,* 30 Food Drug Cosm.L.J. 676, 681 (1975): "Del Monte cannot go to jail. General Mills cannot go to jail. Pillsbury cannot go to jail. Acme Markets cannot go to jail. All four could absorb sizable fines: their financial losses, if any, are in any case borne by the stockholders rather than by the corporate officials who bear ultimate responsibility for the firm's compliance with laws written to protect the consumer. But the fear of being branded a criminal—even though I doubt John Park is a social outcast because of his misdemeanor conviction—and the mere possibility, albeit remote, of a prison term, strikes terror in executive hearts, creating a potent deterrent for which civil sanctions and criminal sanctions against the corporation alone cannot substitute. The mere existence of this sanction helps to create the desired behavior of full compliance with the Act."

(b) William McVisk, *Toward a Rational Theory of Criminal Liability for the Corporate Executive,* 69 J.Crim.L. & Criminology 75, 88 (1978): "By imposing vague and seemingly arbitrary standards of conduct, enforced by criminal sanctions, the Court's doctrine may well discourage responsible people from taking jobs in highly regulated industries. The long run result may be less careful operation of these businesses. Because the Court's system of liability does not specifically provide a defense for individual officers who have taken reasonable steps to prevent violations from occurring, it fails to provide adequate incentive to take these steps. Further, because the standards imposed seem arbitrary and impossible to fulfill, judges are likely to refuse to use the sanction of imprisonment and will probably impose very light fines, thus reducing the effectiveness of the regulation still further. Most importantly, the Court has failed to provide any clear direction which would guide corporate officials in their attempts to comply with the law."

3. Does *Park* include a requirement of culpability, or does it impose strict liability? Compare the views of the following two commentators (who also disagree about many other aspects of *Park*):

(a) Norman Abrams, *Criminal Liability of Corporate Officers for Strict Liability Offenses—A Comment on Dotterweich and Park,* 28 U.C.L.A.L.Rev. 463, 469–70 (1981): "Most courts are likely to agree with Justice Stewart—who in dissent characterized the Chief Justice's opinion as embodying a negligence standard—and conclude that *Park* supports the imposition of criminal liability only where there is a departure from a standard of care. Certainly the Burger opinion is also replete with language which smacks of negligence—'the defendant's ... power, in light of the duty imposed by the Act, to prevent or correct ... some measure of blameworthiness ... the scope of the duty, provide[s] the measure of culpability.' * * *

"Given language that speaks of 'the highest standard of foresight' and that which is not 'objectively impossible', the most plausible interpretation is that the culpability standard thereby established is one of extraordinary care. Under this view, all that must be proved by the government is a deviation from that standard—something certainly less than common law negligence; it can be characterized as 'very slight' or 'slight' negligence to be distinguished from 'ordinary' negligence."

(b) Kathleen F. Brickey, *Criminal Liability of Corporate Officers for Strict Liability Offenses—Another View,* 35 Vand.L.Rev. 1337, 1363–64 (1982): "The Chief Justice explained that proof that the officer had the responsibility and the power to prevent the violation and that he failed to fulfill the duty to do so establishes the required causal link between the officer and the violation. Thus, while a corporate officer cannot be blamed for a violation unless he is factually connected with it, the prosecution may establish the required factual connection without also proving a culpable state of mind.

"That the Court did not intend its reference to blameworthiness in this passage to connote any requirement of a culpable mental state is reinforced by its explicit rejection, in the same passage, of the Fourth Circuit's position regarding the Government's burden of proof. The court of appeals had stated that Park could not be found guilty unless the Government established 'some wrongful action' on his part.''

4. FDA agents inspected a food storage warehouse on the island of Maui, Hawaii, in May and June of 1972. They discovered that birds were flying in and out of the warehouse, perching on overhead sprinkler pipes and on bags of rice, and eating from rice bags. The corporation and its president were charged with violating the Federal Food, Drug and Cosmetic Act. The evidence showed that the president had been aware of the bird infestation problem as early as August 1971, and that numerous devices to prevent birds from gaining entry to the warehouse had been tried, but none of them was completely successful. In the spring of 1972, it was decided to enclose the food storage area of the warehouse in a huge wire cage. The materials necessary to do this were ordered from the mainland, but they had not been received by the time of the inspections. Both the corporation and the president have asked for an "objective impossibility" instruction, but the government contends "that the defense is available only to the corporate officer and not to the corporation itself, and applies only when the officer was in fact powerless to prevent or correct the violation, even by suspending the corporation's food warehousing activity if necessary.''[a] Should the judge give the instruction?

5. Sometimes an officer or employee will escape liability because the statute in question is construed as being applicable only to the organization he serves. Illustrative is *State v. Riley*, 158 W.Va. 823, 215 S.E.2d 460 (1975), overturning the conviction of truck drivers, employees of a motor carrier, found not to have the required identification card displayed in their vehicles. Noting that the statute said it "shall be unlawful for any motor carrier to operate any power unit within this State unless such identification card is displayed" (in contrast to another part of the same statute making it "unlawful for the motor carrier, his agent, servant, or employee, or any other person to use or display said identification card" after it had expired), the court concluded: "The appellants as mere employees do not come within the definition of 'motor carrier' and thus could not be prosecuted individually for failure to display the required identification card.''

Similarly, in *Day v. State*, 168 Ind.App. 68, 341 N.E.2d 209 (1976), the court held that the president of a professional association which employed a lobbyist could not be convicted of failing to file an expense statement within a specified time, as the statute imposed that duty on the "person, firm, corporation or association employing legislative counsel or legislative agents." The court concluded that the "statute clearly imposes the duty on the association as a separate entity—not on the officers or members of the association.''

Can these cases be squared with *Park?* In light of the fact, as we saw earlier, that a person may be an accomplice to a crime he cannot commit directly, are these decisions correct? Is it significant that there was no showing that the truck drivers knew they were driving without the permits, or that the association president knew the expense statement had not been filed? What if such knowledge had been established?

6. If a person has engaged in conduct which would otherwise suffice for personal criminal liability, it is no defense that he was acting on behalf of a corporation. Illustrative is *People v. Cheff*, 37 Mich.App. 1, 194 N.W.2d 401 (1971), where the defendant, president of a mortgage corporation, obtained money under false pretenses with intent to defraud. The court held: "Even though the money was received and misappropriated by the

---

a. See *United States v. Y. Hata & Co., Ltd.*, 535   F.2d 508 (9th Cir.1976), affirming the convictions.

corporation, the scheme for acquisition of the funds was a fraudulent act perpetrated by Mr. Cheff, the president and principal officer of the corporation. Thus, in the light of the generally recognized principle that a corporate officer is criminally responsible for the fraudulent larceny of the property of another through a corporate act where the act was done by the individual officer, at his discretion, or by his permission, it was no defense here that the money was paid to the corporation and not to the defendant, Cheff, personally."

7. A somewhat different contention was made in *United States v. Sain*, 141 F.3d 463 (3d Cir.1998), where Sain and his corporation (AEC) were both convicted under the Major Fraud Act, which proscribes any scheme to defraud the government undertaken by "a prime contractor with the United States." In response to Sain's challenge to his own conviction, the court stated:

"Sain's argument is pure sophistry; its fundamental inconsistency is its fatal flaw. It is inconsistent because, on the one hand, Sain contends that AEC, because it is a corporation, is a separate entity that entered into the contract with the Army, thereby insulating him personally from any criminal liability for the fraud. On the other hand, * * * Sain asserts that given his stock ownership and control of AEC, he and the corporation are actually the same entity and, therefore, he cannot, in essence, aid and abet himself. * * *

"One of the principal reasons why individuals choose the corporate form is that it is a separate entity and offers protection from personal liability for its debts. * * * AEC, because it is a corporation, is a separate legal entity, even though Sain owned all the stock. Thus, it has the capacity of being aided and abetted. To hold otherwise would allow the controlling stockholder of a corporation to enjoy the benefits of the corporate form, protection from personal liability for corporation's debts, without accepting the burden of assuming criminal responsibility when the individual causes the corporation to commit a crime."

SECTION 11. POST–CRIME AID

STEPHENS v. STATE

Supreme Court of Wyoming, 1987.

734 P.2d 555.

Brown, Chief Justice.

This is an appeal from a conviction of accessory after the fact to the commission of a burglary. The issues raised by appellant are whether or not there was sufficient evidence of the element of "rendering assistance" and of the element of "intent" to sustain the conviction. We hold that there was not sufficient evidence of either element, and reverse the conviction.

On December 1, 1985, appellant was at his ex-wife's residence with Harry Van Buren. Appellant agreed to let Van Buren stay with him that evening and in return Van Buren agreed to help appellant look for a part for appellant's truck the following morning. Appellant left the house about three o'clock that afternoon, while Van Buren remained. The next time appellant saw Van Buren was about 8:00 that evening. At that time, Van Buren informed appellant and appellant's girl friend that he had burglarized Yellowstone Electric hours earlier. Appellant told Van Buren he "didn't want to hear about it." The next morning appellant and his girlfriend awoke to find Van Buren gone. He returned around 7:30 a.m., and went with appellant to look for the truck part, as previously arranged.

When appellant was unable to find the truck part he needed he asked Van Buren to give him some money to purchase a car. Van Buren complied, giving appellant $100. Thereafter, an automobile was purchased and the two traveled back to the home, appellant driving the recently purchased car while Van Buren drove the truck. Upon arriving home, appellant noticed that Van Buren, having arrived home already, was being questioned by police officers in a police car. Subsequently, appellant was approached by the police officers.

When the officers questioned appellant about the burglary and Van Buren's possible role in it, appellant replied that he did not know anything about it. Upon further questioning, appellant informed the officers that a few years earlier he had received money from Van Buren from a similar burglary. Appellant told the officers that he had learned his lesson after the earlier burglary and would not get involved in that situation again.

About fifteen minutes later the police confronted appellant with some information they had received from his girlfriend, and appellant then admitted that he knew of the burglary and of Van Buren's role in it. Appellant also told the officers that he had told Van Buren he did not want to know about it.

The statute under which appellant was convicted reads, in part:

"(a) A person is an accessory after the fact if, with intent to hinder, delay or prevent the discovery, detection, apprehension, prosecution, detention, conviction or punishment of another for the commission of a crime, he renders assistance to the person * * *."

The two elements that appellant contends are missing are the elements of intent and rendering assistance.

"Render assistance" is defined in § 6–5–201 as follows:

"(a) As used in this article:

" * * *

"(iv) 'Render assistance' means to:

"(A) Harbor or conceal the person;

"(B) Warn the person of impending discovery or apprehension, excluding an official warning given in an effort to bring the person into compliance with the law;

" * * *

"(D) By force, intimidation or deception, obstruct anyone in the performance of any act which might aid in the discovery, detection, apprehension, prosecution, conviction or punishment of the person."

The state contends that appellant rendered assistance by harboring or concealing Van Buren and by helping Van Buren to avoid discovery and apprehension. The facts that the state relies on are that appellant provided Van Buren a place to stay the night after the burglary and that he denied knowledge of Van Buren's involvement in the burglary. Case law from other jurisdictions does not support this argument.

In the case of *State v. Clifford*, 263 Or. 436, 502 P.2d 1371 (1972), the defendant saw Douglas Wright a day after Wright murdered two people and kidnapped a five-year-old boy. After learning of the murder, defendant was arrested on other charges and asked by the police if he had seen Wright. Defendant told the police either that he had not seen Wright, or that he had not seen him in a long time. The Oregon Supreme Court, after reciting the common-law history of the offense of being an accessory after the fact, concluded that there was no sharp line between conduct which constituted aiding or concealing and that which does not. However, some type of line may be drawn from examples given.

" * * * The examples describing criminal conduct uniformly consist of an affirmative act from which the intention to aid an offender, to escape arrest, conviction or punishment is obvious. None of the examples indicate that a mere denial of knowledge of the whereabouts of an offender at some time in the past would amount to accessorial conduct."

Furthermore, other cases uniformly support the conclusion reached by the Oregon Supreme Court, that is, merely denying knowledge of the principal's involvement in a crime will not give rise to a charge of accessory after the fact. A mere denial of knowledge is to be differentiated from an "[a]ffirmative statement of facts tending to raise any defense for (the principal), or a statement within itself indicating an effort to shield or protect (the principal)." Such an affirmative statement would be such as supplying a false alibi. This amounts to more than passive nondisclosure.

In the case here, appellant did nothing more than passively deny knowledge of Van Buren's involvement in the burglary. When finally confronted by the statement made by his girlfriend, appellant relented and told the police what he really knew. This does not rise to the level of helping Van Buren avoid discovery and detection, especially in light of appellant's probable intent, which will be discussed later.

Further, we question whether appellant actually harbored Van Buren. Again, case law supports appellant. Here, the distinction is between active concealment and merely allowing a person to stay in one's home. This distinction is examined in the case of *United States v. Bissonette*, 586 F.2d 73 (8th Cir.1978). There, the defendant kept several juveniles, including her grandson, in her basement following a shooting and jail break, of which she was aware. "She [the defendant] told [the juveniles] and the others to stay in the basement when she was out of the house, to keep the doors locked, and the blinds drawn. In the following days, she purchased food and cooked for [the juveniles] and cashed a check for [her grandson.]"

The federal court found that the defendant's conduct went beyond merely offering the juveniles the comforts of her home. " * * * [s]he instructed the fugitives to stay in the basement when she was out of the house, to keep the blinds drawn, and the doors locked; she berated them when they tried to contact friends outside the house, lest their discovery result." This all resulted in an affirmative, continuing pattern of conduct establishing the intent of the defendant to prevent apprehension of her grandson by the authorities.

The *Bissonette* case is far different than the case before us. Here, appellant had agreed to let Van Buren spend the night at his home. This agreement was made before appellant had any knowledge of a burglary. Further, appellant did not keep Van Buren concealed, but rather, was accompanied by him in public to look for a truck part, and then to purchase a car. There was no active concealment.

Appellant also contends there was insufficient evidence of intent to uphold his conviction. The requisite intent, from a plain reading of the statute, is to hinder, prevent or delay the discovery or apprehension, etc., of the principal. Once more, case law is in appellant's favor.

"If, however, the act is a mere false denial of knowledge which may have been motivated by self-interest, there must also be evidence from which the jury could infer that the actor told the lie with the intent to aid the offender and that the lie was, under the existing circumstances, likely to aid the offender to escape arrest or punishment. * * * "

The intent evident from the testimony presented at trial was clearly self-motivated. First, Van Buren had already been apprehended by the police when they questioned appellant. Second, appellant knew that he was guilty himself of receiving stolen property (the $100 that Van Buren gave him to buy a car). Further, appellant knew that four years ago when an almost identical situation arose, he ended up with a felony on his record and a two to four year sentence, suspended, with four years probation. Appellant certainly had plenty of self-interest in denying any knowledge of Van Buren's activities in the present instance. Further, no other evidence presented at trial indicated any intent of appellant to benefit Van Buren.

The standard of review with respect to the sufficiency of the evidence is that we examine the evidence in a light most favorable to the state to determine if there is sufficient evidence to uphold the verdict. Even when we apply this standard, we are unable to find evidence sufficient to uphold appellant's conviction, either on the element of intent or of rendering assistance.

The conviction is reversed and the charge of accessory after the fact is dismissed.

Notes and Questions

1. In *Commonwealth v. Devlin*, 366 Mass. 132, 314 N.E.2d 897 (1974), defendant was convicted of being an accessory after the fact[a] to assault with intent to murder. Bartoloni stabbed another inmate in block B–2 of the state prison. Defendant, also an inmate, then entered the block, asked what had happened, was summoned to cell No. 3 as the block representative, and was told a knife had been kicked into the cell. Defendant picked up the knife with a T-shirt, apparently rubbed it with the shirt, and then handed it over to a guard. The court reversed:

"1. We assume, although we need not so decide, that the evidence was sufficient to show that the actions of the defendant constituted aid to the principal felon, presumably by removing his fingerprints from the knife. However, we do not believe there was sufficient evidence that the defendant either knew that a felony had been committed, or that he knew the identity of the principal felon, to warrant submission of the case to the jury. The record does not indicate that the blood later shown by chemical tests to have been present on the knife was visible to the defendant. Even assuming that it was, the Commonwealth presented no testimony that would indicate the defendant knew how the knife had been used. While mere possession of the knife was no doubt a violation of prison regulations, and even assuming it was a crime, it was certainly not a felony to which the defendant could have been an accessory after the fact. The defendant's own testimony was that he was not present when the disturbance began and was inquiring of other inmates as to what had occurred when he was called to the scene of his alleged crime. It would be mere speculation to conclude that he had learned of the felony or such details as who had committed it.

"We hold that knowledge of the particular felony which has occurred is an element of the crime of being an accessory after the fact which must be proved beyond a reasonable doubt. That is to say, one charged as such an accessory must be shown to have been aware,

---

a. The applicable statute reads: "Whoever, after the commission of a felony, harbors, conceals, maintains or assists the principal felon or accessory before the fact, or gives such offender any other aid, knowing that he has committed a felony or has been accessory thereto before the fact, with intent that he shall avoid or escape detention, arrest, trial or punishment, shall be an accessory after the fact, and, except as otherwise provided, be punished by imprisonment in the state prison for not more than seven years or in jail for not more than two and one half years or by a fine of not more than one thousand dollars. The fact that the defendant is the husband or wife, or by consanguinity, affinity or adoption, the parent or grandparent, child or grandchild, brother or sister of the offender, shall be a defence to a prosecution under this section. If such a defendant testifies solely as to the existence of such relationship, he shall not be subject to cross examination on any other subject matter, nor shall his criminal record, if any, except for perjury or subornation of perjury, be admissible to impeach his credibility."

by his observations or by information transmitted to him, of the substantial facts of the felonious crime.[b] Since there was a failure to prove that knowledge in this case, a directed verdict for the defendant is required.

"2. The accessory after the fact must also be shown to have had knowledge of the identity of the principal felon. There was not the slightest showing here that the defendant was aware that the principal, Bartoloni, was concerned in the matter. For that reason too, the defendant must have a directed verdict.

"Since there is total absence of knowledge here, we need not reach discussion of the minimum evidence which might be required to establish sufficient knowledge of identity. Nor need we discuss the nature of such proof.[5]

"The common law emphasized, as a basis for liability, the personal relationship between principal and accessory. In fact, the accessory was often considered 'an accomplice in the original crime.' The accessory was defined by his direct, personal assistance as one who receives and comforts, or conceals the principal felon. This assistance could be provided in a variety of ways: '[G]enerally, any assistance whatever given to a felon, to hinder his being apprehended, tried, or suffering punishment, makes the assistor an accessory. As furnishing him with a horse to escape his pursuers, money or victuals to support him, a house or other shelter to conceal him, or open force and violence to rescue or protect him.' 4 Blackstone, *Commentaries,* 37–38 (1769).

"The requirement that relief or assistance be given to the felon personally is also illustrated by the common law doctrine that one could never be convicted as an accessory after the fact for receiving stolen goods 'because he only received the stolen goods and did nothing to receive the felon.' This crime is, of course, now separately provided for by statute.

"A proper interpretation of G.L. c. 274, § 4, also demands incorporation of this knowledge requirement. The language of the statute is in the common law form. The words themselves require aid to the principal felon 'knowing that he has committed a felony.' The plain meaning of these words requires knowledge of the identity of the principal. * * *

"3. In summary, it is clear that there was insufficient proof of the requisite elements of the statutory crime charged in the indictment. It may be considered that the defendant's acts constituted what is in some jurisdictions called 'obstruction of justice.' He was not so charged and therefore we need not consider whether such a common law crime exists in Massachusetts."

2. Consider the following statement of facts in *Outlaw v. United States,* 632 A.2d 408 (D.C.App.1993), with a view to determining whether the court was correct in deciding, as to the curiously-cognomened Noah Outlaw, that "the evidence was insufficient to prove that he was an accessory after the fact to murder or to any lesser included offense" (which the court did without reaching "the principal question briefed by the parties, namely, whether one may be convicted of being an accessory after the fact to murder on the basis of actions taken while the decedent was still alive"[c]):

b. There is no suggestion here that the knowledge of the accessory must be such that he is able to put a name or label on the felony—only that he is aware of the substantial facts which make up the elements of the felony.

5. For example, suppose a defendant witnessed the flight of a robber, who was a stranger to him, whereupon the defendant wilfully impeded pursuit of the rob-

ber by a police officer. Is this sufficient knowledge by the defendant as to the identity of the felon?

c. The court did, however, drop a footnote stating: "Although we need not and do not take any position on the issue, we do note as a matter of historical fact * * * that the District's statute has remained unchanged at least since the beginning of the century, and that it has been construed as consistent with the common law. As the government has acknowledged in

"The prosecution presented evidence tending to show that at approximately 11:00 a.m. on the day of the murder, Samuel Outlaw was arguing with Walter Jones over a $20 debt which Samuel claimed that Jones owed him. Jones said he did not have any money. Samuel Outlaw left and went into a nearby apartment building. He soon emerged with a small silver-colored pistol in his hand. Samuel Outlaw complained to Jones that 'you ain't going to pay me my fucking money, man,' and fired the handgun into Jones' neck. Jones grabbed his throat and began gasping for air. Jones' half-brother, Anthony Ferguson, held Jones and attempted to assist him.

"At some point during this tragic encounter, but apparently after Samuel Outlaw fired the shot, Noah Outlaw arrived on the scene. Jones was still alive. Samuel Outlaw handed Noah Outlaw the pistol. Noah Outlaw profanely reprimanded his brother because the latter had not killed Jones. He then placed the pistol in his pocket and began to walk towards Jones in a manner that at least two witnesses perceived as threatening. Several individuals immediately interceded, and Noah 'chilled' and backed off, apparently because police officers were arriving on the scene. Noah Outlaw returned the handgun to Samuel, who left the area. One witness testified that Noah had previously stated that his brother was to '[g]o to aunt somebody's house.' Noah Outlaw remained on the scene and watched the police officers as they investigated the shooting. One of the witnesses pointed Noah Outlaw out to the officers, and Noah was arrested."

3. *United States v. Hobson,* 519 F.2d 765 (9th Cir.1975): "Both Hobson and Newman were convicted of being accessories after the fact, in violation of 18 U.S.C. § 3 which provides in part:

'Whoever, knowing that an offense against the United States has been committed, receives, relieves, comforts or assists the offender in order to hinder or prevent his apprehension, trial or punishment is an accessory after the fact. * * * '

They contend that in order for them to have violated the statute they must be shown to have known that Beaty's escape (and shooting of the guard) constituted an offense *against the United States.* The district court rejected Hobson's proposed instruction to this effect and refused to grant a judgment of acquittal. The district court was correct in both rulings.

"Beaty was clearly guilty of escape. He has been convicted and sentenced to life imprisonment for that escape. There is no requirement that he had to have known that he was committing a federal offense in escaping. *See United States v. Fernandez,* 497 F.2d 730, 736–739 (9 Cir.1974). It borders on the ridiculous to suggest that Hobson and Newman could be acquitted, despite knowledge that they were aiding Beaty in hiding from the authorities, because they thought he had *only* committed murder and escape from a *State* prison. In fact, the Supreme Court has recently rejected just such a contention with respect to a conspiracy prosecution. *See United States v. Feola,* [p. 724 of this Book]."

Is this so?

4. In *United States v. Prescott,* 581 F.2d 1343 (9th Cir.1978), federal agents sought to arrest Duvernay, but found his apartment padlocked from the outside. They then asked defendant, a neighbor, if Duvernay was in her apartment. She said no, and the agents then asked permission to search her apartment. She asked if they had a warrant, they said no, and she then refused to admit them. The agents kicked down the door and found Duvernay inside. On reversal of defendant's accessory after the fact conviction, the court held that upon retrial defendant's refusal to admit the police should not be admitted into evidence

its well-researched and scholarly brief, the early common-law commentators almost invariably take the view that a defendant may not be convicted as an accessory after the fact to murder unless the victim was dead at the time the defendant committed the acts of assistance."

because under the Fourth Amendment one has a constitutional right to refuse to consent to a search:

"One cannot be penalized for passively asserting this right, regardless of one's motivation. Just as a criminal suspect may validly invoke his Fifth Amendment privilege in an effort to shield himself from criminal liability, so one may withhold consent to a warrantless search, even though one's purpose be to conceal evidence of wrongdoing.

"Had Prescott forcibly resisted the entry into her apartment, we might have a different case. We express no opinion on that question. We only hold that her passive refusal to consent to a warrantless search is privileged conduct which cannot be considered as evidence of criminal wrongdoing. If the government could use such a refusal against the citizen, an unfair and impermissible burden would be placed upon the assertion of a constitutional right and future consents would not be 'freely and voluntarily given.' "

A dissent reasoned that the refusal did have evidentiary significance and that defendant was merely entitled to a jury instruction that "assertion of Fourth Amendment rights, even if without foundation, cannot constitute the crime with which the defendant is charged."

5.   Carullo and Johnston stole gold coins in Mission, Kansas, and transported them to Kansas City, Missouri, and then to Kansas City, Kansas, to Sol's Loan Office, where Balano and Rosen provided them with clothing to replace that used in the crime and a suitcase within which to hide the coins. Balano and Rosen were charged as accessories after the fact to interstate transportation of stolen goods. On appeal of Balano's conviction, *United States v. Balano,* 618 F.2d 624 (10th Cir.1979), the court stated:

"Balano's argument that Carullo and Johnston were still in the escape phase of their crime when they reached the loan office is similarly without merit. There is no doubt that one who assists in an escape should be charged under 18 U.S.C. § 2 [as a principal] rather than 18 U.S.C. § 3 [as an accessory after the fact]. It is not necessary, however, for the principals to have come to a final resting place for the escape to have ended. The escape phase doctrine was developed to deal with those who are entangled in the consummation of the crime itself, such as getaway car drivers. In contrast, accessories after the fact '[obstruct] justice by rendering assistance to hinder or prevent the arrest of the offender after he has committed the crime.'

"Carullo and Johnston crossed the state line again after leaving Sol's Loan Office, and the sale of the coins took place shortly thereafter. However, sufficient evidence was admitted at Balano's trial to permit the jury to infer that Carullo and Johnston had made prior arrangements to 'fence' the coins at Sol's. Although they did not ultimately fence the coins there, a finding that the events at Sol's were beyond the escape phase is entirely consistent with the testimony of Carullo and Johnston. The getaway car had been abandoned, and no more furtive action was taken. We cannot consider an escape to continue until an ultimate buyer is found. The court's dismissal of the third count, based on 18 U.S.C. § 2, at the end of the first trial was therefore proper, and we cannot say the submission of the second count to the jury was improper."

6.   Exemptions along the lines of those stated in the statute applied in *Devlin* are found in most jurisdictions. Compare *Model Penal Code* § 242.3, Comment (1980): "Section 242.3 does not contain a statutory exemption, in part on the ground that this is a factor that can be taken into account at sentencing. It is hard to justify any particular limitation on an exemption provision. Furthermore, exemption rules create trial difficulties if the government bears the burden of proving that none of the specified relations exist."

Assume now a statute with exemptions like those in *Devlin*. Compare *State v. Williams,* 142 Vt. 81, 451 A.2d 1142 (1982) (where defendant's brother, a juvenile not subject to criminal prosecution, and one Bristol together committed a homicide, the defendant could not be convicted as an accessory after the fact because his acts "consisted entirely of deeds helping both his brother and Bristol"); with *State v. Mobbley,* 98 N.M. 557, 650 P.2d 841 (App.1982) (where police told defendant warrants had been issued for Mobbley and Needham and asked if "both were there" and defendant "denied that the men were there, although she knew that both men were there," defendant—the wife of Mobbley—was properly convicted).

7. In *State v. Cole,* 502 S.W.2d 443 (Mo.App.1973), an appeal of defendant's conviction for armed robbery, defendant noted that the evidence was susceptible to the interpretation that he had not been aware in advance that the passenger in his car would commit the robbery and that thus the trial judge should have given the jury an instruction that they might instead convict him of being an accessory after the fact for his conduct in driving the robber away while being pursued by the police. "Under the evidence he was either guilty as charged or he was not guilty. The crime of accessory after the fact is a distinct and separate offense and not a lesser included offense of Robbery in the First Degree by means of dangerous and deadly weapon. It would therefore have been error for the trial court to instruct on the crime of accessory after the fact."

May the prosecutor *charge* a defendant with both being a principal and an accessory after the fact? See *Thomas v. State,* 275 Ind. 499, 417 N.E.2d 1124 (1981), rejecting the notion a defendant should not have to defend against "two inconsistent theories of prosecution."

8. Most jurisdictions have rejected the old common law view that an accessory after the fact could not be tried until after the principal was found guilty. See, e.g., *State ex rel. Brown v. Thompson,* 149 W.Va. 649, 142 S.E.2d 711 (1965).

But, "the jury in the trial of the accessory must find as a fact that the principal did actually commit the crime involved." *State v. Massey,* 267 S.C. 432, 229 S.E.2d 332 (1976). What then of *State v. Price,* 278 S.C. 266, 294 S.E.2d 426 (1982), where defendant helped conceal the body after her 12–year–old son Randy strangled a playmate, and the court upheld exclusion of testimony that at the time of the killing the son was unconscious due to an epileptic seizure, reasoning that "the defense of Randy's incapacity is not available to appellant" because it "does not constitute a defense to his crime, it only relates to the degree of culpability"?

9. Most jurisdictions prescribe penalties for the accessory after the fact without reference to the penalty attached to the principal offense; five years is the most common maximum, with a range from six months to ten years. See *Osborne v. State,* 304 Md. 323, 499 A.2d 170 (1985).

10. Today, the accessory after the fact situation is dealt with by statute in most jurisdictions. These statutes often retain the accessory terminology, although the more modern approach is to abandon the traditional terminology and to cover the subject by one or more statutes creating such offenses as "hindering prosecution," "obstructing justice," "concealing or aiding a fugitive," "harboring or aiding a felon," "tampering with evidence," and "aiding escape." While some of these statutes do not extend liability beyond that which was possible under the common law accessory after the fact offense, many of them do. In contrast to the common law requirement that the accessory have known that the person aided was a felon, some statutes also cover the case in which the aider only believed that a felony had been committed or had reasonable grounds to believe that a felony had been committed, or where the person aided was in fact a felon. Some of the

statutes cover aid to both felons and misdemeanants. In a few states, the mental element has been broadened to include the situation in which the intent is "to assist a person in profiting or benefiting from the commission" of a felony or any crime.

HOLLAND v. STATE

District Court of Appeal of Florida, Second District, 1974.

302 So.2d 806.

McNULTY, CHIEF JUDGE.

Petitioner seeks review by common law certiorari of an order of the Circuit Court of Pinellas County, sitting in its appellate capacity, which reversed the county court's dismissal of an indictment charging petitioner with the crime of "misprision of felony." We grant certiorari and reinstate the order quashing the indictment.

As far as we know or are able to determine, this is the first case in Florida involving the crime of misprision of felony. Such offense is not proscribed by the statutes of Florida, but was a crime at common law. The circuit court order now under review, as did the county court order before it, recognized it as such common law offense and held it to be a "crime under the laws of the State of Florida" pursuant to the provisions of § 775.01, F.S.1971, which declares common law crimes to be of full force in this state in the absence of a specific statute on the subject. We disagree on this fundamental finding and therefore deem it unnecessary to discuss the factual issues which the circuit court considered viable and upon which he predicated his reversal of the court's dismissal of the indictment.

Before continuing further, and to assist in lighting the path we take, we briefly define the offense as it existed at common law. We will more fully discuss it, *infra;* but for now, let it be said that it was the bare failure of a person with knowledge of the commission of a felony to bring the crime to the attention of the proper authorities.[2]

Now the facts. Petitioner was, at the times material herein, City Manager of the City of Pinellas Park, Florida. On or about the critical date herein, to wit: August 2, 1973, he was attempting to contact his assistant city manager, one Rutherford, and had been unable to do so by telephone. He drove to Rutherford's residence but though Rutherford's car was parked in front he was unable to raise him. He went around to the rear of the house looking for him and, at that time, noticed several plants growing in the rear yard which he suspected to be marijuana. He picked two leaves from two different plants and returned to his office. He contacted one T.W. Kelley, Captain of the Pinellas Park Police Department, to whom he related his findings. The two men then caused the plant samples to be chemically analyzed and their suspicions were confirmed.

Subsequently, Captain Kelley accompanied appellant back to Rutherford's house where they confronted Mr. Rutherford and accused him of the offense of which they suspected he was guilty. After some equivocation Rutherford finally indicated to them his guilt. In Mr. Rutherford's presence, then, appellant and Kelley uprooted a sufficient number of the aforesaid plants to constitute an aggregate of more than five grams of marijuana thus establishing the offense as *felony* possession of marijuana.

Thereafter, appellant requested Rutherford's resignation as assistant city manager, which Rutherford submitted, and then both appellant and Captain Kelley contacted

---

2. * * * We note here that misprision of felony does exist by statute under Federal law. 18 U.S.C. § 4 (1970). However, this statutory crime of misprision includes the added element of a positive act of concealment. In Florida, this type of behavior is proscribed by §§ 776.03 and 843.14, F.S.1971, which respectively condemn such conduct as "accessory after the fact" or "compounding a felony."

Pinellas Park Police Chief Ernest Van Horn to whom they related all of the foregoing. The decision was then made by appellant, and concurred in by Chief Van Horn and Captain Kelley, that the matter would be handled administratively as an internal affair, that they would avoid unfavorable publicity and dishonor to the City of Pinellas Park and that, to preclude further dishonor and disgrace to Rutherford and his family, no criminal prosecution would ensue.

Within several days thereafter appellant related the entire incident, together with a full disclosure of the decision aforesaid, to three city councilmen, the city clerk, six high level city officials, four lower level city officials, one newspaper editor, one newspaper reporter and one prominent clergyman of the city. Each of these seventeen persons filed an identical affidavit herein in which he acknowledges his full and complete knowledge of the matter and each of whom made the following sworn statement:

"Douglas J. Holland * * * advised me what action was taken in this matter, at which time I told him in effect that I felt he had taken the appropriate steps and agreed that this was good so as to avoid unfavorable publicity and dishonor to the City of Pinellas Park and to further avoid any dishonor to Rutherford's career and disgrace and serious harm to his family. I certainly felt that we should not proceed to cause the arrest of Mr. Rutherford."

As hereinabove noted, we chose to decide this case on the fundamental issue of whether misprision of felony is a crime in Florida. We parenthetically insert here, however, that had we not so chosen it is difficult to conclude from the foregoing facts, which are not in dispute, that appellant Holland failed to bring knowledge of the commission of a felony to the "proper authorities" or was guilty of concealing such knowledge in any respect.

In any case, we now get on to the merits of the question we decide today. We begin by pointing out that almost every state in the United States has adopted the Common Law of England to some extent. Many of these states have done so by constitutional or statutory provisions similar to ours. But the nearly universal interpretation of such provisions is that they adopt the common law of England only to the extent that such laws are consistent with the existing physical and social conditions in the country or in the given state. * * *

With the foregoing as a predicate, we now consider the history of the crime of misprision of felony and whether the reasons therefor have ceased to exist, if indeed they ever did exist, in this country. The origin of the crime is well described in 8 U. of Chi.L.Rev. 338, as follows:

"[M]isprision of felony as defined by Blackstone is merely one phase of the system of communal responsibility for the apprehension of criminals which received its original impetus from William I, under pressure of the need to protect the invading Normans in hostile country, and which endured up to the Seventeenth Century in England. In order to secure vigilant prosecution of criminal conduct, the vill or hundred in which such conduct occurred was subject to fine, as was the tithing to which the criminal belonged, and every person who knew of the felony and failed to make report thereof was subject to punishment for misprision of felony. Compulsory membership in the tithing group, the obligation to pursue criminals when the hue and cry was raised, broad powers of private arrest, and the periodic visitations of the General Eyre for the purpose of penalizing laxity in regard to crime, are all suggestive of the administrative background against which misprision of felony developed. With the appearance of specialized and paid law enforcement officers, such as constables and justices of the peace in the Seventeenth Century, there was a movement away from strict communal responsibility, and a growing tendency to rely on professional police * * *."

In short the initial reason for the existence of misprision of felony as a crime at common law was to aid an alien, dictorial sovereign in his forcible subjugation of England's inhabitants. Enforcement of the crime was summary, harsh and oppressive; and commentators note that most prosecutors in this country long ago recognized the inapplicability or obsolescence of the law and its harshness in their contemporary society by simply not charging people with that crime. This very case, in fact, serves well to illustrate the potential mischief of the charge and the possible discriminatory, oppressive or absurd results thereof. For example, should not Captain Kelley have been indicted too? Or Chief Van Horn? And if not, why only Holland? Or, perhaps, should not the three city councilmen have been indicted? Or the city clerk? Or the other city officials, the newspaper people or the clergyman in their turn? Should there be fully nineteen indictments herein, or any given lesser number, when for aught we know the principal felon hasn't even been charged?

Many courts faced with this issue have also found, though with varying degrees of clarity, that the reasons for the proscription of this crime do not exist. Moreover, as early as 1822 in this country Chief Justice John Marshall stated in *Marbury v. Brooks:*[8]

> "It may be the duty of a citizen to accuse every offender, and to proclaim every offense which comes to his knowledge; but the law which would punish him in every case, for not performing this duty, is too harsh for man." * * *

We agree with Chief Justice Marshall and with the above cases and commentaries that the crime of misprision of felony is wholly unsuited to American criminal law. While it may be desirable, even essential, that we encourage citizens to "get involved" to help reduce crime, they ought not be adjudicated criminals themselves if they don't. The fear of such a consequence is a fear from which our traditional concepts of peace and quietude guarantee freedom. We cherish the right to mind our own business when our own best interests dictate. Accordingly, we hold that misprision of felony has not been adopted into, and is not a part of, Florida substantive law. * * *

Notes and Questions

1. Compare George Goldberg, *Misprision of Felony: An Old Concept in a New Context,* 52 A.B.A.J. 148, 149–50 (1966): "The Supreme Court of Vermont in 1907 defined the offense in its traditional sense:

> Misprision of felony is * * * a criminal neglect either to prevent a felony from being committed or to bring the offender to justice after its commission, but without such previous concert with or subsequent assistance of him as will make the concealer an accessory before or after the fact.

"Thus defined, misprision of felony would be a very salutary influence in our distressed society. If limited by its terms to serious crimes, perhaps only serious crimes against the person, few injustices are likely to result. Then Chief Justice Marshall's concern * * * need not deter legislators from passing a much-needed law. In the case which elicited Marshall's compassion, the defendant had advanced money to his son-in-law in an attempt to save him from the consequences of forgery. The law which would punish such behavior and even require a man to report his family's peculations to the police *is* too harsh. Restricting the operation of the law to serious crimes (and perhaps exempting certain degrees of consanguinity) ought to remove this objection.

"Exceptions must also be made for conflicting legal duties. A lawyer is legally obliged not to divulge information confidentially revealed to him by his client regarding a

---

8.   20 U.S. (7 Wheat.) 556, 575–576, 5 L.Ed. 522.

committed felony. Nor may a doctor broadcast his patient's confidential communications, nor a clergyman his parishioner's. Misprision of felony statutes must allow for these obligations to be respected without fear of lawbreaking.

"It may finally be objected that a legal duty to report criminal acts to the authorities would be so novel in most American jurisdictions that even responsible citizens would unavoidably break the law. But all Americans are familiar with their legal duty to report serious traffic accidents to the police. It is about time we consider violent assault on persons as important as automobile crashes."

2. In *United States v. Kuh*, 541 F.2d 672 (7th Cir.1976), a complaint was initially filed against Kuh and Rea for violation of 18 U.S.C.A. § 2113(c),[1] but the grand jury instead indicted them for violation of the misprision of felony statute, 18 U.S.C.A. § 4.[2] Upon their motion to dismiss, the United States attorney indicated the evidence would be that they had buried money taken in a bank robbery. In affirming the dismissal, the court of appeals, after noting "that the defendants could reasonably apprehend that they had violated § 2113(c)," concluded that prosecution was barred by the Fifth Amendment privilege against self-incrimination:

"The privilege guaranteed by the Fifth Amendment not only extends to statements that would in themselves support a conviction but likewise embraces those which would furnish a 'link in the chain of evidence' that could lead to prosecution, provided that the individual has reasonable cause to fear he might thereby be convicted of the crime. An effort to use the misprision statute against persons who have knowingly possessed, received, and concealed the proceeds of a bank robbery clearly raises a serious Fifth Amendment question.

"The Government insists that *United States v. Daddano,* 432 F.2d 1119, 1125 (7th Cir.1970), precludes the defendants' argument that the misprision statute is unconstitutional as applied to them. We do not agree and decline to give such a broad reading to that decision.

"The defendants in *Daddano* relied upon a legal theory akin to that advanced by Kuh and Rea. This court rejected the argument and the holding of *United States v. King,* 402 F.2d 694 (9th Cir.1968), observing that the offense of misprision as defined in 18 U.S.C. § 4 consists of an act of concealment in addition to failure to disclose, so that the statute did not purport to punish one solely for failure to report facts which he has reasonable fear might lead to his conviction of crime.

"The *Daddano* ruling, however, must be read within the context of the facts of that case. Indeed, the opinion noted at the outset that the evidence presented an unusual story. The defendants charged in the misprision count had caused lie detector tests to be administered in order to determine whether certain persons were furnishing information concerning the bank robbery and the perpetrators thereof to governmental authorities investigating the same. It appeared from the evidence that whichever bank robber failed the test would be silenced, *viz.,* the others could shoot him if they wished. The arrangement whereby a member of the Special Investigations Unit of Cook County administered the polygraph tests presented a situation wherein an entirely separate offense from that

---

1. "Whoever receives, possesses, conceals, stores, barters, sells, or disposes of, any property or money or other thing of value knowing the same to have been taken from a bank, credit union, or a savings and loan association, in violation of subsection (b) of this section shall be subject to the punishment provided in said subsection (b) for the taker."

2. "Whoever, having knowledge of the actual commission of a felony cognizable by a court of the United States, conceals and does not as soon as possible make known the same to some judge or other person in civil or military authority under the United States, shall be fined not more than $500 or imprisoned not more than three years, or both."

involved in the original bank robbery was the means employed to mislead the federal authorities. In *Daddano* the polygraph procedures engaged in by the defendants constituted a distinct and separate concealment of the commission of a felony. This as the court observed in *Daddano* is the 'act of concealment in addition to failure to disclose.' The concealment in the present case, while it might incidentally have served to cloak the felony commission, was directly the concealment of the stolen money, a clear violation of 18 U.S.C. § 2113(c).

"Moreover, although the *Daddano* court recognized that defendant Montagna had knowingly received part of the stolen money and, as a professional bondsman, had arranged for the bonds of the four defendants originally charged with the robbery, its characterization of his conduct took place in a context wherein he had not been charged in the indictment with that particular misprision but only with concealing information through the use of the polygraph test. Thus, the rejection of his Fifth Amendment claim focused on Montagna's fear of being convicted as an accessory after the fact. True, the *Daddano* court did make a brief reference to 'some other related offense'; but the absence of any count in the indictment alleging that Montagna had possessed or used funds which he knew to be the fruits of a bank robbery in violation of 18 U.S.C. § 2113(c) points to a conclusion that the quoted phrase was not intended to refer to a subsection (c) violation.

"We are satisfied that *Daddano* is factually and legally distinguishable from the instant case. Here the facts as represented by the prosecutors are that at the time the duty to disclose arose, the defendants Kuh and Rea were simultaneously involved in criminal conduct through the knowing receipt and possession of the stolen money followed by its concealment. The object of the Fifth Amendment is to insure that a person should not be compelled to give information which might tend to show he himself has committed a crime. Under the circumstances of this case, we cannot accept the argument that, although a person who fails to disclose a felony in which he might be implicated is protected from punishment by the Fifth Amendment, his failure to make known the felony, when coupled with an act of concealment, makes him susceptible to prosecution, conviction, and punishment under 18 U.S.C. § 4. If the duty to notify federal authorities is precluded by constitutional privilege, it is difficult to understand how a conviction could be substantiated. The factual allegations were and are sufficient to engender in the defendants reasonable cause to believe that disclosing information as to their knowledge of the Purolator robbery would place them in the position of furnishing the Government with evidence that could lead to their prosecution or conviction."

3. In *United States v. Ciambrone*, 750 F.2d 1416 (9th Cir.1984), defendant contacted a Secret Service agent, showed him a xerox copy of a counterfeit $100 bill and also two actual counterfeit bills and said for $15,000 he would provide further information about a very substantial counterfeiting operation (the counterfeiters were seeking to trade the fruits of their labors for half a million dollars). Upon his refusal to give any further information without such a payoff, he was convicted of misprision of a felony. The court of appeals reversed:

"The starting point of our analysis is the proposition that '[m]ere silence, without some affirmative act, is insufficient evidence' of the crime of misprision of felony. Thus, a person who witnesses a crime does not violate 18 U.S.C. § 4 if he simply remains silent. Here, Ciambrone did not remain silent; rather, he made a truthful, but partial disclosure of what he knew about the counterfeiting operation. The district court viewed Ciambrone's actions as 'tantamount to an affirmative act,' because 'the case goes beyond the defendant sitting at home knowing about it, not doing anything about it.' We disagree. In our view, Ciambrone's partial disclosure did not result in any greater concealment of the crime than would have occurred had he stayed at home and said nothing. Indeed, in stepping forward to make at least a partial disclosure, Ciambrone provided some information and possibly valuable leads that the Secret Service would not have otherwise obtained from him. Thus, Ciambrone not only informed Agent Devaney that he knew a person with large quantities of counterfeit notes, but also gave him a xerox copy of one and showed him two actual counterfeit notes before they were put into circulation. From the Secret Service's standpoint, this partial disclosure had to be better than no disclosure at all. Rather than helping the counterfeiters conceal their criminal activity, Ciambrone's partial disclosure put them at some greater risk of detection than if he had remained silent.

"Since it is undisputed that Ciambrone was truthful, the Secret Service could not have been misled by his statements. This case is thus distinguishable from *Hodges,* where we determined that 'the giving of an untruthful statement [denying knowledge of the crime] to [F.B.I.] authorities is a sufficient act of concealment to sustain a conviction for misprision of felony.' The important distinction is that lying to the authorities can help those who committed a crime by throwing the authorities off the track. Here, although Ciambrone chose to be selectively silent, he did at least convey some information that might have been useful to the Secret Service, which is better than no information at all."

*

Appendix

AMERICAN LAW INSTITUTE
MODEL PENAL CODE
(OFFICIAL DRAFT, 1962)

TABLE OF CONTENTS

MODEL PENAL CODE

PART I. GENERAL PROVISIONS

ARTICLE 1. PRELIMINARY

Section

APPENDIX

PART II. DEFINITION OF SPECIFIC CRIMES

OFFENSES AGAINST EXISTENCE OR STABILITY OF THE STATE

OFFENSES INVOLVING DANGER TO THE PERSON

ARTICLE 210. CRIMINAL HOMICIDE

ARTICLE 211. ASSAULT; RECKLESS ENDANGERING; THREATS

ARTICLE 212. KIDNAPPING AND RELATED OFFENSES; COERCION

ARTICLE 213. SEXUAL OFFENSES

OFFENSES AGAINST PROPERTY

ARTICLE 220. ARSON, CRIMINAL MISCHIEF, AND OTHER PROPERTY DESTRUCTION

ARTICLE 221. BURGLARY AND OTHER CRIMINAL INTRUSION

ARTICLE 222. ROBBERY

ADDITIONAL ARTICLES

PART III. TREATMENT AND CORRECTION [OMITTED]

PART IV. ORGANIZATION OF CORRECTION [OMITTED]

PART I. GENERAL PROVISIONS

ARTICLE 1. PRELIMINARY

Section 1.01. Title and Effective Date.

(1) This Act is called the Penal and Correctional Code and may be cited as P.C.C. It shall become effective on ____.

(2) Except as provided in Subsections (3) and (4) of this Section, the Code does not apply to offenses committed prior to its effective date and prosecutions for such offenses shall be governed by the prior law, which is continued in effect for that purpose, as if this Code were not in force. For the purposes of this Section, an offense was committed prior to the effective date of the Code if any of the elements of the offense occurred prior thereto.

(3) In any case pending on or after the effective date of the Code, involving an offense committed prior to such date:

(a) procedural provisions of the Code shall govern, insofar as they are justly applicable and their application does not introduce confusion or delay;

(b) provisions of the Code according a defense or mitigation shall apply, with the consent of the defendant;

(c) the Court, with the consent of the defendant, may impose sentence under the provisions of the Code applicable to the offense and the offender.

(4) Provisions of the Code governing the treatment and the release or discharge of prisoners, probationers and parolees shall apply to persons under sentence for offenses committed prior to the effective date of the Code, except that the minimum or maximum period of their detention or supervision shall in no case be increased.

Section 1.02. Purposes; Principles of Construction.

(1) The general purposes of the provisions governing the definition of offenses are:

(a) to forbid and prevent conduct that unjustifiably and inexcusably inflicts or threatens substantial harm to individual or public interests;

(b) to subject to public control persons whose conduct indicates that they are disposed to commit crimes;

(c) to safeguard conduct that is without fault from condemnation as criminal;

(d) to give fair warning of the nature of the conduct declared to constitute an offense;

(e) to differentiate on reasonable grounds between serious and minor offenses.

(2) The general purposes of the provisions governing the sentencing and treatment of offenders are:

(a) to prevent the commission of offenses;

(b) to promote the correction and rehabilitation of offenders;

(c) to safeguard offenders against excessive, disproportionate or arbitrary punishment;

(d) to give fair warning of the nature of the sentences that may be imposed on conviction of an offense;

(e) to differentiate among offenders with a view to a just individualization in their treatment;

(f) to define, coordinate and harmonize the powers, duties and functions of the courts and of administrative officers and agencies responsible for dealing with offenders;

(g) to advance the use of generally accepted scientific methods and knowledge in the sentencing and treatment of offenders;

(h) to integrate responsibility for the administration of the correctional system in a State Department of Correction [or other single department or agency].

(3) The provisions of the Code shall be construed according to the fair import of their terms but when the language is susceptible of differing constructions it shall be interpreted to further the general purposes stated in this Section and the special purposes of the particular provision involved. The discretionary powers conferred by the Code shall be exercised in accordance with the criteria stated in the Code and, insofar as such criteria are not decisive, to further the general purposes stated in this Section.

Section 1.03. Territorial Applicability.

(1) Except as otherwise provided in this Section, a person may be convicted under the law of this State of an offense committed by his own conduct or the conduct of another for which he is legally accountable if:

(a) either the conduct which is an element of the offense or the result which is such an element occurs within this State; or

(b) conduct occurring outside the State is sufficient under the law of this State to constitute an attempt to commit an offense within the State; or

(c) conduct occurring outside the State is sufficient under the law of this State to constitute a conspiracy to commit an offense within the State and an overt act in furtherance of such conspiracy occurs within the State; or

(d) conduct occurring within the State establishes complicity in the commission of, or an attempt, solicitation or conspiracy to commit, an offense in another jurisdiction which also is an offense under the law of this State; or

(e) the offense consists of the omission to perform a legal duty imposed by the law of this State with respect to domicile, residence or a relationship to a person, thing or transaction in the State; or

(f) the offense is based on a statute of this State which expressly prohibits conduct outside the State, when the conduct bears a reasonable relation to a legitimate interest of this State and the actor knows or should know that his conduct is likely to affect that interest.

(2) Subsection (1)(a) does not apply when either causing a specified result or a purpose to cause or danger of causing such a result is an element of an offense and the result occurs or is designed or likely to occur only in another jurisdiction where the conduct charged would not constitute an offense, unless a legislative purpose plainly appears to declare the conduct criminal regardless of the place of the result.

(3) Subsection (1)(a) does not apply when causing a particular result is an element of an offense and the result is caused by conduct occurring outside the State which would not constitute an offense if the result had occurred there, unless the actor purposely or knowingly caused the result within the State.

(4) When the offense is homicide, either the death of the victim or the bodily impact causing death constitutes a "result," within the meaning of Subsection (1)(a) and if the body of a homicide victim is found within the State, it is presumed that such result occurred within the State.

(5) This State includes the land and water and the air space above such land and water with respect to which the State has legislative jurisdiction.

Section 1.04. Classes of Crimes; Violations.

(1) An offense defined by this Code or by any other statute of this State, for which a sentence of [death or of] imprisonment is authorized, constitutes a crime. Crimes are classified as felonies, misdemeanors or petty misdemeanors.

(2) A crime is a felony if it is so designated in this Code or if persons convicted thereof may be sentenced [to death or] to imprisonment for a term which, apart from an extended term, is in excess of one year.

(3) A crime is a misdemeanor if it is so designated in this Code or in a statute other than this Code enacted subsequent thereto.

(4) A crime is a petty misdemeanor if it is so designated in this Code or in a statute other than this Code enacted subsequent thereto or if it is defined by a statute other than this Code which now provides that persons convicted thereof may be sentenced to imprisonment for a term of which the maximum is less than one year.

(5) An offense defined by this Code or by any other statute of this State constitutes a violation if it is so designated in this Code or in the law defining the offense or if no other sentence than a fine, or fine and forfeiture or other civil penalty is authorized upon conviction or if it is defined by a statute other than this Code which now provides that the offense shall not constitute a crime. A violation does not constitute a crime and conviction of a violation shall not give rise to any disability or legal disadvantage based on conviction of a criminal offense.

(6) Any offense declared by law to constitute a crime, without specification of the grade thereof or of the sentence authorized upon conviction, is a misdemeanor.

(7) An offense defined by any statute of this State other than this Code shall be classified as provided in this Section and the sentence that may be imposed upon conviction thereof shall hereafter be governed by this Code.

Section 1.05. All Offenses Defined by Statute; Application of General Provisions of the Code.

(1) No conduct constitutes an offense unless it is a crime or violation under this Code or another statute of this State.

(2) The provisions of Part I of the Code are applicable to offenses defined by other statutes, unless the Code otherwise provides.

(3) This Section does not affect the power of a court to punish for contempt or to employ any sanction authorized by law for the enforcement of an order or a civil judgment or decree.

Section 1.06. Time Limitations.

(1) A prosecution for murder may be commenced at anytime.

(2) Except as otherwise provided in this Section, prosecutions for other offenses are subject to the following periods of limitation:

(a) a prosecution for a felony of the first degree must be commenced within six years after it is committed;

(b) a prosecution for any other felony must be commenced within three years after it is committed;

(c) a prosecution for a misdemeanor must be commenced within two years after it is committed;

(d) a prosecution for a petty misdemeanor or a violation must be commenced within six months after it is committed.

(3) If the period prescribed in Subsection (2) has expired, a prosecution may nevertheless be commenced for:

(a) any offense a material element of which is either fraud or a breach of fiduciary obligation within one year after discovery of the offense by an aggrieved party or by a person who has legal duty to represent an aggrieved party and who is himself not a party to the offense, but in no case shall this provision extend the period of limitation otherwise applicable by more than three years; and

(b) any offense based upon misconduct in office by a public officer or employee at any time when the defendant is in public office or employment or within two years thereafter, but in no case shall this provision extend the period of limitation otherwise applicable by more than three years.

(4) An offense is committed either when every element occurs, or, if a legislative purpose to prohibit a continuing course of conduct plainly appears, at the time when the course of conduct or the defendant's complicity therein is terminated. Time starts to run on the day after the offense is committed.

(5) A prosecution is commenced either when an indictment is found [or an information filed] or when a warrant or other process is issued, provided that such warrant or process is executed without unreasonable delay.

(6) The period of limitation does not run:

(a) during any time when the accused is continuously absent from the State or has no reasonably ascertainable place of abode or work within the State, but in no case shall this provision extend the period of limitation otherwise applicable by more than three years; or

(b) during any time when a prosecution against the accused for the same conduct is pending in this State.

Section 1.07. Method of Prosecution When Conduct Constitutes More Than One Offense.

(1) **Prosecution for Multiple Offenses; Limitation on Convictions.** When the same conduct of a defendant may establish the commission of more than one offense, the defendant may be prosecuted for each such offense. He may not, however, be convicted of more than one offense if:

(a) one offense is included in the other, as defined in Subsection (4) of this Section; or

(b) one offense consists only of a conspiracy or other form of preparation to commit the other; or

(c) inconsistent findings of fact are required to establish the commission of the offenses; or

(d) the offenses differ only in that one is defined to prohibit a designated kind of conduct generally and the other to prohibit a specific instance of such conduct; or

(e) the offense is defined as a continuing course of conduct and the defendant's course of conduct was uninterrupted, unless the law provides that specific periods of such conduct constitute separate offenses.

(2) **Limitation on Separate Trials for Multiple Offenses.** Except as provided in Subsection (3) of this Section, a defendant shall not be subject to separate trials for multiple offenses based on the same conduct or arising from the same criminal episode, if such offenses are known to the appropriate prosecuting officer at the time of the commencement of the first trial and are within the jurisdiction of a single court.

(3) **Authority of Court to Order Separate Trials.** When a defendant is charged with two or more offenses based on the same conduct or arising from the same criminal episode, the Court, on application of the prosecuting attorney or of the defendant, may order any such charge to be tried separately, if it is satisfied that justice so requires.

(4) **Conviction of Included Offense Permitted.** A defendant may be convicted of an offense included in an offense charged in the indictment [or the information]. An offense is so included when:

(a) it is established by proof of the same or less than all the facts required to establish the commission of the offense charged; or

(b) it consists of an attempt or solicitation to commit the offense charged or to commit an offense otherwise included therein; or

(c) it differs from the offense charged only in the respect that a less serious injury or risk of injury to the same person, property or public interest or a lesser kind of culpability suffices to establish its commission.

(5) **Submission of Included Offense to Jury.** The Court shall not be obligated to charge the jury with respect to an included offense unless there is a rational basis for a verdict acquitting the defendant of the offense charged and convicting him of the included offense.

Section 1.08. When Prosecution Barred by Former Prosecution for the Same Offense.

When a prosecution is for a violation of the same provision of the statutes and is based upon the same facts as a former prosecution, it is barred by such former prosecution under the following circumstances:

(1) The former prosecution resulted in an acquittal. There is an acquittal if the prosecution resulted in a finding of not guilty by the trier of fact or in a determination that there was insufficient evidence to warrant a conviction. A finding of guilty of a lesser included offense is an acquittal of the greater inclusive offense, although the conviction is subsequently set aside.

(2) The former prosecution was terminated, after the information had been filed or the indictment found, by a final order or judgment for the defendant, which has not been set aside, reversed, or vacated and which necessarily required a determination inconsistent with a fact or a legal proposition that must be established for conviction of the offense.

(3) The former prosecution resulted in a conviction. There is a conviction if the prosecution resulted in a judgment of conviction which has not been reversed or vacated, a verdict of guilty which has not been set aside and which is capable of supporting a judgment, or a plea of guilty accepted by the Court. In the latter two cases failure to enter judgment must be for a reason other than a motion of the defendant.

(4) The former prosecution was improperly terminated. Except as provided in this Subsection, there is an improper termination of a prosecution if the termination is for reasons not amounting to an acquittal, and it takes place after the first witness is sworn but before verdict. Termination under any of the following circumstances is not improper:

(a) The defendant consents to the termination or waives, by motion to dismiss or otherwise, his right to object to the termination.

(b) The trial court finds that the termination is necessary because:

(i) it is physically impossible to proceed with the trial in conformity with law; or

(ii) there is a legal defect in the proceedings which would make any judgment entered upon a verdict reversible as a matter of law; or

(iii) prejudicial conduct, in or outside the courtroom, makes it impossible to proceed with the trial without injustice to either the defendant or the State; or

(iv) the jury is unable to agree upon a verdict; or

(v) false statements of a juror on voir dire prevent a fair trial.

Section 1.09. When Prosecution Barred by Former Prosecution for Different Offense.

Although a prosecution is for a violation of a different provision of the statutes than a former prosecution or is based on different facts, it is barred by such former prosecution under the following circumstances:

(1) The former prosecution resulted in an acquittal or in a conviction as defined in Section 1.08 and the subsequent prosecution is for:

(a) any offense of which the defendant could have been convicted on the first prosecution; or

(b) any offense for which the defendant should have been tried on the first prosecution under Section 1.07, unless the Court ordered a separate trial of the charge of such offense; or

(c) the same conduct, unless (i) the offense of which the defendant was formerly convicted or acquitted and the offense for which he is subsequently prosecuted each requires proof of a fact not required by the other and the law defining each of such offenses is intended to prevent a substantially different harm or evil, or (ii) the second offense was not consummated when the former trial began.

(2) The former prosecution was terminated, after the information was filed or the indictment found, by an acquittal or by a final order or judgment for the defendant which has not been set aside, reversed or vacated and which acquittal, final order or judgment necessarily required a determination inconsistent with a fact which must be established for conviction of the second offense.

(3) The former prosecution was improperly terminated, as improper termination is defined in Section 1.08, and the subsequent prosecution is for an offense of which the

defendant could have been convicted had the former prosecution not been improperly terminated.

Section 1.10. Former Prosecution in Another Jurisdiction: When a Bar.

When conduct constitutes an offense within the concurrent jurisdiction of this State and of the United States or another State, a prosecution in any such other jurisdiction is a bar to a subsequent prosecution in this State under the following circumstances:

(1) The first prosecution resulted in an acquittal or in a conviction as defined in Section 1.08 and the subsequent prosecution is based on the same conduct, unless (a) the offense of which the defendant was formerly convicted or acquitted and the offense for which he is subsequently prosecuted each requires proof of a fact not required by the other and the law defining each of such offenses is intended to prevent a substantially different harm or evil or (b) the second offense was not consummated when the former trial began; or

(2) The former prosecution was terminated, after the information was filed or the indictment found, by an acquittal or by a final order or judgment for the defendant which has not been set aside, reversed or vacated and which acquittal, final order or judgment necessarily required a determination inconsistent with a fact which must be established for conviction of the offense of which the defendant is subsequently prosecuted.

Section 1.11. Former Prosecution Before Court Lacking Jurisdiction or When Fraudulently Procured by the Defendant.

A prosecution is not a bar within the meaning of Sections 1.08, 1.09 and 1.10 under any of the following circumstances:

(1) The former prosecution was before a court which lacked jurisdiction over the defendant or the offense; or

(2) The former prosecution was procured by the defendant without the knowledge of the appropriate prosecuting officer and with the purpose of avoiding the sentence which might otherwise be imposed; or

(3) The former prosecution resulted in a judgment of conviction which was held invalid in a subsequent proceeding on a writ of habeas corpus, coram nobis or similar process.

Section 1.12. Proof Beyond a Reasonable Doubt; Affirmative Defenses; Burden of Proving Fact When Not an Element of an Offense; Presumptions.

(1) No person may be convicted of an offense unless each element of such offense is proved beyond a reasonable doubt. In the absence of such proof, the innocence of the defendant is assumed.

(2) Subsection (1) of this Section does not:

(a) require the disproof of an affirmative defense unless and until there is evidence supporting such defense; or

(b) apply to any defense which the Code or another statute plainly requires the defendant to prove by a preponderance of evidence.

(3) A ground of defense is affirmative, within the meaning of Subsection (2)(a) of this Section, when:

(a) it arises under a section of the Code which so provides; or

(b) it relates to an offense defined by a statute other than the Code and such statute so provides; or

(c) it involves a matter of excuse or justification peculiarly within the knowledge of the defendant on which he can fairly be required to adduce supporting evidence.

(4) When the application of the Code depends upon the finding of a fact which is not an element of an offense, unless the Code otherwise provides:

(a) the burden of proving the fact is on the prosecution or defendant, depending on whose interest or contention will be furthered if the finding should be made; and

(b) the fact must be proved to the satisfaction of the Court or jury, as the case may be.

(5) When the Code establishes a presumption with respect to any fact which is an element of an offense, it has the following consequences:

(a) when there is evidence of the facts which give rise to the presumption, the issue of the existence of the presumed fact must be submitted to the jury, unless the Court is satisfied that the evidence as a whole clearly negatives the presumed fact; and

(b) when the issue of the existence of the presumed fact is submitted to the jury, the Court shall charge that while the presumed fact must, on all the evidence, be proved beyond a reasonable doubt, the law declares that the jury may regard the facts giving rise to the presumption as sufficient evidence of the presumed fact.

(6) A presumption not established by the Code or inconsistent with it has the consequences otherwise accorded it by law.

Section 1.13. General Definitions.

In this Code, unless a different meaning plainly is required:

(1) "statute" includes the Constitution and a local law or ordinance of a political subdivision of the State;

(2) "act" or "action" means a bodily movement whether voluntary or involuntary;

(3) "voluntary" has the meaning specified in Section 2.01;

(4) "omission" means a failure to act;

(5) "conduct" means an action or omission and its accompanying state of mind, or, where relevant, a series of acts and omissions;

(6) "actor" includes, where relevant, a person guilty of an omission;

(7) "acted" includes, where relevant, "omitted to act";

(8) "person," "he" and "actor" include any natural person and, where relevant, a corporation or an unincorporated association;

(9) "element of an offense" means (i) such conduct or (ii) such attendant circumstances or (iii) such a result of conduct as

(a) is included in the description of the forbidden conduct in the definition of the offense; or

(b) establishes the required kind of culpability; or

(c) negatives an excuse or justification for such conduct; or

(d) negatives a defense under the statute of limitations; or

(e) establishes jurisdiction or venue;

(10) "material element of an offense" means an element that does not relate exclusively to the statute of limitations, jurisdiction, venue or to any other matter similarly

unconnected with (i) the harm or evil, incident to conduct, sought to be prevented by the law defining the offense, or (ii) the existence of a justification or excuse for such conduct;

(11) "purposely" has the meaning specified in Section 2.02 and equivalent terms such as "with purpose," "designed" or "with design" have the same meaning;

(12) "intentionally" or "with intent" means purposely;

(13) "knowingly" has the meaning specified in Section 2.02 and equivalent terms such as "knowing" or "with knowledge" have the same meaning;

(14) "recklessly" has the meaning specified in Section 2.02 and equivalent terms such as "recklessness" or "with recklessness" have the same meaning;

(15) "negligently" has the meaning specified in Section 2.02 and equivalent terms such as "negligence" or "with negligence" have the same meaning;

(16) "reasonably believes" or "reasonable belief" designates a belief which the actor is not reckless or negligent in holding.

ARTICLE 2. GENERAL PRINCIPLES OF LIABILITY

Section 2.01. Requirement of Voluntary Act; Omission as Basis of Liability; Possession as an Act.

(1) A person is not guilty of an offense unless his liability is based on conduct which includes a voluntary act or the omission to perform an act of which he is physically capable.

(2) The following are not voluntary acts within the meaning of this Section:

(a) a reflex or convulsion;

(b) a bodily movement during unconsciousness or sleep;

(c) conduct during hypnosis or resulting from hypnotic suggestion;

(d) a bodily movement that otherwise is not a product of the effort or determination of the actor, either conscious or habitual.

(3) Liability for the commission of an offense may not be based on an omission unaccompanied by action unless:

(a) the omission is expressly made sufficient by the law defining the offense; or

(b) a duty to perform the omitted act is otherwise imposed by law.

(4) Possession is an act, within the meaning of this Section, if the possessor knowingly procured or received the thing possessed or was aware of his control thereof for a sufficient period to have been able to terminate his possession.

Section 2.02. General Requirements of Culpability.

(1) **Minimum Requirements of Culpability.** Except as provided in Section 2.05, a person is not guilty of an offense unless he acted purposely, knowingly, recklessly or negligently, as the law may require, with respect to each material element of the offense.

(2) **Kinds of Culpability Defined.**

(a) *Purposely.*

A person acts purposely with respect to a material element of an offense when:

(i) if the element involves the nature of his conduct or a result thereof, it is his conscious object to engage in conduct of that nature or to cause such a result; and

(ii) if the element involves the attendant circumstances, he is aware of the existence of such circumstances or he believes or hopes that they exist.

(b) *Knowingly.*

A person acts knowingly with respect to a material element of an offense when:

(i) if the element involves the nature of his conduct or the attendant circumstances, he is aware that his conduct is of that nature or that such circumstances exist; and

(ii) if the element involves a result of his conduct, he is aware that it is practically certain that his conduct will cause such a result.

(c) *Recklessly.*

A person acts recklessly with respect to a material element of an offense when he consciously disregards a substantial and unjustifiable risk that the material element exists or will result from his conduct. The risk must be of such a nature and degree that, considering the nature and purpose of the actor's conduct and the circumstances known to him, its disregard involves a gross deviation from the standard of conduct that a law-abiding person would observe in the actor's situation.

(d) *Negligently.*

A person acts negligently with respect to a material element of an offense when he should be aware of a substantial and unjustifiable risk that the material element exists or will result from his conduct. The risk must be of such a nature and degree that the actor's failure to perceive it, considering the nature and purpose of his conduct and the circumstances known to him, involves a gross deviation from the standard of care that a reasonable person would observe in the actor's situation.

(3) **Culpability Required Unless Otherwise Provided.** When the culpability sufficient to establish a material element of an offense is not prescribed by law, such element is established if a person acts purposely, knowingly or recklessly with respect thereto.

(4) **Prescribed Culpability Requirement Applies to All Material Elements.** When the law defining an offense prescribes the kind of culpability that is sufficient for the commission of an offense, without distinguishing among the material elements thereof, such provision shall apply to all the material elements of the offense, unless a contrary purpose plainly appears.

(5) **Substitutes for Negligence, Recklessness and Knowledge.** When the law provides that negligence suffices to establish an element of an offense, such element also is established if a person acts purposely, knowingly or recklessly. When recklessness suffices to establish an element, such element also is established if a person acts purposely or knowingly. When acting knowingly suffices to establish an element, such element also is established if a person acts purposely.

(6) **Requirement of Purpose Satisfied if Purpose Is Conditional.** When a particular purpose is an element of an offense, the element is established although such purpose is conditional, unless the condition negatives the harm or evil sought to be prevented by the law defining the offense.

(7) **Requirement of Knowledge Satisfied by Knowledge of High Probability.** When knowledge of the existence of a particular fact is an element of an offense, such knowledge is established if a person is aware of a high probability of its existence, unless he actually believes that it does not exist.

(8) **Requirement of Wilfulness Satisfied by Acting Knowingly.** A requirement that an offense be committed wilfully is satisfied if a person acts knowingly with respect to

the material elements of the offense, unless a purpose to impose further requirements appears.

(9) **Culpability as to Illegality of Conduct.** Neither knowledge nor recklessness or negligence as to whether conduct constitutes an offense or as to the existence, meaning or application of the law determining the elements of an offense is an element of such offense, unless the definition of the offense or the Code so provides.

(10) **Culpability as Determinant of Grade of Offense.** When the grade or degree of an offense depends on whether the offense is committed purposely, knowingly, recklessly or negligently, its grade or degree shall be the lowest for which the determinative kind of culpability is established with respect to any material element of the offense.

Section 2.03. Causal Relationship Between Conduct and Result; Divergence Between Result Designed or Contemplated and Actual Result or Between Probable and Actual Result.

(1) Conduct is the cause of a result when:

(a) it is an antecedent but for which the result in question would not have occurred; and

(b) the relationship between the conduct and result satisfies any additional causal requirements imposed by the Code or by the law defining the offense.

(2) When purposely or knowingly causing a particular result is an element of an offense, the element is not established if the actual result is not within the purpose or the contemplation of the actor unless:

(a) the actual result differs from that designed or contemplated, as the case may be, only in the respect that a different person or different property is injured or affected or that the injury or harm designed or contemplated would have been more serious or more extensive than that caused; or

(b) the actual result involves the same kind of injury or harm as that designed or contemplated and is not too remote or accidental in its occurrence to have a [just] bearing on the actor's liability or on the gravity of his offense.

(3) When recklessly or negligently causing a particular result is an element of an offense, the element is not established if the actual result is not within the risk of which the actor is aware or, in the case of negligence, of which he should be aware unless:

(a) the actual result differs from the probable result only in the respect that a different person or different property is injured or affected or that the probable injury or harm would have been more serious or more extensive than that caused; or

(b) the actual result involves the same kind of injury or harm as the probable result and is not too remote or accidental in its occurrence to have a [just] bearing on the actor's liability or on the gravity of his offense.

(4) When causing a particular result is a material element of an offense for which absolute liability is imposed by law, the element is not established unless the actual result is a probable consequence of the actor's conduct.

Section 2.04. Ignorance or Mistake. *combines — don't be confused*

(1) Ignorance or mistake as to a matter of fact or law is a defense if: *mental state*

(a) the ignorance or mistake negatives the purpose, knowledge, belief, recklessness or negligence required to establish a material element of the offense; or

(b) the law provides that the state of mind established by such ignorance or mistake constitutes a defense.

(2) Although ignorance or mistake would otherwise afford a defense to the offense charged, the defense is not available if the defendant would be guilty of another offense had the situation been as he supposed. In such case, however, the ignorance or mistake of the defendant shall reduce the grade and degree of the offense of which he may be convicted to those of the offense of which he would be guilty had the situation been as he supposed.

(3) A belief that conduct does not legally constitute an offense is a defense to a prosecution for that offense based upon such conduct when:

(a) the statute or other enactment defining the offense is not known to the actor and has not been published or otherwise reasonably made available prior to the conduct alleged; or

(b) he acts in reasonable reliance upon an official statement of the law, afterward determined to be invalid or erroneous, contained in (i) a statute or other enactment; (ii) a judicial decision, opinion or judgment; (iii) an administrative order or grant of permission; or (iv) an official interpretation of the public officer or body charged by law with responsibility for the interpretation, administration or enforcement of the law defining the offense.

(4) The defendant must prove a defense arising under Subsection (3) of this Section by a preponderance of evidence.

Section 2.05. When Culpability Requirements Are Inapplicable to Violations and to Offenses Defined by Other Statutes; Effect of Absolute Liability in Reducing Grade of Offense to Violation.

(1) The requirements of culpability prescribed by Sections 2.01 and 2.02 do not apply to:

(a) offenses which constitute violations, unless the requirement involved is included in the definition of the offense or the Court determines that its application is consistent with effective enforcement of the law defining the offense; or

(b) offenses defined by statutes other than the Code, insofar as a legislative purpose to impose absolute liability for such offenses or with respect to any material element thereof plainly appears.

(2) Notwithstanding any other provision of existing law and unless a subsequent statute otherwise provides:

(a) when absolute liability is imposed with respect to any material element of an offense defined by a statute other than the Code and a conviction is based upon such liability, the offense constitutes a violation; and

(b) although absolute liability is imposed by law with respect to one or more of the material elements of an offense defined by a statute other than the Code, the culpable commission of the offense may be charged and proved, in which event negligence with respect to such elements constitutes sufficient culpability and the classification of the offense and the sentence that may be imposed therefor upon conviction are determined by Section 1.04 and Article 6 of the Code.

Section 2.06. Liability for Conduct of Another; Complicity.

(1) A person is guilty of an offense if it is committed by his own conduct or by the conduct of another person for which he is legally accountable, or both.

(2) A person is legally accountable for the conduct of another person when:

(a) acting with the kind of culpability that is sufficient for the commission of the offense, he causes an innocent or irresponsible person to engage in such conduct; or

(b) he is made accountable for the conduct of such other person by the Code or by the law defining the offense; or

(c) he is an accomplice of such other person in the commission of the offense.

(3) A person is an accomplice of another person in the commission of an offense if:

(a) with the purpose of promoting or facilitating the commission of the offense, he

(i) solicits such other person to commit it; or

(ii) aids or agrees or attempts to aid such other person in planning or committing it; or

(iii) having a legal duty to prevent the commission of the offense, fails to make proper effort so to do; or

(b) his conduct is expressly declared by law to establish his complicity.

(4) When causing a particular result is an element of an offense, an accomplice in the conduct causing such result is an accomplice in the commission of that offense, if he acts with the kind of culpability, if any, with respect to that result that is sufficient for the commission of the offense.

(5) A person who is legally incapable of committing a particular offense himself may be guilty thereof if it is committed by the conduct of another person for which he is legally accountable, unless such liability is inconsistent with the purpose of the provision establishing his incapacity.

(6) Unless otherwise provided by the Code or by the law defining the offense, a person is not an accomplice in an offense committed by another person if:

(a) he is a victim of that offense; or

(b) the offense is so defined that his conduct is inevitably incident to its commission; or

(c) he terminates his complicity prior to the commission of the offense and

(i) wholly deprives it of effectiveness in the commission of the offense; or

(ii) gives timely warning to the law enforcement authorities or otherwise makes proper effort to prevent the commission of the offense.

(7) An accomplice may be convicted on proof of the commission of the offense and of his complicity therein, though the person claimed to have committed the offense has not been prosecuted or convicted or has been convicted of a different offense or degree of offense or has an immunity to prosecution or conviction or has been acquitted.

Section 2.07. Liability of Corporations, Unincorporated Associations and Persons Acting, or Under a Duty to Act, in Their Behalf.

(1) A corporation may be convicted of the commission of an offense if:

(a) the offense is a violation or the offense is defined by a statute other than the Code in which a legislative purpose to impose liability on corporations plainly appears and the conduct is performed by an agent of the corporation acting in behalf of the corporation within the scope of his office or employment, except that if the law defining the offense designates the agents for whose conduct the corporation is accountable or the circumstances under which it is accountable, such provisions shall apply; or

(b) the offense consists of an omission to discharge a specific duty of affirmative performance imposed on corporations by law; or

(c) the commission of the offense was authorized, requested, commanded, performed or recklessly tolerated by the board of directors or by a high managerial agent acting in behalf of the corporation within the scope of his office or employment.

(2) When absolute liability is imposed for the commission of an offense, a legislative purpose to impose liability on a corporation shall be assumed, unless the contrary plainly appears.

(3) An unincorporated association may be convicted of the commission of an offense if:

(a) the offense is defined by a statute other than the Code which expressly provides for the liability of such an association and the conduct is performed by an agent of the association acting in behalf of the association within the scope of his office or employment, except that if the law defining the offense designates the agents for whose conduct the association is accountable or the circumstances under which it is accountable, such provisions shall apply; or

(b) the offense consists of an omission to discharge a specific duty of affirmative performance imposed on associations by law.

(4) As used in this Section:

(a) "corporation" does not include an entity organized as or by a governmental agency for the execution of a governmental program;

(b) "agent" means any director, officer, servant, employee or other person authorized to act in behalf of the corporation or association and, in the case of an unincorporated association, a member of such association;

(c) "high managerial agent" means an officer of a corporation or an unincorporated association, or, in the case of a partnership, a partner, or any other agent of a corporation or association having duties of such responsibility that his conduct may fairly be assumed to represent the policy of the corporation or association.

(5) In any prosecution of a corporation or an unincorporated association for the commission of an offense included within the terms of Subsection (1)(a) or Subsection (3)(a) of this Section, other than an offense for which absolute liability has been imposed, it shall be a defense if the defendant proves by a preponderance of evidence that the high managerial agent having supervisory responsibility over the subject matter of the offense employed due diligence to prevent its commission. This paragraph shall not apply if it is plainly inconsistent with the legislative purpose in defining the particular offense.

(6)(a) A person is legally accountable for any conduct he performs or causes to be performed in the name of the corporation or an unincorporated association or in its behalf to the same extent as if it were performed in his own name or behalf.

(b) Whenever a duty to act is imposed by law upon a corporation or an unincorporated association, any agent of the corporation or association having primary responsibility for the discharge of the duty is legally accountable for a reckless omission to perform the required act to the same extent as if the duty were imposed by law directly upon himself.

(c) When a person is convicted of an offense by reason of his legal accountability for the conduct of a corporation or an unincorporated association, he is subject to the sentence authorized by law when a natural person is convicted of an offense of the grade and the degree involved.

Section 2.08. Intoxication.

(1) Except as provided in Subsection (4) of this Section, intoxication of the actor is not a defense unless it negatives an element of the offense.

(2) When recklessness establishes an element of the offense, if the actor, due to self-induced intoxication, is unaware of a risk of which he would have been aware had he been sober, such unawareness is immaterial.

(3) Intoxication does not, in itself, constitute mental disease within the meaning of Section 4.01.

(4) Intoxication which (a) is not self-induced or (b) is pathological is an affirmative defense if by reason of such intoxication the actor at the time of his conduct lacks substantial capacity either to appreciate its criminality [wrongfulness] or to conform his conduct to the requirements of law.

(5) **Definitions.** In this Section unless a different meaning plainly is required:

(a) "intoxication" means a disturbance of mental or physical capacities resulting from the introduction of substances into the body;

(b) "self-induced intoxication" means intoxication caused by substances which the actor knowingly introduces into his body, the tendency of which to cause intoxication he knows or ought to know, unless he introduces them pursuant to medical advice or under such circumstances as would afford a defense to a charge of crime;

(c) "pathological intoxication" means intoxication grossly excessive in degree, given the amount of the intoxicant, to which the actor does not know he is susceptible.

Section 2.09. Duress.

(1) It is an affirmative defense that the actor engaged in the conduct charged to constitute an offense because he was coerced to do so by the use of, or a threat to use, unlawful force against his person or the person of another, which a person of reasonable firmness in his situation would have been unable to resist.

(2) The defense provided by this Section is unavailable if the actor recklessly placed himself in a situation in which it was probable that he would be subjected to duress. The defense is also unavailable if he was negligent in placing himself in such a situation, whenever negligence suffices to establish culpability for the offense charged.

(3) It is not a defense that a woman acted on the command of her husband, unless she acted under such coercion as would establish a defense under this Section. [The presumption that a woman, acting in the presence of her husband, is coerced is abolished.]

(4) When the conduct of the actor would otherwise be justifiable under Section 3.02, this Section does not preclude such defense.

Section 2.10. Military Orders.

It is an affirmative defense that the actor, in engaging in the conduct charged to constitute an offense, does no more than execute an order of his superior in the armed services which he does not know to be unlawful.

Section 2.11. Consent.

(1) **In General.** The consent of the victim to conduct charged to constitute an offense or to the result thereof is a defense if such consent negatives an element of the offense or

precludes the infliction of the harm or evil sought to be prevented by the law defining the offense.

(2) **Consent to Bodily Injury.** When conduct is charged to constitute an offense because it causes or threatens bodily injury, consent to such conduct or to the infliction of such injury is a defense if:

(a) the bodily injury consented to or threatened by the conduct consented to is not serious; or

(b) the conduct and the injury are reasonably foreseeable hazards of joint participation in a lawful athletic contest or competitive sport or other concerted activity not forbidden by law; or

(c) the consent establishes a justification for the conduct under Article 3 of the Code.

(3) **Ineffective Consent.** Unless otherwise provided by the Code or by the law defining the offense, assent does not constitute consent if:

(a) it is given by a person who is legally incompetent to authorize the conduct charged to constitute the offense; or

(b) it is given by a person who by reason of youth, mental disease or defect or intoxication is manifestly unable or known by the actor to be unable to make a reasonable judgment as to the nature or harmfulness of the conduct charged to constitute the offense; or

(c) it is given by a person whose improvident consent is sought to be prevented by the law defining the offense; or

(d) it is induced by force, duress or deception of a kind sought to be prevented by the law defining the offense.

Section 2.12. De Minimis Infractions.

The Court shall dismiss a prosecution if, having regard to the nature of the conduct charged to constitute an offense and the nature of the attendant circumstances, it finds that the defendant's conduct:

(1) was within a customary license or tolerance, neither expressly negatived by the person whose interest was infringed nor inconsistent with the purpose of the law defining the offense; or

(2) did not actually cause or threaten the harm or evil sought to be prevented by the law defining the offense or did so only to an extent too trivial to warrant the condemnation of conviction; or

(3) presents such other extenuations that it cannot reasonably be regarded as envisaged by the legislature in forbidding the offense.

The Court shall not dismiss a prosecution under Subsection (3) of this Section without filing a written statement of its reasons.

Section 2.13. Entrapment.

(1) A public law enforcement official or a person acting in cooperation with such an official perpetrates an entrapment if for the purpose of obtaining evidence of the commission of an offense, he induces or encourages another person to engage in conduct constituting such offense by either:

(a) making knowingly false representations designed to induce the belief that such conduct is not prohibited; or

(b) employing methods of persuasion or inducement which create a substantial risk that such an offense will be committed by persons other than those who are ready to commit it.

(2) Except as provided in Subsection (3) of this Section, a person prosecuted for an offense shall be acquitted if he proves by a preponderance of evidence that his conduct occurred in response to an entrapment. The issue of entrapment shall be tried by the Court in the absence of the jury.

(3) The defense afforded by this Section is unavailable when causing or threatening bodily injury is an element of the offense charged and the prosecution is based on conduct causing or threatening such injury to a person other than the person perpetrating the entrapment.

ARTICLE 3. GENERAL PRINCIPLES OF JUSTIFICATION

Section 3.01. Justification an Affirmative Defense; Civil Remedies Unaffected.

(1) In any prosecution based on conduct which is justifiable under this Article, justification is an affirmative defense.

(2) The fact that conduct is justifiable under this Article does not abolish or impair any remedy for such conduct which is available in any civil action.

Section 3.02. Justification Generally: Choice of Evils.

(1) Conduct which the actor believes to be necessary to avoid a harm or evil to himself or to another is justifiable, provided that:

(a) the harm or evil sought to be avoided by such conduct is greater than that sought to be prevented by the law defining the offense charged; and

(b) neither the Code nor other law defining the offense provides exceptions or defenses dealing with the specific situation involved; and

(c) a legislative purpose to exclude the justification claimed does not otherwise plainly appear.

(2) When the actor was reckless or negligent in bringing about the situation requiring a choice of harms or evils or in appraising the necessity for his conduct, the justification afforded by this Section is unavailable in a prosecution for any offense for which recklessness or negligence, as the case may be, suffices to establish culpability.

Section 3.03. Execution of Public Duty.

(1) Except as provided in Subsection (2) of this Section, conduct is justifiable when it is required or authorized by:

(a) the law defining the duties or functions of a public officer or the assistance to be rendered to such officer in the performance of his duties; or

(b) the law governing the execution of legal process; or

(c) the judgment or order of a competent court or tribunal; or

(d) the law governing the armed services or the lawful conduct of war; or

(e) any other provision of law imposing a public duty.

(2) The other sections of this Article apply to:

(a) the use of force upon or toward the person of another for any of the purposes dealt with in such sections; and

(b) the use of deadly force for any purpose, unless the use of such force is otherwise expressly authorized by law or occurs in the lawful conduct of war.

(3) The justification afforded by Subsection (1) of this Section applies:

(a) when the actor believes his conduct to be required or authorized by the judgment or direction of a competent court or tribunal or in the lawful execution of legal process, notwithstanding lack of jurisdiction of the court or defect in the legal process; and

(b) when the actor believes his conduct to be required or authorized to assist a public officer in the performance of his duties, notwithstanding that the officer exceeded his legal authority.

Section 3.04. Use of Force in Self–Protection.

(1) **Use of Force Justifiable for Protection of the Person.** Subject to the provisions of this Section and of Section 3.09, the use of force upon or toward another person is justifiable when the actor believes that such force is immediately necessary for the purpose of protecting himself against the use of unlawful force by such other person on the present occasion.

(2) **Limitations on Justifying Necessity for Use of Force.**

(a) The use of force is not justifiable under this Section:

(i) to resist an arrest which the actor knows is being made by a peace officer, although the arrest is unlawful; or

(ii) to resist force used by the occupier or possessor of property or by another person on his behalf, where the actor knows that the person using the force is doing so under a claim of right to protect the property, except that this limitation shall not apply if:

(1) the actor is a public officer acting in the performance of his duties or a person lawfully assisting him therein or a person making or assisting in a lawful arrest; or

(2) the actor has been unlawfully dispossessed of the property and is making a re-entry or recaption justified by Section 3.06; or

(3) the actor believes that such force is necessary to protect himself against death or serious bodily harm.

(b) The use of deadly force is not justifiable under this Section unless the actor believes that such force is necessary to protect himself against death, serious bodily harm, kidnapping or sexual intercourse compelled by force or threat; nor is it justifiable if:

(i) the actor, with the purpose of causing death or serious bodily harm, provoked the use of force against himself in the same encounter; or

(ii) the actor knows that he can avoid the necessity of using such force with complete safety by retreating or by surrendering possession of a thing to a person asserting a claim of right thereto or by complying with a demand that he abstain from any action which he has no duty to take, except that:

(1) the actor is not obliged to retreat from his dwelling or place of work, unless he was the initial aggressor or is assailed in his place of work by another person whose place of work the actor knows it to be; and

(2) a public officer justified in using force in the performance of his duties or a person justified in using force in his assistance or a person justified in using force in making an

arrest or preventing an escape is not obliged to desist from efforts to perform such duty, effect such arrest or prevent such escape because of resistance or threatened resistance by or on behalf of the person against whom such action is directed.

(c) Except as required by paragraphs (a) and (b) of this Subsection, a person employing protective force may estimate the necessity thereof under the circumstances as he believes them to be when the force is used, without retreating, surrendering possession, doing any other act which he has no legal duty to do or abstaining from any lawful action.

(3) **Use of Confinement as Protective Force.** The justification afforded by this Section extends to the use of confinement as protective force only if the actor takes all reasonable measures to terminate the confinement as soon as he knows that he safely can, unless the person confined has been arrested on a charge of crime.

Section 3.05. Use of Force for the Protection of Other Persons.

(1) Subject to the provisions of this Section and of Section 3.09, the use of force upon or toward the person of another is justifiable to protect a third person when:

(a) the actor would be justified under Section 3.04 in using such force to protect himself against the injury he believes to be threatened to the person whom he seeks to protect; and

(b) under the circumstances as the actor believes them to be, the person whom he seeks to protect would be justified in using such protective force; and

(c) the actor believes that his intervention is necessary for the protection of such other person.

(2) Notwithstanding Subsection (1) of this Section:

(a) when the actor would be obliged under Section 3.04 to retreat, to surrender the possession of a thing or to comply with a demand before using force in self-protection, he is not obliged to do so before using force for the protection of another person, unless he knows that he can thereby secure the complete safety of such other person; and

(b) when the person whom the actor seeks to protect would be obliged under Section 3.04 to retreat, to surrender the possession of a thing or to comply with a demand if he knew that he could obtain complete safety by so doing, the actor is obliged to try to cause him to do so before using force in his protection if the actor knows that he can obtain complete safety in that way; and

(c) neither the actor nor the person whom he seeks to protect is obliged to retreat when in the other's dwelling or place of work to any greater extent than in his own.

Section 3.06. Use of Force for the Protection of Property.

(1) **Use of Force Justifiable for Protection of Property.** Subject to the provisions of this Section and of Section 3.09, the use of force upon or toward the person of another is justifiable when the actor believes that such force is immediately necessary:

(a) to prevent or terminate an unlawful entry or other trespass upon land or a trespass against or the unlawful carrying away of tangible, movable property, provided that such land or movable property is, or is believed by the actor to be, in his possession or in the possession of another person for whose protection he acts; or

(b) to effect an entry or re-entry upon land or to retake tangible movable property, provided that the actor believes that he or the person by whose authority he acts or a person from whom he or such other person derives title was unlawfully dispossessed of such land or movable property and is entitled to possession, and provided, further, that:

    (i) the force is used immediately or on fresh pursuit after such dispossession; or

    (ii) the actor believes that the person against whom he uses force has no claim of right to the possession of the property and, in the case of land, the circumstances, as the actor believes them to be, are of such urgency that it would be an exceptional hardship to postpone the entry or re-entry until a court order is obtained.

(2) **Meaning of Possession.** For the purposes of Subsection (1) of this Section:

    (a) a person who has parted with the custody of property to another who refuses to restore it to him is no longer in possession, unless the property is movable and was and still is located on land in his possession;

    (b) a person who has been dispossessed of land does not regain possession thereof merely by setting foot thereon;

    (c) a person who has a license to use or occupy real property is deemed to be in possession thereof except against the licensor acting under claim of right.

(3) **Limitations on Justifiable Use of Force.**

    (a) *Request to Desist.* The use of force is justifiable under this Section only if the actor first requests the person against whom such force is used to desist from his interference with the property, unless the actor believes that:

    (i) such request would be useless; or

    (ii) it would be dangerous to himself or another person to make the request; or

    (iii) substantial harm will be done to the physical condition of the property which is sought to be protected before the request can effectively be made.

    (b) *Exclusion of Trespasser.* The use of force to prevent or terminate a trespass is not justifiable under this Section if the actor knows that the exclusion of the trespasser will expose him to substantial danger of serious bodily harm.

    (c) *Resistance of Lawful Re-entry or Recaption.* The use of force to prevent an entry or re-entry upon land or the recaption of movable property is not justifiable under this Section, although the actor believes that such re-entry or recaption is unlawful, if:

    (i) the re-entry or recaption is made by or on behalf of a person who was actually dispossessed of the property; and

    (ii) it is otherwise justifiable under paragraph (1)(b) of this Section.

    (d) *Use of Deadly Force.* The use of deadly force is not justifiable under this Section unless the actor believes that:

    (i) the person against whom the force is used is attempting to dispossess him of his dwelling otherwise than under a claim of right to its possession; or

    (ii) the person against whom the force is used is attempting to commit or consummate arson, burglary, robbery or other felonious theft or property destruction and either:

(1) has employed or threatened deadly force against or in the presence of the actor; or

(2) the use of force other than deadly force to prevent the commission or the consummation of the crime would expose the actor or another in his presence to substantial danger of serious bodily harm.

(4) **Use of Confinement as Protective Force.** The justification afforded by this Section extends to the use of confinement as protective force only if the actor takes all reasonable measures to terminate the confinement as soon as he knows that he can do so with safety to the property, unless the person confined has been arrested on a charge of crime.

(5) **Use of Device to Protect Property.** The justification afforded by this Section extends to the use of a device for the purpose of protecting property only if:

(a) the device is not designed to cause or known to create a substantial risk of causing death or serious bodily harm; and

(b) the use of the particular device to protect the property from entry or trespass is reasonable under the circumstances, as the actor believes them to be; and

(c) the device is one customarily used for such a purpose or reasonable care is taken to make known to probable intruders the fact that it is used.

(6) **Use of Force to Pass Wrongful Obstructor.** The use of force to pass a person whom the actor believes to be purposely or knowingly and unjustifiably obstructing the actor from going to a place to which he may lawfully go is justifiable, provided that:

(a) the actor believes that the person against whom he uses force has no claim of right to obstruct the actor; and

(b) the actor is not being obstructed from entry or movement on land which he knows to be in the possession or custody of the person obstructing him, or in the possession or custody of another person by whose authority the obstructor acts, unless the circumstances, as the actor believes them to be, are of such urgency that it would not be reasonable to postpone the entry or movement on such land until a court order is obtained; and

(c) the force used is not greater than would be justifiable if the person obstructing the actor were using force against him to prevent his passage.

Section 3.07. Use of Force in Law Enforcement.

(1) **Use of Force Justifiable to Effect an Arrest.** Subject to the provisions of this Section and of Section 3.09, the use of force upon or toward the person of another is justifiable when the actor is making or assisting in making an arrest and the actor believes that such force is immediately necessary to effect a lawful arrest.

(2) **Limitations on the Use of Force.**

(a) The use of force is not justifiable under this Section unless:

(i) the actor makes known the purpose of the arrest or believes that it is otherwise known by or cannot reasonably be made known to the person to be arrested; and

(ii) when the arrest is made under a warrant, the warrant is valid or believed by the actor to be valid.

(b) The use of deadly force is not justifiable under this Section unless:

(i) the arrest is for a felony; and

(ii) the person effecting the arrest is authorized to act as a peace officer or is assisting a person whom he believes to be authorized to act as a peace officer; and

(iii) the actor believes that the force employed creates no substantial risk of injury to innocent persons; and

(iv) the actor believes that:

(1) the crime for which the arrest is made involved conduct including the use or threatened use of deadly force; or

(2) there is a substantial risk that the person to be arrested will cause death or serious bodily harm if his apprehension is delayed.

(3) **Use of Force to Prevent Escape from Custody.** The use of force to prevent the escape of an arrested person from custody is justifiable when the force could justifiably have been employed to effect the arrest under which the person is in custody, except that a guard or other person authorized to act as a peace officer is justified in using any force, including deadly force, which he believes to be immediately necessary to prevent the escape of a person from a jail, prison, or other institution for the detention of persons charged with or convicted of a crime.

(4) **Use of Force by Private Person Assisting an Unlawful Arrest.**

(a) A private person who is summoned by a peace officer to assist in effecting an unlawful arrest, is justified in using any force which he would be justified in using if the arrest were lawful provided that he does not believe the arrest is unlawful.

(b) A private person who assists another private person in effecting an unlawful arrest, or who, not being summoned, assists a peace officer in effecting an unlawful arrest, is justified in using any force which he would be justified in using if the arrest were lawful, provided that (i) he believes the arrest is lawful, and (ii) the arrest would be lawful if the facts were as he believes them to be.

(5) **Use of Force to Prevent Suicide or the Commission of a Crime.**

(a) The use of force upon or toward the person of another is justifiable when the actor believes that such force is immediately necessary to prevent such other person from committing suicide, inflicting serious bodily harm upon himself, committing or consummating the commission of a crime involving or threatening bodily harm, damage to or loss of property or a breach of the peace, except that:

(i) any limitations imposed by the other provisions of this Article on the justifiable use of force in self-protection, for the protection of others, the protection of property, the effectuation of an arrest or the prevention of an escape from custody shall apply notwithstanding the criminality of the conduct against which such force is used; and

(ii) the use of deadly force is not in any event justifiable under this Subsection unless:

(1) the actor believes that there is a substantial risk that the person whom he seeks to prevent from committing a crime will cause death or serious bodily harm to another unless the commission or the consummation of the crime is prevented and that the use of such force presents no substantial risk of injury to innocent persons; or

(2) the actor believes that the use of such force is necessary to suppress a riot or mutiny after the rioters or mutineers have been ordered to disperse

and warned, in any particular manner that the law may require, that such force will be used if they do not obey.

(b) The justification afforded by this Subsection extends to the use of confinement as preventive force only if the actor takes all reasonable measures to terminate the confinement as soon as he knows that he safely can, unless the person confined has been arrested on a charge of crime.

Section 3.08. Use of Force by Persons With Special Responsibility for Care, Discipline or Safety of Others.

The use of force upon or toward the person of another is justifiable if:

(1) the actor is the parent or guardian or other person similarly responsible for the general care and supervision of a minor or a person acting at the request of such parent, guardian or other responsible person and:

(a) the force is used for the purpose of safeguarding or promoting the welfare of the minor, including the prevention or punishment of his misconduct; and

(b) the force used is not designed to cause or known to create a substantial risk of causing death, serious bodily harm, disfigurement, extreme pain or mental distress or gross degradation; or

(2) the actor is a teacher or a person otherwise entrusted with the care or supervision for a special purpose of a minor and:

(a) the actor believes that the force used is necessary to further such special purpose, including the maintenance of reasonable discipline in a school, class or other group, and that the use of such force is consistent with the welfare of the minor; and

(b) the degree of force, if it had been used by the parent or guardian of the minor, would not be unjustifiable under Subsection (1)(b) of this Section; or

(3) the actor is the guardian or other person similarly responsible for the general care and supervision of an incompetent person; and:

(a) the force is used for the purpose of safeguarding or promoting the welfare of the incompetent person, including the prevention of his misconduct, or, when such incompetent person is in a hospital or other institution for his care and custody, for the maintenance of reasonable discipline in such institution; and

(b) the force used is not designed to cause or known to create a substantial risk of causing death, serious bodily harm, disfigurement, extreme or unnecessary pain, mental distress, or humiliation; or

(4) the actor is a doctor or other therapist or a person assisting him at his direction, and:

(a) the force is used for the purpose of administering a recognized form of treatment which the actor believes to be adapted to promoting the physical or mental health of the patient; and

(b) the treatment is administered with the consent of the patient or, if the patient is a minor or an incompetent person, with the consent of his parent or guardian or other person legally competent to consent in his behalf, or the treatment is administered in an emergency when the actor believes that no one competent to consent can be consulted and that a reasonable person, wishing to safeguard the welfare of the patient, would consent; or

(5) the actor is a warden or other authorized official of a correctional institution, and:

(a) he believes that the force used is necessary for the purpose of enforcing the lawful rules or procedures of the institution, unless his belief in the lawfulness of the rule or procedure sought to be enforced is erroneous and his error is due to ignorance or mistake as to the provisions of the Code, any other provision of the criminal law or the law governing the administration of the institution; and

(b) the nature or degree of force used is not forbidden by Article 303 or 304 of the Code; and

(c) if deadly force is used, its use is otherwise justifiable under this Article; or

(6) the actor is a person responsible for the safety of a vessel or an aircraft or a person acting at his direction, and

(a) he believes that the force used is necessary to prevent interference with the operation of the vessel or aircraft or obstruction of the execution of a lawful order, unless his belief in the lawfulness of the order is erroneous and his error is due to ignorance or mistake as to the law defining his authority; and

(b) if deadly force is used, its use is otherwise justifiable under this Article; or

(7) the actor is a person who is authorized or required by law to maintain order or decorum in a vehicle, train or other carrier or in a place where others are assembled, and:

(a) he believes that the force used is necessary for such purpose; and

(b) the force used is not designed to cause or known to create a substantial risk of causing death, bodily harm, or extreme mental distress.

Section 3.09. Mistake of Law as to Unlawfulness of Force or Legality of Arrest; Reckless or Negligent Use of Otherwise Justifiable Force; Reckless or Negligent Injury or Risk of Injury to Innocent Persons.

(1) The justification afforded by Sections 3.04 to 3.07, inclusive, is unavailable when:

(a) the actor's belief in the unlawfulness of the force or conduct against which he employs protective force or his belief in the lawfulness of an arrest which he endeavors to effect by force is erroneous; and

(b) his error is due to ignorance or mistake as to the provisions of the Code, any other provision of the criminal law or the law governing the legality of an arrest or search.

(2) When the actor believes that the use of force upon or toward the person of another is necessary for any of the purposes for which such belief would establish a justification under Sections 3.03 to 3.08 but the actor is reckless or negligent in having such belief or in acquiring or failing to acquire any knowledge or belief which is material to the justifiability of his use of force, the justification afforded by those Sections is unavailable in a prosecution for an offense for which recklessness or negligence, as the case may be, suffices to establish culpability.

(3) When the actor is justified under Sections 3.03 to 3.08 in using force upon or toward the person of another but he recklessly or negligently injures or creates a risk of injury to innocent persons, the justification afforded by those Sections is unavailable in a prosecution for such recklessness or negligence towards innocent persons.

Section 3.10. Justification in Property Crimes.

Conduct involving the appropriation, seizure or destruction of, damage to, intrusion on or interference with property is justifiable under circumstances which would establish a defense of privilege in a civil action based thereon, unless:

(1) the Code or the law defining the offense deals with the specific situation involved; or

(2) a legislative purpose to exclude the justification claimed otherwise plainly appears.

Section 3.11. Definitions.

In this Article, unless a different meaning plainly is required:

(1) "unlawful force" means force, including confinement, which is employed without the consent of the person against whom it is directed and the employment of which constitutes an offense or actionable tort or would constitute such offense or tort except for a defense (such as the absence of intent, negligence, or mental capacity; duress; youth; or diplomatic status) not amounting to a privilege to use the force. Assent constitutes consent, within the meaning of this Section, whether or not it otherwise is legally effective, except assent to the infliction of death or serious bodily harm.

(2) "deadly force" means force which the actor uses with the purpose of causing or which he knows to create a substantial risk of causing death or serious bodily harm. Purposely firing a firearm in the direction of another person or at a vehicle in which another person is believed to be constitutes deadly force. A threat to cause death or serious bodily harm, by the production of a weapon or otherwise, so long as the actor's purpose is limited to creating an apprehension that he will use deadly force if necessary, does not constitute deadly force;

(3) "dwelling" means any building or structure, though movable or temporary, or a portion thereof, which is for the time being the actor's home or place of lodging.

ARTICLE 4. RESPONSIBILITY

Section 4.01. Mental Disease or Defect Excluding Responsibility.

(1) A person is not responsible for criminal conduct if at the time of such conduct as a result of mental disease or defect he lacks substantial capacity either to appreciate the criminality [wrongfulness] of his conduct or to conform his conduct to the requirements of law.

(2) As used in this Article, the terms "mental disease or defect" do not include an abnormality manifested only by repeated criminal or otherwise anti-social conduct.

Section 4.02. Evidence of Mental Disease or Defect Admissible When Relevant to Element of the Offense; [Mental Disease or Defect Impairing Capacity as Ground for Mitigation of Punishment in Capital Cases].

(1) Evidence that the defendant suffered from a mental disease or defect is admissible whenever it is relevant to prove that the defendant did or did not have a state of mind which is an element of the offense.

[(2) Whenever the jury or the Court is authorized to determine or to recommend whether or not the defendant shall be sentenced to death or imprisonment upon conviction, evidence that the capacity of the defendant to appreciate the criminality [wrongfulness] of his conduct or to conform his conduct to the requirements of law was impaired as a result of mental disease or defect is admissible in favor of sentence of imprisonment.]

Section 4.03. Mental Disease or Defect Excluding Responsibility is Affirmative Defense; Requirement of Notice; Form of Verdict and Judgment When Finding of Irresponsibility is Made.

(1) Mental disease or defect excluding responsibility is an affirmative defense.

(2) Evidence of mental disease or defect excluding responsibility is not admissible unless the defendant, at the time of entering his plea of not guilty or within ten days thereafter or at such later time as the Court may for good cause permit, files a written notice of his purpose to rely on such defense.

(3) When the defendant is acquitted on the ground of mental disease or defect excluding responsibility, the verdict and the judgment shall so state.

Section 4.04. Mental Disease or Defect Excluding Fitness to Proceed.

No person who as a result of mental disease or defect lacks capacity to understand the proceedings against him or to assist in his own defense shall be tried, convicted or sentenced for the commission of an offense so long as such incapacity endures.

Section 4.05. Psychiatric Examination of Defendant With Respect to Mental Disease or Defect.

(1) Whenever the defendant has filed a notice of intention to rely on the defense of mental disease or defect excluding responsibility, or there is reason to doubt his fitness to proceed, or reason to believe that mental disease or defect of the defendant will otherwise become an issue in the cause, the Court shall appoint at least one qualified psychiatrist or shall request the Superintendent of the Hospital to designate at least one qualified psychiatrist, which designation may be or include himself, to examine and report upon the mental condition of the defendant. The Court may order the defendant to be committed to a hospital or other suitable facility for the purpose of the examination for a period of not exceeding sixty days or such longer period as the Court determines to be necessary for the purpose and may direct that a qualified psychiatrist retained by the defendant be permitted to witness and participate in the examination.

(2) In such examination any method may be employed which is accepted by the medical profession for the examination of those alleged to be suffering from mental disease or defect.

(3) The report of the examination shall include the following: (a) a description of the nature of the examination; (b) a diagnosis of the mental condition of the defendant; (c) if the defendant suffers from a mental disease or defect, an opinion as to his capacity to understand the proceedings against him and to assist in his own defense; (d) when a notice of intention to rely on the defense of irresponsibility has been filed, an opinion as to the extent, if any, to which the capacity of the defendant to appreciate the criminality [wrongfulness] of his conduct or to conform his conduct to the requirements of law was impaired at the time of the criminal conduct charged; and (e) when directed by the Court, an opinion as to the capacity of the defendant to have a particular state of mind which is an element of the offense charged.

If the examination can not be conducted by reason of the unwillingness of the defendant to participate therein, the report shall so state and shall include, if possible, an opinion as to whether such unwillingness of the defendant was the result of mental disease or defect.

The report of the examination shall be filed [in triplicate] with the clerk of the Court, who shall cause copies to be delivered to the district attorney and to counsel for the defendant.

Section 4.06. Determination of Fitness to Proceed; Effect of Finding of Unfitness; Proceedings if Fitness is Regained [; Post–Commitment Hearing].

(1) When the defendant's fitness to proceed is drawn in question, the issue shall be determined by the Court. If neither the prosecuting attorney nor counsel for the defendant contests the finding of the report filed pursuant to Section 4.05, the Court may make the determination on the basis of such report. If the finding is contested, the Court shall hold a hearing on the issue. If the report is received in evidence upon such hearing, the party who contests the finding thereof shall have the right to summon and to cross-examine the psychiatrists who joined in the report and to offer evidence upon the issue.

(2) If the Court determines that the defendant lacks fitness to proceed, the proceeding against him shall be suspended, except as provided in Subsection (3) [Subsections (3) and (4)] of this Section, and the Court shall commit him to the custody of the Commissioner of Mental Hygiene [Public Health or Correction] to be placed in an appropriate institution of the Department of Mental Hygiene [Public Health or Correction] for so long as such unfitness shall endure. When the Court, on its own motion or upon the application of the Commissioner of Mental Hygiene [Public Health or Correction] or the prosecuting attorney, determines, after a hearing if a hearing is requested, that the defendant has regained fitness to proceed, the proceeding shall be resumed. If, however, the Court is of the view that so much time has elapsed since the commitment of the defendant that it would be unjust to resume the criminal proceeding, the Court may dismiss the charge and may order the defendant to be discharged or, subject to the law governing the civil commitment of persons suffering from mental disease or defect, order the defendant to be committed to an appropriate institution of the Department of Mental Hygiene [Public Health].

(3) The fact that the defendant is unfit to proceed does not preclude any legal objection to the prosecution which is susceptible of fair determination prior to trial and without the personal participation of the defendant.

[Alternative: (3) At any time within ninety days after commitment as provided in Subsection (2) of this Section, or at any later time with permission of the Court granted for good cause, the defendant or his counsel or the Commissioner of Mental Hygiene [Public Health or Correction] may apply for a special post-commitment hearing. If the application is made by or on behalf of a defendant not represented by counsel, he shall be afforded a reasonable opportunity to obtain counsel, and if he lacks funds to do so, counsel shall be assigned by the Court. The application shall be granted only if the counsel for the defendant satisfies the Court by affidavit or otherwise that as an attorney he has reasonable grounds for a good faith belief that his client has, on the facts and the law, a defense to the charge other than mental disease or defect excluding responsibility.

[(4) If the motion for a special post-commitment hearing is granted, the hearing shall be by the Court without a jury. No evidence shall be offered at the hearing by either party on the issue of mental disease or defect as a defense to, or in mitigation of, the crime charged. After hearing, the Court may in an appropriate case quash the indictment or other charge, or find it to be defective or insufficient, or determine that it is not proved beyond a reasonable doubt by the evidence, or otherwise terminate the proceedings on the evidence or the law. In any such case, unless all defects in the proceedings are promptly cured, the Court shall terminate the commitment ordered under Subsection (2) of this Section and order the defendant to be discharged or, subject to the law governing the civil commitment of persons suffering from mental disease or defect, order the defendant to be committed to an appropriate institution of the Department of Mental Hygiene [Public Health].]

Section 4.07. Determination of Irresponsibility on Basis of Report; Access to Defendant by Psychiatrist of His Own Choice; Form of Expert Testimony When Issue of Responsibility is Tried.

(1) If the report filed pursuant to Section 4.05 finds that the defendant at the time of the criminal conduct charged suffered from a mental disease or defect which substantially impaired his capacity to appreciate the criminality [wrongfulness] of his conduct or to conform his conduct to the requirements of law, and the Court, after a hearing if a hearing is requested by the prosecuting attorney or the defendant, is satisfied that such impairment was sufficient to exclude responsibility, the Court on motion of the defendant shall enter judgment of acquittal on the ground of mental disease or defect excluding responsibility.

(2) When, notwithstanding the report filed pursuant to Section 4.05, the defendant wishes to be examined by a qualified psychiatrist or other expert of his own choice, such examiner shall be permitted to have reasonable access to the defendant for the purposes of such examination.

(3) Upon the trial, the psychiatrists who reported pursuant to Section 4.05 may be called as witnesses by the prosecution, the defendant or the Court. If the issue is being tried before a jury, the jury may be informed that the psychiatrists were designated by the Court or by the Superintendent of the Hospital at the request of the Court as the case may be. If called by the Court, the witness shall be subject to cross-examination by the prosecution and by the defendant. Both the prosecution and the defendant may summon any other qualified psychiatrist or other expert to testify, but no one who has not examined the defendant shall be competent to testify to an expert opinion with respect to the mental condition or responsibility of the defendant, as distinguished from the validity of the procedure followed by, or the general scientific propositions stated by, another witness.

(4) When a psychiatrist or other expert who has examined the defendant testifies concerning his mental condition, he shall be permitted to make a statement as to the nature of his examination, his diagnosis of the mental condition of the defendant at the time of the commission of the offense charged and his opinion as to the extent, if any, to which the capacity of the defendant to appreciate the criminality [wrongfulness] of his conduct or to conform his conduct to the requirements of law or to have a particular state of mind which is an element of the offense charged was impaired as a result of mental disease or defect at that time. He shall be permitted to make any explanation reasonably serving to clarify his diagnosis and opinion and may be cross-examined as to any matter bearing on his competency or credibility or the validity of his diagnosis or opinion.

Section 4.08. Legal Effect of Acquittal on the Ground of Mental Disease or Defect Excluding Responsibility; Commitment; Release or Discharge.

(1) When a defendant is acquitted on the ground of mental disease or defect excluding responsibility, the Court shall order him to be committed to the custody of the Commissioner of Mental Hygiene [Public Health] to be placed in an appropriate institution for custody, care and treatment.

(2) If the Commissioner of Mental Hygiene [Public Health] is of the view that a person committed to his custody, pursuant to paragraph (1) of this Section, may be discharged or released on condition without danger to himself or to others, he shall make application for the discharge or release of such person in a report to the Court by which such person was committed and shall transmit a copy of such application and report to the prosecuting attorney of the county [parish] from which the defendant was committed. The Court shall thereupon appoint at least two qualified psychiatrists to examine such person and to report

within sixty days, or such longer period as the Court determines to be necessary for the purpose, their opinion as to his mental condition. To facilitate such examination and the proceedings thereon, the Court may cause such person to be confined in any institution located near the place where the Court sits, which may hereafter be designated by the Commissioner of Mental Hygiene [Public Health] as suitable for the temporary detention of irresponsible persons.

(3) If the Court is satisfied by the report filed pursuant to paragraph (2) of this Section and such testimony of the reporting psychiatrists as the Court deems necessary that the committed person may be discharged or released on condition without danger to himself or others, the Court shall order his discharge or his release on such conditions as the Court determines to be necessary. If the Court is not so satisfied, it shall promptly order a hearing to determine whether such person may safely be discharged or released. Any such hearing shall be deemed a civil proceeding and the burden shall be upon the committed person to prove that he may safely be discharged or released. According to the determination of the Court upon the hearing, the committed person shall thereupon be discharged or released on such conditions as the Court determines to be necessary, or shall be recommitted to the custody of the Commissioner of Mental Hygiene [Public Health], subject to discharge or release only in accordance with the procedure prescribed above for a first hearing.

(4) If, within [five] years after the conditional release of a committed person, the Court shall determine, after hearing evidence, that the conditions of release have not been fulfilled and that for the safety of such person or for the safety of others his conditional release should be revoked, the Court shall forthwith order him to be recommitted to the Commissioner of Mental Hygiene [Public Health], subject to discharge or release only in accordance with the procedure prescribed above for a first hearing.

(5) A committed person may make application for his discharge or release to the Court by which he was committed, and the procedure to be followed upon such application shall be the same as that prescribed above in the case of an application by the Commissioner of Mental Hygiene [Public Health]. However, no such application by a committed person need be considered until he has been confined for a period of not less than [six months] from the date of the order of commitment, and if the determination of the Court be adverse to the application, such person shall not be permitted to file a further application until [one year] has elapsed from the date of any preceding hearing on an application for his release or discharge.

Section 4.09. Statements for Purposes of Examination or Treatment Inadmissible Except on Issue of Mental Condition.

A statement made by a person subjected to psychiatric examination or treatment pursuant to Sections 4.05, 4.06 or 4.08 for the purposes of such examination or treatment shall not be admissible in evidence against him in any criminal proceeding on any issue other than that of his mental condition but it shall be admissible upon that issue, whether or not it would otherwise be deemed a privileged communication [, unless such statement constitutes an admission of guilt of the crime charged].

Section 4.10. Immaturity Excluding Criminal Conviction; Transfer of Proceedings to Juvenile Court.

(1) A person shall not be tried for or convicted of an offense if:

(a) at the time of the conduct charged to constitute the offense he was less than sixteen years of age [, in which case the Juvenile Court shall have exclusive jurisdic-

tion*]; or

    (b) at the time of the conduct charged to constitute the offense he was sixteen or seventeen years of age unless:

        (i) the Juvenile Court has no jurisdiction over him, or,

        (ii) the Juvenile Court has entered an order waiving jurisdiction and consenting to the institution of criminal proceedings against him.

    (2) No court shall have jurisdiction to try or convict a person of an offense if criminal proceedings against him are barred by Subsection (1) of this Section. When it appears that a person charged with the commission of an offense may be of such an age that criminal proceedings may be barred under Subsection (1) of this Section, the Court shall hold a hearing thereon, and the burden shall be on the prosecution to establish to the satisfaction of the Court that the criminal proceeding is not barred upon such grounds. If the Court determines that the proceeding is barred, custody of the person charged shall be surrendered to the Juvenile Court, and the case, including all papers and processes relating thereto, shall be transferred.

ARTICLE 5. INCHOATE CRIMES

Section 5.01. Criminal Attempt.

    (1) **Definition of Attempt.** A person is guilty of an attempt to commit a crime if, acting with the kind of culpability otherwise required for commission of the crime, he:

    (a) purposely engages in conduct which would constitute the crime if the attendant circumstances were as he believes them to be; or

    (b) when causing a particular result is an element of the crime, does or omits to do anything with the purpose of causing or with the belief that it will cause such result without further conduct on his part; or

    (c) purposely does or omits to do anything which, under the circumstances as he believes them to be, is an act or omission constituting a substantial step in a course of conduct planned to culminate in his commission of the crime.

    (2) **Conduct Which May Be Held Substantial Step Under Subsection (1)(c).** Conduct shall not be held to constitute a substantial step under Subsection (1)(c) of this Section unless it is strongly corroborative of the actor's criminal purpose. Without negativing the sufficiency of other conduct, the following, if strongly corroborative of the actor's criminal purpose, shall not be held insufficient as a matter of law:

    (a) lying in wait, searching for or following the contemplated victim of the crime;

    (b) enticing or seeking to entice the contemplated victim of the crime to go to the place contemplated for its commission;

    (c) reconnoitering the place contemplated for the commission of the crime;

    (d) unlawful entry of a structure, vehicle or enclosure in which it is contemplated that the crime will be committed;

    (e) possession of materials to be employed in the commission of the crime, which are specially designed for such unlawful use or which can serve no lawful purpose of the actor under the circumstances;

    (f) possession, collection or fabrication of materials to be employed in the commission of the crime, at or near the place contemplated for its commission, where such

---

* The bracketed words are unnecessary if the Juvenile Court Act so provides or is amended accordingly.

possession, collection or fabrication serves no lawful purpose of the actor under the circumstances;

(g) soliciting an innocent agent to engage in conduct constituting an element of the crime.

(3) **Conduct Designed to Aid Another in Commission of a Crime.** A person who engages in conduct designed to aid another to commit a crime which would establish his complicity under Section 2.06 if the crime were committed by such other person, is guilty of an attempt to commit the crime, although the crime is not committed or attempted by such other person.

(4) **Renunciation of Criminal Purpose.** When the actor's conduct would otherwise constitute an attempt under Subsection (1)(b) or (1)(c) of this Section, it is an affirmative defense that he abandoned his effort to commit the crime or otherwise prevented its commission, under circumstances manifesting a complete and voluntary renunciation of his criminal purpose. The establishment of such defense does not, however, affect the liability of an accomplice who did not join in such abandonment or prevention.

Within the meaning of this Article, renunciation of criminal purpose is not voluntary if it is motivated, in whole or in part, by circumstances, not present or apparent at the inception of the actor's course of conduct, which increase the probability of detection or apprehension or which make more difficult the accomplishment of the criminal purpose. Renunciation is not complete if it is motivated by a decision to postpone the criminal conduct until a more advantageous time or to transfer the criminal effort to another but similar objective or victim.

Section 5.02. Criminal Solicitation.

(1) **Definition of Solicitation.** A person is guilty of solicitation to commit a crime if with the purpose of promoting or facilitating its commission he commands, encourages or requests another person to engage in specific conduct which would constitute such crime or an attempt to commit such crime or which would establish his complicity in its commission or attempted commission.

(2) **Uncommunicated Solicitation.** It is immaterial under Subsection (1) of this Section that the actor fails to communicate with the person he solicits to commit a crime if his conduct was designed to effect such communication.

(3) **Renunciation of Criminal Purpose.** It is an affirmative defense that the actor, after soliciting another person to commit a crime, persuaded him not to do so or otherwise prevented the commission of the crime, under circumstances manifesting a complete and voluntary renunciation of his criminal purpose.

Section 5.03. Criminal Conspiracy.

(1) **Definition of Conspiracy.** A person is guilty of conspiracy with another person or persons to commit a crime if with the purpose of promoting or facilitating its commission he:

(a) agrees with such other person or persons that they or one or more of them will engage in conduct which constitutes such crime or an attempt or solicitation to commit such crime; or

(b) agrees to aid such other person or persons in the planning or commission of such crime or of an attempt or solicitation to commit such crime.

(2) **Scope of Conspiratorial Relationship.** If a person guilty of conspiracy, as defined by Subsection (1) of this Section, knows that a person with whom he conspires to

commit a crime has conspired with another person or persons to commit the same crime, he is guilty of conspiring with such other person or persons, whether or not he knows their identity, to commit such crime.

(3) **Conspiracy With Multiple Criminal Objectives.** If a person conspires to commit a number of crimes, he is guilty of only one conspiracy so long as such multiple crimes are the object of the same agreement or continuous conspiratorial relationship.

(4) **Joinder and Venue in Conspiracy Prosecutions.**

(a) Subject to the provisions of paragraph (b) of this Subsection, two or more persons charged with criminal conspiracy may be prosecuted jointly if:

(i) they are charged with conspiring with one another; or

(ii) the conspiracies alleged, whether they have the same or different parties, are so related that they constitute different aspects of a scheme of organized criminal conduct.

(b) In any joint prosecution under paragraph (a) of this Subsection:

(i) no defendant shall be charged with a conspiracy in any county [parish or district] other than one in which he entered into such conspiracy or in which an overt act pursuant to such conspiracy was done by him or by a person with whom he conspired; and

(ii) neither the liability of any defendant nor the admissibility against him of evidence of acts or declarations of another shall be enlarged by such joinder; and

(iii) the Court shall order a severance or take a special verdict as to any defendant who so requests, if it deems it necessary or appropriate to promote the fair determination of his guilt or innocence, and shall take any other proper measures to protect the fairness of the trial.

(5) **Overt Act.** No person may be convicted of conspiracy to commit a crime, other than a felony of the first or second degree, unless an overt act in pursuance of such conspiracy is alleged and proved to have been done by him or by a person with whom he conspired.

(6) **Renunciation of Criminal Purpose.** It is an affirmative defense that the actor, after conspiring to commit a crime, thwarted the success of the conspiracy, under circumstances manifesting a complete and voluntary renunciation of his criminal purpose.

(7) **Duration of Conspiracy.** For purposes of Section 1.06(4):

(a) conspiracy is a continuing course of conduct which terminates when the crime or crimes which are its object are committed or the agreement that they be committed is abandoned by the defendant and by those with whom he conspired; and

(b) such abandonment is presumed if neither the defendant nor anyone with whom he conspired does any overt act in pursuance of the conspiracy during the applicable period of limitation; and

(c) if an individual abandons the agreement, the conspiracy is terminated as to him only if and when he advises those with whom he conspired of his abandonment or he informs the law enforcement authorities of the existence of the conspiracy and of his participation therein.

Section 5.04. Incapacity, Irresponsibility or Immunity of Party to Solicitation or Conspiracy.

(1) Except as provided in Subsection (2) of this Section, it is immaterial to the liability of a person who solicits or conspires with another to commit a crime that:

(a) he or the person whom he solicits or with whom he conspires does not occupy a particular position or have a particular characteristic which is an element of such crime, if he believes that one of them does; or

(b) the person whom he solicits or with whom he conspires is irresponsible or has an immunity to prosecution or conviction for the commission of the crime.

(2) It is a defense to a charge of solicitation or conspiracy to commit a crime that if the criminal object were achieved, the actor would not be guilty of a crime under the law defining the offense or as an accomplice under Section 2.06(5) or 2.06(6)(a) or (b).

Section 5.05. Grading of Criminal Attempt, Solicitation and Conspiracy; Mitigation in Cases of Lesser Danger; Multiple Convictions Barred.

(1) **Grading.** Except as otherwise provided in this Section, attempt, solicitation and conspiracy are crimes of the same grade and degree as the most serious offense which is attempted or solicited or is an object of the conspiracy. An attempt, solicitation or conspiracy to commit a [capital crime or a] felony of the first degree is a felony of the second degree.

(2) **Mitigation.** If the particular conduct charged to constitute a criminal attempt, solicitation or conspiracy is so inherently unlikely to result or culminate in the commission of a crime that neither such conduct nor the actor presents a public danger warranting the grading of such offense under this Section, the Court shall exercise its power under Section 6.12 to enter judgment and impose sentence for a crime of lower grade or degree or, in extreme cases, may dismiss the prosecution.

(3) **Multiple Convictions.** A person may not be convicted of more than one offense defined by this Article for conduct designed to commit or to culminate in the commission of the same crime.

Section 5.06. Possessing Instruments of Crime; Weapons.

(1) **Criminal Instruments Generally.** A person commits a misdemeanor if he possesses any instrument of crime with purpose to employ it criminally. "Instrument of crime" means:

(a) anything specially made or specially adapted for criminal use; or

(b) anything commonly used for criminal purposes and possessed by the actor under circumstances which do not negative unlawful purpose.

(2) **Presumption of Criminal Purpose from Possession of Weapon.** If a person possesses a firearm or other weapon on or about his person, in a vehicle occupied by him, or otherwise readily available for use, it is presumed that he had the purpose to employ it criminally, unless:

(a) the weapon is possessed in the actor's home or place of business;

(b) the actor is licensed or otherwise authorized by law to possess such weapon; or

(c) the weapon is of a type commonly used in lawful sport.

"Weapon" means anything readily capable of lethal use and possessed under circumstances not manifestly appropriate for lawful uses which it may have; the term includes a firearm which is not loaded or lacks a clip or other component to render it immediately operable, and components which can readily be assembled into a weapon.

(3) **Presumptions as to Possession of Criminal Instruments in Automobiles.** Where a weapon or other instrument of crime is found in an automobile, it shall be presumed to be in the possession of the occupant if there is but one. If there is more than one occupant, it shall be presumed to be in the possession of all, except under the following circumstances:

(a) where it is found upon the person of one of the occupants;

(b) where the automobile is not a stolen one and the weapon or instrument is found out of view in a glove compartment, car trunk, or other enclosed customary depository, in which case it shall be presumed to be in the possession of the occupant or occupants who own or have authority to operate the automobile;

(c) in the case of a taxicab, a weapon or instrument found in the passengers' portion of the vehicle shall be presumed to be in the possession of all the passengers, if there are any, and, if not, in the possession of the driver.

Section 5.07. Prohibited Offensive Weapons.

A person commits a misdemeanor if, except as authorized by law, he makes, repairs, sells, or otherwise deals in, uses, or possesses any offensive weapon. "Offensive weapon" means any bomb, machine gun, sawed-off shotgun, firearm specially made or specially adapted for concealment or silent discharge, any blackjack, sandbag, metal knuckles, dagger, or other implement for the infliction of serious bodily injury which serves no common lawful purpose. It is a defense under this Section for the defendant to prove by a preponderance of evidence that he possessed or dealt with the weapon solely as a curio or in a dramatic performance, or that he possessed it briefly in consequence of having found it or taken it from an aggressor, or under circumstances similarly negativing any purpose or likelihood that the weapon would be used unlawfully. The presumptions provided in Section 5.06(3) are applicable to prosecutions under this Section.

ARTICLE 6. AUTHORIZED DISPOSITION OF OFFENDERS

Section 6.01. Degrees of Felonies.

(1) Felonies defined by this Code are classified, for the purpose of sentence, into three degrees, as follows:

(a) felonies of the first degree;

(b) felonies of the second degree;

(c) felonies of the third degree.

A felony is of the first or second degree when it is so designated by the Code. A crime declared to be a felony, without specification of degree, is of the third degree.

(2) Notwithstanding any other provision of law, a felony defined by any statute of this State other than this Code shall constitute for the purpose of sentence a felony of the third degree.

Section 6.02. Sentence in Accordance With Code; Authorized Dispositions.

(1) No person convicted of an offense shall be sentenced otherwise than in accordance with this Article.

[(2) The Court shall sentence a person who has been convicted of murder to death or imprisonment, in accordance with Section 210.6.]

(3) Except as provided in Subsection (2) of this Section and subject to the applicable provisions of the Code, the Court may suspend the imposition of sentence on a person who

has been convicted of a crime, may order him to be committed in lieu of sentence, in accordance with Section 6.13, or may sentence him as follows:

    (a) to pay a fine authorized by Section 6.03; or

    (b) to be placed on probation [, and, in the case of a person convicted of a felony or misdemeanor to imprisonment for a term fixed by the Court not exceeding thirty days to be served as a condition of probation]; or

    (c) to imprisonment for a term authorized by Sections 6.05, 6.06, 6.07, 6.08, 6.09, or 7.06; or

    (d) to fine and probation or fine and imprisonment, but not to probation and imprisonment [, except as authorized in paragraph (b) of this Subsection].

(4) The Court may suspend the imposition of sentence on a person who has been convicted of a violation or may sentence him to pay a fine authorized by Section 6.03.

(5) This Article does not deprive the Court of any authority conferred by law to decree a forfeiture of property, suspend or cancel a license, remove a person from office, or impose any other civil penalty. Such a judgment or order may be included in the sentence.

Section 6.03. Fines.

A person who has been convicted of an offense may be sentenced to pay a fine not exceeding:

    (1) $10,000, when the conviction is of a felony of the first or second degree;

    (2) $5,000, when the conviction is of a felony of the third degree;

    (3) $1,000, when the conviction is of a misdemeanor;

    (4) $500, when the conviction is of a petty misdemeanor or a violation;

    (5) any higher amount equal to double the pecuniary gain derived from the offense by the offender;

    (6) any higher amount specifically authorized by statute.

Section 6.04. Penalties Against Corporations and Unincorporated Associations; Forfeiture of Corporate Charter or Revocation of Certificate Authorizing Foreign Corporation to Do Business in the State.

(1) The Court may suspend the sentence of a corporation or an unincorporated association which has been convicted of an offense or may sentence it to pay a fine authorized by Section 6.03.

    (2)(a) The [prosecuting attorney] is authorized to institute civil proceedings in the appropriate court of general jurisdiction to forfeit the charter of a corporation organized under the laws of this State or to revoke the certificate authorizing a foreign corporation to conduct business in this State. The Court may order the charter forfeited or the certificate revoked upon finding (i) that the board of directors or a high managerial agent acting in behalf of the corporation has, in conducting the corporation's affairs, purposely engaged in a persistent course of criminal conduct and (ii) that for the prevention of future criminal conduct of the same character, the public interest requires the charter of the corporation to be forfeited and the corporation to be dissolved or the certificate to be revoked.

    (b) When a corporation is convicted of a crime or a high managerial agent of a corporation, as defined in Section 2.07, is convicted of a crime committed in the conduct of the affairs of the corporation, the Court, in sentencing the corporation or the agent, may direct the [prosecuting attorney] to institute proceedings authorized by paragraph (a) of this Subsection.

(c) The proceedings authorized by paragraph (a) of this Subsection shall be conducted in accordance with the procedures authorized by law for the involuntary dissolution of a corporation or the revocation of the certificate authorizing a foreign corporation to conduct business in this State. Such proceedings shall be deemed additional to any other proceedings authorized by law for the purpose of forfeiting the charter of a corporation or revoking the certificate of a foreign corporation.

Section 6.05. Young Adult Offenders.

(1) **Specialized Correctional Treatment.** A young adult offender is a person convicted of a crime who, at the time of sentencing, is sixteen but less than twenty-two years of age. A young adult offender who is sentenced to a term of imprisonment which may exceed thirty days [alternatives: (1) ninety days; (2) one year] shall be committed to the custody of the Division of Young Adult Correction of the Department of Correction, and shall receive, as far as practicable, such special and individualized correctional and rehabilitative treatment as may be appropriate to his needs.

(2) **Special Term.** A young adult offender convicted of a felony may, in lieu of any other sentence of imprisonment authorized by this Article, be sentenced to a special term of imprisonment without a minimum and with a maximum of four years, regardless of the degree of the felony involved, if the Court is of the opinion that such special term is adequate for his correction and rehabilitation and will not jeopardize the protection of the public.

[(3) **Removal of Disabilities; Vacation of Conviction.**

(a) In sentencing a young adult offender to the special term provided by this Section or to any sentence other than one of imprisonment, the Court may order that so long as he is not convicted of another felony, the judgment shall not constitute a conviction for the purposes of any disqualification or disability imposed by law upon conviction of a crime.

(b) When any young adult offender is unconditionally discharged from probation or parole before the expiration of the maximum term thereof, the Court may enter an order vacating the judgment of conviction.]

[(4) **Commitment for Observation.** If, after pre-sentence investigation, the Court desires additional information concerning a young adult offender before imposing sentence, it may order that he be committed, for a period not exceeding ninety days, to the custody of the Division of Young Adult Correction of the Department of Correction for observation and study at an appropriate reception or classification center. Such Division of the Department of Correction and the [Young Adult Division of the] Board of Parole shall advise the Court of their findings and recommendations on or before the expiration of such ninety-day period.]

Subsection (3) should be eliminated if Section 306.6, dealing with removal of disabilities generally, is adopted.

Subsection (4) should be eliminated if Subsection (1) of Section 7.08, dealing with commitments for observation generally, is adopted.

Section 6.06. Sentence of Imprisonment for Felony; Ordinary Terms.

A person who has been convicted of a felony may be sentenced to imprisonment, as follows:

(1) in the case of a felony of the first degree, for a term the minimum of which shall be fixed by the Court at not less than one year nor more than ten years, and the maximum of which shall be life imprisonment;

(2) in the case of a felony of the second degree, for a term the minimum of which shall be fixed by the Court at not less than one year nor more than three years, and the maximum of which shall be ten years;

(3) in the case of a felony of the third degree, for a term the minimum of which shall be fixed by the Court at not less than one year nor more than two years, and the maximum of which shall be five years.

Alternate Section 6.06. Sentence of Imprisonment for Felony; Ordinary Terms.

A person who has been convicted of a felony may be sentenced to imprisonment, as follows:

(1) in the case of a felony of the first degree, for a term the minimum of which shall be fixed by the Court at not less than one year nor more than ten years, and the maximum at not more than twenty years or at life imprisonment;

(2) in the case of a felony of the second degree, for a term the minimum of which shall be fixed by the Court at not less than one year nor more than three years, and the maximum at not more than ten years;

(3) in the case of a felony of the third degree, for a term the minimum of which shall be fixed by the Court at not less than one year nor more than two years, and the maximum at not more than five years.

No sentence shall be imposed under this Section of which the minimum is longer than one-half the maximum, or, when the maximum is life imprisonment, longer than ten years.

Section 6.07. Sentence of Imprisonment for Felony; Extended Terms.

In the cases designated in Section 7.03, a person who has been convicted of a felony may be sentenced to an extended term of imprisonment, as follows:

(1) in the case of a felony of the first degree, for a term the minimum of which shall be fixed by the Court at not less than five years nor more than ten years, and the maximum of which shall be life imprisonment;

(2) in the case of a felony of the second degree, for a term the minimum of which shall be fixed by the Court at not less than one year nor more than five years, and the maximum of which shall be fixed by the Court at not less than ten nor more than twenty years;

(3) in the case of a felony of the third degree, for a term the minimum of which shall be fixed by the Court at not less than one year nor more than three years, and the maximum of which shall be fixed by the Court at not less than five nor more than ten years.

Section 6.08. Sentence of Imprisonment for Misdemeanors and Petty Misdemeanors; Ordinary Terms.

A person who has been convicted of a misdemeanor or a petty misdemeanor may be sentenced to imprisonment for a definite term which shall be fixed by the Court and shall not exceed one year in the case of a misdemeanor or thirty days in the case of a petty misdemeanor.

Section 6.09. Sentence of Imprisonment for Misdemeanors and Petty Misdemeanors; Extended Terms.

(1) In the cases designated in Section 7.04, a person who has been convicted of a misdemeanor or a petty misdemeanor may be sentenced to an extended term of imprisonment, as follows:

(a) in the case of a misdemeanor, for a term the minimum of which shall be fixed by the Court at not more than one year and the maximum of which shall be three years;

(b) in the case of a petty misdemeanor, for a term the minimum of which shall be fixed by the Court at not more than six months and the maximum of which shall be two years.

(2) No such sentence for an extended term shall be imposed unless:

(a) the Director of Correction has certified that there is an institution in the Department of Correction, or in a county, city [or other appropriate political subdivision of the State] which is appropriate for the detention and correctional treatment of such misdemeanants or petty misdemeanants, and that such institution is available to receive such commitments; and

(b) the [Board of Parole] [Parole Administrator] has certified that the Board of Parole is able to visit such institution and to assume responsibility for the release of such prisoners on parole and for their parole supervision.

Section 6.10. First Release of All Offenders on Parole; Sentence of Imprisonment Includes Separate Parole Term; Length of Parole Term; Length of Recommitment and Reparole After Revocation of Parole; Final Unconditional Release.

(1) **First Release of All Offenders on Parole.** An offender sentenced to an indefinite term of imprisonment in excess of one year under Section 6.05, 6.06, 6.07, 6.09 or 7.06 shall be released conditionally on parole at or before the expiration of the maximum of such term, in accordance with Article 305.

(2) **Sentence of Imprisonment Includes Separate Parole Term; Length of Parole Term.** A sentence to an indefinite term of imprisonment in excess of one year under Section 6.05, 6.06, 6.07, 6.09 or 7.06 includes as a separate portion of the sentence a term of parole or of recommitment for violation of the conditions of parole which governs the duration of parole or recommitment after the offender's first conditional release on parole. The minimum of such term is one year and the maximum is five years, unless the sentence was imposed under Section 6.05(2) or Section 6.09, in which case the maximum is two years.

(3) **Length of Recommitment and Reparole After Revocation of Parole.** If an offender is recommitted upon revocation of his parole, the term of further imprisonment upon such recommitment and of any subsequent reparole or recommitment under the same sentence shall be fixed by the Board of Parole but shall not exceed in aggregate length the unserved balance of the maximum parole term provided by Subsection (2) of this Section.

(4) **Final Unconditional Release.** When the maximum of his parole term has expired or he has been sooner discharged from parole under Section 305.12, an offender shall be deemed to have served his sentence and shall be released unconditionally.

Section 6.11. Place of Imprisonment.

(1) When a person is sentenced to imprisonment for an indefinite term with a maximum in excess of one year, the Court shall commit him to the custody of the Department of Correction [or other single department or agency] for the term of his sentence and until released in accordance with law.

(2) When a person is sentenced to imprisonment for a definite term, the Court shall designate the institution or agency to which he is committed for the term of his sentence and until released in accordance with law.

Section 6.12. Reduction of Conviction by Court to Lesser Degree of Felony or to Misdemeanor.

If, when a person has been convicted of a felony, the Court, having regard to the nature and circumstances of the crime and to the history and character of the defendant, is of the view that it would be unduly harsh to sentence the offender in accordance with the Code, the Court may enter judgment of conviction for a lesser degree of felony or for a misdemeanor and impose sentence accordingly.

Section 6.13. Civil Commitment in Lieu of Prosecution or of Sentence.

(1) When a person prosecuted for a [felony of the third degree,] misdemeanor or petty misdemeanor is a chronic alcoholic, narcotic addict [or prostitute] or person suffering from mental abnormality and the Court is authorized by law to order the civil commitment of such person to a hospital or other institution for medical, psychiatric or other rehabilitative treatment, the Court may order such commitment and dismiss the prosecution. The order of commitment may be made after conviction, in which event the Court may set aside the verdict or judgment of conviction and dismiss the prosecution.

(2) The Court shall not make an order under Subsection (1) of this Section unless it is of the view that it will substantially further the rehabilitation of the defendant and will not jeopardize the protection of the public.

ARTICLE 7. AUTHORITY OF COURT IN SENTENCING

Section 7.01. Criteria for Withholding Sentence of Imprisonment and for Placing Defendant on Probation.

(1) The Court shall deal with a person who has been convicted of a crime without imposing sentence of imprisonment unless, having regard to the nature and circumstances of the crime and the history, character and condition of the defendant, it is of the opinion that his imprisonment is necessary for protection of the public because:

(a) there is undue risk that during the period of a suspended sentence or probation the defendant will commit another crime; or

(b) the defendant is in need of correctional treatment that can be provided most effectively by his commitment to an institution; or

(c) a lesser sentence will depreciate the seriousness of the defendant's crime.

(2) The following grounds, while not controlling the discretion of the Court, shall be accorded weight in favor of withholding sentence of imprisonment:

(a) the defendant's criminal conduct neither caused nor threatened serious harm;

(b) the defendant did not contemplate that his criminal conduct would cause or threaten serious harm;

(c) the defendant acted under a strong provocation;

(d) there were substantial grounds tending to excuse or justify the defendant's criminal conduct, though failing to establish a defense;

(e) the victim of the defendant's criminal conduct induced or facilitated its commission;

(f) the defendant has compensated or will compensate the victim of his criminal conduct for the damage or injury that he sustained;

(g) the defendant has no history of prior delinquency or criminal activity or has led a law-abiding life for a substantial period of time before the commission of the present crime;

(h) the defendant's criminal conduct was the result of circumstances unlikely to recur;

(i) the character and attitudes of the defendant indicate that he is unlikely to commit another crime;

(j) the defendant is particularly likely to respond affirmatively to probationary treatment;

(k) the imprisonment of the defendant would entail excessive hardship to himself or his dependents.

(3) When a person who has been convicted of a crime is not sentenced to imprisonment, the Court shall place him on probation if he is in need of the supervision, guidance, assistance or direction that the probation service can provide.

Section 7.02. Criteria for Imposing Fines.

(1) The Court shall not sentence a defendant only to pay a fine, when any other disposition is authorized by law, unless having regard to the nature and circumstances of the crime and to the history and character of the defendant, it is of the opinion that the fine alone suffices for protection of the public.

(2) The Court shall not sentence a defendant to pay a fine in addition to a sentence of imprisonment or probation unless:

(a) the defendant has derived a pecuniary gain from the crime; or

(b) the Court is of opinion that a fine is specially adapted to deterrence of the crime involved or to the correction of the offender.

(3) The Court shall not sentence a defendant to pay a fine unless:

(a) the defendant is or will be able to pay the fine; and

(b) the fine will not prevent the defendant from making restitution or reparation to the victim of the crime.

(4) In determining the amount and method of payment of a fine, the Court shall take into account the financial resources of the defendant and the nature of the burden that its payment will impose.

Section 7.03. Criteria for Sentence of Extended Term of Imprisonment; Felonies.

The Court may sentence a person who has been convicted of a felony to an extended term of imprisonment if it finds one or more of the grounds specified in this Section. The finding of the Court shall be incorporated in the record.

(1) The defendant is a persistent offender whose commitment for an extended term is necessary for protection of the public.

The Court shall not make such a finding unless the defendant is over twenty-one years of age and has previously been convicted of two felonies or of one felony and two misdemeanors, committed at different times when he was over [insert Juvenile Court age] years of age.

(2) The defendant is a professional criminal whose commitment for an extended term is necessary for protection of the public.

The Court shall not make such a finding unless the defendant is over twenty-one years of age and:

(a) the circumstances of the crime show that the defendant has knowingly devoted himself to criminal activity as a major source of livelihood; or

(b) the defendant has substantial income or resources not explained to be derived from a source other than criminal activity.

(3) The defendant is a dangerous, mentally abnormal person whose commitment for an extended term is necessary for protection of the public.

The Court shall not make such a finding unless the defendant has been subjected to a psychiatric examination resulting in the conclusions that his mental condition is gravely abnormal; that his criminal conduct has been characterized by a pattern of repetitive or compulsive behavior or by persistent aggressive behavior with heedless indifference to consequences; and that such condition makes him a serious danger to others.

(4) The defendant is a multiple offender whose criminality was so extensive that a sentence of imprisonment for an extended term is warranted.

The Court shall not make such a finding unless:

(a) the defendant is being sentenced for two or more felonies, or is already under sentence of imprisonment for felony, and the sentences of imprisonment involved will run concurrently under Section 7.06; or

(b) the defendant admits in open court the commission of one or more other felonies and asks that they be taken into account when he is sentenced; and

(c) the longest sentences of imprisonment authorized for each of the defendant's crimes, including admitted crimes taken into account, if made to run consecutively would exceed in length the minimum and maximum of the extended term imposed.

Section 7.04. Criteria for Sentence of Extended Term of Imprisonment; Misdemeanors and Petty Misdemeanors.

The Court may sentence a person who has been convicted of a misdemeanor or petty misdemeanor to an extended term of imprisonment if it finds one or more of the grounds specified in this Section. The finding of the Court shall be incorporated in the record.

(1) The defendant is a persistent offender whose commitment for an extended term is necessary for protection of the public.

The Court shall not make such a finding unless the defendant has previously been convicted of two crimes, committed at different times when he was over [insert Juvenile Court age] years of age.

(2) The defendant is a professional criminal whose commitment for an extended term is necessary for protection of the public.

The Court shall not make such a finding unless:

(a) the circumstances of the crime show that the defendant has knowingly devoted himself to criminal activity as a major source of livelihood; or

(b) the defendant has substantial income or resources not explained to be derived from a source other than criminal activity.

(3) The defendant is a chronic alcoholic, narcotic addict, prostitute or person of abnormal mental condition who requires rehabilitative treatment for a substantial period of time.

The Court shall not make such a finding unless, with respect to the particular category to which the defendant belongs, the Director of Correction has certified that there is a specialized institution or facility which is satisfactory for the rehabilitative treatment of such persons and which otherwise meets the requirements of Section 6.09, Subsection (2).

(4) The defendant is a multiple offender whose criminality was so extensive that a sentence of imprisonment for an extended term is warranted.

The Court shall not make such a finding unless:

(a) the defendant is being sentenced for a number of misdemeanors or petty misdemeanors or is already under sentence of imprisonment for crime of such grades, or admits in open court the commission of one or more such crimes and asks that they be taken into account when he is sentenced; and

(b) maximum fixed sentences of imprisonment for each of the defendant's crimes, including admitted crimes taken into account, if made to run consecutively, would exceed in length the maximum period of the extended term imposed.

Section 7.05. Former Conviction in Another Jurisdiction; Definition and Proof of Conviction; Sentence Taking into Account Admitted Crimes Bars Subsequent Conviction for Such Crimes.

(1) For purposes of paragraph (1) of Section 7.03 or 7.04, a conviction of the commission of a crime in another jurisdiction shall constitute a previous conviction. Such conviction shall be deemed to have been of a felony if sentence of death or of imprisonment in excess of one year was authorized under the law of such other jurisdiction, of a misdemeanor if sentence of imprisonment in excess of thirty days but not in excess of a year was authorized and of a petty misdemeanor if sentence of imprisonment for not more than thirty days was authorized.

(2) An adjudication by a court of competent jurisdiction that the defendant committed a crime constitutes a conviction for purposes of Sections 7.03 to 7.05 inclusive, although sentence or the execution thereof was suspended, provided that the time to appeal has expired and that the defendant was not pardoned on the ground of innocence.

(3) Prior conviction may be proved by any evidence, including fingerprint records made in connection with arrest, conviction or imprisonment, that reasonably satisfies the Court that the defendant was convicted.

(4) When the defendant has asked that other crimes admitted in open court be taken into account when he is sentenced and the Court has not rejected such request, the sentence shall bar the prosecution or conviction of the defendant in this State for any such admitted crime.

Section 7.06. Multiple Sentences; Concurrent and Consecutive Terms.

(1) **Sentences of Imprisonment for More Than One Crime.** When multiple sentences of imprisonment are imposed on a defendant for more than one crime, including a crime for which a previous suspended sentence or sentence of probation has been revoked, such multiple sentences shall run concurrently or consecutively as the Court determines at the time of sentence, except that:

(a) a definite and an indefinite term shall run concurrently and both sentences shall be satisfied by service of the indefinite term; and

(b) the aggregate of consecutive definite terms shall not exceed one year; and

(c) the aggregate of consecutive indefinite terms shall not exceed in minimum or maximum length the longest extended term authorized for the highest grade and degree of crime for which any of the sentences was imposed; and

(d) not more than one sentence for an extended term shall be imposed.

(2) **Sentences of Imprisonment Imposed at Different Times.** When a defendant who has previously been sentenced to imprisonment is subsequently sentenced to another term for a crime committed prior to the former sentence, other than a crime committed while in custody:

(a) the multiple sentences imposed shall so far as possible conform to Subsection (1) of this Section; and

(b) whether the Court determines that the terms shall run concurrently or consecutively, the defendant shall be credited with time served in imprisonment on the prior sentence in determining the permissible aggregate length of the term or terms remaining to be served; and

(c) when a new sentence is imposed on a prisoner who is on parole, the balance of the parole term on the former sentence shall be deemed to run during the period of the new imprisonment.

(3) **Sentence of Imprisonment for Crime Committed While on Parole.** When a defendant is sentenced to imprisonment for a crime committed while on parole in this State, such term of imprisonment and any period of reimprisonment that the Board of Parole may require the defendant to serve upon the revocation of his parole shall run concurrently, unless the Court orders them to run consecutively.

(4) **Multiple Sentences of Imprisonment in Other Cases.** Except as otherwise provided in this Section, multiple terms of imprisonment shall run concurrently or consecutively as the Court determines when the second or subsequent sentence is imposed.

(5) **Calculation of Concurrent and Consecutive Terms of Imprisonment.**

(a) When indefinite terms run concurrently, the shorter minimum terms merge in and are satisfied by serving the longest minimum term and the shorter maximum terms merge in and are satisfied by discharge of the longest maximum term.

(b) When indefinite terms run consecutively, the minimum terms are added to arrive at an aggregate minimum to be served equal to the sum of all minimum terms and the maximum terms are added to arrive at an aggregate maximum equal to the sum of all maximum terms.

(c) When a definite and an indefinite term run consecutively, the period of the definite term is added to both the minimum and maximum of the indefinite term and both sentences are satisfied by serving the indefinite term.

(6) **Suspension of Sentence or Probation and Imprisonment; Multiple Terms of Suspension and Probation.** When a defendant is sentenced for more than one offense or a defendant already under sentence is sentenced for another offense committed prior to the former sentence:

(a) the Court shall not sentence to probation a defendant who is under sentence of imprisonment [with more than thirty days to run] or impose a sentence of probation and a sentence of imprisonment [, except as authorized by Section 6.02(3)(b)]; and

(b) multiple periods of suspension or probation shall run concurrently from the date of the first such disposition; and

(c) when a sentence of imprisonment is imposed for an indefinite term, the service of such sentence shall satisfy a suspended sentence on another count or a prior suspended sentence or sentence to probation; and

(d) when a sentence of imprisonment is imposed for a definite term, the period of a suspended sentence on another count or a prior suspended sentence or sentence to probation shall run during the period of such imprisonment.

(7) **Offense Committed While Under Suspension of Sentence or Probation.** When a defendant is convicted of an offense committed while under suspension of sentence or on probation and such suspension or probation is not revoked:

(a) if the defendant is sentenced to imprisonment for an indefinite term, the service of such sentence shall satisfy the prior suspended sentence or sentence to probation; and

(b) if the defendant is sentenced to imprisonment for a definite term, the period of the suspension or probation shall not run during the period of such imprisonment; and

(c) if sentence is suspended or the defendant is sentenced to probation, the period of such suspension or probation shall run concurrently with or consecutively to the remainder of the prior periods, as the Court determines at the time of sentence.

Section 7.07. Procedure on Sentence; Presentence Investigation and Report; Remand for Psychiatric Examination; Transmission of Records to Department of Correction.

(1) The Court shall not impose sentence without first ordering a pre-sentence investigation of the defendant and according due consideration to a written report of such investigation where:

(a) the defendant has been convicted of a felony; or

(b) the defendant is less than twenty-two years of age and has been convicted of a crime; or

(c) the defendant will be [placed on probation or] sentenced to imprisonment for an extended term.

(2) The Court may order a pre-sentence investigation in any other case.

(3) The pre-sentence investigation shall include an analysis of the circumstances attending the commission of the crime, the defendant's history of delinquency or criminality, physical and mental condition, family situation and background, economic status, education, occupation and personal habits and any other matters that the probation officer deems relevant or the Court directs to be included.

(4) Before imposing sentence, the Court may order the defendant to submit to psychiatric observation and examination for a period of not exceeding sixty days or such longer period as the Court determines to be necessary for the purpose. The defendant may be remanded for this purpose to any available clinic or mental hospital or the Court may appoint a qualified psychiatrist to make the examination. The report of the examination shall be submitted to the Court.

(5) Before imposing sentence, the Court shall advise the defendant or his counsel of the factual contents and the conclusions of any pre-sentence investigation or psychiatric examination and afford fair opportunity, if the defendant so requests, to controvert them. The sources of confidential information need not, however, be disclosed.

(6) The Court shall not impose a sentence of imprisonment for an extended term unless the ground therefor has been established at a hearing after the conviction of the defendant and on written notice to him of the ground proposed. Subject to the limitation of Subsection (5) of this Section, the defendant shall have the right to hear and controvert the evidence against him and to offer evidence upon the issue.

(7) If the defendant is sentenced to imprisonment, a copy of the report of any pre-sentence investigation or psychiatric examination shall be transmitted forthwith to the Department of Correction [or other state department or agency] or, when the defendant is committed to the custody of a specific institution, to such institution.

Section 7.08. Commitment for Observation; Sentence of Imprisonment for Felony Deemed Tentative for Period of One Year; Re-sentence on Petition of Commissioner of Correction.

(1) If, after pre-sentence investigation, the Court desires additional information concerning an offender convicted of a felony or misdemeanor before imposing sentence, it may order that he be committed, for a period not exceeding ninety days, to the custody of the Department of Correction, or, in the case of a young adult offender, to the custody of the Division of Young Adult Correction, for observation and study at an appropriate reception or classification center. The Department and the Board of Parole, or the Young Adult Divisions thereof, shall advise the Court of their findings and recommendations on or before the expiration of such ninety-day period. If the offender is thereafter sentenced to imprisonment, the period of such commitment for observation shall be deducted from the maximum term and from the minimum, if any, of such sentence.

(2) When a person has been sentenced to imprisonment upon conviction of a felony, whether for an ordinary or extended term, the sentence shall be deemed tentative, to the extent provided in this Section, for the period of one year following the date when the offender is received in custody by the Department of Correction [or other state department or agency].

(3) If, as a result of the examination and classification by the Department of Correction [or other state department or agency] of a person under sentence of imprisonment upon conviction of a felony, the Commissioner of Correction [or other department head] is satisfied that the sentence of the Court may have been based upon a misapprehension as to the history, character or physical or mental condition of the offender, the Commissioner, during the period when the offender's sentence is deemed tentative under Subsection (2) of this Section shall file in the sentencing Court a petition to resentence the offender. The petition shall set forth the information as to the offender that is deemed to warrant his resentence and may include a recommendation as to the sentence to be imposed.

(4) The Court may dismiss a petition filed under Subsection (3) of this Section without a hearing if it deems the information set forth insufficient to warrant reconsideration of the sentence. If the Court is of the view that the petition warrants such reconsideration, a copy of the petition shall be served on the offender, who shall have the right to be heard on the issue and to be represented by counsel.

(5) When the Court grants a petition filed under Subsection (3) of this Section, it shall resentence the offender and may impose any sentence that might have been imposed originally for the felony of which the defendant was convicted. The period of his imprisonment prior to re-sentence and any reduction for good behavior to which he is entitled shall be applied in satisfaction of the final sentence.

(6) For all purposes other than this Section, a sentence of imprisonment has the same finality when it is imposed that it would have if this Section were not in force.

(7) Nothing in this Section shall alter the remedies provided by law for vacating or correcting an illegal sentence.

Section 7.09. Credit for Time of Detention Prior to Sentence; Credit for Imprisonment Under Earlier Sentence for the Same Crime.

(1) When a defendant who is sentenced to imprisonment has previously been detained in any state or local correctional or other institution following his [conviction of] [arrest for] the crime for which such sentence is imposed, such period of detention following his [conviction] [arrest] shall be deducted from the maximum term, and from the minimum, if any, of such sentence. The officer having custody of the defendant shall furnish a certificate to the Court at the time of sentence, showing the length of such detention of the defendant prior to sentence in any state or local correctional or other institution, and the certificate shall be annexed to the official records of the defendant's commitment.

(2) When a judgment of conviction is vacated and a new sentence is thereafter imposed upon the defendant for the same crime, the period of detention and imprisonment theretofore served shall be deducted from the maximum term, and from the minimum, if any, of the new sentence. The officer having custody of the defendant shall furnish a certificate to the Court at the time of sentence, showing the period of imprisonment served under the original sentence, and the certificate shall be annexed to the official records of the defendant's new commitment.

PART II. DEFINITION OF SPECIFIC CRIMES

OFFENSES AGAINST EXISTENCE OR STABILITY OF THE STATE

[This category of offenses, including treason, sedition, espionage and like crimes, was excluded from the scope of the Model Penal Code. These offenses are peculiarly the concern of the federal government. The Constitution itself defines treason: "Treason against the United States shall consist only in levying War against them, or in adhering to their Enemies, giving them Aid and Comfort. * * * "Article III, Section 3; cf. Pennsylvania v. Nelson, 350 U.S. 497 (supersession of state sedition legislation by federal law). Also, the definition of offenses against the stability of the state is inevitably affected by special political considerations. These factors militated against the use of the Institute's limited resources to attempt to draft "model" provisions in this area. However we provide at this point in the Plan of the Model Penal Code for an Article 200, where definitions of offenses against the existence or stability of the state may be incorporated.]

OFFENSES INVOLVING DANGER TO THE PERSON

ARTICLE 210. CRIMINAL HOMICIDE

Section 210.0. Definitions.

In Articles 210–213, unless a different meaning plainly is required:

(1) "human being" means a person who has been born and is alive;

(2) "bodily injury" means physical pain, illness or any impairment of physical condition;

(3) "serious bodily injury" means bodily injury which creates a substantial risk of death or which causes serious, permanent disfigurement, or protracted loss or impairment of the function of any bodily member or organ;

(4) "deadly weapon" means any firearm, or other weapon, device, instrument, material or substance, whether animate or inanimate, which in the manner it is used

or is intended to be used is known to be capable of producing death or serious bodily injury.

Section 210.1. Criminal Homicide.

(1) A person is guilty of criminal homicide if he purposely, knowingly, recklessly or negligently causes the death of another human being.

(2) Criminal homicide is murder, manslaughter or negligent homicide.

Section 210.2. Murder.

(1) Except as provided in Section 210.3(1)(b), criminal homicide constitutes murder when:

(a) it is committed purposely or knowingly; or

(b) it is committed recklessly under circumstances manifesting extreme indifference to the value of human life. Such recklessness and indifference are presumed if the actor is engaged or is an accomplice in the commission of, or an attempt to commit, or flight after committing or attempting to commit robbery, rape or deviate sexual intercourse by force or threat of force, arson, burglary, kidnapping or felonious escape.

(2) Murder is a felony of the first degree [but a person convicted of murder may be sentenced to death, as provided in Section 210.6].

Section 210.3. Manslaughter.

(1) Criminal homicide constitutes manslaughter when:

(a) it is committed recklessly; or

(b) a homicide which would otherwise be murder is committed under the influence of extreme mental or emotional disturbance for which there is reasonable explanation or excuse. The reasonableness of such explanation or excuse shall be determined from the viewpoint of a person in the actor's situation under the circumstances as he believes them to be.

(2) Manslaughter is a felony of the second degree.

Section 210.4. Negligent Homicide.

(1) Criminal homicide constitutes negligent homicide when it is committed negligently.

(2) Negligent homicide is a felony of the third degree.

Section 210.5. Causing or Aiding Suicide.

(1) **Causing Suicide as Criminal Homicide.** A person may be convicted of criminal homicide for causing another to commit suicide only if he purposely causes such suicide by force, duress or deception.

(2) **Aiding or Soliciting Suicide as an Independent Offense.** A person who purposely aids or solicits another to commit suicide is guilty of a felony of the second degree if his conduct causes such suicide or an attempted suicide, and otherwise of a misdemeanor.

[Section 210.6. Sentence of Death for Murder; Further Proceedings to Determine Sentence.

(1) **Death Sentence Excluded.** When a defendant is found guilty of murder, the Court shall impose sentence for a felony of the first degree if it is satisfied that:

(a) none of the aggravating circumstances enumerated in Subsection (3) of this Section was established by the evidence at the trial or will be established if further proceedings are initiated under Subsection (2) of this Section; or

(b) substantial mitigating circumstances, established by the evidence at the trial, call for leniency; or

(c) the defendant, with the consent of the prosecuting attorney and the approval of the Court, pleaded guilty to murder as a felony of the first degree; or

(d) the defendant was under 18 years of age at the time of the commission of the crime; or

(e) the defendant's physical or mental condition calls for leniency; or

(f) although the evidence suffices to sustain the verdict, it does not foreclose all doubt respecting the defendant's guilt.

(2) **Determination by Court or by Court and Jury.** Unless the Court imposes sentence under Subsection (1) of this Section, it shall conduct a separate proceeding to determine whether the defendant should be sentenced for a felony of the first degree or sentenced to death. The proceeding shall be conducted before the Court alone if the defendant was convicted by a Court sitting without a jury or upon his plea of guilty or if the prosecuting attorney and the defendant waive a jury with respect to sentence. In other cases it shall be conducted before the Court sitting with the jury which determined the defendant's guilt or, if the Court for good cause shown discharges that jury, with a new jury empanelled for the purpose.

In the proceeding, evidence may be presented as to any matter that the Court deems relevant to sentence, including but not limited to the nature and circumstances of the crime, the defendant's character, background, history, mental and physical condition and any of the aggravating or mitigating circumstances enumerated in Subsections (3) and (4) of this Section. Any such evidence, not legally privileged, which the Court deems to have probative force may be received, regardless of its admissibility under the exclusionary rules of evidence, provided that the defendant's counsel is accorded a fair opportunity to rebut such evidence. The prosecuting attorney and the defendant or his counsel shall be permitted to present argument for or against sentence of death.

The determination whether sentence of death shall be imposed shall be in the discretion of the Court, except that when the proceeding is conducted before the Court sitting with a jury, the Court shall not impose sentence of death unless it submits to the jury the issue whether the defendant should be sentenced to death or to imprisonment and the jury returns a verdict that the sentence should be death. If the jury is unable to reach a unanimous verdict, the Court shall dismiss the jury and impose sentence for a felony of the first degree.

The Court, in exercising its discretion as to sentence, and the jury, in determining upon its verdict, shall take into account the aggravating and mitigating circumstances enumerated in Subsections (3) and (4) and any other facts that it deems relevant, but it shall not impose or recommend sentence of death unless it finds one of the aggravating circumstances enumerated in Subsection (3) and further finds that there are no mitigating circumstances sufficiently substantial to call for leniency. When the issue is submitted to the jury, the Court shall so instruct and also shall inform the jury of the nature of the sentence of imprisonment that may be imposed, including its implication with respect to possible release upon parole, if the jury verdict is against sentence of death.

Alternative formulation of Subsection (2):

(2) **Determination by Court.** Unless the Court imposes sentence under Subsection (1) of this Section, it shall conduct a separate proceeding to determine whether the defendant should be sentenced for a felony of the first degree or sentenced to death. In the proceeding, the Court, in accordance with Section 7.07, shall consider the report of the pre-sentence investigation and, if a psychiatric examination has been ordered, the report of such examination. In addition, evidence may be presented as to any matter that the Court deems relevant to sentence, including but not limited to the nature and circumstances of the crime, the defendant's character, background, history, mental and physical condition and any of the aggravating or mitigating circumstances enumerated in Subsections (3) and (4) of this Section. Any such evidence, not legally privileged, which the Court deems to have probative force may be received, regardless of its admissibility under the exclusionary rules of evidence, provided that the defendant's counsel is accorded a fair opportunity to rebut such evidence. The prosecuting attorney and the defendant or his counsel shall be permitted to present argument for or against sentence of death.

The determination whether sentence of death shall be imposed shall be in the discretion of the Court. In exercising such discretion, the Court shall take into account the aggravating and mitigating circumstances enumerated in Subsections (3) and (4) and any other facts that it deems relevant but shall not impose sentence of death unless it finds one of the aggravating circumstances enumerated in Subsection (3) and further finds that there are no mitigating circumstances sufficiently substantial to call for leniency.

(3) **Aggravating Circumstances.**

(a) The murder was committed by a convict under sentence of imprisonment.

(b) The defendant was previously convicted of another murder or of a felony involving the use or threat of violence to the person.

(c) At the time the murder was committed the defendant also committed another murder.

(d) The defendant knowingly created a great risk of death to many persons.

(e) The murder was committed while the defendant was engaged or was an accomplice in the commission of, or an attempt to commit, or flight after committing or attempting to commit robbery, rape or deviate sexual intercourse by force or threat of force, arson, burglary or kidnapping.

(f) The murder was committed for the purpose of avoiding or preventing a lawful arrest or effecting an escape from lawful custody.

(g) The murder was committed for pecuniary gain.

(h) The murder was especially heinous, atrocious or cruel, manifesting exceptional depravity.

(4) **Mitigating Circumstances.**

(a) The defendant has no significant history of prior criminal activity.

(b) The murder was committed while the defendant was under the influence of extreme mental or emotional disturbance.

(c) The victim was a participant in the defendant's homicidal conduct or consent-ed to the homicidal act.

(d) The murder was committed under circumstances which the defendant believed to provide a moral justification or extenuation for his conduct.

(e) The defendant was an accomplice in a murder committed by another person and his participation in the homicidal act was relatively minor.

(f) The defendant acted under duress or under the domination of another person.

(g) At the time of the murder, the capacity of the defendant to appreciate the criminality [wrongfulness] of his conduct or to conform his conduct to the requirements of law was impaired as a result of mental disease or defect or intoxication.

(h) The youth of the defendant at the time of the crime.]

ARTICLE 211. ASSAULT; RECKLESS ENDANGERING; THREATS

Section 211.0. Definitions.

In this Article, the definitions given in Section 210.0 apply unless a different meaning plainly is required.

Section 211.1. Assault.

(1) **Simple Assault.** A person is guilty of assault if he:

(a) attempts to cause or purposely, knowingly or recklessly causes bodily injury to another; or

(b) negligently causes bodily injury to another with a deadly weapon; or

(c) attempts by physical menace to put another in fear of imminent serious bodily injury.

Simple assault is a misdemeanor unless committed in a fight or scuffle entered into by mutual consent, in which case it is a petty misdemeanor.

(2) **Aggravated Assault.** A person is guilty of aggravated assault if he:

(a) attempts to cause serious bodily injury to another, or causes such injury purposely, knowingly or recklessly under circumstances manifesting extreme indifference to the value of human life; or

(b) attempts to cause or purposely or knowingly causes bodily injury to another with a deadly weapon.

Aggravated assault under paragraph (a) is a felony of the second degree; aggravated assault under paragraph (b) is a felony of the third degree.

Section 211.2. Recklessly Endangering Another Person.

A person commits a misdemeanor if he recklessly engages in conduct which places or may place another person in danger of death or serious bodily injury. Recklessness and danger shall be presumed where a person knowingly points a firearm at or in the direction of another, whether or not the actor believed the firearm to be loaded.

Section 211.3. Terroristic Threats.

A person is guilty of a felony of the third degree if he threatens to commit any crime of violence with purpose to terrorize another or to cause evacuation of a building, place of assembly, or facility of public transportation, or otherwise to cause serious public inconvenience, or in reckless disregard of the risk of causing such terror or inconvenience.

ARTICLE 212. KIDNAPPING AND RELATED OFFENSES; COERCION

Section 212.0. Definitions.

In this Article, the definitions given in Section 210.0 apply unless a different meaning plainly is required.

Section 212.1. Kidnapping.

A person is guilty of kidnapping if he unlawfully removes another from his place of residence or business, or a substantial distance from the vicinity where he is found, or if he unlawfully confines another for a substantial period in a place of isolation, with any of the following purposes:

    (a) to hold for ransom or reward, or as a shield or hostage; or

    (b) to facilitate commission of any felony or flight thereafter; or

    (c) to inflict bodily injury on or to terrorize the victim or another; or

    (d) to interfere with the performance of any governmental or political function.

Kidnapping is a felony of the first degree unless the actor voluntarily releases the victim alive and in a safe place prior to trial, in which case it is a felony of the second degree. A removal or confinement is unlawful within the meaning of this Section if it is accomplished by force, threat or deception, or, in the case of a person who is under the age of 14 or incompetent, if it is accomplished without the consent of a parent, guardian or other person responsible for general supervision of his welfare.

Section 212.2. Felonious Restraint.

A person commits a felony of the third degree if he knowingly:

    (a) restrains another unlawfully in circumstances exposing him to risk of serious bodily injury; or

    (b) holds another in a condition of involuntary servitude.

Section 212.3. False Imprisonment.

A person commits a misdemeanor if he knowingly restrains another unlawfully so as to interfere substantially with his liberty.

Section 212.4. Interference With Custody.

(1) **Custody of Children.** A person commits an offense if he knowingly or recklessly takes or entices any child under the age of 18 from the custody of its parent, guardian or other lawful custodian, when he has no privilege to do so. It is an affirmative defense that:

    (a) the actor believed that his action was necessary to preserve the child from danger to its welfare; or

    (b) the child, being at the time not less than 14 years old, was taken away at its own instigation without enticement and without purpose to commit a criminal offense with or against the child.

Proof that the child was below the critical age gives rise to a presumption that the actor knew the child's age or acted in reckless disregard thereof. The offense is a misdemeanor unless the actor, not being a parent or person in equivalent relation to the child, acted with knowledge that his conduct would cause serious alarm for the child's safety, or in reckless disregard of a likelihood of causing such alarm, in which case the offense is a felony of the third degree.

(2) **Custody of Committed Persons.** A person is guilty of a misdemeanor if he knowingly or recklessly takes or entices any committed person away from lawful custody when he is not privileged to do so. "Committed person" means, in addition to anyone committed under judicial warrant, any orphan, neglected or delinquent child, mentally defective or insane person, or other dependent or incompetent person entrusted to another's custody by or through a recognized social agency or otherwise by authority of law.

Section 212.5. Criminal Coercion.

(1) **Offense Defined.** A person is guilty of criminal coercion if, with purpose unlawfully to restrict another's freedom of action to his detriment, he threatens to:

(a) commit any criminal offense; or

(b) accuse anyone of a criminal offense; or

(c) expose any secret tending to subject any person to hatred, contempt or ridicule, or to impair his credit or business repute; or

(d) take or withhold action as an official, or cause an official to take or withhold action.

It is an affirmative defense to prosecution based on paragraphs (b), (c) or (d) that the actor believed the accusation or secret to be true or the proposed official action justified and that his purpose was limited to compelling the other to behave in a way reasonably related to the circumstances which were the subject of the accusation, exposure or proposed official action, as by desisting from further misbehavior, making good a wrong done, refraining from taking any action or responsibility for which the actor believes the other disqualified.

(2) **Grading.** Criminal coercion is a misdemeanor unless the threat is to commit a felony or the actor's purpose is felonious, in which cases the offense is a felony of the third degree.

ARTICLE 213. SEXUAL OFFENSES

Section 213.0. Definitions.

In this Article, the definitions given in Section 210.0 apply unless a different meaning plainly is required. Sexual intercourse includes intercourse per os or per anum, with some penetration however slight; emission is not required.

Deviate sexual intercourse means sexual intercourse per os or per anum between human beings who are not husband and wife, and any form of sexual intercourse with an animal.

Section 213.1. Rape and Related Offenses.

(1) **Rape.** A male who has sexual intercourse with a female not his wife is guilty of rape if:

(a) he compels her to submit by force or by threat of imminent death, serious bodily injury, extreme pain or kidnapping, to be inflicted on anyone; or

(b) he has substantially impaired her power to appraise or control her conduct by administering or employing without her knowledge drugs, intoxicants or other means for the purpose of preventing resistance; or

(c) the female is unconscious; or

(d) the female is less than 10 years old.

Rape is a felony of the second degree unless (i) in the course thereof the actor inflicts serious bodily injury upon anyone, or (ii) the victim was not a voluntary social companion of the actor upon the occasion of the crime and had not previously permitted him sexual liberties, in which cases the offense is a felony of the first degree.

(2) **Gross Sexual Imposition.** A male who has sexual intercourse with a female not his wife commits a felony of the third degree if:

(a) he compels her to submit by any threat that would prevent resistance by a woman of ordinary resolution; or

(b) he knows that she suffers from a mental disease or defect which renders her incapable of appraising the nature of her conduct; or

(c) he knows that she is unaware that a sexual act is being committed upon her or that she submits because she mistakenly supposes that he is her husband.

Section 213.2. Deviate Sexual Intercourse by Force or Imposition.

(1) **By Force or Its Equivalent.** A person who engages in deviate sexual intercourse with another person, or who causes another to engage in deviate sexual intercourse, commits a felony of the second degree if:

(a) he compels the other person to participate by force or by threat of imminent death, serious bodily injury, extreme pain or kidnapping, to be inflicted on anyone; or

(b) he has substantially impaired the other person's power to appraise or control his conduct, by administering or employing without the knowledge of the other person drugs, intoxicants or other means for the purpose of preventing resistance; or

(c) the other person is unconscious; or

(d) the other person is less than 10 years old.

(2) **By Other Imposition.** A person who engages in deviate sexual intercourse with another person, or who causes another to engage in deviate sexual intercourse, commits a felony of the third degree if:

(a) he compels the other person to participate by any threat that would prevent resistance by a person of ordinary resolution; or

(b) he knows that the other person suffers from a mental disease or defect which renders him incapable of appraising the nature of his conduct; or

(c) he knows that the other person submits because he is unaware that a sexual act is being committed upon him.

Section 213.3. Corruption of Minors and Seduction.

(1) **Offense Defined.** A male who has sexual intercourse with a female not his wife, or any person who engages in deviate sexual intercourse or causes another to engage in deviate sexual intercourse, is guilty of an offense if:

(a) the other person is less than [16] years old and the actor is at least [4] years older than the other person; or

(b) the other person is less than 21 years old and the actor is his guardian or otherwise responsible for general supervision of his welfare; or

(c) the other person is in custody of law or detained in a hospital or other institution and the actor has supervisory or disciplinary authority over him; or

(d) the other person is a female who is induced to participate by a promise of marriage which the actor does not mean to perform.

(2) **Grading.** An offense under paragraph (a) of Subsection (1) is a felony of the third degree. Otherwise an offense under this section is a misdemeanor.

Section 213.4. Sexual Assault.

A person who has sexual contact with another not his spouse, or causes such other to have sexual intercourse with him, is guilty of sexual assault, a misdemeanor, if:

(1) he knows that the contact is offensive to the other person; or

(2) he knows that the other person suffers from a mental disease or defect which renders him or her incapable of appraising the nature of his or her conduct; or

(3) he knows that the other person is unaware that a sexual act is being committed; or

(4) the other person is less than 10 years old; or

(5) he has substantially impaired the other person's power to appraise or control his or her conduct, by administering or employing without the other's knowledge drugs, intoxicants or other means for the purpose of preventing resistance; or

(6) the other person is less than [16] years old and the actor is at least [4] years older than the other person; or

(7) the other person is less than 21 years old and the actor is his guardian or otherwise responsible for general supervision of his welfare; or

(8) the other person is in custody of law or detained in a hospital or other institution and the actor has supervisory or disciplinary authority over him.

Sexual contact is any touching of the sexual or other intimate parts of the person for the purpose of arousing or gratifying sexual desire.

Section 213.5. Indecent Exposure.

A person commits a misdemeanor if, for the purpose of arousing or gratifying sexual desire of himself or of any person other than his spouse, he exposes his genitals under circumstances in which he knows his conduct is likely to cause affront or alarm.

Section 213.6. Provisions Generally Applicable to Article 213.

(1) **Mistake as to Age.** Whenever in this Article the criminality of conduct depends on a child's being below the age of 10, it is no defense that the actor did not know the child's age, or reasonably believed the child to be older than 10. When criminality depends on the child's being below a critical age other than 10, it is a defense for the actor to prove by a preponderance of the evidence that he reasonably believed the child to be above the critical age.

(2) **Spouse Relationships.** Whenever in this Article the definition of an offense excludes conduct with a spouse, the exclusion shall be deemed to extend to persons living as man and wife, regardless of the legal status of their relationship. The exclusion shall be inoperative as respects spouses living apart under a decree of judicial separation. Where the definition of an offense excludes conduct with a spouse or conduct by a woman, this shall not preclude conviction of a spouse or woman as accomplice in a sexual act which he or she causes another person, not within the exclusion, to perform.

(3) **Sexually Promiscuous Complainants.** It is a defense to prosecution under Section 213.3 and paragraphs (6), (7) and (8) of Section 213.4 for the actor to prove by a preponderance of the evidence that the alleged victim had, prior to the time of the offense charged, engaged promiscuously in sexual relations with others.

(4) **Prompt Complaint.** No prosecution may be instituted or maintained under this Article unless the alleged offense was brought to the notice of public authority within [3] months of its occurrence or, where the alleged victim was less than [16] years old or otherwise incompetent to make complaint, within [3] months after a parent, guardian or other competent person specially interested in the victim learns of the offense.

(5) **Testimony of Complainants.** No person shall be convicted of any felony under this Article upon the uncorroborated testimony of the alleged victim. Corroboration may be circumstantial. In any prosecution before a jury for an offense under this Article, the jury shall be instructed to evaluate the testimony of a victim or complaining witness with special care in view of the emotional involvement of the witness and the difficulty of determining the truth with respect to alleged sexual activities carried out in private.

OFFENSES AGAINST PROPERTY

ARTICLE 220. ARSON, CRIMINAL MISCHIEF, AND OTHER PROPERTY DESTRUCTION

Section 220.1. Arson and Related Offenses.

(1) **Arson.** A person is guilty of arson, a felony of the second degree, if he starts a fire or causes an explosion with the purpose of:

(a) destroying a building or occupied structure of another; or

(b) destroying or damaging any property, whether his own or another's, to collect insurance for such loss. It shall be an affirmative defense to prosecution under this paragraph that the actor's conduct did not recklessly endanger any building or occupied structure of another or place any other person in danger of death or bodily injury.

(2) **Reckless Burning or Exploding.** A person commits a felony of the third degree if he purposely starts a fire or causes an explosion, whether on his own property or another's, and thereby recklessly:

(a) places another person in danger of death or bodily injury; or

(b) places a building or occupied structure of another in danger of damage or destruction.

(3) **Failure to Control or Report Dangerous Fire.** A person who knows that a fire is endangering life or a substantial amount of property of another and fails to take reasonable measures to put out or control the fire, when he can do so without substantial risk to himself, or to give a prompt fire alarm, commits a misdemeanor if:

(a) he knows that he is under an official, contractual, or other legal duty to prevent or combat the fire; or

(b) the fire was started, albeit lawfully, by him or with his assent, or on property in his custody or control.

(4) **Definitions.** "Occupied structure" includes a ship, trailer, sleeping car, airplane, or other vehicle, structure or place adapted for overnight accommodation of persons or for carrying on business therein, whether or not a person is actually present. Property is that of another, for the purposes of this section, if anyone other than the actor has a possessory or proprietary interest therein. If a building or structure is divided into separately occupied units, any unit not occupied by the actor is an occupied structure of another.

Section 220.2. Causing or Risking Catastrophe.

(1) **Causing Catastrophe.** A person who causes a catastrophe by explosion, fire, flood, avalanche, collapse of building, release of poison gas, radioactive material or other harmful or destructive force or substance, or by any other means of causing potentially widespread injury or damage, commits a felony of the second degree if he does so purposely or knowingly, or a felony of the third degree if he does so recklessly.

(2) **Risking Catastrophe.** A person is guilty of a misdemeanor if he recklessly creates a risk of catastrophe in the employment of fire, explosives or other dangerous means listed in Subsection (1).

(3) **Failure to Prevent Catastrophe.** A person who knowingly or recklessly fails to take reasonable measures to prevent or mitigate a catastrophe commits a misdemeanor if:

(a) he knows that he is under an official, contractual or other legal duty to take such measures; or

(b) he did or assented to the act causing or threatening the catastrophe.

Section 220.3. Criminal Mischief.

(1) **Offense Defined.** A person is guilty of criminal mischief if he:

(a) damages tangible property of another purposely, recklessly, or by negligence in the employment of fire, explosives, or other dangerous means listed in Section 220.2(1); or

(b) purposely or recklessly tampers with tangible property of another so as to endanger person or property; or

(c) purposely or recklessly causes another to suffer pecuniary loss by deception or threat.

(2) **Grading.** Criminal mischief is a felony of the third degree if the actor purposely causes pecuniary loss in excess of $5,000, or a substantial interruption or impairment of public communication, transportation, supply of water, gas or power, or other public service. It is a misdemeanor if the actor purposely causes pecuniary loss in excess of $100, or a petty misdemeanor if he purposely or recklessly causes pecuniary loss in excess of $25. Otherwise criminal mischief is a violation.

ARTICLE 221. BURGLARY AND OTHER CRIMINAL INTRUSION

Section 221.0. Definitions.

In this Article, unless a different meaning plainly is required:

(1) "occupied structure" means any structure, vehicle or place adapted for overnight accommodation of persons, or for carrying on business therein, whether or not a person is actually present.

(2) "night" means the period between thirty minutes past sunset and thirty minutes before sunrise.

Section 221.1. Burglary.

(1) **Burglary Defined.** A person is guilty of burglary if he enters a building or occupied structure, or separately secured or occupied portion thereof, with purpose to commit a crime therein, unless the premises are at the time open to the public or the actor is licensed or privileged to enter. It is an affirmative defense to prosecution for burglary that the building or structure was abandoned.

(2) **Grading.** Burglary is a felony of the second degree if it is perpetrated in the dwelling of another at night, or if, in the course of committing the offense, the actor:

(a) purposely, knowingly or recklessly inflicts or attempts to inflict bodily injury on anyone; or

(b) is armed with explosives or a deadly weapon.

Otherwise, burglary is a felony of the third degree. An act shall be deemed "in the course of committing" an offense if it occurs in an attempt to commit the offense or in flight after the attempt or commission.

(3) **Multiple Convictions.** A person may not be convicted both for burglary and for the offense which it was his purpose to commit after the burglarious entry or for an attempt to commit that offense, unless the additional offense constitutes a felony of the first or second degree.

Section 221.2. Criminal Trespass.

(1) **Buildings and Occupied Structures.** A person commits an offense if, knowing that he is not licensed or privileged to do so, he enters or surreptitiously remains in any building or occupied structure, or separately secured or occupied portion thereof. An offense under this Subsection is a misdemeanor if it is committed in a dwelling at night. Otherwise it is a petty misdemeanor.

(2) **Defiant Trespasser.** A person commits an offense if, knowing that he is not licensed or privileged to do so, he enters or remains in any place as to which notice against trespass is given by:

(a) actual communication to the actor; or

(b) posting in a manner prescribed by law or reasonably likely to come to the attention of intruders; or

(c) fencing or other enclosure manifestly designed to exclude intruders.

An offense under this Subsection constitutes a petty misdemeanor if the offender defies an order to leave personally communicated to him by the owner of the premises or other authorized person. Otherwise it is a violation.

(3) **Defenses.** It is an affirmative defense to prosecution under this Section that:

(a) a building or occupied structure involved in an offense under Subsection (1) was abandoned; or

(b) the premises were at the time open to members of the public and the actor complied with all lawful conditions imposed on access to or remaining in the premises; or

(c) the actor reasonably believed that the owner of the premises, or other person empowered to license access thereto, would have licensed him to enter or remain.

ARTICLE 222. ROBBERY

Section 222.1. Robbery.

(1) **Robbery Defined.** A person is guilty of robbery if, in the course of committing a theft, he:

(a) inflicts serious bodily injury upon another; or

(b) threatens another with or purposely puts him in fear of immediate serious bodily injury; or

(c) commits or threatens immediately to commit any felony of the first or second degree.

An act shall be deemed "in the course of committing a theft" if it occurs in an attempt to commit theft or in flight after the attempt or commission.

(2) **Grading.** Robbery is a felony of the second degree, except that it is a felony of the first degree if in the course of committing the theft the actor attempts to kill anyone, or purposely inflicts or attempts to inflict serious bodily injury.

ARTICLE 223. THEFT AND RELATED OFFENSES

Section 223.0. Definitions.

In this Article, unless a different meaning plainly is required:

(1) "deprive" means: (a) to withhold property of another permanently or for so extended a period as to appropriate a major portion of its economic value, or with intent to restore only upon payment of reward or other compensation; or (b) to dispose of the property so as to make it unlikely that the owner will recover it.

(2) "financial institution" means a bank, insurance company, credit union, building and loan association, investment trust or other organization held out to the public as a place of deposit of funds or medium of savings or collective investment.

(3) "government" means the United States, any State, county, municipality, or other political unit, or any department, agency or subdivision of any of the foregoing, or any corporation or other association carrying out the functions of government.

(4) "movable property" means property the location of which can be changed, including things growing on, affixed to, or found in land, and documents although the rights represented thereby have no physical location. "Immovable property" is all other property.

(5) "obtain" means: (a) in relation to property, to bring about a transfer or purported transfer of a legal interest in the property, whether to the obtainer or another; or (b) in relation to labor or service, to secure performance thereof.

(6) "property" means anything of value, including real estate, tangible and intangible personal property, contract rights, choses-in-action and other interests in or claims to wealth, admission or transportation tickets, captured or domestic animals, food and drink, electric or other power.

(7) "property of another" includes property in which any person other than the actor has an interest which the actor is not privileged to infringe, regardless of the fact that the actor also has an interest in the property and regardless of the fact that the other person might be precluded from civil recovery because the property was used in an unlawful transaction or was subject to forfeiture as contraband. Property in possession of the actor shall not be deemed property of another who has only a security interest therein, even if legal title is in the creditor pursuant to a conditional sales contract or other security agreement.

Section 223.1. Consolidation of Theft Offenses; Grading; Provisions Applicable to Theft Generally.

(1) **Consolidation of Theft Offenses.** Conduct denominated theft in this Article constitutes a single offense. An accusation of theft may be supported by evidence that it was committed in any manner that would be theft under this Article, notwithstanding the specification of a different manner in the indictment or information, subject only to the power of the Court to ensure fair trial by granting a continuance or other appropriate relief where the conduct of the defense would be prejudiced by lack of fair notice or by surprise.

(2) **Grading of Theft Offenses.**

(a) Theft constitutes a felony of the third degree if the amount involved exceeds $500, or if the property stolen is a fire-arm, automobile, airplane, motorcycle, motorboat or other motor-propelled vehicle, or in the case of theft by receiving stolen property, if the receiver is in the business of buying or selling stolen property.

(b) Theft not within the preceding paragraph constitutes a misdemeanor, except that if the property was not taken from the person or by threat, or in breach of a fiduciary obligation, and the actor proves by a preponderance of the evidence that the amount involved was less than $50, the offense constitutes a petty misdemeanor.

(c) The amount involved in a theft shall be deemed to be the highest value, by any reasonable standard, of the property or services which the actor stole or attempted to steal. Amounts involved in thefts committed pursuant to one scheme or course of conduct, whether from the same person or several persons, may be aggregated in determining the grade of the offense.

(3) **Claim of Right.** It is an affirmative defense to prosecution for theft that the actor:

(a) was unaware that the property or service was that of another; or

(b) acted under an honest claim of right to the property or service involved or that he had a right to acquire or dispose of it as he did; or

(c) took property exposed for sale, intending to purchase and pay for it promptly, or reasonably believing that the owner, if present, would have consented.

(4) **Theft from Spouse.** It is no defense that theft was from the actor's spouse, except that misappropriation of household and personal effects, or other property normally accessible to both spouses, is theft only if it occurs after the parties have ceased living together.

Section 223.2. Theft by Unlawful Taking or Disposition.

(1) **Movable Property.** A person is guilty of theft if he unlawfully takes, or exercises unlawful control over, movable property of another with purpose to deprive him thereof.

(2) **Immovable Property.** A person is guilty of theft if he unlawfully transfers immovable property of another or any interest therein with purpose to benefit himself or another not entitled thereto.

Section 223.3. Theft by Deception.

A person is guilty of theft if he purposely obtains property of another by deception. A person deceives if he purposely:

(1) creates or reinforces a false impression, including false impressions as to law, value, intention or other state of mind; but deception as to a person's intention to perform a promise shall not be inferred from the fact alone that he did not subsequently perform the promise; or

(2) prevents another from acquiring information which would affect his judgment of a transaction; or

(3) fails to correct a false impression which the deceiver previously created or reinforced, or which the deceiver knows to be influencing another to whom he stands in a fiduciary or confidential relationship; or

(4) fails to disclose a known lien, adverse claim or other legal impediment to the enjoyment of property which he transfers or encumbers in consideration for the property obtained, whether such impediment is or is not valid, or is or is not a matter of official record.

The term "deceive" does not, however, include falsity as to matters having no pecuniary significance, or puffing by statements unlikely to deceive ordinary persons in the group addressed.

Section 223.4. Theft by Extortion.

A person is guilty of theft if he purposely obtains property of another by threatening to:

(1) inflict bodily injury on anyone or commit any other criminal offense; or

(2) accuse anyone of a criminal offense; or

(3) expose any secret tending to subject any person to hatred, contempt or ridicule, or to impair his credit or business repute; or

(4) take or withhold action as an official, or cause an official to take or withhold action; or

(5) bring about or continue a strike, boycott or other collective unofficial action, if the property is not demanded or received for the benefit of the group in whose interest the actor purports to act; or

(6) testify or provide information or withhold testimony or information with respect to another's legal claim or defense; or

(7) inflict any other harm which would not benefit the actor.

It is an affirmative defense to prosecution based on paragraphs (2), (3) or (4) that the property obtained by threat of accusation, exposure, lawsuit or other invocation of official action was honestly claimed as restitution or indemnification for harm done in the circumstances to which such accusation, exposure, lawsuit or other official action relates, or as compensation for property or lawful services.

Section 223.5. Theft of Property Lost, Mislaid, or Delivered by Mistake.

A person who comes into control of property of another that he knows to have been lost, mislaid, or delivered under a mistake as to the nature or amount of the property or the identity of the recipient is guilty of theft if, with purpose to deprive the owner thereof, he fails to take reasonable measures to restore the property to a person entitled to have it.

Section 223.6. Receiving Stolen Property.

(1) **Receiving.** A person is guilty of theft if he purposely receives, retains, or disposes of movable property of another knowing that it has been stolen, or believing that it has probably been stolen, unless the property is received, retained, or disposed with purpose to restore it to the owner. "Receiving" means acquiring possession, control or title, or lending on the security of the property.

(2) **Presumption of Knowledge.** The requisite knowledge or belief is presumed in the case of a dealer who:

(a) is found in possession or control of property stolen from two or more persons on separate occasions; or

(b) has received stolen property in another transaction within the year preceding the transaction charged; or

(c) being a dealer in property of the sort received, acquires it for a consideration which he knows is far below its reasonable value.

"Dealer" means a person in the business of buying or selling goods, including a pawnbroker.

Section 223.7. Theft of Services.

(1) A person is guilty of theft if he purposely obtains services which he knows are available only for compensation, by deception or threat, or by false token or other means to avoid payment for the service. "Services" includes labor, professional service, transportation, telephone or other public service, accommodation in hotels, restaurants or elsewhere, admission to exhibitions, use of vehicles or other movable property. Where compensation for service is ordinarily paid immediately upon the rendering of such service, as in the case of hotels and restaurants, refusal to pay or absconding without payment or offer to pay gives rise to a presumption that the service was obtained by deception as to intention to pay.

(2) A person commits theft if, having control over the disposition of services of others, to which he is not entitled, he knowingly diverts such services to his own benefit or to the benefit of another not entitled thereto.

Section 223.8. Theft by Failure to Make Required Disposition of Funds Received.

A person who purposely obtains property upon agreement, or subject to a known legal obligation, to make specified payment or other disposition, whether from such property or its proceeds or from his own property to be reserved in equivalent amount, is guilty of theft if he deals with the property obtained as his own and fails to make the required payment or disposition. The foregoing applies notwithstanding that it may be impossible to identify particular property as belonging to the victim at the time of the actor's failure to make the required payment or disposition. An officer or employee of the government or of a financial institution is presumed: (i) to know any legal obligation relevant to his criminal liability under this Section, and (ii) to have dealt with the property as his own if he fails to pay or account upon lawful demand, or if an audit reveals a shortage or falsification of accounts.

Section 223.9. Unauthorized Use of Automobiles and Other Vehicles.

A person commits a misdemeanor if he operates another's automobile, airplane, motorcycle, motorboat, or other motor-propelled vehicle without consent of the owner. It is an affirmative defense to prosecution under this Section that the actor reasonably believed that the owner would have consented to the operation had he known of it.

ARTICLE 224. FORGERY AND FRAUDULENT PRACTICES

Section 224.0. Definitions.

In this Article, the definitions given in Section 223.0 apply unless a different meaning plainly is required.

Section 224.1. Forgery.

(1) **Definition.** A person is guilty of forgery if, with purpose to defraud or injure anyone, or with knowledge that he is facilitating a fraud or injury to be perpetrated by anyone, the actor:

(a) alters any writing of another without his authority; or

(b) makes, completes, executes, authenticates, issues or transfers any writing so that it purports to be the act of another who did not authorize that act, or to have been executed at a time or place or in a numbered sequence other than was in fact the case, or to be a copy of an original when no such original existed; or

(c) utters any writing which he knows to be forged in a manner specified in paragraphs (a) or (b).

"Writing" includes printing or any other method of recording information, money, coins, tokens, stamps, seals, credit cards, badges, trademarks, and other symbols of value, right, privilege, or identification.

(2) **Grading.** Forgery is a felony of the second degree if the writing is or purports to be part of an issue of money, securities, postage or revenue stamps, or other instruments issued by the government, or part of an issue of stock, bonds or other instruments representing interests in or claims against any property or enterprise. Forgery is a felony of the third degree if the writing is or purports to be a will, deed, contract, release, commercial instrument, or other document evidencing, creating, transferring, altering, terminating, or otherwise affecting legal relations. Otherwise forgery is a misdemeanor.

Section 224.2. Simulating Objects of Antiquity, Rarity, Etc.

A person commits a misdemeanor if, with purpose to defraud anyone or with knowledge that he is facilitating a fraud to be perpetrated by anyone, he makes, alters or utters any object so that it appears to have value because of antiquity, rarity, source, or authorship which it does not possess.

Section 224.3. Fraudulent Destruction, Removal or Concealment of Recordable Instruments.

A person commits a felony of the third degree if, with purpose to deceive or injure anyone, he destroys, removes or conceals any will, deed, mortgage, security instrument or other writing for which the law provides public recording.

Section 224.4. Tampering With Records.

A person commits a misdemeanor if, knowing that he has no privilege to do so, he falsifies, destroys, removes or conceals any writing or record, with purpose to deceive or injure anyone or to conceal any wrongdoing.

Section 224.5. Bad Checks.

A person who issues or passes a check or similar sight order for the payment of money, knowing that it will not be honored by the drawee, commits a misdemeanor. For the purposes of this Section as well as in any prosecution for theft committed by means of a bad check, an issuer is presumed to know that the check or order (other than a post-dated check or order) would not be paid, if:

(1) the issuer had no account with the drawee at the time the check or order was issued; or

(2) payment was refused by the drawee for lack of funds, upon presentation within 30 days after issue, and the issuer failed to make good within 10 days after receiving notice of that refusal.

Section 224.6. Credit Cards.

A person commits an offense if he uses a credit card for the purpose of obtaining property or services with knowledge that:

(1) the card is stolen or forged; or

(2) the card has been revoked or cancelled; or

(3) for any other reason his use of the card is unauthorized.

It is an affirmative defense to prosecution under paragraph (3) if the actor proves by a preponderance of the evidence that he had the purpose and ability to meet all obligations to the issuer arising out of his use of the card. "Credit card" means a writing or other evidence of an undertaking to pay for property or services delivered or rendered to or upon the order of a designated person or bearer. An offense under this Section is a felony of the third degree if the value of the property or services secured or sought to be secured by means of the credit card exceeds $500; otherwise it is a misdemeanor.

Section 224.7. Deceptive Business Practices.

A person commits a misdemeanor if in the course of business he:

(1) uses or possesses for use a false weight or measure, or any other device for falsely determining or recording any quality or quantity; or

(2) sells, offers or exposes for sale, or delivers less than the represented quantity of any commodity or service; or

(3) takes or attempts to take more than the represented quantity of any commodity or service when as buyer he furnishes the weight or measure; or

(4) sells, offers or exposes for sale adulterated or mislabeled commodities. "Adulterated" means varying from the standard of composition or quality prescribed by or pursuant to any statute providing criminal penalties for such variance, or set by established commercial usage. "Mislabeled" means varying from the standard of truth or disclosure in labeling prescribed by or pursuant to any statute providing criminal penalties for such variance, or set by established commercial usage; or

(5) makes a false or misleading statement in any advertisement addressed to the public or to a substantial segment thereof for the purpose of promoting the purchase or sale of property or services; or

(6) makes a false or misleading written statement for the purpose of obtaining property or credit; or

(7) makes a false or misleading written statement for the purpose of promoting the sale of securities, or omits information required by law to be disclosed in written documents relating to securities.

It is an affirmative defense to prosecution under this Section if the defendant proves by a preponderance of the evidence that his conduct was not knowingly or recklessly deceptive.

Section 224.8. Commercial Bribery and Breach of Duty to Act Disinterestedly.

(1) A person commits a misdemeanor if he solicits, accepts or agrees to accept any benefit as consideration for knowingly violating or agreeing to violate a duty of fidelity to which he is subject as:

(a) agent or employee of another;

(b) trustee, guardian, or other fiduciary;

(c) Lawyer, physician, accountant, appraiser, or other professional adviser or informant;

(d) officer, director, manager or other participant in the direction of the affairs of an incorporated or unincorporated association; or

(e) arbitrator or other purportedly disinterested adjudicator or referee.

(2) A person who holds himself out to the public as being engaged in the business of making disinterested selection, appraisal, or criticism of commodities or services commits a misdemeanor if he solicits, accepts or agrees to accept any benefit to influence his selection, appraisal or criticism.

(3) A person commits a misdemeanor if he confers, or offers or agrees to confer, any benefit the acceptance of which would be criminal under this Section.

Section 224.9. Rigging Publicly Exhibited Contest.

(1) A person commits a misdemeanor if, with purpose to prevent a publicly exhibited contest from being conducted in accordance with the rules and usages purporting to govern it, he:

(a) confers or offers or agrees to confer any benefit upon, or threatens any injury to a participant, official or other person associated with the contest or exhibition; or

(b) tampers with any person, animal or thing.

(2) **Soliciting or Accepting Benefit for Rigging.** A person commits a misdemeanor if he knowingly solicits, accepts or agrees to accept any benefit the giving of which would be criminal under Subsection (1).

(3) **Participation in Rigged Contest.** A person commits a misdemeanor if he knowingly engages in, sponsors, produces, judges, or otherwise participates in a publicly exhibited contest knowing that the contest is not being conducted in compliance with the rules and usages purporting to govern it, by reason of conduct which would be criminal under this Section.

Section 224.10. Defrauding Secured Creditors.

A person commits a misdemeanor if he destroys, removes, conceals, encumbers, transfers or otherwise deals with property subject to a security interest with purpose to hinder enforcement of that interest.

Section 224.11. Fraud in Insolvency.

A person commits a misdemeanor if, knowing that proceedings have been or are about to be instituted for the appointment of a receiver or other person entitled to administer property for the benefit of creditors, or that any other composition or liquidation for the benefit of creditors has been or is about to be made, he:

(a) destroys, removes, conceals, encumbers, transfers, or otherwise deals with any property with purpose to defeat or obstruct the claim of any creditor, or otherwise to obstruct the operation of any law relating to administration of property for the benefit of creditors; or

(b) knowingly falsifies any writing or record relating to the property; or

(c) knowingly misrepresents or refuses to disclose to a receiver or other person entitled to administer property for the benefit of creditors, the existence, amount or location of the property, or any other information which the actor could be legally required to furnish in relation to such administration.

Section 224.12. Receiving Deposits in a Failing Financial Institution.

An officer, manager or other person directing or participating in the direction of a financial institution commits a misdemeanor if he receives or permits the receipt of a deposit, premium payment or other investment in the institution knowing that:

(1) due to financial difficulties the institution is about to suspend operations or go into receivership or reorganization; and

(2) the person making the deposit or other payment is unaware of the precarious situation of the institution.

Section 224.13. Misapplication of Entrusted Property and Property of Government or Financial Institution.

A person commits an offense if he applies or disposes of property that has been entrusted to him as a fiduciary, or property of the government or of a financial institution, in a manner which he knows is unlawful and involves substantial risk of loss or detriment to the owner of the property or to a person for whose benefit the property was entrusted. The offense is a misdemeanor if the amount involved exceeds $50; otherwise it is a petty misdemeanor. "Fiduciary" includes trustee, guardian, executor, administrator, receiver and any person carrying on fiduciary functions on behalf of a corporation or other organization which is a fiduciary.

Section 224.14. Securing Execution of Documents by Deception.

A person commits a misdemeanor if by deception he causes another to execute any instrument affecting or purporting to affect or likely to affect the pecuniary interest of any person.

OFFENSES AGAINST THE FAMILY
ARTICLE 230. OFFENSES AGAINST THE FAMILY

Section 230.1. Bigamy and Polygamy.

(1) **Bigamy.** A married person is guilty of bigamy, a misdemeanor, if he contracts or purports to contract another marriage, unless at the time of the subsequent marriage:

    (a) the actor believes that the prior spouse is dead; or

    (b) the actor and the prior spouse have been living apart for five consecutive years throughout which the prior spouse was not known by the actor to be alive; or

    (c) a Court has entered a judgment purporting to terminate or annul any prior disqualifying marriage, and the actor does not know that judgment to be invalid; or

    (d) the actor reasonably believes that he is legally eligible to remarry.

(2) **Polygamy.** A person is guilty of polygamy, a felony of the third degree, if he marries or cohabits with more than one spouse at a time in purported exercise of the right of plural marriage. The offense is a continuing one until all cohabitation and claim of marriage with more than one spouse terminates. This Section does not apply to parties to a polygamous marriage, lawful in the country of which they are residents or nationals, while they are in transit through or temporarily visiting this State.

(3) **Other Party to Bigamous or Polygamous Marriage.** A person is guilty of bigamy or polygamy, as the case may be, if he contracts or purports to contract marriage with another knowing that the other is thereby committing bigamy or polygamy.

Section 230.2. Incest.

A person is guilty of incest, a felony of the third degree, if he knowingly marries or cohabits or has sexual intercourse with an ancestor or descendant, a brother or sister of the whole or half blood [or an uncle, aunt, nephew or niece of the whole blood]. "Cohabit" means to live together under the representation or appearance of being married. The relationships referred to herein include blood relationships without regard to legitimacy, and relationship of parent and child by adoption.

Section 230.3. Abortion.

(1) **Unjustified Abortion.** A person who purposely and unjustifiably terminates the pregnancy of another otherwise than by a live birth commits a felony of the third degree or, where the pregnancy has continued beyond the twenty-sixth week, a felony of the second degree.

(2) **Justifiable Abortion.** A licensed physician is justified in terminating a pregnancy if he believes there is substantial risk that continuance of the pregnancy would gravely impair the physical or mental health of the mother or that the child would be born with grave physical or mental defect, or that the pregnancy resulted from rape, incest, or other felonious intercourse. All illicit intercourse with a girl below the age of 16 shall be deemed felonious for purposes of this subsection. Justifiable abortions shall be performed only in a licensed hospital except in case of emergency when hospital facilities are unavailable. [Additional exceptions from the requirement of hospitalization may be incorporated here to take account of situations in sparsely settled areas where hospitals are not generally accessible.]

(3) **Physicians' Certificates; Presumption from Non–Compliance.** No abortion shall be performed unless two physicians, one of whom may be the person performing the abortion, shall have certified in writing the circumstances which they believe to justify the abortion. Such certificate shall be submitted before the abortion to the hospital where it is to be performed and, in the case of abortion following felonious intercourse, to the prosecuting attorney or the police. Failure to comply with any of the requirements of this Subsection gives rise to a presumption that the abortion was unjustified.

(4) **Self–Abortion.** A woman whose pregnancy has continued beyond the twenty-sixth week commits a felony of the third degree if she purposely terminates her own pregnancy otherwise than by a live birth, or if she uses instruments, drugs or violence upon herself for that purpose. Except as justified under Subsection (2), a person who induces or knowingly aids a woman to use instruments, drugs or violence upon herself for the purpose of terminating her pregnancy otherwise than by a live birth commits a felony of the third degree whether or not the pregnancy has continued beyond the twenty-sixth week.

(5) **Pretended Abortion.** A person commits a felony of the third degree if, representing that it is his purpose to perform an abortion, he does an act adapted to cause abortion in a pregnant woman although the woman is in fact not pregnant, or the actor does not believe she is. A person charged with unjustified abortion under Subsection (1) or an attempt to commit that offense may be convicted thereof upon proof of conduct prohibited by this Subsection.

(6) **Distribution of Abortifacients.** A person who sells, offers to sell, possesses with intent to sell, advertises, or displays for sale anything specially designed to terminate a pregnancy, or held out by the actor as useful for that purpose, commits a misdemeanor, unless:

(a) the sale, offer or display is to a physician or druggist or to an intermediary in a chain of distribution to physicians or druggists; or

(b) the sale is made upon prescription or order of a physician; or

(c) the possession is with intent to sell as authorized in paragraphs (a) and (b); or

(d) the advertising is addressed to persons named in paragraph (a) and confined to trade or professional channels not likely to reach the general public.

(7) **Section Inapplicable to Prevention of Pregnancy.** Nothing in this Section shall be deemed applicable to the prescription, administration or distribution of drugs or other substances for avoiding pregnancy, whether by preventing implantation of a fertilized ovum or by any other method that operates before, at or immediately after fertilization.

Section 230.4. Endangering Welfare of Children.

A parent, guardian, or other person supervising the welfare of a child under 18 commits a misdemeanor if he knowingly endangers the child's welfare by violating a duty of care, protection or support.

Section 230.5. Persistent Non-support.

A person commits a misdemeanor if he persistently fails to provide support which he can provide and which he knows he is legally obliged to provide to a spouse, child or other defendant.

OFFENSES AGAINST PUBLIC ADMINISTRATION
ARTICLE 240. BRIBERY AND CORRUPT INFLUENCE

Section 240.0. Definitions.

In Articles 240–243, unless a different meaning plainly is required:

(1) "benefit" means gain or advantage, or anything regarded by the beneficiary as gain or advantage, including benefit to any other person or entity in whose welfare he is interested, but not an advantage promised generally to a group or class of voters as a consequence of public measures which a candidate engages to support or oppose;

(2) "government" includes any branch, subdivision or agency of the government of the State or any locality within it;

(3) "harm" means loss, disadvantage or injury, or anything so regarded by the person affected, including loss, disadvantage or injury to any other person or entity in whose welfare he is interested;

(4) "official proceeding" means a proceeding heard or which may be heard before any legislative, judicial, administrative or other governmental agency or official authorized to take evidence under oath, including any referee, hearing examiner, commissioner, notary or other person taking testimony or deposition in connection with any such proceeding;

(5) "party official" means a person who holds an elective or appointive post in a political party in the United States by virtue of which he directs or conducts, or participates in directing or conducting party affairs at any level of responsibility;

(6) "pecuniary benefit" is benefit in the form of money, property, commercial interests or anything else the primary significance of which is economic gain;

(7) "public servant" means any officer or employee of government, including legislators and judges, and any person participating as juror, advisor, consultant or otherwise, in performing a governmental function; but the term does not include witnesses;

(8) "administrative proceeding" means any proceeding other than a judicial proceeding the outcome of which is required to be based on a record or documentation prescribed by law, or in which law or regulation is particularized in application to individuals.

Section 240.1. Bribery in Official and Political Matters.

A person is guilty of bribery, a felony of the third degree, if he offers, confers or agrees to confer upon another, or solicits, accepts or agrees to accept from another:

(1) any pecuniary benefit as consideration for the recipient's decision, opinion, recommendation, vote or other exercise of discretion as a public servant, party official or voter; or

(2) any benefit as consideration for the recipient's decision, vote, recommendation or other exercise of official discretion in a judicial or administrative proceeding; or

(3) any benefit as consideration for a violation of a known legal duty as public servant or party official.

It is no defense to prosecution under this section that a person whom the actor sought to influence was not qualified to act in the desired way whether because he had not yet assumed office, or lacked jurisdiction, or for any other reason.

Section 240.2. Threats and Other Improper Influence in Official and Political Matters.

(1) **Offenses Defined.** A person commits an offense if he:

(a) threatens unlawful harm to any person with purpose to influence his decision, opinion, recommendation, vote or other exercise of discretion as a public servant, party official or voter; or

(b) threatens harm to any public servant with purpose to influence his decision, opinion, recommendation, vote or other exercise of discretion in a judicial or administrative proceeding; or

(c) threatens harm to any public servant or party official with purpose to influence him to violate his known legal duty; or

(d) privately addresses to any public servant who has or will have an official discretion in a judicial or administrative proceeding any representation, entreaty, argument or other communication with purpose to influence the outcome on the basis of considerations other than those authorized by law.

It is no defense to prosecution under this Section that a person whom the actor sought to influence was not qualified to act in the desired way, whether because he had not yet assumed office, or lacked jurisdiction, or for any other reason.

(2) **Grading.** An offense under this Section is a misdemeanor unless the actor threatened to commit a crime or made a threat with purpose to influence a judicial or administrative proceeding, in which cases the offense is a felony of the third degree.

Section 240.3. Compensation for Past Official Behavior.

A person commits a misdemeanor if he solicits, accepts or agrees to accept any pecuniary benefit as compensation for having, as public servant, given a decision, opinion, recommendation or vote favorable to another, or for having otherwise exercised a discretion in his favor, or for having violated his duty. A person commits a misdemeanor if he offers, confers or agrees to confer compensation acceptance of which is prohibited by this Section.

Section 240.4. Retaliation for Past Official Action.

A person commits a misdemeanor if he harms another by any unlawful act in retaliation for anything lawfully done by the latter in the capacity of public servant.

Section 240.5. Gifts to Public Servants by Persons Subject to Their Jurisdiction.

(1) **Regulatory and Law Enforcement Officials.** No public servant in any department or agency exercising regulatory functions, or conducting inspections or investigations, or carrying on civil or criminal litigation on behalf of the government, or having custody of prisoners, shall solicit, accept or agree to accept any pecuniary benefit from a person known to be subject to such regulation, inspection, investigation or custody, or against whom such litigation is known to be pending or contemplated.

(2) **Officials Concerned with Government Contracts and Pecuniary Transactions.** No public servant having any discretionary function to perform in connection with contracts, purchases, payments, claims or other pecuniary transactions of the government shall solicit, accept or agree to accept any pecuniary benefit from any person known to be interested in or likely to become interested in any such contract, purchase, payment, claim or transaction.

(3) **Judicial and Administrative Officials.** No public servant having judicial or administrative authority and no public servant employed by or in a court or other tribunal having such authority, or participating in the enforcement of its decisions, shall solicit, accept or agree to accept any pecuniary benefit from a person known to be interested in or likely to become interested in any matter before such public servant or a tribunal with which he is associated.

(4) **Legislative Officials.** No legislator or public servant employed by the legislature or by any committee or agency thereof shall solicit, accept or agree to accept any pecuniary benefit from any person known to be interested in a bill, transaction or proceeding, pending or contemplated, before the legislature or any committee or agency thereof.

(5) **Exceptions.** This Section shall not apply to:

(a) fees prescribed by law to be received by a public servant, or any other benefit for which the recipient gives legitimate consideration or to which he is otherwise legally entitled; or

(b) gifts or other benefits conferred on account of kinship or other personal, professional or business relationship independent of the official status of the receiver; or

(c) trivial benefits incidental to personal, professional or business contacts and involving no substantial risk of undermining official impartiality.

(6) **Offering Benefits Prohibited.** No person shall knowingly confer, or offer or agree to confer, any benefit prohibited by the foregoing Subsections.

(7) **Grade of Offense.** An offense under this Section is a misdemeanor.

Section 240.6. Compensating Public Servant for Assisting Private Interests in Relation to Matters Before Him.

(1) **Receiving Compensation.** A public servant commits a misdemeanor if he solicits, accepts or agrees to accept compensation for advice or other assistance in preparing or promoting a bill, contract, claim, or other transaction or proposal as to which he knows that he has or is likely to have an official discretion to exercise.

(2) **Paying Compensation.** A person commits a misdemeanor if he pays or offers or agrees to pay compensation to a public servant with knowledge that acceptance by the public servant is unlawful.

Section 240.7. Selling Political Endorsement; Special Influence.

(1) **Selling Political Endorsement.** A person commits a misdemeanor if he solicits, receives, agrees to receive, or agrees that any political party or other person shall receive, any pecuniary benefit as consideration for approval or disapproval of an appointment or advancement in public service, or for approval or disapproval of any person or transaction for any benefit conferred by an official or agency of government. "Approval" includes recommendation, failure to disapprove, or any other manifestation of favor or acquiescence. "Disapproval" includes failure to approve, or any other manifestation of disfavor or nonacquiescence.

(2) **Other Trading in Special Influence.** A person commits a misdemeanor if he solicits, receives or agrees to receive any pecuniary benefit as consideration for exerting special influence upon a public servant or procuring another to do so. "Special influence" means power to influence through kinship, friendship or other relationship, apart from the merits of the transaction.

(3) **Paying for Endorsement or Special Influence.** A person commits a misdemeanor if he offers, confers or agrees to confer any pecuniary benefit receipt of which is prohibited by this Section.

ARTICLE 241. PERJURY AND OTHER FALSIFICATION IN OFFICIAL MATTERS

Section 241.0. Definitions.

In this Article, unless a different meaning plainly is required:

(1) the definitions given in Section 240.0 apply; and

(2) "statement" means any representation, but includes a representation of opinion, belief or other state of mind only if the representation clearly relates to state of mind apart from or in addition to any facts which are the subject of the representation.

Section 241.1. Perjury.

(1) **Offense Defined.** A person is guilty of perjury, a felony of the third degree, if in any official proceeding he makes a false statement under oath or equivalent affirmation, or swears or affirms the truth of a statement previously made, when the statement is material and he does not believe it to be true.

(2) **Materiality.** Falsification is material, regardless of the admissibility of the statement under rules of evidence, if it could have affected the course or outcome of the proceeding. It is no defense that the declarant mistakenly believed the falsification to be immaterial. Whether a falsification is material in a given factual situation is a question of law.

(3) **Irregularities No Defense.** It is not a defense to prosecution under this Section that the oath or affirmation was administered or taken in an irregular manner or that the declarant was not competent to make the statement. A document purporting to be made upon oath or affirmation at any time when the actor presents it as being so verified shall be deemed to have been duly sworn or affirmed.

(4) **Retraction.** No person shall be guilty of an offense under this Section if he retracted the falsification in the course of the proceeding in which it was made before it became manifest that the falsification was or would be exposed and before the falsification substantially affected the proceeding.

(5) **Inconsistent Statements.** Where the defendant made inconsistent statements under oath or equivalent affirmation, both having been made within the period of the statute of limitations, the prosecution may proceed by setting forth the inconsistent statements in a single count alleging in the alternative that one or the other was false and not believed by the defendant. In such case it shall not be necessary for the prosecution to prove which statement was false but only that one or the other was false and not believed by the defendant to be true.

(6) **Corroboration.** No person shall be convicted of an offense under this Section where proof of falsity rests solely upon contradiction by testimony of a single person other than the defendant.

Section 241.2. False Swearing.

(1) **False Swearing in Official Matters.** A person who makes a false statement under oath or equivalent affirmation, or swears or affirms the truth of such a statement previously made, when he does not believe the statement to be true, is guilty of a misdemeanor if:

(a) the falsification occurs in an official proceeding; or

(b) the falsification is intended to mislead a public servant in performing his official function.

(2) **Other False Swearing.** A person who makes a false statement under oath or equivalent affirmation, or swears or affirms the truth of such a statement previously made, when he does not believe the statement to be true, is guilty of a petty misdemeanor, if the statement is one which is required by law to be sworn or affirmed before a notary or other person authorized to administer oaths.

(3) **Perjury Provisions Applicable.** Subsections (3) to (6) of Section 241.1 apply to the present Section.

Section 241.3. Unsworn Falsification to Authorities.

(1) **In General.** A person commits a misdemeanor if, with purpose to mislead a public servant in performing his official function, he:

(a) makes any written false statement which he does not believe to be true; or

(b) purposely creates a false impression in a written application for any pecuniary or other benefit, by omitting information necessary to prevent statements therein from being misleading; or

(c) submits or invites reliance on any writing which he knows to be forged, altered or otherwise lacking in authenticity; or

(d) submits or invites reliance on any sample, specimen, map, boundary-mark, or other object which he knows to be false.

(2) **Statements "Under Penalty."** A person commits a petty misdemeanor if he makes a written false statement which he does not believe to be true, on or pursuant to a form bearing notice, authorized by law, to the effect that false statements made therein are punishable.

(3) **Perjury Provisions Applicable.** Subsections (3) to (6) of Section 241.1 apply to the present Section.

Section 241.4. False Alarms to Agencies of Public Safety.

A person who knowingly causes a false alarm of fire or other emergency to be transmitted to or within any organization, official or volunteer, for dealing with emergencies involving danger to life or property commits a misdemeanor.

Section 241.5. False Reports to Law Enforcement Authorities.

(1) **Falsely Incriminating Another.** A person who knowingly gives false information to any law enforcement officer with purpose to implicate another commits a misdemeanor.

(2) **Fictitious Reports.** A person commits a petty misdemeanor if he:

(a) reports to law enforcement authorities an offense or other incident within their concern knowing that it did not occur; or

(b) pretends to furnish such authorities with information relating to an offense or incident when he knows he has no information relating to such offense or incident.

Section 241.6. Tampering With Witnesses and Informants; Retaliation Against Them.

(1) **Tampering.** A person commits an offense if, believing that an official proceeding or investigation is pending or about to be instituted, he attempts to induce or otherwise cause a witness or informant to:

(a) testify or inform falsely; or

(b) withhold any testimony, information, document or thing; or

(c) elude legal process summoning him to testify or supply evidence; or

(d) absent himself from any proceeding or investigation to which he has been legally summoned.

The offense is a felony of the third degree if the actor employs force, deception, threat or offer of pecuniary benefit. Otherwise it is a misdemeanor.

(2) **Retaliation Against Witness or Informant.** A person commits a misdemeanor if he harms another by any unlawful act in retaliation for anything lawfully done in the capacity of witness or informant.

(3) **Witness or Informant Taking Bribe.** A person commits a felony of the third degree if he solicits, accepts or agrees to accept any benefit in consideration of his doing any of the things specified in clauses (a) to (d) of Subsection (1).

Section 241.7. Tampering With or Fabricating Physical Evidence.

A person commits a misdemeanor if, believing that an official proceeding or investigation is pending or about to be instituted, he:

(1) alters, destroys, conceals or removes any record, document or thing with purpose to impair its verity or availability in such proceeding or investigation; or

(2) makes, presents or uses any record, document or thing knowing it to be false and with purpose to mislead a public servant who is or may be engaged in such proceeding or investigation.

Section 241.8. Tampering With Public Records or Information.

(1) **Offense Defined.** A person commits an offense if he:

(a) knowingly makes a false entry in, or false alteration of, any record, document or thing belonging to, or received or kept by, the government for information or record, or required by law to be kept by others for information of the government; or

(b) makes, presents or uses any record, document or thing knowing it to be false, and with purpose that it be taken as a genuine part of information or records referred to in paragraph (a); or

(c) purposely and unlawfully destroys, conceals, removes or otherwise impairs the verity or availability of any such record, document or thing.

(2) **Grading.** An offense under this Section is a misdemeanor unless the actor's purpose is to defraud or injure anyone, in which case the offense is a felony of the third degree.

Section 241.9. Impersonating a Public Servant.

A person commits a misdemeanor if he falsely pretends to hold a position in the public service with purpose to induce another to submit to such pretended official authority or otherwise to act in reliance upon that pretense to his prejudice.

ARTICLE 242. OBSTRUCTING GOVERNMENTAL OPERATIONS; ESCAPES

Section 242.0. Definitions.

In this Article, unless another meaning plainly is required, the definitions given in Section 240.0 apply.

Section 242.1. Obstructing Administration of Law or Other Governmental Function.

A person commits a misdemeanor if he purposely obstructs, impairs or perverts the administration of law or other governmental function by force, violence, physical interference or obstacle, breach of official duty, or any other unlawful act, except that this Section does not apply to flight by a person charged with crime, refusal to submit to arrest, failure to perform a legal duty other than an official duty, or any other means of avoiding compliance with law without affirmative interference with governmental functions.

Section 242.2. Resisting Arrest or Other Law Enforcement.

A person commits a misdemeanor if, for the purpose of preventing a public servant from effecting a lawful arrest or discharging any other duty, the person creates a substantial risk of bodily injury to the public servant or anyone else, or employs means justifying or requiring substantial force to overcome the resistance.

Section 242.3. Hindering Apprehension or Prosecution.

A person commits an offense if, with purpose to hinder the apprehension, prosecution, conviction or punishment of another for crime, he:

(1) harbors or conceals the other; or

(2) provides or aids in providing a weapon, transportation, disguise or other means of avoiding apprehension or effecting escape; or

(3) conceals or destroys evidence of the crime, or tampers with a witness, informant, document or other source of information, regardless of its admissibility in evidence; or

(4) warns the other of impending discovery or apprehension, except that this paragraph does not apply to a warning given in connection with an effort to bring another into compliance with law; or

(5) volunteers false information to a law enforcement officer.

The offense is a felony of the third degree if the conduct which the actor knows has been charged or is liable to be charged against the person aided would constitute a felony of the first or second degree. Otherwise it is a misdemeanor.

Section 242.4. Aiding Consummation of Crime.

A person commits an offense if he purposely aids another to accomplish an unlawful object of a crime, as by safeguarding the proceeds thereof or converting the proceeds into negotiable funds. The offense is a felony of the third degree if the principal offense was a felony of the first or second degree. Otherwise it is a misdemeanor.

Section 242.5. Compounding.

A person commits a misdemeanor if he accepts or agrees to accept any pecuniary benefit in consideration of refraining from reporting to law enforcement authorities the commission or suspected commission of any offense or information relating to an offense. It is an affirmative defense to prosecution under this Section that the pecuniary benefit did not exceed an amount which the actor believed to be due as restitution or indemnification for harm caused by the offense.

Section 242.6. Escape.

(1) **Escape.** A person commits an offense if he unlawfully removes himself from official detention or fails to return to official detention following temporary leave granted for a specific purpose or limited period. "Official detention" means arrest, detention in any facility for custody of persons under charge or conviction of crime or alleged or found to be delinquent, detention for extradition or deportation, or any other detention for law enforcement purposes; but "official detention" does not include supervision of probation or parole, or constraint incidental to release on bail.

(2) **Permitting or Facilitating Escape.** A public servant concerned in detention commits an offense if he knowingly or recklessly permits an escape. Any person who knowingly causes or facilitates an escape commits an offense.

(3) **Effect of Legal Irregularity in Detention.** Irregularity in bringing about or maintaining detention, or lack of jurisdiction of the committing or detaining authority, shall not be a defense to prosecution under this Section if the escape is from a prison or other custodial facility or from detention pursuant to commitment by official proceedings. In the case of other detentions, irregularity or lack of jurisdiction shall be a defense only if:

(a) the escape involved no substantial risk of harm to the person or property of anyone other than the detainee; or

(b) the detaining authority did not act in good faith under color of law.

(4) **Grading of Offenses.** An offense under this Section is a felony of the third degree where:

(a) the actor was under arrest for or detained on a charge of felony or following conviction of crime; or

(b) the actor employs force, threat, deadly weapon or other dangerous instrumentality to effect the escape; or

(c) a public servant concerned in detention of persons convicted of crime purposely facilitates or permits an escape from a detention facility.

Otherwise an offense under this section is a misdemeanor.

Section 242.7. Implements for Escape; Other Contraband.

(1) **Escape Implements.** A person commits a misdemeanor if he unlawfully introduces within a detention facility, or unlawfully provides an inmate with, any weapon, tool or other thing which may be useful for escape. An inmate commits a misdemeanor if he unlawfully procures, makes, or otherwise provides himself with, or has in his possession, any such implement of escape. "Unlawfully" means surreptitiously or contrary to law, regulation or order of the detaining authority.

(2) **Other Contraband.** A person commits a petty misdemeanor if he provides an inmate with anything which the actor knows it is unlawful for the inmate to possess.

Section 242.8. Bail Jumping; Default in Required Appearance.

A person set at liberty by court order, with or without bail, upon condition that he will subsequently appear at a specified time and place, commits a misdemeanor if, without lawful excuse, he fails to appear at that time and place. The offense constitutes a felony of the third degree where the required appearance was to answer to a charge of felony, or for disposition of any such charge, and the actor took flight or went into hiding to avoid apprehension, trial or punishment. This Section does not apply to obligations to appear incident to release under suspended sentence or on probation or parole.

ARTICLE 243. ABUSE OF OFFICE

Section 243.0. Definitions.

In this Article, unless a different meaning plainly is required, the definitions given in Section 240.0 apply.

Section 243.1. Official Oppression.

A person acting or purporting to act in an official capacity or taking advantage of such actual or purported capacity commits a misdemeanor if, knowing that his conduct is illegal, he:

(a) subjects another to arrest, detention, search, seizure, mistreatment, dispossession, assessment, lien or other infringement of personal or property rights; or

(b) denies or impedes another in the exercise or enjoyment of any right, privilege, power or immunity.

Section 243.2. Speculating or Wagering on Official Action or Information.

A public servant commits a misdemeanor if, in contemplation of official action by himself or by a governmental unit with which he is associated, or in reliance on information to which he has access in his official capacity and which has not been made public, he:

(1) acquires a pecuniary interest in any property, transaction or enterprise which may be affected by such information or official action; or

(2) speculates or wagers on the basis of such information or official action; or

(3) aids another to do any of the foregoing.

OFFENSES AGAINST PUBLIC ORDER AND DECENCY

ARTICLE 250. RIOT, DISORDERLY CONDUCT, AND RELATED OFFENSES

Section 250.1. Riot; Failure to Disperse.

(1) **Riot.** A person is guilty of riot, a felony of the third degree, if he participates with [two] or more others in a course of disorderly conduct:

(a) with purpose to commit or facilitate the commission of a felony or misdemeanor;

(b) with purpose to prevent or coerce official action; or

(c) when the actor or any other participant to the knowledge of the actor uses or plans to use a firearm or other deadly weapon.

(2) **Failure of Disorderly Persons to Disperse Upon Official Order.** Where [three] or more persons are participating in a course of disorderly conduct likely to cause substantial harm or serious inconvenience, annoyance or alarm, a peace officer or other public servant engaged in executing or enforcing the law may order the participants and others in the immediate vicinity to disperse. A person who refuses or knowingly fails to obey such an order commits a misdemeanor.

Section 250.2. Disorderly Conduct.

(1) **Offense Defined.** A person is guilty of disorderly conduct if, with purpose to cause public inconvenience, annoyance or alarm, or recklessly creating a risk thereof, he:

    (a) engages in fighting or threatening, or in violent or tumultuous behavior; or

    (b) makes unreasonable noise or offensively coarse utterance, gesture or display, or addresses abusive language to any person present; or

    (c) creates a hazardous or physically offensive condition by any act which serves no legitimate purpose of the actor.

"Public" means affecting or likely to affect persons in a place to which the public or a substantial group has access; among the places included are highways, transport facilities, schools, prisons, apartment houses, places of business or amusement, or any neighborhood.

(2) **Grading.** An offense under this section is a petty misdemeanor if the actor's purpose is to cause substantial harm or serious inconvenience, or if he persists in disorderly conduct after reasonable warning or request to desist. Otherwise disorderly conduct is a violation.

Section 250.3. False Public Alarms.

A person is guilty of a misdemeanor if he initiates or circulates a report or warning of an impending bombing or other crime or catastrophe, knowing that the report or warning is false or baseless and that it is likely to cause evacuation of a building, place of assembly, or facility of public transport, or to cause public inconvenience or alarm.

Section 250.4. Harassment.

A person commits a petty misdemeanor if, with purpose to harass another, he:

    (1) makes a telephone call without purpose of legitimate communication; or

    (2) insults, taunts or challenges another in a manner likely to provoke violent or disorderly response; or

    (3) makes repeated communications anonymously or at extremely inconvenient hours, or in offensively coarse language; or

    (4) subjects another to an offensive touching; or

    (5) engages in any other course of alarming conduct serving no legitimate purpose of the actor.

Section 250.5. Public Drunkenness; Drug Incapacitation.

A person is guilty of an offense if he appears in any public place manifestly under the influence of alcohol, narcotics or other drug, not therapeutically administered, to the degree that he may endanger himself or other persons or property, or annoy persons in his vicinity. An offense under this Section constitutes a petty misdemeanor if the actor has been convicted hereunder twice before within a period of one year. Otherwise the offense constitutes a violation.

Section 250.6. Loitering or Prowling.

A person commits a violation if he loiters or prowls in a place, at a time, or in a manner not usual for law-abiding individuals under circumstances that warrant alarm for the safety of persons or property in the vicinity. Among the circumstances which may be considered in determining whether such alarm is warranted is the fact that the actor takes flight upon appearance of a peace officer, refuses to identify himself, or manifestly endeavors to conceal himself or any object. Unless flight by the actor or other circumstance makes it impracticable, a peace officer shall prior to any arrest for an offense under this section afford the actor an opportunity to dispel any alarm which would otherwise be warranted, by requesting him to identify himself and explain his presence and conduct. No person shall be convicted of an offense under this Section if the peace officer did not comply with the preceding sentence, or if it appears at trial that the explanation given by the actor was true and, if believed by the peace officer at the time, would have dispelled the alarm.

Section 250.7. Obstructing Highways and Other Public Passages.

(1) A person, who, having no legal privilege to do so, purposely or recklessly obstructs any highway or other public passage, whether alone or with others, commits a violation, or, in case he persists after warning by a law officer, a petty misdemeanor. "Obstructs" means renders impassable without unreasonable inconvenience or hazard. No person shall be deemed guilty of recklessly obstructing in violation of this Subsection solely because of a gathering of persons to hear him speak or otherwise communicate, or solely because of being a member of such a gathering.

(2) A person in a gathering commits a violation if he refuses to obey a reasonable official request or order to move:

(a) to prevent obstruction of a highway or other public passage; or

(b) to maintain public safety by dispersing those gathered in dangerous proximity to a fire or other hazard.

An order to move, addressed to a person whose speech or other lawful behavior attracts an obstructing audience, shall not be deemed reasonable if the obstruction can be readily remedied by police control of the size or location of the gathering.

Section 250.8. Disrupting Meetings and Processions.

A person commits a misdemeanor if, with purpose to prevent or disrupt a lawful meeting, procession or gathering, he does any act tending to obstruct or interfere with it physically, or makes any utterance, gesture or display designed to outrage the sensibilities of the group.

Section 250.9. Desecration of Venerated Objects.

A person commits a misdemeanor if he purposely desecrates any public monument or structure, or place of worship or burial, or if he purposely desecrates the national flag or any other object of veneration by the public or a substantial segment thereof in any public place. "Desecrate" means defacing, damaging, polluting or otherwise physically mistreating in a way that the actor knows will outrage the sensibilities of persons likely to observe or discover his action.

Section 250.10. Abuse of Corpse.

Except as authorized by law, a person who treats a corpse in a way that he knows would outrage ordinary family sensibilities commits a misdemeanor.

Section 250.11. Cruelty to Animals.

A person commits a misdemeanor if he purposely or recklessly:

(1) subjects any animal to cruel mistreatment; or

(2) subjects any animal in his custody to cruel neglect; or

(3) kills or injures any animal belonging to another without legal privilege or consent of the owner.

Subsections (1) and (2) shall not be deemed applicable to accepted veterinary practices and activities carried on for scientific research.

Section 250.12. Violation of Privacy.

(1) **Unlawful Eavesdropping or Surveillance.** A person commits a misdemeanor if, except as authorized by law, he:

(a) trespasses on property with purpose to subject anyone to eavesdropping or other surveillance in a private place; or

(b) installs in any private place, without the consent of the person or persons entitled to privacy there, any device for observing, photographing, recording, amplifying or broadcasting sounds or events in such place, or uses any such unauthorized installation; or

(c) installs or uses outside a private place any device for hearing, recording, amplifying or broadcasting sounds originating in such place which would not ordinarily be audible or comprehensible outside, without the consent of the person or persons entitled to privacy there.

"Private place" means a place where one may reasonably expect to be safe from casual or hostile intrusion or surveillance, but does not include a place to which the public or a substantial group thereof has access.

(2) **Other Breach of Privacy of Messages.** A person commits a misdemeanor if, except as authorized by law, he:

(a) intercepts without the consent of the sender or receiver a message by telephone, telegraph, letter or other means of communicating privately; but this paragraph does not extend to (i) overhearing of messages through a regularly installed instrument on a telephone party line or on an extension, or (ii) interception by the telephone company or subscriber incident to enforcement of regulations limiting use of the facilities or incident to other normal operation and use; or

(b) divulges without the consent of the sender or receiver the existence or contents of any such message if the actor knows that the message was illegally intercepted, or if he learned of the message in the course of employment with an agency engaged in transmitting it.

ARTICLE 251. PUBLIC INDECENCY

Section 251.1. Open Lewdness.

A person commits a petty misdemeanor if he does any lewd act which he knows is likely to be observed by others who would be affronted or alarmed.

Section 251.2. Prostitution and Related Offenses.

(1) **Prostitution.** A person is guilty of prostitution, a petty misdemeanor, if he or she:

(a) is an inmate of a house of prostitution or otherwise engages in sexual activity as a business; or

(b) loiters in or within view of any public place for the purpose of being hired to engage in sexual activity.

"Sexual activity" includes homosexual and other deviate sexual relations. A "house of prostitution" is any place where prostitution or promotion of prostitution is regularly carried on by one person under the control, management or supervision of another. An "inmate" is a person who engages in prostitution in or through the agency of a house of prostitution. "Public place" means any place to which the public or any substantial group thereof has access.

(2) **Promoting Prostitution.** A person who knowingly promotes prostitution of another commits a misdemeanor or felony as provided in Subsection (3). The following acts shall, without limitation of the foregoing, constitute promoting prostitution:

(a) owning, controlling, managing, supervising or otherwise keeping, alone or in association with others, a house of prostitution or a prostitution business; or

(b) procuring an inmate for a house of prostitution or a place in a house of prostitution for one who would be an inmate; or

(c) encouraging, inducing, or otherwise purposely causing another to become or remain a prostitute; or

(d) soliciting a person to patronize a prostitute; or

(e) procuring a prostitute for a patron; or

(f) transporting a person into or within this state with purpose to promote that person's engaging in prostitution, or procuring or paying for transportation with that purpose; or

(g) leasing or otherwise permitting a place controlled by the actor, alone or in association with others, to be regularly used for prostitution or the promotion of prostitution, or failure to make reasonable effort to abate such use by ejecting the tenant, notifying law enforcement authorities, or other legally available means; or

(h) soliciting, receiving, or agreeing to receive any benefit for doing or agreeing to do anything forbidden by this Subsection.

(3) **Grading of Offenses Under Subsection (2).** An offense under Subsection (2) constitutes a felony of the third degree if:

(a) the offense falls within paragraph (a), (b) or (c) of Subsection (2); or

(b) the actor compels another to engage in or promote prostitution; or

(c) the actor promotes prostitution of a child under 16, whether or not he is aware of the child's age; or

(d) the actor promotes prostitution of his wife, child, ward or any person for whose care, protection or support he is responsible.

Otherwise the offense is a misdemeanor.

(4) **Presumption from Living off Prostitutes.** A person, other than the prostitute or the prostitute's minor child or other legal dependent incapable of self-support, who is supported in whole or substantial part by the proceeds of prostitution is presumed to be knowingly promoting prostitution in violation of Subsection (2).

(5) **Patronizing Prostitutes.** A person commits a violation if he hires a prostitute to engage in sexual activity with him, or if he enters or remains in a house of prostitution for the purpose of engaging in sexual activity.

(6) **Evidence.** On the issue whether a place is a house of prostitution the following shall be admissible evidence: its general repute; the repute of the persons who reside in or frequent the place; the frequency, timing and duration of visits by non-residents. Testimony of a person against his spouse shall be admissible to prove offenses under this Section.

Section 251.3. Loitering to Solicit Deviate Sexual Relations.

A person is guilty of a petty misdemeanor if he loiters in or near any public place for the purpose of soliciting or being solicited to engage in deviate sexual relations.

Section 251.4. Obscenity.

(1) **Obscene Defined.** Material is obscene if, considered as a whole, its predominant appeal is to prurient interest, that is, a shameful or morbid interest, in nudity, sex or excretion, and if in addition it goes substantially beyond customary limits of candor in describing or representing such matters. Predominant appeal shall be judged with reference to ordinary adults unless it appears from the character of the material or the circumstances of its dissemination to be designed for children or other specially susceptible audience. Undeveloped photographs, molds, printing plates, and the like, shall be deemed obscene notwithstanding that processing or other acts may be required to make the obscenity patent or to disseminate it.

(2) **Offenses.** Subject to the affirmative defense provided in Subsection (3), a person commits a misdemeanor if he knowingly or recklessly:

(a) sells, delivers or provides, or offers or agrees to sell, deliver or provide, any obscene writing, picture, record or other representation or embodiment of the obscene; or

(b) presents or directs an obscene play, dance or performance, or participates in that portion thereof which makes it obscene; or

(c) publishes, exhibits or otherwise makes available any obscene material; or

(d) possesses any obscene material for purposes of sale or other commercial dissemination; or

(e) sells, advertises or otherwise commercially disseminates material, whether or not obscene, by representing or suggesting that it is obscene.

A person who disseminates or possesses obscene material in the course of his business is presumed to do so knowingly or recklessly.

(3) **Justifiable and Non–Commercial Private Dissemination.** It is an affirmative defense to prosecution under this Section that dissemination was restricted to:

(a) institutions or persons having scientific, educational, governmental or other similar justification for possessing obscene material; or

(b) non-commercial dissemination to personal associates of the actor.

(4) **Evidence; Adjudication of Obscenity.** In any prosecution under this Section evidence shall be admissible to show:

(a) the character of the audience for which the material was designed or to which it was directed;

(b) what the predominant appeal of the material would be for ordinary adults or any special audience to which it was directed, and what effect, if any, it would probably have on conduct of such people;

(c) artistic, literary, scientific, educational or other merits of the material;

(d) the degree of public acceptance of the material in the United States;

(e) appeal to prurient interest, or absence thereof, in advertising or other promotion of the material; and

(f) the good repute of the author, creator, publisher or other person from whom the material originated.

Expert testimony and testimony of the author, creator, publisher or other person from whom the material originated, relating to factors entering into the determination of the issue of obscenity, shall be admissible. The Court shall dismiss a prosecution for obscenity if it is satisfied that the material is not obscene.

ADDITIONAL ARTICLES

[At this point, a State enacting a new Penal Code may insert additional Articles dealing with special topics such as narcotics, alcoholic beverages, gambling and offenses against tax and trade laws. The Model Penal Code project did not extend to these, partly because a higher priority on limited time and resources was accorded to branches of the penal law which have not received close legislative scrutiny. Also, in legislation dealing with narcotics, liquor, tax evasion, and the like, penal provisions have been so intermingled with regulatory and procedural provisions that the task of segregating one group from the other presents special difficulty for model legislation.]

*

Index

References are to Pages

References are to Pages

References are to Pages